What Readers Have Said About C++ Primer Plus:

"By far the best C++ book there is. This book is fun to read, is very well set up, and teaches you a lot. I bought other C++ books with this one, but since opening this book I've shelved the others. If you want to learn C++, and have fun doing it, consider this book as your only choice."

—Jan Pittner

"This is by far the best cross-platform book I have ever seen."

—Ivan G. Burch II

"The only book you will need to dive into C++ programming. The reading is easy flowing, and the example programs are excellent.... I recommend this as a "must have" for any person wanting to do serious C++ programming."

—Chris Cox

"*C++ Primer Plus*—hands-down, the best tutorial on C++. Aspiring programmers will find this book to be a treasure trove of clear, concise explanations of C++'s key features. Personally, I came to programming with a liberal arts degree and no more technical expertise than it took to install my new compiler software. Prata's remarkably lucid, friendly style guided me step-by-step to a thorough grasp of the basics. I have purchased and worked through several other recently published books on C++, and can attest that Prata's book is by far the best."

—Tim Mansfield

MITCHELL WAITE
Signature Series

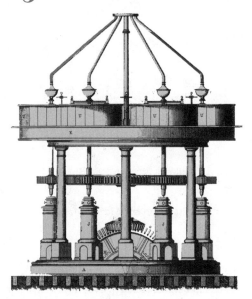

MITCHELL WAITE SIGNATURE SERIES: C++ PRIMER PLUS, THIRD EDITION

STEPHEN PRATA

Waite Group Press™
A Division of Macmillan Computer Publishing
Corte Madera, CA

Publisher: Mitchell Waite
Associate Publisher: Charles Drucker
Executive Editor: Susan Walton
Project Development Editor: Andrea Rosenberg
Content/Technical Editor: Russ Jacobs
Project Editor: Jim Bowie
Copy Editors: Sean Dixon, Kate Givens, San Dee Phillips
Managing Editor: Jodi Jensen
Indexing Manager: Johnna L. VanHoose
Editorial Assistant: Carmela Carvajal
Software Specialist: Dan Scherf
Director of Marketing: Kelli S. Spencer
Product Marketing Manager: Wendy Gilbride
Marketing Coordinator: Linda B. Beckwith
Production Manager: Cecile Kaufman
Production Team Supervisor: Brad Chinn
Cover Designer: Sestina Quarequio, Karen Johnston, Sandra Schroeder, Jean Bisesi
Book Designer: Diana Jean Parks
Interior Illustration: Laura Robbins
Production: Michael Henry, Linda Knose, Tim Osborn, Staci Somers, Mark Walchle

Printed in the United States of America
98 99 00 • 10 9 8 7 6 5 4 3 2 1

Library of Congress Cataloging-in-Publication Data

International Standard Book Number: 1-57169-131-6

Dedication

To my colleagues and students at the College of Marin, with whom it is a pleasure to work.

—*Stephen Prata*

About the Author

Stephen Prata teaches astronomy, physics, and computer science at the College of Marin in Kentfield, California. He received his B.S. from the California Institute of Technology and his Ph.D. from the University of California, Berkeley. Stephen has authored or coauthored over a dozen books for The Waite Group, including *Artificial Life Playhouse* and *Certified Course in Visual Basic 4*. He also wrote The Waite Group's *New C Primer Plus*, which received the Computer Press Association's 1990 Best How-to Computer Book Award and The Waite Group's *C++ Primer Plus*, nominated for the Computer Press Association's Best How-to Computer Book Award in 1991.

Contents

Table of Contents

Acknowledgments to the Third Edition

I'd like to thank Executive Editor Susan Walton for helping get the third edition started, Mitchell Waite for choosing this book to be part of the Signature Series, Project Editor Andrea Rosenberg for managing the project, Dan Scherf for coordinating the contents of the CD, and Russ Jacobs for his content and technical editing. From Metrowerks, I'd like to thank Dave Mark, Alex Harper, and especially Ron Liechty, for their help and cooperation.

Acknowledgments to the Second Edition

I'd like to thank Mitchell Waite and Scott Calamar for supporting a second edition and Joel Fugazzotto and Joanne Miller for guiding the project to completion. Thanks to Michael Marcotty of Metrowerks for dealing with my questions about their beta version CodeWarrior compiler. I'd also like to thank the following instructors for taking the time to give us feedback on the first edition: Jeff Buckwalter, Earl Brynner, Mike Holland, Andy Yao, Larry Sanders, Shahin Momtazi, and Don Stephens. Finally, I wish to thank Heidi Brumbaugh for her helpful content editing of new and revised material.

Acknowledgments to the First Edition

Many people have contributed to this book. In particular, I wish to thank Mitch Waite for his work in developing, shaping, and reshaping this book, and for reviewing the manuscript. I appreciate Harry Henderson's work in reviewing the last few chapters and in testing programs with the Zortech C++ compiler. Thanks to David Gerrold for reviewing the entire manuscript and for championing the needs of less experienced readers. Also, thanks to Hank Shiffman for testing programs using Sun C++ and to Kent Williams for testing programs with AT&T cfront and with G++. Thanks to Nan Borreson of Borland International for her responsive and cheerful assistance with Turbo C++ and Borland C++. Thank you, Ruth Myers and Christine Bush, for handling the relentless paper flow involved with this kind of project. Finally, thanks to Scott Calamar for keeping everything on track.

Preface to the Third Edition

Learning C++ is an adventure of discovery, particularly because C++ is a moving target. Since the second edition of this book, the C++ language has continued to evolve under the guidance of the ISO/ANSI committee, and it has continued to mature as programmers explore the language's features. But now the proposed C++ standard is nearly in place, and no further major changes are expected for a while. Thus, it is a good time to summarize the state of the language, and that is the goal of this third edition of *C++ Primer Plus*.

The main changes in content are these:

- The book reflects changes in and additions to the language since the previous edition, including the expanding role of templates and generic programming.

- A new chapter explores the `string` class and the Standard Template Library (STL). One of the main thrusts of C++ is reusable code, and these class libraries provide useful and efficient examples.

- Some of the discussions have been revised to further simplify and clarify the presentation of ideas.

There also are two significant production changes:

- The book includes a CD with source code for all the examples and limited editions of the Metrowerks CodeWarrior Lite compilers for Macintosh and for Windows.

- The book has ascended to *Mitchell Waite Signature Series* status, enhancing its production values.

Like the previous editions, this book practices generic C++ so that it is not tied to any particular kind of computer, operating system, or compiler. All the programs were tested with CodeWarrior Pro 2 (Macintosh and Windows) and Microsoft Visual C++ 5.0, and most were tested with Borland C++Builder 1.0, Symantic C++ 8.0, Release 5 for the Macintosh, Watcom C++ 10.6 for IBM PC compatibles, and Gnu g++ 2.7.1 running under Linux. None of the implementations were completely consistent with the proposed standard, but that state of affairs is to be expected, at least until the standard is set forth in final form.

C++ offers a lot to the programmer; have fun as you harvest its riches!

Preface to the Second Edition

Learning C++ is not a simple task. Not only is it a very full-featured language, but it also supports a programming style (object-oriented programming) that may require you to learn new ways of thinking about programming. Furthermore, C++ has rules of practice that aren't built into the language. For example, to use the language feature called inheritance correctly, you have to learn the proper language rules so that the compiler will accept your program, but you also have to learn conceptual rules about when it is and isn't appropriate to use inheritance. Also, C++ is a moving target, and it has evolved significantly since the first edition of this book.

This book aims to make learning C++ manageable, even pleasurable. It follows the precepts outlined in the Preface to the First Edition. In addition, the new edition does the following:

- It presents additions to C++, such as templates, exceptions, RTTI, and namespaces.

- It tracks changes in C++, such as in the rules governing reference arguments.

- It reflects the developing draft ANSI/ISO C++ standard.

- It provides more conceptual guidance about when to use particular features, such as using public inheritance to model what are known as *is-a* relationships.

- It illustrates common C++ programming idioms and techniques.

- It has programming exercises at the end of each chapter to provide practice in applying new ideas.

- It devotes greater attention to organizing and explaining C++ classes, dividing the original presentation into more chapters, and revising and expanding the discussion.

Like the first edition, this book practices generic C++. That means you should be able to use it with any contemporary C++ implementation. Towards that end we tested the examples with a variety of compilers, including Borland C++ 3.1, Borland C++ 4.0, GNU C++ 2.0, Metrowerks CodeWarrior CW 3.5, Microsoft Visual C++ 1.0, Symantec C++ 6.0 (PC), and Symantec C++ 7.0 (Mac). Ideally, C++ is C++ is C++, but compilers do differ in how closely they track the draft standard. For example, many of these compilers don't yet support templates or exceptions; naturally, they won't run examples using those features. Aside from that, however, we ran into only a few minor differences, which the book notes. In general, C++ implementations are more consistent with each other now than they were at the time of the first edition, which is good news for programmers.

Learn and enjoy!

Preface to the First Edition

When the Waite Group first released *C Primer Plus* in 1984, the C language had been around for about a decade but was just beginning to boom. We take pride in the important role that our book played in introducing programmers to C. Today the C++ language, which derives from C, has reached a similar stage in its evolution. It's booming because it offers a new paradigm—object-oriented programming, or OOP—well-suited to modern programming needs. Thus, AT&T is rewriting UNIX in C++ because C++ improves the reliability, maintainability, and reusability of the code. Apple is using C++ to develop system software for its Macintosh line for the same reasons and because OOP techniques are a natural match to program features such as windows and dialog boxes. Individual programmers are turning to C++ because its new features bring the thrill back to programming. Naturally, it's time to release *C++ Primer Plus* and help this new boom along.

One difference between now and then is that many more books have been written about C++ than were written about C when it was new. However, none of the new C++ books plays the role that a Waite Group "primer" does. Many C++ books assume that you already know C and know it well. That's of little help to those who wish to move to C++ from, say, Pascal or BASIC, or to those who have enjoyed C recreationally without acquiring expert status. Most of the other C++ books present the full language, not just the new elements, but still assume you are fairly knowledgeable in C and in programming in general. Some C++ books make excellent references but can be rather tough sledding for learning the language. A few C++ titles were rushed out the door. They merely tack on a few new chapters to an old C book and don't fully integrate the new material or really do justice to C++'s exciting new object-oriented features.

Enter The Waite Group's *C++ Primer Plus*. We don't assume you know C, and we integrate discussing the basic C language with presenting the C++ features. We do assume you've had some programming experience, but we don't skip over the basics. We've tried to present C++ in a book instilled with traditional Waite Group primer virtues:

- A primer should be an easy-to-use, friendly guide.

- A primer doesn't assume that you already are familiar with all relevant programming concepts.

- A primer emphasizes hands-on learning with brief, easily typed examples that develop your understanding a concept or two at a time.

- A primer clarifies concepts with illustrations.

- A primer provides exercises to let you test your understanding, making the book suitable for self-learning or for the classroom.

C++ Primer Plus presents C++ fundamentals and illustrates them with short, to-the-point programs that are easy to copy and to experiment with. The book is not intended to provide encyclopedic coverage of all features and nuances of the C++ language, but it does present the most important aspects while laying the foundation for further study. You'll learn about input and output, how to make programs perform repetitive tasks and make choices, the many ways to handle data, and how to use functions. You'll learn about the important object-oriented programming concepts of information hiding (lots of fun), polymorphism (not as bad as it sounds), and inheritance. Besides learning basic techniques, you'll learn about the OOP philosophy. Meanwhile, we'll do our best to keep the presentation short, simple, and fun. Our goal is that by the end you'll be able to write solid, effective programs and enjoy yourself doing so.

Note to Instructors

One of the goals of the third edition is to provide a book that can be used either as a teach-yourself book or as a textbook. Here are some of the features that support using *C++ Primer Plus,* Third Edition as a textbook:

- This book describes generic C++, so it isn't dependent upon some particular implementation.

- The contents track the ISO/ANSI C++ standards committee's work and include discussions of templates, the Standard Template Library, the `string` class, exceptions, RTTI, and namespaces.

- It doesn't assume prior knowledge of C, so it can be used without a C prerequisite. (Some programming background is desirable, however.)

- Topics are arranged so that the early chapters can be covered rapidly as review chapters for courses that do have a C prerequisite.

- Chapters have review questions and programming exercises.

- The book introduces several topics appropriate for computer science courses, including abstract data types, stacks, queues, simple lists, simulations, generic programming, and using recursion to implement a divide-and-conquer strategy.

- Most chapters are short enough to cover in a week or less.

- The book discusses *when* to use certain features as well as *how* to use them. For example, it links public inheritance to *is-a* relationships and composition and private inheritance to *has-a* relationships, and it discusses when to use virtual functions and when not to.

How This Book Is Organized

This book is divided into 16 chapters and 9 appendices summarized here.

Chapter 1: Getting Started

This chapter relates how Bjarne Stroustrup created the C++ programming language by adding object-oriented programming support to the C language. You'll learn the distinctions between procedural languages, such as C, and object-oriented languages, such as C++. You'll read about the joint ANSI/ISO work to develop a C++ standard. The chapter discusses the mechanics of creating a C++ program, outlining the approach for several current C++ compilers. Finally, it describes the conventions used in this book.

Chapter 2: Setting Out to C++

Chapter 2 guides you through the process of creating simple C++ programs. You'll learn about the role of the main() function and about some of the kinds of statements that C++ programs use. You'll use the predefined cout and cin objects for program output and input, and you'll learn about creating and using variables. Finally, you'll be introduced to functions, C++'s programming modules.

Chapter 3: Dealing with Data

C++ provides built-in types for storing two kinds of data: integers (numbers with no fractional parts) and floating-point numbers (numbers with fractional parts). To meet the diverse requirements of programmers, C++ offers several types in each category. This chapter discusses these types, including creating variables and writing constants of various types. You'll also learn how C++ handles implicit and explicit conversions from one type to another.

Chapter 4: Derived Types

C++ lets you construct more elaborate types from the basic built-in types. The most advanced form is the class, discussed in Chapters 9, 10, 11, 12, and 13. This chapter discusses other forms, including arrays, which hold several values of a single type, structures, which hold several values of unlike types, and pointers, which identify locations in memory. You'll also learn how to create and store text strings and to handle text input and output. Finally, you'll learn some of the ways C++ handles memory allocation, including the `new` and `delete` operators for managing memory explicitly.

Chapter 5: Loops and Relational Expressions

Programs often need to perform repetitive actions, and C++ provides three looping structures for that purpose: the `for` loop, the `while` loop, and the `do while` loop. Such loops need to know when they should terminate, and the C++ relational operators enable you to create tests to guide such loops. You'll also learn how to create loops that read and process input character-by-character. Finally, you'll learn how to create two-dimensional arrays and how to use nested loops to process them.

Chapter 6: Branching Statements and Logical Operators

Programs can behave intelligently if they can tailor their behavior to circumstances. In this chapter you'll learn how to control program flow by using the `if`, `if else`, and `switch` statements and the conditional operator. You'll learn how to use logical operators to help express decision-making tests. Also, you'll meet the `cctype` library of functions for evaluating character relations, such as testing whether a character is a digit or a nonprinting character.

Chapter 7: Functions—C++'s Programming Modules

Functions are the basic building blocks of C++ programs. This chapter concentrates on features that C++ functions share with C functions. In particular, you'll review the general format of a function definition and examine how function prototypes increase the reliability of programs. Also, you'll investigate how to write functions to process arrays, character strings, and structures. Next you'll learn about recursion, which is when a function calls itself, and see how it can be used to implement a divide-and-conquer strategy. Finally, you'll meet pointers to functions, which enable you to use a function argument to tell one function to use a second function.

Chapter 8: Adventures in Functions

This chapter explores the new features C++ adds to functions. You'll learn about inline functions, which can speed program execution at the cost of additional program size. You'll work with reference variables, which provide an alternative way to pass information to functions. Default arguments let a function automatically supply values for function arguments that you omit from a function call. Function overloading lets you create functions having the same name but taking different argument lists. All these features have frequent use in class design. Also, you'll learn about function templates, which allow you to specify the design of a family of related functions. You'll learn about putting together multifile programs. Finally, you'll examine storage classes, scope, linkage, and namespaces, which determine what parts of a program know about a variable.

Chapter 9: Objects and Classes

A class is a user-defined type, and an object is an instance of a class, such as a variable. This chapter introduces you to object-oriented programming and to class design. A class declaration describes the information stored in a class object and also the operations (class methods) allowed for class objects. Some parts of an object are visible to the outside world (the public portion), and some are hidden (the private portion). Special class methods (constructors and destructors) come into play when objects are created and destroyed. You will learn about all this and other class details in this chapter, and you'll see how classes can be used to implement abstract data types (ADTs), such as a stack.

Chapter 10: Working with Classes

In this chapter you'll further your understanding of classes. First, you'll learn about operator overloading, which lets you define how operators such as + will work with class objects. You'll learn about friend functions, which can access class data that's inaccessible to the world at large. You'll see how certain constructors and overloaded operator member functions can be used to manage conversion to and from class types.

Chapter 11: Classes and Dynamic Memory Allocation

Often it's useful to have a class member point to dynamically allocated memory. If you use new in a class constructor to allocate dynamic memory, you incur the responsibilities of providing an appropriate destructor, of defining an explicit copy constructor, and of defining an explicit assignment operator. This chapter shows you how and discusses the behavior of the member functions generated implicitly if you fail to provide explicit definitions. You'll also expand your experience with classes by using pointers to objects and studying a queue simulation problem.

Chapter 12: Class Inheritance

One of the most powerful features of object-oriented programming is inheritance, by which a derived class inherits the features of a base class, enabling you to reuse the base class code. This chapter discusses public inheritance, which models *is-a* relationships, meaning that a derived object is a special case of a base object. For instance, a physicist is a special case of a scientist. Implementing *is-a* relationships necessitates using a new kind of member function called a virtual function. This chapter discusses these matters, pointing out when public inheritance is appropriate and when it is not.

Chapter 13: Reusing Code in C++

Public inheritance is just one way to reuse code. This chapter looks at several other ways. Containment is when one class contains members that are objects of another class. It can be used to model *has-a* relationships, in which one class has components of another class. For instance, an automobile has a motor. You also can use private and protected inheritance to model such relationships. This chapter shows you how and points out the differences among the different approaches. Also, you'll learn about class templates, which let you define a class in terms of some unspecified generic type, then use the template to create specific classes in terms of specific types. For instance, a stack template enables you to create a stack of integers or a stack of strings. Finally, you'll learn about multiple public inheritance, whereby a class can derive from more than one class.

Chapter 14: Friends, Exceptions, and More

This chapter extends the discussion of friends to include friend classes and friend member functions. Then it presents several new developments in C++, beginning with exceptions, which provide a mechanism for dealing with unusual program occurrences, such as inappropriate function argument values or running out of memory. Then you'll learn about RTTI (runtime type information), a mechanism for identifying object types. Finally, you'll learn about the safer alternatives to unrestricted type-casting.

Chapter 15: The `string` Class and the Standard Template Library

This chapter discusses some useful class libraries recently added to the language. The `string` class is a convenient and powerful alternative to traditional C-style strings. The `auto_ptr` class helps manage dynamically allocated memory. The Standard Template Library (STL) provides several generic containers, including template representations of arrays, queues, lists, sets, and maps. It also provides an efficient library of generic algorithms that can be used with STL containers and also with ordinary arrays.

Chapter 16: Input, Output, and Files

This chapter reviews C++ I/O and discusses how to format output. You'll learn how to use class methods to determine the state of an input or output stream and to see, for example, if there has been a type mismatch on input or if end-of-file has been detected. C++ uses inheritance to derive classes for managing file input and output. You'll learn how to open files for input and output, how to append data to a file, how to use binary files, and how to get random access to a file. Finally, you'll learn how to apply standard I/O methods to read from and write to strings.

Appendix A: Number Bases

This appendix discusses octal, hexadecimal, and binary numbers.

Appendix B: C++ Keywords

This appendix lists C++ keywords.

Appendix C: The ASCII Character Set

This appendix lists the ASCII character set along with decimal, octal, hexadecimal, and binary representations.

Appendix D: Operator Precedence

This appendix lists the C++ operators in order of decreasing precedence.

Appendix E: Other Operators

This appendix summarizes those C++ operators, such as the bitwise operators, not covered in the main body of the text.

Appendix F: The `string` Template Class

This appendix summarizes `string` class methods and functions.

Appendix G: The STL Methods and Functions

This appendix summarizes the STL container methods and the general STL algorithm functions.

Appendix H: Selected Readings

This appendix lists some books that can further your understanding of C++.

Appendix I: Answers to Review Questions

This appendix contains the answers to the review questions posed at the end of each chapter.

1

Getting Started

Welcome to C++! This exciting language, which blends the C language with support for object-oriented programming, has become one of the most important programming languages of the 1990s and promises to continue strongly into the 2000s. Its C ancestry brings to C++ the tradition of an efficient, compact, fast, and portable language. Its object-oriented heritage brings C++ a fresh programming methodology designed to cope with the escalating complexity of modern programming tasks. Its newly enhanced template features bring yet another new programming methodology, generic programming. This triple heritage is both a blessing and a bane. It makes the language very powerful, but it also means there's more to learn.

In this chapter we'll explore C++'s background further and then go over some of the ground rules for creating C++ programs. The rest of the book teaches you to use the C++ language, from the modest basics of the language to the glory of object-oriented programming (OOP) and its supporting cast of new jargon—objects, classes, encapsulation, data hiding, polymorphism, and inheritance—on to its support of generic programming. (Of course, as you learn C++, these terms will be transformed from buzzwords to the necessary vocabulary of cultivated discourse.)

You will learn about the following in this chapter:

- How C++ adds object-oriented concepts to the C language

- How C++ adds generic programming concepts to the C language

- The history and philosophy of C

- Procedural versus object-oriented programming

- The history and philosophy of C++
- Programming language standards
- The mechanics of creating a program
- Conventions used in this book

Learning C++

C++ joins three separate programming traditions: the procedural language tradition, represented by C; the object-oriented language tradition, represented by the class enhancements C++ adds to C; and generic programming, supported by C++ templates. This chapter will look into those traditions shortly. But first, let's consider what this heritage implies about learning C++. One reason to use C++ is to avail yourself of its object-oriented features. To do so, you need a sound background in standard C, for that language provides the basic types, operators, control structures, and syntax rules. So, if you already know C, you're poised to learn C++. But it's not just a matter of learning a few more keywords and constructs. Going from C to C++ involves about as much work as learning C in the first place. Also, if you know C, you must unlearn some programming habits as you make the transition to C++. If you don't know C, you must master the C components, the OOP components, and the generic components to learn C++, but at least you might not have to unlearn programming habits. If you are beginning to think that learning C++ may involve some mind-stretching effort on your part, you're right. This book will guide you through the process in a clear, helpful manner, one step at a time, so the mind stretching will be sufficiently gentle to leave your brain resilient.

C++ Primer Plus approaches C++ by teaching both its C basis and its new components, so this book assumes you have no prior knowledge of C. You'll start by learning the features C++ shares with C. Even if you know C, you may find this part of the book a good review. Also, it points out concepts that will become important later, and it indicates where C++ differs from C. After you are well-founded in the basics of C, you'll add the C++ superstructure. At this point you'll learn about objects and classes and how C++ implements them. And you will learn about templates.

This book is not intended to be a complete C++ reference; it won't explore every nook and cranny of the language. But you will learn all the major features of the language, including some, like templates, exceptions, and namespaces, that are recent additions.

Now let's take a brief look at some of C++'s background.

A Little History

Computer technology has evolved at an amazing rate during the last few decades. Today a laptop computer can compute faster and store more information than the mainframe computers of 40 years ago. (Quite a few programmers can recall bearing offerings of decks of punched cards to be submitted to a mighty, room-filling computer system with a majestic 100KB of memory—not enough memory to run a good personal computer game today.) Computer languages have evolved, too. The changes might not be as dramatic, but they are important. Bigger, more powerful computers spawn bigger, more complex programs which, in turn, raise new problems in program management and maintenance.

In the 1970s, languages like C and Pascal helped usher in an era of structured programming, a philosophy that brought some order and discipline to a field badly in need of these qualities. Besides providing the tools for structured programming, C also produced compact, fast-running programs along with the capability to address hardware matters, such as managing communication ports and disk drives. These gifts helped make C the dominant programming language in the 1980s. Meanwhile, the 1980s witnessed the growth of a new programming paradigm: object-oriented programming, or OOP, as embodied in languages such as Smalltalk and C++. Let's examine these two developments (C and OOP) a bit more closely.

THE C LANGUAGE

In the early 1970s, Dennis Ritchie of Bell Laboratories was working on a project to develop the UNIX operating system. (An *operating system* is a set of programs that manages a computer's resources and handles its interactions with users. For example, it's the operating system that puts the system prompt onscreen and that runs programs for you.) For this work Ritchie needed a language that was concise, that produced compact, fast programs, and that could control hardware efficiently. Traditionally, programmers met these needs by using assembly language, which is closely tied to a computer's internal machine language. However, assembly language is a *low-level* language; that is, it is specific to a particular computer processor. So if you want to move an assembly program to a different kind of computer, you may have to completely rewrite the program using a different assembly language. It was a bit as if each time you bought a new car, you found that the designers decided to change where the controls went and what they did, forcing you to relearn how to drive. But UNIX was intended to work on a variety of computer types (or *platforms*). That suggested using a high-level language. A *high-level* language is oriented toward problem-solving instead of toward specific hardware. Special programs called *compilers* translate a high-level language to the internal language of a particular computer. Thus, you can use the same high-level language program on different platforms by using a separate compiler for each platform. Ritchie wanted a language that combined low-level efficiency and hardware access with high-level generality and portability. So, building from older languages, he created C.

C PROGRAMMING PHILOSOPHY

Because C++ grafts a new programming philosophy onto C, we should first take a look at the older philosophy that C follows. In general, computer languages deal with two concepts—data and algorithms. The data constitute the information a program uses and processes. The algorithms are the methods the program uses (see Figure 1.1). C, like most mainstream languages to date, is a *procedural* language. That means it emphasizes the algorithm side of programming. Conceptually, procedural programming consists of figuring out the actions a computer should take and then using the programming language to implement those actions. A program prescribes a set of procedures for the computer to follow to produce a particular outcome, much as a recipe prescribes a set of procedures for a cook to follow to produce a cake.

Earlier procedural languages, such as FORTRAN and BASIC, ran into organizational problems as programs grew larger. For example, programs often use branching statements, which route execution to one or another set of instructions depending upon the result of some sort of test. Many older programs had such tangled routing (called "spaghetti programming") that it was virtually impossible to understand a program by reading it, and modifying such a program was an invitation to disaster. In response, computer scientists developed a more disciplined style of programming called *structured programming*. C includes features to facilitate this approach. For instance, structured programming limits branching (choosing which instruction to do next) to a small set of

FIGURE 1.1
Data + algorithms = program

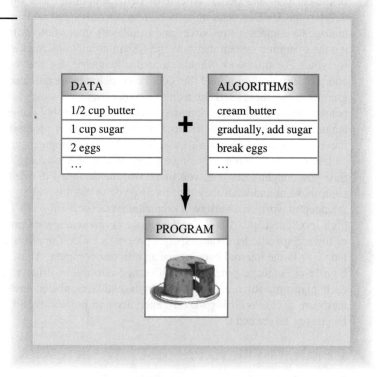

well-behaved constructions. C incorporates these constructions (the for loop, the while loop, the do while loop, and the if else statement) into its vocabulary.

Top-down design was another of the new principles. The idea is to break a large program into smaller, more manageable tasks. If one of these tasks is still too broad, divide it into yet smaller tasks. Continue with this process until the program is compartmentalized into small, easily programmed modules. (Organize your study. Aargh! Well, organize your desk, your table top, your filing cabinet, and your bookshelves. Aargh! Well, start with the desk and organize each drawer, starting with the middle one. Hmmm, perhaps I can manage that task.) C's design facilitates this approach, encouraging you to develop program units called *functions* to represent individual task modules. As you may have noticed, the structured programming techniques reflect a procedural mind-set, thinking of a program in terms of the actions it performs.

OBJECT-ORIENTED PROGRAMMING

Although the principles of structured programming improved the clarity, reliability, and ease of maintenance of programs, large-scale programming still remains a challenge. *Object-oriented programming* (OOP) brings a new approach to that challenge. Unlike procedural programming, which emphasizes algorithms, OOP emphasizes the data. Rather than trying to fit a problem to the procedural approach of a language, OOP attempts to fit the language to the problem. The idea is to design data forms that correspond to the essential features of a problem.

In C++, a *class* is a specification describing such a new data form, and an *object* is a particular data structure constructed according to that plan. For instance, a class could describe the general properties of a corporation executive (name, title, salary, unusual abilities, for example), while an object would represent a specific executive (Guilford Sheepblat, vice president, $325,000, knows how to use a CONFIG.SYS file). In general, a class defines what data are used to represent an object *and* the operations that can be performed upon that data. For example, suppose you were developing a computer drawing program capable of drawing a rectangle. You could define a class to describe a rectangle. The data part of the specification could include such things as the location of the corners, the height and width, the color and style of the boundary line, and the color and pattern used to fill the rectangle. The operations part of the specification could include methods for moving the rectangle, resizing it, rotating it, changing colors and patterns, and copying the rectangle to another location. If you then use your program to draw a rectangle, it will create an object according to the class specification. That object will hold all the data values describing the rectangle, and you can use the class methods to modify that rectangle. If you draw two rectangles, the program will create two objects, one for each rectangle.

The OOP approach to program design is to first design classes that accurately represent those things with which the program deals. A drawing program, for example, might define classes to represent rectangles, lines, circles, brushes, pens, and the like. The class definitions, recall, include a description of permissible operations for each class, such as moving a circle or rotating a line. Then you proceed to design a program using objects of those classes. The process of going from a lower level of organization, such as classes, to a higher level, such as program design, is called *bottom-up* programming.

There's more to OOP programming than the binding of data and methods into a class definition. OOP, for example, facilitates creating reusable code, and that eventually can save a lot of work. Information hiding safeguards data from improper access. Polymorphism lets you create multiple definitions for operators and functions, with the programming context determining which definition is used. Inheritance lets you derive new classes from old ones. As you can see, object-oriented programming introduces many new ideas and involves a different approach to programming than does procedural programming. Instead of concentrating on tasks, you concentrate on representing concepts. Instead of taking a top-down programming approach, you sometimes take a bottom-up approach. This book will guide you through all these points with plenty of easily grasped examples.

Designing a useful, reliable class can be a difficult task. Fortunately, OOP languages make it simple to incorporate existing classes into your own programming. Vendors provide a variety of useful class libraries, including libraries of classes designed to simplify creating programs for environments such as Windows or the Macintosh. One of the real benefits of C++ is that it lets you easily reuse and adapt existing, well-tested code.

GENERIC PROGRAMMING

Generic programming is yet another programming paradigm supported by C++. It shares with OOP the aim of making it simpler to reuse code and the technique of abstracting general concepts. But whereas OOP emphasizes the data aspect of programming, generic programming emphasizes the algorithmic aspect. And its focus is different. OOP is a tool for managing large projects, whereas generic programming provides tools for performing common tasks, such as sorting data or merging lists. The term *generic* means to create code that is type-independent. C++ data comes in many types—integers, numbers with fractional parts, characters, strings of characters, user-defined compound structures of several types. If, for example, you wanted to sort data of these various types, you normally must create a separate sorting function for each type. Generic programming involves extending the language so that you can write a function for a generic (that is, not specified) type once, and use it for a variety of actual types. C++ templates provide a mechanism for doing that.

C++

Like C, C++ began its life at Bell Labs, where Bjarne Stroustrup developed the language in the early 1980s. In his own words, "C++ was designed primarily so that my friends and I would not have to program in assembler, C, or various modern high-level languages. Its main purpose was to make writing good programs easier and more pleasant for the individual programmer" (Bjarne Stroustrup, *The C++ Programming Language*. Third Edition. Reading, MA: Addison-Wesley Publishing Company, 1997).

Stroustrup was more concerned with making C++ useful than with enforcing particular programming philosophies or styles. Real programming needs are more important than theoretical purity in determining language features. Stroustrup based C++ on C because of C's brevity, its suitability to system programming, its widespread availability, and its close ties to the UNIX operating system. C++'s OOP aspect was inspired by a computer simulation language called Simula67. Stroustrup added OOP features to C without significantly changing the C component. Thus, C++ is a superset of C, meaning that any valid C program is a valid C++ program, too. There are some minor discrepancies, but nothing crucial. C++ programs can use existing C software libraries. *Libraries* are collections of programming modules that you can call up from a program. They provide proven solutions to many common programming problems, thus saving you much time and effort. This has helped the spread of C++.

The name C++ comes from the C increment operator ++, which adds 1 to the value of a variable. The name C++ correctly suggests an augmented version of C.

A computer program translates a real-life problem into a series of actions to be taken by a computer. While the OOP aspect of C++ gives the language the capability to relate to concepts involved in the problem, the C part of C++ gives the language the capability to get close to the hardware (see Figure 1.2). This combination of capabilities has helped the spread of C++. It may also involve a mental shift of gears as you turn from one aspect of a program to another. (Indeed, some OOP purists regard adding OOP features to C as akin to adding wings to a pig, albeit a lean, efficient pig.) Also, because C++ grafts OOP onto C, you can ignore C++'s object-oriented features. But you'll miss a lot if that's all you do.

Only after C++ achieved some success did Stroustrup add templates, enabling generic programming. And only after the template feature had been used and enhanced did it become apparent that they were perhaps as significant an addition as OOP—or even more significant, some would argue. The fact that C++ incorporates both OOP and generic programming demonstrates that C++ emphasizes the utilitarian over the ideological approach, and that is one of the reasons for the language's success.

FIGURE 1.2
C++ duality

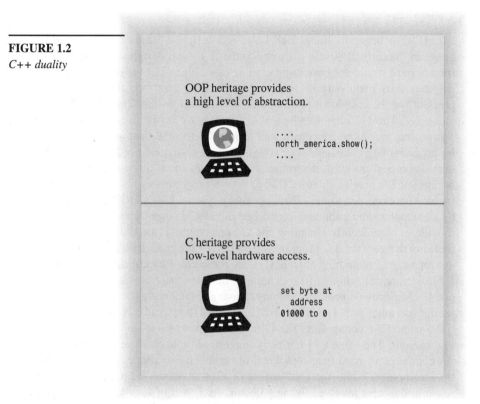

OOP heritage provides
a high level of abstraction.

```
....
north_america.show();
....
```

C heritage provides
low-level hardware access.

```
set byte at
address
01000 to 0
```

Portability and Standards

You've written a handy C++ program for the elderly 286 PC AT computer at work when management decides to replace the machine with a Sun workstation, a computer using a different processor and a different operating system. Can you run your program on the new platform? Of course, you'll have to recompile the program using a C++ compiler designed for the new platform. But will you have to make any changes to the code you wrote? If you can recompile the program without making changes and it runs without a hitch, we say the program is *portable*.

There are a couple of obstacles to portability, the first of which is hardware. A program that is hardware-specific is not likely to be portable. One that takes direct control of an IBM PC VGA video board, for instance, will be speaking gibberish as far as a Sun is concerned. We will avoid that sort of programming in this book. (The Waite Group's *Object-Oriented Programming in C++*, Second Edition, by Robert Lafore covers more hardware-specific issues.)

The second obstacle to portability is language divergence. Certainly, that can be a problem with spoken languages. A Yorkshireman's description of the day's events may not be portable to Brooklyn, even though English is spoken in both areas. Computer languages, too, can develop dialects. Is the IBM PC C++ implementation the same as the Sun implementation? Although most implementers would like to make their versions of C++ compatible with others, it's difficult to do so without a published standard describing exactly how the language works. Therefore, the American National Standards Institute (ANSI) created a committee in 1990 (ANSI X3J16) to develop a standard for C++. (ANSI already has developed a standard for C.) The International Standards Organization (ISO) soon joined the process with its own committee (ISO-WG-21), so now there is a joint ANSI/ISO effort to develop the C++ standard. These committees meet jointly three times a year, and we'll simply lump them together notationally as the ANSI/ISO committee. ANSI/ISO's decision to create a standard emphasizes that C++ has become an important and widespread language. It also indicates C++ has reached a certain level of maturity, for it's not productive to introduce standards while a language is developing rapidly. Nonetheless, C++ has undergone significant changes since the committee began its work.

Work on the ANSI/ISO C++ standard began in 1990. The committee issued some interim working papers in the following years. In April 1995 it released a Committee Draft (CD) for public comment. In December 1996 it released a second version (CD2) for further public review. These documents not only refined the description of existing C++ features but also extended the language with exceptions, RTTI, templates, and the Standard Template Library. The interim working papers and committee drafts often were referred to as the "draft standard," but the first document officially entitled to that label is the Final Draft International Standard (FDIS), issued November 1997. At the time of this writing, the final International Standard (IS) is expected to be ratified by March 1998. This book is based primarily on the CD2, which is very close to the FDIS. Differences between the FDIS and IS, in turn, should just be in the nature of corrections, not addition or alteration of features.

The ANSI/ISO C++ standard additionally draws upon the ANSI C standard, because C++ is supposed to be, as far as possible, a superset of C. That means any valid C program ideally should also be a valid C++ program. There are a few differences between ANSI C and the corresponding rules for C++, but they are minor. Indeed, ANSI C incorporates some features first introduced in C++, such as function prototyping and the const type qualifier.

Prior to the emergence of ANSI C, the C community followed a de facto standard based on the book *The C Programming Language*, by Kernighan and Ritchie (Addison-Wesley Publishing Company, Reading, MA, 1978). This standard often was termed K&R C; with the emergence of ANSI C, the simpler K&R C now sometimes is called *classic C*.

The ANSI C standard not only defines the C language, it also defines a standard C library that ANSI C implementations must support. C++ also uses that library; this book will refer to it as the standard C library or the standard library. In addition, the ANSI/ISO C++ committee has provided a standard library of C++ classes.

Before the ANSI/ISO committee began its work, many people accepted the most recent Bell Labs version of C++ as a standard. For example, a compiler might describe itself as compatible with Release 2.0 or Release 3.0 of C++.

Before getting to the C++ language proper, let's cover some of the groundwork about creating programs and about using this book.

The Mechanics of Creating a Program

Suppose you've written a C++ program. How do you get it running? The exact steps depend upon your computer environment and the particular C++ compiler you use, but they will resemble the following steps (see Figure 1.3):

- Use a text editor of some sort to write the program and save it in a file. This file constitutes the *source code* for your program.

- Compile the source code. This means running a program that translates the source code to the internal language, called *machine language,* used by the host computer. The file containing the translated program is the *object code* for your program.

- Link the object code with additional code. C++ programs, for example, normally use *libraries.* A C++ library contains object code for a collection of computer routines, called *functions,* to perform tasks such as displaying information on the screen or calculating the square root of a number. Linking combines your object code with object code for the functions you use and with some standard startup code to produce a runnable version of your program. The file containing this final product is called the *executable code.*

You will encounter the term *source code* throughout the book, so be sure to file it away in your personal random-access memory.

The programs in this book are generic and should run in any system supporting modern C++. (However, at the time of this writing, many compilers don't support all features. For instance, only some support namespaces and the newest template features.) The steps for putting a program together may differ. Let's look a little further at these steps.

CREATING THE SOURCE CODE

Some C++ implementations, such as Microsoft Visual C++, Borland C++ (various versions), Watcom C++, Symantec C++, and Metrowerks CodeWarrior, provide *integrated development environments (IDEs)* that let you manage all steps of program development, including editing, from one master program. Other implementations, such as AT&T C++ or GNU C++ on UNIX and Linux, just handle the compilation and linking stages and expect you to type commands on the system command line. In such cases, you can use any available text editor to create and modify source code. On

FIGURE 1.3

Programming steps

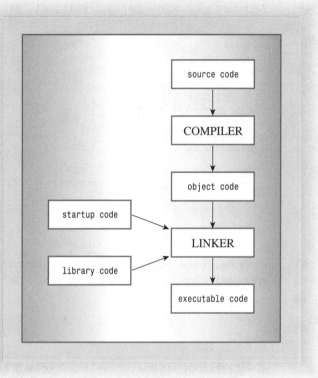

UNIX, for example, you can use vi or ed or ex or emacs. On a DOS system, you can use edlin or edit or any of several available program editors. You can even use a word processor, providing you save the file as a standard DOS ASCII text file instead of in a special word processor format.

In naming a source file, you must use the proper suffix to identify the file as a C++ file. This not only tells you the file is C++ source code, it tells the compiler that, too. (If a UNIX compiler complains to you about a "bad magic number," that's just its endearingly obscure way of saying that you used the wrong suffix.) The suffix consists of a period followed by a character or group of characters called the *extension* (see Figure 1.4).

The extension you use depends on the C++ implementation. Table 1.1 shows some common choices. For example, spiffy.C is a valid AT&T C++ source code file name. Note that UNIX is case sensitive, meaning you should use an uppercase C character. Actually, a lowercase c extension also works, but standard C uses that extension. So, to avoid confusion on UNIX systems, use c with C programs and C with C++ programs. If you don't mind typing an extra character or two, you can also use cc and cxx extensions with some UNIX systems. DOS, being a bit simple-minded compared to

FIGURE 1.4
Source file extension

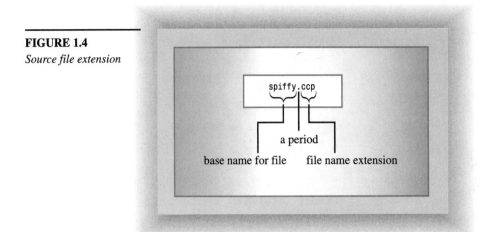

UNIX, doesn't distinguish between uppercase and lowercase, so DOS implementations use additional letters, as shown in Table 1.1, to distinguish between C and C++ programs.

TABLE 1.1
SOURCE CODE EXTENSIONS

C++ IMPLEMENTATION	SOURCE CODE EXTENSION
UNIX AT&T	C, cc, cxx, c
GNU C++	C, cc, cxx, c
Symantec	cpp, cp
Borland C++	cpp
Watcom	cpp
Microsoft Visual C++	cpp, cxx
Metrowerks CodeWarrior	cp, cpp

COMPILATION AND LINKING

Originally, Stroustrup implemented C++ with a C++-to-C compiler program instead of developing a direct C++-to-object code compiler. This program, called `cfront` (for C front end), translated C++ source code to C source code, which could then be compiled by a standard C compiler. This approach simplified introducing C++ to the C community. Other implementations have used this approach to bring C++ to other platforms. As C++ has developed and grown in popularity, more and more implementers have turned to creating C++ compilers that generate object code directly from C++ source code. This direct approach speeds up the compilation process and emphasizes that C++ is a separate, if similar, language.

Often the distinction between a cfront translator and compiler is nearly invisible to the user. For instance, on a UNIX system the CC command may first pass your program to the cfront translator and then automatically pass the translator's output on to the C compiler, which is called cc. Henceforth, we'll use the term *compiler* to include translate-and-compile combinations. The mechanics of compiling depend upon the implementation, and the following sections outline a few common forms. These summaries outline the basic steps, but they are no substitute for consulting the documentation for your system.

UNIX Compiling and Linking

Suppose, for example, that you are on a UNIX system using AT&T Release 3.0 C++. Use the CC command to compile your program. The name is in uppercase letters to distinguish it from the standard UNIX C compiler cc. The CC compiler is a command-line compiler, meaning you type compilation commands on the UNIX command line.

For example, to compile the C++ source code file spiffy.C, you would type this command at the UNIX prompt:

```
CC spiffy.C
```

If, through skill, dedication, or luck, your program has no errors, the compiler generates an object code file with an o extension. In this case, the compiler would produce a spiffy.o file.

Next, the compiler automatically passes the object code file to the system linker, a program that combines your code with library code to produce the executable file. By default, the executable file is called a.out. If you used just one source file, the linker also deletes the spiffy.o file, because it's no longer needed. To run the program, just type the name of the executable file:

```
a.out
```

Note that if you compile a new program, the new a.out executable file replaces the previous a.out. (That's because executable files take a lot of space, so overwriting old executable files helps reduce storage demands.) But if you develop an executable program you want to keep, just use the UNIX mv command to change the name of the executable file.

In C++, as in C, you can spread a program over more than one file. (Many of the programs in this book from Chapters 8 to 16 do this.) In that case, you can compile a program by listing all the files on the command line:

```
CC my.C precious.C
```

If there are multiple source code files, the compiler does not delete the object code files. That way, if you just change the my.C file, you can recompile the program with this command:

```
CC my.C precious.o
```

This recompiles the `my.C` file and links it with the previously compiled `precious.o` file.

You might have to identify some libraries explicitly. For example, to access functions defined in the math library, you might have to add the `-lm` flag to the command line.

```
CC usingmath.C -lm
```

The Free Software Foundation supplies the GNU C++ compiler called g++ that works much like the standard UNIX compiler:

```
g++ spiffy.C
```

Some versions may require that you link in the C++ library:

```
g++ spiffy.C -lg++
```

GNU g++ is available for many platforms, including Linux running on IBM-compatible PCs.

Turbo C++ 2.0 and Borland C++ 3.1 (DOS)

In DOS versions of Turbo C++'s and Borland C++'s integrated environment, which includes a built-in editor, you use a menu bar, accessible through a mouse or through ALT+KEY combinations, to make your desires known. For example, the File menu lets you create, save, and open files. The Edit menu assists in editing your source file. The Compile menu offers several compiling options, and the Run menu presents choices for running the program. After you've used the built-in editor to write a program, the simplest choice is to select Run from the Run menu. This causes Borland C++ or Turbo C++ to compile, link, and run your program. If the compiler catches errors, of course, it won't run the program, but it will display a list of errors and highlight the offending lines in your source code. Also, the integrated environment includes a debugger that lets you step through the program a line at a time and examine any values you want to see.

If you develop a program using more than one source code file, use the Project menu to open a new project. Then you can use further menu options to add the relevant files to a project list. The project file lets Borland C++ or Turbo C++ keep track of what's going on. If you change one of the files in the project list, the compiler knows it should update the executable program. In Borland C++ or Turbo C++ you can have several source code files, each in its own window onscreen simultaneously, and you can easily switch from one file to another.

Both Borland C++ and Turbo C++ come with a tutorial program that shows you the ins and outs of the Borland C++ or Turbo C++ environment. And, of course, you can read the manuals.

Windows Compilers

Windows products are too abundant and too often revised to make it reasonable to describe them all individually. However, they do share some common features.

Typically, you must create a project for a program and add the file or files constituting your program to the project. Each vender will supply an IDE (Integrated Development Environment) with menu options and, possibly, automated assistance in creating a project. One very important matter you have to establish is the kind of program you're creating. Typically, the compiler will offer many choices, such as a Windows application, an MFC Windows application, a dynamic-link library, an ActiveX control, a DOS or character-mode executable, a static library, or a console application. Some of these may be available in both 16-bit and 32-bit versions.

Because the programs in this book are generic, you should avoid choices that require platform-specific code, such as Windows applications. Instead, you want to run in a character-based mode. The choice will depend on the compiler. Some Microsoft versions feature a QuickWin choice that emulates a DOS session; other versions feature a Console option. Some Borland versions feature an EasyWin choice that emulates a DOS session; other versions offer a Console option. In general, look to see whether there is an option labeled Console, character-mode, or DOS executable, and try that.

After you have the project set up, you must compile and link your program. The IDE typically will give you several choices such as Compile, Build, Make, Build All, Link, Execute, and Run (but not necessarily all these choices in the same IDE!).

Compile typically means compile the code in the file currently open.

Build or *Make* typically means compile the code for all the source code files in the project. This typically is an incremental process. That is, if the project has three files, and you change just one, then just that one is recompiled.

Build All typically means compile all the source code files from scratch.

Link means (as described earlier) combine the compiled source code with the necessary library code.

Run or *Execute* means run the program. Typically, if you have not yet done the earlier steps, Run will do them, too, before trying to run a program.

A compiler generates an error message when you violate a language rule and identifies the line with the problem. Unfortunately, when you are new to a language, you may find it difficult to understand the message. Sometimes the actual error may occur before the identified line, and sometimes a single error will generate a chain of error messages.

Remember

When fixing errors, fix the first error first. If you can't find it on the line identified as the line with the error, check the preceding line.

Remember

Occasionally, compilers get confused after incompletely building a program and respond by giving meaningless error messages that cannot be fixed. In such cases, you can clear things up by selecting Build All to restart the process from scratch. Unfortunately, it is difficult to distinguish this situation from the more common one in which the error messages merely seem to be meaningless.

Usually, the IDE will let you run the program in an auxiliary window. Some IDEs close the window as soon as the program finishes execution, some leave it open. If your compiler closes the window, you'll have a hard time seeing the output unless you have quick eyes and a photographic memory. To see the output, you must place some additional code at the end of the program:

```
cin.get();  // add this statement
cin.get();  // and maybe this, too
return 0;
}
```

The cin.get() statement reads the next keystroke, so this statement causes the program to wait until you press the (ENTER) key. (No keystrokes get sent to a program until you press (ENTER), so there's no point in pressing another key.) The second statement is needed if the program otherwise leaves an unprocessed keystroke after its regular input. For example, if you enter a number, you'll type the number and then press (ENTER). The program will read the number but leave the (ENTER) keystroke unprocessed, and it then will be read by the first cin.get().

The Borland C++Builder compiler departs a bit from more traditional designs. Its primary aim is Windows programming. To use it for generic programs, select New from the File menu. Then select Console App. A window will open that includes a skeleton version of main(). Some of the items you can delete, but you should retain the following two non-standard lines:

```
#include <vcl\condefs.h>
#pragma hdrstop
```

Macintosh Compilers

The two best known Macintosh C++ compilers are Metrowerks CodeWarrior and Symantec C++ compiler for the Macintosh. Both provide project-based IDEs similar, in basic concepts, to what you would find in a Windows compiler. (Indeed, both companies offer Windows-based versions of their compilers.) With either product, start by selecting New Project from the File menu. You'll be given a choice of project types. For CodeWarrior, choose MacOS:C/C++:ANSI C++ Console; for Symantec, choose ANSII C++ (Iostreams). You also may have to choose between a 68K version (for the Motorola 680X0 series of processors) or a PowerPC version (for the PowerPC processors).

Both products include a small source code file as part of the initial project. You can try compiling and running that program to see if you have your system set up properly. However, once you provide your own code, you should delete this file from the project. Do so by highlighting the file in the project window and then selecting Remove from the Project menu.

Next, you must add your source code to the project. You can use New from the File menu to create a new file or Open from the File menu to open an existing file. Use a proper suffix, such as .cp or .cpp. Use the Project menu to add this file to the project list. Some programs in this book require that you add more than one source code file. When you are ready, select Run from the Project menu.

Remember

Hint: To save time, you can use just one project for all the sample programs. Delete the previous example source code file from the project list and add the current source code. This saves disk space.

Both compilers include a debugger to help you locate the causes of runtime problems.

Conventions Used in This Book

To help distinguish between different kinds of text, we've used a few typographic conventions. Italic type is used for important words or phrases used for the first time, such as *structured programming*. Monospace type can denote any of the following:

- Names or values used in a program, such as x, starship, and 3.14

- Language keywords, such as int and if else

- Filenames, such as iostream

- Functions, such as main() and puts()

C++ source code is presented as follows:

```
#include <iostream>
using namespace std;
int main()
{
    cout << "What's up, Doc!\n";
    return 0;
}
```

Sample program runs use the same format, except user input appears in boldface:

```
Please enter your name:
Plato
```

You'll find an occasional rule or suggestion in the following format:

Remember

You learn by doing, so try the examples and experiment with them.

By the way, you've just read a real and important suggestion, not just an example of what a rule or suggestion looks like.

Finally, when you enter program input, you normally have to press the RETURN key or the ENTER key to send the input to the program. Some keyboards use one and some the other; this book uses ENTER.

Our System

This book describes the ISO/ANSI CD2 draft definition of C++, so the examples should work with any C++ implementation compatible with that standard. (At least, this is the vision and hope of portability.) However, the C++ standard is still new, and you may find a few discrepancies. For example, at the time of this writing, many C++ compilers lack namespaces or the newest template features. Support for the Standard Template Library described in Chapter 15 is spotty at the time of this writing. Systems that use the Release 2.0 (or later) cfront translator may then pass the translated code to a C compiler that is not fully ANSI compatible, resulting in some language features being left unimplemented and in some standard ANSI library functions and header files not being supported. Also, some things, such as the number of bytes used to hold an integer, are implementation-dependent.

For the record, the examples in this book were developed using Microsoft Visual C++ 5.0 and Metrowerks CodeWarrior Professional Release 1 on a Pentium PC with a hard disk and running under Windows 95. Programs were checked using GNU g++ 2.7.1 on an IBM-compatible 486 running Linux, Watcom 10.6 on a Pentium PC, Metrowerks CodeWarrior Professional Release 1 on a Macintosh 7100 under System 7.5.5 and System 8.0. The book reports discrepancies stemming from lagging behind the standard generically, as in "older implementations use ios::fixed instead of ios_base::fixed." The book reports some bugs and idiosyncrasies that would prove troublesome or confusing; however, these may very well be fixed in subsequent releases.

2

Setting Out to C++

In this chapter you learn

- How to create a C++ program
- The `#include` directive
- The general format for a C++ program
- The `main()` function
- Using the `cout` object for output
- Placing comments in a C++ program
- The newline character `\n`
- Declaring and using variables
- Using the `cin` object for input
- Defining and using simple functions

When you construct a simple home, you begin with the foundation and the framework. If you don't have a solid structure from the beginning, you'll have trouble later filling in the details, such as windows, door frames, observatory domes, and parquet ballrooms. Similarly, when you learn a computer language, you should begin by learning the basic structure for a program. Only then can you move on to the details, such as loops and objects. This chapter gives you an overview of the essential structure of a C++ program and previews some topics—notably functions and classes—that this book covers in much greater detail later. (The idea is to introduce at least some of the basic concepts gradually en route to the great awakenings that come later.)

C++ Initiation

Begin with a simple C++ program that displays a message. Listing 2.1 uses the C++ cout (pronounced cee-out) facility to produce character output. The source code includes several comments to the reader; these lines begin with //, and the compiler ignores them. C++ is *case-sensitive*; that is, it discriminates between uppercase characters and lowercase characters. This means you must be careful to use the same case as in the examples. For instance, this program uses cout. If you substitute Cout or COUT, the compiler rejects your offering and accuses you of using unknown identifiers. (The compiler also is spelling-sensitive, so don't try kout or coot, either.) The cpp filename extension is a common way to indicate a C++ program; you might need to use a different extension, as described in Chapter 1, "Getting Started."

Listing 2.1 myfirst.cpp

```
// myfirst.cpp--displays a message

#include <iostream>                              // a PREPROCESSOR directive
using namespace std;                             // make definitions visible
int main()                                       // function heading
{                                                // start of function body
    cout << "Come up and C++ me some time.";     // message
    cout << "\n";                                // start a new line
    return 0;                                     // terminate main()
}                                                // end of function body
```

Remember

If you're using an older compiler, you might need to use #include <iostream.h> instead of #include <iostream>; in this case, you also would omit the using namespace std; line. That is, replace

```
#include <iostream>      // the way of the future
using namespace std;     // ditto
```

with

```
#include <iostream.h>   // in case the future has not yet
arrived
```

(Some very old compilers use #include <stream.h> instead of #include <iostream.h>; if you have a compiler that old, you should get either a newer compiler or an older book.) The switch from iostream.h to iostream is fairly recent, and, at the time of this writing, many vendors haven't implemented it yet.

Continued...

Remember Continued...

Some windowing environments run the program in a separate window, and then automatically close the window when the program finishes. As discussed in Chapter 1, you can make the window stay open until you strike a key by adding the following line of code before the return statement:

```
cin.get();
```

For some programs you must add two of these lines. You learn what this code does in Chapter 4, "Derived Types."

P R O G R A M   A D J U S T M E N T S

You might find that you must alter the examples in this book to run on your system. The two most common changes are those the first Remember in this chapter mentions. One is a matter of language standards; if your compiler is not up-to-date, you need to include iostream.h instead of iostream and omit the namespace line. The second is a matter of the programming environment; you might need to add one or two cin.get() statements to keep the program output visible onscreen. Because these adjustments apply equally to every example in this book, this Compatibility Note is the only alert to them you get. Don't forget them! Future Compatibility Notes alert you to other possible alterations you might have to make.

After you use your editor of choice to copy this program (or else use the source code file on the CD-ROM that accompanies this book), use your C++ compiler to create the executable code, as Chapter 1 outlined. Here is the output from running the compiled program:

```
Come up and C++ me some time.
```

C   I N P U T   A N D   O U T P U T

If you're used to programming in C, seeing cout instead of the printf() function might come as a minor shock. C++ can, in fact, use printf(), scanf(), and all the other standard C input and output functions, provided that you include the usual C stdio.h file. But this is a C++ book, so you'll use C++'s new input facilities, which improve in many ways upon the C versions.

You construct C++ programs from building blocks called *functions*. Typically, you organize a program into major tasks, and then design separate functions to handle those tasks. The example shown in Listing 2.1 is simple enough to consist of a single function named `main()`. The `myfirst.cpp` example has the following elements:

- Comments, indicated by the `//` prefix
- A preprocessor `#include` directive
- A `using namespace` directive
- A function heading: `int main()`
- A function body, delimited by `{` and `}`
- A statement that uses the C++ `cout` facility to display a message
- A return statement to terminate the `main()` function

Let's look at these various elements in greater detail now. The `main()` function is a good place to start because some of the features that precede `main()`, such as the preprocessor directive, are simpler to understand after you see what `main()` does.

THE `main()` FUNCTION

Stripped of the trimmings, the sample program shown in Listing 2.1 has the following fundamental structure:

```
int main()
{
    statements
    return 0;
}
```

These lines state that you have a function called `main()`, and they describe how the function behaves. Together they constitute a *function definition*. This definition has two parts: the first line, `int main()`, which is called the *function heading*, and the portion enclosed in braces (`{` and `}`), which is the *function body*. Figure 2.1 shows the `main()` function. The function heading is a capsule summary of the function's interface with the rest of the program, and the function body represents your instructions to the computer about what the function should do. In C++ each complete instruction is called a *statement*. You must terminate each statement with a semicolon, so don't omit the semicolons when you type the examples.

The final statement in `main()`, called a *return statement*, terminates the function. You'll learn more about the return statement as you read through this chapter.

FIGURE 2.1
The main() function

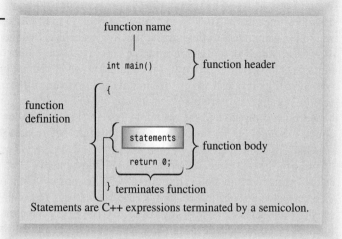

Statements are C++ expressions terminated by a semicolon.

S T A T E M E N T S   A N D   S E M I C O L O N S

A statement represents a complete instruction to a computer. To understand your source code, a compiler must know when one statement ends and another begins. Some languages use a statement separator. FORTRAN, for instance, uses the end of the line to separate one statement from the next. Pascal uses a semicolon to separate one statement from the next. In Pascal you can omit the semicolon in certain cases, such as after a statement just before an END, when you aren't actually separating two statements. (Pragmatists and minimalists will disagree about whether *can* implies *should*.) But C++, like C, uses a *terminator* rather than a separator. The terminator is the semicolon that marks the end of the statement as part of the statement rather than a marker between statements. The practical upshot is that in C++ you never can omit the semicolon.

The Function Heading as an Interface

Right now the main point to remember is that C++ syntax requires that you begin the definition of the main() function with this heading: int main(). This chapter goes into greater detail about this later, but, for those who can't put their curiosity on hold, here's a preview.

In general, a C++ function is activated, or *called*, by another function, and the function heading describes the interface between a function and the function that calls it. The part preceding the function name is called the *function return type*, which

" *In general, a C++ function is activated, or called, by another function, and the function heading describes the interface between a function and the function that calls it.* "

describes information flow from a function back to the function that calls it. The part within the parentheses following the function name is called the *argument list* or *parameter list*, which describes information flow from the calling function to the called function. This general format is a bit confusing when you apply it to `main()`, because you normally don't call `main()` from other parts of your program. Typically, however, `main()` is called by startup code that your compiler adds to your program to mediate between the program and the operating system (UNIX, Windows 95, or whatever). In effect, the function header describes the interface between `main()` and the operating system.

Consider the interface for `main()`, beginning with the `int` part. A C++ function called by another function can return a value to the activating (calling) function. That value is called a *return value*. In this case, `main()` can return an integer value, as indicated by the keyword `int`. Next, note the empty parentheses. In general, one C++ function can pass information to another function when it calls that function. The portion of the function heading enclosed in parentheses describes that information. In this case, the empty parentheses mean that the `main()` function takes no information, or, in the usual terminology, `main()` takes no arguments. (To say that `main()` takes no arguments doesn't mean that `main()` is an unreasonable, authoritarian function. Rather, *argument* is the term computer buffs use to refer to information passed from one function to another.)

In short, the heading

```
int main()
```

states that the `main()` function can return an integer value to the function that calls it and that `main()` takes no information from the function that calls it.

Many existing programs use the classic C heading instead:

```
main()     // original C style
```

Under C, omitting the return type is the same as saying that the function is type `int`. However, C++ is phasing this usage out.

You also can use this variant:

```
int main(void)     // very explicit style
```

Using the keyword `void` in the parentheses is an explicit way of saying that the function takes no arguments. Under C++ (but not C), leaving the parentheses empty is the same as using `void` in the parentheses. (In C, leaving the parentheses empty means you are remaining silent about whether or not there are arguments.)

Some programmers use this heading

```
void main()
```

and omit the return statement. This is logically consistent, because a `void` return type means the function doesn't return a value. This variant works on many systems, but, because it isn't mandated as an option under current standards, it does not work on some systems.

Finally, the ANSI/ISO C++ committee has decided that a

```
return 0;
```

statement implicitly is understood to come at the end of the `main()` function (but of no other function) if you don't explicitly provide it.

Why `main()` by Any Other Name Is Not the Same

There's an extremely compelling reason to name the function in the `myfirst.cpp` program `main()`: you have to do so. Every C++ program requires a function called `main()`. (And not, by the way, `Main()` or `MAIN()` or `mane()`. Remember, case and spelling count.) Because the `myfirst.cpp` program has only one function, that function must bear the responsibility of being `main()`. When you run a C++ program, execution always begins at the beginning of the `main()` function. Therefore, if you don't have `main()`, you don't have a complete program, and the compiler points out that you haven't defined a `main()` function.

There are exceptions. For example, in Windows programming you can write a dynamic link library (`dll`) module. This is code that other Windows programs can use. Because a `dll` module is not a stand-alone program, it doesn't need a `main()`. Programs for specialized environments, such as for a controller chip in a robot, might not need a `main()`. But your ordinary stand-alone program does need a `main()`; this book discusses that kind of program.

C++ COMMENTS

The double slash (`//`) introduces a C++ comment. A *comment* is a remark from the programmer to the reader that usually identifies a section of a program or explains some aspect of the code. The compiler ignores comments. After all, it knows C++ at least as well as you do, and, in any case, it's incapable of understanding comments. As far as the compiler is concerned, Listing 2.1 looks as if it were written without comments:

```cpp
#include <iostream>
using namespace std;
int main()
{
    cout << "Come up and C++ me some time.";
    cout << "\n";
    return 0;
}
```

C++ comments run from the `//` to the end of the line. A comment can be on its own line or it can be on the same line as code. Incidentally, note the first line in Listing 2.1:

```cpp
// myfirst.cpp -- displays a message
```

In this book all programs begin with a comment that gives the filename for the source code and a brief program summary. As mentioned in Chapter 1, the filename extension for source code depends on your C++ system. Other systems might use `myfirst.C` or `myfirst.cxx` for names.

Remember

You should use comments to document your programs. The more complex the program, the more valuable comments become. Not only do they help others to understand what you have done, but also they help you understand what you've done, especially if you haven't looked at the program for a while.

C-STYLE COMMENTS

C++ also recognizes C comments, which are enclosed between /* and */ symbols:

```
#include <iostream> /* a C-style comment */
```

Because the C-style comment is terminated by */ rather than by the end of a line, you can spread it over more than one line. You can use either or both styles in your programs. However, try sticking to the C++ style. That way, a C programmer glancing over your shoulder will know you've advanced to a higher level of programming.

THE C++ PREPROCESSOR AND THE `iostream` FILE

Here's the short version of what you need to know. If your program is to use the usual C++ input or output facilities, provide these two lines:

```
#include <iostream>
using namespace std;
```

If your compiler doesn't like these lines (for example, if it complains that it can't find the file iostream), try the following single line instead:

```
#include <iostream.h >     // compatible with older compilers
```

That's all you really need to know to make your programs work, but now take a more in-depth look.

C++, like C, uses a *preprocessor*. This is a program that processes a source file before the main compilation takes place. (Some C++ implementations, as you might recall from Chapter 1, use a translator program to convert a C++ program to C. Although the translator also is a form of preprocessor, you do not learn here about that preprocessor; instead, you learn about the one that handles directives whose names begin with #.) You don't have to do anything special to invoke this preprocessor. It automatically operates when you compile the program.

The listing uses the #include directive:

```
#include <iostream>     // a PREPROCESSOR directive
```

This directive causes the preprocessor to add the contents of the iostream file to your program. This is a typical preprocessor action: adding or replacing text in the source code before it's compiled.

This raises the question of why you should add the contents of the iostream file to the program. The answer concerns communication between the program and the outside world. The io in iostream refers to *input*, which is information brought into the program, and to *output*, which is information sent out from the program. C++'s input/output scheme involves several definitions found in the iostream file. Your first program needs these definitions to use the cout facility to display a message. The #include directive causes the contents of the iostream file to be sent along with the contents of your file to the compiler. In essence, the contents of the iostream file replace the #include <iostream> line in the program. Your original file is not altered, but a composite file formed from your file and iostream goes on to the next stage of compilation.

Remember

Programs that use cin and cout for input and output must include the iostream file.

HEADER FILENAMES

Files such as iostream are called *include files* (because they are included in other files) or *header files* (because they are included at the beginning of a file). C++ compilers come with many header files, each supporting a particular family of facilities. The C tradition has been to use the h extension with header files as a simple way to identify the type of file by its name. For example, a math.h header file supports various C math functions. Initially, C++ did the same. For instance, the header file supporting input and output was named iostream.h. More recently, however, C++ usage has changed. Now the h extension is reserved for the old C header files (which C++ programs still can use), whereas C++ header files have no extension. There also are C header files that have been converted to C++ header files. These files have been renamed by dropping the h extension (making it a C++ style name) and prefixing the filename with a c (indicating that it supports C features). For example, the C++ version of math.h is the cmath header file. Sometimes the C and C++ versions of C header files are identical, whereas in other cases the new version may have a few changes. For purely C++ header files such as iostream, dropping the h is more than a cosmetic change, for the h-free header files also incorporate namespaces, the next topic in this summary. Table 2.1 summarizes the naming conventions for header files.

TABLE 2.1
HEADER FILE NAMING CONVENTIONS

KIND OF HEADER	CONVENTION	EXAMPLE	COMMENTS
C++ old style	Ends in `.h`	`iostream.h`	Usable by C++ programs
C old style	Ends in `.h`	`math.h`	Usable by C, C++ programs
C++ new style	No extension	`iostream`	Usable by C++ programs, uses namespace `std`
Converted C	`c` prefix, no extension	`cmath`	Usable by C++ programs, might use non-C features such as `namespace std`

In view of the C tradition of using different file extensions to indicate different file types, it appears reasonable to have some special extension to indicate C++ header files. The ANSI/ISO committee felt so, too. The problem was agreeing on which extension to use, so eventually they agreed upon nothing.

NAMESPACES

If you use `iostream` instead of `iostream.h`, you should use the following namespace directive to make the definitions in `iostream` available to your program:

```
using namespace std;
```

This is called a *using directive*. The simplest thing to do is to accept this for now and worry about it later (for instance, in Chapter 8, "Adventures in Functions"). But here's an overview of what's happening, so you won't be left completely in the dark.

Namespace support is a new C++ feature designed to simplify the writing of programs that combine pre-existing code from several vendors. One potential problem is that you might use two prepackaged products that both have, say, a function called `wanda()`. If you then use the `wanda()` function, the compiler won't know which version you mean. The namespace facility lets a vender package its wares in a unit called a *namespace* so that you can use the name of a namespace to indicate which vender's product you want. So, Microflop Industries could place its definitions in a namespace called `Microflop`. Then `Microflop::wanda()` would become the full name for its `wanda()` function. Similarly, `Piscine::wanda()` could denote Piscine Corporation's version of `wanda()`. Thus, your compiler now could use the namespaces to discriminate between various versions:

```
Microflop::wanda("go dancing?");        // use Microflop namespace version
Piscine::wanda("a fish named Desire"); // use Piscine namespace version
```

In this spirit, the classes, functions, and variables that are a standard component of C++ compilers now are placed in a namespace called `std`. This takes place in the h-free header files. This means, for example, that the `cout` variable used for output and defined in `iostream` is really called `std::cout`. However, most users don't feel like converting pre-namespace code, which uses `iostream.h` and `cout`, to namespace code, which uses `iostream` and `std::cout`, unless they can do this without a lot of hassle. This is where the `using` directive comes in. The line

```
using namespace std;
```

means you can use names defined in the `std` namespace without using the `std::` prefix.

C++ OUTPUT WITH cout

Now look at how you display a message. The `myfirst.cpp` program uses the following C++ statement:

```
cout << "Come up and C++ me some time.";
```

The part enclosed within the double quotation marks is the message to print. In C++, any series of characters enclosed in double quotation marks is called a *string*, presumably because it consists of several characters strung together into a larger unit. The `<<` notation indicates that the statement is sending this string to `cout`; the symbols point the way the information flows. And what is `cout`? It's a predefined object that knows how to display a variety of things, including strings, numbers, and individual characters. (An object, as you may remember from Chapter 1, is a particular instance of a class, and a class defines how data is stored and used.)

Well, this is a bit awkward. You won't be in a position to learn about objects for several more chapters, yet here you must use one. Actually, this reveals one of the strengths of objects. You don't have to know the innards of an object in order to use it. All you must know is its interface—that is, how to use it. The `cout` object has a simple interface. If `string` represents a string, do the following to display the string:

```
cout << string;
```

This is all you need to know to display a string, but now take a look at how the C++ conceptual view represents the process. In this view, the output is a stream—that is, a series of characters flowing from the program. The `cout` object, whose properties are defined in the `iostream` file, represents that stream. The object properties for `cout` include an insertion operator (`<<`) that inserts the information on its right into the stream. So the statement (note the terminating semicolon)

```
cout << "Come up and C++ me some time.";
```

inserts the string "Come up and C++ me some time." into the output stream. Thus, rather than say that your program displays a message, you can say that it inserts a string into the output stream. Somehow, that sounds more impressive. (See Figure 2.2.)

If you're coming to C++ from C, you probably noticed that the insertion operator (`<<`) looks just like the bitwise left-shift operator (`<<`). This is an example of *operator overloading*, by which the same operator symbol can have different meanings. The compiler uses the context to figure out which meaning is intended. C itself has some operator overloading. For instance, the `&` symbol represents both the address operator and the bitwise AND operator. The `*` symbol represents both multiplication and dereferencing a pointer. The important point here is not the exact function of these operators

> *" You don't have to know the innards of an object in order to use it. All you need to know is its interface—that is, how to use it. "*

FIGURE 2.2

Displaying a string with
cout

but that the same symbol can have more than one meaning, with the compiler determining the proper meaning from the context. (You do much the same when you determine the meaning of "shoot" in "shoot the breeze" versus "shoot the piano player.") C++ extends the operator overloading concept by letting you redefine operator meanings for the user-defined types called classes.

The Newline Character (\n)

Now examine an odd-looking notation that appears in the second output statement:

```
cout << "\n";
```

The \n is a special C++ (and C) notation representing an important concept dubbed the *newline character*. Although you type the newline character by using two characters (\ and n), these count as a single character. Note that you use the backslash (\), not the regular slash (/). If you display the newline character, the screen cursor moves to the beginning of the next line, and if you send the newline character to a printer, the print head moves to the beginning of the next line. The newline character earns its name.

Note that the `cout` facility does not move automatically to the next line when it prints a string, so the first `cout` statement in Listing 2.1 leaves the cursor positioned just after the period at the end of the output string. To move the cursor to the beginning of the next line, you must send a newline character to the output. Or, to practice C++ lingo, you must insert a newline character into the output stream.

You can use the newline character just like any ordinary character. Listing 2.1 uses it in a separate string, but the listing could have used it in the original string. That is, you can replace the original two output statements with the following:

```
cout << "Come up and C++ me some time.\n";
```

You even can place the newline character in the midst of a string. For instance, consider the following statement:

```
cout << "I am a mighty stream\nof lucid\nclarity.\n";
```

Each newline character moves the cursor to the beginning of the next line, making the output as follows:

```
I am a mighty stream
of lucid
clarity.
```

By leaving out newlines, you can make successive `cout` statements print on the same line. For example, the statements

```
cout << "The Good, the";
cout << "Bad, ";
cout << "and the Ukelele\n";
```

produce the following output:

```
The Good, theBad, and the Ukelele
```

Note that the beginning of one string comes immediately after the end of the preceding string. If you want a space where two strings join, you must include it in one of the strings. (Remember that to try out these output examples, you must place them in a complete program, with a `main()` function heading and opening and closing braces.)

C++ has another way to indicate a newline in output: the word `endl`:

```
cout << "What's next?" << endl;    // endl means start a new line
```

This term is defined in `iostream`. It's a bit easier for most to type than `"\n"`, but you only can use it separately, not as part of a string. That is, the string `"What's next?\n"` includes a newline character, but `"What's next?endl"` is just a string ending in the four letters e, n, d, and l.

C++ SOURCE CODE FORMATTING

Some languages, such as FORTRAN, are line-oriented, with one statement to a line. For these languages, the carriage return serves to separate statements. In C++, however, the semicolon marks the end of each statement. This leaves C++ free to treat the carriage return in the same way as a space or a tab. That is, in C++ you normally can use a space where you would use a carriage return, and vice versa. This means you can spread a single statement over several lines or place several statements on one line. For instance, you could reformat `myfirst.cpp` as follows:

```
#include <iostream>
   using
    namespace
          std;
      int
main
() { cout
            <<
"Come up and C++ me some time.";
    cout << "\n"; return 0; }
```

This is ugly, but valid, code. You do have to observe some rules. In particular, in C and C++ you can't put a space, tab, or carriage return in the middle of an element such as a name, nor can you place a carriage return in the middle of a string.

```
int ma  in()     // INVALID -- space in name
re
turn 0; // INVALID -- carriage return in word
cout << "Behold the Beans
 of Beauty!"; // INVALID -- carriage return in string
```

The indivisible elements in a line of code are called *tokens*. (See Figure 2.3) Generally, you must separate one token from the next by a space, tab, or carriage return, which collectively are termed *white space*.

```
return0;         // INVALID, must be return 0;
return(0);       // VALID, white space omitted
return (0);      // VALID, white space used
int main()       // VALID, white space omitted
int main ( )     // ALSO VALID, white space used
```

C++ Source Code Style

Although C++ gives you much formatting freedom, your programs will be easier to read if you follow a sensible style. Having valid but ugly code should leave you unsatisfied. Most programmers use the style of Listing 2.1, which observes these rules:

- One statement per line

- An opening and a closing brace for a function, each of which is on its own line

- Statements in a function indented from the braces

- No white space around the parentheses associated with a function name

The first three rules have the simple intent to keep the code clean and readable. The fourth helps to differentiate functions from some built-in C++ structures, such as loops, that also use parentheses. The book will alert you to other rules as they come up.

FIGURE 2.3

Tokens and white space

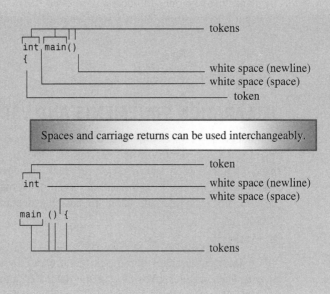

More About C++ Statements

A C++ program is a collection of functions, and each function is a collection of statements. C++ has several kinds of statements, so let's look at some of the possibilities. Listing 2.2 provides two new kinds of statements. First, a declaration statement creates a variable. Second, an assignment statement provides a value for that variable. Also, the program shows a new capability for cout.

```
Listing 2.2 fleas.cpp
// fleas.cpp -- display the value of a variable
#include <iostream>
using namespace std;
int main()
{
    int fleas;              // create an integer variable

    fleas = 38;             // give a value to the variable
    cout << "My cat has ";
    cout << fleas;          // display the value of fleas
    cout << " fleas.\n";
    return 0;
}
```

A blank line separates the declaration from the rest of the program. This practice is the usual C convention, but it's somewhat less common in C++. Here is the program output:

```
My cat has 38 fleas.
```

The next few pages examine this program.

DECLARATION STATEMENTS AND VARIABLES

Computers are precise, orderly machines. To store an item of information in a computer, you must identify both the storage location and how much memory storage space the information requires. One relatively painless way to do this in C++ is to use a *declaration statement* to indicate the type of storage and to provide a label for the location. For example, the program has this declaration statement (note the semicolon):

```
int fleas;
```

This statement declares that the program uses enough storage to hold what is called an int. The compiler takes care of the details of allocating and labeling memory for that task. C++ can handle several kinds, or types, of data, and the int is the most basic data type. It corresponds to an integer, a number with no fractional part. The C++ int type can be positive or negative, but the size range depends on the implementation. Chapter 3, "Dealing with Data," provides the details on int and the other basic types.

Besides giving the type, the declaration statement declares that henceforth the program will use the name fleas to identify the value stored at that location. We call fleas a *variable* because you can change its value. In C++ you must declare all variables. If you were to omit the declaration in fleas.cpp, the compiler would report an error when the program attempts to use fleas further on. (In fact, you might want to try omitting the declaration just to see how your compiler responds. Then, if you see that response in the future, you'll know to check for omitted declarations.)

WHY MUST VARIABLES BE DECLARED?

Some languages, notably BASIC, create a new variable whenever you use a new name, without the aid of explicit declarations. That might seem friendlier to the user, and it is—in the short term. The problem is that by misspelling the name of a variable, you inadvertently can create a new variable without realizing it. That is, in BASIC, you can do something like the following:

```
CastleDark = 34
...
CastleDank = CastleDank + MoreGhosts
```

Continued...

WHY MUST VARIABLES BE DECLARED? Continued...

```
...
PRINT CastleDark
```

Because `CastleDank` is mispelled (the r was typed as an n), the changes you make to it leave `CastleDark` unchanged. This kind of error can be hard to trace because it breaks no rules in BASIC. However, in C++ the equivalent code breaks the rule about the need to declare a variable for you to use it, so the compiler catches the error and stomps the potential bug.

In general, then, a declaration indicates the type of data to be stored and the name the program will use for the data that's stored there. In this particular case, the program creates a variable called `fleas` in which it can store an integer. (See Figure 2.4.)

The declaration statement in the program is called a *defining declaration* statement, or *definition*, for short. This means that its presence causes the compiler to allocate memory space for the variable. In more complex situations, you also can have *reference declarations*. These tell the computer to use a variable that already has been defined elsewhere. In general, a declaration need not be a definition, but in this example it is.

If you're familiar with C or Pascal, you're already familiar with variable declarations. You also may have a modest surprise in store for you. In C and Pascal, all variable declarations normally come at the very beginning of a function or procedure. But C++ has no such restriction. Indeed, the usual C++ style is to declare a variable just before it is first used. That way, you don't have to rummage back through a program to see what the type is. You'll see an example of this later in the chapter. This style does have the disadvantage of not gathering all your variable names in one place; thus, you can't tell at a glance what variables a function uses.

Remember \\
The C++ style for declaring variables is to declare a variable as closely as possible to its first use.

FIGURE 2.4
A variable declaration

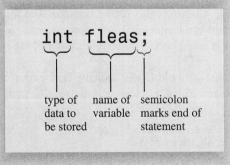

```
int fleas;
```

type of   name of   semicolon
data to   variable   marks end of
be stored   statement

THE ASSIGNMENT STATEMENT

An assignment statement assigns a value to a storage location. For instance, the statement

```
fleas = 38;
```

assigns the integer 38 to the location represented by the variable `fleas`. The = symbol is called the *assignment operator*. One unusual feature of C++ (and C) is that you can use the assignment operator serially. That is, the following is valid code:

```
int steinway;
int baldwin;
int yamaha;
yamaha = baldwin = steinway = 88;
```

The assignment works from right to left. First, `88` is assigned to `steinway`; then the value of `steinway`, which is now 88, is assigned to `baldwin`; then `baldwin`'s value of 88 is assigned to `yamaha`. (C++ follows C's penchant for allowing weird-appearing code.)

NEW TRICK FOR cout

Prior to now, the examples have given `cout` strings to print. Listing 2.2 additionally gives `cout` a variable whose value is an integer:

```
cout << fleas;
```

The program doesn't print the word `fleas`; instead, it prints the integer value stored in `fleas`, which is 38. Actually, this is two tricks in one. First, `cout` replaces `fleas` with its current numeric value of 38. Second, it translates the value to the proper output characters.

As you see, `cout` works with both strings and integers. This may not seem particularly remarkable to you, but keep in mind that the integer 38 is something quite different from the string "38". The string holds the characters with which you write the number; that is, a 3 character and an 8 character. The program internally stores the code for the 3 character and the 8 character. To print the string, `cout` simply prints each character in the string. But the integer 38 is stored as a numeric value. Rather than store each digit separately, the computer stores 38 as a binary number. (Appendix A, "Number Bases," discusses this representation.) The main point here is that `cout` must translate a number in integer form into character form before it can print it. Furthermore, `cout` is smart enough to recognize that `fleas` is an integer requiring conversion.

Perhaps the contrast with old C will indicate how clever `cout` is. To print the string "38" and the integer 38 in C, you could use C's multipurpose output function `printf()`:

```
printf("Printing a string: %s\n", "38");
printf("Printing an integer: %d\n", 38);
```

Without going into the intricacies of `printf()`, note that you must use special codes (`%s` and `%d`) to indicate whether you are going to print a string or an integer. And if you tell printf() to print a string but give it an integer by mistake, printf() is too dumb to notice your mistake. It just goes ahead and displays garbage.

The intelligent way in which cout behaves stems from C++'s object-oriented features. In essence, the C++ insertion operator (<<) adjusts its behavior to fit the type of data that follows it. This is an example of operator overloading. In later chapters, when you take up function overloading and operator overloading, you learn how to implement such smart designs yourself.

cout AND printf()

If you are used to C and printf(), you might think cout looks odd. You might even prefer to cling to your hard-won mastery of printf(). But cout actually is no stranger in appearance than printf() with all of its conversion specifications. More important, cout has significant advantages. Its capability to recognize types reflects a more intelligent and foolproof design. Also, it is *extensible*. That is, you can redefine the << operator so that cout can recognize and display new data types you develop. And if you relish the fine control printf() provides, you can accomplish the same effects with more advanced uses of cout (see Chapter 16, "Input, Output, and Files").

More C++ Statements

Look at a couple more examples of statements. The program in Listing 2.3 expands on the preceding example by allowing you to enter a value while the program is running. To do so, it uses cin (pronounced cee-in), the input counterpart to cout. Also, the program shows yet another way to use that master of versatility, the cout object.

Listing 2.3 yourcat.cpp

```cpp
// yourcat.cpp -- input and output
#include <iostream>
using namespace std;
int main()
{
    int fleas;

    cout << "How many fleas does your cat have?\n";
    cin >> fleas;                    // C++ input
// next line concatenates output
    cout << "Well, that's " << fleas << " fleas too many!\n";

    return 0;
}
```

Here is a sample output:

```
How many fleas does your cat have?
112
Well, that's 112 fleas too many!
```

The program has two new features: using `cin` to read keyboard input and combining three output statements into one. Let's take a look.

USING `cin`

As the output demonstrates, the value typed from the keyboard (112) eventually is assigned to the variable `fleas`. Here is the statement that performs that wonder:

```
cin >> fleas;
```

Looking at this statement, you practically can see information flowing from `cin` into `fleas`. Naturally, there is a slightly more formal description of this process. Just as C++ considers output as a stream of characters flowing out of the program, it considers input as a stream of characters flowing into the program. The `iostream` file defines `cin` as an object that represents this stream. For output, the << operator inserts characters into the output stream. For input, `cin` uses the >> operator to extract characters from the input stream. Typically, you provide a variable to the right of the operator to receive the extracted information. (The symbols << and >> were chosen to suggest visually the direction that information flows.)

Like `cout`, `cin` is a smart object. It converts input, which is just a series of characters typed from the keyboard, into a form acceptable to the variable receiving the information. In this case, the program declared `fleas` to be an integer variable, so the input is converted to the numerical form the computer uses to store integers.

MORE `cout`

The second new feature of `yourcat.cpp` is combining three output statements into one. The `iostream` file defines the << operator so that you can combine (concatenate) output as follows:

```
cout << "Well, that's " << fleas << " fleas too many.\n";
```

This allows you to combine string output and integer output in a single statement. The resulting output is the same as what the following code produces:

```
cout << "Well, that's ";
cout << fleas;
cout << " fleas too many.\n";
```

While you're still in the mood for `cout` advice, you also can rewrite the concatenated version this way, spreading the single statement over three lines:

```
cout    << "Well, that's "
        << fleas
        << " fleas too many.\n";
```

That's because C++'s free format rules treat newlines and spaces between tokens interchangeably. This last technique is convenient when the line width cramps your style.

A TOUCH OF CLASS

You've seen enough of cin and cout to justify your exposure to a little object lore. In particular, you learn some more about the notion of classes. Classes are one of the core concepts for object-oriented programming in C++.

A *class* is a data type the user defines. To define a class, you describe what sort of information it can represent and what sort of actions you can perform with that data. A class bears the same relationship to an object that a type does to a variable. That is, a class definition describes a data form and how it can be used, whereas an object is an entity created according to the data form specification. Or, in noncomputer terms, if a class is analogous to a category such as famous actors, then an object is analogous to a particular example of that category, such as Kermit the Frog. To extend the analogy, a class representation of actors would include definitions of possible actions relating to the class, such as Reading for a Part, Expressing Sorrow, Projecting Menace, Accepting an Award, and the like. If you've been exposed to different OOP terminology, it may help to know that the C++ class corresponds to what some languages term an object type, and the C++ object corresponds to an object instance or instance variable.

Now get a little more specific. Recall this declaration of a variable:

```
int fleas;
```

This creates a particular variable (fleas) that has the properties of the int type. That is, fleas can store an integer and can be used in particular ways—for addition and subtraction, for instance. Now consider cout. It is an object created to have the properties of the ostream class. The ostream class definition (another inhabitant of the iostream file) describes the sort of data an ostream object represents and the operations you can perform with and to it, such as inserting a number or string into an output stream. Similarly, cin is an object created with the properties of the istream class, also defined in iostream.

Remember

The class describes all the properties of a data type, and an object is an entity created according to that description.

You have learned that classes are user-defined types, but as a user you certainly did not design the ostream and istream classes. Just as functions can come in function libraries, classes can come in class libraries. That's the case for the ostream and istream classes. Technically, they are not built into the C++ language, but are examples of classes that happen to come with the language. The class definitions are laid out in the iostream file and are not built into the compiler. You even can modify these class definitions if you like, although that's not a good idea. (More precisely, it is a truly dreadful idea.) The iostream family of classes and the related fstream (or file I/O) family are the only sets of class definitions that came with all early implementations of C++. However, the ANSI/ISO C++ committee added a few more classes to the standard. Also, most implementations provide additional class definitions as part of the package. Indeed, much of the current appeal of C++ is the existence of extensive and useful class libraries supporting UNIX, Macintosh, and Windows programming.

The class description specifies all the operations that can be performed on objects of that class. To perform such an allowed action on a particular object, you send a message to the object. For example, if you want the `cout` object to display a string, you send it a message that says, in effect, "Object! Display this!" C++ provides a couple of ways to send messages. One way, called using a class method, essentially is a function call like the ones you've seen. The other, which is the one used with `cin` and `cout`, is to redefine an operator. Thus, the statement

```
cout << "I am not a crook."
```

uses the redefined << operator to send the "display message" to `cout`. In this case, the message comes with an argument, which is the string to be displayed. (See Figure 2.5.)

Functions

Because functions are the modules from which C++ programs are built and because they are essential to C++ OOP definitions, you should become thoroughly familiar with them. Because some aspects of functions are advanced topics, the main discussion of functions comes later, in Chapters 7, "Functions—C++'s Programming Modules," and 8, "Adventures in Functions." However, if you deal now with some basic characteristics of functions, you'll be more at ease and more practiced with functions later. The rest of this chapter introduces you to these function basics.

C++ functions come in two varieties: those with return values and those with none. You can find examples of each kind in the standard C++ library of functions, and you can create your own functions of each type. Let's look at a library function that has a return value, and then examine how you can write your own simple functions.

FIGURE 2.5

Sending a message to an object

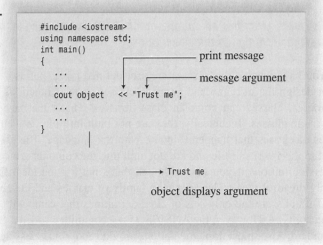

```
#include <iostream>
using namespace std;
int main()
{
                              ┌──────────── print message
    ...
    ...                       ┌──── message argument
    cout object   << "Trust me";
    ...
    ...
}
```

──────► Trust me

object displays argument

USING A FUNCTION WITH A RETURN VALUE

A function that has a return value produces a value that you can assign to a variable. For instance, the standard C/C++ library includes a function called sqrt() that returns the square root of a number. Suppose you want to calculate the square root of 6.25 and assign it to a variable x. You could use the following statement in your program:

```
x = sqrt(6.25); // returns the value 2.5 and assigns it to x
```

The expression sqrt(6.25) invokes, or *calls*, the sqrt() function. The expression sqrt(6.25) is termed a *function call*, the invoked function is termed the *called function*, and the function containing the function call is termed the *calling function*. (See Figure 2.6.)

The value in the parentheses (6.25, in this example) is information sent to the function; it is said to be *passed* to the function. A value sent to a function this way is called an *argument* or *parameter*. (See Figure 2.7.) The sqrt() function calculates the answer to be 2.5 and sends that value back to the calling function; the value sent back is called the *return value* of the function. Think of the return value as what is substituted for the function call in the statement once the function finishes its job. Thus, this example assigns the return value to the variable x. In short, an argument is information sent to the function, and the return value is a value sent back from the function.

That's practically all there is to it, except that before it uses a function, the C++ compiler must know what kind of arguments the function uses and what kind of return value it has. That is, does the function return an integer? A character? A number with a decimal fraction? A guilty verdict? Or something else? If it lacks this information, the compiler won't know how to interpret the return value. The C++ way to convey this information is by using a function prototype statement.

FIGURE 2.6

Calling a function

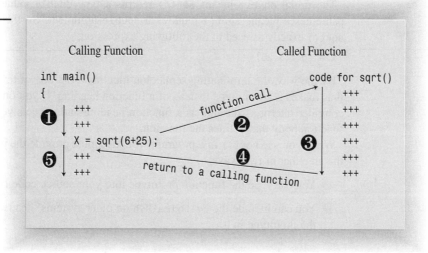

FIGURE 2.7

Function call syntax

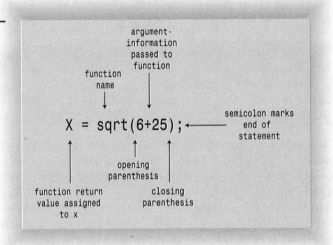

Remember

A C++ program should provide a prototype for each function used in the program.

A function prototype does for functions what a variable declaration does for variables—it tells what types are involved. For instance, the C++ library defines the sqrt() function to take a number with (potentially) a fractional part (like 6.25) as an argument and to return a number of the same type. Some languages refer to such numbers as real numbers, but the name C++ uses for this type is double. (You see more of double in Chapter 3.) The function prototype for sqrt() looks like this:

```
double sqrt(double);   // function prototype
```

The initial double means sqrt() returns a type double value. The double in the parentheses means sqrt() requires a double argument. So this prototype describes sqrt() exactly as used in the following expression:

```
x = sqrt(6.25);
```

By the way, the terminating semicolon identifies this line of text as a statement, and thus makes it a prototype instead of a function heading. If you omit the semicolon, the compiler interprets the line as a function heading and expects you to follow it with a function body that defines the function.

When you use sqrt() in a program, you also must provide the prototype. You can do this in either of two ways:

- You can type the function prototype into your source code file yourself.

- You can include the cmath (math.h on older systems) header file, which has the prototype in it.

> *You should place a function prototype ahead of where you first use the function.*

The second way is better, because the header file is even more likely than you to get the prototype right. Every function in the C++ library has a prototype in one or more header files. Just check the function description in your manual or with online help, if you have it, and the description tells you which header file to use. For example, the description of the sqrt() function should tell you to use the cmath header file. (Again, you might have to use the older math.h header file, which works for both C and C++ programs.)

Don't confuse the function prototype with the function definition. The prototype, as you've seen, only describes the function interface. That is, it describes the information sent to the function and the information sent back. The definition, however, includes the code for the function's workings, for example, the code for calculating the square root of a number. C and C++ divide these two features—prototype and definition—for library functions. The library files contain the compiled code for the functions, whereas the header files contain the prototypes.

You should place a function prototype ahead of where you first use the function. The usual practice is to place prototypes just before the definition of the main() function. Listing 2.4 demonstrates the use of the library function sqrt(); it provides a prototype by including the cmath file.

Listing 2.4 sqrt.cpp

```cpp
// sqrt.cpp -- use a square root function
#include <iostream>
using namespace std;
#include <cmath>          // or math.h
int main()
{
    double cover;         // use double for real numbers

    cout << "How many square feet of sheets do you have?\n";
    cin >> cover;
    double side;          // create another variable
    side = sqrt(cover); // call function, assign return value
    cout << "You can cover a square with sides of " << side;
    cout << " feet\nwith your sheets.\n";
    return 0;
}
```

Remember

If you're using an older compiler, you might have to use #include <math.h> instead of #include <cmath> in Listing 2.4.

USING LIBRARY FUNCTIONS

C++ library functions are stored in library files. When the compiler compiles a program, it must search the library files for the functions you've used. Compilers differ on which library files they search automatically. If you try to run Listing 2.4 and get a message that _sqrt is an undefined external (sounds like a condition to avoid!), chances are that your compiler doesn't automatically search the math library. (Compilers like to add an underscore prefix to function names—another subtle reminder that they have the last say about your program.) If you get such a message, check your compiler documentation to see how to have the compiler search the correct library. The usual UNIX implementations, for example, require that you use a -lm option (for *library math*) at the end of the command line:

```
CC sqrt.C -lm
```

Merely including the cmath header file provides the prototype but does not necessarily cause the compiler to search the correct library file.

Here's a sample run:

```
How many square feet of sheets do you have?
123.21
You can cover a square with sides of 11.1 feet
with your sheets.
```

Because sqrt() works with type double values, the example makes the variables that type. Note that you declare a type double variable by using the same form, or syntax, as when you declare a type int variable:

```
typename variablename;
```

Type double allows the variables cover and side to hold values with decimal fractions, such as 123.21 and 1.1. As you see in Chapter 3, type double encompasses a much greater range of values than type int.

C++ does allow you to declare new variables anywhere in a program, so sqrt.cpp didn't declare side until just before using it. C++ also allows you to assign a value to a variable when you create it, so you also could have done this:

```
double side = sqrt(cover);
```

You return to this process, called *initialization*, in Chapter 3.

Note that cin knows how to convert information from the input stream to type double, and cout knows how to insert type double into the output stream. As noted before, these objects are smart.

FUNCTION VARIATIONS

Some functions require more than one item of information. These functions use multiple arguments separated by commas. For example, the math function pow() takes two arguments and returns a value equal to the first argument raised to the power given by the second argument. It has this prototype:

```
double pow(double, double);  // prototype of a function with two arguments
```

If, say, you wanted to find 5 to the 8th power, you would use the function like this:

```
answer = pow(5.0, 8.0);       // function call with a list of arguments
```

Other functions take no arguments. For instance, one of the C libraries (the one associated with the `cstdlib` or the `stdlib.h` header file) has a `rand()` function that has no arguments and that returns a random integer. Its prototype looks like this:

```
int rand(void);             // prototype of a function that takes no arguments
```

The keyword `void` explicitly indicates that the function takes no arguments. If you omit `void` and leave the parentheses empty, C++ interprets this as an implicit declaration that there are no arguments. You could use the function this way:

```
myGuess = rand();           // function call with no arguments
```

Note that, unlike some computer languages, you must use the parentheses in the function call even if there are no arguments.

There also are functions that have no return value. For example, suppose you wrote a function that displayed a number in dollar-and-cents format. You could send it an argument of, say, 23.5, and it would display $23.50 onscreen. Because this function sends a value to the screen instead of to the calling program, it doesn't return a value. You indicate this in the prototype by using the keyword `void` for the return type:

```
void bucks(double);  // prototype for function with no return value
```

Because it doesn't return a value, you can't use the function as part of an assignment statement or of some other expression. Instead, you have a pure function call statement:

```
bucks(1234.56);       // function call, no return value
```

Some languages reserve the term *function* for functions with return values and use the term *procedure* or *subroutine* for those without return values, but C++, like C, uses the term *function* for both variations.

USER-DEFINED FUNCTIONS

The standard C library provides more than 140 predefined functions. If one fits your needs, by all means use it. But often you must write your own, particularly when you design classes. Anyway, it's a lot more fun to design your own functions, so now you examine that process. You've already used several user-defined functions, and they all have been named `main()`. Every C++ program must have a `main()` function, which the user must define. Suppose you want to add a second user-defined function. Just as with a library function, you can call a user-defined function by using its name. And, as with a library function, you must provide a function prototype before using the function, which you typically do by placing the prototype above the `main()` definition. The new element is that you also have to provide the source code for the new function. The simplest way is to place the code in the same file after the code for `main()`. Listing 2.5 illustrates these elements.

Listing 2.5 ourfunc.cpp

```
// ourfunc.cpp -- defining your own function
#include <iostream>
using namespace std;
void simon(int);    // function prototype for simon()
int main()
{
    simon(3);        // call the simon() function
    cout << "Pick an integer: ";
    int count;
    cin >> count;
    simon(count);    // call it again
    return 0;
}

void simon(int n)    // define the simon() function
{
    cout << "Simon says touch your toes " << n << " times.\n";
}                    // void functions don't need return statements
```

The `main()` function calls the `simon()` function twice, once with an argument of 3 and once with a variable argument count. In between, the user enters an integer that's used to set the value of count. The example doesn't use a newline character in the cout prompting message. This results in the user input appearing on the same line as the prompt. Here is a sample run:

```
Simon says touch your toes 3 times.
Pick an integer: 512
Simon says touch your toes 512 times.
```

Function Form

The definition for the `simon()` function follows the same general form as the definition for `main()`. First, there is a function header. Then, enclosed in braces, comes the function body. You can generalize the form for a function definition as follows:

```
type functionname(argumentlist)
{
    statements
}
```

Note that the source code that defines `simon()` follows the closing brace of `main()`. Like C, and unlike Pascal, C++ does not allow you to embed one function definition inside another. Each function definition stands separately from all others; all functions are created equal. (See Figure 2.8.)

FIGURE 2.8
Function definitions occur sequentially in a file

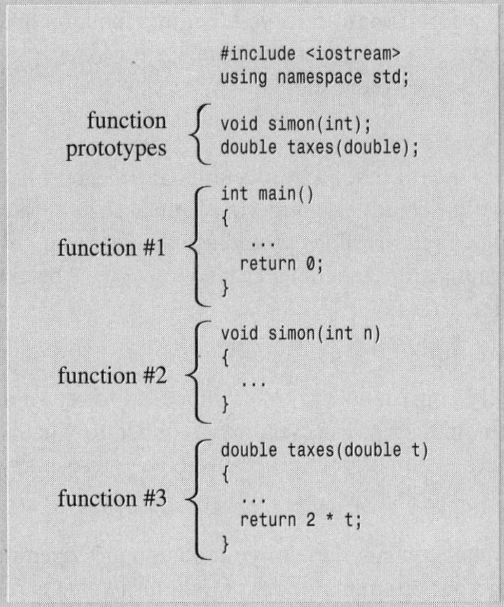

```
                        #include <iostream>
                        using namespace std;
function    {  void simon(int);
prototypes  {  double taxes(double);

                int main()
                {
function #1        ...
                   return 0;
                }

                void simon(int n)
                {
function #2        ...
                }

                double taxes(double t)
                {
function #3        ...
                   return 2 * t;
                }
```

Function Headings

The simon() function has this heading:

```
void simon(int n)
```

The initial void means that simon() has no return value. So, calling simon() doesn't produce a number that you can assign to a variable in main(). Thus, the first function call looks like this:

```
simon(3);              // ok for void functions
```

Because poor simon() lacks a return value, you can't use it this way:

```
simple = simon(3);   // not allowed for void functions
```

The int n within the parentheses means that you are expected to use simon() with a single argument of type int. The n is a new variable assigned the value passed during a function call. Thus, the function call

```
simon(3);
```

assigns the value 3 to the n variable defined in the simon() heading. When the cout statement in the function body uses n, it uses the value passed in the function call. That's why simon(3) displays a 3 in its output. The call to simon(count) in the sample run causes the function to display 512 because that's the value given to count. In short, the heading for `simon()` tells you that this function takes a single type `int` argument and that it doesn't have a return value.

Review `main()`'s function header:

```
int main()
```

The initial `int` means that `main()` returns an integer value. The empty parentheses (which, optionally, could contain `void`) means that `main()` has no arguments. Functions that have return values should use the keyword `return` to provide the return value and to terminate the function. That's why you've been using the following statement at the end of `main()`:

```
return 0;
```

This is logically consistent: `main()` is supposed to return a type `int` value, and you have it return the integer `0`. But, you may wonder, to what are you returning a value? After all, nowhere in any of your programs have you seen anything calling `main()`:

```
squeeze = main();   // absent from our programs
```

The answer is that you can think of your computer's operating system (UNIX, say, or DOS) as calling your program. So `main()`'s return value is returned not to another part of the program but to the operating system. Many operating systems can use the program's return value. For example, UNIX shell scripts and DOS batch files can be designed to run programs and test their return values, usually called exit values. The normal convention is that an exit value of zero means the program ran successfully, whereas a nonzero value means there was a problem. Thus, you can design your C++ program to return a nonzero value if, say, it fails to open a file. You then can design a shell script or batch file to run that program and to take some alternative action if the program signals a failure.

KEYWORDS

Keywords are the vocabulary of a computer language. In this chapter, you've used four C++ keywords: `int`, `void`, `return`, and `double`. Because these keywords are special to C++, you cannot use them for other purposes. That is, you can't use `return` as the name for a variable or `double` as the name of a function. But you can use them as part of a name, as in `painter` (with its hidden `int`) or `return_aces`. Appendix B, "C++ Keywords," provides a complete list of C++ keywords. Incidentally, `main` is not a keyword because it's not part of the language. Rather, it is the name of a required function. You can use `main` as a variable name. (That can cause a problem in circumstances too esoteric to describe here, and because it is confusing in any case, you'd best not.) Similarly, other function names and object names are not keywords. However, using the same name, say `cout`, for both an object and a variable in a program confuses the compiler. That is, you can use `cout` as a variable name in a function that doesn't use the `cout` object for output, but you can't use `cout` both ways in the same function.

USER-DEFINED FUNCTION WITH A RETURN VALUE

" In the U.K., many bathroom scales are calibrated in stone instead of in U.S. pounds or international kilograms. "

Let's go one step further and write a function that uses the return statement. The main() function already illustrates the plan for a function with a return value: give the return type in the function heading and use return at the end of the function body. You can use this form to solve a weighty problem for those visiting the United Kingdom. In the U.K., many bathroom scales are calibrated in *stone* instead of in U.S. pounds or international kilograms. The word *stone* is both singular and plural in this context. (The English language does lack the internal consistency of, say, C++.) One stone is 14 pounds, and the program in Listing 2.6 uses a function to make this conversion.

Listing 2.6 convert.cpp

```cpp
// convert.cpp -- converts stone to pounds
#include <iostream>
using namespace std;
int stonetolb(int);      // function prototype
int main()
{
    int stone;
    cout << "Enter the weight in stone: ";
    cin >> stone;
    int pounds = stonetolb(stone);
    cout << stone << " stone are ";
    cout << pounds << " pounds.\n";
    return 0;
}

int stonetolb(int sts)
{
     return 14 * sts;
}
```

Here's a sample run:

```
Enter the weight in stone: 14
14 stone are 196 pounds.
```

In main(), the program uses cin to provide a value for the integer variable stone. This value is passed to the stonetolb() function as an argument and is assigned to the variable sts in that function. stonetolb() then uses the return keyword to return the value of 14 * sts to main(). This illustrates that you aren't limited to following return with a simple number. Here, by using a more complex expression, you avoid the bother of having to create a new variable to which to assign the value before returning it. The program calculates the value of that expression (196 in this example) and returns the resulting value. If returning the value of an expression bothers you, you can take the longer route:

```cpp
int stonetolb(int sts)
{
     int pounds = 14 * sts;
     return pounds;
}
```

Either version produces the same result, but the second version takes slightly longer to do so.

In general, you can use a function with a return value wherever you would use a simple constant of the same type. For instance, `stonetolb()` returns a type `int` value. This means you can use the function in the following ways:

```
int aunt = stonetolb(20);
int aunts = aunt + stonetolb(10);
cout << "Ferdie weighs " << stonetolb(16) << " pounds.\n";
```

In each case, the program calculates the return value and then uses that number in these statements.

As these examples show, the function prototype describes the function interface—that is, how the function interacts with the rest of the program. The argument list shows what sort of information goes into the function, and the function type shows the type of value returned. Programmers sometimes describe functions as *black boxes* (a term from electronics) specified by the flow of information into and out of them. The function prototype perfectly portrays that point of view. (See Figure 2.9.)

The `stonetolb()` function is short and simple, yet it embodies a full range of functional features:

- It has a heading and a body.

- It accepts an argument.

- It returns a value.

- It requires a prototype.

Consider `stonetolb()` as a standard form for function design. You'll go further into functions in Chapters 7 and 8. In the meantime, the material in this chapter should give you a good feel for how functions work and how they fit into C++.

FIGURE 2.9

The function prototype and the function as a black box

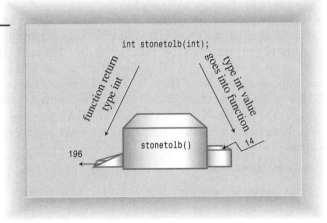

STATEMENT SUMMARY

The following list is a summary of the several kinds of C++ statements you've learned and used in this chapter.

- A declaration statement announces the name and the type of a variable used in a function.

- An assignment statement uses the assignment operator (=) to assign a value to a variable.

- A message statement sends a message to an object, initiating some sort of action.

- A function call activates a function. When the called function terminates, the program returns to the statement in the calling function immediately following the function call.

- A function prototype declares the return type for a function along with the number and type of arguments the function expects.

- A return statement sends a value from a called function back to the calling function.

Summary

A C++ program consists of one or more modules called functions. Programs begin executing at the beginning of the function called `main()`, so you always should have a function by this name. A function, in turn, consists of a heading and a body. The function heading tells you what kind of return value, if any, the function produces and what sort of information it expects to be passed to it by arguments. The function body consists of a series of C++ statements enclosed in paired braces: {}.

C++ statement types include declaration statements, assignment statements, function call statements, object message statements, and return statements. The declaration statement announces the name of a variable and establishes the type of data it can hold. An assignment statement gives a value to a variable. A function call passes program control to the called function. When the function finishes, control returns to the statement in the calling function immediately following the function call. A message instructs an object to perform a particular action. A return statement is the mechanism by which a function returns a value to its calling function.

A class is a user-defined specification for a data type. This specification details how information is to be represented and also the operations that can be performed with the data. An object is an entity created according to a class prescription, just as a simple variable is an entity created according to a data type description.

C++ provides two predefined objects (cin and cout) for handling input and output. They are examples of the istream and ostream classes, which are defined in the iostream file. These classes view input and output as streams of characters. The insertion operator (<<), which is defined for the ostream class, lets you insert data into the output stream, and the extraction operator (>>), which is defined for the istream class, lets you extract information from the input stream. Both cin and cout are smart objects, capable of automatically converting information from one form to another according to the program context.

C++ can use the extensive set of C library functions. To use a library function, you should include the header file that provides the prototype for the function.

Now that you have an overall view of simple C++ programs, you can go on in the next chapters to fill in detail and expand horizons.

Review Questions

You can find the answers to these and subsequent review questions in Appendix I, "Answers to Review Questions."

1. What are the modules of C++ programs called?

2. What does the following preprocessor directive do?

   ```
   #include <iostream>
   ```

3. What does the following statement do?

   ```
   using namespace std;
   ```

4. What statement would you use to print the phrase "Hello, world" and then start a new line?

5. What statement would you use to create an integer variable with the name cheeses?

6. What statement would you use to assign the value 32 to the variable cheeses?

7. What statement would you use to read a value from keyboard input into the variable cheeses?

8. What statement would you use to print "We have X varieties of cheese", where the current value of the cheeses variable replaces X?

9. What does the following function header tell you about the function?

   ```
   int froop(double t)
   ```

10. When do you not use the keyword return when you define a function?

Programming Exercises

1. Write a C++ program that displays your name and address.

2. Write a C++ program that asks for a distance in furlongs and converts it to yards (one furlong is 220 yards).

3. Write a C++ program that uses three user-defined functions (counting `main()` as one) and produces the following output:

```
Three blind mice
Three blind mice
See how they run
See how they run
```

One function, called two times, should produce the first two lines, and the remaining function, also called twice, should produce the remaining output.

4. Write a program that has `main()` call a user-defined function that takes a Celsius temperature value as an argument and then returns the equivalent Fahrenheit value. The program should request the Celsius value as input from the user and display the result, as shown in the following code:

```
Please enter a Celsius value: 20
20 degrees Celsius is 68 degrees Fahrenheit.
```

For reference, here is the formula for making the conversion:

Fahrenheit = 1.8 × Celsius + 32.0

3

Dealing with Data

In this chapter you learn

- Rules for naming C++ variables
- C++'s built-in integer types: `unsigned long`, `long`, `unsigned int`, `int`, `unsigned short`, `short`, `char`, `unsigned char`, `signed char`, and `bool`
- The `climits` file, representing system limits for various integer types
- Numeric constants of various integer types
- Using the `const` qualifier to create symbolic constants
- C++'s built-in floating-point types: `float`, `double`, and `long double`
- The `cfloat` file, representing system limits for various floating-point types
- Numeric constants of various floating-point types
- C++'s arithmetic operators
- Automatic type conversions
- Forced type conversions (type casts)

The essence of object-oriented programming is designing and extending your own data types. Designed types represent an effort to make a type match the data. If you do this properly, you'll find it much simpler to work with the data later. But before you can create your own types, you need to know and understand the types built into C++, for these types will be your building blocks.

The built-in C++ types come in two groups: fundamental types and derived types. In this chapter you'll meet the fundamental types, which represent integers and floating-point numbers. That may sound like just two types; however, C++ recognizes that no one integer type and no one floating-point type match all programming requirements, so it offers several variants on these two data themes. Next, Chapter 4, "Derived Types," follows up by covering several types derived from the basic types; these additional derived types include arrays, strings, pointers, and structures.

Of course, a program also needs a means to identify stored data. You'll examine one method for doing so—using variables. Next, you'll look at how to do arithmetic in C++. Finally, you'll see how C++ converts values from one type to another.

Simple Variables

Programs typically need to store information—perhaps the current price of IBM stock, the average humidity in New York City in August, the most common letter in the Constitution and its relative frequency, or the number of available Elvis imitators. To store an item of information in a computer, the program needs to keep track of three fundamental properties:

- Where the information is stored
- What value is kept there
- What kind of information is stored

The strategy the examples have been using so far is to declare a variable. The type used in the declaration describes the kind of information, and the variable name represents the value symbolically. For instance, suppose Chief Lab Assistant Igor uses the following statements:

```
int braincount;
braincount = 5;
```

These statements tell the program that it is storing an integer and that the name `braincount` represents the integer's value, 5 in this case. In essence, the program locates a chunk of memory large enough to hold an integer, notes the location, assigns the label `braincount` to the location, and copies the value 5 into the location. These statements don't tell you (or Igor) where in memory the value is stored, but the program does keep track of that information, too. Indeed, you can use the & operator to retrieve `braincount`'s address in memory. You'll take up that operator in the next chapter when you investigate a second strategy for identifying data—using pointers.

NAMES FOR VARIABLES

C++ encourages you to use meaningful names for variables. If a variable represents the cost of a trip, call it `costoftrip` or `costOfTrip`, not just x or cot. You do have to follow a few simple C++ naming rules:

- The only characters you can use in names are alphabetic characters, digits, and the underscore (_) character.

- The first character in a name cannot be a digit.

- Uppercase characters are considered distinct from lowercase characters.

- You can't use a C++ keyword for a name.

- Names beginning with two underscore characters or with an underscore character followed by an uppercase letter are reserved for use by the implementation. Names beginning with a single underscore character are reserved for use as global identifiers by the implementation.

- C++ places no limits on the length of a name, and all characters in a name are significant.

The next-to-last point is a bit different from the preceding points because using a name like __time_stop or _Donut doesn't produce a compiler error; instead, it leads to undefined behavior. In other words, there's no telling what the result will be. The reason there is no compiler error is that the names are not illegal but rather are reserved for the implementation to use. The bit about global names refers to where the names are declared; Chapter 4 touches on that topic.

The last point makes C++ different from ANSI C, which guarantees only that the first 31 characters in a name are significant. (In ANSI C, two names that have the same first 31 characters are considered identical, even if the 32nd characters differ.)

Here are some valid and invalid C++ names:

```
int poodle;     // valid
int Poodle;     // valid and distinct from poodle
int POODLE;     // valid and even more distinct
Int terrier;    // invalid -- has to be int, not Int
int my_stars3   // valid
int _Mystars3;  // valid but reserved -- starts with underscore
int 4ever;      // invalid because starts with a digit
int double;     // invalid -- double is a C++ keyword
int begin;      // valid -- begin is a Pascal keyword
int __fools;    // valid but reserved -- starts with two underscores
int the_very_best_variable_i_can_be_version_112;  // valid
int honky-tonk;       // invalid -- no hyphens allowed
```

If you want to form a name from two or more words, the usual practice is to separate the words with an underscore character, as in my_onions, or to capitalize the initial character of each word after the first, as in myEyeTooth. (C veterans tend to use the underscore method in the C tradition, while Pascalians prefer the capitalization approach.) Either form makes it easier to see the individual words and to distinguish between, say, `carDrip` and `cardRip`, or `boat_sport` and `boats_port`.

INTEGER TYPES

Integers are numbers with no fractional part, such as 2, 98, −5286, and 0. There are lots of integers, assuming you consider an infinite number to be a lot, so no finite amount of computer memory can represent all possible integers. Thus, a language only can represent a subset of all integers. Some languages, such as Standard Pascal, offer just one integer type (one type fits all!), but C++ provides several choices. This gives you the option of choosing the integer type that best meets a program's particular requirements. This concern with matching type to data presages the designed data types of OOP.

The various C++ integer types differ in the amount of memory they use to hold an integer. A larger block of memory can represent a larger range in integer values. Also, some types (signed types) can represent both positive and negative values, whereas others (unsigned types) can't represent negative values. C++'s basic integer types, in order of increasing size, are called char, short, int, and long. Each comes in both signed and unsigned versions. That gives you a choice of eight different integer types! Look at these integer types in more detail. Because the char type has some special properties (it's most often used to represent characters instead of numbers), this chapter will cover the other types first.

THE short, int, AND long INTEGER TYPES

Computer memory consists of units called *bits*. (See the following Bits and Bytes note.) By using different numbers of bits to store values, the C++ types of short, int, and long can represent up to three different integer sizes. It would be convenient if each type were always some particular size for all systems, for example, if short were always 16 bits, int always 32 bits, and so on. But life is not that simple. The reason is that no one choice is suitable for all computer designs. C++ offers a flexible standard with some guaranteed minimum sizes. Here's what you get:

- A short integer is at least 16 bits.

- An int integer is at least as big as short.

- A long integer is at least 32 bits and at least as big as int.

BITS AND BYTES

The fundamental unit of computer memory is the *bit*. Think of a bit as an electronic switch that you can set either to off or on. Off represents the value 0, and on represents the value 1. An 8-bit chunk of memory can be set to 256 different combinations. The number 256 comes from the fact that each bit has two possible settings, making the total number of combinations for 8 bits 2 x 2 x 2 x 2 x 2 x 2 x 2 x 2, or 256. Thus, an 8-bit unit can represent, say, the values 0 through 255 or the values –128 through 127. Each additional bit doubles the number of combinations. This means you can set a 16-bit unit to 65,536 different values and a 32-bit unit to 4,294,672,296 different values.

A *byte* usually means an 8-bit unit of memory. Byte in this sense is the unit of measurement that describes the amount of memory in a computer, with a kilobyte equal to 1024 bytes and a megabyte equal to 1024 kilobytes. C++, however, defines a byte differently. The *C++ byte* consists of at least enough adjacent bits to accommodate the basic character set for the implementation. That is, the number of possible values must equal or exceed the number of distinct characters. In the U.S., the basic character sets usually are the ASCII and EBCDIC sets, each of which can be accommodated by 8 bits, so the C++ byte is 8 bits on systems using these character sets. However, international programming can require much larger character sets, such as Unicode, so some implementations may use a 16-bit byte.

Many systems currently use the minimum guarantee, making `short` 16 bits and `long` 32 bits. This still leaves several choices open for `int`. It could be 16, 24, or 32 bits in size and meet the standard. Typically, `int` is 16 bits (the same as `short`) for older IBM PC implementations and 32 bits (the same as `long`) for Windows 95, Windows NT, Macintosh, VAX, and many other minicomputer implementations. Some implementations give you a choice of how to handle `int`. (What does your implementation use? The next example shows you how to determine the limits for your system without your having to open a manual.) The differences between implementations for type sizes can cause problems when you move a C++ program from one environment to another. But a little care, as discussed later in this chapter, can minimize those problems.

You use these type names to declare variables just as you would use `int`:

```
short score;        // creates a type short integer variable
int temperature;    // creates a type int integer variable
long position;      // creates a type long integer variable
```

Actually, `short` is short for `short int` and `long` is short for `long int`, but hardly anyone uses the longer forms.

The three types, `int`, `short`, and `long`, are signed types, meaning each splits its range approximately equally between positive and negative values. For example, a 16-bit `int` might run from –32768 to +32767.

If you want to know how your system's integers size up, C++ offers tools to let you investigate type sizes with a program. First, the `sizeof` operator returns the size, in bytes, of a type or a variable. (An operator is a built-in language element that operates on one or more items to produce a value. For instance, the addition operator, represented by +, adds two values.) Note that the meaning of "byte" is implementation-dependent, so a two-byte `int` could be 16 bits on one system and 32 bits on another. Second, the `climits` header file (or, for older implementations, the `limits.h` header file) contains information about integer type limits. In particular, it defines symbolic names to represent different limits. For instance, it defines `INT_MAX` to be the largest possible `int` value. Listing 3.1 demonstrates how to use these facilities. The program also illustrates *initialization*, which is the use of a declaration statement to assign a value to a variable.

Listing 3.1 limits.cpp

```cpp
// limits.cpp -- some integer limits
#include <iostream>
using namespace std;
#include <climits>                  // use limits.h for older systems
int main()
{
    int n_int = INT_MAX;          // initialize n_int to max int value
    short n_short = SHRT_MAX;    // symbols defined in limits.h file
    long n_long = LONG_MAX;

    // sizeof operator yields size of type or of variable
    cout << "int is " << sizeof (int) << " bytes.\n";
    cout << "short is " << sizeof n_short << " bytes.\n";
    cout << "long is " << sizeof n_long << " bytes.\n\n";

    cout << "Maximum values:\n";
    cout << "int: " << n_int << "\n";
    cout << "short: " << n_short << "\n";
    cout << "long: " << n_long << "\n\n";

    cout << "Minimum int value = " << INT_MIN << "\n";
    return 0;
}
```

Remember

The `climits` header file is the C++ version of the ANSI C `limits.h` header file. Some earlier C++ platforms have neither header file available. If you're using such a system, you must limit yourself to experiencing this example in spirit only.

Here is the output using Microsoft Visual C++ 5.0:

```
int is 4 bytes.
short is 2 bytes.
long is 4 bytes.

Maximum values:
int: 2147483647
short: 32767
long: 2147483647

Minimum int value = -2147483648
```

Here is the output for a second system (Borland C++ 3.1 for DOS):

```
int is 2 bytes.
short is 2 bytes.
long is 4 bytes.

Maximum values:
int: 32767
short: 32767
long: 2147483647

Minimum int value = -32768
```

Program Notes

This section summarizes the chief programming features for this program.

The `sizeof` operator reports that `int` is 4 bytes on the base system, which uses an 8-bit byte. You can apply the `sizeof` operator to a type name or to a variable name. When you use the `sizeof` operator with a type name, such as `int`, you enclose the name in parentheses. But if you use the operator with the name of the variable, such as n_short, parentheses are optional:

```
cout << "int is " << sizeof (int) << " bytes.\n";
cout << "short is " << sizeof n_short << " bytes.\n";
```

The `climits` header file defines symbolic constants (see the Symbolic Constants note) to represent type limits. As mentioned, `INT_MAX` represents the largest value type `int` can hold; this turned out to be 32767 for our DOS system. The compiler manufacturer provides a `climits` file that reflects the values appropriate to that compiler. For instance, the `climits` file for a system using a 32-bit `int` would define `INT_MAX` to represent 2147483647. Table 3.1 summarizes the symbolic constants defined in this file; some pertain to types you have not yet learned.

TABLE 3.1
SYMBOLIC CONSTANTS FROM `climits`

SYMBOLIC CONSTANT	REPRESENTS
CHAR_BIT	number of bits in a char
CHAR_MAX	maximum char value
CHAR_MIN	minimum char value
SCHAR_MAX	maximum signed char value
SCHAR_MIN	minimum signed char value
UCHAR_MAX	maximum unsigned char value
SHRT_MAX	maximum short value
SHRT_MIN	minimum short value
USHRT_MAX	maximum unsigned short value
INT_MAX	maximum int value
INT_MIN	minimum int value

Continued...

TABLE 3.1
SYMBOLIC CONSTANTS FROM `climits` CONTINUED...

SYMBOLIC CONSTANT	REPRESENTS
UINT_MAX	maximum unsigned int value
LONG_MAX	maximum long value
LONG_MIN	minimum long value
ULONG_MAX	maximum unsigned long value

Initialization combines assignment with declaration. For instance, the statement

```
int n_int = INT_MAX;
```

declares the n_int variable and sets it to the largest possible type int value. You also can use regular constants to initialize values. You can initialize a variable to another variable, provided that the other variable has been defined first. You even can initialize a variable to an expression, provided that all the values in the expression are known at compilation time:

```
int uncles = 5;                  // initialize uncles to 5
int aunts = uncles;              // initialize aunts to 5
int chairs = aunts + uncles + 4; // initialize chairs to 14
```

To move the uncles declaration to the end of this list of statements would invalidate the other two initializations, for then the value of uncles wouldn't be known at the time the compiler tried to initialize the other variables.

Remember

If you don't initialize a variable defined inside a function, the variable's value is _undefined_. That means the value is whatever happened to be sitting at that memory location prior to the creation of the variable.

If you know what the initial value of a variable should be, initialize it. True, separating the declaring of a variable from assigning it a value can create momentary suspense:

```
short year;     // what could it be?
year = 1492;    // oh
```

But initializing the variable when you declare it protects you from forgetting to assign the value later.

SYMBOLIC CONSTANTS THE PREPROCESSOR WAY

The `climits` file contains lines similar to the following:

```
#define INT_MAX 32767
```

The C++ compilation process, recall, first passes the source code through a pre-processor. Here #define, like #include, is a preprocessor directive. What this particular directive tells the preprocessor is this: Look through the program for instances of INT_MAX and replace each occurrence with 32767. So the #define directive works like a global search-and-replace command in an editor or word processor. The altered program is compiled after these replacements occur. The preprocessor looks for independent tokens (separate words), skipping embedded words. That is, the preprocessor doesn't replace PINT_MAXIM with P32767IM. You can use #define to define your own symbolic constants, too. (See Listing 3.2.) However, the #define directive is a C relic. C++ has a better way for creating symbolic constants (the const keyword, discussed in a later section), so you won't be using #define much. But some header files, particularly those designed to be used with both C and C++, do use it.

UNSIGNED TYPES

Each of the three integer types you just learned comes in an unsigned variety that can't hold negative values. This has the advantage of increasing the largest value the variable can hold. For instance, if short represents the range –32768 to +32767, then the unsigned version can represent the range 0 to 65535. Of course, you should use unsigned types only for quantities that are never negative, such as populations, inventory counts, and happy face manifestations. To create unsigned versions of the basic integer types, just use the keyword unsigned to modify the declarations:

```
unsigned short change;      // unsigned short type
unsigned int rovert;        // unsigned int type
unsigned quarterback;       // also unsigned int
unsigned long gone;         // unsigned long type
```

Note that unsigned by itself is short for unsigned int.

Listing 3.2 illustrates the use of unsigned types. It also shows what might happen if your program tries to go beyond the limits for integer types. Finally, it gives you one last look at the preprocessor #define statement.

Listing 3.2 exceed.cpp

```
// exceed.cpp -- exceeding some integer limits
#include <iostream>
using namespace std;
#define ZERO 0      // makes ZERO symbol for 0 value
#include <climits>  // defines INT_MAX as largest int value
int main()
{
    short sam = SHRT_MAX;      // initialize a variable to max value
    unsigned short sue = sam;// okay if variable sam already defined

    cout << "Sam has " << sam << " dollars and Sue has " << sue;
    cout << " dollars deposited.\nAdd $1 to each account.\nNow ";
    sam = sam + 1;
```

```
        sue = sue + 1;
        cout << "Sam has " << sam << " dollars and Sue has " << sue;
        cout << " dollars deposited.\nPoor Sam!\n";
        sam = ZERO;
        sue = ZERO;
        cout << "Sam has " << sam << " dollars and Sue has " << sue;
        cout << " dollars deposited.\n";
        cout << "Take $1 from each account.\nNow ";
        sam = sam - 1;
        sue = sue - 1;
        cout << "Sam has " << sam << " dollars and Sue has " << sue;
        cout << " dollars deposited.\nLucky Sue!\n";          return 0;
}
```

Remember

Listing 3.2, like Listing 3.1, uses the `climits` file; older compilers might need to use `limits.h`, and some very old compilers might not have either file available.

Here's the output:

```
Sam has 32767 dollars and Sue has 32767 dollars deposited.
Add $1 to each account.
Now Sam has -32768 dollars and Sue has 32768 dollars deposited.
Poor Sam!
Sam has 0 dollars and Sue has 0 dollars deposited.
Take $1 from each account.
Now Sam has -1 dollars and Sue has 65535 dollars deposited.
Lucky Sue!
```

The program sets a short variable (sam) and an unsigned short variable (sue) to the largest short value, which is 32767 on our system. Then, it adds 1 to each value. This causes no problems for sue, for the new value still is much less than the maximum value for an unsigned integer. But sam goes from 32767 to –32768! Similarly, subtracting 1 from 0 creates no problems for sam, but it makes the unsigned variable sue go from 0 to 65535. As you can see, these integers behave much like an odometer or a VCR counter. If you go past the limit, the values just start over at the other end of the range. See Figure 3.1. C++ guarantees that unsigned types behave in this fashion. However, C++ doesn't guarantee that integer types can exceed their limits (overflow and underflow) without complaint, but that is the most common behavior on current implementations.

WHICH TYPE?

With this richness of C++ integer types, which should you use? Generally, int is set to the most "natural" integer size for the target computer. *Natural size* means the integer form the computer handles most efficiently. If there is no compelling reason to choose another type, use int.

FIGURE 3.1

Typical overflow behavior for integers

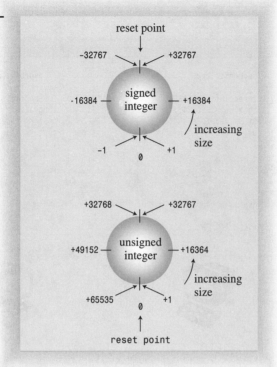

Now look at reasons you might use another type. If a variable represents something that never is negative, such as the number of words in a document, you can use an unsigned type; that way the variable can represent higher values.

If you know that the variable might have to represent integer values too great for a 16-bit integer, use long. This is true even if int is 32 bits on your system. That way, if you transfer your program to a system with a 16-bit int, your program won't embarrass you by suddenly failing to work properly. See Figure 3.2.

Using short can conserve memory if short is smaller than int. Most typically, this is important only if you have a large array of integers. (An *array* is a data structure that stores several values of the same type sequentially in memory.) If it is important to conserve space, you should use short instead of int, even if the two are the same size. Suppose, for example, you move your program from a 16-bit int DOS PC system to a 32-bit int Windows NT system. That doubles the amount of memory needed to hold an int array, but it doesn't affect the requirements for a short array. Remember, a bit saved is a bit earned.

If you need only a single byte, you can use char. You'll examine that possibility soon.

> **"** *If you know that the variable might have to represent integer values too great for a 16-bit integer, use* long*. This is true even if* int *is 32 bits on your system.* **"**

FIGURE 3.2

For portability, use *long* *for big integers*

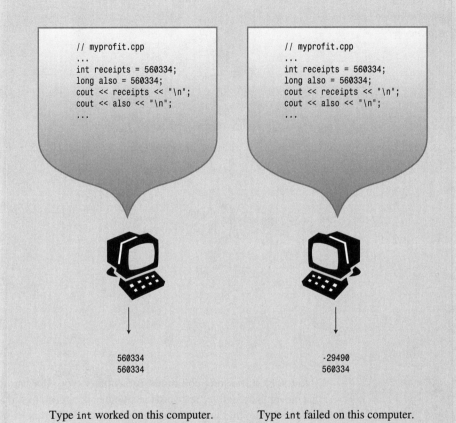

```
// myprofit.cpp
...
int receipts = 560334;
long also = 560334;
cout << receipts << "\n";
cout << also << "\n";
...
```

```
// myprofit.cpp
...
int receipts = 560334;
long also = 560334;
cout << receipts << "\n";
cout << also << "\n";
...
```

```
560334
560334
```

```
-29490
560334
```

Type int worked on this computer.   Type int failed on this computer.

INTEGER CONSTANTS

An integer constant is one you write out explicitly, such as 212 or 1776. C++, like C, lets you write integers in three different number bases: base 10 (the public favorite), base 8 (the old UNIX favorite), and base 16 (the hardware hacker's favorite). Appendix A, "Number Bases," describes these bases; here we'll look at the C++ representations. C++ uses the first digit or two to identify the base of a number constant. If the first digit is in the range 1–9, the number is base 10 (decimal); thus 93 is base 10. If the first digit is 0 and the second digit is in the range 1–7, the number is base 8 (octal); thus 042 is octal and equal to 34 decimal. If the first two characters are 0x or 0X, the number is base 16 (hexadecimal); thus 0x42 is hex and equal to 66 decimal. For hexadecimal values, the characters a–f and A–F represent the hexadecimal digits corresponding to the values 10–15. 0xF is 15 and 0xA5 is 165 (10 sixteens plus 5 ones). Listing 3.3 is tailor-made to show the three bases.

Listing 3.3 hexoct.cpp

```
// hexoct.cpp -- shows hex and octal constants
#include <iostream>
using namespace std;
int main()
{
    int chest = 42;      // decimal integer constant
    int waist = 0x42;    // hexadecimal integer constant
    int inseam = 042;    // octal integer constant

    cout << "Monsieur cuts a striking figure!\n";
    cout << "chest = " << chest << "\n";
    cout << "waist = " << waist << "\n";
    cout << "inseam = " << inseam << "\n";
    return 0;
}
```

By default, cout displays integers in decimal form, regardless of how they are written in a program, as the following output shows:

```
Monsieur cuts a striking figure!
chest = 42
waist = 66
inseam = 34
```

Keep in mind that these notations are merely notational conveniences. For instance, if you read that the CGA video memory segment is B000 in hexadecimal, you don't have to convert the value to base ten 45056 before using it in your program. Instead, simply use 0xB000. But whether you write the value ten as 10, 012, or 0xA, it's stored the same way in the computer—as a binary (base two) value.

By the way, if you want to display a value in hexadecimal or octal form, you can use some special features of cout. Let's not get into that now, but you can find this information in Chapter 16, "Input, Output, and Files." (You can skim the chapter for that information and ignore the explanations.) On input, cin recognizes the C++ notation for different number bases. So if you type 0x20, cin interprets that as a hex value, the equivalent of 32.

HOW C++ DECIDES WHAT TYPE A CONSTANT IS

A program's declarations tell the C++ compiler the type of a particular integer variable. But what about constants? That is, suppose you represent a number with a constant in a program:

```
cout << "Year = " << 1492 << "\n";
```

Does the program store 1492 as an int, a long, or some other integer type? The answer is that C++ stores integer constants as type int unless there is a reason to do otherwise. Two such reasons are if you use a special suffix to indicate a particular type or if a value is too large to be an int.

First, look at the suffixes. These are letters placed at the end of a numeric constant to indicate the type. An l or L suffix on an integer means the integer is a type long constant, a u or U suffix indicates an unsigned int constant, and ul (in any combination of orders and uppercase and lowercase) indicates a type unsigned long constant. (Because a lowercase l can look much like the digit 1, you should use the uppercase L for suffixes.) For example, on a system using a 16-bit int and a 32-bit long, the number 22022 is stored in 16 bits as an int, and the number 22022L is stored in 32 bits as a long. Similarly, 22022LU and 22022UL are unsigned long.

Next, look at size. C++ has slightly different rules for decimal integers than it has for hexadecimal and octal integers. (Here decimal means base 10, just as hexadecimal means base 16; the term does not necessarily imply a decimal point.) A decimal integer without a suffix is represented by the smallest of the following types that can hold it: int, long, or unsigned long. On a computer system using a 16-bit int and a 32-bit long, 20000 is represented as type int, 40000 is represented as long, and 3000000000 is represented as unsigned long. A hexadecimal or octal integer without a suffix is represented by the smallest of the following types that can hold it: int, unsigned int, long, unsigned long. The same computer system that represents 40000 as long represents the hexadecimal equivalent 0x9C40 as an unsigned int. That's because hexadecimal frequently is used to express memory addresses, which intrinsically are unsigned. So unsigned int is more appropriate than long for a 16-bit address.

THE char TYPE: CHARACTERS AND SMALL INTEGERS

It's time to turn to the final integer type, type char. As you probably suspect from its name, the char type is designed to store characters, such as letters and digits. Now, whereas storing numbers is no big deal for computers, storing letters is another matter. Programming languages take the easy way out by using a number code for letters. Thus, the char type is another integer type. It's guaranteed to be large enough to represent the entire range of basic symbols—all the letters, digits, punctuation, and the like—for the target computer system. In practice, most systems support fewer than 256 kinds of characters, so a single byte can represent the whole range. Therefore, although char most often is used to handle characters, you also can use it as an integer type typically smaller than short.

The most common symbol set in the United States is the ASCII (pronounced askey) character set described in Appendix C, "The ASCII Character Set." A numeric code (the ASCII code) represents the characters in the set. For example, 65 is the code for the character A. For convenience, this book assumes ASCII code in its examples. However, a C++ implementation uses whatever code is native to its host system—for instance, EBCDIC (pronounced eb-se-dik) on an IBM mainframe. Neither ASCII nor EBCDIC serve international needs that well, and C++ supports a wide-character type that can hold a larger range of values, such as are used by the international Unicode character set. You'll learn about this wchar_t type later in this chapter.

Try the char type in Listing 3.4.

Listing 3.4 chartype.cpp

```cpp
// chartype.cpp -- the char type
#include <iostream>
using namespace std;
int main( )
{
    char ch;          // declare a char variable

    cout << "Enter a character:\n";
    cin >> ch;
    cout << "Holla! ";
    cout << "Thank you for the " << ch << " character.\n";
    return 0;
}
```

As usual, the \n notation is the C++ representation of the newline character. Here's the output:

```
Enter a character:
M
Holla! Thank you for the M character.
```

The interesting thing is that you type an M, not the corresponding character code of 77. Also, the program prints an M, not a 77. Yet if you peer into memory, you find that 77 is the value stored in the ch variable. The magic, such as it is, lies not in the char type but in cin and cout. These worthy facilities make conversions on your behalf. On input, cin converts the keystroke input M to the value 77. On output, cout converts the value 77 to the displayed character of M; cin and cout are guided by the type of variable. If you place the same value of 77 into an int variable, then cout displays it as 77. (That is, cout displays two 7 characters.) Listing 3.5 illustrates this point. It also shows how to write a character constant in C++: Enclose the character within two single quotation marks, as in 'M'. (Note that the example doesn't use double quotation marks. C++ uses single quotation marks for a character and double quotation marks for a string. As Chapter 4 discusses, the two are quite different.) Finally, the program introduces a cout feature, the cout.put() function, which displays a single character.

Listing 3.5 morechar.cpp

```cpp
// morechar.cpp -- the char type and int type contrasted
#include <iostream>
using namespace std;
int main()
{
    char c = 'M';         // assign ASCII code for M to c
    int i = c;            // store same code in an int
    cout << "The ASCII code for " << c << " is " << i << "\n";

    cout << "Add one to the character code:\n";
    c = c + 1;
    i = c;
    cout << "The ASCII code for " << c << " is " << i << '\n';

    // using the cout.put() member function to display a char
    cout << "Displaying char c using cout.put(c): ";
```

```
        cout.put(c);

        // using cout.put() to display a char constant
        cout.put('!');

        cout << "\nDone\n";
        return 0;
    }
```

Here is the output:

```
The ASCII code for M is 77
Add one to the character code:
The ASCII code for N is 78
Displaying char c using cout.put(c): N!
Done
```

Program Notes

The notation `'M'` represents the numeric code for the M character, so initializing the char variable c to `'M'` sets c to the value 77. The program then assigns the identical value to the int variable i. Both c and i have the value 77. Next, cout displays c as M and i as 77. As previously stated, a value's type guides cout as it chooses how to display that value—just another example of smart objects.

Because c is really an integer, you can apply integer operations to it, such as adding 1. This changes the value of c to 78. The program then resets i to the new value. (Equivalently, you simply can add 1 to i.) Again, cout displays the char version of that value as a character and the int version as a number.

The fact that C++ represents characters as integers is a genuine convenience that makes it easy to manipulate character values. You don't have to use awkward conversion functions to convert characters to ASCII and back.

Finally, the program uses the `cout.put()` function to display both c and a character constant.

A Member Function: `cout.put()`

Just what is `cout.put()`, and why does it have a period in its name? The `cout.put()` function is your first example of an important C++ OOP concept, the *member function*. A class, remember, defines how to represent data and how to manipulate it. A member function belongs to a class and describes a method for manipulating class data. The `ostream` class, for instance, has a `put()` member function designed to output characters. You can use a member function only with a particular object of that class, such as the cout object, in this case. To use a class member function with an object like cout, you use a period to combine the object name (cout) with the function name (put()). The period is called the *membership operator*. The notation `cout.put()` means to use the class member function put() with the class object cout. Of course, you'll learn about this in greater detail when you reach classes in Chapter 9, "Objects and Classes." Now, the only classes you have are the istream and ostream classes, and you can experiment with their member functions to get more comfortable with the concept.

The `cout.put()` member function provides an alternative to using the `<<` operator to display a character. At this point you might wonder why there is any need for `cout.put()`. Much of the answer is historical. Prior to Release 2.0 of C++, cout would display character variables as characters but display character constants, such as `'M'` and `'\n'`, as numbers. The problem was that earlier versions of C++, like C, stored character constants as type `int`. That is, the code 77 for `'M'` would be stored in a 16-bit or 32-bit unit. Meanwhile, `char` variables typically occupied 8 bits. A statement like

```
char c = 'M';
```

copied 8 bits (the important 8 bits) from the constant `'M'` to the variable c. Unfortunately, this meant that `'M'` and c looked quite different to cout, even though both held the same value. So a statement like

```
cout << '$';
```

would print the ASCII code for the $ character rather than simply display $. But

```
cout.put('$');
```

would print the character, as desired. Now, after Release 2.0, C++ stores single character constants as type `char`, not type `int`. That means cout now correctly handles character constants. C++ always could use the string `"\n"` to start a new line; now it also can use the character constant `'\n'`:

```
cout << "\n"; // using a string
cout << '\n'; // using a character constant
```

A string is enclosed in double quotation marks instead of single quotation marks and can hold more than one character. Strings, even one-character strings, are not the same as type `char`. You come back to strings in the next chapter.

The `cin` object has a couple of different ways of reading characters from input. You more easily explore these by using a program that uses a loop to read several characters, so you go into the matter when you cover loops in Chapter 5, "Loops and Relational Expressions."

`char` Constants

You have several options for writing character constants in C++. The simplest choice for ordinary characters, such as letters, punctuation, and digits, is to enclose the character in single quotation marks. This notation stands for the numeric code for the character. For instance, an ASCII system has the following correspondences:

```
'A' is 65, the ASCII code for A
'a' is 97, the ASCII code for a
'5' is 53, the ASCII code for the digit 5
' ' is 32, the ASCII code for the space character
'!' is 33, the ASCII code for the exclamation mark
```

Using this notation is better than using the numeric codes explicitly. It's clearer, and it doesn't assume a particular code. If a system uses EBCDIC, then 65 is not the code for A, but `'A'` still represents the character.

You can't enter some characters into a program directly from the keyboard. For instance, you can't make the newline character part of a string by pressing the Enter key; instead, the program editor interprets that keystroke as a request for it to start a new line in your source code file. Other characters have difficulties because the C++ language imbues them with special significance. For instance, the double quotation mark character delimits strings, so you can't just stick one in the middle of a string. C++ has special notations, called *escape sequences*, for several of these characters, as shown in Table 3.2. For instance, \a represents the alert character, which beeps your terminal's speaker or rings its bell. And \" represents the double quotation mark as an ordinary character instead of a string delimiter. You can use these notations in strings or in character constants:

```cpp
char alarm = '\a';
cout << alarm << "Don't do that again!\a\n";
cout << "Ben \"Buggsie\" Hacker was here!\n";
```

The last line produces the following output:

```
Ben "Buggsie" Hacker was here!
```

Note that you treat an escape sequence, such as \a, just as a regular character, such as Q. That is, you enclose it in single quotes to create a character constant and don't use single quotes when including it as part of a string.

TABLE 3.2
C++ ESCAPE SEQUENCE CODES

CHARACTER NAME	ASCII SYMBOL	C++ CODE	ASCII DECIMAL CODE	ASCII HEX CODE
newline	NL (LF)	\n	10	0xA
horizontal tab	HT	\t	9	0x9
vertical tab	VT	\v	11	0xB
backspace	BS	\b	8	0x8
carriage return	CR	\r	13	0xD
alert	BEL	\a	7	0x7
backslash	\	\\	92	0x5C
question mark	?	\?	63	0x3F
single quote	´	\'	39	0x27
double quote	″	\"	34	0x22

Finally, you can use escape sequences based on the octal or hexadecimal codes for a character. For instance, CTRL-Z has an ASCII code of 26, which is 032 in octal and 0x1a in hexadecimal. You can represent this character by either of the following escape sequences: \032 or \x1a. You can make character constants out of these by enclosing them in single quotes, as in '\032', and you can use them as parts of a string, as in "hi\x1a there".

When you have a choice between using a numeric escape sequence or a symbolic escape sequence, as in \0x8 versus \b, use the symbolic code. The numeric representation is tied to a particular code, such as ASCII, but the symbolic representation works with all codes and is more readable.

Listing 3.6 demonstrates a few escape sequences. It uses the alert character to get your attention, the newline character to advance the cursor (one small step for a cursor, one giant step for cursorkind), and the backspace character to back the cursor one space to the left. (Houdini once painted a picture of the Hudson River using only escape sequences; he was, of course, a great escape artist.)

Listing 3.6 bondini.cpp

```
// bondini.cpp -- using escape sequences
#include <iostream>
using namespace std;
int main()
{
    cout << "\aOperation \"HyperHype\" is now activated!\n";
    cout << "Enter your agent code:_____\b\b\b\b\b\b\b\b";
    long code;
    cin >> code;
    cout << "\aYou entered " << code << "...\n";
    cout << "\aCode verified! Proceed with Plan Z3!\n";
    return 0;
}
```

Some C++ systems based on pre-ANSI C compilers don't recognize \a. You can substitute \007 for \a on systems that use the ASCII character code. Some systems might behave differently, displaying the \b as a small rectangle rather than backspacing, for example, or perhaps erasing as backspacing.

When you start the program, it puts the following text on the screen:

```
Operation "HyperHype" is now activated!
Enter your agent code:_____
```

After printing the underscore characters, the program uses the backspace character to back up the cursor to the first underscore. You then can enter your secret code and continue. Here's a complete run:

```
Operation "HyperHype" is now activated!
Enter your agent code:42007007
You entered 42007007...
Code verified! Proceed with Plan Z3!
```

signed char and unsigned char

Unlike int, char is not signed by default. Nor is it unsigned by default. The choice is left to the C++ implementation in order to allow the compiler developer to best fit the type to the hardware properties. If it is vital to you that char has a particular behavior, you can use signed char or unsigned char explicitly as types:

```
char fodo;             // may be signed, may be unsigned
unsigned char bar;     // definitely unsigned
signed char snark;     // definitely signed
```

These distinctions are particularly important if you use char as a numeric type. The unsigned char type typically represents the range 0 to 255, and signed char typically represents the range -128 to 127. For example, suppose you want to use a char variable to hold values as large as 200. That works on some systems but fails on others. You can, however, successfully use unsigned char for that purpose on any system. On the other hand, if you use a char variable to hold a standard ASCII character, it doesn't really matter whether char is signed or unsigned, so you simply can use char.

For When You Need More: wchart_t

Programs might have to handle character sets that don't fit within the confines of a single 8-bit byte; for instance, the Japanese kanja system. C++ handles this in a couple of ways. First, if a large set of characters is the basic character set for an implementation, a compiler vender can define char as a 16-bit byte or larger. Second, an implementation can support both a small basic character set and a larger extended character set. The usual 8-bit char can represent the basic character set, and a new type, called wchar_t (for *w*ide *char*acter *t*ype), can represent the extended character set. The wchar_t type is an integer type with sufficient space to represent the largest extended character set used on the system. This type has the same size and sign properties as one of the other integer types, which is called the *underlying* type. The choice of underlying type depends on the implementation, so it could be unsigned short on one system and int on another.

The cin and cout family consider input and output as consisting of streams of chars, so they are not suitable for handling the wchar_t type. The latest version of the iostream header file provides parallel facilities in the form of wcin and wcout for handling wchar_t streams. Also, you can indicate a wide-character constant or string by preceding it with an L.

```
wchar_t bob = L'P';          // a wide-character constant
wcout << L"tall" << endl;     // outputting a wide-character string
```

On a system with a two-byte `wchar_t`, this code stores each character in a two-byte unit of memory. This book won't use the wide-character type, but you should be aware of it, particularly if you become involved in international programming or in using Unicode.

UNICODE

Unicode provides a solution to the representation of various character sets by providing standard numeric codes for a great number of characters and symbols, grouping them by type. For example, the ASCII code is incorporated as a subset of Unicode, so U.S. Latin characters such as A and Z have the same representation under both systems. But Unicode also incorporates other Latin characters, such as are used in European languages; characters from other alphabets, including Greek, Cyrillic, Hebrew, Arabic, Thai, and Bengali; and ideographs, such as those used for Chinese and Japanese. So far Unicode represents over 38,000 symbols, and it still is under development. If you want to know more, you can check the Unicode Consortium's Web site at `www.unicode.org`.

THE NEW bool TYPE

The ANSI/ISO C++ standards committee has accepted a new type (new to C++, that is), called `bool`. It's named in honor of the English mathematician George Boole, who developed a mathematical representation of the laws of logic. In computing, a *Boolean variable* is one whose value can be either true or false. In the past, C++, like C, has not had a Boolean type. Instead, as you can see in greater detail in Chapters 5, "Loops and Relational Expressions," and 6, "Branching Statements and Logical Operators," C++ used to interpret nonzero values as true and zero values as false. Now, however, you can use the `bool` type to represent true and false, and the predefined literals `true` and `false` represent those values. That is, you can make statements like the following:

```
bool isready = true;
```

The literals `true` and `false` can be converted to type `int` by promotion, with `true` converting to 1 and `false` to 0:

```
int ans = true;              // ans assigned 1
int promise = false;         // promise assigned 0
```

Also, any numeric or pointer value can be converted implicitly (that is, without an explicit type cast) to a `bool` value. Any nonzero value converts to `true`, whereas a zero value converts to `false`:

```
bool start = -100;      // start assigned true
bool stop = 0;          // stop assigned false
```

Later chapters illustrate how this type can come in handy.

The `const` Qualifier

Now let's return to the topic of symbolic names for constants. A symbolic name can suggest what the constant represents. Also, if the program uses the constant in several places and you need to change the value, you can just change the single symbol definition. The note about #define statements earlier in this chapter (Symbolic Constants the Preprocessor Way) promised that C++ has a better way to handle symbolic constants. That way is to use the `const` keyword to modify a variable declaration and initialization. Suppose, for instance, that you want a symbolic constant for the number of months in a year. Enter this line in a program:

```
const int MONTHS = 12;  // Months is symbolic constant for 12
```

Now you can use MONTHS in a program instead of 12. (A bare 12 in a program might represent the number of inches in a foot or the number of donuts in a dozen, but the name MONTHS tells you what it represents.) After you initialize a constant like MONTHS, its value is set. The compiler does not let you subsequently change the value MONTHS. For instance, Borland C++ gives an error message stating that an Lvalue is required. This is the same message you get if you try, say, to assign the value 4 to 3. (An Lvalue is a value, such as a variable, that appears on the left side of the assignment operator.) The keyword `const` is termed a *qualifier* because it qualifies the meaning of a declaration.

Capitalize the name to help remind yourself that MONTHS is a constant. This is by no means a universal convention, but it helps separate the constants from the variables when you read a program. Another convention is capitalizing just the first character in the name. Yet another convention is to begin constant names with the letter k, as in kmonths. And there are yet other conventions. Many organizations have particular coding conventions they expect their programmers to follow.

The general form for creating a constant is this:

```
const type name = value;
```

Note that you initialize a const in the declaration. The following sequence is no good:

```
const int toes;    // value of toes undefined at this point
toes = 10;         // too late!
```

If you don't provide a value when you declare the constant, it ends up with an unspecified value that you cannot modify.

If your background is in C, you might feel that the #define statement, which was discussed earlier, already does the job adequately. But const is better. For one thing, it lets you specify the type explicitly. Second, you can use C++'s scoping rules to limit the definition to particular functions or files. (Scoping rules describe how widely known a name is to different modules; you learn about this in more detail in Chapter 8, "Adventures in Functions.") Third, you can use const with more elaborate types, such as the arrays and structures coming up in the next chapter.

Remember

If you are coming to C++ from C and you are about to use #define to define a symbolic constant, use const instead.

ANSI C also uses the const qualifier. If you're familiar with the ANSI C version, you should be aware that the C++ version is slightly different. One difference relates to the scope rules, and Chapter 8 covers that point. The other main difference is that in C++ (but not in C) you can use a const value to declare the size of an array. You'll see examples in the next chapter.

Floating-Point Numbers

Now that you have seen the complete line of C++ integer types, let's look at the floating-point types, which compose the second major group of fundamental C++ types. These numbers let you represent numbers with fractional parts, such as the gas mileage of an M1 tank (0.56 MPG). They also provide a much greater range in values. If a number is too large to be represented as type long, for instance, the number of stars in our galaxy (an estimated 400,000,000,000), you can use one of the floating-point types.

With floating-point types, you can represent numbers like 2.5 and 3.14159 and 122442.32, that is, numbers with a fractional part. A computer stores such values in two parts. One part represents a value, and the other part scales that value up or down. Here's an analogy. Consider the two numbers 34.1245 and 34124.5. They're identical except for scale. You can represent the first one as 0.341245 (the base value) and 100 (the scaling factor). You can represent the second as 0.341245 (the same base value) and 100000 (a bigger scaling factor). The scaling factor serves to move the decimal point, hence the term floating-point. C++ uses a similar method to represent floating-point numbers internally, except it's based on binary numbers, so the scaling is by factors of 2 instead of by factors of 10. Fortunately, you don't have to know much about the internal representation. The main points are that floating-point numbers let you represent fractional, very large, and very small values, and they have an internal representation much different from that of integers.

WRITING FLOATING-POINT NUMBERS

C++ has two ways of writing floating-point numbers. The first is to use the standard decimal-point notation you've been using much of your life:

```
12.34            // floating-point
939001.32        // floating-point
0.00023          // floating-point
8.0              // still floating-point
```

Even if the fractional part is 0, as in 8.0, the decimal point ensures that the number is stored in floating-point format and not as an integer.

The second method for representing floating-point values is called E notation, and it looks like this: `3.45E6`. This means that the value 3.45 is multiplied by 1,000,000; the E6 means 10 to the 6th power, which is 1 followed by 6 zeros. Thus `3.45E6` means 3,450,000. The 6 is called an *exponent*, and the 3.45 is termed the *mantissa*. Here are more examples:

```
2.52e+8              // can use E or e, + is optional
8.33E-4              // exponent can be negative
7E5                  // same as 7.0E+05
-18.32e13            // can have + or - sign in front
2.857e12             // US public debt, 1989
5.98E24              // mass of Earth in kilograms
9.11e-31             // mass of an electron in kilograms
```

As you may have noticed, E notation is most useful for very large and very small numbers.

E notation guarantees that the number is stored in floating-point format, even if no decimal point is used. Note that you can use either E or e, and the exponent can have a positive or negative sign (see Figure 3.3). However, you can't have spaces in the number: `7.2 E6` is invalid.

To use a negative exponent means to divide by a power of 10 instead of multiplying by a power of 10. So 8.33E-4 means 8.33 ÷ 10^4, or 0.000833. Similarly, the electron mass of 9.11e-31 kg means:

`0.000000000000000000000000000000911 kg`

Take your choice. (Incidentally, note that 911 is the usual emergency telephone number in the United States and that telephone messages are carried by electrons.

FIGURE 3.3

E notation

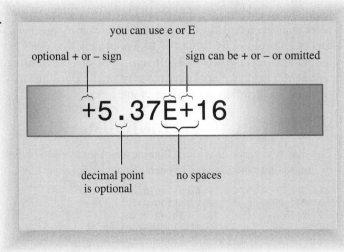

Coincidence or scientific conspiracy? You be the judge.) Note that –8.33E4 means –83300. A sign in front applies to the number value, while a sign in the exponent applies to the scaling.

Remember

The form d.dddE+n means move the decimal point n places to the right, and the form d.dddE-n means move the decimal point n places to the left.

FLOATING-POINT TYPES

"Significant figures are the meaningful digits in a number... writing the height of Mt. Shasta in California as 14,162 feet uses five significant figures, [but] writing the height of Mt. Shasta as about 14,000 feet tall uses two significant figures..."

Like ANSI C, C++ has three floating-point types: `float`, `double`, and `long double`. These types are described in terms of the number of significant figures they can represent and the minimum allowable range of exponents. *Significant figures* are the meaningful digits in a number. For example, writing the height of Mt. Shasta in California as 14,162 feet uses five significant figures, for it specifies the height to the nearest foot. But writing the height of Mt. Shasta as about 14,000 feet tall uses two significant figures, for the result is rounded to the nearest thousand feet. In this case, the remaining three digits are just placeholders. The number of significant figures doesn't depend on the location of the decimal point. For instance, you can write the height as 14.162 thousand feet. Again, this uses five significant digits, because the value is accurate to the fifth digit.

In effect, the C and C++ requirements for significant digits amount to `float` being at least 32 bits, `double` being at least 48 bits and certainly no smaller than `float`, and `long double` being at least as big as `double`. All three can be the same size. Typically, however, `float` is 32 bits, `double` is 64 bits, and `long double` is 80, 96, or 128 bits. Also, the range in exponents for all three types is at least -37 to +37. You can look in the `cfloat` or `float.h` header files to find the limits for your system. (The `cfloat` is the C++ version of the C `float.h` file.) Here, for example, are some annotated entries from the `float.h` file for Borland C++Builder:

```
// the following are the minimum number of significant digits
#define DBL_DIG 15          // double
#define FLT_DIG 6           // float
#define LDBL_DIG 18         // long double

// the following are the number of bits used to represent
// the mantissa
#define DBL_MANT_DIG      53
#define FLT_MANT_DIG      24
#define LDBL_MANT_DIG     64

// the following are the maximum and minimum exponent values
#define DBL_MAX_10_EXP    +308
#define FLT_MAX_10_EXP    +38
#define LDBL_MAX_10_EXP   +4932

#define DBL_MIN_10_EXP    -307
#define FLT_MIN_10_EXP    -37
#define LDBL_MIN_10_EXP   -4931
```

Listing 3.7 examines types `float` and `double` and how they can differ in the precision to which they represent numbers (that's the significant figure aspect). The program previews an `ostream` method called `setf()` from Chapter 16, "Input, Output, and Files." This particular call forces output to stay in fixed-point notation so that you can better see the precision. It prevents the program from switching to E notation for large values and causes the program to display six digits to the right of the decimal. The arguments `ios_base::fixed` and `ios_base::floatfield` are constants provided by including `iostream`.

Listing 3.7 floatnum.cpp

```cpp
// floatnum.cpp -- floating-point types
#include <iostream>
using namespace std;
int main()
{
    cout.setf(ios_base::fixed, ios_base::floatfield); // fixed-point
    float tub = 10.0 / 3.0;      // good to about 6 places
    double mint = 10.0 / 3.0;    // good to about 15 places
    const float million = 1.0e6;

    cout << "tub = " << tub;
    cout << ", a million tubs = " << million * tub;
    cout << ",\nand ten million tubs = ";
    cout << 10 * million * tub << "\n";

    cout << "mint = " << mint << " and a million mints = ";
    cout << million * mint << "\n";
    return 0;
}
```

Here is the output:

```
tub = 3.333333, a million tubs = 3333333.250000,
and ten million tubs = 33333332.000000
mint = 3.333333 and a million mints = 3333333.333333
```

The default setting also suppresses trailing zeros, displaying 23.4500 as 23.45. Implementations differ in how they respond to using the setf() statement to override the default settings. Older versions, such as Borland C++ 3.1 for DOS, suppress trailing zeros in this mode as well. More recent versions, such as Microsoft Visual C++, Metrowerks CodeWarrior, and Borland C++ Builder, display the zeros, as shown in Listing 3.7.

Program Notes

Normally cout drops trailing zeros. For example, it would display 3333333.250000 as 3333333.25. The call to cout.setf() overrides that behavior, at least in new implementations. The main thing to note here is how float has less precision than double. Both tub and mint are initialized to 10.0 / 3.0. That should evaluate to 3.33333333333333333...(etc.). Because cout prints six figures to the right of the decimal, you can see that both tub and mint are accurate that far. But, after the program multiplies each number by a million, you see that tub diverges from the proper value after the seventh 3. tub is good to seven significant figures. (This system guarantees six significant figures for float, but that's the worst-case scenario.) The type double variable, however, shows thirteen 3s, so it's good to at least thirteen significant figures. Because the system guarantees fifteen, this shouldn't surprise you. Also, note that multiplying a million tubs by ten didn't quite result in the correct answer; this again points out the limitations of float precision.

The ostream class to which cout belongs has class member functions that give you precise control on how the output is formatted—field widths, places to the right of the decimal point, decimal form or E form, and so on. Chapter 16 outlines those choices. This book's examples keep it simple and usually just use the << operator. Occasionally, this practice displays more digits than necessary, but that causes only esthetic harm. If you do mind, you can skim through Chapter 16 to see how to use the formatting methods. Don't, however, expect to follow fully the explanations at this point.

FLOATING-POINT CONSTANTS

When you write a floating-point constant in a program, in which floating-point type does the program store it? By default, floating-point constants such as 8.24 and 2.4E8 are type double. If you want a constant to be type float, use an f or F suffix. For type long double, use an l or L suffix.

```
1.234f          // a float constant
2.45E20F        // a float constant
2.345324E28     // a double constant
2.2L            // a long double constant
```

FLOATING-POINT ADVANTAGES AND DISADVANTAGES

Floating-point numbers have two advantages over integers. First, they can represent values between integers. Second, because of the scaling factor, they can represent a much greater range of values. On the other hand, floating-point operations are slower than integer operations, at least on computers without math coprocessors, and you can lose precision. Listing 3.8 illustrates the last point.

Listing 3.8 fltadd.cpp

```cpp
// fltadd.cpp -- precision problems with float
#include <iostream>
using namespace std;
int main()
{
    float a = 2.34E+22f;
    float b = a + 1.0f;

    cout << "a = " << a << "\n";
    cout << "b - a = " << b - a << "\n";
    return 0;
}
```

Remember

Some ancient C++ implementations based on pre-ANSI C compilers don't support the f suffix for floating-point constants. If you find yourself facing this problem, you can replace 2.34E+22f with 2.34E+22 and replace 1.0f with (float) 1.0.

The program takes a number, adds 1, and then subtracts the original number. That should result in a value of 1. Does it? Here is the output for one system:

```
a = 2.34e+022
b - a = 0
```

The problem is that 2.34E+22 represents a number with 23 digits to the left of the decimal place. By adding 1, you are attempting to add 1 to the 23rd digit in that number. But type float only can represent the first 6 or 7 digits in a number, so trying to change the 23rd digit has no effect on the value.

CLASSIFYING THE TYPES

C++ brings some order to its basic types by classifying them into families. Types `signed char`, `short`, `int`, and `long` are termed *signed integer* types. The unsigned versions are termed *unsigned integer* types. The `bool`, `char`, `wchar_t`, signed integer, and unsigned integer types together are termed *integral* types or *integer* types. The `float`, `double`, and `long double` are termed *floating-point* types. Integer and floating-point types collectively are termed *arithmetic* types.

C++ Arithmetic Operators

Perhaps you have warm memories of doing arithmetic drills in grade school. You can give that same pleasure to your computer. C++ uses operators to do arithmetic. It provides operators for five basic arithmetic calculations: addition, subtraction, multiplication, division, and taking the modulus. Each of these operators uses two values (called *operands*) to calculate a final answer. Together, the operator and its operands constitute an *expression*. For instance, consider the following statement:

```
int wheels = 4 + 2;
```

The values 4 and 2 are operands, the + symbol is the addition operator, and 4 + 2 is an expression whose value is 6.

Here are C++'s five basic arithmetic operators:

- The + operator adds its operands. For instance, 4 + 20 evaluates to 24.

- The - operator subtracts the second operand from the first. For instance, 12 - 3 evaluates to 9.

- The * operator multiplies its operands. For instance, 28 * 4 evaluates to 112.

- The / operator divides its first operand by the second. For instance, 1000 / 5 evaluates to 200. If both operands are integers, the result is the integer portion of the quotient. For instance, 17 / 3 is 5, with the fractional part discarded.

- The % operator finds the modulus of its first operand with respect to the second. That is, it produces the remainder of dividing the first by the second. For instance, 19 % 6 is 1, because 6 goes into 19 three times with a remainder of 1. Both operands must be integer types. If one of the operands is negative, the sign of the result depends on the implementation.

Of course, you can use variables as well as constants for operands. Listing 3.9 does just that. Because the % operator works only with integers, we'll use it in a later example.

Listing 3.9 arith.cpp

```cpp
// arith.cpp -- some C++ arithmetic
#include <iostream>
using namespace std;
int main()
{
    float hats, heads;

    cout.setf(ios_base::fixed, ios_base::floatfield); // fixed-point
    cout << "Enter a number: ";
    cin >> hats;
    cout << "Enter another number: ";
    cin >> heads;

    cout << "hats = " << hats << "; heads = " << heads << "\n";
    cout << "hats + heads = " << hats + heads << "\n";
    cout << "hats - heads = " << hats - heads << "\n";
    cout << "hats * heads = " << hats * heads << "\n";
    cout << "hats / heads = " << hats / heads << "\n";
    return 0;
}
```

Remember

> If your compiler does not accept the `ios_base` forms in `setf()`, try using the older `ios` forms instead.

Here's sample output. As you can see, you can trust C++ to do simple arithmetic:

```
Enter a number: 50.25
Enter another number: 11.17
hats = 50.250000; heads = 11.170000
hats + heads = 61.419998
hats - heads = 39.080002
hats * heads = 561.292480
hats / heads = 4.498657
```

Well, maybe you can't trust it completely. Adding 11.17 to 50.25 should yield 61.42, but the output reports 61.419998. This is not an arithmetic problem; it's a problem with the limited capacity of type `float` to represent significant figures.

Remember, C++ guarantees just six significant figures for `float`. If you round 61.419998 to six figures, you get 61.4200, which is the correct value to the guaranteed precision. The moral is that if you need greater accuracy, use `double` or `long double`.

WHICH ORDER: OPERATOR PRECEDENCE AND ASSOCIATIVITY

Can you trust C++ to do complicated arithmetic? Yes, but you need to know the rules C++ uses. For instance, many expressions involve more than one operator. That can raise questions about which operator gets applied first. For example, consider this statement:

```
int flyingpigs = 3 + 4 * 5;   // 35 or 23?
```

The 4 appears to be an operand for both the + and the * operators. When more than one operator can be applied to the same operand, C++ uses *precedence* rules to decide which operator is used first. The arithmetic operators follow the usual algebraic precedence, with multiplication, division, and the taking of the modulus done before addition and subtraction. Thus 3 + 4 * 5 means 3 + (4 * 5), not (3 + 4) * 5. So the answer is 23, not 35. Of course, you can use parentheses to enforce your own priorities. Appendix D, "Operator Precedence," shows precedence for all the C++ operators. In it, note that *, /, and % all are in the same row. That means they have equal precedence. Similarly, addition and subtraction share a lower precedence.

Sometimes the precedence list is not enough. Consider the next statement:

```
float logs = 120 / 4 * 5;      // 150 or 6?
```

> " *When more than one operator can be applied to the same operand, C++ uses* precedence *rules to decide which operator is used first.* "

Once again 4 is an operand for two operators. But the / and * operators have the same precedence, so precedence alone doesn't tell the program whether first to divide 120 by 4 or to multiply the 4 by 5. Because the first choice leads to a result of 150 and the second to a result of 6, the choice is an important one. When two operators have the same precedence, C++ looks at whether the operators have a left-to-right *associativity* or a right-to-left associativity. Left-to-right associativity means that if two operators acting upon the same operand have the same precedence, apply the left-hand operator first. For right-to-left associativity, apply the right-hand operator first. The associativity information, too, is in Appendix D. There you see that multiplication and division associate left-to-right. That means you use 4 with the leftmost operator first. That is, you divide 120 by 4, get 30 as a result, and then multiply the result by 5 to get 150.

Note that the precedence and associativity rules only come into play when two operators share the same operand. Consider the following expression:

```
int dues = 20 * 5 + 24 * 6;
```

Operator precedence tells you two things: the program must evaluate 20 * 5 before doing addition, and the program must evaluate 24 * 6 before doing addition. But neither precedence nor associativity says which multiplication takes place first. You might think that associativity says to do the leftmost multiplication first, but in this case, the two * operators do not share a common operand, so the rules don't apply. In fact, C++ leaves it to the implementation to decide which order works best on a system. For your example, either order gives the same result, but there are circumstances in which the order can make a difference. You see one when Chapter 5 discusses the increment operator.

DIVISION DIVERSIONS

You have yet to see the rest of the story about the division operator. The behavior of this operator depends on the type of the operands. If both operands are integers, C++

performs integer division. That means any fractional part of the answer is discarded, making the result an integer. If one or both operands are floating-point values, the fractional part is kept, making the result floating-point. Listing 3.10 illustrates how C++ division works with different types of values. Like Listing 3.8, this invokes the `setf()` member function to modify how the data are displayed.

Listing 3.10 divide.cpp

```
// divide.cpp -- integer and floating-point division
#include <iostream>
using namespace std;
int main()
{
    cout.setf(ios_base::fixed, ios_base::floatfield);
    cout << "Integer division: 9/5 = " << 9 / 5  << "\n";
    cout << "Floating-point division: 9.0/5.0 = ";
    cout << 9.0 / 5.0 << "\n";
    cout << "Mixed division: 9.0/5 = " << 9.0 / 5  << "\n";
    cout << "double constants: 1e7/9.0 = ";
    cout << 1.e7 / 9.0 <<   "\n";
    cout << "float constants: 1e7f/9.0f = ";
    cout << 1.e7f / 9.0f <<   "\n";
    return 0;
}
```

Remember

If your compiler does not accept the `ios_base` forms in `setf()`, try using the older `ios` forms instead.

Some C++ implementations based on pre-ANSI C compilers don't support the `f` suffix for floating-point constants. If you find yourself facing this problem, you can replace `1.e7f / 9.0f` with `(float) 1.e7 /(float) 9.0`.

Some implementations suppress trailing zeros.

Here is the output for one implementation:

```
Integer division: 9/5 = 1
Floating-point division: 9.0/5.0 = 1.800000
Mixed division: 9.0/5 = 1.800000
double constants: 1e7/9.0 = 1111111.111111
float constants: 1e7f/9.0f = 1111111.125000
```

The first output line shows that dividing the integer 9 by the integer 5 yields the integer 1. The fractional part of 4 / 5 (or 0.8) is discarded. You see a practical use for this kind of division when you learn about the modulus operator. The next two lines show that when at least one of the operands is floating-point, you get a floating-point answer of 1.8. Actually, when you try to combine mixed types, C++ converts all the concerned types to the same type. You learn about these automatic conversions later in the chapter. The relative precisions of the last two lines show that the result is type `double` if both operands are `double` and that it is `float` if both operands are `float`. Remember, floating-point constants are type `double` by default.

A GLIMPSE OF OPERATOR OVERLOADING

In Listing 3.10, the division operator represents three distinct operations: `int` division, `float` division, and `double` division. C++ uses the context, in this case the type of operands, to determine which operator is meant. The process of using the same symbol for more than one operation is called *operator overloading*. C++ has a few examples of overloading built into the language. C++ also lets you extend operator overloading to user-defined classes, so what you see here is a precursor of an important OOP property (see Figure 3.4).

THE MODULUS OPERATOR

Most people are more familiar with addition, subtraction, multiplication, and division than with the modulus operator, so take a moment to look at this operator in action. The modulus operator, recall, returns the remainder of an integer division. In combination with integer division, the modulus operator is particularly useful in problems that

FIGURE 3.4
Different divisions

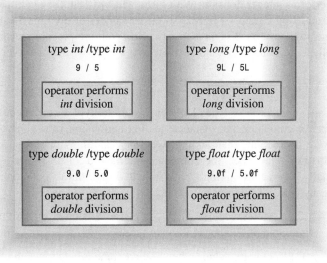

require dividing a quantity into different integral units, such as converting inches to feet and inches or converting dollars to quarters, dimes, nickels, and pennies. In Chapter 2, "Setting Out to C++," Listing 2.6 converted weight in British stone to pounds. Listing 3.11 reverses the process, converting weight in pounds to stone. A stone, you remember, is 14 pounds, and most British bathroom scales are calibrated in this unit. The program uses integer division to find the largest number of whole stone in the weight, and it uses the modulus operator to find the number of pounds left over.

Listing 3.11 modulus.cpp

```
// modulus.cpp -- uses % operator to convert lbs to stone
#include <iostream>
using namespace std;
int main()
{
    const int Lbs_per_stn = 14;
    int lbs;

    cout << "Enter your weight in pounds: ";
    cin >> lbs;
    int stone = lbs / Lbs_per_stn;      // whole stone
    int pounds = lbs % Lbs_per_stn;     // remainder in pounds
    cout << lbs << " pounds are " << stone;
    cout << " stone, " << pounds << " pound(s).\n";
    return 0;
}
```

Here is a sample run:

```
Enter your weight in pounds: 184
184 pounds are 13 stone, 2 pound(s).
```

In the expression lbs / Lbs_per_stn, both operands are type int, so the computer performs integer division. With a lbs value of 184, the expression evaluates to 13. The product of 13 and 14 is 182, so the remainder of dividing 14 into 184 is 2, and that's the value of lbs % Lbs_per_stn. Now you are prepared technically, if not emotionally, to respond to questions about your weight when you travel in Great Britain.

TYPE CONVERSIONS

C++'s profusion of types lets you match the type to the need. It also complicates life for the computer. For instance, adding two short values may involve different hardware instructions than adding two long values. With eleven integral types and three floating-point types, the computer can have a lot of different cases to handle, especially if you start mixing types. To help deal with this potential mishmash, C++ makes many type conversions automatically:

- C++ converts values when you assign a value of one arithmetic type to a variable of another arithmetic type.

- C++ converts values when you combine mixed types in expressions.

- C++ converts values when you pass arguments to functions.

If you don't understand what happens in these automatic conversions, you might find some program results baffling, so let's take a more detailed look at the rules.

Conversion on Assignment

C++ is fairly liberal in allowing you to assign a numeric value of one type to a variable of another type. Whenever you do so, the value is converted to the type of the receiving variable. For instance, suppose so_long is type long, thirty is type short, and you have the following statement in a program:

```
so_long = thirty;          // assigning a short to a long
```

The program takes the value of thirty (typically a 16-bit value) and expands it to a long value (typically a 32-bit value) upon making this assignment. Note that the expansion takes place when a value is created to place in so_long; the contents of thirty are unaltered.

Assigning a value to a type with a greater range usually poses no problem. For instance, assigning a short value to a long variable doesn't change the value; it just gives the value a few more bytes in which to laze about. However, assigning a large long value like 2111222333 to a float variable results in the loss of some precision. Because float can have just six significant figures, the value can be rounded to 2.11122E9. Table 3.3 points out some possible conversion problems.

A zero value assigned to a bool variable is converted to false, and a non-zero value is converted to true.

Assigning floating-point values to integer types poses a couple of problems. First, converting floating-point to integer results in truncating the number (discarding the fractional part). Second, a float value may be too big to fit in a cramped int variable. In that case, C++ doesn't define what the result should be; that means different implementations can respond differently. Listing 3.12 shows a few conversions by assignment.

TABLE 3.3
POTENTIAL CONVERSION PROBLEMS

CONVERSION	POTENTIAL PROBLEMS
Bigger floating-point type to smaller floating-point type, such as double to float	Loss of precision (significant figures), value might be out of range for target type, in which case result is undefined
Floating-point type to integer type	Loss of fractional part, original value might be out of range for target type, in which case result is undefined
Bigger integer type to smaller integer type, such as long to short	Original value might be out of range for target type, typically just the low-order bytes are copied

Listing 3.12 assign.cpp

```cpp
// assign.cpp -- type changes on assignment
#include <iostream>
using namespace std;
int main()
{
    float tree = 3;      // int converted to float
    int guess = 3.9832; // float converted to int
    int debt = 3.0E12;  // result not defined in C++
    cout << "tree = " << tree << "\n";
    cout << "guess = " << guess << "\n";
    cout << "debt = " << debt << "\n";
    return 0;
}
```

Here is the output for one system:

```
tree = 3
guess = 3
debt = 0
```

Here `tree` is assigned the floating-point value 3.0. However, because cout drops trailing zeros on output, it displays 3.0 as 3. Assigning 3.9832 to the int variable `guess` causes the value to be truncated to 3; C++ uses truncation (discarding the fractional part) and not rounding (finding the closest integer value) when converting floating-point types to integer types. Finally, note that the int variable `debt` is unable to hold the value 3.0E12. This creates a situation in which C++ doesn't define the result. On this system, `debt` ends up with the value 0. Well, that's a novel way to solve massive indebtedness!

Some compilers warn you of possible data loss for those statements that initialize integer variables to floating-point values. Also, the value displayed for `debt` varies from compiler to compiler. For example, running the same program on a second system produced a value of 2112827392.

Conversions in Expressions

Next, consider what happens when you combine two different arithmetic types in one expression. C++ makes two kinds of automatic conversions in that case. First, some types automatically are converted whenever they occur. Second, some types are converted when they are combined with other types in an expression.

First, examine the automatic conversions. When it evaluates expressions, C++ converts bool, char, unsigned char, signed char, and short values to int. In particular, true is promoted to 1 and false to 0. These conversions are termed *integral promotions*. For instance, consider the following fowl statements:

```cpp
short chickens = 20;            // line 1
short ducks = 35;              // line 2
short fowl = chickens + ducks; // line 3
```

To execute the statement on line 3, a C++ program takes the values of `chickens` and `ducks` and converts both to int. Then, the program converts the result back to type short, because the answer is assigned to a type short variable. You might find this a bit roundabout, but it does make sense. The `int` type generally is chosen to be the computer's most natural type, which means the computer probably does calculations fastest for that type.

There's some more integral promotion: the `unsigned short` type is converted to `int` if `short` is smaller than `int`. If the two types are the same size, `unsigned short` is converted to `unsigned int`. This rule ensures that there's no data loss in promoting `unsigned short`. Similarly, `wchar_t` is promoted to the first of the following types big enough to accommodate its range: `int`, `unsigned int`, `long`, or `unsigned long`.

Then there are the conversions that take place when you arithmetically combine different types, such as by adding an `int` to a `float`. When an operation involves two types, the smaller is converted to the larger. For instance, the program in Listing 3.10 divides 9.0 by 5. Because 9.0 is type `double`, the program converts 5 to type `double` before it does the division. More generally, the compiler goes through a checklist to determine which conversions to make in an arithmetic expression. Here's the list—the compiler goes through it in order:

1. If either operand is type `long double`, the other operand is converted to `long double`.

2. Otherwise, if either operand is `double`, the other operand is converted to `double`.

3. Otherwise, if either operand is `float`, the other operand is converted to `float`.

4. Otherwise the operands are integer types and the integral promotions are made.

5. In that case, if either operand is `unsigned long`, the other operand is converted to `unsigned long`.

6. Otherwise, if one operand is `long int` and the other is `unsigned int`, the conversion depends on the relative sizes of the two types. If `long` can represent possible `unsigned int` values, `unsigned int` is converted to `long`.

7. Otherwise, both operands are converted to `unsigned long`.

8. Otherwise, if either operand is `long`, the other is converted to `long`.

9. Otherwise, if either operand is `unsigned int`, the other is converted to `unsigned int`.

10. If the compiler reaches this point in the list, both operands should be `int`.

ANSI C follows the same rules as C++, but classic K&R C had slightly different rules. For instance, classic C always promoted `float` to `double` even if both operands were `float`.

Conversions in Passing Arguments

Normally, C++ function prototyping controls type conversions for the passing of arguments, as you learn in Chapter 7, "Functions—C++'s Programming Modules." However, it is possible, although usually unwise, to waive prototype control for argument passing. In that case, C++ applies the integral promotions to the char and short types (signed and unsigned). Also, to preserve compatibility with huge amounts of code in classic C, C++ promotes float arguments to double when passing them to a function unless the argument has been prototyped as type float.

Type Casts

" C++ also empowers you to force type conversions explicitly via the type cast mechanism. "

C++ also empowers you to force type conversions explicitly via the type cast mechanism. (C++ is such a masterful language.) The type cast comes in two forms. For example, to convert an int value stored in a variable called thorn to type long, you can use either of the following expressions:

```
(long) thorn      // makes the value of thorn type long
long (thorn)      // makes the value of thorn type long
```

The type cast doesn't alter the thorn variable itself; rather, it creates a new value of the indicated type, which you then can use in an expression.

More generally, you can do the following:

```
(typeName) value    // converts value to typeName type
typeName (value)    // converts value to typeName type
```

The first form is straight C. The second form is pure C++. The idea behind the new form is to make a type cast look like a function call. This makes type casts for the built-in types look like the type conversions you can design for user-defined classes.

Listing 3.13 gives a short illustration of both forms. Imagine that the first section of this listing is part of a powerful ecological modeling program that does floating-point calculations that are converted to integral numbers of birds and animals. The results you get depend on when you convert. The calculation for auks first adds the floating-point values and then converts the sum to int upon assignment. But the calculations for bats and coots first use type casts to convert the floating-point values to int and then sum the values. The final part of the program shows how you can use a type cast to display the ASCII code for a type char value.

Listing 3.13 typecast.cpp

```cpp
// typecast.cpp -- forcing type changes
#include <iostream>
using namespace std;
int main()
{
    int auks, bats, coots;

    // the following statement adds the values as double,
    // then converts the result to int
    auks = 19.99 + 11.99;

    // these statements add values as int
    bats = (int) 19.99 + (int) 11.99;   // old C syntax
    coots = int (19.99) + int (11.99);  // new C++ syntax
    cout << "auks = " << auks << ", bats = " << bats;
    cout << ", coots = " << coots << '\n';
```

```
        char ch = 'Z';
        cout << "The code for " << ch << " is ";      // print as char
        cout << int(ch) << '\n';                       // print as int
        return 0;
}
```

Here is the result:

```
auks = 31, bats = 30, coots = 30
The code for Z is 90
```

First, adding 19.99 to 11.99 yields 31.98. When this value is assigned to the `int` variable `auks`, it's truncated to 31. But using type casts truncates the same two values to 19 and 11 before addition, making 30 the result for both the `bats` and `coots`. The final `cout` statement uses a type cast to convert a type `char` value to `int` before it displays the result. This causes `cout` to print the value as an integer rather than as a character.

The program illustrates two reasons to use type casting. First, you might have values that are stored as type `double` but are used to calculate a type `int` value. For instance, you might be fitting a position to a grid or modeling integer values, such as populations, with floating-point numbers. You might want the calculations to treat the values as `int`. Type casting enables you to do so directly. Notice that you get a different result, at least for these values, when you convert to `int` and add than you do when you add first and then convert to `int`.

The second part of the program shows the most common reason to use a type cast—the capability to compel data in one form to meet a different expectation. In this listing, for instance, the `char` variable `ch` holds the code for the letter Z. Using `cout` with `ch` displays the character Z, because `cout` zeros in on the fact that `ch` is type `char`. But by type casting `ch` to type `int`, you get `cout` to shift to `int` mode and print the ASCII code stored in `ch`.

Summary

C++'s basic types fall into two groups. One group consists of values that are stored as integers. The second group consists of values that are stored in a floating-point format. The integer types differ from each other in the amount of memory used to store values and in whether they are signed or unsigned. From smallest to largest, the integer types are `bool`, `char`, `signed char`, `unsigned char`, `short`, `unsigned short`, `int`, `unsigned int`, `long`, and `unsigned long`. There also is a `wchar_t` type whose placement in this sequence of size depends on the implementation. C++ guarantees that `char` is large enough to hold any member of the system's basic character set, `wchar_t` can hold any member of the system's extended character set, `short` is at least 16 bits, `int` is at least as big as `short`, and `long` is at least 32 bits and at least as large as `int`. The exact sizes depend on the implementation.

Characters are represented by their numeric codes. The I/O system determines whether a code is interpreted as a character or as a number.

The floating-point types can represent fractional values and values much larger than integers can represent. The three floating-point types are called `float`, `double`, and long double. C++ guarantees that float is no larger than double, and that double is no larger than long double. Typically, float uses 32 bits of memory, double uses 64 bits, and long double uses 80 to 128 bits.

By providing a variety of types in different sizes and in both signed and unsigned varieties, C++ lets you match the type to particular data requirements.

C++ uses operators to provide the usual arithmetical support for numeric types: addition, subtraction, multiplication, division, and taking the modulus. When two operators seek to operate on the same value, C++'s precedence and associativity rules determine which operation takes place first.

C++ converts values from one type to another when you assign values to a variable, mix types in arithmetic, and use type casts to force type conversions. Many type conversions are "safe," meaning you can make them with no loss or alteration of data. For instance, you can convert an int value to a long value with no problems. Others, such as conversions of floating-point types to integer types, require more care.

At first, you might find the large number of basic C++ types a little excessive, particularly when you take the various conversion rules into account. But most likely you eventually will find occasions when one of the types is just what you need at the time, and you'll thank C++ for having it.

Review Questions

1. Why does C++ have more than one integer type?

2. Define the following:

   a. A short integer with the value 80

   b. An unsigned int integer with the value 42110

   c. An integer with the value 3000000000

3. What safeguards does C++ provide to keep you from exceeding the limits of an integer type?

4. What is the distinction between 33L and 33?

5. Consider the two C++ statements that follow. Are they equivalent?

```
char grade = 65;
char grade = 'A';
```

6. How could you use C++ to find out which character the code 88 represents? Come up with at least two ways.

7. Assigning a long value to a float can result in a round-off error. What about assigning long to double?

8. Evaluate the following expressions as C++ would:

   a. 8 * 9 + 2

   b. 6 * 3 / 4

   c. 3 / 4 * 6

   d. 6.0 * 3 / 4

   e. 15 % 4

9. Suppose x1 and x2 are two type double variables that you want to add as integers and assign to an integer variable. Construct a C++ statement for doing so.

Programming Exercises

1. Write a short program that asks for your height in integer inches and then converts your height to feet and inches. Have the program use the underscore character to indicate where to type the response. Also, use a const symbolic constant to represent the conversion factor.

2. Write a short program that asks for your height in feet and inches and your weight in pounds. (Use three variables to store the information.) Have the program report your BMI (Body Mass Index). To calculate the BMI, first convert your height in feet and inches to your height in inches. Then, convert your height in inches to your height in meters by multiplying by 0.0254. Then, convert your weight in pounds into your mass in kilograms by dividing by 2.2. Finally, compute your BMI by dividing your mass in kilograms by the square of your height in meters. Use symbolic constants to represent the various conversion factors.

3. Write a program that asks how many miles you have driven and how many gallons of gasoline you used and then reports the miles per gallon your car got. Or, if you prefer, the program can request distance in kilometers and petrol in liters and then report the result European style, in liters per 100 kilometers. (Or, perhaps, you can use litres per 100 kilometres.)

4

Derived Types

In this chapter, you learn

- Creating and using arrays
- Creating and using strings
- The `getline()` and `get()` methods for reading strings
- Mixing string and numeric input
- Creating and using structures
- Creating and using unions
- Creating and using enumerations
- Creating and using pointers
- Managing dynamic memory with `new` and `delete`
- Creating dynamic arrays
- Creating dynamic structures
- Automatic, static, and dynamic storage

You've developed a computer game called User-Hostile in which players match wits with a cryptic and abusive computer interface. Now you need to write a program that keeps track of your monthly game sales for a five-year period. Or you want to inventory your accumulation of hacker-hero trading cards. You soon conclude you need something more than C++'s simple basic types to meet these data requirements, and C++ offers something more—derived types. These are types built from the basic integer and floating-point types. The most far-reaching derived type is the class, that bastion of OOP toward which we are progressing. But C++ also supports several more modest derived types taken from C. The array, for example, can hold several values of the same type. A particular kind of array can hold a string, which is a series of characters. Structures can hold several values of differing types. Then there are pointers, which are variables that tell a computer where data is placed. You'll examine all these derived forms (except classes) in this chapter and also take a first look at `new` and `delete` and how you can use them to manage data.

Introducing Arrays

An *array* is a data form that can hold several values all of one type. For instance, an array can hold 60 type `int` values that represent five years of game sales data, 12 `short` values that represent the number of days in each month, or 365 `float` values that indicate your food expenses for each day of the year. Each value is stored in a separate array element, and the computer stores all the elements of an array consecutively in memory.

To create an array, you use a declaration statement. An array declaration should indicate three things:

- The type of value to be stored in each element
- The name of the array
- The number of elements in the array

You accomplish this in C++ by modifying the declaration for a simple variable, adding brackets that contain the number of elements. For example, the declaration

```
short months[12];     // creates array of 12 short
```

creates an array named `months` that has 12 elements, each of which can hold a type `short` value. Each element, in essence, is a variable that you can treat as a simple variable.

The general form for declaring an array is this:

```
typeName arrayName[arraySize];
```

The expression *arraySize*, which is the number of elements, must be a constant, such as 10 or a `const` value, or a constant expression, such as 8 * `sizeof` (`int`), for which all values are known at the time compilation takes place. In particular, *arraySize* cannot be a variable whose value is set while the program is running. However, later this chapter shows you how to use the `new` operator to get around that restriction.

THE ARRAY AS DERIVED TYPE

An array is called a derived type because it is based on some other type. You can't simply declare that something is an array; it always must be an array of some particular type. There is no generalized array type. Instead, there are many specific array types, such as array of char or array of long. For example, consider this declaration:

```
float loans[20];
```

The type for loans is not "array"; rather, it is "array of float." This emphasizes that the loans array is derived from the float type.

Much of the usefulness of the array comes from the fact that you can access the array elements individually. The way to do this is to use a *subscript*, or *index*, to number the elements. C++ array numbering starts with 0. (This is nonnegotiable; you have to start at 0. Pascal and BASIC users will have to adjust.) C++ uses a bracket notation with the index to specify an array element. For example, months[0] is the first element of the months array, and months[11] is the last element. Note that the index of the last element is one less than the size of the array. See Figure 4.1. Thus, an array declaration enables you to create a lot of variables with a single declaration, and you then can use an index to identify individual elements.

The yam analysis program in Listing 4.1 demonstrates a few properties of arrays, including declaring an array, assigning values to array elements, and initializing an array.

FIGURE 4.1

Creating an array

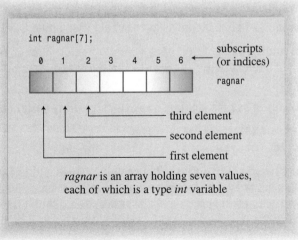

Listing 4.1 arrayone.cpp

```cpp
// arrayone.cpp _ small arrays of integers
#include <iostream>
using namespace std;
int main()
{
    int yams[3];      // creates array with three elements
    yams[0] = 7;      // assign value to first element
    yams[1] = 8;
    yams[2] = 6;

    int yamcosts[3] = {20, 30, 5}; // create, initialize array
// NOTE: If your C++ compiler or translator can't initialize
// this array, use static int yamcosts[3] instead of
// int yamcosts[3]

    cout << "Total yams = ";
    cout << yams[0] + yams[1] + yams[2] << "\n";
    cout << "The package with " << yams[1] << " yams costs ";
    cout << yamcosts[1] << " cents per yam.\n";
    int total = yams[0] * yamcosts[0] + yams[1] * yamcosts[1];
    total = total + yams[2] * yamcosts[2];
    cout << "The total yam expense is " << total << " cents.\n";

    cout << "\nSize of yams array = " << sizeof yams;
    cout << " bytes.\n";
    cout << "Size of one element = " << sizeof yams[0];
    cout << " bytes.\n";
    return 0;
}
```

Remember

Current versions of C++, as well as ANSI C, allow you to initialize ordinary arrays defined in a function. However, in some older implementations that use a C++ translator instead of a true compiler, the C++ translator creates C code for a C compiler that is not fully ANSI C–compliant. In that case, you can get an error message like the following example from a Sun C++ 2.0 system:

```
"arrayone.cc", line 10: sorry, not implemented:
initialization of yamcosts (automatic aggregate) Compilation
failed
```

The fix is to use the keyword `static` in the array declaration:

```cpp
// pre-ANSI initialization
static int yamcosts[3] = {20, 30, 5};
```

The keyword `static` causes the compiler to use a different memory scheme for storing the array, one that allows initialization even under pre-ANSI C. Chapter 8, "Adventures in Functions," discusses `static` in the section about storage classes.

Here is the output:

```
Total yams = 21
The package with 8 yams costs 30 cents per yam.
The total yam expense is 410 cents.

Size of yams array = 12 bytes.
Size of one element = 4 bytes.
```

Program Notes

First, the program creates a three-element array called yams. Because yams has three elements, the elements are numbered from 0 to 2, and arrayone.cpp uses index values of 0–2 to assign values to the three individual elements. Each individual yam element is an int with all the rights and privileges of an int type, so arrayone.cpp can, and does, assign values to elements, add elements, multiply elements, and display elements.

The program uses the long way to assign values to the yam elements. C++ also lets you initialize array elements within the declaration statement. Listing 4.1 uses this shortcut to assign values to the yamcosts array:

```
int yamcosts[3] = {20, 30, 5};
```

Simply provide a comma-separated list of values (the *initialization list*) enclosed in braces. The spaces in the list are optional. If you don't initialize an array that's defined inside a function, the element values remain undefined. That means the element takes on whatever value previously resided at that location in memory.

Next, the program uses the array values in a few calculations. This part of the program looks cluttered with all the subscripts and brackets. The for loop, coming up in Chapter 5, "Loops and Relational Expressions," provides a powerful way to deal with arrays and eliminates the need to write each element explicitly. Meanwhile, we'll stick to small arrays.

The sizeof operator, you recall, returns the size, in bytes, of a type or data object. Note that if you use the sizeof operator with an array name, you get the number of bytes in the whole array. But if you use sizeof with an array element, you get the size, in bytes, of the element. This illustrates that yams is an array, but yams[1] is just an int.

More on Array Initialization

C++ has several rules about initializing an array. They restrict when you can do it, and they determine what happens if the number of array elements doesn't match the number of values in the initializer. Let's examine these rules.

You can use the initialization form *only* when defining the array. You cannot use it later, and you cannot assign one array wholesale to another:

```
int cards[4] = {3, 6, 8, 10};     // okay
int hand[4];                      // okay
hand[4] = {5, 6, 7, 9};           // not allowed
hand = cards;                     // not allowed
```

" You can use the initialization form only when defining the array. You cannot use it later, and you cannot assign one array wholesale to another. "

However, you always can use subscripts and assign values to the elements of an array individually.

When initializing an array, you can provide fewer values than array elements. For example, the following statement initializes only the first two elements of `hotelTips`:

```
float hotelTips[5] = {5.0, 2.5};
```

If you partially initialize an array, the compiler sets the remaining elements to zero. Thus, it's easy to initialize all the elements of an array to zero—just initialize the first element explicitly to zero and then let the compiler initialize the remaining elements to zero:

```
float totals[500] = {0};
```

If you leave the square brackets empty when you initialize an array, the C++ compiler counts the elements for you. Suppose, for instance, you make this declaration:

```
short things[] = {1, 5, 3, 8};
```

The compiler makes `things` an array of four elements.

LETTING THE COMPILER DO IT

Normally, letting the compiler count the number of elements is poor practice, because its count can be different from what you think it is. However, this approach can be safer for initializing a character array to a string, as you'll soon see. And if your main concern is that the program, not you, knows how large an array is, you can do something like this:

```
short things[] = {1, 5, 3, 8};
int num_elements = sizeof things / sizeof (short);
```

Whether this is useful or lazy depends on the circumstances.

Strings

A *string* is a series of characters stored in consecutive bytes of memory. C++ has two ways of dealing with strings. The first, taken from C and often called a *C-style string*, is the method you'll learn here. Chapter 15, "The String Class and the Standard Template Library," takes up an alternative method based on a `string` class library. Meanwhile, the idea of a series of characters stored in consecutive bytes implies that you can store a string in an array of `char`, with each character kept in its own array element. Strings provide a convenient way to store text information, such as messages to the user (*"Please tell me your secret Swiss bank account number:"*) or responses from the user (*"You must be joking"*). C-style strings have a special feature: The last character of every string is the *null character*. This character, written \0, is the character with ASCII code 0, and it serves to mark the string's end. For instance, consider the following two declarations:

```
char dog [5] = { 'b', 'e', 'a', 'u', 'x'};     // not a string!
char cat[5] = {'f', 'a', 't', 's', '\0'};      // a string!
```

Both arrays are arrays of `char`, but only the second is a string. The null character plays a fundamental role in C-style strings. For example, C++ has many functions that handle strings, including those used by `cout`. They all work by processing a string character-by-character until they reach the null character. If you ask `cout` to display a nice string like `cat` above, it displays the first four characters, detects the null character, and stops. But if you are ungracious enough to tell `cout` to display the `dog` array above, which is not a string, `cout` prints the five letters in the array and then keeps marching through memory byte-by-byte, interpreting each byte as a character to print, until it reaches a null character. Because null characters, which really are bytes set to zero, tend to be common in memory, the damage usually is contained quickly; nonetheless, you should not treat nonstring character arrays as strings.

The `cat` array example makes initializing an array to a string look tedious—all those single quotes and then having to remember the null character. Don't worry. There is a better way to initialize a character array to a string. Just use a quoted string, called a *string constant* or *string literal*, as in the following:

```
char bird[10] = "Mr. Cheep";   // the \0 is understood
char fish[] = "Bubbles";       // let the compiler count
```

Quoted strings always include the terminating null character implicitly, so you don't have to spell it out. See Figure 4.2. Also, the various C++ input facilities for reading a string from keyboard input into a `char` array automatically add the terminating null character for you. (If, when you run the program in Listing 4.1, you discover you have to use the keyword `static` to initialize an array, you have to use it with these `char` arrays, too.)

FIGURE 4.2

*Initializing an array
to a string*

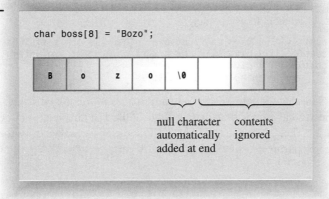

Of course, you should make sure the array is large enough to hold all the characters of the string, including the null character. Initializing a character array with a string constant is one case where it may be safer to let the compiler count the number of elements for you. There is no harm, other than wasted space, in making an array larger than the string. That's because functions that work with strings are guided by the location of the null character, not by the size of the array. C++ imposes no limits on the length of a string.

Remember

When determining the minimum array size necessary to hold a string, remember to include the terminating null character in your count.

Note that a string constant (double quotes) is not interchangeable with a character constant (single quotes). A character constant, such as `'S'`, is a shorthand notation for the code for a character. On an ASCII system, `'S'` is just another way of writing 83. Thus, the statement

```
char shirt_size = 'S';          // this is fine
```

assigns the value 83 to `shirt_size`. But `"S"` represents the string consisting of two characters, the S and the \0 characters. Even worse, `"S"` actually represents the memory address at which the string is stored. So, a statement like

```
char shirt_size = "S";          // illegal type mismatch
```

attempts to assign a memory address to `shirt_size`! Because an address is a separate type in C++, a C++ compiler won't allow this sort of nonsense. (We'll return to this point later, after we've discussed pointers.) But C, which is more lenient about checking type agreement, lets this statement pass with a warning, and the result is garbage.

STRING CONCATENATION

Sometimes a string may be too long to conveniently fit on one line of code. C++ enables you to concatenate string constants; that is, to combine two quoted strings into one. Indeed, any two string constants separated only by white space (spaces, tabs, and newlines) automatically are joined into one. Thus, all the following output statements are equivalent to each other:

```
cout << "I'd give my right arm to be" " a great violinist.\n";
cout << "I'd give my right arm to be a great violinist.\n";
cout << "I'd give my right ar"
        "m to be a great violinist.\n";
```

Note that the join doesn't add any spaces to the joined strings. The first character of the second string immediately follows the last character, not counting \0, of the first string. The \0 character from the first string is replaced by the first character of the second string.

USING STRINGS IN AN ARRAY

The two most common ways of getting a string into an array are to initialize an array to a string constant and to read keyboard or file input into an array. Listing 4.2 demonstrates these approaches by initializing one array to a quoted string and using cin to place an input string in a second array. The program also uses the standard library function strlen() to get the length of a string. The standard cstring header file (or string.h for older implementations) provides declarations for this and many other string-related functions.

Listing 4.2 strings.cpp

```cpp
// strings.cpp _ storing strings in an array
#include <iostream>
#include <cstring>  // for the strlen() function
using namespace std;
int main()
{
    const int Size = 15;
    char name1[Size];                   // empty array
    char name2[Size] = "C++owboy";   // initialized array
// NOTE: some implementations may require the static keyword
// to initialize the array name2

    cout << "Howdy! I'm " << name2;
    cout << "! What's your name?\n";
    cin >> name1;
    cout << "Well, " << name1 << ", your name has ";
    cout << strlen(name1) << " letters and is stored\n";
    cout << "in an array of " << sizeof name1 << " bytes.\n";
    cout << "Your initial is " << name1[0] << ".\n";
    name2[3] = '\0';                    // null character
    cout << "Here are the first 3 characters of my name: ";
    cout << name2 << "\n";
    return 0;
}
```

Remember

> If your system doesn't provide the cstring header file, try the older string.h version.

Here is a sample run:

```
Howdy! I'm C++owboy! What's your name?
Basicman
Well, Basicman, your name has 8 letters and is stored
in an array of 15 bytes.
Your initial is B.
Here are the first 3 characters of my name: C++
```

Program Notes

What can you learn from this example? First, note that the `sizeof` operator gives the size of the entire array, 15 bytes, but the `strlen()` function returns the size of the string stored in the array and not the size of the array itself. Also, `strlen()` counts just the visible characters and not the null character. Thus, it returns a value of 8, not 9, for the length of `Basicman`. If cosmic is a string, the minimum array size for holding that string is `strlen(cosmic) + 1`.

Because `name1` and `name2` are arrays, you can use an index to access individual characters in the array. For instance, the program uses `name1[0]` to find the first character in that array. Also, the program sets `name2[3]` to the null character. That makes the string end after three characters even though more characters remain in the array. See Figure 4.3.

Note that the program uses a symbolic constant for the array size. Often, the size of an array appears in several statements in a program. Using a symbolic constant to represent the size of an array simplifies revising the program to use a different array size; you just have to change the value once, where the symbolic constant is defined.

ADVENTURES IN STRING INPUT

The `strings.cpp` program has a blemish that was concealed through the often useful technique of carefully selected sample input. Listing 4.3 removes the veils and shows that string input can be tricky.

FIGURE 4.3

Shortening a string with \0

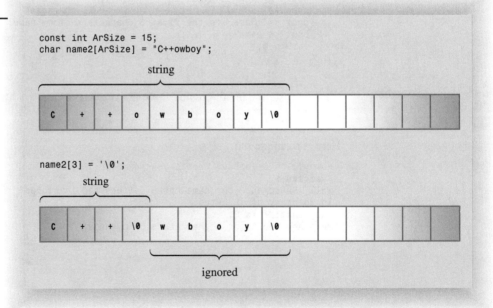

Listing 4.3 instr1.cpp

```cpp
// instr1.cpp -- reading more than one string
#include <iostream>
using namespace std;
int main()
{
    const int ArSize = 20;
    char name[ArSize];
    char dessert[ArSize];

    cout << "Enter your name:\n";
    cin >> name;
    cout << "Enter your favorite dessert:\n";
    cin >> dessert;
    cout << "I have some delicious " << dessert;
    cout << " for you, " << name << ".\n";
    return 0;
}
```

The intent is simple: Read a user's name and favorite dessert from the keyboard and then display the information. Here is a sample run:

```
Enter your name:
Alistair Dreeb
Enter your favorite dessert:
I have some delicious Dreeb for you, Alistair.
```

We didn't even get a chance to respond to the dessert prompt! The program showed it and then immediately moved on to display the final line.

The problem lies with how cin determines when you've finished entering a string. You can't enter the null character from the keyboard, so cin needs some other means for locating the end of a string. The cin technique is to use white space —spaces, tabs, and newlines—to delineate a string. This means cin reads just one word when it gets input for a character array. After it reads this word, cin automatically adds the terminating null character when it places the string into the array.

The practical result in this example is that cin reads Alistair as the entire first string and puts it into the name array. This leaves poor Dreeb still sitting in the input queue. When cin searches the input queue for the response to the favorite dessert question, it finds Dreeb still there. Then cin gobbles up Dreeb and puts it into the dessert array. See Figure 4.4.

Another problem, which didn't surface in the sample run, is that the input string might turn out to be longer than the destination array. Using cin as this example did offers no protection against placing a 30-character string in a 20-character array.

Many programs depend on string input, so it's worth while to explore this topic further. We'll have to draw upon some of the more advanced features of cin, which are described in Chapter 16, "Input, Output, and Files."

FIGURE 4.4

The cin view of string input

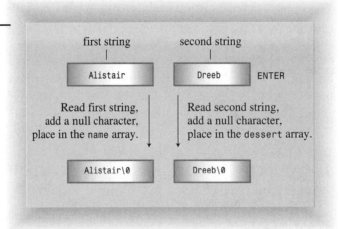

Line-Oriented Input: `getline()` and `get()`

To be able to enter whole phrases instead of single words as a string, you need a different approach to string input. Specifically, you need a line-oriented method instead of a word-oriented method. You are in luck, for the `istream` class, of which `cin` is an example, has some line-oriented class member functions. The `getline()` function, for example, reads a whole line, using the newline character transmitted by the [ENTER] key to mark the end of input. You invoke this method by using `cin.getline()` as a function call. The function takes two arguments. The first argument is the name of the array destined to hold the line of input, and the second argument is a limit on the number of characters to be read. If this limit is, say, 20, the function reads no more than 19 characters, leaving room to automatically add the null character at the end. The `getline()` member function stops reading input when it reaches this numeric limit or when it reads a newline, whichever comes first.

For example, suppose you want to use `getline()` to read a name into the 20-element `name` array. You would use this call:

```
cin.getline(name,20);
```

This reads the entire line into the `name` array, provided that the line consists of 19 or fewer characters. (The `getline()` member function also has an optional third argument, which Chapter 16 discusses.)

Listing 4.4 modifies Listing 4.3 to use `cin.getline()` instead of a simple `cin`. Otherwise, the program is unchanged.

Listing 4.4 instr2.cpp

```cpp
// instr2.cpp _ reading more than one word with getline
#include <iostream>
using namespace std;
int main()
{
    const int ArSize = 20;
    char name[ArSize];
    char dessert[ArSize];

    cout << "Enter your name:\n";
    cin.getline(name, ArSize);  // reads through newline
    cout << "Enter your favorite dessert:\n";
    cin.getline(dessert, ArSize);
    cout << "I have some delicious " << dessert;
    cout << " for you, " << name << ".\n";
    return 0;
}
```

Remember

Some early C++ versions don't fully implement all facets of the current C++ I/O package. In particular, the `getline()` member function isn't always available. If this affects you, just read about this example and go on to the next one, which uses a member function that predates `getline()`. Early releases of Turbo C++ implement `getline()` slightly differently so that it does store the newline character in the string. Microsoft Visual C++ 5.0 has a bug in `getline()` as implemented in the `iostream` header file but not in the `ostream.h` version.

Here is some sample output:

```
Enter your name:
Melanie Ploops
Enter your favorite dessert:
Raspberry Torte
I have some delicious Raspberry Torte for you, Melanie Ploops.
```

The program now reads complete names and delivers the user her just desserts! The `getline()` function conveniently gets a line at a time. It reads input through the newline character marking the end of the line, but it doesn't save the newline character. Instead, it replaces it with a null character when storing the string. See Figure 4.5.

Let's try another approach. The `istream` class has another member function, called `get()`, which comes in several variations. One variant works much like `getline()`. It takes the same arguments, interprets them the same way, and reads to the end of a line. But rather than read and discard the newline character, `get()` leaves that character in the input queue. Suppose we use two calls to `get()` in a row:

```cpp
cin.get(name, ArSize);
cin.get(dessert, Arsize);   // a problem
```

FIGURE 4.5

getline( ) reads and
replaces the newline

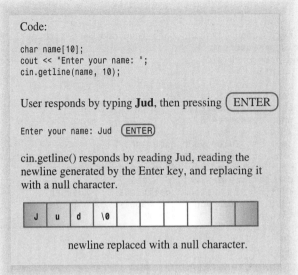

```
Code:

char name[10];
cout << "Enter your name: ";
cin.getline(name, 10);
```

User responds by typing **Jud**, then pressing ⟨ENTER⟩

Enter your name: Jud ⟨ENTER⟩

cin.getline() responds by reading Jud, reading the
newline generated by the Enter key, and replacing it
with a null character.

| J | u | d | \0 | | | | | |

newline replaced with a null character.

Because the first call leaves the newline in the input queue, that newline is the first character the second call sees. Thus, get() concludes that it's reached the end of line without having found anything to read. Without help, get() just can't get past that newline.

Fortunately, there is help in the form of a variation of get(). The call cin.get() (no arguments) reads the single next character, even if it is a newline, so you can use it to dispose of the newline and prepare for the next line of input. That is, this sequence works:

```
cin.get(name, ArSize);    // read first line
cin.get();                // read newline
cin.get(dessert, Arsize); // read second line
```

Another way to use get() is to *concatenate*, or join, the two class member functions as follows:

```
cin.get(name, ArSize).get(); // concatenate member functions
```

What makes this possible is that cin.get(name, ArSize) returns the cin object, which then is used as the object that invokes the get() function. Similarly, the statement

```
cin.getline(name1, ArSize).getline(name2, ArSize);
```

reads two consecutive input lines into the arrays name1 and name2; it's equivalent to making two separate calls to cin.getline().

Listing 4.5 uses concatenation. In Chapter 10, "Working With Classes," you'll learn how to incorporate this feature into your class definitions.

Listing 4.5 instr3.cpp

```cpp
// instr3.cpp _ reading more than one word with get() & get()
#include <iostream>
using namespace std;
int main()
{
    const int ArSize = 20;
    char name[ArSize];
    char dessert[ArSize];

    cout << "Enter your name:\n";
    cin.get(name, ArSize).get();    // read string, newline
    cout << "Enter your favorite dessert:\n";
    cin.get(dessert, ArSize).get();
    cout << "I have some delicious " << dessert;
    cout << " for you, " << name << ".\n";
    return 0;
}
```

Remember

Some older C++ versions don't implement the `get()` variant having no arguments. They do, however, implement yet another `get()` variant, one that takes a single `char` argument. To use it instead of the argumentless `get()`, you first must declare a `char` variable:

```cpp
char ch;
cin.get(name, ArSize).get(ch);
```

You can use this code instead of what is found in Listing 4.5. Chapters 5, 6, "Branching Statements and Logical Operators," and 16 further discuss the `get()` variants.

Here is a sample run:

```
Enter your name:
Mai Parfait
Enter your favorite dessert:
Chocolate Mousse
I have some delicious Chocolate Mousse for you, Mai Parfait.
```

One thing to note is how C++ allows multiple versions of functions provided that they have different argument lists. If you use, say, `cin.get(name, ArSize)`, the compiler notices you're using the form that puts a string into an array and sets up the appropriate member function. If, instead, you use `cin.get()`, the compiler realizes you want the form that reads one character. Chapter 8 will explore this feature, called function overloading.

Why use get() instead of getline() at all? First, older implementations may not have getline(). Second, get() lets you be a bit more careful. Suppose, for example, you used get() to read a line into an array. How can you tell if it read the whole line rather than stopped because the array was filled? Look at the next input character. If it is a newline, then the whole line was read. If it is not a newline, then there is still more input on that line. Chapter 16 investigates this technique. In short, getline() is a little simpler to use, but get() makes error-checking simpler.

Empty Lines and Other Problems

What happens after getline() or get() reads an empty line? The original practice was that the next input statement picked up where the last getline() or get() left off. However, the current practice after you read an empty line with get() (but not getline()) is to set something called the *failbit*. The implications of this act are that further input is blocked but you can restore input with the following command:

```
cin.clear();
```

Another potential problem is that the input string could be longer than the allocated space. If the input line is longer than the number of characters specified, both getline() and get() leave the remaining characters in the input queue. However, getline() additionally sets the failbit and turns off further input.

Chapters 5, 6, and 16 investigate these properties and how to utilize them.

MIXING STRING AND NUMERIC INPUT

Mixing numeric input with line-oriented string input can cause problems. Consider the simple program in Listing 4.6.

Listing 4.6 numstr.cpp

```cpp
// numstr.cpp -- following number input with line input
#include <iostream>
using namespace std;
int main()
{
    cout << "What year was your house built?\n";
    int year;
    cin >> year;
    cout << "What is its street address?\n";
    char address[80];
    cin.getline(address, 80);
    cout << "Year built: " << year << "\n";
    cout << "Address: " << address << "\n";
    return 0;
}
```

Running this program would look something like this:

```
What year was your house built?
1966
What is its street address?
```

```
Year built: 1966
Address:
```

You never get the opportunity to enter the address. The problem is that when `cin` reads the year, it leaves the newline generated by the ENTER key in the input queue. Then, `cin.getline()` reads the newline as an empty line and assigns a null string to the `address` array. The fix is to read and discard the newline before reading the address. This can be done several ways, including using `get()` with no argument or with a `char` argument, as described in the preceding example. You can make this call separately:

```
cin >> year;
cin.get();    // or cin.get(ch);
```

Or, you can concatenate the call, making use of the fact that the expression `cin >> year` returns the `cin` object:

```
(cin >> year).get();   // or (cin >> year).get(ch);
```

If you make one of these changes to Listing 4.6, it works properly:

```
What year was your house built?
1966
What is its street address?
43821 Unsigned Short Street
Year built: 1966
Address: 43821 Unsigned Short Street
```

C++ programs frequently use pointers instead of arrays to handle strings. We'll take up that aspect of strings after learning a bit about pointers. Meanwhile, let's take a look at another derived type, the structure.

Introducing Structures

Suppose you want to store information about a basketball player. You might want to store his or her name, salary, height, weight, scoring average, free-throw percentage, assists, and so on. You'd like some sort of data form that could hold all this information in one unit. An array won't do. Although an array can hold several items, each item has to be the same type. That is, one array can hold 20 `int`s and another can hold 10 `float`s, but a single array can't store `int`s in some elements and `float`s in other elements.

The answer to your desire (the one about storing information about a basketball player) is the C++ *structure*. The structure is a more versatile data form than an array, because a single structure can hold items of more than one data type. This enables you to unify your data representation by storing all the related basketball information in a single structure variable. If you want to keep track of a whole team, you can use an array of structures. The structure type also is a stepping-stone to that bulwark of C++ OOP, the class. Learning a little about structures now takes us that much closer to the OOP heart of C++.

A structure is a user-definable type, with a structure declaration serving to define the type's data properties. After you define the type, you can create variables of that type. Thus, creating a structure is a two-part process. First, you define a structure description. It describes and labels the different types of data that can be stored in a structure. Then, you can create structure variables, or, more generally, structure data objects, that follow the description's plan.

For example, suppose that Bloataire, Inc., wants to create a type to describe members of its product line of designer inflatables. In particular, the type should hold the name of the item, its volume in cubic feet, and its selling price. Here is a structure description meeting those needs:

```
struct inflatable      // structure description
{
    char name[20];     // an array member
    float volume;      // a float member
    double price;      // a double member
};
```

The keyword `struct` indicates that the code defines the layout for a structure. The identifier `inflatable` is the name, or *tag*, for this form; this makes `inflatable` the name for the new type. Thus, you now can create variables of type `inflatable` just as you create variables of type `char` or `int`. Next, between braces, comes the list of data types to be held in the structure. Each list item is a declaration statement. You can use any of the C++ types here, including arrays and other structures. This example uses an array of `char`, suitable for storing a string, a `float` and a `double`. Each individual item in the list is called a structure *member*, so the `inflatable` structure has three members. See Figure 4.6.

FIGURE 4.6

Parts of a structure description

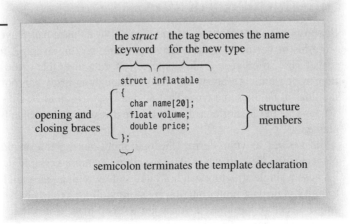

After you have the template, you can create variables of that type:

```
inflatable hat;              // hat is a structure variable of type
inflatable
inflatable woopie_cushion;   // type inflatable variable
inflatable mainframe;        // type inflatable variable
```

If you're familiar with C structures, you'll notice (probably with pleasure) that C++ allows you to drop the keyword struct when you declare structure variables:

```
struct inflatable goose;     // keyword struct required in C
inflatable vincent;          // keyword struct not required in C++
```

In C++, the structure tag is used just like a fundamental type name. This change emphasizes that a structure declaration defines a new type. It also removes omitting struct from the list of curse-inducing errors.

Given that hat is type inflatable, you use the membership operator (.) to access individual members. For instance, hat.volume refers to the volume member of the structure, and hat.price refers to the price member. Similarly, vincent.price is the price member of a vincent variable. In short, the member names enable you to access members of a structure much as indices enable you to access elements of an array. Because the price member is declared as type double, hat.price and vincent.price both are equivalent to type double variables and can be used in any manner an ordinary type double variable can. hat is a structure, but hat.price is a double. By the way, the method used to access class member functions like cin.getline() has its origins in the method used to access structure member variables like vincent.price.

Listing 4.7 illustrates these points about a structure. Also, it shows how to initialize one.

Listing 4.7 structur.cpp

```cpp
// structur.cpp -- a simple structure
#include <iostream>
using namespace std;
struct inflatable    // structure template
{
    char name[20];
    float volume;
    double price;
};

int main()
{
    inflatable guest =
    {
        "Glorious Gloria",  // name value
        1.88,               // volume value
        29.99               // price value
    }; // guest is a structure variable of type inflatable
       // It's initialized to the indicated values
    inflatable pal =
    {
        "Audacious Arthur",
```

```
        3.12,
        32.99
    };  // pal is a second variable of type inflatable
// NOTE: some implementations require using
// static inflatable guest =

    cout << "Expand your guest list with " << guest.name;
    cout << " and " << pal.name << "!\n";
    // pal.name is the name member of the pal variable
    cout << "You can have both for $";
    cout << guest.price + pal.price << "!\n";
    return 0;
}
```

Remember

> **Just as some implementations do not yet implement the capability to initialize an ordinary array defined in a function, they also do not implement the capability to initialize an ordinary structure defined in a function. Again, the solution is to use the keyword `static` in the declaration.**

Here is the output:

```
Expand your guest list with Glorious Gloria and Audacious Arthur!
You can have both for $62.98!
```

PROGRAM NOTES

One important matter is where to place the structure declaration. There are two choices for `structur.cpp`. You could place the declaration inside the `main()` function, just after the opening brace. The second choice, and the one made here, is to place it outside of and preceding `main()`. When a declaration occurs outside of any function, it's called an *external declaration*. For this program, there is no practical difference between the two choices. But for programs consisting of two or more functions, the difference can be crucial. The external declaration can be used by all the functions following it, whereas the internal declaration can be used only by the function in which the declaration is found. Most often, you want an external structure declaration so that all the functions can use structures of that type. See Figure 4.7.

Variables, too, can be defined internally or externally, with external variables shared among functions. (Chapter 8 looks further into that topic.) C++ practices discourage the use of external variables but encourage the use of external structure declarations. Also, it often makes sense to declare symbolic constants externally.

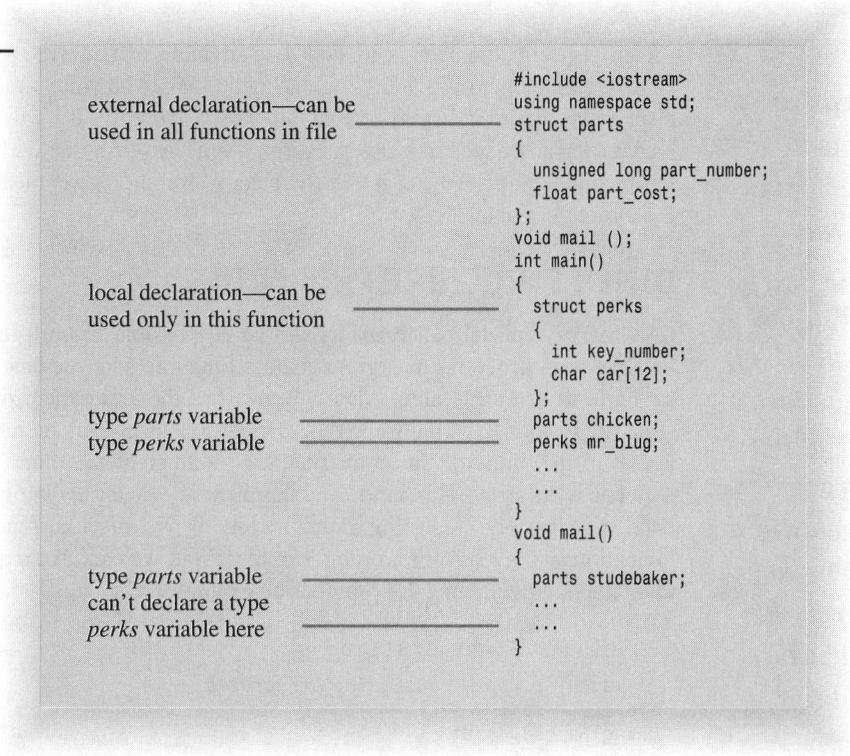

FIGURE 4.7

Local and external structure declarations

external declaration—can be used in all functions in file ─────────

local declaration—can be used only in this function ─────────

type *parts* variable ─────────
type *perks* variable ─────────

type *parts* variable can't declare a type *perks* variable here ─────────

```cpp
#include <iostream>
using namespace std;
struct parts
{
    unsigned long part_number;
    float part_cost;
};
void mail ();
int main()
{
    struct perks
    {
        int key_number;
        char car[12];
    };
    parts chicken;
    perks mr_blug;
    ...
    ...
}
void mail()
{
    parts studebaker;
    ...
    ...
}
```

Next, notice the initialization procedure:

```cpp
inflatable guest =
{
    "Glorious Gloria",   // name value
    1.88,                // volume value
    29.99                // price value
};
```

As with arrays, you use a comma-separated list of values enclosed within a pair of braces. The program places one value per line, but you can place them all on the same line. Just remember to separate items with a comma:

```cpp
inflatable duck = {"Daphne", 0.12, 9.98};
```

You can initialize each member of the structure to the appropriate kind of datum. For instance, the name member is a character array, so you can initialize it to a string.

Each structure member is treated as a variable of that type. Thus, `pal.price` is a `double` variable and `pal.name` is an array of `char`. And when the program uses `cout` to display `pal.name`, it displays the member as a string. By the way, because `pal.name` is a character array, you can use subscripts to access individual characters in the array. For example, `pal.name[0]` is the character A. But `pal[0]` is meaningless, because `pal` is a structure, not an array.

OTHER STRUCTURE PROPERTIES

C++ makes user-defined types as similar as possible to built-in types. For example, you can pass structures as arguments to a function, and you can have a function use a structure as a return value. Also, you can use the assignment operator to assign one structure to another of the same type. Doing so causes each member of one structure to be set to the value of the corresponding member in the other structure, even if the member is an array. This kind of assignment is called *memberwise assignment*. We'll defer passing and returning structures until we discuss functions in Chapter 7, "Functions—C++'s Programming Modules," but we can take a quick look at structure assignment now. Listing 4.8 provides an example.

Listing 4.8 assgn_st.cpp

```cpp
// assgn_st.cpp -- assigning structures
#include <iostream>
using namespace std;
struct inflatable
{
    char name[20];
    float volume;
    double price;
};
int main()
{
    inflatable bouquet =
    {
        "sunflowers",
        0.20,
        12.49
    };
    inflatable choice;
    cout << "bouquet: " << bouquet.name << " for $";
    cout << bouquet.price << "\n";

    choice = bouquet;  // assign one structure to another
    cout << "choice: " << choice.name << " for $";
    cout << choice.price << "\n";
    return 0;
}
```

Here's the output:

```
bouquet: sunflowers for $12.49
choice: sunflowers for $12.49
```

As you can see, memberwise assignment is at work, because the members of the `choice` structure are assigned the same values stored in the `bouquet` structure.

You can combine the definition of a structure form with the creation of structure variables. To do so, follow the closing brace with the variable name or names:

```
struct perks
{
     int key_number;
     char car[12];
} mr_smith, ms_jones;    // two perks variables
```

You even can initialize a variable you create in this fashion:

```
struct perks
{
     int key_number;
     char car[12];
} mr_glitz =
{
     7,              // value for mr_glitz.key_number member
     "Packard"       // value for mr_glitz.car member
};
```

However, keeping the structure definition separate from the variable declarations usually makes a program easier to read and follow.

Another thing you can do with structures is create a structure with no type name. You do this by omitting a tag name while simultaneously defining a structure form and a variable:

```
struct     // no tag
{
     int x;  // 2 members
     int y;
} position;  // a structure variable
```

This creates one structure variable called `position`. You can access its members with the membership operator, as in `position.x`, but there is no general name for the type. You subsequently can't create other variables of the same type. This book won't be using this limited form of structure.

Aside from the fact a C++ program can use the structure tag as a type name, C structures have all the features we've discussed so far for C++ structures. But C++ structures go further. Unlike C structures, for instance, C++ structures can have member functions in addition to member variables. But these more advanced features most typically are used with classes rather than structures, so we'll discuss them when we cover classes.

ARRAYS OF STRUCTURES

The `inflatable` structure contains an array (the `name` array). It's also possible to create arrays whose elements are structures. The technique is exactly the same as for creating arrays of the fundamental types. For example, to create an array of 100 `inflatable` structures, do the following:

```
inflatable gifts[100];  // array of 100 inflatable structures
```

This makes `gifts` an array of `inflatables`. Hence, each element of the array, such as `gifts[0]` or `gifts[99]`, is an `inflatable` object and can be used with the membership operator:

```
cin >> gifts[0].volume;       // use volume member of first struct
cout << gifts[99].price << endl; // display price member of last struct
```

Keep in mind that `gifts` itself is an array, not a structure, so constructions such as `gifts.price` are not valid.

To initialize an array of structures, combine the rule for initializing arrays (a brace-enclosed, comma-separated list of values for each element) with the rule for structures (a brace-enclosed, comma-separated list of values for each member). Because each element of the array is a structure, its value is represented by a structure initialization. Thus, you wind up with a brace-enclosed, comma-separated list of values, each of which itself is a brace-enclosed, comma-separated list of values:

```
inflatable guests[2] =           // initializing an array of structs
    {
        {"Bambi", 0.5, 21.99},   // first structure in array
        {"Godzilla", 2000, 565.99} // next structure in array
    };
```

As usual, you can format this the way you like. Both initializations can be on the same line, or each separate structure member initialization can get a line of its own, for example.

BIT FIELDS

C++, like C, enables you to specify structure members that occupy a particular number of bits. This can be handy for creating a data structure that corresponds, say, to a register on some hardware device. The field type should be an integral or enumeration type (enumerations are discussed later this chapter), and a colon followed by a number indicates the actual number of bits to be used. You can use unnamed fields to provide spacing. Each member is termed a *bit field*. Here's an example:

```
struct torgle_register
{
    int SN : 4;          // 4 bits for SN value
    int : 4;             // 4 bits unused
    bool goodIn : 1;     // valid input (1 bit)
    bool goodTorgle : 1; // successful torgling
};
```

You use standard structure notation to access bit fields:

```
torgle_register tr;
...
if (tr.goodIn)
    ...
```

Bit fields typically are used in low-level programming. Often, using an integral type and the bitwise operators of Appendix E, "Other Operators," provides an alternative approach.

Unions

A *union* is a data format that can hold different data types but only one type at a time. That is, whereas a structure can hold, say, an int *and* a long *and* a double, a union can hold an int *or* a long *or* a double. The syntax is like that for a structure, but the meaning is different. For example, consider the following declaration:

```
union one4all
{
    int int_val;
    long long_val;
    double double_val;
};
```

You can use a one4all variable to hold an int, a long, or a double, just as long as you do so at different times:

```
one4all pail;
pail.int_val = 15;          // store an int
cout << pail.int_val;
pail.double_val = 1.38;     // store a double, int value is lost
cout << pail.double_val;
```

Thus, pail can serve as an int variable on one occasion and as a double variable on another. The member name identifies the capacity in which the variable is acting. Because a union holds only one value at a time, it has to have space enough to hold its largest member. Hence, the size of the union is the size of its largest member.

One use for the union is to save space when a data item can use two or more formats but never simultaneously. For instance, suppose you manage a mixed inventory of widgets, some of which have an integer ID, and some of which have a string ID. Then, you could do the following:

```
struct widget
{
    char brand[20];
    union id              // format depends on widget type
    {
        long id_num;       // type 1 widgets
        char id_char[20]; // other widgets
    };
    int type;
};
...
widget prize;
...
if (prize.type == 1)
    cin >> prize.id.id_num;     // use member name to indicate mode
else
    cin >> prize.id.id_char;
```

An *anonymous union* has no name; in essence, its members become variables that share the same address. Naturally, only one member can be current at one time:

```cpp
struct widget
{
    char brand[20];
    union                       // format depends on widget type
    {
        long id_num;        // type 1 widgets
        char id_char[20]; // other widgets
    };
    int type;
};
...
widget prize;
...
if (prize.type == 1)
    cin >> prize.id_num;
else
    cin >> prize.id_char;
```

Because the union is anonymous, `id_num` and `id_char` are treated as two members of `prize` that share the same address. The need for an intermediate identifier id is eliminated. It is up to the program to keep track of which choice is active.

Enumerations

The C++ enum facility provides an alternative means to `const` for creating symbolic constants. It also lets you define new types but in a fairly restricted fashion. The syntax for using enum resembles structure syntax. For instance, consider the following statement:

```cpp
enum spectrum {red, orange, yellow, green, blue, violet, indigo,
               ultraviolet};
```

This statement does two things:

- It makes `spectrum` the name of a new type; `spectrum` is termed an *enumeration*, much as a `struct` variable is called a structure.

- It establishes `red`, `orange`, `yellow`, and so on as symbolic constants for the integer values 0–7. These constants are called *enumerators*.

By default, enumerators are assigned integer values starting with 0 for the first enumerator, 1 for the second enumerator, and so forth. You can override the default by explicitly assigning integer values. We'll show you how later.

You can use an enumeration name to declare a variable of that type:

```cpp
spectrum band;
```

An enumeration variable has some special properties, which we'll examine now.

The only valid values that you can assign to an enumeration variable without a type cast are the enumerator values used in defining the type. Thus, we have the following:

```
band = blue;        // valid, blue is an enumerator
band = 2000;        // invalid, 2000 not an enumerator
```

Thus, a `spectrum` variable is limited to just eight possible values. Some compilers issue a compiler error if you attempt to assign an invalid value, whereas others issue a warning. For maximum portability, you should regard assigning a non-enum value to an enum variable as an error.

Only the assignment operator is defined for enumerations. In particular, arithmetic operations are not defined:

```
band = orange;      // valid
++band;             // not valid
band = orange + red;    // not valid
...
```

However, some implementations do not honor this restriction. That can make it possible to violate the type limits. For example, if band has the value `ultraviolet`, or 7, then `++band`, if valid, increments band to 8, which is not a valid value for a `spectrum` type. Again, for maximum portability, you should adopt the stricter limitations.

Enumerators are of integer type and can be promoted to type `int`, but `int` types are not converted automatically to the enumeration type:

```
int color = blue;   // valid, spectrum type promoted to int
band = 3;           // invalid, int not converted to spectrum
color = 3 + red;    // valid, red converted to int
...
```

Note that even though 3 corresponds to the enumerator green, assigning 3 to band is a type error. But assigning `green` to band is fine because they both are type `spectrum`. Again, some implementations do not enforce this restriction. In the expression 3 + red, addition isn't defined for enumerators. However, `red` is converted to type `int`, and the result is type `int`. Although addition is not defined for enumerations, you can use enumerations in arithmetic expressions.

You can assign an `int` value to an `enum` provided that the value is valid and that you use an explicit type cast:

```
band = spectrum(3);     // type cast 3 to type spectrum
```

What if you try to type cast an inappropriate value? The result is undefined, meaning that the attempt won't be flagged as an error but that you can't rely upon the value of the result:

```
band = spectrum(40003);   // undefined
```

As you can see, the rules governing enumerations are fairly restrictive. In practice, enumerations are used more often as a way of defining related symbolic constants than as a means of defining a new type. For instance, you might use an enumeration to define symbolic constants for a `switch` statement. (See Chapter 6 for an example.) If you plan to use just the constants and not create variables of the enumeration type, you can omit an enumeration type name:

```
enum {red, orange, yellow, green, blue, violet, indigo, ultraviolet};
```

SETTING ENUMERATOR VALUES

You can set enumerator values explicitly by using the assignment operator:

```
enum bits{one = 1, two = 2, four = 4, eight = 8};
```

The assigned values must be integers. You also can define just some of the enumerators explicitly:

```
enum bigstep{first, second = 100, third};
```

In this case, `first` is 0 by default. Subsequent uninitialized enumerators are larger by one than their predecessors. So, `third` would have the value 101.

Finally, you can create more than one enumerator with the same value:

```
enum {zero, null = 0, one, numero_uno = 1};
```

Here, both `zero` and `null` are 0, and both `one` and `numero_uno` are 1. In earlier versions of C++, you could assign only `int` values (or values that promote to `int`) to enumerators, but that restriction has been removed so that you can use type `long` values.

VALUE RANGES FOR ENUMERATIONS

Originally, the only valid values for an enumeration were those named in the declaration. However, C++ now supports a refined concept by which you validly can assign values by a type cast to an enumeration variable. Each enumeration has a *range*, and you can assign any integer value in the range, even if it's not an enumerator value, by using a type cast to an enumeration variable. For instance, suppose `myflag` is a type `bits` variable (as previously defined). Then, the following is valid:

```
myflag = bits(6);     // valid, because 6 is in bits range
```

Here, 6 is not one of the enumerations, but it lies in the range the enumerations define.

The range is defined as follows. First, to find the upper limit, take the largest enumerator value. Find the smallest power of two greater than this largest value, subtract one, and that is the upper end of the range. For example, the largest `bigstep` value, as previously defined, is 101. The smallest power of two greater than this is 128, so the upper end of the range is 127. Next, to find the lower limit, find the smallest enumerator value. If it is zero or greater, the lower limit for the range is zero. If the smallest enumerator is negative, use the same approach as for finding the upper limit, but toss in a minus sign. For example, if the smallest enumerator is –6, the next power of two (times a minus sign) is –8, and the lower limit is –7.

The idea is that the compiler can choose how much space to hold an enumeration. It might use one byte or less for an enumeration with a small range and four bytes for an enumeration with type long values.

Pointers and the Free Store

The beginning of Chapter 3, "Dealing with Data," mentions three fundamental properties of which a computer program must keep track when it stores data. To save the book the wear and tear of your thumbing back to that chapter, here are those properties again:

- Where the information is stored
- What value is kept there
- What kind of information is stored

You've used one strategy to accomplish these ends: defining a simple variable. The declaration statement provides the type and a symbolic name for the value. It also causes the program to allocate memory for the value and to keep track of the location internally.

Let's look at a second strategy now, one that becomes particularly important in developing C++ classes. This strategy is based on pointers, which are variables that store addresses of values rather than the values themselves. But before discussing pointers, let's see how to find addresses explicitly for ordinary variables. Just apply the address operator, represented by &, to a variable to get its location; for example, if home is a variable, &home is its address. Listing 4.9 demonstrates this operator.

Listing 4.9 address.cpp

```
// address.cpp _ using the & operator to find addresses
#include <iostream>
using namespace std;
int main()
{
    int donuts = 6;
    double cups = 4.5;

    cout << "donuts value = " << donuts;
    cout << " and donuts address = " << &donuts << "\n";
// NOTE: you may need to use unsigned (&donuts)
//    and unsigned (&cups)
    cout << "cups value = " << cups;
    cout << " and cups address = " << &cups << "\n";
    return 0;
}
```

Remember

Cout is a smart object, but some versions are smarter than others. Thus, some implementations might fail to recognize pointer types. In that case, you must type cast the address to a recognizable type, such as unsigned int. The appropriate type cast depends on the memory model. The default DOS memory model uses a 2-byte address, hence unsigned int is the proper cast. Some DOS memory models, however, use a 4-byte address, which requires a cast to unsigned long.

Here is the output on one system:

```
donuts value = 6 and donuts address = 0x8566fff4
cups value = 4.5 and cups address = 0x8566ffec
```

When it displays addresses, cout uses hexadecimal notation because that is the usual notation used to describe memory. Our implementation stores cups at a lower memory location than donuts. The difference between the two addresses is 0x8566fff4–0x8566ffec, or 8. This makes sense because cups is type double, which uses eight bytes. In case you're interested, these particular representations of addresses reflect the PC method of describing an address by a segment value and an offset. The segment value, 8566 in this case, identifies the block of memory used to store the data; it's the actual address divided by 16. The offsets, ffec and fff4 in this case, represent memory position relative to the beginning of the segment. PC programs can use 2-byte pointers that hold just the offset, if all the data is in one segment. Or, they can use 4-byte pointers, with the first two bytes holding the segment value and the second two bytes holding the offset.

Using ordinary variables, then, treats the value as a named quantity and the location as a derived quantity. Now look at the pointer strategy, one that is essential to the C++ programming philosophy of memory management. (See the following note.)

POINTERS AND THE C++ PHILOSOPHY

Object-oriented programming differs from traditional procedural programming in OOP's emphasis on making decisions during run time instead of compile time. *Run time* means while a program is running, and *compile time* means when the compiler is putting a program together. A runtime decision is like, when on vacation, choosing what sights to see depending on the weather and your mood at the moment, whereas a compile-time decision is more like adhering to a preset schedule regardless of the conditions.

Runtime decisions provide the flexibility to adjust to current circumstances. For example, consider allocating memory for an array. The traditional way is to declare an array. To declare an array in C++, you have to commit yourself to a particular array size. Thus, the array size is set when the program is compiled; it is a compile-time decision. Perhaps you think an array of 20 elements is sufficient 80% of the time, but that occasionally the program will need to handle 200 elements. To be safe, you use an array with 200 elements. This results in your program wasting memory most of the time it's used. OOP tries to make a program more flexible by delaying such decisions until run time. That way, after the program is running, you can tell it you need only 20 elements one time or that you need 205 elements another time.

In short, you make the array size a runtime decision. To make this approach possible, the language has to allow you to create an array—or the equivalent—while the program runs. The C++ method, as you soon see, involves using the keyword new to request the correct amount of memory and using pointers to keep track of where the newly allocated memory is found.

The new strategy for handling stored data switches things around by treating the location as the named quantity and the value as a derived quantity. A special type of variable—the *pointer*—holds the address of a value. Thus, the name of the pointer represents the location. Applying the * operator, called the *indirect value* or the *dereferencing* operator, yields the value at the location. (Yes, this is the same * symbol used for multiplication; C++ uses the context to determine whether you mean multiplication or dereferencing.) Suppose, for example, that manly is a pointer. Then, manly represents an address, and *manly represents the value at that address. The combination *manly becomes equivalent to an ordinary type int variable. Listing 4.10 demonstrates these points. It also shows how to declare a pointer.

Listing 4.10 pointer.cpp

```cpp
// pointer.cpp _ our first pointer variable
#include <iostream>
using namespace std;
int main()
{
    int updates = 6;       // declare a variable
    int * p_updates;       // declare pointer to an int

    p_updates = &updates;    // assign address of int to pointer

    // express values two ways
    cout << "Values: updates = " << updates;
    cout << ", *p_updates = " << *p_updates << "\n";

    // express address two ways
    cout << "Addresses: &updates = " << &updates;
    cout << ", p_updates = " << p_updates << "\n";

    // use pointer to change value
    *p_updates = *p_updates + 1;
    cout << "Now updates = " << updates << "\n";
    return 0;
}
```

Here is the output:

```
Values: updates = 6, *p_updates = 6
Addresses: &updates = 0x85b0fff4, p_updates = 0x85b0fff4
Now updates = 7
```

As you can see, the int variable updates and the pointer variable p_updates are just two sides of the same coin. The updates variable represents the value as primary and uses the & operator to get the address, whereas the p_updates variable represents the address as primary and uses the * operator to get the value. See Figure 4.8. Because p_updates points to updates, *p_updates and updates are completely equivalent. You can use *p_updates exactly as you would use a type int variable. As the program shows, you even can assign values to *p_updates. Doing so changes the value of the pointed-to value, updates.

DECLARING AND INITIALIZING POINTERS

Let's examine the process of declaring pointers. A computer must keep track of the type of value to which a pointer refers. For instance, the address of a char looks the same as the address of a double, but char and double use different numbers of bytes and different internal formats for storing values. Therefore, a pointer declaration must specify what type of data it is to which the pointer points.

For example, the last example has this declaration:

```
int * p_updates;
```

FIGURE 4.8

Two sides of a coin

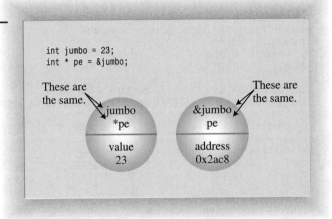

This states that the combination * p_updates is type int. Because the * operator is used by applying it to a pointer, the p_updates variable itself must *be* a pointer. We say that p_updates points to type int. We also say that the type for p_updates is pointer-to-int or, more concisely, int *. To repeat: p_updates is a pointer (an address), and *p_updates is an int and not a pointer. See Figure 4.9.

Incidentally, the use of spaces around the * operator are optional. Traditionally, C programmers have used this form:

```
int *ptr;
```

This accentuates the idea that the combination *ptr is a type int value. Many C++ programmers, on the other hand, use this form:

```
int* ptr;
```

This emphasizes the idea that int* is a type, pointer-to-int. Where you put the spaces makes no difference to the compiler. Be aware, however, that the declaration

```
int* p1, p2;
```

creates one pointer (p1) and one ordinary int (p2). You need an * for each pointer variable name.

In C++, the combination int * is a derived type, pointer-to-int.

FIGURE 4.9

Pointers store addresses

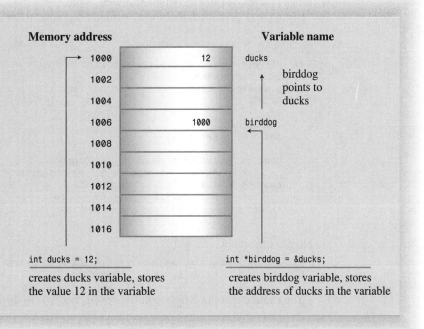

Memory address		Variable name
1000	12	ducks
1002		birddog points to ducks
1004		
1006	1000	birddog
1008		
1010		
1012		
1014		
1016		

int ducks = 12;
creates ducks variable, stores the value 12 in the variable

int *birddog = &ducks;
creates birddog variable, stores the address of ducks in the variable

> *A pointer variable is never simply a pointer. It always is a pointer to a specific type.*

You use the same syntax to declare pointers to other types:

```
double * tax_ptr; // tax_ptr points to type double
char * str;       // str points to type char
```

Because you declare tax_ptr as a pointer-to-double, the compiler knows that *tax_ptr is a type double value. That is, it knows that *tax_ptr represents a number stored in floating-point format that occupies (on most systems) eight bytes. A pointer variable is never simply a pointer. It always is a pointer to a specific type. tax_ptr is type pointer-to-double (or type double *) and str is type pointer-to-char (or char *). Although both are pointers, they are pointers of two different types. Like arrays, pointers are derived from other types.

Note that whereas tax_ptr and str point to data types of two different sizes, the two variables tax_ptr and str themselves typically are the same size. That is, the address of a char is the same size as the address of a double, much as 1016 might be the street address for a department store, whereas 1024 could be the street address of a small cottage. The size or value of an address doesn't really tell you anything about the size or kind of variable or building you find at that address. Usually, addresses require two or four bytes, depending on the computer system. (Some systems might have larger addresses, and a system can use different address sizes for different types.)

You can use a declaration statement to initialize a pointer. In that case, the pointer, not the pointed-to value, is initialized. That is, the statements

```
int higgens = 5;
int * pi = &higgens;
```

set pi and not *pi to the value &higgens.

Listing 4.11 demonstrates how to initialize a pointer to an address.

Listing 4.11 init_ptr.cpp

```
// init_ptr.cpp -- initialize a pointer
#include <iostream>
using namespace std;
int main()
{
    int higgens = 5;
    int * pi = &higgens;

    cout << "Value of higgens = " << higgens
        << "; Address of higgens = " << &higgens << "\n";
    cout << "Value of *pi = " << *pi
        << "; Value of pi = " << pi << "\n";
    return 0;
}
```

Here is the output:

```
Value of higgens = 5; Address of higgens = 0068FDF0
Value of *pi = 5; Value of pi = 0068FDF0
```

You can see that the program initializes pi, not *pi, to the address of higgens.

Danger awaits those who incautiously use pointers. One extremely important point is that when you create a pointer in C++, the computer allocates memory to hold an address, but it does not allocate memory to hold the data to which the address points. Creating space for the data involves a separate step. Omitting that step, as in the following, is an invitation to disaster:

```
long * fellow;           // create a pointer-to-long
*fellow = 223323;        // place a value in never-never land
```

Sure, `fellow` is a pointer. But where does it point? The code failed to assign an address to `fellow`. So where is the value 223323 placed? We can't say. Because `fellow` wasn't initialized, it could have any value. Whatever that value is, the program interprets it as the address at which to store 223323. If `fellow` happens to have the value 1200, then the computer attempts to place the data at address 1200, even if that happens to be an address in the middle of your program code. Chances are that wherever `fellow` points, that is not where you want to put the number 223323. This kind of error can produce some of the most insidious and hard-to-trace bugs.

Pointer Golden Rule: ALWAYS initialize a pointer to a definite and appropriate address before you apply the dereferencing operator (*) to it.

POINTERS AND NUMBERS

Pointers are not integer types, even though computers typically handle addresses as integers. Conceptually, pointers are distinct types from integers. Integers are numbers you can add, subtract, divide, and so on. But a pointer describes a location, and it doesn't make sense, for example, to multiply two locations by each other. In terms of the operations you can perform with them, pointers and integers are different from each other. Consequently, you can't simply assign an integer to a pointer:

```
int * pi;
pi = 0xB8000000;  // type mismatch
```

Here, the left side is a pointer to `int`, so you can assign it an address, but the right side is just an integer. You might know that 0xB8000000 is the combined segment-offset address of video memory on your system, but nothing in the statement tells the program that this number is an address. C lets you make assignments like this. But C++ more stringently enforces type agreement, and the compiler will give you an error message saying you have a type mismatch. If you want to use a numeric value as an address, you should use a type cast to convert the number to the appropriate address type:

```
int * pi;
pi = (int *) 0xB8000000; // types now match
```

Now both sides of the assignment statement represent addresses of integers, so the assignment is valid. Note that just because it is the address of a type int value doesn't mean that pi itself is type int. For instance, in the large memory model on an IBM PC, type int is a 2-byte value, whereas addresses are 4-byte values.

Pointers have some other interesting properties that we'll discuss as they become relevant. Meanwhile, let's look at how pointers can be used to manage runtime allocation of memory space.

ALLOCATING MEMORY WITH new

Now that you have some feel for how pointers work, let's see how they can implement that important OOP technique of allocating memory as a program runs. So far, we've initialized pointers to the addresses of variables; the variables are *named* memory allocated during compile time, and the pointers merely provide an alias for memory you could access directly by name anyway. The true worth of pointers comes into play when you allocate *unnamed* memory during run time to hold values. In this case, pointers become the only access to that memory. In C, you could allocate memory with the library function malloc(). You still can do so in C++, but C++ also has a better way, the new operator.

Let's try out this new technique by creating unnamed, runtime storage for a type int value and accessing the value with a pointer. The key is the C++ new operator. You tell new for what data type you want memory; new finds a block of the correct size and returns the address of the block. Assign this address to a pointer, and you're in business. Here's a sample of the technique:

```
int * pn = new int;
```

The new int part tells the program you want some new storage suitable for holding an int. The new operator uses the type to figure out how many bytes are needed. Then, it finds the memory and returns the address. Next, assign the address to pn, which is declared to be of type pointer-to-int. Now pn is the address and *pn is the value stored there. Compare this with assigning the address of a variable to a pointer:

```
int higgens;
int * pi = &higgens;
```

In both cases (pn and pi) you assign the address of an int to a pointer. In the second case, you also can access the int by name: higgens. In the first case, your only access is via the pointer. That raises a question: Because the memory to which pn points lacks a name, what do you call it? We say that pn points to a *data object*. This is not "object" in the sense of "object-oriented programming"; it's just "object" in the sense of "thing." The term "data object" is more general than the term "variable," because it means any block of memory allocated for a data item. Thus, a variable also is a data object, but the memory to which pn points is not a variable. The pointer method for handling data objects may seem more awkward at first, but it offers greater control over how your program manages memory.

The general form for obtaining and assigning memory for a single data object, which can be a structure as well as a fundamental type, is this:

```
typeName pointer_name = new typeName;
```

You use the data type twice: once to specify the kind of memory requested and once to declare a suitable pointer. Of course, if you've already declared a pointer of the correct type, you can use it rather than declare a new one. Listing 4.12 illustrates using new with two different types.

Listing 4.12 use_new.cpp

```cpp
// use_new.cpp _ using the new operator
#include <iostream>
using namespace std;
int main()
{
    int * pi = new int;        // allocate space for an int
    *pi = 1001;                // store a value there

    cout << "int ";
    cout << "value = " << *pi << ": location = " << pi << "\n";

    double * pd = new double;  // allocate space for a double
    *pd = 10000001.0;          // store a double there

    cout << "double ";
    cout << "value = " << *pd << ": location = " << pd << "\n";
    cout << "size of pi = " << sizeof pi;
    cout << ": size of *pi = " << sizeof *pi << "\n";
    cout << "size of pd = " << sizeof pd;
    cout << ": size of *pd = " << sizeof *pd << "\n";
    return 0;
}
```

Here is the output:

```
int value = 1001: location = 007B0A60
double value = 1e+007: location = 007B0CD0
size of pi = 4: size of *pi = 4
size of pd = 4: size of *pd = 8
```

Program Notes

The program uses new to allocate memory for the type int and type double data objects. This occurs while the program is running. The pointers pi and pd point to these two data objects. Without them, you cannot access those memory locations. With them, you can use *pi and *pd just as you would use variables. You assign values to *pi and *pd to assign values to the new data objects. Similarly, you print *pi and *pd to display those values.

The program also demonstrates one of the reasons you have to declare the type a pointer points to. An address in itself reveals only the beginning address of the object stored, not its type or the number of bytes used. Look at the addresses of the two values.

They are just numbers with no type or size information. Also, note that the size of a pointer-to-int is the same as the size of a pointer-to-double. Both are just addresses. But because use_new.cpp declared the pointer types, the program knows that *pd is a double value of 8 bytes, whereas *pi is an int value of 4 bytes. When use_new.cpp prints the value of *pd, cout can tell how many bytes to read and how to interpret them.

OUT OF MEMORY?

It's possible that the computer might not have sufficient memory available to satisfy a new request. When that is the case, new returns the value 0. In C++, a pointer with the value 0 is called the *null pointer*. C++ guarantees that the null pointer never points to valid data, so it often is used to indicate failure for operators or functions that otherwise return usable pointers. After you learn about if statements (in Chapter 6), you can check to see whether new returns the null pointer and thus protects your program from attempting to exceed its bounds. In addition to returning the null pointer upon failure to allocate memory, new might throw a bad_alloc exception. Chapter 14 discusses the exception mechanism.

FREEING MEMORY WITH delete

Using new to request memory when you need it is just the more glamorous half of the C++ memory-management package. The other half is the delete operator, which enables you to return memory to the memory pool when you are finished with it. That is an important step toward making the most effective use of memory. Memory that you return, or *free*, then can be reused by other parts of your program. You use delete by following it with a pointer to a block of memory originally allocated with new:

```
int * ps = new int; // allocate memory with new
delete ps;          // free memory with delete
```

This removes the memory to which ps points; it doesn't remove the pointer ps itself. You can reuse ps, for example, to point to another new allocation. You always should balance a use of new with a use of delete; otherwise, you can wind up with a *memory leak;* that is, memory that has been allocated but no longer can be used. If a memory leak grows too large, it can bring a program seeking more memory to a halt.

You should not attempt to free a block of memory that you already have freed. The result of such an attempt is not defined. Also, you cannot use delete to free memory created by declaring variables:

```
int * ps = new int;    // ok
delete ps;............// ok
delete ps;............// not ok now
int jugs = 5;          // ok
int * pi = & jugs;     // ok
delete pi;             // not allowed, memory not allocated by new
```

Remember

Use `delete` only to free memory allocated with `new`. However, it is safe to apply `delete` to a null pointer.

Note that the critical test for using `delete` is that you use it with memory allocated by `new`. This doesn't mean you must use the same pointer you used with `new`; instead, you must use the same address:

```
int * ps = new int;    // allocate memory
int * pq = ps;         // set second pointer to same block
delete pq;             // delete with second pointer
```

Ordinarily, you won't create two pointers to the same block of memory because that raises the possibility you mistakenly will try to delete the same block twice. But, as you soon see, using a second pointer does make sense when you work with a function that returns a pointer.

USING new TO CREATE DYNAMIC ARRAYS

If all a program needs is a single value, you might as well declare a simple variable, for that is simpler, if less impressive, than using `new` and a pointer to manage a single small data object. More typically, you use `new` with larger chunks of data, such as arrays, strings, and structures. This is where `new` is useful. Suppose, for example, you're writing a program that might or might not need an array, depending on information given to the program while it is running. If you create an array by declaring it, the space is allocated when the program is compiled. Whether or not the program finally uses the array, the array is there, using up memory. Allocating the array during compile time is called *static binding,* meaning the array is built into the program at compilation time. But with `new`, you can create an array during run time if you need it and skip creating the array if you don't need it. Or, you can select an array size after the program is running. This is called *dynamic binding*, meaning that the array is created while the program is running. Such an array is called a *dynamic array*. With static binding, you must specify the array size when you write the program. With dynamic binding, the program can decide upon an array size while the program runs.

For now, we'll look at two basic matters concerning dynamic arrays: how to use C++'s `new` operator to create an array and how to use a pointer to access array elements.

Creating a Dynamic Array with new

It's easy to create a dynamic array in C++; you tell `new` the type of array element and number of elements you want. The syntax requires that you follow the type name with the number of elements in brackets. For instance, if you need an array of 10 `int`s, do this:

```
int * psome = new int [10]; // get a block of 10 ints
```

The new operator returns the address of the first element of the block. In this example, that value is assigned to the pointer psome. You should balance the call to new with a call to delete when the program is finished using that block of memory.

When you use new to create an array, you should use an alternative form of delete that indicates you are freeing an array:

```
delete [] psome;                      // free a dynamic array
```

The presence of the brackets tells the program that it should free the whole array, not just the element pointed to by the pointer. Note that the brackets are between delete and the pointer. If you use new without brackets, use delete without brackets. If you use new with brackets, use delete with brackets. Earlier versions of C++ might not recognize the bracket notation. With current versions, however, the effect of mismatching new and delete forms is undefined, meaning you can't rely upon some particular behavior.

```
int * pi = new int;
short * ps = new short [500];
delete [] pi;  // effect is undefined, don't do it
delete ps;     // effect is undefined, don't do it
```

In short, observe these rules when you use new and delete:

- Don't use delete to free memory that new didn't allocate.

- Don't use delete to free the same block of memory twice in succession.

- Use delete [] if you used new [] to allocate an array.

- Use delete (no brackets) if you used new to allocate a single entity.

- It's safe to apply delete to the null pointer (nothing happens).

Now let's return to the dynamic array. Note that psome is a pointer to a single int, the first element of the block. It's your responsibility to keep track of how many elements are in the block. That is, because the compiler doesn't keep track of the fact that psome points to the first of 10 integers, you have to write your program so that it keeps track of the number of elements.

Actually, the program does keep track of the amount of memory allocated so that it can be correctly freed at a later time when you use the delete [] operator. But that information isn't publicly available; you can't use the sizeof operator, for example, to find the number of bytes in a dynamically allocated array.

The general form for allocating and assigning memory for an array is this:

```
type_name pointer_name = new type_name [num_elements];
```

Invoking the new operator secures a block of memory large enough to hold *num_elements* elements of type *type_name*, with *pointer_name* pointing to the first element. As you're about to see, you can use *pointer_name* in many of the same ways you can use an array name.

Using a Dynamic Array

After you create a dynamic array, how do you use it? First, think about the problem conceptually. The statement

```
int * psome = new int [10]; // get a block of 10 ints
```

creates a pointer, psome, that points to the first element of a block of 10 int values. Think of it as a finger pointing to that element. Suppose an int occupies four bytes. Then, by moving your finger four bytes in the correct direction, you can point to the second element. Altogether, there are 10 elements, which is the range over which you can move your finger. Thus, the new statement supplies you with all the information you need to identify every element in the block.

Now think about the problem practically. How do you access one of these elements? The first element is no problem. Because psome points to the first element of the array, *psome is the value of the first element. That leaves nine more elements to access. The simplest way may surprise you if you haven't worked with C: Just use the pointer as if it were an array name. That is, you can use psome[0] instead of *psome for the first element, psome[1] for the second element, and so on. It turns out to be very simple to use a pointer to access a dynamic array, even though why the method works might not immediately be obvious. The reason you can do this is that C and C++ handle arrays internally by using pointers anyway. This near equivalence of arrays and pointers is one of the beauties of C and C++. We'll elaborate on this equivalence in a moment. First, Listing 4.13 shows how you can use new to create a dynamic array and then use array notation to access the elements. It also points out a fundamental difference between a pointer and a true array name.

Listing 4.13 arraynew.cpp

```
// arraynew.cpp _ using the new operator for arrays
#include <iostream>
using namespace std;
int main()
{
    double * p3 = new double [3]; // space for 3 doubles
    p3[0] = 0.2;                  // treat p3 like an array name
    p3[1] = 0.5;
    p3[2] = 0.8;
    cout << "p3[1] is " << p3[1] << ".\n";
    p3 = p3 + 1;                  // increment the pointer
    cout << "Now p3[0] is " << p3[0] << " and ";
    cout << "p3[1] is " << p3[1] << ".\n";
    p3 = p3 - 1;                  // point back to beginning
    delete [] p3;                 // free the memory
    return 0;
}
```

Here is the output:

```
p3[1] is 0.5.
Now p3[0] is 0.5 and p3[1] is 0.8.
```

As you can see, `arraynew.cpp` uses the pointer p3 as if it were the name of an array, with p3[0] as the first element, and so on. The fundamental difference between an array name and a pointer shows in the following line:

```
p3 = p3 + 1; // okay for pointers, wrong for array names
```

You can't change the value of an array name. But a pointer is a variable, hence you can change its value. Note the effect of adding 1 to p3. The expression p3[0] now refers to the former second element of the array. Thus, adding 1 to p3 causes it to point to the second element instead of the first. Subtracting one takes the pointer back to its original value so that the program can provide delete [] with the correct address.

The actual addresses of consecutive ints typically differ by two or four bytes, so the fact that adding 1 to p3 gives the address of the next element suggests that there is something special about pointer arithmetic. There is.

Pointers, Arrays, and Pointer Arithmetic

The near equivalence of pointers and array names stems from *pointer arithmetic* and how C++ handles arrays internally. First, let's check out the arithmetic. Adding 1 to an integer variable increases its value by 1, but adding 1 to a pointer variable increases its value by the number of bytes of the type to which it points. Adding 1 to a pointer to double adds 8 to the numerical value on systems with 8-byte double, whereas adding 1 to a pointer-to-short adds 2 to the pointer value if short is 2 bytes. Listing 4.14 demonstrates this amazing point. It also shows a second important point: C++ interprets the array name as an address.

Listing 4.14 addpntrs.cpp
```
#include <iostream>
using namespace std;
int main()
{
    double wages[3] = {10000.0, 20000.0, 30000.0};
    short stacks[3] = {3, 2, 1};

// Here are two ways to get the address of an array
    double * pw = wages;     // name of an array = address
    short * ps = &stacks[0]; // or use address operator
                             // with array element
    cout << "pw = " << pw << ", *pw = " << *pw << "\n";
    pw = pw + 1;
    cout << "add 1 to the pw pointer:\n";
    cout << "pw = " << pw << ", *pw = " << *pw << "\n\n";

    cout << "ps = " << ps << ", *ps = " << *ps << "\n";
    ps = ps + 1;
    cout << "add 1 to the ps pointer:\n";
    cout << "ps = " << ps << ", *ps = " << *ps << "\n\n";
```

```
        cout << "access two elements with array notation\n";
        cout << stacks[0] << " " << stacks[1] << "\n";
        cout << "access two elements with pointer notation\n";
        cout << *stacks << " " << *(stacks + 1) << "\n";

        cout << sizeof wages << " = size of wages array\n";
        cout << sizeof pw << " = size of pw pointer\n";
        return 0;
}
```

Here is the output:

```
pw = 0068FDE0, *pw = 10000
add 1 to the pw pointer:
pw = 0068FDE8, *pw = 20000

ps = 0068FDD0, *ps = 3
add 1 to the ps pointer:
ps = 0068FDD2, *ps = 2

access two elements with array notation
3 2
access two elements with pointer notation
3 2
24 = size of wages array
4 = size of pw pointer
```

PROGRAM NOTES

In most contexts, C++ interprets the name of an array as the address of its first element. Thus, the statement

```
double * pw = wages;
```

makes pw a pointer to type double and then initializes pw to wages, which is the address of the first element of the wages array. For wages, as with any array, we have the following equality:

```
wages = &wages[0] = address of first element of array
```

Just to show that this is no jive, the program explicitly uses the address operator in the expression &stacks[0] to initialize the ps pointer to the first element of the stacks array.

Next, the program inspects the values of pw and *pw. The first is an address and the second is the value at that address. Because pw points to the first element, the value displayed for *pw is that of the first element, 10000. Then, the program adds 1 to pw. As promised, this adds 8 (E0 + 8 = E8 in hexadecimal) to the numeric address value, because double on our system is 8 bytes. This makes pw equal to the address of the second element. Thus, *pw now is 20000, the value of the second element. See Figure 4.10. (The address values in the figure are adjusted to make the figure clearer.)

FIGURE 4.10

Pointer addition

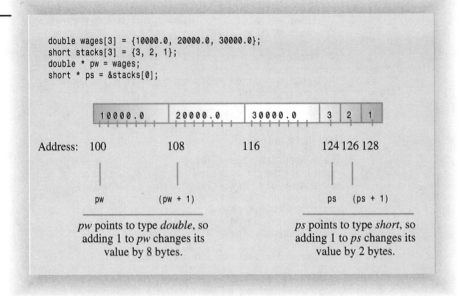

```
double wages[3] = {10000.0, 20000.0, 30000.0};
short stacks[3] = {3, 2, 1};
double * pw = wages;
short * ps = &stacks[0];
```

After this, the program goes through similar steps for ps. This time, because ps points to type short and because short is 2 bytes, adding 1 to the pointer increases its value by 2. Again, the result is to make the pointer point to the next element of the array.

Remember

Remember, adding 1 to a pointer variable increases its value by the number of bytes of the type to which it points.

Now consider the array expression stacks[1]. The C++ compiler treats this expression exactly as if you wrote it as *(stacks + 1). The second expression means calculate the address of the second element of the array and then find the value stored there. The end result is precisely what stacks[1] means. (Operator precedence requires that you use the parentheses. Without them, 1 would be added to *stacks instead of to stacks.)

The program output demonstrates that *(stacks + 1) and stacks[1] are the same. Similarly, *(stacks + 2) is the same as stacks[2]. In general, wherever you use array notation, C++ makes the following conversion:

```
arrayname[i] becomes *(arrayname + i)
```

And if you use a pointer instead of an array name, C++ makes the same conversion:

```
pointername[i] becomes *(pointername + i)
```

Thus, in many respects you can use pointer names and array names in the same way. You can use the array brackets notation with either. You can apply the dereferencing operator (*) to either. In most expressions, each represents an address. One difference is that you can change the value of a pointer while an array name is a constant:

```
pointername = pointername + 1; // valid
arrayname = arrayname + 1;     // not allowed
```

The second difference is that applying the `sizeof` operator to an array name yields the size of the array, but applying `sizeof` to a pointer yields the size of the pointer, even if the pointer points to the array. For instance, in Listing 4.15, both `pw` and `wages` refer to the same array. But applying the `sizeof` operator to them produces the following results:

```
24 = size of wages array // displaying sizeof wages
4 = size of pw pointer   // displaying sizeof pw
```

This is one case in which C++ doesn't interpret the array name as an address.

In short, using `new` to create an array and using a pointer to access the different elements is a simple matter. Just treat the pointer as an array name. Understanding why this works, however, is an interesting challenge. If you actually want to understand arrays and pointers, you should review their mutual relationships carefully. In fact, you've been exposed to quite a bit of pointer knowledge lately, so let's summarize what's been revealed about pointers and arrays to date.

Summarizing Pointer Points

Declaring Pointers: To declare a pointer to a particular type, use this form:

```
typeName * pointerName;
```

Examples:

```
double * pn;    // pn points to a double value
char * pc;      // pc points to a char value
```

Here, `pn` and `pc` are pointers, and `double *` and `char *` are the C++ notations for the types pointer-to-double and pointer-to-char.

Assigning Values to Pointers: You should assign a pointer a memory address. You can apply the & operator to a variable name to get an address of named memory, and the `new` operator returns the address of unnamed memory.

Examples:

```
double bubble = 3.2;
pn = &bubble;   // assign address of bubble to pn
pc = new char;  // assign address of newly allocated char memory to pc
```

Dereferencing Pointers: Dereferencing a pointer means referring to the pointed-to value. Apply the dereferencing, or indirect value, operator (*) to a pointer to dereference it. Thus, if `pn` is a pointer to `bubble`, as in the last example, then `*pn` is the pointed-to value, or 3.2, in this case.

> *Thus, in many respects you can use pointer names and array names the same way. You can use the array brackets notation with either. You can apply the dereferencing operator (*) to either.*

Examples:

```
cout << *pn; // print the value of bubble
*pc = 'S';   // place 'S' into the memory location whose address is pc
```

Never dereference a pointer that has not been initialized to a proper address.

Distinguishing Between a Pointer and the Pointed-to Value: Remember, if pi is a pointer-to-int, that *pi is not a pointer-to-int; instead, *pi is the complete equivalent to a type int variable. It is pi that is the pointer.

Examples:

```
int * pi = new int;     // assigns an address to the pointer pi
*pi = 5;                // stores the value 5 at that address
```

Array Names: In most contexts, C++ treats the name of an array as equivalent to the address of the first element of an array.

Example:

```
int tacos[10];          // now tacos is the same as &tacos[0]
```

One exception is when you use the name of an array with the sizeof operator. In that case, sizeof returns the size of the entire array, in bytes.

Pointer Arithmetic: C++ allows you to add an integer to a pointer. The result of adding 1 equals the original address value plus a value equal to the number of bytes in the pointed-to object. You also can subtract an integer from a pointer and take the difference between two pointers. The last operation, which yields an integer, is meaningful only if the two pointers point into the same array (pointing to one position past the end is allowed, too); it then yields the separation between the two elements.

Examples:

```
int tacos[10] = {5,2,8,4,1,2,2,4,6,8};
int * pt = tacos;       // suppose pf and fog are the address 3000
pt = pt + 1;            // now pt is 3004 if a int is four bytes
int *pe = &tacos[9];    // pe is 3036 if an int is four bytes
pe = pe -1;             // now pe is 3032, the address of tacos[8]
int diff = pe - pt;     // diff is 7, the separation between
                        // tacos[8] and tacos[1]
```

Dynamic Binding and Static Binding for Arrays: Use an array declaration to create an array with static binding; that is, an array whose size is set during compilation time:

```
int tacos[10]; // static binding, size fixed at compile time
```

Use the new [] operator to create an array with dynamic binding (a dynamic array), that is, an array that is allocated and whose size can be set during run time. Free the memory with delete [] when you are finished:

```
int size;
cin >> size;
int * pz = new int [size];   // dynamic binding, size set at run time
...
delete [] pz;                // free memory when finished
```

Array Notation and Pointer Notation: Using bracket array notation is equivalent to dereferencing a pointer:

```
tacos[0] means *tacos means the value at address tacos
tacos[3] means *(tacos + 3) means the value at address tacos + 3
```

This is true for both array names and pointer variables, so you can use either pointer notation or array notation with pointers and array names.

Examples:

```
int * pi = new int [10];    // pi points to block of 10 ints
*pi = 5;                    // set zero element to 5
pi[0] = 6;                  // reset zero element to 6
pi[9] = 44;                 // set tenth element to 44
int tacos[10];
*(tacos + 4) = 12;          // set tacos[4] to 12
```

POINTERS AND STRINGS

The special relationship between arrays and pointers extends to strings. Consider the following code:

```
char flower[10] = "rose";
cout << flower << "s are red\n";
```

The name of an array is the address of its first element, so flower in the cout statement is the address of the char element containing the character r. The cout object assumes that the address of a char is the address of a string, so it prints the character at that address and then continues printing characters until it runs into the null character (\0). In short, if you give cout the address of a character, it prints everything from that character to the first null character that follows it.

The crucial element here is not that flower is an array name but that flower acts as the address of a char. This implies that you can use a pointer-to-char variable as an argument to cout, also, because it, too, is the address of a char. Of course, that pointer should point to the beginning of a string. We'll check that out in a moment.

But first, what about the final part of the preceding cout statement? If flower actually is the address of the first character of a string, what is the expression "s are red\n"? To be consistent with cout's handling of string output, this quoted string also should be an address. And it is, for in C++ a quoted string, like an array name, serves as the address of its first element. The preceding code doesn't really send a whole string to cout, it just sends the string address. This means strings in an array, quoted string constants, and strings described by pointers all are handled equivalently. Each really is passed along as an address. That's certainly less work than passing each and every character in a string.

Remember

With cout and with most C++ expressions, the name of an array of char, a pointer-to-char, and a quoted string constant all are interpreted as the address of the first character of a string.

Listing 4.15 illustrates using the different forms of strings. It uses two functions from the string library. The strlen() function, which we've used before, returns the length of a string. The strcpy() function copies a string from one location to another. Both have function prototypes in the cstring header file (or string.h, on less up-to-date implementations). The program also showcases some pointer misuses that you should try to avoid.

Listing 4.15   ptrstr.cpp

```cpp
// ptrstr.cpp _ using pointers to strings
#include <iostream>
using namespace std;
#include <cstring>                    // declare strlen(), strcpy()
int main()
{
    char animal[20] = "bear";    // animal holds bear
    const char * bird = "wren"; // bird holds address of string
    char * ps;                   // uninitialized

    cout << animal << " and ";   // display bear
    cout << bird << "\n";        // display wren
    cout << ps << "\n";          // blunder - display garbage

    cout << "Enter a kind of animal: ";
    cin >> animal;               // ok if input < 20 chars
    // cin >> ps; Too horrible a blunder to try; ps doesn't
    //            point to allocated space

    ps = animal;                 // set ps to point to string
    cout << ps << "s!\n";        // ok, same as using animal
    cout << "Before using strcpy():\n";
    cout << animal << " at " << (int *) animal << endl;
    cout << ps << " at " << (int *) ps << endl;

    ps = new char[strlen(animal) + 1];  // get new storage
    strcpy(ps, animal);          // copy string to new storage
    cout << "After using strcpy():\n";
    cout << animal << " at " << (int *) animal << endl;
    cout << ps << " at " << (int *) ps << endl;
    delete [] ps;
    return 0;
}
```

Remember

If your system doesn't have the cstring header file, use the older string.h version. The first attempt to display ps might lead to a runtime error.

Here is a sample run:

```
bear and wren
                " output from cout << ps << "\n";
Enter a kind of animal: fox
foxs!
Before using strcpy():
fox at 0068FDE4
fox at 0068FDE4
After using strcpy():
fox at 0068FDE4
fox at 007B0D80
```

Program Notes

The program in Listing 4.15 creates one char array (animal) and two pointers-to-char variables (bird and ps). The program begins by initializing the animal array to the "bear" string, just as we've initialized arrays before. Then, the program does something new. It initializes a pointer-to-char to a string:

```
const char * bird = "wren"; // bird holds address of string
```

Remember, "wren" actually represents the address of the string, so this statement assigns the address of "wren" to the bird pointer. (Typically, a compiler sets aside an area in memory to hold all the strings used in the program source code, associating each stored string with its address.) This means you can use the pointer bird just as you would use the string "wren", as in cout << "A concerned " << bird << " speaks\n". String literals are constants, which is why the code uses the const keyword in the declaration. Using const in this fashion means you can use bird to access the string but not to change it. Chapter 7 takes up the topic of const pointers in greater detail. Finally, the pointer ps remains uninitialized, so it doesn't point to any string. (This, you recall, usually is a bad idea, and this example is no exception.)

Next, the program illustrates that you can use the array name animal and the pointer bird equivalently with cout. Both, after all, are the addresses of strings, and cout displays the two strings ("bear" and "wren") stored at those addresses. When the code makes the error of attempting to display ps, we get a blank line. Creating an uninitialized pointer is a bit like distributing a blank signed check; you lack control over how it will be used. We are a little lucky here, for ps, being uninitialized, might have pointed accidentally to some awkward location. As it is, it points to a location that contains a zero, so nothing is displayed. Otherwise, you might get some garbage output.

For input, the situation is a bit different. It's safe to use the array animal for input as long as the input is short enough to fit into the array. It would not be proper to use bird for input, however:

- Some compilers treat string literals as read-only constants, leading to a runtime error if you try to write new data over them. That string literals be constant is the mandated behavior in C++, but not all compilers have made that change from older behavior yet.

🍂 Some compilers use just one copy of a string literal to represent all
occurrences of that literal in a program.

Let's amplify the second point. C++ doesn't guarantee that string literals are stored
uniquely. That is, if you use a string literal "wren" several times in the program, the
compiler might store several copies of the string or just one copy. If it does the latter,
then setting bird to point to one "wren" makes it point to the only copy of that string.
Reading a value into one string could affect what you thought was an independent
string elsewhere. In any case, because the bird pointer is declared as const, the compiler prevents any attempt to change the contents of the location pointed to by bird.

Worse yet is trying to read information into the location to which ps points. Because
ps is not initialized, you don't know where the information will wind up. It might even
overwrite information already in memory. Fortunately, it's easy to avoid these problems—just use a sufficiently large char array to receive input. Don't use string constants to receive input or uninitialized pointers to receive input.

Remember

**When you read a string into a program, you always should use the address of
previously allocated memory. This address can be in the form of an array name
or of a pointer that has been initialized using new.**

Next, notice what the following code accomplishes:

```
ps = animal;                    // set ps to point to string
...
    cout << animal << " at " << (int *) animal << endl;
    cout << ps << " at " << (int *) ps << endl;
```

It produces the following output:

```
fox at 0068FDE4
fox at 0068FDE4
```

Normally, if you give cout a pointer, it prints an address. But if the pointer is type
char *, cout displays the pointed-to string. If you want to see the address of the
string, you have to type cast the pointer to another pointer type, such as int *, which
this code does. So, ps displays as the string "fox", but (int *) ps displays as the
address where the string is found. Note that assigning animal to ps does not copy the
string, it copies the address. This results in two pointers (animal and ps) to the same
memory location and string.

To get a copy of a string, you need to do more. First, you need to allocate memory to
hold the string. You can do this by declaring a second array or by using new. The second approach enables you to custom fit the storage to the string:

```
ps = new char[strlen(animal) + 1]; // get new storage
```

The string "fox" doesn't completely fill the animal array, so we're wasting space.
This bit of code uses strlen() to find the length of the string; it adds 1 to get the
length including the null character. Then, the program uses new to allocate just enough
space to hold the string.

Next, you need a way to copy a string from the `animal` array to the newly allocated space. It doesn't work to assign `animal` to `ps` because that just changes the address stored in `ps` and thus loses the only way the program had to access the newly allocated memory. Instead, you need to use the `strcpy()` library function:

```
strcpy(ps, animal);                    // copy string to new storage
```

The `strcpy()` function takes two arguments. The first is the destination address, and the second is the address of the string to be copied. It's up to you to make certain that the destination really is allocated and has sufficient space to hold the copy. That's accomplished here by using `strlen()` to find the correct size and using `new` to get free memory.

> **Often you encounter the need to place a string into an array. Use the = operator when you initialize an array; otherwise, use `strcpy()` or `strncpy()`.**

Often you encounter the need to place a string into an array. Use the = operator when you initialize an array; otherwise, use `strcpy()` or `strncpy()`. You've seen the `strcpy()` function:

```
char food[20] = "carrots"; // initialization
strcpy(food, "flan");      // otherwise
```

Note that something like

```
strcpy(food, "a picnic basket filled with many goodies");
```

can cause problems because the `food` array is smaller than the string. In this case, the function copies the rest of the string into the memory bytes immediately following the array, which can overwrite other memory your program is using. To avoid that problem, use `strncpy()` instead. It takes a third argument: the maximum number of characters to be copied. Be aware, however, that if this function runs out of space before it reaches the end of the string, it doesn't add the null character. Thus, you should use the function like this:

```
strncpy(food, "a picnic basket filled with many goodies", 19);
food[19] = '\0';
```

This copies up to 19 characters into the array and then sets the last element to the null character. If the string is shorter than 19 characters, `strncpy()` adds a null character earlier to mark the true end of the string.

USING new TO CREATE DYNAMIC STRUCTURES

You've seen how it can be advantageous to create arrays during run time rather than compile time. The same holds true for structures. You must allocate space for only as many structures as a program needs during a particular run. Again, the `new` operator is the tool to use. With it, you can create dynamic structures. Again, "dynamic" means the memory is allocated during run time, not during compilation. Incidentally, because classes are much like structures, you are able to use the techniques you learn for structures with classes, too.

Using new with structures has two parts: creating the structure and accessing its members. To create a structure, use the structure type with new. For example, to create an unnamed structure of the `inflatable` type and assign its address to a suitable pointer, you can do the following:

```
inflatable * ps = new inflatable;
```

This assigns to ps the address of a chunk of free memory large enough to hold a structure of the `inflatable` type. Note that the syntax is exactly the same as it is for C++'s built-in types.

The tricky part is accessing members. When you create a dynamic structure, you can't use the dot membership operator with the structure name, because the structure has no name. All you have is its address. C++ provides an operator just for this situation: the arrow membership operator (`->`). This operator, formed by typing a hyphen and then a greater-than symbol, does for pointers to structures what the dot operator does for structure names. For instance, if ps points to a type `inflatable` structure, then `ps->price` is the `price` member of the pointed-to structure. See Figure 4.11.

Remember

Sometimes new users become confused about when to use the dot operator and when to use the arrow operator to specify a structure member. The rule is simple. If the structure identifier is the name of a structure, use the dot operator. If the identifier is a pointer to the structure, use the arrow operator.

FIGURE 4.11
Identifying structure members

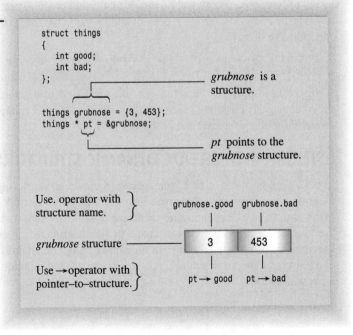

A second, uglier approach is to realize that if ps is a pointer to a structure, then *ps represents the pointed-to value—the structure itself. Then, because *ps is a structure, (*ps).price is the price member of the structure. C++'s operator precedence rules require that you use parentheses in this construction.

Listing 4.16 uses new to create an unnamed structure and demonstrates both pointer notations for accessing structure members.

Listing 4.16 newstrct.cpp

```cpp
// newstrct.cpp _ using new with a structure
#include <iostream>
using namespace std;
struct inflatable    // structure template
{
    char name[20];
    float volume;
    double price;
};
int main()
{
    inflatable * ps = new inflatable; // allot structure space

    cout << "Enter name of inflatable item: ";
    cin.get(ps->name, 20);          // method 1 for member access
    cout << "Enter volume in cubic feet: ";
    cin >> (*ps).volume;            // method 2 for member access
    cout << "Enter price: $";
    cin >> ps->price;
    cout << "Name: " << (*ps).name << "\n";  // method 2
    cout << "Volume: " << ps->volume << " cubic feet\n";
    cout << "Price: $" << ps->price << "\n"; // method 1
    return 0;
}
```

Here is a sample run:

```
Enter name of inflatable item: Fabulous Frodo
Enter volume in cubic feet: 1.4
Enter price: $17.99
Name: Fabulous Frodo
Volume: 1.4 cubic feet
Price: $17.99
```

A new and delete Example

Let's look at an example using new and delete to manage storing string input from the keyboard. Listing 4.17 defines a function that returns a pointer to an input string. This function reads the input into a large temporary array and then uses new [] to create a chunk of memory sized to fit to the input string. Then, the function returns the pointer to the block. This approach could conserve a lot of memory for programs that read in a large number of strings.

Suppose your program has to read 1000 strings and that the largest string might be 79 characters long, but most of the strings are much shorter. If you used char arrays to hold the strings, you'd need 1000 arrays of 80 characters each. That's 80,000 bytes, and much of that block of memory would wind up unused. Alternatively, you could create an array of 1000 pointers to char and then use new to allocate only the amount of memory needed for each string. That could save tens of thousands of bytes. Instead of having to use a large array for every string, you fit the memory to the input. Even better, you also could use new to find space to store only as many pointers as needed. Well, that's a little too ambitious for right now. Even using an array of 1000 pointers is a little too ambitious for right now, but Listing 4.17 illustrates some of the technique. Also, just to illustrate how delete works, the program uses it to free memory for reuse.

Listing 4.17 delete.cpp

```cpp
// delete.cpp _ using the delete operator
#include <iostream>
#include <cstring>        // or string.h
using namespace std;
char * getname(void);     // function prototype
int main()
{
    char * name;          // create pointer but no storage

    name = getname();     // assign address of string to name
    cout << name << " at " << (int *) name << "\n";
    delete [] name;       // memory freed

    name = getname();     // reuse freed memory
    cout << name << " at " << (int *) name << "\n";
    delete [] name;       // memory freed again
    return 0;
}

char * getname()          // return pointer to new string
{
    char temp[80];        // temporary storage

    cout << "Enter last name: ";
    cin >> temp;
    char * pn = new char[strlen(temp) + 1];
    strcpy(pn, temp);     // copy string into smaller space

    return pn;            // temp lost when function ends
}
```

Here is a sample run:

```
Enter last name: Fredeldumpkin
Fredeldumpkin at 007B0B40
Enter last name: Pook
Pook at 007B0DC0
```

Program Notes

First, consider the function getname(). It uses cin to place an input word into the temp array. Next, it uses new to allocate new memory to hold the word. Including the null character, the program needs strlen(temp) + 1 characters to store the string, so that's the value given to new. After the space becomes available, getname() uses the standard library function strcpy() to copy the string from temp to the new block. The function doesn't check to see whether the string fits or not, but getname() covers that by requesting the right number of bytes with new. Finally, the function returns pn, the address of the string copy.

In main(), the return value (the address) is assigned to the pointer name. This pointer is defined in main(), but it points to the block of memory allocated in the getname() function. The program then prints the string and the address of the string.

Next, after it frees the block pointed to by name, main() calls getname() a second time. C++ doesn't guarantee that newly freed memory is the first to be chosen the next time new is used, and in this sample run, it isn't.

To appreciate some of the more subtle aspects of this program, you should know a little more about how C++ handles memory. So let's preview some material that's covered more fully in Chapter 8.

AUTOMATIC STORAGE, STATIC STORAGE, THE FREE STORE

C++ has three ways of managing memory for data, depending on the method used to allocate memory: *automatic storage, static storage*, and the *free store*. Data objects allocated in these three ways differ from each other in how long they remain in existence. We'll take a quick look at each type.

Automatic Variables

Ordinary variables defined inside a function are called *automatic variables*. They come into existence automatically when the function containing them is invoked, and they expire when the function terminates. For example, the temp array in Listing 4.17 exists only while the getname() function is active. When program control returns to main(), the memory used for temp is freed automatically. If getname() had returned the address of temp, the name pointer in main() would have been left pointing to a memory location that soon would be reused. That's one reason we had to use new in getname().

Actually, automatic values are local to the block containing them. A block is a section of code enclosed between braces. So far, all our blocks have been entire functions. But, as you'll see in the next chapter, you can have blocks within a function. If you define a variable inside one of those blocks, it exists only while the program is executing statements inside the block.

Static Storage

Static storage is storage that exists throughout the execution of an entire program. There are two ways to make a variable static. One is to define it externally, outside a function. The other is to use the keyword `static` when declaring a variable:

```
static double fee = 56.50;
```

Under K&R C, you only can initialize static arrays and structures, whereas C++ Release 2.0 (and later) and ANSI C allow you to initialize automatic arrays and structures, too. However, as some of you may have discovered, some C++ implementations do not yet implement initialization for automatic arrays and structures.

Chapter 8 takes up static storage in more detail. The main point here about automatic and static storage is that these methods rigidly define the lifetime of a variable. Either the variable exists for the entire duration of a program (the static variable) or else it exists only while a particular function is being executed (the automatic variable).

The Free Store

The `new` and `delete` operators, however, provide a more flexible approach. They manage a pool of memory, which C++ refers to as the free store. This pool is separate from the memory used for static and automatic variables. As Listing 4.17 shows, `new` and `delete` enable you to allocate memory in one function and free it in another. Thus, the lifetime of the data is not tied arbitrarily to the life of the program or the life of a function. Using `new` and `delete` together gives you much more control over how a program uses memory than does using ordinary variables.

 Remember

Pointers are among the most powerful of C++ tools. They also are the most dangerous because they permit computer-unfriendly actions, such as using an uninitialized pointer to access memory or attempting to free the same memory block twice. Furthermore, until practice makes you used to pointer notation and pointer concepts, pointers can be confusing. This book returns to pointers several more times in the hopes that each exposure makes you more comfortable with them.

Summary

The array, the structure, and the pointer are three C++ derived types. The array can hold several values all of the same type in a single data object. By using an index, or subscript, you can access the individual elements in an array.

The structure can hold several values of different types in a single data object, and you can use the membership operator (.) to access individual members. The first step in using structures is creating a structure template defining what members the structure holds. The name, or tag, for this template then becomes a new type identifier. You then can declare structure variables of that type.

A union can hold a single value, but it can be of a variety of types, with the member name indicating which mode is being used.

Pointers are variables designed to hold addresses. We say a pointer points to the address it holds. The pointer declaration always states to what type of object a pointer points. Applying the dereferencing operator (*) to a pointer yields the value at the location to which the pointer points.

A string is a series of characters terminated by a null character. A string can be represented by a quoted string constant, in which case the null character is implicitly understood. You can store a string in an array of char, and you can represent a string by a pointer-to-char that is initialized to point to the string. The strlen() function returns the length of a string, not counting the null character. The strcpy() function copies a string from one location to another. When using these functions, include the cstring or the string.h header file.

The new operator lets you request memory for a data object while a program is running. The operator returns the address of the memory it obtains, and you can assign that address to a pointer. The only means to access that memory is to use the pointer. If the data object is a simple variable, you can use the dereferencing operator (*) to indicate a value. If the data object is an array, you can use the pointer as if it were an array name to access the elements. If the data object is a structure, you can use the pointer dereferencing operator (->) to access structure members.

Pointers and arrays are closely connected. If ar is an array name, then the expression ar[i] is interpreted as *(ar + i), with the array name interpreted as the address of the first element of the array. Thus, the array name plays the same role as a pointer. In turn, you can use a pointer name with array notation to access elements in an array allocated by new.

The new and delete operators let you explicitly control when data objects are allocated and when they are returned to the memory pool. Automatic variables, which are those declared within a function, and static variables, which are defined outside a function or with the keyword static, are less flexible. An automatic variable comes into being when the block containing it (typically a function definition) is entered, and it expires when the block is left. A static variable persists for the duration of a program.

Review Questions

1. How would you declare each of the following?

    a. actors is an array of 30 char.

    b. betsie is an array of 100 short.

    c. chuck is an array of 13 float.

    d. dipsea is an array of 64 long double.

2. Declare an array of five `int`s and initialize it to the first five odd integers.

3. Write a statement that assigns the sum of the first and last elements of the array in question 2 to the variable `even`.

4. Write a statement that displays the value of the second element in the `float` array `ideas`.

5. Declare an array of `char` and initialize it to the string `"cheeseburger"`.

6. Devise a structure declaration that describes a fish. The structure should include the kind, the weight in whole ounces, and the length in fractional inches.

7. Declare a variable of the type defined in question 6 and initialize it.

8. Use `enum` to define a type called `Response` with the possible values of `Yes`, `No`, and `Maybe`. `Yes` should be 1, `No` should be 0, and `Maybe` should be 2.

9. Suppose `ted` is a `double` variable. Declare a pointer that points to `ted` and use the pointer to display `ted`'s value.

10. Suppose `treacle` is an array of 10 `float`s. Declare a pointer that points to the first element of `treacle` and use the pointer to display the first and last elements of the array.

11. Write a code fragment that asks the user to enter a positive integer and then creates a dynamic array of that many `int`s.

12. Is the following valid code? If so, what does it print?

```
cout << (int *) "Home of the jolly bytes";
```

13. Write a code fragment that dynamically allocates a structure of the type described in question 6 and then reads a value for the kind member of the structure.

14. Listing 4.6 illustrates a problem with the following numeric input with line-oriented string input. How would replacing

```
cin.getline(address,80);
```

with

```
cin >> address;
```

affect the working of this program?

Programming Exercises

1. Write a C++ program that requests and displays information as shown below. Note that the program should be able to accept first names of more than one word. Also note that the program adjusts the grade downward, that is, up one

letter. Assume the user requests an A, B, or C so that you don't have to worry about the gap between a D and an F.

```
What is your first name? Betty Sue
What is your last name? Yew
What letter grade do you deserve? B
What is your age? 22
Name: Yew, Betty Sue
Grade: C
Age: 22
```

2. The CandyBar structure contains three members. The first member holds the brand name of a candy bar. The second member holds the weight (which may have a fractional part) of the candy bar, and the third member holds the number of calories (an integer value) in the candy bar. Write a program that declares such a structure and creates a CandyBar variable called snack, initializing its members to "Mocha Munch", 2.3, and 350, respectively. The initialization should be part of the declaration for snack. Finally, the program should display the contents of the snack variable.

3. The CandyBar structure contains three members, as described in programming exercise 2. Write a program that creates an array of three CandyBar structures, initializes them to values of your choice, and then displays the contents of each structure.

4. William Wingate runs a pizza-analysis service. For each pizza, he must record the following information:

   ◈ The name of the pizza company, which can consist of more than one word

   ◈ The diameter of the pizza

   ◈ The weight of the pizza

   Devise a structure that can hold this information and write a program using a structure variable of that type. The program should ask the user to enter each of the preceding items of information, and then the program should display that information. Use cin (or its methods) and cout.

5. Do programming exercise 2, but use new to allocate a structure instead of declaring a structure variable. Also, have the program request the pizza diameter before it requests the pizza company name.

5

Loops and Relational Expressions

In this chapter you learn

- The for loop
- Expressions and statements
- The increment and decrement operators: ++ and - -
- Combination assignment operators
- Compound statements (blocks)
- The comma operator
- Relational operators: >, >=, ==, <=, <, and !=
- The while loop
- The typedef facility
- The do while loop
- The get() character input method
- The end-of-file condition
- Nested loops and two-dimensional arrays

Computers do more than store data. They analyze, consolidate, rearrange, extract, modify, extrapolate, synthesize, and otherwise manipulate data. Sometimes they even distort and trash data, but we'll try to steer clear of that kind of behavior. To perform their manipulative miracles, programs need tools for performing repetitive actions and for making decisions. C++, of course, provides such tools. Indeed, it uses the same for loops, while loops, do while loops, if statements, and switch statements that regular C employs, so if you know C, you can zip through this and the next chapter. (But don't zip too fast—you don't want to miss how cin handles character input!) These various program control statements often use relational expressions and logical expressions to govern their behavior. This chapter discusses loops and relational expressions, and the next chapter follows up with branching statements and logical expressions.

Introducing the for Loop

Circumstances often call upon a program to perform repetitive tasks, such as adding together the elements of an array one by one or printing some paean to productivity 20 times. The C++ for loop makes such tasks easy to do. Let's look at a loop in Listing 5.1, see what it does, and then discuss how it works.

Listing 5.1 forloop.cpp

```
// forloop.cpp -- introducing the for loop
#include <iostream>
using namespace std;
int main()
{
    int i;  // create a counter
    //   initialize; test ; update
    for (i = 0; i < 5; i++)
        cout << "C++ knows loops.\n";
    cout << "C++ knows when to stop.\n";
    return 0;
}
```

Here is the output:

```
C++ knows loops.
C++ knows loops.
C++ knows loops.
C++ knows loops.
C++ knows loops.
C++ knows when to stop.
```

This loop begins by setting the integer i to 0:

```
i = 0
```

This is the *loop initialization* part of the loop. Then, in the *loop test*, the program tests to see if i is less than 5:

```
i < 5
```

If so, the program executes the following statement, which is termed the *loop body*:

```
cout << "C++ knows loops.\n";
```

Then, the program uses the *loop update* part of the loop to increase i by 1:

```
i++
```

This uses the ++ operator, called the *increment operator*. It increments the value of its operand by 1. (The increment operator is not restricted to for loops. For instance, you can use

```
i++;
```

instead of

```
i = i + 1;
```

as a statement in a program.) Incrementing i completes the first cycle of the loop.

Next, the loop begins a new cycle by comparing the new i value with 5. Because the new value (1) also is less than 5, the loop prints another line and then finishes by incrementing i again. That sets the stage for a fresh cycle of testing, executing a statement, and updating the value of i. The process continues until the loop updates i to 5. Then, the next test fails, and the program moves on to the next statement after the loop.

for LOOP PARTS

A for loop, then, provides a step-by-step recipe for performing repeated actions. Let's take a more detailed look at how it's set up. The usual parts of a for loop handle these steps:

- Setting a value initially
- Performing a test to see if the loop should continue
- Executing the loop actions
- Updating value(s) used for the test

The C++ loop design positions these elements so that you can spot them at a glance. The initialization, test, and update actions constitute a three-part control section enclosed in parentheses. Each part is an expression, and semicolons separate the expressions from each other. The statement following the control section is called the *body* of the loop, and it is executed as long as the test expression remains true:

```
for (initialization; test-expression; update-expression)
    body
```

C++ syntax counts a complete for statement as a single statement, even though it can incorporate one or more statements in the body portion.

The loop performs initialization just once. Typically, programs use this expression to set a variable to a starting value and then use the variable to count loop cycles.

The *test-expression* determines whether the loop body gets executed. Typically, this expression is a relational expression, that is, one that compares two values. Our example, for instance, compares the value of i to 5, checking to see if i is less than 5.

If the comparison is true, the program executes the loop body. Actually, C++ doesn't limit *test-expression* to true-false comparisons. You can use any expression. If the expression evaluates to zero, the loop terminates. If the expression evaluates to nonzero, the loop continues. Listing 5.2 demonstrates this by using the expression i as the test condition. (In the update section, i-- is similar to i++ except that it decreases the value of i by 1 each time it's used.)

Listing 5.2 num_test.cpp

```cpp
// num_test.cpp -- use numeric test in for loop
#include <iostream>
using namespace std;
int main()
{
    cout << "Enter the starting countdown value: ";
    int limit;
    cin >> limit;
    int i;
    for (i = limit; i; i--)       // quits when i is 0
        cout << "i = " << i << "\n";
    cout << "Done now that i = " << i << "\n";
    return 0;
}
```

Here is the output:

```
Enter the starting countdown value: 4
i = 4
i = 3
i = 2
i = 1
Done now that i = 0
```

Note that the loop terminates when i reaches 0.

How do relational expressions, such as i < 5, fit into this framework of terminating a loop with a 0 value? Originally, relational expressions evaluated to 1 if true and 0 if false. Thus, the value of the expression 3 < 5 was 1 and the value of 5 < 5 was 0. Now that C++ has added the bool type, however, relational expressions evaluate to the bool literals true and false instead of 1 and 0. This change doesn't lead to incompatibilities, however, for a C++ program converts true and false to 1 and 0 where integer values are expected, and it converts 0 to false and nonzero to true where bool values are expected.

The for loop is an entry-condition loop. This means the test expression is evaluated *before* each loop cycle. The loop never executes the loop body when the test expression is false. For instance, suppose you rerun the program in Listing 5.2 but give 0 as a starting value. Because the test condition fails the very first time it's evaluated, the loop body never gets executed:

```
Enter the starting countdown value: 0
Done now that i = 0
```

This look-before-you-loop attitude can help keep a program out of trouble.

The *update-expression* is evaluated at the end of the loop, after the body has been executed. Typically, it's used to increase or decrease the value of the variable keeping track of the number of loop cycles. However, it can be any valid C++ expression, as can the other control expressions. This makes the for loop capable of much more than simply counting from 0 to 5, the way the first loop example did. You'll see some examples later.

The for loop body consists of a single statement, but you'll soon learn how to stretch that rule. Figure 5.1 summarizes the for loop design.

A for statement looks something like a function call because it uses a name followed by paired parentheses. However, for's status as a C++ keyword prevents the compiler from thinking for is a function. It also prevents you from naming a function for.

FIGURE 5.1

The for loop

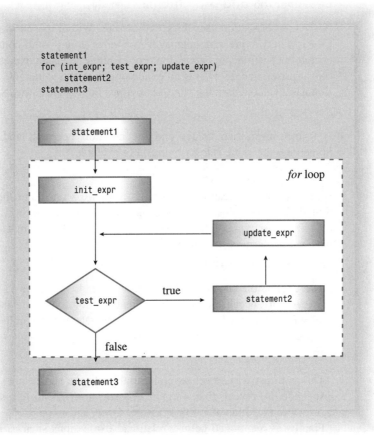

Remember

Common C++ style is to place a space between `for` and the following parentheses and to omit space between a function name and the following parentheses:

```
for (int i = 6; i < 10; i++)
    smart_function(i);
```

Other control statements, such as `if` and `while`, are treated similarly to `for`. This serves to reinforce visually the distinction between a control statement and a function call. Also, common practice is to indent the body of a `for` statement to make it stand out visually.

Expressions and Statements

A `for` control section uses three expressions. Within its self-imposed limits of syntax, C++ is a very expressive language. Any value or any valid combination of values and operators constitute an expression. For example, 10 is an expression with the value 10 (no surprise), and 28 * 20 is an expression with the value 560. In C++, every expression has a value. Often the value is obvious. For instance, the expression

```
22 + 27
```

is formed from two values and the addition operator, and it has the value 49. Sometimes the value is less obvious. For example,

```
x = 20
```

is an expression because it's formed from two values and the assignment operator. C++ defines the value of an assignment expression to be the value of the member on the left, so the expression above has the value 20. The fact that assignment expressions have values permits statements such as the following:

```
maids = (cooks = 4) + 3;
```

The expression `cooks = 4` has the value 4, so `maids` is assigned the value 7. However, just because C++ permits this behavior doesn't mean you should encourage it. But the same rule that makes this peculiar statement possible also makes the following useful statement possible:

```
x = y = z = 0;
```

This is a fast way to set several variables to the same value. The precedence table (Appendix D) reveals that assignment associates right-to-left, so first 0 is assigned to z, and then the value of z = 0 is assigned to y, and so on.

Finally, as mentioned before, relational expressions such as x < y evaluate to the `bool` values `true` or `false`. The short program in Listing 5.3 illustrates some points about expression values. The << operator has higher precedence than the operators used in the expressions, so the code uses parentheses to enforce the correct order.

Listing 5.3 express.cpp

```cpp
// express.cpp -- values of expressions
#include <iostream>
using namespace std;
int main()
{
    int x;

    cout << "The expression x = 100 has the value ";
    cout << (x = 100) << "\n";
    cout << "Now x = " << x << "\n";
    cout << "The expression x < 3 has the value ";
    cout << (x < 3) << "\n";
    cout << "The expression x > 3 has the value ";
    cout << (x > 3) << "\n";
    cout.setf(ios_base::boolalpha);
    cout << "The expression x < 3 has the value ";
    cout << (x < 3) << "\n";
    cout << "The expression x > 3 has the value ";
    cout << (x > 3) << "\n";
    return 0;
}
```

Remember

> Older implementations of C++ may require using `ios::boolalpha` instead of `ios_base::boolalpha` as the argument for `cout.setf()`. Yet older implementations may not recognize either form.

Here is the output:

```
The expression x = 100 has the value 100
Now x = 100
The expression x < 3 has the value 0
The expression x > 3 has the value 1
The expression x < 3 has the value false
The expression x > 3 has the value true
```

Normally, cout converts bool values to int before displaying them, but the `cout.setf(ios::boolalpha)` function call sets a flag that instructs cout to display the words true and false instead of 1 and 0.

Remember

> A C++ expression is a value or a combination of values and operators, and every C++ expression has a value.

To evaluate the expression x = 100, C++ must assign the value 100 to x. When the very act of evaluating an expression changes the value of data in memory, we say the evaluation has a *side effect*. Thus, evaluating an assignment expression has the side effect of changing the assignee's value. You might think of assignment as the intended effect, but from the standpoint of how C++ is constructed, evaluating the expression is the primary effect. Not all expressions have side effects. For instance, evaluating x + 15 calculates a new value, but it doesn't change the value of *x*. But evaluating ++x + 15 does have a side effect, because it involves incrementing x.

From expression to statement is a short step; just add a semicolon. Thus,

```
age = 100
```

is an expression, whereas

```
age = 100;
```

is a statement. Any expression can become a statement if you add a semicolon, but the result might not make programming sense. For instance, if `rodents` is a variable, then

```
rodents + 6;      // valid, but useless, statement
```

is a valid C++ statement. The compiler allows it, but the statement doesn't accomplish anything useful. The program merely calculates the sum, does nothing with it, and goes on to the next statement. (A smart compiler might even skip the statement.)

Nonexpressions and Statements

Some concepts, such as knowing the structure of a `for` loop, are crucial to understanding C++. But there also are relatively minor aspects of syntax that suddenly can bedevil you just when you think you understand the language. We'll look at a couple of them now.

Although it is true that adding a semicolon to any expression makes it a statement, the reverse is not true. That is, removing a semicolon from a statement does not necessarily convert it to an expression. Of the kinds of statements we've used so far, return statements, declaration statements, and `for` statements don't fit the *statement = expression + semicolon* mold. For instance, although

```
int toad;
```

is a statement, the fragment `int toad` is not an expression and does not have a value. This makes code such as the following invalid:

```
eggs = int toad * 1000;    // invalid, not an expression
cin >> int toad;           // can't combine declaration with cin
```

Similarly, you can't assign a `for` loop to a variable:

```
int fx = for (int i = 0; i< 4; i++)
    cout >> i;    // not possible
```

Here the `for` loop is not an expression, so it has no value and you can't assign it.

Bending the Rules

C++ adds a feature to C loops that requires some artful adjustments to the `for` loop syntax. This was the original syntax:

```
for (expression; expression; expression)
    statement
```

In particular, the control section of a for structure consisted of three expressions, as defined earlier, separated by semicolons. C++ loops allow you do to things like the following, however:

```
for (int i = 0; i < 5; i++)
```

That is, you can declare a variable in the initialization area of a for loop. This can be convenient, but it doesn't fit the original syntax because a declaration is not an expression. This lawless behavior originally was accommodated by defining a new kind of expression, the *declaration-statement expression*, which was a declaration stripped of the semicolon, and which only could appear in a for statement. That adjustment has been dropped, however. Instead, the syntax for the for statement has been modified to the following:

```
for (for-init-statement condition; expression)
    statement
```

At first glance, this looks odd because there is just one semicolon instead of two. But that's okay because the *for-init-statement* is identified as a statement, and a statement has its own semicolon. As for the *for-init-statement*, it's identified as either an expression-statement or a declaration. This syntax rule replaces an expression followed by a semicolon with a statement, which has its own semicolon. What this boils down to is that C++ programmers want to be able to declare and initialize a variable in a for loop initialization, and they'll do whatever is necessary to C++ syntax and to the English language to make it possible.

There's a practical aspect to declaring a variable in a *for-init-statement* about which you should know. Such a variable exists only within the for statement. That is, once the program leaves the loop, the variable is eliminated:

```
for (int i = 0; i < 5; i++)
    cout << "C++ knows loops.\n";
cout << i << endl;  // oops! i no longer defined
```

Another thing you should know is that some C++ implementations follow an earlier rule and treat the preceding loop as if i were declared before the loop, thus making it available after the loop terminates. Use of this new option for declaring a variable in a for loop initialization results, at least at this time, in different behaviors on different systems.

Remember

At the time of writing, not all compilers have caught up with the current rule that a variable declared in a for loop control section expires when the loop terminates.

BACK TO THE for LOOP

Let's be a bit more ambitious with loops. Listing 5.4 uses a loop to calculate and store the first 16 factorials. Factorials, which are handy for computing odds, are calculated the following way. Zero factorial, written as 0!, is defined to be 1. Then, 1! is 1 * 0!, or

1. Next, 2! is 2 * 1!, or 2. Then, 3! is 3 * 2!, or 6, and so on, with the factorial of each integer being the product of that integer with the preceding factorial. (One of the pianist Victor Borge's best-known monologues features phonetic punctuation, in which the exclamation mark is pronounced something like phffft pptz, with a moist accent. However, in this case, "!" is pronounced "factorial.") The program uses one loop to calculate the values of successive factorials, storing them in an array. Then, it uses a second loop to display the results. Also, the program introduces the use of external declarations for values.

Listing 5.4 formore.cpp

```cpp
// formore.cpp -- more looping with for
#include <iostream>
using namespace std;
const int ArSize = 16;      // example of external declaration
int main()
{
    double factorials[ArSize];
    factorials[1] = factorials[0] = 1.0;
    int i;
    for (i = 2; i < ArSize; i++)
        factorials[i] = i * factorials[i-1];
    for (i = 0; i < ArSize; i++)
        cout << i << "! = " << factorials[i] << "\n";
    return 0;
}
```

Here is the output:

```
0! = 1
1! = 1
2! = 2
3! = 6
4! = 24
5! = 120
6! = 720
7! = 5040
8! = 40320
9! = 362880
10! = 3.6288e+006
11! = 3.99168e+007
12! = 4.79002e+008
13! = 6.22702e+009
14! = 8.71783e+010
15! = 1.30767e+012
```

Factorials get big fast!

Program Notes

The program creates an array to hold the factorial values. Element 0 is 0!, element 1 is 1!, and so on. Because the first two factorials equal 1, the program sets the first two elements of the factorials array to 1.0. (Remember, the first element of an array has an index value of 0.) After that, the program uses a loop to set each factorial to the product of the index with the previous factorial. The loop illustrates that you can use the loop counter as a variable in the body of the loop.

The program demonstrates how the for loop works hand in hand with arrays by providing a convenient means to access each array member in turn. Also, formore.cpp uses const to create a symbolic representation (ArSize) for the array size. Then, it uses ArSize wherever the array size comes into play, such as in the array definition and in the limits for the loops handling the array. Now, if you wish to extend the program to, say, 20 factorials, you just have to set ArSize to 20 in the program and recompile. By using a symbolic constant, you avoid having to change every occurrence of 16 to 20 individually.

Remember

It's usually a good idea to define a const value to represent the number of elements in an array. Use the const value in the array declaration and in all other references to the array size, such as in a for loop.

The limit i < ArSize expression reflects the fact that subscripts for an array with ArSize elements run from 0 to ArSize - 1, so the array index should stop 1 short of ArSize. You could use the test i <= ArSize - 1 instead, but it looks awkward in comparison.

One program sidelight is that it declares the const int variable ArSize outside the body of main(). As the end of Chapter 4, "Derived Types," mentions, this makes ArSize external data. The two consequences of declaring ArSize in this fashion are that ArSize exists for the duration of the program and that all functions in the program files can use it. In this particular case, the program has just one function, so declaring ArSize externally has little practical effect. But multifunction programs often benefit from sharing external constants, so we'll practice using them now.

"...the for loop works hand in hand with arrays by providing a convenient means to access each array member in turn."

CHANGING THE STEP SIZE

So far the loop examples have increased or decreased the loop counter by 1 each cycle. You can change that by changing the update expression. The program in Listing 5.5, for example, increases the loop counter by a user-selected step size. Rather than use i++ as the update expression, it uses the expression i = i + by, where by is the user-selected step size.

Listing 5.5 bigstep.cpp

```
// bigstep.cpp -- count as directed
#include <iostream>
using namespace std;
int main()
{
    cout << "Enter an integer: ";
    int by;
    cin >> by;
    cout << "Counting by " << by << "s:\n";
    for (int i = 0; i < 100; i = i + by)
```

```
        cout << i << "\n";
    return 0;
}
```

Here is a sample run:

```
Enter an integer: 17
Counting by 17s:
0
17
34
51
68
85
```

Once i reaches the value 102, the loop quits. The main point here is that the update expression can be any valid expression. For instance, if you want to square i and add 10 each cycle, you can use i = i * i + 10.

INSIDE STRINGS WITH THE for LOOP

The for loop provides a direct way to access each character in a string in turn. Listing 5.6, for example, enables you to enter a string and then displays the string character-by-character in reverse order. The strlen() yields the number of characters in the string; the loop uses that value in its initializing expression to set i to the index of the last character in the string, not counting the null character. To count backwards, the program uses the decrement operator (--) to decrease the array subscript by 1 each loop. Also, Listing 5.6 uses the greater than or equal to relational operator (>=) to test whether the loop has reached the first element. We summarize all the relational operators soon.

Listing 5.6 forstr1.cpp

```
// forstr1.cpp -- using for with a string
#include <iostream>
#include <cstring>
using namespace std;
const int ArSize = 20;
int main()
{
    cout << "Enter a word: ";
    char word[ArSize];
    cin >> word;

    // display letters in reverse order
    for (int i = strlen(word) - 1; i >= 0; i--)
        cout << word[i];
    cout << "\n";
    return 0;
}
```

Remember

You might have to use `string.h` instead of `cstring` if your implementation has not yet added the new header files.

Here is a sample run:

```
Enter a word: animal
lamina
```

Yes, the program succeeds in printing animal backwards; choosing animal as a test word more clearly illustrates the effect of this program than choosing, say, redder or stats.

THE INCREMENT (++) AND DECREMENT (- -) OPERATORS

C++ features several operators that frequently are used in loops, so let's take a little time to examine them now. You've already seen two: the increment operator (++), which inspired the name C++, and the decrement operator (- -). These perform two exceedingly common loop operations: increasing or decreasing a loop counter by 1. However, there's more to their story than you've seen to date. Each operator comes in two varieties. The *prefix* version comes before the operand, as in ++x. The *postfix* version comes after the operand, as in x++. The two versions have the same effect upon the operand, but they differ in when they take place. It's like getting paid for mowing the lawn in advance or afterwards; both methods have the same final effect on your wallet, but they differ in when the money gets added. Listing 5.7 demonstrates this difference for the increment operator.

Listing 5.7 plus_one.cpp

```cpp
// plus_one.cpp -- the increment operator
#include <iostream>
using namespace std;
int main()
{
    int a = 20;
    int b = 20;

    cout << "a   = " << a << ":   b = " << b << "\n";
    cout << "a++ = " << a++ << ": ++b = " << ++b << "\n";
    cout << "a   = " << a << ":   b = " << b << "\n";
    return 0;
}
```

Here is the output:

```
a     = 20:   b = 20
a++   = 20: ++b = 21
a     = 21:   b = 21
```

Roughly speaking, the notation a++ means "use the current value of a in evaluating an expression, and then increment the value of a." Similarly, the notation ++b means "first increment the value of b, and then use the new value in evaluating the expression." For example, we have the following relationships:

```
int x = 5;
int y = ++x;      // change x, then assign to y
                  // y is 6, x is 6

int z = 5;
int y = z++;      // assign to y, then change z
                  // y is 5, z is 6
```

The increment and decrement operators are a concise, convenient way to handle the common task of increasing or decreasing values by 1. You can use them with pointers as well as with basic variables. Recall that adding 1 to a pointer increases its value by the number of bytes in the type it points to. The same rule holds for incrementing and decrementing pointers.

Remember

Incrementing and decrementing pointers follow pointer arithmetic rules. Thus, if pt points to the first member of an array, ++pt changes pt so that it points to the second member.

The increment and decrement operators are nifty little operators, but don't get carried away and increment or decrement the same value more than once in the same statement. The problem is that the use-then-change and change-then-use rules can become ambiguous. That is, a statement such as

```
x = 2 * x++ * (3 - ++x);     // don't do it
```

can produce quite different results on different systems. C++ does not define correct behavior for this sort of statement.

COMBINATION ASSIGNMENT OPERATORS

Listing 5.5 uses the following expression to update a loop counter:

```
i = i + by
```

C++ has a combined addition and assignment operator that accomplishes the same result more concisely:

```
i += by
```

The += operator adds the values of its two operands and assigns the result to the operand on the left. This implies that the left operand must be something to which you can assign a value, such as a variable, an array element, a structure member, or data you identify by dereferencing a pointer:

```
int k = 5;
k += 3;                  // ok, k set to 8
int *pa = new int[10];   // pa points to pa[0]
pa[4] = 12;
pa[4] += 6;              // ok, pa[4] set to 18
*(pa + 4) += 7;          // ok, pa[4] set to 25
pa += 2;                 // ok, pa points to the former pa[2]
34 += 10;                // quite wrong
```

Each arithmetic operator has a corresponding assignment operator, as summarized in Table 5.1. Each operator works analogously to +=. Thus, the statement

```
k *= 10;
```

replaces the current value of k with a value ten times greater.

TABLE 5.1
COMBINED ASSIGNMENT OPERATORS

OPERATOR	EFFECT (L=LEFT OPERAND, R=RIGHT OPERAND)
+=	assigns L + R to L
-=	assigns L – R to L
*=	assigns L * R to L
/=	assigns L / R to L
%=	assigns L % R to L

COMPOUND STATEMENTS, OR BLOCKS

" The block consists of paired braces and the statements they enclose and, for the purposes of syntax, counts as a single statement."

The format, or syntax, for writing a C++ for statement might seem restrictive to you because the body of the loop must be a single statement. That's awkward if you want the loop body to contain several statements. Fortunately, C++ provides a syntax loophole through which you may stuff as many statements as you like into a loop body. The trick is to use paired braces to construct a *compound statement*, or *block*. The block consists of paired braces and the statements they enclose and, for the purposes of syntax, counts as a single statement. For instance, the program in Listing 5.8 uses braces to combine three separate statements into a single block. This enables the body of the loop to prompt the user, read input, and do a calculation. The program calculates the running sum of the numbers you enter, and this provides a natural occasion for using the += operator.

Listing 5.8 block.cpp

```cpp
// block.cpp -- use a block statement
#include <iostream>
using namespace std;
int main()
{
    cout << "The Amazing Accounto will sum and average ";
    cout << "five numbers for you.\n";
    cout << "Please enter five values:\n";
    double number;
    double sum = 0.0;
    for (int i = 1; i <= 5; i++)
    {                                       // block starts here
        cout << "Value " << i << ": ";
        cin >> number;
        sum += number;
    }                                       // block ends here
    cout << "Five exquisite choices indeed! ";
    cout << "They sum to " << sum << "\n";
    cout << "and average to " << sum / 5 << ".\n";
    cout << "The Amazing Accounto bids you adieu!\n";
    return 0;
}
```

Here is a sample run:

```
The Amazing Accounto will sum and average five numbers for you.

Please enter five values:
Value 1: 1942
Value 2: 1948
Value 3: 1957
Value 4: 1974
Value 5: 1980
Five exquisite choices indeed! They sum to 9801
and average to 1960.2.
The Amazing Accounto bids you adieu!
```

Suppose you leave in the indentation but omit the braces:

```cpp
for (int i = 1; i <= 5; i++)
        cout << "Value " << i << ": ";       // loop ends here
    cin >> number;                           // after the loop
    sum += number;
cout << "Five exquisite choices indeed! ";
```

The compiler ignores indentation, so only the first statement would be in the loop. Thus, the loop would print the five prompts and do nothing more. After the loop completed, the program would move to the following lines, reading and summing just one number.

Compound statements have another interesting property. If you define a new variable inside a block, the variable persists only as long as the program is executing statements within the block. When execution leaves the block, the variable is deallocated. That means the variable is known only within the block:

```cpp
#include  <iostream>
using namespace std;
int main()
```

```
{
    int x = 20;
    {                           // block starts
        int y = 100;
        cout << x << "\n";      // ok
        cout << y << "\n";      // ok
    }                       // block ends
    cout << x << "\n";   // ok
    cout << y << "\n";              // invalid, won't compile
    return 0;
}
```

Note that a variable defined in an outer block still is defined in the inner block.

What happens if you declare a variable in a block that has the same name as one outside the block? The new variable hides the old one from its point of appearance until the end of the block. Then, the old one becomes visible again.

```
int main()
{
    int x = 20;             // original x
    {                       // block starts
        cout << x << "\n";  // use original x
        int x = 100;        // new x
        cout << x << "\n";  // use new x
    }                       // block ends
    cout << x << "\n";      // use original x
    return 0;
}
```

THE COMMA OPERATOR (OR MORE SYNTAX TRICKS)

The block, as you saw, enables you to sneak two or more statements into a place where C++ syntax allows just one statement. The comma operator does the same for expressions, enabling you to sneak two expressions into a place where C++ syntax allows only one expression. For instance, suppose you have a loop in which one variable increases by 1 each cycle and a second variable decreases by 1 each cycle. Doing both in the update part of a for loop control section would be convenient, but the loop syntax allows just one expression there. The solution is to use the comma operator to combine the two expressions into one:

```
j++, i--   // two expressions count as one for syntax purposes
```

The comma is not always a comma operator. For instance, the comma in the declaration

```
int i, j; // comma is a separator here, not an operator
```

serves to separate adjacent names in a list of variables.

Listing 5.9 uses the comma operator twice in a program that reverses the contents of a character array. Note that Listing 5.6 displays the contents of an array in reverse order, but Listing 5.9 actually moves characters around in the array. The program also uses a block to group several statements into one.

Listing 5.9 forstr2.cpp

```cpp
// forstr2.cpp -- reversing an array
#include <iostream>
#include <cstring>
using namespace std;
const int ArSize = 20;
int main()
{
    cout << "Enter a word: ";
    char word[ArSize];
    cin >> word;

    // physically modify array
    char temp;
    int i, j;
    for (j = 0, i = strlen(word) - 1; j < i; i--, j++)
    {                          // start block
        temp = word[i];
        word[i] = word[j];
        word[j] = temp;
    }                          // end block
    cout << word << "\n";
    return 0;
}
```

Here is a sample run:

```
Enter a word: parts
strap
```

Program Notes

Look at the `for` control section:

```cpp
for (j = 0, i = strlen(word) - 1; j < i; i--, j++)
```

First, it uses the comma operator to squeeze two initializations into one expression for the first part of the control section. Then, it uses the comma operator again to combine two updates into a single expression for the last part of the control section.

Next, look at the body. The program uses braces to combine several statements into a single unit. In the body, the program reverses the word by switching the first element of the array with the last element. Then, it increments j and decrements i so that they now refer to the next-to-the-first element and the next-to-the-last element. After this is done, the program swaps those elements. Note that the test condition j<i makes the loop stop when it reaches the center of the array. If it were to continue past this point, it would begin swapping the switched elements back to their original positions. See Figure 5.2.

FIGURE 5.2

Reversing a string

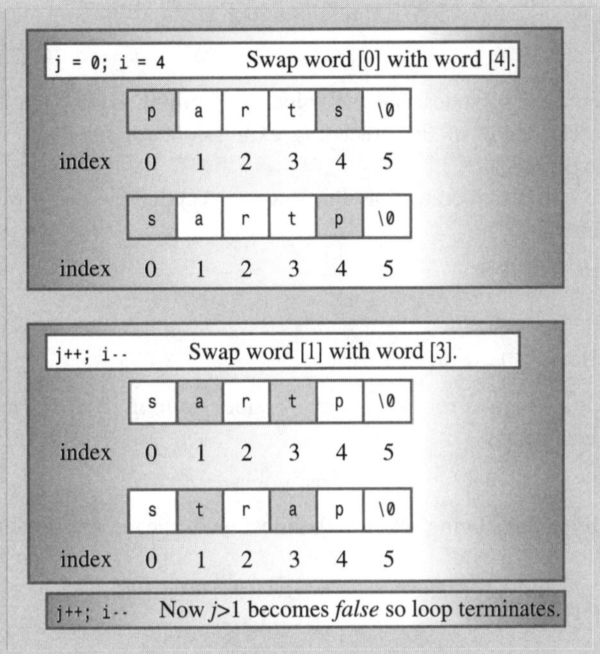

Another thing to note is the location for declaring the variables temp, i, and j. The code declares i and j before the loop, because you can't combine two declarations with a comma operator. That's because declarations already use the comma for another purpose—separating items in a list. You can use a single declaration-statement expression to create and initialize two variables, but it's a bit confusing visually:

```
int j = 0, i = strlen(word) - 1;
```

In this case the comma is just a list separator, not the comma operator, so the expression declares and initializes both j and i. However, it looks as if it declares only j. Incidentally, you can declare temp inside the for loop:

```
int temp = word[i];
```

This results in temp being allocated and deallocated each loop cycle. This might be a bit slower than declaring temp once before the loop. On the other hand, after the loop is finished, temp is discarded if it's declared inside the loop.

Comma Operator Tidbits

By far the most common use for the comma operator is to fit two or more expressions into a single for loop expression. But C++ does provide the operator with two additional properties. First, it guarantees that the first expression is evaluated before the second expression. Expressions such as the following are safe:

```
i = 20, j = 2 * i      // i set to 20, j set to 40
```

Second, C++ states that the value of a comma expression is the value of the second part. The value of the preceding expression, for instance, is 40, because that is the value of j = 2 * i.

The comma operator has the lowest precedence of any operator. For example, the statement

```
cata = 17,240;
```

gets read as

```
(cats = 17), 240;
```

That is, `cats` is set to 17, and 240 does nothing. But, because parentheses have high precedence,

```
cats = (17,240);
```

results in `cats` being set to 240, the value of the expression on the right.

Relational Expressions

Computers are more than relentless number crunchers. They have the capability to compare values, and this capability is the foundation of computer decision-making. In C++, relational operators embody this ability. C++ provides six relational operators to compare numbers. Because characters are represented by their ASCII code, you can use these operators with characters, too, but they don't work with C-style strings. Each relational expression reduces to the `bool` value `true` if the comparison is true and to the `bool` value `false` if the comparison is false, so they are well suited for use in a loop test expression. (Older implementations evaluate true relational expressions to `1` and false relational expressions to `0`.) Table 5.2 summarizes these operators.

The six relational operators exhaust the comparisons C++ enables you to make for numbers. If you want to compare two values to see which is the more beautiful or the luckier, you have to look elsewhere.

TABLE 5.2
RELATIONAL OPERATORS

OPERATOR	MEANING
<	is less than
<=	is less than or equal to
==	is equal to
>	is greater than
>=	is greater than or equal to
!=	is not equal to

Here are some sample tests:

```
for (x = 20; x > 5; x--) // continue while x is greater than 5
for (x = 1; y != x; x++) // continue while y is not equal to x
for (cin >> x; x == 0; cin >> x)) // continue while x is 0
```

The relational operators have a lower precedence than the arithmetic operators. That means the expression

```
x + 3 > y - 2                      // expression 1
```

corresponds to

```
(x + 3) > (y - 2)                  // expression 2
```

and not the following:

```
x + (3 > y) - 2                    // expression 3
```

Because the expression (3 > y) is either 1 or 0 after the bool value is promoted to int, expressions 2 and 3 both are valid. But most of us would want expression 1 to mean expression 2, and that is what C++ does.

THE MISTAKE YOU'LL PROBABLY MAKE

Don't confuse testing the is-equal-to operator (==) with the assignment operator (=). The expression

```
musicians == 4     // comparison
```

asks the musical question, is musicians equal to 4? The expression has the value true or false. The expression

```
musicians = 4      // assignment
```

assigns the value 4 to musicians. The whole expression, in this case, has the value 4, because that's the value of the left side.

The flexible design of the for loop creates an interesting opportunity for error. If you accidentally drop an equal sign (=) from the == operator and use an assignment expression instead of a relational expression for the test part of a for loop, you still produce valid code. That's because you can use any valid C++ expression for a for loop test condition. Remember, nonzero values test as true and zero tests as false. An expression that assigns 4 to musicians has the value 4 and is treated as true. If you come from a language, such as Pascal or BASIC, that uses = to test for equality, you might be particularly prone to this slip.

Listing 5.10 shows a situation in which you can make this sort of error. The program attempts to examine an array of quiz scores and stop when it reaches the first score that's not a 20. It shows a loop that correctly uses comparison and then one that mistakenly uses assignment in the test condition. The program also has another egregious design error that you'll see how to fix later. (You learn from your mistakes, and Listing 5.10 is happy to help in that respect.)

Listing 5.10 equal.cpp

```cpp
// equal.cpp -- equality vs assignment
#include <iostream>
using namespace std;
int main()
{
    int quizscores[10] =
        { 20, 20, 20, 20, 20, 19, 20, 18, 20, 20};

    cout << "Doing it right:\n";
    int i;
    for (i = 0; quizscores[i] == 20; i++)
        cout << "quiz " << i << " is a 20\n";

    cout << "Doing it dangerously wrong:\n";
    for (i = 0; quizscores[i] = 20; i++)
        cout << "quiz " << i << " is a 20\n";

    return 0;
}
```

Because this program has a serious problem, you might prefer reading about it to actually running it. Here is some sample output:

```
Doing it right:
quiz 0 is a 20
quiz 1 is a 20
quiz 2 is a 20
quiz 3 is a 20
quiz 4 is a 20
Doing it dangerously wrong:
quiz 0 is a 20
quiz 1 is a 20
quiz 2 is a 20
quiz 3 is a 20
quiz 4 is a 20
quiz 5 is a 20
quiz 6 is a 20
quiz 7 is a 20
quiz 8 is a 20
quiz 9 is a 20
quiz 10 is a 20
quiz 11 is a 20
quiz 12 is a 20
quiz 13 is a 20
...
```

The first loop correctly halts after displaying the first five quiz scores. But the second starts by displaying the whole array. Worse than that, it says every value is 20. Worse than that, it doesn't stop at the end of the array!

Where things go wrong, of course, is with the following test expression:

```cpp
quizscores[i] = 20
```

First, simply because it assigns a nonzero value to the array element, the expression always is nonzero, hence always true. Second, because the expression assigns values to the array elements, it actually changes the data. Third, because the test expression remains true, the program continues changing data beyond the end of the array. It just keeps putting more and more 20s into memory! This is not good.

The difficulty with this kind of error is that the code is syntactically correct, so the compiler won't tag it as an error. (However, years and years of C and C++ programmers making this error eventually has led many compilers to issue a warning asking if that's what you really meant to do.)

Remember

Don't use = to compare for equality; use ==.

Like C, C++ grants you more freedom than most programming languages. This comes at the cost of requiring greater responsibility on your part. Nothing but your own good planning prevents a program from going beyond the bounds of a standard C++ array. However, with C++ classes, you can design a protected array type that prevents this sort of nonsense. Chapter 12, "Class Inheritance," provides an example. In the meantime, you should build the protection into your programs when you need it. For instance, the loop should have included a test that kept it from going past the last member. That's true even for the "good" loop. If all the scores had been 20s, it, too, would have exceeded the array bounds. In short, the loop needed to test the values of the array and the array index. Chapter 6 shows you how to use logical operators to combine two such tests into a single condition.

COMPARING STRINGS

> *C++ grants you more freedom than most programming languages. This comes at the cost of requiring greater responsibility on your part.*

Suppose you want to see if a string in a character array is the word `mate`. If `word` is the array name, the following test might not do what you think:

```
word == "mate"
```

Remember that the name of an array is a synonym for its address. Similarly, a quoted string constant is a synonym for its address. Thus, the preceding relational expression doesn't test to see if the strings are the same—it checks to see if they are stored at the same address. The answer to that is no, even if the two strings have the same characters.

Because C++ handles strings as addresses, you get little satisfaction if you try to use the relational operators to compare strings. Instead, you can go to the C-style string library and use the `strcmp()` function to compare strings. This function takes two string addresses as arguments. That means the arguments can be pointers, string constants, or character array names. If the two strings are identical, the function returns the value zero. If the first string precedes the second alphabetically, `strcmp()` returns a negative value, and if the first string follows the second alphabetically, `strcmp()` returns a positive value. Actually, "in the system collating sequence" is more accurate than "alphabetically." This means that characters are compared according to the system code for characters. For instance, in ASCII code, all uppercase letters have smaller codes than the lowercase letters, so uppercase precedes lowercase in the collating sequence. Therefore, the string `"Zoo"` precedes the string `"aviary"`. That comparisons are based on code values also means that uppercase and lowercase letters differ, so the string "FOO" is different from the "foo" string.

In some languages, such as BASIC and standard Pascal, strings stored in differently sized arrays are necessarily unequal to each other. But C-style strings are defined by the terminating null character, not by the size of the containing array. This means that two strings can be identical even if they are contained in differently sized arrays:

```
char big[80] = "Daffy";        // 5 letters plus \0
char little[6] = "Daffy";      // 5 letters plus \0
```

By the way, although you can't use relational operators to compare strings, you can use them to compare characters, because characters actually are integer types. So,

```
for (ch = 'a'; ch <= 'z'; ch++)
    cout << ch;
```

is valid code, at least for the ASCII character set, for displaying the characters of the alphabet.

Listing 5.11 uses strcmp() in the test condition of a for loop. The program displays a word, changes its first letter, displays the word again, and keeps going until strcmp() determines the word is the same as the string "mate". Note that the listing includes the cstring file because it provides a function prototype for strcmp().

Listing 5.11 compstr.cpp

```
// compstr.cpp -- comparing strings
#include <iostream>
#include <cstring>       // prototype for strcmp()
using namespace std;
int main()
{
    char word[5] = "?ate";

    for (char ch = 'a'; strcmp(word, "mate"); ch++)
    {
        cout << word << "\n";
        word[0] = ch;
    }
    cout << "After loop ends, word is " << word << "\n";
    return 0;
}
```

Remember

You might have to use string.h instead of cstring. Also, the code assumes the system uses the ASCII character code set. In this set, the codes for the letters a through z are consecutive, and the code for the ? character immediately precedes the code for a.

Here is the output:

```
?ate
aate
bate
cate
```

```
date
eate
fate
gate
hate
iate
jate
kate
late
After loop ends, word is mate
```

Program Notes

The program has some interesting points. One, of course, is the test. We want the loop to continue as long as word is not mate. That is, we want the test to continue as long as strcmp() says the two strings are not the same. The most obvious test for that is this:

```
strcmp(word, "mate") != 0     // strings are not the same
```

This statement has the value 1 (true) if the strings are unequal and the value 0 (false) if they are equal. But what about strcmp(word, "mate") by itself? It has a nonzero value (true) if the strings are unequal and the value 0 (false) if the strings are equal. In essence, the function returns true if the strings are different and false if they are the same. You can use just the function instead of the whole relational expression. This produces the same behavior and involves less typing. Also, it's the way C and C++ programmers traditionally have used strcmp().

Next, compstr.cpp uses the increment operator to march the variable ch through the alphabet:

```
ch++
```

You can use the increment and decrement operators with character variables, because type char really is an integer type, so the operation actually changes the integer code stored in the variable. Also, note that using an array index makes it simple to change individual characters in a string:

```
word[0] = ch;
```

Finally, unlike most of the for loops to date, this loop isn't a counting loop. That is, it doesn't execute a block of statements a specified number of times. Instead, the loop watches for a particular circumstance (word being "mate") to signal that it's time to stop. More typically, C++ programs use while loops for this second kind of test, so let's examine that form now.

The while Loop

The while loop is a for loop stripped of the initialization and update parts; it has just a test condition and a body:

```
while (test-condition)
        body
```

First, a program evaluates the *test-condition* expression. If the expression evaluates to `true`, the program executes the statement(s) in the body. As with a `for` loop, the body consists of a single statement or a block defined by paired braces. After it finishes with the body, the program returns to the test-condition and reevaluates it. If the condition is nonzero, the program executes the body again. This cycle of testing and execution continues until the test-condition evaluates to `false`. See Figure 5.3. Clearly, if you want the loop to terminate eventually, something within the loop body must do something to affect the test-condition expression. For example, the loop can increment a variable used in the test condition or read a new value from keyboard input. Like the `for` loop, the `while` loop is an entry-condition loop. Thus, if the test-condition evaluates to false at the beginning, the program never executes the body of the loop.

Listing 5.12 puts the `while` loop to work. The loop cycles through each character in a string and displays the character and its ASCII code. The loop quits when it reaches the null character. This technique of stepping through a string character-by-character until reaching the null character is a standard C++ method for processing strings. Because a string contains its own termination marker, programs often don't need explicit information about how long a string is.

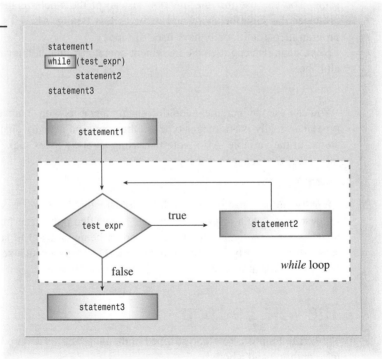

FIGURE 5.3
The `while` *loop*

Listing 5.12 while.cpp

```cpp
// while.cpp -- introducing the while loop
#include <iostream>
using namespace std;
const int ArSize = 20;
int main()
{
    char name[ArSize];

    cout << "Your first name, please: ";
    cin >> name;
    cout << "Here is your name, verticalized and ASCIIized:\n";
    int i = 0;                  // start at beginning of string
    while (name[i] != '\0')     // process to end of string
    {
        cout << name[i] << ": " << int(name[i]) << '\n';
        i++;                    // don't forget this step
    }
    return 0;
}
```

Here is a sample run:

```
Your first name, please: Muffy
Here is your name, verticalized and ASCIIized:
M: 77
u: 117
f: 102
f: 102
y: 121
```

(No, verticalized and ASCIIized are not real words or even good would-be words. But they do add a technoid tone to the output.)

Program Notes

The while condition looks like this:

```cpp
while (name[i] != '\0')
```

It tests whether a particular character in the array is the null character. For this test eventually to succeed, the loop body needs to change the value of i. It does so by incrementing i at the end of the loop body. Omitting this step keeps the loop stuck on the same array element, printing the character and its code until you manage to kill the program. Such an infinite loop is one of the most common problems with loops. Often you can cause it when you forget to update some value within the loop body.

You can rewrite the while line this way:

```cpp
while (name[i])
```

With this change, the program works just as it did before. That's because when name[i] is an ordinary character, its value is the character code, which is nonzero, or true. But when name[i] is the null character, its character-code value is 0, or false. This notation is more concise but less clear than what we used. Dumb compilers might produce faster code for the second version, but smart compilers will produce the same code for both.

To get the program to print the ASCII code for a character, the program uses a type cast to convert `name[i]` to an integer type. Then, `cout` prints the value as an integer rather than interprets it as a character code.

for VERSUS while

In C++ the `for` and `while` loops essentially are equivalent. For instance, the `for` loop

```
for (init-expression; test-expression; update-expression)
{
    statement(s)
}
```

> " *Because the for loop and while loop are nearly equivalent, the one you use is a matter of style.* "

could be rewritten this way:

```
init-expression;
while (test-expression)
{
    statement(s)
    update-expression;
}
```

Similarly, the `while` loop

```
while (test-expression)
    body
```

could be rewritten this way:

```
for ( ;test-expression;)
    body
```

The `for` loop requires three expressions, (or, more technically, one statement followed by two expressions) but they can be empty expressions (or statements). Only the two semicolons are mandatory. Incidentally, a missing test expression in a `for` loop is construed as true, so the loop

```
for ( ; ; )
    body
```

runs forever.

Because the `for` loop and `while` loop are nearly equivalent, the one you use is a matter of style. (There is a slight difference if the body includes a `continue` statement, which is discussed in Chapter 6, "Branching Statements and Logical Operators.") Typically, programmers use the `for` loop for counting loops because the `for` loop format enables you to place all the relevant information—initial value, terminating value, and method of updating the counter—in one place. You most often use the `while` loop when you don't know in advance precisely how many times the loop will execute.

You should keep in mind the following guidelines when you design a loop:

1. Identify the condition that terminates loop execution.

2. Initialize that condition before the first test.

3. Update the condition each loop cycle before the condition is tested again.

One nice thing about the `for` loop is that its structure provides a place to implement these three guidelines, thus helping you to remember to do so.

BAD PUNCTUATION

Both the `for` loop and the `while` loop have bodies consisting of the *single* statement following the parenthesized expressions. As you've seen, that single statement can be a block, which can contain several statements. Keep in mind that braces, not indentation, define a block. Consider the following loop, for example:

```
i = 0;
while (name[i] != '\0')
      cout << name[i] << "\n";
      i++;
cout << "Done\n";
```

The indentation tells us the program author intended the `i++;` statement to be part of the loop body. The absence of braces, however, tells the compiler that the body consists solely of the first `cout` statement. Thus, the loop keeps printing the first character of the array indefinitely. The program never reaches the `i++;` statement because it is outside the loop.

The next example shows another potential pitfall:

```
i = 0;
while (name[i] != '\0');    // problem semicolon
{
      cout << name[i] << "\n";
      i++;
}
cout << "Done\n";
```

This time the code got the braces right, but it also inserted an extra semicolon. Remember, a semicolon terminates a statement, so this semicolon terminates the `while` loop. In other words, the body of the loop is a *null statement*, that is, nothing followed by a semicolon. All the material in braces now comes *after* the loop. It never is reached. Instead, the loop cycles doing nothing forever. Beware the straggling semicolon.

JUST A MOMENT

Sometimes it's useful to build a time delay into a program. For instance, you might have encountered programs that flash a message onscreen and then go on to something else before you can read it. You're left with the fear that you've missed irretrievable information of vital importance. It would be so much nicer if the program paused five seconds before moving on. The while loop is handy for producing this effect. One of the earlier techniques was to make the computer count for a while to use up time:

```
long wait = 0;
while (wait < 10000)
    wait++;                // counting silently
```

The problem with this approach is that you have to change the counting limit when you change computer processor speed. Several games written for the original IBM PC, for instance, became unmanageably fast when run on its faster successors. A better approach is to let the system clock do the timing for you.

The ANSI C and the C++ libraries have a function to help you do this. The function is called clock(), and it returns the system time elapsed since a program started execution. There are a couple of complications. First, clock() doesn't necessarily return the time in seconds. Second, the function's return type might be long on some systems, unsigned long on others, or perhaps some other type.

But the ctime header file (time.h on less current implementations) provides solutions to these problems. First, it defines a symbolic constant, CLOCKS_PER_SEC, that equals the number of system time units per second. So dividing the system time by this value yields seconds. Or, you can multiply seconds by CLOCKS_PER_SEC to get time in the system units. Second, ctime establishes clock_t as an alias for the clock() return type. (See the note about Type Aliases.) This means you can declare a variable as type clock_t and the compiler then converts that to long or unsigned int or whatever the proper type is for your system.

Remember

Systems that haven't added the ctime header file can use time.h instead. Some C++ implementations might have problems with waiting.cpp if the implementation's library component is not fully ANSI C-compliant. That's because the clock() function is an ANSI addition to the traditional C library. Also, some premature implementations of ANSI C used CLK_TCK or TCK_CLK instead of the longer CLOCKS_PER_SEC. Some older versions of g++ don't recognize any of these defined constants. Some environments (such as MSVC++ 1.0 but not MSVC++ 5.0) have problems with the alarm character \a and coordinating the display with the time delay.

Listing 5.13 shows how to use clock() and the ctime header to create a time-delay loop.

Listing 5.13 waiting.cpp

```
// waiting.cpp -- using clock() in a time-delay loop
#include <iostream>
#include <ctime> // describes clock() function, clock_t type
using namespace std;
int main()
{
    cout << "Enter the delay time, in seconds: ";
```

```
    float secs; cin >> secs;
    clock_t delay = secs * CLOCKS_PER_SEC;  // convert to clock ticks
    cout << "starting\a\n";
    clock_t start = clock();
    while (clock() - start < delay )         // wait until time elapses
        ;                                    // note the semicolon
    cout << "done \a\n";
    return 0;
}
```

By calculating the delay time in system units instead of in seconds, the program avoids having to convert system time to seconds each loop cycle.

TYPE ALIASES

C++ has two ways to establish a new name as an alias for a type. One is to use the preprocessor:

```
#define BYTE char // preprocessor replaces BYTE with char
```

The preprocessor then replaces all occurrences of BYTE with char when you compile a program, thus making BYTE an alias for char.

The second method is to use the C++ (and C) keyword typedef to create an alias. For instance, to make byte an alias for char, do this:

```
typedef char byte;    // makes byte an alias for char
```

Here's the general form:

```
typedef typeName aliasName;
```

In other words, if you want aliasName to be an alias for a particular type, declare aliasName as if it were a variable of that type and then prefix the declaration with the typedef keyword. For example, to make byte_pointer an alias for pointer-to-char, declare byte_pointer as a pointer-to-char and then stick typedef in front:

```
typedef char * byte_pointer; // pointer to char type
```

You could try something similar with #define, but that won't work if you declare a list of variables. For instance, consider the following:

```
#define FLOAT_POINTER float *
FLOAT_POINTER pa, pb;
```

Preprocessor substitution converts the declaration to this:

```
float * pa, pb;  // pa a pointer to float, pb just a float
```

The typedef approach doesn't have that problem.

Notice that typedef doesn't create a new type. It just creates a new name for an old type. If you make word an alias for int, cout treats a type word value as the int it really is.

The `do while` Loop

You've now seen the `for` loop and the `while` loop. The third C++ loop is the `do while`. It's different from the other two because it's an *exit-condition* loop. That means this devil-may-care loop first executes the body of the loop and only then evaluates the test expression to see if it should continue looping. If the condition evaluates to false, the loop terminates; otherwise, a new cycle of execution and testing begins. Such a loop always executes at least once because its program flow has to pass through the body of the loop before reaching the test. Here's the syntax:

```
do
        body
while (test-expression);
```

The body portion can be a single statement or a brace-delimited statement block. Figure 5.4 summarizes the program flow for the `do while` loop.

FIGURE 5.4

The `do while` loop

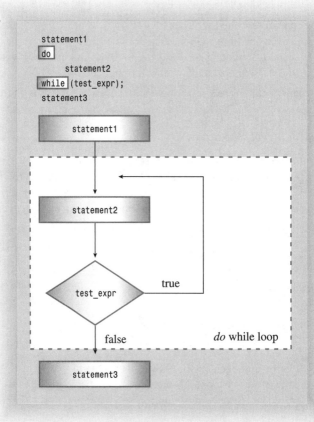

Usually, an entry-condition loop is a better choice than an exit-condition loop because the entry-condition loop checks before looping. For instance, suppose Listing 5.12 had used do while instead of while. Then, the loop would have printed the null character and its code before it found it already had reached the end of the string. But sometimes a do while test does make sense. For instance, if you're requesting user input, the program has to obtain the input before testing it. Listing 5.14 shows how to use do while in that situation.

Listing 5.14 dowhile.cpp

```
// dowhile.cpp -- exit-condition loop
#include <iostream>
using namespace std;
int main()
{
    int n;

    cout << "Enter numbers in the range 1-10 to find ";
    cout << "my favorite number\n";
    do
    {
        cin >> n;          // execute body
    } while (n != 7);    // then test
    cout << "Yes, 7 is my favorite.\n" ;
    return 0;
}
```

Here's a sample run:

```
Enter numbers in the range 1-10 to find my favorite number
9
4
7
Yes, 7 is my favorite.
```

Loops and Text Input

Now that you've seen how loops work, let's look at one of the most common and important tasks assigned to loops: reading text character-by-character from a file or from the keyboard. For instance, you might want to write a program that counts the number of characters, lines, and words in the input. Traditionally, C++, like C, uses the while loop for this sort of task. We'll investigate now how that is done. If you already know C, don't skim through this part too fast. Although the C++ while loop is the same as C's, C++'s I/O facilities are different. This can give the C++ loop a somewhat different look. In fact, the cin object supports three distinct modes of single-character input, each with a different user interface. Look at how to use these choices with while loops.

"...the cin object supports three distinct modes of single-character input, each with a different user interface."

USING UNADORNED `cin` FOR INPUT

If a program is going to use a loop to read input from the keyboard, it has to have some way of knowing when to stop. How can it know when to stop? One way is to choose some special character, sometimes called a *sentinel character*, to act as a stop sign. For instance, Listing 5.15 stops reading input when the program encounters a # character. The program counts the number of characters it reads and it echoes them. That is, it redisplays the characters that have been read. (Pressing a keyboard key doesn't automatically place a character on the screen; programs have to do that drudge work by echoing the input character.) When finished, it reports the total number of characters processed. Listing 5.15 shows the program.

Listing 5.15 textin1.cpp

```
// textin1.cpp -- reading chars with a while loop
#include <iostream>
using namespace std;
int main()
{
    char ch;
    int count = 0;          // use basic input

    cin >> ch;              // get a character
    while (ch != '#')       // test the character
    {
        cout << ch;         // echo the character
        count++;            // count the character
        cin >> ch;          // get the next character
    }
    cout << "\n" << count << " characters read\n";
    return 0;
}
```

Here's a sample run:

see ken run#really fast
seekenrun
9 characters read

Apparently Ken runs so fast, he obliterates space itself—or at least the space characters in the input.

Program Notes

First, note the structure. The program reads the first input character before it reaches the loop. That way, the first character can be tested when the program reaches the loop statement. This is important, for the first character might be #. Because `textin1.cpp` uses an entry-condition loop, the program correctly skips the entire loop in that case. And because the variable `count` previously was set to zero, `count` has the correct value.

Suppose the first character read is not a #. Then, the program enters the loop, displays the character, increments the count, and reads the next character. This last step is vital. Without it, the loop repeatedly processes the first input character forever. With it, the program advances to the next character.

Note the loop design follows the guidelines mentioned earlier. The condition that terminates the loop is if the last character read is #. The condition is initialized by reading a character before the loop starts. The condition is updated by reading a new character at the end of the loop.

This all sounds reasonable. So why does the program omit the spaces on output? Blame `cin`. When reading type `char` values, just as when reading other basic types, `cin` skips over spaces and newlines. The spaces in the input are not echoed, and so they are not counted.

To further complicate things, the input to `cin` is buffered. That means the characters you type don't get sent to the program until you press ENTER. This is why we were able to type characters after the #. After we pressed ENTER, the whole sequence of characters was sent to the program, but the program quit processing the input after it reached the # character.

`cin.get(char)` TO THE RESCUE

Usually, programs that read input character-by-character need to examine every character, including spaces, tabs, and newlines. The `istream` class (defined in `iostream`), to which `cin` belongs, includes member functions that meet this need. In particular, the member function `cin.get(ch)` reads the next character, even if it is a space, from the input and assigns it to the variable `ch`. By replacing `cin>>ch` with this function call, you can fix Listing 5.15. Listing 5.16 shows the result.

Listing 5.16 textin2.cpp

```
#include <iostream>
using namespace std;
int main()
{
    char ch;
    int count = 0;

    cin.get(ch);        // use the cin.get(ch) function
    while (ch != '#')
    {
        cout << ch;
        count++;
        cin.get(ch);    // use it again
    }
    cout << "\n" << count << " characters read\n";
    return 0;
}
```

Here is a sample run:

Did you use a #2 pencil?
Did you use a
14 characters read

Now the program echoes and counts every character, including the spaces. Input still is buffered, so it still is possible to type more input than what eventually reaches the program.

If you are familiar with C, this program may strike you as terribly wrong! The cin.get(ch) call places a value in the ch variable, which means it alters the value of the variable. In C, you must pass the address of a variable to a function if you want to change the value of that variable. But the call to cin.get() in Listing 5.16 passes ch, not &ch. In C, code like this won't work. In C++ it can, provided that the function declares the argument as a *reference*. This is a derived type new to C++. The iostream header file declares the argument to cin.get(ch) as a reference type, so this function can alter the value of its argument. We get to the details in Chapter 8, "Adventures in Functions." Meanwhile, the C mavens among you can relax—ordinarily, argument passing in C++ works just as it does in C. For cin.get(ch), however, it doesn't.

WHICH cin.get()?

Chapter 4 uses this code:

```
char name[ArSize];
...

cout << "Enter your name:\n";
cin.get(name, ArSize).get();
```

The last line is equivalent to two consecutive function calls:

```
cin.get(name, ArSize).get();
cin.get();
```

One version of cin.get() takes two arguments: the array name, which is the address of the string (technically, type char*), and ArSize, which is an integer of type int. (Recall that the name of an array is the address of its first element, so the name of a character array is type char*.) Then, the program uses cin.get() with no arguments. And, most recently, we've used cin.get() this way:

```
char ch;
cin.get(ch);
```

This time cin.get() has one argument, and it is type char.

Once again it is time for those of you familiar with C to get excited or confused. In C, if a function takes a pointer-to-char and an int as arguments, you can't success-fully use the same function with a single argument of a different type. But you can do so in C++ because the language supports an OOP feature called *function overloading*. Function overloading allows you to create different functions that have the same name provided that they have different argument lists. If, for instance, you use cin.get(name, ArSize) in C++, the compiler finds the version of cin.get() that uses a char* and an int as arguments. But if you use cin.get(ch), the compiler fetches the version that uses a single type char argument. And if the code provides no arguments, the compiler uses the version of cin.get() that takes no arguments. Function overloading enables you to use the same name for related functions that perform the same basic task in different ways or for different types. This is another topic awaiting you in Chapter 8. Meanwhile, you can get accustomed to function overloading by using the examples that come with the istream class. To distinguish between the different function versions, we'll include the argument list when referring to them. Thus, cin.get() means the version that takes no arguments and cin.get(char) means the version that takes one argument.

THE END-OF-FILE CONDITION

As Listing 5.16 shows, using a symbol such as # to signal the end of input is not always satisfactory, because such a symbol might be part of legitimate input. The same is true of other arbitrarily chosen symbols, such as @ or %. If the input comes from a file, you can employ a much more powerful technique—detecting the end-of-file (EOF). C++ input facilities cooperate with the operating system to detect when input reaches the end of a file and report that information back to a program.

At first glance, reading information from files seems to have little to do with cin and keyboard input, but there are two connections. First, many operating systems, including UNIX and MS-DOS, support *redirection*, which enables you to substitute a file for keyboard input. For instance, suppose in MS-DOS that you have an executable program called gofish.exe and a text file called fishtale. Then, you can give this command line at the DOS prompt:

```
gofish <fishtale
```

This causes the program to take input from the fishtale file instead of from the keyboard. The < symbol is the redirection operator for both UNIX and DOS. Second, many operating systems allow you to simulate the end-of-file condition from the keyboard. In UNIX you do so by pressing CTRL-D at the beginning of a line. In DOS, you press CTRL-Z, ENTER anywhere on the line. Some implementations support similar behavior even though the underlying operating system doesn't. The end-of-file concept for keyboard entry actually is a legacy of command-line environments. However, Symantec C++ for the Mac imitates UNIX and recognizes CTRL-D as a simulated EOF. The Microsoft Visual C++ 5.0 and the Borland C++Builder Windows environments support a console mode in which CTRL-Z works without an ENTER. However, here the mechanism is a bit different. The console mode catches the CTRL-Z before it ever reaches the program and terminates further I/O interaction, so this technique is of limited usefulness in that environment. The Metrowerks compilers don't provide a simulated EOF.

If your program can test for the end of a file, you can use the program with redirected files and you can use it for keyboard input in which you simulate end-of-file. That sounds useful, so let's see how it's done.

When cin detects the end-of-file (EOF), it sets a bit (the *eofbit*) to 1. You can use a member function named eof() to see whether the bit has been set; the call cin.eof() returns the bool value true if EOF has been detected and false otherwise. Note that the eof() method reports the result of the most recent attempt to read; that is, it reports on the past rather than looks ahead. So the `cin.eof()` test always should follow an attempt to read. The design of Listing 5.17 reflects this fact.

Remember

Some systems, including Metrowerks CodeWarrior, do not support simulated EOF from the keyboard. Other systems, including Microsoft Visual C++ 5.0 and Borland C++Builder, support it imperfectly.

Listing 5.17 textin3.cpp

```cpp
// textin3.cpp -- reading chars to end of file
#include <iostream>
using namespace std;
int main()
{
    char ch;
    int count = 0;
    cin.get(ch);            // attempt to read a char
    while (cin.eof() == false)  // test for EOF
    {
        cout << ch;         // echo character
        count++;
        cin.get(ch);        // attempt to read another char
    }
    cout << count << " characters read\n";
    return 0;
}
```

Here is sample output. Because we ran the program on a Windows 95 system, we pressed CTRL-Z to simulate the end-of-file condition. DOS users would press CTRL-Z, ENTER instead. UNIX and Symantec C++ for the Mac users would press CTRL-D instead.

```
The green bird sings in the winter.ENTER
The green bird sings in the winter.
Yes, but the crow flies in the dawn.ENTER
Yes, but the crow flies in the dawn.
CTRL Z
73 characters read
```

By using redirection, you can use this program to display a text file and report how many characters it has. This time, we have a program read, echo, and count a two-line file on a UNIX system (the $ is a UNIX prompt):

```
$ textin3 < stuff
I am a UNIX file. I am proud
to be a UNIX file.
49 characters read
$
```

End-of-File Ends Input

When a `cin` method detects end-of-file, recall, it sets a flag in the `cin` object indicating the end-of-file condition. When this flag is set, `cin` does not read any more input, and further calls to `cin` have no effect. For file input, this makes sense because you shouldn't read past the end of a file. For keyboard input, however, you might use a simulated end-of-file to terminate a loop but then want to read more input later. The `cin.clear()` method clears the end-of-file flag and lets input proceed again. Chapter 16, "Input, Output, and Files," discusses this further. Keep in mind, however, that in a Windows 95 console emulation mode, typing CTRL-Z effectively terminates both input and output beyond the powers of `cin.clear()` to restore them.

Common Idioms

The essential design of the input loop is this:

```
cin.get(ch);            // attempt to read a char
while (cin.eof() == false)  // test for EOF
{
    ...                 // do stuff
    cin.get(ch);        // attempt to read another char
}
```

There are some short cuts you can make. Chapter 6 introduces the `!` operator, which toggles `true` to `false` and vice versa. You can use it to rewrite the `while` test to look like this:

```
while (!cin.eof())     // while not at eof
```

The return value for the `cin.get(char)` method is `cin`, an object. However, the `istream` class provides a function that can convert an `istream` object such as `cin` to a `bool` value; this conversion function is called when `cin` occurs in a location where a `bool` is expected, such as in the test condition of a `while` loop. Furthermore, the `bool` value for the conversion is `true` if the last attempted read was successful and `false` otherwise. This means you can rewrite the `while` test to look like this:

```
while (cin)      // while input is successful
```

This is a bit more general than using `!cin.eof()`, for it detects other possible causes of failure, such a disk failure.

Finally, because the return value of `cin.get(char)` is `cin`, you can condense the loop to this format:

```
while (cin.get(ch))   // while input is successful
{
    ...                // do stuff
}
```

To evaluate the loop test, the program first has to execute the call to `cin.get(ch)`, which, if successful, places a value into `ch`. Then, the program obtains the return value from the function call, which is `cin`. Then, it applies the `bool` conversion to `cin`, which yields `true` if input worked, `false` otherwise. The three guidelines (identifying the termination condition, initializing the condition, and updating the condition) all are compressed into one loop test condition.

YET ANOTHER `cin.get()`

The more nostalgic of the C users among you might yearn for C's character I/O functions, getchar() and putchar(). They still are available if you want them. Just use the stdio.h header file as you would in C (or use the more current cstdio). Or, you can use member functions from the istream and ostream classes that work in much the same way. We look at that approach now.

Remember

Some older implementations don't support the `cin.get()` member function (no arguments) discussed here.

The cin.get() member function with no arguments returns the next character from the input. That is, you use it in this way:

```
ch = cin.get();
```

(Recall that cin.get(ch) returns an object, not the character read.) This function works much the same as C's getchar(), returning the character code as a type int value. Similarly, you can use the cout.put() function (see Chapter 3, "Dealing with Data") to display the character:

```
cout.put(ch);
```

It works much like C's putchar(), except that its argument should be type char instead of type int.

Remember

Originally, the `put()` member had a single prototype of `put(char)`. You could pass it an `int` argument, which then would be type cast to `int`. The draft standard also calls for a single prototype. However, many current implementations provide three prototypes: `put(char)`, `put(signed char)`, and `put(unsigned char)`. Using `put()` with an `int` argument in these implementations generates an error message because there is more than one choice for converting the `int`. An explicit type cast, such as `cin.put(char(c))`, works for int types.

To use cin.get() successfully, you need to know how it handles the end-of-file condition. When the function reaches the end of a file, there are no more characters to be returned. Instead, cin.get() returns a special value represented by the symbolic constant EOF. This constant is defined in the iostream header file. The EOF value must be different from any valid character value so that the program won't confuse EOF with a regular character. Typically, EOF is defined as the value –1, because no character has an ASCII code of −1, but you don't need to know the actual value. Just use EOF in the program. For instance, the heart of Listing 5.15 looked like this:

```
cin >> ch;
while (ch != '#')
{
    cout << ch;
    count++;
    cin >> ch;
}
```

You can replace cin with cin.get(), cout with cout.put(), and '#' with EOF:

```
ch = cin.get();
while (ch != EOF)
{
    cout.put(ch);     // cout.put(char(ch)) for some implementations
    count++;
    ch = cin.get();
}
```

If ch is a character, the loop displays it. If ch is EOF, the loop terminates.

Remember

> **You should realize that EOF does not represent a character in the input. Rather, it's a signal that there are no more characters.**

There's a subtle but important point about using cin.get() beyond the changes made so far. Because EOF represents a value outside the valid character codes, it's possible that it might not be compatible with the char type. For instance, on some systems type char is unsigned, so a char variable could never have the usual EOF value of −1. For this reason, if you use cin.get() (no argument) and test for EOF, you need to assign the return value to type int instead of type char. Also, if you make ch type int instead of type char, you might have to do a type cast to char when displaying ch.

Listing 5.18 incorporates the cin.get() approach into a new version of Listing 5.15. It also condenses the code by combining character input with the while loop test.

Listing 5.18 textin4.cpp

```
// textin4.cpp -- reading chars with cin.get()
#include <iostream.h>
int main(void)
{
    int ch;                          // should be int, not char
    int count = 0;

    while ((ch = cin.get()) != EOF)  // test for end-of-file
    {
        cout.put(char(ch));
        count++;
    }
    cout << count << " characters read\n";
    return 0;
}
```

Some systems either do not support simulated EOF from the keyboard or support it imperfectly.

Here's a sample run:

```
The sullen mackerel sulks in the shadowy shallows. ENTER
The sullen mackerel sulks in the shadowy shallows.
Yes, but the blue bird of happiness harbors secrets. ENTER
Yes, but the blue bird of happiness harbors secrets.
^Z

104 characters read
```

Let's analyze the loop condition:

```
while ((ch = cin.get()) != EOF)
```

The parentheses that enclose the subexpression ch=cin.get() cause the program to evaluate that expression first. To do the evaluation, the program first has to call the cin.get() function. Next, it assigns the function return value to ch. Because the value of an assignment statement is the value of the left operand, the whole subexpression reduces to the value of ch. If this value is EOF, the loop terminates; otherwise, it continues. The test condition needs all the parentheses. Suppose we leave some out:

```
while (ch = cin.get() != EOF)
```

The != operator has higher precedence than =, so first the program compares cin.get()'s return value to EOF. A comparison produces a false or true result; that bool value is converted to 0 or 1, and that's the value that gets assigned to ch.

Using cin.get(ch) (with an argument) for input, on the other hand, doesn't create any type problems. The cin.get(char) function, recall, doesn't assign a special value to ch on end-of-file. In fact it doesn't assign anything to ch in that case. ch is never called upon to hold a non-char value. Table 5.3 summarizes the differences between cin.get(char) and cin.get().

So which should you use, cin.get() or cin.get(char)? The form with the character argument is integrated more fully into the object approach because its return value is an istream object. This means, for example, that you can chain uses. For instance, the following code means read the next input character into ch1 and the following input character into ch2:

```
cin.get(ch1).get(ch2);
```

This works because the function call cin.get(ch1) returns the cin object, which then acts as the object to which get(ch2) is attached.

Probably the main use for the get() form is to let you make quick-and-dirty conversions from the getchar() and putchar() functions of stdio.h to the cin.get() and cout.put() methods of iostream. Just replace one header file with the other and globally replace getchar() and putchar() with their act-alike method equivalents. (If the old code uses a type int variable for input, you have to make further adjustments if your implementation has multiple prototypes for put().)

TABLE 5.3
`cin.get(ch)` VERSUS `cin.get()`

PROPERTY	`cin.get(ch)`	`ch=cin.get()`
Method for conveying input character	Assign to argument `ch`	Use function return value to assign to `ch`
Function return value for character input	A class `istream` object (`true` after `bool` conversion)	Code for character as type `int` value
Function return value at end-of-file	A class `istream` object (`false` after `bool` conversion)	EOF

Nested Loops and Two-Dimensional Arrays

Earlier you saw how the `for` loop is a natural tool for processing arrays. Let's go a step further and look at how a `for` loop within a `for` loop (nested loops) serves to handle two-dimensional arrays.

First, let's examine what a two-dimensional array is. The arrays used so far are termed one-dimensional arrays because you can visualize each array as a single row of data. You can visualize a two-dimensional array as being more like a table, having both rows and columns of data. You can use a two-dimensional array, for instance, to represent quarterly sales figures for six separate districts, with one row of data for each district. Or, you can use a two-dimensional array to represent the position of RoboDork on a computerized game board.

"You can visualize a two-dimensional array as being more like a table, having both rows and columns of data."

C++ doesn't provide a special two-dimensional array type. Instead, you create an array for which each element is itself an array. For example, suppose you want to store maximum temperature data for five cities over a four-year period. In that case, you can declare an array as follows:

```
int maxtemps[4][5];
```

This declaration means that `maxtemps` is an array with four elements. Each of these elements is an array of five integers. See Figure 5.5. You can think of the `maxtemps` array as representing four rows of five temperature values each.

The expression `maxtemps[0]` is the first element of the `maxtemps` array; hence, `maxtemps[0]` is itself an array of five `int`s. The first element of the `maxtemps[0]` array is `maxtemps[0][0]`, and this element is a single `int`. Thus, you need to use two subscripts to access the `int` elements. You can think of the first subscript as representing the row and the second subscript as representing the column. See Figure 5.6.

FIGURE 5.5

An array of arrays

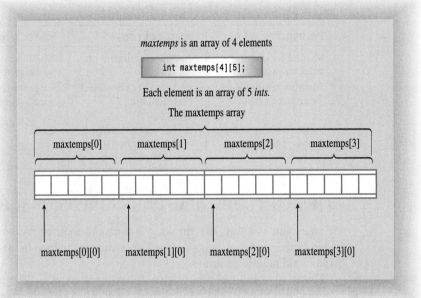

maxtemps is an array of 4 elements

```
int maxtemps[4][5];
```

Each element is an array of 5 *ints*.

The maxtemps array

| maxtemps[0] | maxtemps[1] | maxtemps[2] | maxtemps[3] |

maxtemps[0][0]   maxtemps[1][0]   maxtemps[2][0]   maxtemps[3][0]

FIGURE 5.6

Accessing array elements with subscripts

```
int maxtemps[4][5];
```

The maxtemps array viewed as a table:

		0	1	2	3	4
maxtemps[0]	0	maxtemps[0][0]	maxtemps[0][1]	maxtemps[0][2]	maxtemps[0][3]	maxtemps[0][4]
maxtemps[1]	1	maxtemps[1][0]	maxtemps[1][1]	maxtemps[1][2]	maxtemps[1][3]	maxtemps[1][4]
maxtemps[2]	2	maxtemps[2][0]	maxtemps[2][1]	maxtemps[2][2]	maxtemps[2][3]	maxtemps[2][4]
maxtemps[3]	3	maxtemps[3][0]	maxtemps[3][1]	maxtemps[3][2]	maxtemps[3][3]	maxtemps[3][4]

Suppose that you want to print all the array contents. Then, you can use one for loop to change rows and a second, nested for loop to change columns:

```
for (int row = 0; row < 4; row++)
{
    for (int col = 0; col < 5; col++)
        cout << maxtemps[row][col] << "\t";
    cout << "\n";
}
```

For each value of row, the inner for loop cycles through all the col values. This example prints a tab character (\t in C++ notation) after each value and a newline character after each complete row.

INITIALIZING A TWO-DIMENSIONAL ARRAY

When you create a two-dimensional array, you have the option of initializing each element. The technique is based on that for initializing a one-dimensional array. That method, you remember, is to provide a comma-separated list of values enclosed in braces:

```
// initializing a one-dimensional array
int btus[5] = { 23, 26, 24, 31, 28};
```

For a two-dimensional array, each element is itself an array, so you can initialize each element by using a form like that above. Thus, the initialization consists of a comma-separated series of one-dimensional initializations all enclosed in a set of braces:

```
int maxtemps[4][5] =            // 2-D array
{
    {94, 98, 87, 103, 101},     // values for maxtemps[0]
    {98, 99, 91, 107, 105},     // values for maxtemps[1]
    {93, 91, 90, 101, 104},     // values for maxtemps[2]
    {95, 100, 88, 105, 103}     // values for maxtemps[3]
};
```

The term {94, 98, 87, 103, 101} initializes the first row, represented by maxtemps[0]. As a matter of style, placing each row of data on its own line, if possible, makes the data easier to read.

Listing 5.19 incorporates an initialized two-dimensional array and a nested loop into a program. This time the program reverses the order of the loops, placing the column loop (city index) on the outside and the row loop (year index) on the inside. Also, it uses a common C++ practice of initializing an array of pointers to a set of string constants. That is, cities is declared as an array of pointers-to-char. That makes each element, such as cities[0], a pointer-to-char that can be initialized to the address of a string. The program initializes cities[0] to the address of the "Gribble City" string, and so on. Thus, this array of pointers essentially is an array of strings.

Listing 5.19 nested.cpp

```cpp
// nested.cpp -- nested loops and 2-D array
#include <iostream>
using namespace std;
const int Cities = 5;
const int Years = 4;
int main()
{
    const char * cities[Cities] =     // array of pointers
    {                                 // to 5 strings
        "Gribble City",
        "Gribbleton",
        "New Gribble",
        "San Gribble",
        "Gribble Vista"
    };

    int maxtemps[Years][Cities] =     // 2-D array
    {
        {94, 98, 87, 103, 101}, // values for maxtemps[0]
        {98, 99, 91, 107, 105}, // values for maxtemps[1]
        {93, 91, 90, 101, 104}, // values for maxtemps[2]
        {95, 100, 88, 105, 103} // values for maxtemps[3]
    };

    cout << "Maximum temperatures for 1995 - 1998\n\n";
    for (int city = 0; city < Cities; city++)
    {
        cout << cities[city] << ":\t";
        for (int year = 0; year < Years; year++)
            cout << maxtemps[year][city] << "\t";
        cout << "\n";
    }

    return 0;
}
```

Here is the program output:

```
Maximum temperatures for 1995 - 1998
Gribble City:     94      98      93      95
Gribbleton:       98      99      91      100
New Gribble:      87      91      90      88
San Gribble:      103     107     101     105

Gribble Vista:    101     105     104     103
```

Using tabs in the output spaces the data more regularly than using spaces would. Chapter 16 presents more precise, but more complex, methods for formatting output.

Summary

C++ offers three varieties of loops: the for loop, the while loop, and the do while loop. A loop cycles through the same set of instructions repetitively as long as the loop test condition evaluates to true or nonzero, and the loop terminates execution when the test condition evaluates to false or zero. The `for` loop and the `while` loop are entry-condition loops, meaning they examine the test condition before executing the statements in the body of the loop. The `do while` loop is an exit-condition loop, meaning it examines the test condition after executing the statements in the body of the loop.

The syntax for each loop calls for the loop body to consist of a single statement. However, that statement can be a compound statement, or block, formed by enclosing several statements within paired curly braces.

Relational expressions, which compare two values, are often used as loop test conditions. Relational expressions are formed by using one of the six relational operators: `<`, `<=`, `==`, `>=`, `>`, or `!=`. Relational expressions evaluate to the type `bool` values `true` and `false`.

Many programs read text input or text files character-by-character. The `istream` class provides several ways to do this. If `ch` is a type `char` variable, the statement

```
cin >> ch;
```

reads the next input character into `ch`. However, it skips over spaces, newlines, and tabs. The member function call

```
cin.get(ch);
```

reads the next input character, regardless of its value, and places it in `ch`. The member function call `cin.get()` returns the next input character, including spaces, newlines, and tabs, so it can be used as follows:

```
ch = cin.get();
```

The `cin.get(char)` member function call reports encountering the end-of-file condition by returning a value with the `bool` conversion of `false`, whereas the `cin.get()` member function call reports end-of-file by returning the value `EOF`, which is defined in the `iostream` file.

A nested loop is a loop within a loop. Nested loops provide a natural way to process two-dimensional arrays.

Review Questions

1. What's the difference between an entry-condition loop and an exit-condition loop? Which kind is each of the C++ loops?

2. What would the following code fragment print if it were part of a valid program?

```
int i;
for (i = 0; i < 5; i++)
     cout << i;
     cout << "\n";
```

3. What would the following code fragment print if it were part of a valid program?

```
int j;
for (j = 0; j < 11; j += 3)
        cout << j;
cout << "\n" << j << "\n";
```

4. What would the following code fragment print if it were part of a valid program?

```
int j = 5;
while ( ++j < 9)
        cout << j++ << "\n";
```

5. What would the following code fragment print if it were part of a valid program?

```
int k = 8;
do
        cout <<" k = " << k << "\n";
while (k++ < 5);
```

6. Write a `for` loop that prints the values 1 2 4 8 16 32 64 by increasing the value of a counting variable by a factor of 2 each cycle.

7. How do you make a loop body include more than one statement?

8. Is the following statement valid? If not, why not? If so, what does it do?

```
int x = (1,024);
```

   What about the following?

```
int y;
y = 1,024;
```

9. How does `cin>>ch` differ from `cin.get(ch)` and `ch=cin.get()` in how it views input?

Programming Exercises

1. Write a program that requests the user to enter two integers. The program then should calculate and report the sum of all the integers between and including the two integers. At this point, assume that the smaller integer is entered first. For instance, if the user enters 2 and 9, the program reports that the sum of all the integers from 2 through 9 is 44.

2. Write a program that asks you to type in numbers. After each entry, the number reports the cumulative sum of the entries to date. The program terminates when you enter a zero.

3. Daphne invests $100 at 10% simple interest. That is, every year, the investment earns 10% of the original investment, or $10 each and every year:

interest = 0.10 x original balance

At the same time, Cleo invests $100 at 5% compound interest. That is, interest is 5% of the current balance, including previous additions of interest:

interest = 0.05 x current balance

Cleo earns 5% of $100 the first year, giving her $105. The next year she earns 5% of $105, or $5.25, and so on. Write a program that finds how many years it takes for the value of Cleo's investment to exceed the value of Daphne's investment and then displays the value of both investments at that time.

4. You sell *C++ For Fools*. Write a program that has you enter a year's worth of monthly sales (in terms of number of books, not of money). The program should use a loop to prompt you by month, using an array of char * initialized to the month strings and storing the input data in an array of int. Then, the program should find the sum of the array contents and report the total sales for the year.

5. Do Programming Exercise 4 but use a two-dimensional array to store input for three years of monthly sales. Report the total sales for each individual year and for the combined years.

6. Design a structure called car that holds the following information about an automobile: its make as a string in a character array and the year it was built as an integer. Write a program that asks the user how many cars to catalog. The program then should use new to create a dynamic array of that many car structures. Next, it should prompt the user to input the make (which might consist of more than one word) and year information for each structure. Note that this requires some care, for it alternates reading strings with numeric data (see Chapter 4). Finally, it should display the contents of each structure. A sample run should look something like the following:

```
How many cars do you wish to catalog? 2
Car #1:
Please enter the make: Hudson Hornet
Please enter the year made: 1952
Car #2:
Please enter the make: Kaiser
Please enter the year made: 1951
Here is your collection:
1952 Hudson Hornet
1951 Kaiser
```

6

Branching Statements and Logical Operators

In this chapter you learn

- The `if` statement
- The `if else` statement
- Logical operators: `&&`, `¦¦`, and `!`
- The `cctype` library of character functions
- The conditional operator: `?:`
- The `switch` statement
- The `continue` and `break` statements
- Number-reading loops

One of the keys to designing intelligent programs is to give them the ability to make decisions. Chapter 5, "Loops and Relational Expressions," shows you one kind of decision making—looping—in which a program decides whether to continue looping. Now you investigate how C++ lets you use branching statements to decide among alternative actions. Which vampire-protection scheme (garlic or cross) should the program use? What menu choice has the user selected? Did the user enter a zero? C++ provides the `if` and `switch` statements to implement decisions, and they are this chapter's main topics. You also look at the conditional operator, which provides another way to make a choice, and the logical operators, which let you combine two tests into one.

The `if` Statement

When a C++ program must choose whether to take a particular action, you can use the `if` statement. The `if` comes in two forms: `if` and `if else`. Let's investigate the simple `if` first. It's modeled after ordinary English, as in "If you have a Captain Cookie card, you get a free cookie." The `if` statement directs a program to execute a statement or statement block if a test condition is true and to skip that statement or block if the condition is false. The syntax is similar to the `while` syntax:

```
if (test-condition)
    statement
```

A true or nonzero *test-condition* causes the program to execute *statement*, which can be a single statement or a block. A false or zero *test-condition* causes the program to skip *statement*. See Figure 6.1. The entire `if` construction counts as a single *statement*.

FIGURE 6.1

The if statement

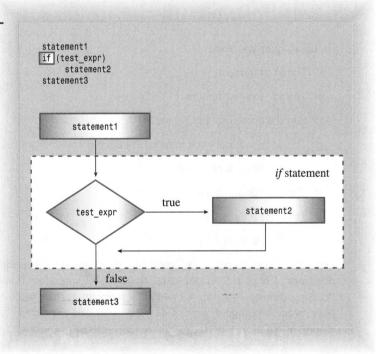

Usually, *test-condition* is a relational expression such as those used to control loops. Suppose, for instance, you want a program that counts the spaces in the input as well as the total number of characters. You can use cin.get(char) in a while loop to read the characters and then use an if statement to identify and count the space characters. Listing 6.1 does just that, using the period to recognize the end of a sentence.

Listing 6.1 if.cpp

```
// if.cpp -- using the if statement
#include <iostream>
using namespace std;
int main()
{
    char ch;
    int spaces = 0;
    int total = 0;
    cin.get(ch);
    while (ch != '.')    // quit at end of sentence
    {
        if (ch == ' ')   // check if ch is a space
            spaces++;
        total++;         // done every time
        cin.get(ch);
    }
    cout << spaces << " spaces, " << total;
    cout << " characters total in sentence\n";
    return 0;
}
```

Here's some sample output:

```
The balloonist was an airhead
with lofty goals.
6 spaces, 46 characters total in sentence
```

As the comments indicate, the spaces++; statement is executed only when ch is a space. Because it is outside the if statement, the total++; statement is executed every loop cycle. Note that the total count includes the newline character generated by pressing ENTER.

THE if else STATEMENT

The if statement lets a program decide whether a *particular* statement or block is executed. The if else statement lets a program decide which of *two* statements or blocks is executed. It's an invaluable statement for creating alternative courses of action. The C++ if else is modeled after simple English, as in "If you have a Captain Cookie card, you get a Cookie Plus Plus, else you just get a Cookie d'Ordinaire." The if else statement has this general form:

```
if (test-condition)
    statement1
else
    statement2
```

If *test-condition* is true or nonzero, the program executes *statement1* and skips over *statement2*. Otherwise, when *test-condition* is false or zero, the program skips *statement1* and executes *statement2* instead. So the code fragment

```
if (answer == 1492)
    cout << "That's right!\n";
else
        cout << "You'd better review Chapter 1 again.\n";
```

prints the first message if answer is 1492 and prints the second message otherwise. Each statement can be either a single statement or a statement block delimited by braces. See Figure 6.2. The entire `if else` construct counts syntactically as a single statement.

For instance, suppose you want to alter incoming text by scrambling the letters while keeping the newline character intact. That way, each line of input is converted to an output line of equal length. This means you want the program to take one course of action for newline characters and a different course of action for all other characters. As Listing 6.2 shows, `if else` makes this task easy.

FIGURE 6.2

The if else statement

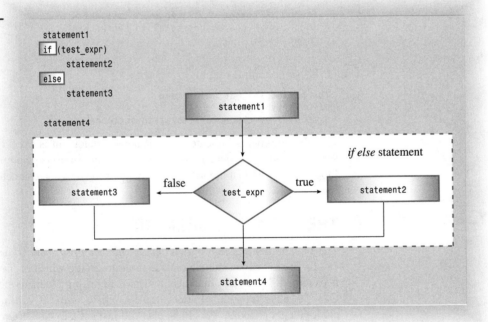

Listing 6.2 ifelse.cpp

```cpp
// ifelse.cpp -- using the if else statement
#include <iostream>
using namespace std;
int main()
{
    char ch;

    cout << "Type, and I shall repeat.\n";
    cin.get(ch);
    while (ch != '.')
    {
        if (ch == '\n')
            cout << ch;       // done if newline
        else
            cout << ++ch;     // done otherwise
        cin.get(ch);
    }
// try ch + 1 instead of ++ch for interesting effect
    cout << "\nPlease excuse the slight confusion.\n";
    return 0;
}
```

Here's some sample output:

```
Type, and I shall repeat.
I am extraordinarily pleased
J!bn!fyusbpsejobsjmz!qmfbtfe
to use such a powerful computer.
up!vtf!tvdi!b!qpxfsgvm!dpnqvufs
Please excuse the slight confusion.
```

Note that one of the program comments suggests that changing ++ch to ch+1 has an interesting effect. Can you deduce what it will be? If not, try it out and then see if you can explain what's happening. (Hint: Think about how cout handles different types.)

FORMATTING YOUR if else STATEMENTS

Keep in mind that the two if else alternatives must be single statements. If you need more than one statement, use braces to collect them into a single block statement. Unlike some languages, such as BASIC or FORTRAN, C++ does not automatically consider everything between if and else a block, so you must use braces to make the statements a block. The following code, for instance, produces a compiler error. The compiler sees it as a simple if statement that ends with the zorro++; statement. Then there is a cout statement. So far, so good. But then there is what the compiler perceives as an unattached else, and that is flagged as a syntax error.

```cpp
if (ch == 'Z')
    zorro++;            // if ends here
    cout << "Another Zorro candidate\n";
else                    // wrong
    dull++;
    cout << "Not a Zorro candidate\n";
```

Add the braces to convert the code to what you want:

```
if (ch == 'Z')
{                              // if true block
    zorro++;
    cout << "Another Zorro candidate\n";
}
else
{                              // if false block
    dull++;
    cout << "Not a Zorro candidate\n";
}
```

Because C++ is a free-form language, you can arrange the braces as you like, as long as they enclose the statements. The preceding code shows one popular format. Here's another:

```
if (ch == 'Z') {
    zorro++;
    cout << "Another Zorro candidate\n";
    }
else {
    dull++;
    cout << "Not a Zorro candidate\n";
    }
```

The first form emphasizes the block structure for the statements, whereas the second form more closely ties the blocks to the keywords if and else. Either style should serve you well unless you encounter a passionate advocate for some particular style.

THE if else if else CONSTRUCTION

Computer programs, like life, might present you with a choice of more than two selections. You can extend the C++ if else statement to meet that need. The else, you've seen, should be followed by a single statement, which can be a block. Because an if else statement itself is a single statement, it can follow an else:

```
if (ch == 'A')
    a_grade++;                 // alternative # 1
else
    if (ch == 'B')            // alternative # 2
        b_grade++;            // subalternative # 2a
    else
        soso++;              // subalternative # 2b
```

If ch is not 'A', the program goes to the else. There, a second if else subdivides that alternative into two more choices. C++'s free formatting enables you to arrange these elements into an easier-to-read format:

```
if (ch == 'A')
    a_grade++;                 // alternative # 1
else if (ch == 'B')
    b_grade++;                 // alternative # 2
else
    soso++;                   // alternative # 3
```

" Computer programs, like life, might present you with a choice of more than two selections. You can extend the C++ if else statement to meet that need. "

This looks like a new control structure—an if else if else structure. But actually it is one if else contained within a second. This revised format looks much cleaner, and it enables you to skim through the code to pick out the different alternatives. This entire construction still counts as one statement.

Listing 6.3 uses this preferred formatting to construct a modest quiz program.

Listing 6.3 ifelseif.cpp

```cpp
// ifelseif.cpp -- using if else if else
#include <iostream>
using namespace std;
const int Fave = 27;
int main()
{
    int n;

    cout << "Enter a number in the range 1-100 to find ";
    cout << "my favorite number: ";
    do
    {
        cin >> n;
        if (n < Fave)
            cout << "Too low -- guess again: ";
        else if (n > Fave)
            cout << "Too high -- guess again: ";
        else
            cout << Fave << " is right!\n";
    } while (n != Fave);
    return 0;
}
```

Here's some sample output:

```
Enter a number in the range 1-100 to find my favorite number: 50
Too high -- guess again: 25
Too low -- guess again: 37
Too high -- guess again: 31
Too high -- guess again: 28
Too high -- guess again: 27
27 is right!
```

Logical Expressions

Often you must test for more than one condition. For example, for a character to be a lowercase letter, its value must be greater than or equal to 'a' and less than or equal to 'z'. Or, if you ask a user to respond with a y or an n, you want to accept uppercase (Y and N) as well as lowercase. To meet this kind of need, C++ provides three logical operators to combine or modify existing expressions. The operators are logical OR, written ¦¦; logical AND, written &&; and logical NOT, written !. Let's examine them now.

THE LOGICAL OR OPERATOR: ¦¦

In English, the word *or* can indicate when one or both of two conditions satisfy a requirement. For instance, you can go to the MegaMicro company picnic if you *or* your spouse work for MegaMicro, Inc. The C++ equivalent is the logical OR operator, written ¦¦. This operator combines two expressions into one. If either or both of the original expressions are true, or nonzero, the resulting expression has the value true; otherwise, the expression has the value false. Here are some examples:

```
5 ==5 ¦¦ 5 == 9      // true because first expression is true
5 > 3 ¦¦ 5 > 10      // true because first expression is true
5 > 8 ¦¦ 5 < 10      // true because second expression is true
5 < 8 ¦¦ 5 > 2       // true because both expressions are true
5 > 8 ¦¦ 5 < 2       // false because both expressions are false
```

Because the ¦¦ has a lower precedence than the relational operators, you don't need to use parentheses in these expressions. Table 6.1 summarizes how the ¦¦ operator works.

C++ provides that the ¦¦ operator is a *sequence point*. That is, any value changes indicated in the left side take place before the right side is evaluated. For instance, consider the following expression:

```
i++ < 6 ¦¦ i == j
```

Suppose i originally has the value 10. By the time the comparison with j takes place, i has the value 11. Also, C++ won't bother evaluating the expression on the right if the expression on the left is true, because only one true expression makes the whole logical expression true.

Listing 6.4 uses the ¦¦ operator in an if statement to check for both uppercase and lowercase versions of a character. Also, it uses C++'s string concatenation feature (see Chapter 4, "Derived Types") to spread a single string over three lines.

TABLE 6.1
THE ¦¦ OPERATOR

THE VALUE OF EXPR1 ¦¦ EXPR2		
	expr1 == true	expr1 == false
expr2 == true	true	true
expr2 == false	true	false

Listing 6.4 or.cpp

```cpp
// or.cpp -- use logical OR operator
#include <iostream>
using namespace std;
int main()
{
    cout << "This program may reformat your hard disk\n"
            "and destroy all your data.\n"
            "Do you wish to continue? <y/n> ";
    char ch;
    cin >> ch;
    if (ch == 'y' || ch == 'Y')             // y or Y
        cout << "You were warned!\a\a\n";
    else if (ch == 'n' || ch == 'N')        // n or N
        cout << "A wise choice ... bye\n";
    else
        cout << "That wasn't a y or an n, so I guess I'll "
                "trash your disk anyway.\n";
    return 0;
}
```

Here is a sample run:

```
This program may reformat your hard disk
and destroy all your data.
Do you wish to continue? <y/n> N
A wise choice ... bye
```

The program reads just one character, so only the first character in the response matters. That means the user could have replied NO! instead of N. The program would just read the N. But if the program tried to read more input later, it would start at the O.

THE LOGICAL AND OPERATOR: &&

The logical AND operator, written &&, also combines two expressions into one. The resulting expression has the value true only if both of the original expressions are true. Here are some examples:

```
5 == 5 && 4 == 4    // true because both expressions are true
5 == 3 && 4 == 4    // false because first expression is false
5 > 3 && 5 > 10     // false because second expression is false
5 > 8 && 5 < 10     // false because first expression is false
5 < 8 && 5 > 2      // true because both expressions are true
5 > 8 && 5 < 2      // false because both expressions are false
```

Because the && has a lower precedence than the relational operators, you don't need to use parentheses in these expressions. Like the || operator, the && operator acts as a sequence point, so the left side is evaluated and any side effects are carried out before the right side is evaluated. If the left side is false, the whole logical expression must be false, so C++ doesn't bother evaluating the right side in that case. Table 6.2 summarizes how the && operator works.

TABLE 6.2
THE *&&* OPERATOR

THE VALUE OF EXPR1 && EXPR2		
	expr1 == true	expr1 == false
expr2 == true	true	false
expr2 == false	false	false

Listing 6.5 shows how to use *&&* to cope with a common situation, terminating a *while* loop, for two different reasons. In the listing, a *while* loop reads values into an array. One test (*i < ArSize*) terminates the loop when the array is full. The second test (*temp >= 0*) gives the user the option of quitting early by entering a negative number. The *&&* operator lets you combine the two tests into a single condition. The program also uses two *if* statements, an *if else* statement, and a *for* loop, so it demonstrates several topics from this and the preceding chapter.

Listing 6.5 and.cpp

```cpp
// and.cpp -- use logical AND operator
#include <iostream>
using namespace std;
const int ArSize = 6;
int main()
{
    float naaq[ArSize];
    cout << "Enter the NAAQs (New Age Awareness Quotients) "
         << "of\nyour neighbors. Program terminates "
         << "when you make\n" << ArSize << " entries "
         << "or enter a negative value.\n";

    int i = 0;
    float temp;
    cin >> temp;
    while (i < ArSize && temp >= 0) // 2 quitting criteria
    {
        naaq[i++] = temp;
        if (i < ArSize)                 // room left in the array,
            cin >> temp;                // so get next value
    }
    if (i == 0)
        cout << "No data--bye\n";
    else
    {
        cout << "Enter your NAAQ: ";
        float you;
        cin >> you;
        int count = 0;
        for (int j = 0; j < i; j++)
            if (naaq[j] > you)
                count++;
        cout << count;
        cout << " of your neighbors have greater awareness of\n"
             << "the New Age than you do.\n";
```

```
        }
        return 0;
    }
```

Note that the program places input into a temporary variable temp. Only after it verifies that the input is valid does the program assign the value to the array.

Here are a couple of sample runs. One terminates after six entries, and the second terminates after a negative value is entered:

```
Enter the NAAQs (New Age Awareness Quotients) of
your neighbors. Program terminates when you make
6 entries or enter a negative value.
28 72 19
6
130 145
Enter your NAAQ: 50
3 of your neighbors have greater awareness of
the New Age than you do.

Enter the NAAQs (New Age Awareness Quotients) of
your neighbors. Program terminates when you make
6 entries or enter a negative value.
123 119
4
89
-1
Enter your NAAQ: 123.027
0 of your neighbors have greater awareness of
the New Age than you do.
```

Program Notes

Look at the input part of the program:

```
cin >> temp;
while (i < ArSize && temp >= 0)        // 2 quitting criteria
{
    naaq[i++] = temp;
    if (i < ArSize)                    // room left in the array,
        cin >> temp;                   // so read next value
}
```

The program begins by reading the first input value into a temporary variable called temp. Then, the while test condition checks to see whether there still is room left in the array (i < ArSize) and whether the input value is nonnegative (temp >= 0). If so, it copies the temp value to the array and increases the array index by 1. At this point, because array numbering starts at 0, i equals the total number of entries to date. That is, if i starts out at 0, the first cycle through the loop assigns a value to naaq[0] and then sets i to 1.

The loop terminates when the array is filled or when the user enters a negative number. Note that the loop reads another value into temp only if i is less than ArSize, that is, only if there still is room left in the array.

After it gets data, the program uses an `if else` statement to comment if no data were entered (that is, if the first entry was a negative number) and to process the data if any is present.

Setting Up Ranges with &&

The `&&` operator also lets you set up a series of `if else if else` statements with each choice corresponding to a particular range of values. Listing 6.6 illustrates the approach. It also shows a useful technique for handling a series of messages. Just as a pointer-to-char variable can identify a single string by pointing to its beginning, an array of pointers-to-char can identify a series of strings. Simply assign the address of each string to a different array element. Listing 6.6 uses the `qualify` array to hold the addresses of four strings. For instance, `qualify[1]` holds the address of the string `"mud tug-of-war\n"`. The program then can use `qualify[1]` like any other pointer to a string—for example, with `cout` or with `strlen()` or `strcmp()`. Using the `const` qualifier protects these strings from accidental alterations.

Listing 6.6 more_and.cpp

```cpp
// more_and.cpp -- use logical AND operator
#include <iostream>
using namespace std;
const char * qualify[4] =        // an array of pointers
{                                // to strings
    "10,000-meter race.\n",
    "mud tug-of-war.\n",
    "masters canoe jousting.\n",
    "pie-throwing festival.\n"
};
int main()
{
    int age;
    cout << "Enter your age in years: ";
    cin >> age;
    int index;

    if (age > 17 && age < 35)
        index = 0;
    else if (age >= 35 && age < 50)
        index = 1;
    else if (age >= 50 && age < 65)
        index = 2;
    else
        index = 3;

    cout << "You qualify for the " << qualify[index];
    return 0;
}
```

You might recall that some C++ implementations require that you use the keyword `static` in an array declaration in order to make it possible to initialize that array. That restriction, as Chapter 8 discusses, applies to arrays declared inside a function body. When an array is declared outside a function body, as is `qualify` in Listing 6.6, it's termed an *external* array and can be initialized even in pre-ANSI C implementations.

Here is a sample run:

```
Enter your age in years: 87
You qualify for the pie-throwing festival.
```

The entered age didn't match any of the test ranges, so the program set `index` to 3 and then printed the corresponding string.

Program Notes

The expression `age > 17 && age < 35` tests for ages between the two values; that is, ages in the range 18–34. The expression `age >= 35 && age < 50` uses the `<=` operator to include 35 in its range, which is 35–49. If the program had used `age > 35 && age < 50`, the value 35 would have been missed by all the tests. When you use range tests, you should check that the ranges don't have holes between them and that they don't overlap. Also, be sure to set up each range correctly; see the note on Range Tests.

The `if else` statement serves to select an array index, which, in turn, identifies a particular string.

RANGE TESTS

Note that each part of a range test should use the AND operator to join two complete relational expressions:

```
if (age > 17 && age < 35)    // OK
```

Don't borrow from mathematics and use the following notation:

```
if (17 < age < 35)            // Don't do this!
```

If you make this error, the compiler won't catch it, for it still is valid C++ syntax. The `<` operator associates from left to right, so the previous expression means the following:

```
if ( (17 < age) < 35)
```

But `17 < age` is either `true`, or 1, or else `false`, or 0. In either case, the expression `17 < age` is less than 35, so the entire test is always true!

THE LOGICAL NOT OPERATOR: !

The ! operator negates, or reverses the truth value of, the expression that follows it. That is, if *expression* is true, then *!expression* is false, and vice versa. More precisely, if *expression* is true *or* nonzero, then !expression is false. Incidentally, many people call the exclamation point *bang*, making !x bang-exe and !!x bang-bang-exe.

Usually you more clearly can express a relationship without using this operator:

```
if (!(x > 5))                    // if (x <= 5) is clearer
```

But the ! operator can be useful with functions that return true-false values or values that can be interpreted that way. For instance, strcmp(s1,s2) returns a nonzero (true) value if the two strings s1 and s2 are different from each other and a zero value if they are the same. This implies that !strcmp(s1,s2) is true if the two strings are equal.

Listing 6.7 uses this technique (applying the ! operator to a function return value) to screen numeric input for suitability to be assigned to type int. The function is_int(), which we discuss further in a moment, returns true if its argument is within the range of values that can be assigned to type int. The program then uses the test while(!is_int(num)) to reject values that don't fit in the range.

Listing 6.7 not.cpp

```cpp
// not.cpp -- using the not operator
#include <iostream>
#include <climits>
using namespace std;
bool is_int(double);
int main()
{
    double num;

    cout << "Yo, dude! Enter an integer value: ";
    cin >> num;
    while (!is_int(num))      // continue while num is not int-able
    {
        cout << "Out of range -- please try again: ";
        cin >> num;
    }
    int val = num;
    cout << "You've entered the integer " << val << "\n";
    return 0;
}

bool is_int(double x)
{
```

```
        if (x <= INT_MAX && x >= INT_MIN)    // use climits values
            return true;
        else
            return false;
    }
```

Remember

If your system doesn't provide `climits`, **use** `limits.h`.

Here is a sample run on a system with a 32-bit int:

```
Yo, dude! Enter an integer value: 6234128679
Out of range -- please try again: -8000222333
Out of range -- please try again: 99999
You've entered the integer 99999
```

Program Notes

If you enter a too-large value to a program reading a type int, most implementations simply truncate the value to fit without informing you that data was lost. This program avoids that by first reading the potential int as a double. The double type has more than enough precision to hold a typical int value, and its range is much greater.

The Boolean function is_int() uses the two symbolic constants (INT_MAX and INT_MIN) defined in the climits file (discussed in Chapter 3, "Dealing with Data") to determine whether its argument is within the proper limits. If so, the program returns a value of true; otherwise, it returns false.

The main() program uses a while loop to reject invalid input until the user gets it right. You could make the program friendlier by displaying the int limits when the input is out of range. After the input has been validated, the program assigns it to an int variable.

LOGICAL OPERATOR FACTS

As we mentioned, the C++ logical OR and logical AND operators have a lower precedence than relational operators. That means an expression such as

```
x > 5 && x < 10
```

is read this way:

```
(x > 5) && (x < 10)
```

The ! operator, on the other hand, has a higher precedence than any of the relational or arithmetic operators. Therefore, to negate an expression, you should enclose the expression in parentheses:

```
!(x > 5)      // is it false that x is greater than 5
!x > 5        // is !x greater than 5
```

The second expression, incidentally, is always false, for !x can have only the values true or false, which get converted to 1 or 0.

The logical AND operator has a higher precedence than the logical OR operator. Thus, the expression

```
age > 30 && age < 45 ¦¦ weight > 300
```

means the following:

```
(age > 30 && age < 45) ¦¦ weight > 300
```

That is, one condition is that age be in the range 31 to 44, and the second condition is that weight be greater than 300. The entire expression is true if one or the other or both of these conditions are true.

You can, of course, use parentheses to tell the program the interpretation you want. For instance, suppose you want to use && to combine the condition that age be greater than 50 or weight be greater than 300 with the condition that donation be greater than 1000. You must enclose the OR part within parentheses:

```
(age > 50 ¦¦ weight > 300) && donation > 1000
```

Otherwise, the compiler combines the weight condition with the donation condition instead of with the age condition. The simplest course of action is to use parentheses to group the tests, whether or not the parentheses are needed. It makes the code easier to read.

C++ guarantees that when a program evaluates a logical expression, it evaluates it from left to right and stops evaluation as soon as it knows what the answer is. Suppose, for instance, you have this condition:

```
x != 0  && 1.0 / x > 100.0
```

If the first condition is false, then the whole expression must be false. That's because for this expression to be true, each individual condition must be true. Knowing the first condition is false, the program doesn't bother evaluating the second condition. That's fortunate in this example, because evaluating the second condition would result in dividing by 0, which is not in a computer's realm of possible actions.

The cctype Library of Character Functions

C++ has inherited from C a handy package of character-related functions, prototyped in the cctype header file (ctype.h, in the older style), that simplify such tasks as determining whether a character is an uppercase letter or a digit or punctuation, and the like. For example, the isalpha(ch) function returns a nonzero value if ch is a letter and a zero value otherwise. Similarly, ispunct(ch) returns a true value only if ch is a punctuation character, such as a comma or period. (These functions have return type int rather than bool, but the usual bool conversions allow you to treat them as type bool.)

Using these functions is more convenient than using the AND and OR operators. For instance, here's how you might use AND and OR to test whether a character ch is an alphabetic character:

```
if ((ch >= 'a' && ch <= 'z') || (ch >= 'A' && ch <= 'Z'))
```

Compare that to using isalpha():

```
if (isalpha(ch))
```

Not only is isalpha() easier to use, it is more general. The AND, OR form assumes that character codes for A through Z are in sequence, with no other characters having codes in that range. This assumption is true for the ASCII code, but it need not be true in general.

Listing 6.8 demonstrates some functions from this family. In particular, it uses isalpha(), which tests for alphabetic characters; isdigits(), which tests for digit characters, such as 3; isspace(), which tests for white-space characters, such as newlines, spaces, and tabs; and ispunct(), which tests for punctuation characters. The program also reviews the if else if structure and using a while loop with cin.get(char).

Listing 6.8 cctypes.cpp

```cpp
// cctypes.cpp--use ctype.h library
#include <iostream>
#include <cctype>                    // prototypes for character functions
using namespace std;
int main()
{
    cout << "Enter text for analysis, and type @"
            " to terminate input.\n";
    char ch;
    int whitespace = 0;
    int digits = 0;
    int chars = 0;
    int punct = 0;
    int others = 0;

    cin.get(ch);                    // get first character
    while(ch != '@')                // test for sentinal
    {
        if(isalpha(ch))             // is it an alphabetic character?
            chars++;
        else if(isspace(ch))        // is it a whitespace character?
            whitespace++;
        else if(isdigit(ch))        // is it a digit?
            digits++;
        else if(ispunct(ch))        // is it punctuation?
            punct++;
```

```
            else
                others++;
            cin.get(ch);                // get next character
        }
        cout << chars << " letters, "
            << whitespace << " whitespace, "
            << digits << " digits, "
            << punct << " punctuations, "
            << others << " others.\n";
        return 0;
    }
```

Here is a sample run; note that the white-space count includes newlines:

```
Enter text for analysis, and type @ to terminate input.
Jody "Java-Java" Joystone, noted restaurant critic,
celebrated her 39th birthday with a carafe of 1982
Chateau Panda.@
89 letters, 16 whitespace, 6 digits, 6 punctuations, 0 others.
```

Table 6.3 summarizes the functions available in the `cctype` package. Some systems may lack some of these functions or have additional ones.

TABLE 6.3
THE `cctype` CHARACTER FUNCTIONS

FUNCTION NAME	RETURN VALUE
isalnum()	True if argument is alphanumeric, that is, a letter or a digit
isalpha()	True if argument is alphabetic
iscntrl()	True if argument is a control character
isdigit()	True if argument is a decimal digit (0–9)
isgraph()	True if argument is any printing character other than a space
islower()	True if argument is a lowercase letter
isprint()	True if argument is any printing character, including a space
ispunct()	True if argument is a punctuation character
isspace()	True if argument is a standard white-space character, that is, a space, formfeed, newline, carriage return, horizontal tab, or vertical tab
isupper()	True if argument is an uppercase letter
isxdigit()	True if argument is a hexadecimal digit character, that is, 0–9, a–f, or A–F
tolower()	If the argument is an uppercase character, `tolower()` returns the lowercase version of that character; otherwise, it returns the argument unaltered
toupper()	If the argument is a lowercase character, `toupper()` returns the uppercase version of that character; otherwise, it returns the argument unaltered

The ? : Operator

C++ has an operator that often can be used instead of the `if else` statement. This operator is called the *conditional operator*, written ?:, and, for you trivia buffs, it is the only C++ operator that requires three operands. The general form looks like this:

```
expression1 ? expression2 : expression3
```

If *expression1* is true, then the value of the whole conditional expression is the value of *expression2*. Otherwise, the value of the whole expression is the value of *expression3*. Here are two examples showing how the operator works:

```
5 > 3 ? 10 : 12  // 5 > 3 is true, so expression value is 10
3 == 9? 25 : 18  // 3 == 9 is false, so expression value is 18
```

We can paraphrase the first example this way: If 5 is greater than 3, the expression evaluates to 10; otherwise, it evaluates to 12. In real programming situations, of course, the expressions would involve variables.

Listing 6.9 uses the conditional operator to determine the larger of two values.

```
Listing 6.9 condit.cpp
// condit.cpp -- using the conditional operator
#include <iostream>
using namespace std;
int main()
{
    int a, b;
    cout << "Enter two integers: ";
    cin >> a >> b;
    cout << "The larger of " << a << " and " << b;
    int c = a > b ? a : b;   // c = a if a > b, else c = b
    cout << " is " << c << "\n";
    return 0;
}
```

Here is a sample run:

```
Enter two numbers: 25 27
The larger of 25 and 27 is 27
```

The key part of the program is this statement:

```
int c = a > b ? a : b;
```

It produces the same result as the following statements:

```
int c;
if (a > b)
    c = a;
else
    c = b;
```

Compared to the `if else` sequence, the conditional operator is more concise but, at first, less obvious. One difference between the two approaches is that the conditional operator produces an expression and hence a single value that can be assigned or incorporated into a larger expression, as the program did when it assigned the value of the conditional expression to the variable c. The conditional operator's concise form, unusual syntax, and overall weird appearance make it a great favorite among programmers who appreciate those qualities. One favorite trick for the reprehensible goal of concealing the purpose of code is to nest conditional expressions within one another, as the following mild example shows:

```
const char x[2] [20] = {"Jason ","at your service\n"};
const char * y = "Quillstone ";

for (int i = 0; i < 3; i++)
    cout << ((i < 2)? !i ? x [i] : y : x[1]);
```

This is merely an obscure (but, by no means, maximally obscure) way to print the three strings in the following order:

```
Jason Quillstone at your service
```

The `switch` Statement

Suppose you create a screen menu that asks the user to select one of five choices, for example, Cheap, Moderate, Expensive, Extravagant, and Excessive. You can extend an `if else if else` sequence to handle five alternatives, but the C++ `switch` statement more easily handles selecting a choice from an extended list. Here's the general form for a `switch` statement:

```
switch (integer-expression)
{
    case label1 : statement(s)
    case label2 : statement(s)
    ...
    default    : statement(s)
}
```

A C++ `switch` statement acts as a routing device that tells the computer which line of code to execute next. On reaching a `switch`, the program jumps to the line labeled with the value corresponding to the value of *integer-expression*. For instance, if *integer-expression* has the value 4, the program goes to the line having a `case 4:` label. The value *integer-expression*, as the name suggests, must be an expression that reduces to an integer value. Also, each label must be an integer constant expression. Most often, labels are simple `int` or `char` constants, such as 1 or q, or enumerators. If *integer-expression* doesn't match any of the labels, the program jumps to the line labeled `default`. The `default` label is optional. If you omit it and there is no match, the program jumps to the next statement following the `switch`. See Figure 6.3.

FIGURE 6.3

The switch statement

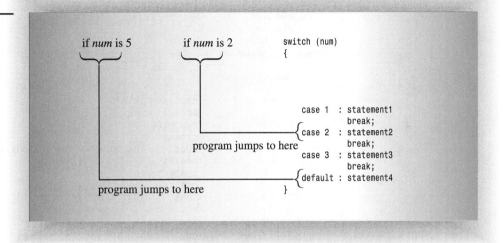

The switch statement is different from similar statements in languages such as Pascal in a very important way. Each C++ case label functions only as a line label, not as a boundary between choices. That is, after a program jumps to a particular line in a switch, it then sequentially executes all the statements following that line in the switch unless you explicitly direct it otherwise. Execution does NOT automatically stop at the next case. To make execution stop at the end of a particular group of statements, you must use the break statement. This causes execution to jump to the statement following the switch.

Listing 6.10 shows how to use switch and break together to implement a simple menu for executives. The program uses a showmenu() function to display a set of choices. A switch statement then selects an action based on the user's response.

Remember

Some implementations treat the \a escape sequence as silent.

Listing 6.10 switch.cpp

```cpp
// switch.cpp -- use the switch statement
#include <iostream>
using namespace std;
void showmenu();    // function prototypes
void report();
void comfort();
```

```cpp
int main()
{
    showmenu();
    int choice;
    cin >> choice;
    while (choice != 5)
    {
        switch(choice)
        {
            case 1 :    cout << "\a\n";
                        break;
            case 2 :    report();
                        break;
            case 3 :    cout << "The boss was in all day.\n";
                        break;
            case 4 :    comfort();
                        break;
            default :   cout << "That's not a choice.\n";
        }
        showmenu();
        cin >> choice;
    }
    cout << "Bye!\n";
    return 0;
}

void showmenu()
{
    cout << "Please enter 1, 2, 3, 4, or 5:\n"
            "1) alarm            2) report\n"
            "3) alibi            4) comfort\n"
            "5) quit\n";
}
void report()
{
    cout << "It's been an excellent week for business.\n"
         "Sales are up 120%. Expenses are down 35%.\n";
}
void comfort()
{
    cout << "Your employees think you are the finest CEO\n"
         "in the industry. The board of directors think\n"
         "you are the finest CEO in the industry.\n";
}
```

Here is a sample run of the executive menu program:

```
Please enter 1, 2, 3, 4, or 5:
1) alarm            2) report
3) alibi            4) comfort
5) quit
4
Your employees think you are the finest CEO
in the industry. The board of directors think
you are the finest CEO in the industry.
Please enter 1, 2, 3, 4, or 5:
1) alarm            2) report
3) alibi            4) comfort
5) quit
2
```

```
It's been an excellent week for business.
Sales are up 120%. Expenses are down 35%.
Please enter 1, 2, 3, 4, or 5:
1) alarm            2) report
3) alibi            4) comfort
5) quit
6
That's not a choice.
Please enter 1, 2, 3, 4, or 5:
1) alarm            2) report
3) alibi            4) comfort
5) quit
5
Bye!
```

The while loop terminates when the user enters 5. Entering 1 through 4 activates the corresponding choice from the switch list, and entering 6 triggers the default statements.

As noted before, this program needs the break statements to confine execution to a particular portion of a switch. To see that this is so, you can remove the break statements from Listing 6.10 and see how it works afterward. You'll find, for example, that entering 2 causes the program to execute *all* the statements associated with case labels 2, 3, 4, and the default. C++ works this way because that sort of behavior can be useful. For one thing, it makes it simple to use multiple labels. For example, suppose you rewrote Listing 6.10 using characters instead of integers as menu choices and switch labels. Then, you could use both an uppercase and a lowercase label for the same statements:

```
char choice;
cin >> choice;
while (choice != 'Q' && choice != 'q')
{
    switch(choice)
    {
        case 'a':
        case 'A': cout << "\a\n";
                  break;
        case 'r':
        case 'R': report();
                  break;
        case 'l':
        case 'L': cout << "The boss was in all day.\n";
                  break;
        case 'c'
        case 'C': comfort();
                  break;
        default : cout << "That's not a choice.\n";
    }
    showmenu();
    cin >> choice;
}
```

Because there is no break immediately following case 'a', program execution passes to the next line, which is the statement following case 'A'.

Using Enumerators as Labels

Listing 6.11 illustrates using enum to define a set of related constants and then using the constants in a switch. In general, cin doesn't recognize enumerated types (it can't know how you will define them), so the program reads the choice as an int. When the switch statement compares the int value to an enumerator case label, it promotes the enumerator to int. Also, the enumerators are promoted to type int in the while loop test condition.

Listing 6.11 enum.cpp

```cpp
// enum.cpp -- use enum
#include <iostream>
using namespace std;
// create named constants for 0 - 6
enum {red, orange, yellow, green, blue, violet, indigo};

int main()
{
    cout << "Enter color code (0-6): ";
    int code;
    cin >> code;
    while (code >= red && code <= indigo)
    {
        switch (code)
        {
            case red    : cout << "Her lips were red.\n"; break;
            case orange : cout << "Her hair was orange.\n"; break;
            case yellow : cout << "Her shoes were yellow.\n"; break;
            case green  : cout << "Her nails were green.\n"; break;
            case blue   : cout << "Her sweatsuit was blue.\n"; break;
            case violet : cout << "Her eyes were violet.\n"; break;
            case indigo : cout << "Her mood was indigo.\n"; break;
        }
        cout << "Enter color code (0-6): ";
        cin >> code;
    }
    cout << "Bye\n";
    return 0;
}
```

Here's a sample output:

```
Enter color code (0-6): 3
Her nails were green.
Enter color code (0-6): 5
Her eyes were violet.
Enter color code (0-6): 2
Her shoes were yellow.
Enter color code (0-6): 8
Bye
```

switch AND if else

Both the `switch` statement and the `if else` statement let a program select from a list of alternatives. The `if else` is the more versatile of the two. For instance, it can handle ranges, as in the following:

```
if (age > 17 && age < 35)
        index = 0;
    else if (age >= 35 && age < 50)
        index = 1;
    else if (age >= 50 && age < 65)
        index = 2;
    else
        index = 3;
```

The `switch`, however, isn't designed to handle ranges. Each `switch` case label must be a single value. Also, that value must be an integer (which includes `char`), so a `switch` won't handle floating-point tests. And the case label value must be a constant. If your alternatives involve ranges or floating-point tests or comparing two variables, use `if else`.

If, however, all the alternatives can be identified with integer constants, you can use a `switch` or an `if else` statement. Because that's precisely the situation that the `switch` statement is designed to process, the `switch` statement usually is the more efficient choice in terms of code size and execution speed, unless there are only a couple of alternatives from which to choose.

Remember

If you can use either an `if else if` sequence or a `switch` statement, the usual rule is to use a `switch` if you have three or more alternatives.

The break and continue Statements

The `break` and `continue` statements enable a program to skip over parts of the code. You can use the `break` statement in a `switch` statement and in any of the loops. It causes program execution to pass to the next statement following the `switch` or the loop. The `continue` statement is used in loops and causes a program to skip the rest of the body of the loop and then start a new loop cycle. See Figure 6.4.

Listing 6.12 shows how the two statements work. The program lets you enter a line of text. The loop echoes each character and uses `break` to terminate the loop if the character is a period. This shows how you can use `break` to terminate a loop from within when some condition becomes true. Next, the program counts spaces, but not other characters. The loop uses `continue` to skip over the counting part of the loop when the character isn't a space.

FIGURE 6.4

*The break and
continue statements*

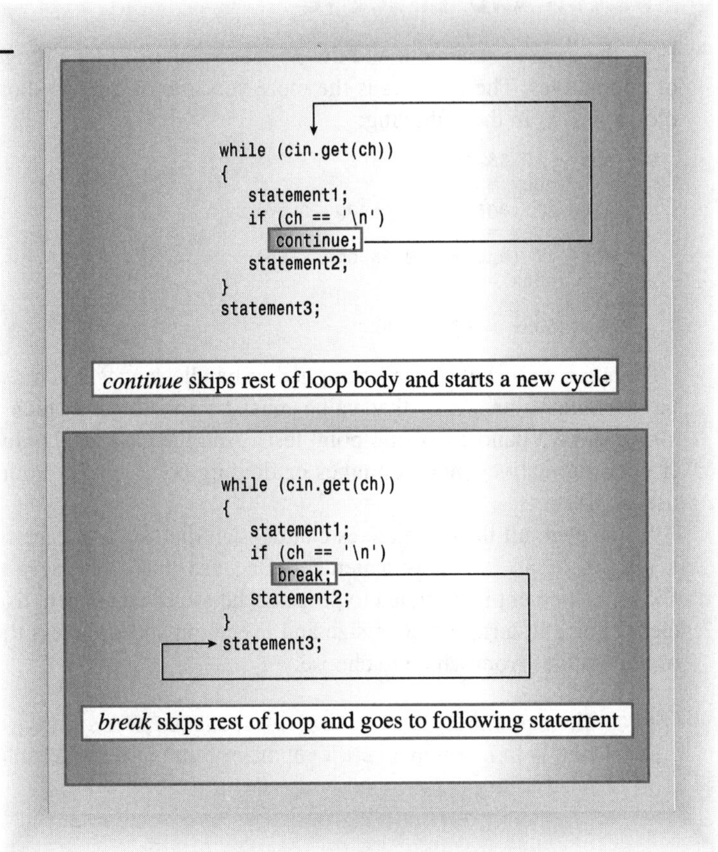

```
          ┌──────────────────────┐
          ↓                      │
while (cin.get(ch))              │
{                                │
    statement1;                  │
    if (ch == '\n')              │
    │continue;│──────────────────┘
    statement2;
}
statement3;
```

continue skips rest of loop body and starts a new cycle

```
while (cin.get(ch))
{
    statement1;
    if (ch == '\n')
    │break;│───────────────────┐
    statement2;                 │
}                               │
statement3;  ←──────────────────┘
```

break skips rest of loop and goes to following statement

Listing 6.12 jump.cpp

```cpp
// jump.cpp -- using continue and break
#include <iostream>
using namespace std;
const int ArSize = 80;
int main()
{
    char line[ArSize];
    int spaces = 0;

    cout << "Enter a line of text:\n";
    cin.get(line, ArSize);
    for (int i = 0; line[i] != '\0'; i++)
    {
        cout << line[i];    // display character
        if (line[i] == '.') // quit if it's a period
            break;
        if (line[i] != ' ') // skip rest of loop
            continue;
        spaces++;
```

```
    }
    cout << "\n" << spaces << " spaces\n";
    return 0;
}
```

Here's a sample run:

Let's do lunch today. You can pay!
Let's do lunch today.
3 spaces

Program Notes

Note that whereas the `continue` statement causes the program to skip the rest of the loop body, it doesn't skip the loop update expression. In a `for` loop, the `continue` statement makes the program skip directly to the update expression and then to the test expression. For a `while` loop, however, `continue` makes the program go directly to the test expression. Therefore, any update expression in a `while` loop body following the `continue` would be skipped. In some cases, that could be a problem.

This program didn't have to use `continue`. Instead, it could have used this code:

```
if (line[i] == ' ')
    spaces++;
```

However, the `continue` statement can make the program more readable when several statements follow the `continue`. That way, you don't need to make all those statements part of an `if` statement.

C++, like C, also has a `goto` statement. A statement like

```
goto paris
```

means to jump to the location bearing `paris:` as a label. That is, you can have code like this:

```
char ch;
cin >> ch;
if (ch == 'P')
    goto paris;
cout < ...
...
paris: cout << "You've just arrived at Paris.\n";
```

In most circumstances, using a `goto` is a bad hack, and you should use structured controls, such as `if else`, `switch`, `continue`, and the like, to control program flow.

Number-Reading Loops

You're preparing a program to read a series of numbers into an array. You want to give the user the option to terminate input before filling the array. One way is to utilize how `cin` behaves. Consider the following code:

```
int n;
cin >> n;
```

What happens if the user responds by entering a word instead of a number? Four things occur in such a mismatch:

- The value of n is left unchanged.

- The mismatched input is left in the input queue.

- An error flag is set in the cin object.

- The call to the cin method, if converted to type bool, returns false.

The fact that the method returns false means that you can use non-numeric input to terminate a number-reading loop. The fact that non-numeric input sets an error flag means that you must reset the flag before the program can read more input. The clear() method, which also resets the end-of-file condition (see Chapter 5), resets the bad input flag. (Either bad input or end-of-file can cause cin to return false. Chapter 16, "Input, Output, and Files," discusses how to distinguish between the two cases.) Let's look at a couple of examples illustrating these techniques.

You want to write a program to calculate the average weight of your day's catch of fish. There's a five-fish limit, so a five-element array can hold all the data, but it's possible that you could catch fewer fish. Listing 6.13 uses a loop that terminates if the array is full or if you enter non-numeric input.

Listing 6.13 cinfish.cpp

```cpp
// cinfish.cpp -- non-numeric input terminates loop
#include <iostream>
using namespace std;
const int Max = 5;
int main()
{
// get data
    double fish[Max];
    cout << "Please enter the weights of your fish.\n";
    cout << "You may enter up to " << Max
            << " fish <q to terminate>.\n";
    cout << "fish #1: ";
    int i = 0;
    while (i < Max && cin >> fish[i]) {
        if (++i < Max)
            cout << "fish #" << i+1 << ": ";
    }
// calculate average
    double total = 0.0;
    for (int j = 0; j < i; j++)
        total += fish[j];
// report results
    if (i == 0)
        cout << "No fish\n";
    else
        cout << total / i << " = average weight of "
            << i << " fish\n";
    return 0;
}
```

The expression cin >> fish[i] really is a cin method function call, and the function returns cin. If cin is part of a test condition, it's converted to type bool. The conversion value is true if input succeeds and false otherwise. A false value for the expression terminates the loop. By the way, here's a sample run:

```
Please enter the weights of your fish.
You may enter up to 5 fish <q to terminate>.
fish #1: 30
fish #2: 35
fish #3: 25
fish #4: 40
fish #5: q
32.5 = average weight of 4 fish
```

Note the following line of code:

```
while (i < Max && cin >> fish[i]) {
```

Recall that C++ doesn't evaluate the right side of a logical AND expression if the left side is false. In this case, evaluating the right side means using cin to place input into the array. If i does equal Max, the loop terminates without trying to read a value into a location past the end of the array.

The last example didn't attempt to read any input after non-numeric input. Let's look at a case that does. Suppose you are required to submit exactly five golf scores to a C++ program to establish your average. If a user enters non-numeric input, the program should object, insisting on numeric input. As you've seen, you can use the value of a cin input expression to test for non-numeric input. Suppose you find the user did enter the wrong stuff. You need to take three steps:

- Reset cin to accept new input.

- Get rid of the bad input.

- Prompt the user to try again.

Note that you must reset cin before getting rid of the bad input. Listing 6.14 shows how these tasks can be accomplished.

Listing 6.14 cingolf.cpp

```cpp
// cingolf.cpp -- non-numeric input skipped
#include <iostream>
using namespace std;
const int Max = 5;
int main()
{
// get data
    int golf[Max];
    cout << "Please enter your golf scores.\n";
    cout << "You must enter " << Max << " rounds.\n";
    int i;
    for (i = 0; i < Max; i++)
    {
        cout << "round #" << i+1 << ": ";
        while (!(cin >> golf[i])) {
```

```
                    cin.clear();      // reset input
                    while (cin.get() != '\n')
                        continue;     // get rid of bad input
                    cout << "Please enter a number: ";
                }
            }
    // calculate average
        double total = 0.0;
        for (i = 0; i < Max; i++)
            total += golf[i];
    // report results
        cout << total / Max << " = average score "
                << Max << " rounds\n";
        return 0;
}
```

Here is a sample run:

```
Please enter your golf scores.
You must enter 5 rounds.
round #1: 88
round #2: 87
round #3: must i?
Please enter a number: 103
round #4: 94
round #5: 86
91.6 = average score 5 rounds
```

Program Notes

The heart of the error-handling code is the following:

```
while (!(cin >> golf[i])) {
    cin.clear();       // reset input
    while (cin.get() != '\n')
        continue; // get rid of bad input
    cout << "Please enter a number: ";
}
```

If the user enters 88, the cin expression is true, a value is placed in the array, the expression !(cin >> golf[i]) is false, and this inner loop terminates. But if the user enters must i?, the cin expression is false, nothing is placed into the array, the expression !(cin >> golf[i]) is true, and the program enters the inner while loop. The first statement in the loop uses the clear() method to reset input. If you omit this statement, the program refuses to read any more input. Next, the program uses cin.get() in a while loop to read the remaining input through the end of the line. This gets rid of the bad input along with anything else on the line. Another approach is to read to the next white space, which would get rid of bad input one word at a time instead of one line at a time. Finally, the program tells the user to enter a number.

Summary

Programs and programming become more interesting when you introduce statements that guide the program through alternative actions. (Whether this also makes the programmer more interesting is a point we've not fully researched.) C++ provides the `if` statement, the `if else` statement, and the `switch` statements as means for managing choices. The C++ `if` statement lets a program execute a statement or statement block conditionally. That is, the program executes the statement or block if a particular condition is met. The C++ `if else` statement lets a program select from two choices which statement or statement block to execute. You can append additional `else ifs` to the statement to present a series of choices. The C++ `switch` statement directs the program to a particular case in a list of choices.

C++ also provides operators to help in decision making. Chapter 5 discusses the relational expressions, which compare two values. The `if` and `if else` statements typically use relational expressions as test conditions. By using C++'s logical operators (`&&`, `¦¦`, and `!`), you can combine or modify relational expressions, constructing more elaborate tests. The conditional operator (`?:`) provides a compact way to choose from two values.

The `cctype` library of character functions provides a convenient and powerful set of tools for analyzing character input.

With C++'s loops and decision-making statements, you have the tools for writing interesting, intelligent, and powerful programs. But we've only begun to investigate the real powers of C++. Next, we look at functions.

Review Questions

1. Consider the following two code fragments for counting spaces and newlines:

```
// Version 1
while (cin.get(ch))     // quit on eof
{
    if (ch == ' ')
        spaces++;
    if (ch == '\n')
        newlines++;
}
// Version 2
while (cin.get(ch))     // quit on eof
{
    if (ch == ' ')
        spaces++;
    else if (ch == '\n')
        newlines++;
}
```

What advantages, if any, does the second form have over the first?

2. In Listing 6.2, what is the effect of replacing ++ch with ch+1?

3. Consider carefully the following program:

```cpp
#include <iostream>
using namespace std;
int main()
{
    char ch;
    int ct1, ct2;

    ct1 = ct2 = 0;
    while ((ch = cin.get()) != '$')
    {
        cout << ch;
        ct1++;
        if (ch = '$')
            ct2++;
        cout << ch;
    }
    cout <<"ct1 = " << ct1 << ", ct2 = " << ct2 << "\n";
    return 0;
}
```

Suppose we provide the following input, where ø represents pressing ENTER:

```
Hi!ø
Send $10 or $20 now!ø
```

What is the output? (Recall that input is buffered.)

4. Construct logical expressions to represent the following conditions:

   a. weight is greater than or equal to 115 but less than 125.

   b. ch is q or Q.

   c. x is even but is not 26.

   d. donation is in the range 1000–2000 or guest is 1.

   e. ch is a lowercase letter or an uppercase letter (assume the lowercase letters are coded sequentially and that the uppercase letters are coded sequentially but that there is a gap in the code between uppercase and lowercase).

5. In English the statement "I will not not speak" means the same as "I will speak." In C++, is !!x the same as x?

6. Construct a conditional expression that is equal to the absolute value of a variable. That is, if a variable x is positive, the value of the expression is just x, but if x is negative, the value of the expression is -x, which is positive.

7. Rewrite the following fragment using switch:

```cpp
if (ch == 'A')
    a_grade++;
else if (ch == 'B')
    b_grade++;
else if (ch == 'C')
    c_grade++;
else if (ch == 'D')
    d_grade++;
```

```
        else
            f_grade++;
```

8. In Listing 6.10, what advantage would there be in using character labels, such as a and c, instead of numbers for the menu choices and switch cases? (Hint: Think about what happens if the user types q in either case and what happens if the user types 5 in either case.)

9. Consider the following code fragment:

```
int line = 0;
char ch;
while (cin.get(ch))
{
    if (ch == 'Q')
            break;
    if (ch != '\n')
            continue;
    line++;
}
```

Rewrite this code without using break or continue.

Programming Exercises

1. Write a program that reads keyboard input to the @ symbol and that echoes the input except for digits, converting each uppercase character to lowercase, and vice versa. (Don't forget the cctype family.)

2. Write a program that reads up to 10 donation values into an array of double. The program should terminate input on non-numeric input. It should report the average of the numbers and also report how many numbers in the array are larger than the average.

3. Write a precursor to a menu-driven program. The program should display a menu offering four choices, each labeled with a letter. If the user responds with a letter other than one of the four valid choices, the program should prompt the user to enter a valid response until the user complies. Then, the program should use a switch to select a simple action based on the user's selection. A program run could look something like this:

```
Please enter one of the following choices:
c) carnivore           p) pianist
t) tree                g) game
f
Please enter a c, p, t, or g: q
Please enter a c, p, t, or g: t
A maple is a tree.
```

4. When you join the Benevolent Order of Programmers, you can be known at BOP meetings by your real name, your job title, or by your secret BOP name. Write a program that can list members by real name, by job title, by secret name, or by a member's preference. Base the program on the following structure:

```
// Benevolent Order of Programmers name structure
struct bop {
    char fullname[strsize]; // real name
    char title[strsize];    // job title
    char bopname[strsize];  // secret BOP name
    int preference;         // 0 = fullname, 1 = title, 2 = bopname
};
```

In the program, create a small array of such structures and initialize it to suitable values. Have the program run a loop that lets the user select from different alternatives:

```
a. display by name       b. display by title
c. display by bopname    d. display by preference
q. quit
```

A sample run may look something like the following:

```
Benevolent Order of Programmers Report
a. display by name       b. display by title
c. display by bopname    d. display by preference
q. quit
Enter your choice: a
Wimp Macho
Raki Rhodes
Celia Laiter
Hoppy Hipman
Pat Hand
Next choice: d
Wimp Macho
Junior Programmer
MIPS
Analyst Trainee
LOOPY
Next choice: q
Bye!
```

5. The Kingdom of Neutronia, where the unit of currency is the tvarp, has the following income tax code:

first 5000 tvarps: 0% tax

next 10000 tvarps: 10% tax

next 20000 tvarps: 15% tax

tvarps after 35000: 20% tax

For example, someone earning 38000 tvarps would owe 5000 × 0.00 + 10000 × 0.10 + 20000 × 0.15 + 3000 × .020, or 4600 tvarps. Write a program that uses a loop to solicit incomes and to report tax owed. The loop terminates when the user enters a negative number or nonnumeric input.

7

Functions– C++'s Programming Modules

In this chapter you learn

- 💧 Function basics (review)
- 💧 Function prototypes
- 💧 Passing function arguments by value
- 💧 Designing functions to process arrays
- 💧 Using `const` pointer arguments
- 💧 Designing functions to process text strings
- 💧 Designing functions to process structures
- 💧 Functions that call themselves (recursion)
- 💧 Pointers to functions

Fun is where you find it. Look closely, and you can find it in functions. C++ comes with a large library of useful functions (the standard ANSI C library plus several C++

classes), but real programming pleasure comes with writing your own. In this and the next chapter you'll examine how to define functions, convey information to them, and retrieve information from them. After reviewing how functions work, this chapter concentrates on how to use functions in conjunction with arrays, strings, and structures. Finally, it touches on recursion and pointers to functions. If you've paid your C dues, you'll find much of this chapter familiar. But don't be lulled into a false sense of expertise. C++ has made several additions to what functions can do, and the next chapter deals primarily with those. Meanwhile, let's attend to the fundamentals.

Function Review

First, let's review what you've already learned about functions. To use a C++ function, you must do the following:

- Provide a function definition.
- Provide a function prototype.
- Call the function.

If you're using a library function, the function already has been defined and compiled for you. Also, you can use a standard library header file to provide the prototype. All that's left to do is to call the function properly. The examples in this book have done that several times. For example, the standard C library includes the `strlen()` function for finding the length of the string. The associated standard header file `cstring` contains the function prototype for `strlen()` and several other string-related functions. This advance work allows you to use the `strlen()` function in programs without further worries.

But when you create your own functions, you have to handle all three aspects—defining, prototyping, and calling—yourself. Listing 7.1 shows these steps in a short example.

Listing 7.1 calling.cpp

```
// calling.cpp -- defining, prototyping, and calling a function
#include <iostream>
using namespace std;

void simple();     // function prototype

int main()
{
    cout << "main() will call the simple() function:\n";
    simple();     // function call
    return 0;
}

// function definition
void simple()
{
    cout << "I'm but a simple function.\n";
}
```

Here's the output:

```
main() will call the simple() function:
I'm but a simple function.
```

Let's take a more detailed look at these steps now.

DEFINING A FUNCTION

You can group functions into two categories: functions that don't have return values and functions that do have return values. Functions without return values are termed type `void` functions and have the following general form:

```
void functionName(argumentList)
{
    statement(s)
    return;         // optional
}
```

Here `argumentList` specifies the types and number of arguments passed to the function. This chapter more fully investigates this list later. The optional return statement marks the end of the function. Otherwise, the function terminates at the closing brace. Type `void` functions correspond to Pascal procedures, FORTRAN subroutines, and modern BASIC subprogram procedures. Typically, you use a `void` function to perform some type of action. For instance, a function to print Cheers! a given number (n) of times can look like this:

```
void cheers(int n)            // no return value
{
    for (int i = 0; i < n; i++)
        cout << "Cheers! ";
    cout << "\n";
}
```

The `int n` argument list means that `cheers()` expects to be passed an `int` value as an argument when you call this function.

A function with a return value produces a value that it returns to the function that called it. In other words, if the function returns the square root of 9.0 (`sqrt(9.0)`), then the function call is replaced by the value 3.0. Such a function is declared as having the same type as the value it returns. Here is the general form:

```
typeName functionName(argumentList)
{
    statements
    return value;   // value is of type typename
}
```

Functions with return values require that you use a return statement so that the value is returned to the calling function. The value itself can be a constant, a variable, or a more general expression. The only requirement is that the expression reduce to a value that has, or is convertible to, the `typeName` type. (If the declared return type is, say, `double`, and the function returns an `int` expression, the `int` value is typecast to type `double`.) The function then returns the final value to the function that called it. C++

does place a restriction on what types you can use for a return value: The return value cannot be an array. Everything else is possible—integers, floating-point numbers, pointers, even structures and objects! (Interestingly, even though a C++ function can't return an array directly, it can return an array that's part of a structure or object.)

As a programmer, you don't need to know how a function returns a value, but knowing the method might clarify the concept for you. (Also, it gives you something to talk about with your friends and family.) Typically, a function returns a value by copying the return value to a specified CPU register or memory location. Then, the calling program examines that location. Both the returning function and the calling function have to agree on the type of data at that location. The function prototype tells the calling program what to expect, and the function definition tells the called program what to return. See Figure 7.1. Providing the same information in the prototype as in the definition might seem like extra work, but it does make good sense. Certainly, if you want a courier to pick up something from your desk at the office, you enhance the odds of the task being done right if you provide a description of what you want both to the courier and to someone at the office.

FIGURE 7.1

Typical return value mechanism

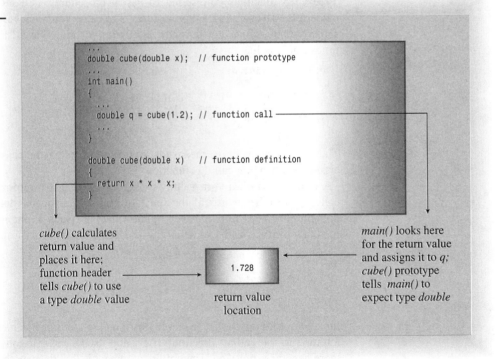

```
...
double cube(double x);  // function prototype
...
int main()
{
    ...
    double q = cube(1.2); // function call
    ...
}

double cube(double x)   // function definition
{
    return x * x * x;
}
```

cube() calculates return value and places it here; function header tells *cube()* to use a type *double* value

1.728

return value location

main() looks here for the return value and assigns it to *q*; *cube()* prototype tells *main()* to expect type *double*

A function terminates after executing a return statement. If a function has more than one return statement—for example, as alternatives to different `if else` selections—the function terminates after it executes the first return statement it reaches:

```
int bigger(int a, int b)
{
    if (a > b )
        return a;  // if a > b, function terminates here
    else
        return b;  // otherwise, function terminates here
}
```

Here the `else` isn't needed, but it does help the casual reader understand the intent.

Functions with return values are much like functions in Pascal, FORTRAN, and BASIC. They return a value to the calling program, which then can assign that value to a variable, display the value, or otherwise use it. Here's a simple example that returns the cube of a type `double` value:

```
double cube(double x)     // x times x times x
{
    return x * x * x; // a type double value
}
```

For instance, the function call `cube(1.2)` returns the value 1.728. Note that this return statement uses an expression. The function computes the value of the expression (`1.728`, in this case) and returns the value.

FUNCTION PROTOTYPING AND FUNCTION CALLS

By now you are familiar with making function calls, but you may be less comfortable with function prototyping because that's often been hidden in the include files. Let's use the `cheers()` and `cube()` functions in a program (Listing 7.2); notice the function prototypes.

Listing 7.2 protos.cpp

```
// protos.cpp -- use prototypes and function calls
#include <iostream>
using namespace std;
void cheers(int);        // prototype: no return value
double cube(double x);   // prototype: returns a double
int main(void)
{
    cheers(5);           // function call
    cout << "Give me a number: ";
    double side;
    cin >> side;
    double volume = cube(side);    // function call
    cout << "A " << side <<"-foot cube has a volume of ";
    cout << volume << " cubic feet.\n";
    cheers(cube(2));     // prototype protection at work
    return 0;
}
```

```
void cheers(int n)
{
    for (int i = 0; i < n; i++)
        cout << "Cheers! ";
    cout << "\n";
}

double cube(double x)
{
    return x * x * x;
}
```

Here's a sample run:

```
Cheers! Cheers! Cheers! Cheers! Cheers!
Give me a number: 5
A 5-foot cube has a volume of 125 cubic feet.
Cheers! Cheers! Cheers! Cheers! Cheers! Cheers! Cheers! Cheers!
```

Note that `main()` calls the type `void` function `cheers()` by using the function name and arguments followed by a semicolon: `cheers(5);`. That's an example of a function call statement. But because `cube()` has a return value, `main()` can use it as part of an assignment statement:

```
double volume = cube(side);
```

But we said you should concentrate on the prototypes. What should you know about prototypes? First, you should understand why C++ requires prototypes. Then, because C++ requires prototypes, you should know the proper syntax. Finally, you should appreciate what the prototype does for you. Let's look at these points in turn, using Listing 7.2 as a basis for discussion.

Why Prototypes?

The prototype describes the function interface to the compiler. That is, it tells the compiler what type of return value, if any, the function has, and it tells the compiler the number and type of function arguments. Consider, for example, how a prototype affects this function call from Listing 7.2:

```
double volume = cube(side);
```

First, the prototype tells the compiler that `cube()` should have one type `double` argument. If the program fails to provide one, prototyping allows the compiler to catch the error. Second, when the `cube()` function finishes its calculation, it places its return value at some specified location—perhaps in a CPU register, perhaps in memory. Then, the calling function, `main()` in this case, retrieves the value from that location. Because the prototype states that `cube()` is type `double`, the compiler knows how many bytes to retrieve and how to interpret them. Without that information, the compiler could only guess.

Still, you might wonder, why does the compiler need a prototype? Can't it just look further in the file and see how the functions are defined?

Still, you might wonder, why does the compiler need a prototype? Can't it just look further in the file and see how the functions are defined? One problem with that approach is that it is less efficient. The compiler would have to put compiling `main()` on hold while searching the rest of the file. An even more serious problem is the fact that the function might not even be in the file. C++ allows you to spread a program over several files, which you can compile independently and then combine later. If that's the case, the compiler might not have access to the function code when it's compiling `main()`. The same is true if the function is part of a library. The only way to avoid using a function prototype is to place the function definition before its first use. That is not always possible. Also, the C++ programming style is to put `main()` first because it generally provides the structure for the whole program.

Prototype Syntax

A function prototype is a statement, so it must have a terminating semicolon. The simplest way to get a prototype is to copy the function heading from the function definition and add a semicolon. That's what the program does for `cube()`:

```
double cube(double x); // add ; to heading to get prototype
```

However, the function prototype does not require that you provide names for the variables; a list of types is enough. The program prototypes `cheers()` by using only the argument type:

```
void cheers(int); // okay to drop variable names in prototype
```

In general, you either can include or exclude variable names in the argument lists for prototypes. The variable names in the prototype just act as placeholders, so if you do use names, they don't have to match the names in the function definition.

C++ VERSUS ANSI C PROTOTYPING

ANSI C borrowed prototyping from C++, but the two languages do have some differences. The most important is that ANSI C, to preserve compatibility with classic C, made prototyping optional, whereas C++ makes prototyping mandatory. For instance, consider the following function declaration:

```
void say_hi();
```

In C++, leaving the parentheses empty is the same as using the keyword `void` within the parentheses. It means the function has no arguments. In ANSI C, leaving the parentheses empty means that you are declining to state what the arguments are. That is, it means you're foregoing prototyping the argument list.

What Prototypes Do for You

You've seen that prototypes help the compiler, but what do they do for you? They greatly reduce the chances for program errors. In particular, prototypes ensure the following:

- The compiler correctly handles the function return value.

- The compiler checks that you use the correct number of function arguments.

- The compiler checks that you use the correct type of arguments. If not, it converts the arguments to the correct type, if possible.

We've already discussed how to handle correctly the return value. Let's look now at what happens when you use the wrong number of arguments. For instance, suppose you made the following call:

```
double z = cube();
```

Without function prototyping, the compiler lets this go by. When the function is called, it looks where the call to cube() should have placed a number and uses whatever value happens to be there. This, for instance, is how C worked before ANSI C borrowed prototyping from C++. Because prototyping is optional for ANSI C, this still is how some C programs work. But in C++ prototyping is not optional, so you are guaranteed protection from that sort of error.

Next, suppose you provide an argument but it is the wrong type. In C, this could create weird errors. For instance, if a function expects a type int value (assume that's 16 bits) and you pass a double (assume that's 64 bits), the function looks at just the first 16 bits of the 64 and tries to interpret them as an int value. C++, however, automatically converts the value you pass to the type specified in the prototype, provided that both are arithmetic types. For instance, Listing 7.2 manages to get two type mismatches in one statement:

```
cheers(cube(2));
```

First, the program passes the int value of 2 to cube(), which expects type double. The compiler, noting that the cube() prototype specifies a type double argument, converts 2 to 2.0, a type double value. Then, cube() returns a type double value (8.0) to be used as an argument to cheers(). Again, the compiler checks the prototypes and notes that cheers() requires an int. It converts the return value to the integer 8. In general, prototyping produces automatic type casts to the expected types. (Function overloading, discussed in Chapter 8, "Adventures in Functions," can create ambiguous situations, however, that prevent some automatic type casts.)

Automatic type conversion doesn't head off all possible errors. For instance, if you pass a value of 8.33E27 to a function that expects an int, such a large value cannot be converted correctly to a mere int. Some compilers warn you of possible data loss when there is an automatic conversion from a larger type to a smaller.

Also, prototyping results in type conversion only when it makes sense. It won't, for example, convert an integer to a structure or pointer.

Prototyping takes place during compile time and is termed *static type checking*. Static type checking, as we've just seen, catches many errors that are much more difficult to catch during run time.

Function Arguments and Passing by Value

It's time to take a closer look at function arguments. C++ normally passes arguments *by value*. That means the numeric value of the argument is passed to the function, where it is assigned to a new variable. For instance, Listing 7.2 has this function call:

```
double volume = cube(side);
```

Here side is a variable that, in the sample run, had the value 5. The function heading for cube(), recall, was this:

```
double cube(double x)
```

When this function is called, it creates a new type double variable called x and assigns the value 5 to it. This insulates data in main() from actions that take place in cube(), for cube() works with a copy of side rather than with the original data. You'll see an example of this protection soon. A variable that's used to receive passed values is called a *formal argument* or *parameter*. The value passed to the function is called the *actual argument* or *parameter*. Thus, argument passing assigns the actual argument to the formal argument. See Figure 7.2.

FIGURE 7.2

Passing by value

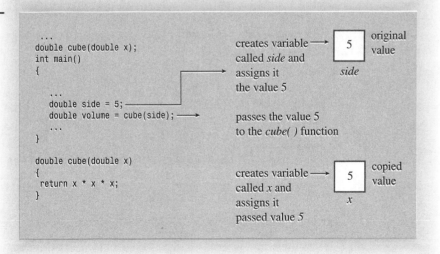

Variables, including formal parameters, declared within a function are private to the function. When a function is called, the computer allocates the memory needed for these variables. When the function terminates, the computer frees the memory that was used for those variables. (Some C++ literature refers to this allocating and freeing of memory as creating and destroying variables. That does make it sound much more exciting.) Such variables are called *local variables* because they are localized to the function. As we mentioned, this helps preserve data integrity. It also means that if you declare a variable called x in main() and another variable called x in some other function, these are two distinct, unrelated variables, much as the Albany in California is distinct from the Albany in New York. See Figure 7.3.

FIGURE 7.3
Local variables

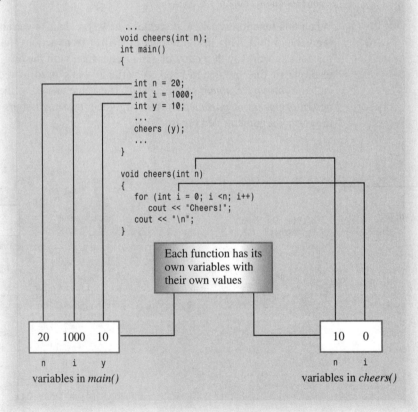

MULTIPLE ARGUMENTS

Functions can have more than one argument. In the function call, just separate the arguments with commas:

```
n_chars('R', 25);
```

This passes two arguments to the function n_chars(), which will be defined shortly.

Similarly, when you define the function, you use a comma-separated list of declarations in the function heading:

```
void n_chars(char c, int n)   // two arguments
```

This function heading states that the function n_chars() takes one type char argument and one type int argument. The variables c and n are assigned the values passed to the function. If a function takes two arguments of the same type, you have to give the type of each argument separately. You can't combine declarations the way you can when you declare regular variables:

```
void fifi(float a, float b) // declare each variable separately
void fifi(float a, b)       // NOT acceptable
```

As with other functions, just add a semicolon to get a prototype:

```
void n_chars(char c, int n); // prototype, style 1
```

As with single arguments, you don't have to use the same variable names in the prototype as in the definition, and you can omit the variable names in the prototype:

```
void n_chars(char, int);     // prototype, style 2
```

However, providing variable names can make the prototype more understandable, particularly if two parameters are the same type. Then, the names can remind you which argument is which:

```
double melon_density(double weight, double volume);
```

Listing 7.3 shows an example of a function with two arguments. It also illustrates how changing the value of a formal argument in a function has no effect on the data in the calling program.

Listing 7.3 twoarg.cpp

```
// twoarg.cpp -- a function with 2 arguments
#include <iostream>
using namespace std;
void n_chars(char, int);
int main()
{
    int times;
    char ch;

    cout << "Enter a character: ";
    cin >> ch;
    while (ch != 'q')          // q to quit
    {
```

```
        cout << "Enter an integer: ";
        cin >> times;
        n_chars(ch, times); // function with two arguments
        cout << "\nEnter another character or press the"
                " q-key to quit: ";
            cin >> ch;
    }
    cout << "The value of times is " << times << ".\n";
    cout << "Bye\n";
    return 0;
}

void n_chars(char c, int n) // displays c n times
{
    while (n-- > 0)              // continue until n reaches 0
        cout << c;
}
```

Here is a sample run:

```
Enter a character: W
Enter an integer: 50
WWWWWWWWWWWWWWWWWWWWWWWWWWWWWWWWWWWWWWWWWWWWWWWWWWWW
Enter another character or press the q-key to quit: a
Enter an integer: 20
aaaaaaaaaaaaaaaaaaaa
Enter another character or press the q-key to quit: q
The value of times is 20.
Bye
```

Program Notes

The main() function uses a while loop to keep loops fresh in your mind. Note that it uses cin >> ch to read a character rather than cin.get(ch) or cin = cin.get(). There's a good reason for doing so. The cin.get() pair of functions, you recall, read all input characters, including spaces and newlines, whereas cin >> skips spaces and newlines. When you respond to the program prompt, you have to press [ENTER] at the end of each line, thus generating a newline character. The cin >> ch approach conveniently skips over these newlines, but the cin.get() siblings read the newline following each number entered as the next character to display. You can program around this nuisance, but it's simpler to use cin as the program does.

The n_chars() function takes two arguments: a character c and an integer n. It then uses a loop to display the character the number of times the integer specifies:

```
while (n-- > 0)              // continue until n reaches 0
    cout << c;
```

Notice that the program keeps count by decrementing the n variable, where n is the formal parameter from the argument list. This variable is assigned the value of the times variable in main(). The while loop then decreases n to zero, but, as the sample run demonstrates, changing the value of n has no effect on times.

ANOTHER TWO-ARGUMENT FUNCTION

" Our function will calculate the probability that you have a winning pick. (Yes, a function that successfully predicts the winning picks themselves would be more useful, but C++, although powerful, has yet to implement psychic faculties.)"

Let's create a more ambitious function, one that performs a nontrivial calculation. Also, the function will illustrate the use of local variables other than the function's formal arguments.

Many states in the United States now sponsor a lottery with some form of Lotto game. Lotto lets you pick a certain number of choices from a card. For instance, you might get to pick six numbers from a card having 51 numbers. Then, the Lotto managers pick six numbers at random. If your choice exactly matches theirs, you win a few million dollars or so. Our function will calculate the probability that you have a winning pick. (Yes, a function that successfully predicts the winning picks themselves would be more useful, but C++, although powerful, has yet to implement psychic faculties.)

First, we need a formula. Suppose you have to pick six values out of 51. Then, mathematics says you have one chance in R of winning, where the following formula gives R:

$$ R = \frac{51 \times 50 \times 49 \times 48 \times 47 \times 46}{6 \times 5 \times 4 \times 3 \times 2 \times 1} $$

For six choices the denominator is the product of the first six integers, or six factorial. The numerator also is the product of six consecutive numbers, this time starting with 51 and going down. More generally, if you pick `picks` values out of `numbers` numbers, the denominator is `picks` factorial and the numerator is the product of `picks` integers starting with the value `numbers` and working down. You can use a `for` loop to make that calculation:

```
long double result = 1.0;
for (n = numbers, p = picks; p > 0; n--, p--)
    result = result * n / p ;
```

Rather than multiplying all the numerator terms first, the loop begins by multiplying 1.0 by the first numerator term and then dividing by the first denominator term. Then, in the next cycle, the loop multiplies and divides by the second numerator and denominator terms. This keeps the running product smaller than if you did all the multiplication first. For instance, compare

```
(10 * 9) / (2 * 1)
```

with the following:

```
(10 / 2) * (9 / 1)
```

The first evaluates to 90 / 2 and then to 45, whereas the second evaluates to 5 * 9 and then to 45. Both give the same answer, but the first method produces a larger intermediate value (90) than does the second. The more factors you have, the bigger the difference gets. For large numbers, this strategy of alternating multiplication with division can keep the calculation from overflowing the maximum possible floating-point value.

Listing 7.4 incorporates this formula into an `odds()` function. Because the number of picks and the total number of choices should be positive values, the program uses the `unsigned int` type (unsigned, for short) for those quantities. Multiplying several integers together can produce pretty large results, so `lotto.cpp` uses the `long double` type for the function's return value. Also, terms such as 49 / 6 produce a truncation error for integer types.

Remember

Some C++ implementations don't support type `long double`. If your implementation falls into that category, try ordinary `double` instead.

Listing 7.4 `lotto.cpp`

```cpp
// lotto.cpp -- odds against winning
#include <iostream>
using namespace std;
// Note: some implementations require double instead of long double
long double odds(unsigned numbers, unsigned picks);
int main()
{
    double total, choices;
    cout << "Enter total number of game card choices and\n"
            "number of picks allowed:\n";
    while ((cin >> total >> choices) && choices <= total)
    {
        cout << "You have one chance in ";
        cout << odds(total, choices);        // compute the odds
        cout << " of winning.\n";
        cout << "Next two numbers (q to quit): ";
    }
    cout << "bye\n";
    return 0;
}

// the following function calculates the odds of picking picks
// numbers correctly from numbers choices
long double odds(unsigned numbers, unsigned picks)
{
    long double result = 1.0;  // here come some local variables
    long double n;
    unsigned p;

    for (n = numbers, p = picks; p > 0; n--, p--)
        result = result * n / p ;
    return result;
}
```

Here's a sample run. Notice that increasing the number of choices on the game card greatly increases the odds against winning.

```
Enter total number of game card choices and
number of picks allowed:
49 6
```

```
You have one chance in 1.39838e+007 of winning.
Next two numbers (q to quit): 51 6
You have one chance in 1.80095e+007 of winning.
Next two numbers (q to quit): 38 6
You have one chance in 2.76068e+006 of winning.
Next two numbers (q to quit): q
bye
```

Program Notes

The odds() function illustrates two kinds of local variables you can have in a function. First, there are the formal parameters (numbers and picks), which are declared in the function heading before the opening brace. Then come the other local variables (result, n, and p). They are declared in between the braces bounding the function definition. The main difference between the formal parameters and the other local variables is that the formal parameters get their values from the function that calls odds(), whereas the other variables get values from within the function.

Functions and Arrays

So far the sample functions have been simple, using only the basic types for arguments and return values. But functions can be the key to handling more involved types, such as arrays and structures. Let's take a look now at how arrays and functions get along with each other.

Suppose you use an array to keep track of how many cookies each person has eaten at the family picnic. (Each array index corresponds to a person, and the value of the element corresponds to the number of cookies that person ate.) Now you want the total. That's easy to do; just use a loop to add all the array elements. But adding array elements is such a common task that it makes sense to design a function to do the job. Then, you won't have to write a new loop every time you have to sum an array.

Let's consider what the function interface involves. Because the function calculates a sum, it should return the answer. If you keep your cookies intact, you can use a function with a type int return value. So that the function knows what array to sum, you want to pass the array name as an argument. And to make the function general so that it is not restricted to an array of a particular size, you pass the size of the array. The only new ingredient here is that you have to declare that one of the formal arguments is an array name. Let's see what that and the rest of the function heading look like:

```
int sum_arr(int arr[], int n) // arr = array name, n = size
```

This looks plausible. The brackets seem to indicate that arr is an array, and the fact that the brackets are empty seems to indicate you can use the function with an array of any size. But things are not always what they seem: arr is not really an array; it's a pointer! The good news is that you can write the rest of the function just as if arr were an array. First, let's see that this approach works, and then let's look into why it works.

> *The key is that C++, like C, in most contexts treats the name of an array as if it were a pointer.*

Listing 7.5 illustrates using a pointer as if it were an array name. The program initializes the array to some values and uses the `sum_arr()` function to calculate the sum. Note that the `sum_arr()` function uses `arr` as if it were an array name.

Listing 7.5 arrfun1.cpp

```
// arrfun1.cpp -- functions with an array argument
#include <iostream>
using namespace std;
const int ArSize = 8;
int sum_arr(int arr[], int n);        // prototype
int main()
{
    int cookies[ArSize] = {1,2,4,8,16,32,64,128};
// some systems require preceding int with static to
// enable array initialization

    int sum = sum_arr(cookies, ArSize);
    cout << "Total cookies eaten: " << sum <<  "\n";
    return 0;
}

// return the sum of an integer array
int sum_arr(int arr[], int n)
{
    int total = 0;

    for (int i = 0; i < n; i++)
        total = total + arr[i];
    return total;
}
```

Here is the program output:

```
Total cookies eaten: 255
```

As you can see, the program works. Now let's look at why it works.

ARRAYS AND POINTERS (AGAIN)

The key is that C++, like C, in most contexts treats the name of an array as if it were a pointer. Recall from Chapter 4 that C++ interprets an array name as the address of its first element:

```
cookies == &cookies[0]  // array name is address of first element
```

(There are two exceptions to this rule. First, the array declaration uses the array name to label the storage. Second, applying `sizeof` to an array name yields the size of the whole array, in bytes.)

Listing 7.5 makes the following function call:

```
int sum = sum_arr(cookies, ArSize);
```

Here `cookies` is the name of an array, hence by C++ rules `cookies` is the address of its first element. The function passes an address. Because the array has type `int` elements, `cookies` must be type pointer-to-int, or `int *`. That suggests that the correct function heading should be this:

```
int sum_arr(int * arr, int n) // arr = array name, n = size
```

Here `int *arr` has replaced `int arr[]`. It turns out that both headings are correct, for in C++ the notations `int *arr` and `int arr[]` have the identical meaning when (and *only* when) used in a function heading or function prototype. Both mean that `arr` is a pointer-to-int. However, the array notation version (`int arr[]`) symbolically reminds us that `arr` not only points to an `int`, it points to the first `int` in an array of `int`s. We'll use the array notation when the pointer is to the first element of an array, and we'll use the pointer notation when the pointer is to an isolated value. Don't forget that the notations `int *arr` and `int arr[]` are not synonymous in any other context. For instance, you can't use the notation `int tip[]` to declare a pointer in the body of a function.

Given that the variable `arr` actually is a pointer, the rest of the function makes sense. As you might recall from the discussion of dynamic arrays in Chapter 4, you can use the bracket array notation equally well with array names or with pointers to access elements of an array. Whether `arr` is a pointer or an array name, the expression `arr[3]` means the fourth element of the array. And it probably will do no harm at this point to remind you of the following two identities:

```
arr[i] == *(ar + i)     // values in two notations
&arr[i] == ar + I       // addresses in two notations
```

Remember, adding 1 to a pointer, including an array name, actually adds a value equal to the size, in bytes, of the type to which the pointer points. Pointer addition and array subscription are two equivalent ways of counting elements from the beginning of an array.

IMPLICATIONS OF USING ARRAYS AS ARGUMENTS

Let's look at the implications of Listing 7.5. The function call `sum_arr(cookies, ArSize)` passes the address of the first element of the `cookies` array and the number of elements of the array to the `sum_arr()` function. The `sum_arr()` function assigns the `cookies` address to the pointer variable `arr` and assigns `ArSize` to the `int` variable n. This means Listing 7.5 doesn't really pass the array contents to the function. Instead, it tells the function where the array is (the address), what kind of elements it has (the type), and how many elements it has (the n variable). See Figure 7.4. Armed with this information, the function then uses the original array. Pass an ordinary variable, and the function works with a copy. But pass an array, and the function works with the original. Actually, this difference doesn't violate C++'s pass-by-value approach. The `sum_arr()` function still passes a value that's assigned to a new variable. But that value is a single address, not the contents of an array.

Is the correspondence between array names and pointers a good thing? Indeed, it is. The design decision to use array addresses as arguments saves the time and memory needed to copy an entire array. The overhead for using copies can be prohibitive if you're working with large arrays. Not only does a program need more computer memory, but it has to spend time copying large blocks of data. On the other hand, working with the original data raises the possibility of inadvertent data corruption. That's a real problem in classic C, but ANSI C and C++'s const modifier provides a remedy. We'll soon show an example. But first, let's alter Listing 7.5 to illustrate some points about how array functions operate. Listing 7.6 demonstrates that cookies and arr have the same value. It also shows how the pointer concept makes the sum_arr function more versatile than it may have appeared at first.

Listing 7.6 arrfun2.cpp

```cpp
// arrfun2.cpp -- functions with an array argument
#include <iostream>
using namespace std;
const int ArSize = 8;
int sum_arr(int arr[], int n);
int main()
{
    int cookies[ArSize] = {1,2,4,8,16,32,64,128};
//  some systems require preceding int with static to
//  enable array initialization

    cout << cookies << " = array address, ";
//  some systems require a type cast: unsigned (cookies)

    cout << sizeof cookies << " = sizeof cookies\n";
    int sum = sum_arr(cookies, ArSize);
    cout << "Total cookies eaten: " << sum <<  "\n";
    sum = sum_arr(cookies, 3);        // a lie
    cout << "First three eaters ate " << sum << " cookies.\n";
    sum = sum_arr(cookies + 4, 4);    // another lie
    cout << "Last four eaters ate " << sum << " cookies.\n";
    return 0;
}

// return the sum of an integer array
int sum_arr(int arr[], int n)
{
    int total = 0;
    cout << arr << " = arr, ";
// some systems require a type cast: unsigned (arr)

    cout << sizeof arr << " = sizeof arr\n";
    for (int i = 0; i < n; i++)
        total = total + arr[i];
    return total;
}
```

FIGURE 7.4

Telling a function about an array

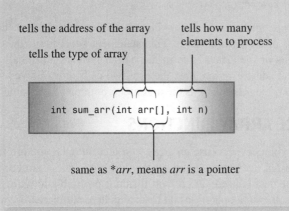

Here's the output (the address values and the array and integer sizes will vary from system to system):

```
0068FDD4 = array address, 32 = sizeof cookies
0068FDD4 = arr, 4 = sizeof arr
Total cookies eaten: 255
0068FDD4 = arr, 4 = sizeof arr
First three eaters ate 7 cookies.
0068FDE4 = arr, 4 = sizeof arr
Last four eaters ate 240 cookies.
```

Program Notes

Listing 7.6 illustrates some very interesting points about array functions. First, note that `cookies` and `arr` both evaluate to the same address, exactly as claimed. But `sizeof cookies` is 16, whereas `sizeof arr` is only 4. That's because `sizeof cookies` is the size of the whole array, whereas `sizeof arr` is the size of the pointer variable. (This program execution takes place on a system using 4-byte addresses.) By the way, that's why you have to pass explicitly the size of the array rather than use `sizeof arr` in `sum_arr()`.

Because the only way `sum_arr()` knows the number of elements in the array is through what you tell it with the second argument, you can lie to the function. For instance, the second time the program uses the function, it makes this call:

```
sum = sum_arr(cookies, 3);
```

By telling the function that `cookies` has but three elements, you get the function to calculate the sum of the first three elements.

Why stop there? You also can lie about where the array starts:

```
sum = sum_arr(cookies + 4, 4);
```

Because `cookies` acts as the address of the first element, `cookies + 4` acts as the address of the fifth element. This statement sums the fifth, sixth, seventh, and eighth elements of the array. Note in the output how the third call to the function assigns a different address to `arr` than the first two calls did. And yes, you can use `&cookies[4]` instead of `cookies + 4` as the argument; both mean the same thing.

MORE ARRAY FUNCTIONS

When you choose to use an array to represent data, you are making a design decision. But design decisions should go beyond how data is stored; they also should involve how the data is used. Often, you'll find it profitable to write specific functions to handle specific data operations. (The profits here are increased program reliability, ease of modification, and ease of debugging.) Also, when you begin integrating storage properties with operations when you think about a program, you are taking an important step toward the OOP mind-set; that, too, might prove profitable in the future.

Let's examine a simple case. Suppose you want to use an array to keep track of the dollar values of your real estate. (If necessary, suppose you have real estate.) You have to decide what type to use. Certainly, `double` is less restrictive in its range than `int` or `long`, and it provides enough significant digits to represent the values precisely. Next, you have to decide on the number of array elements. (With dynamic arrays created with `new`, you can put off that decision, but let's keep things simple.) Suppose that you have no more than five properties, so you can use an array of five `doubles`.

Now consider the possible operations you might want to execute with the real estate array. Two very basic ones are reading values into the array and displaying the array contents. Let's add one more operation to the list: reassessing the value of the properties. For simplicity, assume that all your properties increase or decrease in value at the same rate. (Remember, this is a book on C++, not on real estate management.) Next, fit a function to each operation and then write the code accordingly. We go through these steps next.

Filling the Array

Because a function with an array name argument accesses the original array, not a copy, you can use a function call to assign values to array elements. One argument to the function will be the name of the array to be filled. In general, a program might manage more than one person's investments, hence more than one array, so you won't want to build the array size into the function. Instead, pass the array size as a second argument, as in the previous example. Also, it's possible that you might want to quit reading data before filling the array, so you want to build that feature into the function. Because you might enter fewer than the maximum number of elements, it makes sense to have the function return the actual number of values entered. These considerations suggest the following function prototype:

```
int fill_array(double ar[], int limit);
```

The function takes an array name argument and an argument specifying the maximum number of items to be read, and the function returns the actual number of items read. For instance, if you use this function with an array of five elements, you pass 5 as the second argument. If you enter only three values, the function returns 3.

You can use a loop to read successive values into the array, but how can you terminate the loop early? One way is use a special value to indicate the end of input. Because no property should have a negative value, you can use a negative number to indicate the end of input. Given this, you can code the function as follows:

```
int fill_array(double ar[], int limit)
{
    double temp;
    int i;
    for (i = 0; i < limit; i++)
    {
        cout << "Enter value #" << i + 1 << ": ";
        cin >> temp;
        if (temp < 0)       // signal to terminate
            break;
        ar[i] = temp;
    }
    return i;
}
```

Note that the code includes a prompt to the user in the program. If the user enters a non-negative value, the value is assigned to the array. Otherwise, the loop terminates. If the user enters only valid values, the loop terminates after it reads limit values. The last thing the loop does is increment i, so after the loop terminates, i is 1 greater than the last array index, hence it's equal to the number of filled elements. The function then returns that value.

Showing the Array and Protecting It with `const`

Building a function to display the array contents is simple. You pass the name of the array and the number of filled elements to the function, which then uses a loop to display each element. But there is another consideration—guaranteeing that the display function doesn't alter the original array. Unless the purpose of a function is to alter data passed to it, you should safeguard it from doing so. That protection comes automatically with ordinary arguments because C++ passes them by value and the function works with a copy. But functions that use an array work with the original. After all, that's why the fill_array() function is able to do its job. To keep a function from accidentally altering the contents of an array argument, you can use the keyword const (discussed in Chapter 3, "Dealing with Data") when you declare the formal argument:

```
void show_array(const double ar[], int n);
```

The declaration states that the pointer ar points to constant data. This means that you can't use ar to change the data. That is, you can use a value such as ar[0], but you can't change that value. Note that this doesn't mean that the original array must be constant; it just means that you can't use ar in the show_array() function to change the data. Thus, show_array() treats the array as read-only data. Suppose you accidentally violate this restriction by doing something like the following in the show_array() function:

```
ar[0] += 10;
```

Then, the compiler will put a stop to your wrongful ways. Borland C++, for example, gives an error message like this (edited slightly):

```
Cannot modify a const object in function
        show_array(const double *,int)
```

The message reminds us that C++ interprets the declaration const double ar[] to mean const double *ar. Thus, the declaration really says that ar points to a constant value. We'll discuss this in detail when we finish with the current example. Meanwhile, here is the code for the show_array() function:

```
void show_array(const double ar[], int n)
{
    for (int i = 0; i < n; i++)
    {
        cout << "Property #" << i + 1 << ": $";
        cout << ar[i] << "\n";
    }
}
```

Modifying the Array

The third operation for our array is multiplying each element by the same revaluation factor. You need to pass three arguments to the function: the factor, the array, and the number of elements. No return value is needed, so the function can look like this:

```
void reassess(double r, double ar[], int n)
{
    for (int i = 0; i < n; i++)
        ar[i] *= r;
}
```

Because this function is supposed to alter the array values, you don't use const when you declare ar.

Putting the Pieces Together

Now that we've defined the data type in terms of how it's stored (an array) and how it's used (three functions), we can put together a program that uses the design. Because we've already built all the array-handling tools, we've greatly simplified programming main(). Most of the remaining programming work consists of having main() call the functions we've just developed. Listing 7.7 shows the result.

Listing 7.7 arrfun3.cpp

```cpp
// arrfun3.cpp -- array functions and const
#include <iostream>
using namespace std;
const int Max = 5;

// function prototypes
int fill_array(double ar[], int limit);
void show_array(const double ar[], int n);  // don't change data
void reassess(double r, double ar[], int n);

int main()
{
    double properties[Max];

    int size = fill_array(properties, Max);
    show_array(properties, size);
    cout << "Enter reassessment rate: ";
    double rate;
    cin >> rate;
    reassess(rate, properties, size);
    show_array(properties, size);
    return 0;
}

int fill_array(double ar[], int limit)
{
    double temp;
    int i;
    for (i = 0; i < limit; i++)
    {
        cout << "Enter value #" << i + 1 << ": ";
        cin >> temp;
        if (temp < 0)
            break;
        ar[i] = temp;
    }
    return i;
}

// the following function can use, but not alter,
// the array whose address is ar
void show_array(const double ar[], int n)
{
    for (int i = 0; i < n; i++)
    {
        cout << "Property #" << i + 1 << ": $";
        cout << ar[i] << "\n";
    }
}

// multiplies each element of ar[] by r
void reassess(double r, double ar[], int n)
{
    for (int i = 0; i < n; i++)
        ar[i] *= r;
}
```

Here are two sample runs. Recall that input should quit when the user enters five properties or enters a negative number, whichever comes first. The first example illustrates reaching the five-property limit, and the second example illustrates entering a negative value.

```
Enter value #1: 100000
Enter value #2: 80000
Enter value #3: 222000
Enter value #4: 240000
Enter value #5: 118000
Property #1: $100000
Property #2: $80000
Property #3: $222000
Property #4: $240000
Property #5: $118000
Enter reassessment rate: 1.10
Property #1: $110000
Property #2: $88000
Property #3: $244200
Property #4: $264000
Property #5: $129800

Enter value #1: 200000
Enter value #2: 84000
Enter value #3: 160000
Enter value #4: -2
Property #1: $200000
Property #2: $84000
Property #3: $160000
Enter reassessment rate: 1.20
Property #1: $240000
Property #2: $100800
Property #3: $192000
```

Program Notes

We've already discussed the important programming details, so let's reflect on the process. We began by thinking about the data type and designed appropriate functions to handle the data. Then, we assembled these functions into a program. This sometimes is called bottom-up programming, because the design process moves from the component parts to the whole. This approach is well suited to OOP, which concentrates on data representation and manipulation first. Traditional procedural programming, on the other hand, leans toward top-down programming, in which you develop a modular grand design first and then turn your attention to the details. Both methods are useful, and both lead to modular programs.

POINTERS AND const

Using const with pointers has some subtle aspects (pointers always seem to have subtle aspects), so let's take a closer look. You can use the const keyword two different ways with pointers. The first way is to make a pointer point to a constant object, and that prevents you from using the pointer to change the pointed-to value. The second way is to make the pointer itself constant, and that prevents you from changing where the pointer points. Now for the details.

First, let's declare a pointer pt that points to a constant:

```
int age = 39;
const int * pt = &age;
```

This declaration states that pt points to a const int (39, in this case). Therefore, you can't use pt to change that value. In other words, the value *pt is const and cannot be modified:

```
*pt += 1;           // INVALID because pt points to a const int
cin >> *pt;         // INVALID for the same reason
```

Now for a subtle point. Our declaration for pt doesn't necessarily mean that the value to which it points is really a constant; it just means the value is a constant insofar as pt is concerned. For instance, pt points to age, and age is not const. You can change the value of age directly by using the age variable, but you can't change the value indirectly via the pt pointer:

```
*pt = 20;           // INVALID because pt points to a const int
age = 20;           // VALID because age is not declared to be const
```

In the past, we've assigned the address of a regular variable to a regular pointer. Now we've assigned the address of a regular variable to a pointer-to-const. That leaves two other possibilities: assigning the address of a const variable to a pointer-to-const and assigning the address of a const to a regular pointer. Are they both possible? The first is, and the second isn't:

```
const float g_earth = 9.80;
const float * pe = &g_earth;    // VALID

const float g_moon = 1.63;
float * pm = &g_moon;           // INVALID
```

For the first case, you can use neither g_earth nor pe to change the value 9.80. C++ doesn't allow the second case for a simple reason—if you can assign the address of g_moon to pm, then you can cheat and use pm to alter the value of g_moon. That makes a mockery of g_moon's const status, so C++ prohibits you from assigning the address of a const to a non-const pointer.

Remember

You can assign either the address of const data or non-const data to a pointer-to-const, but you only can assign the address of non-const data to a non-const pointer.

Suppose that you have an array of const data:

```
const int months[12] = {31,28,31,30,31,30, 31, 31,30,31,30,31};
```

The prohibition against assigning the address of a constant array means that you cannot pass the array name as an argument to a function using a non-constant formal argument:

```
int sum(int arr[], int n);  // should have been const int arr[]
...
int j = sum(months, 12);    // not allowed
```

The function call attempts to assign a `const` pointer (`months`) to a non-const pointer (`arr`), and the compiler disallows the function call.

USE **const** WHEN YOU CAN

There are two strong reasons to declare pointer arguments as pointers to constant data:

🖐 This protects you against programming errors that inadvertently alter data.

🖐 Using const allows a function to process both const and non-const actual arguments, whereas a function omitting const in the prototype can accept only non-const data.

You should declare formal pointer arguments as pointers to const whenever it's appropriate to do so.

Now another subtle point: the declarations

```
int age = 39;
const int * pt = &age;
```

only prevent you from changing the value to which pt points, which is 39. It doesn't prevent you from changing the value of pt itself. That is, you can assign a new address to pt:

```
int sage = 80;
pt = &sage; // okay to point to another location
```

But you still can't use pt to change the value to which it points (now 80).

The second way to use const makes it impossible to change the value of the pointer itself:

```
int sloth = 3;
const int * ps = &sloth;      // a pointer to const int
int * const finger = &sloth;  // a const pointer to int
```

Note that the last declaration has repositioned the keyword const. This form of declaration constrains finger to point only to sloth. However, it does allow you to use finger to alter the value of sloth. The middle declaration does not allow you to use ps to alter the value of sloth, but it does permit you to have ps point to another location. In short, finger and *ps are both const, and *finger and ps are not const. See Figure 7.5.

FIGURE 7.5

*Pointers-to-const and
const pointers.*

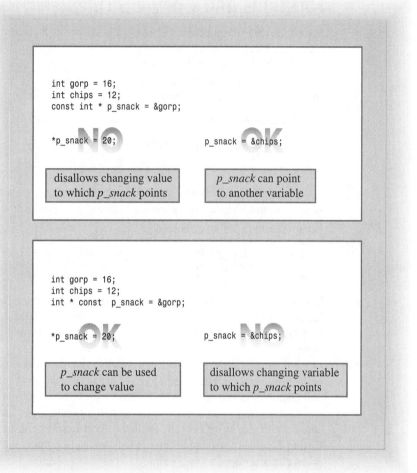

If you like, you can declare a const pointer to a const object:

```
double trouble = 2.0E30;
const double * const stick = &trouble;
```

Here stick can point only to trouble, and stick cannot be used to change the value of trouble. In short, both stick and *stick are const.

Usually you use the pointer-to-const form to protect data when you pass pointers as function arguments. For example, recall the show_array() prototype from Listing 7.5:

```
void show_array(const double ar[], int n);
```

Using const in that declaration means that show_array() cannot alter the values in any array passed to it.

Functions and C-Style Strings

A C-style string, you recall, consists of a series of characters terminated by the null character. Much of what you've learned about designing array functions applies to string functions, too. But there are a few special twists to strings that we unravel now. Suppose that you want to pass a string as an argument to a function. You have three choices for representing a string:

- An array of char
- A quoted string constant (also called a string literal)
- A pointer-to-char set to the address of a string

All three choices, however, are type pointer-to-char (more concisely, type char *), so you can use all three as arguments to string-processing functions:

```
char ghost[15] = "galloping";
char * str = "galumphing";
int n1 = strlen(ghost);          // ghost is &ghost[0]
int n2 = strlen(str);            // pointer to char
int n3 = strlen("gamboling");    // address of string
```

Informally, you can say you're passing a string as an argument, but you're really passing the address of the first character in the string. This implies that a string function prototype should use type char * as the type for the formal parameter representing a string.

One important difference between a string and a regular array is that the string has a built-in terminating character. (Recall that a char array containing characters but no null character is just an array and not a string.) That means you don't have to pass the size of the string as an argument. Instead, the function can use a loop to examine each character in the string in turn until the loop reaches the terminating null character. Listing 7.8 illustrates that approach with a function that counts the number of times a given character appears in a string.

Listing 7.8 strgfun.cpp

```
// strgfun.cpp -- functions with a string argument
#include <iostream>
using namespace std;
int c_in_str(const char * str, char ch);
int main()
{
    char mmm[15] = "minimum";       // string in an array
// some systems require preceding char with static to
// enable array initialization

    char *wail = "ululate";         // wail points to string

    int ms = c_in_str(mmm, 'm');
    int us = c_in_str(wail, 'u');
    cout << ms << " m characters in " << mmm << "\n";
    cout << us << " u characters in " << wail << "\n";
    return 0;
```

```
}

// this function counts the number of ch characters
// in the string str
int c_in_str(const char * str, char ch)
{
    int count = 0;

    while (*str)            // quit when *str is '\0'
    {
        if (*str == ch)
            count++;
        str++;              // move pointer to next char
    }
    return count;
}
```

Here's the output:

```
3 m characters in minimum
2 u characters in ululate
```

Program Notes

Because the `c_int_str()` function shouldn't alter the original string, it uses the `const` modifier when it declares the formal parameter `str`. Then, if you mistakenly let the function alter part of the string, the compiler catches your error. Of course, you can use array notation instead to declare `str` in the function heading:

```
int c_in_str(const char str[], char ch) // also okay
```

However, using pointer notation reminds you that the argument doesn't have to be the name of an array but can be some other form of pointer.

The function itself demonstrates a standard way to process the characters in a string:

```
while (*str)
{
    statements
    str++;
}
```

Initially, `str` points to the first character in the string, so `*str` represents the first character itself. For instance, immediately after the first function call, `*str` has the value `m`, the first character in minimum. As long as the character is not the null character (`\0`), `*str` is nonzero, so the loop continues. At the end of each loop the expression `str++` increments the pointer by one byte so that it points to the next character in the string. Eventually, `str` points to the terminating null character, making `*str` equal to `0`, which is the numeric code for the null character. That condition terminates the loop. (Why are string-processing functions ruthless? Because they stop at nothing.)

FUNCTIONS THAT RETURN STRINGS

Now suppose you want to write a function that returns a string. Well, a function can't do that. But it can return the address of a string, and that's even better. Listing 7.9 for instance, defines a function called `buildstr()` that returns a pointer. This function takes two arguments: a character and a number. Using `new`, the function creates a string whose length equals the number, and then it initializes each element to the character. Then, it returns a pointer to the new string.

Listing 7.9 strgback.cpp

```cpp
// strgback.cpp -- a function returning a pointer to char
#include <iostream>
using namespace std;
char * buildstr(char c, int n);      // prototype
int main()
{
    int times;
    char ch;

    cout << "Enter a character: ";
    cin >> ch;
    cout << "Enter an integer: ";
    cin >> times;
    char *ps = buildstr(ch, times);
    cout << ps << "\n";
    delete [] ps;                    // free memory
    ps = buildstr('+', 20);          // reuse pointer
    cout << ps << "-DONE-" << ps << "\n";
    delete [] ps;                    // free memory
    return 0;
}

// builds string made of n c characters
char * buildstr(char c, int n)
{
    char * pstr = new char[n + 1];
    pstr[n] = '\0';                  // terminate string
    while (n— > 0)
        pstr[n] = c;                 // fill rest of string
    return pstr;
}
```

Here's a sample run:

```
Enter a character: V
Enter an integer: 46
VVVVVVVVVVVVVVVVVVVVVVVVVVVVVVVVVVVVVVVVVVVVVVVV
++++++++++++++++++++-DONE-++++++++++++++++++++
```

Program Notes

To create a string of n visible characters, you need storage for n + 1 characters in order to have space for the null character. So the function asks for n + 1 bytes to hold the string. Next, it sets the final byte to the null character. Then, it fills in the rest of the array from back to front. The loop

```
while (n-- > 0)
    pstr[n] = c;
```

cycles n times as n decreases to zero, filling n elements. At the start of the final cycle, n has the value 1. Because n-- means use the value and then decrement it, the while loop test condition compares 1 to 0, finds the test to be true, and continues. But after making the test, the function decrements n to 0, so pstr[0] is the last element set to c. The reason for filling the string from back to front instead of front to back is to avoid using an additional variable. Using the other order would involve something like this:

```
int i = 0;
while (i < n)
    pstr[i++] = c;
```

Note that the variable pstr is local to the buildstr function, so when that function terminates, the memory used for pstr (but not for the string) is freed. But because the function returns the value of pstr, the program is able to access the new string through the ps pointer in main().

The program uses delete to free memory used for the string after the string is no longer needed. Then, it reuses ps to point to the new block of memory obtained for the next string and frees that memory. The disadvantage to this kind of design (having a function return a pointer to memory allocated by new) is that it makes it the programmer's responsibility to remember to use delete. The auto_ptr template, discussed in Chapter 15, "The String Class and the Standard Template Library," can help automate the process.

> *Although structure variables resemble arrays in that both can hold several data items, structure variables behave like basic, single-valued variables when it comes to functions. You can pass structures by value, [and] a function can return a structure.*

Functions and Structures

Let's move from arrays to structures. It's easier to write functions for structures than for arrays. Although structure variables resemble arrays in that both can hold several data items, structure variables behave like basic, single-valued variables when it comes to functions. You can pass structures by value, just as you do with ordinary variables. In that case, the function works with a copy of the original structure. Also, a function can return a structure. There's no funny business like the name of an array being the address of its first element. The name of a structure is simply the name of the structure, and if you want its address, you have to use the & address operator.

The most direct way to program by using structures is to treat them as you would treat the basic types; that is, pass them as arguments and use them, if necessary, as return values. However, there is one disadvantage to passing structures by value. If the structure is large, the space and effort involved in making a copy of a structure can increase memory requirements and slow the system down. For those reasons (and because, at first, C didn't allow the passing of structures by value), many C programmers prefer passing the address of a structure and then using a pointer to access the structure contents. C++ provides a third alternative, called passing by reference, that we discuss in Chapter 8. We examine the other two choices now, beginning with passing and returning entire structures.

PASSING AND RETURNING STRUCTURES

Passing structures by value makes the most sense when the structure is relatively compact, so let's develop a couple of examples along those lines. The first example deals with travel time (not to be confused with time travel). Some maps will tell you that it is three hours, 50 minutes, from Thunder Falls to Bingo City and one hour, 25 minutes, from Bingo City to Grotesquo. You can use a structure to represent such times, using one member for the hour value and a second member for the minute value. Adding two times is a little tricky because you might have to transfer some of the minutes to the hours part. For instance, the two preceding times sum to four hours, 75 minutes, which should be converted to five hours, 15 minutes. Let's develop a structure to represent a time value and then a function that takes two such structures as arguments and returns a structure that represents their sum.

Defining the structure is simple:

```
struct travel_time
{
    int hours;
    int mins;
};
```

Next, consider the prototype for a sum() function that returns the sum of two such structures. The return value should be type travel_time, and so should the two arguments. Thus, the prototype should look like this:

```
travel_time sum(travel_time t1, travel_time t2);
```

To add two times, first add the minute members. Integer division by 60 yields the number of hours to carry over, and the modulus operator (%) yields the number of minutes left. Listing 7.10 incorporates this approach into the sum() function and adds a show_time() function to display the contents of a travel_time structure.

Listing 7.10 travel.cpp

```
// travel.cpp -- using structures with functions
#include <iostream>
using namespace std;
struct travel_time
{
    int hours;
    int mins;
};
const int Mins_per_hr = 60;

travel_time sum(travel_time t1, travel_time t2);
void show_time(travel_time t);

int main()
{
    travel_time day1 = {5, 45};    // 5 hrs, 45 min
```

```
    travel_time day2 = {4, 55};     // 4 hrs, 55 min

    travel_time trip = sum(day1, day2);
    cout << "Two-day total: ";
    show_time(trip);

    travel_time day3= {4, 32};
    cout << "Three-day total: ";
    show_time(sum(trip, day3));

    return 0;
}
travel_time sum(travel_time t1, travel_time t2)
{
    travel_time total;

    total.mins = (t1.mins + t2.mins) % Mins_per_hr;
    total.hours = t1.hours + t2.hours +
                 (t1.mins + t2.mins) / Mins_per_hr;
    return total;
}

void show_time(travel_time t)
{
    cout << t.hours << " hours, "
         << t.mins << " minutes\n";
}
```

Here, `travel_time` acts just like a standard type name; you can use it to declare variables, function return types, and function argument types. Because variables like `total` and `t1` are `travel_time` structures, you can apply the dot membership operator to them. Note that because the `sum()` function returns a `travel_time` structure, you can use it as an argument for the `show_time()` function. Because C++ functions, by default, pass arguments by value, the `show_time(sum(trip, day3))` function call first evaluates the `sum(trip, day3)` function call in order to find its return value. The `show_time()` call then passes `sum()`'s return value, not the function itself, to `show_time()`. Here's the program output:

```
Two-day total: 10 hours, 40 minutes
Three-day total: 15 hours, 12 minutes
```

ANOTHER EXAMPLE

Much of what you learn about functions and C++ structures carries over to C++ classes, so it's worth looking at a second example. This time we deal with space instead of time. In particular, the example defines two structures representing two different ways of describing positions and then develops functions to convert one form to the other and show the result. This example is a bit more mathematical than the last, but you don't have to follow the mathematics to follow the C++.

Suppose you want to describe the position of a point on the screen or a location on a map relative to some origin. One way is to state the horizontal offset and the vertical offset of the point from the origin. Traditionally, mathematicians use the symbol x to represent the horizontal offset and y to represent the vertical offset. See Figure 7.6. Together, x and y constitute rectangular coordinates. You can define a structure consisting of two coordinates to represent a position:

```
struct rect
{
    double x;           // horizontal distance from origin
    double y;           // vertical distance from origin
};
```

A second way to describe the position of a point is to state how far it is from the origin and in what direction it is (for example, 40 degrees north of east). Traditionally, mathematicians measure the angle counterclockwise from the positive horizontal axis. See Figure 7.7. The distance and angle together constitute polar coordinates. You can define a second structure to represent this view of a position:

```
struct Polar
{
    double distance;    // distance from origin
    double angle;       // direction from origin
};
```

FIGURE 7.6
Rectangular coordinates

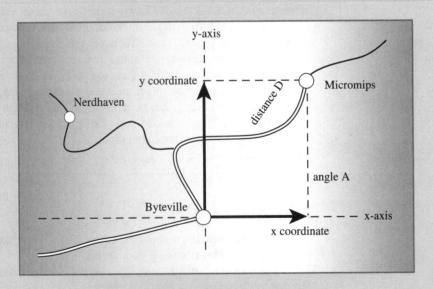

polar coordinates of Micromips relative to Byteville

FIGURE 7.7
Polar coordinates

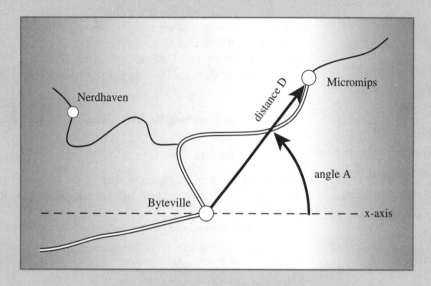

polar coordinates of Micromips relative to Byteville

Let's construct a function that displays the contents of a type `Polar` structure. The math functions in the C++ library assume angles are in radians, so we measure angles in that unit. But for display purposes, we convert radian measure to degrees. That means multiplying by $180/\pi$, which is approximately 57.29577951. Here's the function:

```
// show polar coordinates, converting angle to degrees
void show_polar (Polar dapos)
{
    const double Rad_to_deg = 57.29577951;

    cout << "distance = " << dapos.distance;
    cout << ", angle = " << dapos.angle * Rad_to_deg;
    cout << " degrees\n";
}
```

Notice that the formal variable is type `Polar`. When you pass a `Polar` structure to this function, the structure contents are copied into the `dapos` structure, and the function then uses that copy in its work. Because `dapos` is a structure, the function uses the membership (dot) operator (see Chapter 4) to identify structure members.

Next, let's try something more ambitious and write a function that converts rectangular coordinates to polar coordinates. Write the function so that it passes a rect structure to the function and have the function return a Polar structure to the calling program. This involves using functions from the math library, so the program has to include the math.h header file. Also, on some systems you have to tell the compiler to load the math library (see Chapter 1, "Getting Started"). You can use the Pythagorean theorem to get the distance from the horizontal and vertical components:

```
distance = sqrt( x * x + y * y)
```

The atan2() function from the math library calculates the angle from the x and y values:

```
angle = atan2(y, x)
```

(There's also an atan() function, but it doesn't distinguish between angles 180 degrees apart. That uncertainty is no more desirable in a math function than it is in a wilderness guide.)

Given these formulas, you can write the function as follows:

```
// convert rectangular to polar coordinates
Polar rect_to_polar(rect xypos)    // type polar
{
    Polar answer;

    answer.distance =
        sqrt( xypos.x * xypos.x + xypos.y * xypos.y);
    answer.angle = atan2(xypos.y, xypos.x);
    return answer;        // returns a Polar structure
}
```

Now that the functions are ready, writing the rest of the program is straightforward. Listing 7.11 presents the result.

Listing 7.11 strctfun.cpp

```
// strctfun.cpp -- functions with a structure argument
#include <iostream>
#include <cmath>
using namespace std;

// structure templates
struct Polar
{
    double distance;// distance from origin
    double angle;   // direction from origin
};
struct rect
{
    double x;       // horizontal distance from origin
    double y;       // vertical distance from origin
};

// prototypes
Polar rect_to_polar(rect xypos);
void show_polar(Polar dapos);
```

```
int main()
{
    rect rplace;
    Polar pplace;

    cout << "Enter the x and y values: ";
    while (cin >> rplace.x >> rplace.y)  // slick use of cin
    {
        pplace = rect_to_polar(rplace);
        show_polar(pplace);
        cout << "Next two numbers (q to quit): ";
    }
    return 0;
}

// convert rectangular to polar coordinates
Polar rect_to_polar(rect xypos)
{
    Polar answer;

    answer.distance =
        sqrt( xypos.x * xypos.x + xypos.y * xypos.y);
    answer.angle = atan2(xypos.y, xypos.x);
    return answer;        // returns a Polar structure
}

// show polar coordinates, converting angle to degrees
void show_polar (Polar dapos)
{
    const double Rad_to_deg = 57.29577951;

    cout << "distance = " << dapos.distance;
    cout << ", angle = " << dapos.angle * Rad_to_deg;
    cout << " degrees\n";
}
```

Remember

> **S**ome implementations still use `math.h` instead of the newer `cmath` header
> file. Some compilers require explicit instructions to search the math library. For
> instance, older versions of g++ use this command line:
>   `g++ structfun.C -lm`

Here is a sample run:

```
Enter the x and y values: 30 40
distance = 50, angle = 53.1301 degrees
Next two numbers (q to quit): -100 100
distance = 141.421, angle = 135 degrees
Next two numbers (q to quit): q
```

Program Notes

We've already discussed the two functions, so let's review how the program uses `cin`
to control a `while` loop:

```
while (cin >> rplace.x >> rplace.y)
```

Recall that `cin` is an object of the `istream` class. The extraction operator (`>>`) is designed in such a way that `cin >> rplace.x` also is an object of that type. As you'll see in Chapter 10, "Working with Classes," class operators are implemented with functions. What really happens when you use `cin >> rplace.x` is that the program calls a function that returns a type `istream` value. Apply the extraction operator to the `cin >> rplace.x` object (as in `cin >> rplace.x >> rplace.y`), and you again get an object of the `istream` class. Thus, the entire `while` loop test expression eventually evaluates to `cin`, which, as you may recall, when used in the context of a test expression is converted to a `bool` value of `true` or `false`, depending on whether input succeeded or not. In this loop, for example, `cin` expects the user to enter two numbers. If, instead, you enter q, as we did, `cin >>` recognizes that q is not a number. It leaves the q in the input queue and returns a value that's converted to `false`, terminating the loop.

Compare this approach for reading numbers to the one in Listing 7.7:

```
for (i = 0; i < limit; i++)
    {
        cout << "Enter value #" << i + 1 << ": ";
        cin >> temp;
        if (temp < 0)
            break;
        ar[i] = temp;
    }
```

To terminate that loop early, you enter a negative number. That restricts input to non-negative values. That restriction fits the needs of that program, but more typically you would want a means of terminating a loop that didn't exclude certain numeric values. Using `cin >>` as the test condition eliminates such restrictions, for it accepts all valid numeric input. Keep this trick in mind when you need an input loop for numbers. Also, keep in mind that non-numeric input sets an error condition that prevents the reading of any more input. If your program needs input subsequent to the input loop, you must use `cin.clear()` to reset input, as described in Chapters 6 and 16, and you might then need to get rid of the offending input by reading it.

PASSING STRUCTURE ADDRESSES

Suppose that you want to save time and space by passing the address of a structure instead of passing the entire structure. This requires rewriting the functions so that they use pointers to structures. First, let's see how to rewrite the `show_polar()` function. You need to make three changes:

- When calling the function, pass it the address of the structure (`&pplace`) rather than the structure itself (`pplace`).

- Declare the formal parameter to be a pointer-to-`Polar`, that is, type `Polar *`. Because the function shouldn't modify the structure, use the `const` modifier.

- Because the formal parameter is a pointer instead of a structure, use the indirect membership operator (`->`) rather than the membership operator (dot).

After the changes, the function looks like this:

```
// show Polar coordinates, converting angle to degrees
void show_polar (const Polar * pda)
{
    const double Rad_to_deg = 57.29577951;

    cout << "distance = " << pda->distance;
    cout << ", angle = " << pda->angle * Rad_to_deg;
    cout << " degrees\n";
}
```

Next, let's alter `rect_to_polar`. This is more involved because the original `rect_to_polar` function returns a structure. To take full advantage of pointer efficiency, you should use a pointer instead of a return value. The way to do this is to pass two pointers to the function. The first points to the structure to be converted, and the second points to the structure that's to hold the conversion. Instead of *returning* a new structure, the function *modifies* an existing structure in the calling function. Hence, although the first argument is `const` pointer, the second is not `const`. Otherwise, apply the same principles used to convert `show_polar()` to pointer arguments. Listing 7.12 shows the reworked program.

Listing 7.12 strctptr.cpp

```
// strctptr.cpp -- functions with pointer to structure arguments
#include <iostream>
#include <cmath>
using namespace std;

// structure templates
struct Polar
{
    double distance;    // distance from origin
    double angle;       // direction from origin
};
struct rect
{
    double x;           // horizontal distance from origin
    double y;           // vertical distance from origin
};

// prototypes
void rect_to_polar(const rect * pxy, Polar * pda);
void show_Polar (const Polar * pda);

int main()
{
    rect rplace;
    Polar pplace;

    cout << "Enter the x and y values: ";
    while (cin >> rplace.x >> rplace.y)
    {
```

```
        rect_to_polar(&rplace, &pplace);    // pass addresses
        show_polar(&pplace);         // pass address
        cout << "Next two numbers (q to quit): ";
    }
    return 0;
}

// convert rectangular to polar coordinates
void rect_to_polar(const rect * pxy, Polar * pda)
{
    pda->distance =
        sqrt(pxy->x * pxy->x + pxy->y * pxy->y);
    pda->angle = atan2(pxy->y, pxy->x);
}
```

" A C++ function has the interesting characteristic that it can call itself. "

Remember

Some implementations still use `math.h` instead of the newer `cmath` header file. Some compilers require explicit instructions to search the math library.

From the user's standpoint, the program in Listing 7.12 behaves like that in Listing 7.11. The hidden difference is that 7.11 works with copies of structures, whereas 7.12 uses pointers to the original structures.

Recursion

And now for something completely different. A C++ function has the interesting characteristic that it can call itself. (Unlike C, however, C++ does not let `main()` call itself.) This capability is termed *recursion*. Recursion is an important tool in certain types of programming, such as artificial intelligence, but we'll just take a superficial look (artificial shallowness) at how it works.

If a recursive function calls itself, then the newly called function calls itself, and so on ad infinitum unless the code includes something to terminate the chain of calls. The usual method is to make the recursive call part of an `if` statement. For instance, a type void recursive function called `recurs()` can have a form like this:

```
void recurs(argumentlist)
{
    statements1
    if (test)
        recurs(arguments)
    statements2
}
```

With luck or foresight, *test* eventually becomes false, and the chain of calls is broken.

Recursive calls produce an intriguing chain of events. As long as the `if` statement remains true, each call to `recurs()` executes *statements1* and then invokes a new incarnation of `recurs()` without reaching *statements2*. When the `if` statement becomes false, the current call then proceeds to *statements2*. Then, when the current call terminates, program control returns to the previous version of recurs() that called it. Then, that version of recurs() completes executing its *statements2* section and terminates, returning control to the prior call, and so on. Thus, if recurs() undergoes five recursive calls, first the *statements1* section is executed five times in the order in which the functions were called, and then the *statements2* section is executed five times in the opposite order in which the functions were called. After going in five levels of recursion, the program then has to back out through the same five levels. Listing 7.13 illustrates this behavior.

Listing 7.13 recur.cpp

```cpp
// recur.cpp -- use recursion
#include <iostream>
using namespace std;
void countdown(int n);

int main()
{
    countdown(4);            // call the recursive function
    return 0;
}

void countdown(int n)
{
    cout << "Counting down ... " << n << "\n";
    if (n > 0)
        countdown(n-1);      // function calls itself
    cout << n << ": Kaboom!\n";
}
```

Here's the output:

```
Counting down ... 4    ← level 1--beginning to add levels of recursion
Counting down ... 3    ← level 2
Counting down ... 2    ← level 3
Counting down ... 1    ← level 4
Counting down ... 0    ← level 5
0: Kaboom!             ← level 5--beginning to back out through the series of calls
1: Kaboom!             ← level 4
2: Kaboom!             ← level 3
3: Kaboom!             ← level 2
4: Kaboom!             ← level 1
```

Note that each recursive call creates its own set of variables, so by the time the program reaches the fifth call, it has five separate variables called n, each with a different value.

Recursion is particularly useful for situations that call for repeatedly subdividing a task into two smaller, similar tasks. For instance, consider this approach to drawing a ruler. Mark the two ends, locate the midpoint and mark it. Then, apply this same procedure to the left half of the ruler and then to the right half. If you want more subdivisions, apply the same procedure to each of the current subdivisions. This recursive approach sometimes is called the *divide-and-conquer strategy*. Listing 7.14 illustrates this approach with the recursive function subdivide(). It uses a string initially filled with spaces except for a ¦ character at each end. The main program uses a loop to call the subdivide() function six times, each time increasing the number of recursion levels and printing the resulting string. Thus, each line of output represents an additional level of recursion.

Listing 7.14 ruler.cpp

```cpp
// ruler.cpp - use recursion to subdivide a ruler
#include <iostream>
using namespace std;
const int Len = 66;
const int Divs = 6;
void subdivide(char ar[], int low, int high, int level);
int main()
{
    char ruler[Len];
    int i;
    for (i = 1; i < Len - 2; i++)
        ruler[i] = ' ';
    ruler[Len - 1] = '\0';
    int max = Len - 2;
    int min = 0;
    ruler[min] = ruler[max] = '¦';
    cout << ruler << "\n";
    for (i = 1; i <= Divs; i++)
    {
        subdivide(ruler,min,max, i);
        cout << ruler << "\n";
        for (int j = 1; j < Len - 2; j++)
            ruler[j] = ' ';  // reset to blank ruler
    }

    return 0;
}
void subdivide(char ar[], int low, int high, int level)
{
    if (level == 0)
        return;
    int mid = (high + low) / 2;
    ar[mid] = '¦';
    subdivide(ar, low, mid, level - 1);
    subdivide(ar, mid, high, level - 1);
}
```

Here is the program's output:

Program Notes

The `subdivide()` function uses a variable called `level` to control the recursion level. When the function calls itself, it reduces `level` by 1, and the function with a `level` of 0 terminates. Note that `subdivide()` calls itself twice, once for the left subdivision and once for the right subdivision. The original midpoint becomes the right end for one call and the left end for the other call. Notice that the number of calls grows geometrically. That is, one call generates two, which generate four calls, which generate eight, and so on. That's why the level 6 call is able to fill in 64 elements ($2^6 = 64$).

Pointers to Functions

No discussion of C or C++ functions would be complete without mention of pointers to functions. We'll take a quick look at this topic and leave the full exposition of the possibilities to more advanced texts.

Functions, like data items, have addresses. A function's address is the memory address at which the stored machine language code for the function begins. Normally, it's neither important nor useful for us or the user to know that address, but it can be useful to a program. For example, it's possible to write a function that takes the address of another function as an argument. That enables the first function to find the second function and run it. This approach is more awkward than simply having the first function call the second one directly, but it leaves open the possibility of passing different function addresses at different times. That means the first function can use different functions at different times.

FUNCTION POINTER BASICS

Let's clarify this process with an example. Suppose you want to design an `estimate()` function that estimates the amount of time necessary to write a given number of lines of code, and you want different programmers to use the function. Part of the code for `estimate()` will be the same for all users, but the function will allow each programmer to provide his or her own algorithm for estimating time. The mechanism for that will be to pass to `estimate()` the address of the particular algorithm function the programmer wants to use. To implement this plan, you need to be able to do the following:

- Take the address of a function.
- Declare a pointer to a function.
- Use a pointer to a function to invoke the function.

Obtaining the Address of a Function

Taking the address of a function is simple: just use the function name without trailing parentheses. That is, if think() is a function, then think is the address of the function. To pass a function as an argument, pass the function name. Be sure you distinguish between passing the address of a function and passing the return value of a function:

```
process(think);    // passes address of think() to process()
thought(think());  // passes return value of think() to thought()
```

The process() call enables the process() function to invoke the think() function from within process(). The thought() call first invokes the think() function and then passes the return value of think() to the thought() function.

Declaring a Pointer to a Function

When you've declared pointers to data types, the declaration has had to specify exactly to what type the pointer points. Similarly, a pointer to a function has to specify to what type of function the pointer points. This means the declaration should identify the function's return type and the function's signature (its argument list). That is, the declaration should tell us the same things about a function that a function prototype does. For instance, suppose Pam LeCoder has written a time-estimating function with the following prototype:

```
double pam(int);  // prototype
```

Here's what a declaration of an appropriate pointer type looks like:

```
double (*pf)(int);    // pf points to a function that takes
                      // one int argument and that
                      // returns type double
```

Note that this looks just like the pam() declaration, with (*pf) playing the part of pam. Because pam is a function, so is (*pf). And if (*pf) is a function, then pf is a pointer to a function.

Remember

In general, to declare a pointer to a particular kind of function, you first can write a prototype for a regular function of the desired kind and then replace the function name by an expression in the form of (*pf). That makes pf a pointer to a function of that type.

The declaration requires the parentheses around *pf to provide the proper operator precedence. Parentheses have a higher precedence than the * operator, so *pf(int) means pf() is a function that returns a pointer, whereas (*pf)(int) means pf is a pointer to a function:

```
double (*pf)(int); // pf points to a function that returns double
double *pf(int);   // pf() a function that returns a pointer-to-double
```

Once you've declared pf properly, you can assign it the address of a matching function:

```
double pam(int);
double (*pf)(int);
pf = pam;                // pf now points to the pam() function
```

Note that pam() has to match pf in both signature and return type. The compiler rejects nonmatching assignments:

```
double ned(double);
int ted(int);
double (*pf)(int);
pf = ned;          // invalid -- mismatched signature
pf = ted;          // invalid -- mismatched return types
```

Let's return to the estimate() function we mentioned earlier. Suppose you want to pass it the number of lines of code to be written and the address of an estimating algorithm, such as the pam() function. Then, it could have the following prototype:

```
void estimate(int lines, double (*pf)(int));a
```

This declaration says the second argument is a pointer to a function that has an int argument and a double return value. To have estimate() use the pam() function, pass it pam()'s address:

```
estimate(50, pam); // function call telling estimate() to use pam()
```

Clearly, the tricky part about using pointers to functions is writing the prototypes, whereas passing the address is very simple.

Using a Pointer to Invoke a Function

Now we get to the final part of the technique, which is using a pointer to call the pointed-to function. The clue comes in the pointer declaration. There, recall, (*pf) played the same role as a function name. Thus, all we have to do is use (*pf) as if it were a function name:

```
double pam(int);
double (*pf)(int);
pf = pam;                // pf now points to the pam() function
double x = pam(4);   // call pam() using the function name
double y = (*pf)(5); // call pam() using the pointer pf
```

Actually, C++ also allows you to use pf as if it were a function name:

```
double y = pf(5);      // also call pam() using the pointer pf
```

We'll use the first form. It is uglier, but it provides a strong visual reminder that the code is using a function pointer.

HISTORY VERSUS LOGIC

Holy syntax! How can pf and (*pf) be equivalent? Historically, one school of thought maintains that because pf is a pointer to a function, *pf is a function; hence you should use (*pf)() as a function call. A second school maintains that because the name of a function is a pointer to that function, a pointer to that function should act like the name of a function; hence you should use pf() as a function call. C++ takes the compromise view that both forms are correct, or at least can be allowed, even though they are logically inconsistent with each other. Before you judge that compromise too harshly, reflect that the ability to hold views that are not logically self-consistent is a hallmark of the human mental process.

Listing 7.15 demonstrates how to use function pointers in a program. It calls the estimate() function twice, once passing the betsy() function address and once passing the pam() function address. In the first case, estimate() uses betsy() to calculate the number of hours necessary, and in the second case, estimate() uses pam() for the calculation. This design facilitates future program development. When Ralph develops his own algorithm for estimating time, he doesn't have to rewrite estimate(). Instead, he merely needs to supply his own ralph() function, making sure it has the correct signature and return type. Of course, rewriting estimate() isn't a difficult task, but the same principle applies to more complex code. Also, the function pointer method allows Ralph to modify the behavior of estimate() even if he doesn't have access to the source code for estimate().

Listing 7.15 fun_ptr.cpp

```cpp
// fun_ptr.cpp -- pointers to functions
#include <iostream>
using namespace std;
double betsy(int);
double pam(int);

// second argument is pointer to a type double function that
// takes a type int argument
void estimate(int lines, double (*pf)(int));

int main()
{
    int code;

    cout << "How many lines of code do you need? ";
    cin >> code;
    cout << "Here's Betsy's estimate:\n";
    estimate(code, betsy);
    cout << "Here's Pam's estimate:\n";
    estimate(code, pam);
    return 0;
}
```

```
double betsy(int lns)
{
    return 0.05 * lns;
}

double pam(int lns)
{
    return 0.03 * lns + 0.0004 * lns * lns;
}

void estimate(int lines, double (*pf)(int))
{
    cout << lines << " lines will take ";
    cout << (*pf)(lines) << " hour(s)\n";
}
```

Here are two sample runs:

```
How many lines of code do you need? 30
Here's Betsy's estimate:
30 lines will take 1.5 hour(s)
Here's Pam's estimate:
30 lines will take 1.26 hour(s)

How many lines of code do you need? 100
Here's Betsy's estimate:
100 lines will take 5 hour(s)
Here's Pam's estimate:
100 lines will take 7 hour(s)
```

Summary

Functions are the C++ programming modules. To use a function, you need to provide a definition and a prototype, and you have to use a function call. The function definition is the code that implements what the function does. The function prototype describes the function interface: how many and what kinds of values to pass to the function and what sort of return type, if any, to get from it. The function call causes the program to pass the function arguments to the function and to transfer program execution to the function code.

By default, C++ functions pass arguments by value. This means that the formal parameters in the function definition are new variables that are initialized to the values provided by the function call. Thus, C++ functions protect the integrity of the original data by working with copies.

C++ treats an array name argument as the address of the first element of the array. Technically, this still is passing by value because the pointer is a copy of the original address, but the function uses the pointer to access the contents of the original array. When declaring formal parameters for a function (and only then), the following two declarations are equivalent:

```
typeName arr[];
typeName * arr;
```

Both mean arr is a pointer to *typeName*. When you write the function code, however, you can use arr as if it were an array name in order to access elements: arr[i]. Even when passing pointers, you can preserve the integrity of the original data by declaring the formal argument to be a pointer to a const type. Because passing the address of an array conveys no information about the size of the array, you normally would pass the array size as a separate argument.

C++ provides three ways to represent strings: a character array, a string constant, and a pointer to a string. All are type char* (pointer-to-char), so they are passed to a function as a type char* argument. C++ uses the null character (\0) to terminate strings, and string functions test for the null character to determine the end of any string they are processing.

C++ treats structures the same as basic types, meaning that you can pass them by value and use them as function return types. However, if the structure is large, it might be more efficient to pass a pointer to the structure and let the function work with the original data.

A C++ function can be recursive; that is, the code for a particular function can include a call of itself.

The name of a C++ function acts as the address of the function. By using a function argument that is a pointer to a function, you can pass to a function the name of a second function that you want the first function to evoke.

Review Questions

1. What are the three steps in using a function?

2. Construct function prototypes that match the following descriptions:

   a. igor() takes no arguments and has no return value.

   b. tofu() takes an int argument and returns a float.

   c. mpg() takes two type double arguments and returns a double.

   d. summation() takes the name of a long array and an array size as values and returns a long value.

   e. doctor() takes a string argument (the string is not to be modified) and returns a double value.

   f. ofcourse() takes a boss structure as an argument and returns nothing.

   g. plot() takes a pointer to a map structure as an argument and returns a string.

3. Write a function that takes three arguments: the name of an int array, the array size, and an int value. Have the function set each element of the array to the int value.

4. Write a function that takes a double array name and an array size as arguments and returns the largest value in that array. Note that this function shouldn't alter the contents of the array.

5. Why don't we use the const qualifier for function arguments that are one of the fundamental types?

6. Listing 7.7 uses a negative property value to terminate the input loop. Suppose, instead, that it used non-numeric input to terminate the input loop. Rewrite fill_array() to meet this new design goal.

7. What are the three forms a C-style string can take in a C++ program?

8. Write a function that has this prototype:

```
int replace(char * str, char c1, char c2);
```

Have the function replace every occurrence of c1 in the string str with c2, and have the function return the number of replacements it makes.

9. What does the expression *"pizza" mean? What about "taco"[2]?

10. C++ enables you to pass a structure by value and it lets you pass the address of a structure. If glitz is a structure variable, how would you pass it by value? How would you pass its address? What are the trade-offs of the two approaches?

11. The function judge() has a type int return value. As an argument, it takes the address of a function that takes a pointer to a const char as an argument and that also returns an int. Write the function prototype.

Programming Exercises

1. Write a program that repeatedly asks you to enter pairs of numbers until at least one of the pair is zero. For each pair, the program should use a function to calculate the harmonic mean of the numbers. The function should return the answer to main(), which reports the result. The harmonic mean of the numbers is the inverse of the average of the inverses and can be calculated as follows:

harmonic mean = 2.0 * x * y / (x + y)

2. Write a program that asks you to enter up to 10 golf scores, which are to be stored in an array. You should provide a means for the user to terminate input before entering 10 scores. The program should display all the scores on one line and report the average score. Handle input, display, and the average calculation with three separate array-processing functions.

3. Here is a structure template:

```
struct box
{
    char maker[40];
    float height;
    float width;
    float length;
    float volume;
};
```

   a. Write a function that passes a box structure by value and that displays the value of each member.

   b. Write a function that passes the address of a box structure and that sets the volume member to the product of the other three dimensions.

   c. Write a simple program that uses these two functions.

4. Define a recursive function that takes an integer argument and returns the factorial of that argument. Recall that 3 factorial, written 3!, equals 3 x 2!, and so on, with 0! defined as 1. In general, n! = n * (n - 1)!. Test it in a program that uses a loop to allow the user to enter various values for which the program reports the factorial.

5. Write a program that uses the following functions:

   Fill_array() takes as arguments the name of an array of double and an array size. It prompts the user to enter double values to be entered in the array. It ceases taking input when the array is full or when the user enters non-numeric input, and it returns the actual number of entries.

   Show_array() takes as arguments the name of an array of double and an array size and displays the contents of the array.

   Reverse_array() takes as arguments the name of an array of double and an array size and reverses the order of the values stored in the array.

   The program should fill an array, show the array, reverse the array, show the array, reverse all but the first and last elements of the array, and then show the array.

6. This exercise provides practice in writing functions dealing with arrays and structures. The following is a program skeleton. Complete it by providing the described functions.

```
#include <iostream>
using namespace std;

const int SLEN = 30;
struct student {
    char fullname[SLEN];
    char hobby[SLEN];
    int ooplevel;
};
// getinfo() has two arguments: a pointer to the first element of
// an array of student structures and an int representing the
// number of elements of the array. The function solicits and
// stores data about students. It terminates input upon filling
// the array or upon encountering a blank line for the student
// name. The function returns the actual number of array elements
// filled.
int getinfo(student pa[], int n);

// display1() takes a student structure as an argument
// and displays its contents
```

```
void display1(student st);

// display2() takes the address of student structure as an
// argument and displays the structure's contents
void display2(const student * ps);

// display3() takes the address of the first element of an array
// of student structures and the number of array elements as
// arguments and displays the contents of the structures
void display3(const student pa[], int n);

int main()
{
    cout << "Enter class size: ";
    int class_size;
    cin >> class_size;
    while (cin.get() != '\n')
        continue;

    student * ptr_stu = new student[class_size];
    int entered = getinfo(ptr_stu, class_size);
    for (int i = 0; i < entered; i++)
    {
        display1(ptr_stu[i]);
        display2(&ptr_stu[i]);
    }
    display3(ptr_stu, entered);
    delete [] ptr_stu;
    cout << "Done\n";
    return 0;
}
```

7. Design a function `calculate()` that takes two type `double` values and a pointer to a function that takes two `double` arguments and returns a `double`. The `calculate()` function also should be type `double`, and it should return the value that the pointed-to function calculates using the double arguments to `calculate()`. For example, suppose we have this definition for the `add()` function:

```
double add(double x, double y)
{
    return x + y;
}
```

Then, the function call in

```
double q = calculate(2.5, 10.4, add);
```

would cause `calculate()` to pass the values `2.5` and `10.4` to the `add()` function and then return the `add()` return value (`12.9`).

Use these functions and at least one additional function in the `add()` mold in a program. The program should use a loop that allows the user to enter pairs of numbers. For each pair, use `calculate()` to invoke `add()` and at least one other function. If you are feeling adventurous, try creating an array of pointers to add()-style functions and use a loop to successively apply calculate() to a series of functions by using these pointers. Hint: Here's how to declare such an array of three pointers:

```
double (*pf[3])(double, double);
```

You can initialize such an array by using the usual array initialization syntax and function names as addresses.

8

Adventures in Functions

In this chapter you learn

- Inline functions
- Reference variables
- Passing function arguments by reference
- Default arguments
- Function overloading
- Function templates
- Function template specializations
- Separate compilation
- Storage classes, scope, and linkage
- Namespaces

With the last chapter under your belt, you now know a lot about C++ functions, but there's much more to come. C++ provides many new function features that separate C++ from its C heritage. The new features include inline functions, passing variables by reference, default argument values, function overloading (polymorphism), and template functions. This chapter discusses these C++ enhancements to functions. Also, it examines multifile programs and C++'s varieties of storage classes, including namespaces. This chapter, more than any other you've read so far, explores features found in C++ but not C, so it marks your first major foray into plus-plussedness.

Inline Functions

Let's begin by examining inline functions, a C++ enhancement designed to speed up programs. The primary distinction between normal functions and inline functions is not in how you code them but in how the C++ compiler incorporates them into a program. To understand the distinction between inline functions and normal functions, you need to peer more deeply into a program's innards than we have so far. Let's do that now.

The final product of the compilation process is an executable program, which consists of a set of machine language instructions. When you start a program, the operating system loads these instructions into the computer's memory, so each instruction has a particular memory address. The computer then goes through these instructions step-by-step. Sometimes, as when you have a loop or a branching statement, program execution will skip over instructions, jumping back or forward to a particular address. Normal function calls also involve having a program jump to another address (the function's address) and then jump back when the function terminates. Let's look at a typical implementation of that process in a little more detail. When the program reaches the function call instruction, the program stores the memory address of the instruction immediately following the function call, copies arguments to the stack (a block of memory reserved for that purpose), jumps to the memory location that marks the beginning of the function, executes the function code (perhaps placing a return value in a register), and then jumps back to the instruction whose address it saved.[1] Jumping back and forth and keeping track of where to jump means that there is an overhead in elapsed time to using functions.

The C++ inline function provides an alternative. This is a function whose compiled code is "in line" with the other code in the program. That is, the compiler replaces the function call with the corresponding function code. With inline code, the program doesn't have to jump to another location to execute the code and then jump back. Inline functions thus run a little faster than regular functions, but there is a memory penalty. If a program calls an inline function ten times, then the program winds up with ten copies of the function inserted into the code. See Figure 8.1.

You should be selective about using inline functions. The speed gain usually is minimal unless the function itself is so short that the time needed to execute the function is comparable to the time spent jumping to and from the function. In that case, the function already is fast, so about the only time you would get much of a benefit is if the function were the main time-consumer in a crucial loop.

To use this feature, you have to do two things:

- Preface the function definition with the keyword `inline`.

- Place the function definition above all functions that call it.

---

[1] It's a bit like having to leave off reading some text to find out what a footnote says and then, upon finishing the footnote, returning to where you were reading in the text.

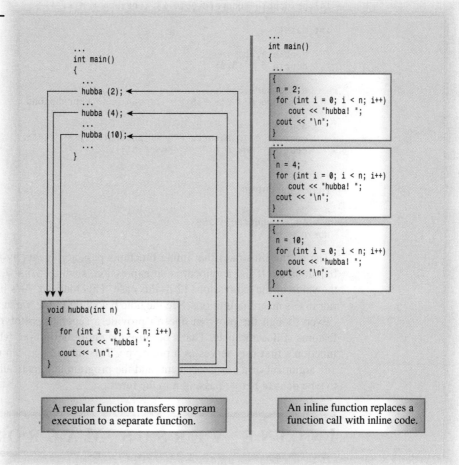

FIGURE 8.1

Inline functions versus regular functions

A regular function transfers program execution to a separate function.

An inline function replaces a function call with inline code.

Note that you have to place the entire definition (meaning the function header and all the function code), not just the prototype, above the other functions.

The compiler does not have to honor your request to make a function inline. It might decide the function is too large or notice that it calls itself (recursion is not allowed for inline functions), or the feature might not be implemented for your particular compiler. Listing 8.1 illustrates the inline technique with an inline `square()` function that squares its argument. Note that we've placed the entire definition on one line. That's not required, but if the definition doesn't fit on one line, the function probably is a poor candidate for an inline function.

Listing 8.1 inline.cpp

```
// inline.cpp -- use an inline function
#include <iostream>
using namespace std;
```

```
// an inline function must be defined before first use
inline double square(double x) { return x * x; }

int main()
{
    double a, b;
    double c = 13.0;

    a = square(5.0);
    b = square(4.5 + 7.5);    // can pass expressions
    cout << "a = " << a << ", b = " << b << "\n";
    cout << "c = " << c;
    cout << ", c squared = " << square(c++) << "\n";
    cout << "Now c = " << c << "\n";
    return 0;
}
```

Here's the output:

```
a = 25, b = 144
c = 13, c squared = 169
Now c = 14
```

The output illustrates that inline functions pass arguments by value just like regular functions do. If the argument is an expression, such as 4.5 + 7.5, the function passes the value of the expression, 12 in this case. This makes C++'s inline facility far superior to C's macro definitions. See the note below on Inline Versus Macros.

Even though the program doesn't provide a separate prototype, C++'s prototyping features still are in play. That's because the entire definition, which comes before the function's first use, serves as a prototype. This means you can use square() with an int argument or a long argument, and the program automatically type casts the value to type double before passing it to the function.

INLINE VERSUS MACROS

The inline facility is a C++ addition. C uses the preprocessor #define statement to provide *macros*, a crude implementation of inline code. For instance, here's a macro for squaring a number:

```
#define SQUARE(X) X*X
```

This works not by passing arguments but by text substitution, with the X acting as a symbolic label for the "argument":

```
a = SQUARE(5.0); is replaced by a = 5.0*5.0;
b = SQUARE(4.5 + 7.5); is replaced by b = 4.5 + 7.5 * 4.5 + 7.5;
d = SQUARE(c++); is replaced by d = c++*c++;
```

Only the first example works properly. You can improve matters with a liberal application of parentheses:

```
#define SQUARE(X) ((X)*(X))
```

Still, the problem remains that macros don't pass by value. Even with this new definition, SQUARE(c++) increments c twice, but the inline square() function in Listing 8.1 evaluates c, passes that value to be squared, and then increments c once.

The intent here is not to show you how to write C macros. Rather, it is to suggest that if you have been using C macros to perform function-like services, consider converting them to C++ inline functions.

Reference Variables

C++ adds a new derived type to the language—the reference variable. A *reference* is a name that acts as an alias, or alternative name, for a previously defined variable. For instance, if you make twain a reference to the clemens variable, you can use twain and clemens interchangeably to represent that variable. Of what use is such an alias? Is it to help people who are embarrassed by their choice of variable names? Maybe, but the main use for a reference is as a formal argument to a function. By using a reference as an argument, the function works with the original data instead of with a copy. References provide a convenient alternative to pointers for processing large structures with a function, and they are essential for designing classes. Before you see how to use references with functions, however, let's examine the basics of defining and using a reference.

CREATING A REFERENCE VARIABLE

You might recall that C and C++ use the & symbol to indicate the address of a variable. C++ assigns an additional meaning to the & symbol and presses it into service for declaring references. For example, to make rodents an alternative name for the variable rats, do the following:

```
int rats;
int & rodents = rats;      // makes rodents an alias for rats
```

In this context, & is not the address operator. Instead, it serves as part of the type identifier. Just as char * in a declaration means pointer-to-char, int & means reference-to-int. The reference declaration allows you to use rats and rodents interchangeably; both refer to the same value and the same memory location. Listing 8.2 illustrates the truth of this claim.

Listing 8.2 firstref.cpp

```
// firstref.cpp -- defining and using a reference
#include <iostream>
using namespace std;
int main()
{
    int rats = 101;
    int & rodents = rats;    // rodents is a reference
```

```
    cout << "rats = " << rats;
    cout << ", rodents = " << rodents << "\n";
    rodents++;
    cout << "rats = " << rats;
    cout << ", rodents = " << rodents << "\n";

// some implementations require type casting the following
// addresses to type unsigned
    cout << "rats address = " << &rats;
    cout << ", rodents address = " << &rodents << "\n";
    return 0;
}
```

Note that the & operator in the statement

```
int & rodents = rats;
```

is not the address operator but declares that rodents is of type int &, that is, a reference to an int variable. But the & operator in the statement

```
cout<<", rodents address ="<< &rodents << "\n";
```

is the address operator, with &rodents representing the address of the variable to which rodents refers. Here is the program's output:

```
rats = 101, rodents = 101
rats = 102, rodents = 102
rats address = 0068FDF4, rodents address = 0068FDF4
```

As you can see, both rats and rodents have the same value and the same address. Incrementing rodents by 1 affects both variables. More precisely, the rodents++ operation increments a single variable for which we have two names. (Keep in mind that although this example shows you how a reference works, it doesn't represent the typical use for a reference, which is as a function parameter, particularly for structure and object arguments. We look into these uses pretty soon.)

References tend to be a bit confusing at first to C veterans coming to C++ because they are tantalizingly reminiscent of pointers, yet somehow different. For instance, you can create both a reference and a pointer to refer to rats:

```
int rats = 101;
int & rodents = rats;    // rodents a reference
int * prats = &rats;     // prats a pointer
```

Then, you could use the expressions rodents and *prats interchangeably with rats and use the expressions &rodents and prats interchangeably with &rats. From this standpoint, a reference looks a lot like a pointer in disguised notation in which the * dereferencing operator is understood implicitly. And, in fact, that's more or less what a reference is. But there are differences besides those of notation. For one, it is necessary to initialize the reference when you declare it; you can't declare the reference and then assign it a value later the way you can with a pointer:

```
int rat;
int & rodent;
rodent = rat;    // No, you can't do this.
```

> *" References tend to be a bit confusing at first to C veterans coming to C++ because they are tantalizingly reminiscent of pointers, yet somehow different. "*

You should initialize a reference variable when you declare it.

A reference is more like a const pointer; you have to initialize it when you create it, and once a reference pledges its allegiance to a particular variable, it sticks to its pledge. That is,

```
int & rodents = rats;
```

is, in essence, a disguised notation for something like this:

```
int * const pr = &rats;
```

Here rodents plays the same role as *pr.

Listing 8.3 shows what happens if you try to make a reference change allegiance from a rats variable to a bunnies variable.

Listing 8.3 secref.cpp
```
// secref.cpp -- defining and using a reference
#include <iostream>
using namespace std;
int main()
{
    int rats = 101;
    int & rodents = rats;    // rodents is a reference

    cout << "rats = " << rats;
    cout << ", rodents = " << rodents << "\n";

    cout << "rats address = " << &rats;
    cout << ", rodents address = " << &rodents << "\n";

    int bunnies = 50;
    rodents = bunnies;        // can we change the reference?
    cout << "bunnies = " << bunnies;
    cout << ", rats = " << rats;
    cout << ", rodents = " << rodents << "\n";

    cout << "bunnies address = " << &bunnies;
    cout << ", rodents address = " << &rodents << "\n";
    return 0;
}
```

Here's the output:
```
rats = 101, rodents = 101
rats address = 0068FDF4, rodents address = 0068FDF4
bunnies = 50, rats = 50, rodents = 50
bunnies address = 0068FDF0, rodents address = 0068FDF4
```

Initially, rodents refers to rats, but then the program attempts to make rodents a reference to bunnies:

```
rodents = bunnies;
```

For a moment, it looks as if this attempt has succeeded, for the value of rodents changes from 101 to 50. But closer inspection reveals that rats also has changed to 50 and that rats and rodents still share the same address, which differs from the bunnies address. Because rodents is an alias for `rats`, the assignment statement really means the same as the following:

```
rats = bunnies;
```

That is, it means "assign the value of the bunnies variable to the rat variable." In short, you can set a reference by an initializing declaration, not by assignment.

Suppose you tried the following:

```
int rats = 101;
int * pi = &rats;
int & rodents = *pi;
int bunnies = 50;
pi = &bunnies;
```

Initializing `rodents` to `*pi` makes `rodents` refer to `rats`. Subsequently altering `pi` to point to `bunnies` does not alter the fact that `rodents` refers to `rats`.

REFERENCES AS FUNCTION PARAMETERS

Most often, references are used as function parameters, making a variable name in the function an alias for a variable in the calling program. This method of passing arguments is called *passing by reference*. Passing by reference allows a called function to access variables in the calling function. C++'s addition of the feature is a break from C, which passes only by value. Passing by value, recall, results in the called function working with copies of values from the calling program. See Figure 8.2. Of course, C lets you get around the passing by value limitation by using pointers.

Let's compare using references and using pointers in a common computer problem: swapping the values of two variables. A swapping function has to be able to alter values of variables in the calling program. That means the usual approach of passing variables by value won't work, because the function will end up swapping the contents of copies of the original variables instead of the variables themselves. If you pass references, however, the function can work with the original data. Alternatively, you can pass pointers in order to access the original data. Listing 8.4 shows all three methods, including the one that doesn't work, so that you can compare them.

Listing 8.4 swaps.cpp

```cpp
// swaps.cpp -- swapping with references and with pointers
#include <iostream>
using namespace std;
void swapr(int & a, int & b);    // a, b are aliases for ints
void swapp(int * p, int * q);    // p, q are addresses of ints
void swapv(int a, int b);        // a, b are new variables
int main()
{
    int wallet1 = 300;
    int wallet2 = 350;
```

```
        cout << "wallet1 = $" << wallet1;
        cout << " wallet2 = $" << wallet2 << "\n";

        cout << "Using references to swap contents:\n";
        swapr(wallet1, wallet2);    // pass variables
        cout << "wallet1 = $" << wallet1;
        cout << " wallet2 = $" << wallet2 << "\n";

        cout << "Using pointers to swap contents:\n";
        swapp(&wallet1, &wallet2); // pass addresses of variables
        cout << "wallet1 = $" << wallet1;
        cout << " wallet2 = $" << wallet2 << "\n";

        cout << "Trying to use passing by value:\n";
        swapv(wallet1, wallet2);    // pass values of variables
        cout << "wallet1 = $" << wallet1;
        cout << " wallet2 = $" << wallet2 << "\n";
        return 0;
    }

void swapr(int & a, int & b)      // use references
    {
        int temp;

        temp = a;         // use a, b for values of variables
        a = b;
        b = temp;
    }

void swapp(int * p, int * q)      // use pointers
    {
        int temp;

        temp = *p;        // use *p, *q for values of variables
        *p = *q;
        *q = temp;
    }

void swapv(int a, int b)          // try using values
    {
        int temp;

        temp = a;         // use a, b for values of variables
        a = b;
        b = temp;
    }
```

Here's the output:

```
wallet1 = $300 wallet2 = $350          ← original values
Using references to swap contents:
wallet1 = $350 wallet2 = $300          ← values swapped
Using pointers to swap contents:
wallet1 = $300 wallet2 = $350          ← values swapped again
Trying to use passing by value:
wallet1 = $300 wallet2 = $350          ← swap failed
```

FIGURE 8.2

Passing by value and passing by reference

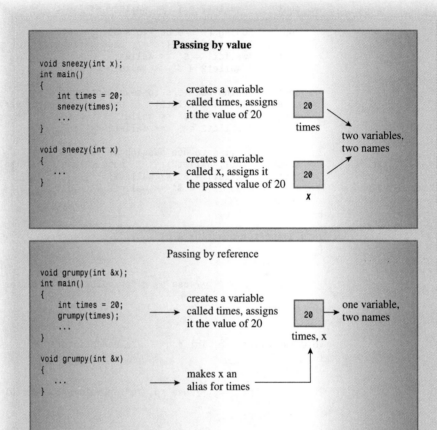

As we expected, the reference and pointer methods both successfully swap the contents of the two wallets, whereas the passing by value method fails.

Program Notes

First, note how each function is called:

```
swapr(wallet1, wallet2);        // pass variables
swapp(&wallet1, &wallet2);      // pass addresses of variables
swapv(wallet1, wallet2);        // pass values of variables
```

Passing by reference (swapr(wallet1, wallet2)) and passing by value (swapv(wallet1, wallet2)) look identical. The only way you can tell that swapr() passes by reference is by looking at the prototype or the function definition. However, the presence of the address operator (&) makes it obvious when a function passes by address ((swapp(&wallet1, &wallet2)). (Recall that the type declaration int *p means that p is a pointer to an int and therefore the argument corresponding to p should be an address, such as &wallet1.)

Next, compare the code for the functions swapr() (passing by reference) and swapv() (passing by value). The only outward difference between the two is how the function parameters are declared:

```
void swapr(int & a, int & b)
void swapv(int a, int b)
```

The internal difference, of course, is that in swapr() the variables a and b serve as aliases for wallet1 and wallet2, so swapping a and b swaps wallet1 and wallet2. But in swapv(), the variables a and b are new variables that copy the values of wallet1 and wallet2, so swapping a and b has no effect on wallet1 and wallet2.

Finally, compare the functions swapr() (passing a reference) and swapp() (passing a pointer). The first difference is in how the function parameters are declared:

```
void swapr(int & a, int & b)
void swapp(int * p, int * q)
```

The second difference is that the pointer version requires using the * dereferencing operator throughout when the function uses p and q.

Earlier, we said you should initialize a reference variable when you define it. You can consider reference function arguments as being initialized to the argument passed by the function call. That is, the function call

```
swapr(wallet1, wallet2);
```

initializes the formal parameter a to wallet1 and the formal parameter b to wallet2.

" Using reference arguments has several twists about which you need to know. "

REFERENCE PROPERTIES AND ODDITIES

Using reference arguments has several twists about which you need to know. First, consider Listing 8.5. It uses two functions to cube an argument. One takes a type double argument, whereas the other takes a reference to double. The actual code for cubing is purposefully a bit odd to illustrate a point.

Listing 8.5 cubes.cpp

```cpp
// cubes.cpp -- regular and reference arguments
#include <iostream>
using namespace std;
double cube(double a);
double refcube(double &ra);
int main ()
{
    double x = 3.0;

    cout << cube(x);
    cout << " = cube of " << x << "\n";
    cout << refcube(x);
    cout << " = cube of " << x << "\n";
```

```
    return 0;
}

double cube(double a)
{
    a *= a * a;
    return a;
}

double refcube(double &ra)
{
    ra *= ra * ra;
    return ra;
}
```

Here is the output:

```
27 = cube of 3
27 = cube of 27
```

Note that the `refcube()` function modifies the value of x in `main()` whereas `cube()` doesn't, which reminds us of why passing by value is the norm. The variable a is local to `cube()`. It is initialized to the value of x, but changing a has no effect on x. But because `refcube()` uses a reference argument, the changes it makes to ra actually are made to x. If your intent is that a function use the information passed to it without modifying the information, and if you're using a reference, you should use a constant reference. Here, for example, we should have used const in the function prototype and function heading:

```
double refcube(const double &ra);
```

Had we done this, the compiler would have generated an error message when it found code altering the value of ra.

Incidentally, if you need to write a function along the lines of this example, use passing by value rather than the more exotic passing by reference. Reference arguments become useful with larger data units, such as structures and classes, as you soon see.

Functions that pass by value, such as the `cube()` function in Listing 8.5, can use many kinds of actual arguments. For instance, all the following calls are valid:

```
double z = cube(x + 2.0);    // evaluate x + 2.0, pass value
z = cube(8.0);               // pass the value 8.0
int k = 10;
z = cube(k);        // convert value of k to double, pass value
double yo[3] = { 2.2, 3.3, 4.4};
z = cube (yo[2]);            // pass the value 4.4
```

Suppose you try similar arguments for a function with a reference parameter. It would seem that passing a reference should be more restrictive. After all, if ra is the alternative name for a variable, then the actual argument should be that variable. Something like

```
double z = refcube(x + 3.0);  // may not compile
```

doesn't appear to make sense because the expression x + 3.0 is not a variable. For instance, you can't assign a value to such an expression:

```
x + 3.0 = 5.0;  // nonsensical
```

What happens if you try a function call like refcube(x + 3.0)? In contemporary C++, that's an error, and some compilers will tell you so. Others give you a warning along the following lines:

```
Warning: Temporary used for parameter 'ra' in call to refcube(double &)
```

The reason for this milder response is that C++, in its early years, did allow you to pass expressions to a reference variable. In some cases, it still does. What happens is this: Because x + 3.0 is not a type double variable, the program creates a temporary, nameless variable, initializing it to the value of the expression x + 3.0. Then, ra becomes a reference to that temporary variable. Let's take a closer look at temporary variables and see when they are and are not created.

Temporary Variables, Reference Arguments, and `const`

C++ can generate a temporary variable if the actual argument doesn't match a reference argument. Currently, C++ permits this only if the argument is a const reference, but this is a new restriction. Let's look at the cases in which C++ does generate temporary variables and see why the restriction to a const reference makes sense.

First, when is a temporary variable created? Provided that the reference parameter is a const, the compiler generates a temporary variable in two kinds of situations:

- The actual argument is the correct type, but isn't an Lvalue

- The actual argument is of the wrong type, but of a type that can be converted to the correct type

An argument that's an *Lvalue* is a data object that can be referenced. For instance, a variable, an array element, a structure member, a reference, and a dereferenced pointer are Lvalues. Non-Lvalues include literal constants and expressions with multiple terms. For example, suppose we redefine refcube() so that it has a constant reference argument:

```
double refcube(const double &ra)
{
    return ra * ra * ra;
}
```

Now consider the following code:

```
double side = 3.0;
double * pd = &side;
double & rd = side;
long edge = 5L;
double lens[4] = { 2.0, 5.0, 10.0, 12.0};
double c1 = refcube(side);        // ra is side
double c2 = refcube(lens[2]);     // ra is lens[2]
double c3 = refcube(rd);          // ra is rd is side
```

```
double c4 = refcube(*pd)            // ra is *pd is side
double c4 = refcube(edge);          // ra is temporary variable
double c5 = refcube(7.0);           // ra is temporary variable
double c6 = refcube(side + 10.0);   // ra is temporary variable
```

The arguments side, lens[2], rd, and *pd are type double data objects with names, so it is possible to generate a reference for them, and no temporary variables are needed. (Recall that an element of an array behaves like a variable of the same type as the element.) But edge, although a variable, is of the wrong type. A reference to a double can't refer to a long. The arguments 7.0 and side + 10.0, on the other hand, are the right type, but are not named data objects. In each of these cases, the compiler generates a temporary, anonymous variable and makes ra refer to it. These temporary variables last for the duration of the function call, but then the compiler is free to dump them.

So why is this behavior okay for constant references but not otherwise? Recall the swapr() function of Listing 8.4:

```
void swapr(int & a, int & b)  // use references
{
    int temp;

    temp = a;       // use a, b for values of variables
    a = b;
    b = temp;
}
```

What would happen if we did the following under the freer rules of early C++?

```
long a = 3, b = 5;
swapr(a, b);
```

Here there is a type mismatch, so the compiler would create two temporary int variables, initialize them to 3 and 5, and then swap the contents of the temporary variables, leaving a and b unaltered.

In short, if the intent of a function with reference arguments is to modify variables passed as arguments, situations that create temporary variables thwart that purpose. The solution is to prohibit creating temporary variables in these situations, and that is what C++ now does.

Now think about the refcube() function. Its intent is merely to use passed values, not to modify them, so temporary variables cause no harm and make the function more general in the sorts of arguments that it can handle. Therefore, if the declaration states that a reference is const, C++ generates temporary variables when necessary. In essence, a C++ function with a const reference formal argument and a nonmatching actual argument mimics the traditional passing by value behavior, guaranteeing that the original data is unaltered and using a temporary variable to hold the value.

Remember

If a function call argument isn't an Lvalue or does not match the type of the corresponding const reference parameter, C++ creates an anonymous variable of the correct type, assigns the value of the function call argument to the anonymous variable, and has the parameter refer to that variable.

USE const WHEN YOU CAN

There are three strong reasons to declare reference arguments as references to constant data:
- Using const protects you against programming errors that inadvertently alter data.
- Using const allows a function to process both const and non-const actual arguments, while a function omitting const in the prototype can accept only non-const data.
- Using a const reference allows the function to generate and use a temporary variable appropriately.

You should declare formal reference arguments as const whenever it's appropriate.

USING REFERENCES WITH A STRUCTURE

References work wonderfully with structures and classes, C++'s user-defined types. Indeed, references were introduced primarily for use with these types, not for use with the basic built-in types.

The method for using a reference to a structure is the same as the method for using a reference to a basic variable; just use the & reference operator when declaring a structure parameter. The program in Listing 8.6 does exactly that. It also adds an interesting twist by having a function return a reference. This makes it possible to use a function invocation as an argument to a function. Well, that's true of any function with a return value. But it also makes it possible to assign a value to a function invocation, and that's possible only with a reference return type. We'll explain these points after showing the program's output. The program has a use() function that displays two members of a structure and increments a third member. Thus, the third member can keep track of how many times a particular structure has been handled by the use() function.

Listing 8.6 strtref.cpp

```cpp
// strtref.cpp -- using structure references
#include <iostream>
using namespace std;
struct sysop
{
    char name[26];
    char quote[64];
    int used;
};

sysop & use(sysop & sysopref);   // function with a reference return type
```

```
int main()
{
// NOTE: some implementations require using the keyword static
// in the two structure declarations to enable initialization
    sysop looper =
    {
        "Rick \"Fortran\" Looper",
        "I'm a goto kind of guy.",
        0
    };

    use(looper);              // looper is type sysop
    cout << looper.used << " use(s)\n";

    use (use(looper));        // use(looper) is type sysop
    cout << looper.used << " use(s)\n";

    sysop morf =
    {
        "Polly Morf",
        "Polly's not a hacker.",
        0
    };
    use(looper) = morf;       // can assign to function!
    cout << looper.name << " says:\n" << looper.quote << '\n';
    return 0;
}

// use() returns the reference passed to it
sysop & use(sysop & sysopref)
{
    cout << sysopref.name << " says:\n";
    cout << sysopref.quote << "\n";
    sysopref.used++;
    return sysopref;
}
```

Here's the output:

```
Rick "Fortran" Looper says:
I'm a goto kind of guy.
1 use(s)
Rick "Fortran" Looper says:
I'm a goto kind of guy.
Rick "Fortran" Looper says:
I'm a goto kind of guy.
3 use(s)
Rick "Fortran" Looper says:
I'm a goto kind of guy.
Polly Morf says:
Polly's not a hacker.
```

Program Notes

The program ventures into three new areas. The first is using a reference to a structure, illustrated by the first function call:

```
use(looper);
```

It passes the structure looper by reference to the use() function, making sysopref a synonym for looper. When the use() function displays the name and quote members of sysopref, it really displays the members of looper. Also, when the function increments sysopref.used to 1, it really increments looper.used, as the program output shows:

```
Rick "Fortran" Looper says:
I'm a goto kind of guy.
1 use(s)
```

The second new area is using a reference as a return value. Normally, the return mechanism copies the returned value to a temporary storage area, which the calling program then accesses. Returning a reference, however, means that the calling program accesses the return value directly without there being a copy. Typically, the reference refers to a reference passed to the function in the first place, so the calling function actually winds up directly accessing one of its own variables. Here, for example, sysopref is a reference to looper, so the return value is the original looper variable in main().

Because use() returns a type sysop reference, it can be used as an argument to any function expecting either a sysop argument or a reference-to-sysop argument, such as use() itself. Thus, the next function call in Listing 8.6 is really two function calls, with one function's return value serving as the argument for the second:

```
use(use(looper));
```

The inner function call prints the name and quote members and increments the used member to 2. The function returns sysopref, reducing what's left to the following:

```
use(sysopref);
```

Because sysopref is a reference to looper, this function call is equivalent to the following:

```
use(looper);
```

Therefore, use() displays the two string members again and increments the used member to 3.

Remember

A function that returns a reference is actually an alias for the referred-to variable.

The third new area the program explores is that you can assign a value to a function if that function has a reference type return value:

```
use(looper) = morf;
```

For nonreference return values, this assignment is a syntax error, but it's okay for use(). This is the order of events. First, the use() function is evaluated. That means looper is passed by reference to use(). As usual, the function displays two members and increments the used member to 4. Then, the function returns the reference.

Because the return value refers to `looper`, this makes the final step equivalent to the following:

```
looper = morf;
```

C++ allows you to assign one structure to another, so this copies the contents of the `morf` structure into `looper`, as is shown when displaying `looper.name` produces Morf's name and not Looper's. In short, the statement

```
use(looper) = morf;  // return value a reference to looper
```

is equivalent to the following:

```
use(looper);
looper = morf;
```

Remember

> You can assign a value (including a structure or a class object) to a C++ function only if the function returns a reference to a variable or, more generally, to a data object. In that case, the value is assigned to the referred-to variable or data object.

This is another property that enables certain forms of operator redefinition. You can use it, for instance, to redefine the array subscript operator `[ ]` for a class that defines a more powerful version of the array.

Considerations When Returning a Reference or a Pointer

When a function returns a reference or a pointer to a data object, that object had better continue to exist after the function terminates. The simplest way to do that is to have the function return a reference or pointer that was passed to it as an argument. That way, the reference or pointer already refers to something in the calling program. The `use()` function in Listing 8.6 uses this technique.

A second method is to use `new` to create new storage. You've already seen examples in which `new` creates space for a string and the function returns a pointer to that space. Here's how you could do something similar with a reference:

```
sysop & clone(sysop & sysopref)
{
    sysop * psysop = new sysop;
    *psysop = sysopref;   // copy info
    return *psysop;       // return reference to copy
}
```

The first statement creates a nameless `sysop` structure. The pointer `psysop` points to the structure, so `*psysop` is the structure. The code appears to return the structure, but the function declaration indicates the function really returns a reference to this structure. You then could use the function this way:

```
sysop & jolly = clone(looper);
```

This makes `jolly` a reference to the new structure. There is a problem with this approach, which is that you should use `delete` to free memory allocated by `new` when the memory is no longer needed. A call to clone() hides the call to new, making it simpler to forget to use delete later. The auto_ptr template discussed in Chapter 15, "The String Class and the Standard Template Library," can help automate the deletion process.

What you want to avoid is code along these lines:

```
sysop & clone2(sysop & sysopref)
{
     sysop newguy;               // first step to big error
     newguy = sysopref;          // copy info
     return newguy;              // return reference to copy
}
```

This has the unfortunate effect of returning a reference to a temporary variable (newguy) that passes from existence as soon as the function terminates. (This chapter discusses the persistence of various kinds of variables later, in the section on storage classes.) Similarly, you should avoid returning pointers to such temporary variables.

When to Use Reference Arguments

" So, when should you use a reference? Use a pointer? Pass by value?"

There are two main reasons for using reference arguments:

- To allow you to alter a data object in the calling function

- To speed up a program by passing a reference instead of an entire data object

The second reason is most important for larger data objects, such as structures and class objects. These two reasons are the same reasons one might have for using a pointer argument. This makes sense, for reference arguments are really just a different interface for pointer-based code. So, when should you use a reference? Use a pointer? Pass by value? Here are some guidelines.

A function uses passed data without modifying it

- If the data object is small, such as a built-in data type or a small structure, pass it by value.

- If the data object is an array, use a pointer because that's your only choice. Make the pointer a pointer to const.

- If the data object is a good-sized structure, use a const pointer or a const reference to increase program efficiency. You save the time and space needed to copy a structure or a class design. Make the pointer or reference const.

- If the data object is a class object, use a const reference. The semantics of class design often require using a reference, which is the main reason why C++ added this feature. Thus, the standard way to pass class object arguments is by reference.

A function modifies data in the calling function

- If the data object is a built-in data type, use a pointer. If you spot code like fixit(&x), where x is an int, it's pretty clear that this function intends to modify x.

- If the data object is an array, use your only choice, a pointer.

- If the data object is a structure, use a reference or a pointer.

- If the data object is a class object, use a reference.

Of course, these are just guidelines, and there might be reasons for making different choices. For instance, cin uses references for basic types so that you can use cin >> n instead of cin >> &n.

Default Arguments

Let's look at another topic from C++'s bag of new tricks—the default argument. A default argument is a value that's used automatically if you omit the corresponding actual argument from a function call. For example, if you set up void wow(int n) so that n has a default value of 1, then the function call wow() is the same as wow(1). This gives you greater flexibility in how you use a function. Suppose you have a function called left() that returns the first n characters of a string, with the string and n as arguments. More precisely, the function returns a pointer to a new string consisting of the selected portion of the original string. For instance, the call left("theory", 3) constructs a new string "the" and returns a pointer to it. Now suppose you establish a default value of 1 for the second argument. The call left("theory", 3) would work as before, with your choice of 3 overriding the default. But the call left("theory"), instead of being an error, would assume a second argument of 1 and return a pointer to the string "t". This kind of default is helpful if your program often needs to extract a one-character string but occasionally needs to extract longer strings.

How do you establish a default value? You must use the function prototype. Because the compiler looks at the prototype to see how many arguments a function uses, the function prototype also has to alert the program to the possibility of default arguments. The method is to assign a value to the argument in the prototype. For instance, here's the prototype fitting this description of left():

```
char * left(const char * str, int n = 1);
```

We want the function to return a new string, so its type is char*, or pointer-to-char. We want to leave the original string unaltered, so we use the const qualifier for the first argument. We want n to have a default value of 1, so we assign that value to n. A default argument value is an initialization value. Thus, the prototype above initializes n to the value 1. If you leave n alone, it has the value 1, but if you pass an argument, the new value overwrites the 1.

When you use a function with an argument list, you must add defaults from right to left. That is, you can't provide a default value for a particular argument unless you also provide defaults for all the arguments to its right:

```
int harpo(int n, int m = 4, int j = 5);      // VALID
int chico(int n, int m = 6, int j);          // INVALID
int groucho(int k = 1, int m = 2, int n = 3);  // VALID
```

The `harpo()` prototype, for example, permits calls with one, two, or three arguments:

```
beeps = harpo(2);       // same as harpo(2,4,5)
beeps = harpo(1,8);     // same as harpo(1,8,5)
beeps = harpo (8,7,6);  // no default arguments used
```

The actual arguments are assigned to the corresponding formal arguments from left to right; you can't skip over arguments. Thus, the following isn't allowed:

```
beeps = harpo(3, ,8);   // invalid, doesn't set m to 4
```

Default arguments aren't a major programming breakthrough; rather, they are a convenience. When you get to class design, you'll find they can reduce the number of constructor methods you have to define.

Listing 8.7 puts default arguments to use. Note that only the prototype indicates the default. The function definition is the same as it would have been without default arguments.

Listing 8.7 left.cpp

```cpp
// left.cpp -- string function with a default argument
#include <iostream>
using namespace std;
const int ArSize = 80;
char * left(const char * str, int n = 1);
int main()
{
    char sample[ArSize];
    cout << "Enter a string:\n";
    cin.get(sample,ArSize);
    char *ps = left(sample, 4);
    cout << ps << "\n";
    delete [] ps;        // free old string
    ps = left(sample);
    cout << ps << "\n";
    delete [] ps;        // free new string
    return 0;
}

// This function returns a pointer to a new string
// consisting of the first n characters in the str string.
char * left(const char * str, int n)
{
    if(n < 0)
        n = 0;
    char * p = new char[n+1];
    int i;
    for (i = 0; i < n && str[i]; i++)
        p[i] = str[i]; // copy characters
```

```
    while (i <= n)
        p[i++] = '\0';  // set rest of string to '\0'
    return p;
}
```

Here's a sample run:

```
Enter a string:
forthcoming
fort
f
```

PROGRAM NOTES

The program uses new to create a new string for holding the selected characters. One awkward possibility is that an uncooperative user requests a negative number of characters. In that case, the function sets the character count to zero and eventually returns the null string. Another awkward possibility is that an irresponsible user requests more characters than the string contains. The function protects against this by using a combined test:

```
i < n && str[i]
```

The i < n test stops the loop after n characters have been copied. The second part of the test, the expression str[i], is the code for the character about to be copied. If the loop reaches the null character, the code is zero, and the loop terminates. The final while loop terminates the string with the null character and then sets the rest of the allocated space, if any, to null characters.

Another approach for setting the size of the new string is to set n to the smaller of the passed value and the string length:

```
int len = strlen(str);
n = (n < len) ? n : len;     // the lesser of n and len
char * p = new char[n+1];
```

This ensures that new doesn't allocate more space than what's needed to hold the string. That can be useful if you make a call like left("Hi!", 32767). The first approach copies the "Hi!" into an array of 32767 characters, setting all but the first three characters to the null character. The second approach copies "Hi!" into an array of four characters. But, by adding another function call (strlen()), it increases the program size, slows the process, and requires that you remember to include the cstring (or string.h) header file. C programmers have tended to opt for faster running, more compact code and leave a greater burden on the programmer to use functions correctly. The C++ tradition, however, places greater weight on reliability. After all, a slower program working correctly is better than a fast program that works incorrectly. If the time taken to call strlen() turns out to be a problem, you can let left() determine the lesser of n and the string length directly. For instance, the following loop quits when m reaches n or the end of the string, whichever comes first:

```
int m = 0;
while ( m <= n && str[m] != '\0')
```

```
    m++;
char * p = new char[m+1]:
// use m instead of n in rest of code
```

Function Polymorphism (Function Overloading)

Function polymorphism is a neat C++ addition to C's capabilities. While default arguments let you call the same function using varying numbers of arguments, *function polymorphism*, also called *function overloading*, lets you use multiple functions sharing the same name. The word "polymorphism" means having many forms, so function polymorphism lets a function have many forms. Similarly, the expression "function overloading" means you can attach more than one function to the same name, thus overloading the name. Both expressions boil down to the same thing, but we'll usually use the expression function overloading—it sounds harder working. You can use function overloading to design a family of functions that do essentially the same thing, but using different argument lists.

Overloaded functions are analogous to verbs having more than one meaning. For instance, Miss Piggy can root at the ball park for the home team, or she can root in the soil for truffles. The context (one hopes) tells you which meaning of root is intended in each case. Similarly, C++ uses the context to decide which version of an overloaded function is intended.

The key to function overloading is a function's argument list, also called the *function signature*. If two functions use the same number and types of arguments in the same order, they have the same signature; the variable names don't matter. C++ enables you to define two functions by the same name provided that the functions have different signatures. The signature can differ in the number of arguments or in the type of arguments, or both. For instance, you can define a set of print() functions with the following prototypes:

```
void print(const char * str, int width);   // #1
void print(double d, int width);           // #2
void print(long l, int width);             // #3
void print(int i, int width);              // #4
void print(const char *str);               // #5
```

When you then use a print() function, the compiler matches your use to the prototype that has the same signature:

```
print("Pancakes", 15);      // use #1
print("Syrup");             // use #5
print(1999.0, 10);          // use #2
print(1999, 12);            // use #4
print(1999L, 15);           // use #3
```

For instance, print("Pancakes", 15) uses a string and an integer as arguments, and that matches prototype #1.

When you use overloaded functions, be sure you use the proper argument types in the function call. For instance, consider the following statements:

```
unsigned int year = 3210;
print(year, 6);           // ambiguous call
```

Which prototype does the print() call match here? It doesn't match any of them! A lack of a matching prototype doesn't automatically rule out using one of the functions, because C++ will try to use standard type conversions to force a match. If, say, the only print() prototype were #2, the function call print(year, 6) would convert the year value to type double. But in the code above there are three prototypes that take a number as the first argument, providing three different choices for converting year. Faced with this ambiguous situation, C++ rejects the function call as an error.

Some signatures that appear different from each other can't coexist. For instance, consider these two prototypes:

```
double cube(double x);
double cube(double & x);
```

You might think this is a place you could use function overloading because the function signatures appear to be different. But consider things from the compiler's standpoint. Suppose you have code like this:

```
cout << cube(x);
```

The x argument matches both the double x prototype and the double &x prototype. Thus, the compiler has no way of knowing which function to use. Therefore, to avoid such confusion, when it checks function signatures, the compiler considers a reference to a type and the type itself to be the same signature.

The function matching process does discriminate between const and non-const variables. Consider the following prototypes:

```
void dribble(char * bits);        // overloaded
void dribble (const char *cbits); // overloaded
void dabble(char * bits);         // not overloaded
void drivel(const char * bits);   // not overloaded
```

Here's what various function calls would match:

```
const char p1[20] = "How's the weather?";
char p2[20] = "How's business?";
dribble(p1);    // dribble(const char *);
dribble(p2);    // dribble(char *);
dabble(p1);     // no match
dabble(p2);     // dabble(char *);
drivel(p1);     // drivel(char *);
drivel(p2);     // drivel(char *);
```

The dribble() function has two prototypes, one for const pointers and one for regular pointers, and the compiler selects one or the other depending on whether or not the actual argument is const. The dabble() function only matches a call with a non-const argument, but the drivel() function matches calls with either const or non-const arguments. The reason for this difference in behavior between `drivel()` and `dabble()` is that it's valid to assign a non-const value to a const variable, but not vice versa.

Keep in mind that it's the signature, not the function type, that enables function overloading. For instance, the following two declarations are incompatible:

```
long gronk(int n, float m);      // same signatures,
double gronk(int n, float m);    // hence not allowed
```

Therefore, C++ won't permit you to overload `gronk()` in this fashion. You can have different return types, but only if the signatures also are different:

```
long gronk(int n, float m);      // different signatures,
double gronk(float n, float m);  // hence allowed
```

After we discuss templates later in this chapter, we'll further discuss function matching.

> *Keep in mind that it's the signature, not the function type, that enables function overloading.*

AN OVERLOADING EXAMPLE

We've already developed a `left()` function that returns a pointer to the first n characters in a string. Let's add a second `left()` function, one that returns the first n digits in an integer. You can use it, for example, to examine the first three digits of a U.S. postal zip code stored as an integer, a useful act if you want to sort for urban areas.

The integer function is a bit more difficult to program than the string version, because we don't have the benefit of each digit being stored in its own array element. One approach is first to compute the number of digits in the number. Dividing a number by 10 lops off one digit, so you can use division to count digits. More precisely, you can do so with a loop like this:

```
unsigned digits = 1;
while (n /= 10)
    digits++;
```

This loop counts how many times you can remove a digit from n until none are left. Recall that n /= 10 is short for n = n / 10. If n is 8, for example, the test condition assigns to n the value 8 / 10, or 0, because it's integer division. That terminates the loop, and `digits` remains at 1. But if n is 238, the first loop test sets n to 238 / 10, or 23. That's nonzero, so the loop increases `digits` to 2. The next cycle sets n to 23 / 10, or 2. Again, that's nonzero, so `digits` grows to 3. The next cycle sets n to 2 / 10, or 0, and the loop quits, leaving `digits` set to the correct value, 3.

Now suppose you know the number has five digits, and you want to return the first three digits. You can get that value by dividing the number by 10 and then dividing the answer by 10 again. Each division by 10 lops one more digit off the right end. To calculate the number of digits to lop, just subtract the number of digits to be shown from the total number of digits. For instance, to show four digits of a nine-digit number, lop off the last five digits. You can code this approach as follows:

```
ct = digits - ct;
while (ct--)
    num /= 10;
return num;
```

Listing 8.8 incorporates this code into a new left() function. The function includes some additional code to handle special cases, such as asking for zero digits or asking for more digits than the number possesses. Because the signature of the new left() differs from that of the old left(), we can, and do, use both functions in the same program.

Listing 8.8 leftover.cpp

```cpp
// leftover.cpp -- overloading the left() function
#include <iostream>
using namespace std;
unsigned long left(unsigned long num, unsigned ct);
char * left(const char * str, int n = 1);

int main()
{
    char * trip = "Hawaii!!";   // test value
    unsigned long n = 12345678; // test value
    int i;
    char * temp;

    for (i = 1; i < 10; i++)
    {
        cout << left(n, i) << "\n";
        temp = left(trip,i);
        cout << temp << "\n";
        delete [] temp; // point to temporary storage
    }
    return 0;

}

// This function returns the first ct digits of the number num.
unsigned long left(unsigned long num, unsigned ct)
{
    unsigned digits = 1;
    unsigned long n = num;

    if (ct == 0 || num == 0)
        return 0;       // return 0 if no digits
    while (n /= 10)
        digits++;
    if (digits > ct)
    {
    ct = digits - ct;
    while (ct--)
        num /= 10;
    return num;         // return left ct digits
    }
    else                // if ct >= number of digits
        return num;     // return the whole number
}

// This function returns a pointer to a new string
// consisting of the first n characters in the str string.
char * left(const char * str, int n)
{
    if(n < 0)
```

```
        n = 0;
    char * p = new char[n+1];
    int i;
    for (i = 0; i < n && str[i]; i++)
        p[i] = str[i];   // copy characters
    while (i <= n)
        p[i++] = '\0';   // set rest of string to '\0'
    return p;
}
```

Here's the output:

```
1
H
12
Ha
123
Haw
1234
Hawa
12345
Hawai
123456
Hawaii
1234567
Hawaii!
12345678
Hawaii!!
12345678
Hawaii!!
```

WHEN TO USE FUNCTION OVERLOADING

You might find function overloading fascinating, but don't overuse the facility. You should reserve function overloading for functions that perform basically the same task but with different forms of data. Also, you might want to check whether you can accomplish the same end with default arguments. For example, you could replace the single, string-oriented left() function with two overloaded functions:

```
char * left(const char * str, unsigned n);   // two arguments
char * left(const char * str);               // one argument
```

But using the single function with a default argument is simpler. There's just one function to write, instead of two, and the program requires memory for just one function, instead of two. If you decide to modify the function, there's only one you have to edit. However, if you require different types of arguments, default arguments are of no avail, so then you should use function overloading.

Function Templates

Contemporary C++ compilers implement one of the newer C++ additions, *function templates*. Function templates are a generic function description; that is, they define a function in terms of a generic type for which a specific type, such as int or double, can be substituted. By passing a type as a parameter to a template, you cause the compiler to generate a function for that particular type. Because templates let you program in terms of a generic type instead of a specific type, the process is sometimes termed *generic programming*. Because types are represented by parameters, the template feature is sometimes referred to as *parameterized types*. Let's see why such a feature is useful and how it works.

Earlier we defined a function that swapped two `int` values. Suppose you want to swap two `double` values instead. One approach is to duplicate the original code but replace each `int` with `double`. If you need to swap two `char` values, you can use the same technique again. Still, it's wasteful of your valuable time to have to make these petty changes, and there's always the possibility of making an error. If you make the changes by hand, you might overlook an `int`. If you do a global search-and-replace, you might do something such as converting

```
int integer;
```

to the following:

```
double doubleeger;
```

C++'s function template capability automates the process, saving you time and providing greater reliability.

Function templates enable you to define a function in terms of some arbitrary type. For instance, you can set up a swapping template like this:

```
template <class Any>
void Swap(Any &a, Any &b)
{
    Any temp;
    temp = a;
    a = b;
    b = temp;
}
```

> *" Function templates enable you to define a function in terms of some arbitrary type. "*

The first line specifies that you are setting up a template and that you're naming the arbitrary type *Any*. The keywords `template` and `class` (alternatively, `typename`) are obligatory, as are the angle brackets. The type name is your choice, as long as you follow the usual C++ naming rules; many programmers use simple names like `T`. The rest of the code describes the algorithm for swapping two values of type `Any`. The template does not create any functions. Instead, it provides the compiler with directions about how to define a function. If you want a function to swap `int`s, then the compiler creates a function following the template pattern, substituting `int` for `Any`. Similarly, if you need a function to swap `double`s, the compiler follows the template, substituting the `double` type for `Any`.

Recently, C++ added a new keyword, `typename`, that you can use instead of the keyword `class` in this particular context. That is, you can write the template definition this way:

```
template <typename Any>
void Swap(Any &a, Any &b)
{
    Any temp;
```

```
        temp = a;
        a = b;
        b = temp;
    }
```

The typename keyword makes it a bit more obvious that the parameter Any represents a type; however, large libraries of code already have been developed by using the older keyword class. Up-to-date compilers treat the two keywords identically when they are used in this context.

Remember

Use templates if you need functions that apply the same algorithm to a variety of types. If you aren't concerned with backward compatibility and can put up with the effort of typing a longer word, use the keyword typename rather than class when you declare type parameters.

To let the compiler know that you need a particular form of swap function, just use a function called Swap() in your program. The compiler checks the argument types you use and then generates the corresponding function. Listing 8.9 shows how this works. The program layout follows the usual pattern for ordinary functions with a template function prototype near the top of the file and the template function definition following main().

Remember

Non-current versions of C++ compilers might not support templates. New versions accept the keyword typename as an alternative to class. Version 2.71 of g++ requires that the template definition appears before the template is used.

Listing 8.9 funtemp.cpp

```cpp
// funtemp.cpp -- using a function template
#include <iostream>
using namespace std;
// function template prototype
template <class Any>  // or typename Any
void Swap(Any &a, Any &b);

int main()
{
    int i = 10;
    int j = 20;
    cout << "i, j = " << i << ", " << j << ".\n";
    cout << "Using compiler-generated int swapper:\n";
    Swap(i,j);  // generates void Swap(int &, int &)
    cout << "Now i, j = " << i << ", " << j << ".\n";

    double x = 24.5;
    double y = 81.7;
    cout << "x, y = " << x << ", " << y << ".\n";
    cout << "Using compiler-generated double swapper:\n";
    Swap(x,y);  // generates void Swap(double &, double &)
    cout << "Now x, y = " << x << ", " << y << ".\n";
```

```
    return 0;
}

// function template definition
template <class Any>  // or typename Any
void Swap(Any &a, Any &b)
{
    Any temp;   // temp a variable of type Any
    temp = a;
    a = b;
    b = temp;
}
```

The first Swap() function has two int arguments, so the compiler generates an int version of the function. That is, it replaces each use of Any with int, producing a definition that looks like this:

```
void Swap(int &a, int &b)
{
    int temp;
    temp = a;
    a = b;
    b = temp;
}
```

You don't see this code, but the compiler does. The second Swap() function has two double arguments, so the compiler generates a double version. That is, it replaces Any with double, generating this code:

```
void Swap(double &a, double &b)
{
    double temp;
    temp = a;
    a = b;
    b = temp;
}
```

Here's the program output; you can see the process has worked:

```
i, j = 10, 20.
Using compiler-generated int swapper:
Now i, j = 20, 10.
x, y = 24.5, 81.7.
Using compiler-generated double swapper:
Now x, y = 81.7, 24.5.
```

Note that function templates don't make your executable programs any shorter. In Listing 8.9, you still wind up with two separate function definitions, just as if you had defined each function manually. And the final code doesn't contain any templates; it just contains the actual functions generated for your program. The benefits of templates are that they make generating multiple function definitions simpler and more reliable.

OVERLOADED TEMPLATES

You use templates when you need functions that apply the same algorithm to a variety of types, as in Listing 8.8. It might be, however, that not all types would use the same algorithm. To meet this possibility, you can overload template definitions, just as you overload regular function definitions. As with ordinary overloading, overloaded templates need distinct function signatures. For instance, Listing 8.10 adds a new swapping template, one for swapping elements of two arrays. The original template has the signature (Any &, Any &), whereas the new template has the signature (Any [], Any [], int). Note that the final argument is a specific type (int) rather than a generic type. Not all function arguments have to be template parameter types.

When, in twotemps.cpp, the compiler encounters the first use of Swap(), it notices that it has two int arguments and matches it to the original template. The second use, however, has two int arrays and an int value as arguments, and this matches the new template.

```
Listing 8.10 twotemps.cpp
// twotemps.cpp -- using overloaded template functions
#include <iostream>
using namespace std;
template <class Any>      // original template
void Swap(Any &a, Any &b);

template <class Any>      // new template
void Swap(Any *a, Any *b, int n);

void Show(int a[]);
const int Lim = 8;
int main()
{
    int i = 10, j = 20;
    cout << "i, j = " << i << ", " << j << ".\n";
    cout << "Using compiler-generated int swapper:\n";
    Swap(i,j);                 // matches original template
    cout << "Now i, j = " << i << ", " << j << ".\n";

    int d1[Lim] = {0,7,0,4,1,7,7,6};
    int d2[Lim] = {0,6,2,0,1,9,6,9};
    cout << "Original arrays:\n";
    Show(d1);
    Show(d2);
    Swap(d1,d2,Lim);           // matches new template
    cout << "Swapped arrays:\n";
    Show(d1);
    Show(d2);

    return 0;
}

template <class Any>
void Swap(Any &a, Any &b)
{
    Any temp;
    temp = a;
```

```
        a = b;
        b = temp;
    }

    template <class Any>
    void Swap(Any a[], Any b[], int n)
    {
        Any temp;
        for (int i = 0; i < n; i++)
        {
            temp = a[i];
            a[i] = b[i];
            b[i] = temp;
        }
    }

    void Show(int a[])
    {
        cout << a[0] << a[1] << "/";
        cout << a[2] << a[3] << "/";
        for (int i = 4; i < Lim; i++)
            cout << a[i];
        cout << "\n";
    }
```

Remember 〉 **Non-current versions of C++ compilers might not support templates. New versions might accept the keyword `typename` instead of `class`. Older versions of C++ are more picky about type matching and require the following code to make the `const int Lim` match the template requirement for an ordinary int:**

```
Swap(d1,d2, int (Lim));          // typecast Lim to non-const int
```

Version 2.71 of g++ requires that the template definitions be placed ahead of `main()`.

Here is the program's output:

```
i, j = 10, 20.
Using compiler-generated int swapper:
Now i, j = 20, 10.
Original arrays:
07/04/1776
07/20/1969
Swapped arrays:
07/20/1969
07/04/1776
```

EXPLICIT SPECIALIZATIONS

Suppose you define a structure like the following:

```
struct job
{
    char name[40];
```

```
        double salary;
        int floor;
};
```

Also, suppose you want to be able to swap the contents of two such structures. The original template uses the following code to effect a swap:

```
temp = a;
a = b;
b = temp;
```

Because C++ allows you to assign one structure to another, this works fine, even if type Any is a job structure. But suppose you only want to swap the salary and floor members. This requires different code, but the arguments to Swap() would be the same as for the first case (references to two job structures), so you can't use template overloading to supply the alternative code.

However, you can supply a specialized function definition, called an *explicit specialization*, with the required code. If the compiler finds a specialized definition that exactly matches a function call, it uses that definition without looking for templates.

The specialization mechanism has changed with the evolution of the language. We look at the original form, supported by older compilers, an intermediate form, and then the current form.

First Generation Approach

Originally, a regular function declaration that exactly matched a function call overrode a template definition. For instance, consider the following code fragments:

```
template <class Any>
void Swap(Any &a, Any &b);      // template prototype
void Swap(int & n, int & m);    // regular prototype
int main()
{
    double u, v;
    ...
    Swap(u,v);  // use template
    int a, b;
    ...
    Swap(a,b);  // use void Swap(int &, int &)
```

> *"However, you can supply a specialized function definition, called an explicit specialization, with the required code. If the compiler finds a specialized definition that exactly matches a function call, it uses that definition without looking for templates."*

When the compiler reaches the Swap(a,b) function call, it has the choice of generating a function definition using the template or of using the nontemplate Swap(int &, int &) function. The original template facility called for the compiler to use the nontemplate version, treating it as a specialization of the template.

Second Generation

For a while, C++ (the non-official predraft version) called for different treatment. In the case of the code above, the compiler used the template and ignored the regular function prototype and definition. Making this change, however, didn't remove the need for explicit specializations. Therefore, C++ introduced a new syntax for declaring and defining explicit specializations. The idea is to follow the function name with angle brackets containing the specialized type. For instance, a specialized prototype of Swap() for ints would look like this:

```
void Swap<int>(int &a, int & b);    // a specialization
```

This prototype has to appear before the first function call with matching arguments:

```
template <class Any>
void Swap(Any &a, Any &b);         // template prototype
void Swap<int>(int & n, int & m);  // specialization prototype
int main()
{
    double u, v;
    ...
    Swap(u,v); // use template
    int a, b;
    ...
    Swap(a,b); // use void Swap<int>(int &, int &)
}
void Swap<int>(int & n, int & m)   // specialization definition
{...}
```

Note that the <int> appears in the prototype and the function definition. It can, but doesn't have to, appear in the function call:

```
Swap<int>(a, b); // also a choice
```

Third Generation

The latest developments are that

1. The non-template function overrides the template again, but it is not considered a specialization

2. The prototype and definition for an explicit specialization should be preceded by template <>:

A specialization overrides the regular template, and a non-template function overrides both.

Thus, a non-template version is chosen over explicit specializations and template versions, and an explicit specialization is chosen over a version generated from a template.

```
template <class Any>
void Swap(Any &a, Any &b);              // template prototype
template <> void Swap<int>(int & n, int & m);   // specialization
prototype
int main()
{
    double u, v;
    ...
    Swap(u,v); // use template
    int a, b;
    ...
    Swap(a,b); // use void Swap<int>(int &, int &)
}
```

```
template <> void Swap<int>(int & n, int & m)    // specialization
definition
{...}
```

The <int> in Swap<int> is optional, for the function argument types indicate that this is a specialization for int. Thus, the prototype also can be written this way:

```
template <> void Swap(int & n, int & m);    // simpler form
```

The template function heading also can be simplified by omitting the <int> part.
In a bit we look at the reason for this escalation in syntax complexity, but first, let's look at an example.

An Example

Listing 8.11 illustrates how explicit specialization works. It's set up to work in the newest manner, but you can delete and insert comment marks to choose one of the other versions.

Listing 8.11 twoswap.cpp

```cpp
// twoswap.cpp -- specialization overrides a template
#include <iostream>
using namespace std;
template <class Any>
void Swap(Any &a, Any &b);

struct job
{
    char name[40];
    double salary;
    int floor;
};

//void Swap(job &j1, job &j2);        // first generation
//void Swap<job>(job &j1, job &j2); // second generation
template <> void Swap(job &j1, job &j2); // third generation
void Show(job &j);

int main()
{
    cout.precision(2);
    cout.setf(ios::fixed, ios::floatfield);
    int i = 10, j = 20;
    cout << "i, j = " << i << ", " << j << ".\n";
    cout << "Using compiler-generated int swapper:\n";
    Swap(i,j);    // generates void Swap(int &, int &)
    cout << "Now i, j = " << i << ", " << j << ".\n";

    job sue = {"Susan Yaffee", 63000.60, 7};
    job sidney = {"Sidney Taffee", 66060.72, 9};
    cout << "Before job swapping:\n";
    Show(sue);
    Show(sidney);
    Swap(sue, sidney); // uses void Swap(job &, job &)
    cout << "After job swapping:\n";
    Show(sue);
```

```
    Show(sidney);

    return 0;
}

template <class Any>
void Swap(Any &a, Any &b)      // general version
{
    Any temp;
    temp = a;
    a = b;
    b = temp;
}

// swaps just the salary and floor fields of a job structure

//void Swap(job &j1, job &j2)         // first generation
//void Swap<job>(job &j1, job &j2)   // second generation
template <> void Swap(job &j1, job &j2)   // third generation
{
    double t1;
    int t2;
    t1 = j1.salary;
    j1.salary = j2.salary;
    j2.salary = t1;
    t2 = j1.floor;
    j1.floor = j2.floor;
    j2.floor = t2;
}

void Show(job &j)
{
    cout << j.name << ": $" << j.salary
         << " on floor " << j.floor << "\n";
}
```

Remember

Some compilers recognize the `template <> void Swap()` form, some recognize the `void Swap<job>()` form, and some recognize the `void Swap()` form.

Here's the program output:

```
i, j = 10, 20.
Using compiler-generated int swapper:
Now i, j = 20, 10.
Before job swapping:
Susan Yaffee: $63000.60 on floor 7
Sidney Taffee: $66060.72 on floor 9
After job swapping:
Susan Yaffee: $66060.72 on floor 9
Sidney Taffee: $63000.60 on floor 7
```

INSTANTIATIONS AND SPECIALIZATIONS

Keep in mind that including a function template in your code does not in itself generate a function definition. It's merely a plan for generating a function definition. When the compiler uses the template to generate a function definition for a particular type, the result is termed an *instantiation* of the template. For example, in Listing 8.11, the function call Swap(i,j) causes the compiler to generate an instantiation of the Swap() using int as the type. The template is not a function definition, but the specific instantiation using int is a function definition. This type of instantiation is termed an *implicit instantiation*, because the compiler deduces the necessity for making the definition by noting that the program uses a Swap() function with int parameters.

Originally, implicit instantiation was the only way the compiler generated function definitions from templates, but now C++ allows for *explicit instantiation*. That means you can instruct the compiler to create a particular instantiation, for instance Swap<int>(), directly. The syntax is to declare the particular variety you want, using the <> notation to indicate the type and prefixing the declaration with the keyword template:

```
template Swap<int>(int, int);  // explicit instantiation
```

A compiler that implements this feature will, upon seeing this declaration, use the Swap() template to generate an instantiation using the int type.

Contrast the explicit instantiation with the explicit specialization, which uses one or the other of these equivalent declarations:

```
template <> Swap<int>(int, int);  // explicit specialization
template <> Swap(int, int);       // explicit specialization
```

The difference is that these declarations mean "Don't use the Swap() template to generate a function definition. Instead, use a separate, specialized function definition explicitly defined for the int type." These prototypes have to be coupled with their own function definitions.

Remember

It is an error to try to use both an explicit instantiation and an explicit specialization for the same type(s) in the same programming unit.

Implicit instantiations, explicit instantiations, and explicit specializations collectively are termed *specializations*. What they all have in common is that they represent a function definition based on specific types rather than one that is a generic description.

The addition of the explicit instantiation led to the new syntax of using template and template <> prefixes in declarations to distinguish between the explicit instantiation and the explicit specialization. Often, the cost of doing more is more syntax rules.

WHICH FUNCTION?

What with function overloading, function templates, and function template overloading, C++ needs, and has, a well-defined strategy for deciding which function definition to use for a function call, particularly when there are multiple arguments. The process is called *overload resolution*. Detailing the complete strategy would take a small chapter, so let's take an overview of how the process works:

◆ Phase 1: Assemble a list of candidate functions. These are functions and template functions with the same name as the called function.

◆ Phase 2: From the candidate functions, assemble a list of viable functions. These are functions with the correct number of arguments and for which there is an implicit conversion sequence, which includes the case of an cxact match for each type of actual argument to the type of the corresponding formal argument. For example, a function call with a type `float` argument could have that value converted to a `double` to match a type `double` formal parameter, and a template could generate an instantiation for `float`.

◆ Phase 3: Determine if there is a best viable function. If so, use that function. Otherwise, the function call is an error.

Consider a case with just one function argument, for example, the following call:

```
may('B');    // actual argument is type char
```

First, the compiler rounds up the suspects, which are functions and function templates having the name may(). Then, it finds those that can be called with one argument. For example, the following will pass muster:

```
void may(int);                            // #1
float may(float, float = 3);              // #2
void may(char);                           // #3
char * may(const char *);                 // #4
template<class T> void may(const T &);    // #5
template<class T. void may(T *);          // #6
```

Note that just the signatures and not the return types are considered. Two of these candidates (#4 and #6), however, are not viable because an intregal type cannot be converted implicitly (that is, without an explicit type cast) to a pointer type. That leaves four viable functions, each of which could be used if it were the only function declared.

Next, the compiler has to determine which of the viable functions is best. It looks at the conversion required to make the function call argument match the viable candidate's argument. In general, the ranking from best to worst is this:

1. Exact match

2. Conversion by promotion (the automatic conversions of `char` and `short` to `int` and of `float` to `double`, for example)

3. Conversion by standard conversion (converting `int` to `char` or `long` to `double`, for example)

4. User-defined conversions, such as those defined in class declarations

For example, function #1 is better than function #2 because char-to-int is a promotion (Chapter 3, "Dealing with Data"), whereas char-to-float is a standard conversion (Chapter 3). Functions #3 and #5 are better than either #1 or #2, because both are exact matches. This raises a couple of questions. What is an exact match, and what happens if you get two of them?

Exact Matches and Best Matches

C++ allows some "trivial conversions" when making an exact match. Table 8.1 lists them, with *Type* standing for some arbitrary type. For example, an int actual argument is an exact match to an int & formal parameter. Note that *Type* can be something like char &, so these rules include converting char & to const char &. The *Type* (*argument-list*) entry means that a function name as an actual argument matches a function pointer as a formal argument as long as both have the same return type and argument list. (Remember function pointers from Chapter 7, "Functions—C++'s Programming Modules," and how you can pass the name of a function as an argument to a function expecting a pointer to a function.) We discuss the volatile keyword later in this chapter.

Anyway, suppose you have the following function code:

```
struct blot {int a; char b[10];};
blot ink = {25, "spots"};
...
recycle(ink);
```

Then, all the following prototypes would be exact matches:

```
void recycle(blot);         // #1  blot-to-blot
void recycle(const blot);   // #2  blot-to-(const blot)
void recycle(blot &);       // #3  blot-to-(blot &)
void recycle(const blot &); // #4  blot-to-(const blot &)
```

As you might expect, the result of having several matching prototypes is that the compiler cannot complete the overload resolution process. There is no best viable function, and the compiler generates an error message, probably using words like "ambiguous."

TABLE 8.1
TRIVIAL CONVERSIONS ALLOWED FOR AN EXACT MATCH

FROM AN ACTUAL ARGUMENT	TO A FORMAL ARGUMENT
Type	*Type* &
Type &	*Type*
Type []	* *Type*
Type (*argument-list*)	*Type* (*)(*argument-list*)
Type	const *Type*
Type	volatile *Type*
Type *	const *Type* *
Type *	volatile *Type* *

However, sometimes there can be overload resolution even if two functions are an exact match. First, pointers and references to non-const data preferentially are matched to non-const pointer and reference parameters. That is, if only functions #3 and #4 were available in the preceding example, #3 would be chosen because ink wasn't declared as const. However, this discrimination between const and non-const applies just to data referred to by pointers and references. That is, if only #1 and #2 were available, you would get an ambiguity error.

Another case where one exact match is better than another is when one function is a non-template function and the other isn't. In that case, the non-template is considered better than a template, including explicit specializations.

If you wind up with two exact matches that both happen to be template functions, the template function that is the more specialized, if either, is the better function. That means, for example, that an explicit specialization is chosen over one generated implicitly from the template pattern:

```
struct blot {int a; char b[10];};
template <class Type> void recycle (Type t); // template
template <> void recycle<blot> (blot & t);    // specialization for blot
...
blot ink = {25, "spots"};
...
recycle(ink); // use specialization
```

The term "most specialized" doesn't necessarily imply an explicit specialization; more generally, it indicates that fewer conversions take place when the compiler deduces what type to use. For example, consider the following two templates:

```
template <class Type> void recycle (Type t);    #1
template <class Type> void recycle (Type * t);..#2
```

Suppose the program that contains these templates also contains the following code:

```
struct blot {int a; char b[10];};
blot ink = {25, "spots"};
...
recycle(&ink); // address of a structure
```

The recycle(&ink) call matches template #1 with Type interpreted as blot *. The recycle(&ink) function call also matches template #2, this time with Type being ink. This combination sends two implicit instantiations, recycle<blot *>(blot *) and recycle<blot>(blot *), to the viable function pool.

Of these two template functions, recycle<blot *>(blot *) is considered the more specialized because it underwent fewer conversions in being generated. That is, template #2 already explicitly said the function argument was pointer-to-*Type*, so *Type* could be directly identified with blot. Template #1, however, had *Type* as the function argument, so *Type* had to be interpreted as pointer-to-blot. That is, in template #2, *Type* already was specialized as a pointer, hence the term "more specialized."

The rules for finding the most specialized template are called the *partial ordering rules* for function templates. Like explicit instantiations, they are new additions to the language.

In short, the overload resolution process looks for a function that's the best match. If there's just one, that function is chosen. If there are more than one otherwise tied, but only one is a non-template function, that's chosen. If there are more than one candidates otherwise tied, and all are template functions, but one template is more specialized than the rest, that is chosen. If there are two or more equally good non-template functions, or if there are two or more equally good template functions, none of which is more specialized than the rest, the function call is ambiguous and an error. If there are no matching calls, of course, that also is an error.

Functions with Multiple Arguments

Where matters really get involved is when a function call with multiple arguments is matched to prototypes with multiple arguments. The compiler must look at matches for all the arguments. If it can find a function that is better than all the other viable functions, it's the chosen one. For one function to be better than another function, it has to provide at least as good a match for all arguments and a better match for at least one argument.

This book does not intend to challenge the matching process with complex examples. The rules are there so that there is a well-defined result for any possible set of function prototypes and templates.

Separate Compilation

C++, like C, allows you, even encourages you, to locate the component functions to a program in separate files. As Chapter 1, "Getting Started," describes, you can compile the files separately and then link them into the final executable program. (A C++ compiler typically compiles programs and also manages the linker program.) If you modify just one file, you can recompile just that one file and then link it to the previously compiled versions of the other files. This facility makes it easier to manage large programs. Furthermore, most C++ environments provide additional facilities to help with the management. UNIX systems, for example, have the make program; it keeps track of which files a program depends upon and when they were last modified. If you run make and it detects you've changed one or more source files since the last compilation, make remembers the proper steps needed to reconstitute the program. The Symantec C++, Turbo C++, Borland C++, Watcom C++, Microsoft Visual C++, and Metrowerks CodeWarrior environments provide similar facilities with their Project menus.

Let's look at a simple example. Instead of looking at compilation details, which depend on the implementation, let's concentrate on more general aspects, such as design.

Suppose, for example, you decide to break up the program in Listing 7.11 by placing the functions in a separate file. That listing, recall, converted rectangular coordinates to polar coordinates and then displayed the result. You can't simply cut the original file on a dotted line after the end of main(). The problem is that main() and the other two functions all use the same structure declarations, so you need to put the declarations in both files. Simply typing them in is an invitation to err. Even if you copy the structure declarations correctly, you have to remember to modify both sets of declarations if you make changes later. In short, spreading a program over multiple files creates new problems.

Who wants more problems? The developers of C and C++ didn't, so they've provided the #include facility to deal with this sort of situation. Instead of placing the structure declarations in each file, you can place them in a header file and then include that header file in each source code file. That way, if you modify the structure declaration, you can do so just once, in the header file. Also, you can place the function prototypes in the header file. Thus, you can divide the original program into three parts:

- A header file that contains the structure declarations and prototypes for functions using those structures

- A source code file that contains the code for the structure-related functions

- A source code file that contains the code that calls upon those functions

This is a useful strategy for organizing a program. If, for instance, you write another program that uses those same functions, just include the header file and add the function file to the project or make list. Also, this organization reflects the OOP approach. One file, the header file, contains the definition of the user-defined types. A second file contains the function code for manipulating the user-defined types. Together, they form a package you can use for a variety of programs.

Don't put function definitions or variable declarations into a header file. It might work for a simple setup, but usually it leads to trouble. For example, if you had a function definition in a header file and then included the header file in two other files that are part of a single program, you'd wind up with two definitions of the same function in a single program, which is an error. Here are some things commonly found in header files:

- Function prototypes

- Symbolic constants defined using #define or const

- Structure declarations

- Class declarations

- Template declarations

- Inline functions

It's okay to put structure declarations in a header file because they don't create variables; they just tell the compiler how to create a structure variable when you declare one in a source code file. Similarly, template declarations aren't code to be compiled; they are instructions to the compiler on how to generate function definitions to match function calls found in the source code. Data declared const and inline functions have special linkage properties (coming up soon) that allow them to be placed in header files without causing problems.

> " *This is a useful strategy for organizing a program.* "

Listings 8.12, 8.13, and 8.14 show the result of dividing Listing 7.11 into separate parts. Note that we use "coordin.h" instead of <coordin.h> when including the header file. If the filename is enclosed in brackets, the C++ compiler looks at the part of the host system's file system that holds the standard header files. But if the filename is enclosed in double quotation marks, the compiler first looks at the current working directory or at the source code directory (or some such choice, depending upon the compiler). If it doesn't find the header file there, it then looks in the standard location. So use quotation marks, not angle brackets, when including your own header files.

Figure 8.3 outlines the steps for putting this program together on a UNIX system. Note that you just give the CC compile command and the other steps follow automatically. Symantec C++, Borland C++, Turbo C++, Metrowerks CodeWarrior, Watcom C++, and Microsoft Visual C++ go through essentially the same steps, but, as outlined in Chapter 1, you initiate the process differently, using menus that let you create a project and associate source code files with it. Note that you only add source code files, not header files to projects. That's because the #include directive manages the header files. Also, don't use #include to include source code files because that can lead to multiple declarations.

Remember

In Integrated Development Environments, don't add header files to the project list, and don't use #include to include source code files in other source code files.

Listing 8.12 coordin.h

```cpp
// coordin.h -- structure templates and function prototypes
// structure templates
struct Polar
{
    double distance;    // distance from origin
    double angle;       // direction from origin
};
struct rect
{
    double x;           // horizontal distance from origin
    double y;           // vertical distance from origin
};

// prototypes
Polar rect_to_polar(rect xypos);
void show_polar(Polar dapos);
```

FIGURE 8.3

Compiling a multifile C++ program on a UNIX system

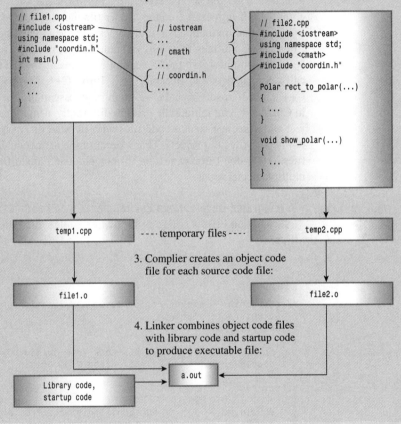

Listing 8.13 file1.cpp

```cpp
// file1.cpp -- example of a two-file program
#include <iostream>
#include "coordin.h" // structure templates, function prototypes
using namespace std;
int main()
{
    rect rplace;
    Polar pplace;

    cout << "Enter the x and y values: ";
```

```
    while (cin >> rplace.x >> rplace.y)  // slick use of cin
    {
        pplace = rect_to_polar(rplace);
        show_polar(pplace);
        cout << "Next two numbers (q to quit): ";
    }
    return 0;
}
```

Listing 8.14 file2.cpp

```
// file2.cpp -- contains functions called in file1.cpp
#include <iostream>
#include <cmath>
#include "coordin.h" // structure templates, function prototypes
using namespace std;

// convert rectangular to polar coordinates
Polar rect_to_polar(rect xypos)
{
    Polar answer;

    answer.distance =
        sqrt( xypos.x * xypos.x + xypos.y * xypos.y);
    answer.angle = atan2(xypos.y, xypos.x);
    return answer;        // returns a Polar structure
}

// show polar coordinates, converting angle to degrees
void show_polar (Polar dapos)
{
    const double Rad_to_deg = 57.29577951;

    cout << "distance = " << dapos.distance;
    cout << ", angle = " << dapos.angle * Rad_to_deg;
    cout << " degrees\n";
}
```

By the way, although we've discussed separate compilation in terms of files, the language description uses the term *translation unit* instead of file in order to preserve greater generality; the file metaphor is not the only possible way to organize information for a computer.

Storage Classes, Scope, and Linkage

Now that you've seen a multifile program, it's a good time to extend the discussion of storage classes in Chapter 4, "Derived Types" because storage classes affect how information can be shared across files. It might have been awhile since you last read Chapter 4, so let's review what it said about storage classes. C++ uses three separate schemes for storing data, and the schemes differ in how long they preserve data in memory.

🢒 Automatic variables are those declared inside a function definition; that includes function parameters. They are created when program execution enters the function or block in which they are defined, and the memory used for them is freed when execution leaves the function or block.

🢒 Static variables are those defined outside a function definition or else by using the keyword `static`. They persist for the entire time a program is running.

🢒 Dynamic storage allocated by the `new` operator persists until freed with the `delete` operator or until the program ends, whichever comes first.

We get the rest of the story now, including fascinating details about when variables of different types are in scope, or visible (usable by the program), and about linkage, which determines what information is shared across files.

SCOPE AND LINKAGE

Scope describes how widely visible a name is in a file (translation unit). For instance, a variable defined in a function can be used in that function, but not in another, whereas a variable defined in a file above the function definitions can be used in all the functions. *Linkage* describes how a name can be shared in different units. A name with *external linkage* can be shared across files, and a name with *internal linkage* can be shared by functions within a single file. Names of automatic variables have no linkage because they are not shared.

A C++ variable can have one of several scopes. A variable having *local scope* (also termed *block scope*) is known only within the block in which it is defined. A block, remember, is a series of statements enclosed in braces. A function body, for example, is a block, but you can have other blocks nested within the function body. A variable having *global scope* (also termed *file scope*) is known throughout the file after the point where it is defined. Automatic variables have local scope, and a static variable can have either scope, depending on how it is defined. Names used in a *function proto-type scope* are known just within the parentheses enclosing the argument list. (That's why it doesn't really matter what they are or if they are even present.) Members declared in a class have *class scope* (see Chapter 9, "Objects and Classes"). Variables declared in a namespace have *namespace scope*. (Now that namespaces have been added to the language, the global scope has become a special case of namespace scope.)

C++ functions can have class scope or namespace scope, including global scope, but they can't have local scope. (Because a function can't be defined inside a block, if a function were to have local scope, it could only be known to itself, and hence couldn't be called by another function. Such a function couldn't function.)

Let's look in more detail at the scope and linkage properties of C++'s various storage classes. We begin by examining the situation before namespaces were added to the mix, and then see how namespaces modify the picture.

AUTOMATIC VARIABLES

> *"If you define a variable inside a block, the variable's persistence and scope is confined to that block."*

Function parameters and variables declared inside a function belong, by default, to the automatic storage class. These variables have local visibility, or scope. That is, if you declare a variable called `texas` in `main()` and declare another variable with the same name in a function called `oil()`, you've created two independent variables, each known only in the function in which it's defined. Anything you do to the `texas` in `oil()` has no effect on the `texas` in `main()`, and vice versa. Also, each variable is allocated when its function begins execution, and each fades from existence when its function terminates.

If you define a variable inside a block, the variable's persistence and scope is confined to that block. Suppose, for instance, you define a variable called `teledeli` at the beginning of `main()`. Now suppose you start a new block within `main()` and define a new variable, called `websight`, in the block. Then, `teledeli` is visible in both the outer and inner block, whereas `websight` is visible only in the inner block and exists only from its point of definition until program execution passes the end of the block:

```
int main()
{
    int teledeli = 5;
    {
        int websight = -2;
        cout << websight << ' ' << teledeli << endl;
    } // websight expires
    cout << teledeli << endl;
    ...
}
```

But what if you name the variable in the inner block `teledeli` instead of `websight` so that you have two variables of the same name, with one in the outer block and one in the inner block? In this case, the program interprets the `teledeli` name to mean the local block variable while the program executes statements within the block. We say the new definition *hides* the prior definition. The new definition is in scope, and the old definition temporarily is out of scope. When the program leaves the block, the original definition comes back into scope. See Figure 8.4.

Listing 8.15 illustrates how automatic variables are localized to the function or block that contains them.

FIGURE 8.4

Blocks and scope

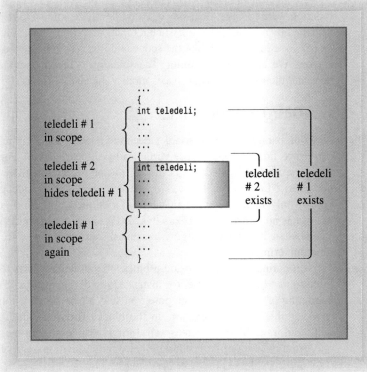

Listing 8.15 auto.cpp

```cpp
// auto.cpp -- illustrating scope of automatic variables
#include <iostream>
using namespace std;
void oil(int x);
int main()
{
// NOTE: some implementations require that you type cast the
// addresses in this program to type unsigned

    int texas = 31;
    int year = 1999;
    cout << "In main(), texas = " << texas << ", &texas =";
    cout << &texas << "\n";
    cout << "In main(), year = " << year << ", &year =";
    cout << &year << "\n";
    oil(texas);
    cout << "In main(), texas = " << texas << ", &texas =";
    cout << &texas << "\n";
```

```
        cout << "In main(), year = " << year << ", &year =";
        cout << &year << "\n";
        return 0;
}

void oil(int x)
{
    int texas = 5;

    cout << "In oil(), texas = " << texas << ", &texas =";
    cout << &texas << "\n";
    cout << "In oil(), x = " << x << ", &x =";
    cout << &x << "\n";
    {                                    // start a block
        int texas = 113;
        cout << "In block, texas = " << texas;
        cout << ", &texas = " << &texas << "\n";
            cout << "In block, x = " << x << ", &x =";
        cout << &x << "\n";
    }                                    // end a block
    cout << "Post-block texas = " << texas;
    cout << ", &texas = " << &texas << "\n";
}
```

Here is the output:

```
In main(), texas = 31, &texas =0068FDF0
In main(), year = 1999, &year =0068FDF4
In oil(), texas = 5, &texas =0068FDE0
In oil(), x = 31, &x =0068FDEC
In block, texas = 113, &texas = 0068FDDC
In block, x = 31, &x =0068FDEC
Post-block texas = 5, &texas = 0068FDE0
In main(), texas = 31, &texas =0068FDF0
In main(), year = 1999, &year =0068FDF4
```

Notice how each of the three texas variables has its own distinct address and how the program uses only the particular variable in scope at the moment, so assigning the value 113 to the texas in the inner block in oil() has no effect on the other variables of the same name.

Let's summarize the sequence of events. When main() starts, the program allocates space for texas and year, and these variables come into scope. When the program calls oil(), these variables remain in memory but pass out of scope. Two new variables, x and texas, are allocated and come into scope. When program execution reaches the inner block in oil(), the new texas passes out of scope as it is superseded by an even newer definition. The variable x, however, stays in scope because the block doesn't define a new x. When execution exits the block, the memory for the newest texas is freed, and texas number 2 comes back into scope. When the oil() function terminates, that texas and x expire, and the original texas and year come back into scope.

Incidentally, you can use the C++ (and C) keyword `auto` to indicate the storage class explicitly:

```
int froob(int n)
{
    auto float ford;
    ...
}
```

Because you can use the `auto` keyword only with variables that already are automatic by default, programmers rarely bother using it. Occasionally, it's used to clarify code to the reader. For example, you can use it to indicate that you purposely are creating an automatic variable that overrides a global definition, such as those we discuss shortly.

Automatic Variables and the Stack

You might gain a better understanding of automatic variables by seeing how a typical C++ compiler implements them. Because the number of automatic variables grows and shrinks as functions start and terminate, the program has to manage automatic variables as it runs. The usual means is to set aside a section of memory and treat it as a stack for managing the flow and ebb of variables. It's called a stack because new data figuratively is stacked atop old data (that is, at an adjacent location, not at the same location) and then removed from the stack when a program is finished with it. The default size of the stack depends on the implementation, but a compiler generally provides the option of changing the size. The program keeps track of the stack by using two pointers. One points to the base of the stack, where the memory set aside for the stack begins, and one points to the top of the stack, which is the next free memory location. When a function is called, its automatic variables are added to the stack, and the pointer to the top points to the next available free space following the variables. When the function terminates, the top pointer is reset to the value it had before the function was called, effectively freeing the memory that had been used for the new variables.

A stack is a LIFO (last in-first out) design, meaning the last variables added to the stack are the first to go. The design simplifies argument passing. The function call places the values of its arguments on top of the stack and resets the top pointer. The called function uses the description of its formal arguments to determine the addresses of each argument. Figure 8.5, for example, shows a `fib()` function that, when called, passes a 2-byte `int` and a 4-byte `long`. These values go on the stack. When `fib()` begins execution, it associates the names `real` and `tell` with the two values. When `fib()` terminates, the top-of-stack pointer is relocated to its former position. The new values aren't erased, but they no longer are labeled, and the space they occupy will be used by the next process that places values on the stack. (The figure is somewhat simplified, for function calls may pass additional information, such as a return address.)

FIGURE 8.5

Passing arguments with a stack

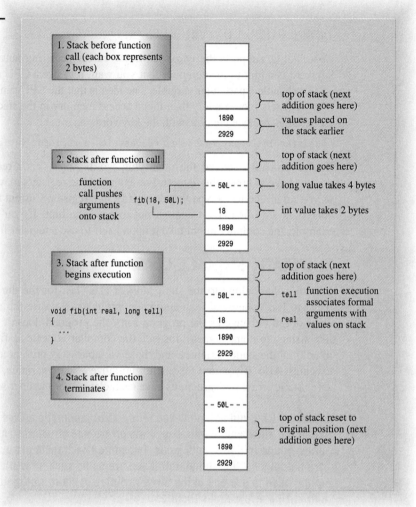

You might have noticed that addresses in Listing 8.15 decrease rather than increase as new variables are added. That's because this particular C++ compiler implements the stack upside down. This changes the direction the stack grows, but it retains the basic concept.

Type `register` Variables

C++, like C, supports the `register` keyword for declaring automatic variables. This keyword is a hint to the compiler that you want it to use a CPU register instead of the stack to handle a particular variable. The idea is that the CPU can access a value in one of its registers more rapidly than it can access memory in the stack. To declare a register variable, preface the type with the keyword `register`:

```
register int count_fast;  // request for a register variable
```

You've probably noticed the qualifying words "hint" and "request." The compiler doesn't have to honor the request. For example, the registers may already be occupied, or you might request a type that doesn't fit in a register. Current feeling is that modern compilers are often smart enough not to need the hint. If you write a `for` loop, for example, the compiler might take it upon itself to use a register for the loop index.

THE STATIC STORAGE CLASS

Variables that belong to the static storage class last for the duration of the program; they are less ephemeral than automatic variables. Because the number of static variables doesn't change as the program runs, the program doesn't need a special device like a stack to manage them. Instead, the compiler allocates a fixed block of memory to hold all the static variables, and those variables stay present as long as the program executes. Also, if you don't explicitly initialize a static variable, the compiler sets it to zero. Static arrays and structures have each element or member set to zero by default.

Remember

Classic K&R C did not allow you to initialize automatic arrays and structures, but it did allow you to initialize static arrays and structures. ANSI C and C++ allow you to initialize both kinds, but some C++ translators use C compilers that are not fully ANSI C-compliant. If you are using such an implementation, you might need to use one of the three varieties of static storage classes for initializing arrays and structures.

C++, like C, provides three varieties of static variables: external, static, and external static. If that looks a little confusing to you, you're right. Unfortunately, C++ uses the word *static* in two different senses. One is that of a variable that persists for the duration of the program. In that sense, all three varieties are static. The second sense limits how widely known the variable is; it affects the scope and linkage. The external variable is available to all files of a program (global scope, external linkage); the external static variable is available to all the functions in a single file (global scope, internal linkage); and the static variable declared within a block is confined to a single block (block scope, internal linkage). Table 8.2 summarizes the storage class features as used in the pre-namespace era; you've seen some of this information already, but we take a closer look now.

TABLE 8.2
STORAGE CLASSES

STORAGE CLASS	HOW CREATED	SCOPE	LINKAGE	DURATION
Automatic block	Default for function parameters and variables declared inside a function	Local	Internal	While defining is being executed
External	Default for variables declared outside any function	Global	External	While program is running
Static	By applying the static keyword to a variable declared inside a function	Local	Internal	While program is running
Extern static	By applying the static keyword to a variable declared outside any function	Global	Internal	While program is running

External Variables

> *"C++, like C, provides three varieties of static variables: external, static, and external static. If that looks a little confusing to you, you're right."*

External variables are called external because they are defined outside of, and hence external to, any function. For example, they could be declared above the main() function. You can use an external variable in any function that follows the external variable's definition in the file. Thus, external variables also are termed global variables in contrast to automatic variables, which are local variables. However, if you define an automatic variable having the same name as an external variable, the automatic variable is the one in scope when the program executes that particular function. Listing 8.16 illustrates these points. It also shows how you can use the keyword extern to redeclare an external variable defined earlier and how you can use C++'s scope resolution operator to access an otherwise hidden external variable.

Listing 8.16 external.cpp

```cpp
// external.cpp -- external variables
#include <iostream>
using namespace std;
// external variable
double warming = 0.3;

// function prototypes
void update(double dt);
void local();

int main()                   // uses global variable
{
    cout << "Global warming is " << warming << " degrees.\n";
    update(0.1);             // call function to change warming
    cout << "Global warming is " << warming << " degrees.\n";
    local();                 // call function with local warming
```

```
        cout << "Global warming is " << warming << " degrees.\n";
        return 0;
    }

    void update(double dt)        // modifies global variable
    {
        extern double warming;  // optional redeclaration
        warming += dt;
        cout << "Updating global warming to " << warming;
        cout << " degrees.\n";
    }

    void local()                   // uses local variable
    {
        double warming = 0.8;    // new variable hides external one

        cout << "Local warming = " << warming << " degrees.\n";
            // Access global variable with the
            // scope resolution operator
        cout << "But global warming = " << ::warming;
        cout << " degrees.\n";
    }
```

Here is the output:

```
Global warming is 0.3 degrees.
Updating global warming to 0.4 degrees.
Global warming is 0.4 degrees.
Local warming = 0.8 degrees.
But global warming = 0.4 degrees.
Global warming is 0.4 degrees.
```

Program Notes

The program output illustrates that both main() and update() can access the external variable warming. Note that the change that update() makes to warming shows up in subsequent uses of the variable.

The update() function redeclares the warming variable by using the keyword extern. This keyword means "use the variable by this name previously defined externally." Because that is what update() would do anyway if you omitted the entire declaration, this declaration is optional. It serves to document that the function is designed to use the external variable. The original declaration

```
double warming = 0.3;
```

is called a *defining declaration*, or, simply, a *definition*. It causes storage for the variable to be allocated. The redeclaration

```
extern double warming;
```

is called a *referencing declaration*, or, simply, a *declaration*. It does not cause storage to be allocated because it refers to an existing variable. You can use the extern keyword only in declarations referring to variables defined elsewhere (or functions—more on that later). Also, you cannot initialize a variable in a referencing declaration:

```
extern double warming = 0.5;   // INVALID
```

You can initialize a variable in a declaration only if the declaration allocates the variable, that is, only in a defining declaration. After all, the term initialization means assigning a value to a memory location when that location is allocated.

The `local()` function demonstrates that when you define a local variable having the same name as a global variable, the local version hides the global version. The `local()` function, for example, uses the local definition of `warming` when it displays `warming`'s value.

C++ takes a step beyond C by offering the *scope resolution operator* (`::`). When prefixed to the name of a variable, this operator means to use the global version of that variable. Thus, `local()` displays `warming` as 0.8, but it displays `::warming` as 0.4. You'll encounter this operator again in namespaces and classes.

GLOBAL OR LOCAL?

Now that you have a choice of using global or local variables, which should you use? At first, global variables have a seductive appeal—because all functions have access to a global variable, you don't have to bother passing arguments. But this easy access has a heavy price—unreliable programs. Computing experience has shown that the better job your program does of isolating data from unnecessary access, the better job the program does in preserving the integrity of the data. Most often, you should use local variables and pass data to functions on a need-to-know basis rather than make data available indiscriminately with global variables. As you will see, OOP takes this data isolation a step further.

Global variables do have their uses, however. For example, you might have a block of data that's to be used by several functions, such as an array of month names or the atomic weights of the elements. The external storage class is particularly suited to representing constant data, for then you can use the keyword `const` to protect the data from change.

```
const char * const months[12] =
{
    "January", "February", "March", "April", "May",
    "June", "July", "August", "September", "October",
    "November", "December"
};
```

The first `const` protects the strings from change, and the second `const` makes sure that each pointer in the array remains pointing to the same string to which it pointed initially.

THE `static` MODIFIER (LOCAL VARIABLES)

The `static` modifier can be used either with a local variable or with a global variable. We look at the local case now. When you use it inside a block, `static` makes a local variable have the static storage class. That means that even though the variable is known within that block, it exists even while the block is inactive. Thus, a static local variable can preserve its value between function calls. (Static variables would be useful for reincarnation—you could use them to pass secret account numbers for a Swiss bank to your next appearance.) Also, if you initialize a static local variable, the program initializes the variable once, when the program starts up. Subsequent calls to the function don't reinitialize the variable the way they do for automatic variables. Listing 8.17 illustrates these points.

Incidentally, the program shows one way to deal with line input that may exceed the size of the destination array. The `cin.get(input,ArSize)` input method, recall, reads up to the end of the line or up to `ArSize` - 1 characters, whichever comes first. It leaves the newline character in the input queue. This program reads the character that follows the line input. If it is a newline character, then the whole line was read. If it isn't a newline character, more characters are left on the line. This program then uses a loop to reject the rest of the line, but you can modify the code to use the rest of the line for the next input cycle. The program also uses the fact that attempting to read an empty line with `get(char *, int)` causes `cin` to test as false.

Listing 8.17 static.cpp

```cpp
// static.cpp -- using a static local variable
#include <iostream>
using namespace std;
// constants
const int ArSize = 10;

// function prototype
void strcount(const char * str);

int main()
{
    char input[ArSize];
    char next;

    cout << "Enter a line:\n";
    cin.get(input, ArSize);
    while (cin)
    {
        cin.get(next);
        while (next != '\n')       // string didn't fit!
            cin.get(next);
        strcount(input);
        cout << "Enter next line (empty line to quit):\n";
        cin.get(input, ArSize);
    }
    cout << "Bye\n";
    return 0;
}
```

```
void strcount(const char * str)
{
    static int total = 0;       // static local variable
    int count = 0;              // automatic local variable

    cout << "\"" << str <<"\" contains ";
    while (*str++)                  // go to end of string
        count++;
    total += count;
    cout << count << " characters\n";
    cout << total << " characters total\n";
}
```

Remember

Some older compilers don't implement the requirement that when `cin.get(char *,int)` reads an empty line, it sets the failbit error flag, causing `cin` to test as false. In that case, you can replace the test

```
while (cin)
```

with this:

```
while (input[0])
```

Or, for a test that works for both old and new implementations, do this:

```
while (cin && input[0])
```

Here is the program's output:

```
Enter a line:
nice pants
"nice pant" contains 9 characters
9 characters total
Enter next line (empty line to quit):
thanks
"thanks" contains 6 characters
15 characters total
Enter next line (empty line to quit):
parting is such sweet sorrow
"parting i" contains 9 characters
24 characters total
Enter next line (empty line to quit):
ok
"ok" contains 2 characters
26 characters total
Enter next line (empty line to quit):

Bye
```

Note that because the array size is 10, the program does not read more than 9 characters per line. Also note that the automatic variable count is reset to 0 each time the function is called. However, the static variable total is set to 0 once, at the beginning. After that, total retains its value between function calls, so it's able to maintain a running total.

LINKAGE AND EXTERNAL VARIABLES

Applying the static modifier to an external variable becomes meaningful in multifile programs. In that context, a static external variable is local to the file containing it. It has internal linkage. But a regular external variable has external linkage, meaning it can be used in different files. For external linkage, only one file can contain the external definition for the variable. Other files that want to use that variable must use the keyword extern in a reference declaration. See Figure 8.6.

If a file doesn't provide the extern declaration of a variable, it can't use an external variable defined elsewhere:

```
// file1
int errors = 20;        // global declaration
...
------------------------------------------------
// file 2
...                           // missing an extern int errors declaration
void froobish()
{
    cout << errors;   // doomed attempt to use errors
..
```

If a file attempts to define a second external variable by the same name, that's an error:

```
// file1
int errors = 20;           // external declaration
...
------------------------------------------------
// file 2
int errors;                // invalid declaration
void froobish()
{
    cout << errors;      // doomed attempt to use errors
..
```

The correct approach is to use the keyword extern in the second file:

```
// file1
int errors = 20;           // external declaration
...
------------------------------------------------
// file 2
extern int errors;         // refers to errors from file1
void froobish()
{
    cout << errors;      // uses errors defined in file1
..
```

But if a file declares a static external variable having the same name as an ordinary external variable declared in another file, the static version is the one in scope for that file:

```
// file1
int errors = 20;           // external declaration
...
------------------------------------------------
```

```
// file2
static int errors = 5;  // known to file2 only
void froobish()
{
     cout << errors;   // uses errors defined in file2
     ...
```

> **Remember**
>
> In a multifile program, you can define an external variable in only one file. All other files using that variable have to declare that variable with the `extern` keyword.

Use a regular external variable to share data among different parts of a multifile program. Use a static external variable to share data among functions found in just one file. (Namespaces offer an alternative method for this.) Also, if you make an external variable static, you needn't worry about its name conflicting with external variables found in other files.

Listings 8.18 and 8.19 show how C++ handles external and static external variables. Listing 8.18 (`twofile1.cpp`) defines the external variables `tom` and `dick` and the static external variable `harry`. The `main()` function in that file displays the addresses of the

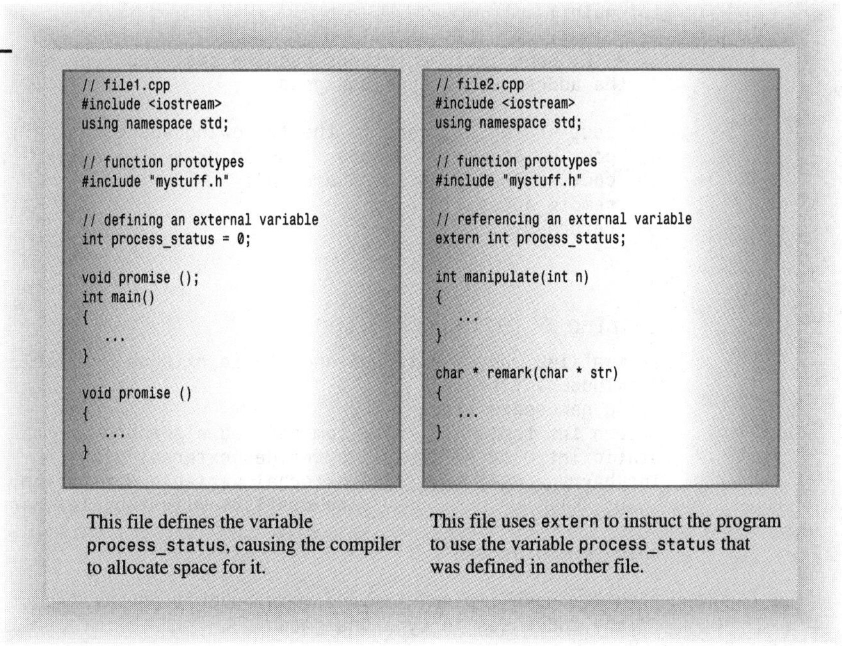

FIGURE 8.6

Defining declaration and referencing declaration

```
// file1.cpp
#include <iostream>
using namespace std;

// function prototypes
#include "mystuff.h"

// defining an external variable
int process_status = 0;

void promise ();
int main()
{
    ...
}

void promise ()
{
    ...
}
```

```
// file2.cpp
#include <iostream>
using namespace std;

// function prototypes
#include "mystuff.h"

// referencing an external variable
extern int process_status;

int manipulate(int n)
{
    ...
}

char * remark(char * str)
{
    ...
}
```

This file defines the variable `process_status`, causing the compiler to allocate space for it.

This file uses `extern` to instruct the program to use the variable `process_status` that was defined in another file.

three variables and then calls the `remote_access()` function, which is defined in a second file. Listing 8.19 (`twofile2.cpp`) shows that file. In addition to defining `remote_access()`, the file uses the `extern` keyword to share `tom` with the first file. Next, the file defines a static variable called `dick`. The `static` modifier makes this variable local to the file and overrides the global definition. Then, the file defines an external variable called `harry`. It can do so without conflicting with the `harry` of the first file because the first `harry` has internal linkage only. Then, the `remote_access()` function displays the addresses of these three variables so that you can compare them with the addresses of the corresponding variables in the first file. Remember to compile both files and link them together to get the complete program.

Listing 8.18 `twofile1.cpp`

```
// twofile1.cpp -- external and static external variables
#include <iostream>       // to be compiled with two file2.cpp
using namespace std;
int tom = 3;              // external variable definition
int dick = 30;            // external variable definition
static int harry = 300;   // static external variable definition

// function prototype
void remote_access();

int main()
{
// NOTE: some implementations require that you type cast
// the addresses to type unsigned

    cout << "main() reports the following addresses:\n";
    cout << &tom << " = &tom, " << &dick << " = &dick, ";
    cout << &harry << " = &harry\n";
    remote_access();
    return 0;
}
```

Listing 8.19 `twofile2.cpp`

```
// twofile2.cpp -- external and static external variables
#include <iostream>
using namespace std;
extern int tom;          // tom defined elsewhere
static int dick = 10;    // overrides external dick
int harry = 200;         // external variable definition,
                         // no conflict with twofile1 harry

void remote_access()
{
// NOTE: some implementations require that you type cast
// the addresses to type unsigned

    cout << "remote_access() reports the following addresses:\n";
    cout << &tom << " = &tom, " << &dick << " = &dick, ";
    cout << &harry << " = &harry\n";
}
```

Here is the output:

```
main() reports the following addresses:
00450E50 = &tom, 00450E54 = &dick, 00450E58 = &harry
remote_access() reports the following addresses:
00450E50 = &tom, 00450F40 = &dick, 00450F44 = &harry
```

As you can see, both files use the same `tom` variable but different `dick` and `harry` variables.

STORAGE CLASS QUALIFIERS: `const`, `volatile`, AND `mutable`

Certain C++ keywords, called *qualifiers*, provide additional information about storage. The most commonly used is `const`, and you've already seen its purpose. It indicates that memory, once initialized, should not be altered by a program. We come back to `const` in a moment.

The `volatile` keyword indicates that the value in a memory location can be altered even though nothing in the program code modifies the contents. This is less mysterious than it sounds. For example, you could have a pointer to a hardware location that contains the time or information from a serial port. Here the hardware, not the program, changes the contents. The intent of this keyword is to improve the optimization abilities of compilers. For instance, suppose the compiler notices that a program uses the value of a particular variable twice within a few statements. Rather than have the program look up the value twice, the compiler might cache the value in a register. This optimization assumes that the value of the variable doesn't change between the two uses. If you don't declare a variable to be `volatile`, then the compiler can feel free to make this optimization. If you do declare the variable to be `volatile`, you're telling the compiler not to make that sort of optimization.

C++ recently added a new qualifier: `mutable`. You can use it to indicate that a particular member of a structure (or class) can be altered even if a particular structure (or class) variable is a `const`. For example, consider the following code:

```
struct data
{
    char name[30];
    mutable int accesses;
    ...
};
const data veep = {"Claybourne Clodde", 0, ... };
strcpy(veep.name, "Joye Joux");   // not allowed
veep.accesses++;                  // allowed
```

The `const` qualifier to `veep` prevents a program from changing `veep`'s members, but the `mutable` qualifier to the `accesses` member shields `accesses` from that restriction. This book won't be using `volatile` or `mutable`, but there is more to learn about `const`.

More About `const`

In C++ (but not C), the `const` modifier alters the default storage classes slightly. Whereas a global variable has external linkage by default, a `const` global variable has internal linkage by default. That is, C++ treats a global `const` definition like a static global definition. You can think of the keyword `const`, when used in an external definition, as being preceded by an implicit static keyword.

```
const int fingers = 10;     // same as static const int fingers;
int main(void)
{
    ...
```

C++ altered the rules for constant types to make life easier for you. Suppose, for instance, you have a set of constants that you'd like to place in a header file and that you use this header file in several files in the same program. After the preprocessor includes the header file contents in each source file, each source file will contain definitions like this:

```
const int fingers = 10;
const char * warning = "Wak!";
```

If global `const` declarations had external linkage like regular variables, this would be an error because you can define a global variable in one file only. That is, only one file can contain the preceding declaration, whereas the other files have to provide reference declarations using the `extern` keyword. Moreover, only the declarations without the `extern` keyword can initialize values:

```
// extern would be required if const had external linkage
extern const int fingers;       // can't be initialized
extern const char * warning;
```

So, you need one set of definitions for one file and a different set of declarations for the other files. But, because externally defined `const` data have internal linkage, you can use the same declarations in all files.

Internal linkage also means that each file gets its own set of constants rather than sharing them. Each definition is private to the file containing it. This is why it's a good idea to put constant definitions in a header file. That way, as long as you include the same header file in two source code files, they receive the same set of constants.

If, for some reason, you want to make a constant have external linkage, you can use the `extern` keyword to override the default internal linkage:

```
extern const states = 50;   // external linkage
```

You must use the `extern` keyword to declare the constant in all files using the constant. This differs from regular external variables, in which you don't use the keyword `extern` when you define a variable, but use `extern` in other files using that variable. Also, unlike regular variables, you can initialize an `extern` `const` value. Indeed, you have to because `const` data requires initialization.

When you declare a `const` within a function or block, it has block scope, meaning the constant is usable only when the program is executing code within the block. This means that you can create constants within a function or block and not have to worry about the name conflicting with constants defined elsewhere.

STORAGE CLASSES AND FUNCTIONS

Functions, too, have storage classes, although the selection is more limited than for variables. C++, like C, does not allow you to define one function inside another, so all functions automatically have a static storage class, meaning they are all present as long as the program is running. By default, functions are external, meaning they have external linkage and can be shared across files. You can, in fact, use the keyword `extern` in a function prototype to indicate the function is defined in another file, but that is optional. (For the program to find the function in another file, that file must be one of the files being compiled as part of the program or a library file searched by the linker.) You also can use the keyword `static` to give a function internal linkage, confining its use to a single file. You would apply this keyword to the prototype and to the function definition:

```
static int private(double x);
...
static int private(double x)
{
    ...
}
```

That means the function is known only in that file. It also means you can use the same name for another function in a different file. As with variables, a static function overrides an external definition for the file containing the static declaration. If you define your own `strlen()` function in one file of a multifile program and declare the function `static`, that one file uses your definition of `strlen()`, whereas the other files use the library version. If you define your own `strlen()` function and do not declare it as `static`, then the compiler uses your version in all the files of your program. See the note on Where C++ Finds Functions.

Inline functions behave differently from regular functions. By default, they have internal linkage and hence are local to the file containing them. For this reason, it's okay to place inline function definitions in a header file.

WHERE C++ FINDS FUNCTIONS

Suppose you call a function in a particular file in a program. Where does C++ look for the function definition? If the function prototype in that file indicates that function is static, the compiler looks only in that file for the function. Otherwise, the compiler (including the linker, too) looks in all the program files. If it finds two definitions, the compiler sends you an error message, for you can have only one definition for an external function. If it fails to find any definition in your files, the function then searches the libraries. This implies that if you define a function having the same

Continues...

WHERE C++ FINDS FUNCTIONS continued...

name as a library function, the compiler uses your version rather than the library version. (However, there are problems if you use a header file declaring the library function and if that prototype doesn't match your version.) Some compiler-linkers need explicit instructions to identify which libraries to search.

LANGUAGE LINKING

There is another form of linking, called *language linking*, that affects functions. First, a little background. A linker needs a different symbolic name for each distinct function. In C, this was simple to implement because there could be only one C function by a given name. So, for internal purposes, a C compiler might translate a C function name such as `spiff` to `_spiff`. The C approach is termed *C language linkage*. C++, however, can have several functions with the same C++ name that have to be translated to separate symbolic names. Thus, the C++ compiler indulged in a process called *name mangling* to generate different symbolic names for overloaded functions. For example, it could convert `spiff(int)` to, say, `_spiff_i`, and `spiff(double, double)` to `_spiff_d_d`. The C++ approach is *C++ language linkage*.

When the linker looks for a function to match a C++ function call, it uses a different look-up method than it does to match a C function call. But suppose you want to use a precompiled function from a C library in a C++ program? For instance, suppose you have this code:

```
spiff(22); // want spiff(int) from a C library
```

Its symbolic name in the C library file is `_spiff`, but, for our hypothetical linker, the C++ look-up convention is to look for the symbolic name `_spiff_i`. To get around this problem, you can use the function prototype to indicate which protocol to use:

```
extern "C" void spiff(int);   // use C protocol for name look-up
extern void spoff(int);       // use C++ protocol for name look-up
extern "C++" void spaff(int); // use C++ protocol for name look-up
```

The first uses C language linkage. The second and third use C++ language linkage. The second does so by default, and the third explicitly.

STORAGE CLASSES AND DYNAMIC ALLOCATION

Storage classes describe memory allocated for variables (including arrays and structures) and functions. They don't apply to memory allocated by using the C++ `new` operator (or by the older C `malloc()` function). We call that kind of memory *dynamic memory*. As you saw in Chapter 4, dynamic memory is controlled by the `new` and `delete` operators, not by scope and linkage rules. Thus, dynamic memory can be allocated from one function and freed from another function. Unlike automatic memory, dynamic memory is not LIFO; the order of allocation and freeing depends on when and how `new` and `delete` are used. Typically, the compiler uses three separate memory chunks: one for static variables (this chunk might be subdivided), one for automatic variables, and one for dynamic storage.

Although storage class concepts don't apply to dynamic memory, they do apply to the pointer variables used to keep track of dynamic memory. For instance, suppose you have the following statement inside a function:

```
float * p_fees = new float [20];
```

The 80 bytes (assuming a float is four bytes) of memory allocated by new remains in memory until the delete operator frees it. But the p_fees pointer passes from existence when the function containing this declaration terminates. If you want to have the 80 bytes of allocated memory available to another function, you need to pass or return its address to that function. On the other hand, if you make the same declaration externally, then the p_fees pointer will be available to all the functions following that declaration in the file. And by using

```
extern float * p_fees;
```

in a second file, you make that same pointer available in the second file.

Remember

Memory allocated by new typically is freed when the program terminates. However, this is not always true. Under DOS, for example, in some circumstances a request for a large block of memory can result in a block that is not deleted automatically when the program terminates.

Namespaces

Names in C++ can refer to variables, functions, structures, enumerations, classes, and class and structure members. When programming projects grow large, the potential for name conflicts increases. When you use class libraries from more than one source, you can get name conflicts. For instance, two libraries might both define classes named List, Tree, and Node, but in incompatible ways. You might want the List class from one library and the Tree from the other, and each might expect its own version of Node. Such conflicts are termed namespace problems.

C++ provides namespace facilities to provide greater control over the scope of names. At the time of this writing, these facilities are still working their way into the marketplace, and you might be using a compiler that doesn't support them. But if the current release of your compiler doesn't support namespaces, probably the next one will.

TRADITIONAL C++ NAMESPACES

Before looking at the new facilities, let's review the namespace properties that already exist in C++ and introduce some terminology. This can help make the idea of namespaces seem more familiar.

The first term is *declarative region*. A declarative region is a region in which declarations can be made. For example, you can declare a global variable outside any function. The declarative region for that variable is the file in which it is declared. If you declare a variable inside a function, its declarative region is the innermost block in which it is declared.

The second term is *potential scope*. The potential scope for a variable begins at its point of declaration and extends to the end of its declarative region. So the potential scope is more limited than the declarative region because you can't use a variable above the point it is first defined.

A variable, however, might not be visible everywhere in its potential scope. For example, it can be hidden by another variable of the same name declared in a nested declarative region. For example, a local variable declared in a function (the declarative region is the function) hides a global variable declared in the same file (the declarative region is the file). The portion of the program that actually can see the variable is termed the *scope*, which is the way we've been using the term all along. Figures 8.7 and 8.8 illustrate the terms declarative region, potential scope, and scope.

FIGURE 8.7

Declarative regions

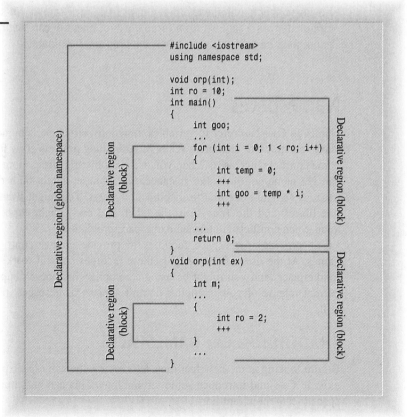

FIGURE 8.8

Potential scope and scope

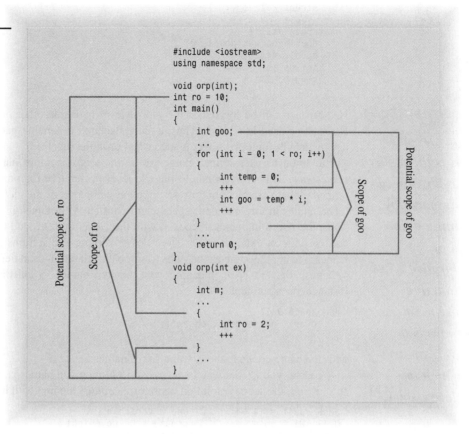

C++'s rules about global and local variables define a kind of namespace heirarchy. Each declarative region can declare names that are independent of names declared in other declarative regions. A local variable declared in one function doesn't conflict with a local variable declared in a second function.

NEW NAMESPACE FEATURES

What C++ now adds is the ability to create named namespaces by defining a new kind of declarative region, one whose main purpose is to provide an area in which to declare names. The names in one namespace don't conflict with the same names declared in other namespaces, and there are mechanisms for letting other parts of programs use items declared in a namespace. The following code, for instance, uses the new keyword namespace to create two namespaces, Jack and Jill.

```
namespace Jack {
    double pail;
    void fetch();
    int pal;
```

```
    struct Well { ... };
}
namespace Jill {
    double bucket(double n) { ... }
    double fetch;
    int pal;
    struct Hill { ... };
}
```

Namespaces can be located at the global level or inside other namespaces, but they cannot be placed in a block. Thus, a name declared in a namespace has external linkage by default (unless it refers to a constant or inline function).

In addition to user-defined namespaces, there is one more namespace, the *global namespace*. This corresponds to the file-level declarative region, so what used to be termed global variables are now described as being part of the global namespace.

The names in any one namespace can't conflict with names in another namespace. Thus, the fetch in Jack can coexist with the fetch in Jill, and the Hill in Jill can coexist with an external Hill. The rules governing declarations and definitions in a namespace are the same as the rules for global declarations and definitions.

Namespaces are *open*, meaning you can add names to existing namespaces. For instance, the statement

```
namespace Jill {
    char * goose(const char *);
}
```

adds the name goose to the existing list of names in Jill.

Of course, you need a way to access names in a given namespace. The simplest way is to use ::, the scope resolution operator, to *qualify* a name with its namespace:

```
Jack::pail = 12.34;     // use a variable
Jill::Hill mole;        // create a Queue object
Jack::fetch();          // use a function
```

An unadorned name, such as pail, is termed the *unqualified name*, whereas a name with the namespace, as in Jack::pail, is termed a *qualified name*.

Using-Declarations and Using-Directives

Having to qualify names every time they are used is not an appealing prospect, so C++ provides two mechanisms to simplify using namespace names. The first is called a *using-declaration*, which consists of preceding a qualified name with the new keyword using:

```
using Jill::fetch;     // a using-declaration
```

A using-declaration adds a particular name to the declarative region in which it occurs. For instance, a using-declaration of Jill::fetch in main() adds fetch to the declarative region defined by main(). After making this declaration, you can use the name fetch instead of Jill::fetch.

```
namespace Jill {
    double bucket(double n) { ... }
```

```
        double fetch;
        struct Hill { ... };
    }
    char fetch;
    int main()
    {
        using Jill::fetch;    // put fetch into local namespace
    /*  double fetch;         // Error! Already have a local fetch
        cin >> fetch;         // read a value into Jill::fetch
        cin >> ::fetch;       // read a value into global fetch
        ...
    }
```

Because a using-declaration adds the name to the local declarative region, this example precludes creating another local variable by the name of `fetch`. Also, like any other local variable, `fetch` would override a global variable by the same name. Placing a using-declaration at the external level adds the name to the global namespace.

The second new mechanism is called a *using-directive*. It consists of preceding a namespace name with the keywords `using namespace`, and it makes all the names in the namespace available without using the scope resolution operator:

```
using namespace Jack;   // make all the names in Jack available
```

Placing a using directive at the global level makes the namespace names available globally. You've seen this in action many a time:

```
#include <iostream>     // places names in namespace std
using namespace std;    // make names available globally
```

You can make namespace names available locally by placing a using directive in a local declarative region.

Using a using-directive to import all the names wholesale is *not* the same as using multiple using-declarations. It's more like the mass application of a scope resolution operator. When you use a using-declaration, it is as if the name is declared at the location of the using-declaration. If a particular name already is declared in a function, you can't import the same name with a using-declaration. When you use a using-directive, however, it is as if you declared the names in the smallest declarative region containing both the using-declaration and the namespace itself. For the following example, that would be the global namespace. You can use a using-directive to import a name that already is declared in a function, but the local name will hide the namespace name, just as it would hide a global variable of the same name. However, you still can use the scope resolution operator:

> *" Using a using-directive to import all the names wholesale is not the same as using multiple using-declarations. "*

```
namespace Jill {
    double bucket(double n) { ... }
    double fetch;
    struct Hill { ... };
}
char fetch;                     // global namespace
int main()
{
    using namespace Jill;       // import namespace names
    struct Hill Thrill;         // create a Jill::Hill
```

```
    double water = bucket(2);   // use Jill::bucket();
    double fetch;               // not an error; hides Jill::fetch
    cin >> fetch;               // read a value into the local fetch
    cin >> ::fetch;             // read a value into global fetch
    cin >> Jill::fetch;         // read a value into Jill::fetch
    ...
}
```

Here, the Jill::fetch is placed in the local namespace. It doesn't have local scope, so it doesn't override the global fetch. However, both fetch variables are available if you use the scope resolution operator. You might want to compare this example to the preceding one, which used a using-declaration.

Remember

> **Suppose a namespace and a declarative region both define the same name. If you attempt to use a using-declaration to bring the namespace name into the declarative region, the two names conflict, and you get an error. If you use a using-directive to bring the namespace name into the declarative region, the local version of the name hides the namespace version.**

Generally speaking, the using-declaration is safer to use because it shows exactly what names you are making available. And if the name conflicts with a local name, the compiler lets you know. The using-directive adds all names, even ones you might not need. If a local name conflicts, it overrides the namespace version, and you won't be warned. Also, the open nature of namespaces means that the complete list of names in a namespace might be spread over several locations, making it difficult to know exactly which names you are adding.

What about the approach used for this book's examples?

```
#include <iostream>
using namespace std;
```

First, the iostream header file puts everything in the std namespace. Then, the next line exports everything in that namespace into the global namespace. Thus, this approach merely reproduces the pre-namespace era. The main rationale for this approach is expediency. It's easy to do, and if your system doesn't have namespaces, you can replace the preceding two lines with the original form:

```
#include <iostream.h>
```

However, the hope of namespace proponents is that you will be more selective and use either the resolution operator or the using-declaration. That is, don't use the following:

```
using namespace std;   // avoid as too indiscriminate
```

Instead, do this:

```
int x;
std::cin >> x;
std::cout << x << std::endl;
```

Or else do this:

```
using std::cin;
using std::cout;
using std::endl;
int x;
cin >> x;
cout << x << endl;
```

More Namespace Features

You can nest namespace declarations:

```
namespace elements
{
    namespace fire
    {
        int flame;
        ...
    }
    float water;
}
```

In this case, you refer to the `flame` variable as `elements::fire::flame`. Similarly, you can make the inner names available with this using-directive:

```
using namespace elements::fire;
```

Also, you can use using-directives and using-declarations inside namespaces:

```
namespace myth
{
    using Jill::fetch;
    using namespace elements;
}
```

Suppose you want to access `Jill::fetch`. Because `Jill::fetch` is now part of the `myth` namespace, where it can be called `fetch`, you can access it this way:

```
cin >> myth::fetch;
```

Of course, because it also is part of the `Jill` namespace, you still can call it `Jill::fetch`:

```
cout << Jill:fetch;   // display value read into myth::fetch
```

Or you can do this, providing no local variables conflict:

```
using namespace myth;
cin >> fetch;       // really Jill::fetch
```

Now consider applying a using-directive to the `myth` namespace. The using-directive is *transitive*. We say an operation *op* is transitive if A *op* B and B *op* C implies A *op* C. For example, the > operator is transitive. (That is, A bigger than B and B bigger than C implies A bigger than C.) In this context, the upshot is that the statement

```
using namespace myth;
```

results in the elements namespace being added via a using-directive also, so it's the same as the following:

```
using namespace myth;
using namespace elements;
```

You can create an alias for a namespace. For example, suppose you have a namespace defined as follows:

```
namespace my_very_favorite_things { ... };
```

You can make mvft an alias for my_very_favorite_things with the following statement:

```
namespace mvft = my_very_favorite_things;
```

You can use this technique to simplify using nested namespaces:

```
namespace MEF = myth::elements::fire;
using MEF::flame;
```

Unnamed Namespaces

You can create an unnamed namespace by omitting the namespace name:

```
namespace          // unnamed namespace
{
    int ice;
    int bandycoot;
}
```

This behaves as if it were followed by a using-directive; that is, the names declared in this namespace are in potential scope until the end of the declarative region containing the unnamed namespace. In this respect, they are like global variables. However, because the namespace has no name, you can't explicitly use a using-directive or using-declaration to make the names available elsewhere. In particular, you can't use names from an unnamed namespace in a file other than the one containing the namespace declaration. This provides an alternative to using static external variables.

NAMESPACES AND THE FUTURE

As programmers become familiar with namespaces, common programming idioms will emerge. In particular, many hope that use of the global namespace will wither away and that class libraries will be designed by using the namespace mechanisms. Indeed, current C++ already calls for placing standard library functions in a namespace called std.

As mentioned before, changes in the header filenames reflect these changes. The older style header files, such as iostream.h, do not use namespaces, but the newer iostream header file should use the std namespace.

Summary

C++ has expanded C function capabilities. By using the inline keyword with a function definition and by placing that definition ahead of the first call to that function, you suggest to the C++ compiler that it make the function inline. That is, instead of having the program jump to a separate section of code to execute the function, the compiler replaces the function call with the corresponding code inline. An inline facility should be used only when the function is short.

A reference variable is a kind of disguised pointer that lets you create an alias (a second name) for a variable. Reference variables primarily are used as arguments to functions processing structures and class objects.

C++ prototypes enable you to define default values for arguments. If a function call omits the corresponding argument, the program uses the default value. If the function includes an argument value, the program uses that value instead of the default. Default arguments can be provided only from right to left in the argument list. Thus, if you provide a default value for a particular argument, you also must provide default values for all arguments to the right of that argument.

A function's signature is its argument list. You can define two functions having the same name provided that they have different signatures. This is called function polymorphism, or function overloading. Typically, you overload functions to provide essentially the same service to different data types.

Function templates automate the process of overloading functions. You define a function using a generic type and a particular algorithm, and the compiler generates appropriate function definitions for the particular argument types you use in a program.

C++ encourages you to use multiple files in developing programs. An effective organizational strategy is to use a header file to define user types and provide function prototypes for functions to manipulate the user types. Use a separate source code file for the function definitions. Together, the header file and the source file define and implement the user-defined type and how it can be used. Then, main() and other functions using those functions can go into a third file.

C++'s storage classes determine how long variables remain in memory and what parts of a program have access to them (scope and linkage). Automatic variables are those defined within a block, such as a function body or a block within the body. They exist and are known only while the program executes statements in the block that contains the definition.

Static variables exist for the duration of the program. A variable defined outside any function has external storage class. It's known to all functions in the file following its definition (file scope) and is made available to other files in the program (external linkage). For another file to use such a variable, it must declare it by using the extern keyword. A variable defined outside any function but qualified with the keyword static has file scope but is not made available to other files (internal linkage). A variable defined inside a block but qualified with the keyword static is local to that block but retains its value for the duration of the program.

C++ functions, by default, have external storage class, so they can be shared across files. But inline functions and functions qualified with the keyword `static` have internal linkage and are confined to the defining file.

Namespaces let you define named regions in which you can declare identifiers. The intent is to reduce name conflicts, particularly in large programs using code from several vendors. Identifiers in a namespace can be made available by using the scope resolution operator, by using a using-declaration, or by using a using-directive.

Review Questions

1. What kinds of functions are good candidates for inline status?

2. Suppose the `song()` function has this prototype:

```
void song(char * name, int times);
```

    a. How would you modify the prototype so that the default value for times is 1?

    b. What changes would you make in the function definition?

    c. Can you provide a default value of "O, My Papa" for `name`?

3. Write overloaded versions of `iquote()`, a function that displays its argument enclosed in double quotation marks. Write three versions: one for an `int` argument, one for a `double` argument, and one for a `string` argument.

4. Here is a structure template:

```
struct box
{
    char maker[40];
    float height;
    float width;
    float length;
    float volume;
};
```

    a.   Write a function that has a reference to a box structure as its formal argument and displays the value of each member.

    b.   Write a function that has a reference to a box structure as its formal argument and sets the `volume` member to the product of the other three dimensions.

5. Here are some desired effects. Indicate whether each can be accomplished with default arguments, function overloading, both, or neither. Provide appropriate prototypes.

    a. `mass(density, volume)` returns the mass of an object having a density of `density` and a volume of `volume`, whereas `mass(density)` returns the mass having a density of `density` and a volume of 1.0 cubic meters. All quantities are type `double`.

    b. repeat(10, "I'm OK") displays the indicated string ten times, whereas repeat("But you're kind of stupid") displays the indicated string five times.

    c. average(3,6) returns the int average of two int arguments, whereas average(3.0, 6.0) returns the double average of two double values.

    d. mangle("I'm glad to meet you") returns the character I or a pointer to the string "I'm mad to gleet you" depending on whether you assign the return value to a char variable or to a char* variable.

    e. average(3,6) returns an int average of the two int arguments when called in one file, and it returns a double average of the two int arguments when called in a second file in the same program.

6. Write a function template that returns the larger of its two arguments.

7. Given the template of Review Question 6 and the box structure of Review Question 4, provide a template specialization that takes two box arguments and returns the one with the larger volume.

8. What storage class would you use for the following situations?

    a. homer is a formal argument (parameter) to a function.

    b. The secret variable is to be shared by two files.

    c. The topsecret variable is to be shared by the functions in one file but hidden from other files.

    d. beencalled keeps track of how many times the function containing it has been called.

9. Discuss the differences between a using-declaration and a using-directive.

Programming Exercises

1. Write a function that normally takes one argument, the address of a string, and prints that string once. However, if a second, type int argument is provided and is nonzero, the function prints the string a number of times equal to the number of times that function has been called to at that point. (Note that the number of times the string is printed is not equal to the value of the second argument; it's equal to the number of times the function has been called.) Yes, this is a silly function, but it makes you use some of the techniques discussed in this chapter. Use the function in a simple program that demonstrates how the function works.

2. The CandyBar structure contains three members. The first member holds the brand name of a candy bar. The second member holds the weight (which may have a fractional part) of the candy bar, and the third member holds the number of calories (an integer value) in the candy bar. Write a program that

uses a function that takes as arguments a reference to a `CandyBar`, a pointer-to-char, a double, and an `int` and uses the last three values to set the corresponding members of the structure. The last three arguments should have default values of "Millennium Munch", 2.85, and 350. Also, the program should use a function taking a reference to a `CandyBar` as an argument and display the contents of the structure. Use `const` where appropriate.

3. Below is a program skeleton. Complete it by providing the described functions and prototypes. Note that there should be two `show()` functions, each using default arguments. Use `const` arguments when appropriate. Note that `set()` should use `new` to allocate sufficient space to hold the designated string. The techniques used here are similar to those used in designing and implementing classes. (You might have to alter the header filenames and delete the using-directive, depending upon your compiler.)

```cpp
#include <iostream>
using namespace std;
#include <cstring>        // for strlen(), strcpy()
struct stringy {
    char * str;          // points to a string
    int ct;              // length of string (not counting '\0')
    };

// prototypes for set(), show(), and show() go here
int main()
{
    stringy beany;
    char testing[] = "Reality isn't what it used to be.";

    set(beany, testing);     // first argument is a reference,
                    // allocates space to hold copy of testing,
                    // sets str member of beany to point to the
                    // new block, copies testing to new block,
                    // and sets ct member of beany
    show(beany);        // prints member string once
    show(beany, 2);     // prints member string twice
    testing[0] = 'D';
    testing[1] = 'u';
    show(testing);      // prints testing string once
    show(testing, 3);   // prints testing string thrice
    show("Done!");
    return 0;
}
```

4. Here is a header file:

```cpp
// golf.h -- for pe8-3.cpp

const int Len = 40;
struct golf
{
    char fullname[Len];
    int handicap;
};

//  function solicits name and handicap from user
```

```
//  and sets the members of g to the values entered
//  returns 1 if name is entered, 0 if name is empty string
int setgolf(golf & g);

//  function sets golf structure to provided name, handicap
//   using values passed as arguments to the function
void setgolf(golf & g, const char * name, int hc);

// function resets handicap to new value
void handicap(golf & g, int hc);

// function displays contents of golf structure
void showgolf(const golf & g);
```

Put together a multifile program based on this header. One file, named golf.cpp, should provide suitable function definitions to match the prototypes in the header file. A second file should contain main() and demonstrate all the features of the prototyped functions. For example, a loop should solicit input for an array of golf structures and terminate when the array is full or the user enters an empty string for the golfer's name. The main() function should use only the prototyped functions to access the golf structures.

5. Write a template function max5() that takes as its argument an array of five items of type T and returns the largest item in the array. (Because the size is fixed, it can be hard-coded into the loop instead of passed as an argument.) Test it in a program that uses the function with an array of 5 int value and an array of 5 double values.

6. Write a template function maxn() that takes as its arguments an array of items of type T and an integer representing the number of elements in the array and which returns the largest item in the array. Test it in a program that uses the function template with an array of 6 int value and an array of 4 double values. The program also should include a specialization that takes an array of pointers-to-char as an argument and the number of pointers as a second argument and which returns the address of longest string. If there are more than one string having the longest length, the function returns the address of the first one tied for longest. Test the specialization with an array of 5 string pointers.

9

Objects
and
Classes

In this chapter you learn:

- Procedural and object-oriented programming
- The class concept
- How to define and implement a class
- Public and private class access
- Class data members
- Class methods (class function members)
- Creating and using class objects
- Class constructors and destructors
- `const` member functions
- The `this` pointer
- Creating arrays of objects
- Class scope
- Abstract data types (ADTs)

Object-oriented programming (OOP) is a particular conceptual approach to designing programs, and C++ has enhanced C with features that ease the way to applying that approach. The most important OOP features are these:

● Abstraction

● Encapsulation and data hiding

● Polymorphism

● Inheritance

● Reusable code

The class is the single most important C++ enhancement for implementing these features and tying them together. This chapter begins our examination of classes. It explains abstraction, encapsulation, and data hiding, and shows how classes implement these features. It discusses how to define a class, provide a class with public and private sections, and create member functions that work with the class data. Also, the chapter acquaints you with constructors and destructors, which are special member functions for creating and disposing of objects belonging to a class. Finally, you meet the this pointer, an important component of some class programming. The following chapters extend the discussion to operator overloading (another variety of polymorphism) and inheritance, the basis for reusing code.

Procedural and Object-Oriented Programming

Although we have explored the OOP perspective on programming every so often, we've usually stuck pretty close to the standard procedural approach of languages such as C, Pascal, and BASIC. Let's look at an example that clarifies how the OOP outlook differs from that of procedural programming.

As the newest member of the Genre Giants softball team, you've been asked to keep the team statistics. Naturally, you turn to your computer for help. If you were a procedural programmer, you might think along these lines:

Let's see, I want to enter the name, times at bat, number of hits, batting averages (for those who don't follow baseball or softball, the batting average is the number of hits divided by the player's official number of times at bat. An at bat terminates when a player gets on base or makes an out, but certain events, such as getting a walk, don't count as official times at bat), and all those other great basic statistics for each player. Wait, the computer is supposed to make life easier for me, so let's have it figure out some of that stuff, such as the batting average. Also, I want the program to report the results. How should I organize this? I guess I should do things right and use functions. Yeah, I'll make main() call a function to get the input, call a function to make the calculations, and then call a function to report the results. Hmmm, what happens when I get data from the next game? I don't want to start from scratch again. Okay, I can add a function to update the statistics. Golly, maybe I'll need a menu in `main()` to select between entering, calculating, updating, and showing the data. Hmmm—how am I going to represent the data? I could use an array of strings to hold the players' names, another array to hold the at bats for each player, yet another array to hold the hits, and so on. No, that's dumb. I can design a structure to hold all the information for a single player and then use an array of those structures to represent the whole team.

In short, you first concentrate on the procedures you will follow and then think about how to represent the data. (Note: So that you don't have to keep the program running the whole season, you probably also want to be able to save data to a file and read data from a file. But because we haven't covered files yet, we ignore that complication for now.)

Now let's see how your perspective changes when you don your OOP hat (an attractive polymorphic design). You begin by thinking about the data. Furthermore, you think about the data not only in terms of how to represent it, but in terms of how it's to be used:

Let's see—what am I keeping track of? A ball player, of course. So, I want an object that represents the whole player, not just his or her batting average or times at bat. Yeah, that'll be my fundamental data unit, an object representing the name and statistics for a player. I'll need some methods to handle this object. Hmmm, I guess I need a method to get basic information into this unit. The computer should calculate some of the stuff, like the batting averages—I can add methods to do calculations. And the program should do those calculations automatically, without the user having to remember to ask to have them done. Also, I'll need methods for updating and displaying the information. So, the user gets three ways to interact with the data: initialization, updating, and reporting. That's the user interface.

In short, you concentrate on the object as the user perceives it, thinking about the data you need in order to describe the object and the operations that will describe the user's interaction with the data. After you develop a description of that interface, you move on to decide how to implement the interface and data storage. Finally, you put together a program to use your new design.

Abstraction and Classes

Life is full of complexities, and one way we cope with complexity is to frame simplifying abstractions. You are a collection of more than an octillion atoms. Some students of the mind would say your mind is a collection of semiautonomous agents. But it's much simpler to think of yourself as a single entity. In computing, abstraction is the crucial step of representing information in terms of its interface with the user. That is, you abstract the essential operational features of a problem and express a solution in those terms. In the softball statistics example, the interface describes how the user initializes, updates, and displays the data. From abstraction, it is a short step to the user-defined type, which in C++ is a class design that implements that interface.

WHAT'S A TYPE?

Let's think a little more about what constitutes a type. For example, what is a nerd? If you subscribe to the popular stereotype, you might think of a nerd in visual terms—thick black-rimmed glasses, pocket protector full of pens, and so on. After a little reflection, you might conclude that a nerd is better defined operationally, for example, by how he or she responds to an awkward social situation. We have a similar situation, if you don't mind stretched analogies, with a procedural language like C. At first, you tend to think of a data type in terms of its appearance—how it is stored in memory. A char, for example, is one byte of memory, and a double often is eight bytes of memory. But a little reflection leads us to conclude that a data type also is defined in terms of the operations that can be performed upon it. For instance, the int type can use all the arithmetic operations. You can add, subtract, multiply, and divide integers. You also can use the modulus operator (%) with them.

On the other hand, consider pointers. A pointer might very well require the same amount of memory as an int. It might even be represented internally as an integer. But a pointer doesn't allow the same operations that an integer does. You can't, for example, multiply two pointers times each other. The concept makes no sense, so C++ doesn't implement it. Thus, when you declare a variable as an int or as a pointer-to-float, you're not just allocating memory—you also are establishing which operations can be performed with the variable. In short, specifying a basic type does two things:

- It determines how much memory is needed for a data object.

- It determines what operations, or methods, can be performed using the data object.

For built-in types, this information is built into the compiler. But when you define a user-defined type in C++, you have to provide the same kind of information yourself. In exchange for this extra work, you gain the power and flexibility to custom fit new data types to match real-world requirements.

THE CLASS

The *class* is the C++ vehicle for translating an abstraction to a user-defined type. It combines data representation and methods for manipulating that data into one neat package. Let's look at a class that represents stocks.

First, we have to think a bit about how to represent stocks. We could take one share of stock as the basic unit and define a class to represent a share. However, that implies that you would need 100 objects to represent 100 shares, and that's not practical. Instead, let's represent a person's current holdings in a particular stock as a basic unit. The number of shares owned would be part of the data representation. A realistic approach would have to maintain records of such things as initial purchase price and date of purchase, for tax purposes. Also, it would have to manage events such as stock splits. That seems a bit ambitious for our first effort at defining a class, so let's take an idealized, simplified view of matters. In particular, let's limit the operations we can perform to the following:

- Acquire stock in a company.

- Buy more shares of the same stock.

- Sell stock.

- Update the per-share value of a stock.

- Display information about the holdings.

We can use this list to define the public interface for the stock class, leaving additional features as exercises for the interested. To support this interface, we need to store some information. Again, we use a simplified approach. For example, we won't worry about the standard U.S. practice of evaluating stocks in multiples of eighths of a dollar. We will store the following information:

- Name of company

- Number of stocks owned

- Value of each share

- Total value of all shares

Next, let's define the class. Generally, a class specification has two parts:

- A *class declaration*, which describes the data component in terms of data members, and the public interface, in terms of member functions

- The *class method definitions*, which describe how certain class member functions are implemented

Roughly speaking, the class declaration provides a class overview, whereas the method definitions supply the details.

Listing 9.1 presents a tentative class declaration for a Stock class. (To help identify classes, we follow a common, but not universal, convention of capitalizing class names.) You'll notice it looks like a structure declaration with a few additional wrinkles, such as member functions and public and private sections. We'll improve on this declaration shortly (so don't use it as a model), but first let's see how this definition works.

Listing 9.1 stocks.cpp

```
// beginning of stocks.cpp file
class Stock   // class declaration
{
private:
    char company[30];
    int shares;
    double share_val;
    double total_val;
    void set_tot() { total_val = shares * share_val; }
public:
    void acquire(const char * co, int n, double pr);
```

```
      void buy(int num, double price);
      void sell(int num, double price);
      void update(double price);
      void show();
};     // note semicolon at the end
```

You'll get a closer look at the class details later, but first let's examine the more general features. To begin, the C++ keyword `class` identifies this code as defining the design of a class. The syntax identifies `Stock` as the type name for this new class. This declaration enables us to declare variables, called *objects* or *instances*, of the `Stock` type. Each individual object represents a single holding. For example, the declarations

```
Stock sally;
Stock solly;
```

create two `Stock` objects called `sally` and `solly`. The `sally` object, for example, could represent Sally's stock holdings in a particular company.

Next, notice that the information we decided to store appears in the form of class data members, such as `company` and `shares`. The `company` member of `sally`, for example, holds the name of the company, the `share` member holds the number of shares Sally owns, the `share_val` member holds the value of each share, and the `total_val` member holds the total value of all the shares. Similarly, the operations that we want appear as class function members, such as `sell()` and `update()`. Class member functions are also termed *class methods*. A member function can be defined in place, like `set_tot()`, or it can be represented by a prototype, like the other member functions in this class. The full definitions for the other member functions come later, but the prototypes suffice to describe the function interfaces. The binding of data and methods into a single unit is the most striking feature of the class. Because of this design, creating a `Stock` object automatically establishes the rules governing how that object can be used.

You've already seen how the `istream` and `ostream` classes have member functions, such as `get()` and `getline()`. The function prototypes in the `Stock` class declaration demonstrate how member functions are established. The `iostream` header file, for example, has a `getline()` prototype in the `istream` class declaration.

Also new are the keywords `private` and `public`. These labels describe access control for class members. Any program that uses an object of a particular class can access the public portions directly. A program can access the private members of an object only by using the public member functions (or, as you see in Chapter 10, "Working with Classes," via a friend function). For instance, the only way to alter the `shares` member of the `Stock` class is to use one of the `Stock` member functions. Thus, the public member functions act as go-betweens for a program and an object's private members; they provide the interface between object and program. This insulation of data from direct access by a program is called `data hiding`. (C++ provides a third access-control keyword, `protected`, which we discuss when we cover class inheritance in Chapter 12, "Class Inheritance.") See Figure 9.1. Whereas data hiding might be an unscrupulous act in, say, a stock fund prospectus, it's a good practice in computing because it preserves the integrity of the data.

FIGURE 9.1

The Stock class

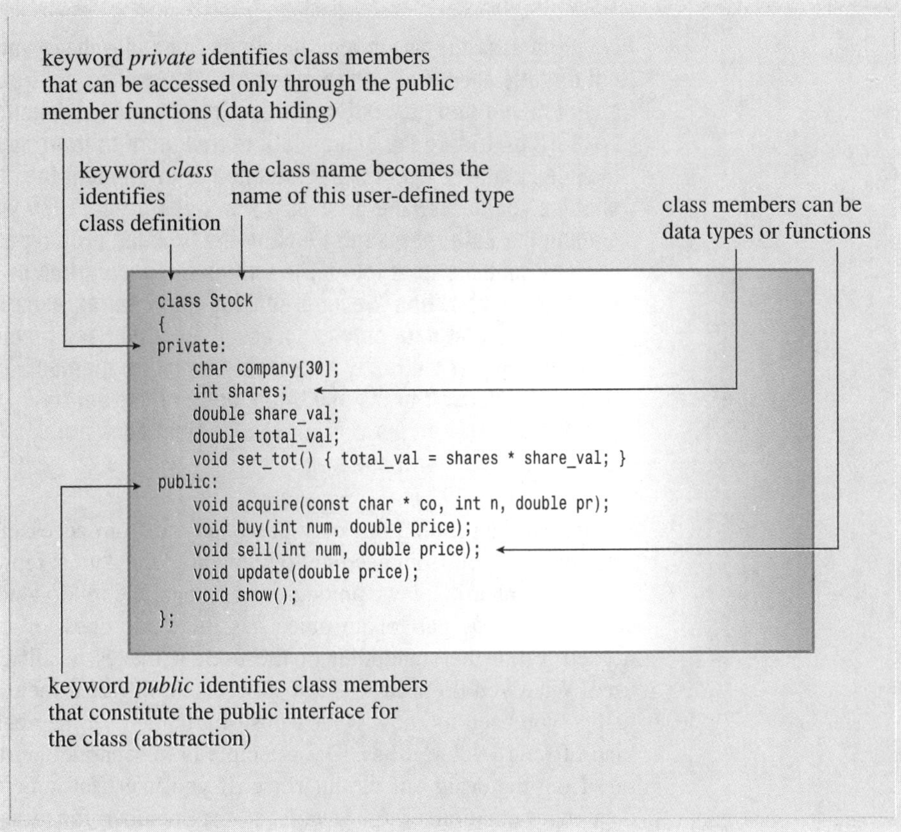

keyword *private* identifies class members
that can be accessed only through the public
member functions (data hiding)

keyword *class*   the class name becomes the
identifies   name of this user-defined type
class definition

class members can be
data types or functions

```
class Stock
{
private:
    char company[30];
    int shares;
    double share_val;
    double total_val;
    void set_tot() { total_val = shares * share_val; }
public:
    void acquire(const char * co, int n, double pr);
    void buy(int num, double price);
    void sell(int num, double price);
    void update(double price);
    void show();
};
```

keyword *public* identifies class members
that constitute the public interface for
the class (abstraction)

A class design attempts to separate the public interface from the specifics of the implementation. The public interface represents the abstraction component of the design. Gathering the implementation details together and separating them from the abstraction is called *encapsulation*. *Data hiding* (putting data into the private section of a class) is an example of encapsulation and so is hiding functional details of an implementation in the private section, as the Stock class does with set_tot(). Another example of encapsulation is the usual practice of placing class function definitions in a separate file from the class declaration.

Remember

Object-oriented programming is a programming style that you can use to some degree with any language. Certainly, you can incorporate many OOP ideas into ordinary C programs. For instance, Chapter 8, "Adventures in Functions," provides an example (Listings 8.12, 13, 14) in which a header file contains a structure prototype along with the prototypes for functions to manipulate that structure. Thus, the main() function simply defines variables of that structure type and uses the associated functions to handle those variables; `main()` does not directly access structure members. In essence, that example defines an abstract type that places the storage format and the function prototypes in a header file, hiding the actual data representation from `main()`. C++, however, includes features specifically intended to implement the OOP approach, so it enables you to take the process a few steps further than you can with C. First, placing the data representation and the function prototypes into a single class declaration instead of into a file unifies the description by placing everything in one class declaration. Second, making the data representation private enforces the stricture that data only is accessed by authorized functions. If, in the C example, `main()` directly accesses a structure member, it violates the spirit of OOP, but it doesn't break any C language rules. But trying to access directly, say, the `shares` member of a `Stock` object does break a C++ language rule, and the compiler will catch it.

Note that data hiding not only prevents you from accessing the data directly, but it also absolves you from needing to know how the data is represented. For example, the `show()` member displays, among other things, the total value of a holding. This value can be stored as part of an object, as this code does, or it can be calculated when needed. From the standpoint of the user, it makes no difference which approach is used. What you do need to know is what the different member functions accomplish; that is, you need to know what kinds of arguments a member function takes and what kind of return value it has. The principle is to separate the details of the implementation from the design of the interface. If you later find a better way to implement the data representation or the details of the member functions, you can change those details without changing the program interface, and that makes programs much easier to maintain.

Public or Private?

You can declare class members, whether they are data items or member functions, either in the public or the private section of a class. But because one of the main OOP precepts is to hide the data, data items normally go into the private section. The member functions that constitute the class interface go into the public section; otherwise, you can't call those functions from a program. As the `Stock` declaration shows, you also can put member functions in the private section. You can't call such functions directly from a program, but the public methods can use them. Typically, you use private member functions to handle implementation details that don't form part of the public interface.

You don't have to use the keyword `private` in class declarations, for that is the default access control for class objects:

```
class World
{
    float mass;          // private by default
    char name[20];       // private by default
```

```
public:
    void tellall(void);
    ...
};
```

However, we'll explicitly use the `private` label in order to emphasize the concept of data hiding.

CLASSES AND STRUCTURES

Class descriptions look much like structure declarations with the addition of member functions and the `public` and `private` visibility labels. In fact, C++ extends to structures the same features classes have. The only difference is that the default access type for a structure is `public`, whereas the default type for the class is `private`. C++ programmers commonly use classes to implement class descriptions while restricting structures to representing pure data objects or, occasionally, classes with no private component.

IMPLEMENTING CLASS MEMBER FUNCTIONS

We still have the second part of the class specification to do: providing code for those member functions represented by a prototype in the class declaration. Let's look at that next. Member function definitions are much like regular function definitions. They have a function heading and a function body. They can have return types and arguments. But they also have two special characteristics:

- When you define a member function, you use the scope operator (::) to identify the class to which the function belongs.

- Class methods can access the `private` components of the class.

Let's look at these points now.

First, the function heading for a member function uses the scope operator (::) to indicate to which class the function belongs. For example, the heading for the update() member function looks like this:

```
void Stock::update(double price)
```

This notation means we are defining the `update()` function that is a member of the `Stock` class. Not only does this identify `update()` as a member function, it means we can use the same name for a member function for a different class. For instance, an `update()` function for a `Buffoon` class would have this function heading:

```
void Buffoon::update()
```

Thus, the scope resolution operator resolves the question of which class a method definition applies. We say that the identifier `update()` has *class scope*. Other member functions of the `Stock` class can, if necessary, use the `update()` method without using the scope resolution operator. That's because they belong to the same class, making `update()` in scope. Using `update()` outside of the class declaration and method definitions, however, requires special measures, which we get to soon.

One way of looking at method names is that the complete name of a class method includes the class name. We say that `Stock::update()` is the *qualified name* of the function. A simple *update()*, on the other hand, is an abbreviation (the *unqualified name*) for the full name, one that can be used just in class scope.

The second special characteristic of methods is that a method can access the private members of a class. For instance, the `show()` method can use code like this:

```
cout << "Company: " << company
     << "  Shares: " << shares << '\n'
     << "  Share Price: $" << share_val
     << "  Total Worth: $" << total_val << '\n';
```

Here `company`, `shares`, and so on, are private data members of the `Stock` class. If you try to use a nonmember function to access these data members, the compiler stops you cold in your tracks. (However, friend functions, which Chapter 10 discusses, provide an exception.)

With these two points in mind, we can implement the class methods as shown in Listing 9.2. These method definitions can go in a separate file or in the same file with the class declaration. Because we are beginning simply, we assume that these definitions follow the class declaration in the same file. This is the easiest, although not the best, way to make the class declaration available to the method definitions. (The best way, which we apply later in this chapter, is to use a header file for the class declaration and a source code file for the class member function definitions.)

Listing 9.2 stocks.cpp

```
//more stocks.cpp -- implementing the class member functions
#include <iostream>
using namespace std;
#include <cstdlib>  // --or stdlib.h--for exit()
#include <cstring>  // --or string.h--for strncpy()

void Stock::acquire(const char * co, int n, double pr)
{
    strncpy(company, co, 29); // truncate co to fit if needed
    company[29] = '\0';
    shares = n;
    share_val = pr;
    set_tot();
}

void Stock::buy(int num, double price)
{
    shares += num;
    share_val = price;
    set_tot();
```

```
    }

void Stock::sell(int num, double price)
{
    if (num > shares)
    {
        cerr << "You can't sell more than you have!\n";
        exit(1);
    }
    shares -= num;
    share_val = price;
    set_tot();
}

void Stock::update(double price)
{
    share_val = price;
    set_tot();
}

void Stock::show()
{
    cout << "Company: " << company
        << "  Shares: " << shares << '\n'
        << "  Share Price: $" << share_val
        << "  Total Worth: $" << total_val << '\n';
}
```

Member Function Notes

The acquire() function manages the first acquisition of stock for a given company, whereas buy() and sell() manage adding to or subtracting from an existing holding. If the user attempts to sell more shares than he or she has, the sell() function calls the exit() function, which terminates the program. (Exceptions, discussed in Chapter 14, "Friends, Exceptions, and More," allow a more flexible response.) Four of the member functions set or reset the total_val member value. Rather than write this calculation four times, the class has each function call the set_tot() function. Because this function is merely the means of implementing the code and not part of the public interface, the class makes set_tot() a private member function. If the calculation were lengthy, this could save some typing and code space. Here, however, the main value is that by using a function call instead of retyping the calculation each time, you insure that the exact same calculation gets done. Also, if you have to revise the calculation (not likely in this particular case), you have to revise it in just one location.

The acquire() method uses strncpy() to copy the string. In case you've forgotten, the call strncpy(s2, s1, n) copies s1 to s2 or else up to n characters from s1 to s2, whichever comes first. If s1 contains fewer characters than n, the strncpy() function pads s2 with null characters. That is, strncpy(firstname,"Tim", 6) copies the characters T, i, and m to firstname and then adds three null characters to bring the total to six characters. But if s1 is longer than n, no null characters are appended. That is, strncpy(firstname, "Priscilla", 4) just copies the characters P, r, i, and s to

firstname, making it a character array but, because it lacks a terminating null character, not a string. Therefore, acquire() places a null character at the end of the array to
guarantee that it is a string.

cerr AND exit()

The cerr object, like cout, is an ostream object. The difference is that operating
system redirection affects cout but not cerr. The cerr object is used for error
messages. Thus, if you redirect program output to a file and there is an error, you still
get the error message onscreen. The exit() function terminates a program.
Commonly, nonzero arguments are used to indicate that the program terminated abnor-
mally, and a zero argument is used to indicate normal termination. However, for maximum ANSI portability, you can use EXIT_SUCCESS and EXIT_FAILURE as return values.
Calling exit() from main() has the same effect as calling return from main(), but,
unlike return, exit() terminates a program regardless of the function from which it's
called. The cstdlib header file (formerly stdlib.h) provides the function prototype
and defines the portable return values.

Inline Methods

Any function with a definition in the class declaration automatically becomes an inline
function. Thus, Stock::set_tot() is an inline function. Class declarations often use
inline functions for short member functions, and set_tot() qualifies on that account.

You can, if you like, define a member function outside the class declaration and still
make it inline. To do so, just use the inline qualifier when you define the function in
the class implementation section:

```
class Stock
{
private:
    ...
    void set_tot();  // definition kept separate
public:
    ...
};

inline void Stock::set_tot()  // use inline in definition
{
    total_val = shares * share_val;
}
```

Because inline functions have internal linkage, they are known only to the file in
which they are declared. The easiest way to make sure that inline definitions are available to all files in a multifile program is to include the inline definition in the same

header file in which the corresponding class is defined. (Some development systems might have smart linkers that allow the inline definitions to go into a separate implementation file.)

Incidentally, according to the *rewrite rule*, defining a method in a class declaration is equivalent to replacing the method definition with a prototype and then rewriting the definition as an inline function immediately after the class declaration. That is, the original definition of set_tot() is equivalent to the one just shown.

> *" Any function with a definition in the class declaration automatically becomes an inline function. "*

Which Object?

Now we come to one of the most important aspects of using objects: how you apply a class method to an object. Code such as

```
shares += num;
```

uses the shares member of an object. But which object? That's an excellent question! To answer it, first consider how you create an object. The simplest way is to declare class variables:

```
Stock kate, joe;
```

This creates two objects of the Stock class, one named kate and one named joe.

Next, consider how to use a member function with one of these objects. The answer, as with structures and structure members, is to use the membership operator:

```
kate.show();    // the kate object calls the member function
joe.show();     // the joe object calls the member function
```

The first call invokes show() as a member of the kate object. This means the method interprets shares as kate.shares and share_val as kate.share_val. Similarly, the call joe.show() makes the show() method interpret shares and share_val as joe.shares and joe.share_val, respectively.

Remember

When you call a member function, it uses the data members of the particular object that invokes the member function.

Similarly, the function call kate.sell() invokes the set_tot() function as if it were kate.set_tot(), causing that function to get its data from the kate object.

Each new object you create contains storage for its own internal variables, the class members. But all objects of the same class share the same set of class methods. Suppose, for instance, that kate and joe are Stock objects. Then, kate.shares occupies one chunk of memory and joe.shares occupies a second chunk of memory. But kate.show() and joe.show() both invoke the same method; that is, both execute the same block of code. They just apply the code to different data. Calling a member function is what some OOP languages term *sending a message*. Thus, sending the same message to two different objects invokes the same method but applies it to two different objects. See Figure 9.2.

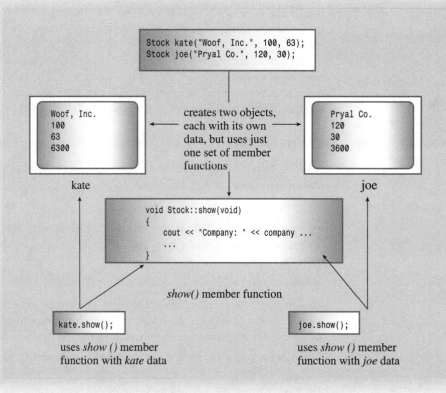

FIGURE 9.2

Objects, data, and member functions

USING A CLASS

Now you've seen how to define a class and its class methods. The next step is to produce a program that creates and uses objects of a class. The C++ goal is to make using classes as similar as possible to using the basic, built-in types, such as int and char. You can create a class object by declaring a class variable or using new to allocate an object of a class type. You can pass objects as arguments, return them as function return values, and assign one object to another. C++ provides facilities for initializing objects, teaching cin and cout to recognize objects, and even providing automatic type conversions between objects of similar classes. It will be a while before you can do all these things, but let's start now with the simpler properties. Indeed, you've already seen how to declare a class object and call a member function. Listing 9.3 combines those techniques with the class declaration and the member function definitions to form a complete program. It creates a Stock object named stock1. The program is simple, but it does test the features we built into the class.

" *The C++ goal is to make using classes as similar as possible to using the basic, built-in types, such as* int *and* char.*"*

Listing 9.3 stocks.cpp

```cpp
// stocks.cpp
#include <iostream>
using namespace std;
#include <cstdlib>  // --or stdlib.h--for exit()
#include <cstring>  // --or string.h--for strncpy()

class Stock
{
private:
    char company[30];
    int shares;
    double share_val;
    double total_val;
    void set_tot() { total_val = shares * share_val; }
public:
    void acquire(const char * co, int n, double pr);
    void buy(int num, double price);
    void sell(int num, double price);
    void update(double price);
    void show();
};

void Stock::acquire(const char * co, int n, double pr)
{
    strncpy(company, co, 29); // truncate co to fit if needed
    company[29] = '\0';
    shares = n;
    share_val = pr;
    set_tot();
}

void Stock::buy(int num, double price)
{
    shares += num;
    share_val = price;
    set_tot();
}

void Stock::sell(int num, double price)
{
    if (num > shares)
    {
        cerr << "You can't sell more than you have!\n";
        exit(1);
    }
    shares -= num;
    share_val = price;
    set_tot();
}

void Stock::update(double price)
{
    share_val = price;
    set_tot();
}
```

```
void Stock::show()
{
    cout << "Company: " << company
         << "  Shares: " << shares << '\n'
         << "  Share Price: $" << share_val
         << "  Total Worth: $" << total_val << '\n';
}

int main()
{
    Stock stock1;

    stock1.acquire("NanoSmart", 20, 12.50);
    cout.precision(2);                     // #.## format
    cout.setf(ios_base::fixed);            // #.## format
    cout.setf(ios_base::showpoint);        // #.## format
    stock1.show();
    stock1.buy(15, 18.25);
    stock1.show();
    return 0;
}
```

The program uses three formatting commands. The net effect is to display two digits to the right of the decimal, including trailing zeros. Actually, only the first two are needed according to current practices, and older implementations just need the first and third. Using all three produces the same output for both implementations. See Chapter 16, "Input, Output, and Files," for the details. Meanwhile, here is the program output:

```
Company: NanoSmart  Shares: 20
  Share Price: $12.50  Total Worth: $250.00
Company: NanoSmart  Shares: 35
  Share Price: $18.25  Total Worth: $638.75
```

Note that main() is just a vehicle for testing the design of the Stock class. Given that the class works as we like, we now can use the Stock class as a user-defined type in other programs. The critical point in using the new type is understanding what the member functions do; you shouldn't have to think about the implementation details. See the following note regarding the Client-Server Model.

THE CLIENT-SERVER MODEL

OOP programmers often discuss program design in terms of a client-server model. In this conceptualization, the *client* is a program that uses the class. The class declaration, including the class methods, constitutes the *server*, which is a resource available to the programs that need it. The client uses the server through the publicly defined interface only. This means the client's only responsibility—and, by extension, the client's programmer's only responsibility—is to know that interface. The server's responsibility—and, by extension, the server's designer's responsibility—is to see that the server reliably and accurately performs according to that interface. Any changes the server designer makes to the class design should be to details of implementation, not to the interface. This allows programmers to improve the client and the server independently of each other, without changes in the server having unforeseen repercussions in the client's behavior.

OUR STORY TO DATE

The first step in specifying a class design is providing a class declaration. The class declaration is modeled after a structure declaration and can include data members and function members. The declaration has a private section, and members declared in that section can be accessed only through the member functions. The declaration also has a public section, and members declared there can be accessed directly by a program using class objects. Typically, data members go into the private section and member functions go into the public section, so a typical class declaration has this form:

```
class className
{
private:
    data member declarations
public:
    member function prototypes
};
```

The contents of the public section constitute the abstract part of the design, the public interface. Encapsulating data in the private section protects the integrity of the data and is called *data hiding*. Thus, the class is the C++ way of making it easy to implement the OOP goals of abstraction, data hiding, and encapsulation.

The second step in specifying the class design is to implement the class member functions. You can use a complete function definition instead of a function prototype in the class declaration, but the usual practice, except for very brief functions, is to provide the function definitions separately. In that case, you need to use the scope operator to indicate to which class a member function belongs. For instance, suppose the Bozo class has a member function called retort() that returns a pointer to a char. Then, the function heading would look like this:

```
char * Bozo::retort()
```

In other words, retort() is not just a type char * function; it is a type char * function that belongs to the Bozo class. The full, or qualified, name of the function is Bozo::retort(). The name retort(), on the other hand, is an abbreviation of the qualified name, and it can be used only in certain circumstances, such as in class method code. Another way of describing this situation is to say the name retort has class scope, so the scope resolution operator is needed to qualify the name when it is used outside the class declaration and a class method.

To create an object, which is a particular instance, or example, of a class, use the class name as if it were a type name:

```
Bozo bozetta;
```

This works because a class *is* a user-defined type.

A class member function, or method, can be invoked only by a class object. You can do so by using the dot membership operator:

```
cout << Bozetta.retort();
```

This invokes the `retort()` member function, and whenever the code for that function refers to a particular data member, the function uses the value that member has in the `bozetta` object.

Class Constructors and Destructors

Meanwhile, there's more to be done with the `Stock` class. There are certain standard functions, called *constructors* and *destructors*, you normally should provide for a class. Let's see why they are needed and how to write them.

One of C++'s aims is to make using class objects similar to using standard types. However, you can't yet initialize a `Stock` object the way you can an ordinary `int` or `struct`:

```
int year = 2001                                    // okay
struct thing
{
    char * pn;
    int m;
};
thing amabob = {"wodget", -23};                    //okay
Stock hot = {"Sukie's Autos, Inc.", 200, 50.25};   // NO!
```

The reason you can't initialize a `Stock` object this way is because the data parts have private access status, which means a program cannot access the data members directly. As you've seen, the only way a program can access the data members is through a member function. Therefore, you need to devise an appropriate member function if you're to succeed in initializing an object. (You could initialize a class object as shown if you made the data members public instead of private, but making the data public goes against one of the main justifications for classes, that is, data hiding.)

In general, it's best that all objects be initialized when they are created. For example, consider the following code:

```
Stock gift;
gift.buy(10, 24.75);
```

With the current implementation of the `Stock` class, the `gift` object has no value for the `company` member. The class design assumes that the user calls `acquire()` before calling any other member functions, but there is no way to enforce that assumption. One way around this difficulty is to have objects initialized automatically when they are created. To accomplish this, C++ provides for special member functions, called class constructors, especially for constructing new objects and assigning values to their data members. More precisely, C++ provides a name for these member functions and a syntax for using them, and you provide the method definition. The name is the same as the class name. For instance, a possible constructor for the Stock class is a member function called Stock(). The constructor prototype and heading have an interesting property—although the constructor has no return value, it's not declared type void. In fact, a constructor has no declared type.

DECLARING AND DEFINING CONSTRUCTORS

Let's build a Stock constructor. Because a Stock object has three values to be provided from the outside world, you give the constructor three arguments. (The fourth value, the total_val member, is calculated from shares and share_val, so you don't have to provide it to the constructor.) Possibly, you just want to set the company member and set the other values to zero; this can be done with default arguments (see Chapter 8, "Adventures in Functions"). Thus, the prototype would look like this:

```
// constructor prototype with some default arguments
Stock(const char * co, int n = 0, double pr = 0.0);
```

The first argument is a pointer to the string that is used to initialize the company character array class members. The n and pr arguments provide values for the shares and share_val members. Note that there is no return type. The prototype goes in the public section of the class declaration.

Next, here's one possible definition for the constructor:

```
// constructor definition
Stock::Stock(const char * co, int n, double pr)
{
    strncpy(company, co, 29);
    company[29] = '\0';
    shares = n;
    share_val = pr;
    set_tot();
}
```

This is the same code that we used for the acquire() function. The difference is that a program automatically invokes the constructor when it declares an object.

Remember

Often those new to constructors try to use the class member names as arguments to the constructor:

```
Stock::Stock(const char * company, int shares, double
share_val)  // no!
{
...
}
```

This is wrong. The constructor arguments don't represent the class members; they represent values that are assigned to the class members. Thus, they must have distinct names.

USING A CONSTRUCTOR

C++ provides two ways to initialize an object by using the constructor. The first is to call the constructor explicitly:

```
Stock food = Stock("World Cabbage", 250, 1.25);
```

This sets the company member of the food object to the string "World Cabbage", the shares member to 250, and so on.

The second way is to call the constructor implicitly:

```
Stock garment("Furry Mason", 50, 2.5);
```

This more compact form is equivalent to the following explicit call:

```
Stock garment = Stock("Furry Mason", 50, 2.5));
```

C++ uses a class constructor whenever you create an object of that class, even when you use new for dynamic memory allocation. Here's how to use the constructor with new:

```
Stock *pstock = new Stock("Electroshock Games", 18, 19.0);
```

This statement creates a Stock object, initializes it to the values provided by the arguments, and assigns the address of the object to the pstock pointer. In this case, the object doesn't have a name, but you can use the pointer to manage the object. We put off further discussion of pointers to objects until Chapter 10, "Working with Classes."

Constructors are used differently from the other class methods. Normally, you use an object to invoke a method:

```
stock1.show();  // stock1 object invokes show() method
```

However, you can't use an object to invoke a constructor because, until the constructor finishes its work of making the object, there is no object. Rather than being invoked by an object, the constructor is used to create the object.

THE DEFAULT CONSTRUCTOR

The *default constructor* is the constructor used to create an object when you don't provide explicit initialization values. That is, it's the constructor used for declarations like this:

```
Stock stock1;  // uses the default constructor
```

Hey, Listing 9.3 already did that! The reason this statement works is that if you fail to provide any constructors, C++ automatically supplies a default constructor. It's a default version of a default constructor, and it does nothing. For the Stock class, it would look like this:

```
Stock::Stock() { }
```

The net result is that the stock1 object is created with its members uninitialized, just as

```
int x;
```

creates x without providing it a value. The fact that the default constructor has no arguments reflects the fact that no values appear in the declaration.

A curious fact about the default constructor is that the compiler provides one only if you don't define any constructors. After you define any constructor for a class, the responsibility for providing a default constructor for that class passes from the compiler to you. If you provide a non-default constructor, such as `Stock(const char * co, int n, double pr)` and don't provide your own version of a default constructor, then a declaration like

```
Stock stock1;   // not possible with current constructor
```

becomes an error. The reason for this behavior is that you might want to make it impossible to create uninitialized objects. On the other hand, you might want to be able to create objects without explicit initialization. If so, you must define your own default constructor. This is a constructor that takes no arguments. You can define a default constructor two ways. One is to provide default values for all the arguments to the existing constructor:

```
Stock(const char * co = "Error", int n = 0, double pr = 0.0);
```

The second is to use function overloading to define a second constructor, one that has no arguments:

```
Stock();
```

(With early versions of C++, you could use only the second method for creating a default constructor.)

Actually, you usually should initialize objects in order to ensure that all members begin with known, reasonable values. Thus, the default constructor typically provides implicit initialization for all member values. Here, for example, is how you might define one for the `Stock` class:

```
Stock::Stock()
{
    strcpy(company, "no name");
    shares = 0;
    share_val = 0.0;
    total_val = 0.0;
}
```

When you design a class, you usually should provide a default constructor that implicitly initializes all class members.

After you've used either method (no arguments or default values for all arguments) to create the default constructor, you can declare object variables without initializing them explicitly:

```
Stock first;            // calls default constructor implicitly
Stock first = Stock();  // calls it explicitly
Stock *prelief = new Stock; // calls it implicitly
```

However, don't be misled by the implicit form of the nondefault constructor:

```
Stock first("Concrete Conglomerate");    // calls constructor
Stock second();                          // declares a function

Stock third;                             // calls default constructor
```

The first declaration calls the nondefault constructor, that is, the one that takes arguments. The second declaration states that second() is a function that returns a Stock object. When you implicitly call the default constructor, don't use parentheses.

DESTRUCTORS

When you use a constructor to create an object, the program undertakes the responsibility of tracking that object until it expires. At that time, the program automatically calls a special member function bearing the formidable title of *destructor*. The destructor should clean up any debris, so it actually serves a constructive purpose. For instance, if your constructor uses new to allocate memory, the destructor should use delete to free that memory. The Stock constructor doesn't do anything fancy like using new, so it doesn't really need a destructor. But it's a good idea to provide one anyway in case a future class revision needs one.

Like a constructor, the destructor has a special name: the class name preceded by a tilde (~). Thus, the destructor for the Stock class is called ~Stock(). Also, like a constructor, a destructor can have no return value and has no declared type. Unlike the constructor, the destructor must have no arguments. Thus, the prototype for a Stock destructor must be this:

```
~Stock();
```

Because a Stock destructor has no vital duties, we can code it as a do-nothing function:

```
Stock::~Stock()
{
}
```

However, just so that you can see when the destructor is called, we'll code it this way:

```
Stock::~Stock()    // class destructor
{
    cout << "Bye, " << company << "!\n";

}
```

When should a destructor be called? This is a decision handled by the compiler; your code shouldn't explicitly call the destructor. If you create a static storage class object, its destructor is called automatically when the program terminates. If you create an automatic storage class object, as we have been doing, its destructor is called automatically when the program exits the block of code in which the object is defined. If the object is created by using new, it resides in heap memory, or the free store, and its destructor is called automatically when you use delete to free the memory. Finally, a program can create temporary objects to carry out certain operations; in that case, the program automatically calls the destructor for the object when it has finished using it.

Because the destructor is called automatically when a class object expires, there has to be a destructor. If you don't provide one, the compiler provides a default destructor that does nothing.

IMPROVING THE stock CLASS

The next step is to incorporate the constructors and the destructor into the class and method definitions. This time we follow the usual C++ practice and organize the program into separate files. We place the class declaration in a header file called stock1.h. (As the name suggests, we have future revisions in mind.) The class methods go into a file called stock1.cpp. In general, the header file containing the class declaration and the source code file containing the methods definitions should have the same base name so that you can keep track of which files belong together. Using separate files for the class declaration and the member functions separates the abstract definition of the interface (the class declaration) from the details of implementation (the member functions). You could, for example, distribute the class declaration as a text header file but distribute the function definitions as compiled code. Finally, we place the program using these resources in a third file, which we call usestok1.cpp.

The Header File

Listing 9.4 shows the header file. It adds prototypes for the constructor and destructor functions to the original class declaration. Also, it dispenses with the acquire() function, which no longer is necessary now that the class has constructors.

Listing 9.4 stock1.h

```
// stock1.h
#ifndef _STOCK1_H_
#define _STOCK1_H_

class Stock
{
private:
    char company[30];
    int shares;
    double share_val;
    double total_val;
    void set_tot() { total_val = shares * share_val; }
public:
    Stock();          // default constructor
    Stock(const char * co, int n = 0, double pr = 0.0);
    ~Stock();         // noisey destructor
    void buy(int num, double price);
    void sell(int num, double price);
    void update(double price);
    void show();
};

#endif
```

HEADER FILE MANAGEMENT

You should include a header file just once in a file. That might seem to be an easy thing to remember, but it's possible to include a header file several times without knowing you did so. For instance, you might use a header file that includes another header file. There's a standard C/C++ technique for avoiding multiple inclusions of header files. It's based on the preprocessor #ifndef (for *if n*ot *def*ined) directive. A code segment like

```
#ifndef _STOCK1_H_
...
#endif
```

means process the statements between the #ifndef and #endif only if the name _STOCK1_H_ has not been defined previously by the preprocessor #define directive.

Normally, you use the #define statement to create symbolic constants, as in the following:

```
#define MAXIMUM 4096
```

But simply using #define with a name is enough to establish that a name is defined, as in the following:

```
#define _STOCK1_H_
```

The technique, which Listing 9.4 uses, is to wrap the file contents in an #ifndef:

```
#ifndef _STOCK1_H_
#define _STOCK1_H_
// place include file contents here
#endif
```

The first time the compiler encounters the file, the name _STOCK1_H_ should be undefined. (We chose a name based on the include file name with a few underscore characters tossed in so as to create a name unlikely to be defined elsewhere.) That being the case, the compiler looks at the material between the #ifndef and the #endif, which is what we want. In the process of looking at the material, the compiler reads the line defining _STOCK1_H_. If it then encounters a second inclusion of stock1.h in the same file, the compiler notes that _STOCK1_H_ is defined and skips to the line following the #endif. Note that this method doesn't keep the compiler from including a file twice. Instead, it makes it ignore the contents of all but the first inclusion. Most of the standard C and C++ header files use this scheme.

The Implementation File

Listing 9.5 provides the method definitions. It includes the stock1.h file in order to provide the class declaration. (Recall that enclosing the file name in double quotation marks instead of in brackets means the compiler searches for it at the same location your source files are found.) Also, the listing includes the iostream and cstring files, because the methods use cin, cout, and strncpy(). This file adds the constructor and destructor method definitions to the prior methods.

Listing 9.5 stock1.cpp

```cpp
// stock1.cpp          // Stock class methods
#include <iostream>
#include <cstdlib>      // (or stdlib.h) for exit()
#include <cstring>      // (or string.h) for strncpy()
using namespace std;
#include "stock1.h"

// constructors
Stock::Stock()          // default constructor
{
    strcpy(company, "no name");
    shares = 0;
    share_val = 0.0;
    total_val = 0.0;
}

Stock::Stock(const char * co, int n, double pr)
{
    strncpy(company, co, 29);
    company[29] = '\0';
    shares = n;
    share_val = pr;
    set_tot();
}

// class destructor
Stock::~Stock()         // verbose class destructor
{
    cout << "Bye, " << company << "!\n";
}

// other methods
void Stock::buy(int num, double price)
{
    shares += num;
    share_val = price;
    set_tot();
}

void Stock::sell(int num, double price)
{
    if (num > shares)
    {
        cerr << "You can't sell more than you have!\n";
        exit(1);
    }
    shares -= num;
    share_val = price;
    set_tot();
}

void Stock::update(double price)
{
```

```
        share_val = price;
        set_tot();
}

void Stock::show()
{
    cout << "Company: " << company
         << "  Shares: " << shares << '\n'
         << "  Share Price: $" << share_val
         << "  Total Worth: $" << total_val << '\n';
}
```

Remember

You might have to use `stdlib.h` and `string.h` rather than `cstdlib` and `cstring`.

A Client File

Listing 9.6 provides a short program for testing the new methods. Like stock1.cpp, it includes the stock1.h file to provide the class declaration. The program demonstrates constructors and destructors. It also uses the same formatting commands invoked by Listing 9.3. To compile the complete program, use the techniques for multifile programs described in Chapters 1 and 8.

Listing 9.6 usestok1.cpp

```
// usestok1.cpp -- use the Stock class
#include <iostream>
using namespace std;
#include "stock1.h"

int main()
{
// using constructors to create new objects
    Stock stock1("NanoSmart", 12, 20.0);          // syntax 1
    Stock stock2 = Stock ("Boffo Objects", 2, 2.0); // syntax 2

    cout.precision(2);                            // #.## format
    cout.setf(ios::fixed, ios::floatfield);       // #.## format
    cout.setf(ios::showpoint);                    // #.## format

    stock1.show();
    stock2.show();
    stock2 = stock1;                              // object assignment

// using a constructor to reset an object
    stock1 = Stock("Nifty Foods", 10, 50.0);      // temp object

    cout << "After stock reshuffle:\n";
    stock1.show();
    stock2.show();
    return 0;
}
```

Here's the program output:

```
Company: NanoSmart  Shares: 12
  Share Price: $20.00  Total Worth: $240.00
```

```
Company: Boffo Objects  Shares: 2
  Share Price: $2.00  Total Worth: $4.00
Bye, Nifty Foods!
After stock reshuffle:
Company: Nifty Foods  Shares: 10
  Share Price: $50.00  Total Worth: $500.00
Company: NanoSmart  Shares: 12
  Share Price: $20.00  Total Worth: $240.00
Bye, NanoSmart!
Bye, Nifty Foods!
```

Program Notes

The statement

```
Stock stock1("NanoSmart", 12, 20.0);
```

creates a Stock object called stock1 and initializes its data members to the indicated values. The statement

```
Stock stock2 = Stock ("Boffo Objects", 2, 2.0);
```

uses the second variety of syntax to create and initialize an object called stock2.

You can use the constructor for more than initializing a new object. For instance, the program has this statement in main():

```
stock1 = Stock("Nifty Foods", 10, 50.0);
```

The stock1 object already exists. Thus, instead of initializing stock1, this statement assigns new values to the object. It does so by having the constructor create a new, temporary object and then copy the contents of the new object to stock1.

The statement

```
stock2 = stock1;      // object assignment
```

illustrates that you can assign one object to another of the same type. As with structure assignment, class object assignment, by default, copies the members of one object to the other. In this case, the original contents of stock2 are overwritten.

Remember

When you assign one object to another of the same class, C++, by default, copies the contents of each data member of the source object to the corresponding data member of the target object.

Note that output shows the program saying Bye, Nifty Foods! before it displays the new stock1 contents. Later, at the end, the program says Bye, NanoSmart! and Bye, Nifty Foods!. Where do these farewells come from? Recall that the destructor has an output statement to this effect so that you can see when the destructor is invoked. (This is a learning device, not a normal design feature!) The final two farewells happen when the main() terminates and the two local objects the program declares (stock1 and stock2) pass from our plane of existence. Because such automatic variables go on the stack, the last object created is the first deleted, and the first created is the last deleted. (Note that `"NanoSmart"` originally was in `stock1` but later was transferred to `stock2`.)

But what about the first farewell to Nifty Foods? When the program uses the constructor to reassign the Nifty Food values to the `stock1` object, recall, the program first creates a temporary, nameless object that has the provided values. Then, those values are copied to the `stock1` object. Finally, when the temporary object expires, the program calls the destructor function for it. The first Nifty Foods deleted is the temporary object, and the second Nifty Foods deleted is the `stock1` object. Incidentally, C++ doesn't really specify when a temporary object is disposed. This implementation (Microsoft Visual C++ 5.0) deletes it as soon as it no longer is needed, whereas Turbo C++ 2.0 deletes the temporary object when the function terminates.

This little episode points out that there is a fundamental difference between the following two statements:

```
Stock stock2 = Stock ("Boffo Objects", 2, 2.0);
stock1 = Stock("Nifty Foods", 10, 50.0); // temp object
```

The first statement is initialization; it creates an object with the indicated value. The second statement is assignment. It creates a temporary object and then copies it to an existing object. This clearly is less efficient than initialization. (However, a compiler is allowed to implement the initialization form shown above for `stock2` by creating a temporary object first and copying its contents to `stock2`.)

Remember

If you can set object values either by initialization or by assignment, choose initialization. It usually is more efficient.

The `show()` output near the end of the program demonstrates that both object assignment and object resetting by using a constructor and assignment worked.

`const` Member Functions

Consider the following code snippets:

```
const Stock land = Stock("Kludgehorn Properties");
land.show();
```

With current C++, the compiler should object to the second line. Why? Because the code for `show()` fails to guarantee that it won't modify the invoking object, which, because it is `const`, should not be altered. You've solved this kind of problem before by declaring a function's argument to be a `const` reference or a pointer to `const`. But here we have a syntax problem: The `show()` method doesn't have any arguments. Instead, the object it uses is provided implicitly by the method invocation. What's needed is a new syntax, one that says a function promises not to modify the invoking object. The C++ solution is to place the `const` keyword after the function parentheses. That is, the `show()` declaration should look like this:

```
void show() const;          // promises not to change invoking object
```

Similarly, the beginning of the function definition should look like this:

```
void stock::show() const    // promises not to change invoking object
```

Class functions declared and defined this way are called `const` member functions. Just as you should use `const` references and pointers as formal function arguments whenever appropriate, you should make class methods `const` whenever they don't modify the invoking object. We follow this rule from here on out.

> *Just as you should use `const` references and pointers as formal function arguments whenever appropriate, you should make class methods `const` whenever they don't modify the invoking object.*

CONSTRUCTORS AND DESTRUCTORS IN REVIEW

Now that we've gone through a few examples of constructors and destructors, you might wish to pause and assimilate what has passed. To help you, here is a summary of these methods.

A constructor is a special class member function that's called whenever an object of that class is created. A class constructor has the same name as its class, but, through the miracle of function overloading, you can have more than one constructor with the same name, provided that each has its own signature, or argument list. Also, a constructor has no declared type. Usually, the constructor is used to initialize members of a class object. Your initialization should match the constructor's argument list. For instance, suppose the `Bozo` class has the following prototype for a class constructor:

```
Bozo(char * fname, char * lname);    // constructor prototype
```

Then, you would use it to initialize new objects as follows:

```
Bozo bozetta = bozo("Bozetta", "Biggens");    // primary form
Bozo fufu("Fufu", "O'Dweeb");                 // short form
Bozo *pc = new Bozo("Popo", "Le Peu");        // dynamic object
```

If a constructor has just one argument, that constructor is invoked if you initialize an object to a value that has the same type as the constructor argument. For instance, suppose you have this constructor prototype:

```
Bozo(int age);
```

Then, you can use any of the following forms to initialize an object:

```
Bozo dribble = bozo(44);    // primary form
Bozo roon(66);              // secondary form
Bozo tubby = 32;            // special form for one-argument constructors
```

Actually, the third example is a new point, not a review point, but it seemed like a nice time to tell you about it. Chapter 10 mentions a way to turn off this feature.

Remember

A constructor that you can use with a single argument allows you to use assignment syntax to initialize an object to a value:

```
Classname object = value;
```

The default constructor has no arguments, and it is used if you create an object without explicitly initializing it. If you fail to provide any constructors, the compiler defines a default constructor for you. Otherwise, you have to supply your own default constructor. It can have no arguments or else have default values for all arguments:

```
Bozo();        // default constructor prototype
Bistro(const char * s = "Chez Zero");    // default for Bistro class
```

The program uses the default constructor for uninitialized objects:

```
Bozo bubi;            // use default
Bozo *pb = new Bozo;  // use default
```

Just as a program invokes a constructor when an object is created, it invokes a destructor when an object is destroyed. You can have only one destructor per class. It has no return type, not even void; it has no arguments; and its name is the class name preceded by a tilde. The Bozo class destructor, for example, has the following prototype:

```
~Bozo();    // class destructor
```

Class destructors become necessary when class constructors use new.

Knowing Your Objects: The `this` Pointer

There's still more to be done with the Stock class. So far, each class member function has dealt with but a single object, which has been the object that invokes it. Sometimes, however, a method might need to deal with two objects, and doing so may involve a curious C++ pointer called this. Let's see how this need can unfold.

Although the Stock class declaration displays data, it's deficient in analytic power. For instance, by looking at the show() output you can tell which of your holdings has the greatest value, but the program can't tell because it can't access total_val directly. The most direct way of letting a program know about stored data is to provide methods to return values. Typically, you use inline code for this:

```
class Stock
{
private:
    ...
    double total_val;
    ...
public:
    double total() const { return total_val; }
    ...
};
```

This definition, in effect, makes total_val read-only memory as far as a direct program access is concerned.

By adding this function to the class declaration, you can let a program investigate a series of stocks to find the one with the greatest value. However, let's take a different approach, mainly so you can learn about the this pointer. The approach is to define a member function that looks at two Stock objects and returns a reference to the larger of the two. Attempting to implement this approach raises some interesting questions, and we look into them now.

First, how do you provide the member function with two objects to compare? Suppose, for example, you decide to name the method topval(). Then, the function call stock1.topval() accesses the data of the stock1 object, whereas the message stock2.topval() accesses the data of the stock2 object. If you want the method to compare two objects, you have to pass the second object as an argument. For efficiency, pass the argument by reference. That is, have the topval() method use a type const Stock & argument.

Second, how do you communicate the method's answer back to the calling program? The most direct way is to have the method return a reference to the object that has the larger total value. Thus, the comparison method should have the following prototype:

```
const Stock & topval(const Stock & s) const;
```

This function accesses one object implicitly and one object explicitly, and it returns a reference to one of those two objects. The const in the parentheses states that the function won't modify the explicitly accessed object, and the const that follows the parentheses states that the function won't modify the implicitly accessed object. Because the function returns a reference to one of the two const objects, the return type also has to be a const reference.

Suppose, then, that you want to compare Stock objects stock1 and stock2 and assign the one with the greater total value to the object top. You can use either of the following statements:

```
top = stock1.topval(stock2);
top = stock2.topval(stock1);
```

The first form accesses stock1 implicitly and stock2 explicitly, whereas the second accesses stock1 explicitly and stock2 implicitly. See Figure 9.3. Either way, the method compares the two objects and returns a reference to the one with the higher total value.

Actually, this notation is a bit confusing. It would be clearer if you could somehow use the relational operator > to compare the two objects. You can do so with operator overloading, which Chapter 10 discusses.

Meanwhile, there's still the implementation of topval() to attend to. That raises a slight problem. Here's a partial implementation that highlights the problem:

```
const Stock & Stock::topval(const Stock & s) const
{
    if (s.total_val > total_val)
        return s;                    // argument object
    else
        return ?????;                // invoking object
}
```

FIGURE 9.3

Accessing two objects with a member function

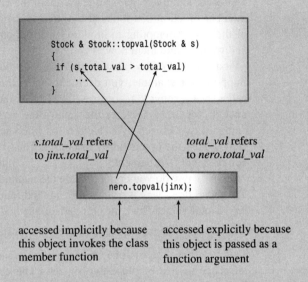

```
Stock & Stock::topval(Stock & s)
{
  if (s.total_val > total_val)
    ...
}
```

s.total_val refers to *jinx.total_val*

total_val refers to *nero.total_val*

```
nero.topval(jinx);
```

accessed implicitly because this object invokes the class member function

accessed explicitly because this object is passed as a function argument

> *The this pointer points to the object used to invoke a member function.*

Here s.total_val is the total value for the object passed as an argument, and total_val is the total value for the object to which the message is sent. If s.total_val is greater than total_val, the function returns s. Otherwise, it returns the object used to evoke the method. (In OOP talk, that is the object to which the topval message is sent.) The problem is, what do you call that object? If you make the call stock1.topval(stock2), then s is a reference for stock2 (that is, an alias for stock2), but there is no alias for stock1.

The C++ solution to this problem is a special pointer called this. The this pointer points to the object used to invoke a member function. (Basically, this is passed as a hidden argument to the method.) Thus, the function call stock1.topval(stock2) sets this to the address of the stock1 object and makes that pointer available to the topval() method. Similarly, the function call stock2.topval(stock1) sets this to the address of the stock2 object. In general, all class methods have a this pointer set to the address of the object invoking the method. Indeed, total_val in topval() is just shorthand notation for this->total_val. (Recall from Chapter 4 that you use the -> operator to access structure members via a pointer. The same is true for class members.) See Figure 9.4.

FIGURE 9.4

this points to the invoking object

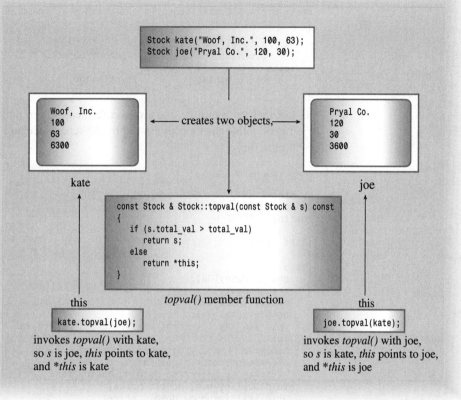

```
Stock kate("Woof, Inc.", 100, 63);
Stock joe("Pryal Co.", 120, 30);
```

| Woof, Inc.
100
63
6300 | ←— creates two objects,—→ | Pryal Co.
120
30
3600 |

kate   joe

```
const Stock & Stock::topval(const Stock & s) const
{
    if (s.total_val > total_val)
        return s;
    else
        return *this;
}
```

topval( ) member function

this   this

`kate.topval(joe);`   `joe.topval(kate);`

invokes *topval( )* with kate,   invokes *topval( )* with joe,
so *s* is joe, *this* points to kate,   so *s* is kate, *this* points to joe,
and *this is kate   and *this is joe

THE **this** POINTER

Each member function, including constructors and destructors, has a `this` pointer. The special property of the `this` pointer is that it points to the invoking object. If a method needs to refer to the invoking object as a whole, it can use the *this. If you use the `const` qualifier after the function argument parentheses, you can't use `this` to change the object's value.

What you want to return, however, is not `this`, because `this` is the address of the object. You want to return the object itself, and that is symbolized by *this. (Recall that applying the dereferencing operator * to a pointer yields the value to which the pointer points.) Now you can complete the method definition by using *this as an alias for the invoking object.

```
const Stock & Stock::topval(const Stock & s) const
{
    if (s.total_val > total_val)
        return s;               // argument object
    else
        return *this;           // invoking object
}
```

The fact that the return type is a reference means the returned object is the invoking object itself rather than a copy passed by the return mechanism. Listing 9.7 shows the new header file.

Listing 9.7 stock2.h

```
// stock2.h
#ifndef _STOCK2_H_
#define _STOCK2_H_

class Stock
{
private:
    char company[30];
    int shares;
    double share_val;
    double total_val;
    void set_tot() { total_val = shares * share_val; }
public:
    Stock();          // default constructor
    Stock(const char * co, int n, double pr);
    ~Stock() {}       // do-nothing destructor
    void buy(int num, double price);
    void sell(int num, double price);
    void update(double price);
    void show() const;
    const Stock & topval(const Stock & s) const;
};

#endif
```

Listing 9.8 presents the revised class methods file. It includes the new `topval()` method. Also, now that you've seen how the destructor method works, let's replace it with a silent version.

Listing 9.8 stock2.cpp

```
// stock2.cpp      // Stock class methods
#include <iostream>
using namespace std;
#include <cstdlib>    // for exit()
#include <cstring> // for strcpy()
#include "stock2.h"

// constructors
Stock::Stock()
{
    strcpy(company, "no name");
    shares = 0;
    share_val = 0.0;
```

```
    total_val = 0.0;
}

Stock::Stock(const char * co, int n, double pr)
{
    strcpy(company, co);
    shares = n;
    share_val = pr;
    set_tot();
}

void Stock::buy(int num, double price)
{
    shares += num;
    share_val = price;
    set_tot();
}

void Stock::sell(int num, double price)
{
    if (num > shares)
    {
        cerr << "You can't sell more than you have!\n";
        exit(1);
    }
    shares -= num;
    share_val = price;
    set_tot();
}

void Stock::update(double price)
{
    share_val = price;
    set_tot();
}

void Stock::show() const
{
    cout << "Company: " << company
        << "  Shares: " << shares << '\n'
        << "  Share Price: $" << share_val
        << "  Total Worth: $" << total_val << '\n';
}

const Stock & Stock::topval(const Stock & s) const
{
    if (s.total_val > total_val)
        return s;
    else
        return *this;
}
```

Of course, we want to see whether the this pointer works, and a natural place to use the new method is in a program with an array of objects, which leads us to the next topic.

An Array of Objects

Often, as with the Stock examples so far, you want to create several objects of the same class. You can create separate object variables, as the examples have done so far, but it might make more sense to create an array of objects. That might sound like a major leap into the unknown, but, in fact, you declare an array of objects the same way you would an array of any of the standard types:

```
Stock mystuff[4]; // creates an array of 4 Stock objects
```

Recall that a program always calls the default class constructor when it creates class objects that aren't explicitly initialized. This declaration requires either that the class explicitly defines no constructors at all, in which case the implicit do-nothing default constructor is used, or, as in this case, that an explicit default constructor is defined.

Each element—mystuff[0], mystuff[1], and so on—is a Stock object and thus can be used with the Stock methods:

```
mystuff[0].update();       // apply update() to 1st element
mystuff[3].show();         // apply show() to 4th element
Stock tops = mystuff[2].topval(mystuff[1]);
                           // compare 3rd and 2nd elements
```

You can use a constructor to initialize the array elements. In that case, you have to call the constructor for each individual element:

```
const int STKS = 4;
Stock stocks[STKS] = {
    Stock("NanoSmart", 12.5, 20),
    Stock("Boffo Objects", 200, 2.0),
    Stock("Monolithic Obelisks", 130, 3.25),
    Stock("Fleep Enterprises", 60, 6.5)
    };
```

Here the code uses the standard form for initializing an array: a comma-separated list of values enclosed in braces. In this case, a call to the constructor method represents each value. If the class has more than one constructor, you can use different constructors for different elements.

This format for initializing an array of objects still initially uses the default constructor to create the array elements. Then, the constructors in the braces create temporary objects whose contents are copied to the vector. Thus, a class must have a default constructor if you want to create arrays of class objects.

Remember

If you want to create an array of class objects, the class must have a default constructor.

Listing 9.9 applies these principles to a short program that initializes four array elements, displays their contents, and tests the elements to find the one with the highest total value. Because topval() examines just two objects at a time, the program uses a for loop to examine the whole array. Use the header file and methods file shown in Listings 9.7 and 9.8, respectively.

Listing 9.9 usestok2.cpp

```
// usestok2.cpp -- use the Stock class
#include <iostream>
using namespace std;
```

```
#include "stock2.h"

const int STKS = 4;
int main()
{
// create an array of initialized objects
    Stock stocks[STKS] = {
        Stock("NanoSmart", 12, 20.0),
        Stock("Boffo Objects", 200, 2.0),
        Stock("Monolithic Obelisks", 130, 3.25),
        Stock("Fleep Enterprises", 60, 6.5)
        };

    cout.precision(2);                        // #.## format
    cout.setf(ios::fixed, ios::floatfield);   // #.## format
    cout.setf(ios::showpoint);                // #.## format

    cout << "Stock holdings:\n";
    int st;
    for (st = 0; st < STKS; st++)
        stocks[st].show();

    Stock top = stocks[0];
    for (st = 1; st < STKS; st++)
        top = top.topval(stocks[st]);
    cout << "\nMost valuable holding:\n";
    top.show();

    return 0;
}
```

Remember

You might have to use `stdlib.h` and `string.h` rather than `cstdlib` and `cstring`.

Here is the output:

```
Stock holdings:
Company: NanoSmart  Shares: 12
  Share Price: $20.00  Total Worth: $240.00
Company: Boffo Objects  Shares: 200
  Share Price: $2.00  Total Worth: $400.00
Company: Monolithic Obelisks  Shares: 130
  Share Price: $3.25  Total Worth: $422.50
Company: Fleep Enterprises  Shares: 60
  Share Price: $6.50  Total Worth: $390.00

Most valuable holding:
Company: Monolithic Obelisks  Shares: 130
  Share Price: $3.25  Total Worth: $422.50
```

One thing to note is how most of the work goes into designing the class. When that's done, writing the program itself is rather simple.

Incidentally, knowing about the `this` pointer makes it easier to see how C++ works under the skin. For instance, the C++ front end `cfront` converts C++ programs to C programs. To handle method definitions, all it has to do is convert a C++ method definition like

```
void Stock::show() const
{
```

```
        cout << "Company: " << company
             << "  Shares: " << shares << '\n'
             << "  Share Price: $" << share_val
             << "  Total Worth: $" << total_val << '\n';
}
```

to the following C definition:

```
void show(const Stock * this)
{
        cout << "Company: " << this->company
             << "  Shares: " << this->shares << '\n'
             << "  Share Price: $" << this->share_val
             << "  Total Worth: $" << this->total_val << '\n';
}
```

That is, it converts a Stock:: qualifier to a function argument that is a pointer to Stock and then uses the pointer to access class members.

Similarly, the front end converts function calls like

```
top.show();
```

to:

```
show(&top);
```

In this fashion, the this pointer is assigned the address of the invoking object. (The actual details might be more involved.)

Class Scope

Chapter 8 discusses global, or file, scope and local, or block, scope. You can use a variable with global scope, recall, anywhere in the file that contains its definition, whereas a variable with local scope is local to the block that contains its definition. Function names, too, can have global scope, but they never have local scope. C++ classes introduce a new kind of scope: *class scope*. Class scope applies to names defined in a class, such as the names of class data members and class member functions. Items that have class scope are known within the class but not outside the class. Thus, you can use the same class member names in different classes without conflict: The shares member of the Stock class is a variable distinct from the shares member of a JobRide class. Also, class scope means you can't directly access members of a class from the outside world. This is true even for public function members. That is, to invoke a public member function, you have to use an object:

```
Stock sleeper("Exclusive Ore", 100, 0.25);  // create object
sleeper.show();      // use object to invoke a member function
show();              // invalid — can't call method directly
```

Similarly, you have to use the scope resolution operator when you define member functions:

```
void Stock::update(double price)
{
    ...
}
```

In short, within a class declaration or a member function definition you can use an unadorned member name (the unqualified name), as when `sell()` calls the `set_tot()` member function. Otherwise, you must use the direct membership operator (`.`), the indirect membership operator (`->`), or the scope resolution operator (`::`), depending on the context, when you use a class member name.

Sometimes it would be nice to have symbolic constants of class scope. For instance, the `Stock` class declaration used a literal 30 to specify the array size for `company`. You might think the following would be a solution:

```
class Stock
{
private:
    const int Len = 30;     // declare a constant?
    char company[Len];
    ...
```

But this won't work, because declaring a class describes what an object looks like but doesn't create an object. Hence, until you create an object, there's no place to store a value. There are, however, a couple of ways to achieve essentially the same desired effect.

First, you can declare an enumeration within a class. An enumeration given in a class declaration has class scope, so you can use enumerations to provide class scope symbolic names for integer constants. That is, you can start off the `Stock` declaration this way:

```
class Stock
{
private:
    enum {Len = 30};  // class-specific constant
    char company[Len];
    ...
```

Because this uses the enumeration merely to create a symbolic constant with no intent of creating variables of the enumeration type, you needn't provide an enumeration tag. Incidentally, for many implementations, the `ios_base` class does something similar in its public section; that's the source of identifiers such as `ios_base::fixed`. Here `fixed` is an enumerator defined in the `ios_base` class.

More recently, C++ has introduced a second way of defining a constant within a class—using the keyword `static`:

```
class Stock
{
private:
    static const int Len = 30;     // declare a constant!
    char company[Len];
    ...
```

This creates a single constant called `Len` that is stored with other static variables rather than in an object. Thus, there is only one `Len` constant shared by all `Stock` objects. Chapter 11, "Classes and Dynamic Memory Allocation," looks further into static class members. You only can use this technique for declaring static constants with integral and enumeration values. You can't store a `double` constant this way.

An Abstract Data Type

The Stock class is pretty specific. Often, however, programmers define classes to represent more general concepts. For instance, classes are a good way to implement what computer scientists describe as *abstract data types*, or ADTs, for short. As the name suggests, an ADT describes a data type in a general fashion, without bringing in language or implementation details. Consider, for example, the stack. The stack is a way of storing data in which data is always added to or deleted from the top of the stack. C++ programs, for example, use a stack to manage automatic variables. As new automatic variables are generated, they are added to the top of the stack. When they expire, they are removed from a stack.

Let's describe the properties of a stack in a general, abstract way. First, a stack holds a number of items. It's a particular case of an even more general abstraction, the container. Next, a stack is characterized by the operations you can perform on one.

- You can create an empty stack.

- You can add an item to the top of a stack (*push* an item).

- You can remove an item from the top (*pop* an item).

- You can check to see whether the stack is full.

- You can check to see whether the stack is empty.

You can match this description with a class declaration in which the public member functions provide an interface that represents the stack operations. The private data members take care of storing the stack data. The class concept is a nice match to the ADT approach.

The private section has to commit itself to how to hold the data. For instance, you can use an ordinary array, a dynamically allocated array, or some more advanced data structure, such as a linked list. The public interface, however, should hide the exact representation. Instead, it should be expressed in general terms, such as creating a stack, pushing an item, and so on. Listing 9.10 shows one approach. It assumes that the bool type has been implemented. If it hasn't been on your system, you can use int, 0, and 1 rather than bool, false, and true.

Listing 9.10 stack.h

```
// stack.h -- class definition for the stack ADT
#ifndef _STACK_H_
#define _STACK_H_
typedef unsigned long Item;

class Stack
{
private:
    enum {MAX = 10};    // constant specific to class
    Item items[MAX];    // holds stack items
    int top;            // index for top stack item
public:
    Stack();
```

```
    bool isempty() const;
    bool isfull() const;
    // push() returns false if stack already is full, true otherwise
    bool push(const Item & item);   // add item to stack
    // pop() returns false if stack already is empty, true otherwise
    bool pop(Item & item);          // pop top into item
};
#endif
```

Remember

If your system hasn't implemented the `bool` type, you can use `int`, `0`, and `1` rather than `bool`, `false`, and `true`. Alternatively, your system might support an earlier, non-standard form, such as `boolean` or `Boolean`.

In this example, the private section shows that the stack is implemented by using an array, but the public section doesn't reveal that fact. Thus, you can replace the array with, say, a dynamic array without changing the class interface. That means changing the stack implementation doesn't require that you recode programs using the stack. You just recompile the stack code and link it with existing program code.

The interface is slightly redundant in that pop() and push() return information about the stack status (full or empty) instead of being type void. This provides the programmer with a couple of options as to how to handle exceeding the stack limit or emptying the stack. He or she can use isempty() and isfull() to check before attempting to modify the stack, or else use the return value of push() and pop() to determine whether the operation is successful.

Rather than define the stack in terms of some particular type, the class describes it in terms of a general Item type. In this case, the header file uses typedef to make Item the same as unsigned long. If you want, say, a stack of double or of a structure type, you can change the typedef and leave the class declaration and method definitions unaltered. Class templates (see Chapter 13, "Reusing Code in C++") provide a more powerful method for isolating the type of data stored from the class design.

Next, let's implement the class methods. Listing 9.11 shows one possibility.

Listing 9.11 stack.cpp

```
// stack.cpp -- Stack member functions
#include "stack.h"
Stack::Stack()    // create an empty stack
{
    top = 0;
}

bool Stack::isempty() const
{
    return top == 0;
}

bool Stack::isfull() const
{
    return top == MAX;
}
```

```
bool Stack::push(const Item & item)
{
    if (top < MAX)
    {
        items[top++] = item;
        return true;
    }
    else
        return false;
}

bool Stack::pop(Item & item)
{
    if (top > 0)
    {
        item = items[—top];
        return true;
    }
    else
        return false;
}
```

The default constructor guarantees that all stacks are created empty. The code for pop() and push() guarantees that the top of the stack is managed properly. Guarantees like this are one of the things that make object-oriented programming more reliable. Suppose, instead, you create a separate array to represent the stack and an independent variable to represent the index of the top. Then, it is your responsibility to get the code right each time you create a new stack. Without the protection that private data offers, there's always the possibility of making some program blunder that alters data unintentionally.

Let's test this stack. Listing 9.12 models the life of a clerk who processes purchase orders from the top of his in-basket, using the LIFO (*last in-first out*) approach of a stack.

Listing 9.12 stacker.cpp

```
// stacker.cpp -- test Stack class
#include <iostream>
using namespace std;
#include <cctype>  // or ctype.h
#include "stack.h"
int main()
{
    Stack st; // create an empty stack
    char c;
    unsigned long po;
    cout << "Please enter A to add a purchase order,\n"
         << "P to process a PO, or Q to quit.\n";
    while (cin >> c && toupper(c) != 'Q')
    {
        while (cin.get() != '\n')
            continue;
        if (!isalpha(c))
        {
            cout << '\a';
            continue;
        }
```

```
        switch(c)
        {
            case 'A':
            case 'a': cout << "Enter a PO number to add: ";
                      cin >> po;
                      if (st.isfull())
                          cout << "stack already full\n";
                      else
                          st.push(po);
                      break;
            case 'P':
            case 'p': if (st.isempty())
                          cout << "stack already empty\n";
                      else {
                          st.pop(po);
                          cout << "PO #" << po << " popped\n";
                      }
                      break;
        }
        cout << "Please enter A to add a purchase order,\n"
             << "P to process a PO, or Q to quit.\n";
    }
    cout << "Bye\n";
    return 0;
}
```

The little `while` loop that gets rid of the rest of the line isn't needed here, but it comes in handy in a modification of this program in Chapter 13. Here's a sample run:

```
Please enter A to add a purchase order,
P to process a PO, or Q to quit.
A
Enter a PO number to add: 17885
Please enter A to add a purchase order,
P to process a PO, or Q to quit.
P
PO #17885 popped
Please enter A to add a purchase order,
P to process a PO, or Q to quit.
A
Enter a PO number to add: 17965
Please enter A to add a purchase order,
P to process a PO, or Q to quit.
A
Enter a PO number to add: 18002
Please enter A to add a purchase order,
P to process a PO, or Q to quit.
P
PO #18002 popped
Please enter A to add a purchase order,
P to process a PO, or Q to quit.
P
PO #17965 popped
Please enter A to add a purchase order,
P to process a PO, or Q to quit.
P
stack already empty
Please enter A to add a purchase order,
P to process a PO, or Q to quit.
Q
Bye
```

Summary

Object-oriented programming emphasizes how a program represents data. The first step toward solving a programming problem by using the OOP approach is describing the data in terms of its interface with the program, specifying how the data is used. Next, design a class that implements the interface. Typically, private data members store the information, whereas public member functions, also called methods, provide the only access to the data. The class combines data and methods into one unit, and the private aspect accomplishes data hiding.

Usually, you separate the class declaration into two parts, typically kept in separate files. The class declaration proper goes into a header file, with the methods represented by function prototypes. The source code that defines the member functions goes into a methods file. This approach separates the description of the interface from the details of the implementation. In principle, you only need to know the public class interface to use the class. Of course, you can look at the implementation (unless it's been supplied to you in compiled form only), but your program shouldn't rely on details of the implementation, such as knowing a particular value is stored as an int. As long as a program and a class communicate only through methods defining the interface, you are free to improve either part separately without worrying about unforeseen interactions.

A class is a user-defined type, and an object is an instance of a class. That means an object is a variable of that type or the equivalent of a variable, such as memory allocated by new according to the class specification. C++ tries to make user-defined types as similar as possible to standard types, so you can declare objects, pointers to objects, and arrays of objects. You can pass objects as arguments, return them as function return values, and assign one object to another of the same type. If you provide a constructor method, you can initialize objects when they are created. If you provide a destructor method, the program executes that method when the object expires.

Each object holds its own copies of the data portion of a class declaration, but they share the class methods. If mr_object is the name of a particular object and try_me() is a member function, you invoke the member function by using the dot membership operator: mr_object.try_me(). OOP terminology describes this function call as sending a try_me message to the mr_object object. Any reference to class data members in the try_me() method then applies to the data members of the mr_object object. Similarly, the function call i_object.try_me() accesses the data members of the i_object object.

If you want a member function to act on more than one object, you can pass additional objects to the method as arguments. If a method needs to refer explicitly to the object that evoked it, it can use the this pointer. The this pointer is set to the address of the evoking object, so *this is an alias for the object itself.

Classes are well matched to describing abstract data types (ADTs). The public member function interface provides the services described by an ADT, and the class's private section and the code for the class methods provide an implementation hidden from clients of the class.

Review Questions

1. What is a class?
2. How does a class accomplish abstraction, encapsulation, and data hiding?
3. What is the relationship between an object and a class?
4. In what way, aside from being functions, are class function members different from class data members?
5. Define a class to represent a bank account. Data members should include the depositor's name, the account number (use a string), and the balance. Member functions should allow the following:

  - Creating an object and initializing it
  - Assigning starting values to the data members
  - Displaying the depositor's name, account number, and balance
  - Depositing an amount of money given by an argument
  - Withdrawing an amount of money given by an argument

   Just show the class declaration, not the method implementations. (Programming exercise 1 provides you with an opportunity to write the implementation.)
6. When are class constructors named? When are class destructors named?
7. Provide code for a constructor for the bank account class of question 5.
8. What is a default constructor and what's the advantage of having one?
9. Modify the Stock class (the version in stock2.h) so that it has member functions that return the values of the individual data members. Note: A member that returns the company name should not provide a weapon for altering the array. That is, it can't simply return a char *. It could return a const pointer, or it could return a pointer to a copy of the array, manufactured by using new.
10. What are this and *this?

Programming Exercises

1. Provide method definitions for the class described in review question 5 and write a short program illustrating all the features.
2. Do programming exercise 4 from Chapter 8, but replace the code shown there with an appropriate golf class declaration. Use a constructor with the appropriate argument for providing initial values.

3. Consider the following structure declaration:

```
struct customer {
    char fullname[35];
    double payment;
  };
```

Write a program that adds and removes customer structures from a stack, represented by a class declaration. Each time a customer is removed, his payment is added to a running total and the running total is reported.

4. Here's a class declaration:

```
class Move
{
private:
    double x;
    double y;
public:
    Move(double a = 0, double b = 0);    // sets x, y to a, b
    showmove() const;                    // shows current x, y values
    Move add(const Move & m) const;
// this function adds x of m to x of invoking object to get new x,
// adds y of m to y of invoking object to get new y, creates a new
// move object initialized to new x, y values and returns it
    reset(double a = 0, double b = 0);   // resets x,y to a, b
};
```

Supply member function definitions and a program that exercises the class.

5. A Betelgeusean plorg has these properties:

Data

A plorg has a name of no more than 19 letters.

A plorg has a contentment index (CI), which is an integer.

Operations

A new plorg starts out with a name and a CI value of 50.

A plorg's CI can change.

A plorg can report its name and CI.

The default plorg has a name of "Plorga".

Write a Plorg class declaration (data members and member function prototypes) that represents a plorg. Write the function definitions for the member functions. Write a short program that demonstrates all the features of the Plorg class.

6. We can describe a simple list as follows:

- A simple list can hold zero or more items of some particular type.

- You can create an empty list.

- You can add items to a list.

- You can determine whether the list is empty.

- You can determine whether the list is full.

- You can visit each item in a list and perform some action upon it.

As you can see, this list really is simple, not allowing insertion or deletion, for example. The main use of such a list is to provide a simplified programming project. In this case, create a class matching this description. You can implement the list as an array or, if you're familiar with the data type, as a linked list. But the public interface should not depend on your choice. That is, the public interface should not have array indices, pointers to nodes, and so on. It should be expressed in the general concepts of creating a list, adding an item to the list, and so on. The usual way to handle visiting each item and performing an action is to use a function that takes a function pointer as an argument:

```
void visit(void (*pf)(Item &));
```

Here `pf` points to a function (not a member function) that takes a reference to `Item` argument, where `Item` is the type for items in the list. The `visit()` function applies this function to each item in the list.

You also should provide a short program utilizing your design.

10

Working with Classes

You will learn about the following in this chapter:

- Operator overloading
- Friend functions
- Overloading the << operator for output
- State members
- Using rand() to generate random values
- Automatic conversions and type casts for classes
- Class conversion functions

C++ classes are feature-rich, complex, and powerful. In Chapter 9, you began a journey toward object-oriented programming by learning to define and use a simple class. You saw how a class defines a data type by defining the type of data to be used to represent an object and by also defining, through member functions, the operations that can be performed with that data. And you learned about two special member functions, the constructor and the destructor, that manage creating and discarding objects made to a class specification. This chapter will take you a few steps further in the exploration of class properties, concentrating on class design techniques rather than on general principles. You'll probably find some of the features covered here straightforward, some a bit more subtle. To best understand these new features, you should try the examples and experiment with them. What happens if I use a regular argument instead of a reference argument for this function? What happens if I leave something out of a destructor? Don't be afraid to make mistakes; usually you can learn more from unraveling an error than by doing something correctly, but by rote. (However, don't assume that a maelstrom of mistakes inevitably leads to incredible insight.) In the end, you'll be rewarded with a fuller understanding of how C++ works and of what C++ can do for you.

This chapter starts with operator overloading, which lets you use standard C++ operators such as = and + with class objects. Then it examines friends, the C++ mechanism for letting nonmember functions access private data. Finally, it looks at how you can instruct C++ to perform automatic type conversions with classes. As you go through this and the next chapter, you'll gain a greater appreciation of the roles class constructors and class destructors play. Also, you'll see some of the stages you may go through as you develop and improve a class design.

One difficulty with learning C++, at least by the time you've gotten this far into the subject, is that there is an awful lot to remember. And it's unreasonable to expect to remember it all until you've logged enough experience on which to hang your memories. Learning C++, in this respect, is like learning a feature-laden word processor or spreadsheet program. No one feature is that daunting, but, in practice, most people really know well only those features they use regularly, such as searching for text or italicizing. You may recall having read somewhere how to generate alternative characters or create a table of contents, but those skills probably won't be part of your daily repertoire until you find yourself in a situation in which you need them frequently. Probably the best approach to absorbing the wealth of material in this chapter is to begin incorporating just some of these new features into your own C++ programming. As your experiences enhance your understanding and appreciation of these features, begin adding other C++ features. As Bjarne Stroustrup, the creator of C++, suggested at a C++ conference for professional programmers: "Ease yourself into the language. Don't feel you have to use all of the features, and don't try to use them all on the first day."

Operator Overloading

Let's look at a technique for giving object operations a prettier look. *Operator overloading* is another example of C++ polymorphism. In Chapter 8, you saw how C++ enables you to define several functions having the same name as long as they have different signatures (argument lists). That was function overloading, or functional polymorphism. Its purpose is to let you use the same function name for the same basic operation even though you apply the operation to different data types. (Imagine how awkward English would be if you had to use a different verb form for each different type of object—lift_lft your left foot, but lift_sp your spoon.) Operator overloading extends the overloading concept to operators, letting you assign multiple meanings to C++ operators. Actually, many C++ (and C) operators already are overloaded. For instance, the * operator, when applied to an address, yields the value stored at that address. But applying * to two numbers yields the product of the values. C++ uses the number and type of operands to decide which action to take.

C++ lets you extend operator overloading to user-defined types, permitting you, say, to use the + symbol to add two objects. Again, the compiler will use the number and type of operands to determine which definition of addition to use. Overloaded operators often can make code look more natural. For instance, a common computing task is adding two arrays. Usually, this winds up looking like the following for loop:

```
for (int i = 0; i < 20; i++)
        evening[i] = sam[i] + janet[i];  // add element by element
```

But in C++, you can define a class that represents arrays and that overloads the + operator so that you can do this:

```
evening = sam + janet;                     // add two array objects
```

We'll do just that in Chapter 12. (Why not now? Because you also have to overload the [] operator, and that's a bit more involved than overloading the + operator.) This simple addition notation conceals the mechanics and emphasizes what is essential, and that is another OOP goal.

To overload an operator, you use a special function form called an *operator function*. An operator function has the form:

```
operatorop(argument-list)
```

where *op* is the symbol for the operator being overloaded. The *op* has to be a valid C++ operator; you can't just make up a new symbol. For instance, you can't have an operator@() function because C++ has no @ operator. But the operator+() function would overload the + operator. Suppose, for example, that you have a Salesperson class for which you define an operator+() member function to overload the + operator so that it adds sales figures of one salesperson object to another. Then, if district2, sid, and sara all are objects of the Salesperson class, you can write this equation:

```
district2 = sid + sara;
```

The compiler, recognizing the operands as belonging to the Salesperson class, will replace the operator with the corresponding operator function:

```
district2 = sid.operator+(sara);
```

The function will then use the sid object implicitly (because it invoked the method) and the sara object explicitly (because it's passed as an argument) to calculate the sum, which it then returns. Of course, the nice part is that you can use the nifty + operator notation instead of the clunky function notation.

C++ imposes some restrictions on operator overloading, but they're easier to understand after you've seen how overloading works. So let's develop a few examples first to clarify the process and then discuss the limitations.

A VECTOR CLASS WITH OPERATOR OVERLOADING

To show how overloading is useful in real applications, we'll develop an example based on vectors. Not only will the example present operator overloading, it will also illustrate further aspects of class design, such as incorporating two different ways of describing the same thing into an object. Even if you don't care for vectors, you can use many of the new techniques in other contexts. A *vector*, as the term is used in engineering and physics, is a quantity having both a magnitude (size) and a direction. For instance, if you push something, the effect depends on how hard you push (the magnitude) and in what direction you push. A push in one direction can save a tottering vase, whereas a push in the opposite direction can hasten its rush to doom. To fully describe the motion of your car, you should give both the speed (the magnitude) and the direction; arguing with the highway patrol that you were driving under the speed limit carries little weight if you were traveling in the wrong direction. (Immunologists and computer scientists may use the term vector differently; ignore them, at least until Chapter 15, which looks at the computer science version.) The following note tells you more about vectors, but understanding them completely isn't necessary for following the C++ aspects of the examples.

Remember

Although the author may hope you open your heart to vectors, the only feature you really need to appreciate is that vectors are things that can be added.

V E C T O R S

> *[A]rguing with the highway patrol that you were driving under the speed limit carries little weight if you were traveling in the wrong direction.*

You're a worker bee that has discovered a marvelous nectar cache. You rush back to the hive and announce you've found nectar 120 yards away. "Not enough information," buzz the other bees. "You have to tell us the direction, too!" You answer, "It's 30 degrees north of the sun direction." Knowing both the distance (magnitude) and the direction, the other bees rush to the sweet site. Bees know vectors.

Many quantities involve both a magnitude and a direction. The effect of a push, for instance, depends on both its strength and direction. Moving an object on a computer screen involves a distance and a direction. You can describe such things using vectors. For example, you can describe moving (displacing) an object on the screen with a vector, which you can visualize as an arrow drawn from the starting position to the final position. The length of the vector is its magnitude, and that describes how far the point has been displaced. The orientation of the arrow describes the direction. See Figure 10.1. A vector representing such a change in position is called a *displacement vector*.

Now you're Lhanappa, the great mammoth hunter. Scouts report a mammoth herd 14.1 kilometers to the northwest. But, because of a southeast wind, you don't want to approach from the southeast. So you go 10 kilometers west, then 10 kilometers north, approaching the herd from the south. You know these two displacement vectors bring you to the same location as the single 14.1-kilometer vector pointing northwest. Lhanappa, the great mammoth hunter, also knows how to add vectors.

Adding two vectors has a simple geometric interpretation. First, draw one vector. Then draw the second vector starting from the arrow-end of the first vector. Finally, draw a vector from the starting point of the first vector to the end point of the second vector. This third vector represents the sum of the first two. See Figure 10.2. Note that the length of the sum can be less than the sum of the individual lengths.

FIGURE 10.1

*Describing a displace-
ment with a vector*

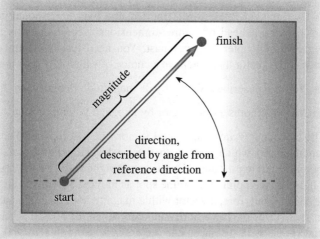

FIGURE 10.2

Adding two vectors

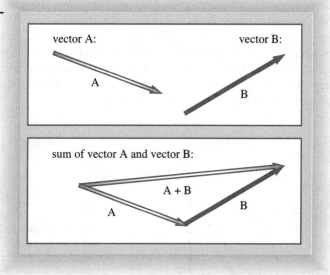

Vectors make a natural choice for operator overloading. First, you can't represent a vector with a single number, so it makes sense to create a class to represent vectors. Second, vectors have analogs to ordinary arithmetic operations such as addition and subtraction. This parallel suggests overloading the corresponding operators so you can use them with vectors.

To keep things simple, we'll implement a two-dimensional vector, such as a screen displacement, instead of a three-dimensional vector, such as might represent movement of a helicopter or a gymnast. You need just two numbers to describe a two-dimensional vector, but you have a choice of what set of two numbers:

- You can describe a vector by its magnitude (length) and direction (an angle).

- You can represent the vector by its x and y components.

The components are a horizontal vector (the x component) and a vertical vector (the y component), which add up to the final vector. For instance, you can describe a motion as moving a point 30 units to the right and 40 units up. See Figure 10.3. That motion puts the point at the same spot as moving 50 units at an angle of 53.1° from the horizontal. Therefore, a vector with a magnitude of 50 and an angle of 53.1° is equivalent to a vector having a horizontal component of 30 and a vertical component of 40. What counts with displacement vectors is where you start and where you end up, not the exact route taken to get there. This choice of representation is basically the same thing we covered with the Chapter 7 program that converted between rectangular and polar coordinates.

Sometimes one form is more convenient, sometimes the other, so we'll incorporate both representations into the class description. See the note on Multiple Representations and Classes coming up shortly. Also, we'll design the class so that if you alter one representation of a vector, the object automatically updates the other representation. The ability to build such intelligence into an object is another C++ class virtue. Listing 10.1 presents a preliminary class declaration that doesn't yet include operator overloading.

FIGURE 10.3

x and y components of a vector

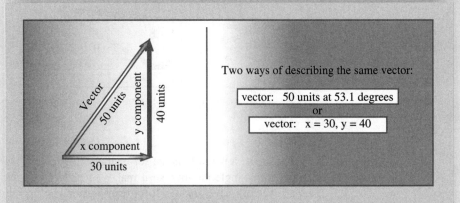

Two ways of describing the same vector:

vector: 50 units at 53.1 degrees
or
vector: x = 30, y = 40

Listing 10.1 vector0.h

```
// vector0.h -- vector class before operator overloading
#ifndef _VECTOR0_H_
#define _VECTOR0_H_
class Vector
{
private:
    double x;                       // horizontal value
    double y;                       // vertical value
    double mag;                     // length of vector
    double ang;                     // direction of vector
    void set_mag();
    void set_ang();
public:
    Vector();
    Vector(double h, double v);     // set x, y values
    ~Vector();
    void set_by_polar(double m, double a);
    double xval() const {return x;} // report x value
    double yval() const {return y;} // report y value
    double magval() const {return mag;} // report magnitude
    double angval() const {return ang;} // report angle
    void show_polar() const;        // show polar values
    void show_vector() const;       // show rectangular values
};
#endif
```

Notice that the four functions that report component values are defined in the class declaration. This automatically makes them inline functions. The fact that these functions are so short makes them excellent candidates for inlining. None of them should alter object data, so they are declared using the const modifier. As you may recall from Chapter 9, this is the syntax for declaring a function that doesn't modify the object it implicitly accesses.

MULTIPLE REPRESENTATIONS AND CLASSES

Quantities having different, but equivalent, representations are common. For example, you can measure gasoline consumption in miles per gallon, as done in the United States, or in liters per 100 kilometers, as done in Europe. You can represent a number in string form or numeric form, and you can represent intelligence as an IQ or in kiloturkeys. Classes lend themselves nicely to encompassing different aspects and representations of an entity in a single object. First, you can store multiple representations in one object. Second, you can write the class functions so that assigning values for one representation automatically assigns values for the other representation(s). For instance, the set_by_polar() method for the Vector class sets the mag and ang members to the function arguments, but it also sets the x and y members. By handling conversions internally, a class can help you think of a quantity in terms of its essential nature rather than in terms of its representation.

This particular class declaration emphasizes the rectangular coordinate approach, with a class constructor that takes arguments representing the horizontal and vertical values. The constructor implementation will call the private functions set_mag() and set_ang() to set the corresponding magnitude and angle values. However, if you want to specify a vector by its polar coordinates (magnitude and angle), you can use the set_by_polar() method. Provide the method with magnitude and angle arguments, and it sets the x and y horizontal values. Also, the declaration provides methods for displaying both vector representations.

You may have wondered why we didn't provide a third constructor, one that initializes a vector using the magnitude and angle values. The problem is that magnitude and angle require the same function signature (double, double) as x and y, but C++ requires distinct function signatures for overloading. So we have a choice of providing a constructor for one or the other representation, but not both. Later, we'll refine this example and show a way around that problem.

Note that it is the public interface, not the private data representation, that shows the class deals with both representations. For example, it isn't really necessary to simultaneously store both representations in the private section. Instead, for instance, the private section of the class can store just the rectangular representation. In that case, functions like show_polar() would calculate the polar values instead of just looking them up. This would slow up the show_polar() function, but it would speed up the constructor, for it would just have to construct the rectangular coordinates. Also, this approach would make a Vector object smaller, because it would hold less data. Which approach is better depends on what a program does. If it has to make frequent conversions from polar to rectangular representations and vice versa, then storing both forms most likely is the better choice. If a program needs polar forms only rarely, then storing just the rectangular coordinates makes more sense. As long as you keep the same public interface, you can use different implementations with different programs, matching the implementation to a program's needs.

Overloading the + Operator

Meanwhile, let's add operator overloading. Adding two vectors is simple in rectangular coordinates. Just add the two x components together to get the new x component, and add the two y components together to get the new y component. Here is a sample prototype for a class operator overloading method (it goes into the class declaration) and its implementation (it goes into the class member function file):

```
Vector operator+(const Vector & b) const;          // prototype
Vector Vector::operator+(const Vector & b) const    // definition
{
    double sx, sy;
    sx = x + b.x;                  // x component of sum
    sy = y + b.y;                  // y component of sum
    Vector sum = Vector(sx, sy);
    return sum;
}
```

The prototype defines a function named operator+(). The function returns a Vector and it takes a Vector argument. To save time and memory, we pass the vector by reference (type Vector &), making b an alias for the vector passed to the function. Because the function should not alter the value of the vectors it is adding, we declare the argument as a const type and declare the function a const method. Because operator+() is a class method, it uses the invoking object implicitly. For instance, suppose move1 and move2 are two vectors and that we use the operator+() function to add them:

```
Vector q = move1.operator+(move2);
```

The operator+() function definition contains the following statement:

```
sx = x + b.x;      // x component of sum
```

In this statement, the term b.x refers to the object passed as an argument (move2, in this case), and x refers to the object invoking the member function (move1, in this case), making the statement equivalent to the following:

```
sx = move1.x + move2.x;    // x component of sum
```

After calculating the x and y components of the sum, the method uses the Vector(sx,sy) constructor to initialize the vector sum to the proper values:

```
Vector sum = Vector(sx, sy);
```

As you'll see soon, this constructor also sets the mag and ang members. Thus, sum is a Vector object having both its rectangular representation and its polar representation set to the correct values. Then the operator+() function returns the sum vector to the calling program.

 Remember

If a method needs to compute a new class object, see if you can use a class constructor to do the work. Not only does that save you trouble, it insures that the new object is constructed in the proper fashion.

You may wonder why the function uses reference arguments but doesn't return a reference. After all, if reference arguments save time and memory, shouldn't a reference return value do the same? The answer is yes, returning a reference can save time and memory. However, there is a more important consideration. The object sum is a local variable, so it expires when the function terminates. Thus, a returned reference would be a reference to an object that no longer exists. Returning sum instead of a reference to sum means the value of sum gets copied and saved, which is much more useful.

Remember

Don't return a reference to a local variable or other temporary object.

Incidentally, by using the fact that the arguments to a function, including a constructor, can be expressions, it's possible to shorten the method a bit to the following:

```
Vector Vector::operator+(const Vector & b) const   // definition
{
    return Vector(x + b.x, y + b.y); // return the constructed Vector
}
```

Here the code avoids intermediate variables and feeds the new component values directly to a constructor, which then constructs the object to be returned.

So far, `operator+()` looks like a regular class member function with a funny name. We could have just as easily called the method `Sum()` and used it like this:

```
Vector q = move1.Sum(move2);
```

Here, however, is where C++ gets cute by offering an alternative syntax for the function call that makes it look as if you were using an operator. The alternative syntax for

```
Vector q = move1.operator+(move2);   // function call syntax
```

is this:

```
Vector q = move1 + move2;            // alternative syntax
```

Both mean the same thing, but the second form is easier on the eyes and on the mind, and it is the one we'll use.

Let's take one more look at the planning steps in overloading the + operator for the `Vector` class:

- Create a member function named `operator+()`.

- Addition requires two operands. Invoking the function with an object provides one operand, so use an argument to provide the second operand. This operand can be type `Vector`, or, in the interests of efficiency, type `const Vector &`.

- The sum of two `Vector` objects is also a `Vector` object, so give the function a `Vector` return type. (Don't use a reference in this case.)

- Put the following prototype in the class declaration:

  ```
  Vector operator+(const Vector & b) const;   // prototype
  ```

- Use the following function heading in the methods definition file:

  ```
  Vector Vector::operator+(const Vector & b) const   // definition
  ```

- Write code to handle the intended operation.

At this point, if you're programming a Bobo the Space Barbarian game, you can write code like the following:

```
#include <iostream>
using namespace std;
#include "vector0.h"                 // class declaration
int main ()
{
    ...
    Vector movebobo1(20,30);
    Vector movebobo2(50, 10);
    Vector bobo = movebobo1 + movebobo2;   // add 2 vectors
    bobo.showpolar();                      // display result
    ...
}
```

But, having gone this far, it's worth the extra effort to add a few more features to the class declaration. In particular, we'll investigate how to overload an overloaded operator and when friends are useful for overloading.

More Refinement: Overloading an Overloaded Operator

Let's start by overloading the - operator. In ordinary C++, this operator already has two meanings. First, when used with two operands, it's the subtraction operator. The subtraction operator is termed a *binary operator* because it has exactly two operands. Second, when used with one operand, as in -x, it's a minus sign operator. This form is termed a *unary operator*, meaning it has exactly one operand. Both operations—subtraction and sign reversal—make sense for vectors, too, so we'll extend them to the Vector class, beginning with subtraction. To subtract vector B from vector A, you simply subtract components, so the definition for overloading subtraction is quite similar to the one for addition:

```
Vector operator-(const Vector & b) const;          // prototype
Vector Vector::operator-(const Vector & b) const    // definition
{
    return Vector(x - b.x, y - b.y);  // return the constructed Vector
}
```

Here, it's important to get the correct order. Consider the following statement:

```
diff = v1 - v2;
```

It's converted to a member function call:

```
diff = v1.operator-(v2);
```

This means the vector passed as the explicit argument is subtracted from the implicit vector argument, so we should use x - b.x and not b.x - x.

Next, let's overload the unary minus operator, which takes just one operand. Applying this operator to a regular number, as in -x, changes the sign of the value. We'll want to define it so that applying it to a vector reverses the sign of each component. More precisely, we'll have the function return a new vector that is the reverse of the original. (In polar terms, negation leaves the magnitude unchanged, but reverses the direction. Many politicians with little or no mathematical training, nonetheless, have an intuitive mastery of this operation.) Here are the prototype and definition for overloading negation:

```
Vector operator-() const;
Vector Vector::operator-() const
{
    return Vector (-x, -y);
}
```

Note that now there are two separate definitions for operator-(). That's fine, because the two definitions have different signatures. You can define both binary and unary versions of the - operator because C++ provides both binary and unary versions of that operator to begin with. An operator having only a binary form, such as division (/), can only be overloaded as a binary operator.

Remember

> Because operator overloading is implemented with functions, you can overload the same operator many times, as long as each operator function has a distinct signature and as long as each operator function has the same number of operands as the corresponding built-in C++ operator.

As with overloading functions, you should use sensible restraint in overloading operators. For instance, don't overload the * operator so that it swaps the components of a Vector object. Nothing in the notation would suggest what the operator did, so it would be better to define a class method with an explanatory name like Swap().

FRIENDS AND OPERATOR OVERLOADING

As you've seen, C++ controls access to the private portions of a class object. Usually public class methods serve as the only access, but sometimes this restriction is too rigid to fit particular programming problems. In such cases, C++ provides another form of access, the *friend*. Friends come in three varieties:

- Friend functions
- Friend classes
- Friend member functions

By making a function a friend to a class, you allow the function the same access privileges that a member function of the class has. We'll look into friend functions now, leaving the other two varieties to Chapter 14.

Before seeing how to make friends, let's look into why they might be needed. Often overloading a binary operator (one with two arguments) for a class generates a need for friends. Multiplying a vector by a real number provides just such a situation, so let's study that case.

In visual terms, multiplying a vector by a number makes the vector longer or shorter by that factor. So multiplying a vector by 3 produces a vector with three times the length, but still pointed in the same direction. It's easy to translate that image into how the class represents a vector. In polar terms, multiply the magnitude and leave the angle alone. In rectangular terms, you multiply a vector by a number by multiplying its x and y components separately by the number. That is, if a vector has components of 5 and 12, multiplying by 3 makes the components 15 and 36. Here are the prototype (goes in the class declaration) and the implementation (goes in the methods file) for multiplication:

```
Vector operator*(double n) const;        // prototype
// multiplies invoking vector by n
Vector Vector::operator*(double n) const // definition (long form)
{
    double mx, my;
    mx = n * x;
    my = n * y;
    Vector mult = Vector(mx, my);
    return mult;
}
```

Again, we can shorten the code by eliminating intermediate temporary variables:

```
Vector Vector::operator*(double n) const // definition (shrt form)
{
    return Vector(n * x, n * y);
}
```

This code (either implementation) works fine for multiplying a vector times a number, but it fails for multiplying a number times a vector. To see this, first consider multiplying a vector times a number:

```
Vector borge = piano * 2.0;          // valid code
```

This translates to the following function call:

```
Vector borge = piano.operator*(2.0);
```

That statement requires that `operator*()` be a member function of the `Vector` class, for it is invoked by a `Vector` object. It also requires that the function take a type `double` argument. These two requirements match the function just defined, so the program automatically uses that definition.

But suppose you reverse the order of the operands while writing a program:

```
Vector borge = 2.0 * piano;          // not supported
```

That would correspond to a meaningless function call:

```
Vector borge = 2.0.operator*(piano);   // nonsense
```

That is, this demands a function that is a member of the `double` class (which doesn't even exist) and that takes a type `Vector` argument. But our definition of multiplication requires that a `Vector` object (`piano`, in this case) be the first operand and the `double` value (2.0) be the second operand.

One way around this difficulty is to tell everyone (and to remember yourself) that you can only write `piano * 2.0` but never write `2.0 * piano`. This is a programmer-friendly, user-beware solution, and that's not what OOP is about.

Can you write a second member function to handle this reverse-order problem? No, you can't, because the invoking object is always the first operand; the `piano` object must come before the 2.0 *if* you use a member function. What you need is a *nonmember* function such as the following:

```
Vector operator*(double n, const Vector & a);
```

Because it is an ordinary, nonmember function, you don't need an object to invoke it. There are no hidden implicit arguments. For a nonmember operator function called `operator+()`, C++ interprets the first argument as the left operand of the + operator and the second argument as the right operand. That means the expression

```
2.0 * piano
```

becomes the following function call:

```
operator*(2.0, piano);   // non-member function
```

This appears to be just what we need, but there is a big problem: nonmember functions don't access the private data of an object. Here's where friend functions come into play.

" This is a programmer-friendly, user-beware solution, and that's not what OOP is about."

Making Friends

A friend function is a nonmember function that is allowed access to an object's private section. To indicate that a function is a friend, declare the function in the class declaration using the keyword friend. In this particular case, place the following prototype in the Vector declaration:

```
friend Vector operator*(double n, const Vector & a);   //nonmember friend
```

Note that a friend function has to supply an object explicitly, by an argument. You use the friend keyword only in the prototype found in the class declaration. You don't use it in the function definition.

The most direct way to implement this particular friend function is this:

```
Vector operator*(double n, const Vector & a)
{
    return Vector(n * a.x, n * a.y);
}
```

Because operator*() is a friend function to the Vector class, it can access the a.x and a.y members.

A trickier implementation is to have it reverse the order of its arguments and then call the original function:

```
Vector operator*(double n, const Vector & a)
{
    return a * n;       // calls original operator function
}
```

Thus the friend function translates

```
Vector borge = 2.0 * piano;   // now supported
```

to the following:

```
Vector borge = piano * 2.0;
```

Using a friend function to reverse the operand order is a common and useful technique for overloading an operator that takes two different types of operands.

By the way, this second approach doesn't require that operator*() be a friend function. The reason is that it accesses the Vector object a as a whole without directly accessing the private members. However, making it a friend better documents the fact that this method is part of the class design. It also leaves open the possibility of rewriting the method so that it does access class members.

 Remember

If you want to overload an operator for a class and you want to use the operator with a nonclass term as the first operand, you have to use a friend function to reverse the operand order.

By the way, we didn't have the kind of problem raised by defining operator*() when defining the operator+() member function because, in that case, both arguments were type Vector, so either could come first.

Friends Versus Class Member Functions

Incidentally, you can define all the `Vector` operator functions as friend functions. In that case, each binary operator function would require two `Vector` arguments, and the unary `operator-()` function would take a single `Vector` argument. (A friend function always requires one more argument than the equivalent member function; the extra argument explicitly represents the object that a member function uses implicitly.)

For instance, you can define subtraction this way:

```
// prototype
friend Vector operator-(const Vector & a, const Vector & b);
// definition
Vector operator-(const Vector & a, const Vector & b)
{
    return Vector(a.x - b.x, a.y - b.y);  // use two explicit Vectors
}
```

Calling this version would look different from calling the first version if you used function notation:

```
a = b.operator-(c);   // - defined as class method
a = operator-(b, c);  // - defined as friend function
```

But either definition would let you use the same operator notation:

```
a = b - c;     // permitted by either definition
```

There is an advantage to using the friend method if conversions to the `Vector` class are available. We'll return to this point later in the chapter when we discuss type conversions.

ARE FRIENDS UNFAITHFUL TO OOP?

At first glance, it may seem that friends violate the OOP principle of data hiding, for the friend mechanism allows nonmember functions to access private data. However, that's an overly narrow view. Instead, think of friend functions as part of an extended interface for a class. For instance, from a conceptual point of view, multiplying a `double` times a `Vector` is pretty much the same as multiplying a `Vector` times a `double`. That the first requires a friend function whereas the second can be done with a member function is the result of C++ syntax, not of a deep conceptual difference. By using both a friend function and a class method, you can express either operation with the same user interface. Also, keep in mind that only a class declaration can decide which functions are friends, so the class declaration still controls which functions access private data. In short, class methods and friends are just two different mechanisms for expressing a class interface.

Defining the Vector Class: Nearly the Final Version

Now that we have the operator functions ready, we can put together a full Vector class declaration. Listing 10.2 presents the complete declaration for the Vector class.

Listing 10.2 vector1.h

```
// vector1.h -- Vector class, introduce operator overloading
#ifndef _VECTOR1_H_
#define _VECTOR1_H_
class Vector
{
private:
    double x;                            // horizontal value
    double y;                            // vertical value
    double mag;                          // length of vector
    double ang;                          // direction of vector
    void set_mag();
    void set_ang();
public:
    Vector();
    Vector(double h, double v);
    ~Vector();
    double xval() const {return x;}      // report x value
    double yval() const {return y;}      // report y value
    double magval() const {return mag;}  // report magnitude
    double angval() const {return ang;}  // report angle
    void set_by_polar(double m, double a);
    void show_polar() const;             // show polar values
    void show_vector() const;            // show rectilinear values
// operator overloading
    Vector operator+(const Vector & b) const;
    Vector operator-(const Vector & b) const;
    Vector operator-() const;
    Vector operator*(double n) const;
// friend function
    friend Vector operator*(double n, const Vector & a);
};
#endif
```

Listing 10.3 defines the class member functions declared in Listing 10.2. Note how the constructor functions and the set_by_polar() function each set both the rectangular and the polar representations of the vector. Thus, either set of values is available immediately without further calculation should you need them. Also, as mentioned in Chapters 4 and 7, C++'s built-in math functions use angles in radians, so we've built conversion to and from degrees into the methods. The implementation hides such things as converting from polar coordinates to rectangular coordinates or converting radians to degrees from the user. All the user needs to know is that the class uses angles in degrees and that it makes a vector available in two equivalent representations.

These design decisions follow the OOP tradition of having the class interface concentrate on the essentials (the abstract model) while hiding the details. Thus, when you use the Vector class, you can think about a vector's general features, such as that they can represent displacements and that you can add two vectors. Whether you express a vector in component notation or in magnitude, direction notation becomes secondary, for you can set a vector's values and display them in whichever format is most convenient at the time.

 Remember

Some systems may still use math.h instead of cmath. Also, some C++ systems don't automatically search the math library. For instance, some UNIX systems require that you do the following:

```
$ CC source_file(s) -lm
```

The -lm option instructs the linker to search the math library. So, when you eventually compile programs using the Vector class, if you get a message about undefined externals, try the -lm option or check to see if your system requires something similar.

Listing 10.3 vector1.cpp

```cpp
// vector1.cpp -- methods for Vector class
#include <iostream>
#include <cmath>
using namespace std;
#include "vector1.h"
const double Rad_to_deg = 57.2957795130823;

// private methods
// calculates magnitude from x and y
void Vector::set_mag()
{
    mag = sqrt(x * x + y * y);
}

// calculates angle from x and y
void Vector::set_ang()
{
    ang = atan2(y, x);
}

// public methods
Vector::Vector()    // default constructor
{
    x = y = mag = ang = 0.0;
}

// constructs a Vector from rectangular coordinates
Vector::Vector(double h, double v)
{
    x = h;
    y = v;
    set_mag();
    set_ang();
}

Vector::~Vector()    // destructor
{
}
```

```
// sets Vector members from polar coordinates
void Vector::set_by_polar(double m, double a)
{
    mag = m;
    ang = a / Rad_to_deg;
    x = m * cos(ang);
    y = m * sin(ang);
}

// shows magnitude and direction of vector
void Vector::show_polar() const
{
    cout << "(" << mag << ", ";
    cout << ang * Rad_to_deg << ")\n";
}

// shows x and y components of vector
void Vector::show_vector() const
{
    cout << "(" << x << ", " << y << ")\n";
}

// operator overloading
// add two Vectors
Vector Vector::operator+(const Vector & b) const
{
    return Vector(x + b.x, y + b.y);
}

// subtract Vector b from a
Vector Vector::operator-(const Vector & b) const
{
    return Vector(x - b.x, y - b.y);
}

// reverse sign of Vector
Vector Vector::operator-() const
{
    return Vector(-x, -y);
}

// multiple vector by n
Vector Vector::operator*(double n) const
{
    return Vector(n * x, n * y);;
}

// friend method
// multiply n by Vector a
Vector operator*(double n, const Vector & a)
{
    return a * n;
}
```

The next step, of course, is to use these definitions in a program. Listing 10.4 does that using vectors representing movements. It demonstrates using both the rectangular and polar representations, and it shows addition and multiplication. All in all, it is pretty dull, but the test program for the next refinement will investigate the fabulous random walk problem. Remember to compile Listing 10.3 along with Listing 10.4.

Listing 10.4 use_vect.cpp

```cpp
// use_vect.cpp -- use the Vector class
// compile with vector1.cpp
#include <iostream>
using namespace std;
#include "vector1.h"
int main()
{
    Vector first_move(120, 50);
    Vector second_move(50, 120);
    Vector result;
    cout.precision(3);                          // format output
    cout.setf(ios_base::fixed, ios_base::floatfield);
    cout.setf(ios_base::showpoint);

    result = first_move + second_move;  // adding objects!
    cout << "First move: ";
    first_move.show_vector();                   // display first_move
    cout << "Magnitude, angle = ";
    first_move.show_polar();
    cout << "Second move: ";
    second_move.show_vector();
    cout << "Magnitude, angle = ";
    second_move.show_polar();
    cout << "Result: ";
    result.show_vector();
    cout << "Magnitude, angle = ";
    result.show_polar();

    Vector twotimes = result * 2.0;     // member function
    cout << "Doubled result: ";
    twotimes.show_vector();

    result = 0.5 * result;                      // friend function
    cout << "Halved result: ";
    result.show_vector();

    return 0;
}
```

Here is the program's output:

```
First move: (120.000, 50.000)
Magnitude, angle = (130.000, 22.620)
Second move: (50.000, 120.000)
Magnitude, angle = (130.000, 67.380)
Result: (170.000, 170.000)
Magnitude, angle = (240.416, 45.000)
Doubled result: (340.000, 340.000)
Halved result: (85.000, 85.000)
```

Program Notes

The first_move vector represents moving 120 units to the right and 50 units up. The net result is the same as moving 130 units in a direction 22.62 degrees counterclockwise from the x-axis. The first two output lines display these two descriptions of the first_move vector. Similarly, the second move of 50 units to the right and 120 units up is the same as a move of 130 units in a direction 67.38 degrees from the x-axis. The combined effect of the two moves is moving 170 units to the right (120 + 50) and 170 units up, just as the output for the result vector shows. And that is equivalent to moving 240.42 units at an angle of 45 degrees from the x-axis, as the sixth line of output shows. Note that you can't simply add the magnitudes of two vectors to get the magnitude of the sum. That's why we used rectangular coordinates rather than polar coordinates to calculate the sum. Finally, the program illustrates that both overloadings of the * function work.

OVERLOADING RESTRICTIONS

C++ does impose some limits on user-defined operator overloading as follows:

1. The overloaded operator must have at least one operand that is a user-defined type. This prevents you from overloading operators for the standard types. Thus, you can't redefine the minus operator (-) so that it yields the sum of two double values instead of their difference. This restriction preserves program sanity, although it may hinder creative accounting.

2. You can't use an operator in a manner that violates the syntax rules for the original operator. For instance, you can't overload the modulus operator (%) so that it can be used with a single operand:

> " *The overloaded operator must have at least one operand that is a user-defined type.* "

```
int x;
Vector shiva;
% x;      // invalid for modulus operator
% shiva;  // invalid for overloaded operator
```

Similarly, you can't alter operator precedence. So if you overload the addition operator to let you add two classes, the new operator has the same precedence as ordinary addition.

3. You can't create new operator symbols. For instance, you can't use the combination ** to denote exponentiation.

4. You cannot overload the following operators:

sizeof	the sizeof operator
.	membership operator
.*	pointer-to-member operator
::	scope resolution operator
?:	conditional operator
typeid	an RTTI operator
const_cast	a type cast operator
dynamic_cast	a type cast operator
reinterpret_cast	a type cast operator
static_cast	a type cast operator

This still leaves all the operators in Table 10.1 available for overloading.

5. Most of the operators in Table 10.1 can be overloaded by using either member or nonmember functions. However, you can use *only* member functions to overload the following operators:

=   assignment operator

()   function call operator

[]   subscripting operator

->   class member access by pointer operator

Remember

Note: We have not covered, nor will we cover, every operator mentioned in the list of restrictions or in Table 10.1. However, Appendix E does summarize those operators not covered in the main body of this text.

OVERLOADING THE << OPERATOR

One of the more useful features of classes is that you can overload the << operator so that you can use it with `cout` to display an object's contents. In some ways, this over-loading is a bit trickier than the earlier examples, so we'll develop it in two steps instead of in one.

Suppose `hector` is a `Vector` object. To display `Vector` values, we've been using `show_vector()` and `show_polar()`. Wouldn't it be nice, however, if you could do the following?

```
cout << hector;  // make cout recognize Vector class?
```

You can, because << is one of the C++ operators that can be overloaded. In fact, it already is heavily overloaded. In its most basic incarnation, the << operator is one of C and C++'s bit manipulation operators; it shifts bits left in a value (see Appendix E). But the `ostream` class overloads the operator, converting it into an output tool. Recall that `cout` is an `ostream` object and that it is smart enough to recognize all the basic C++ types. That's because the `ostream` class declaration includes an overloaded `oper-ator<<()` definition for each of the basic types. That is, one definition uses an `int` argument, one uses a `double` argument, and so on. So, one way to teach `cout` to

TABLE 10.1
OPERATORS THAT CAN BE OVERLOADED

+	-	*	/	%	^	&	|
~!	!	=	<	>	+=	-=	*=
/=	%=	^=	&=	|=	<<	>>	>>=
<<=	==	!=	<=	>=	&&	||	++
--	,	->*	->	()	[]	new	delete
new []	delete []						

recognize a `Vector` object is to add a new function operator definition to the `ostream` class declaration. But it's not a good idea to alter the `iostream` file and mess around with a standard interface. It's better to use the `Vector` class declaration to teach the Vector `class` how to use `cout`.

First Version of Overloading <<

To teach the `Vector` class to use `cout`, you'll have to use a friend function. Why? Because a statement like

```
cout << hector;
```

uses two objects, with the `ostream` class object (`cout`) first. If you use a `Vector` member function to overload `<<`, the `Vector` object would come first, as it did when we overloaded the `*` operator with a member function. That means you would have to use the `<<` operator this way:

```
hector << cout;    // if operator<<() were a Vector member function
```

That would be confusing. But by using a friend function, you can overload the operator this way:

```
void operator<<(ostream & os, const Vector & v)
{
    os << "(x,y) = (" << v.x << "," << v.y <<")";
}
```

This lets you use

```
cout << hector;
```

to print data in the following format:

```
(x,y) = (120,50)
```

Note that the new `operator<<()` definition uses an `ostream` reference os as its first argument. Normally, os will refer to the `cout` object, as it does in the expression `cout << hector`. But you could use the operator with other `ostream` objects, in which case os would refer to those objects. (What? You don't know of any other `ostream` objects? Don't forget `cerr`, introduced in Chapter 9. Also, in Chapter 16, you'll learn how to create new objects to manage output to files, and these objects can use `ostream` methods. You then can use the `operator<<()` definition to write `Vector` data to files as well as to the screen.) Furthermore, the call `cout << hector` should use the `cout` object itself, not a copy, so the function passes the object as a reference instead of by value. Thus, the expression `cout << hector` causes os to be an alias for `cout`, and the expression `cerr << hector` causes os to be an alias for `cerr`. The `Vector` object can be passed by value or by reference, because either form makes the object values available to the function. Again, passing by reference uses less memory and time than passing by value.

Second Version of Overloading <<

The implementation we just presented has a problem. Statements such as

```
cout << hector;
```

work fine, but the implementation doesn't allow you to combine the redefined << operator with the ones cout normally uses:

```
cout << "hector value: " << hector << "\n"; // can't do
```

To understand why this doesn't work and what must be done to make it work, you first need to know a bit more about how cout operates. Consider the following statements:

```
int x = 5;
int y = 8;

cout << x << y;
```

C++ reads the output statement from left to right, meaning it is equivalent to the following:

```
(cout << x) << y;
```

The << operator, as defined in iostream, takes an ostream object to its left. Clearly, the expression cout << x satisfies that requirement because cout is an ostream object. But the output statement also requires that the whole expression (cout << x) be a type ostream object, because that expression is to the left of << y. Therefore, the ostream class implements the operator<<() function so that it returns an ostream object. In particular, it returns the invoking object, cout, in this case. Thus, the expression (cout << x) is itself an ostream object, and it can be used to the left of the << operator.

You can take the same approach with the friend function. Just revise the operator<<() function so that it returns a reference to an ostream object:

```
ostream & operator<<(ostream & os, const Vector & v)
{
    os << "(x,y) = (", << v.x << "," << v.y <<")";
    return os;
}
```

Note that the return type is ostream &. That means, recall, that the function returns a reference to an ostream object. Because a program passes an object reference to the function to begin with, the net effect is that the function's return value is just the object passed to it. That is, the statement

```
cout << hector;
```

becomes the following function call:

```
operator<<(cout, hector);
```

And that call returns the cout object. So now the following statement does work:

```
cout << "hector value: " << hector << "\n"; // can do
```

Let's break this into separate steps to see how it works. First,

```
cout << "hector value: "
```

invokes the particular ostream definition of << that displays a string and returns the cout object, so the expression cout << "hector value: " displays the string and then is replaced by its return value, cout. This reduces the original statement to the following one:

```
cout << hector << "\n";
```

Next, the program uses the Vector declaration of << to display the hector values and to return the cout object again. This reduces the statement to the following:

```
cout << "\n";
```

The program now finishes up by using the ostream definition of << for strings to display the final string.

Remember

In general, to overload the << operator to display an object of class c_name, use a friend function with a definition of this form:

```
ostream & operator<<(ostream & os, const c_name & obj)
{
    os << ... ;  // display object contents
    return os;
}
```

A Friendless Approach

If a class has member functions that access class contents, you may use cout without using a friend function. For example, you can do the following for the Vector class:

```
void operator<<(ostream & os, const Vector & v)
{
    os << "(x,y) = (" << v.xval() << "," << v.yval() <<")";
}
```

Because this version uses member functions rather than directly accessing an object's data, it need not be a friend function. This would be the better choice, for it's more in accord with the need-to-know policy. However, if a class doesn't provide member function access to needed information, then a friend function is your only choice.

IMPROVING THE CLASS BY ADDING A STATE MEMBER

Once you start playing with class declarations, it can be hard to stop, so let's add one more improvement. The definition of the << operator displays just the rectangular representation of a vector. Can you overload the definition so that the operator can also display the polar representation? No. Separate definitions require separate function signatures. The operator takes two operands, so the friend operator function takes two arguments, and they have to be an ostream object and a Vector object. So you have no freedom to select another function signature.

But you can change the class declaration. The idea is to add a *state member*. This is a variable that affects how the object behaves, sort of like a switch on a printer that lets you set which printer emulation to use. For instance, you can add a type char member that can be set to 'p' or 'r'. The object will display in polar mode if the state member is 'p' and in rectangular mode if the state member is 'r'. (The ostream class, incidentally, uses the same state member technique to control the various formatting options discussed in Chapter 16.) Suppose that you call this state member mode. Then you can rewrite operator<<() this way:

```
ostream & operator<<(ostream & os, const Vector & v)
{
    if (v.mode == 'r')
       os << "(x,y) = (" << v.x << ", " << v.y << ")";
    else if (v.mode == 'p')
    {
        os << "(m,a) = (" << v.mag << ", "
            << v.ang * Rad_to_deg << ")";
    }
    else
        os << "Vector object mode is invalid";
    return os;
}
```

The program labels its output with (x,y) or (m,a) so that you can readily see if the output is in x- and y-coordinates or in magnitude and angle values. That way, you don't have to check the program code in order to interpret the program output. (Keep that output user-friendly!)

To use this approach, you need to alter the Vector class declarations and rewrite several member functions. First, of course, you have to add the mode member to the private part of the class. Then you have to add methods to set the mode to the desired value. Also, you should make it impossible to set an invalid mode. True, the operator<<() definition prints an error message if the mode isn't a 'p' or an 'r', but that's more a debugging tool. If a program generates that error message, you know you should work more on the class design. The most direct way to prevent invalid modes is to modify the constructors so that they always initialize a new object to a correct mode. For instance, you can define the default constructor this way:

```
Vector::Vector()                    // default constructor
{
    x = y = mag = ang = 0.0;
    mode = 'r';                      // default mode
}
```

Yet Another Trick

Remember how the other constructor is biased toward the x-y view of vectors? The prohibition on duplicate signatures prevented making another constructor using the magnitude-angle view. But now you can use the new mode member to rewrite the other constructor so that it can initialize a vector either to x-y values or to magnitude-angle values. The trick is to add the mode as the third argument to the constructor:

```
Vector::Vector(double n1, double n2, char form)
{
    mode = form;        // set mode member to form argument
    if (form == 'r')
    {
        x = n1;
        y = n2;
        set_mag();
        set_ang();
    }
    else if (form == 'p')
    {
        mag = n1;
        ang = n2 / Rad_to_deg;
        set_x();        // add to class declaration
        set_y();        // add to class declaration
    }
    else
    {
        cout << "Incorrect 3rd argument to Vector() -- ";
        cout << "vector set to 0\n";
        x = y = mag = ang = 0.0;
         mode = 'r';
    }
}
```

Further, you can use `'r'` as the default value for the third argument. This lets you continue to use the two-argument form to initialize vectors in the x-y mode.

Listing 10.5 shows the revised class declaration. It adds a `mode` member and private functions for setting the `x` and `y` member values from the polar values. It provides a new prototype for one of the constructors. Note that the prototype provides a default value of `'r'` for mode. Because the new constructor can set either polar or rectangular values, we drop the old `set_to_polar()` function. Next, the `operator<<()` method replaces the old `show_vector()` and `show_polar()` methods.

Listing 10.5 vector2.h

```cpp
// vector2.h -- Vector class with <<, mode state
#ifndef _VECTOR2_H_
#define _VECTOR2_H_
class Vector
{
private:
    double x;          // horizontal value
    double y;          // vertical value
    double mag;        // length of vector
    double ang;        // direction of vector
    char mode;         // 'r' = rectangular, 'p' = polar
    void set_mag();
    void set_ang();
    void set_x();
    void set_y();
public:
    Vector();
    Vector(double n1, double n2, char form = 'r');
    void set(double n1, double n2, char form = 'r');
    ~Vector();
```

```
    double xval() const {return x;}        // report x value
    double yval() const {return y;}        // report y value
    double magval() const {return mag;}    // report magnitude
    double angval() const {return ang;}    // report angle
    void polar_mode();
    void rect_mode();
// operator overloading
    Vector operator+(const Vector & b) const;
    Vector operator-(const Vector & b) const;
    Vector operator-() const;
    Vector operator*(double n) const;
// friends
    friend Vector operator*(double n, const Vector & a);
    friend ostream& operator<<(ostream& os, const Vector & v);
};
#endif
```

FRIEND OR NO FRIEND?

The new Vector class declaration makes the operator<<() function a friend function to the Vector class. But this function, although not inimical to the ostream class, is not a friend to it. The operator<<() function takes an ostream argument and a Vector argument, so it might seem this function has to be friends to both classes. If you look at the code for the function, however, you'll notice that the function accesses individual members of the Vector object but only uses the ostream object as a whole. Because operator<<() accesses private Vector object members directly, it has to be a friend to the Vector class. But because it does not directly access private ostream object members, the function does not have to be a friend to the ostream class. That's nice because it means you don't have to tinker with the ostream definition.

Listing 10.6 lists the revised methods for the Vector class. We've already discussed most of these changes individually. Keep in mind that default values appear only in the prototypes in Listing 10.5, not in the methods file.

Listing 10.6 vector2.cpp

```
// vector2.cpp -- methods for Vector class
#include <iostream>
#include <cmath>
using namespace std;
#include "vector2.h"
const double Rad_to_deg = 57.2957795130823;

// private methods
// calculates magnitude from x and y
void Vector::set_mag()
{
    mag = sqrt(x * x + y * y);
}
```

```
void Vector::set_ang()
{
    if (x == 0.0 && y == 0.0)
        ang = 0.0;
    else
        ang = atan2(y, x);
}
// set x from polar coordinate
void Vector::set_x()
{
    x = mag * cos(ang);
}

// set y from polar coordinate
void Vector::set_y()
{
    y = mag * sin(ang);
}

// public methods
Vector::Vector()                    // default constructor
{
    x = y = mag = ang = 0.0;
    mode = 'r';
}

// construct vector from rectangular coordinates if form is r
// or else from polar coordinates if form is p
Vector::Vector(double n1, double n2, char form)
{
    mode = form;
    if (form == 'r')
     {
        x = n1;
        y = n2;
        set_mag();
        set_ang();
    }
    else if (form == 'p')
    {
        mag = n1;
        ang = n2 / Rad_to_deg;
        set_x();
        set_y();
    }
    else
    {
        cout << "Incorrect 3rd argument to Vector() -- ";
        cout << "vector set to 0\n";
        x = y = mag = ang = 0.0;
        mode = 'r';
    }
}

// set vector from rectangular coordinates if form is r
// or else from polar coordinates if form is p
void Vector:: set(double n1, double n2, char form)
{
    mode = form;
```

```
        if (form == 'r')
         {
             x = n1;
             y = n2;
             set_mag();
             set_ang();
         }
        else if (form == 'p')
         {
             mag = n1;
             ang = n2 / Rad_to_deg;
             set_x();
             set_y();
         }
        else
         {
             cout << "Incorrect 3rd argument to Vector() -- ";
             cout << "vector set to 0\n";
             x = y = mag = ang = 0.0;
             mode = 'r';
         }
    }

Vector::~Vector()     // destructor
{
}

void Vector::polar_mode()      // set to polar mode
{
    mode = 'p';
}

void Vector::rect_mode()          // set to rectangular mode
{
    mode = 'r';
}

// operator overloading
// add two Vectors
Vector Vector::operator+(const Vector & b) const
{
    return Vector(x + b.x, y + b.y);
}

// subtract Vector b from a
Vector Vector::operator-(const Vector & b) const
{
    return Vector(x - b.x, y - b.y);
}

// reverse sign of Vector
Vector Vector::operator-() const
{
    return Vector(-x, -y);
}

// multiple vector by n
Vector Vector::operator*(double n) const
{
```

```
        return Vector(n * x, n * y);;
}

// friend methods
// multiply n by Vector a
Vector operator*(double n, const Vector & a)
{
    return a * n;
}

// display rectangular coordinates if mode is r,
// else display polar coordinates if mode is p
ostream& operator<<(ostream & os, const Vector & v)
{
    if (v.mode == 'r')
        os << "(x,y) = (" << v.x << ", " << v.y << ")";
    else if (v.mode == 'p')
    {
        os << "(m,a) = (" << v.mag << ", "
            << v.ang * Rad_to_deg << ")";
    }
    else
        os << "Vector object mode is invalid";
    return os;
}
```

Listing 10.7 provides a short program using the revised class. It simulates the famous Drunkard's Walk problem. Actually, now that the drunk is recognized as someone with a serious health problem rather than as a source of amusement, it's usually called the Random Walk problem. The idea is that you place someone at a lamp post. The subject begins walking, but the direction of each step varies randomly from the preceding step. One way of phrasing the problem is, how many steps does it take the random walker to travel, say, 50 feet away from the post. In terms of vectors, this amounts to adding a bunch of randomly oriented vectors until the sum exceeds 50 feet.

Listing 10.7 lets you select the target distance to be traveled and the length of the wanderer's step. It maintains a running total representing the position after each step (represented as a vector), and reports the number of steps needed to reach the target distance along with the walker's location (in both formats). As you'll see, the walker's progress is quite inefficient. A journey of a thousand steps, each two feet long, may carry the walker only 50 feet from the starting point. The program divides the net distance traveled (50 feet in this case) by the number of steps to provide a measure of the walker's inefficiency. All the random direction changes make this average much smaller than the length of a single step. To select directions randomly, the program uses the standard library functions rand(), srand(), and time(), described in the Program Notes. Remember to compile Listing 10.6 along with Listing 10.7.

Listing 10.7 randwalk.cpp

```
// randwalk.cpp -- use the revised Vector class
// compile with the vector2.cpp file
#include <iostream>
#include <cstdlib>        // rand(), srand() prototypes
```

> *The idea is that you place someone at a lamp post. The subject begins walking, but the direction of each step varies randomly from the preceding step.*

```cpp
#include <ctime>          // time() prototype
using namespace std;
#include "vector2.h"
int main()
{
    srand(time(0));        // seed random-number generator
    double direction;
    Vector step;
    Vector result(0.0, 0.0);
    unsigned long steps = 0;
    double target;
    double dstep;
    cout << "Enter target distance (q to quit): ";
    while (cin >> target)
    {
        cout << "Enter step length: ";
        if (!(cin >> dstep))
            break;

        while (result.magval() < target)
        {
            direction = rand() % 360;
            step.set(dstep, direction, 'p');
            result = result + step;
            steps++;
        }
        cout << "After " << steps << " steps, the subject "
            "has the following location:\n";
        cout << result << "\n";
        result.polar_mode();
        cout << " or\n" << result << "\n";
        cout << "Average outward distance per step = "
            << result.magval()/steps << "\n";
        steps = 0;
        result.set(0.0, 0.0);
        cout << "Enter target distance (q to quit): ";
    }
    cout << "Bye!\n";

    return 0;
}
```

Remember

You may have to use `stdlib.h` instead of `cstdlib` and `time.h` instead of `ctime`.

Here is a sample run:

```
Enter target distance (q to quit): 50
Enter step length: 2
After 253 steps, the subject has the following location:
(x,y) = (46.1512, 20.4902)
 or
(m,a) = (50.495, 23.9402)
Average outward distance per step = 0.199587
Enter target distance (q to quit): 50
Enter step length: 2
```

```
After 951 steps, the subject has the following location:
(x,y) = (-21.9577, 45.3019)
 or
(m,a) = (50.3429, 115.8593)
Average outward distance per step = 0.0529362
Enter target distance (q to quit): 50
Enter step length: 1
After 1716 steps, the subject has the following location:
(x,y) = (40.0164, 31.1244)
 or
(m,a) = (50.6956, 37.8755)
Average outward distance per step = 0.0295429
Enter target distance (q to quit): q
```

The random nature of the process produces considerable variation from trial to trial, even if the initial conditions are the same. On the average, however, halving the step size quadruples the number of steps needed to cover a given distance. Probability theory suggests that, on the average, the number of steps (N) of length s needed to reach a net distance of D is given by the following equation:

```
N = (D/s)²
```

This is just an average, but there will be considerable variations from trial to trial. For example, a thousand trials of attempting to travel 50 feet in 2-foot steps yielded an average of 636 steps (close to the theoretical value of 625) to travel that far, but the range was from 91 to 3951. Similarly, a thousand trials of traveling 50 feet in 1-foot steps averaged 2557 steps (close to the theoretical value of 2500) with a range of 345 to 10882. So if you find yourself walking randomly, be confident and take long steps. You still won't have any control over the direction you wind up going, but at least you'll get farther.

Program Notes

First, let's talk about random numbers. The standard ANSI C library, which also comes with C++, includes a rand() function that returns a random integer in the range from 0 to some implementation-dependent value. Our program uses the modulus operator to get an angle value in the range 0–359. The rand() function works by applying an algorithm to an initial seed value to get a random value. That value is used as the seed for the next function call, and so on. The numbers are really *pseudorandom*, for ten consecutive calls normally produce the same set of ten random numbers. (The exact values will depend on the implementation.) However, the srand() function lets you override the default seed value and initiate a different sequence of random numbers. This program uses the return value of time(0) to set the seed. The time(0) function returns the current calendar time, often implemented as the number of seconds since some specific date. (More generally, time() takes the address of a type time_t variable and puts the time into that variable and also returns it. Using a 0 address argument obviates the need for an otherwise unneeded time_t variable.) Thus, the statement

```
srand(time(0));
```

" So if you find yourself walking randomly, be confident and take long steps. You still won't have any control over the direction you wind up going, but at least you'll get farther."

sets a different seed each time you run the program, making the random output appear even more random. The `cstdlib` header file (formerly `stdlib.h`) contains the prototypes for `srand()` and `rand()`, whereas `ctime` (formerly `time.h`) contains the `time()` prototype.

The program uses the `result` vector to keep track of the walker's progress. Each cycle of the inner loop, the program sets the `step` vector to a new direction and adds it to the current `result` vector. When the magnitude of `result` exceeds the target distance, the loop terminates.

By setting the vector mode, the program displays the final position in rectangular terms and in polar terms.

Incidentally, the statement

```
result = result + step;
```

has the effect of placing `result` in the `'r'` mode regardless of the initial modes of `result` and `step`. Here's why. First, the addition operator function creates and returns a new vector holding the sum of the two arguments. The function creates that vector using the default constructor, which creates vectors in the `'r'` mode. Thus, the vector being assigned to result is in the `'r'` mode. By default, assignment assigns each member variable individually, so `'r'` is assigned to `result.mode`. If you would prefer some other behavior, such as `result` retaining its original mode, you can override default assignment by defining an assignment operator for the class. The next chapter shows examples of this.

We've used the `Vector` class to illustrate operator overloading with member functions and with friend functions. We've used it to illustrate overloading the `<<` operator to display `Vector` values, and we've used it to illustrate how a state variable can add flexibility to a design. This entire sequence of examples shows how a class declaration can grow in flexibility and power as you work with it. When developing a new class, it's usually a good idea to proceed as these examples did, starting with a basic implementation, getting it to work, and then expanding the class. By now, however, the `Vector` class is getting too involved to add new features without risking the new ideas being buried in the clutter. So, we'll retire the `Vector` class and return to simpler classes as we explore still more class concepts and techniques. Before proceeding to new material, you may want to pause to take a deep, relaxing breath and reward yourself with a treat, perhaps a cookie, perhaps a good movie, perhaps a short trip to Tahiti.

Automatic Conversions and Type Casts for Classes

The next topic on the class menu is type conversion. We'll look into how C++ handles conversions to and from user-defined types. To set the stage, let's first review how C++ handles conversions for its built-in types. When you make a statement assigning a value of one standard type to a variable of another standard type, C++ automatically will convert the value to the same type as the receiving variable, providing the two types are compatible. For instance, the following statements all generate numeric type conversions:

```
long count = 8;      // int value 8 converted to type long
double time = 11;    // int value 11 converted to type double
int side = 3.33;     // double value 3.33 converted to type int 3
```

These assignments work because C++ recognizes that the diverse numeric types all represent the same basic thing, a number, and because C++ incorporates built-in rules for making the conversions. Recall, however (from your reading of Chapter 3), that you can lose some precision in these conversions. For instance, assigning 3.33 to the int variable side results in side getting the value 3, losing the 0.33 part.

The C++ language does not automatically convert types that are not compatible. For instance, the statement

```
int * p = 10;   // type clash
```

fails because the left side is a pointer-type, whereas the right side is a number. And even though a computer may represent an address internally with an integer, integers and pointers conceptually are quite different. For instance, you wouldn't square a pointer. However, when automatic conversions fail, you may use a type cast:

```
int * p = (int *) 10;   // ok, p and (int *) 10 both pointers
```

This sets a pointer to the address 10 by type casting 10 to type pointer-to-int (that is, type int *).

You may define a class sufficiently related to a basic type or to another class that it makes sense to convert from one form to another. In that case, you can instruct C++ how to make such conversions automatically or, perhaps, via a type cast. To show how that works, let's recast the pounds-to-stone program from Chapter 3 into class form. First, design an appropriate type. Fundamentally, we're representing one thing (a weight) two ways (pounds and stone). A class provides an excellent way to incorporate two representations of one concept into a single entity. Therefore, it makes sense to place both representations of weight into the same class and then to provide class methods for expressing the weight in different forms. Listing 10.8 provides the class header.

Listing 10.8 stonewt.h

```
// stonewt.h -- definition for Stonewt class
#ifndef _STONEWT_H_
#define _STONEWT_H_
class Stonewt
{
private:
    enum {Lbs_per_stn = 14};        // pounds per stone
    int stone;                       // whole stones
    double pds_left;                 // fractional pounds
    double pounds;                   // entire weight in pounds
public:
    Stonewt(double lbs);             // constructor for double pounds
    Stonewt(int stn, double lbs);    // constructor for stone, lbs
    Stonewt();                       // default constructor
```

```
    ~Stonewt();
    void show_lbs() const;        // show weight in pounds format
    void show_stn() const;        // show weight in stone format
};
#endif
```

Note that the class has three constructors. They allow you to initialize a Stonewt object to a floating-point number of pounds, or to a stone and pound combination. Or you can create a Stonewt object without initializing it.

Also, the class provides two display functions. One displays the weight in pounds, and the other displays the weight in stone and pounds. Listing 10.9 shows the class methods implementation. Note that each constructor assigns values to all three private members. Thus, creating a Stonewt object automatically sets both representations of weight.

As mentioned in Chapter 9, enum provides a convenient way to define class-specific constants, providing that they are integers.

Listing 10.9 stonewt.cpp

```
include <iostream>
using namespace std;
#include "stonewt.h"

// construct Stonewt object from double value
Stonewt::Stonewt(double lbs)
{
    stone = int (lbs) / Lbs_per_stn;    // integer division
    pds_left = int (lbs) % Lbs_per_stn + lbs - int(lbs);
    pounds = lbs;
}

// construct Stonewt object from stone, double values
Stonewt::Stonewt(int stn, double lbs)
{
    stone = stn;
    pds_left = lbs;
    pounds =  stn * Lbs_per_stn +lbs;
}

Stonewt::Stonewt()             // default constructor, wt = 0
{
    stone = pounds = pds_left = 0;
}

Stonewt::~Stonewt()           // destructor
{
}

// show weight in stones
void Stonewt::show_stn() const
{
    cout << stone << " stone, " << pds_left << " pounds\n";
}

// show weight in pounds
void Stonewt::show_lbs() const
```

```
{
    cout << pounds << " pounds\n";
}
```

Because a Stonewt object represents a single weight, it makes sense to provide ways to convert an integer or a floating-point value to a Stonewt object. And we have already done so! In C++, any constructor taking a single argument acts as a blueprint for converting a value of that argument type to the class type. Thus the constructor

```
Stonewt(double lbs);  // template for double-to-Stonewt conversion
```

serves as instructions for converting type double values to a type Stonewt value. That is, you can write code like the following:

```
Stonewt myCat;      // create a Stonewt object
myCat = 19.6;       // use Stonewt(double) to convert 19.6 to Stonewt
```

The program will use the Stonewt(double) constructor to construct a temporary Stonewt object, using 19.6 as the initialization value. Then memberwise assignment will copy the contents of the temporary object into myCat. This process is termed an implicit conversion because it happens automatically without the need of an explicit type cast.

Only a constructor that can be used with just one argument works as a conversion function. The constructor

```
Stonewt(int stn, double lbs);
```

has two arguments, so it cannot be used to convert types.

Having a constructor work as an automatic type-conversion function seems like a nice feature. As programmers acquired more experience working with C++, however, they found that the automatic aspect isn't always desirable, for it can lead to unexpected conversions. So recent C++ implementations have a new keyword, explicit, to turn off the automatic aspect. That is, you can declare the constructor this way:

```
explicit Stonewt(double lbs);  // no implicit conversions allowed
```

This turns off implicit conversions such as the example above but still allows explicit conversions; that is, conversions using explicit type casts:

```
Stonewt myCat;          // create a Stonewt object
myCat = 19.6;           // not valid if Stonewt(double) is declared as
                        // explicit
mycat = Stonewt(19.6);  // ok, an explicit conversion
mycat = (Stonewt) 19.6; // ok, old form for explicit typecast
```

Remember

A C++ constructor containing one argument defines a type conversion from the argument type to the class type. If the constructor is qualified with the keyword explicit, the constructor is used for explicit conversions only; otherwise, it also is used for implicit conversions.

When will the compiler use the Stonewt(double) function? It will use the constructor in the circumstances listed next. If the keyword explicit is used in the declaration, `Stonewt(double)` will be used only for an explicit type cast; otherwise, it also will be used for implicit conversions.

- When you initialize a `Stonewt` object to a type `double` value.

- When you assign a type `double` value to a `Stonewt` object.

- When you pass a type `double` value to a function expecting a `Stonewt` argument.

- When a function that's declared to return a value tries to return a `double` value.

- When any of the situations above uses a built-in type that unambiguously can be converted to type `double`.

Let's look at the last point in more detail. The argument-matching process provided by function prototyping will let the `Stonewt(double)` constructor act as conversions for other numerical types. That is, both of the following statements work by first converting `int` to `double` and then using the `Stonewt(double)` constructor.

```
Stonewt Jumbo(7000);    // uses Stonewt(double), converting int to double
Jumbo = 7300;           // uses Stonewt(double), converting int to double
```

However, this two-step conversion process works only if there is an unambiguous choice. That is, if the class also defined a `Stonewt(long)` constructor, the compiler would reject these statements, probably pointing out that an `int` can be converted to either a `long` or a `double`, so the call is ambiguous.

Listing 10.10 uses the class constructors to initialize some `Stonewt` objects and to handle type conversions. Remember to compile Listing 10.9 along with Listing 10.10.

Listing 10.10 stone.cpp

```cpp
// stone.cpp -- user-defined conversions
// compile with stonewt.cpp
#include <iostream>
using namespace std;
#include "stonewt.h"
void display(Stonewt st, int n);
int main()
{
    Stonewt pavarotti = 260;           // uses constructor to initialize
    Stonewt wolfe((double)285.7);      // same as Stonewt wolfe = 285.7;
    Stonewt taft(21, 8);

    cout << "The tenor weighed ";
    pavarotti.show_stn();
    cout << "The detective weighed ";
    wolfe.show_stn();
    cout << "The President weighed ";
    taft.show_lbs();
    pavarotti = double(265.8);         // uses constructor for conversion
    taft = 325;                        // same as taft = Stonewt(325);
    cout << "After dinner, the tenor weighed ";
    pavarotti.show_stn();
```

```
    cout << "After dinner, the President weighed ";
    taft.show_lbs();
    display(taft, 2);
    cout << "The wrestler weighed even more.\n";
    display(422, 2);
    cout << "No stone left unearned\n";
    return 0;
}

void display(Stonewt st, int n)
{
    for (int i = 0; i < n; i++)
    {
        cout << "Wow! ";
        st.show_stn();
    }
}
```

Here is the output:

```
The tenor weighed 18 stone, 8 pounds
The detective weighed 20 stone, 5.7 pounds
The President weighed 302 pounds
After dinner, the tenor weighed 18 stone, 13.8 pounds
After dinner, the President weighed 325 pounds
Wow! 23 stone, 3 pounds
Wow! 23 stone, 3 pounds
The wrestler weighed even more.
Wow! 30 stone, 2 pounds
Wow! 30 stone, 2 pounds
No stone left unearned
```

Program Notes

First, note that when a constructor has a single argument, you can use the following form when initializing a class object:

```
// a syntax for initializing a class object when
// using a constructor with one argument
Stonewt pavarotti = 260;
```

This is equivalent to the other two forms we've used:

```
// standard syntax forms for initializing class objects
Stonewt pavarotti(260);
Stonewt pavarotti = Stonewt(260);
```

However, the last two forms can also be used with constructors having multiple arguments.

Next, note the following two assignments from Listing 10.10:

```
pavarotti = 265.8;
taft = 325;
```

The first assignment uses the constructor with a type double argument to convert 265.8 to a type Stonewt value. This sets the pounds member of pavarotti to 265.8. Because it uses the constructor, this assignment also sets the stone and pds_left members of the class. Similarly, the second assignment converts a type `int` value to type `double` and then uses `Stonewt(double)` to set all three member values in the process.

Finally, note the following function call:

```
display(422, 2);    // convert 422 to double, then to Stonewt
```

The prototype for `display()` indicates that its first argument should be the `Stonewt` object. Confronted with an `int` argument, the compiler looks for a `Stonewt(int)` constructor to convert the `int` to the desired `Stonewt` type. Failing to find that constructor, the compiler looks for a constructor with some other built-in type to which an `int` can be converted. The `Stonewt(double)` constructor fits the bill. So the compiler converts `int` to `double` and then uses `Stonewt(double)` to convert the result to a `Stonewt` object.

CONVERSION FUNCTIONS

Listing 10.10 converts a number to a `Stonewt` object. Can you do the reverse? That is, can you convert a `Stonewt` object to a `double` value, as in the following?

```
Stonewt wolfe(285.7);
double host = wolfe;  // ?? possible ??
```

The answer is that you can do this, but not by using constructors. Constructors only provide for converting another type to the class type. To do the reverse, you have to use a special form of C++ operator function called a *conversion function*.

Conversion functions resemble user-defined type casts, and you can use them the way you would use a type cast. For instance, if you define a `Stonewt`-to-`double` conversion function, you can use the following conversions:

```
Stonewt wolfe(285.7);
double host = double (wolfe);        // syntax #1
double thinker = (double) wolfe;     // syntax #2
```

Or you can let the compiler figure out what to do:

```
Stonewt wells(20, 3);
double star = wells;    // implicit use of conversion function
```

The computer, noting that the right side is type `Stonewt` and the left side is type `double`, looks to see if you've defined a conversion function matching that description.

So how do you create a conversion function? To convert to type *typeName*, use a conversion function of this form:

```
operator typeName();
```

Note the following points:

- The conversion function must be a class method.

- The conversion function must not specify a return type.

- The conversion function must have no arguments.

For instance, a function to convert to type `double` would have this prototype:

```
operator double();
```

The *typeName* part tells the conversion the type to which to convert, so no return type is needed. The fact that the function is a class method means it has to be invoked by a particular class object, and that tells the function which value to convert. Thus, the function doesn't need arguments.

To add functions converting `stone_wt` objects to type `int` and to type `double`, then, requires adding the following prototypes to the class declaration:

```
operator int();
operator double();
```

Listing 10.11 shows the modified class declaration.

Listing 10.11 stonewt1.h

```
// stonewt1.h -- revised definition for Stonewt class
#ifndef _STONEWT1_H_
#define _STONEWT1_H_
class Stonewt
{
private:
    enum {Lbs_per_stn = 14};        // pounds per stone
int stone;                          // whole stones
    double pds_left;                // fractional pounds
    double pounds;                  // entire weight in pounds
public:
    Stonewt(double lbs);            // construct from double pounds
    Stonewt(int stn, double lbs);   // construct from stone, lbs
    Stonewt();                      // default constructor
    ~Stonewt();
    void show_lbs() const;          // show weight in pounds format
    void show_stn() const;          // show weight in stone format
// conversion functions
    operator int() const;
    operator double() const;
};
#endif
```

Next, Listing 10.12 shows the definitions for these two conversion functions; these definitions should be added to the class member function file. Note that each function does return the desired value even though there is no declared return type. Also note the `int` conversion definition rounds to the nearest integer rather than truncating. For example, if pounds is 114.4, then pounds + `0.5` is 114.9, and int (114.9) is 114. But if pounds is 114.6, then pounds + `0.5` is 115.1, and int (115.1) is 115.

Listing 10.12 stonewt1.cpp

```
// stonewt1.cpp -- Stonewt class methods + conversion functions
#include <iostream>
using namespace std;
#include "stonewt1.h"

// previous definitions go here
```

```
// conversion functions
Stonewt::operator int() const
{

    return int (pounds + 0.5);

}

Stonewt::operator double()const
{
    return pounds;
}
```

Listing 10.13 tests the new conversion functions. The assignment statement in the program uses an implicit conversion, whereas the final cout statement uses an explicit type cast. Remember to compile Listing 10.12 along with Listing 10.13.

Listing 10.13 stone1.cpp

```
// stone1.cpp -- user-defined conversion functions
// compile with stonewt1.cpp
#include <iostream>
using namespace std;
#include "stonewt1.h"

int main()
{
    Stonewt poppins(9,2.8);     // 9 stone, 2.8 pounds
    double p_wt = poppins;      // implicit conversion
        cout << "Convert to double => ";
    cout << "Poppins: " << p_wt << " pounds.\n";
    cout << "Convert to int => ";
        cout << "Poppins: " << int (poppins) << " pounds.\n";
    return 0;
}
```

Here's the program output; it shows the result of converting the type Stonewt object to type double and to type int:

```
Convert to double => Poppins: 128.8 pounds.
Convert to int => Poppins: 129 pounds.
```

Applying Type Conversions Automatically

The last example used int (poppins) with cout. Suppose, instead, it omitted the explicit type cast:

```
cout << "Poppins: " << poppins << " pounds.\n";
```

Would the program use an implicit conversion, as it did in the following statement?

```
double p_wt = poppins;
```

The answer is no. In the p_wt example, the context indicates that poppins should be converted to type double. But in the cout example, nothing indicates whether the conversion should be to int or to double. Facing this lack of information, the compiler would complain that you were using an ambiguous conversion. Nothing in the statement indicates what type to use.

Interestingly, if the class had defined only the `double` conversion function, the compiler would accept our statement. That's because with only one conversion possible, there is no ambiguity.

You can have a similar situation with assignment. With the current class declarations, the compiler rejects the following statement as ambiguous.

```
long gone = poppins;   // ambiguous
```

In C++, you can assign both `int` and `double` values to a `long` variable, so the compiler legitimately can use either conversion function. The compiler doesn't want the responsibility of choosing which. But if you eliminate one of the two conversion functions, the compiler accepts the statement. For example, suppose you omit the `double` definition. Then the compiler will use the `int` conversion to convert `poppins` to a type `int` value. Then it converts the `int` value to type `long` when assigning it to gone.

When the class defines two or more conversions, you can still use an explicit type cast to indicate which conversion function to use. You can use either type cast notation:

```
long gone = (double) poppins;   // use double conversion
long gone = int (poppins);      // use int conversion
```

The first statement converts `poppins` weight to a `double` value, and then assignment converts the `double` value to type `long`. Similarly, the second statement converts `poppins` first to type `int`, and then to `long`.

Like conversion constructors, conversion functions can be a mixed blessing. The problem with providing functions that make automatic, implicit conversions is that they may make conversions when you don't expect them. Suppose, for example, you happen to write the following sleep-deprived code:

```
int ar[20];
...
Stonewt temp(14, 4);
...
int Temp;
...
cout << ar[temp] << "!\n";   // used temp instead of Temp
```

> *" The moral is that often it's better to use explicit conversions and exclude the possibility of implicit conversions. "*

Normally, you'd expect the compiler to catch a blunder such as using an object instead of an integer as an array index. But the `Stonewt` class defines an `operator int()`, so the `Stonewt` object `temp` will be converted to the `int` 200 and be used as an array index. The moral is that often it's better to use explicit conversions and exclude the possibility of implicit conversions. The keyword `explicit` doesn't work with conversion functions, but all you have to do is replace a conversion function with a nonconversion function that does the same task, but only if called explicitly. That is, you can replace

```
Stonewt::operator int() { return int (pounds + 0.5); }
```

with

```
int Stonewt::Stone_to_Int() { return int (pounds + 0.5); }
```

This will disallow

```
int plb = poppins;
```

but, if you really need a conversion, allow the following:

```
int plb = poppins.Stone_to_Int();
```

Remember

Use implicit conversion functions with care. Often a function that can only be invoked explicitly is the better choice.

In summary, then, C++ provides the following type conversions for classes:

- A class constructor that has but a single argument serves as an instruction for converting a value of the argument type to the class type. For example, the Stonewt class constructor with a type int argument is invoked automatically when you assign a type int value to a Stonewt object. Using explicit in the constructor declaration, however, eliminates implicit conversions, allowing only explicit conversions.

- A special class member operator function called a conversion function serves as an instruction for converting a class object to some other type. The conversion function is a class member, has no declared return type, has no arguments, and is called operator *typeName*(), where *typeName* is the type to which the object is to be converted. This conversion function is invoked automatically when you assign a class object to a variable of that type or use the type cast operator to that type.

CONVERSIONS AND FRIENDS

Let's bring addition to the Stonewt class. As we mentioned when discussing the Vector class, you can use either a member function or a friend function to overload addition. (To simplify matters, assume that no conversion functions of the operator double() form are defined.) You can implement addition with the following member function:

```
Stonewt Stonewt::operator+(const Stonewt & st) const
{
    double pds = pounds + st.pounds;
    Stonewt sum(pds);
    return sum;
}
```

Or you can implement addition as a friend function this way:

```
Stonewt operator+(const Stonewt & st1, const Stonewt & st2)

{
    double pds = st1.pounds + st2.pounds;
    Stonewt sum(pds);
    return sum;
}
```

Either form lets you do the following:

```
Stonewt jenny(9, 12);
Stonewt benny(12, 8);
Stonewt total;
total = jenny + benny;
```

Also, given the `Stonewt(double)` constructor, each form lets you do the following:

```
Stonewt jenny(9, 12);
double kenny = 176.0;
Stonewt total;
total = jenny + kenny;
```

But only the friend function lets you do this:

```
Stonewt jenny(9, 12);
double penny = 146.0;
Stonewt total;
total = penny + jenny;
```

To see why, translate each addition into the corresponding function calls. First,

```
total = jenny + benny;
```

becomes

```
total = jenny.operator+(benny);    // member function
```

or else

```
total = operator+(jenny, benny);   // friend function
```

In either case, the actual argument types match the formal arguments. Also, the member function is invoked, as required, by a `Stonewt` object.

Next,

```
total = jenny + kenny;
```

becomes

```
total = jenny.operator+(kenny);    // member function
```

or else

```
total = operator+(jenny, kenny);   // friend function
```

Again, the member function is invoked, as required, by a `Stonewt` object. This time, in each case, one argument is type `double`, which invokes the `Stonewt(double)` constructor to convert the argument to a `Stonewt` object.

By the way, having an `operator double()` member function defined would create confusion at this point, for that would create another option for interpretation. Instead of converting `kenny` to `double` and performing `Stonewt` addition, the compiler could convert `jenny` to `double` and perform `double` addition. Too many conversion functions create ambiguities.

Finally,

```
total = penny + jenny;
```

becomes

```
total = operator+(penny, jenny);   // friend function
```

Here, both arguments are type `double`, which invokes the `Stonewt(double)` constructor to convert them to `Stonewt` objects. The member function cannot be invoked, however.

```
total = penny.operator+(jenny);    // not meaningful
```

The reason is that only a class object can invoke a member function. C++ will not attempt to convert `penny` to a `Stonewt` object. Conversion takes place for member function arguments, not for member function invokers.

The lesson here is that defining addition as a friend makes it easier for a program to accommodate automatic type conversions. The reason is that both operands become function arguments, so function prototyping comes into play for both operands.

A Choice

Given that you want to add `double` quantities to `Stonewt` quantities, you have a couple of choices. The first, which we just outlined, is to define `operator+(const Stonewt &, const Stonewt &)` as a friend function and have the `Stonewt(double)` constructor handle conversions of type `double` arguments to type `Stonewt` arguments.

The second choice is to further overload the addition operator with functions that explicitly use one type `double` argument:

```
Stonewt operator+(double x);   // member function
friend Stonewt operator+(double x, Stonewt & s);
```

That way, the statement

```
total = jenny + kenny; // Stonewt + double
```

exactly matches the `operator+(double x)` member function, and the statement

```
total = penny + jenny; // double + Stonewt
```

exactly matches the `operator+(double x, Stonewt &s)` friend function. Earlier, we did something similar for `Vector` multiplication.

Each choice has its advantages. The first choice results in a shorter program because you define fewer functions. That also implies less work for you and fewer chances to mess up. The disadvantage is the added overhead in time and memory needed to invoke the conversion constructor whenever a conversion is needed. The second choice, however, is the mirror image. It makes for a longer program and more work on your part, but it runs a bit faster.

If your program makes intensive use of adding `double` values to `Stonewt` objects, it may pay to overload addition to handle such cases directly. If the program just uses such addition occasionally, it's simpler to rely on automatic conversions, or, if you want to be more careful, upon explicit conversions.

Summary

This chapter covers many important aspects of defining and using classes. Some of the material in this chapter may seem vague to you until your own experiences enrich your understanding. Meanwhile, let's summarize the chapter.

Normally, the only way you can access private class members is by using a class method. C++ alleviates that restriction with friend functions. To make a function a friend function, declare the function in the class declaration and preface the declaration with the keyword `friend`.

C++ extends overloading to operators by letting you define special operator functions that describe how particular operators relate to a particular class. An operator function can be a class member function or a friend function. (A few operators can only be class member functions.) C++ lets you invoke an operator function either by calling the function or by using the overloaded operator with its usual syntax. An operator function for the operator *op* has this form:

```
operatorop(argument-list)
```

The argument-list represents operands for the operator. If the operator function is a class member function, then the first operand is the invoking object and isn't part of the argument-list. For instance, we overloaded addition by defining an `operator+()` member function for the `Vector` class. If up, `right`, and `result` are three vectors, you can use either of the following statements to invoke vector addition:

```
result = up.operator+(right);
result = up + right;
```

For the second version, the fact that the operands up and `right` are type `Vector` tells C++ to use the `Vector` definition of addition.

When an operator function is a member function, the first operand is the object invoking the function. In the statements above, for example, the up object is the invoking object. If you want to define an operator function so that the first operand is not a class object, you must use a friend function. Then you can pass the operands to the function definition in whichever order you want.

One of the most common tasks for operator overloading is defining the << operator so that it can be used in conjunction with the `cout` object to display an object's contents. To allow an `ostream` object to be the first operand, define the operator function as a friend. To allow the redefined operator to be concatenated with itself, make the return type `ostream` &. Here's a general form satisfying those requirements:

```
ostream & operator<<(ostream & os, const c_name & obj)
{
    os << ... ;  // display object contents
    return os;
}
```

If, however, the class has methods that return values for the data members you want to display, you can use those methods instead of direct access in `operator<<()`. In that case, the function needn't (and shouldn't) be a friend.

C++ lets you establish conversions to and from class types. First, any class constructor taking a single argument acts as a conversion function, converting values of the argument type to the class type. C++ invokes the constructor automatically if you assign a value of the argument type to an object. For instance, suppose you have a String class with a constructor that takes char * value as its sole argument. Then, if bean is a String object, you can use the following statement:

```
bean = "pinto";   // converts type char * to type String
```

If, however, you precede the constructor declaration with the keyword explicit, then the constructor can be used only for explicit conversions:

```
bean = String("pinto");   // converts type char * to type String
explicitly
```

To convert from a class to another type, you must define a conversion function providing instruction about how to make the conversion. A conversion function must be a member function. If it is to convert to type *typeName*, it should have the following prototype:

```
operator typeName();
```

Note that it must have no declared return type, must have no arguments, and must (despite having no declared return type) return the converted value. For instance, a function to convert type Vector to type double would have this function form:

```
Vector::operator double()
{
    ...
    return a_double_value;
}
```

Experience has shown that often it is better not to rely upon such implicit conversion functions.

As you may have noticed, classes require much more care and attention to detail than do simple C-style structures. In return, they do much more for you.

Review Questions

1. Use a member function to overload the multiplication operator for the Stonewt class; have the operator multiply the data members by a type double value. Note that this will require carryover for the stone-pound representation. That is, twice 10 stone 8 pounds is 21 stone 2 pounds.

2. What are the differences between a friend function and a member function?

3. Does a nonmember function have to be a friend to access a class's members?

4. Use a friend function to overload the multiplication operator for the Stonewt class; have the operator multiply the double value by the Stone value.

5. Which operators cannot be overloaded?

6. What restriction applies to overloading the following operators? = () [] ->

7. Define a conversion function for the `Vector` class that converts a `Vector` to a type `double` value representing the vector's magnitude.

Programming Exercises

1. Modify Listing 10.7 so that instead of reporting the results of a single trial for a particular target-step combination, it reports the highest, lowest, and average number of steps for *N* trials, where *N* is an integer entered by the user.

2. Rewrite the `Stonewt` class so that it has a state member governing whether the object is interpreted in stone form, integer pounds form, or floating-point pounds form. Overload the `<<` operator to replace the `show_stn()` and `show_lbs()` methods. Overload the addition, subtraction, and multiplication operators so that one can add, subtract, and multiply `Stonewt` values. Test your class with a short program.

3. Rewrite the `Stonewt` class so that it overloads the relational operators. Write a program that declares an array of six `Stonewt` objects and initializes the first three objects in the array declaration. Then it should use a loop to read in values used to set the remaining three array elements. Then it should report the smallest element, the largest element, and how many elements are greater or equal to 11 stone.

4. A complex number has two parts: a real part and an imaginary part. One way to write an imaginary number is this: (3.0, 4.0i). Here 3.0 is the real part and 4.0 is the imaginary part. Suppose a = (A,Bi) and c = (C,Di). Here are some complex operations:

   ● Addition: a + c = (A + C, (B + D)i)

   ● Subtraction: a – c = (A – C, (B – D)i)

   ● Multiplication: a * c = (A * C – B*D, (A*D + B*C)i)

   ● Multiplication: (x a real number): x * c = (x*C,x*Di)

   ● Conjugation: ~a = (A, – Bi)

Define a complex class so that the following program can use it with correct results. Note that you have to overload the `<<` and `>>` operators. Many systems already have complex support in a `complex.h` header file, so use `complex0.h` to avoid conflicts. Use `const` whenever warranted.

```
#include <iostream>
using namespace std;
#include "complex0.h"            // to avoid confusion with complex.h
int main()
{
```

```
        complex a(3.0, 4.0);    // initialize to (3,4i)
        complex c;
        cout << "Enter a complex number (q to quit):\n";
        while (cin >> c)
        {
            cout << "c is " << c << '\n';
            cout << "complex conjugate is " << ~c << '\n';
            cout << "a + c is " << a + c << '\n';
            cout << "a - c is " << a - c << '\n';
            cout << "a * c is " << a * c << '\n';
            cout << "2 * c is " << 2 * c << '\n';
            cout << "Enter a complex number (q to quit):\n";
        }
        cout << "Done!\n";
        return 0;
    }
```

Here is a sample run. Note that cin >> c, through overloading, now prompts for real and imaginary parts:

```
Enter a complex number (q to quit):
real: 10
imaginary: 12
c is (10,12i)
complex conjugate is (10,-12i)
a + c is (13,16i)
a - c is (13,16i)
a * c is (-18,76i)
2 * c is (20,24i)
Enter a complex number (q to quit):
real: q
Done!
```

11

Classes
and
Dynamic
Memory
Allocation

You will learn about the following in this chapter:

- Using dynamic memory allocation for class members

- Implicit and explicit copy constructors

- Implicit and explicit overloaded assignment operators

- What you must do if you use `new` in a constructor

- Using `static` class members

- Using pointers to objects

- Implementing a queue ADT

This chapter looks at how to use new and delete with classes and how to deal with some of the subtle problems that using dynamic memory can cause. This may sound like a short list of topics, but these topics affect constructor design, destructor design, and operator overloading.

Let's look at a specific example of how C++ can add to your memory load. Suppose you want to create a class with a member representing someone's last name. The simplest way is to use a character array member to hold the name. But this has some drawbacks. You might use a 14-character array and then run into Bartholomew Smeadsbury-Crafthovingham. Or, to be safer, you may use a 40-character array. But, if you then create an array of 2000 such objects, you'll waste a lot of memory with character arrays that are only partly filled. (At this point, we're adding to the computer's memory load.) There is an alternative.

Often it is much better to decide many matters, such as how much storage to use, when a program runs than when it's compiled. The usual C++ approach to storing a name in an object is to use the new operator in a class constructor to allocate the correct amount of memory while the program is running. But introducing new to a class constructor raises several new problems unless you remember to take a series of additional steps, such as expanding the class destructor, bringing all constructors into harmony with the new destructor, and writing additional class methods to facilitate correct initialization and assignment. (This chapter, of course, will explain all these steps.) If you're just learning C++, you may be better off sticking initially to the simple, if inferior, character array approach. Then, when a class design works well, you can return to your OOP workbench and enhance the class declaration by using new. In short, grow gradually into C++.

Dynamic Memory and Classes

What would you like for breakfast, lunch, and dinner for the next month? How many ounces of milk for dinner on the third day? How many raisins in your cereal for breakfast on the fifteenth day? If you're like most people, you'd rather postpone some of those decisions until the actual mealtimes. Part of C++ strategy is to take the same attitude toward memory allocation, letting the program decide about memory during runtime rather than during compile time. That way, memory use can depend on the needs of a program instead of upon a rigid set of storage-class rules. To gain dynamic control of memory, you remember, C++ utilizes the new and delete operators. Unhappily, using these operators with classes can pose some new programming problems. As you'll see, destructors can become necessary instead of merely ornamental. And sometimes, you have to overload the assignment operator to get programs to behave properly. We'll look into these matters now.

REVIEW EXAMPLE AND STATIC CLASS MEMBERS

We haven't used new and delete for a while, so let's review them with a short program. While we're at it, we'll introduce a new storage class: the static class member. The vehicle will be a String class. (C++ now comes with a string class library, supported by the string header file, and Chapter 15 discusses that class. Meanwhile, the humble String class in this chapter will provide some insight into what underlies such a class.) A String class object will hold a pointer to a string and a value representing the string length. We'll use the String class primarily to give an inside look at how new, delete, and static class members operate. For that reason, the constructors and destructors will display messages when called so that you can follow the action. Also, we'll omit several useful member and friend functions, such as overloaded + and >> operators and a conversion function, in order to simplify the class interface. (But rejoice! The review questions for this chapter give you the opportunity to add those useful support functions.) Listing 11.1 shows the class declaration. We've called the file strng1.h instead of string.h to avoid conflicting with the standard library file string.h. (Recent C++ implementations include a string.h header file supporting C functions like strcpy() that work with C-style strings, a cstring header file based on string.h, and a string header file supporting the C++ string class.)

Listing 11.1 strng1.h

```
// strng1.h -- string class definition
#include <iostream>
using namespace std;
#ifndef _STRNG1_H_
#define _STRNG1_H_
class String
{
private:
    char * str;             // pointer to string
    int len;                // length of string
    static int num_strings; // number of objects
public:
    String(const char * s); // constructor
    String();               // default constructor
    ~String();              // destructor
// friend function
    friend ostream & operator<<(ostream & os, const String & st);
};
#endif
```

You should note two points about this declaration. First, it uses a pointer-to-char instead of a char array to represent a name. This means that the class declaration does not allocate storage space for the string itself. Instead, it will use new in the constructors to allocate space for the string. This arrangement avoids straitjacketing the class declaration with a predefined limit to the string size.

Second, the definition declares the num_strings member as belonging to the static storage class. A *static class member* has a special property: a program creates only one copy of a static class variable regardless of the number of objects created. That is, a static member is shared among all objects of that class, much as a phone number might be shared among all members of a family. If, say, you create ten String objects, there would be ten str members and ten len members, but just one shared num_strings member (see Figure 11.1). This is convenient for data that should be private to a class but that should have the same value for all class objects. The num_strings member, for example, is intended to keep track of the number of objects created.

FIGURE 11.1

The static data member

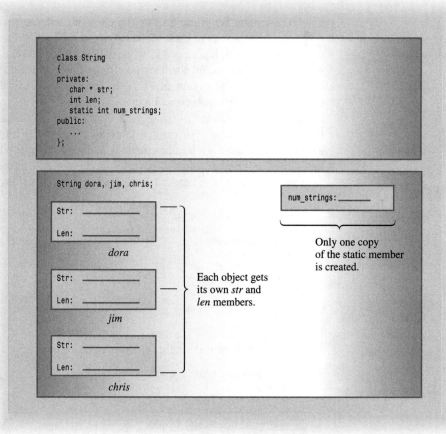

By the way, we've used the num_strings member as a convenient means of illustrating static data members. In general, a String class doesn't need such a member. If you did need such a facility, a better approach would be to define a more general String class, and then use class inheritance (Chapter 12) to add this feature to a derived class. (Class inheritance lets you create a new class that extends an existing class.)

Let's look at the implementation of the class methods in Listing 11.2. There, you'll see how these two points (using a pointer and using a static member) are handled.

Listing 11.2 strng1.cpp

```
// strng1.cpp -- String class methods
#include <iostream>
#include <cstring>                      // string.h for some
#include "strng1.h"
using namespace std;

// initializing static class member
```

```
int String::num_strings = 0;

// class methods
String::String(const char * s)      // construct String from C string
{
    len = strlen(s);                // set size
    str = new char[len + 1];        // allot storage
    strcpy(str, s);                 // initialize pointer
    num_strings++;                  // set object count
    cout << num_strings << ": \"" << str
        << "\" object created\n";   // For Your Information
}

String::String()                    // default constructor
{
    len = 4;
    str = new char[4];
    strcpy(str, "C++");             // default string
    num_strings++;
    cout << num_strings << ": \"" << str
        << "\" default object created\n";   // FYI
}

String::~String()                           // necessary destructor
{
    cout << "\"" << str << "\" object deleted, ";      // FYI
    --num_strings;                  // required
    cout << num_strings << " left\n"; // FYI
    delete [] str;                  // required
}

ostream & operator<<(ostream & os, const String & st)
{
    os << st.str;
    return os;
}
```

First, notice the following statement from Listing 11.2:

```
int String::num_strings = 0;
```

This statement initializes the static num_strings member to zero. Note that you cannot initialize a static member variable inside the class declaration. That's because the declaration is a description of how memory is to be allocated, but it doesn't allocate memory. You allocate and initialize memory by creating an object using that format. In the case of a static class member, you initialize the static member independently with a separate statement outside the class declaration. That's because the static class member is stored separately rather than as part of an object. Note that the initialization statement gives the type and uses the scope operator:

```
int String::num_strings = 0;
```

This initialization goes in the methods file, not in the class declaration file. That's because the class declaration is in a header file, and a program may include a header file in several other files. That would result in multiple copies of the initialization statement, which is an error.

The exception (see Chapter 9) to the noninitialization of a static data member inside the class declaration is if the static data member is a const of integral or enumeration type.

Remember

A static data member is declared in the class declaration and is initialized in the file containing the class methods. The scope operator is used in the initialization to indicate to which class the static member belongs. However, if the static member is a constant of an integral or enumeration type, it can be initialized in the class declaration itself.

Next, notice that each constructor contains the expression num_strings++. This ensures that each time a program creates a new object, the shared variable num_strings increases by one, keeping track of the total number of String objects. Also, the destructor contains the expression --num_strings. Thus, the String class also keeps track of deleted objects, keeping the value of the num_strings member current.

STATIC CLASS MEMBER FUNCTIONS

It's also possible to declare a member function as being static. (The keyword static should appear in the function declaration but not in the function definition, if the latter is separate.) This has two important consequences. First, a static member function doesn't have to be invoked by an object; in fact, it doesn't even get a this pointer to play with. If the static member function is declared in the public section, it can be invoked using the class name and the scope resolution operator. For example, if the Person class had a static member function called SetMode(), it could be invoked like this:

```
Person::SetMode(1);   // invoking a static member function
```

Second, because a static member function is not associated with a particular object, the only data members it can use are the static data members. For example, a static member function can be used to set a class-wide flag that controls the format in which dates stored in objects of that class are displayed.

Now look at the first constructor, which initializes a String object with a regular C string:

```
String::String(const char * s)     // construct String from C string
{
    len = strlen(s);               // set size
    str = new char[len + 1];       // allot storage
    strcpy(str, s);                // initialize pointer
    num_strings++;                 // set object count
```

```
    cout << num_strings << ": \"" << str
        << "\" object created\n"; // For Your Information
}
```

The class `str` member, you recall, is just a pointer, so the constructor has to provide the memory for holding a string. You can pass a string pointer to the constructor when you initialize an object:

```
String boston("Boston");
```

The constructor then must allocate enough memory to hold the string, and then copy the string to that location. Let's go through the process step-by-step.

First, the function initializes the `len` member, using the `strlen()` function to compute the length of the string. Next, it uses `new` to allocate sufficient space to hold the string, and then assigns the address of the new memory to the `str` member. (Recall that `strlen()` returns the length of a string not counting the terminating null character, so the constructor adds 1 to `len` to allow space for the string including the null character.)

Next, the constructor uses `strcpy()` to copy the passed string into the new memory. Then it updates the object count. Finally, to help us monitor what's going on, the constructor displays the current number of objects and the string stored in the object. This feature will come in handy later, when we deliberately lead the `String` class into trouble.

Note that you do not do this:

```
str = s;  // not the way to go
```

This merely stores the address without making a copy of the string.

The default constructor behaves similarly, except that it provides a default string of `"C++"`.

The destructor contains the example's most important addition to our handling of classes:

```
String::~String()                    // necessary destructor
{
    cout << "\"" << str << "\" object deleted, ";    // FYI
    --num_strings;                   // required
    cout << num_strings << " left\n"; // FYI
    delete [] str;                   // required
}
```

The destructor begins by announcing when the destructor gets called. This part is informative, but not essential. The `delete` statement, however, is vital. Recall that the `str` member points to memory allocated with `new`. When a `String` object expires, the `str` pointer expires. But the memory `str` pointed to remains allocated unless you use `delete` to free it. Deleting an object frees the memory occupied by the object itself, but it does not automatically free memory pointed to by pointers that were object members. For that, you need to use the destructor. By placing the `delete` statement in the destructor, you ensure that the memory allocated with `new` by a constructor is freed when the object expires.

Remember

Whenever you use new in a constructor to allocate memory, you should use delete in the corresponding destructor to free that memory. If you use new [] (with brackets), then you should use delete [] (with brackets).

Listing 11.3, taken from a program under development at *The Daily Vegetable*, illustrates when and how the String constructors and destructor work. Remember to compile Listing 11.2 along with Listing 11.3.

Listing 11.3 vegnews.cpp

```cpp
// vegnews.cpp -- using new and delete with classes
// compile with strng1.cpp
#include <iostream>
using namespace std;
#include "strng1.h"

String sports("Spinach Leaves Bowl for Dollars");
                            // sports an external object
void callme1();             // creates local object
String * callme2();         // creates dynamic object

int main()
{
    cout << "Top of main()\n";
    String headlines[2] =   // local object array
    {
        String("Celery Stalks at Midnight"),
        String("Lettuce Prey")
    };
    cout << headlines[0] << "\n";
    cout << headlines[1] << "\n";
    callme1();
    cout << "Middle of main()\n";
    String *pr = callme2(); // set pointer to object
    cout << sports << "\n";
    cout << *pr << "\n";       // invoke class method
    delete pr;              // delete object
    cout << "End of main()\n";
    return 0;
}

void callme1()
{
    cout << "Top of callme1()\n";
    String grub;            // local object
    cout << grub << "\n";
    cout << "End of callme1()\n";
}

String * callme2()
{
    cout << "Top of callme2()\n";
    String *pveg = new String("Cabbage Heads Home");
            // dynamic object uses constructor
    cout << *pveg << "\n";
    cout << "End of callme2()\n";
    return pveg;            // pveg expires, object lives
}
```

This first draft of a design for `String` has some deliberate flaws, which, for many compilers, don't show up at this stage. However, the class flaws do affect some compilers, and they won't reproduce the following output. The subsequent section about revising the `String` class discusses and remedies the class problems. Also, some implementations may not call the final destructor until after terminating output, so its message may not be visible.

Here is the output:

```
1: "Spinach Leaves Bowl for Dollars" object created
Top of main()
2: "Celery Stalks at Midnight" object created
3: "Lettuce Prey" object created
Celery Stalks at Midnight
Lettuce Prey
Top of callme1()
4: "C++" default object created
C++
End of callme1()
"C++" object deleted, 3 left
Middle of main()
Top of callme2()
4: "Cabbage Heads Home" object created
Cabbage Heads Home
End of callme2()
Spinach Leaves Bowl for Dollars
Cabbage Heads Home
"Cabbage Heads Home" object deleted, 3 left
End of main()
"Lettuce Prey" object deleted, 2 left
"Celery Stalks at Midnight" object deleted, 1 left
"Spinach Leaves Bowl for Dollars" object deleted, 0 left
```

Program Notes

You should make sure you understand the sequence of events in this example program, so let's run through them now. The `sports` object is an external variable, so it's created before `main()` begins execution. The next objects created are the two elements of the headlines array. The program calls the constructor twice—once to initialize each array element. Each element is a class object, so the calls

```
cout << headlines[0] << "\n";
cout << headlines[1] << "\n";
```

evoke the friend method `operator<<()` for the two objects `headlines[0]` and `headlines[1]`.

Next, the program calls the `callme1()` function. This function uses the default constructor to create a local object called `grub`. The default constructor initializes the `str` member to `"C++"`. This object expires when the `callme1()` function finishes execution, as is shown by the following output lines:

```
Top of callme1()
4: "C++" default object created
```

```
C++
End of callme1()
"C++" object deleted, 3 left
```

In addition to printing its farewell message, the destructor also frees the memory that held the string `"C++"`.

Now we come to the thorniest part of the example. The program calls `callme2()`, and this function uses `new` to create and initialize a `String` object:

```
String *pveg = new String("Cabbage Heads Home");
```

The function assigns the address of this new object to the `pveg` pointer. Because the function provides `new` `String` with a string argument, the program calls the corresponding constructor to initialize the object. Figure 11.2 summarizes the statement.

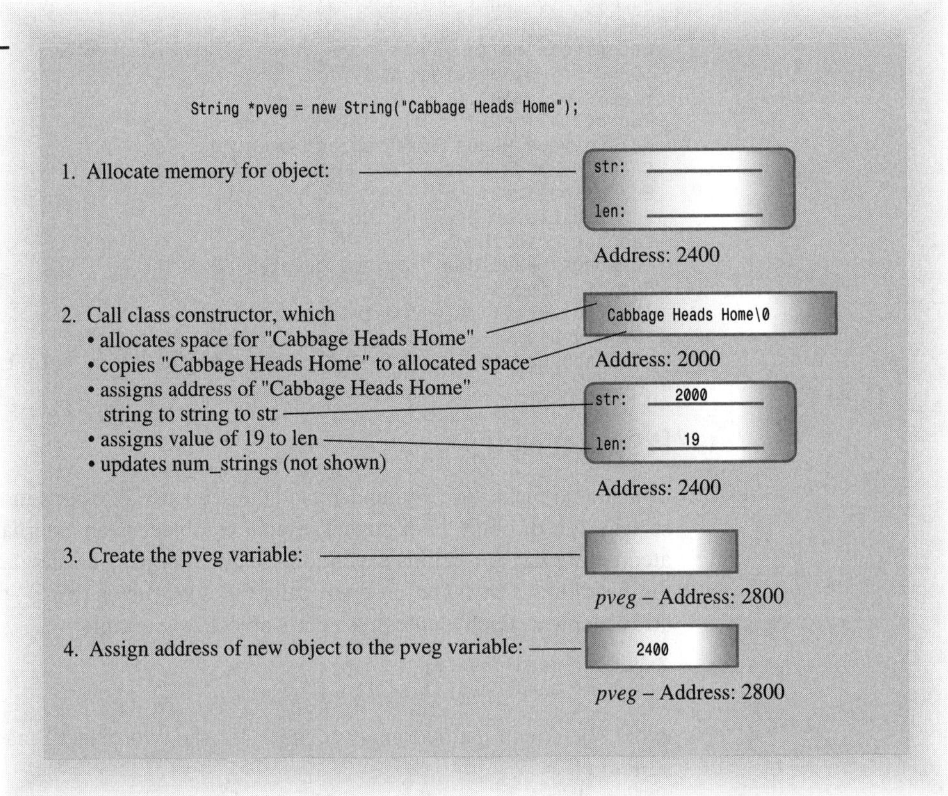

FIGURE 11.2

Creating an object with new

Note that because pveg is a pointer to an object, *pveg is an object. That means you can use *pveg in the same way that you use a declared object:

```
cout << *pveg << "\n";
```

This causes the function to display the "Cabbage Heads Home" string.

Then the function terminates, automatically freeing the memory used by its variables. This means the memory used to hold the pointer pveg is freed. But because callme2() doesn't use delete pveg, the memory holding the object to which pveg pointed is still allocated. Note that there is no destructor message when callme2() terminates; that shows the object still is present—the string "Cabbage Heads Home" lives on! But because pveg has expired, the program no longer can access that object with pveg. However, the program passes the value of pveg back to the calling program and assigns it to the pointer pr. In short, at first pveg pointed to the String object. Then pveg expired, but meanwhile the program set pr to point to the String object. Thus, the program now can use pr to access the dynamic object. And it does so after first displaying the sports object:

```
Top of callme2()
4: "Cabbage Heads Home" object created
Cabbage Heads Home              ← uses pveg pointer in callme2()
End of callme2()
Spinach Leaves Bowl for Dollars
Cabbage Heads Home              ← uses pr pointer in main()
```

Now the program moves to the sad tasks of deleting the remaining objects. Because it created the cabbage object with new, it can remove it with delete:

```
delete pr;
```

Recall that this frees the memory that pr points to and not pr itself. In short, this statement deleted the object. Deleting the object, in turn, activates the class destructor, which then deletes the memory occupied by the "Cabbage Heads Home" string:

```
"Cabbage Heads Home" object deleted, 3 left
```

Scoping rules control the existence of the remaining objects. The two array elements are automatic variables, so they expire when execution leaves the block in which they are defined. In this case, the block is the body of the main() function, so these two objects are freed when main() terminates. Last of all, the external object expires when the program terminates:

```
End of main()
"Celery Stalks at Midnight" object deleted, 2 left
"Lettuce Prey" object deleted, 1 left
"Spinach Leaves Bowl for Dollars" object deleted, 0 left
```

(As mentioned before, some compilers don't call constructors for external objects until after terminating output, so they wouldn't show the final line.)

Looking Again at `new` and `delete`

Note that the program uses `new` and `delete` on two levels. First, it uses `new` to allocate storage space for the name strings for each object that is created. This happens in the constructor functions, so the destructor function uses `delete` to free that memory. Because each string is an array of characters, the destructor uses `delete` with brackets. Thus, memory used to store the string contents is freed automatically when an object is destroyed. Second, the program uses `new` to allocate an entire object in the `callme2()` function. This allocates space not for the name string but for the object, that is, for the `str` pointer that holds the address of the string and for the `len` member. (It does not allocate space for the `num_strings` member because that is a static member stored separately from the objects.) Creating the object, in turn, calls the constructor, which allocates space for storing the string and assigns the string's address to `str`. The program then uses `delete` to delete this object when it is finished with it. The object is a single object, so the program uses `delete` without brackets. Again, this frees only the space used to hold the `str` pointer and the `len` member. It doesn't free the memory used to hold the string `str` points to, but the destructor takes care of that final task.

Let's emphasize again when destructors get called (see Figure 11.3).

FIGURE 11.3

When destructors are called

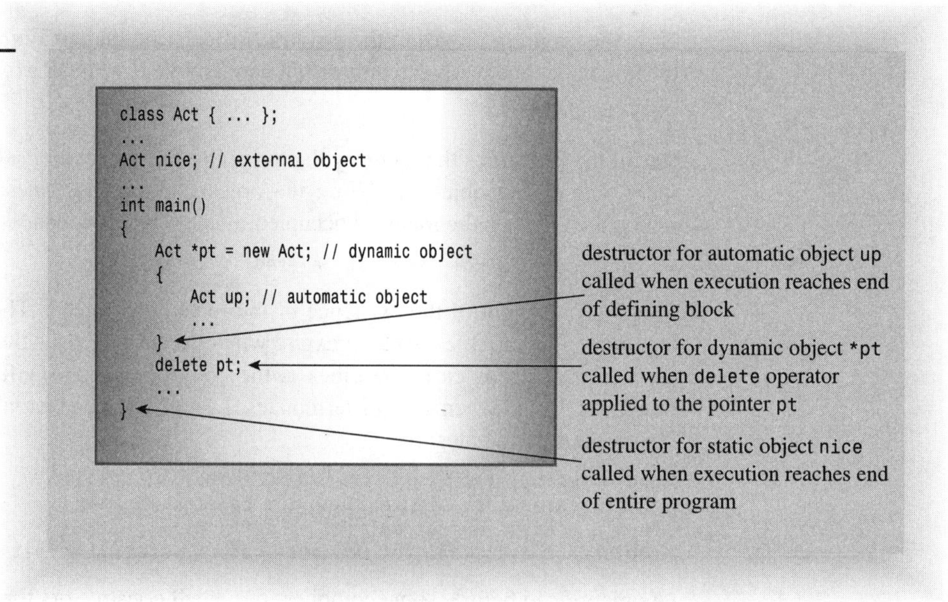

```
class Act { ... };
...
Act nice; // external object
...
int main()
{
    Act *pt = new Act; // dynamic object
    {
        Act up; // automatic object
        ...
    }
    delete pt;
    ...
}
```

destructor for automatic object up called when execution reaches end of defining block

destructor for dynamic object *pt called when `delete` operator applied to the pointer pt

destructor for static object nice called when execution reaches end of entire program

- If an object is an automatic variable, the object's destructor is called when the program exits the block in which the object is defined. Thus, the destructor is called for `headlines[0]` and `headlines[1]` when the program exits `main()`, and the destructor for `grub` is called when the program exits `callme1()`.

- If an object is a static variable (external, static, static external, or from a namespace), its destructor is called when the program terminates. This is what happened for the `sports` object.

- If an object is created by `new`, its destructor is called only when you explicitly `delete` the object, as is the case for the object created in `callme2()` and deleted in `main()`.

> *" If an object is created by new, its destructor is called only when you explicitly delete the object...."*

The way this example uses `new` to create an object in one function and deletes the object in another function is a potential problem source, for it relies upon the programmer to remember to delete the object. For instance, consider the following hideous variation:

```
String * ps;
for (int i = 0; i < 100; i++)
{
    ps = callme2();
    cout << *ps << "\n";
}
delete ps;
```

This code creates 100 distinct objects. Each loop cycle sets `ps` to point to the most recent object, losing track of the location of the preceding object. Finally, the code deletes only the last object created. The other 99 wind up occupying memory to which the program has no access. This sort of programming bumbling is called a *memory leak*. Properly designed destructors prevent internal memory leaks in an object once an object is destroyed, but you still have to explicitly delete objects you explicitly create by using `new`. In this case, the `delete` statement should have been placed inside the `for` loop.

Trouble in String City

This definition of a `String` class is incomplete. Of course, for brevity's sake, it fails to implement many useful methods, such as overloading the < , ==, and > operators to facilitate string comparisons. But the class flaws are more fundamental than that. As proof, consider this simple program (Listing 11.4), using the current `String` implementation.

Listing 11.4 problem1.cpp

```
// problem1.cpp -- uses a function with a String argument
// compile with strng1.cpp
#include <iostream>
using namespace std;
#include "strng1.h"
```

```
void showit(String s, int n);
int main()
{
    String motto("Home Sweet Home");
    showit(motto, 3);
    return 0;
}

void showit(String s, int n)     // show String s n times
{
    for (int i = 0; i < n; i++)
        cout << s << "\n";
}
```

Remember

Because this and the next two programs demonstrate a design flaw, the output will vary from compiler to compiler. The samples shown here are from Borland C++ 3.1.

The example passes a `String` object to the `showit()` function, which then displays the string the indicated number of times. Here is the output for one system:

```
1: "Home Sweet Home" object created
Home Sweet Home
Home Sweet Home
Home Sweet Home
"Home Sweet Home" object deleted, 0 left
"Home Sweet Home" object deleted, -1 left
Null pointer assignment
```

You'll note a couple of peculiar features. First, the program shows just one object being created but two objects being destroyed, leaving a total of -1 objects in memory. (Your implementation may also show gibberish instead of `"Home Sweet Home"` for the final output statement.) Then there is the cryptic message about a null pointer assignment. (Whether you get this message or some other message or no message at all depends upon your compiler, but regardless of the message, there is an underlying problem.)

Here's another simple program (Listing 11.5) that falters.

Listing 11.5 problem2.cpp

```cpp
// problem2.cpp -- initializes one string to another
// compile with strng1.cpp
#include <iostream>
using namespace std;
#include "strng1.h"

int main()
{
    String motto("Home Sweet Home");
    String ditto(motto);    // initialize ditto to motto

    cout << motto << "\n";
    cout << ditto << "\n";
    return 0;
}
```

It attempts to do something that the class declaration apparently doesn't handle: using one String object to initialize another. However, as the following output shows, it succeeds in doing so. The program also exhibits the same weird behavior that the preceding example did:

```
1: "Home Sweet Home" object created
Home Sweet Home
Home Sweet Home
"Home Sweet Home" object deleted, 0 left
"Home Sweet Home" object deleted, -1 left
Null pointer assignment
```

IMPLICIT MEMBER FUNCTIONS

What these two examples have in common is that they invoke implicit member functions that are defined automatically and whose behavior is inappropriate to this particular class design. In particular, C++ automatically provides the following member functions:

- A default constructor if you define no constructors

- A copy constructor if you don't define one

- An assignment operator if you don't define one

- A default destructor if you don't define one

- An address operator if you don't define one

The implicit address operator returns the address of the invoking object (that is, the value of the this pointer). That's fine for our purposes, and we won't discuss this member function further. The default destructor does nothing, and we won't discuss it, either. But the others do warrant more discussion.

The Default Constructor

If you fail to provide any constructors at all, C++ provides you with a default constructor. For instance, suppose you define a Klunk class and omit any constructors. Then the compiler will supply the following default:

```
Klunk::Klunk() { }  // implicit default constructor
```

That is, it supplies a constructor that takes no arguments and that does nothing. It's needed because creating an object always invokes a constructor:

```
Klunk lunk;  // invokes default constructor
```

The default constructor makes lunk like an ordinary automatic variable; that is, its value at initialization is unknown.

Once you define any constructor, C++ doesn't bother to define a default constructor. If you want to create objects that aren't initialized explicitly, or if you want to create an array of objects, you then have to define a default constructor explicitly. It's the constructor with no arguments, but you can use it to set particular values:

```
Klunk::Klunk()  // explicit default constructor
{
    klunk_ct = 0;
    ...
}
```

A constructor with arguments still can be a default constructor if all its arguments have default values. For instance, the Klunk class could have the following inline constructor:

```
Klunk(int n = 0) { klunk_ct = n; }
```

However, you can have only one default constructor. That is, you can't do this:

```
Klunk() { klunk_ct = 0 }
Klunk(int n = 0) { klunk_ct = n; }   // ambiguous
```

The Copy Constructor

The copy constructor is used to copy an object to a newly created object. That is, it's used during initialization, not during ordinary assignment. The copy constructor for a class has this prototype:

```
Class_name(const Class_name &);
```

Note that it takes a constant reference to a class object as its argument. For instance, the copy constructor for the String class would have this prototype:

```
String(const String &);
```

You need to know two things about the copy constructor: when it's used and what it does.

When the Copy Constructor Is Used   The copy constructor is invoked whenever a new object is created and initialized to an existing object of the same kind. This happens in several situations. The most obvious situation is when you explicitly initialize a new object to an existing object. For instance, given that motto is a String object, the following four defining declarations invoke the copy constructor:

```
String ditto(motto);                  // calls String(const String &)
String metoo = motto;                 // calls String(const String &)
String also = String(motto);          // calls String(const String &)
String * pstring = new String(motto); // calls String(const String &)
```

Depending upon the implementation, the middle two declarations may use the copy constructor directly to create metoo and also, or they may use the copy constructor to generate temporary objects whose contents are then assigned to metoo and also. The last example initializes an anonymous object to motto and assigns the address of the new object to the pstring pointer.

Less obviously, the compiler uses the copy constructor whenever a program generates copies of an object. In particular, it's used when a function passes an object by value or when it returns an object. Remember, passing by value means creating a copy of the original variable. The compiler also uses the copy constructor whenever it generates temporary objects. For instance, a compiler might generate a temporary `Vector` object to hold an intermediate result when adding three `Vector` objects. Compilers will vary as to when they generate temporary objects, but all will invoke the copy constructor when passing objects by value and when returning them. In particular, the function call in Listing 11.4 invoked the copy constructor:

```
showit(motto, 3);  // creates and passes copy of motto object
```

The program uses the copy constructor to initialize `st`, the formal `String`-type parameter for the `showit()` function.

By the way, the fact that passing an object by value involves invoking a copy constructor is a good reason for passing by reference instead. That saves the time of invoking the constructor and the space for storing the new object.

What the Copy Constructor Does The default copy constructor performs a member-by-member copy of the nonstatic members (memberwise copying). Each member is copied by value. In Listing 11.5, this amounts to the following:

```
ditto.str = motto.str;
ditto.len = motto.len;
```

If a member is itself a class object, the copy constructor for that class is used to copy one member object to another. Static members, such as `num_strings`, are unaffected, for they belong to the class as a whole instead of to individual objects. Figure 11.4 illustrates the action of the implicit copy constructor.

Where We Went Wrong

We are now in a position to understand the threefold weirdness of Listings 11.4 and 11.5. The first weirdness is that the program output showed one object constructed but two destroyed. The explanation is that each program did create two objects, with the second object being created by the copy constructor. The default copy constructor doesn't vocalize its activities, so it didn't announce its creations. This weirdness in communication is merely cosmetic in nature and doesn't affect the reliability of the program.

The second weirdness is that each program reported that –1 objects were left. The explanation for this is that the default constructor doesn't affect static members. Thus, the copy constructor didn't update the `num_strings` count. The destructor, however, does update the count, and it's invoked upon the demise of all objects, regardless of how they were constructed. This weirdness is a problem, for it means the program doesn't keep an accurate object count. The solution is to provide an explicit copy constructor that does update the count:

> " *[T]he fact that passing an object by value involves invoking a copy constructor is a good reason for passing by reference instead. That saves the time of invoking the constructor and the space for storing the new object.* "

FIGURE 11.4

Memberwise copying

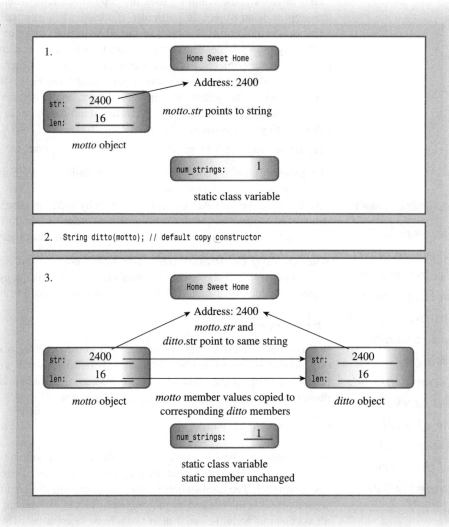

String ditto(motto); // default copy constructor

```
String::String(const String & s)
{
    num_strings++;
    .../ // important stuff to go here
}
```

Remember

If your class has a static data member whose value changes when new objects are created, provide an explicit copy constructor that handles the accounting.

The third weirdness is the most subtle and dangerous of the bunch. The symptom, for Borland 3.1, was the following message, which appeared after the program terminated:

```
Null pointer assignment
```

Microsoft Visual C++ 5.0 (debug mode) displayed an error message window saying that the Debug Assertion _CtrlsValidHeapPointer(pUserData) failed. Other systems might provide different messages or even no message, but the same evil lurks within the programs.

The cause is that the implicit copy constructor copies by value. Consider Listing 11.5, for example. The effect, recall, is this:

```
ditto.str = motto.str;
```

This does not copy the string; it copies the pointer to a string. That is, after ditto is initialized to motto, you wind up with two pointers to the same string. That's not a problem when the operator<<() function uses the pointer to display the string. It *is* a problem when the destructor is called. The String destructor, you recall, frees the memory pointed to by the str pointer. The effect of destroying ditto is this:

```
delete [] ditto.str;      // delete the string that ditto.str points to
```

This frees the memory occupied by the string "Home Sweet Home". Next, the effect of destroying motto is this:

```
delete [] motto.str;      // effect is undefined
```

Here, motto.str points to a memory location that has already been freed, and this results in undefined, possibly harmful, behavior. In our case, the program produced the null pointer warning, which usually is a sign of memory mismanagement.

The cure is to make a *deep copy*. That is, rather than just copying the address of the string, the copy constructor should duplicate the string and assign the address of the duplicate to the str member. That way, each object gets its own string rather than referring to another object's string. And each call of the destructor frees a different string rather than having duplicate attempts at freeing the same string. Here's how you can code the String copy constructor:

```
String::String(const String & st)
{
    num_strings++;              // handle static member update
    len = st.len;               // same length
    str = new char [len + 1];   // allot space
    strcpy(str, st.str);        // copy string to new location
    cout << num_strings << ": \"" << str
        << "\" object created\n"; // For Your Information
}
```

What makes defining the copy constructor necessary is the fact that some class members were new-initialized pointers to data rather than the data themselves. Figure 11.5 illustrates deep copying.

FIGURE 11.5

Deep copying

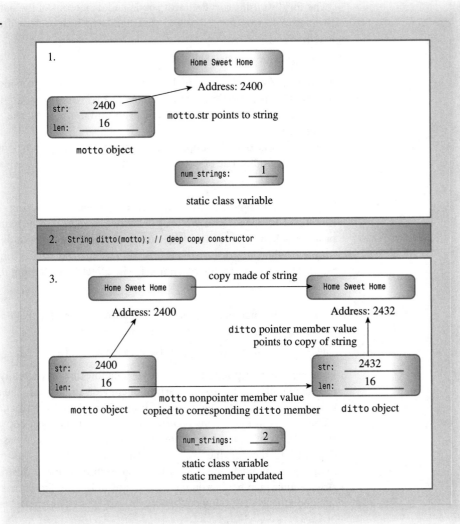

Remember

If a class contains members that are pointers initialized by new, then you should define a copy constructor that copies the pointed-to data instead of copying the pointers themselves. This is termed *deep copying*.

We'll test the new copy constructor soon, but first, let's look at yet another problem, one demonstrated by the short, but flawed, program of Listing 11.6. It assigns one object to another.

```
Listing 11.6 problem3.cpp
// problem3.cpp -- assigns one object to another
// compile with strng1.cpp
#include <iostream>
using namespace std;
#include "strng1.h"

int main()
{
    String motto("Home Sweet Home");
    String ditto;          // default constructor
    ditto = motto;         // object assignment
    cout << motto << "\n";
    cout << ditto << "\n";
    return 0;
}
```

Here's what happens when we run it (the exact consequences are compiler-dependent):

```
1: "Home Sweet Home" object created
2: "C++" object created
Home Sweet Home
Home Sweet Home
"Home Sweet Home" object deleted, 1 left
 Sweet Home" object deleted, 0 left
Null pointer assignment
```

Here at least the destructions balance the creations. However, one destruction seems to have messed up the string in the other object, because it reports a different string when it's destroyed. And once more the null pointer message disturbs our peace of mind. Again, the details of the output depend upon the compiler, but even if your output winds up looking correct, there still is a hidden, potentially dangerous problem.

The Assignment Operator

Just as ANSI C allows structure assignment, C++ allows class object assignment. It does so by automatically overloading the assignment operator for a class. It has the following prototype:

```
Class_name & Class_name::operator=(const Class_name &);
```

That is, it takes and returns a reference to an object of the class. For example, here's the prototype for the String class:

```
String & String::operator=(const String &);
```

When the Assignment Operator Is Used The overloaded assignment operator is used when you assign one object to another existing object:

```
string motto("Home Sweet Home");
string ditto;
ditto = motto;  // use overloaded assignment operator
```

It is not necessarily used when initializing an object:

```
string metoo = ditto; // use copy constructor
```

Here `metoo` is a newly created object being initialized to `ditto`'s values; hence the copy constructor is used. However, as mentioned before, implementations have the option of handling this statement in two steps: using the copy constructor to create a temporary object, and then using assignment to copy the values to the new object. That is, initialization always invokes the copy constructor, and forms using the = operator may also invoke the assignment operator.

What the Assignment Operator Does Like the copy constructor, the implicit implementation of the assignment operator performs a member-to-member copy. If a member is itself an object of some class, the program uses the assignment operator defined for that class to do the copying for that particular member. Static data members are unaffected.

Where We Went Wrong

Listing 11.6 showed two oddities. First, the second call to the destructor displayed a string that had been altered mysteriously. Second, upon terminating, the program generated a null pointer assignment message. Both are indications of memory mismanagement. The problem is the same one we saw for the copy constructor: member-by-member copying copies the values of pointers instead of the pointed-to data. Thus, when the destructor is called for `ditto`, it deletes the string `"Home Sweet Home"`; and when it's called for `motto`, it attempts to delete the previously deleted string. As mentioned earlier, the effect of attempting to delete previously deleted data is undefined. Also, the effect of deleting memory may change the memory contents. In Listings 11.4 and 11.5, the first `delete` actually left the string unchanged, because the second call to the destructor displayed the string correctly. In Listing 11.6, however, the initial deletion modified the string. As some like to point out, if the effect of a particular operation is undefined, your compiler can do anything it wants, including displaying the Declaration of Independence or freeing your hard disk of unsightly files.

Fixing Assignment

The solution for the problems created by an inappropriate default assignment operator is to provide your own assignment operator definition, one that makes a deep copy. The implementation is similar to that of the copy constructor, but there are some differences.

1. Because the target object may already refer to previously allocated data, the function should use `delete` to free former obligations.

2. The function should protect against assigning an object to itself; otherwise, the freeing of memory described above could erase the object's contents before they are reassigned.

3. The function returns a reference to the invoking object.

By returning an object, the function can emulate the way ordinary assignment for built-in types can be chained. That is, if A, B, and C are `String` objects, you can write the following:

```
A = B = C;
```

> *" The solution for the problems created by an inappropriate default assignment operator is to provide your own assignment operator definition, one that makes a deep copy. "*

In function notation, this becomes the following:

```
A.operator=(B.operator=(C));
```

Thus, the return value of `B.operator=(C)` becomes the argument of the `A.operator=()` function. Because the return value is a reference to a `String` object, it is the correct argument type.

Here's how you could write an assignment operator for the `String` class:

```
String & String::operator=(const String & st)
{
    if (this == &st)               // object assigned to itself
        return *this;              // all done
    delete [] str;                 // free old string
    len = st.len;
    str = new char [len + 1];      // get space for new string
    strcpy(str, st.str);           // copy the string
    return *this;                  // return reference to invoking object
}
```

First, the code checks for self-assignment. It does so by seeing if the address of the right-hand side of the assignment (`&s`) is the same as the address of the receiving object (`this`). If so, the program returns `*this` and terminates. You may recall from Chapter 10 that the assignment operator is one of the operators that can be overloaded only by a class member function.

Otherwise, the function proceeds to free the memory that `str` pointed to. The reason for this is that shortly thereafter `str` will be assigned the address of a new string. If you don't first apply the `delete` operator, the previous string would remain in memory. Because the program no longer has a pointer to the old string, that memory would be wasted.

Next, the program proceeds like the copy constructor, allocating enough space for the new string, then copying the string from the right-hand object to the new location.

Once finished, the program returns `*this` and terminates.

Assignment does not create a new object, so you don't have to adjust the value of the static data member `num_strings`.

THE NEW, IMPROVED `String` CLASS

Now that we are a bit wiser, let's revise the `String` class. First, we'll add the copy constructor and the assignment operator we just discussed so that the class correctly manages the memory used by class objects. Next, now that we've seen when objects are constructed and destroyed, we can mute the class constructors and destructors so that they no longer announce each time they are used. Also, now that we're no longer watching the constructors at work, let's simplify the default constructor so that it constructs an empty string instead of `"C++"`. And now that we've seen how a static data member works, we can remove the object-counting feature.

Next, let's add a few capabilities to the class. A useful `String` class would incorporate all the functionality of the standard `cstring` library of string functions, but we'll add only enough to show the way. (Keep in mind that this `String` class is an illustrative example and that the C++ standard string class is much more extensive.) In particular, we'll add the following methods:

```
int length () const { return len; }
friend bool operator>(const String &st1, const String &st2);
friend bool operator<(const String &st, const String &st2);
friend bool operator==(const String &st, const String &st2);
friend operator>>(istream & is, String & st);
```

The first new method returns the length of the stored string, and the next three allow you to compare strings. The `operator>()` function, for example, returns `true` if the first string comes after the second string alphabetically (or, more precisely, in the machine collating sequence). The simplest way to implement the string comparison functions is to use the standard `strcmp()` function, which returns a negative value if its first argument precedes the second alphabetically, zero if the strings are the same, and a positive value if the first follows the second alphabetically. So you can use `strcmp()` like this:

```
bool operator>(const String &st1, const String &st2)
{
    if (strcmp(st1.str, st2.str) > 0)
        return true;
    else
        return false;
}
```

Making the comparison functions friends facilitates comparisons between `String` objects and regular C strings. For instance, suppose `answer` is a `String` object and that you have the following code:

```
if ("love" == answer)
```

This gets translated to the following:

```
if (operator==("love", answer))
```

The compiler then uses one of the constructors to convert the code, in effect, to this:

```
if (operator==(String("love"), answer))
```

And this matches the prototype.

The new default constructor merits notice. It will look like this:

```
String::String()
{
    len = 0;
    str = new char[1];
    str[0] = '\0';                    // default string
}
```

You may wonder why the code does this:

```
str = new char[1];
```

and not this:

```
str = new char;
```

Both forms allocate the same amount of memory. The difference is that the first form is compatible with the class destructor and the second is not. The destructor, you recall, contains this code:

```
delete [] str;
```

Using `delete` with brackets is compatible with pointers initialized by using `new` with brackets and with the null pointer. Its effect is undefined for pointers initialized any other way.

Before looking at the new listings, let's consider another matter. Suppose you want to copy an ordinary string to a `String` object. For instance, suppose you use `getline()` to read a string and you want to place it in a `String` object. The class methods already allow you to do the following:

```
String name;
char temp[40];
cin.getline(temp, 40);
name = temp;  // use constructor to convert type
```

However, this may not be a satisfactory solution if you have to do it often. To see why, let's review how the final statement works:

1. The program uses the `String(const char *)` constructor to construct a temporary `String` object containing a copy of the string stored in `temp`. Remember (Chapter 10) that a constructor with a single argument serves as a conversion function.

2. The program uses the `String & String::operator=(const String &)` function to copy information from the temporary object to the name object.

3. The program calls the `~String()` destructor to delete the temporary object.

> " *The simplest way to make the process more efficient is to overload the assignment operator so that it works directly with ordinary strings.* "

The simplest way to make the process more efficient is to overload the assignment operator so that it works directly with ordinary strings. This removes the extra steps of creating and destroying a temporary object. Here's one possible implementation:

```
String & String::operator=(const char * s)
{
    delete [] str;
    len = strlen(s);
    str = new char[len + 1];
    strcpy(str, s);
    return *this;
}
```

As usual, you need to deallocate memory formerly managed by `str` and allocate enough memory for the new string.

Listing 11.7 shows the revised class declaration.

Listing 11.7 strng2.h

```
// strng2.h -- String class definition
#ifndef _STRNG2_H_
#define _STRNG2_H_
#include <iostream>
using namespace std;
```

```
class String
{
private:
    char * str;                     // pointer to string
    int len;                        // length of string
public:
    String(const char * s);         // constructor
    String();                       // default constructor
    String(const String & st);
    ~String();                      // destructor
    int length() const { return len; }
// overloaded operators
    String & operator=(const String & st); // Assignment operator
    String & operator=(const char * s);    // Assignment operator #2
// friend functions
    friend bool operator>(const String &st1, const String &st2);
    friend bool operator<(const String &st, const String &st2);
    friend bool operator==(const String &st, const String &st2);
    friend ostream & operator<<(ostream & os, const String & st);
    friend istream & operator>>(istream & is, String & st);
};
#endif
```

Remember

You may have a compiler that has not implemented **bool**. In that case, you can use **int** instead of **bool**, **0** instead of **false**, and **1** instead of **true**.

Next, Listing 11.8 presents the revised method definitions.

Listing 11.8 strng2.cpp

```
// strng2.cpp -- String class methods
#include <iostream>
#include <cstring>
using namespace std;
#include "strng2.h"

// class methods

String::String(const char * s)  // make String from C string
{
    len = strlen(s);
    str = new char[len + 1];    // allot storage
    strcpy(str, s);             // initialize pointer
}

String::String()                // default constructor
{
    len = 0;
    str = new char[1];
    str[0] = '\0';              // default string
}

String::String(const String & st)// copy constructor
{
    len = st.len;
    str = new char[len + 1];
    strcpy(str, st.str);
}
```

```
String::~String()              // destructor
{
    delete [] str;             // required
}

    // assign a String to a String
String & String::operator=(const String & st)
{
    if (this == &st)
        return *this;
    delete [] str;
    len = st.len;
    str = new char[len + 1];
    strcpy(str, st.str);
    return *this;
}

    // assign a C string to a String
String & String::operator=(const char * s)
{
    delete [] str;
    len = strlen(s);
    str = new char[len + 1];
    strcpy(str, s);
    return *this;
}

    // true if st1 follows st2 in collating sequence
bool operator>(const String &st1, const String &st2)
{
    if (strcmp(st1.str, st2.str) > 0)
        return true;
    else
        return false;
}

    // true if st1 precedes st2 in collating sequence
bool operator<(const String &st1, const String &st2)
{
    if (strcmp(st1.str, st2.str) < 0)
        return true;
    else
        return false;
}

// friends
    // true if st1 is the same as st2
bool operator==(const String &st1, const String &st2)
{
    if (strcmp(st1.str, st2.str) == 0)
        return true;
    else
        return false;
}

    // display string
ostream & operator<<(ostream & os, const String & st)
{
    os << st.str;
```

```
        return os;
}

    // quick and dirty String input
istream & operator>>(istream & is, String & st)
{
    char temp[80];
    is.get(temp, 80);
    if (is)
        st = temp;
    while (is && is.get() != '\n')
        continue;
    return is;
}
```

The overloaded >> operator provides a simple way to read a line of keyboard input into a String object. However, it's not foolproof, for it assumes an input line of 79 characters or fewer. Keep in mind that the value of an istream object in an if condition evaluates to false if input fails for some reason, such as encountering an end-of-file condition, or, in the case of get(char *, int), reading an empty line.

Let's exercise the class with a short program that lets you enter a few strings. The program has the user enter sayings, puts the strings into String objects, displays them, and reports which string is the shortest and which comes first alphabetically. Listing 11.9 shows the program.

Listing 11.9 sayings1.cpp

```cpp
// sayings1.cpp -- uses expanded string class
// compile with strng2.cpp
#include <iostream>
using namespace std;
#include "strng2.h"
const ArSize = 10;
const MaxLen =81;
int main()
{
    String name;
    cout <<"Hi, what's your name?\n>> ";
    cin >> name;

    cout << name << ", please enter up to " << ArSize
        << " short sayings <empty line to quit>:\n";
    String sayings[ArSize];     // array of objects
    char temp[MaxLen];          // temporary string storage
    int i;
    for (i = 0; i < ArSize; i++)
    {
        cout << i+1 << ": ";
        cin.get(temp, MaxLen);
        while (cin && cin.get() != '\n')
            continue;
        if (!cin || temp[0] == '\0')    // empty line?
            break;                      // i not incremented
        else
            sayings[i] = temp;  // overloaded assignment
    }
```

```
    int total = i;                 // total # of lines read

    cout << "Here are your sayings:\n";
    for (i = 0; i < total; i++)
        cout << sayings[i] << "\n";

    int shortest = 0;
    int first = 0;
    for (i = 1; i < total; i++)
    {
        if (sayings[i].length() < sayings[shortest].length())
            shortest = i;
        if (sayings[i] < sayings[first])
            first = i;
    }
    cout << "Shortest saying:\n" << sayings[shortest] << "\n";
    cout << "First alphabetically:\n" << sayings[first] << "\n";
    return 0;
}
```

Remember

Older versions of `get(char *, int)` don't evaluate to `false` upon reading an empty line. For those versions, however, the first character in the string will be a null if an empty line is entered. This example uses the following code:

```
if (!cin || temp[0] == '\0')     // empty line?
    break;                       // i not incremented
```

If the implementation follows the current standard, the first test in the `if` statement will detect an empty line, whereas the second test will detect the empty line for older implementations.

The program asks the user to enter up to ten sayings. Each saying is read into a temporary character array and then copied to a `String` object. If the user enters a blank line, a break statement terminates the input loop. After echoing the input, the program uses the `length()` and `operator<()` member functions to locate the shortest string and the alphabetically earliest string. Here's a sample run:

```
Hi, what's your name?
>> Misty Gutz
Misty Gutz, please enter up to 10 short sayings <empty line to quit>:
1: a fool and his money are soon parted
2: penny wise, pound foolish
3: the love of money is the root of much evil
4: out of sight, out of mind
5: absence makes the heart grow fonder
6: absinthe makes the hart grow fonder
7:
Here are your sayings:
a fool and his money are soon parted
penny wise, pound foolish
the love of money is the root of much evil
out of sight, out of mind
absence makes the heart grow fonder
absinthe makes the hart grow fonder
Shortest saying:
```

```
penny wise, pound foolish
First alphabetically:
a fool and his money are soon parted
```

WHEN USING new IN CONSTRUCTORS

By now you've noticed that you must take special care when using new to initialize pointer members of an object. In particular, you should do the following:

- If you use new to initialize a pointer member in a constructor, you should use delete in the destructor.

- The uses of new and delete should be compatible. Pair new with delete and new [ ] with delete [ ].

- If there are multiple constructors, all should use new the same way—either all with brackets or all without brackets. There's only one destructor, so all constructors have to be compatible to that destructor. It is, however, permissible to initialize a pointer with new in one constructor and with the null pointer (NULL or 0) in another constructor because it's okay to apply the delete operation (with or without brackets) to the null pointer.

NULL OR 0 ?

The null pointer can be represented by 0 or by NULL—a symbolic constant defined as 0 in several header files. C programmers often use NULL instead of 0 as a visual reminder that the value is pointer value, just as they use '\0' instead of 0 for the null character as a visual reminder that this value is a character. The C++ tradition, however, seems to favor using a simple 0 instead of the equivalent NULL.

- You should define a copy constructor that initializes one object to another by doing deep copying. Typically, the constructor would emulate the following example:

```
String::String(const String & st)
{
    num_strings++;             // handle static member update if
                               // necessary
    len = st.len;              // same length
    str = new char [len + 1];  // allot space
    strcpy(str, st.str);       // copy string to new location
}
```

" If you use new to initialize a pointer member in a constructor ... the copy constructor should allocate space to hold the copied data, and it should copy the data, not just the address of the data. "

🔹 In particular, the copy constructor should allocate space to hold the copied data, and it should copy the data, not just the address of the data. Also, it should update any static class members whose value would be affected by the process.

🔹 You should define an assignment operator that copies one object to another by doing deep copying. Typically, the class method would emulate the following example:

```
String & String::operator=(const String & st)
{
    if (this == &st)            // object assigned to itself
        return *this;           // all done
    delete [] str;              // free old string
    len = st.len;
    str = new char [len + 1];   // get space for new string
    strcpy(str, st.str);        // copy the string
    return *this;               // return reference to invoking object
}
```

🔹 In particular, the method should check for self-assignment; it should free memory formerly pointed to by the member pointer; it should copy the data, not just the address of the data; and it should return a reference to the invoking object.

The following excerpt contains two examples of what not to do and one example of a good constructor:

```
String::String()
{
   str = "default string";    // oops, no new []
   len = strlen(str);
}

String::String(const char * s)
{
   len = strlen(s);
   str = new char;            // oops, no []
   strcpy(str, s);            // oops, no room
}

String::String(const String & st)
{
   len = st.len;
   str = new char[len + 1];   // good, allocate space
   strcpy(str, st.str);       // good, copy value
}
```

The first constructor fails to use new to initialize str. The destructor, when called for a default object, will apply delete to str. The result of applying delete to a pointer not initialized by new is undefined, but probably bad. Any of the following would be okay:

```
String::String()
{
    len = 0;
    str = new char[1];  // uses new with []
    str[0] = '\0';
}

String::String()
{
    len = 0;
    str = NULL;  // or the equivalent str = 0;
}

String::String()
{
    static const char * s = "C++";     // initialized just once
    len = strlen(s);
    str = new char[len + 1];           // uses new with []
    strcpy(str, s);
}
```

The second constructor in the original excerpt applies new, but it fails to request the correct amount of memory; hence new will return a block containing space for but one character. Attempting to copy a longer string to that location is asking for memory problems. Also, the use of new without brackets is inconsistent with the correct form of the other constructors.

The third constructor is fine.

Finally, here's a destructor that *won't* work correctly with the previous constructors.

```
String::~String()
{
    delete str;     // oops, should be delete [] str;
}
```

The destructor uses delete incorrectly. Because the constructors request arrays of characters, the destructor should delete an array.

USING POINTERS TO OBJECTS

C++ programs often use pointers to objects, so let's get in a bit of practice. Listing 11.9 used array index values to keep track of the shortest string and of the first string alphabetically. Another approach is to use pointers to point to the current leaders in these categories. Listing 11.10 implements this approach, using two pointers to String. Initially, the shortest pointer points to the first object in the array. Each time the program finds an object with a shorter string, it resets shortest to point to that object. Similarly, a first pointer tracks the alphabetically earliest string. Note that these two pointers do not create new objects; they merely point to existing objects.

For variety, the program uses a pointer that does keep track of a new object:

```
String * favorite = new String(sayings[choice]);
```

Here the pointer favorite provides the only access to the nameless object created by new. This particular syntax means to initialize the new String object by using the object `sayings[choice]`. That invokes the copy constructor because the argument type for the copy constructor (`const String &`) matches the initialization value (`sayings[choice]`). The program uses `srand()`, `rand()`, and `time()` to select a value for choice at random.

OBJECT INITIALIZATION WITH new

In general, if *Class_name* is a class and if *value* is of type *Type_name*, the statement

```
Class_name * pclass = new Class_name(value);
```

invokes the

```
Class_name(Type_name);
```

constructor. There may be trivial conversions, such as to:

```
Class_name(const Type_name &);
```

Also, the usual conversions invoked by prototype matching, such as from `int` to `double`, will take place as long as there is no ambiguity. An initialization of the form

```
Class_name * ptr = new Class_name;
```

invokes the default constructor.

Listing 11.10 sayings2.cpp

```cpp
// sayings2.cpp -- uses pointers to objects
// compile with strng2.cpp
#include <iostream>
using namespace std;
#include <cstdlib>      // (or stdlib.h) for rand(), srand()
#include <ctime>        // (or time.h) for time()
#include "strng2.h"
const ArSize = 10;
const MaxLen = 81;
int main()
{
    String name;
    cout <<"Hi, what's your name?\n>> ";
    cin >> name;

    cout << name << ", please enter up to " << ArSize
        << " short sayings <empty line to quit>:\n";
    String sayings[ArSize];
    char temp[MaxLen];              // temporary string storage
    int i;
    for (i = 0; i < ArSize; i++)
    {
```

```
        cout << i+1 << ": ";
        cin.get(temp, MaxLen);
        while (cin && cin.get() != '\n')
            continue;
        if (!cin || temp[0] == '\0')  // empty line?
            break;                    // i not incremented
        else
            sayings[i] = temp;        // overloaded assignment
    }
    int total = i;                    // total # of lines read

    cout << "Here are your sayings:\n";
    for (i = 0; i < total; i++)
        cout << sayings[i] << "\n";

// use pointers to keep track of shortest, first strings
    String * shortest = &sayings[0]; // initialize to first object
    String * first = &sayings[0];
    for (i = 1; i < total; i++)
    {
        if (sayings[i].length() < shortest->length())
            shortest = &sayings[i];
        if (sayings[i] < *first)       // compare values
            first = &sayings[i];       // assign address
    }
    cout << "Shortest saying:\n" << * shortest << "\n";
    cout << "First alphabetically:\n" << * first << "\n";

    srand(time(0));
    int choice = rand() % total;      // pick index at random
// use new to create, initialize new String object
    String * favorite = new String(sayings[choice]);
    cout << "My favorite saying:\n" << *favorite << "\n";
    delete favorite;
    return 0;
}
```

Remember

Older implementations may require including `stdlib.h` instead of `cstdlib` and `time.h` instead of `ctime`.

Here's a sample run:

```
Hi, what's your name?
>> Kirt Rood
Kirt Rood, please enter up to 10 short sayings <empty line to quit>:
1: a friend in need is a friend indeed
2: neither a borrower nor a lender be
3: a stitch in time saves nine
4: a niche in time saves stine
5: it takes a crook to catch a crook
6: cold hands, warm heart
7:
Here are your sayings:
a friend in need is a friend indeed
neither a borrower nor a lender be
a stitch in time saves nine
a niche in time saves stine
```

```
it takes a crook to catch a crook
cold hands, warm heart
Shortest saying:
cold hands, warm heart
First alphabetically:
a friend in need is a friend indeed
My favorite saying:
a stitch in time saves nine
```

You should note several points about using pointers to objects (see Figure 11.6).

🖐 You declare a pointer to an object using the usual notation:

```
String * glamour;
```

FIGURE 11.6

Pointers and objects

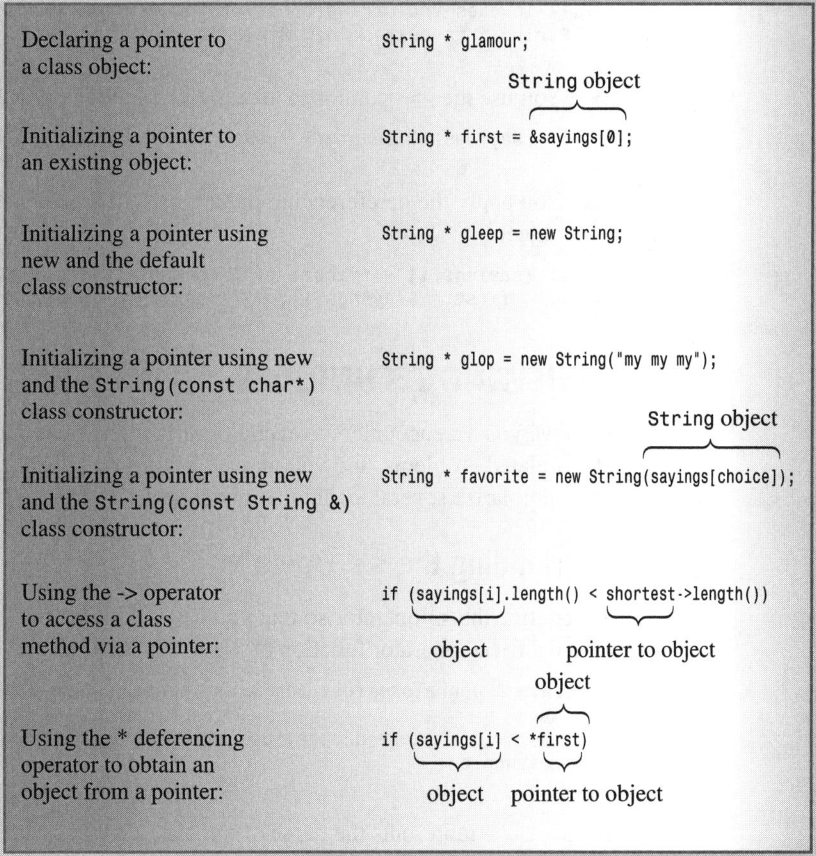

Declaring a pointer to a class object:	`String * glamour;`
Initializing a pointer to an existing object:	`String object` `String * first = &sayings[0];`
Initializing a pointer using new and the default class constructor:	`String * gleep = new String;`
Initializing a pointer using new and the String(const char*) class constructor:	`String * glop = new String("my my my");`
Initializing a pointer using new and the String(const String &) class constructor:	`String object` `String * favorite = new String(sayings[choice]);`
Using the -> operator to access a class method via a pointer:	`if (sayings[i].length() < shortest->length())` object pointer to object
Using the * dereferencing operator to obtain an object from a pointer:	object `if (sayings[i] < *first)` object pointer to object

Using new with a class invokes the appropriate class constructor to initialize the newly created object....

◈ You can initialize a pointer to point to an existing object:

```
String * first = &sayings[0];
```

◈ You can initialize a pointer using new; this creates a new object:

```
String * favorite = new String(sayings[choice]);
```

◈ Using new with a class invokes the appropriate class constructor to initialize the newly created object:

```
// invokes default constructor
String * gleep = new String;

// invokes the String(const char *) constructor
String * glop = new String("my my my");

// invokes the String(const String &) constructor
String * favorite = new String(sayings[choice]);
```

◈ You use the -> operator to access a class method via a pointer:

```
if (sayings[i].length() < shortest->length())
```

◈ You apply the dereferencing operator (*) to a pointer to an object to obtain an object:

```
if (sayings[i] < *first)     // compare object values
    first = &sayings[i];     // assign object address
```

REVIEWING TECHNIQUES

By now, you've encountered several programming techniques for dealing with various class-related problems, and you may be having trouble keeping track of all of them. So let's summarize several techniques and when they are used.

Overloading the << Operator

To redefine the << operator so that you use it with cout to display an object's contents, define a friend operator function of the following form:

```
ostream & operator<<(ostream & os, const c_name & obj)
{
    os << ... ;  // display object contents
    return os;
}
```

Here *c_name* represents the name of the class. If the class provides public methods that return the required contents, you can use those methods in the operator function and dispense with the friend status.

Conversion Functions

To convert a single value to a class type, create a class constructor of the following form of prototype:

```
c_name(type_name value);
```

Here *c_name* represents the class name, and *type_name* represents the name of the type that you want to convert.

To convert a class type to some other type, create a class member function having the following prototype:

```
operator type_name();
```

Although the function has no declared return type, it should return a value of the desired type.

Remember, use conversions functions with care. You can use the keyword explicit when declaring a constructor to prevent it from being used for implicit conversions.

Classes Whose Constructors Use new

Classes that use the new operator to allocate memory pointed to by a class member require several precautions in the design. (Yes, we summarized these precautions recently, but the rules are very important to remember, particularly because the compiler does not know them and, thus, won't catch your mistakes.)

1. Any class member pointing to memory allocated by new should have the delete operator applied to it in the class destructor. This frees the allocated memory.

2. If a destructor frees memory by applying delete to a pointer that is a class member, then every constructor for that class should initialize that pointer either by using new or by setting the pointer to the null pointer.

3. Constructors should settle on using either new [] or new, but not a mixture of both. The destructor should use delete [] if the constructors use new [], and it should use delete if the constructors use new.

4. You should define a copy constructor that allocates new memory rather than copying a pointer to existing memory. This enables a program to initialize one class object to another. The constructor normally should have the following form of prototype:

```
className(const className &)
```

5. You should define a class member function overloading the assignment operator and having the following form of function definition (here

c_pointer is a member of the *c_name* class and has the type pointer-to-*type_name*):

```
c_name & c_name::operator=(const c_name & cn)
{
    if (this == & cn_)
        return *this;      // done if self-assignment
    delete c_pointer;
    c_pointer = new type_name[size];
    // then copy data pointed to by cn.c_pointer to
    // location pointed to by c_pointer
    ...
    return *this;
}
```

A Queue Simulation

Let's apply our improved understanding of classes to a programming problem. The Bank of Heather wants to open an automatic teller in the Food Heap supermarket. The Food Heap management is concerned about lines at the automatic teller interfering with traffic flow in the market and may want to impose a limit on the number of people allowed to line up at the teller machine. The Bank of Heather people want estimates of how long customers will have to wait in line. Your task is to prepare a program to simulate the situation so that management can see what the effect of the automatic teller might be.

A rather natural way of representing the problem is to use a queue of customers. A *queue* is an abstract data type (ADT) that holds an ordered sequence of items. New items are added to the rear of the queue, and items can be removed from the front. A queue is a bit like a stack, except that a stack has additions and removals at the same end. This makes a stack a LIFO (last in-first out) structure, whereas the queue is a FIFO (first in-first out) structure. Conceptually, a queue is like a line at a checkout stand or automatic teller, so it's ideally suited to the task. So, one part of your project will be to define a Queue class.

The items in the queue will be customers. A Bank of Heather representative tells you that, on the average, a third of the customers will take one minute to be processed, a third will take two minutes, and a third will take three minutes. Furthermore, customers arrive at random intervals, but the average number of customers per hour is fairly constant. Two more parts of your project will be to design a class representing customers and to put together a program simulating the interactions between customers and the queue (see Figure 11.7).

FIGURE 11.7
A queue

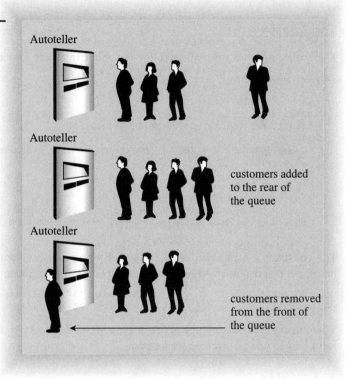

FIGURE 11.7
A queue

A QUEUE CLASS

The first order of business is designing a Queue class. First, let's list the attributes of the kind of queue we'll need:

- A queue holds an ordered sequence of items.

- A queue has a limit to the number of items it can hold.

- You should be able to create an empty queue.

- You should be able to check if a queue is empty.

- You should be able to check if a queue is full.

- You should be able to add an item to the end of a queue.

- You should be able to remove an item from the front of the queue.

- You should be able to determine the number of items in the queue.

As usual when designing a class, you'll need to develop a public interface and a private implementation.

The Interface

The queue attributes suggest the following public interface for a queue class:

```
class Queue
{
    enum {Q_SIZE = 10};
private:
// private representation to be developed later
public:
    Queue(int qs = Q_SIZE); // create queue with a qs limit
    ~Queue();
    bool isempty() const;
    bool isfull() const;
    int queuecount() const;
    bool enqueue(const Item &item); // add item to end
    bool dequeue(Item &item);       // remove item from front
};
```

The constructor creates an empty queue. By default, the queue can hold up to ten items, but that can be overridden with an explicit initialization argument:

```
Queue line1;            // queue with 10-item limit
Queue line2(20);        // queue with 20-item limit
```

When using the queue, you can use a `typedef` to define `Item`. (In Chapter 13, you'll learn how to use class templates instead.)

The Implementation

Next, let's implement the interface. First, you have to decide how to represent the queue data. One approach is to use new to dynamically allocate an array with the required number of elements. However, arrays aren't a good match to queue operations. For instance, removing an item from the front of the array should be followed up by shifting every remaining element one unit closer to the front. Or else you'll need to do something more elaborate, such as treating the array as circular. The *linked list*, however, is a good fit to the requirements of a queue. A linked list consists of a sequence of *nodes*. Each node contains the information to be held in the list plus a pointer to the next node in the list. For this queue, each data part will be a type `Item` value, and you can use a structure to represent a node:

```
struct Node
{
    Item item;              // data stored in the node
    struct Node * next;     // pointer to next node
};
```

Figure 11.8 illustrates a linked list. This particular form of linked list is called a *singly linked list* because each node has a single link, or pointer, to another node. If you have the address of the first node, you can follow the pointers to each subsequent node in the list. Commonly, the pointer in the last node in the list is set to NULL (or, equivalently, to 0) to indicate that there are no further nodes. To keep track of a linked list, you need to know the address of the first node. You can use a data member of the

FIGURE 11.8

A linked list

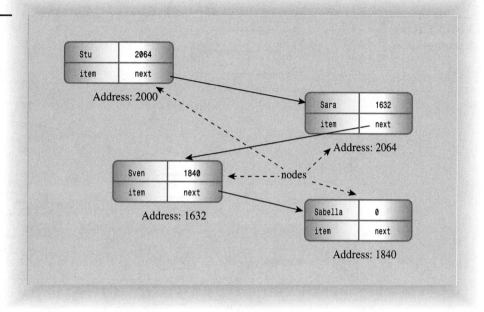

Queue class to point to the beginning of the list. In principle, that's all the information you need, for you can trace down the chain of nodes to find any other node. However, because a queue always adds a new item to the end of the queue, it will be convenient to have a data member pointing to the last node, too (see Figure 11.9). In addition, you can use data members to keep track of the maximum number of items allowed in the queue and of the current number of items. Thus, the private part of the class declaration can look like this:

```
class Queue
{
// class scope definitions
    // Node is a nested structure definition local to this class
    struct Node { Item item; struct Node * next;};
    enum {Q_SIZE = 10};
private:
    Node * front;          // pointer to front of Queue
    Node * rear;           // pointer to rear of Queue
    int items;             // current number of items in Queue
    const int qsize;       // maximum number of items in Queue
    ...
public:
//...
};
```

FIGURE 11.9
A Queue object

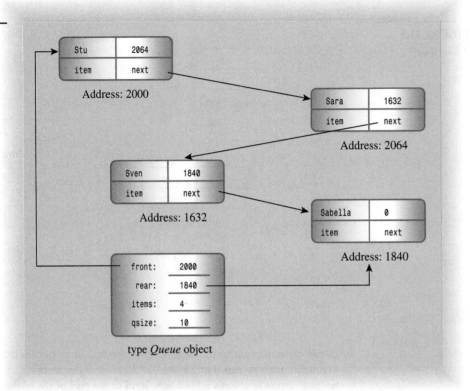

type *Queue* object

The declaration uses a new C++ feature: the ability to nest a structure or class declaration inside a class. By placing the Node declaration inside the Queue class, you give it class scope. That is, Node is a type that you can use to declare class members and as a type name in class methods, but the type is restricted to the class. That way, you don't have to worry about this declaration of Node conflicting with some global declaration or with a Node declared inside some other class. Not all compilers currently support nested structures and classes. If yours doesn't, then you'll have to define a Node structure globally, giving it file scope.

NESTED STRUCTURES AND CLASSES

A structure, class, or enumeration declared within a class declaration is said to be nested in the class. It has class scope. Such a declaration doesn't create a data object. Rather, it specifies a type that can be used internally within the class. If the declaration is made in the private section of the class, then the declared type can be used only within the class. If the declaration is made in the public section, then the declared type also can be used out of the class by using the scope resolution operator. For instance, if Node were declared in the public section of the Queue class, then you could declare variables of type Queue::Node outside the class.

Once you settle upon a data representation, the next step is to code the class methods.

The Class Methods

The class constructor should provide values for the class members. Because the queue begins in an empty state, you should set the front and rear pointers to NULL (or 0) and items to 0. Also, you should set the maximum queue size qsize to the constructor argument qs. Here's an implementation that does not work:

```
Queue::Queue(int qs)
{
    front = rear = NULL;
    items = 0;
    qsize = qs;    // not acceptable!
}
```

The problem is that qsize is a const, so it can be initialized to a value, but it can't be assigned a value. Conceptually, calling a constructor creates an object before the code within the brackets is executed. Thus, calling the Queue(int qs) constructor causes the program to first allocate space for the four member variables. Then program flow enters the brackets and uses ordinary assignment to place values into the allocated space. Therefore, if you want to initialize a const data member, you have to do so when the object is created, before execution reaches the body of the constructor. C++ provides a special syntax for doing just that. It's called an *initializer list*. The initializer list consists of a comma-separated list of initializers preceded by a colon. It's placed after the closing parenthesis of the argument list and before the opening bracket of the function body. If a data member is named mdata and if it's to be initialized to value val, the initializer has the form mdata(val). Using this notation, you can write the Queue constructor like this:

```
Queue::Queue(int qs) : qsize(qs)    // initialize qsize to qs
{
    front = rear = NULL;
    items = 0;
}
```

In general, the initial value can involve constants and arguments from the constructor's argument list. The technique is not limited to initializing constants; you also can write the Queue constructor like this:

```
Queue::Queue(int qs) : qsize(qs), front(NULL), rear(NULL), items(0)
{
}
```

> " *Therefore, if you want to initialize a const data member, you have to do so when the object is created, before execution reaches the body of the constructor. C++ provides a special syntax for doing just that. It's called an initializer list.* "

Only constructors can use this initializer-list syntax. As you've seen, you have to use this syntax for const class members. You also have to use it for class members that are declared as references:

```
class Agency {...};
class Agent
{
private:
    Agency & belong;      // must use initializer list to initialize
    ...
};
Agent::Agent(Agency & a) : belong(a) {...}
```

That's because references, like const data, can be initialized only when created. For simple data members, such as front and items, it doesn't make much difference whether you use an initializer list or use assignment in the function body. As you'll see in Chapter 13, however, it's more efficient to use the initializer list for members that are themselves class objects.

THE INITIALIZER LIST SYNTAX

If Classy is a class and if mem1, mem2, and mem3 are class data members, a class constructor can use the following syntax to initialize the data members:

```
Classy::Classy(int n, int m) :mem1(n), mem2(0), mem3(n*m + 2)
{
//...
}
```

This initializes mem1 to n, mem2 to 0, and mem3 to n*m + 2. Conceptually, these initializations take place when the object is created and before any code within the brackets is executed. Note the following:

◈ This form can be used only with constructors.

◈ You must use this form to initialize a nonstatic const data member.

◈ You must use this form to initialize a reference data member.

Data members get initialized in the order in which they appear in the class declaration, not in the order in which initializers are listed.

Remember

You can't use the initializer list syntax with class methods other than constructors.

Incidentally, the initialization form used in the initializer list can be used elsewhere. That is, if you like, you can replace code like

```
int games = 162;
double talk = 2.71828;
```

with

```
int games(162);
double talk(2.71828);
```

This lets initializing built-in types look like initializing class objects.

The code for isempty(), isfull(), and queuecount() is simple. If items is 0, the queue is empty. If items is qsize, the queue is full. Returning the value of items answers the question of how many items are in the queue. We'll show the code in a header file later.

Adding an item to the rear of the queue (enqueuing) is more involved. Here is one approach:

```
bool Queue::enqueue(const Item & item)
{
    if (isfull())
        return false;
    Node * add = new Node;   // create node
    if (add == NULL)
        return false;        // quit if none available
    add->item = item;        // set node pointers
    add->next = NULL;
    items++;
    if (front == NULL)       // if queue is empty,
        front = add;         // place item at front
    else
        rear->next = add;    // else place at rear
    rear = add;              // have rear point to new node
    return true;
}
```

In brief, the method goes through the following phases (see Figure 11.10):

1. Terminate if the queue is already full.

2. Create a new node, terminating if it can't do so—for example, if the request for more memory fails.

3. Place proper values into the node. In this case, the code copies an Item value into the data part of the node and sets the node's next pointer to NULL. This prepares the node to be the last item in the queue.

4. Increase the item count (items) by one.

5. Attach the node to the rear of the queue. There are two parts to this process. The first is linking the node to the other nodes in the list. This is done by having the next pointer of the currently rear node point to the new rear node. The second part is to set the Queue member pointer rear to point to the new node so that the queue can access the last node directly. If the queue is empty, you also need to set the front pointer to point to the new node. (If there's just one node, it's both the front and the rear node.)

FIGURE 11.10

Enqueuing an item

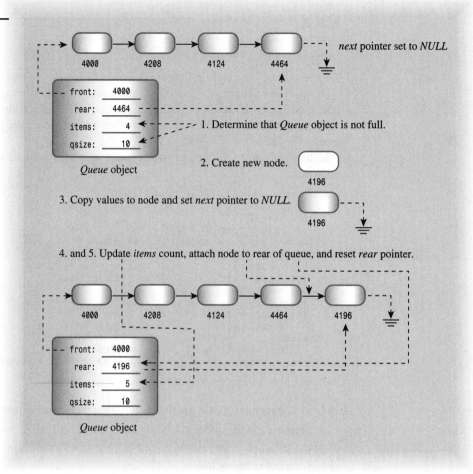

Removing an item from the front of the queue (dequeuing) also has several steps.

```
bool Queue::dequeue(Item & item)
{
    if (front == NULL)
        return false;
    item = front->item;     // set item to first item in queue
    items--;
    Node * temp = front;    // save location of first item
    front = front->next;    // reset front to next item
    delete temp;            // delete former first item
    if (items == 0)
        rear = NULL;
    return true;
}
```

In brief, the method goes through the following phases (see Figure 11.11):

FIGURE 11.11

Dequeuing an item

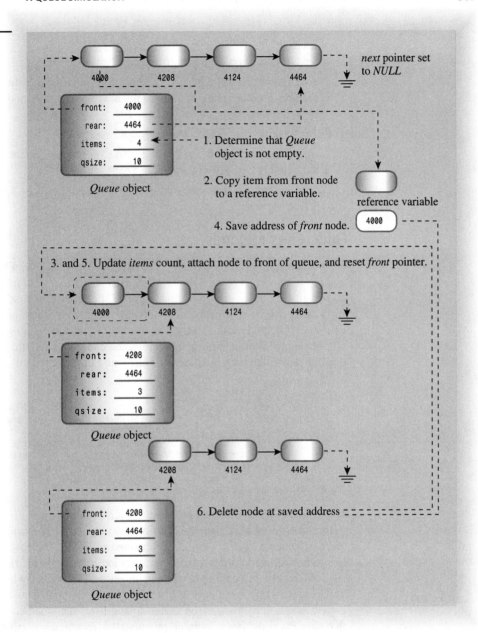

1. Terminate if the queue is already empty.

2. Provide the first item in the queue to the calling function. This is accomplished by copying the data portion of the current `front` node into the reference variable passed to the method.

3. Decrease the item count (items) by one.

4. Save the location of the front node for later deletion.

5. Take the node off the queue. This is accomplished by setting the Queue member pointer front to point to the next node, whose address is provided by front->next.

6. To conserve memory, delete the former first node.

7. If the list is now empty, set rear to NULL. (The front pointer already would be NULL in this case after being set to front->next.)

The reason step 4 is necessary is that step 5 erases the queue's memory of where the former first node is.

Other Class Methods?

Do you need any more methods? The class constructor doesn't use new, so, at first glance, it may appear you don't have to worry about the special requirements of classes that do use new in the constructors. Of course, that first glance is misleading, for adding objects to a queue does invoke new to create new nodes. It's true that the dequeue() method cleans up by deleting nodes, but there's no guarantee that a queue will be empty when it expires. Therefore, the class does require an explicit destructor, one that deletes all remaining nodes. Here's an implementation:

```
Queue::~Queue()
{
    Node * temp;
    while (front != NULL)    // while queue is not yet empty
    {
        temp = front;        // save address of front item
        front = front->next;// reset pointer to next item
        delete temp;         // delete former front
    }
}
```

It starts at the front of the list and deletes each node in turn.

Hmmm. You've seen that classes using new usually require explicit copy constructors and assignment operators that do deep copying. Is that the case here? The first question to answer is, does the default memberwise copying do the right thing? The answer is no. Memberwise copying of a Queue object would produce a new object that pointed to the front and rear of the same linked list as the original. Thus, adding an item to the copy Queue object changes the shared linked list. That's bad enough. What's worse is that only the copy's rear pointer gets updated, essentially corrupting the list from the standpoint of the original object. Clearly, then, cloning or copying queues requires providing a copy constructor and an assignment constructor that do deep copying.

Of course, that raises the question of why would you want to copy a queue? Well, perhaps you would want to save snapshots of a queue during different stages of a simulation. Or you would like to provide identical input to two different strategies. Actually, it might be useful to have operations that split a queue, the way supermarkets sometimes do when opening an additional checkout stand. Similarly, you might want to combine two queues into one or truncate a queue.

But we don't want to do any of these things in this simulation. Can't you simply ignore those concerns and use the methods you already have? Of course you can. However, at some time in the future, you may need to use a queue again, this time with copying. And you might forget that you failed to provide proper code for copying. Your programs will compile and run, but will generate puzzling results and crashes. So maybe you'd better provide a copy constructor and an assignment operator, even though you don't need them now.

Fortunately, there is a sneaky way to avoid doing this extra work while still protecting yourself from future program crashes. The idea is to define the required methods as dummy private methods:

> " *Fortunately, there is a sneaky way to avoid doing this extra work while still protecting yourself from future program crashes.* "

```
class Queue
{
private:
    Queue(const Queue & q) : qsize(0) { }   // preemptive definition
    Queue & operator=(const Queue & q) { return *this;}
//...
};
```

This has two effects. First, it overrides the default method definitions that otherwise would be generated automatically. Second, because these methods are private, they can't be used by the world at large. That is, if nip and tuck are Queue objects, the compiler won't allow the following:

```
Queue snick(nip);     // not allowed
tuck = nip;           // not allowed
```

Therefore, instead of being faced with mysterious runtime malfunctions in the future, you'll get an easier-to-trace compiler error stating that these methods aren't accessible. Also, this trick is useful when you define a class whose objects should not be copied.

Are there any other effects to note? Yes. Recall that the copy constructor is invoked when objects are passed (or returned) by value. However, this is no problem if you follow the preferred practice of passing objects as references. Also, the copy constructor is used to create other temporary objects. But the Queue definition lacks operations that lead to temporary objects, such as overloading the addition operator.

THE CUSTOMER CLASS

Next, you need to design a customer class. In general, a teller machine customer has many properties, such as a name, account numbers, and account balances. However, the only properties you need for the simulation are when a customer joins the queue and the time required for the customer's transaction. When the simulation produces a new customer, the program will create a new customer object, storing in it the customer's time of arrival and a randomly generated value for the transaction time. When the customer reaches the front of the queue, the program will note the time and subtract the queue-joining time to get the customer's waiting time. Here's how you can define and implement the Customer class:

```
class Customer
{
private:
    long arrive;        // arrival time for customer
    int processtime;    // processing time for customer
public:
    Customer() { arrive = processtime = 0; }
    void set(long when);
    long when() const { return arrive; }
    int ptime() const { return processtime; }
};
void Customer::set(long when)
{
    processtime = rand() % 3 + 1;
    arrive = when;
}
```

The default constructor creates a null customer. The set() member function sets the arrival time to its argument and randomly picks a value from 1 through 3 for the processing time.

Listing 11.11 gathers together the Queue and Customer class declarations, and Listing 11.12 provides the methods.

Listing 11.11 queue.h

```
// queue.h -- interface for a queue
#ifndef _QUEUE_H_
#define _QUEUE_H_
// This queue will contain Customer items
class Customer
{
private:
    long arrive;        // arrival time for customer
    int processtime;    // processing time for customer
public:
    Customer() { arrive = processtime = 0; }
    void set(long when);
    long when() const { return arrive; }
    int ptime() const { return processtime; }
};

typedef Customer Item;

class Queue
{
// class scope definitions
    // Node is a nested structure definition local to this class
    struct Node { Item item; struct Node * next;};
    enum {Q_SIZE = 10};
private:
    Node * front;       // pointer to front of Queue
    Node * rear;        // pointer to rear of Queue
    int items;          // current number of items in Queue
    const int qsize;    // maximum number of items in Queue
    // preemptive definitions to prevent public copying
    Queue(const Queue & q) : qsize(0) { }
    Queue & operator=(const Queue & q) { return *this;}
public:
```

```
        Queue(int qs = Q_SIZE); // create queue with a qs limit
        ~Queue();
        bool isempty() const;
        bool isfull() const;
        int queuecount() const;
        bool enqueue(const Item &item); // add item to end
        bool dequeue(Item &item);       // remove item from front
};
#endif
```

Listing 11.12 queue.cpp

```
// queue.cpp -- Queue and Customer methods
#include "queue.h"
#include <cstdlib>          // (or stdlib.h) for rand()

// Queue methods
Queue::Queue(int qs) : qsize(qs)
{
    front = rear = NULL;
    items = 0;
}

Queue::~Queue()
{
    Node * temp;
    while (front != NULL)   // while queue is not yet empty
    {
        temp = front;       // save address of front item
        front = front->next;// reset pointer to next item
        delete temp;        // delete former front
    }
}

bool Queue::isempty() const
{
    return items == 0;
}

bool Queue::isfull() const
{
    return items == qsize;
}

int Queue::queuecount() const
{
    return items;
}

// Add item to queue
bool Queue::enqueue(const Item & item)
{
    if (isfull())
        return false;
    Node * add = new Node;  // create node
    if (add == NULL)
        return false;       // quit if none available
    add->item = item;       // set node pointers
    add->next = NULL;
```

```
    items++;
    if (front == NULL)      // if queue is empty,
        front = add;        // place item at front
    else
        rear->next = add;   // else place at rear
    rear = add;             // have rear point to new node
    return true;
}

// Place front item into item variable and remove from queue
bool Queue::dequeue(Item & item)
{
    if (front == NULL)
        return false;
    item = front->item;     // set item to first item in queue
    items--;
    Node * temp = front;    // save location of first item
    front = front->next;    // reset front to next item
    delete temp;            // delete former first item
    if (items == 0)
        rear = NULL;
    return true;
}

// customer method

// when is the time at which the customer arrives
// the arrival time is set to when and the processing
// time set to a random value in the range 1 - 3
void Customer::set(long when)
{
    processtime = rand() % 3 + 1;
    arrive = when;
}
```

 Remember

You may have a compiler that has not implemented **bool**. In that case, you can use **int** instead of **bool**, **0** instead of **false**, and **1** instead of **true**. You may have to use **stdlib.h** instead of the newer **cstdlib**.

THE SIMULATION

We now have the tools needed for the automatic teller simulation. The program will allow the user to enter three quantities: the maximum queue size, the number of hours the program will simulate, and the average number of customers per hour. The program will use a loop in which each cycle represents one minute. During each minute cycle, the program will do the following:

1. Determine if a new customer has arrived. If so, add the customer to the queue if there is room; otherwise, turn the customer away.

2. If no one is being processed, take the first person from the queue. Determine how long the person has been waiting, and sct a wait_time counter to the processing time that the new customer will need.

3. If a customer is being processed, decrement the wait_time counter one minute.

4. Track various quantities, such as the number of customers served, customers turned away, cumulative time spent waiting in line, and cumulative queue length.

Once the simulation cycle is finished, the program will report various statistical findings.

An interesting matter is how the program determines if a new customer has arrived. Suppose, on the average, ten customers arrive an hour. That, on the average, amounts to a customer every six minutes. The program computes and stores that value in the variable min_per_cust. However, having a customer show up exactly every six minutes is unrealistic. What we really want (at least most of the time) is a more random process that averages to a customer every six minutes. The program uses this function to determine if a customer shows up during a cycle:

```
bool newcustomer(double x)
{
    return (rand() * x / RAND_MAX < 1);
}
```

Here's how it works. The value RAND_MAX is defined in the cstdlib file (formerly stdlib.h) and represents the largest value the rand() function can return (0 is the lowest value). Suppose that x, the average time between customers, is 6. Then the value of rand() * x / RAND_MAX will be somewhere between 0 and 6. In particular, it will be less than 1 a sixth of the time, on the average. However, it's possible that this function might yield two customers spaced one minute apart one time, or 20 minutes apart another time. This behavior leads to the clumpiness that often distinguishes real processes from the clocklike regularity of exactly one customer every six minutes. This particular method breaks down if the average time between arrivals drops below one minute, but the simulation is not intended to handle that scenario. If you did need to deal with such a case, you'd use a finer time resolution, perhaps letting each cycle represent ten seconds.

Remember

Some compilers don't define RAND_MAX. If you face that situation, you can define a value for RAND_MAX yourself by using #define or else a const int. If you can't find the correct value documented, try using the largest possible int value, given by INT_MAX in the climits or the limits.h header file.

Listing 11.13 presents the details of the simulation. Running the simulation for a long time period provides insight into long-term averages, and running it for short times provides insight into short-term variations.

Listing 11.13 bank.cpp

```
// bank.cpp -- use the Queue interface
#include <iostream>
using namespace std;
#include <cstdlib> // for rand() and srand()
#include <ctime>   // for time()
```

```cpp
#include "queue.h"
const int MIN_PER_HR = 60;

bool newcustomer(double x); // is there a new customer?

int main()
{
// setting things up
    srand(time(0));          //  random initializing of rand()

    cout << "Case Study: Bank of Heather Automatic Teller\n";
    cout << "Enter maximum size of queue: ";
    int qs;
    cin >> qs;
    Queue line(qs);          // line queue holds up to qs people

    cout << "Enter the number of simulation hours: ";
    int hours;               //  hours of simulation
    cin >> hours;
    // simulation will run 1 cycle per minute
    long cyclelimit = MIN_PER_HR * hours; // # of cycles

    cout << "Enter the average number of customers per hour: ";
    double perhour;          //  average # of arrival per hour
    cin >> perhour;
    double min_per_cust;     //  average time between arrivals
    min_per_cust = MIN_PER_HR / perhour;

    Item temp;               //  new customer data
    long turnaways = 0;      //  turned away by full queue
    long customers = 0;      //  joined the queue
    long served = 0;         //  served during the simulation
    long sum_line = 0;       //  cumulative line length
    int wait_time = 0;       //  time until autoteller is free
    long line_wait = 0;      //  cumulative time in line


// running the simulation
    for (int cycle = 0; cycle < cyclelimit; cycle++)
    {
        if (newcustomer(min_per_cust))  // have newcomer
        {
            if (line.isfull())
                turnaways++;
            else
            {
                customers++;
                temp.set(cycle);     // cycle = time of arrival
                line.enqueue(temp); // add newcomer to line
            }
        }
        if (wait_time <= 0 && !line.isempty())
        {
            line.dequeue (temp);        // attend next customer
            wait_time = temp.ptime(); // for wait_time minutes
            line_wait += cycle - temp.when();
            served++;
        }
        if (wait_time > 0)
```

```
                wait_time--;
            sum_line += line.queuecount();
        }

//  reporting results
        if (customers > 0)
        {
            cout << "customers accepted: " << customers << '\n';
            cout << "   customers served: " << served << '\n';
            cout << "              turnaways: " << turnaways << '\n';
            cout << "average queue size: ";
            cout.precision(2);
            cout.setf(ios_base::fixed, ios_base::floatfield);
            cout.setf(ios_base::showpoint);
            cout << (double) sum_line / cyclelimit << '\n';
            cout << " average wait time: "
                  << (double) line_wait / served << " minutes\n";
        }
        else
            cout << "No customers!\n";

        return 0;
}

//  x = average time, in minutes, between customers
//  return value is true if customer shows up this minute
bool newcustomer(double x)
{
        return (rand() * x / RAND_MAX < 1);
}
```

Remember

You may have a compiler that has not implemented `bool`. In that case, you can use `int` instead of `bool`, `0` instead of `false`, and `1` instead of `true`. You may have to use `stdlib.h` and `time.h` instead of the newer `cstdlib` and `ctime`. You may have to define `RAND_MAX` yourself.

Here are a few sample runs for a longer time period:

```
Case Study: Bank of Heather Automatic Teller
Enter maximum size of queue: 10
Enter the number of simulation hours: 100
Enter the average number of customers per hour: 15
customers accepted: 1485
  customers served: 1485
         turnaways: 0
average queue size: 0.15
 average wait time: 0.63 minutes

Case Study: Bank of Heather Automatic Teller
Enter maximum size of queue: 10
Enter the number of simulation hours: 100
Enter the average number of customers per hour: 30
customers accepted: 2896
  customers served: 2888
         turnaways: 101
average queue size: 4.64
 average wait time: 9.63 minutes
```

```
Case Study: Bank of Heather Automatic Teller
Enter maximum size of queue: 20
Enter the number of simulation hours: 100
Enter the average number of customers per hour: 30
customers accepted: 2943
  customers served: 2943
         turnaways: 93
average queue size: 13.06
 average wait time: 26.63 minutes
```

" [G]oing from 15 customers an hour to 30 customers an hour doesn't double the average wait time—it increases it by about a factor of 15. "

Note that going from 15 customers an hour to 30 customers an hour doesn't double the average wait time—it increases it by about a factor of 15. Allowing a longer queue just makes matters worse. However, the simulation doesn't allow for the fact that many customers, frustrated with a long wait, would simply leave the queue.

Here are a few more sample runs. These illustrate the short-term variations one might see, even though the average number of customers per hour is kept constant.

```
Case Study: Bank of Heather Automatic Teller
Enter maximum size of queue: 10
Enter the number of simulation hours: 4
Enter the average number of customers per hour: 30
customers accepted: 114
  customers served: 110
         turnaways: 0
average queue size: 2.15
 average wait time: 4.52 minutes

Case Study: Bank of Heather Automatic Teller
Enter maximum size of queue: 10
Enter the number of simulation hours: 4
Enter the average number of customers per hour: 30
customers accepted: 121
  customers served: 116
         turnaways: 5
average queue size: 5.28
 average wait time: 10.72 minutes

Case Study: Bank of Heather Automatic Teller
Enter maximum size of queue: 10
Enter the number of simulation hours: 4
Enter the average number of customers per hour: 30
customers accepted: 112
  customers served: 109
         turnaways: 0
average queue size: 2.41
 average wait time: 5.16 minutes
```

Summary

This chapter covers many important aspects of defining and using classes. Several of these aspects are subtle, even difficult, concepts. If some of them seem obscure or unusually complex to you, don't feel bad—they affect most newcomers to C++ that way. Often, the way you come to really appreciate concepts like copy constructors is through getting into trouble by ignoring them. So some of the material in this chapter may seem vague to you until your own experiences enrich your understanding. Meanwhile, let's summarize the chapter.

You can use `new` in a class constructor to allocate memory for data and then assign the address of the memory to a class member. This enables a class, for example, to handle strings of various sizes without committing the class design in advance to a fixed array size. Using `new` in class constructors also raises potential problems when an object expires. If an object has member pointers pointing to memory allocated by `new`, freeing the memory used to hold the object does not automatically free the memory pointed to by the object member pointers. Therefore, if you use `new` in a class constructor to allocate memory, you should use `delete` in the class destructor to free that memory. That way, the demise of an object automatically triggers the deletion of pointed-to memory.

Objects having members pointing to memory allocated by `new` also have problems with initializing one object to another or assigning one object to another. By default, C++ uses memberwise initialization and assignment, which means that the initialized or the assigned-to object winds up with exact copies of the original object's members. If an original member points to a block of data, the copy member points to the same block. When the program eventually deletes the two objects, the class destructor will attempt to delete the same block of memory twice, which is an error. The solution is to define a special copy constructor that redefines initialization and to overload the assignment operator. In each case, the new definition should create duplicates of any pointed-to data and have the new object point to the copies. That way, both the old and the new object refer to separate, but identical, data with no overlap. The same reasoning applies to defining an assignment operator. In each case, the goal is making a deep copy, that is, copying the real data and not just pointers to them.

C++ allows you to place structure, class, and enumeration definitions inside a class. Such nested types have class scope, meaning that they are local to the class and don't conflict with structures, classes, and enumerations of the same name defined elsewhere.

C++ provides a special syntax for class constructors that can be used to initialize data members. This syntax consists of a colon followed by a comma-separated list of initializers. This is placed after the closing parenthesis of the constructor arguments and before the opening brace of the function body. Each initializer consists of the name of the member being initialized followed by parentheses containing the initialization value. Conceptually, these initializations take place when the object is created and before any statements in the function body are executed. The syntax looks like this:

```
queue(int qs) : qsize(qs), items(0), front(NULL), rear(NULL) { }
```

This form is obligatory if the data member is a nonstatic const member or a reference.

As you may have noticed, classes require much more care and attention to detail than do simple C-style structures. In return, they do much more for you.

Review Questions

1. Suppose a `String` class has the following private members:

```
class String
{
private:
    char * str;     // points to string allocated by new
    int len;        // holds length of string
//...
};
```

a. What's wrong with this default constructor?

```
String::String() {}
```

b. What's wrong with this constructor?

```
String::String(const char * s)

{
    str = s;
    len = strlen(s);
}
```

c. What's wrong with this constructor?

```
String::String(const char * s)
{
    strcpy(str, s);
    len = strlen(s);
}
```

2. Name three problems that may arise if you define a class in which a pointer member is initialized using `new` and indicate how they can be remedied.

3. What class methods does the compiler generate automatically if you don't provide them explicitly? Describe how these implicitly generated functions behave.

4. Identify and correct errors in the following class declaration:

```
class nifty
{
// data
    char personality[];
    int talents;
// methods
    nifty();
    nifty(char * s);
    ostream & operator<<(ostream & os, nifty & n);
}

nifty:nifty()
{
    personality = NULL;
    talents = 0;
}
```

```
nifty:nifty(char * s)
{
    personality = new char [strlen(s)];
    personality = s;
    talents = 0;
}

ostream & nifty:operator<<(ostream & os, nifty & n)
{
    os << n;
}
```

5. Consider the following class declaration:

```
class Golfer
{
private:
    char * fullname;        // points to string containing golfer's
name
    int games;              // holds number of golf games played
    int * scores;           // points to first element of array of golf
scores
public:
    Golfer();
    Golfer(const char * name, int g= 0);
     // creates empty dynamic array of g elements if g > 0
    Golfer(const Golfer & g);
    ~Golfer();
};
```

    a. What class methods would be invoked by each of the following statements?

```
Golfer nancy;                           // #1
Golfer lulu("Little Lulu");             // #2
Golfer roy("Roy Hobbs", 12);            // #3
Golfer * par = new Golfer;              // #4
Golfer next = lulu;                     // #5
Golfer hazzard = "Weed Thwacker";       // #6
*par = nancy;                           // #7
nancy = "Nancy Putter";                 // #8
```

    b. Clearly, the class requires several more methods to make it useful, but what additional method does it require to protect against data corruption?

Programming Exercises

1. Consider the following class declaration:

```
class Cow {
    char name[20];
    char * hobby;
    double weight;
public:
    Cow();
    Cow(const char * nm, const char * ho, double wt);
```

```
    Cow(const Cow c&);
    ~Cow();
    Cow operator=(const Cow & c);
    void ShowCow();  // display name, hobby, and weight of a cow
};
```

Provide the implementation for this class and write a short program that uses all the member functions.

2. Enhance the `String` class declaration (that is, upgrade `strng2.h` to `string3.h`) by doing the following:

a. Overload the + operator to allow you to join two strings into one.

b. Provide a `stringlow()` member function that converts all alphabetic characters in a string to lowercase. (Don't forget the `cctype` family of character functions.)

c. Provide a `stringup()` member function that converts all alphabetic characters in a string to uppercase.

d. Provide a member function that takes a char argument and returns the number of times that character appears in the string.

Test your work in the following program:

```
// pe11_1.cpp
#include <iostream>
using namespace std;
#include "strng3.h"
int main()
{
    String s1(" and I am a C++ student.");
    String s2 = "Please enter your name: ";
    String s3;
    cout << s2;                 // overloaded << operator
    cin >> s3;                  // overloaded >> operator
    s2 = "My name is " + s3;    // overloaded =, + operators
    cout << s2 << ".\n";
    s2 = s2 + s1;
    s2.stringup();              // converts string to uppercase
    cout << "The string\n" << s2 << "\ncontains " << s2.has('A')
            << " 'A' characters in it.\n";
    s1 = "red";        // String(const char *), then String &
operator=(const String&)
    String rgb[3] = { String(s1), String("green"), String("blue")};
    cout << "Enter the name of a primary color for mixing light: ";
    String ans;
    bool success = false;
    while (cin >> ans)
    {
        ans.stringlow();        // converts string to lowercase
        for (int i = 0; i < 3; i++)
        {
            if (ans == rgb[i])  // overloaded == operator
            {
                cout << "That's right!\n";
                success = true;
                break;
```

```
            }
        }
        if (success)
            break;
        else
            cout << "Try again!\n";
    }
    cout << "Bye\n";
    return 0;
}
```

Your output should look like this sample run:

```
Please enter your name: Fretta Farbo
My name is Fretta Farbo.
The string
MY NAME IS FRETTA FARBO AND I AM A C++ STUDENT.
contains 6 'A' characters in it.
Enter the name of a primary color for mixing light: yellow
Try again!
BLUE
That's right!
Bye
```

3. Rewrite the Stock class, as described in Listings 9.7 and 9.8, so that it uses dynamically allocated memory instead of fixed arrays to hold the stock names. Also, replace the show() member function with an overloaded operator<<() definition. Test the new definition program in Listing 9.9.

4. Consider the following variation of the Stack class defined in Listing 9.10.

```
// stack.h -- class declaration for the stack ADT
typedef unsigned long Item;

class Stack
{
private:
    enum {MAX = 10};        // constant specific to class
    Item  * pitems;         // holds stack items
    int size;               // number of elements in stack
    int top;                // index for top stack item
public:
    Stack(int n = 10);      // creates stack with n elements
    Stack(const Stack & st);
    ~Stack();
    bool isempty() const;
    bool isfull() const;
    // push() returns False if stack already is full, True otherwise
    bool push(const Item & item); // add item to stack
    // pop() returns False if stack already is empty, True otherwise
    bool pop(Item & item);  // pop top into item
    Stack operator=(const Stack & st);
};
```

As the private members suggest, this class uses a dynamically allocated array to hold the stack items. Rewrite the methods to fit this new representation, and write a program that demonstrates all the methods, including the copy constructor and assignment operator.

5. The Bank of Heather has performed a study showing that autoteller customers won't wait more than one minute in line. Using the simulation of Listing 11.13, find a value for number of customers per hour that leads to an average wait time of one minute. (Use at least a 100-hour trial period.)

6. The Bank of Heather would like to know what would happen if it added a second automatic teller. Modify the simulation so that it has two queues. Assume a customer will join the first queue if it has fewer people in it than the second queue and that he will join the second queue otherwise. Again, find a value for number of customers per hour that leads to an average wait time of one minute. (Note: This is a nonlinear problem in that doubling the number of machines doesn't double the number of customers that can be handled per hour with a one-minute wait maximum.)

12

Class
Inheritance

One of the main goals of object-oriented programming is providing reusable code. When you develop a new project, particularly if the project is large, it's nice to be able to reuse proven code rather than to reinvent it. Employing old code saves time and, because it has already been used and tested, can help suppress the introduction of bugs into a program. Also, the less you have to concern yourself with details, the better you can concentrate upon overall program strategy.

Traditional C function libraries provide reusability through predefined, precompiled functions, such as `strlen()` and `rand()`, that you can use in your programs. Many vendors furnish specialized C libraries providing functions beyond those of the standard C library. For example, you can purchase libraries of database management functions and of screen control functions. However, function libraries have a limitation. Unless the vendor supplies the source code for its library functions (and often it doesn't), you can't extend or modify the functions to meet your particular needs. Instead, you have to shape your program to meet the workings of the library. Even if the vendor does supply the source code, you run the risk of unintentionally modifying how part of a function works or of altering the relationships among library functions as you add your changes.

C++ classes bring you a higher level of reusability. Many vendors now offer class libraries, which consist of class declarations and implementations. Because a class combines data representation with class methods, it provides a more integrated package than does a function library. A single class, for example, may provide all the resources for managing a dialog box. Often, class libraries are available in source code, meaning that you can modify them to meet your needs. But C++ has a better method than code modification for extending and modifying classes. This method,

533

called *class inheritance*, lets you derive new classes from old ones, with the derived class inheriting the properties, including the methods, of the old class, called a base class. Just as inheriting a fortune is usually easier than earning one from scratch, deriving a class through inheritance is usually easier than designing a new one. Here are some things you can do with inheritance:

- You can add functionality to an existing class. For instance, given a basic array class, you could add arithmetic operations.

- You can add to the data that a class represents. For instance, given a basic string class, you could derive a class that adds a data member representing a color to be used when displaying the string.

- You can modify how a class method behaves. For instance, given a Passenger class that represents the services provided to an airline passenger, you can derive an Upgrade class that provides a higher level of services.

Of course, you could accomplish the same aims by duplicating the original class code and modifying it, but the inheritance mechanism allows you to proceed by just providing the new features. You don't even need access to the source code to derive a class. Thus, if you purchase a class library that provides only the header files and the compiled code for class methods, you still can derive new classes based upon the library classes. Conversely, you can distribute your own classes to others, keeping parts of your implementation secret, yet still giving your clients the option of adding features to your classes.

Inheritance is a splendid concept, and its basic implementation is quite simple. But managing inheritance so that it works properly in all situations requires some adjustments. This chapter looks at both the simple and the subtle aspects of inheritance.

You will learn about the following in this chapter:

- Inheritance as an *is-a* relationship

- How to publicly derive one class from another

- Protected access

- Constructor initialization lists

- Upcasting and downcasting

- Virtual member functions

- Early (static) binding and late (dynamic) binding

- Pure virtual functions

- When and how to use public inheritance

Beginning with a Simple Base Class

When one class inherits from another, the original class is called a *base class* and the inheriting class is called a *derived class*. So, to illustrate inheritance, we need to begin with a base class. Fortunately, the Pontoon National Bank needs a class to represent its basic checking plan, the Brass Account. Listing 12.1 shows a header for a streamlined BankAccount class meeting this need. It has data members representing a client's name, account number, and balance. It has methods for creating an account, making deposits, making withdrawals, and displaying account data. The class falls short of representing a real bank account, but it has enough features to satisfy the imaginary Pontoon National Bank and to begin our study of inheritance.

Listing 12.1 bankacct.h

```cpp
// bankacct.h--a simple BankAccount class
#ifndef _BANKACCT_H_
#define _BANKACCT_H_

class BankAccount
{
private:
    enum {MAX = 35};
    char fullName[MAX];
    long acctNum;
    double balance;
public:
    BankAccount(const char *s = "Nullbody", long an = -1,
                double bal = 0.0);
    void Deposit(double amt);
    void Withdraw(double amt);
    double Balance() const;
    void ViewAcct() const;
};
#endif
```

The class uses the technique of creating a class scope constant with enum. Next come the class methods, as shown in Listing 12.2.

Listing 12.2 bankacct.cpp

```cpp
// bankacct.cpp--methods for BankAccount class
#include <iostream>
using namespace std;
#include "bankacct.h"
#include <cstring>

BankAccount::BankAccount(const char *s, long an, double bal)
{
    strncpy(fullName, s, MAX - 1);
    fullName[MAX - 1] = '\0';
```

```
        acctNum = an;
        balance = bal;
}

void BankAccount::Deposit(double amt)
{
    balance += amt;
}

void BankAccount::Withdraw(double amt)
{
    if (amt <= balance)
        balance -= amt;
    else
        cout << "Withdrawal amount of $" << amt
             << " exceeds your balance.\n"
             << "Withdrawal canceled.\n";
}

double BankAccount::Balance() const
{
    return balance;
}

void BankAccount::ViewAcct() const
{
    // set up ###.## format
    ios_base::fmtflags initialState =
        cout.setf(ios_base::fixed, ios_base::floatfield);
    cout.setf(ios_base::showpoint);
    cout.precision(2);
    cout << "Client: " << fullName << endl;
    cout << "Account Number: " << acctNum << endl;
    cout << "Balance: $" << balance << endl;
    cout.setf(initialState); // restore original format
}
```

Remember

Use **string.h** if your compiler doesn't support **cstring**. If your compiler doesn't support **ios_base**, use **ios** instead. In that case, use **long** instead of **ios_base::fmtflago** as the type for **initialState**.

There a couple of things to note about the implementation. First, the Withdraw() method checks that the balance is large enough to cover the withdrawal. If not, the withdrawal is not allowed. This is an example of an interface offering protection that would be missing if direct access to data members were allowed.

Second, the ViewAcct() method uses formatting commands to display money in a $2356.32 format. Earlier examples have used similar settings (which Chapter 16 discusses in more detail), but this goes further by saving the original formatting information:

```
ios_base::fmtflags initialState =
    cout.setf(ios_base::fixed, ios_base::floatfield);
```

Here `ios_base::fmtflags` is a type defined in the `ios_base` class. (Libraries that use the older `ios` class use type `long` instead.) This call to the `setf()` method sets output to the fixed decimal point format and returns the format flag setting that existed prior to the call. This allows the function to restore the original settings when it finishes:

```
cout.setf(initialState); // restore original format
```

Next, Listing 12.3 presents a short program illustrating the class's short list of features.

Listing 12.3 usebank.cpp

```
// usebank.cpp
// compile with bankacct.cpp
#include <iostream>
using namespace std;
#include <cstring>
#include "bankacct.h"

int main()
{
    BankAccount Porky("Porcelot Pigg", 381299, 4000.00);

    Porky.ViewAcct();
    Porky.Deposit(5000.00);
    cout << "New balance: $" << Porky.Balance() << endl;
    Porky.Withdraw(8000.00);
    cout << "New balance: $" << Porky.Balance() << endl;
    Porky.Withdraw(1200.00);
    cout << "New balance: $" << Porky.Balance() << endl;

    return 0;
}
```

Remember

Use `string.h` if your compiler doesn't support `cstring`.

Here is the program's output:

```
Client: Porcelot Pigg
Account Number: 381299
Balance: $4000.00
New balance: $9000.00
New balance: $1000.00
Withdrawal amount of $1200.00 exceeds your balance.
Withdrawal canceled.
New balance: $1000.00
```

Inheritance—An *Is-A* Relationship

" Anything you do with a base-class object, you should be able to do with a derived-class object. "

Now that BankAccount has joined the ranks of the working class, you can derive a new class from it. Before doing so, however, let's examine the underlying model for C++ inheritance. Actually, C++ has three varieties of inheritance: public, protected, and private. Public inheritance is the most common form, and it models an *is-a* relationship. This is shorthand for saying that an object of a derived class should also be an object of the base class. Anything you do with a base-class object, you should be able to do with a derived-class object. Suppose, for instance, you have a Fruit class. It could store, say, the weight and caloric content of a fruit. Because a banana is a particular kind of fruit, you could derive a Banana class from the Fruit class. The new class would inherit all the data members of the original class, so a Banana object would have members representing the weight and caloric content of a banana. The new Banana class also might add members that apply particularly to bananas and not to fruit in general, such as the Banana Institute Peel Index. Because the derived class can add features, it's probably more accurate to describe the relationship as an *is-a-kind-of* relationship, but *is-a* is the usual term.

To clarify the *is-a* relationship, let's look at some examples that don't match that model. Public inheritance doesn't model a *has-a* relationship. A lunch, for instance, might contain a fruit. But a lunch, in general, is not a fruit. Therefore, you should not derive a Lunch class from the Fruit class in an attempt to place fruit in a lunch. The correct way to handle putting fruit into a lunch is to consider the matter as a *has-a* relationship: a lunch has a fruit. As you'll see in Chapter 13, that's most easily modeled by including a Fruit object as a data member of a Lunch class (see Figure 12.1).

Public inheritance doesn't model an *is-like-a* relationship, that is, it doesn't do similes. It's often pointed out that lawyers are like sharks. But it is not literally true that a lawyer is a shark. For instance, sharks can live underwater. Therefore, you shouldn't derive a Lawyer class from a Shark class. Inheritance can add properties to a base class; it doesn't remove properties from a base class. In some cases, shared characteristics can be handled by designing a class encompassing those characteristics and then using that class, either in an *is-a* or *has-a* relationship, to define the related classes.

Public inheritance doesn't model an *is-implemented-as-a* relationship. For instance, you could implement a stack using an array. However, it wouldn't be proper to derive a Stack class from an Array class. A stack is not an array. For example, array indexing is not a stack property. Also, a stack could be implemented in some other way, such as by using a linked list. A proper approach would be to hide the array implementation by giving the stack a private Array object member.

FIGURE 12.1

Is-a *and* has-a *relationships*

Public inheritance doesn't model a *uses-a* relationship. For example, a computer can use a laser printer, but it doesn't make sense to derive a `Printer` class from a `Computer` class or vice versa. One might, however, devise friend functions or classes to handle communication between `Printer` objects and `Computer` objects.

Nothing in the C++ language prevents you from using public inheritance to model *has-a*, *is-implemented-as-a*, or *uses-a* relationships. However, doing so usually leads to programming problems. So let's stick to the *is-a* relationships. Fortunately, again, it turns out that the Pontoon National Bank also offers the Brass Plus checking account.

This account has all the features of the regular Brass account, plus it offers overdraft protection. That is, if you write a check larger (but not too much larger) than your balance, the bank will cover the check, charging you for the excess payment and adding a penalty. You'd like to use the BankAccount class, but it doesn't support the new feature. What you can do is define a new class that inherits all the properties of the BankAccount class and that additionally has the new functionality needed. By basing the new class on BankAccount instead of starting from scratch, you take advantage of the work that already has gone into developing BankAccount , and you take advantage of the fact that BankAccount has already been tested. In other words, you reuse proven code. The net result is less work and, perhaps, a better product.

Does the new class (call it Overdraft) meet the *is-a* test? Sure. Everything that is true of an BankAccount object will be true for an Overdraft object. That is, you can make deposits and withdrawals and display account information. Note that the *is-a* relationship is not, in general, reversible. A fruit, in general, is not a banana. An BankAccount object won't have all the capabilities of an Overdraft object.

DECLARING A DERIVED CLASS

A derived class has to identify the class from which it is derived. The C++ way is to include the base class name in the derived class declaration. If you derive an Overdraft class from the BankAccount class, you would begin the class declaration like this:

```
class Overdraft : public BankAccount
{
```

The colon indicates the Overdraft class is based upon the BankAccount class. This particular heading indicates that BankAccount is a public base class; this is termed *public derivation*. An object of a derived class incorporates a base-class object. With public derivation, the public members of the base class become public members of the derived class. The private portions of a base class become part of the derived class, but they can be accessed only through public and protected methods of the base class. (We'll get to protected members in a bit.)

For instance, the Deposit() function becomes a public function of the Overdraft class, too. The balance member of BankAccount becomes part of an Overdraft object, but it can be accessed only through BankAccount methods, such as Deposit() and the BankAccount constructors. In short, the Overdraft class inherits public members from the base class along with access to them. You don't have to redefine them for the new class. A derived class contains the private members of a base class, but can't access them except by using the public and protected base-class methods (see Figure 12.2).

FIGURE 12.2

*Base-class and
derived-class objects*

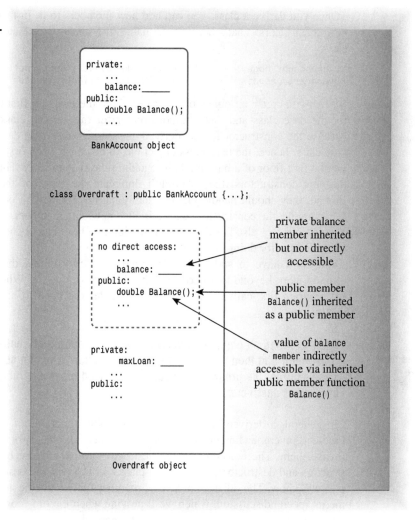

C++ also supports protected derivations and private derivations:

```
class Computer : protected HardDisk
{...};
class House : private Study
{...};
```

We'll discuss these forms in Chapter 13. The main point to know now is that if you omit the access keyword, C++ makes the derivation private:

```
class House : Study  // same as private Study
{...};
```

Once you derive a class, you can add new members to it. In fact, you must provide new constructors. That's because the name of a constructor matches the name of the class:

```
BankAccount bogey;      // needs BankAccount() constructor
Overdraft orson;        // needs Overdraft() constructor
```

When you create an object of a derived class, the program first calls the constructor for the base class and then the constructor for the derived class. This makes sense because the constructor for the derived class may build upon data members from the base class; hence, the base-class object has to be constructed first. It's a bit like building the first floor of a building before adding the second story. Thus, when you define the new constructors, they shouldn't duplicate the work of the base constructors. Instead, they should handle just the additional details that the derived class requires. For example, the constructor could initialize new data members. In general, a derived-class constructor also has to pass information to a base-class constructor; we'll look at the technique for doing so shortly.

You don't have to add a new destructor explicitly unless the new class requires cleanup work beyond that performed by the base destructor. When an object expires, the program first calls the destructor for the derived class, if any, and then the base destructor.

Remember

When creating an object of a derived class, a program first calls the base-class constructor and then the derived-class constructor. When an object of a derived class expires, the program first calls the derived-class destructor and then the base-class destructor.

In general, a derived class inherits the member functions of the base class. If the base-class member functions are public or protected, objects of the derived class can invoke them. The constructors and destructor are exceptions, but derived-class constructors and destructors can use base-class constructors and destructors, as the examples will show. The other noninherited member function is the assignment operator. It merits special discussion, which we'll provide when the time comes. Note that friends are not member functions, so they are not inherited.

You know how to start the declaration of a derived class:

```
class Overdraft : public BankAccount
{
```

Before completing the declaration, however, you need to know precisely what features the Brass Plus account adds. A discussion with the friendly Pontoon National Bank representative reveals the following features:

- A Brass Plus account limits how much money the bank will lend you to cover overdrafts. The default value is $500, but some customers may start with a different limit.

- The bank may change a customer's overdraft limit.

A Brass Plus account charges interest on the loan. The default value is 10%, but some customers may start with a different rate.

The bank may change a customer's interest rate.

The account keeps track of how much the customer owes the bank (overdraft loans plus interest). The user cannot pay off this amount by a regular deposit or by a transfer from another account. Instead, he must pay in cash to a special bank officer, who will, if necessary, seek out the customer. Once the debt is paid, the account can reset the amount owed to 0.

The last feature is an unusual way for a bank to do business, but it has the fortunate side effect of keeping the programming problem simpler.

This list suggests the new class needs data members to hold a maximum debt value, an interest rate, and the current debt. It needs constructors that provide account information and that include a debt limit with a default value of $500 and an interest rate with a default value of 10%. Also, there should be methods for resetting the debt limit, interest rate, and current debt. These are all things to be added to the BankAccount class, and they will be declared in the Overdraft class declaration.

Also, there are BankAccount methods whose behavior should change. In particular, the Withdraw() method and ViewAcct() method need to do more than they did before. Public inheritance allows a derived class to redefine base-class methods, so the Overdraft class declaration will have to redefine the Withdraw() and ViewAcct() methods.

The Deposit() method, however, works the same for both classes. A derived class uses the base-class method unless it is redefined, so to retain use of the base-class Deposit() method, the Overdraft class declaration needs to do nothing. The same holds for the Balance() method.

Listing 12.4 shows a class declaration guided by these points. Note that you don't have to do a thing to the base class to derive a class. All the derivation takes place in defining the new class and its methods. Thus you can derive a class even if you don't have access to the source code for the base class.

" [Y]ou don't have to do a thing to the base class to derive a class. All the derivation takes place in defining the new class and its methods. "

Listing 12.4 overdrft.h

```
// overdrft.h  -- Overdraft class declaration
#ifndef _OVERDRFT_H_
#define _OVERDRFT_H_
#include "bankacct.h"

class Overdraft : public BankAccount
{
private:
    double maxLoan;
    double rate;
    double owesBank;
public:
    Overdraft(const char *s = "Nullbody", long an = -1,
            double bal = 0.0, double ml = 500,
            double r = 0.10);
```

```
    Overdraft(const BankAccount & ba, double ml = 500, double r = 0.1);
    void ViewAcct()const;
    void Withdraw(double amt);
    void ResetMax(double m) { maxLoan = m; }
    void ResetRate(double r) { rate = r; };
    void ResetOwes() { owesBank = 0; }
};

#endif
```

IMPLEMENTING THE DERIVED CLASS

Let's examine how to implement the derived class and look at the rationale for some of the methods, beginning with the constructors. First, let's think about the construction process. The program can't construct an Overdraft object until it first constructs a BankAccount object. So the base constructor has to be called before the program enters the code for the derived constructor. On the other hand, the base constructor can't be called until after the derived constructor is called because calling the derived constructor is what tells the program it needs the base constructor. Consider the following Overdraft constructor:

```
Overdraft(const char *s = "Nullbody", long an = -1,
        double bal = 0.0, double ml = 500,
        double r = 0.10);
```

It has five arguments, three of which provide values for the BankAccount part and two of which provide values for the Overdraft part. It is simple enough to use the final two arguments:

```
// incomplete version
Overdraft::Overdraft(const char *s, long an, double bal, double ml,
                     double r)
{
    maxLoan = ml;
    owesBank = 0.0; // start out debt-free
    rate = r;
}
```

But what about the BankAccount component? First, consider what would happen if you used this incomplete version of the constructor. The base-class object is constructed before the derived component is added. In terms of syntax of this constructor, that means a base-class object is created before program execution reaches the statements in the constructor body. Because no constructor is mentioned explicitly, this means the default BankAccount constructor is used to create the base-class component. Let's rephrase that: Unless instructed to do otherwise, a derived-class constructor calls the default base constructor before entering the body of the derived-class constructor.

In this case, however, the default constructor is the wrong one because it uses the default values instead of the desired values. C++ offers a special syntax that lets you specify which constructor should be used. It's a variation on the initialization-list syntax you saw in Chapter 11, except that you use a class name instead of a member name:

```
Overdraft::Overdraft(const char *s, long an, double bal, double ml,
                     double r) : BankAccount(s, an, bal)
{
    maxLoan = ml;
    owesBank = 0.0;
    rate = r;
}
```

Here the

```
: BankAccount(s, an, bal)
```

part means, "Call the `BankAccount(const char *, double, double)` constructor to construct the base-class portion of the `Overdraft` object." Using this mechanism, the values of the first three arguments to the `Overdraft` constructor are passed on to the `BankAccount` constructor. So the `BankAccount` constructor sets the inherited members, and the body of the `Overdraft` constructor sets the new members (see Figure 12.3).

FIGURE 12.3

Passing arguments through to a base-class constructor

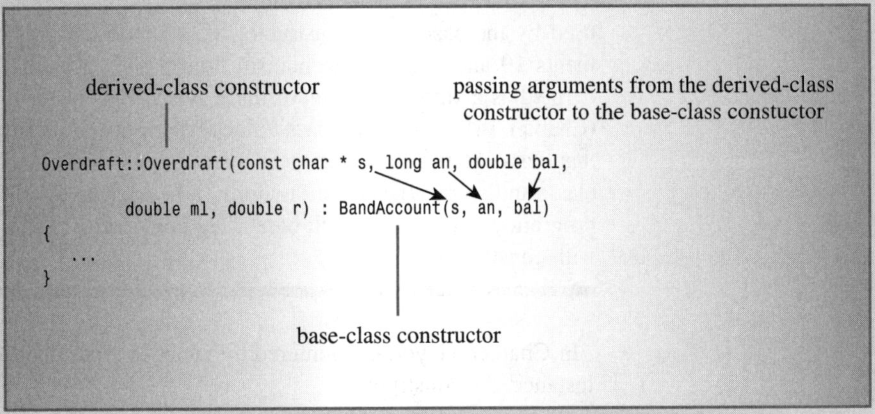

In short, a derived-class constructor always calls a base-class constructor before executing the statements in the derived-class constructor body. The program will use the default base constructor unless you explicitly indicate another constructor by using the initialization-list syntax. In that case, you can use arguments from the derived-class constructor as arguments to the base-class constructor.

Remember

The derived-class constructors are responsible for initializing any data members added to those inherited from the base class. The base-class constructors are responsible for initializing the inherited data members. You can use the initialization-list syntax to indicate which base-class constructor to use. Otherwise, the default base-class constructor is used.

INITIALIZER LISTS

A constructor for a derived class can use the initializer list mechanism to pass values along to a base-class constructor.

```
derived::derived(type1 x, type2 y) : base(x,y) // initializer list
{
    ...
}
```

Here, `derived` is the derived class, `base` is the base class, and x and y are variables used by the base-class constructor. If, say, the derived constructor receives the arguments 10 and 12, this mechanism then passes 10 and 12 on to the base constructor defined as taking arguments of these types. Except for the case of virtual base classes (Chapter 14), a class can pass values back only to its immediate base class. However, that class can use the same mechanism to pass back information to its immediate base class, and so on. If you don't supply a base-class constructor in an initializer list, the program will use the default base-class constructor. The initializer list can be used *only* with constructors.

In Chapter 11 you encountered a syntax for initializing specific class members. For instance, the constructor

```
Queue::Queue(int qs) : qsize(qs)  // initialize qsize to qs
{
    front = rear = NULL;
    items = 0;
}
```

initializes the qsize member of a Queue object to qs. The syntax we've used here is a variant of this earlier form. The difference is that you use the name of a class member to initialize a particular member of an object, but you use the name of a base class to initialize the base-class component of an object.

Initializing Objects to Objects

Let's look at the second Overdraft constructor:

```
Overdraft(const BankAccount & ba, double ml = 500, double r = 0.1);
```

Its intent is to allow conversion from a Brass account to a Brass Plus account. Here the ba argument provides the old account information and the remaining arguments provide information for the new data members. The question is how to use the BankAccount argument to initialize the BankAccount portion. Because this act creates a copy of a BankAccount object, you should use the copy constructor:

```
Overdraft::Overdraft(const BankAccount & ba, double ml, double r)
              : BankAccount(ba)
{
    maxLoan = ml;
    owesBank = 0.0;
    rate = r;
}
```

True, the BankAccount declaration does not explicitly define a copy constructor. However, recall that the compiler provides a default copy constructor if a copy constructor is needed and none is defined. It performs member-wise copying, which is fine for a BankAccount object.

Other Member Functions

The Overdraft class doesn't define a Deposit() function, which means that an Overdraft object will use BankAccount::Deposit(). The same behavior holds for the Balance() function. But the new class does define a ViewAcct() method, which means than an Overdraft object will use Overdraft::ViewAcct(). Let's see how to implement it. First, here is something that will not work:

```
void Overdraft::ViewAcct() const    // INVALID VERSION
{
    // set up ###.## format
    ios_base::fmtflags initialState =
        cout.setf(ios_base::fixed, ios_base::floatfield);
    cout.setf(ios_base::showpoint);
    cout.precision(2);

    cout << "Client: " << fullName << endl;         // not valid
    cout << "Account Number: " << acctNum << endl;  // not valid
    cout << "Balance: $" << balance << endl;        // not valid
```

```
    cout << "Maximum loan: $" << maxLoan << endl;
    cout << "Owed to bank: $" << owesBank << endl;
    cout.setf(initialState);
}
```

The problem is one that you should make sure you understand: A derived class cannot directly access private data and methods of the base class. So an Overdraft object contains a BankAccount object with fullName, acctNum, and balance members, but it cannot access them by name. However, it can access them by using the public interface of the base class. For example, an Overdraft method can use the BankAccount::ViewAcct() method:

```
void Overdraft::ViewAcct() const
{
    // set up ###.## format
    ios_base::fmtflags initialState =
        cout.setf(ios_base::fixed, ios_base::floatfield);
    cout.setf(ios_base::showpoint);
    cout.precision(2);

    BankAccount::ViewAcct();    // display base portion
    cout << "Maximum loan: $" << maxLoan << endl;
    cout << "Owed to bank: $" << owesBank << endl;
    cout.setf(initialState);
}
```

You just have to be sure to use the scope resolution operator. If you omit it, you would get Overdraft::ViewAcct() making a recursive call to itself:

```
void Overdraft::ViewAcct() const
{
    ...
    ViewAcct();      // NO! a recursive call to Overdraft::ViewAcct()
    BankAccount::ViewAcct();                // call base-class version
    ...
}
```

" *If a derived class does not redefine a base-class method, a derived-class object uses the base-class method. If the derived class does redefine the method, the derived-class objects use the new definition.* "

Let's review when which methods are used. If a derived class does not redefine a base-class method, a derived-class object uses the base-class method. If the derived class does redefine the method, the derived-class objects use the new definition. We say the derived-class definition *overrides* the base-class definition:

```
BankAccount bretta;
Overdraft ophelia;
bretta.Deposit(20);     // use BankAccount::Deposit()
ophelia.Deposit(40);    // use BankAccount::Deposit()
bretta.ViewAcct();      // use BankAccount::ViewAcct()
ophelia.ViewAcct();     // use Overdraft::ViewAcct()
```

There's one more function to redefine. The new version of `Withdraw()` has to handle the overdraft protection. Remember that it can use the base-class version of `Withdraw()` but that it cannot access the `balance` member directly. This suggests the following design:

```cpp
void Overdraft::Withdraw(double amt)
{
    double bal = Balance();
    if (amt <= bal)
        BankAccount::Withdraw(amt);
    else if ( amt <= bal + maxLoan - owesBank)
    {
        double advance = amt - bal;
        owesBank += advance * (1.0 + rate);
        cout << "Bank advance: $" << advance << endl;
        cout << "Finance charge: $" << advance * rate << endl;
        Deposit(advance);
        BankAccount::Withdraw(amt);
    }
    else
        cout << "Credit limit exceeded. Transaction cancelled.\n";
}
```

If the balance covers the withdrawal amount, use the base-class version of `Withdraw()`. If overdraft protection is needed and is small enough to be handled by the Brass Plus account, advance the client the amount needed, charge the client for the advance plus interest, then make the withdrawal. Listing 12.5 provides the complete implementation for the `Overdraft` class.

Listing 12.5 overdrft.cpp

```cpp
// overdrft.cpp -- Overdraft class methods
#include <iostream>
using namespace std;
#include "overdrft.h"

Overdraft::Overdraft(const char *s, long an, double bal,
            double ml, double r) : BankAccount(s, an, bal)
{
    maxLoan = ml;
    owesBank = 0.0;
    rate = r;
}

Overdraft::Overdraft(const BankAccount & ba, double ml, double r)
            : BankAccount(ba)    // uses default copy constructor
{
    maxLoan = ml;
    owesBank = 0.0;
    rate = r;
}

// redefine how ViewAcct() works
```

```cpp
void Overdraft::ViewAcct() const
{
    // set up ###.## format
    ios_base::fmtflags initialState =
        cout.setf(ios_base::fixed, ios_base::floatfield);
    cout.setf(ios_base::showpoint);
    cout.precision(2);

    BankAccount::ViewAcct();    // display base portion
    cout << "Maximum loan: $" << maxLoan << endl;
    cout << "Owed to bank: $" << owesBank << endl;
    cout.setf(initialState);
}

// redefine how Withdraw() works
void Overdraft::Withdraw(double amt)
{
    // set up ###.## format
    ios_base::fmtflags initialState =
        cout.setf(ios_base::fixed, ios_base::floatfield);
    cout.setf(ios_base::showpoint);
    cout.precision(2);

    double bal = Balance();
    if (amt <= bal)
        BankAccount::Withdraw(amt);
    else if ( amt <= bal + maxLoan - owesBank)
    {
        double advance = amt - bal;
        owesBank += advance * (1.0 + rate);
        cout << "Bank advance: $" << advance << endl;
        cout << "Finance charge: $" << advance * rate << endl;
        Deposit(advance);
        BankAccount::Withdraw(amt);
    }
    else
        cout << "Credit limit exceeded. Transaction cancelled.\n";
    cout.setf(initialState);
}
```

The next step is to test the derived class. The short program in Listing 12.6 does that. It should be compiled with `overdrft.cpp` and with `bankacct.cpp` because the derived class uses the base-class definitions.

Listing 12.6 useover.cpp

```cpp
// useover.cpp -- test Overdraft class
// compile with bankacct.cpp and overdrft.cpp
#include <iostream>
using namespace std;
#include "overdrft.h"

int main()
{
    BankAccount Porky("Porcelot Pigg", 381299, 4000.00);
// convert Porcelot to new account type
    Overdraft Porky2(Porky);
```

```
Porky2.ViewAcct();
cout << "Depositing $5000:\n";
Porky2.Deposit(5000.00);
cout << "New balance: $" << Porky2.Balance() << "\n\n";
cout << "Withdrawing $8000:\n";
Porky2.Withdraw(8000.00);
cout << "New balance: $" << Porky2.Balance() << "\n\n";
cout << "Withdrawing $1200:\n";
Porky2.Withdraw(1200.00);
Porky2.ViewAcct();
cout << "\nWithdrawing $500:\n";
Porky2.Withdraw(500.00);
Porky2.ViewAcct();

return 0;
}
```

Here is the program output:

```
Client: Porcelot Pigg
Account Number: 381299
Balance: $4000.00
Maximum loan: $500.00
Owed to bank: $0.00
Depositing $5000:
New balance: $9000.00

Withdrawing $8000:
New balance: $1000.00

Withdrawing $1200:
Bank advance: $200.00
Finance charge: $20.00
Client: Porcelot Pigg
Account Number: 381299
Balance: $0.00
Maximum loan: $500.00
Owed to bank: $220.00

Withdrawing $500:
Credit limit exceeded. Transaction cancelled.
Client: Porcelot Pigg
Account Number: 381299
Balance: $0.00
Maximum loan: $500.00
Owed to bank: $220.00
```

Program Notes

Let's examine parts of the program more closely. First, the statement

```
Overdraft Porky2(Porky);
```

creates an `Overdraft` object, initializing the `BankAccount` base component to the values stored in the `Porky` object. The default values ($500 and 10%) are used to initialize the new `maxLoan` and `rate` members.

The

```
Porky2.ViewAcct();
```

statements all invoke the `Overdraft::ViewAcct()` method, which, in turn, explicitly invokes the `BankAccount::ViewAcct()` method to display the base-class members.

The

```
Porky2.Deposit(5000.00);
```

statement invokes `BankAccount::Deposit()` to add $5000 to the account.

The

```
cout << "Withdrawing $1200:\n";
```

statement invokes `Overdraw::Withdraw()`, which advances $200 to the user, debits the user $220, and then has `BankAccount::Withdraw()` make the actual withdrawal.

ACCESS CONTROL—protected

So far the class examples have used the keywords `public` and `private` to control access to class members. There is one more access category, denoted with the keyword `protected`. The `protected` keyword is like `private` in that the outside world can access class members in a `protected` section only by using class members. The difference between `private` and `protected` comes into play only within classes derived from the base class. Members of a derived class can access protected members of a base class directly, but they cannot directly access private members of the base class. So members in the protected category behave like private members as far as the outside world is concerned but behave like public members as far as derived classes are concerned.

For example, suppose the `BankAccount` class declared the `balance` member as protected:

```
class BankAccount
{
protected:
    double balance;
...
};
```

Then the Overdraft class could access balance directly without using BankAccount methods. For example, the core of Overdraft::Withdraw() could be written this way:

```
void Overdraft::Withdraw(double amt)
{
    if (amt <= balance)          // access balance directly
        balance -= amt;
    else if ( amt <= balance + maxLoan - owesBank)
    {
        double advance = amt - balance;
        owesBank += advance * (1.0 + rate);
        cout << "Bank advance: $" << advance << endl;
        cout << "Finance charge: $" << advance * rate << endl;
        Deposit(advance);
        balance -= amt;
    }
    else
        cout << "Credit limit exceeded. Transaction cancelled.\n";
}
```

Using protected data members may simplify writing the code, but it has a design defect. For instance, continuing with the Overdraft example, if balance were protected, you could write code like this:

```
void Overdraft::Reset(double amt)
{
    balance = amt;
}
```

The BankAccount class was designed so that the Deposit() and Withdraw() interface provided the only means for altering balance. But the Reset() method essentially makes balance a public variable as far as Overdraft objects are concerned, ignoring, for example, the safeguards found in Withdraw().

Remember

Prefer private to protected access control for class data members, and use base-class methods to provide derived classes access to base-class data.

However, protected access control can be quite useful for member functions, giving derived classes access to internal functions that are not available publicly.

THE *is-a* RELATIONSHIP, REFERENCES, AND POINTERS

One way public inheritance models the *is-a* relationship is in how it handles pointers and references to objects. Normally, C++ does not allow you to assign an address of one type to a pointer of another type. Nor does it let a reference to one type refer to another type:

```
double x = 2.5;
int * pi = &x;     // invalid assignment, mismatched pointer types
long & rl = x;     // invalid assignment, mismatched reference type
```

However, a reference or a pointer to a base class can refer to a derived-class object without using an explicit type cast. For example, the following assignments are allowed:

```
Overdraft dilly ("Annie Dill", 493222, 2000);
BankAccount * pb = &dilly;   // ok
BankAccount & rb = dilly;    // ok
```

Converting a derived-class reference or pointer to a base-class reference or pointer is called *upcasting*, and it is always allowed for public inheritance without the need for an explicit type cast. This rule is part of expressing the *is-a* relationship. An `Overdraft` object is a `BankAccount` object in that it inherits all the data members and member functions of a `BankAccount` object. Therefore, anything that you can do to a `BankAccount` object, you can do to an `Overdraft` object. So a function designed to handle a `BankAccount` reference can, without fear of creating problems, perform the same acts upon an `Overdraft` object. The same idea applies if you pass a pointer to an object as a function argument.

The opposite process, converting a base-class pointer or reference to a derived-class pointer or reference, is called *downcasting*, and it is not allowed without an explicit type cast. The reason for this restriction is that the *is-a* relationship is not, in general, reversible. A derived class could add new data members, and the class member functions that used these data members wouldn't apply to the base class. For example, suppose you derive a `Singer` class from an `Employee` class, adding a data member representing a singer's vocal range and a member function, called `range()`, that reports the value for the vocal range. It wouldn't make sense to apply the `range()` method to an `Employee` object. But if implicit downcasting were allowed, you could accidentally set a pointer-to-`Singer` to the address of an `Employee` object and use the pointer to invoke the `range()` method (see Figure 12.4).

> *" Converting a derived-class reference or pointer to a base-class reference or pointer is called **upcasting**, and it is always allowed for public inheritance without the need for an explicit type cast."*

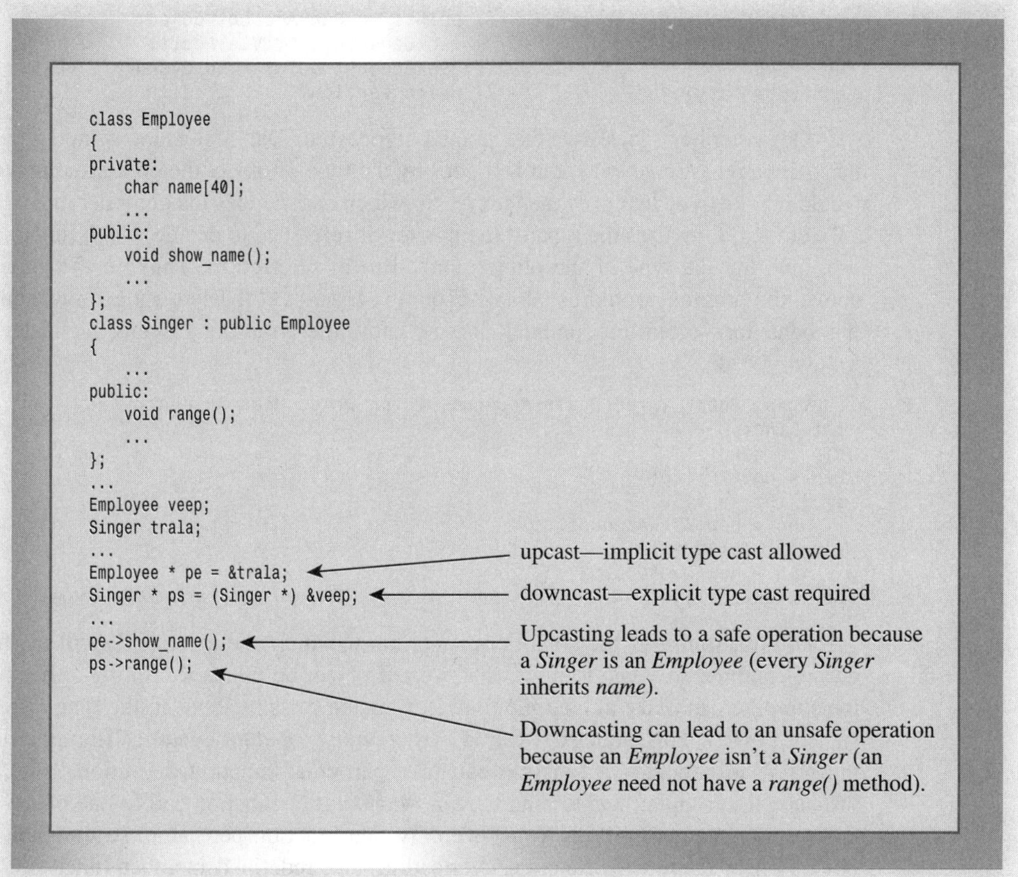

```
class Employee
{
private:
    char name[40];
    ...
public:
    void show_name();
    ...
};
class Singer : public Employee
{
    ...
public:
    void range();
    ...
};
...
Employee veep;
Singer trala;
...
Employee * pe = &trala;        ◄──── upcast—implicit type cast allowed
Singer * ps = (Singer *) &veep; ◄──── downcast—explicit type cast required
...
pe->show_name();   ◄────────────  Upcasting leads to a safe operation because
ps->range();                      a *Singer* is an *Employee* (every *Singer*
                                  inherits *name*).

                                  Downcasting can lead to an unsafe operation
                                  because an *Employee* isn't a *Singer* (an
                                  *Employee* need not have a *range()* method).
```

FIGURE 12.4
*Upcasting and
downcasting*

Virtual Member Functions

Let's take a closer look at which methods are invoked when a derived class redefines a base-class method. Earlier, you learned that the type of object invoking a method determined which method was used:

```
BankAccount bretta;    // base-class object
Overdraft ophelia;     // derived-class object
bretta.ViewAcct();     // use BankAccount::ViewAcct()
ophelia.ViewAcct();    // use Overdraft::ViewAcct()
```

Suppose, however, you use a pointer to invoke a method:

```
BankAccount * bp = &bretta;    // points to BankAccount object
bp->ViewAcct();                // use BankAccount::ViewAcct()
bp = &ophelia;                 // BankAccount pointer to Overdraft object
bp->ViewAcct();                // which version?
```

If the compiler goes by the pointer type, the last statement would invoke `BankAccount::ViewAcct()`, but if it goes by the type of object the pointer points to, it would invoke `Overdraft::ViewAcct()`. So which choice does the compiler make?

By default, C++ uses the type of the pointer or reference to decide which function to use, ignoring the type of the object pointed to or referred to. Thus, in the example above, the program would use `BankAccount::ViewAcct()`. There's a good reason for this behavior—often the compiler doesn't know the type. For instance, consider the following code:

```
cout << "Enter 1 for Brass Account, 2 for Brass Plus Account: ";
int kind;
cin >> kind;
BankAccount * bp;
if (kind == 1)
    bp = new BankAccount;
else if (kind == 2)
    bp = new Overdraft;
bp->ViewAcct();
```

At compilation time, the compiler cannot know which choice (1 or 2) will be made during runtime, so it can't know what type of object bp points to. So the only choice the compiler can make at compile time is to match class methods to the type of reference or pointer. This strategy is called *early binding*, or *static binding*. The term binding refers to attaching a function call to a particular function definition. Here, for instance, the compiler has to bind the `bp->ViewAcct()` function call to one of the two `ViewAcct()` methods. (In C, you have only one function per name, so the choice is obvious. But C++, with function overloading and redefined member functions, can have more than one function matching a given name.)

```
// with static binding
bp = &ophelia;                 // BankAccount pointer to Overdraft object
bp->ViewAcct();                // use BankAccount::ViewAcct()
```

Well, it doesn't hurt to use `BankAccount::ViewAcct()` with an `Overdraft` object; it just doesn't display all the available data. So it would be nice if `bp->ViewAcct()` could somehow key in on the object type instead of the pointer type and invoke `Overdraft::ViewAcct()` instead. C++ offers a second strategy, called *late binding*, or *dynamic binding*, that accomplishes this goal. With this strategy, the compiler doesn't make the decision of which class method to use. Instead, it passes responsibility to the program, which then makes a runtime decision whenever it actually executes a method function call. If you use this strategy, you can have a program choose a method based on the type of object to which a reference or pointer refers:

```
// with dynamic binding
BankAccount * bp = &bretta;    // points to BankAccount object
bp->ViewAcct();                // use BankAccount::ViewAcct()
bp = &ophelia;                 // BankAccount pointer to Overdraft object
bp->ViewAcct();                // use Overdraft::ViewAcct()
```

In most cases, dynamic binding is a good thing.

This discussion should raise some questions in your mind:

- How do you activate dynamic binding?

- Why have two kinds of binding?

- If dynamic binding is so good, why isn't it the default?

- How does it work?

We'll look at answers to these questions next.

ACTIVATING DYNAMIC BINDING

You can turn on dynamic binding *only* for member functions. To do so, precede the function prototype with the keyword `virtual` in the base class declaration. You then term the method a *virtual method*. If you then redefine the function in a derived class, a program will use dynamic binding to determine which definition to use. Once you've made a method virtual, it remains virtual for all classes derived from the base class, along with any classes derived from the derived classes, and so on. For a given method, you only have to use the keyword `virtual` once, in the base class.

Remember

> Virtual member functions are created by preceding the prototype with the keyword `virtual`. C++ programs use dynamic, or late, binding for virtual methods, and static, or early, binding for nonvirtual methods. For virtual functions, the type of object referred to or pointed to determines which method a pointer or reference invokes.

Listing 12.7 shows the `BankAccount` declaration after the change to virtual functions has been made. The listing is identical to Listing 12.1 except that the keyword `virtual` has been inserted twice, once when declaring `Deposit()`, and once when declaring `ViewAcct()`. Changing these two declarations are the only changes you need to make. The other three files supporting the two classes remain unchanged.

Listing 12.7 bankvirt.h

```cpp
// bankvirt.h - a simple BankAccount class with virtual functions
#ifndef _BANKACCT_H_
#define _BANKACCT_H_

class BankAccount
{
private:
    enum {MAX = 35};
    char fullName[MAX];
    long acctNum;
    double balance;
public:
    BankAccount(const char *s = "Nullbody", long an = -1,
                double bal = 0.0);
    void Deposit(double amt);
    virtual void Withdraw(double amt);    // virtual method
    double Balance() const;
    virtual void ViewAcct() const;        // virtual method
};
#endif
```

To show the difference between virtual and non-virtual functions, run the program in Listing 12.8 twice. The first time, compile the program using the original, non-virtual version of bankacct.h (Listing 12.4). The second time, compile the program using the new, virtual version of bankacct.h (Listing 12.7). The program itself uses a small array of pointers-to-BankAccount. Each pointer in the array, as a result of a runtime decision, can point either to a BankAccount object or an Overdraft object. This use of an array of base-class pointers is a common programming technique. If you have a mixture of BankAccount and Overdraft objects, you can't put them in the same array because every element of an array has to be of the same type. But because of the upcasting feature of C++, you can create an array of base-class pointers that can point to either base-class objects or derived-class objects. Thus, you can use a single array of base-class pointers to manage a mixture of object types.

Listing 12.8 useover1.cpp

```cpp
// useover1.cpp -- test Overdraft class
// compile with bankacct.cpp and overdrft.cpp
#include <iostream>
using namespace std;
#include "overvirt.h"
const int SIZE = 3;
const int MAX = 35;
inline void EatLine() {while (cin.get() != '\n') continue;}

int main()
{
    BankAccount * baps[SIZE];
    char name[MAX];
    long acctNum;
    double balance;
    int acctType;
```

```
    int i;
    for (i = 0; i < SIZE; i++)
    {
        cout << "Enter client's name: ";
        cin.get(name,MAX);
        EatLine();
        cout << "Enter client's account number: ";
        cin >> acctNum;
        cout << "Enter client's initial balance: ";
        cin >> balance;
        cout << "Enter 1 for Brass Account, 2 for Brass Plus "
             << "Account: ";
        cin >> acctType;
        EatLine();
        if (acctType == 2)
            baps[i] = new Overdraft(name, acctNum, balance);
        else
        {
            baps[i] = new BankAccount(name, acctNum, balance);
            if (acctType != 1)
                cout << "I'll interpret that as a 1.\n";
        }
    }
    for (i = 0; i < SIZE; i++)
    {
        baps[i]->ViewAcct();
        cout << endl;
    }
    cout << "Bye!\n";
    return 0;
}
```

First, here is a sample run using the non-virtual functions:

```
Enter client's name: Rufus Overbeam
Enter client's account number: 123984
Enter client's initial balance: 3000
Enter 1 for Brass Account, 2 for Brass Plus Account: 2
Enter client's name: Lily Goldleaf
Enter client's account number: 829302
Enter client's initial balance: 4000
Enter 1 for Brass Account, 2 for Brass Plus Account: 1
Enter client's name: Harry Grub
Enter client's account number: 111223
Enter client's initial balance: 22480
Enter 1 for Brass Account, 2 for Brass Plus Account: 1
Client: Rufus Overbeam
Account Number: 123984
Balance: $3000.00

Client: Lily Goldleaf
Account Number: 829302
Balance: $4000.00

Client: Harry Grub
Account Number: 111223
Balance: $22480.00
```

Notice that even though Rufus Overhead has a Brass Plus account and is represented by an `Overdraft` object, using the `BankAccount` pointer causes the `BankAccount::ViewAcct()` method to be used. The method matches the pointer type; static binding holds.

Next, here is a sample run using the same input data but using the virtual version (Listing 12.7) of the header file:

```
Enter client's name: Rufus Overbeam
Enter client's account number: 123984
Enter client's initial balance: 3000
Enter 1 for Brass Account, 2 for Brass Plus Account: 2
Enter client's name: Lily Goldleaf
Enter client's account number: 829302
Enter client's initial balance: 4000
Enter 1 for Brass Account, 2 for Brass Plus Account: 1
Enter client's name: Harry Grub
Enter client's account number: 111223
Enter client's initial balance: 22480
Enter 1 for Brass Account, 2 for Brass Plus Account: 1
Client: Rufus Overbeam
Account Number: 123984
Balance: $3000.00
Maximum loan: $500.00
Owed to bank: $0.00

Client: Lily Goldleaf
Account Number: 829302
Balance: $4000.00

Client: Harry Grub
Account Number: 111223
Balance: $22480.00
```

Again, Rufus Overhead has a Brass Plus account and is represented by an `Overdraft` object, but this time the program uses the `Overdraft::ViewAcct()`. The method matches the object type; dynamic binding holds.

WHY TWO KINDS OF BINDING?

Because dynamic binding allows you to redefine class methods while static binding makes a partial botch of it, why have static binding at all? There are two reasons: efficiency and a conceptual model.

First, consider efficiency. For a program to be able to make a runtime decision, it has to have some way to keep track of what sort of object a base-class pointer or reference refers to, and that entails some extra processing overhead. (We'll describe one method of dynamic binding later.) If, for example, you design a class that won't be used as a base class for inheritance, you don't need the dynamic binding feature. In that case, it makes more sense to use static binding and gain a little efficiency. The fact that static binding is more efficient is why it is the default choice for C++. Stroustrup says one of the guiding principles of C++ is that you shouldn't have to pay (in memory usage or processing time) for those features you don't use. Go to virtual functions only if your program design needs them.

Next, consider the conceptual model. When you design a class, you may have member functions that you don't want redefined in derived classes. For instance, the `BankAccount::Balance()` function, which returns the account balance, seems like a function that shouldn't be redefined. By making this function nonvirtual, you accomplish two things. First, you make it more efficient. Second, you announce that it is your intention that this function not be redefined. That suggests the following rule of thumb.

Remember

If a method in a base class will be redefined in a derived class, make it virtual.
If the method should not be redefined, make it nonvirtual.

Of course, when you design a class, it's not always obvious into which category a method falls. Like many aspects of real life, class design is not a linear process.

HOW VIRTUAL FUNCTIONS WORK

C++ specifies how virtual functions should behave, but it leaves the implementation up to the compiler writer. You don't need to know the implementation method to use virtual functions, but seeing how it is done may help you understand the concepts better, so let's take a look.

The usual way compilers handle virtual functions is to add a hidden member to each object. The hidden member holds a pointer to an array of function addresses. Such an array usually is termed a *table*. The table holds the addresses of the virtual functions declared for objects of that class. For instance, an object of a base class will contain a pointer to a table of addresses of all the virtual functions for that class. An object of a derived class will contain a pointer to a separate table of addresses. If the derived class provides a new definition of a virtual function, the table holds the address of the new function. If the derived class doesn't redefine the virtual function, the table holds the address of the original version of the function. If the derived class defines a new function and makes it virtual, its address is added to the table (see Figure 12.5). Note that whether you define one or ten virtual functions for a class, you add just one address member to an object; it's the table size that varies.

When you call a virtual function, the program looks at the table address stored in an object and goes to the corresponding table of function addresses. If you use the first virtual function defined in the class declaration, the program will use the first function address in the array and execute the function having that address. If you use the third virtual function in the class declaration, the program will use the function whose address is in the third element of the array.

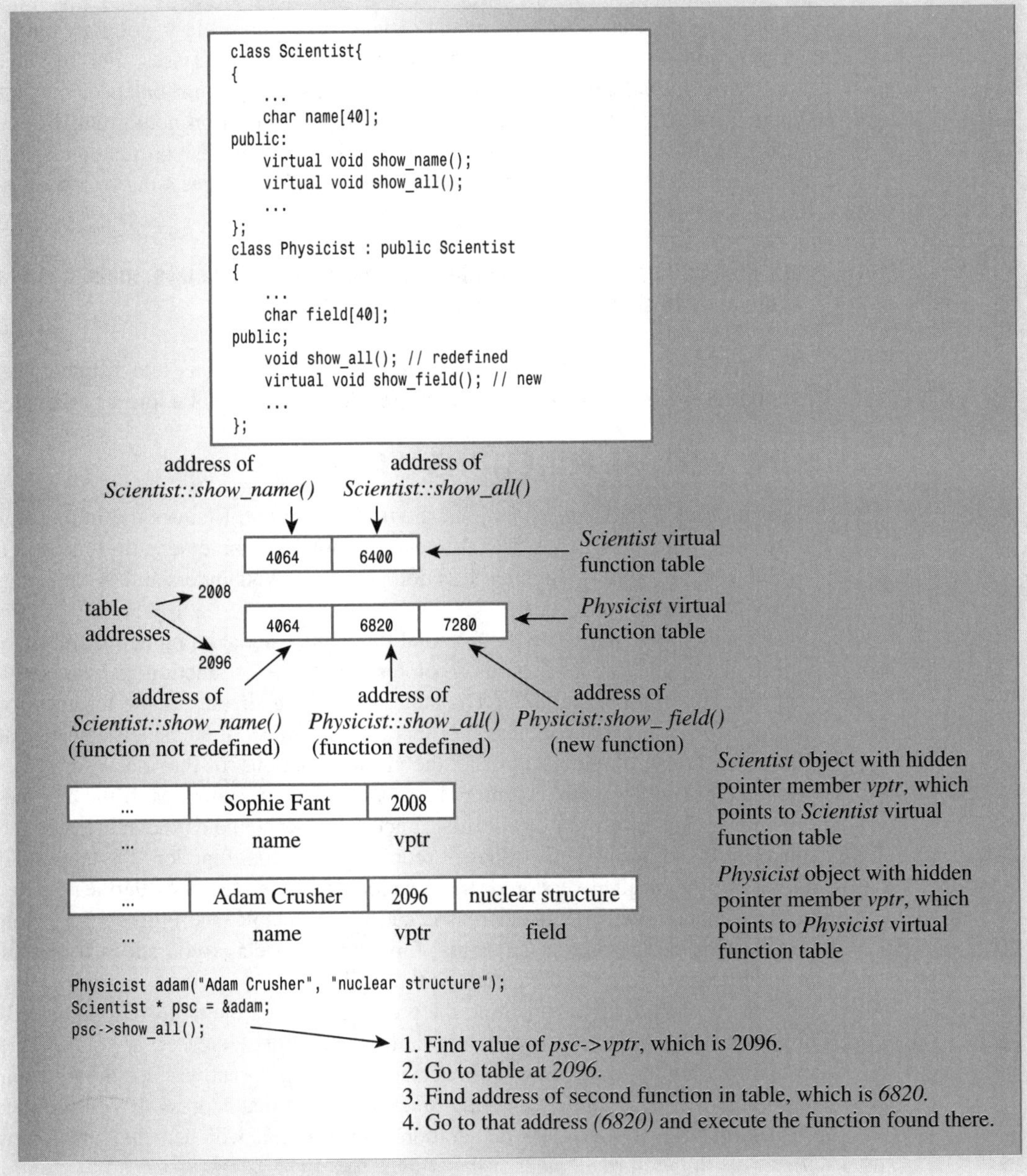

```
class Scientist{
{
    ...
    char name[40];
public:
    virtual void show_name();
    virtual void show_all();
    ...
};
class Physicist : public Scientist
{
    ...
    char field[40];
public;
    void show_all(); // redefined
    virtual void show_field(); // new
    ...
};
```

address of   address of
Scientist::show_name()   *Scientist::show_all()*

| 4064 | 6400 | *Scientist* virtual function table

table
addresses   2008

| 4064 | 6820 | 7280 | *Physicist* virtual function table

            2096

address of   address of   address of
Scientist::show_name()   *Physicist:show_all()*   *Physicist:show_ field()*
(function not redefined)   (function redefined)   (new function)

| ... | Sophie Fant | 2008 |
| ... | name | vptr |

Scientist object with hidden pointer member *vptr*, which points to *Scientist* virtual function table

| ... | Adam Crusher | 2096 | nuclear structure |
| ... | name | vptr | field |

Physicist object with hidden pointer member *vptr*, which points to *Physicist* virtual function table

```
Physicist adam("Adam Crusher", "nuclear structure");
Scientist * psc = &adam;
psc->show_all();
```

1. Find value of *psc->vptr*, which is 2096.
2. Go to table at *2096.*
3. Find address of second function in table, which is *6820.*
4. Go to that address *(6820)* and execute the function found there.

FIGURE 12.5

A virtual function mechanism

In short, using virtual functions has the following modest costs in memory and execution speed:

- Each object has its size increased by the amount needed to hold an address.
- For each class, the compiler creates a table (an array) of addresses of virtual functions.
- For each function call, there's an extra step of going to a table to look up an address.

Keep in mind that although nonvirtual functions are slightly more efficient than virtual functions, they don't provide dynamic binding.

VIRTUAL THINGS TO KNOW

We've already discussed the main points about virtual functions:

- Beginning a class method declaration with the keyword `virtual` in a base class makes the function virtual for the base class and all classes derived from the base class, including classes derived from the derived classes, and so on.
- If a virtual method is invoked by using a reference to an object or by a pointer to an object, the program will use the method defined for the object type rather than the method defined for the reference or pointer type. This is called dynamic, or late, binding. This behavior is important because it's always valid for a base class pointer or reference to refer to an object of a derived type.
- If you're defining a class that will be used as a base class for inheritance, declare as virtual functions those class methods that may have to be redefined in derived classes.

There are several other things you may need to know about virtual functions, some of which have been mentioned in passing already. Let's look at them next.

Constructors

Constructors can't be virtual. A derived class doesn't inherit the base class constructors, so usually there's not much point to making them virtual, anyway.

Destructors

Destructors should be virtual unless a class isn't to be used as a base class. For instance, suppose `Employee` is a base class and `Singer` is a derived class that adds a char * member that points to memory allocated by new. Then, when a `Singer` object expires, it's vital that the `~Singer()` destructor be called to free that memory.

Now consider the following code:

```
Employee * pe = new Singer; // legal because Employee is base for Singer
...
delete pe;                           // ~Employee() or ~Singer()?
```

If the default static binding applies, the delete statement will invoke the `~Employee()` destructor. This will free memory pointed to by the `Employee` components of the `Singer` object but not memory pointed to by the new class members. However, if the destructors are virtual, the same code invokes the `~Singer()` destructor, which frees memory pointed to by the `Singer` component, and then calls the `~Employee()` destructor to free memory pointed to by the `Employee` component.

Note that this implies that even if a base class doesn't require the services of an explicit destructor, you shouldn't rely upon the default constructor. Instead, provide a virtual destructor, even if it has nothing to do:

```
~virtual ~BaseClass() { }
```

Friends

Friends can't be virtual functions because friends are not class members, and only members can be virtual functions. If this poses a problem for a design, you may be able to sidestep it by having the friend function use virtual member functions internally.

No Redefinition

If a derived class fails to redefine a virtual function, the class will use the base class version of the function. If a derived class is part of a long chain of derivations, it will use the most recently defined version of the virtual function. The exception is if the base versions are hidden, as described next.

Redefinition Hides Methods

Suppose you create something like the following:

```
class Dwelling
{
public:
     virtual void showperks(int a) const;
...
};
class Hovel : public Dwelling
{
{
public:
     void showperks();
```

```
   ...
};
```

This causes a problem. You may get a compiler warning similar to the following:

```
Warning: Hovel::showperks(void) hides Dwelling::showperks(int)
```

Or perhaps you won't get a warning. Either way, the code has the following implications:

```
Hovel trump;
trump.showperks();      // valid
trump.showperks(5);     // invalid
```

The new definition defines a showperks() that takes no arguments. Rather than resulting in two overloaded versions of the function, this redefinition *hides* the base-class version that takes an int argument. In short, redefining inherited methods is not a variation of overloading. If you redefine a function in a derived class, it doesn't just override the base class declaration with the same function signature. Instead, it hides *all* base-class methods of the same name, regardless of the argument signatures.

This fact of life leads to a couple of rules of thumb. First, if you redefine an inherited method, make sure you match the original prototype exactly. One exception is that a return type that is a reference or pointer to a base class can be replaced by a reference or pointer to the derived class. (This exception is new, and not all compilers recognize it yet. Also, note that this exception applies only to return values, not to arguments.) Second, if the base-class declaration is overloaded, redefine all the base-class versions in the derived class:

```
class Dwelling
{
public:
// three overloaded showperks()
    virtual void showperks(int a) const;
    virtual void showperks(double x) const;
    virtual void showperks() const;
    ...
};
class Hovel : public Dwelling
{
public:
// three redefined showperks()
    void showperks(int a) const;
    void showperks(double x) const;
    void showperks() const;
    ...
};
```

If you redefine just one version, the other two become hidden and cannot be used by objects of the derived class. Note that if no change is needed, the redefinition can simply call the base-class version.

Inheritance and Assignment

The assignment operator, as mentioned earlier, is one member function that is not inherited. Let's look more closely at the topic of assignment and inheritance. First, some basics. Consider the following code:

```
BankAccount darf("Darfa Flemwit", 121234, 100);
BankAccount temp1;
Overdraft bip("Bipp Fardbag", 212143, 200);
Overdraft temp2;
temp1 = darf;
temp2 = bip;
```

The assignments to `temp1` and `temp2` are equivalent to the following function calls:

```
temp1.operator=(darf);  // call #1
temp2.operator=(bip);   // call #2
```

Because call #1 is invoked by a `BankAccount` object, the compiler will look for a `BankAccount::operator=()` function. Because the argument also is a `BankAccount` object, the compiler will look for a function that accepts a `BankAccount` argument. Both requirements are met by the default assignment operator which, you will recall, has this prototype:

```
BankAccount & BankAccount::operator=(const BankAccount &);
```

Similarly, call #2 is matched by the following prototype:

```
Overdraft & Overdraft::operator=(const Overdraft &);
```

Again, this is the `operator=()` function generated by default for the `Overdraft` class. This has the correct function signature for assigning one `Overdraft` object to another. But if the `Overdraft` class inherited the `BankAccount operator=()` function, the inherited version would have the wrong function signature for handling `Overdraft` objects because its argument is a `BankAccount` reference. Thus, instead of letting a derived class inherit an assignment operator, the compiler defines a new one for the class automatically.

MIXED ASSIGNMENT

Okay, you can assign one `BankAccount` object to another and one `Overdraft` object to another using the default assignment operators. What about assigning an `Overdraft` object to a `BankAccount` object and vice versa? Let's look first at assigning a derived object to a base object:

```
BankAccount temp;
Overdraft bip("Bipp Fardbag", 212143, 200);
temp = bip;  // possible?
```

The answer here is that assignment works, although in a slightly roundabout fashion. First, the compiler puts this into function notation:

```
temp.operator=(bip);
```

Next, the compiler tries to find an assignment operator that matches the function call. Because the invoking object is of the BankAccount class and the argument is of the Overdraft class, the ideal match is this:

```
BankAccount & BankAccount::operator=(const Overdraft &);
```

Note that the function necessarily is a member of the BankAccount class. Well, this is not the default assignment operator, nor is it declared in the BankAccount class, so there is no exact match. Therefore, the compiler looks to see if there is an operator function that will work after a type conversion for the argument. And that does exist:

```
BankAccount & BankAccount::operator=(const BankAccount &);
```

Recall that a base-class reference can refer to a derived-class object (upcasting) without an explicit typecast. Thus, the default assignment operator for the base class will accept a derived-class object. And this means yes, you can assign a derived-class object to a base-class object. The result is that just the base-class portion of the derived object is copied.

Remember

You can assign a derived-class object to a base-class object. The compiler will use the base-class assignment operator and copy just the base-class portion.

Next, let's try assigning a base-class object to a derived-class object:

```
BankAccount darf("Darfa Flemwit", 121234, 100);
Overdraft temp;
temp = darf;    // possible?
```

This time the answer is maybe. This assignment statement translates to the following call:

```
temp.operator=(darf);
```

Because the invoking object is an Overdraft object, the matching assignment function, if it exists, must be an Overdraft member with a BankAccount argument:

```
Overdraft & Overdraft::operator=(const BankAccount &);
```

There is no such function, but there is the default assignment operator:

```
Overdraft & Overdraft::operator=(const Overdraft &);
```

Can it be used? That would require having an Overdraft reference referring to a BankAccount object. That would be making a derived-class reference refer to a base-class object. Normally, such a downcast is allowed only with an explicit typecast, so normally this assignment is not allowed. However, in this case, there is a single-argument constructor that provides an implicit conversion from BankAccount to Overdraft:

```
Overdraft(const BankAccount & ba, double ml = 500, double r = 0.1);
```

So, in this particular case, the program calls the constructor Overdraft(darf) to generate a temporary Overdraft object that's used as an argument to the default Overdraft operator=() function. If the constructor had been declared as explicit, the assignment would be disallowed.

Remember

> You cannot, in general, assign a base-class object to a derived class object. However, such an assignment will work if there is a constructor that defines a base class to derived class conversion.

ASSIGNMENT AND DYNAMIC MEMORY ALLOCATION

Now let's look at how dynamic memory allocation interacts with assignment and inheritance. First, let's modify the BankAccount class so that it uses dynamic memory allocation. Listing 12.9 shows the new class declaration, and Listing 12.10 shows the new implementation. As usual, adding dynamic memory allocation required adding an explicit destructor, copy constructor, and assignment operator.

Listing 12.9 bankdyn.h

```cpp
// bankdyn.h - a simple BankAccountD class with DMA
#ifndef _BANKACCT_H_
#define _BANKACCT_H_

class BankAccountD
{
private:
    char * fullName;
    long acctNum;
    double balance;
public:
    BankAccountD(const char *s = "Nullbody", long an = -1,
                double bal = 0.0);
    BankAccountD(const BankAccountD & ba);
    virtual ~BankAccountD();
    void Deposit(double amt);
    virtual void Withdraw(double amt);    // virtual method
    double Balance() const;
    virtual void ViewAcct() const;        // virtual method
    BankAccountD & operator=(const BankAccountD & ba);
};
#endif
```

Listing 12.10 bankdyn.cpp

```cpp
// bankdyn.cpp -- methods for BankAccountD class
#include <iostream>
using namespace std;
#include "bankdyn.h"
#include <cstring>

BankAccountD::BankAccountD(const char *s, long an, double bal)
{
    fullName = new char[strlen(s) + 1];
    strcpy(fullName, s);
    acctNum = an;
    balance = bal;
}
```

```cpp
BankAccountD::BankAccountD(const BankAccountD & ba)
{
    fullName = new char[strlen(ba.fullName) + 1];
    strcpy(fullName, ba.fullName);
    acctNum = ba.acctNum;
    balance = ba.balance;;
}

BankAccountD::~BankAccountD()
{
    delete [] fullName;
}

void BankAccountD::Deposit(double amt)
{
    balance += amt;
}

void BankAccountD::Withdraw(double amt)
{
    if (amt <= balance)
        balance -= amt;
    else
        cout << "Withdrawal amount of $" << amt
             << " exceeds your balance.\n"
             << "Withdrawal canceled.\n";
}

double BankAccountD::Balance() const
{
    return balance;
}

void BankAccountD::ViewAcct() const
{
    // set up ###.## format
    ios_base::fmtflags initialState =
        cout.setf(ios_base::fixed, ios_base::floatfield);
    cout.setf(ios_base::showpoint);
    cout.precision(2);
    cout << "Client: " << fullName << endl;
    cout << "Account Number: " << acctNum << endl;
    cout << "Balance: $" << balance << endl;
    cout.setf(initialState); // restore original format
}

BankAccountD & BankAccountD::operator=(const BankAccountD & ba)
{
    if (this == &ba)
        return *this;
    delete [] fullName;
    fullName = new char[strlen(ba.fullName) + 1];
    strcpy(fullName, ba.fullName);
    acctNum = ba.acctNum;
    balance = ba.balance;
    return *this;
}
```

" But copying a class member or an inherited class component is done using the copy constructor for that class. "

Case 1—Derived Class Doesn't Use new

Suppose you derive the Overdraft class from BankAccountD instead of from BankAccount. Do you now have to define an explicit destructor, copy constructor, and assignment operator for the Overdraft class? Providing you don't add new features to the Overdraft class that require these methods, the answer is no.

First, consider the need for a destructor. If you don't define one, the compiler will define a default constructor that does nothing. Actually, the default constructor for a derived class always does something; it calls the base-class destructor after executing its own code. Because the Overdraft members don't require any special action, the default destructor is fine.

Next, consider the copy constructor. You've seen that the default copy constructor does memberwise copying, which is inappropriate for dynamic memory allocation. However, memberwise copying is fine for the three new Overdraft members. That leaves the matter of the inherited BankAccountD object. What you need to know is that memberwise copying uses the form of copying that is defined for the data type in question. So copying a long to a long is done using ordinary assignment. But copying a class member or an inherited class component is done using the copy constructor for that class. Thus, the default copy constructor for the Overdraft class uses the explicit BankAccountD copy constructor to copy the BankAccountD portion of an Overdraft object. So if the default copy constructor is fine for the new Overdraft members, it's also fine for the inherited BankAccountD object.

Essentially the same situation holds for assignment. The default assignment operator for a class automatically uses the base-class assignment operator for the base-class component. So it, too, is fine.

Case 2—Derived Class Does Use new

Suppose, however, that the derived class does use new. Then you do have to define an explicit destructor, copy constructor, and assignment operator for the derived class. Let's see how this is done. Suppose it is decided that holders of the Brass Plus Account get a code name, so a new pointer member is added to handle that. Listing 12.11 shows a revised class declaration, indicating the new members.

Listing 12.11 overdyn2.h

```
// overdyn2.h  -- OverdraftD class declaration with DMA
#ifndef _OVERDRFT_H_
#define _OVERDRFT_H_
#include "bankdyn.h"

class OverdraftD : public BankAccountD
{
private:
    double maxLoan;
    double rate;
    double owesBank;
    char * codeName;                              // new
public:
```

```
    OverdraftD(const char * s = "Nullbody", const char *cn = "cent",
        long an = -1, double bal = 0.0, double ml = 500,
        double r = 0.10);
    OverdraftD(const BankAccountD & ba,const char * cn = "cent",
        double ml = 500, double r = 0.1);
    OverdraftD(const OverdraftD & od);                // new
    ~OverdraftD();                                    // new
    void ViewAcct()const;
    void Withdraw(double amt);
    void ResetMax(double m) { maxLoan = m; }
    void ResetRate(double r) { rate = r; };
    void ResetOwes() { owesBank = 0; }
    OverdraftD & operator=(const OverdraftD & od);   // new
};

#endif
```

The original constructors have to be revised in the usual way to allocate space for a string, and `ViewAcct()` will have to add code to display the new member; you'll find these details in Listing 12.12. Meanwhile, let's concentrate on the new member functions.

First, there is the copy constructor. It can be coded this way:

```
OverdraftD::OverdraftD(const OverdraftD & od) : BankAccountD(od)
{
    codeName = new char[strlen(od.codeName) + 1];
    strcpy(codeName, od.codeName);
    maxLoan = od.maxLoan;
    owesBank = od.owesBank;
    rate = od.rate;
}
```

It is the responsibility of the `OverdraftD` constructor to construct the `OverdraftD` portion of the object, and the function body handles memory allocation for the `codeName` string in the usual fashion. Constructing the base-class portion is the responsibility of the base-class constructors. Here, the method uses the initialization-list syntax to invoke the base-class copy constructor. Note that the `OverdraftD` copy constructor passes a reference to an `OverdraftD` object to the `BankAccountD` copy constructor. The argument of the latter is declared as type const `BankAccountD &`; however, because implicit upcasting is the rule, the `BankAccountD` reference can refer to an `OverdraftD` object. In particular, it will refer to the `BankAccountD` component of the `Overdraft` object.

Next, there is the destructor. It need only manage the `OverdraftD` component:

```
OverdraftD::~OverdraftD()
{
    delete [] codeName;
}
```

Remember, after it's called, the base-class destructor is called automatically, freeing the memory pointed to by `fullName`.

Finally, there is the assignment operator. The important point to bear in mind here is that if you define an assignment operator for a derived class, it has to see to it that assignment is handled for both the derived-class *and* the base-class portions.

Furthermore, you can't use the initialization-list syntax for the base-class portion, for that syntax can only be used in constructors. So what you have to do is invoke the base-class assignment operator in the body of the function. This is done most easily by using the function notation for the assignment operator:

```
OverdraftD & OverdraftD::operator=(const OverdraftD & od)
{
    if (this == &od)
        return *this;
    BankAccountD::operator=(od);    // base-class assignment
    delete [] codeName;
    codeName = new char[strlen(od.codeName) + 1];
    strcpy(codeName, od.codeName);
    maxLoan = od.maxLoan;
    owesBank = od.owesBank;
    rate = od.rate;
    return *this;
}
```

The statement:

```
BankAccountD::operator=(od);    // base-class assignment
```

is short for this:

```
this->BankAccountD::operator=(od);    // base-class assignment
```

In other words, use the `BankAccountD` version of assignment to assign od to `*this`. This will copy the `BankAccountD` portion of the od object to the `BankAccountD` portion of the `*this` object. Listing 12.12 shows the full implementation.

Listing 12.12 overdyn2.cpp

```
// overdyn2.cpp -- OverdraftD class methods with DMA
#include <iostream>
using namespace std;
#include "overdyn2.h"

OverdraftD::OverdraftD(const char * s, const char * cn,
          long an, double bal,
          double ml, double r) : BankAccountD(s, an, bal)
{
    codeName = new char[strlen(cn) + 1];
    strcpy(codeName, cn);
    maxLoan = ml;
    owesBank = 0.0;
    rate = r;
}

OverdraftD::OverdraftD(const BankAccountD & ba, const char * cn,
          double ml, double r)
            : BankAccountD(ba)    // uses explicit copy constructor
{
    codeName = new char[strlen(cn) + 1];
    strcpy(codeName, cn);
    maxLoan = ml;
    owesBank = 0.0;
    rate = r;
}
```

```cpp
OverdraftD::OverdraftD(const OverdraftD & od) : BankAccountD(od)
{
    codeName = new char[strlen(od.codeName) + 1];
    strcpy(codeName, od.codeName);
    maxLoan = od.maxLoan;
    owesBank = od.owesBank;
    rate = od.rate;
}

OverdraftD::~OverdraftD()
{
    delete [] codeName;
}

// redefine how ViewAcct() works
void OverdraftD::ViewAcct() const
{
    // set up ###.## format
    ios_base::fmtflags initialState =
        cout.setf(ios_base::fixed, ios_base::floatfield);
    cout.setf(ios_base::showpoint);
    cout.precision(2);

    BankAccountD::ViewAcct();   // display base portion
    cout << "Code Name: " << codeName << endl;
    cout << "Maximum loan: $" << maxLoan << endl;
    cout << "Owed to bank: $" << owesBank << endl;
    cout.setf(initialState);
}

// redefine how Withdraw() works
void OverdraftD::Withdraw(double amt)
{
    // set up ###.## format
    ios_base::fmtflags initialState =
        cout.setf(ios_base::fixed, ios_base::floatfield);
    cout.setf(ios_base::showpoint);
    cout.precision(2);

    double bal = Balance();
    if (amt <= bal)
        BankAccountD::Withdraw(amt);
    else if ( amt <= bal + maxLoan - owesBank)
    {
        double advance = amt - bal;
        owesBank += advance * (1.0 + rate);
        cout << "Bank advance: $" << advance << endl;
        cout << "Finance charge: $" << advance * rate << endl;
        Deposit(advance);
        BankAccountD::Withdraw(amt);
    }
    else
        cout << "Credit limit exceeded. Transaction cancelled.\n";
    cout.setf(initialState);
}

OverdraftD & OverdraftD::operator=(const OverdraftD & od)
{
```

```
    if (this == &od)
        return *this;
    BankAccountD::operator=(od);    // base-class assignment
    delete [] codeName;
    codeName = new char[strlen(od.codeName) + 1];
    strcpy(codeName, od.codeName);
    maxLoan = od.maxLoan;
    owesBank = od.owesBank;
    rate = od.rate;
    return *this;
}
```

Listing 12.13, which should be compiled with Listings 12.10 and 12.12, tests the revised classes.

Listing 12.13 usedyn2.cpp

```cpp
// usedyn2.cpp -- test OverdraftD class
// compile with bankdyn.cpp and overdyn2.cpp
#include <iostream>
using namespace std;
#include "overdyn2.h"

int main()
{
    BankAccountD dolly("Dahlia Dahl", 453216, 6000);
    BankAccountD temp;
    temp = dolly;
    temp.ViewAcct();
    cout << endl;
    OverdraftD rolly("Roland Rayleigh", "Rocky", 223391, 8000);
    OverdraftD dup;
    dup = rolly;
    dup.ViewAcct();
    cout << endl;
    dup = dolly;
    dup.ViewAcct();
    cout << "Bye!\n";
    return 0;
}
```

Here is the output:

```
Client: Dahlia Dahl
Account Number: 453216
Balance: $6000.00

Client: Roland Rayleigh
Account Number: 223391
Balance: $8000.00
Code Name: Rocky
Maximum loan: $500.00
Owed to bank: $0.00

Client: Dahlia Dahl
Account Number: 453216
Balance: $6000.00
Code Name: cent
Maximum loan: $500.00
Owed to bank: $0.00
Bye!
```

As you can see, assignment worked for both classes, and even cross-assignment worked, thanks to the constructor in `OverdraftD` that acts as an implicit `BankAccountD-to-OverdraftD` conversion function. Note that assigning `dolly` to `dup` resulted in `dup` getting the default values for the `OverDraftD` members, because that is what the conversion constructor does:

```
OverdraftD(const BankAccountD & ba,const char * cn = "cent",
           double ml = 500, double r = 0.1);
```

Abstract Base Classes

Sometimes the application of the *is-a* rule is not as simple as it might appear. Suppose, for example, you are developing a graphics program that is supposed to represent, among other things, circles and ellipses. A circle is a special case of an ellipse; it's an ellipse whose long axis is the same as its short axis. Therefore, all circles are ellipses, and it is tempting to derive a `Circle` class from an `Ellipse` class. But once you get to the details, you may find problems.

To see this, first consider what you might include as part of an `Ellipse` class. Data members could include the coordinates of the center of the ellipse, the semimajor axis (half the long diameter), the semiminor axis (half the short diameter), and an orientation angle giving the angle from the horizontal coordinate axis to the semimajor axis. Also, the class could include methods to move the ellipse, to return the area of the ellipse, to rotate the ellipse, and to scale the semimajor and semiminor axes:

```
class Ellipse
{
private:
    double x;      // x-coordinate of the ellipse's center
    double y;      // y-coordinate of the ellipse's center
    double a;      // semimajor axis
    double b;      // semiminor axis
    double angle;  // orientation angle in degrees
    ...
public:
    ...
    void Move(int nx, ny) { x = nx; y = ny; }
    virtual double Area() const { return 3.14159 * a * b; }
    virtual void Rotate(double nang) { angle = nang; }
    virtual void Scale(double sa, double sb)  { a *= sa; b *= sb; }
    ...
};
```

Now suppose you derive a `Circle` class:

```
class Circle : public Ellipse
{
    ...
};
```

Although a circle is an ellipse, this derivation is awkward. For example, a circle only needs a single value, its radius, to describe its size and shape instead of having a semi-major axis (a) and semiminor axis (b). The `Circle` constructors can take care of that by assigning the same value to the a and b members, but then you have redundant representation of the same information. The `angle` parameter and the `Rotate()` method don't really make sense for a circle, and the `Scale()` method, as it stands, can change a circle to a non-circle by scaling the two axes differently. You can try fixing things with tricks, such as putting a redefined `Rotate()` method in the private section of the `Circle` class so that `Rotate()` can't be used publicly with a circle, but, on the whole, it seems simpler to define a `Circle` class without using inheritance:

```cpp
class Circle        // no inheritance
{
private:
    double x;      // x-coordinate of the circle's center
    double y;      // y-coordinate of the circle's center
    double r;      // radius
    ...
public:
    ...
    void Move(int nx, ny) { x = nx; y = ny; }
    double Area() const { return 3.14159 * r * r; }
    void Scale(double sr)  { r *= sr; }
    ...
};
```

Now the class has only the members it needs. Yet this solution also seems weak. The `Circle` and `Ellipse` classes have a lot in common, but defining them separately ignores that fact.

There is another solution, and that is to abstract from the `Ellipse` and `Circle` classes what they have in common and place those features in an *abstract base class* (ABC). Next, derive both the `Circle` and `Ellipse` classes from the ABC. Then, for example, you can use an array of base-class pointers to manage a mixture of `Ellipse` and `Circle` objects. In this case, what the two classes have in common are the coordinates of the center of the shape, a `Move()` method, which is the same for both, and an `Area()` method, which works differently for the two classes. Indeed, the `Area()` method can't even be implemented for the ABC because it doesn't have the necessary data members. C++ has a way to provide an unimplemented function by using a *pure virtual function*. A pure virtual function has = `0` at the end of its declaration, as shown below:

```cpp
class BaseEllipse  // abstract base class
{
private:
    double x;    // x-coordinate of center
    double y;    // y-coordinate of center
    ...
private:
    BaseEllipse(double x0 = 0, double y0 = 0) : x(x0),y(y0) {}
    virtual ~BaseEllipse() {}
    void Move(int nx, ny) { x = nx; y = ny; }
    virtual Area() const = 0;    // a pure virtual function
    ...
}
```

When a class declaration contains a pure virtual function, you can't create an object of that class. The idea is that classes with pure virtual functions exist solely to serve as base classes. For a class to be a genuine abstract base class, it has to have at least one pure virtual function.

Now you can derive the `Ellipse` class and `Circle` class from the `BaseEllipse` class, adding the members needed to complete each class. One point to note is that the `Circle` class always represents circles, while the `Ellipse` class represents ellipses that also can be circles. However, an `Ellipse` class circle can be rescaled to a non-circle, while a `Circle` class circle must remain a circle.

A program using these classes will be able to create `Ellipse` objects and `Circle` objects, but no `BaseEllipse` objects. Because `Circle` and `Ellipse` objects have the same base class, a collection of such objects can be managed with an array of `BaseEllipse` pointers.

In short, an ABC describes an interface using a least one pure virtual function, and classes derived from an ABC use regular virtual functions to implement the interface in terms of the properties of the particular derived class.

Class Design Review

C++ can be applied to a wide variety of programming problems, and you can't reduce class design to some paint-by-the-numbers routine. However, there are some guidelines that often apply, and this is as good a time as any to go over them, by reviewing and amplifying earlier discussions.

MEMBER FUNCTIONS THAT THE COMPILER GENERATES FOR YOU

As first discussed in Chapter 11, the compiler automatically generates certain public member functions. The fact that it does suggests that these member functions are particularly important. Let's look again at some of them now.

The Default Constructor

A default constructor is one with no arguments, or else one for which all the arguments have default arguments. If you don't define any constructors, the compiler defines a default constructor for you. It doesn't do anything, but it must exist for you to do certain things. For instance, suppose `Star` is a class. You need a default constructor to do the following:

```
Star rigel;        // create an object without explicit initialization
Star pleiades[6];  // create an array of objects
```

Also, if you write a derived class constructor without explicitly invoking a base class constructor in the initialization list, the compiler will use the base class default constructor to construct the base class portion of the new object.

If you do define a constructor of any kind, the compiler will not define a default constructor for you. In that case, it's up to you to provide a default constructor if one is needed.

Note that one of the motivations for having constructors is to ensure that objects always are properly initialized. Also, if your class has any pointer members, they certainly should be initialized. Thus, it's a good idea to supply an explicit default constructor that initializes all class data members to reasonable values.

The Copy Constructor

The copy constructor is a constructor that takes a constant reference to the class type as its argument. For instance, the copy constructor for a Star class would have this prototype:

```
Star(const Star &);
```

The class copy constructor is used in the following situations:

- When a new object is initialized to an object of the same class

- When an object is passed to a function by value

- When a function returns an object by value

- When the compiler generates a temporary object

If your program doesn't use a copy constructor (explicitly or implicitly), the compiler provides a prototype, but not a function definition. Otherwise, the program defines a copy constructor that performs memberwise initialization. That is, each member of the new object is initialized to the value of the corresponding member of the original object.

In some cases, memberwise initialization is undesirable. For example, member pointers initialized with new generally require that you institute deep copying, as with the BankAccountD class. Or a class may have a static variable that needs to be modified. In such cases, you need to define your own copy constructor.

The Assignment Operator

The default assignment operator handles assigning one object to another of the same class. Don't confuse assignment with initialization. If the statement creates a new object, it's using initialization, and if it alters the value of an existing object, it's assignment:

```
Star sirius;
Star alpha = sirius;      // initialization (one notation)
Star dogstar;
dogstar = sirius;         // assignment
```

If you need to define the copy constructor explicitly, you also need, for the same reasons, to define the assignment operator explicitly. The prototype for a Star class assignment operator is this:

```
Star & Star::operator=(const Star &);
```

Note that the assignment operator function returns a reference to a `Star` object. The `BankAccountD` class shows a typical example of an explicit assignment operator function.

The compiler doesn't generate assignment operators for assigning one type to another. Suppose you want to be able to assign a string to a `Star` object. One approach is to define such an operator explicitly:

```
Star & Star::operator=(const char *) {...}
```

A second approach is to rely upon a conversion function (see "Conversions" in the next section) to convert a string to a `Star` object and use the `Star`-to-`Star` assignment function. The first approach runs more quickly, but requires more code. The conversion function approach can lead to compiler-befuddling situations.

OTHER CLASS METHOD CONSIDERATIONS

There are several other points to keep in mind as you define a class. The following sections list some of these.

Constructors

> " Constructors are different from other class methods in that they create new objects, while other methods are invoked by existing objects. "

Constructors are different from other class methods in that they create new objects, while other methods are invoked by existing objects.

Destructors

Remember to define an explicit destructor that deletes any memory allocated by `new` in the class constructors and takes care of any other special bookkeeping that destroying a class object requires. If the class is to be used as a base class, make the destructor virtual.

Conversions

Any constructor that can be invoked with exactly one argument defines conversion from the argument type to the class type. For instance, consider the following constructor prototypes for a `Star` class:

```
Star(const char *);                        // converts char * to Star
Star(const Spectral &, int members = 1);   // converts Spectral to Star
```

Conversion constructors get used, for example, when a convertible type is passed to a function defined as taking a class argument. For example, suppose you have the following:

```
Star north;
north = "polaris";
```

The second statement would invoke the `Star::operator=(const Star &)` function, using `Star::Star(const char *)` to generate a `Star` object to be used as an argument for the assignment operator function. This assumes that you haven't defined a `(char *)`-to-`Star` assignment operator.

Using `explicit` in the prototype for a one-argument constructor disables implicit conversions, but still allows explicit conversions:

```
class Star
{
...
public:
    explicit Star(const char *);
...
};
Star north;
north = "polaris";         // not allowed
north = Star ("polaris");  // allowed
```

To convert from a class object to some other type, define a conversion function (Chapter 10). A conversion function is a class member function with no arguments or declared return type that has the name of the type to be converted to. Despite having no declared return type, the function should return the desired conversion value. Here are some samples:

```
Star::Star double() {...}         // converts star to double
Star::Star const char * () {...}  // converts to const char
```

You should be judicious with such functions, only using them if they make good sense. Also, with some class designs, having conversion functions increases the likelihood of writing ambiguous code. For instance, suppose you had defined a `double` conversion for the `vector` type of Chapter 10, and suppose you had the following code:

```
vector ius(6.0, 0.0);
vector lux = ius + 20.2;        // ambiguous
```

The compiler could convert `ius` to `double` and use `double` addition, or else convert `20.2` to `vector` (using one of the constructors) and use `vector` addition. Instead, it would do neither and inform you of an ambiguous construction.

Passing an Object by Value Versus Passing a Reference

In general, if you write a function using an object argument, you should pass the object by reference rather than by value. One reason for this is efficiency. Passing an object by value involves generating a temporary copy, which means calling the copy constructor and then later calling the destructor. Calling these functions takes time, and copying a large object can be quite a bit slower than passing a reference. If the function doesn't modify the object, declare the argument as a `const` reference.

Another reason for passing objects by reference is that, in the case of inheritance using virtual functions, a function defined as accepting a base class reference argument can also be used successfully with derived classes, as you saw earlier in this chapter. Also see the discussion of virtual methods later this chapter.

Returning an Object Versus Returning a Reference

Some class methods return objects. You've probably noticed that some of these members return objects directly while others return references. Sometimes a method must return an object, but if it isn't necessary, you should use a reference instead. Let's look at this more closely.

First, the only coding difference between returning an object directly and returning a reference is in the function prototype and header:

```
Star nova1(const Star &);      // returns a Star object
Star & nova2(const Star &);    // returns a reference to a Star
```

Next, the reason that you should return a reference rather than an object is that returning an object involves generating a temporary copy of the returned object. It's the copy that's made available to the calling program. Thus, returning an object involves the time cost of calling a copy constructor to generate the copy and of calling the destructor to get rid of the copy. Returning a reference saves time and memory use. Returning an object directly is analogous to passing an object by value: both processes generate temporary copies. Similarly, returning a reference is analogous to passing an object by reference: both the calling and the called function operate upon the same object.

However, it's not always possible to return a reference. A function shouldn't return a reference to a temporary object created in the function, for the reference becomes invalid when the function terminates and the object disappears. In this case, the code should return an object in order to generate a copy that will be available to the calling program.

As a rule of thumb, if a function returns a temporary object created in the function, don't use a reference. For example, the following method uses a constructor to create a new object, and it then returns a copy of that object:

```
Vector Vector::operator+(const Vector & b) const
{
    return Vector(x + b.x, y + b.y);
}
```

If a function returns an object that was passed to it via a reference or pointer, return the object by reference. For example, the following code returns, by reference, either the object that invokes the function or else the object passed as an argument:

```
const Stock & Stock::topval(const Stock & s) const
{
    if (s.total_val > total_val)
       return s;           // argument object
    else
       return *this;       // invoking object
}
```

Using `const`

Be alert to opportunities to use `const`. You can use it to guarantee that a method doesn't modify an argument:

```
Star::Star(const char * s) {...} // won't change the string to which s
                                 // points
```

You can use `const` to guarantee that a method won't modify the object that invokes it:

```
void Star::show() const {...} // won't change invoking object
```

Here `const` means `const Star * this`, where `this` points to the invoking object.

Normally, a function that returns a reference can be on the left side of an assignment statement, which really means you can assign a value to the object referred to. But you can use `const` to ensure that a reference or pointer return value can't be used to modify data in an object:

```
const Stock & Stock::topval(const Stock & s) const
{
    if (s.total_val > total_val)
        return s;                // argument object
    else
        return *this;            // invoking object
}
```

Here the method returns a reference either to `this` or to `s`. Because `this` and `s` are both declared `const`, the function is not allowed to change them, which means the returned reference also must be declared `const`.

Note that if a function declares an argument as a reference or pointer to a `const`, it cannot pass along that argument to another function unless that function also guarantees not to change the argument.

PUBLIC INHERITANCE CONSIDERATIONS

Naturally, adding inheritance to a program brings in more things to keep in mind. Let's look at a few.

The *is-a* Relationship

> *" In some cases the best approach may be to create an abstract data class with pure virtual functions and to derive other classes from it. "*

Be guided by the *is-a* relationship. If your proposed derived class is not a particular kind of the base class, don't use public derivation. For instance, don't derive a `Brain` class from a `Programmer` class. If you want to represent the belief that a programmer has a brain, use a `Brain` class object as a member of the `Programmer` class.

In some cases the best approach may be to create an abstract data class with pure virtual functions and to derive other classes from it.

Remember that one expression of the *is-a* relationship is that a base class pointer can point to a derived class object and that a base class reference can refer to a derived class object without an explicit type cast. Also remember that the reverse is not true; thus, you cannot have a derived class pointer or reference refer to a base class object without an explicit type cast. Depending upon the class declarations, such an explicit type cast (a downcast) may or may not make sense.

What's Not Inherited

Constructors are not inherited. However, derived class constructors typically use the initialization-list syntax to call upon base class constructors to construct the base class portion of a derived object. If the derived class constructor doesn't explicitly call a base constructor in using the initialization-list syntax, it will use the base class's default constructor. In an inheritance chain, each class can use an initialization list to pass back information to its immediate base class.

Destructors are not inherited. When an object is destroyed, the program first calls the derived destructor, and then the base destructor. If there is a default base class destructor, the compiler generates a default derived class destructor. Generally speaking, if a class serves as a base class, its destructor should be virtual.

The assignment operator is not inherited. It does have some interesting properties that we'll look at next.

The Assignment Operator

The compiler automatically supplies every class with an assignment operator for assigning one object to another of the same class. The default version of this operator uses memberwise assignment, with each member of the target object being assigned the value of the corresponding member of the source object. However, if the object belongs to a derived class, the compiler uses the base class assignment operator to handle assignment for the base class portion of the derived object. If you've explicitly provided an assignment operator for the base class, that operator is used. Similarly, if a class contains a member that is an object of another class, the assignment operator for that class is used for that member.

As you've seen several times, you need to provide an explicit assignment operator if class constructors use new to initialize pointers. Because C++ uses the base class assignment operator for the base part of derived objects, you don't need to redefine the assignment operator for a derived class *unless* it adds data members that require special care. For example, the BankAccountD class defined assignment explicitly, but the derived Overdraft class uses the default assignment operator generated for that class.

Suppose, however, that a derived class does use new, and you have to provide an explicit assignment operator. The operator must provide for every member of the class, not just the new members. The OverdraftD class illustrates how this can be done:

```
OverdraftD & OverdraftD::operator=(const OverdraftD & od)
{
    if (this == &od)
        return *this;
    BankAccountD::operator=(od);    // base-class assignment
    delete [] codeName;
    codeName = new char[strlen(od.codeName) + 1];
    strcpy(codeName, od.codeName);
    maxLoan = od.maxLoan;
    owesBank = od.owesBank;
    rate = od.rate;
    return *this;
}
```

What about assigning a derived object to a base object? (Note: This is not the same as initializing a base class reference to a derived object.)

```
BankAccountD blips;                                          // base class
OverdraftD snips("Ranele Posh", "Topper", 222333,3993); // derived class
blips = snips;                          // assign derived object to base object
```

Which assignment operator is used? Remember that the assignment statement is translated into a method invoked by the left-hand object:

```
blips.operator=(snips);
```

Here the left-hand object is a `BankAccountD` object, so it invokes the `BankAccountD::operator=(const BankAccountD &)` function. The *is-a* relationship allows the `BankAccountD` reference to refer to a derived class object, such as `snips`. The assignment operator only deals with base class members, so the `codeName` member and other `OverdraftD` members of `snips` are ignored in the assignment. In short, you can assign a derived object to a base object, and only the base class members are involved.

What about the reverse? Can you assign a base class object to a derived object?

```
BankAccount gp("Griff Parker", 21234, 1200);   // base class
Overdraft temp;                                 // derived class
temp = gp;   // possible?
```

Here the assignment statement would be translated as follows:

```
temp.operator=(gp);
```

The left-hand object is an `Overdraft` object, so it invokes the `Overdraft::operator=(const Overdraft &)` function. However, a derived class reference cannot automatically refer to a base object, so this code *won't* run unless there also is a conversion constructor:

```
Overdraft(const BankAccount &);
```

(It could be, as in this case, that there is a constructor with additional arguments, provided they have default values.) In that case, the program will use this constructor to create a temporary `Overdraft` object from `gp`, which will then be used as an argument to the assignment operator.

Alternatively, you could define an assignment operator for assigning a base class to a derived class:

```
Overdraft & Overdraft ::operator=(const BankAccount &) {...}
```

Here the types match the assignment statement exactly, and no type conversions are needed.

Private Versus Protected

Remember that protected members act like public members as far as a derived class is concerned, but like private members for the world at large. A derived class can access protected members of a base class directly, but can access private members only via base class member functions. Thus, making base class members private offers more security, while making them protected simplifies coding and speeds up access. Stroustrup feels that it's better to use private data members than protected data members, but that protected methods are useful. (Bjarne Stroustrup, *The Design and Evolution of C++*. Reading, MA: Addison-Wesley Publishing Company, 1994.)

Virtual Methods

" Note that inappropriate code can circumvent dynamic binding. "

When you design a base class, you have to decide whether to make class methods virtual or not. If you want a derived class to be able to redefine a method, define the method as virtual in the base class. This enables late, or dynamic, binding. If you don't want the method redefined, don't make it virtual. This doesn't prevent someone from redefining the method, but it should be interpreted as meaning that you don't want it redefined.

Note that inappropriate code can circumvent dynamic binding. Consider, for example, the following two functions:

```
void show(const BankAccount & rba)
{
    rba.ViewAcct();
    cout << endl;
}

void sloppy(BankAccount ba)
{
    ba.ViewAcct();
    cout << endl;
}
```

The first passes an object by reference, and the second passes an object by value. Now suppose you use each with a derived class argument:

```
Overdraft buzz("Buzz Parsec", 00001111, 4300);
show(buzz);
sloppy(buzz);
```

The show() function call results in the rba argument being a reference to the Overdraft object buzz, so rba.ViewAcct() is interpreted as the Overdraft version, as it should be. But in the sloppy() function, which passes an object by value, ba is a BankAccount object constructed by the BankAccount(const BankAccount &) constructor. (Automatic upcasting allows the constructor argument to refer to an Overdraft object.) Thus, in sloppy(), ba.ViewAcct() is the BankAccount version, so only the BankAccount component of buzz is displayed.

Destructors

As mentioned before, a base class destructor should be virtual. That way, when you delete a derived object via a base class pointer or reference to the object, the program uses the derived class destructor followed by the base class destructor rather than using only the base class destructor.

CLASS FUNCTION SUMMARY

C++ class functions come in many variations. Some can be inherited, some can't. Some operator functions can be either member functions or friends, while others can only be member functions. Table 12.1, based on a similar table from the ARM (*Annotated Reference Manual*), summarizes these properties. In it, the notation *op=* stands for assignment operators of the form +=, *=, and so on. Note that the properties for the *op=* operators are no different from those of the "other operators" category. The reason for listing *op=* separately is to point out that these operators don't behave like the = operator.

TABLE 12.1
MEMBER FUNCTION PROPERTIES

Function	Inherited	Member or friend	Generated by default	Can be virtual	Can have a return type
constructor	no	member	yes	no	no
destructor	no	member	yes	yes	no
=	no	member	yes	yes	yes
&	yes	either	yes	yes	yes
conversion	yes	member	no	yes	no
( )	yes	member	no	yes	yes
[ ]	yes	member	no	yes	yes
->	yes	member	no	yes	yes
op=	yes	either	no	yes	yes
new	yes	static member	no	no	void *
delete	yes	static member	no	no	void
other operators	yes	either	no	yes	yes
other members	yes	member	no	yes	yes
friends	no	friend	no	no	yes

Summary

Inheritance enables you to adapt programming code to your particular needs by defining a new class (a derived class) from an existing class (the base class). Public inheritance models an *is-a* relationship, meaning a derived-class object also should be a kind of base-class object. As part of the *is-a* model, a derived class inherits the data members and most methods of the base class. However, a derived class doesn't inherit the base class constructors, destructor, and assignment operator. A derived class can access the public and protected members of the base class directly and the private base class members via the public and protected base-class methods. You then can add new data members and methods to the class, and you can use the derived class as a base class for further development. Each derived class requires its own constructors. When a program creates a derived class object, it first calls a base class constructor and then the derived class constructor. When a program deletes an object, it first calls the derived class destructor and then the base class destructor.

If a class is meant to be a base class, you may choose to use protected members instead of private members so that derived classes can access those members directly. However, using private members will, in general, reduce the scope for programming bugs. If you intend that a derived class can redefine a base class method, make it a virtual function by declaring it with the keyword `virtual`. This enables objects accessed by pointers or references to be handled on the basis of the object type rather than on the basis of the reference type or pointer type. In particular, the destructor for a base class normally should be virtual.

You may want to define an ABC (abstract base class) that defines an interface without getting into implementation matters. For instance, you could define an abstract `Shape` class from which particular shape classes, such as `Circle` and `Square`, will be derived. An abstract base class must include at least one pure virtual method. You can declare a pure virtual method by placing `= 0` before the closing semicolon of the declaration.

```
virtual double area() const = 0;
```

You don't define pure virtual methods, and you can't create an object of a class containing pure virtual members. Instead, they serve to define a common interface to be used by derived classes.

Review Questions

1. What does a derived class inherit from a base class?

2. What doesn't a derived class inherit from a base class?

3. Suppose the return type for the `BankAccountD::operator=()` function were defined as `BankAccountD` instead of `BankAccountD &`. What effect, if any, would that have?

4. In what order are class constructors and class destructors called when a derived class object is created and deleted?

5. If a derived class doesn't add any data members to the base class, does the derived class require constructors?

6. Suppose a base class and a derived class both define a method of the same name and a derived class object invokes the method. What method is called?

7. When does a derived class have to define an assignment operator?

8. Can you assign the address of an object of a derived class to a pointer to the base class? Can you assign the address of an object of a base class to a pointer to the derived class?

9. Can you assign an object of a derived class to an object of the base class? Can you assign an object of a base class to an object of the derived class?

10. Suppose you define a function that takes a reference to a base class object as an argument. Why can this function also use a derived class object as an argument?

11. Suppose you define a function that takes a base class object as an argument (that is, the function passes a base class object by value). Why can this function also use a derived class object as an argument?

12. Why is it usually better to pass objects by reference than by value?

13. Suppose `Corporation` is a base class and `PublicCorporation` is a derived class. Also suppose that each class defines a `head()` member function, that `ph` is a pointer to the `Corporation` type, and that `ph` is assigned the address of a `PublicCorporation` object. How is `ph->head()` interpreted if the base class defines `head()` as a

   a. Regular function

   b. Virtual function

14. What's wrong, if anything, with the following code?

```
class Kitchen
{
private:
    double kit_sq_ft;
public:
    Kitchen() {kit_sq_ft = 0.0; }
    virtual double area() { return kit_sq_ft * kit_sq_ft; }
};
class House : public Kitchen
{
private:
    double all_sq_ft;
public:
    House() {all_sq_ft += kit_sq_ft;}
    double area(const char *s) { cout << s; return all_sq_ft; }
};
```

Exercises

1. Start with the following class declaration:

```
// base class
class Cd {  // represents a CD disk
private:
    char performers[50];
    char label[20];
    int selections;    // number of selections
    double playtime;   // playing time in minutes
public:
    Cd(char * s1, char * s2, int n, double x);
    Cd(const Cd & d);
    Cd();
    ~Cd();
    void Report() const;  // reports all CD data
    Cd & operator=(const Cd & d);
};
```

Derive a `Classic` class that adds an array of `char` members that will hold a string identifying the primary work on the CD. If the base class requires that any functions be virtual, modify the base class declaration to make it so. Test your product with the following program:

```
#include <iostream>
using namespace std;
#include "classic.h"      // which will contain #include cd.h
void Bravo(const Cd & disk);
int main()
{
    Cd c1("Beatles", "Capitol", 14, 35.5);
    Classic c2 = Classic("Piano Sonata in B flat, Fantasia in C",
                    "Alfred Brendel", "Philips", 2, 57.17);
    Cd *pcd = &c1;

    cout << "Using object directly:\n";
    c1.Report();    // use Cd method
    c2.Report();    // use Classic method

    cout << "Using type cd * pointer to objects:\n";
    pcd->report();  // use Cd method for cd object
    pcd = &c2;
    pcd->Report();  // use Classic method for classic object

    cout << "Calling a function with a Cd reference argument:\n";
    Bravo(c1);
    Bravo(c2);

    cout << "Testing assignment: ";
    Classic copy;
    copy = c2;
    copy.Report()

    return 0;
}

void bravo(Cd & disk)
{
    disk.report();
}
```

2. Repeat exercise 1, but this time use dynamic memory allocation instead of fixed-size arrays for the various strings tracked by the two classes.

3. Revise the `BankAccount-Overdraft` class hierarchy so that both classes are derived from an abstract base class. Test the result with a program similar to the one in Listing 12.8.

4. The Benevolent Order of Programmers maintains a collection of bottled port. To describe it, the BOP Portmaster has devised a `Port` class as declared below:

```cpp
#include <iostream>
using namespace std;
class Port
{
private:
    char * brand;
    char style[20]; // i.e., tawny, ruby, vintage
    int bottles;
public:
    Port(const char * br = "none", const char * st = "none",
        int b = 0);
    Port(const Port & p);                   // copy constructor
    virtual ~Port() { delete [] brand; }
    Port & operator=(const Port & p);
    Port & operator+=(int b);               // adds b to bottles
    Port & operator-=(int b);// subtracts b from bottles, if available
    int BottleCount() const { return bottles; }
    virtual void Show() const;
    friend ostream & operator<<(ostream & os, const Port & p);
};
```

The `Show()` method presents information in the following format:

```
Brand: Gallo
Kind: tawny
Bottles: 20
```

The `operator<<()` function presents information in the following format (no newline at the end):

```
Gallo, tawny, 20
```

The Portmaster completed the method definitions for the `Port` class and then derived the `VintagePort` class as follows before being relieved of his position for accidentally routing a bottle of '45 Cockburn to someone preparing an experimental barbecue sauce.

```cpp
class VintagePort : public Port // style necessarily = "vintage"
{
private:
    char * nickname;         // i.e., "The Noble" or "Old Velvet", etc.
```

```
    int year;                      // vintage year
public:
    VintagePort();
    VintagePort(const char * br, int b, const char * nn, int y);
    VintagePort(const VintagePort & vp);
    ~VintagePort() { delete [] nickname; }
    VintagePort & operator=(const VintagePort & vp);
    void Show() const;
    friend ostream & operator<<(ostream & os, const VintagePort & vp);
};
```

You get the job of completing the VintagePort work.

    a. Your first task is to re-create the Port method definitions, because the former Portmaster immolated his upon being relieved.

    b. Your second task is to explain why certain methods are redefined and others are not.

    c. Your third task is to explain why operator=() and operator<<() are not virtual.

    d. Your fourth task is to provide definitions for the VintagePort methods.

13

Reusing Code in C++

One of the main goals of C++ is to facilitate the reuse of code. Public inheritance is one mechanism for achieving this goal, but not the only one. This chapter will investigate other choices. One technique is using class members that are themselves objects of another class. This is referred to as *containment*, or *composition*, or *layering*. Another option is using private or protected inheritance. Containment, private inheritance, and protected inheritance typically are used to implement *has-a* relationships, that is, relationships for which the new class has an object of another class. For instance, a `Stereo` class might have a `CdPlayer` object. Multiple inheritance lets you create classes that inherit from two or more base classes, combining their functionality.

Chapter 9 introduced function templates. Now we'll look at class templates, which provide another way of reusing code. Class templates let you define a class in generic terms. Then you can use the template to create specific classes defined for specific types. For instance, you could define a general stack template and then use the template to create one class representing a stack of `int` values and another class representing a stack of `double` values. You could even generate a class representing a stack of stacks.

You will learn about the following in this chapter:

- *Has-a* relationships

- Classes with member objects (containment)

- Private and protected inheritance

- Creating class templates

- Using class templates

- Template specializations
- Multiple inheritance
- Virtual base classes

Classes with Object Members

Let's begin with classes that include class objects as members. Some classes, such as the `String` class of Chapter 11 or the standard C++ classes and templates of Chapter 15, offer convenient ways of representing components of a more extensive class. We'll look at a particular example now.

What is a student? Someone enrolled in a school? Someone engaged in thoughtful investigation? A refugee from the harsh exigencies of the real world? Someone with an identifying name and a set of quiz scores? Clearly, the last definition is a totally inadequate characterization of a person, but it is well-suited for a simple computer representation. So let's develop a `Student` class based on that definition.

Simplifying a student to a name and a set of quiz scores suggests using a `String` class object (Chapter 11) to hold the name and an array class object (coming up soon) to hold the scores (assumed to be type `double`). (Once you learn about the library classes discussed in Chapter 15, you probably would use the standard `string` and `vector` classes.) You might be tempted to publicly derive a `Student` class from these two classes. That would be an example of multiple public inheritance, which C++ allows, but it would be inappropriate here. The reason is that the relationship of a student to these classes doesn't fit the *is-a* model. A student is not a name. A student is not an array of quiz scores. What we have here is a *has-a* relationship. A student has a name, and a student has an array of quiz scores. The usual C++ technique for modeling *has-a* relationships is to use composition or containment; that is, to create a class composed of, or containing, members that are objects of another class. For example, we can begin a `Student` class declaration like this:

```
class Student
{
private:
        String name;        // use a String object for name
        ArrayDb scores;     // use an ArrayDb object for scores
        ...
};
```

As usual, the class makes the data members private. This implies that the `Student` class member functions can use the public interfaces of the `String` and `ArrayDb` (for *array* of `double`) classes to access and modify the `name` and `scores` objects, but that the outside world cannot do so. The only access the outside world will have to `name` and `scores` is through the public interface defined for the `Student` class (see Figure 13.1). A common way of describing this is saying that the `Student` class acquires the implementation of its member objects but doesn't inherit the interface. For instance, a

FIGURE 13.1
Containment

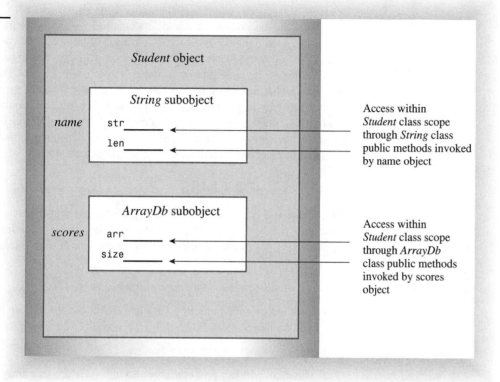

Student object uses the `String` implementation rather than a `char * name` or a `char name[26]` implementation for holding the name. But a `Student` object does not innately have the ability to use the `String operator==()` function.

INTERFACES AND IMPLEMENTATIONS

With public inheritance, a class inherits an interface, and, perhaps, an implementation. (Pure virtual functions in a base class provide an interface without an implementation.) Acquiring the interface is part of the *is-a* relationship. With composition, on the other hand, a class acquires the implementation without the interface. Not inheriting the interface is part of the *has-a* relationship.

The fact that a class object doesn't automatically acquire the interface of a contained object is a good thing for a *has-a* relationship. For instance, one could extend the String class to overload the + operator to allow concatenating two strings together, but, conceptually, it doesn't make sense to concatenate two Student objects. That's one reason not to use public inheritance in this case. On the other hand, parts of the interface for the contained class may make sense for the new class. For instance, you might want to use the operator<() method from the String interface to sort Student objects by name. You can do so by defining a Student::Operator<() member function that, internally, uses the String::Operator<() function. Let's move on to some details.

THE ArrayDb CLASS

The first detail is developing the ArrayDb class so that the Student class can use it. This class will be quite similar to the String class because the latter is an array, too, in this case, of char. First, let's list some necessary or desirable features for the ArrayDb class.

- It should be able to store several double values.
- It should provide random access to individual values using bracket notation with an index.
- One can assign one array to another.
- The class will perform bounds checking to ensure that array indices are valid.

The first two features are the essence of an array. The third feature is not true of built-in arrays but is true for class objects, so creating an array class will provide that feature. The final feature, again, is not true for built-in arrays, but can be added as part of the second feature.

At this point, much of the design can ape the String declaration. That is, you can do this:

```
class ArrayDb
{
private:
    unsigned int size;                 // number of array elements
    double * arr;                      // address of first element
public:
    ArrayDb();                         // default constructor
    // create an ArrayDb of n elements, set each to val
    ArrayDb(unsigned int n, double val = 0.0);
    // create an ArrayDb of n elements, initialize to array pn
    ArrayDb(const double * pn, unsigned int n);
    ArrayDb(const ArrayDb & a);        // copy constructor
    virtual ~ArrayDb();                // destructor
        // other stuff to be added here
    ArrayDb & operator=(const ArrayDb & a);
    friend ostream & operator<<(ostream & os, const ArrayDb & a);
};
```

The class will use dynamic memory allocation to create an array of the desired size. Therefore, it also will provide a destructor, a copy constructor, and an assignment operator. For convenience, it will have a few more constructors.

The main new feature is providing random access using array notation. That is, suppose you have the following declaration:

```
ArrayDb scores(5, 20.0); // 5 elements, each set to 20.0
```

If scores really acts like an array, you should be able to do the following:

```
double temp = scores[3];
scores[3] = 16.5:
```

What this requires is a way to make the public expression scores[3] correspond to the private representation scores.arr[3]. This can be done easily because [] is just another C++ operator, like <<, so it can be overloaded. Like <<, [] has two operands. The main peculiarity is that one of the operands goes inside the brackets. Anyway, an expression like

```
scores[3]
```

maps to the following overloaded operator function call:

```
scores.operator[](3)
```

Here, the function name is operator[]. Because the left operand is an object of the ArrayDb class and the right operand is an int, this would correspond to an ArrayDb::operator[](int) member function.

The statement

```
temp = scores[2];
```

corresponds to the following:

```
temp = scores.operator[](2);
```

This means the function should return the value of scores.arr[2] or else a reference to that element of the array. However, a statement like

```
scores[2] = 19.0;
```

translates to the following:

```
scores.operator[](2) = 19.0;
```

Assigning to a function requires that the function return a reference, not a value, so that's the only route open. The simplest implementation would be this:

```
double & ArrayDb::operator[](int i)
{
    return arr[i];
}
```

Basically, it converts scores[i] to scores.arr[i], allowing public access to the private internal array elements. Because the main purpose of an array is to allow random access to its elements, this particular exposure of private element to public modification is desirable. As the next section shows, using the [ ] operator instead of allowing direct access via public data members can provide better protection.

Tweaking operator[]()

The overloaded [ ] operator lets you access individual elements, but only through this particular operator. This gives you the opportunity to build in some safety checks. In particular, the method can check to see whether the proposed array index is in bounds. That is, you can rewrite the operator this way:

```
double & ArrayDb::operator[](int i)
{
    // check index before continuing
    if (i < 0 || i >= size)
    {
        cerr << "Error in array limits: "
            << i << " is a bad index\n";
        exit(1);
    }
    return arr[i];
}
```

This slows down a program, for it requires evaluating an if statement every time the program accesses an array element. But it adds safety, preventing a program from placing a value in the 2000th element of a 5-element array.

The const Alternative

The preceding definition has a weak point. Consider the following code:

```
const ArrayDb noChanges(5, 0.4);   // 5 elements each set to 0.4
cout << noChanges[2];              // not valid!
```

The problem is that noChanges is const, but operator[]() doesn't promise to not change values, and you can't invoke a non-const method with a const object. Fortunately, there is a simple fix. You can overload functions whose signatures are otherwise identical if one function uses a const reference or pointer and the other one doesn't. That is, the class needs the following function, too:

```
const double & ArrayDb::operator[](int i) const
{
    // check index before continuing
    if (i < 0 || i >= size)
    {
        cerr << "Error in array limits: "
            << i << " is a bad index\n";
        exit(1);
    }
    return arr[i];
}
```

Notice that because the return reference is const, you can't use this version to assign to an array element. That is the proper behavior for accessing a const array. You can use it only to fetch the value in the element. So

```
cout << noChanges[2];    // allowed for a const object
```

> **You can overload functions whose signatures are otherwise identical if one function uses a const reference or pointer and the other one doesn't.**

is valid, and the following statement is not valid:

```
noChanges[2] = 300.4;   // not allowed for a const object
```

The compiler will select the const version of operator[]() for use with const ArrayDb objects and use the other version for non-const ArrayDb objects.

Listing 13.1 shows the header file for the ArrayDb class. For extra convenience, the class definition includes an Average() method that returns the average of the array elements.

Listing 13.1 arraydb.h

```cpp
// arraydb.h -- array class
#ifndef _ARRAYDB_H_
#define _ARRAYDB_H_
#include <iostream>
using namespace std;

class ArrayDb
{
private:
    unsigned int size;              // number of array elements
    double * arr;                   // address of first element
public:
    ArrayDb();                      // default constructor
    // create an ArrayDb of n elements, set each to val
    explicit ArrayDb(unsigned int n, double val = 0.0);
    // create an ArrayDb of n elements, initialize to array pn
    ArrayDb(const double * pn, unsigned int n);
    ArrayDb(const ArrayDb & a);     // copy constructor
    virtual ~ArrayDb();             // destructor
    unsigned int ArSize() const {return size;}// returns array size
    double Average() const;         // return array average
// overloaded operators
    virtual double & operator[](int i); // array indexing
    virtual const double & operator[](int i) const; // array indexing
    ArrayDb & operator=(const ArrayDb & a);
    friend ostream & operator<<(ostream & os, const ArrayDb & a);
};

#endif
```

 Remember

Older implementations don't support the explicit keyword.

One point of interest is that one of the constructors uses explicit:

```cpp
explicit ArrayDb(unsigned int n, double val = 0.0);
```

A constructor that can be called with one argument, recall, serves as an implicit conversion function from the argument type to the class type. In this case, the first argument represents the number of elements in the array rather than a value for the array, so having the constructor serve as an int-to-ArrayDb conversion function does not make sense. Using explicit turns off implicit conversions. If this keyword were omitted, then code like the following would be possible:

```
ArrayDb doh(20,100);  // array of 20 elements, each set to 100
doh = 5;   // set doh to an array of 5 elements, each set to 0
```

Here, the inattentive programmer typed doh instead of doh[0]. If the constructor were explicit free, 5 would be converted to a temporary ArrayDb object using the constructor call ArrayDb(5), with the default value of 0 being used for the second argument. Then, assignment would replace the original doh with the temporary object. Listing 13.2 shows the implementation.

Listing 13.2 arraydb.cpp

```cpp
// arraydb.cpp -- ArrayDb class methods
#include <iostream>
using namespace std;
#include <cstdlib>    // exit() prototype
#include "arraydb.h"

// default constructor -- no arguments
ArrayDb::ArrayDb()
{
    arr = NULL;
    size = 0;
}

// constructs array of n elements, each set to val
ArrayDb::ArrayDb(unsigned int n, double val)
{
    arr = new double[n];
    size = n;
    for (int i = 0; i < size; i++)
        arr[i] = val;
}

// initialize ArrayDb object to a non-class array
ArrayDb::ArrayDb(const double *pn, unsigned int n)
{
    arr = new double[n];
    size = n;
    for (int i = 0; i < size; i++)
        arr[i] = pn[i];
}

// initialize ArrayDb object to another ArrayDb object
ArrayDb::ArrayDb(const ArrayDb & a)
{
    size = a.size;
    arr = new double[size];
    for (int i = 0; i < size; i++)
        arr[i] = a.arr[i];
}

ArrayDb::~ArrayDb()
{
    delete [] arr;
}

double ArrayDb::Average() const
{
```

```
    double sum = 0;
    int i;
    int lim = ArSize();
    for (i = 0; i < lim; i++)
        sum += arr[i];
    if (i > 0)
        return sum / i;
    else
    {
        cerr << "No entries in score array\n";
        return 0;
    }
}

// let user access elements by index (assignment allowed)
double & ArrayDb::operator[](int i)
{
    // check index before continuing
    if (i < 0 || i >= size)
    {
        cerr << "Error in array limits: "
            << i << " is a bad index\n";
        exit(1);
    }
    return arr[i];
}

// let user access elements by index (assignment disallowed)
const double & ArrayDb::operator[](int i) const
{
    // check index before continuing
    if (i < 0 || i >= size)
    {
        cerr << "Error in array limits: "
            << i << " is a bad index\n";
        exit(1);
    }
    return arr[i];
}

// define class assignment
ArrayDb & ArrayDb::operator=(const ArrayDb & a)
{
    if (this == &a)        // if object assigned to self,
        return *this;      // don't change anything
    delete [] arr;
    size = a.size;
    arr = new double[size];
    for (int i = 0; i < size; i++)
        arr[i] = a.arr[i];
    return *this;
}

// quick output, 5 values to a line
ostream & operator<<(ostream & os, const ArrayDb & a)
{
    int i;
    for (i = 0; i < a.size; i++)
    {
```

```
        os << a.arr[i] << " ";
        if (i % 5 == 4)
            os << "\n";
    }
    if (i % 5 != 0)
        os << "\n";
    return os;
}
```

THE Student CLASS EXAMPLE

With the ArrayDb class now in hand, let's proceed to provide the Student class declaration. It should, of course, include constructors and at least a few functions to provide
an interface for the Student class. Listing 13.3 does this, defining all the constructors
inline.

Listing 13.3 studentc.h

```
// studentc.h -- defining a Student class using containment
#ifndef _STUDNTC_H_
#define _STUDENTC_H_

#include <iostream>
using namespace std;
#include "arraydb.h"
#include "strng2.h"      // from Chapter 11

class Student
{
private:
    String name;
    ArrayDb scores;
public:
    Student() : name("Null Student"), scores() {}
    Student(const String & s)
        : name(s), scores() {}
    Student(int n) : name("Nully"), scores(n) {}
    Student(const String & s, int n)
        : name(s), scores(n) {}
    Student(const String & s, const ArrayDb & a)
        : name(s), scores(a) {}
    Student(const char * str, const double * pd, int n)
        : name(str), scores(pd, n) {}
    ~Student() {}
    double & operator[](int i);
    const double & operator[](int i) const;
    double Average() const;

// friends
    friend ostream & operator<<(ostream & os, const Student & stu);
    friend istream & operator>>(istream & is, Student & stu);
};

#endif
```

Initializing Contained Objects

Note that constructors all use the by-now familiar initializer-list syntax to initialize the `name` and `scores` member objects. In some past cases, the constructors used it to initialize members that were built-in types:

```
Queue::Queue(int qs) : qsize(qs)  {...} // initialize qsize to qs
```

This code uses the name of the data member (`qsize`) in the initializer list. Also, constructors from previous examples have used the initializer list to initialize the base class portion of a derived object:

```
OverdraftD::OverdraftD(const OverdraftD & od) : BankAccountD(od) {...}
```

For inherited objects, constructors used the class name in the initializer list to invoke a specific base class constructor. For member objects, constructors use the member name. For example, look at the last constructor in Listing 13.3:

```
Student(const char * str, const double * pd, int n)
        : name(str), scores(pd, n) {}
```

Because it initializes member objects, not inherited objects, it uses the member names, not the class names, in the initializer list. Each item in this initializer list invokes the matching constructor. That is, `name(str)` invokes the `String(const char *)` constructor, and `scores(pd, n)` invokes the `ArrayDb(const double *, int)` constructor.

What happens if you don't use the initializer-list syntax? As with inherited components, C++ requires that all member objects be constructed before the rest of an object is constructed. So if you omit the initializer list, C++ will use the default constructors defined for the member objects' classes.

Using an Interface for a Contained Object

The interface for a contained object isn't public, but it can be used within the class methods. For instance, here is how you can define a function that returns the average of a student's scores:

```
double Student::Average() const
{
    return scores.Average();
}
```

This defines a function that can be invoked by a `Student` object. Internally, it uses the `ArrayDb::Average()` function. That's because `scores` is an `ArrayDb` object, so it can invoke the member functions of the `ArrayDb` class.

Similarly, you can define a friend function that uses both the `String` and the `ArrayDb` versions of the << operator:

```
ostream & operator<<(ostream & os, const Student & stu)
{
    os << "Scores for " << stu.name << ":\n";
    os << stu.scores;
    return os;
}
```

Because `stu.name` is a `String` object, it invokes the `operator<<(ostream &, const String &)` function. Similarly, the `ArrayDb` object `stu.scores` invokes the `operator <<(ostream &, const ArrayDb &)` function. Note that the new function must be a friend to the `Student` class so that it can access the `name` and `scores` member of a `Student` object.

Listing 13.4 shows the class methods file for the `Student` class. It includes methods that allow you to use the `[ ]` operator to access individual scores in a `Student` object.

Listing 13.4 studentc.cpp

```cpp
// studentc.cpp -- Student class using containment
#include "studentc.h"

double Student::Average() const
{
    return scores.Average();  // use ArrayDb::Average()
}

double & Student::operator[](int i)
{
    return scores[i];            // use ArrayDb::operator[]()
}

const double & Student::operator[](int i) const
{
    return scores[i];
}

// friends

// use String and ArrayDb versions
ostream & operator<<(ostream & os, const Student & stu)
{
    os << "Scores for " << stu.name << ":\n";
    os << stu.scores;
    return os;
}

// use String version
istream & operator>>(istream & is, Student & stu)
{
    is >> stu.name;
    return is;
}
```

This hasn't required much new code. Using containment allows you to take advantage of the code you've already written.

Using the New Class

Let's put together a small program to test the new class. To keep things simple, it will use an array of just three `Student` objects, each holding five quiz scores. And it'll use an unsophisticated input cycle that doesn't verify input and that doesn't let you cut the input process short. Listing 13.5 presents the test program. Compile it along with studentc.cpp, strng2.cpp, and arrayDb.cpp.

Listing 13.5 use_stuc.cpp

```cpp
// use_stuc.cpp -- use a composite class
// compile with studentc.cpp, strng2.cpp, arraydb.cpp
#include <iostream>
using namespace std;
#include "studentc.h"

void set(Student & sa, int n);

const int pupils = 3;
const int quizzes = 5;

int main()
{
    Student ada[pupils] = {quizzes, quizzes, quizzes};

    int i;
    for (i = 0; i < pupils; i++)
        set(ada[i], quizzes);
    for (i = 0; i < pupils; i++)
    {
        cout << "\n" << ada[i];
        cout << "average: " << ada[i].Average() << "\n";
    }
    return 0;
}

void set(Student & sa, int n)
{
    cout << "Please enter the student's name: ";
    cin >> sa;
    cout << "Please enter " << n << " quiz scores:\n";
    for (int i = 0; i < n; i++)
        cin >> sa[i];
    while (cin.get() != '\n')
        continue;
}
```

Here is a sample run:

```
Please enter the student's name: Gil Bayts
Please enter 5 quiz scores:
92 94 96 93 95
Please enter the student's name: Pat Roone
Please enter 5 quiz scores:
83 89 72 78 95
Please enter the student's name: Fleur O'Day
Please enter 5 quiz scores:
92 89 96 78 64

Scores for Gil Bayts:
92 94 96 93 95
average: 94
```

```
Scores for Pat Roone:
83 89 72 78 95
average: 83.4

Scores for Fleur O'Day
92 89 96 78 64
average: 83.8
```

Private Inheritance

C++ has a second means of implementing the *has-a* relationship—*private inheritance*. With private inheritance, public and protected members of the base class become private members of the derived class. This means the methods of the base class do not become part of the public interface of the derived object. They can be used, however, inside the member functions of the derived class.

Let's look at the interface topic more closely. With public inheritance, the public methods of the base class become public methods of the derived class. In short, the derived class inherits the base class interface. This is part of the *is-a* relationship. With private inheritance, the public methods of the base class become private methods of the derived class. In short, the derived class does not inherit the base class interface. As you saw with contained objects, this lack of inheritance is part of the *has-a* relationship.

With private inheritance, a class does inherit the implementation. That is, if you base a Student class on a String class, the Student class winds up with an inherited String class component that can be used to store a string. Furthermore, the Student methods can use the String methods internally to access the String component.

Containment adds an object to a class as a named member object, while private inheritance adds an object to a class as an unnamed inherited object. We'll use the term *subobject* to denote an object added by inheritance or by containment.

Private inheritance, then, provides the same features as containment: acquire the implementation, don't acquire the interface. Therefore it, too, can be used to implement a *has-a* relationship. Let's see how you can use private inheritance to redesign the Student class.

THE Student CLASS EXAMPLE (NEW VERSION)

To get private inheritance, use the keyword private instead of public when defining the class. (Actually, private is the default, so omitting an access qualifier also leads to private inheritance.) The Student class should inherit from two classes, so the declaration will list both:

```
class Student : private String, private ArrayDb
{
public:
    ...
};
```

Having more than one base class is called *multiple inheritance*, or MI. In general, multiple inheritance, particularly public multiple inheritance, can lead to problems that must be resolved with additional syntax rules. We'll talk about such matters later in this chapter. But in this particular case, MI causes no problems.

Note that the new class won't need a private section. That's because the two inherited base classes already provide all the needed data members. Containment provided two explicitly named objects as members. Private inheritance, however, provides two nameless subobjects as inherited members. This is the first of the main differences in the two approaches.

" Containment provided two explicitly named objects as members. Private inheritance, however, provides two nameless subobjects as inherited members. "

Initializing Base Class Components

Having implicitly inherited components instead of member objects will affect the coding, for you no longer can use name and scores to describe the objects. Instead, you must go back to the techniques you used for public inheritance. For instance, consider constructors. Containment used this constructor:

```
Student(const char * str, const double * pd, int n)
   : name(str), scores(pd, n) {}     // use object names for containment
```

The new version will use the initializer syntax for inherited classes, which uses the *class* name instead of a *member* name to identify constructors:

```
Student(const char * str, const double * pd, int n)
   : String(str), ArrayDb(pd, n) {}  // use class names for inheritance
```

That is, the initializer list uses terms like String(str) instead of name(str). This is the second main difference in the two approaches.

Listing 13.6 shows the new class declaration. The only changes are the omission of explicit object names and the use of class names instead of member names in the inline constructors.

Listing 13.6 studenti.h

```
// studenti.h -- defining a Student class using private inheritance
#ifndef _STUDNTI_H_
#define _STUDENTI_H_

#include <iostream>
using namespace std;
#include "arraydb.h"
#include "strng2.h"

class Student : private String, private ArrayDb
{
public:
    Student() : String("Null Student"), ArrayDb() {}
    Student(const String & s)
        : String(s), ArrayDb() {}
    Student(int n) : String("Nully"), ArrayDb(n) {}
    Student(const String & s, int n)
        : String(s), ArrayDb(n) {}
```

```
        Student(const String & s, const ArrayDb & a)
            : String(s), ArrayDb(a) {}
        Student(const char * str, const double * pd, int n)
            : String(str), ArrayDb(pd, n) {}
        ~Student() {}
        double & operator[](int i);
        const double & operator[](int i) const;
        double Average() const;
// friends
        friend ostream & operator<<(ostream & os, const Student & stu);
        friend istream & operator>>(istream & is, Student & stu);
    };

    #endif
```

Using Base Class Methods

Private inheritance limits the use of base class methods to within derived class methods. Sometimes, however, you might like to make a base class facility available publicly. For instance, the class declaration suggests the ability to use an Average() function. As with containment, the technique for doing this is to use the private ArrayDb::Average() function within a public Student::average() function (see Figure 13.2). Containment invoked the method with an object:

```
double Student::Average() const
{
    return scores.Average();   // use ArrayDb::Average()
}
```

Here, however, inheritance lets you use the class name and the scope resolution operator to invoke a base-class function:

```
double Student::Average() const
{
    return ArrayDb::Average();
}
```

Omitting the ArrayDb:: qualifier would have caused the compiler to interpret the Average() function call as Student::Average(), leading to a highly undesirable recursive function definition. In short, the containment approach used object names to invoke a method, while private inheritance uses the class name and the scope resolution operator instead.

This technique of explicitly qualifying a function name with its class name doesn't work for friend functions because they don't belong to a class. However, you can use an explicit type cast to the base class to invoke the correct functions. For example, consider the following friend function definition:

FIGURE 13.2

Private inheritance

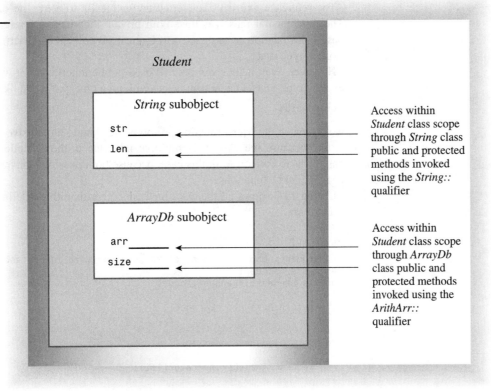

```
ostream & operator<<(ostream & os, const Student & stu)
{
    os << "Scores for " << (const String &) stu << ":\n";
    os << (const ArrayDb &) stu;
    return os;
}
```

If plato is a Student object, then the statement

```
cout << plato;
```

will invoke this function, with stu being a reference to plato and os being a reference to cout. Within the code, the type cast in

```
os << "Scores for " << (const String &) stu << ":\n";
```

explicitly converts stu to a reference to a type String object, and that matches the operator<<(ostream &, const String &) function. Similarly, the type cast in

```
os << (const ArrayDb &) stu;
```

invokes the operator<<(ostream &, const ArrayDb &) function.

The reference stu isn't converted automatically to a String or ArrayDb reference. The fundamental reason is this: With private inheritance, a reference or pointer to a base class cannot be assigned a reference or pointer to a derived class without an explicit type cast.

However, even if the example had used public inheritance, it would have had to use explicit type casts. One reason is that without a type cast, code like

```
os << stu;
```

would match the friend function prototype, leading to a recursive call. A second reason is that because the class uses multiple inheritance, the compiler couldn't tell which base class to convert to in this case, because both possible conversions match existing operator<<() functions.

Listing 13.7 shows all the class methods, other than those defined inline in the class declaration.

Listing 13.7 studenti.cpp
```
// studenti.cpp -- Student class using private inheritance
#include "studenti.h"
double Student::Average() const
{
    return ArrayDb::Average();
}

double & Student::operator[](int i)
{
    return  ArrayDb::operator[](i);
}

const double & Student::operator[](int i) const
{
    return ArrayDb::operator[](i);
}

// friends
ostream & operator<<(ostream & os, const Student & stu)
{
    os << "Scores for " << (const String &) stu << ":\n";
    os << (const ArrayDb &) stu;
    return os;
}

istream & operator>>(istream & is, Student & stu)
{
    is >> (String &) stu;
    return is;
}
```

Using the Revised Student Class

Once again it's time to test a new class. Note that the two versions of the Student class have exactly the same public interface, so you can test it with exactly the same program. The only difference is that you must include studenti.h instead of studentc.h, and you must link the program with studenti.cpp instead of with studentc.cpp. Listing 13.8 shows the program. Compile it along with studenti.cpp, strng2.cpp, and arrayDb.cpp.

Listing 13.8 use_stui.cpp

```cpp
// use_stui.cpp -- use a class with private derivation
// compile with studenti.cpp, strng2.cpp, arraydb.cpp
#include <iostream>
using namespace std;
#include "studenti.h"

void set(Student & sa, int n);

const int pupils = 3;
const int quizzes = 5;

int main()
{
    Student ada[pupils] = {quizzes, quizzes, quizzes};

    int i;
    for (i = 0; i < pupils; i++)
        set(ada[i], quizzes);
    for (i = 0; i < pupils; i++)
    {
        cout << "\n" << ada[i];
        cout << "average: " << ada[i].Average() << "\n";
    }
    return 0;
}

void set(Student & sa, int n)
{
    cout << "Please enter the student's name: ";
    cin >> sa;
    cout << "Please enter " << n << " quiz scores:\n";
    for (int i = 0; i < n; i++)
        cin >> sa[i];
    while (cin.get() != '\n')
        continue;
}
```

Here is a sample run:

```
Please enter the student's name: Gil Bayts
Please enter 5 quiz scores:
92 94 96 93 95
Please enter the student's name: Pat Roone
Please enter 5 quiz scores:
83 89 72 78 95
Please enter the student's name: Fleur O'Day
```

```
Please enter 5 quiz scores:
92 89 96 78 64

Scores for Gil Bayts:
92 94 96 93 95
average: 94

Scores for Pat Roone:
83 89 72 78 95
average: 83.4

Scores for Fleur O'Day
92 89 96 78 64
average: 83.8
```

The same input as before leads to the same output as before.

Containment or Private Inheritance?

Given that you can model a *has-a* relationship either with containment or with private inheritance, which should you use? Most C++ programmers prefer containment. First, it's easier to follow. When you look at the class declaration, you see explicitly named objects representing the contained classes, and your code can refer to these objects by name. Using inheritance makes the relationship appear more abstract. Second, inheritance can raise problems, particularly if a class inherits from more than one base class. You might have to deal with issues such as separate base classes having methods of the same name or of separate base classes sharing a common ancestor. All in all, you're less likely to run into trouble using containment. Also, containment allows you to include more than one subobject of the same class. If a class needs three String objects, you can declare three separate String members using the containment approach. But inheritance limits you to a single object. (It would be difficult to tell objects apart if they all were nameless.)

However, private inheritance does offer features beyond those provided by containment. Suppose, for example, that a class has protected members, which could either be data members or member functions. Such members are available to derived classes, but not to the world at large. If you include such a class in another class using composition, the new class is part of the world at large, not a derived class. Hence, it can't access protected members. But using inheritance makes the new class a derived class, so it can access protected members.

Another situation that calls for using private inheritance is if you want to redefine virtual functions. Again, this is a privilege accorded to a derived class but not to a containing class. With private inheritance, the redefined functions would be usable just within the class, not publicly.

Remember

> In general, use containment to model a *has-a* relationship. Use private inheritance if the new class must access protected members in the original class or if it must redefine virtual functions.

Protected Inheritance

Protected inheritance is a variation on private inheritance. It uses the keyword pro-tected when listing a base class:

```
class Student : protected String, protected ArrayDb {...};
```

With protected inheritance, public and protected members of a base class become protected members of the derived class. As with private inheritance, the interface for the base class is available to the derived class, but not to the outside world. The main difference between private and protected inheritance occurs when you derive another class from the derived class. With private inheritance, this third-generation class does not get the internal use of the base class interface. That's because the public base class methods become private in the derived class, and private members and methods can't be directly accessed by the next level of derivation. With protected inheritance, public base methods become protected in the second generation and so are available internally to the next level of derivation.

Table 13.1 summarizes public, private, and protected inheritance. The term *implicit upcasting* means that you can have a base class pointer or reference refer to a derived class object without using an explicit type cast.

> *" The main difference between private and protected inheritance occurs when you derive another class from the derived class. "*

TABLE 13.1
VARIETIES OF INHERITANCE

PROPERTY	PUBLIC INHERITANCE	PROTECTED INHERITANCE	PRIVATE INHERITANCE
public members become	public members of the derived class	protected members of the derived class	private members of the derived class
protected members become	protected members of the derived class	protected members of the derived class	private members of the derived class
private members become	accessible only through the base class interface	accessible only through the base class interface	accessible only through the base class interface
implicit upcasting	yes	yes (but only within the derived class)	no

Redefining Access With `using`

Public members of a base class become protected or private when you use protected or private derivation. The last example showed how the derived class can make a base class method available by having a derived class method use the base class method:

```
double Student::Average() const
{
    return ArrayDb::Average();
}
```

There is an alternative to wrapping one function call in another, and that is to use a using-declaration (like those used with namespaces) to announce a particular base class member can be used by the derived class, even though the derivation is private. For example, in studenti.h, you can omit the declaration for `Student::Average()` and replace it with a using-declaration:

```
class Student : private String, private ArrayDb
{
public:
    using ArrayDb::Average;
    ...
};
```

The using-declaration makes the `ArrayDb::Average()` method available as if it were a public `Student` method. That means you can drop the `Student::Average()` definition from studenti.cpp and still use `Average()` as before:

```
cout << "average: " << ada[i].Average() << "\n";
```

The difference is that now `ArrayDb::Average()` is called directly rather than through an intermediate call to `Student::Average()`.

Note that the using-declaration just uses the member name—no parentheses, no function signatures, no return types. For example, to make the `ArrayDB operator[]()` method available to the `Student` class, you'd place the following using-declaration in the public section of the `Student` class declaration:

```
using ArrayDb::operator[];
```

This would make both versions (const and non-const) available. The using-declaration approach works only for inheritance and not for containment.

There is an older way to redeclare base-class methods in a privately derived class, and that's to place the method name in the public section of the derived class. Here's how that would be done:

```
class Student : private String, private ArrayDb
{
public:
    ArrayDb::operator[];  // redeclare as public, just use name
    ...

};
```

It looks like a using-declaration without the `using` keyword. This approach is *deprecated*, meaning that the intention is to phase it out. So if your compiler supports the using-declaration, use it to make a method from a private base class available to the derived class.

Class Templates

Inheritance (public, private, or protected) and containment aren't always the answer to a desire to reuse code. Consider, for instance, the `Stack` class (Chapter 9), the `Queue` class (Chapter 11), and the `ArrayDb` class (this chapter). These are all examples of *container classes*, which are classes designed to hold other objects or data types. The `Stack` class, for example, stored `unsigned long` values. You could just as easily define a stack class for storing `double` values or `String` objects. The code would be identical other than for the type of object stored. However, rather than writing new class declarations, it would be nice if you could define a stack in a generic (that is, type-independent) fashion and then provide a specific type as a parameter to the class. Then you could use the same generic code to produce stacks of different kinds of values. In Chapter 9, the `Stack` example used `typedef` as a first pass at dealing with this desire. However, that approach has a couple of drawbacks. First, you must edit the header file each time you change the type. Second, you can use the technique to generate just one kind of stack per program. That is, you can't have a `typedef` represent two different types simultaneously, so you can't use the method to define a stack of `int`s and a stack of `String`s in the same program.

C++'s class templates provide a better way to generate generic class declarations. (C++ originally did not support templates, and, since their introduction, templates have continued to evolve, so it is possible that your compiler might not support all the features presented here.) Templates provide *parameterized* types; that is, the capability of passing a type name as an argument to a recipe for building a class or a function. By feeding the type name `int` to a `Queue` template, for example, you can get the compiler to construct a `Queue` class for queuing `int`s.

C++'s Standard Template Library (STL), which Chapter 15 discusses in part, provides powerful and flexible template implementations of several container classes. This chapter will explore designs of a more elementary nature.

DEFINING A CLASS TEMPLATE

Let's use the `Stack` class from Chapter 9 as the basis from which to build a template. Here's the original class declaration:

```
typedef unsigned long Item;

class Stack
{
private:
    enum {MAX = 10};    // constant specific to class
    Item items[MAX];    // holds stack items
```

```
    int top;              // index for top stack item
public:
    Stack();
    bool isempty() const;
    bool isfull() const;
    // push() returns false if stack already is full, true otherwise
    bool push(const Item & item);   // add item to stack
    // pop() returns false if stack already is empty, true otherwise
    bool pop(Item & item);          // pop top into item
};
```

The template approach will replace the Stack definition with a template definition and the Stack member functions with template member functions. As with template functions, you preface a template class with code of the following form:

```
template <class Type>
```

The keyword template informs the compiler that you're about to define a template. The part in angle brackets is analogous to an argument list to a function. You can think of the keyword class as serving as a type name for a variable that accepts a type as a value, and of Type representing a name for this variable.

Using class here doesn't mean that Type must be a class; it just means that Type serves as a generic type specifier for which a real type will be substituted when the template is used. Newer implementations allow you to use the less confusing keyword typename instead of class in this context:

```
template <typename Type>  // newer choice
```

You can use your choice of generic type name in the Type position. Popular choices include T and Type; we'll use the latter. When a template is invoked, Type will be replaced with a specific type value, such as int or String. Within the template definition, use the generic type name to identify the type to be stored in the stack. For the Stack case, that would mean using Type wherever the old declaration formerly used the typedef identifier Item. For instance,

```
Item items[MAX];  // holds stack items
```

becomes the following:

```
Type items[MAX];  // holds stack items
```

Similarly, you can replace the class methods of the original class with template member functions. Each function heading will be prefaced with the same template announcement:

```
template <class Type>
```

Again, replace the typedef identifier Item with the generic type name Type. One more change is that you need to change the class qualifier from Stack:: to Stack<Type>::. For instance,

```
bool Stack::push(const Item & item)
{
...
}
```

becomes the following:

```
template <class Type>                          // or template <typename Type>
bool Stack<Type>::push(const Type & item)
{
...
}
```

If you define a method within the class declaration (an inline definition), you can omit the template preface and the class qualifier.

Listing 13.9 shows the combined class and member function templates. It's important to realize that these templates are not class and member function definitions. Rather, they are instructions to the C++ compiler about how to generate class and member function definitions. A particular actualization of a template, such as a stack class for handling String objects, is called an *instantiation* or *specialization*. Unless you have a very clever compiler, placing the template member functions in a separate implementation file won't work. Because the templates aren't functions, they can't be compiled separately. Templates have to be used in conjunction with requests for particular instantiations of templates. The simplest way to make this work is to place all the template information in a header file and to include the header file in the file that will use the templates.

" It's important to realize that these templates are not class and member function definitions. Rather, they are instructions to the C++ compiler about how to generate class and member function definitions. "

Listing 13.9 stacktp.h

```
// stacktp.h -- a stack template

template <class Type>
class Stack
{
private:
    enum {MAX = 10};     // constant specific to class
    Type items[MAX];     // holds stack items
    int top;             // index for top stack item
public:
    Stack();
    bool isempty();
    bool isfull();
    bool push(const Type & item); // add item to stack
    bool pop(Type & item);        // pop top into item
};

template <class Type>
Stack<Type>::Stack()
{
    top = 0;
}

template <class Type>
bool Stack<Type>::isempty()
{
    return top == 0;
}

template <class Type>
bool Stack<Type>::isfull()
```

```
{
    return top == MAX;
}

template <class Type>
bool Stack<Type>::push(const Type & item)
{
    if (top < MAX)
    {
        items[top++] = item;
        return true;
    }
    else
        return false;
}

template <class Type>
bool Stack<Type>::pop(Type & item)
{
    if (top > 0)
    {
        item = items[--top];
        return true;
    }
    else
        return false;
}
```

USING A TEMPLATE CLASS

Merely including a template in a program doesn't generate a template class. You have to ask for an instantiation. To do this, declare an object of the template class type, replacing the generic type name with the particular type you want. For instance, here's how you would create two stacks, one for stacking `ints` and one for stacking `String` objects:

```
Stack<int> kernels;      // create a stack of ints
Stack<String> colonels;  // create a stack of String objects
```

Seeing these two declarations, the compiler will follow the `Stack<Type>` template to generate two separate class declarations and two separate sets of class methods. The `Stack<int>` class declaration will replace `Type` throughout with `int`, while the `Stack<String>` class declaration will replace `Type` throughout with `String`. Of course, the algorithms you use have to be consistent with the types. The stack class, for example, assumes that you can assign one item to another. This assumption is true for basic types, structures, and classes (unless you make the assignment operator private), but not for arrays.

Generic type identifiers such as `Type` in the example above are called *type parameters*, meaning that they act something like a variable, but instead of assigning a numeric value to them, you assign a type to them. So in the `kernel` declaration above, the type parameter `Type` has the value `int`.

Notice that you must provide the desired type explicitly. This is different from ordinary function templates, for which the compiler can use the argument types to a function to figure out what kind of function to generate:

```
Template <class T>
void simple(T t) { cout << t << '\n';}
...
simple(2);        // generate void simple(int)
simple("two")     // generate void simple(char *)
```

Listing 13.10 modifies the original stack-testing program (Listing 9.13) to use string purchase order IDs instead of unsigned long values. Because it uses our String class, compile it with strng2.cpp.

Listing 13.10 stacktem.cpp

```
// stacktem.cpp -- test template stack class
// compiler with strng2.cpp
#include <iostream>
using namespace std;
#include <cctype>
#include "stacktp.h"
#include "strng2.h"
int main()
{
    Stack<String> st;   // create an empty stack
    char c;
    String po;
    cout << "Please enter A to add a purchase order,\n"
         << "P to process a PO, or Q to quit.\n";
    while (cin >> c && toupper(c) != 'Q')
    {
        while (cin.get() != '\n')
            continue;
        if (!isalpha(c))
        {
            cout << '\a';
            continue;
        }
        switch(c)
        {
            case 'A':
            case 'a': cout << "Enter a PO number to add: ";
                      cin >> po;
                      if (st.isfull())
                          cout << "stack already full\n";
                      else
                          st.push(po);
                      break;
            case 'P':
            case 'p': if (st.isempty())
                          cout << "stack already empty\n";
                      else {
                          st.pop(po);
                          cout << "PO #" << po << " popped\n";
                          break;
                      }
        }
    }
```

```
            cout << "Please enter A to add a purchase order,\n"
                 << "P to process a PO, or Q to quit.\n";
        }
        cout << "Bye\n";
        return 0;
    }
```

Remember

Use the older `ctype.h` header file if your implementation doesn't provide `cctype`.

Here's a sample run:

```
Please enter A to add a purchase order,
P to process a PO, or Q to quit.
A
Enter a PO number to add: red911porsche
Please enter A to add a purchase order,
P to process a PO, or Q to quit.
A
Enter a PO number to add: green328bmw
Please enter A to add a purchase order,
P to process a PO, or Q to quit.
A
Enter a PO number to add: silver747boeing
Please enter A to add a purchase order,
P to process a PO, or Q to quit.
P
PO #silver747boeing popped
Please enter A to add a purchase order,
P to process a PO, or Q to quit.
P
PO #green328bmw popped
Please enter A to add a purchase order,
P to process a PO, or Q to quit.
P
PO #red911porsche popped
Please enter A to add a purchase order,
P to process a PO, or Q to quit.
P
stack already empty
Please enter A to add a purchase order,
P to process a PO, or Q to quit.
Q
Bye
```

A CLOSER LOOK AT THE TEMPLATE CLASS

You can use a built-in type or a class object as the type for the `Stack<Type>` class template. What about a pointer? For example, can you use a pointer to a `char` instead of a `String` object in Listing 13.10? After all, such pointers are the built-in way to handle C++ strings. The answer is that you can create a stack of pointers, but it won't work very well without major modifications in the program. The compiler can create the class, but it's your task to see that it's used sensibly. Let's see why such a stack of pointers doesn't work very well with Listing 13.10, then let's look at an example where a stack of pointers is useful.

Using a Stack of Pointers Incorrectly

We'll quickly look at three simple, but flawed, attempts to adapt Listing 13.10 to use a stack of pointers. These attempts illustrate the lesson that you should keep the design of a template in mind and not just use it blindly. All three begin with this perfectly valid invocation of the Stack<Type> template:

```
Stack<char *> st; // create a stack for pointers-to-char
```

Version 1 then replaces

```
String po;
```

with:

```
char * po;
```

The idea is to use a char pointer instead of a String object to receive the keyboard input. This approach fails immediately because merely creating a pointer doesn't create space to hold the input strings.

Version 2 replaces

```
String po;
```

with:

```
char po[40];
```

This allocates space for an input string. Furthermore, po is of type char *, so it can be placed on the stack. But an array is fundamentally at odds with the assumptions made for the pop() method:

```
template <class Type>
bool Stack<Type>::pop(Type & item)
{
    if (top > 0)
    {
        item = items[--top];
        return true;
    }
    else
        return false;
}
```

First, the reference variable item has to refer to an Lvalue of some sort, not to an array name. Second, the code assumes that you can assign to item. Even if item could refer to an array, you can't assign to an array name. So this approach fails, too.

Version 3 replaces

```
String po;
```

with:

```
char * po = new char[40];
```

This allocates space for an input string. Furthermore, po is a variable and hence compatible with the code for pop(). Here, however, we come up against the most fundamental problem. There is only one po variable, and it always points to the same memory location. True, the contents of the memory change each time a new string is read, but every push operation puts exactly the same address onto the stack. So when you pop the stack, you always get the same address back, and it always refers to the last string read into memory. In particular, the stack is not storing each new string as it comes in, and it serves no useful purpose.

Using a Stack of Pointers Correctly

One way to use a stack of pointers is to have the calling program provide an array of pointers, with each pointer pointing to a different string. Putting these pointers on a stack then makes sense, for each pointer will refer to a different string.

For example, suppose we have to simulate the following situation. Someone has delivered a cart of folders to Plodson. If Plodson's in-basket is empty, he removes the top folder from the cart and places it in his in-basket. If his in-basket is full, Plodson removes the top file from the basket, processes it, and places it in his out-basket. If the in-basket is neither empty nor full, Plodson may process the top file in the in-basket, or he may take the next file from the cart and put it into his in-basket. In what he secretly regards as a bit of madcap self-expression, he flips a coin to decide which of these actions to take. We'd like to investigate the effects of his method on the original file order.

We can model this with an array of pointers to strings representing the files on the cart. Each string will contain the name of the person described by the file. We can use a stack to represent the in-basket, and we can use a second array of pointers to represent the out-basket. Adding a file to the in-basket is represented by pushing a pointer from the input array onto the stack, and processing a file is represented by popping an item from the stack and adding it to the out-basket.

Given the importance of examining all aspects of this problem, it would be useful to be able to try different stack sizes. Listing 13.11 redefines the `Stack<Type>` class slightly so that the `Stack` constructor accepts an optional size argument. This involves using a dynamic array internally, so the class now needs a destructor, a copy constructor, and an assignment operator. Also, the definition shortens the code by making several of the methods inline.

> *If the in-basket is neither empty nor full, Plodson may process the top file in the in-basket, or he may take the next file from the cart and put it into his in-basket. In what he secretly regards as a bit of madcap self-expression, he flips a coin to decide which of these actions to take.*

Listing 13.11 stcktp1.h

```
// stcktp1.h -- modified Stack template

template <class Type>
class Stack
{
private:
    enum {MAX = 10};      // constant specific to class
    int stacksize;
    Type * items;         // holds stack items
    int top;              // index for top stack item
public:
    explicit Stack(int ss = MAX);
    Stack(const Stack & st);
    ~Stack() { delete [] items; }
    bool isempty() { return top == 0; }
```

```cpp
    bool isfull() { return top == stacksize; }
    bool push(const Type & item);   // add item to stack
    bool pop(Type & item);          // pop top into item
    Stack & operator=(const Stack & st);
};

template <class Type>
Stack<Type>::Stack(int ss) : stacksize(ss), top(0)
{
    items = new Type [stacksize];
}

template <class Type>
Stack<Type>::Stack(const Stack & st)
{
    stacksize = st.stacksize;
    top = st.top;
    items = new Type [stacksize];
    for (int i = 0; i < top; i++)
        items[i] = st.items[i];
}

template <class Type>
bool Stack<Type>::push(const Type & item)
{
    if (top < stacksize)
    {
        items[top++] = item;
        return true;
    }
    else
        return false;
}

template <class Type>
bool Stack<Type>::pop(Type & item)
{
    if (top > 0)
    {
        item = items[--top];
        return true;
    }
    else
        return false;
}

template <class Type>
Stack<Type> & Stack<Type>::operator=(const Stack<Type> & st)
{
    if (this == &st)
        return *this;
    delete [] items;
    stacksize = st.stacksize;
    top = st.top;
    items = new Type [stacksize];
    for (int i = 0; i < top; i++)
        items[i] = st.items[i];
    return *this;
}
```

Some implementations may not recognize explicit.

Notice that the prototype declares the return type for the assignment operator function to be a reference to Stack while the actual template function definition identifies the type as Stack<Type>. The former is an abbreviation for the latter, but it can be used only within the class scope. That is, you can use Stack inside the template declaration and inside the template function definitions, but outside the class, as when identifying return types and when using the scope resolution operator, you must use the full Stack<Type> form.

The program in Listing 13.12 uses the new stack template to implement the Plodson simulation. It uses rand(), srand(), and time() in the same way previous simulations have to generate random numbers. Here, randomly generating a 0 or a 1 simulates the coin toss.

Listing 13.12 stkoptr1.cpp

```cpp
// stkoptr1.cpp -- test stack of pointers
#include <iostream>
using namespace std;
#include <cstdlib>      // for rand(), srand()
#include <ctime>        // for time()
#include "stcktp1.h"
const int Stacksize = 4;
const int Num = 10;
int main()
{
    srand(time(0)); // randomize rand()
    cout << "Please enter stack size: ";
    int stacksize;
    cin >> stacksize;
    Stack<char *> st(stacksize); // create an empty stack with 4 slots

    char * in[Num] = {
            " 1: Hank Gilgamesh", " 2: Kiki Ishtar",
            " 3: Betty Rocker", " 4: Ian Flagranti",
            " 5: Wolfgang Kibble", " 6: Portia Koop",
            " 7: Joy Almondo", " 8: Xaverie Paprika",
            " 9: Juan Moore", "10: Misha Mache"
            };
    char * out[Num];

    int processed = 0;
    int nextin = 0;
    while (processed < Num)
    {
        if (st.isempty())
            st.push(in[nextin++]);
        else if (st.isfull())
            st.pop(out[processed++]);
        else if (rand() % 2  && nextin < Num)    // 50-50 chance
            st.push(in[nextin++]);
        else
            st.pop(out[processed++]);
    }
```

```
    for (int i = 0; i < Num; i++)
        cout << out[i] << "\n";

    cout << "Bye\n";
    return 0;
}
```

Some implementations require `stdlib.h` instead of `cstdlib` and `time.h` instead of `ctime`.

Two sample runs follow. Note that the final file ordering can differ quite a bit from one trial to the next, even when the stack size is kept unaltered.

```
Please enter stack size: 5
 2: Kiki Ishtar
 1: Hank Gilgamesh
 3: Betty Rocker
 5: Wolfgang Kibble
 4: Ian Flagranti
 7: Joy Almondo
 9: Juan Moore
 8: Xaverie Paprika
 6: Portia Koop
10: Misha Mache
Bye

Please enter stack size: 5
 3: Betty Rocker
 5: Wolfgang Kibble
 6: Portia Koop
 4: Ian Flagranti
 8: Xaverie Paprika
 9: Juan Moore
10: Misha Mache
 7: Joy Almondo
 2: Kiki Ishtar
 1: Hank Gilgamesh
Bye
```

PROGRAM NOTES

The strings themselves never move. Pushing a string onto the stack really creates a new pointer to an existing string. That is, it creates a pointer whose value is the address of an existing string. And popping a string off the stack copies that address value into the `out` array.

What effect does the stack destructor have upon the strings? None. The class constructor uses `new` to create an array for holding pointers. The class destructor eliminates that array, not the strings to which the array elements pointed.

AN ARRAY TEMPLATE EXAMPLE AND NON-TYPE ARGUMENTS

Templates frequently are used for container classes, because the idea of type parameters matches well with the need to apply a common storage plan to a variety of types. Indeed, the desire to provide reusable code for container classes was the main motivation for introducing templates, so let's look at another example, exploring a few more facets of template design and use. In particular, we'll look at non-type, or expression, arguments and at using an array to handle an inheritance family.

Let's begin with a simple array template that lets you specify an array size. One technique, which the `Stack` template used, is using a dynamic array within the class and a constructor argument to provide the number of elements. Another approach is using a template argument to provide the size for a regular array. Listing 13.13 shows how this can be done.

Listing 13.13 arraytp.h

```
//arraytp.h  -- Array Template
#include <iostream>
using namespace std;
#include <cstdlib>

template <class T, int n>
class ArrayTP
{
private:
    T ar[n];
public:
    ArrayTP();
    explicit ArrayTP(const T & v);
    virtual T & operator[](int i);
    virtual const T & operator[](int i) const;
};

template <class T, int n>
ArrayTP<T,n>::ArrayTP()
{
    for (int i = 0; i < n; i++)
        ar[i] = 0;
}

template <class T, int n>
ArrayTP<T,n>::ArrayTP(const T & v)
{
    for (int i = 0; i < n; i++)
        ar[i] = v;
}

template <class T, int n>
T & ArrayTP<T,n>::operator[](int i)
{
```

```
        if (i < 0 || i >= n)
        {
            cerr << "Error in array limits: " << i
                 << " is out of range\n";
            exit(1);
        }
        return ar[i];
    }

    template <class T, int n>
    const T & ArrayTP<T,n>::operator[](int i) const
    {
        if (i < 0 || i >= n)
        {
            cerr << "Error in array limits: " << i
                 << " is out of range\n";
            exit(1);
        }
        return ar[i];
    }
```

Note the template heading:

```
template <class T, int n>
```

The keyword `class` identifies `T` as a type parameter, or type argument. The `int` identifies `n` as being an `int` type. This second kind of parameter, one which specifies a particular type instead of acting as a generic name for a type, is called a *non-type* or *expression argument*. Suppose you have the following declaration:

```
ArrayTP<double, 12> eggweights;
```

This causes the compiler to define a class called `ArrayTP<double,12>` and to create an `eggweights` object of that class. When defining the class, the compiler replaces `T` with `double` and `n` with `12`.

Expression arguments have some restrictions. An expression argument can be an integral type, an enumeration type, a reference, or a pointer. Thus, `double m` is ruled out, but `double & rm` or `double * pm` is allowed. Also, the template code can't alter the value of the argument or take its address. Thus, in the `ArrayTP` template, expressions such as `n++` or `&n` would not be allowed. Also, when you instantiate a template, the value used for the expression argument should be a constant expression.

This approach for sizing an array has one advantage over the constructor approach used in `Stack`. The constructor approach uses heap memory managed by `new` and `delete`, while the expression argument approach uses the memory stack maintained for automatic variables. This provides faster execution time, particularly if you have a lot of small arrays.

The main drawback to the expression argument approach is that each array size generates its own template. That is, the declarations

```
ArrayTP<double, 12> eggweights;
ArrayTP(double, 13> donuts;
```

generate two separate class declarations. However, the declarations

```
Stack<int> eggs(12);
Stack<int> dunkers(13);
```

generate just one class declaration, and the size information is passed to the constructor for that class.

Another difference is that the constructor approach is more versatile because the array size is stored as a class member rather than being hard-coded into the definition. This makes it possible, for example, to define assignment from an array of one size to an array of another size or to build a class that allows resizable arrays.

USING THE TEMPLATE WITH A FAMILY OF CLASSES

Suppose you have a family of classes. In particular, suppose you have a base class along with several derived classes. Now suppose you have several objects of these classes that you'd like to store in an array. One problem is that all elements of an array should be of the same type, but an object of a derived class is a different type from the base class or from another derived class. It may not even be the same size as an object of the base class, so lying to the compiler about its type won't work. In short, with the array, you have a tool suited for homogeneous elements (elements all of the same kind), but with a class family, you have a heterogeneous collection of objects (objects of various kinds).

It's in situations like this where the *is-a* relationship and virtual functions come in handy. As Listing 12.8 illustrated briefly, you can create an array of base class pointers. Public inheritance means you can assign the address of any derived class object to a base class pointer, so such an array can hold addresses of a variety of types. The sizes of the types may differ, but the pointers are all the same size. Furthermore, if you use these pointers to invoke class methods, virtual functions ensure that a base class pointer to a derived object will invoke the derived object's class methods.

Let's try this out using the ArrayTP template. First, you need a family of classes. For illustrative purposes, let's keep the classes simple. Listing 13.14 defines a Worker class, a Waiter class, a Singer class, and a Greeter class. A Worker class provides a name and an identification number. The Waiter class, derived from Worker, adds a panache rating. The Singer class, derived from Worker, adds a vocal range descriptor. And the Greeter class, derived from Worker, adds a cheerfulness rating.

```
Listing 13.14 worker.h
// worker.h  -- working classes
#include "strng2.h"

class Worker    // an abstract base class
{
private:
    String fullname;
    long id;
public:
    Worker() : fullname("no one"), id(0L) {}
    Worker(const String & s, long n)
```

```
                     : fullname(s), id(n) {}
        virtual ~Worker() = 0;    // pure virtual destructor
        virtual void Set();
        virtual void Show() const;
};

class Waiter : public Worker
{
private:
    int panache;
public:
    Waiter() : Worker(), panache(0) {}
    Waiter(const String & s, long n, int p = 0)
            : Worker(s, n), panache(p) {}
    Waiter(const Worker & wk, int p = 0)
            : Worker(wk), panache(p) {}
    void Set();
    void Show() const;
};

class Singer : public Worker
{
protected:
    enum {other, alto, contralto, soprano,
                    bass, baritone, tenor};
    enum {Vtypes = 7};
private:
    static char *pv[Vtypes];     // string equivs of voice types
    int voice;
public:
    Singer() : Worker(), voice(other) {}
    Singer(const String & s, long n, int v = other)
            : Worker(s, n), voice(v) {}
    Singer(const Worker & wk, int v = other)
            : Worker(wk), voice(v) {}
    void Set();
    void Show() const;
};

class Greeter : public Worker
{
private:
    int cheer;
public:
    Greeter() : Worker(), cheer(0) {}
    Greeter(const String & s, long n, int c = 0)
            : Worker(s, n), cheer(c) {}
    Greeter(const Worker & wk, int c = 0)
            : Worker(wk), cheer(c) {}
    void Set();
    void Show() const;
};
```

In this arrangement, everyone is some particular type of worker (waiter, singer, greeter) and not a generic worker. Thus, Worker can be made into an abstract base class. Recall that this requires at least one pure virtual function. This class lets the destructor assume that role. (Because Worker is a base class, it should have a virtual destructor, even if it does nothing. If Worker also is to be an abstract base class, you may as well make the destructor a pure virtual function.)

There is one special point about making the destructor pure. Usually, a pure virtual function is implemented in a derived class, but a destructor has to be implemented in its own class. So, in the case of a pure virtual destructor, you still need to provide a base-class implementation, which Listing 13.15 will do. However, declaring the destructor as a pure virtual function is sufficient to make the base class abstract and to prevent the creation of `Worker` objects.

Another point to note is that some of the derived class constructors call upon the `Worker(const Worker &)` constructor even though the class didn't define one. Recall, however, that the compiler generates this constructor (the copy constructor) if we don't. The default constructor is fine for this particular description.

Next, you need to define those functions that don't already have inline definitions. Listing 13.15 provides that information. It also initializes a class-scope array of pointers to data used by the `Singer` class. In service of brevity, the example doesn't make a serious effort to check the validity of all input.

Listing 13.15 worker.cpp

```cpp
// worker.cpp -- working class methods
#include "worker.h"
#include <iostream>
using namespace std;
// Worker methods

    // must implement virtual destructor, even if pure
Worker::~Worker() {}

void Worker::Set()
{
    cout << "Enter worker's name: ";
    cin >> fullname;
    cout << "Enter worker's ID: ";
    cin >> id;
    while (cin.get() != '\n')
        continue;
}

void Worker::Show() const
{
    cout << "Name: " << fullname << "\n";
    cout << "Employee ID: " << id << "\n";
}

// Waiter methods
void Waiter::Set()
{
    Worker::Set();
    cout << "Enter waiter's panache rating: ";
    cin >> panache;
    while (cin.get() != '\n')
        continue;
}

void Waiter::Show() const
{
    cout << "Category: waiter\n";
```

```
        Worker::Show();
        cout << "Panache rating: " << panache << "\n";
}

// Singer methods

char * Singer::pv[] = {"other", "alto", "contralto",
            "soprano", "bass", "baritone", "tenor"};

void Singer::Set()
{
    Worker::Set();
    cout << "Enter number for singer's vocal range:\n";
    int i;
    for (i = 0; i < Vtypes; i++)
    {
        cout << i << ": " << pv[i] << "    ";
        if ( i % 4 == 3)
            cout << '\n';
    }
    if (i % 4 != 0)
        cout << '\n';
    cin >> voice;
    while (cin.get() != '\n')
        continue;
}

void Singer::Show() const
{
    cout << "Category: singer\n";
    Worker::Show();
    cout << "Vocal range: " << pv[voice] << "\n";
}

// Greeter methods
void Greeter::Set()
{
    Worker::Set();
    cout << "Enter greeter's cheerfulness rating: ";
    cin >> cheer;
    while (cin.get() != '\n')
        continue;
}

void Greeter::Show() const
{
    cout << "Category: greeter\n";
    Worker::Show();
    cout << "Cheerfulness rating: " << cheer << "\n";
}
```

Finally, Listing 13.16 provides a program to test the scheme of using an array of base class pointers to manage a family of classes. In it, the Cafe Lola hires its first employees.

Remember

If your system doesn't support templates, you can use an ordinary array of pointers to Worker instead. See the instructions in the listing.

Listing 13.16 workarr.cpp

```cpp
// workarr.cpp -- array of workers
// compile with worker.cpp, strng2.cpp
#include <iostream>
using namespace std;
#include <cstring>
#include "worker.h"
#include "arraytp.h"     // omit if templates not implemented
const int SIZE = 5;
int main()
{
    ArrayTP<Worker *, SIZE> lolas;
    // if no templates, omit the above line and use the one below
    // Worker * lolas[SIZE];

    cout << "Enter staff for Lola's: \n";
    int ct;
    for (ct = 0; ct < SIZE; ct++)
    {
        char choice;
        cout << "Enter the employee category:\n"
             << "g: greeter  w: waiter  s: singer  "
             << "q: quit\n";
        cin >> choice;
        while (strchr("gwsq", choice) == NULL)
        {
            cout << "Please enter an g, w, s, or q: ";
            cin >> choice;
        }
        if (choice == 'q')
            break;
        switch(choice)
        {
            case 'g':   lolas[ct] = new Greeter;
                        break;
            case 'w':   lolas[ct] = new Waiter;
                        break;
            case 's':   lolas[ct] = new Singer;
                        break;
        }
        cin.get();
        lolas[ct]->Set();
    }

    cout << "\nHere is your staff:\n";
    int i;
    for (i = 0; i < ct; i++)
    {
        cout << '\n';
        lolas[i]->Show();
    }
    for (i = 0; i < ct; i++)
        delete lolas[i];
    return 0;
}
```

Here is a sample run:

```
Enter staff for Lola's:
Enter the employee category:
g: greeter  w: waiter  s: singer  q: quit
w
Enter worker's name: Fran Godot
Enter worker's ID: 1004
Enter waiter's panache rating: 6
Enter the employee category:
g: greeter  w: waiter  s: singer  q: quit
s
Enter worker's name: Igor Tunefree
Enter worker's ID: 1009
Enter number for singer's vocal range:
0: other   1: alto   2: contralto   3: soprano
4: bass    5: baritone   6: tenor
4
Enter the employee category:
g: greeter  w: waiter  s: singer  q: quit
g
Enter worker's name: Hap Gladfoote
Enter worker's ID: 1003
Enter greeter's cheerfulness rating: 8
Enter the employee category:
g: greeter  w: waiter  s: singer  q: quit
w
Enter worker's name: Walt Wiltcress
Enter worker's ID: 1022
Enter waiter's panache rating: 5
Enter the employee category:
g: greeter  w: waiter  s: singer  q: quit
q

Here is your staff:

Category: waiter
Name: Fran Godot
Employee ID: 1004
Panache rating: 6

Category: singer
Name: Igor Tunefree
Employee ID: 1009
Vocal range: bass

Category: greeter
Name: Hap Gladfoote
Employee ID: 1003
Cheerfulness rating: 8

Category: waiter
Name: Walt Wiltcress
Employee ID: 1022
Panache rating: 5
```

Program Notes

The ANSI C standard function strchr(const char * str, char ch) searches for the character ch in the string str. It returns the address of the first occurrence of ch if it finds it; otherwise, the function returns the null pointer. Thus, the code

```
while (strchr("ewsq", choice) == NULL)
```

provides a convenient way to see that the entered character is a valid choice.

The switch statement assigns the address of a new object to one of the pointer-to-Worker elements of the array:

```
switch(choice)
{
    case 'g':   lolas[ct] = new Greeter;
                break;
    case 'w':   lolas[ct] = new Waiter;
                break;
    case 's':   lolas[ct] = new Singer;
                break;
}
```

Depending upon the user's input, the pointer may point to a Worker object, a Waiter object, or a Greeter object. Because a base pointer may point to an object of any descendant class, no type casts are needed.

Because Set() and Show() are defined as virtual functions, invoking these functions with a pointer-to-Worker invokes the function appropriate to the pointed-to class:

```
lolas[ct]->Set();
...
lolas[i]->Show();
```

Thus, you can use a homogeneous collection of pointers to manage a heterogeneous collection of objects. This is an example of polymorphism at work: one function call can activate different functions, depending upon the context.

Note the following code:

```
for (i = 0; i < ct; i++)
    delete lolas[i];
```

Memory allocated by new should be freed using delete. It's not the job of the ArrayTP class to do this, for the lolas object neither creates nor destroys the Worker-family objects. It merely stores the addresses of the objects.

TEMPLATE VERSATILITY

You can apply the same techniques to template classes as you do to regular classes. Template classes can serve as base classes, and they can be component classes. They can themselves be type arguments to other templates. For example, you can implement a stack template using an array template, or you can have an array template used to construct an array whose elements are stacks based on a stack template. That is, you can have code along the following lines:

```
template <class T>
class Array
{
private:
    T entry;
    ...
};

template <class Type>
class GrowArray : public Array<Type> {...};  // inheritance

template <class Tp>
class Stack
{
        Array<Tp> ar;          // use an Array<> as a component
        ...
};
...
Array < Stack<int> > asi;  // an array of stacks of int
```

In the last statement, you must separate the two > symbols by at least one white-space character in order to avoid confusion with the >> operator.

Another example of template versatility is that you can use templates recursively. For example, given the earlier definition of an array template, you can use it as follows:

```
ArrayTP< ArrayTP<int,20>, 10> twodee;
```

This makes twodee an array of 10 elements, each of which is an array of 20 ints.

You can have templates with more than one type parameter. For instance, suppose you want a class that holds two kinds of values. You can create and use a Pair template class for holding two disparate values. (Incidentally, the Standard Template Library provides a similar template called pair.) The short program in Listing 13.17 shows an example.

Listing 13.17 pairs.cpp

```
// pairs.cpp -- define and use a Pair template
#include <iostream>
using namespace std;

template <class T1, class T2>
class Pair
{
private:
    T1 a;
    T2 b;
public:
    T1 & first(const T1 & f);
    T2 & second(const T2 & s);
    T1 first() const { return a; }
    T2 second() const { return b; }
    Pair(const T1 & f, const T2 & s) : a(f), b(s) { }
};

template<class T1, class T2>
T1 & Pair<T1,T2>::first(const T1 & f)
{
```

```
        a = f;
        return a;
}
template<class T1, class T2>
T2 & Pair<T1,T2>::second(const T2 & s)
{
        b = s;
        return b;
}

int main()
{
    Pair<char *, int> ratings[4] =
    {
        Pair<char *, int>("The Purple Duke", 5),
        Pair<char *, int>("Jake's Frisco Cafe", 4),
        Pair<char *, int>("Mont Souffle", 5),
        Pair<char *, int>("Gertie's Eats", 3)
    };

    int joints = sizeof(ratings) / sizeof (Pair<char *, int>);
    cout << "Rating:\t Eatery\n";
    for (int i = 0; i < joints; i++)
        cout << ratings[i].second() << ":\t "
             << ratings[i].first() << "\n";

    ratings[3].second(6);
    cout << "Oops! Revised rating:\n";
    cout << ratings[3].second() << ":\t "
         << ratings[3].first() << "\n";

    return 0;;
}
```

One thing to note is that in main(), you have to use Pair<char *,int> to invoke the constructors and as an argument for sizeof. That's because Pair<char *,int> and not Pair is the class name. Also, Pair<String,ArrayDb> would be the name of an entirely different class.

Here's the program output:

```
Rating:  Eatery
5:       The Purple Duke
4:       Jake's Frisco Cafe
5:       Mont Souffle
3:       Gertie's Eats
Oops! Revised rating:
6:       Gertie's Eats
```

Another new class template feature is that you can provide default values for type parameters:

```
template <class T1, class T2 = int> class Map {...};
```

This causes the compiler to use int for the type T2 if a value for T2 is omitted:

```
Map<double, double> m1; // T1 is double, T2 is double
Map<double> m2;         // T1 is double, T2 is int
```

The Standard Template Library (Chapter 15) often uses this feature, with the default type being a class.

Although you can provide default values for class template type parameters, you can't do so for function template parameters. However, you can provide default values for non-type parameters for both class and function templates.

TEMPLATE SPECIALIZATIONS

Class templates are like function templates in that you can have implicit instantiations, explicit instantiations, and explicit specializations, collectively known as specializations. That is, a template describes a class in terms of a general type, while a specialization is a class declaration generated using a specific type.

The examples that you have seen so far used implicit instantiations. That is, you declare one or more objects indicating the desired type, and the compiler generates a specialized class definition using the recipe provided by the general template:

```
ArrayTb<int, 100> stuff; // implicit instantiation
```

The compiler doesn't generate an implicit instantiation of the class until it needs an object:

```
ArrayTb<double, 30> * pt;      // a pointer, no object needed yet
pt = new ArrayTb<double, 30>; // now an object is needed
```

The compiler generates an explicit instantiation of a class declaration when you declare a class using the keyword `template` and indicating the desired type or types:

```
template ArrayTb<String, 100>; // generate ArrayTB<String, 100> class
```

This declares ArrayTb<String, 100> to be a class. In this case the compiler generates the class definition even though no object of the class has yet been created or mentioned. However, just as with the implicit instantiation, the general template is used as a guide to generate the specialization.

The explicit specialization is a definition for a particular type or types that is to be used instead of the general template. Sometimes you may need or want to modify a template to behave differently when instantiated for a particular type; in that case you can create an explicit specialization. Suppose, for instance, that you've defined a template for a class representing a sorted array for which items are sorted as they are added to the array:

```
template <class T>
class SortedArray
{
    ...// details omitted
};
```

Also, suppose the template uses the > operator to compare values. This works well for numbers. It will work if T represents a class type, too, provided that you've defined a T::operator>() method. But it won't work if T is a string represented by type char *. Actually, the template will work, but the strings will wind up sorted by address rather than alphabetically. What is needed is a class definition that uses strcmp() instead of >.

In such a case, you can provide an explicit template specialization. This takes the form of a template defined for one specific type instead of for a general type. When faced with the choice of a specialized template and a general template that both match an instantiation request, the compiler will use the specialized version.

A specialized class template definition has the following form:

```
template <> class Classname<specialized-type-name> { ... };
```

Older compilers may only recognize the older form, which dispenses with the template <>:

```
class Classname<specialized-type-name> { ... };
```

To provide a SortedArray template specialized for the char * type using the new notation, you would use code like the following:

```
template <> class SortedArray<char *>
{
    ...// details omitted
};
```

Here the implementation code would use strcmp() instead of > to compare array values. Now, requests for a SortedArray of char * will use this specialized definition instead of the more general template definition:

```
SortedArray<int> scores;      // use general definition
SortedArray<char *> dates;    // use specialized definition
```

C++ also allows for *partial specializations*, which partially restrict the generality of a template. A partial specialization, for example, can provide a specific type for one of the type parameters:

```
template <class T1, class T2> class Pair {...};  // general template
template <class T1> class Pair<T1, int> {...};    // specialization with
                                                  // T2 set to int
```

The <> following the keyword template declare the type parameters that are still unspecialized. So the second declaration specializes T2 to int but leaves T1 open. Note that specifying all the types leads to an empty bracket pair and a complete explicit specialization:

```
template <> class Pair<int, int> {...};  // specialization with
                                         // T1 and T2 set to int
```

The compiler uses the most specialized template if there is a choice:

```
Pair<double, double> p1; // use general Pair template
Pair<double, int> p2;    // use Pair<T1, int> partial specialization
Pair<int, int> p3;       // use Pair<int, int> explicit specialization
```

Or you can partially specialize an existing template by providing a special version for pointers:

```
template<class T>     // general version
class Feeb { ... };
template<class T*>    // pointer partial specialization
class Feeb { ... };   // modified code
```

If you provide a non-pointer type, the compiler will use the general version; if you provide a pointer, the compiler will use the pointer specialization:

```
Feeb<char> fb1;         // use general Feeb template, T is char
Feeb<char *> fb2;       // use Feeb T* specialization, T is char
```

Without the partial specialization, the second declaration would have used the general template, interpreting T as type char *. With the partial specialization, it uses the specialized template, interpreting T as char.

The partial specialization feature allows for making a variety of restrictions. For instance, you can do the following:

```
template <class T1, class T2, class T3> class Trio{...};
        // general template
template <class T1, class T2> class Trio<T1, T2, T2> {...};
        // specialization with T3 set to T2
template <class T1> class Trio<T1, T1*, T1*> {...};
        // specialization with T3 and T2 set to T1*
```

Given these declarations, the compiler would make the following choices:

```
Trio<int, short, char *> t1; // use general template
Trio<int, short> t2; // use Trio<T1, T2, T2>
Trio<char, char *, char *> t3; use Trio<T1, T1*, T1*>
```

Multiple Inheritance

Multiple inheritance (MI) describes a class that has more than one immediate base class. As with single inheritance, public multiple inheritance should express an *is-a* relationship. For example, if you have a Waiter class and a Singer class, you could derive a SingingWaiter class from the two:

```
class SingingWaiter : public Waiter, public Singer {...};
```

Note that you have to qualify each base class with the keyword public. That's because the compiler assumes private derivation unless instructed otherwise:

```
class SingingWaiter : public Waiter, Singer {...}; // Singer is a private
base
```

As discussed earlier in this chapter, private and protected MI can express a *has-a* relationship. We'll concentrate on public inheritance now.

Multiple inheritance can introduce new problems for the programmer. The two chief problems are inheriting different methods of the same name from two different base classes and inheriting multiple instances of a class via two or more related immediate base classes. Meeting these problems involves introducing a few new rules and syntax variations. Thus, using multiple inheritance can be more difficult and problem-prone than using single inheritance. For this reason, many in the C++ community object strongly to MI; some want it removed from the language. Others love MI and argue that it's very useful, even necessary, for particular projects. Still others suggest using MI cautiously and in moderation.

" The two chief problems are inheriting different methods of the same name from two different base classes and inheriting multiple instances of a class via two or more related immediate base classes. "

Let's explore a particular example and see what the problems and solutions are. We'll use a variation of the Worker class example (Listings 13.14 through 13.16). It has a Waiter class and a Singer class derived from an abstract Worker base class. So you can use MI to derive a SingingWaiter class from the Waiter and Singer classes (see Figure 13.3). This is a case in which a base class (Worker) is inherited via two separate derivations, which is the circumstance that causes the most difficulties with MI. To keep the example shorter, let's drop the Greeter class at this point. Suppose, then, you start with Listing 13.14 (worker.h), after deleting the Greeter section, as the basis for creating a SingingWaiter class that will serve to illustrate some problems. In particular, you'll need to face the following questions:

- How many workers?

- Which method?

FIGURE 13.3

Multiple inheritance with a shared ancestor

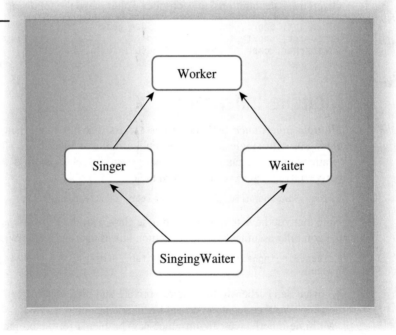

HOW MANY WORKERS?

Suppose you begin by publicly deriving SingingWaiter from Singer and Waiter:

```
class SingingWaiter: public Singer, public  Waiter {...};
```

Because both Singer and Waiter inherit a Worker component, a Singing Waiter winds up with two Worker components (see Figure 13.4).

As you might expect, this raises problems. For example, ordinarily you can assign the address of a derived class object to a base class pointer, but this becomes ambiguous now:

```
SingingWaiter ed;
Worker * pw = &ed;    // ambiguous
```

FIGURE 13.4

Inheriting two base objects

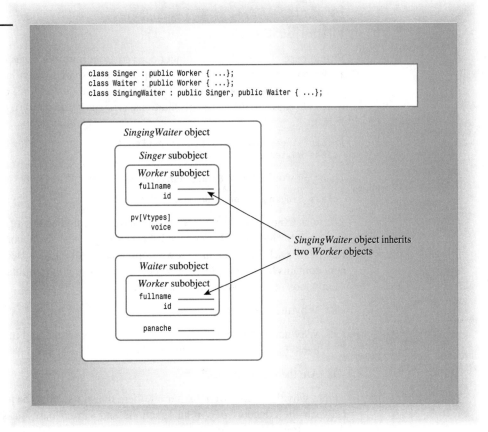

```
class Singer : public Worker { ...};
class Waiter : public Worker { ...};
class SingingWaiter : public Singer, public Waiter { ...};
```

SingingWaiter object

Singer subobject

Worker subobject
fullname _____
id _____

pv[Vtypes] _____
voice _____

SingingWaiter object inherits two *Worker* objects

Waiter subobject

Worker subobject
fullname _____
id _____

panache _____

Normally, such an assignment sets a base class pointer to the address of the base class object within the derived object. But `ed` contains two `Worker` objects, hence there are two addresses from which to choose. You could specify which object by using a type cast:

```
Worker * pw1 = (Waiter *) &ed;    // the Worker in Waiter
Worker * pw2 = (Singer *) &ed;    // the Worker in Singer
```

This certainly complicates the technique of using an array of base class pointers to refer to a variety of objects (polymorphism).

Having two copies of a `Worker` object causes other problems, too. However, the real issue is why should you have two copies of a `Worker` object at all? A singing waiter, like any other worker, should have just one name and one ID. When C++ added multiple inheritance to its bag of tricks, it added a new technique, the *virtual base class*, to make this possible.

Virtual Base Classes

Virtual base classes allow an object derived from multiple bases that themselves share a common base to inherit just one object of that shared base class. For this example, you would make `Worker` a virtual base class to `Singer` and `Waiter` by using the keyword `virtual` in the class declarations (`virtual` and `public` can appear in either order):

```
class Singer : virtual public Worker {...};
class Waiter : public virtual Worker {...};
```

Then you would define `SingingWaiter` as before:

```
class SingingWaiter: public Singer, public  Waiter {...};
```

Now a `SingingWaiter` object will contain a single copy of a `Worker` object. In essence, the inherited `Singer` and `Waiter` objects share a common `Worker` object instead of each bringing in its own copy (see Figure 13.5). Because `SingingWaiter` now contains but one `Worker` subobject, you can use polymorphism again.

Let's look at some questions you may have:

- Why the term *virtual*?

- Why not dispense with declaring base classes virtual and make virtual behavior the norm for multiple inheritance?

- Are there any catches?

First, why the term *virtual*? After all, there doesn't seem to be an obvious connection between the concepts of virtual functions and virtual base classes. It turns out that there is strong pressure from the C++ community to resist the introduction of new keywords. It would be awkward, for example, if a new keyword corresponded to the name of some important function or variable in a major program. So C++ merely recycled the keyword `virtual` for the new facility—a bit of keyword overloading.

FIGURE 13.5

Inheritance with a virtual base class

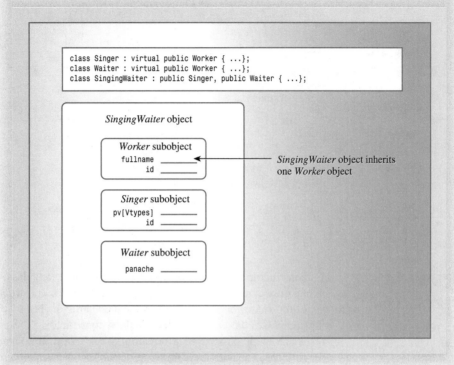

```
class Singer : virtual public Worker { ...};
class Waiter : virtual public Worker { ...};
class SingingWaiter : public Singer, public Waiter { ...};
```

SingingWaiter object

Worker subobject
fullname _____
id _____

SingingWaiter object inherits one *Worker* object

Singer subobject
pv[Vtypes] _____
id _____

Waiter subobject
panache _____

Next, why not dispense with declaring base classes virtual and make virtual behavior the norm for multiple inheritance? First, there are cases for which one might want multiple copies of a base. Second, making a base class virtual requires that a program do some additional accounting, and you shouldn't have to pay for that facility if you don't need it. Third, there are the matters brought up in the next paragraph.

Finally, are there catches? Yes. Making virtual base classes work requires adjustments to C++ rules, and you have to code some things differently. Also, using virtual base classes may involve changing existing code. For instance, adding the `SingingWaiter` class to the `Worker` hierarchy required that you go back and add the `virtual` keyword to the `Singer` and `Waiter` classes.

New Constructor Rules

Having virtual base classes requires a new approach to class constructors. With non-virtual base classes, the *only* constructors that can appear in an initializer list are constructors for the immediate base classes. But these constructors can, in turn, pass information on to their bases. For example, you can have the following organization of constructors:

```
class A
{
    int a;
public:
    A(int n = 0) { a = n; }
    ...
};
class B: public A
{
    int b;
public:
    B(int m = 0, int n = 0) : A(n) : { b = m; }
    ...
};
class C : public B
{
    int c;
public:
    C(int q = 0, int m = 0, int n = 0) : B(m, n) { c = q; }
    ...
};
```

A C constructor can invoke only constructors from the B class, and a B constructor can invoke only constructors from the A class. Here the C constructor uses the q value and passes the values of m and n back to the B constructor. The B constructor uses the value of m and passes the value of n back to the A constructor.

This automatic passing of information doesn't work if Worker is a virtual base class. For instance, consider the following possible constructor for the multiple inheritance example:

```
SingingWaiter(const Worker & wk, int p = 0, int v = Singer::other)
                : Waiter(wk,p), Singer(wk,v) {}
```

The problem is that automatic passing of information would pass wk to the Worker object via two separate paths (Waiter and Singer). To avoid this potential conflict, C++ disables the automatic passing of information through an intermediate class to a base class *if* the base class is virtual. Thus, the above constructor will initialize the panache and voice members, but the information in the wk argument *won't* get to the Waiter subobject. However, the compiler must construct a base object component before constructing derived objects; in the above case, it will use the default Worker constructor.

If you want to use something other than the default constructor for a virtual base class, you need to invoke the base constructor explicitly. Thus, the constructor should look like this:

```
SingingWaiter(const Worker & wk, int p = 0, int v = Singer::other)
                : Worker(wk), Waiter(wk,p), Singer(wk,v) {}
```

Here the code explicitly invokes the Worker(const Worker &) constructor. Note that this usage is legal and often necessary for virtual base classes and illegal for nonvirtual base classes.

If a class has an indirect virtual base class, a constructor for that class should explicitly invoke a constructor for the virtual base class unless all that is needed is the default constructor for the virtual base class.

WHICH METHOD?

In addition to introducing changes in class constructor rules, MI often requires other coding adjustments. Consider the problem of extending the Show() method to the SingingWaiter class. Because a SingingWaiter object has no new data members, you might think the class could just use the inherited methods. This brings up the first problem. Suppose you do omit a new version of Show() and try to use a SingingWaiter object to invoke an inherited Show() method:

```
SingingWaiter newhire("Elise Hawks", 2005, 6, soprano);
newhire.Show();  // ambiguous
```

With single inheritance, failing to redefine Show() results in using the most recent ancestral definition. In this case, each direct ancestor has a Show() function, making this call ambiguous.

Multiple inheritance can result in ambiguous function calls. For instance, a BadDude class could inherit two quite different Draw() methods from a Gunslinger class and a PokerPlayer class.

You can use the scope resolution operator to clarify what you mean:

```
SingingWaiter newhire("Elise Hawks", 2005, 6, soprano);
newhire.Singer::Show();  // use Singer version
```

However, a better approach is to redefine Show() for SingingWaiter and to have it specify which Show() to use. For instance, if you want a SingingWaiter object to use the Singer version, do this:

```
void SingingWaiter::Show()
{
    Singer::Show();
}
```

This method of having the derived method call the base method works well enough for single inheritance. For instance, suppose the HeadWaiter class derives from the Waiter class. You could use a sequence of definitions like this, with each derived class adding to the information displayed by its base class:

```
void Worker::Show() const
{
    cout << "Name: " << fullname << "\n";
    cout << "Employee ID: " << id << "\n";
}

void Waiter::Show() const
{
```

```
    Worker::Show();
    cout << "Panache rating: " << panache << "\n";
}
void HeadWaiter::Show() const
{
    Waiter::Show();
    cout << "Presence rating: " << presence << "\n";
}
```

This incremental approach fails for the `SingingWaiter` case, however. The method

```
void SingingWaiter::Show()
{
    Singer::Show();
}
```

fails because it ignores the `Waiter` component. You can remedy that by calling the `Waiter` version also:

```
void SingingWaiter::Show()
{
    Singer::Show();
    Waiter::Show();
}
```

This displays the person's name and ID twice, for `Singer::Show()` and with `Waiter::Show()` both call `Worker::Show()`.

How can this be fixed? One way is to use a modular approach instead of an incremental approach. That is, provide a method that displays only `Worker` components, another method that displays only `Waiter` components (instead of `Waiter` plus `Worker` components), and another that displays only `Singer` components. Then the `SingingWaiter::Show()` method can put those components together. For instance, you can do this:

```
void Worker::Data() const
{
    cout << "Name: " << fullname << "\n";
    cout << "Employee ID: " << id << "\n";
}

void Waiter::Data() const
{
    cout << "Panache rating: " << panache << "\n";
}

void Singer::Data() const
{
    cout << "Vocal range: " << pv[voice] << "\n";
}

void SingingWaiter::Data() const
{
    Singer::Data();
    Waiter::Data();
}

void SingingWaiter::Show() const
{
```

```
    cout << "Category: singing waiter\n";
    Worker::Data();
    Data();
}
```

Similarly, the other `Show()` methods would be built from the appropriate `Data()` components.

With this approach, objects would still use the `Show()` method publicly. The `Data()` methods, on the other hand, should be internal to the classes, helper methods used to facilitate the public interface. However, making the `Data()` methods private would prevent, say, `Waiter` code from using `Worker::Data()`. Here is just the kind of situation for which the protected access class is useful. If the `Data()` methods are protected, they can by used internally by all the classes in the hierarchy while being kept hidden from the outside world.

Another approach would have been to make all the data components protected instead of private, but using protected methods instead of protected data puts tighter control on the allowable access to the data.

The `Set()` methods, which solicit data for setting object values, present a similar problem. `SingingWaiter::Set()`, for example, should ask for `Worker` information once, not twice. The same solution works. You can provide protected `Get()` methods that solicit information for just a single class, then put together `Set()` methods that use the `Get()` methods as building blocks.

In short, introducing multiple inheritance with a shared ancestor requires introducing virtual base classes, altering the rules for constructor initialization lists, and possibly recoding the classes if they had not been written with MI in mind. Listing 13.18 shows the modified class declarations instituting these changes, and Listing 13.19 shows the implementation.

Listing 13.18 workermi.h

```
// workermi.h  -- working classes with MI
#include "strng2.h"

class Worker    // an abstract base class
{
private:
    String fullname;
    long id;
protected:
    virtual void Data() const;
    virtual void Get();
public:
    Worker() : fullname("no one"), id(0L) {}
    Worker(const String & s, long n)
            : fullname(s), id(n) {}
    virtual ~Worker() = 0; // pure virtual function
    virtual void Set() = 0;
    virtual void Show() const = 0;
};

class Waiter : virtual public Worker
{
```

> *Introducing multiple inheritance with a shared ancestor requires introducing virtual base classes, altering the rules for constructor initialization lists, and possibly recoding the classes if they had not been written with MI in mind.*

```
private:
    int panache;
protected:
    void Data() const;
    void Get();
public:
    Waiter() : Worker(), panache(0) {}
    Waiter(const String & s, long n, int p = 0)
            : Worker(s, n), panache(p) {}
    Waiter(const Worker & wk, int p = 0)
            : Worker(wk), panache(p) {}
    void Set();
    void Show() const;
};

class Singer : virtual public Worker
{
protected:
enum {other, alto, contralto, soprano,
                    bass, baritone, tenor};
    enum {Vtypes = 7};
    void Data() const;
    void Get();
private:
    static char *pv[Vtypes];    // string equivs of voice types
    int voice;
public:
    Singer() : Worker(), voice(other) {}
    Singer(const String & s, long n, int v = other)
            : Worker(s, n), voice(v) {}
    Singer(const Worker & wk, int v = other)
            : Worker(wk), voice(v) {}
    void Set();
    void Show() const;
};

// multiple inheritance
class SingingWaiter : public Singer, public Waiter
{
protected:
    void Data() const;
    void Get();
public:
    SingingWaiter()  {}
    SingingWaiter(const String & s, long n, int p = 0,
                                int v = Singer::other)
            : Worker(s,n), Waiter(s, n, p), Singer(s, n, v) {}
    SingingWaiter(const Worker & wk, int p = 0, int v = Singer::other)
            : Worker(wk), Waiter(wk,p), Singer(wk,v) {}
    SingingWaiter(const Waiter & wt, int v = other)
            : Worker(wt),Waiter(wt), Singer(wt,v) {}
    SingingWaiter(const Singer & wt, int p = 0)
            : Worker(wt),Waiter(wt,p), Singer(wt) {}
    void Set();
    void Show() const;
};
```

Listing 13.19 workermi.cpp

```cpp
// workermi.cpp -- working class methods with MI
#include "workermi.h"
#include <iostream>
using namespace std;
// Worker methods
Worker::~Worker() { }

// protected methods
void Worker::Data() const
{
    cout << "Name: " << fullname << "\n";
    cout << "Employee ID: " << id << "\n";
}

void Worker::Get()
{
    cin >> fullname;
    cout << "Enter worker's ID: ";
    cin >> id;
    while (cin.get() != '\n')
        continue;
}

// Waiter methods
void Waiter::Set()
{
    cout << "Enter waiter's name: ";
    Worker::Get();
    Get();
}

void Waiter::Show() const
{
    cout << "Category: waiter\n";
    Worker::Data();
    Data();
}

// protected methods
void Waiter::Data() const
{
    cout << "Panache rating: " << panache << "\n";
}

void Waiter::Get()
{
    cout << "Enter waiter's panache rating: ";
    cin >> panache;
    while (cin.get() != '\n')
        continue;
}

// Singer methods

char * Singer::pv[Singer::Vtypes] = {"other", "alto", "contralto",
            "soprano", "bass", "baritone", "tenor"};

void Singer::Set()
```

```
{
    cout << "Enter singer's name: ";
    Worker::Get();
    Get();
}

void Singer::Show() const
{
    cout << "Category: singer\n";
    Worker::Data();
    Data();
}

// protected methods
void Singer::Data() const
{
    cout << "Vocal range: " << pv[voice] << "\n";
}

void Singer::Get()
{
    cout << "Enter number for singer's vocal range:\n";
    int i;
    for (i = 0; i < Vtypes; i++)
    {
        cout << i << ": " << pv[i] << "    ";
        if ( i % 4 == 3)
            cout << '\n';
    }
    if (i % 4 != 0)
        cout << '\n';
    cin >>  voice;
    while (cin.get() != '\n')
        continue;
}

// SingingWaiter methods
void SingingWaiter::Data() const
{
    Singer::Data();
    Waiter::Data();
}

void SingingWaiter::Get()
{
    Waiter::Get();
    Singer::Get();
}

void SingingWaiter::Set()
{
    cout << "Enter singing waiter's name: ";
    Worker::Get();
    Get();
}

void SingingWaiter::Show() const
{
    cout << "Category: singing waiter\n";
    Worker::Data();
    Data();
}
```

Of course, curiosity demands we test these classes, and Listing 13.20, based on Listing 13.16, provides code to do so. Note that the program makes use of the polymorphic property by assigning the addresses of various kinds of classes to base class pointers. Compile it along with `workermi.cpp` and `strng2.cpp`. Also make sure the `arraytp.h` header file (the one containing our array template definition) is present.

Remember

If your system doesn't support templates, you can use a regular array instead. Just make the minor changes suggested in the listing.

Listing 13.20 workmi.cpp

```cpp
// workmi.cpp -- multiple inheritance
// compile with workermi.cpp, strng2.cpp
#include <iostream>
using namespace std;
#include <cstring>
#include "workermi.h"
#include "arraytp.h"  // omit if no template support
const int SIZE = 5;
int main()
{
    ArrayTP<Worker *, SIZE> lolas;
    // if no template support, omit the above and use the following:
    // Worker * lolas[SIZE];

    int ct;
    for (ct = 0; ct < SIZE; ct++)
    {
        char choice;
        cout << "Enter the employee category:\n"
            << "w: waiter   s: singer   "
            << "t: singing waiter   q: quit\n";
        cin >> choice;
        while (strchr("ewstq", choice) == NULL)
        {
            cout << "Please enter a w, s, t, or q: ";
            cin >> choice;
        }
        if (choice == 'q')
            break;
        switch(choice)
        {
            case 'w':   lolas[ct] = new Waiter;
                        break;
            case 's':   lolas[ct] = new Singer;
                        break;
            case 't':   lolas[ct] = new SingingWaiter;
                        break;
        }
        cin.get();
        lolas[ct]->Set();
    }

    cout << "\nHere is your staff:\n";
    int i;
```

```
        for (i = 0; i < ct; i++)
        {
            cout << '\n';
            lolas[i]->Show();
        }
        for (i = 0; i < ct; i++)
            delete lolas[i];
        return 0;
}
```

Here is a sample run:

```
Enter the employee category:
w: waiter  s: singer  t: singing waiter  q: quit
w
Enter waiter's name: Wally Snipeside
Enter worker's ID: 1020
Enter waiter's panache rating: 5
Enter the employee category:
w: waiter  s: singer  t: singing waiter  q: quit
t
Enter singing waiter's name: Natasha Gargalova
Enter worker's ID: 1021
Enter waiter's panache rating: 6
Enter number for singer's vocal range:
0: other   1: alto   2: contralto   3: soprano
4: bass    5: baritone   6: tenor
3
Enter the employee category:
w: waiter  s: singer  t: singing waiter  q: quit
q

Here is your staff:

Category: waiter
Name: Wally Snipeside
Employee ID: 1020
Panache rating: 5

Category: singing waiter
Name: Natasha Gargalova
Employee ID: 1021
Vocal range: soprano
Panache rating: 6
```

Let's look at a few more matters concerning multiple inheritance.

Mixed Virtual and Nonvirtual Bases

Consider again the case of a derived class that inherits a base class by more than one route. If the base class is virtual, the derived class contains one subobject of the base class. If the base class is not virtual, the derived class contains multiple subobjects. What if there is a mixture? Suppose, for example, that class B is a virtual base class to classes C and D and a nonvirtual base class to classes X and Y. Furthermore, suppose class M is derived from C, D, X, and Y. In this case, class M contains one class B subobject for all the virtually derived ancestors (that is, classes C and D) and a separate class

" When a class inherits a particular base class through several virtual paths and several non-virtual paths, the class has one base class subobject to represent all the virtual paths and a separate base-class subobject to represent each non-virtual path."

B subobject for each nonvirtual ancestor (that is, classes X and Y). So, all told, it would contain three class B subobjects. When a class inherits a particular base class through several virtual paths and several non-virtual paths, the class has one base-class subobject to represent all the virtual paths and a separate base-class subobject to represent each non-virtual path.

Virtual Base Classes and Dominance

Using virtual base classes alters how C++ resolves ambiguities. With nonvirtual base classes the rules are simple. If a class inherits two or more members (data or methods) of the same name from different classes, using that name without qualifying it with a class name is ambiguous. If virtual base classes are involved, however, such a use may or may not be ambiguous. In this case, if one name *dominates* all others, it can be used unambiguously without a qualifier.

So how does one member name dominate another? A name in a derived class dominates the same name in any ancestor class, direct or indirect. For example, consider the following definitions:

```
class B
{
public:
        short q();
        ...
};

class C : virtual public B
{
public:
        long q();
        int omb()
        ...
};

class D : public C
{
        ...
};

class E : virtual public B
{
private:
        int omb();
        ...
};

class F:  public D, public E
{
        ...
};
```

Here the definition of q() in class C dominates the definition in class B because C is derived from B. Thus, methods in F can use q() to denote C::q(). On the other hand, neither definition of omb() dominates the other because neither C nor E is a base class to the other. Therefore, an attempt by F to use an unqualified omb() would be ambiguous.

The virtual ambiguity rules pay no attention to access rules. That is, even though `E::omb()` is private and hence not directly accessible to class `F`, using `omb()` is ambiguous. Similarly, even if `C::q()` were private, it would dominate `D::q()`. In that case, you could call `B::q()` in class `F`, but an unqualified `q()` for that would refer to the inaccessible `C::q()`.

MULTIPLE INHERITANCE SYNOPSIS

First, let's review multiple inheritance without virtual base classes. This form of MI imposes no new rules. However, if a class inherits two members of the same name but from different classes, you need to use class qualifiers in the derived class to distinguish between the two members. That is, methods in the `BadDude` class, derived from `Gunslinger` and `PokerPlayer`, would use `Gunslinger::draw()` and `PokerPlayer::draw()` to distinguish between `draw()` methods inherited from the two classes. Otherwise, the compiler should complain about ambiguous usage.

If one class inherits from a non-virtual base class by more than one route, then the class inherits one base class object for each nonvirtual instance of the base class. In some cases this may be what you want, but more often multiple instances of a base class are a problem.

Next, let's look at MI with virtual base classes. A class becomes a virtual base class when a derived class uses the keyword `virtual` when indicating derivation:

```
class marketing : public virtual reality { ... };
```

The main change, and the reason for virtual base classes, is that a class that inherits from one or more instances of a virtual base class inherits just one base class object. Implementing this feature entails other requirements:

- A derived class with an indirect virtual base class should have its constructors invoke the indirect base class constructors directly, something that is illegal for indirect nonvirtual base classes.

- Name ambiguity is resolved by the dominance rule.

As you can see, multiple inheritance can introduce programming complexities. However, most of these complexities arise when a derived class inherits from the same base class by more than one route. If you avoid that situation, about the only thing you need to watch for is qualifying inherited names when necessary.

Summary

C++ provides several means for reusing code. Public inheritance, described in Chapter 12, enables you to model *is-a* relationships, with derived classes being able to reuse the code of base classes. Private and protected inheritance also let you reuse base class code, this time modeling *has-a* relationships. With private inheritance, public and protected members of the base class become private members of the derived class. With protected inheritance, public and protected members of the base class become protected members of the derived class. Thus, in either case, the public interface of the base class becomes an internal interface for the derived class. This sometimes is described as inheriting the implementation but not the interface, because a derived object can't explicitly use the base class interface. Thus, you can't view a derived object as a kind of base object. Because of this, a base class pointer or reference is not allowed to refer to a derived object without an explicit type cast.

You also can reuse class code by developing a class with members that are themselves objects. This approach, called containment, layering, or composition, also models the *has-a* relationship. Containment is simpler to implement and use than private or protected inheritance, so it usually is preferred. However, private and protected inheritance have slightly greater capabilities. For instance, inheritance allows a derived class access to protected members of a base class. Also, it allows a derived class to redefine a virtual function inherited from the base class. Because containment is not a form of inheritance, neither of these capabilities are options when you reuse class code by containment. On the other hand, containment is more suitable if you need several objects of a given class. For instance, a `State` class could contain an array of `County` objects.

Multiple inheritance (MI) allows you to reuse code for more than one class in a class design. Private or protected MI models the *has-a* relationship, whereas public MI models the *is-a* relationship. Multiple inheritance can create problems with multi-defined names and multi-inherited bases. You can use class qualifiers to resolve name ambiguities and virtual base classes to avoid multi-inherited bases. However, using virtual base classes introduces new rules for writing initialization lists for constructors and for resolving ambiguities.

Class templates let you create a generic class design in which a type, usually a member type, is represented by a type parameter. A typical template looks like this:

```
template <class T>
class Ic
{
      T v;
      ...
public:
      Ic(const T & val) : v(val) { }
      ...
};
```

Here the `T` is the type parameter and acts as a stand-in for a real type to be specified at a later time. (This parameter can have any valid C++ name, but `T` and `Type` are common choices.) You also can use `typename` instead of `class` in this context:

```
template <typename T>  // same as template <class T>
class Rev {...} ;
```

Class definitions (instantiations) are generated when you declare a class object, specifying a particular type. For instance, the declaration

```
class Ic<short> sic;     // implicit instantiation
```

causes the compiler to generate a class declaration in which every occurrence of the type parameter `T` in the template is replaced by the actual type `short` in the class declaration. In this case the class name is `Ic<short>`, not `Ic`. `Ic<short>` is termed a specialization of the template. In particular, it is an implicit instantiation.

*" Class templates
can be partially
specialized. "*

An explicit instantiation occurs when you declare a specific specialization of the class using the keyword `template`:

```
template class IC<int>;  // explicit instantiation
```

In this situation, the compiler uses the general template to generate an `int` specialization `Ic<int>` even though no objects have yet been requested of that class.

You can provide explicit specializations which are specialized class declarations that override a template definition. Just define the class, starting with `template<>`, then the template class name followed by angle brackets containing the type for which you want a specialization. For example, you could provide a specialized `Ic` class for character pointers as follows:

```
template <> class Ic<char *>.
{
    char * str;
    ...
public:
    Ic(const char * s) : str(s) { }
    ...
};
```

Then a declaration of the form

```
class Ic<char *> chic;
```

would use the specialized definition for `chic` rather than using the general template.

A class template can specify more than one generic type and can also have non-type parameters:

```
template <class T, class TT, int n>
class Pals {…};
```

The declaration

```
Pals<double, String, 6> mix;
```

would generate an implicit instantiation using `double` for T, `String` for TT, and 6 for n.

Class templates can be partially specialized:

```
template <class T> Pals<T, T, 10> {...};
template <class T, class TT> Pals<T, TT, 100> {...};
template <class T, int n> Pals <T, T*, n> {...};
```

The first creates a specialization in which both types are the same and n has the value 6. Similarly, the second creates a specialization for n equal to 100, and the third creates a specialization for which the second type is a pointer to the first type.

The goal of all these methods is to allow you to reuse tested code without having to copy it manually. This simplifies the programming task and makes programs more reliable.

Review Questions

1. For each of the following sets of classes, indicate whether public or private derivation is more appropriate for the second column:

```
class Bear                          class PolarBear
class Kitchen                       class Home
class Person                        class Programmer
class Person                        class HorseAndJockey
class Person,                       class Driver
class Automobile
```

2. Suppose we have the following definitions:

```
class Frabjous {
private:
     char fab[20];
public:
     Frabjous(const char * s = "C++") : fab(s) { }
     virtual void tell() { cout << fab; }
};

class Gloam {
private:
     int glip;
     Frabjous fb;
public:
     Gloam(int g = 0, const char * s = "C++");
     Gloam(int g, const Frabjous & f);
     void tell();
};
```

Given that the Gloam version of tell() should display the values of glip and fb, provide definitions for the three Gloam methods.

3. Suppose we have the following definitions:

```
class Frabjous {
private:
     char fab[20];
public:
     Frabjous(const char * s = "C++") : fab(s) { }
     virtual void tell() { cout << fab; }
};

class Gloam : private Frabjous{
private:
     int glip;
public:
     Gloam(int g = 0, const char * s = "C++");
     Gloam(int g, const Frabjous & f);
     void tell();
};
```

Given that the Gloam version of tell() should display the values of glip and fab, provide definitions for the three Gloam methods.

4. Suppose we have the following definition, based on the `Stack` template of Listing 13.9 and the `Worker` class of Listing 13.18:

```
Stack<Worker *> sw;
```

Write out the class declaration that will be generated. Just do the class declaration, not the non-inline class methods.

5. Use the template definitions in this chapter to define the following:

- An array of `String` objects

- A stack of arrays of `double`

- An array of stacks of pointers to `Worker` objects

6. Describe the differences between virtual and nonvirtual base classes.

Programming Exercises

1. The `Wine` class has a `String` class object (Chapter 11) holding the name of a wine and an `ArrayDb` class object (this chapter) holding the number of available bottles for each of several consecutive years. Implement the `Wine` class using containment and test it with a simple program. The program should prompt you to enter a wine name, the size of the array, the first year for the array, and the number of bottles for each year. The program should use this data to construct a `Wine` object, then display the information stored in the object.

2. The `Wine` class has a `String` class object (Chapter 11) holding the name of a wine and an `ArrayDb` class object (this chapter) holding the number of available bottles for each of several consecutive years. Implement the Wine class using private inheritance and test it with a simple program. The program should prompt you to enter a wine name, the size of the array, the first year for the array, and the number of bottles for each year. The program should use this data to construct a `Wine` object, then display the information stored in the object.

3. Define a `QueueTp` template. Test it by creating a queue of pointers-to-`Worker` (as defined in Listing 13.18) and using the queue in a program similar to that of Listing 13.20.

4. A `Person` class holds the first name and the last name of a person. In addition to its constructors, it has a `Show()` method that displays both names. A `Gunslinger` class derives virtually from the `Person` class. It has a `Draw()` member that returns a type `double` value representing a gunslinger's draw time. The class also has an `int` member representing the number of notches on a gunslinger's gun. Finally, it has a `Show()` function that displays all this information.

A `PokerPlayer` class derives virtually from the `Person` class. It has a `Draw()` member that returns a random number in the range 1 through 52 representing a card value. (Optionally, you could define a `Card` class with suit and face value members and use a `Card` return value for `Draw()`). The `PokerPlayer` class uses the `Person` `show()` function. The `BadDude` class derives publicly from the `Gunslinger` and `PokerPlayer` classes. It has a `Gdraw()` member that returns a bad dude's draw time and a `Cdraw()` member that returns the next card drawn. It has an appropriate `Show()` function. Define all these classes and methods, along with any other necessary methods (such as methods for setting object values), and test them in a simple program similar to that of Listing 13.20.

5. Here are some class declarations:

```cpp
// emp.h -- header file for employee class and children
#include <cstring>
#include <iostream>
using namespace std;

const int SLEN = 20;
class employee
{
protected:
    char fname[SLEN];
    char lname[SLEN];
    char job[SLEN];
public:
    employee();
    employee(char * fn, char * ln, char * j);
    employee(const employee & e);
    virtual void ShowAll() const;
    virtual void SetAll();  // prompts user for values
    friend ostream & operator<<(ostream & os, const employee & e);
};

class manager:  virtual public employee
{
protected:
    int inchargeof;
public:
    manager();
    manager(char * fn, char * ln, char * j, int ico = 0);
    manager(const employee & e, int ico);
    manager(const manager & m);
    void ShowAll() const;
    void SetAll();
};

class fink: virtual public employee
{
protected:
    char reportsto[SLEN];
public:
    fink();
    fink(char * fn, char * ln, char * j, char * rpo);
    fink(const employee & e, char * rpo);
    fink(const fink & e);
    void ShowAll() const;
```

```
        void SetAll();
};


class highfink: public manager, public fink
{
public:
    highfink();
    highfink(char * fn, char * ln, char * j, char * rpo, int ico);
    highfink(const employee & e, char * rpo, int ico);
    highfink(const fink & f, int ico);
    highfink(const manager & m, char * rpo);
    highfink(const highfink & h);
    void ShowAll() const;
    void SetAll();
};
```

Note that the class hierarchy uses multiple inheritance with a virtual base
class, so keep in mind the special rules for constructor initialization lists for
that case. Also note that the data members are declared protected instead of
private. This simplifies the code. However, you might want to use private
data and provide additional protected methods in the manner of the Worker
class with MI. Provide the class method implementations and test the classes
in a program. Here is a minimal test program. You should add at least one test
of a SetAll() member function.

```
// useemp1.cpp -- use employee classes
#include <iostream>
using namespace std;
#include "emp.h"

int main()
{
    employee th("Trip", "Harris", "Thumper");
    cout << th << '\n';
    th.ShowAll();


    manager db("Debbie", "Bolt", "Twigger", 5);
    cout << db << '\n';
    db.ShowAll();

    cout << "Press a key for next batch of output:\n";
    cin.get();

    fink mo("Matt", "Oggs", "Oiler", "Debbie Bolt");
    cout << mo << '\n';
    mo.ShowAll();
    highfink hf(db, "Curly Kew");
    hf.ShowAll();

    cout << "Using an employee * pointer:\n";
    employee  * tri[4] = { &th, &db, &mo, &hf };
    for (int i = 0; i < 4; i++)
        tri[i]->ShowAll();

    return 0;;
}
```

Remember

Symantec C++ requires that the elements of the `tri` array be assigned object addresses individually rather than through an initialization statement.

Why is no assignment operator defined?

Why are `showall()` and `setall()` virtual?

Why is `employee` a virtual base class?

Why does the `highfink` class have no data section?

Why is only one version of `operator<<()` needed?

What would happen if the end of the program were replaced with this code?

```
employee  tri[4] = {th, db, mo, hf};
for (int i = 0; i < 4; i++)
    tri[i].showall();
```

14

Friends, Exceptions, and More

This chapter ties up some loose ends and then ventures into some of the most recent additions to the C++ language. The loose ends include friend classes, friend member functions, and nested classes, which are classes declared within other classes. The recent additions discussed here are exceptions, RTTI, and improved type cast control. C++ exception handling provides a mechanism for dealing with unusual occurrences that otherwise would bring a program to a halt. RTTI, or runtime type information, is a mechanism for identifying object types. The new type cast operators improve the safety of type casts. These last three facilities are fairly new to C++, and many compilers do not yet support them.

You will learn about the following in this chapter:

- Friend classes
- Friend class methods
- Nested classes
- Throwing exceptions, try blocks, and catch blocks
- Exception classes
- RTTI (runtime type information)
- `dynamic_cast` and `typeid`
- `static_cast`, `const_cast`, and `reinterpret_cast`

Friends

Several examples in this book have used friend functions as part of the extended interface for a class. Such functions are not the only kinds of friends a class can have. A class also can be a friend. In that case, any method of the friend class can access private and protected members of the original class. You also can be more restrictive and designate only particular member functions of a class to be friends to another class. A class defines which functions, member functions, or classes are friends; friendship cannot be imposed from the outside. Thus, although friends do grant outside access to a class's private portion, they don't really violate the spirit of object-oriented programming. Instead, they provide more flexibility to the public interface.

FRIEND CLASSES

When would you want to make one class a friend to another? Let's look at an example. Suppose you need to program a simple simulation of a television and a remote control. You decide to define a `Tv` class representing a television and a `Remote` class representing a remote control. Clearly, there should be some sort of relationship between these classes, but what kind? A remote control is not a television and vice versa, so the *is-a* relationship of public inheritance doesn't apply. Nor is either class a component of the other, so the *has-a* relationship of containment or of private or protected inheritance doesn't apply. What is true is that a remote control can modify the state of a television, and this suggests making the `Remote` class a friend to the `Tv` class.

First, let's define the `Tv` class. You can represent a television with a set of state members, that is, variables that describe various aspects of the television. Here are some of the possible states:

- On-off
- Channel setting
- Volume setting
- Cable or antenna tuning mode
- TV tuner or VCR input

The tuning mode reflects the fact that, in the U.S., the spacing between channels for channels 14 and above is different for cable reception than it is for UHF broadcast reception. The input selection chooses between TV, which could be either cable or broadcast TV, and a VCR. Some sets may offer more choices, but this list is enough for our purposes.

Also, a television has some parameters that aren't state variables. For instance, televisions vary in the number of channels they can receive, and you can include a member to track that value.

Next, you need to provide the class with methods for altering these settings. Many television sets these days hide their controls behind panels, but it's still possible with most televisions to change channels, and so on, without a remote control. However, often you can move up or down one channel at a time, but you can't select a channel at random. Similarly, there's usually a button for increasing the volume and one for decreasing the volume.

A remote control should duplicate the controls built into the television. Many of its methods can be implemented by using Tv methods. In addition, a remote control typically provides random access channel selection. That is, you can go directly from channel 2 to channel 20 without going through all the intervening channels. Also, many remotes can work in two modes—as a television controller and as a VCR controller.

These considerations suggest a definition like that shown in Listing 14.1. The definition includes several constants defined as enumerations. The statement making Remote a friend class is this:

```
friend class Remote;
```

A friend declaration can appear in a public, private, or protected section; the location makes no difference. Because the Remote class mentions the Tv class, the compiler has to know about the Tv class before it can handle the Remote class. The simplest way to accomplish this is to define the Tv class first. Alternatively, you can use a forward declaration; we'll discuss that option soon.

Remember

If your compiler doesn't support the bool type, use int, 0, and 1 instead of bool, false, and true.

```
Listing 14.1 tv.h
// tv.h -- Tv and Remote classes
#ifndef _TV_H_
#define _TV_H_

class Tv
{
public:
    friend class Remote;    // Remote can access Tv private parts
    enum State{Off, On};
    enum {MinVal,MaxVal = 20};
    enum {Antenna, Cable};
    enum {TV, VCR};

    Tv(State s = Off, int mc = 100) : state(s), volume(5),
        maxchannel(mc), channel(2), mode(Cable), input(TV) {}
    void onoff() {state = (state == On)? Off : On;}
    bool ison() const {return state == On;}
    bool volup();
    bool voldown();
    void chanup();
    void chandown();
    void set_mode() {mode = (mode == Antenna)? Cable : Antenna;}
    void set_input() {input = (input == TV)? VCR : TV;}
```

```
        void settings() const; // display all settings
    private:
        State state;           // on or off
        int volume;            // assumed to be digitized
        int maxchannel;        // maximum number of channels
        int channel;           // current channel setting
        int mode;              // broadcast or cable
        int input;             // TV or VCR
    };

    class Remote
    {
    private:
        int mode;                   // controls TV or VCR
    public:
        Remote(int m = Tv::TV) : mode(m) {}
        bool volup(Tv & t) { return t.volup();}
        bool voldown(Tv & t) { return t.voldown();}
        void onoff(Tv & t) { t.onoff(); }
        void chanup(Tv & t) {t.chanup();}
        void chandown(Tv & t) {t.chandown();}
        void set_chan(Tv & t, int c) {t.channel = c;}
        void set_mode(Tv & t) {t.set_mode();}
        void set_input(Tv & t) {t.set_input();}
    };
    #endif
```

Most of the class methods are defined inline. Note that each Remote method other than the constructor takes a reference to a Tv object as an argument. That reflects that a remote has to be aimed at a particular TV. Listing 14.2 shows the remaining definitions. The volume-setting functions change the volume member by one unit unless the sound has reached its minimum or maximum setting. The channel selection functions use wraparound, with the lowest channel setting, taken to be 1, immediately following the highest channel setting, maxchannel.

Many of the methods use the conditional operator to toggle a state between two settings:

```
void onoff() {state = (state == On)? Off : On;}
```

Provided that the two state values are 0 and 1, this can be done more compactly using the combined bitwise exclusive OR and assignment operator (^=) discussed in Appendix E:

```
void onoff() {state ^= 1;}
```

In fact, you could store up to eight bivalent state settings in a single unsigned char variable and toggle them individually, but that's another story, one made possible by the bitwise operators discussed in Appendix E.

Listing 14.2 tv.cpp

```
// tv.cpp -- methods for the Tv class (Remote methods are inline)
#include <iostream>
using namespase std;
```

```
#include "tv.h"

bool Tv::volup()
{
    if (volume < MaxVal)
    {
        volume++;
        return true;
    }
    else
        return false;
}
bool Tv::voldown()
{
    if (volume > MinVal)
    {
        volume--;
        return true;
    }
    else
        return false;
}

void Tv::chanup()
{
    if (channel < maxchannel)
        channel++;
    else
        channel = 1;
}

void Tv::chandown()
{
    if (channel > 1)
        channel--;
    else
        channel = maxchannel;
}

void Tv::settings() const
{
    cout << "TV is " << (state == Off? "Off" : "On") << endl;
    if (state == On)
    {
        cout << "Volume setting = " << volume << endl;
        cout << "Channel setting = " << channel << endl;
        cout << "Mode = "
            << (mode == Antenna? "antenna" : "cable") << endl;
        cout << "Input = "
            << (input == TV? "TV" : "VCR") << endl;
    }
}
```

Next, Listing 14.3 is a short program that tests some of the features. The same controller is used to control two separate televisions.

Listing 14.3 use_tv.cpp

```cpp
//use_tv.cpp
#include <iostream>
using namespace std;
#include "tv.h"

int main()
{
    Tv s20;
    cout << "Initial settings for 20\" TV:\n";
    s20.settings();
    s20.onoff();
    s20.chanup();
    cout << "\nAdjusted settings for 20\" TV:\n";
    s20.settings();

    Remote grey;

    grey.set_chan(s20, 10);
    grey.volup(s20);
    grey.volup(s20);
    cout << "\n20\" settings after using remote:\n";
    s20.settings();

    Tv s27(Tv::On);
    s27.set_mode();
    grey.set_chan(s27,28);
    cout << "\n27\" settings:\n";
    s27.settings();

    return 0;
}
```

Here is the program output:

```
Initial settings for 20" TV:
TV is Off

Adjusted settings for 20" TV:
TV is On
Volume setting = 5
Channel setting = 3
Mode = cable
Input = TV

20" settings after using remote:
TV is On
Volume setting = 7
Channel setting = 10
Mode = cable
Input = TV

27" settings:
TV is On
Volume setting = 5
Channel setting = 28
Mode = antenna
Input = TV
```

The main point to this exercise is that class friendship is a natural idiom in which to express some relationships. Without some form of friendship, you would either have to make the private parts of the Tv class public or construct some awkward, larger class that encompasses both a television and a remote control. The latter solution wouldn't reflect the fact that a single remote control can be used with several televisions.

FRIEND MEMBER FUNCTIONS

Looking at the code for the last example, you may notice that most of the Remote methods are implemented using the public interface for the Tv class. This means that those methods don't really need friend status. Indeed, the only Remote method that accesses a private Tv member directly is Remote::set_chan(), so that's the only method that needs to be a friend. Making selected class members friends to another class is an option, but it's a bit more awkward. You need to be careful about the order in which you arrange the various declarations and definitions. Let's see why.

The way to make Remote::set_chan() a friend to the Tv class is to declare it as a friend in the Tv class declaration:

```
class Tv
{
    friend void Remote::set_chan(Tv & t, int c);
    ...
};
```

However, for the compiler to process this statement, it needs to have already seen the Remote definition. Otherwise, it won't know that Remote is a class and that set_chan() is a method of that class. That suggests putting the Remote definition above the Tv definition. But the fact that Remote methods mention Tv objects means that the Tv definition should come above the Remote definition. Part of the way around the circular dependence is to use a *forward declaration*. That means inserting the statement

```
class Tv;                 // forward declaration
```

above the Remote definition. This provides the following arrangement:

```
class Tv;  // forward declaration
class Remote { ... };
class Tv { ... };
```

Could you use the following arrangement instead?

```
class Remote;             // forward declaration
class Tv { ... };
class Remote { ... };
```

The answer is no. The reason, as mentioned earlier, is that when the compiler sees that a Remote method is declared as a friend in the Tv class declaration, the compiler needs to have already viewed the declaration of the Remote class in general and of the set_chan() method in particular.

Another difficulty remains. In Listing 14.1, the `Remote` declaration contained inline code such as the following:

```
void onoff(Tv & t) { t.onoff(); }
```

Because this calls a `Tv` method, the compiler needs to have seen the `Tv` class declaration at this point so that it knows what methods `Tv` has. But, as you've seen, that declaration necessarily follows the `Remote` declaration. The solution to this problem is to restrict `Remote` to method *declarations* and to place the actual *definitions* after the `Tv` class. This leads to the following ordering:

```
class Tv;              // forward declaration
class Remote { ... };  // Tv-using methods as prototypes only
class Tv { ... };
// put Remote method definitions here
```

The prototypes look like this:

```
void onoff(Tv & t);
```

All the compiler needs to know when inspecting this prototype is that `Tv` is a class, and the forward declaration supplies that information. By the time the compiler reaches the actual method definitions, it has already read the `Tv` class declaration and has the added information needed to compile those methods. By using the `inline` keyword in the method definitions, you still can make the methods inline methods. Listing 14.4 shows the revised header file.

```
Listing 14.4 tvfm.h
// tvfm.h -- Tv and Remote classes using a friend member
#ifndef _TVFM_H_
#define _TVFM_H_

class Tv;                          // forward declaration

class Remote
{
public:
    enum State{Off, On};
    enum {MinVal,MaxVal = 20};
    enum {Antenna, Cable};
    enum {TV, VCR};
private:
    int mode;
public:
    Remote(int m = TV) : mode(m) {}
    bool volup(Tv & t);            // prototype only
    bool voldown(Tv & t);
    void onoff(Tv & t) ;
    void chanup(Tv & t) ;
    void chandown(Tv & t) ;
    void set_mode(Tv & t) ;
    void set_input(Tv & t);
```

```
        void set_chan(Tv & t, int c);

};

class Tv
{
public:
    friend void Remote::set_chan(Tv & t, int c);
    enum State{Off, On};
    enum {MinVal,MaxVal = 20};
    enum {Antenna, Cable};
    enum {TV, VCR};

    Tv(State s = Off, int mc = 100) : state(s), volume(5),
        maxchannel(mc), channel(2), mode(Cable), input(TV) {}
    void onoff() {state = (state == On)? Off : On;}
    bool ison() const {return state == On;}
    bool volup();
    bool voldown();
    void chanup();
    void chandown();
    void set_mode() {mode = (mode == Antenna)? Cable : Antenna;}
    void set_input() {input = (input == TV)? VCR : TV;}
    void settings() const;
private:
    State state;
    int volume;
    int maxchannel;
    int channel;
    int mode;
    int input;
};

// Remote methods as inline functions
inline bool Remote::volup(Tv & t) { return t.volup();}
inline bool Remote::voldown(Tv & t) { return t.voldown();}
inline void Remote::onoff(Tv & t) { t.onoff(); }
inline void Remote::chanup(Tv & t) {t.chanup();}
inline void Remote::chandown(Tv & t) {t.chandown();}
inline void Remote::set_mode(Tv & t) {t.set_mode();}
inline void Remote::set_input(Tv & t) {t.set_input();}
inline void Remote::set_chan(Tv & t, int c) {t.channel = c;}
#endif
```

This version behaves the same as the original. The difference is that just one Remote method is a friend to the Tv class instead of all the Remote methods. Figure 14.1 illustrates this difference.

By the way, making the entire Remote class a friend doesn't need a forward declaration because the friend statement itself identifies Remote as a class:

```
friend class Remote;
```

FIGURE 14.1

Class friends versus class member friends

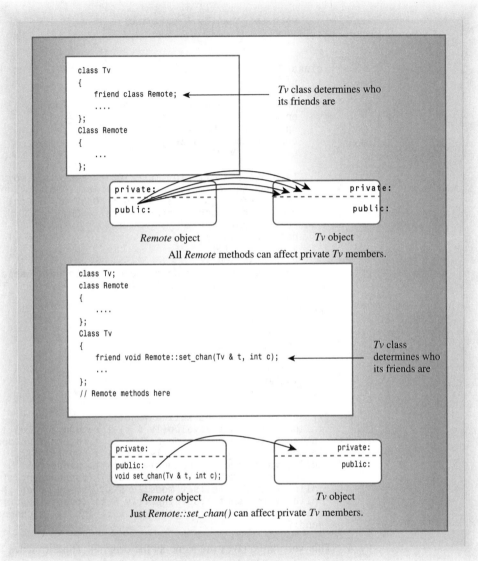

All *Remote* methods can affect private *Tv* members.

Just *Remote::set_chan()* can affect private *Tv* members.

OTHER FRIENDLY RELATIONSHIPS

Other combinations of friends and classes are possible. Let's take a brief look at some of them now. Suppose the advance of technology brings interactive remote controllers. For instance, an interactive remote control unit might let you enter a response to some question posed on a television program, and the television might activate a buzzer in your controller if your response was wrong. Ignoring the possibility of television using such facilities to program the viewers, let's just look at the C++ programming aspects.

The new setup would benefit from mutual friendship, with some `Remote` methods being able to affect a `Tv` object, as before, and with some `Tv` methods being able to affect a `Remote` object. This can be accomplished by making the classes friends to each other. That is, `Tv` will be a friend to `Remote` in addition to `Remote` being a friend to `Tv`. One point to keep in mind is that a `Tv` method that uses a `Remote` object can be prototyped *before* the `Remote` class declaration but must be defined *after* the declaration so that the compiler will have enough information to compile the method. The setup would look like this:

```
class Tv
{
friend class Remote;
public:
    void buzz(Remote & r);
    ...
};
class Remote
{
friend class Tv;
public:
    void Bool volup(Tv & t) { t.volup(); }
    ...
};
inline void Tv::buzz(Remote & r)
{
    ...
}
```

Because the `Remote` declaration follows the `Tv` declaration, `Remote::volup()` can be defined in the class declaration. The `Tv::buzz()` method, however, has to be defined outside the `Tv` declaration so that the definition can follow the `Remote` declaration. If you don't want `buzz()` to be inline, define it in a separate method definitions file.

Shared Friends

Another use for friends is when a function needs to access private data in two separate classes. Logically, such a function should be a member function of each class, but that's impossible. It could be a member of one class and a friend to the other, but sometimes it's more reasonable to make the function friends to both. Suppose, for example, that you have a `Probe` class representing some sort of programmable measuring device and an `Analyzer` class representing some sort of programmable analyzing device. Each has an internal clock, and you would like to be able to synchronize the two clocks. You could do something along the following lines:

```
class Analyzer;  // forward declaration
class Probe
{
    friend void sync(Analyzer & a, const Probe & p);  // sync a to p
    friend void sync(Probe & p, const Analyzer & a);  // sync p to a
    ...
};
class Analyzer
{
```

```
    friend void sync(Analyzer & a, const Probe & p);  // sync a to p
    friend void sync(Probe & p, const Analyzer & a);  // sync p to a
    ...
};

// define the friend functions
inline void sync(Analyzer & a, const Probe & p)
{
    ...
}
inline void sync(Probe & p, const Analyzer & a)
{
    ...
}
```

The forward declaration enables the compiler to know that Analyzer is a type when it reaches the friend declarations in the Probe class declaration.

Templates and Friends

Template class declarations can have friends, too. We can classify friends to templates in three categories:

- Nontemplate friends

- Bound template friends, meaning that the type of the friend is determined by the type of the class when a class is instiantiated

- Unbound template friends, meaning that all instantiations of the friend are friends to each instantiation of the class

Let's look at examples of each. First, here's an example of a template with nontemplate friends:

```
template <class Type>
class HasFriend
{
    friend void date();  // friend to all HasFriend instantiations
    ...
};
```

The date() function will be a friend to all possible instantiations of the template. For instance, it would be a friend to the HasFriend<int> class and the HasFriend<String> class.

Suppose you want to provide a template class argument to the friend. Can you alter the friend declaration to look like this, for example:

```
friend void date(HasFriend &);   // possible?
```

The answer is no. There is no such thing as a HasFriend object. There are only particular instantiations, such as HasFriend<short>. To provide a template class argument, then, you have to indicate an instantiation. For instance, you can do this:

```
template <class Type>
class HasFriend
```

```
{
    friend void date(HasFriend<Type> &); // bound template friend
    ...
};
```

This would require that a template function be defined:

```
template <class A>
void date(A &) { ... };
```

This combination of code results in date<short>() being a friend to HasFriend<short>, and so on. Each class instantiation has one corresponding friend function instantiation. This is an example of *bound template friendship*. The same technique can be used to create bound template friend classes.

Now suppose you alter the class declaration slightly:

```
template <class Type>
class HasFriend
{
    friend void date(HasFriend<T> &); // unbound template friend
    ...
};
```

The original used the same generic type name (Type) in the class heading and in the friend prototype. This version uses a different generic type name (T) for the prototype. The effect of this format is to make all instantiations of date() friends to each HasFriend instantiation. That is, date<int>(), date<double>(), and date<HasFriend<String> >() all are friends to HasFriend<char *>. This is an example of *unbound template friendship*. The same technique can be used to create unbound template friend classes.

Can templates be friends to nontemplate classes? No, they can't, but specific instantiations can be.

```
class Pal
{
    friend class HasFriend<long>;  // ok
    friend class HasFriend;        // not allowed
};
```

Uninstantiated template names like HasFriend can only appear in templates. Regular code can use only specific instantiations such as HasFriend<Complex>.

Nested Classes

In C++, you can place a class declaration inside another class. The class declared within another is called a *nested class*, and it helps avoid name clutter by giving the new type class scope. Member functions of the class containing the declaration can create and use objects of the nested class. The outside world can use the nested class only if the declaration is in the public section and if you use the scope resolution operator. (Older versions of C++, however, don't allow nested classes or implement the concept incompletely.)

Nesting classes is not the same as containment. Containment, you may recall, means having a class object as a member of another class. Nesting a class, on the other hand, does not create a class member. Instead, it defines a type that is known just locally to the class containing the nested class declaration.

The usual reasons for nesting a class are to assist the implementation of another class and to avoid name conflicts. The Queue class example (Chapter 11, Listing 11.11) provided a disguised case of nested classes by nesting a structure definition:

```
class Queue
{
// class scope definitions
    // Node is a nested structure definition local to this class
    struct Node {Item item; struct Node * next;};
    ...
};
```

Because a structure is a class whose members are public by default, Node really is a nested class. However, this definition doesn't take advantage of class abilities. In particular, it lacks an explicit constructor. Let's remedy that now.

First, let's find where Node objects are created in the Queue example. Examining the class declaration (Listing 11.11) and the methods definitions (Listing 11.12) reveals that the only place in which Node objects are created is in the enqueue() method:

```
bool Queue::enqueue(const Item & item)
{
    if (isfull())
        return false;
    Node * add = new Node;   // create node
    if (add == NULL)
        return false;         // quit if none available
    add->item = item;         // set node pointers
    add->next = NULL;
    ...
}
```

Here the code explicitly assigns values to the Node members after creating a Node. This is the sort of work that more properly is done by a constructor.

Knowing where and how a constructor should be used, you can now provide an appropriate constructor definition:

```
class Queue
{
// class scope definitions
    // Node is a nested class definition local to this class
    class Node
    {
    public:
        Item item;
        Node * next;
        Node(const Item & i) : item(i), next(0) { }
    };
    ...
};
```

This constructor initializes the node's item member to i and sets the next pointer to 0, which is one way of writing the null pointer in C++. (Using NULL would require including a header file that defines NULL.) Because all nodes created by the Queue class have next initially set to the null pointer, this is the only constructor the class needs.

Next, rewrite enqueue() using the constructor:

```
bool Queue::enqueue(const Item & item)
{
    if (isfull())
        return false;
    Node * add = new Node(item);  // create, initialize node
    if (add == 0)
        return fFalse;            // quit if none available
    ...
}
```

This makes the code for enqueue() a bit shorter and a bit safer because it automates initialization rather than requiring that the programmer remember correctly what should be done.

This example defined the constructor in the class declaration. Suppose you wanted to define it in a methods file instead. The definition must reflect that the Node class is defined within the Queue class. This is accomplished by using the scope resolution operator twice:

```
Queue::Node::Node(const Item & i) : item(i), next(0) { }
```

NESTED CLASSES AND ACCESS

Two kinds of access pertain to nested classes. First, where a nested class is declared controls the scope of the nested class; that is, it establishes which parts of a program can create objects of that class. Second, as with any class, the public, protected, and private sections of a nested class provide access control to class members. Where and how a nested class can be used depends on both scope and access control. Let's examine these points further.

Scope

If the nested class is declared in a private section of a second class, it is known only to that second class. This applies, for instance, to the Node class nested in the Queue declaration in the last example. (It may appear that Node was defined before the private section, but remember that private is the default access for classes.) Hence, Queue members can use Node objects and pointers to Node objects, but other parts of a program won't even know that the Node class exists. If you were to derive a class from Queue, Node would be invisible to that class, too, because a derived class can't directly access the private parts of a base class.

If the nested class is declared in a protected section of a second class, it is visible to that class but invisible to the outside world. However, in this case, a derived class would know about the nested class and could directly create objects of that type.

If a nested class is declared in a public section of a second class, it is available to the second class, to classes derived from the second class, and, because it's public, to the outside world. However, because the nested class has class scope, it has to be used with a class qualifier in the outside world. For example, suppose you have this declaration:

```
class Team
{
public:
        class Coach { ... };
        ...
};
```

Now suppose you have an unemployed coach, one who belongs to no team. To create a Coach object outside of the Team class, you can do this:

```
Team::Coach forhire; // create a Coach object outside the Team class
```

These same scope considerations apply to nested structures and enumerations, too. Indeed, many programmers use public enumerations to provide class constants that can be used by client programmers. For instance, the many implementations of classes defined to support the iostream facility use this technique to provide various formatting options, as we touched on earlier and will explore more fully in Chapter 16. Table 14.1 summarizes scope properties for nested classes, structures, and enumerations.

Access Control

> *" The same rules govern access to a nested class that govern access to a regular class."*

Once a class is in scope, access control comes into play. The same rules govern access to a nested class that govern access to a regular class. Declaring the Node class in the Queue class declaration does not grant the Queue class any special access privileges to the Node class, nor does it grant the Node class any special access privileges to the Queue class. Thus, a Queue class object can access only the public members of a Node object explicitly. For that reason, the Queue example made all the members of the Node class public. This violates the usual practice of making data members private, but the Node class is an internal implementation feature of the Queue class and is not visible to the outside world. That's because the Node class is declared in the private section of the Queue class. Thus, although Queue methods can access Node members directly, a client using the Queue class cannot do so.

TABLE 14.1
SCOPE PROPERTIES FOR NESTED CLASSES, STRUCTURES, AND ENUMERATIONS

Where Declared in Nesting Class	Available to Nesting Class	Available to Classes Derived from the Nesting Class	Available to the Outside World
Private section	Yes	No	No
Protected section	Yes	Yes	No
Public section	Yes	Yes	Yes, with class qualifier

In short, the location of a class declaration determines the scope or visibility of a class. Given that a particular class is in scope, the usual access control rules (public, protected, private, friend) determine the access a program has to members of the nested class.

NESTING IN A TEMPLATE

You've seen that templates are a good choice for implementing container classes such as the Queue class. You may be wondering if having a nested class poses any problems to converting the Queue class definition to a template. The answer is no. Listing 14.5 shows how this conversion can be made. As usual for class templates, the header file includes the class template along with method function templates.

Listing 14.5 queuetp.h

```
// queuetp.h -- queue template with a nested class
template <class Item>
class QueueTP
{
private:
    enum {Q_SIZE = 10};
    // Node is a nested class definition
    class Node
    {
    public:
        Item item;
        Node * next;
        Node(const Item & i):item(i), next(0){ }
    };
    Node * front;       // pointer to front of Queue
    Node * rear;        // pointer to rear of Queue
    int items;          // current number of items in Queue
    const int qsize;    // maximum number of items in Queue
    QueueTP(const QueueTP & q) : qsize(0) {}
    QueueTP & operator=(const QueueTP & q) { return *this; }
public:
    QueueTP(int qs = Q_SIZE);
    ~QueueTP();
    bool isempty() const
    {
        return items == 0;
    }
    bool isfull() const
    {
        return items == qsize;
    }
    int queuecount() const
    {
        return items;
    }
    bool enqueue(const Item &item); // add item to end
    bool dequeue(Item &item);       // remove item from front
};

// QueueTP methods
template <class Item>
```

```
QueueTP<Item>::QueueTP(int qs) : qsize(qs)
{
    front = rear = 0;
    items = 0;
}

template <class Item>
QueueTP<Item>::~QueueTP()
{
    Node * temp;
    while (front != 0)      // while queue is not yet empty
    {
        temp = front;        // save address of front item
        front = front->next;// reset pointer to next item
        delete temp;         // delete former front
    }
}

// Add item to queue
template <class Item>
bool QueueTP<Item>::enqueue(const Item & item)
{
    if (isfull())
        return false;
    Node * add = new Node(item);    // create node
    if (add == NULL)
        return false;        // quit if none available
    items++;
    if (front == 0)          // if queue is empty,
        front = add;         // place item at front
    else
        rear->next = add;    // else place at rear
    rear = add;              // have rear point to new node
    return true;
}

// Place front item into item variable and remove from queue
template <class Item>
bool QueueTP<Item>::dequeue(Item & item)
{
    if (front == 0)
        return false;
    item = front->item;      // set item to first item in queue
    items--;
    Node * temp = front;     // save location of first item
    front = front->next;     // reset front to next item
    delete temp;             // delete former first item
    if (items == 0)
        rear = 0;
    return true;
}
```

One interesting thing about this template is that Node is defined in terms of the generic type Item. Thus, a declaration like

```
QueueTp<double> dq;
```

leads to a Node defined to hold type double values, while

```
QueueTp<char> cq;
```

leads to a Node defined to hold type char values. These two Node classes are defined in two separate QueueTP classes, so there is no name conflict between the two. That is, one node is type QueueTP<double>::Node and the other is type QueueTP<char>::Node.

Listing 14.6 offers a short program for testing the new class. It creates a queue of String objects, so it should be compiled in conjunction with strng2.cpp (Chapter 11).

Listing 14.6 nested.cpp

```cpp
// nested.cpp -- use queue having a nested class
// compile along with strng2.cpp
#include <iostream>
using namespace std;
#include "strng2.h"
#include "queuetp.h"

int main()
{
    QueueTP<String> cs(5);
    String temp;

    while(!cs.isfull())
    {
        cout << "Please enter your name. You will be "
                "served in the order of arrival.\n"
                "name: ";
        cin >> temp;
        cs.enqueue(temp);
    }
    cout << "The queue is full. Processing begins!\n";

    while (!cs.isempty())
    {
        cs.dequeue(temp);
        cout << "Now processing " << temp << "...\n";
    }
    return 0;
}
```

Here is a sample run:

```
Please enter your name. You will be served in the order of arrival.
name: Kinsey Millhone
Please enter your name. You will be served in the order of arrival.
name: Adam Dalgliesh
Please enter your name. You will be served in the order of arrival.
name: Andrew Dalziel
Please enter your name. You will be served in the order of arrival.
name: Kay Scarpetta
Please enter your name. You will be served in the order of arrival.
name: Richard Jury
The queue is full. Processing begins!
Now processing Kinsey Millhone...
Now processing Adam Dalgliesh...
Now processing Andrew Dalziel...
Now processing Kay Scarpetta...
Now processing Richard Jury...
```

Exceptions

Programs sometimes encounter runtime problems that prevent the program from continuing normally. For example, a program may try to open an unavailable file, or it may request more memory than is available, or it may encounter values it cannot abide. Usually, programmers try to anticipate such calamities. C++ exceptions provide a powerful and flexible tool for dealing with these situations. Exceptions were added to C++ recently, and not all compilers have implemented them yet.

Before examining exceptions, let's look at some of the more rudimentary options available to the programmer. As a test case, take a function that calculates the harmonic mean of two numbers. The harmonic mean of two numbers is defined as the inverse of the average of the inverses. This can be reduced to the following expression:

```
2.0 * x * y / (x + y)
```

Note that if y is the negative of x, this formula results in division by zero, a rather undesirable operation. One way to handle this is to have the function call the abort() function if one argument is the negative of the other. The abort() function has its prototype in the cstdlib (or stdlib.h) header file. A typical implementation, if called, sends a message like "abnormal program termination" to the standard error stream (the same as the one used by cerr) and terminates the program. It also returns an implementation-dependent value indicating failure to the operating system or, if the program was initiated by another program, to the parent process. Whether abort() flushes file buffers (memory areas used to store material for transfers to and from files) depends on the implementation. If you prefer, you can use exit(), which flushes file buffers without displaying a message. Listing 14.7 shows a short program using abort().

```
Listing 14.7 error1.cpp
//error1.cpp -- use the abort() function
#include <iostream>
using namespace std;
#include <cstdlib>
double hmean(double a, double b);

int main()
{
    double x, y, z;

    cout << "Enter two numbers: ";
    while (cin >> x >> y)
    {
        z = hmean(x,y);
        cout << "Harmonic mean of " << x << " and " << y
            << " is " << z << "\n";
        cout << "Enter next set of numbers <q to quit>: ";
    }
    cout << "Bye!\n";
    return 0;
}

double hmean(double a, double b)
{
```

```
    if (a == -b)
    {
        cout << "untenable arguments to hmean()\n";
        abort();
    }
    return 2.0 * a * b / (a + b);
}
```

Here's a sample run:

```
Enter two numbers: 3 6
Harmonic mean of 3 and 6 is 4
Enter next set of numbers <q to quit>: 10 -10
untenable arguments to hmean()
abnormal program termination
```

Note that calling the abort() function from hmean() terminates the program directly without returning first to main().

The program could avoid aborting by checking the values of x and y before calling the hmean() function. However, it's not safe to rely on a program to know (or care) enough to perform such a check.

A more flexible approach than aborting is to use a function's return value to indicate a problem. For example, the get(void) member of the ostream class ordinarily returns the ASCII code for the next input character, but it returns the special value EOF if it encounters the end of a file. This approach doesn't work for hmean(). Any numeric value could be a valid return value, so there's no special value available to indicate a problem. In this kind of situation, you can use a pointer argument or reference argument to get a value back to the calling program and use the function return value to indicate success or failure. The istream family of overloaded >> operators uses a variant of this technique. By informing the calling program of the success or failure, you give the program the option of taking actions other than aborting. Listing 14.8 shows an example of this approach. It redefines hmean() as a bool function whose return value indicates success or failure. It adds a third argument for obtaining the answer.

Listing 14.8 error2.cpp

```
//error2.cpp -- return an error code
#include <iostream>
using namespace std;
#include <cfloat>  // (or float.h) for DBL_MAX

bool hmean(double a, double b, double * ans);

int main()
{
    double x, y, z;

    cout << "Enter two numbers: ";
    while (cin >> x >> y)
    {
        if (hmean(x,y,&z))
            cout << "Harmonic  mean of " << x << " and " << y
                << " is " << z << "\n";
        else
            cout << "One value should not be the negative "
```

```
                        << "of the other - try again.\n";
            cout << "Enter next set of numbers <q to quit>: ";
    }
    cout << "Bye!\n";
    return 0;
}

bool hmean(double a, double b, double * ans)
{
    if (a == -b)
    {
        *ans = DBL_MAX;
        return false;
    }
    else
    {
        *ans = 2.0 * a * b / (a + b);
        return true;
    }
}
```

Here's a sample run:

```
Enter two numbers: 3 6
Harmonic mean of 3 and 6 is 4
Enter next set of numbers <q to quit>: 10 -10
One value should not be the negative of the other - try again.
Enter next set of numbers <q to quit>: 1 19
Harmonic mean of 1 and 19 is 1.9
Enter next set of numbers <q to quit>: q
Bye!
```

PROGRAM NOTES

> *A C++ exception is a response to an exceptional circumstance that arises while a program is running, such as an attempt to divide by zero.*

Here the program design allowed the user to continue, bypassing the effects of bad input. Of course, the design does rely on the user to check the function return value, something that programmers don't always do. For instance, to keep the sample programs short, most of the listings in this book don't check to see if new returns the null pointer or if cout was successful in handling output.

You could use either a pointer or a reference for the third argument. Many programmers prefer using pointers for arguments of the built-in types, because pointers make it obvious which argument is being used for the answer.

THE EXCEPTION MECHANISM

Now let's see how you can handle problems with the exception mechanism. A C++ *exception* is a response to an exceptional circumstance that arises while a program is running, such as an attempt to divide by zero. Exceptions provide a way to transfer control from one part of a program to another. Handling an exception has three components:

- Throwing an exception
- Catching an exception with a handler
- Using a try block

You throw an exception when a problem shows up. For instance, you can modify hmean() in Listing 14.7 to throw an exception instead of calling the abort() function. A throw statement, in essence, is a jump; that is, it tells a program to jump to statements at another location. The throw keyword indicates the throwing of an exception. It's followed by a value, such as a character string or an object, indicating the nature of the exception.

You catch an exception with an *exception handler* at the place in a program where you wish to handle the problem. The catch keyword indicates the catching of an exception. A handler begins with the keyword catch followed, in parentheses, by a type declaration indicating the type of exception to which it responds. That, in turn, is followed by a brace-enclosed block of code indicating the actions to take. The catch keyword, along with the exception type, serves as a label identifying the point in a program to which execution should jump when an exception is thrown. An exception handler also is called a *catch block*.

A *try block* identifies a block of code for which particular exceptions will be activated. It's followed by one or more catch blocks. The try block itself is indicated by the keyword try followed by a brace-enclosed block of code indicating the code for which exceptions will be noticed.

The easiest way to see how these three elements fit together is to look at a short example, such as that provided in Listing 14.9.

Listing 14.9 error3.cpp

```
//error3.cpp
#include <iostream>
using namespace std;
double hmean(double a, double b);

int main()
{
    double x, y, z;

    cout << "Enter two numbers: ";
    while (cin >> x >> y)
    {
        try {                        // start of try block
            z = hmean(x,y);
        }                            // end of try block
        catch (char * s)             // start of exception handler
        {
            cout << s << "\n";
            cout << "Enter a new pair of numbers: ";
            continue;
        }                                    // end of handler
        cout << "Harmonic mean of " << x << " and " << y
             << " is " << z << "\n";
        cout << "Enter next set of numbers <q to quit>: ";
    }
    cout << "Bye!\n";
    return 0;
}

double hmean(double a, double b)
{
    if (a == -b)
        throw "bad hmean() arguments: a = -b not allowed";
```

```
        return 2.0 * a * b / (a + b);
    }
```

Here's a sample run:

```
Enter two numbers: 3 6
Harmonic mean of 3 and 6 is 4
Enter next set of numbers <q to quit>: 10 -10
bad hmean() arguments: a = -b not allowed
Enter a new pair of numbers: 1 19
Harmonic mean of 1 and 19 is 1.9
Enter next set of numbers <q to quit>: q
Bye!
```

PROGRAM NOTES

The try block looks like this:

```
try {                       // start of try block
    z = hmean(x,y);
}                           // end of try block
```

If any statement in this block leads to an exception being thrown, the catch blocks after this block will handle the exception. If the program called `hmean()` somewhere outside this (and any other) try block, it wouldn't have the opportunity to handle an exception.

Throwing an exception looks like this:

```
if (a == -b)
    throw "bad hmean() arguments: a = -b not allowed";
```

In this case, the thrown exception is the string `"bad hmean() arguments: a = -b not allowed"`. Executing the throw is a bit like executing a return statement in that it terminates function execution. However, instead of returning control to the calling program, a throw causes a program to back up through the sequence of current function calls until it finds the function containing the try block. In Listing 14.9, that function is the same as the calling function. Soon you'll see an example involving backing up more than one function. Meanwhile, in this case, the throw passes program control back to `main()`. There the program looks for an exception handler (following the try block) that matches the type of exception thrown.

The handler, or catch block, looks like this:

```
catch (char * s)  // start of exception handler
{
    cout << s << "\n";
    cout << "Enter a new pair of numbers: ";
    continue;
}                           // end of handler
```

It looks a bit like a function definition, but it's not. The keyword `catch` identifies this as a handler, and the `char * s` means that this handler matches a thrown exception that is a string. This declaration of s acts much like a function argument definition in that a matching thrown exception is assigned to s. Also, if an exception does match this handler, the program executes the code within the braces.

If a program completes executing statements in a try block without any exceptions being thrown, it skips the catch block or blocks after the try block and goes to the first statement following the handlers. So when the sample run processed the values 3 and 6, program execution went directly to the output statement reporting the result.

Let's trace through the events in the sample run after the values 10 and -10 are passed to the hmean() function. The if test causes hmean() to throw an exception. This terminates execution of hmean(). Searching back, the program determines that hmean() was called from within a try block in main(). It then looks for a catch block with a type matching the exception type. The single catch block present has a char * parameter, so it does match. Detecting the match, the program assigns the string "bad hmean() arguments: a = -b not allowed" to the variable s. Next, the program executes the code in the handler. First, it prints s, which is the caught exception. Then it prints instructions to the user to enter new data. Finally, it executes a continue statement, which causes the program to skip the rest of the while loop and jump to its beginning again. The fact that the continue takes the program to the beginning of the loop illustrates the fact that handler statements are part of the loop and that the catch line acts like a label directing program flow (see Figure 14.2).

FIGURE 14.2

Program flow with exceptions

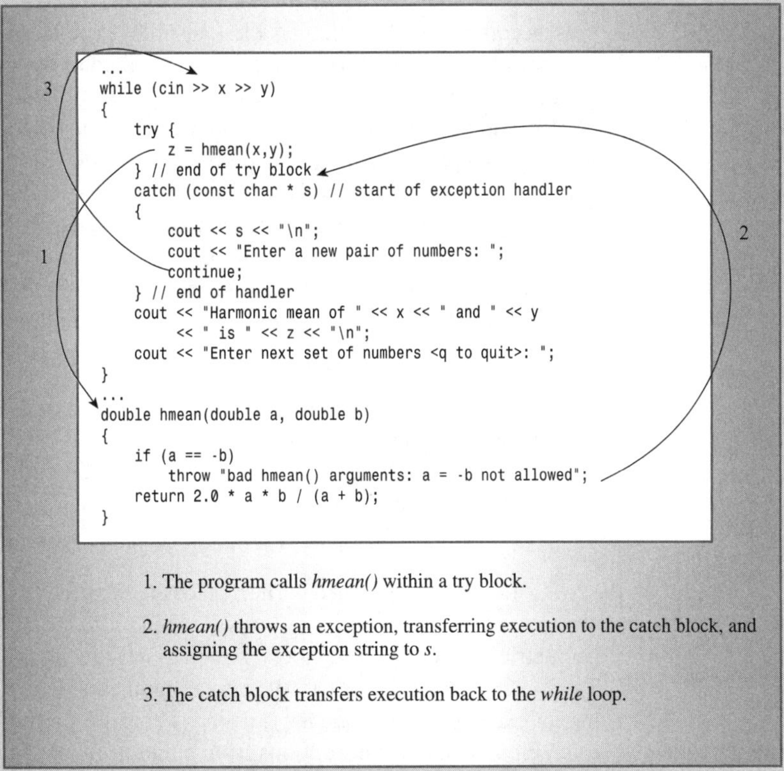

```
...
while (cin >> x >> y)
{
    try {
        z = hmean(x,y);
    } // end of try block
    catch (const char * s) // start of exception handler
    {
        cout << s << "\n";
        cout << "Enter a new pair of numbers: ";
        continue;
    } // end of handler
    cout << "Harmonic mean of " << x << " and " << y
         << " is " << z << "\n";
    cout << "Enter next set of numbers <q to quit>: ";
}
...
double hmean(double a, double b)
{
    if (a == -b)
        throw "bad hmean() arguments: a = -b not allowed";
    return 2.0 * a * b / (a + b);
}
```

1. The program calls *hmean()* within a try block.

2. *hmean()* throws an exception, transferring execution to the catch block, and assigning the exception string to *s*.

3. The catch block transfers execution back to the *while* loop.

You may be wondering what happens if a function throws an exception and there's no try block or no matching handler. By default, the program eventually calls the `abort()` function, but you can modify that behavior. We'll return to this topic later.

EXCEPTION VERSATILITY

C++ exceptions offer versatility because the try block lets you select which code gets checked for exceptions and the handlers let you specify what gets done. For example, in Listing 14.9, the try block was inside the loop, so program execution continued inside the loop after the exception was handled. By placing the loop inside the try block, you can make an exception transfer execution to outside the loop, thus terminating the loop. Listing 14.10 illustrates that. It also demonstrates two more points:

- You can qualify a function definition with an exception specification to indicate which kinds of exceptions it throws.

- A catch block can handle more than one source of exceptions.

To qualify a function prototype to indicate the kinds of exceptions it throws, append an exception specification, which consists of the keyword `throw` followed by a comma-separated list of exception types enclosed in parentheses:

```
double hmean(double a, double b) throw(char *);
```

This accomplishes two things. First, it tells the compiler what sort of exception or exceptions a function throws. If the function then throws some other type of exception, the program will react to the *faux pas* by calling (eventually) the `abort()` function. (We'll examine this behavior and how it can be modified in more detail later.) Second, using an exception specification alerts anyone who reads the prototype that this particular function throws an exception, reminding the reader that he or she may want to provide a try block and a handler. Functions that throw more than one kind of exception can provide a comma-separated list of exception types; the syntax imitates that of an argument list for a function prototype. For example, the following prototype indicates a function that can throw either a `char *` exception or a `double` exception:

```
double multi_err(double z) throw(char *, double);
```

The same information that appears in a prototype, as you can see in Listing 14.10, also should appear in the function definition.

Using empty parentheses in the exception specification indicates that the function does not throw exceptions:

```
double simple(double z) throw(); // doesn't throw an exception
```

Listing 14.10, as mentioned earlier, places the entire `while` loop inside the try block. It also adds a second exception-throwing function, `gmean()`. This function returns the geometric mean of two numbers, which is defined as the square root of their product. This function isn't defined for negative arguments, which provides grounds for throwing an exception. Like `hmean()`, `gmean()` throws a string-type exception, so the same catch block will catch exceptions from either of these two functions.

Listing 14.10 error4.cpp

```cpp
//error4.cpp
#include <iostream>
using namespace std;
#include <cmath> // or math.h, unix users may need -lm flag
double hmean(double a, double b) throw(char *);
double gmean(double a, double b) throw(char *);

int main()
{
    double x, y, z;

    cout << "Enter two numbers: ";
    try {                      // start of try block
        while (cin >> x >> y)
        {
            z = hmean(x,y);
            cout << "Harmonic mean of " << x << " and " << y
                << " is " << z << "\n";
            cout << "Geometric mean of " << x << " and " << y
                << " is " << gmean(x,y) << "\n";
            cout << "Enter next set of numbers <q to quit>: ";
        }
    }                          // end of try block
    catch (char * s)           // start of catch block
    {
        cout << s << "\n";
        cout << "Sorry, you don't get to play any more. ";
    }                          // end of catch block
    cout << "Bye!\n";
    return 0;
}

double hmean(double a, double b) throw(char *)
{
    if (a == -b)
        throw "bad hmean() arguments: a = -b not allowed";
    return 2.0 * a * b / (a + b);
}

double gmean(double a, double b) throw(char *)
{
    if (a < 0 || b < 0)
        throw "bad gmean() arguments: negative values not allowed";
    return sqrt(a * b);
}
```

Here's a sample run that is terminated by bad input for the hmean() function:

```
Enter two numbers: 1 100
Harmonic mean of 1 and 100 is 1.9802
Geometric mean of 1 and 100 is 10
Enter next set of numbers <q to quit>: 10 -10
bad hmean() arguments: a = -b not allowed
Sorry, you don't get to play any more. Bye!
```

Because the exception handler is outside the loop, bad input terminates the loop. After the program finishes the code in the handler, it proceeds to the next line in the program, which prints Bye!.

For comparison, here's a sample run that is terminated by bad input for the `gmean()` function:

```
Enter two numbers: 1 100
Harmonic mean of 1 and 100 is 1.9802
Geometric mean of 1 and 100 is 10
Enter next set of numbers <q to quit>: 3 -15
Harmonic mean of 3 and -15 is 7.5
bad gmean() arguments: negative values not allowed
Sorry, you don't get to play any more. Bye!
```

The message reveals which exception was handled.

Multiple Try Blocks

You have many choices about setting up try blocks. For example, you could handle the two function calls individually, placing each within its own try block. That allows you to program a different response for the two possible exceptions, as the following code shows:

```
while (cin >> x >> y)
{
    try {                          // try block #1
        z = hmean(x,y);
    }                              // end of try block #1
    catch (char * s)    // start of catch block #1
    {
        cout << s << "\n";
        cout << "Enter a new pair of numbers: ";
        continue;
    }                              // end of catch block #1
    cout << "Harmonic mean of " << x << " and " << y
        << " is " << z << "\n";
    try {                          // try block #2
        z = gmean(x,y);
    }                              // end of try block #2
    catch (char * s)    // start of catch block #2
    {
        cout << s << "\n";
        cout << "Data entry terminated!\n";
        break;
    }                              // end of catch block #2
    cout << "Enter next set of numbers <q to quit>: ";
}
```

Another possibility is to nest try blocks, as the next sample shows:

```
try {                              // outer try block
    while (cin >> x >> y)
    {
    try {                              // inner try block
        z = hmean(x,y);
    }                                  // end of inner try block
    catch (char * s)        // inner catch block
    {
    cout << s << "\n";
        cout << "Enter a new pair of numbers: ";
        continue;
    }                                  // end of inner catch block
        cout << "Harmonic mean of " << x << " and " << y
```

```
                << " is " << z << "\n";
        cout << "Geometric mean of " << x << " and " << y
                << " is " << gmean(x,y) << "\n";
        cout << "Enter next set of numbers <q to quit>: ";
    }
}                                      // end of outer try block
catch (char * s)                       // outer catch block
{
    cout << s << "\n";
    cout << "Sorry, you don't get to play any more. ";
}                                      // end of outer catch block
```

Here an exception thrown by hmean() is caught by the inner exception handler, which allows the loop to continue. But an exception thrown by gmean() is caught by the outer exception handler, which terminates the loop.

Unwinding the Stack

Suppose a try block doesn't contain a direct call to a function throwing an exception but that it calls a function that calls a function that throws an exception. Execution still jumps from the function in which the exception is thrown to the function containing the try block and handlers. Doing so involves *unwinding the stack*, which we'll discuss now.

First, let's look at how C++ normally handles function calls and returns. C++ typically handles function calls by placing information on a stack (Chapter 8). In particular, a program places the address of a calling function instruction (a *return address*) on the stack. When the called function has finished, the program uses this address to determine where to continue with program execution. Also the function call places any function arguments on the stack, where they are treated as automatic variables. If the called function creates any new automatic variables, they, too, are added to the stack. If a called function calls another function, its information is added to the stack, and so on. When a function terminates, program execution passes to the address stored when the function was called, and the top of the stack is freed. Thus, a function normally returns to the function that called it, and so on, with each function liberating its automatic variables as it terminates. If an automatic variable is a class object, then the class destructor, if any, is called.

Now suppose a function terminates via an exception throw instead of via a return call. Again, the program frees memory from the stack. But instead of stopping at the first return address on the stack, the program continues freeing the stack until it reaches a return address that resides in a try block (see Figure 14.3). Control then passes to the exception handlers at the end of the block rather than to the first statement following the function call. This is the process called *unwinding the stack*. One very important feature of the throw mechanism is that, just as with function returns, the class destructors are called for any automatic class objects on the stack. However, a function return processes only objects put on the stack by that function, while the throw statement processes only objects put on the stack by the entire sequence of function calls between the try block and the throw. Without the unwinding-the-stack feature, a throw would leave destructors uncalled for automatic class objects placed on the stack by intermediate function calls.

FIGURE 14.3

throw versus return

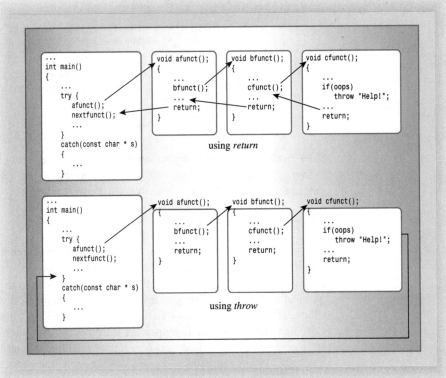

Listing 14.11 provides an example of unwinding the stack. In it, main() calls details(), and details() calls hmean(). When hmean() throws an exception, control returns all the way to main(), where it is caught. In the process, the automatic variables representing the arguments to hmean() and details() are freed.

Listing 14.11 error5.cpp

```cpp
//error5.cpp
#include <iostream>
using namespace std;
double hmean(double a, double b) throw(char *);
void details(double a, double b) throw(char *);
int main()
{
    double x, y;

    cout << "Enter two numbers: ";
    try {
        while (cin >> x >> y)
            details(x,y);
    }
    catch (char * s)
```

```
    {
        cout << s << "\n";
        cout << "Sorry, you can't play anymore. ";
    }
    cout << "Bye!\n";
    return 0;
}

void details(double a, double b) throw(char *){
    cout << "Harmonic mean of " << a << " and " << b
        << " is " << hmean(a,b) << "\n";
    cout << "Enter next set of numbers <q to quit>: ";
}

double hmean(double a, double b) throw(char *)
{
    if (a == -b)
        throw "bad hmean() arguments: a = -b not allowed";
    return 2.0 * a * b / (a + b);
}
```

Here's a sample run; note that throwing the exception skips directly to `main()`, keeping `details()` from displaying the text that otherwise would have been displayed had `hmean()` terminated normally.

```
Enter two numbers: 3 15
Harmonic mean of 3 and 15 is 5
Enter next set of numbers <q to quit>: 20 -20
bad hmean() arguments: a = -b not allowed
Sorry, you can't play anymore. Bye!
```

More Options

You can set up a handler to catch any kind of exception. Also, if a try block is nested, you can have its handlers pass control on up to the handlers for the containing try block.

To catch any exception, use the ellipsis for the exception type:

```
catch (...) { // statements }
```

To pass control to a containing try block, use `throw` without a following exception:

```
catch (char * s)
{
    cout << "Exception caught in inner loop.\n";
    throw;  // send to containing try block
}
```

This sample, for instance, prints a message, then passes control to the containing try block, where the program once again will look for a handler matching the original thrown exception.

Note that there is more than one way for one try block to contain another. One way is to nest one within another, as discussed earlier. Another way is for one try block to contain a function call that invokes a function containing a try block. In the first case, the sample code above would pass control to the outer try block. In the second case, the sample code would cause the program to unwind the stack to find the next try block.

EXCEPTIONS AND CLASSES

Exceptions aren't just for handling error conditions in regular functions. They also can be part of a class design. For example, a constructor could throw an exception if a call to the new operator fails. Or the overloaded [] operator for an array class can throw an exception if an index is out of range. Often it's useful if the exception can carry information with it, such as the value of an invalid index. One could use, say, a type int exception in that case, but it's more useful to throw an exception that's an object. The type of object will help identify the source of the exception, and the object itself can carry the needful information.

In fact, the usual practice in using exceptions is to throw objects as exceptions and to catch them by reference:

```
class problem {...};
...
void super()
{
    ...
    if (oh_no)
    {
        problem oops(); // construct object
        throw oops;     // throw it
    ...
}
...
try {
    super();
}
catch(problem & p)
{
...
}
```

Incidentally, while the throw-catch mechanism is much like function argument passing, there are a few differences. For example, the compiler always creates a temporary copy when throwing an exception, so in the preceeding sample code, p would refer to a copy of oops rather than oops. That's a good thing, because oops no longer exists after super() terminates. Often it is simpler to combine construction with the throw:

```
throw oops();     // construct and throw object
```

When exceptions refer to class processes, it's often useful if the exception type is defined as a nested class. Not only does this make the exception type indicate the class originating an exception, it helps prevent name conflicts. For instance, suppose you have a class called ArrayDbE in which you publicly declare another class called BadIndex. If the [] operator finds a bad index value, it can throw an exception of type BadIndex. Then a handler for this exception would look like this:

```
catch (const ArrayDbE::BadIndex &) { ...}
```

The ArrayDbE:: qualifier identifies BadIndex as being declared in the ArrayDbE class. It also informs a reader that this handler is intended for exceptions generated by ArrayDbE objects. The BadIndex name gives the reader a pretty good idea as to the nature of the exception. This sounds rather attractive, so let's develop the idea. In particular, let's add exceptions to the ArrayDb class first developed in Chapter 13.

To the header file, add an exception BadIndex class, that is, a class defining objects to be thrown as exceptions. As outlined above, it will be used for bad index values, and it will hold the value of the bad index. Note that the nested class declaration just describes the class; it doesn't create objects. The class methods will create objects of this class if they throw exceptions of the BadIndex type. Also note that the nested class is public. This allows the catch blocks to have access to the type. Listing 14.12 shows the new header file. The rest of the definition, aside from changing the class name, is the same as the definition of ArrayDb in Chapter 13, except that it qualifies the method prototypes to indicate which exceptions they can throw. That is, it replaces

```
virtual double & operator[](int i);
```

with

```
virtual double & operator[](int i) throw(BadIndex &);
```

and so on. (As with ordinary function arguments, it's usually better to pass references instead of objects when throwing exceptions.)

Listing 14.12 arraydbe.h

```cpp
// arraydbe.h -- define array class with exceptions
#ifndef _ARRAYDBE_H_
#define _ARRAYDBE_H_
#include <iostream>
using namespace std;

class ArrayDbE
{
private:
    unsigned int size;   // number of array elements
protected:
    double * arr;        // address of first element
public:
    class BadIndex       // exception class for indexing problems
    {
    public:
        int badindex;    // problematic index value
        BadIndex(int i) : badindex(i) {}
    };
    ArrayDbE();                               // default constructor
    // create an ArrayDbE of n elements, set each to val
    ArrayDbE(unsigned int n, double val = 0.0);
    // create an ArrayDbE of n elements, initialize to array pn
    ArrayDbE(const double * pn, unsigned int n);
    // copy constructor
    ArrayDbE(const ArrayDbE & a);
    virtual ~ArrayDbE();                      // destructor
    unsigned int ArSize() const;             // returns array size
    double Average() const;                  // return array average
// overloaded operators
        // array indexing, allowing assignment
    virtual double & operator[](int i) throw(BadIndex &);
        // array indexing (no =)
```

```
    virtual const double & operator[](int i) const throw(BadIndex &);
    ArrayDbE & operator=(const ArrayDbE & a);
    friend ostream & operator<<(ostream & os, const ArrayDbE & a);
};

#endif
```

Next, you have to provide the class methods. These are the same methods used in Chapter 12 with the addition of some exception throwing. Because the overloaded [] operators throw exceptions instead of calling the exit() function, the program no longer needs to include the cstdlib file. Listing 14.13 shows the result.

Listing 14.13 arraydbe.cpp

```cpp
// arraydbe.cpp -- ArrayDbE class methods
#include <iostream>
using namespace std;
#include "arraydbe.h"

// default constructor -- no arguments
ArrayDbE::ArrayDbE()
{
    arr = NULL;
    size = 0;
}

// constructs array of n elements, each set to val
ArrayDbE::ArrayDbE(unsigned int n, double val)
{
    arr = new double[n];
    size = n;
    for (int i = 0; i < size; i++)
       arr[i] = val;
}

// initialize ArrayDbE object to a non-class array
ArrayDbE::ArrayDbE(const double *pn, unsigned int n)
{
    arr = new double[n];
    size = n;
    for (int i = 0; i < size; i++)
       arr[i] = pn[i];
}

// initialize ArrayDbE object to another ArrayDbE object
ArrayDbE::ArrayDbE(const ArrayDbE & a)
{
    size = a.size;
    arr = new double[size];
    for (int i = 0; i < size; i++)
       arr[i] = a.arr[i];
}

ArrayDbE::~ArrayDbE()
{
    delete [] arr;
}

double ArrayDbE::Average() const
```

```cpp
{
    double sum = 0;
    int i;
    int lim = ArSize();
    for (i = 0; i < lim; i++)
        sum += arr[i];
    if (i > 0)
        return sum / i;
    else
    {
        cerr << "No entries in score array\n";
        return 0;
    }
}

// return array size
unsigned int ArrayDbE::ArSize() const
{
    return size;
}

// let user access elements by index (assignment allowed)
double & ArrayDbE::operator[](int i) throw(BadIndex &)
{
    // check index before continuing
    if (i < 0 || i >= size)
        throw BadIndex(i);
    return arr[i];
}

// let user access elements by index (assignment disallowed)
const double & ArrayDbE::operator[](int i)const throw(BadIndex &)
{
    // check index before continuing
    if (i < 0 || i >= size)
        throw BadIndex(i);
    return arr[i];
}

// define class assignment
ArrayDbE & ArrayDbE::operator=(const ArrayDbE & a)
{
    if (this == &a)         // if object assigned to self,
        return *this;       // don't change anything
    delete arr;
    size = a.size;
    arr = new double[size];
    for (int i = 0; i < size; i++)
        arr[i] = a.arr[i];
    return *this;
}

// quick output, 5 values to a line
ostream & operator<<(ostream & os, const ArrayDbE & a)
{
    int i;
    for (i = 0; i < a.size; i++)
    {
        os << a.arr[i] << " ";
```

```
        if (i % 5 == 4)
            os << "\n";
    }
    if (i % 5 != 0)
        os << "\n";
    return os;
}
```

Note that the exceptions now are objects instead of strings. Also note that these exception throws use the exception class constructor to create and initialize the exception objects:

```
if (i < 0 || i >= size)
        throw BadIndex(i);      // create, initialize a BadIndex object
```

What about catching this kind of exception? The exceptions are objects, not character strings, so the catch block has to reflect that fact. Also, because the exception is a nested type, the code needs to use the scope resolution operator.

```
try {
    . . .
}
catch(ArrayDbE::BadIndex &) {
    . . .
}
```

Listing 14.14 provides a short program demonstrating the process.

```
Listing 14.14 exceptar.cpp
// exceptar.cpp -- use the ArrayDbE class
// Compile with arraydbe.cpp
#include <iostream>
using namespace std;
#include "arraydbe.h"

const int Players = 5;
int main()
{
    try {
        ArrayDbE Team(Players);
        cout << "Enter free-throw percentages for your 5 "
                "top players as a decimal fraction:\n";
        int player;
        for (player = 0; player < Players; player++)
        {
            cout << "Player " << (player + 1) << ": % = ";
            cin >> Team[player];
        }
        cout.precision(1);
        cout.setf(ios_base::showpoint);
        cout.setf(ios_base::fixed,ios_base::floatfield);
        cout << "Recapitulating, here are the percentages:\n";
        for (player = 0; player <= Players; player++)
            cout << "Player #" << (player + 1) << ": "
                 << 100.0 * Team[player] << "%\n";
    }                                   // end of try block
    catch (ArrayDbE::BadIndex & bi)     // start of handler
    {
        cout << "ArrayDbE exception: "
```

```
                        << bi.badindex << " is a bad index value\n";
        }                                            // end of handler
      cout << "Bye!\n";
      return 0;
}
```

Note the second `for` loop deliberately exceeds the array bounds, triggering an exception. Here is a sample run:

```
Enter free-throw percentages for your 5 top players as a decimal
fraction:
Player 1: % = 0.923
Player 2: % = 0.858
Player 3: % = 0.821
Player 4: % = 0.744
Player 5: % = 0.697
Recapitulating, here are the percentages:
Player #1: 92.3%
Player #2: 85.8%
Player #3: 82.1%
Player #4: 74.4%
Player #5: 69.7%
ArrayDbe exception: 5 is a bad index value
Bye!
```

Because the loop is inside the try block, throwing the exception terminates the loop as control passes to the second catch block following the try block.

By the way, remember that variables defined in a block, including a try block, are local to the block. For example, the variable `player` is undefined once program control passes beyond the try block in Listing 14.14.

EXCEPTIONS AND INHERITANCE

" Second, you can derive new exception classes from existing ones."

Inheritance interacts with exceptions in a couple of ways. First, if a class has publicly nested exception classes, a derived class inherits those exception classes. Second, you can derive new exception classes from existing ones. We'll look at both these possibilities in the next example.

First, derive a `LimitArE` class from the `ArrayDbE` class. The `LimitArE` class will allow for array indexing to begin with values other than 0. This can be accomplished by storing a value representing the starting index and by redefining the functions. Internally, the array indexing still will begin with 0. But if, say, you specify 1900 as the starting index, the `operator[]()` method will translate an external index of 1908 to an internal index 1908–1900, or 8. Listing 14.15 shows the details.

The `BadIndex` exception declared in the `ArrayDbE` class stored the offending index value. With variable index limits, it would be nice if the exception also stored the correct range for indices. You can accomplish this by deriving a new exception class from `BadIndex`:

```
class SonOfBad : public ArrayDbe::BadIndex
{
public:
      int l_lim;  // lower index limit
```

```
        int u_lim;  // upper index limit
        SonOfBad(int i, int l, int u) : BadIndex(i),
                         l_lim(l), u_lim(u) {}
};
```

You can nest the `SonOfBad` declaration in the `LimitArE` declaration. Listing 14.15 shows the result.

Listing 14.15 limarre.h

```
// limarre.h -- LimitArE class with exceptions

#ifndef _LIMARRE_H_
#define _LIMARRE_H_

#include "arraydbe.h"

class LimitArE : public ArrayDbE
{
public:
    class SonOfBad : public ArrayDbE::BadIndex
    {
    public:
        int l_lim;
        int u_lim;
        SonOfBad(int i, int l, int u) : BadIndex(i),
                   l_lim(l), u_lim(u) {}
    };
private:
    unsigned int low_bnd;             // new data member
protected:
    // handle bounds checking
    virtual void ok(int i) const throw(SonOfBad &);
public:
// constructors
    LimitArE() : ArrayDbE(), low_bnd(0) {}
    LimitArE(unsigned int n, double val = 0.0)
                : ArrayDbE(n,val), low_bnd(0) {}
    LimitArE(unsigned int n, int lb, double val = 0.0)
                : ArrayDbE(n, val), low_bnd(lb) {}
    LimitArE(const double * pn, unsigned int n)
                : ArrayDbE(pn, n), low_bnd(0) {}
    LimitArE(const ArrayDbE & a) : ArrayDbE(a), low_bnd(0) {}
// new methods
    void new_lb(int lb) {low_bnd = lb;}     // reset lower bound
    int lbound() {return low_bnd;}          // return lower bound
    int ubound() {return ArSize() + low_bnd - 1;} // upper bound
// redefined operators
    double & operator[](int i);
    const double & operator[](int i) const;
};
#endif
```

This design moves index checking from the overloaded `[]` methods to an `ok()` method that's called by the overloaded `[]` methods. Therefore, it is the `LimitArE::ok()` method that throws a `SonOfBad` exception. Listing 14.16 shows the class methods.

Listing 14.16 limarre.cpp

```cpp
// limarre.cpp
#include "limarre.h"
#include <iostream>
using namespace std;

// private method
    // lower bound for array index is now low_bnd, and
    // upper bound is now low_bnd + size - 1
void LimitArE::ok(int i) const throw(SonOfBad &)
{
    unsigned long size = ArSize();
    if (i < low_bnd || i >= size + low_bnd)
        throw SonOfBad(i, low_bnd, low_bnd + size - 1);
}

// redefined operators
double & LimitArE::operator[](int i)
{
    ok(i);
    return arr[i - low_bnd];
}

const double & LimitArE::operator[](int i) const
{
    ok(i);
    return arr[i - low_bnd];
}
```

Suppose you have a program with both ArrayDbE and LimitArE objects. Then you would want a try block that catches the two possible exceptions: BadIndex and SonOfBad. You can do that by following the try block with two consecutive catch blocks:

```cpp
try {
    LimitArE income(Years, FirstYear);
    ArrayDbE busywork(Years);
    ...
}   // end of try block
catch (LimitArE::SonOfBad & bi)   // 1st handler
{
    ...
}
catch (LimitArE::BadIndex & bi)   // 2nd handler
{
    ...
}
```

When there is a sequence of catch blocks, a program attempts to match a thrown exception to the first catch block, then the second catch block, and so on. As soon as there's a match, the program executes that catch block. Providing the code in the catch block doesn't terminate the program or generate another throw; the program jumps to the statement following the final catch block after completing any one catch block in the sequence.

This particular sequence of catch blocks has an interesting property—a catch block with a `BadIndex` reference can catch either a `BadIndex` exception or a `SonOfBad` exception. That's because a base class reference can refer to a derived object. However, a catch block with a `SonOfBad` reference can't catch a `BadIndex` object. That's because a derived object reference can't refer to a base class object without an explicit type cast. This state of affairs suggests placing the `SonOfBad` catch block above the `BadIndex` catch block. That way, the `SonOfBad` catch block will catch a `SonOfBad` exception while passing a `BadIndex` exception on to the next catch block. The program in Listing 14.17 illustrates this approach.

Listing 14.17 excptinh.cpp

```cpp
// excptinh.cpp -- use the ArrayDbE and LimitArE classes
// Compile with arraydbe.cpp, limarre.h
#include <iostream>
using namespace std;
#include "arraydbe.h"
#include "limarre.h"

const int Years = 4;
const int FirstYear = 1998;
int main()
{
    int year;
    double total = 0;
    try {
        LimitArE income(Years, FirstYear);
        ArrayDbE busywork(Years);
        cout << "Enter your income for the last " << Years
                << " years:\n";
        for (year = FirstYear; year < FirstYear + Years; year++)
        {
            cout << "Year " << year << ": $";
            cin >> income[year];
            busywork[year - FirstYear] = 0.2 * income[year];
        }
        cout.precision(2);
        cout.setf(ios_base::showpoint);
        cout.setf(ios_base::fixed,ios_base::floatfield);
        cout << "Recapitulating, here are the figures:\n";
        for (year = FirstYear; year <= FirstYear + Years; year++)
        {
            cout << year << ": $" << income[year] << "\n";
            total += income[year];
        }
        cout << "busywork values: " << busywork;
    }   // end of try block
    catch (LimitArE::SonOfBad & bi)   // 1st handler
    {
        cout << "LimitArE exception: "
                << bi.badindex << " is a bad index value.\n";
        cout << "Index should be in the range " << bi.l_lim
                << " to " << bi.u_lim << ".\n";
    }
    catch (LimitArE::BadIndex & bi)   // 2nd handler
    {
```

```
            cout << "ArrayDbE exception: "
                    << bi.badindex << " is a bad index value.\n";
        }
    cout << "Total income for " << (year - FirstYear)
            << " years is $" << total << ".\n";
    cout << "Bye!\n";
    return 0;
}
```

Here is a sample run (note that the program is not affected by the infamous year 2000 bug):

```
Enter your income for the last 4 years:
Year 1998: $35000
Year 1999: $34000
Year 2000: $33000
Year 2001: $38000
Recapitulating, here are the figures:
1998: $35000.00
1999: $34000.00
2000: $33000.00
2001: $38000.00
LimitArE exception: 2002 is a bad index value.
Index should be in the range 1998 to 2001.
Total income for 4 years is $140000.00.
```

The SonOfBad exception terminated execution of the try block and transferred execution to the second catch block. Once the program finished processing the catch block, it jumped to the first statement following the catch blocks.

The following tip summarizes this example's main lesson.

Remember

If you have an inheritance hierarchy of exception classes, arrange the order of the catch blocks so the most derived class exception is caught first and the base class exception is caught last.

THE exception CLASS

The main intent for C++ exceptions is to provide language-level support for designing fault-tolerant programs. That is, exceptions make it easier to incorporate error handling into a program design rather than tacking on some more rigid form of error handling as an afterthought. The flexibility and relative convenience of exceptions should encourage programmers to integrate fault handling into the program design process, if appropriate. In short, exceptions are the kind of feature that, like classes, can modify your approach to programming.

Newer C++ compilers are incorporating exceptions into the language. For example, the exception header file (formerly exception.h or except.h) defines an exception class that C++ uses as a base class for other exception classes used to support the language. Your code, too, can throw an exception object or use the exception class as a base class. One virtual member function is named what(), and it returns a string, the nature of which is implementation dependent. But if you derive a class, you then can

> *The main intent for C++ exceptions is to provide language-level support for designing fault-tolerant programs.*

choose what string you want returned. For example, you could replace the BadIndex declaration with one based on the exception class. Because the contents of the exception header file are part of the std namespace, you can make them available with a using directive:

```
#include <exception>
using namespace std;
class ArrayDbE
{
private:
    unsigned int size;   // number of array elements
protected:
    double * arr;        // address of first element
public:
    class OutOfBounds : public exception
    {
    public:
        OutOfBounds() : exception() {};
        const char * what() {return "Array limit out of bounds\n";}
    };
    ...
};
```

Then you could have the overloaded [] methods throw an OutOfBounds exception, have a program using the class catch that type of exception, and use the what() method to identify the problem:

```
catch (ArrayDbE::OutOfBounds & ob)    //  handler
{
    cout << "ArrayDbE exception: "
            << ob.what() << endl;
}
```

By the way, instead of making all the exception class declarations available with a using directive, you could use the scope resolution operator:

```
class OutOfBounds : public std::exception
```

THE bad_alloc EXCEPTION AND new

C++ gives implementations two choices for handling memory allocation problems when using new. The first choice, and once the only choice, is to have new return the null pointer if it can't satisfy a memory request. The second choice is to have new throw a bad_alloc exception. The new header (formerly new.h) includes a declaration for the bad_alloc class, which is publicly derived from the exception class. An implementation may offer just one choice or, perhaps by using a compiler switch or some other method, let you choose the approach you prefer.

Listing 14.18 straddles the issue by trying both approaches. If the exception is caught, the program displays the implementation-dependent message returned by the inherited what() method and terminates early. Otherwise, it proceeds to see if the return value was the null pointer. (The purpose here is to show the two ways to check for memory allocation errors, not to suggest that a typical program would actually use both methods.)

Listing 14.18 newexcp.cpp

```cpp
// newexcp.cpp -- the bad_alloc exception
#include <iostream>
using namespace std;
#include <new>
#include <cstdlib>

struct Big
{
    double stuff[2000];
};

int main()
{
    Big * pb;
    try {
        cout << "Trying to get a big block of memory:\n";
        pb = new Big[10000];
        cout << "Got past the new request:\n";
    }
    catch (bad_alloc & ba)
    {
        cout << "Caught the exception!\n";
        cout << ba.what() << endl;
        exit(1);
    }
    if (pb != 0)
    {
        pb[0].stuff[0] = 4;
        cout << pb[0].stuff[0] << endl;
    }
    else
        cout << "pb is null pointer\n";
    delete [] pb;
    return 0;
}
```

WHEN EXCEPTIONS GO ASTRAY

Once an exception has been thrown, it has two opportunities to cause problems. First, if it is thrown in a function having an exception specification, it has to match one of the types in the specification list. If it doesn't, the unmatched exception is branded an *unexpected exception*, and, by default, it causes the program to abort. If the exception passes this first hurdle (or avoids it because the function lacks an exception specification), it then has to be caught. If it isn't, which can happen if there is no containing try block or no matching catch block, the exception is branded an *uncaught exception*, and, by default, it causes the program to abort. However, you can alter a program's response to unexpected and uncaught exceptions. Let's see how, beginning with uncaught exceptions.

An uncaught expression doesn't initiate an immediate abort. Instead, the program first calls a function called terminate(). By default, terminate() calls the abort() function. You can modify the behavior of terminate() by *registering* a function that terminate() should call instead of abort(). To do this, call the set_terminate()

function. Both set_terminate() and terminate() are declared in the exception header file:

```
typedef void (*terminate_handler)();
terminate_handler set_terminate(terminate_handler f) throw();
void terminate();
```

The set_terminate() function takes, as its argument, the name of a function (that is, its address) having no arguments and the void return type. It returns the address of the previously registered function. If you call the set_terminate() function more than once, terminate() calls the function set by the most recent call to set_terminate().

Let's look at an example. Suppose you want an uncaught exception to cause a program to print a message to that effect and then call the exit() function, providing an exit status value of 5. First, include the exception header file and make its declarations available with a using directive:

```
#include <exception>
using namespace std;
```

Next, design a function that does the two required actions and has the proper prototype:

```
void myQuit()
{
    cout << "Terminating due to uncaught exception\n";
    exit(5);
}
```

Finally, at the start of your program, designate this function as your chosen termination action:

```
set_terminate(myQuit);
```

Next, let's look at unexpected exceptions. By using exception specifications for a function, you provide the means for users of the functions to know which exceptions to catch. That is, suppose you have the following prototype:

```
double Argh(double, double) throw(exception &);
```

Then you might use the function this way:

```
try {
    x = Argh(a, b);
}
catch(exception & ex)
{
    ...
}
```

It's good to know which exceptions to catch; recall that an uncaught exception, by default, aborts the program.

However, there's a bit more to the story. In principle, the exception specification should include exceptions thrown by functions called by the function in question. For instance, if Argh() calls a Duh() function that can throw a retort object exception, then retort should appear in the Argh() exception specification as well as in the Duh() exception specification. Unless you write all the functions yourself and are careful, there's no guarantee this will get done correctly. You might, for example, use an older commercial library whose functions don't have exception specifications. This suggests looking more closely at what happens if a function does throw an exception not in its exception specification.

The behavior is much like that for uncaught exceptions. If there is an unexpected exception, the program calls the `unexpected()` function. (You didn't expect the `unexpected()` function? No one expects the `unexpected()` function!) This function, in turn, calls `terminate()`, which, by default, calls `abort()`. Just as there is a `set_terminate()` function that modifies the behavior of `terminate()`, there is a `set_unexpected()` function that modifies the behavior of `unexpected()`; these new functions also are declared in the exception header file:

```
typedef void (*unexpected_handler)();
unexpected_handler set_unexpected(unexpected_handler f) throw();
void unexpected();
```

However, the behavior of the function you supply `set_unexpected()` is more regulated than that of a function for `set_terminate()`. In particular, the `unexpected_handler` function has the following choices:

- It can end the program by calling `terminate()` (the default behavior), `abort()`, or `exit()`.

- It can throw an exception.

The result of throwing an exception (the second choice) depends upon the exception thrown by the replacement `unexpected_handler` function and the exception specification:

- If the newly thrown exception matches the exception specification, then the program proceeds normally from there; that is, it will look for a catch block matching the newly thrown exception.

- If the newly thrown exception does not match the exception specification and if the exception specification does not include the `std::bad_exception` type, the program calls `terminate()`. The `bad_exception` type derives from the `exception` type and is declared in the `exception` header file.

- If the newly thrown exception does not match the exception specification and if the exception specification does include the `std::bad_exception` type, the unmatched exception is replaced with an exception of the `std::bad_exception` type.

In short, if you'd like catch all exceptions, expected or otherwise, you can do something along these lines:

First, make sure the exception header file declarations are available:

```
#include <exception>
using namespace std;
```

Next, design a replace function that converts unexpected exceptions to the `bad_exception` type and that has the proper prototype:

```
void myUnexpected()
{
    throw std::bad_exception();  //or just throw;
}
```

Just using `throw` without an exception rethrows the original exception. However, it will be replaced with a `bad_exception` object if the exception specification includes that type.

Next, at the start of your program, designate this function as your chosen unexpected exception action:

```
set_unexpected(myUnexpeced);
```

Finally, include the `bad_exception` type in exception specifications and catch block sequences:

```
double Argh(double, double) throw(exception &, bad_exception &);
...
try {
    x = Argh(a, b);
}
catch(exception & ex)
{
    ...
}
catch(bad_exception & ex)
{
    ...
}
```

EXCEPTION CAUTIONS

From the preceding discussion of using exceptions, you might gather (and gather correctly) that exception handling should be designed into a program rather than tacked on. It has some disadvantages. For example, using exceptions adds to the size and subtracts from the speed of a program. Exception specifications don't work well with templates, because template functions might throw different kinds of exceptions depending upon the particular specialization used. Exceptions and dynamic memory allocation don't always work that well together.

Let's look a little further at dynamic memory allocation and exceptions. First, consider the following function:

```
void test1(int n)
{
    String mesg("I'm trapped in an endless loop");
    ...
    if (oh_no)
        throw exception();
    ...
    return;
}
```

The `String` class, recall, used dynamic memory allocation. Normally, the `String` destructor for `mesg` would be called when the function reached return and terminated. Thanks to stack unwinding, the `throw` statement, even though it terminates the function prematurely, still allows the destructor to be called. So here memory is managed properly.

Now consider this function:

```
void test2(int n)
```

```
    {
        double * ar = new double[n];
        ...
        if (oh_no)
            throw exception();
        ...
        delete [] ar;
        return;
    }
```

Here there is a problem. Unwinding the stack removes the variable ar from the stack. But the premature termination of the function means the delete [] statement at the end of the function is skipped. The pointer is gone, but the memory block it pointed to is still intact and inaccessible. In short, there is a memory leak.

The leak can be avoided. For instance, you can catch the exception in the same function that throws it, put some cleanup code into the catch block, then rethrow the exception:

```
    void test3(int n)
    {
        double * ar = new double[n];
        ...
        try {
            if (oh_no)
                throw exception();
        }
        catch(exception & ex)
        {
            delete [] ar;
            throw;
        }
        ...
        delete [] ar;
        return;
    }
```

However, this clearly enhances the opportunities for oversights and other errors. Another solution is to use the auto_ptr template discussed in Chapter 15.

In short, while exception handling is extremely important for some projects, it does have costs in programming effort, program size, and program speed. Also, compiler exception support and user experience has not yet reached the mature level. So you may wish to use this feature with moderation.

RTTI

RTTI is short for runtime type information. It's one of the more recent additions to C++ and isn't supported by many older implementations. Other implementations may have compiler settings for turning RTTI on and off. The intent of RTTI is to provide a standard way for a program to determine the type of object during runtime. Many class libraries have already provided ways to do so for their own class objects, but in the absence of built-in support in C++, each vendor's mechanism typically is incompatible with those of other vendors. Creating a language standard for RTTI should allow future libraries to be compatible with each other.

WHAT'S IT FOR?

Suppose you have a hierarchy of classes descended from a common base. You can set a base class pointer to point to an object of any of the classes in this hierarchy. Next, you call a function that, after processing some information, selects one of these classes, creates an object of that type, and returns its address, which is assigned to a base class pointer. How can you tell what kind of object it points to?

Before answering this question, let's think about why you would want to know the type. Perhaps you want to invoke the correct version of a class method. If that's the case, you don't really need to know the object type as long as that function is a virtual function possessed by all members of the class hierarchy. But it could be that a derived object has an uninherited method. In that case, only some objects could use the method. Or maybe, for debugging purposes, you would like to keep track of which kinds of objects were generated. For these last two cases, RTTI provides an answer.

> *" Before answering this question, let's think about why you would want to know the type. "*

HOW DOES IT WORK?

C++ has three components supporting RTTI:

- The `dynamic_cast` operator generates a pointer to a derived type from a pointer to a base type, if possible. Otherwise, the operator returns 0, the null pointer.

- The `typeid` operator returns a value identifying the exact type of an object.

- A `type_info` structure holds information about a particular type.

You can use RTTI only with a class hierarchy having virtual functions. The reason for this is that these are the only class hierarchies for which you should be assigning the addresses of derived objects to base class pointers.

 Remember

RTTI works only for classes with virtual functions.

Let's examine the three components of RTTI.

The `dynamic_cast` Operator

The `dynamic_cast` operator is intended to be the most heavily used RTTI component. It doesn't answer the question of what type of object a pointer points to. Instead, it answers the question of whether you can safely assign the address of the object to a pointer of a particular type. Let's see what that means. Suppose you have the following hierarchy:

```
class Grand { // has virtual methods};
class Superb : public Grand { ... };
class Magnificent : public Superb { ... };
```

Next, suppose you have the following pointers:

```
Grand * pg = new Grand;
Grand * ps = new Superb;
Grand * pm = new Magnificent;
```

Finally, consider the following type casts:

```
Magnificent * p1 = (Magnificent *) pm;          // #1
Magnificent * p2 = (Magnificent *) pg;          // #2
Superb * p3 = (Magnificent *) pm;               // #3
```

Which of the above type casts are safe? Depending upon the class declarations, all of them could be safe, but the only ones guaranteed to be safe are the ones in which the pointer is the same type as the object or else a direct or indirect base type for the object. For example, type cast #1 is safe because it sets a type Magnificent pointer to point to a type Magnificent object. Type cast #2 is not safe because it assigns the address of a base object (Grand) to a derived class (Magnificent) pointer. Thus the program would expect the base class object to have derived class properties, and that, in general, is false. A Magnificent object, for instance, might have data members that a Grand object would lack. Type cast #3, however, is safe, because it assigns the address of a derived object to a base class pointer. That is, public derivation promises that a Magnificent object also is a Superb object (direct base) and a Grand object (indirect base). Thus, it's safe to assign its address to pointers of all three types. Virtual functions ensure that using pointers of any of the three types to a Magnificent object will invoke Magnificent methods.

Note that the question of whether a type conversion is safe is both more general and more useful than the question of what kind of object is pointed to. The usual reason for wanting to know the type is so that you can know if it's safe to invoke a particular method. You don't necessarily need an exact type match to invoke a method. The type can be a base type for which a virtual version of the method is defined. The next example will illustrate this point.

First, however, let's look at the dynamic_cast syntax. The operator is used like this, where pg points to an object:

```
Superb pm = dynamic_cast<Superb *>(pg);
```

This asks the question, can the pointer pg be type cast safely (as described above) to the type Superb *? If it can, the operator returns the address of the object. Otherwise it returns 0, the null pointer.

Remember

In general, the expression

```
dynamic_cast<Type *>(pt)
```

converts the pointer pt to a pointer of type Type * if the pointed-to object (*pt) is of type Type or else derived directly or indirectly from type Type. Otherwise, the expression evaluates to 0, the null pointer.

Listing 14.19 illustrates the process. First, it defines three classes, coincidentally named Grand, Superb, and Magnificent. The Grand class defines a virtual Speak() function, which each of the other classes redefines. The Superb class defines a virtual Say() function, which Magnificent redefines (see Figure 14.4). The program defines a GetOne() function that randomly creates and initializes an object of one of these three types, then returns the address as a type Grand * pointer. (The GetOne() function

simulates an interactive user making decisions.) A loop assigns this pointer to a type
Grand * variable called pg, then uses pg to invoke the Speak() function. Because this
function is virtual, the code correctly invokes the Speak() version appropriate to the
pointed-to object:

```
for (int i = 0; i < 5; i++)
{
    pg = GetOne();
    pg->Speak();
    ...
}
```

However, you can't use this exact approach to invoke the Say() function; it's not
defined for the Grand class. However, you can use the dynamic_cast operator to see if
pg can be type cast to a pointer to Superb. This will be true if the object is either type
Superb or Magnificent. In either case, you can invoke the Say() function safely:

```
if (ps = dynamic_cast<Superb *>(pg))
    ps->Say();
```

FIGURE 14.4

*The Grand family of
classes*

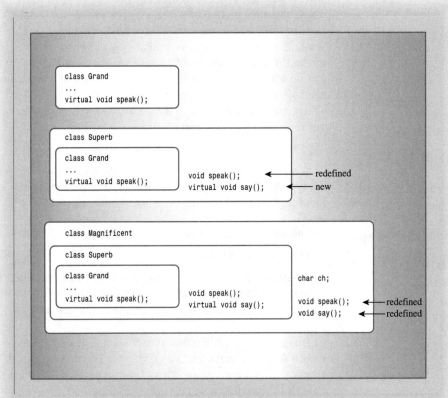

Recall that the value of an assignment expression is the value of its left side. Thus, the value of the if condition is ps. If the type cast succeeds, ps is nonzero, or true. If the type cast fails, which it will if pg points to a Grand object, pm is zero, or false. Listing 14.19 shows the full code.

Listing 14.19 rtti1.cpp

```cpp
// rtti1.cpp -- use the RTTI dynamic_cast operator
#include <iostream>
using namespace std;
#include <cstdlib>
#include <ctime>

class Grand
{
private:
    int hold;
public:
    Grand(int h = 0) : hold(h) {}
    virtual void Speak() const { cout << "I am a grand class!\n";}
    virtual int Value() const { return hold; }
};

class Superb : public Grand
{
public:
    Superb(int h = 0) : Grand(h) {}
    void Speak() const {cout << "I am a superb class!!\n"; }
    virtual void Say() const
        { cout << "I hold the superb value of " << Value() <<
"!\n";}
};

class Magnificent : public Superb
{
private:
    char ch;
public:
    Magnificent(int h = 0, char c = 'A') : Superb(h), ch(c) {}
    void Speak() const {cout << "I am a magnificent class!!!\n";}
    void Say() const {cout << "I hold the character " << ch <<
                " and the integer "  << Value() << "!\n"; }
};

Grand * GetOne();
int main()
{
    srand(time(0));
    Grand * pg;
    Superb * ps;
    for (int i = 0; i < 5; i++)
    {
        pg = GetOne();
        pg->Speak();
        if( ps = dynamic_cast<Superb *>(pg))
            ps->Say();
    }
    return 0;
}
```

```
Grand * GetOne()    // generate one of three kinds of objects
randomly
{
    Grand * p;
    switch( rand() % 3)
    {
        case 0: p = new Grand(rand() % 100);
                    break;
        case 1: p = new Superb(rand() % 100);
                    break;
        case 2: p = new Magnificent(rand() % 100, 'A' + rand() %
26);
                    break;
    }
    return p;
}
```

Remember

Even if your compiler supports RTTI, it may have that feature turned off by default, so you should check your documentation or explore the menu options.

This program illustrates an important point. You should use virtual functions when possible and RTTI only when necessary. Here is a sample output:

```
I am a superb class!!
I hold the superb value of 68!
I am a magnificent class!!!
I hold the character R and the integer 68!
I am a magnificent class!!!
I hold the character D and the integer 12!
I am a magnificent class!!!
I hold the character V and the integer 59!
I am a grand class!
```

As you can see, the Say() methods were invoked just for the Superb and the Magnificent classes.

You can use dynamic_cast with references, too. The usage is slightly different; there is no reference value corresponding to the null-pointer type, hence there's no special reference value that can be used to indicate failure. Instead, when goaded by an improper request, dynamic_cast throws a type bad_cast exception, which is derived from the exception class and defined in the typeinfo header file. Thus, the operator can be used as follows, where rg is a reference to a Grand object:

```
#include <typeinfo> // for bad_cast
...
try {
    Superb & rs = dynamic_cast<Superb &>(rg);
    ...
}
catch(bad_cast &){
    ...
};
```

The `typeid` Operator and `type_info` Class

The `typeid` operator lets you determine if two objects are the same type. Somewhat like `sizeof`, it accepts two kinds of arguments:

- The name of a class

- An expression that evaluates to an object

The `typeid` operator returns a reference to a `type_info` object, where `type_info` is a class defined in the `typeinfo` header file (formerly `typeinfo.h`). The `type_info` class overloads the `==` and `!=` operators so that you can use these operators to compare types. For example, the expression

```
typeid(Magnificent) == typeid(*pg)
```

evaluates to the `bool` value `true` if `pg` points to a `Magnificent` object and to `false` otherwise. If `pg` happens to be a null pointer, the program will throw a `bad_typeid` exception. This exception type is derived from the exception class and is declared in the `typeinfo` header file.

The implementation of the `type_info` class will vary among vendors, but it will include a `name()` member that returns an implementation-dependent string that typically would be the name of the class. For instance, the statement

```
cout << "Now processing type " << typeid(*pg).name() << ".\n";
```

displays the string defined for class of the object to which the pointer `pg` points.

Listing 14.20 modifies Listing 14.19 so that it uses the `typeid` operator and the `name()` member function. Note that they are used for situations that `dynamic_cast` and `virtual` functions don't handle. The `typeid` test is used to select an action that isn't even a class method, so it can't be invoked by a class pointer. The `name()` method statement shows how the method can be used in debugging. Note that the program includes the `typeinfo` header file.

```
Listing 14.20 rtti2.cpp
// rtti2.cpp  -- use dynamic_cast, typeid, and type_info
#include <iostream>
using namespace std;
#include <cstdlib>
#include <ctime>
#include <typeinfo>

class Grand
{
private:
    int hold;
public:
    Grand(int h = 0) : hold(h) {}
    virtual void Speak() const { cout << "I am a grand class!\n";}
    virtual int Value() const { return hold; }
};

class Superb : public Grand
```

```
{
public:
    Superb(int h = 0) : Grand(h) {}
    void Speak() const {cout << "I am a superb class!!\n"; }
    virtual void Say() const
    { cout << "I hold the superb value of " << Value() << "!\n";}
};

class Magnificent : public Superb
{
private:
    char ch;
public:
    Magnificent(int h = 0, char c = 'A') : Superb(h), ch(c) {}
    void Speak() const {cout << "I am a magnificent class!!!\n";}
    void Say() const {cout << "I hold the character " << ch <<
                " and the integer "  << Value() << "!\n"; }
};

Grand * GetOne();
int main()
{
    srand(time(0));
    Grand * pg;
    Superb * ps;
    for (int i = 0; i < 5; i++)
    {
        pg = GetOne();
        cout << "Now processing type " << typeid(*pg).name()
            << ".\n";
        pg->Speak();
        if( ps = dynamic_cast<Superb *>(pg))
            ps->Say();
        if (typeid(Magnificent) == typeid(*pg))
            cout << "Yes, you're really magnificent.\n";
    }
    return 0;
}

Grand * GetOne()
{
    Grand * p;

    switch( rand() % 3)
    {
        case 0: p = new Grand(rand() % 100);
                    break;
        case 1: p = new Superb(rand() % 100);
                    break;
        case 2: p = new Magnificent(rand() % 100, 'A' + rand() % 26);
                    break;
    }
    return p;
}
```

Here's a sample run:

```
Now processing type Magnificent.
I am a magnificent class!!!
I hold the character P and the integer 52!
Yes, you're really magnificent.
```

```
Now processing type Superb.
I am a superb class!!
I hold the superb value of 37!
Now processing type Grand.
I am a grand class!
Now processing type Superb.
I am a superb class!!
I hold the superb value of 18!
Now processing type Grand.
I am a grand class!
```

Misusing RTTI

RTTI has many vocal critics within the C++ community. They view RTTI as unnecessary, a potential source of program inefficiency, and as a possible contributor to bad programming practices. Without delving into the debate over RTTI, let's look at the sort of programming that you should avoid.

Consider the core of Listing 14.19:

```
Grand * pg;
Superb * ps;
for (int i = 0; i < 5; i++)
{
    pg = GetOne();
    pg->Speak();
    if( ps = dynamic_cast<Superb *>(pg))
        ps->Say();
}
```

By using typeid and ignoring dynamic_cast and virtual functions, you can rewrite this code as follows:

```
Grand * pg;
Superb * ps;
Magnificent * pm;
for (int i = 0; i < 5; i++)
{
    pg = GetOne();
    if (typeid(Magnificent) == typeid(*pg))
    {
        pm = (Magnificent *) pg;
        pm->Speak();
        pm->Say();
    }
    else if (typeid(Superb) == typeid(*pg))
    {
        ps = (Superb *) pg;
        ps->Speak();
        ps->Say();
    }
    else
        pg->Speak();
}
```

Not only is this uglier and longer than the original, it has the serious flaw of naming each class explicitly. Suppose, for example, that you find it necessary to derive an Insufferable class from the Magnificent class. The new class redefines Speak() and

Say(). With the version that uses typeid to test explicitly for each type, you would have to modify the for loop code, adding a new else if section. The original version, however, requires no changes at all. The

```
pg->Speak();
```

statement works for all classes derived from Grand, and the

```
if( ps = dynamic_cast<Superb *>(pg))
    ps->Say();
```

statement works for all classes derived from Superb.

Remember

If you find yourself using typeid in an extended series of if else statements, check to see whether you should have been using virtual functions and dynamic_cast.

Type Cast Operators

The C cast operator, in Bjarne Stroustrup's view, is too lax. For instance, consider the following:

```
struct Data
{
    double data[200];
};

struct Junk
{
    int junk[100];
};
Data d = {2.5e33, 3.5e-19, 20.2e32};
char * pch = (char *) (&d);// typecast #1 - convert to string
char ch = char (&d);       // typecast #2 - convert address to a char
Junk * pj = (Junk *) (&d); // typecast #3 - convert to Junk pointer
```

First, which of these three type casts makes any sense? Unless you resort to the implausible, none of them make much sense. Second, which of these three type casts are valid? All of them are.

Stroustrup's response to this laxity was to add four type cast operators that provide more discipline for the casting process:

```
dynamic_cast
const_cast
static_cast
reinterpret_cast
```

Instead of using a general type cast, you can select an operator suited to a particular purpose. This documents the intended reason for the type cast and gives the compiler a chance to check that you did what you thought you did.

You've already seen the dynamic_cast operator. To summarize, suppose High and Low are two classes, that ph is type High* and pl is type Low*. Then the statement

```
pl = dynamic_cast<Low *> ph;
```

assigns a `Low*` pointer to `pl` only if `Low` is an accessible base class (direct or indirect) to `High`. Otherwise, the statement assigns the null pointer to `pl`. In general, the operator has this syntax:

```
dynamic_cast < type-name > (expression)
```

The purpose of this operator is to allow upcasts within a class hierarchy (such type casts being safe because of the *is-a* relationship) and to disallow other casts.

The `const_cast` operator is for making a type cast with the sole purpose of changing whether a value is `const` or `volatile` or not. It has the same syntax as the `dynamic_cast` operator:

```
const_cast < type-name > (expression)
```

The result making such a cast is an error if any other aspect of the type is altered. That is, *type_name* and *expression* must be of the same type except they can differ in the presence or absence of `const` of `volatile`. Again, suppose `High` and `Low` are two classes:

```
const High bar;
  ...
High * pb = const_cast<High *> (&bar);     // valid
Low * pl = const_cast<Low *> (& bar);      // invalid
```

The first type cast makes `*pb` a pointer that can be used to alter the value of the bar object; it removes the `const` label. The second type cast is invalid, because it also attempts to change the type from `High *` to `Low *`.

The reason for this operator is that occasionally you may have a need for a value that is constant most of the time but which can be changed occasionally. Then you can declare the value as `const` and use `const_cast` when you need to alter the value. This could be done using the general cast, but the general cast can also simultaneously change the type:

```
const High bar;
...
High * pb = (const High *) (&bar);   // valid
Low * pl = (const Low *) (&bar);     // also valid
```

Because the simultaneous change of type and constantness may be an unintentional programming slip, using the `const_cast` operator is safer.

The `static_cast` operator has the same syntax as the others:

```
static_cast < type-name > (expression)
```

It's valid only if *type-name* can be converted implicitly to the same type *expression* has or vice versa. Otherwise, the cast is an error. Suppose `High` is a base class to `Low` and that `Pond` is an unrelated class. Then conversions from `High` to `Low` and `Low` to `High` are valid, but a conversion from `Low` to `Pond` is disallowed:

```
const High bar;
const Low blow;
...
High * pb = static_cast<High *> (&blow);     // valid upcast
Low * pl = static_cast<Low *> (&bar);        // valid downcast
Pond * pmer = static_cast<Pond *> (&blow);   // invalid
```

The first conversion is valid because an upcast can be done explicitly. The second conversion, from a base-class pointer to a derived-class pointer can't be done without an explicit type conversion. But because the type cast in the other direction can be made without a type cast, it's valid to use a static_cast for a downcast.

Similarly, because an enumeration value can be converted to an integral type without a type cast, an integral type can be converted to an enumeration value with static_cast.

The reinterpret_cast operator is for inherently risky type casts. It won't let you cast away const, but it will do other unsavory things. Sometimes a programmer has to do implementation-dependent, unsavory things, and using the reinterpret_cast operator makes it simpler to keep track of such acts. It has the same syntax as the other three:

```
reinterpret_cast < type-name > (expression)
```

Here is a sample use:

```
struct dat {short a; short b};
long value = 0xA224B118;
dat * pd = reinterpret_cast< dat *) (&value);
cout << pd->a;    // display first 2 bytes of value
```

Typically, such casts would be used for low-level, implementation-dependent programming.

Summary

Friends allow you to develop a more flexible interface for classes. A class can have other functions, other classes, and member functions of other classes as friends. In some cases, you may need to use forward declarations and to exert care in the ordering of class declarations and methods in order to get friends to mesh properly.

Nested classes are classes declared within other classes. Nested classes facilitate the design of helper classes that implement other classes but needn't be part of a public interface.

The C++ exception mechanism provides a flexible way to deal with awkward programming events such as inappropriate values, failed I/O attempts, and the like. Throwing an exception terminates the function currently executing and transfers control to a matching catch block. Catch blocks immediately follow a try block, and for an exception to be caught, the function call that directly or indirectly led to the exception must be in the try block. The program then executes the code in the catch block. This code may attempt to fix the problem or it can terminate the program. A class can be designed with nested exception classes that can be thrown when problems specific to the class are detected. A function can include an exception specification identifying those exceptions that can be thrown in that function. Uncaught exceptions (those with no matching catch block), by default, terminate a program. So do unexpected exceptions (those not matching an exception specification).

The RTTI (runtime type information) features allow a program to detect the type of an object. The dynamic_cast operator is used to cast a derived-class pointer to a base-class pointer; its main purpose is to ensure that it's okay to invoke a virtual function call. The typeid operator returns a type_info object. Two typeid return values can be compared to determine if an object is of a specific type, and the returned type_info object can be used to obtain information about an object.

The dynamic_cast operator, along with static_cast, const_cast, and reinterpret_cast, provide safer, better documented type casts than the general cast mechanism.

Review Questions

1. What's wrong with the following attempts at establishing friends?

a.
```
class snap {
    friend clasp;
    ...
};
class clasp { ... };
```

b.
```
class cuff {
public:
    void snip(muff &) { ... }
    ...
};
class muff {
    friend void cuff::snip(muff &);
    ...
};
```

c.
```
class muff {
    friend void cuff::snip(muff &);
    ...
};
class cuff {
public:
    void snip(muff &) { ... }
    ...
};
```

2. You've seen how to create mutual class friends. Can you create a more restricted form of friendship in which only some members of class B are friends to class A and some members of A are friends to B? Explain.

3. What problems might the following nested class declaration have?

```
class Ribs
{
private:
    class Sauce
    {
            int soy;
            int sugar;
    public:
            Sauce(int s1, int s2) : soy(s1), sugar(s2) { }
    };
    ...
};
```

4. How does `throw` differ from `return`?

5. Suppose you have a hierarchy of exception classes derived from a base exception class. In what order should you place catch blocks?

6. Consider the `Grand`, `Superb`, and `Magnificent` classes defined in this chapter. Suppose pg is a type `Grand *` pointer assigned the address of an object of one of these three classes and that ps is a type `Superb *` pointer. What is the difference in how the following two code samples behave?

```
if (ps = dynamic_cast<Superb *>(pg))
        ps->say();  // sample #1
    if (typeid(*pg) == typeid(Superb))
        (Superb *) pg)->say();  // sample #2
```

7. How is the `static_cast` operator different from the `dynamic_cast` operator?

Programming Exercises

1. Modify the `Tv` and `Remote` classes as follows:

   a. Make them mutual friends.

   b. Add a state variable member to the `Remote` class that describes whether the remote control is in normal or interactive mode.

   c. Add a `Remote` method that displays the mode.

   d. Provide the `Tv` class with a method for toggling the new `Remote` member. This method should work only if the `Tv` is in the on state.

   Write a short program testing these new features.

2. Modify Listing 14.10 so that hmean() throws an exception of type hmeanexcp and gmean() throws an exception of type gmeanexcp. Both of these exception types are to be derived from the exception class. Also, upon catching an hmeanexcp exception, the program should prompt for a new data pair and continue, while upon catching a gmeanexcp exception, the program should continue with the code following the loop.

15

The String Class and the Standard Template Library

By now you are familiar with the C++ goal of reusable code. One of the big payoffs is when you can reuse code written by others. That's where class libraries come in. There are many commercially available C++ class libraries, and there also are the libraries that come as part of the C++ package. For example, you've been using the input/output classes supported by the `ostream` header file. This chapter will look at other reusable code available for your programming pleasure. First, the chapter examines the `string` class, which simplifies programming with strings. Then it looks at `auto_ptr`, a "smart pointer" template class that makes managing dynamic memory a bit easier. Finally, it looks at the Standard Template Library (or STL), a collection of useful templates for handling various kinds of container objects. STL exemplifies a recent programming paradigm called generic programming.

You will learn about the following in this chapter:

- The standard C++ string class
- The `auto_ptr` template
- The Standard Template Library (STL)
- Container classes
- Iterators
- Function objects (functors)
- STL algorithms

The `string` Class

" After all, one of the most important things to know about a class is what your options are when creating objects of that class. "

Chapter 11 introduced a modest `String` class to illustrate some aspects of class design. C++ itself provides a more powerful version called the `string` class. It is supported by the `string` header file. (Note that the `string.h` and `cstring` header files support the C library string functions for C-style strings, not the `string` class.) The key to using a class is knowing its public interface, and the string class has an extensive set of methods, including several constructors, overloaded operators for assigning strings, concatenating strings, comparing strings, and accessing individual elements, as well as utilities for finding characters and substrings in a string, and more. In short, the `string` class has lots of stuff.

CONSTRUCTING A `string`

Let's begin with looking at the `string` constructors. After all, one of the most important things to know about a class is what your options are when creating objects of that class. Listing 15.1 uses all six of the `string` constructors (labeled *ctor*, the traditional C++ abbreviation for constructor). Table 15.1 briefly describes the constructors in the order used in the program. The constructor representations are simplified in that they conceal the fact that `string` really is a `typedef` for a template specialization `basic_string<char>` and that they omit an optional argument relating to memory management. (This aspect is discussed later this chapter and in Appendix F.) The type `size_type` is an implementation-dependent integral type defined in the `string` header file. The class defines `string::npos` as the maximum possible length of the string. Typically, this would equal the maximum value of an `unsigned int`. Also, the table uses the common abbreviation NBTS for null-byte-terminated string, that is, the traditional C string, which is terminated with a null character.

TABLE 15.1
string CLASS CONSTRUCTORS

CONSTRUCTOR	DESCRIPTION
string(const char * s)	Initializes string object to NBTS pointed to by s.
string(size_type n, char c)	Creates a string object of n elements, each initialized to the character c.
string(const string * str, size_type pos = 0, size_type n = npos)	Initializes string object to the string object str, starting at position pos in str and going to end of str or using n characters, whichever comes first.
string()	Creates a default string object of 0 size.
string(const char * s, size_type n)	Initializes string object to NBTS pointed to by s and continues for n characters even if that exceeds the size of the NBTS.
template<class Iter> string(Iter begin, Iter end)	Initializes string object to the values in the range [begin, end), where begin and end act like pointers and specify locations; the range includes begin and is up to but not including end.

The program also uses the overloaded += operator, which appends one string to another, the overloaded = operator for assigning one string to another, the overloaded << operator for displaying a string object, and the overloaded [ ] operator for accessing an individual character in a string.

Listing 15.1 str1.cpp

```cpp
// str1.cpp -- introducing the string class
#include <iostream>
#include <string>
using namespace std;
// using string constructors

int main()
{
    string one("Lottery Winner!");     // ctor #1
    cout << one << endl;               // overloaded <<
    string two(20, '$');               // ctor #2
    cout << two << endl;
    string three(one);                 // ctor #3
    cout << three << endl;
    one += " Oops!";                   // overloaded +=
    cout << one << endl;
    two = "Sorry! That was ";
    three[0] = 'P';
    string four;                       // ctor #4
    four = two + three;                // overloaded +, =
    cout << four << endl;
    char alls[] = "All's well that ends well";
```

```
string five(alls,20);              // ctor #5
cout << five << "!\n";
string six(alls+6, alls + 10);     // ctor #6
cout << six  << ", ";
string seven(&five[6], &five[10]);// ctor #6 again
cout << seven << "...\n";

return 0;
}
```

Remember

Some older string implementations do not support ctor #6.

Here is the program's output:

```
Lottery Winner!
$$$$$$$$$$$$$$$$$$$$
Lottery Winner!
Lottery Winner! Oops!
Sorry! That was Pottery Winner!
All's well that ends!
well, well...
```

PROGRAM NOTES

The start of the program illustrates that you can initialize a string object to a regular C-style string and display it using the overloaded << operator:

```
string one("Lottery Winner!");    // ctor #1
cout << one << endl;              // overloaded <<
```

The next constructor initializes the string object two to a string consisting of 20 $ characters:

```
string two(20, '$');             // ctor #2
```

The copy constructor initializes the string object three to the string object one:

```
string three(one);               // ctor #3
```

The overloaded += operator appends the string " Oops!" to the string one:

```
one += " Oops!";                 // overloaded +=
```

This particular example appends a C-style string to a string object. However, the += operator is multiply overloaded so that you also can append string objects and single characters:

```
one += two;   // append a string object (not in program)
one += '!';   // append a type char value (not in program)
```

Similarly, the = operator is overloaded so that you can assign a string object to a string object, a C-style string to a string object, or a simple char value to a string object:

```
two = "Sorry! That was "; // assign a C-style string
two = one;                 // assign a string object (not in program)
two = '?';                 // assign a char value (not in program)
```

Overloading the [] operator, as the ArrayDb example in Chapter 13 did, permits access to individual characters in a string object by using array notation:

```
three[0] = 'P';
```

A default constructor creates an empty string which later can be given a value:

```
string four;               // ctor #4
four = two + three;        // overloaded +, =
```

The second line uses the overloaded + operator to create a temporary string object which is then assigned, using the overloaded = operator, to the four object. As you might expect, the + operator concatenates its two operands into a single string object. The operator is multiply overloaded so the second operand can be a string object or a C-style string or a char value.

The fifth constructor takes a C-style string and an integer as arguments, with the integer indicating how many characters to copy:

```
char alls[] = "All's well that ends well";
string five(alls,20);                  // ctor #5
```

Here, as the output shows, just the first 20 characters ("All's well that ends") are used to initialize the five object. As Table 15.1 notes, if the character count exceeds the length of the C-style string, the requested number of characters are still copied. So replacing 20 with 40 in the above example would result in 15 junk characters being copied at the end of five. (That is, the constructor would interpret the contents in memory following the string "All's well that ends well" as character codes.)

The sixth constructor has a template argument:

```
template<class Iter> string(Iter begin, Iter end);
```

The intent is that begin and end act like pointers pointing to two locations in memory. (In general, begin and end can be iterators, generalizations of pointers extensively used in the STL.) The constructor then uses the values between the locations pointed to by begin and end to initialize the string object it constructs. The notation [begin,end), borrowed from mathematics, means the range includes begin but doesn't include end. That is, end points to a location one past the last value to be used. Consider the following statement:

```
string six(alls+6, alls + 10);    // ctor #6
```

Because the name of an array is a pointer, both alls + 6 and alls + 10 are type char *, so the template is used with Iter replaced by type char *. The first argument points to the first w in the alls array, and the second argument points to the space following the first well. Thus, six is initialized to the string "well". Figure 15.1 shows how the constructor works.

FIGURE 15.1

*string constructor
using a range*

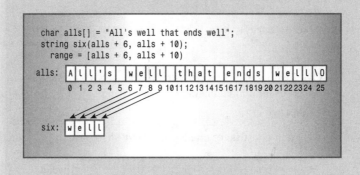

Now suppose you want to use this constructor to initialize an object to part of another `string` object, say, the object `five`. The following does not work:

```
string seven(five + 6, five + 10);
```

The reason is that the name of an object, unlike the name of an array, is not treated as the address of an object, hence `five` is not a pointer and `five + 6` is meaningless. However, `five[6]` is a `char` value, so `&five[6]` is an address and can be used as an argument to the constructor:

```
string seven(&five[6], &five[10]);// ctor #6 again
```

string CLASS INPUT

Another useful thing to know about a class is what input options are available. For C-style strings, recall, you have three options:

```
char info[100];
cin >> info;              // read a word
cin.getline(info, 100);   // read a line, discard \n
cin.get(info, 100);       // read a line, leave \n in queue
```

So what are the input options for a `string` object? First, the `string` class overloads the `>>` operator, much as the `String` class did in Chapter 11. Because the first operand is not a string object, the overloaded `>>` operator function is not a class method. Instead, it is a general function taking an `istream` object as its first argument and a `string` object as its second argument. To be consistent with how the `>>` operator treats C-strings, the string version also reads a single word, terminating input upon reaching a whitespace character, detecting end of file, or reaching the maximum allowable number of characters that can be stored in a string object. The function works by first erasing the contents of the target string and then reading and appending one character at a time. As long as the input sequence is shorter than the maximum allowable number of characters for a string object, the operator>>(istream &, string &) function automatically dimensions the string object to fit the input string. The upshot is that you can use >> with string objects just as you do with C-style strings, but without worrying about overrunning the array size:

```
char fname[10];
cin >> fname;        // could be a problem if input size > 9 characters
string lname;
cin >> lname;        // can read a very, very long word
```

Providing a getline() equivalent is a bit less transparent, for getline(), unlike operator>>(), can't be used with operator notation. Instead, it uses membership notation:

```
cin.getline(fname, 10);
```

To get the same syntax to work with a string object would require adding a new member function to the istream class, which would not be wise. Instead, the string library defines a non-member function getline() that takes an istream object as its first argument and a string object as its second argument. Thus, it's used as follows to read a line of input into a string object:

```
string fullName;
getline(cin, fullName);  // instead of cin.getline(fname, 10);
```

The getline() function first erases the contents of the destination string and then reads one character at a time from the input queue, appending it to the string. This continues until the function reaches the end of the line, detects the end of file, or reaches maximum capacity of a string object. The newline character, if detected, is read but not stored in the string. Note that unlike the istream version, the string version doesn't have a size parameter indicating the maximum number of characters to read. Listing 15.2 illustrates using the two input options.

> *" The upshot is that you can use >> with string objects just as you do with C-style strings, but without worrying about over-running the array size."*

Listing 15.2 str2.cpp

```
// str2.cpp -- string input
#include <iostream>
#include <string>
using namespace std;

int main()
{
    string word;
    cout << "Enter a line: ";
    cin >> word;
    while (cin.get() != '\n')
        continue;
    cout << word << " is all I wanted.\n";

    string line;
    cout << "Enter a line (really!): ";
    getline(cin, line);
    cout << "Line: " << line << endl;
    return 0;
}
```

Remember

Microsoft Visual C++ 5.0 has a bug in its `getline()` implementation that causes output following `getline()` not to appear until something is entered again. Borland C++Builder 1.0's `getline()` requires an explicit delimiter argument: `getline(cin, line, '\n')`.

Here is a sample run:

```
Enter a line: Time and tide wait for no one.
Time is all I wanted.
Enter a line (really!): All things come to he who waits.
Line: All things come to he who waits.
```

WORKING WITH STRINGS

So far, you've learned that you can create `string` objects in a variety of ways, display the contents of a `string` object, read data into a `string` object, append to a `string` object, assign to a `string` object, and concatenate two `string` objects. What else can you do?

You can compare strings. All six relational operators are overloaded for `string` objects, with one object being considered less than another if it occurs earlier in the machine collating sequence. If the machine collating sequence is the ASCII code, that implies that digits are less than uppercase characters and uppercase characters are less than lowercase characters. Each relational operator is overloaded three ways so that you can compare a `string` object with another `string` object, compare a `string` object with a C-style string, and compare a C-style string with a string object:

```
string snake1("cobra");
string snake2("coral");
char snake3[20] = "anaconda";
if (snake1 < snake 2)          // operator<(const string &, const string &)
    ...
if (snake1 == snake3)          // operator==(const string &, const char *)
    ...
if (snake3 != snake2)          // operator!=(const char *, const string &)
    ...
```

You can determine the size of a string. Both the `size()` and `length()` member functions return the number of characters in a string:

```
if (snake1.length() == snake2.size())
    cout << "Both strings have the same length.\n"
```

Why two functions that do the same thing? The `length()` member comes from earlier versions of the `string` class, while `size()` was added for STL compatibility.

You can search a string for a given substring or character in a variety of ways. Table 15.2 provides a short description of four variations of a find() method. Recall that string::npos is the maximum possible number of characters in a string, typically the largest unsigned int or unsigned long value.

The library also provides the related methods rfind(), find_first_of(), find_last_of(), find_first_not_of(), and find_last_not_of(), each with the same set of overloaded function signatures as the find() method. The rfind() finds the last occurrence of a substring or character. The find_first_of() finds the first occurrence in the invoking string of any of the characters in the argument. For example, the statement:

```
int where = snake1.find_first_of("hark");
```

would return the location of the r in "cobra" (i.e., the index 3) because that's the first occurrence of any of the letters in "hark" in "cobra". The find_last_of() method works the same, except it finds the last occurrence. Thus, the statement:

```
int where = snake1.last_first_of("hark");
```

would return the location of the a in "cobra". The find_first_not_of() method finds the first character in the invoking string that is not a character in the argument. So

```
int where = snake1.find_first_not_of("hark");
```

would return the location of the c in cobra, for c is not found in hark. We leave the description of find_last_not_of() as an exercise for the reader.

TABLE 15.2
THE OVERLOADED find() METHOD

METHOD PROTOTYPE	DESCRIPTION
size_type find(const string & str, size_type pos = 0) const	Finds the first occurrence of the substring str, starting the search at location pos in the invoking string. Returns the index of the first character of the substring if found, and returns string::npos otherwise.
size_type find(const char * s, size_type pos = 0) const	Finds the first occurrence of the substring s, starting the search at location pos in the invoking string. Returns the index of the first character of the substring if found, and returns string::npos otherwise.
size_type find(const char * s, size_type pos = 0, size_type n) const	Finds the first occurrence of the substring consisting of the first n characters in s, starting the search at location pos in the invoking string. Returns the index of the first character of the substring if found, and returns string::npos otherwise.
size_type find(char ch, size_type pos = 0) const	Finds the first occurrence of the character ch, starting the search at location pos in the invoking string. Returns the index of the character if found, and returns string::npos otherwise.

There are many more methods, but these are enough to put together a sample program that's a graphically impaired version of the word game Hangman. It stores a list of words in an array of `string` objects, picks a word at random, and lets you guess letters in the word. Six wrong guesses, and you lose. The program uses the `find()` function to check your guesses and the `+=` operator to build a `string` object to keep track of your wrong guesses. To keep track of your good guesses, the program creates a word the same length as the mystery word but consisting of hyphens. The hyphens are then replaced by correct guesses. Listing 15.3 shows the program.

Listing 15.3 str3.cpp

```cpp
// str3.cpp -- some string methods
#include <iostream>
#include <string>
#include <cstdlib>
#include <ctime>
#include <cctype>
using namespace std;

const int NUM = 26;
const string wordlist[NUM] = {"apiary", "beetle", "cereal",
    "danger", "ensign", "florid", "garage", "health", "insult",
    "jackal", "keeper", "loaner", "manage", "nonce", "onset",
    "plaid", "quilt", "remote", "stolid", "train", "useful",
    "valid", "whence", "xenon", "yearn", "zippy"};

int main()
{
    srand(time(0));
    char play;
    cout << "Will you play a word game? <y/n> ";
    cin >> play;
    play = tolower(play);
    while (play == 'y')
    {
        string target = wordlist[rand() % NUM];
        int length = target.length();
        string attempt(length, '-');
        string badchars;
        int guesses = 6;
        cout << "Guess my secret word. It has " << length
            << " letters, and you guess\n"
            << "one letter at a time. You get " << guesses
            << " wrong guesses.\n";
        cout << "Your word: " << attempt << endl;
        while (guesses > 0 && attempt != target)
        {
            char letter;
            cout << "Guess a letter: ";
            cin >> letter;
            if (badchars.find(letter) != string::npos
                || attempt.find(letter) != string::npos)
            {
                cout << "You already guessed that. Try again.\n";
                    continue;
            }
            int loc = target.find(letter);
```

```
                    if (loc == string::npos)
                    {
                        cout << "Oh, bad guess!\n";
                        --guesses;
                        badchars += letter; // add to string
                    }
                    else
                    {
                        cout << "Good guess!\n";
                        attempt[loc]=letter;
                        // check if letter appears again
                        loc = target.find(letter, loc + 1);
                        while (loc != string::npos)
                        {
                            attempt[loc]=letter;
                            loc = target.find(letter, loc + 1);
                        }
                    }
                    cout << "Your word: " << attempt << endl;
                    if (attempt != target)
                    {
                        if (badchars.length() > 0)
                            cout << "Bad choices: " << badchars << endl;
                        cout << guesses << " bad guesses left\n";
                    }
                }
                if (guesses > 0)
                    cout << "That's right!\n";
                else
                    cout << "Sorry, the word is " << target << ".\n";

                cout << "Will you play another? <y/n> ";
                cin >> play;
                play = tolower(play);
            }

            cout << "Bye\n";

            return 0;
        }
```

Here's a sample run.

```
Will you play a word game? <y/n> y
Guess my secret word. It has 6 letters, and you guess
one letter at a time. You get 6 wrong guesses.
Your word: ------
Guess a letter: e
Oh, bad guess!
Your word: ------
Bad choices: e
5 bad guesses left
Guess a letter: a
Good guess!
Your word: a--a--
Bad choices: e
5 bad guesses left
Guess a letter: t
Oh, bad guess!
Your word: a--a--
```

```
Bad choices: et
4 bad guesses left
Guess a letter: r
Good guess!
Your word: a--ar-
Bad choices: et
4 bad guesses left
Guess a letter: y
Good guess!
Your word: a--ary
Bad choices: et
4 bad guesses left
Guess a letter: i
Good guess!
Your word: a-iary
Bad choices: et
4 bad guesses left
Guess a letter: p
Good guess!
Your word: apiary
That's right!
Will you play another? <y/n> n
Bye
```

PROGRAM NOTES

> *"The fact that the relational operators are overloaded lets you treat strings in the same fashion you would treat numeric variables."*

The fact that the relational operators are overloaded lets you treat strings in the same fashion you would treat numeric variables:

```
while (guesses > 0 && attempt != target)
```

This is easier to follow than, say, using strcmp() with C-style strings.

The program uses find() to check if a character has been selected earlier; if it has been selected, it will be found in either the badchars string (bad guesses) or in the attempt string (good guesses):

```
if (badchars.find(letter) != string::npos
    ¦¦ attempt.find(letter) != string::npos)
```

The npos variable is a static member of the string class. Its value, recall, is the maximum allowable number of characters for a string object. Therefore, because indexing begins at 0, it is 1 greater than the largest possible index and can be used to indicate failure to find a character or a string.

The program makes use of the fact that one of the overloaded versions of the += operator lets you append individual characters to a string:

```
badchars += letter;  // append a char to a string object
```

The heart of the program begins by checking if the chosen letter is in the mystery word:

```
int loc = target.find(letter);
```

If loc is a valid value, the letter can be placed in the corresponding location in the answer string:

```
attempt[loc]=letter;
```

However, a given letter may occur more than once in the mystery word, so the program has to keep checking. Here the program uses the optional second argument to find(), which lets you specify a starting place in the string from which to begin the search. Because the letter was found at location loc, the next search should begin at loc + 1. A while loop keeps the search going until no more occurrences of that character are found. Note that find() indicates failure if loc is after the end of the string:

```
// check if letter appears again
loc = target.find(letter, loc + 1);
while (loc != string::npos)
{
    attempt[loc]=letter;
    loc = target.find(letter, loc + 1);
}
```

WHAT ELSE?

The string library supplies many other facilities. There are functions for erasing part or all of a string, for replacing part or all of one string with part or all of another string, for inserting material into a string or removing material from a string, for comparing part or all of one string with part or all of another string, and for extracting a substring from a string. There's a function for copying part of one string to another string, and a function for swapping the contents of two strings. Most of these functions are overloaded so that they can work with C-style strings as well as with string objects. Appendix F describes the string library function briefly.

This section has treated the string class as if it were based on the char type. In fact, as mentioned earlier, the string library really is based on a template class:

```
template<class charT, class traits = char _traits<charT>,
        class Allocator = allocator<charT> >
basic_string {...};
```

The class includes the following two typedefs:

```
typedef basic_string<char> string;
typedef basic_string<wchar_t> wstring;
```

This allows you to use strings based on the wchar_t as well as the char type. You even could develop some sort of character-like class and use the basic_string class template with it, providing your class met certain requirements. The traits class is a class that describes specific facts about the chosen character type, such as how to compare values. There are predefined specializations of the char_traits template for the char and wchar_t types, and these are the default values for traits. The Allocator class represents a class to manage memory allocation. There are predefined specializations of the allocator template for the char and wchar_t types, and these are the defaults. They use new and delete in the usual fashion, but you could reserve a chunk of memory and provide your own allocation methods.

The `auto_ptr` Class

The `auto_ptr` class is a template class for managing the use of dynamic memory allocation. Let's take a look at what might be needed and how it can be accomplished. Consider the following function:

```
void remodel(string & str)
{
    string * ps = new string(str);
    ...
    str = ps;
    return;
}
```

You probably see its flaw. Each time the function is called, it allocates memory from the heap but never returns it, creating a memory leak. You also know the solution—just remember to free the allocated memory by adding the following statement just before the return statement:

```
delete ps;
```

However, a solution involving the phrase "just remember to" seldom is the best solution. Sometimes you won't remember. Or you will remember but accidentally remove or comment out the code. And even if you do remember, there still can be problems. Consider the following variation:

```
void remodel(string & str)
{
    string * ps = new string(str);
    ...
    if (weird_thing())
        throw exception();
    str = *ps;
    delete ps;
    return;
}
```

"However, a solution involving the phrase 'just remember to' seldom is the best solution."

If the exception is thrown, the `delete` statement isn't reached, and again there is a memory leak

You can fix that oversight, as illustrated in Chapter 14, but it would be nice if there were a neater solution. Let's think about what is needed. When a function like `remodel()` terminates, either normally or by throwing an exception, local variables are removed from the stack memory—so the memory occupied by the pointer ps is freed. What would be nice is if the memory pointed to by ps were also freed. That means that you would want the program to take an additional action when ps expires. That extra service is not provided for basic types, but it can be provided for classes via the destructor mechanism. Thus, the problem with ps is that it is just an ordinary pointer and not a class object. If it were an object, you could have its destructor delete the pointed-to memory when the object expires. And that is the idea behind `auto_ptr`.

USING AN auto_ptr

The auto_ptr template defines a pointer-like object intended to be assigned an address obtained (directly or indirectly) by new. When an auto_ptr object expires, its destructor uses delete to free the memory. Thus, if you assign an address returned by new to an auto_ptr object, you don't have to remember to free the memory later; it will be freed automatically when the auto_ptr object expires. Figure 15.2 illustrates the behavioral difference between an auto_ptr and a regular pointer.

To create an auto_ptr object, include the memory header file, which includes the auto_ptr template. Then use the usual template syntax to instantiate the kind of pointer you require. The template includes the following:

```
template<class X> class auto_ptr {
public:
    explicit auto_ptr(X* p =0) throw();
...};
```

(The throw() notation, recall, means this constructor doesn't throw an exception.) Thus, asking for an auto_ptr of type X gives you an auto_ptr pointing to type X:

```
auto_ptr<double> pd(new double);   // an auto_ptr to double
                                   // (use in place of double *)
auto_ptr<string> ps(new string);   // an auto_ptr to string
                                   // (use in place of string *)
```

Thus, to convert the remodel() function, you would follow these three steps:

1. Include the memory header file.

2. Replace the pointer-to-string with an auto_ptr to string.

3. Remove the delete statement.

Here's the function with those changes made:

```
#include <memory>
void remodel(string & str)
{
    auto_ptr<string> ps (new string(str));
    ...
    if (weird_thing())
        throw exception();
    str = *ps;
    // delete ps;  NO LONGER NEEDED
    return;
}
```

Note that auto_ptr constructor is explicit, meaning there is no implicit type cast from a pointer to an auto_ptr:

```
auto_ptr<double> pd;
double *p_reg = new double;
pd = p_reg;                     // not allowed (implicit conversion)
pd = auto_ptr<double>(p_reg);   // allowed (explicit conversion)
auto_ptr<double> pauto = pd;    // not allowed (implicit conversion)
auto_ptr<double> pauto(pd);     // allowed (explicit conversion
```

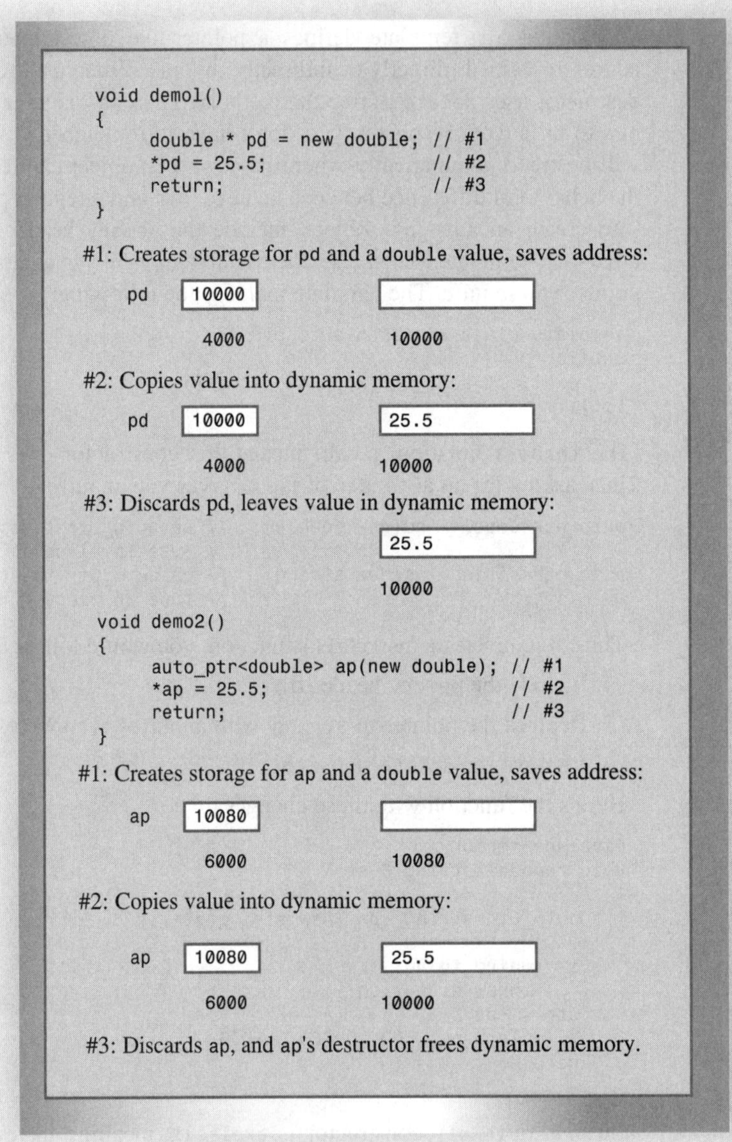

FIGURE 15.2

Regular pointer versus
auto_ptr

```
void demo1()
{
    double * pd = new double; // #1
    *pd = 25.5;               // #2
    return;                   // #3
}
```

#1: Creates storage for pd and a double value, saves address:

pd `10000`   `            `

      4000   10000

#2: Copies value into dynamic memory:

pd `10000`   `25.5`

      4000   10000

#3: Discards pd, leaves value in dynamic memory:

                    `25.5`

                     10000

```
void demo2()
{
    auto_ptr<double> ap(new double); // #1
    *ap = 25.5;                      // #2
    return;                          // #3
}
```

#1: Creates storage for ap and a double value, saves address:

ap `10080`   `            `

      6000   10080

#2: Copies value into dynamic memory:

ap `10080`   `25.5`

      6000   10000

#3: Discards ap, and ap's destructor frees dynamic memory.

The auto_ptr is an example of a *smart pointer*, an object that acts like a pointer, but with additional features. The auto_ptr class is defined so that, in most respects, it acts like a regular pointer. For example, given that ps is an auto_ptr, you can dereference it (*ps), increment it (++ps), use it to access structure members (ps->puffIndex), and assign it to a regular pointer that points to the same type. You also can assign one auto_ptr to another of the same type, but that raises an issue that the next section will face.

The template allows you to initialize an auto_ptr object to an ordinary pointer via a constructor:

auto_ptr CONSIDERATIONS

The auto_ptr is not a panacea. For example, consider the following code:

```
auto_ptr<int> pi(new int [200]);    // NO!
```

Remember, you must pair delete with new and delete [] with new []. The auto_ptr template uses delete, not delete [], so it only can be used with new, not new []. There is no auto_ptr equivalent for using with dynamic arrays. You could copy the auto_ptr template from the memory header file, rename it auto_arr_ptr, and convert the copy to use delete [] instead of delete. In that case, you would want to add support for the [] operator.

What about this?

```
string vacation("I wandered lonely as a cloud.");
auto_ptr<string> pvac(&vacation);  // NO!
```

This would apply the delete operator to non-heap memory, which is wrong.

Remember

> Use an auto_ptr object only for memory allocated by new, not for memory allocated by new [] or by simply declaring a variable.

Now consider assignment:

```
auto_ptr<string> ps (new string("I reigned lonely as a cloud."));
auto_ptr<string> vocation;
vocation = ps;
```

What should the assignment statement accomplish? If ps and vocation were ordinary pointers, the result would be two pointers pointing to the same string object. That is not acceptable here, for then the program would wind up attempting to delete the same object twice, once when ps expires, and once when vocation expires. There are ways to avoid this problem:

- Define the assignment operator so that it makes a deep copy. This results in two pointers pointing to two distinct objects, one of which is a copy of the other.

- Institute the concept of *ownership*, with only one smart pointer allowed to own a particular object. Only if the smart pointer owns the object will its constructor delete the object. Then have assignment transfer ownership. This is the strategy used for auto_ptr.

◆ Create an even smarter pointer that keeps track of how many smart pointers refer to a particular object. This is called *reference counting*. Assignment, for example, would increase the count by one, and the expiration of a pointer would decrease the count by one. Only when the final pointer expires would delete be invoked.

The same strategies, of course, would also be applied to the copy constructors.

Each approach has its uses. Here's a situation, for example, that may not work properly using auto_ptr objects:

```
auto_ptr<string> films[5] =
{
    auto_ptr<string> (new string("Fowl Balls")),
    auto_ptr<string> (new string("Duck Walks")),
    auto_ptr<string> (new string("Chicken Runs")),
    auto_ptr<string> (new string("Turkey Errors")),
    auto_ptr<string> (new string("Goose Eggs"))
};
auto_ptr<string> pwin(films[2]);
int i;
cout << "The nominees for best avian baseball film are\n";
for (i = 0; i < 5; i++)
    cout << *films[i] << endl;
cout << "The winner is " << *pwin << "!\n";
```

The problem is that transferring ownership from films[2] to pwin may cause films[2] to no longer refer to the string. That is, after an auto_ptr object gives up ownership, it may no longer be usable. Whether it's usable or not is an implementation choice.

The Standard Template Library

The Standard Template Library, or STL, provides a collection of templates representing *containers*, *iterators*, *function objects*, and *algorithms*. A container is a unit, like an array, that can hold several values. STL containers are homogeneous, that is, they hold values all of the same kind. Algorithms are recipes for accomplishing particular tasks, such as sorting an array or finding a particular value in a list. Iterators are objects that let you move through a container much as pointers let you move through an array; they are generalizations of pointers. Function objects are objects that act like functions; they can be class objects or function pointers (which includes function names because a function name acts as a pointer). The STL lets you construct a variety of containers, including arrays, queues, and lists, and lets you perform a variety of operations, including searching, sorting, and randomizing.

Alex Stepanov and Meng Lee developed STL at Hewlett-Laboratories, releasing the implementation in 1994. The ISO/ANSI C++ committee voted to incorporate it as a part of the C++ standard. The STL is not an example of object-oriented programming. Instead, it represents a different programming paradigm called *generic programming*. This makes STL interesting both in terms of what it does and in its approach. There's too much information about the STL to present in a single chapter, so we'll look at some representative examples and examine the spirit of the approach. We'll begin by looking at a few specific examples. Then, once you have a hands-on appreciation for containers, iterators, and algorithms, we'll look at the underlying design philosophy, and then take an overview of whole STL. Appendix G summarizes the various STL methods and functions.

THE `vector` TEMPLATE CLASS

In computing, the term *vector* corresponds to an array rather than to the mathematical vector discussed in Chapter 10. A vector holds a set of like values that can be accessed randomly. That is, you can use, say, an index to directly access the tenth element of a vector without having to access the preceding nine elements first. So a `vector` class would provide operations similar to that of the `arrayDb` class of Chapter 13. That is, you could create a `vector` object, assign one `vector` object to another, and use the `[ ]` operator to access `vector` elements. To make the class generic, make it a template class. That's what the STL does, defining a `vector` template in the `vector` (formerly `vector.h`) header file.

To create a `vector` template object, you use the usual `<type>` notation to indicate the type to be used. Also, the `vector` template uses dynamic memory allocation, and you can use an initialization argument to indicate how many vector elements you want:

```
#include vector
using namespace std;
vector<int> ratings(5);        // a vector of 5 ints
int n;
cin >> n;
vector<double> scores(n);      // a vector of n doubles
```

Once you create a vector object, operator overloading for `[ ]` makes it possible to use the usual array notation for accessing individual elements:

```
ratings[0] = 9;
for (int i = 0; i < n; i++)
    cout << scores[i] << endl;
```

ALLOCATORS AGAIN

Like the `string` class, the various STL container templates take an optional template argument specifying what allocator object to use to manage memory. For example, the `vector` template begins like this:

```
template <class T, class Allocator = allocator<T> >
    class vector {...
```

If you omit a value for this template argument, the container template uses the `allocator<T>` class by default. This class uses `new` and `delete` in the standard ways.

Listing 15.4 uses this class in an undemanding application. This particular program creates two `vector` objects, one an `int` specialization and one a `string` specialization; each has five elements.

Listing 15.4 vect1.cpp

```cpp
// vect1.cpp -- introducing the vector template
#include <iostream>
#include <string>
#include <vector>
using namespace std;

const int NUM = 5;
int main()
{
    vector<int> ratings(NUM);
    vector<string> titles(NUM);
    cout << "You will do exactly as told. You will enter\n"
         << NUM << " book titles and your ratings (0-10).\n";
    int i;
    for (i = 0; i < NUM; i++)
    {
        cout << "Enter title #" << i + 1 << ": ";
        getline(cin,titles[i]);
        cout << "Enter your rating (0-10): ";
        cin >> ratings[i];
        cin.get();
    }
    cout << "Thank you. You entered the following:\n"
         << "Rating\tBook\n";
    for (i = 0; i < NUM; i++)
    {
        cout << ratings[i] << "\t" << titles[i] << endl;
    }

    return 0;
}
```

Remember

Older implementations use `vector.h` instead of the `vector` header file. Although the order of include files shouldn't matter, g++ 2.7.1 required the string header file to appear before STL header files. The Microsoft Visual C++ 5.0 `getline()` has a bug that messes up synchronization of input and output, and Borland C++Builder 1.0's `getline()` requires an explicit delimiter argument.

Here's a sample run:

```
You will do exactly as told. You will enter
5 book titles and your ratings (0-10).
Enter title #1: The Cat Who Knew C++
```

```
Enter your rating (0-10): 6
Enter title #2: Felonious Felines
Enter your rating (0-10): 4
Enter title #3: Warlords of Wonk
Enter your rating (0-10): 3
Enter title #4: Don't Touch That Metaphor
Enter your rating (0-10): 5
Enter title #5: Panic Oriented Programming
Enter your rating (0-10): 8
Thank you. You entered the following:
Rating  Book
6       The Cat Who Knew C++
4       Felonious Felines
3       Warlords of Wonk
5       Don't Touch That Metaphor
8       Panic Oriented Programming
```

All this program does is use the `vector` template as a convenient way to create a dynamically allocated array. Let's see an example that uses more of the class methods.

THINGS TO DO TO YOUR VECTORS

What else can the `vector` template do for you? All the STL containers provide certain basic methods, including `size()`, which returns the number of elements in a container, `swap()`, which exchanges the contents of two containers, `begin()`, which returns an iterator referring to the first element in a container, and `end()`, which returns an iterator representing *past-the-end* for the container.

What's an iterator? It's a generalization of a pointer. In fact, it can be a pointer. Or it can be an object for which pointer-like operations such as dereferencing (`operator*()`) and incrementing (`operator++()`) have been defined. As you'll see later, generalizing pointers to iterators allows the STL to provide a uniform interface for a variety of container classes, including ones for which simple pointers wouldn't work. Each container class defines a suitable iterator. The type name for this iterator is a class scope `typedef` called `iterator`. For instance, to declare an iterator for a type `double` specialization of `vector`, you would do this:

```
vector<double>::iterator pd;   // pd an iterator
```

Suppose `scores` is a `vector<double>` object:

```
vector<double> scores;
```

Then you can use the iterator pd do things like the following:

```
pd = scores.begin();  // have pd point to the first element
*pd = 22.3;           // dereference pd and assign value to first element
++pd;                 // make pd point to the next element
```

As you can see, an iterator behaves like a pointer.

What's *past-the-end*? It is an iterator referring to an element one past the last element in a container. The idea is similar to the null character being one element past the last actual character in a C-style string, except that null character is the value in the element and past-the-end is a pointer (or iterator) to the element. The `end()` member

> *"What's an iterator? It's a generalization of a pointer."*

function identifies the past-the-end location. If you set an iterator to the first element in a container and keep incrementing it, eventually it will reach past-the-end, and you will have traversed the entire contents of the container. Thus, if `scores` and `pd` are defined as above, you can display the contents with this code:

```
for (pd = scores.begin(); pd != scores.end(); pd++)
    cout << *pd << endl;;
```

All containers have the methods just discussed. The `vector` template class also has some methods that only some STL containers have. One handy method, called `push_back()` adds an element to the end of a vector. While doing so, it attends to memory management so that the vector size increases to accommodate added members. This means you can write code like the following:

```
vector<double> scores;  // create an empty vector
double temp;
while (cin >> temp && temp >= 0)
    scores.push_back(temp);
cout << "You entered " << scores.size() << " scores.\n";
```

Each loop cycle adds one more element to the `scores` vector. You don't have to pick the number of element when you write the program or when you run the program. As long as the program has access to sufficient memory, it will expand the size of `scores` as necessary.

There is an `erase()` method that removes a given range of a vector. It takes two iterator arguments defining the range to be removed. It's important to understand how the STL defines ranges using two iterators. The first iterator refers to the beginning of the range, and the second iterator is one beyond the end of the range. For example:

```
scores.erase(scores.begin(), scores.begin() + 2);
```

erases the first and second elements, that is, those referred to by `begin()` and `begin() + 1`. (Because `vector` provides random access, operations like `begin() + 2` are defined for the `vector` class iterators.) If `it1` and `it2` are two iterators, the STL literature uses the notation [p1,p2) to indicate a range starting with p1 and going up to, but not including, p2. Thus, the range [begin(), end()) encompasses the entire contents of a collection (see Figure 15-3). Also, the range [p1,p1) is an empty range. The [) notation is not part of C++, so it doesn't appear in code; it just appears in documentation.

Remember

A range [`it1`, `it2`) is specified by two iterators `it1` and `it2`, and it runs from `it1` up to, but not including, `it2`.

An `insert()` method complements `erase()`. It takes three iterator arguments. The first gives the position ahead of which new elements are to be inserted. The second and third iterator parameters define the range to be inserted. This range typically is part of another object. For example, the code:

```
vector<int> old;
vector<int> new;
...
old.insert(old.begin(), new.begin() + 1, new.end());
```

FIGURE 15.3

The STL range concept

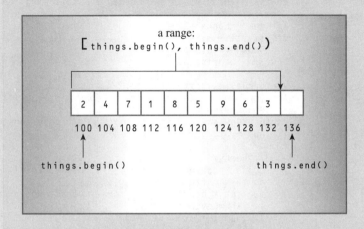

inserts all but the first element of the new vector ahead of the first element of the old vector. Incidentally, this is a case where having a past-the-end element is handy, for it makes it simple to append something to the end of a vector:

```
old.insert(old.end(), new.begin() + 1, new.end());
```

Here the new material is inserted ahead of `old.end()`, meaning it's placed *after* the last element in the vector.

Listing 15.5 illustrates the use of `size()`, `begin()`, `end()`, `push_back()`, `erase()`, and `insert()`. To simplify data-handling, the `rating` and `title` components of Listing 15.4 are incorporated into a single `Review` structure, and `FillReview()` and `ShowReview()` functions provide input and output facilities for `Review` objects.

```
Listing 15.5 vect2.cpp
// vect2.cpp -- methods and iterators
#include <iostream>
#include <string>
#include <vector>
using namespace std;

struct Review {
    string title;
    int rating;
};
bool FillReview(Review & rr);
void ShowReview(const Review & rr);
int main()
{
    vector<Review> books;
```

```
    Review temp;
    while (FillReview(temp))
        books.push_back(temp);
    cout << "Thank you. You entered the following:\n"
         << "Rating\tBook\n";
    int num = books.size();
    for (int i = 0; i < num; i++)
        ShowReview(books[i]);
    cout << "Reprising:\n"
         << "Rating\tBook\n";
    vector<Review>::iterator pr;
    for (pr = books.begin(); pr != books.end(); pr++)
        ShowReview(*pr);
    vector <Review> oldlist(books);      // copy constructor used
    if (num > 3)
    {
        // remove 2 items
        books.erase(books.begin() + 1, books.begin() + 3);
        cout << "After erasure:\n";
        for (pr = books.begin(); pr != books.end(); pr++)
            ShowReview(*pr);
        // insert 1 item
        books.insert(books.begin(), oldlist.begin() + 1,
                        oldlist.begin() + 2);
        cout << "After insertion:\n";
        for (pr = books.begin(); pr != books.end(); pr++)
            ShowReview(*pr);
    }
    books.swap(oldlist);
    cout << "Swapping oldlist with books:\n";
    for (pr = books.begin(); pr != books.end(); pr++)
        ShowReview(*pr);
    return 0;
}

bool FillReview(Review & rr)
{
    cout << "Enter book title (quit to quit): ";
    getline(cin,rr.title);
    if (rr.title == "quit")
        return false;
    cout << "Enter book rating: ";
    cin >> rr.rating;
    if (!cin)
        return false;
    cin.get();
    return true;
}

void ShowReview(const Review & rr)
{
    cout << rr.rating << "\t" << rr.title << endl;
}
```

Remember

Older implementations use `vector.h` instead of the `vector` header file. Although the order of include files shouldn't matter, g++ 2.7.1 required the `string` header file to appear before STL header files. Microsoft Visual C++ 5.0 has a bug in its `getline()` implementation that the following output to not appear until something is entered again. Also, Microsoft Visual C++ 5.0 requires that `<` and `==` be defined for the type stored in a `vector` object. That means you would have to add definitions for `operator<()` and `operator==()` for the `Review` type. The Borland C++Builder 1.0 `getline()` requires an explicit delimiter argument.

Here is a sample program run:

```
Enter book title (quit to quit): The Cat Who Knew Vectors
Enter book rating: 5
Enter book title (quit to quit): Candid Canines
Enter book rating: 7
Enter book title (quit to quit): Warriors of Wonk
Enter book rating: 4
Enter book title (quit to quit): Quantum Manners
Enter book rating: 8
Enter book title (quit to quit): quit
Thank you. You entered the following:
Rating  Book
5       The Cat Who Knew Vectors
7       Candid Canines
4       Warriors of Wonk
8       Quantum Manners
Reprising:
Rating  Book
5       The Cat Who Knew Vectors
7       Candid Canines
4       Warriors of Wonk
8       Quantum Manners
After erasure:
5       The Cat Who Knew Vectors
8       Quantum Manners
After insertion:
7       Candid Canines
5       The Cat Who Knew Vectors
8       Quantum Manners
Swapping oldlist with books:
5       The Cat Who Knew Vectors
7       Candid Canines
4       Warriors of Wonk
8       Quantum Manners
```

MORE THINGS TO DO TO YOUR VECTORS

There are many things programmers commonly do with arrays, such as search them, sort them, randomize the order, and so on. Does the vector template class have methods for these common operations? No! The STL takes a broader view, defining *non-member* functions for these operations. Thus, instead of defining a separate find() member function for each container class, it defines a single find() non-member function that can be used for all container classes. This design philosophy saves a lot of duplicate work. For example, suppose you had 8 container classes and 10 operations to support. If each class had its own member function, you'd need 8*10 or 80 separate member function definitions. But with the STL approach, you'd need just 10 separate non-member function definitions. And if you defined a new container class, providing you followed the proper guidelines, it, too, could use the existing 10 non-member functions to find, sort, and so on.

Let's examine three representative STL functions: for_each(), random_shuffle(), and sort(). The for_each() function can be used with any container class. It takes three arguments. The first two are iterators defining a range in the container, and the last is a pointer to a function. (More generally, the last argument is a function object; you'll learn about them presently.) The for_each() function then applies the pointed-to function to each container element in the range. The pointed-to function must not alter the value of the container elements. You can use the for_each() function instead of a for loop. For instance, you can replace the code:

```
vector<Review>::iterator pr;
for (pr = books.begin(); pr != books.end(); pr++)
    ShowReview(*pr);
```

with the following:

```
for_each(books.begin(), books.end(), ShowReview);
```

This enables you to avoid dirtying your hands (and code) with explicit use of iterator variables.

The random_shuffle() function takes two iterators specifying a range and rearranges the elements in that range in random order. For example, the statement

```
random_shuffle(books.begin(), books.end());
```

randomly rearranges the order of all the elements in the books vector. Unlike for_each, which works with any container class, this function requires that the container class allow random access, which the vector class does.

The sort() function, too, requires that the container support random access. It comes in two versions. The first version takes two iterators defining a range, and it sorts that range using the < operator defined for the type element stored in the container. For example,

```
vector<int> coolstuff;
...
sort(coolstuff.begin(), coolstuff.end());
```

> *" This enables you to avoid dirtying your hands (and code) with explicit use of iterator variables. "*

sorts the contents of `coolstuff` in ascending order, using the built-in < operator to compare values.

If the container elements are user-defined objects, then there has to be an opera-tor<() function defined that works with that type object in order to use `sort()`. For example, you could sort a vector containing `Review` objects if you provided either a `Review` member function or a non-member function for operator<(). Because `Review` is a structure, its members are public, and a non-member function like this would serve:

```
bool operator<(const Review & r1, const Review & r2)
{
    if (r1.title < r2.title)
        return true;
    else if (r1.title == r2.title && r1.rating < r2.rating)
        return true;
    else
        return false;
}
```

With a function like this in place, you then could sort a vector of `Review` objects (such as `books`):

```
sort(books.begin(), books.end());
```

This version of the operator<() function sorts in lexicographic order of the title members. If two objects have the same title members, they then are sorted in ratings order. But suppose you want to sort in decreasing order or in order of ratings instead of titles? Then you can use the second form of `sort()`. It takes three arguments. The first two, again, are iterators indicating the range. The final argument is a pointer to function (more generally, a function object) to be used instead of operator<() for making the comparison. The return value should be convertible to `bool`, with `false` meaning the two arguments are in the wrong order. Here's an example of such a function:

```
bool WorseThan(const Review & r1, const Review & r2)
{
    if (r1.rating < r2.rating)
        return true;
    else
        return false;
}
```

With this function in place, you can use the following statement to sort the `books` vector of `Review` objects in order of increasing rating values:

```
sort(books.begin(), books.end(), WorseThan);
```

Note that the `WorseThan()` function does a less complete job than operator<() of ordering `Review` objects. If two objects have the same title member, the operator<() function sorts using the rating member. But if two objects have the same rating member, `WorseThan()` treats them as equivalent. The first kind of ordering is called *total ordering*, and the second kind is called *strict weak ordering*. With total ordering, if both $a < b$ and $b < a$ are false, then a and b must be identical. With strict weak ordering, that's not so. They might be identical, or they might just have one aspect that is the same, such as the `rating` member in the `WorseThan()` example. So instead of saying the two objects are identical, the best you can say for strict weak ordering is that they are *equivalent*.

Listing 15.6 illustrates the use of these STL functions.

Listing 15.6 vect3.cpp

```cpp
// vect3.cpp -- using STL functions
#include <iostream>
#include <string>
#include <vector>
#include <algorithm>
using namespace std;

struct Review {
    string title;
    int rating;
};

bool operator<(const Review & r1, const Review & r2);
bool worseThan(const Review & r1, const Review & r2);
bool FillReview(Review & rr);
void ShowReview(const Review & rr);
int main()
{
    vector<Review> books;
    Review temp;
    while (FillReview(temp))
        books.push_back(temp);
    cout << "Thank you. You entered the following "
         << books.size() << " ratings:\n"
           << "Rating\tBook\n";
    for_each(books.begin(), books.end(), ShowReview);

    sort(books.begin(), books.end());
    cout << "Sorted by title:\nRating\tBook\n";
    for_each(books.begin(), books.end(), ShowReview);

    sort(books.begin(), books.end(), worseThan);
    cout << "Sorted by rating:\nRating\tBook\n";
    for_each(books.begin(), books.end(), ShowReview);

    random_shuffle(books.begin(), books.end());
    cout << "After shuffling:\nRating\tBook\n";
    for_each(books.begin(), books.end(), ShowReview);

    return 0;
}

bool operator<(const Review & r1, const Review & r2)
{
    if (r1.title < r2.title)
        return true;
    else if (r1.title == r2.title && r1.rating < r2.rating)
        return true;
    else
        return false;
}
```

```
bool worseThan(const Review & r1, const Review & r2)
{
    if (r1.rating < r2.rating)
        return true;
    else
        return false;
}

bool FillReview(Review & rr)
{
    cout << "Enter book title (quit to quit): ";
    getline(cin,rr.title);
    if (rr.title == "quit")
        return false;
    cout << "Enter book rating: ";
    cin >> rr.rating;
    if (!cin)
        return false;
    cin.get();
    return true;
}

void ShowReview(const Review & rr)
{
    cout << rr.rating << "\t" << rr.title << endl;
}
```

Remember

Older implementations use `vector.h` instead of the `vector` header file and `algo.h` instead of the `algorithm` header file. Although the order of include files shouldn't matter, g++ 2.7.1 required the `string` header file to appear before STL header files. The Microsoft Visual C++ 5.0 `getline()` has a bug that delays the next output line appearing until after the next input. Also, Microsoft Visual C++ 5.0 requires you to define `operator==()` in addition to `operator<()`. The Borland C++Builder 1.0 `getline()` requires an explicit delimiter argument.

Here's a sample run:

```
Enter book title (quit to quit): The Cat Who Can Teach You Weight Loss
Enter book rating: 8
Enter book title (quit to quit): The Dogs of Dharma
Enter book rating: 6
Enter book title (quit to quit): The Wimps of Wonk
Enter book rating: 3
Enter book title (quit to quit): Farewell and Delete
Enter book rating: 7
Enter book title (quit to quit): quit
Thank you. You entered the following 4 ratings:
Rating  Book
8       The Cat Who Can Teach You Weight Loss
```

```
6        The Dogs of Dharma
3        The Wimps of Wonk
7        Farewell and Delete
Sorted by title:
Rating   Book
7        Farewell and Delete
8        The Cat Who Can Teach You Weight Loss
6        The Dogs of Dharma
3        The Wimps of Wonk
Sorted by rating:
Rating   Book
3        The Wimps of Wonk
6        The Dogs of Dharma
7        Farewell and Delete
8        The Cat Who Can Teach You Weight Loss
After shuffling:
Rating   Book
7        Farewell and Delete
3        The Wimps of Wonk
6        The Dogs of Dharma
8        The Cat Who Can Teach You Weight Loss
```

Generic Programming

> *Just as templates make the algorithms independent of the type of data stored, iterators make the algorithms independent of the type of container used.*

Now that you have some experience using the STL, let's look at the underlying philosophy. The STL is an example of *generic programming*. Object-oriented programming concentrates on the data aspect of programming, while generic programming concentrates on algorithms. The main things the two approaches have in common are abstraction and the creation of reusable code, but the philosophies are quite different

A goal of generic programming is to write code that is independent of data types. Templates are the C++ tools for doing generic programs. Templates, of course, let you define a function or class in terms of a generic type. The STL goes further by providing a generic representation of algorithms. Templates make this possible, but not without the added element of careful and conscious design. To see how this mixture of templates and design works, let's see why iterators are needed.

WHY ITERATORS?

Understanding iterators is perhaps the key to understanding the STL. Just as templates make the algorithms independent of the type of data stored, iterators make the algorithms independent of the type of container used. Thus, they are an essential component of the STL's generic approach.

To see why iterators are needed, let's look at how you might implement a find function for two different data representations and then see how you could generalize the approach. First, consider a function that searches an ordinary array of double for a particular value. You could write the function like this:

```
double * find_ar(double * ar, int n, const double & val)
{
```

```
        for (int i = 0; i < n; i++)
            if (ar[i] == val)
                return &ar[i];
        return 0;
    }
```

If the function finds the value in the array, it returns the address in the array where the value is found; otherwise it returns the null pointer. It uses subscript notation to move through the array. You could use a template to generalize to arrays of any type having an == operator. Nonetheless, this algorithm is still tied to one particular data structure—the array.

So let's look at searching another kind of data structure, the linked list. (Chapter 11 used a linked list to implement a Queue class.) The list consists of linked Node structures:

```
struct Node
{
    double item;
    Node * p_next;
};
```

Suppose you have a pointer pointing to the first node in the list. The p_next pointer in each node points to the next node, and the p_next pointer for the last node in the list is set to 0. You could write a find_ll() function this way:

```
Node* find_ll(Node * head, const double & val)
{
    Node * start;
    for (start = head; start!= 0; start = start->next)
        if (start->item == val)
            return start;
    return 0;
}
```

Again, you could use a template to generalize this to lists of any data type supporting the == operator. Nonetheless, this algorithm is still tied to one particular data structure—the linked list.

If you consider details of implementation, the two find functions use different algorithms: one uses array indexing to move through a list of items, the other resets start to start->next. But broadly, the two algorithms are the same: compare the value with each value in the container in sequence until you find a match.

The goal of generic programming would be to have a single find function that would work with arrays or linked lists or any other container type. That is, not only should the function be independent of the data type stored in the container, it should be independent of the data structure of the container itself. Templates provide a generic representation for the data type stored in a container. What's needed is a generic representation of the process of moving through the values in a container. The iterator is that generalized representation.

What properties should an iterator have in order to implement a find function? Here's a short list:

- You should be able to dereference an iterator in order to access the value to which it refers. That is, if p is an iterator, *p should be defined.

- You should be able to assign one iterator to another. That is, if p and q are iterators, the expression p = q should be defined.

- You should be able to compare one iterator to another for equality. That is, if p and q are iterators, the expressions p == q and p != q should be defined.

- You should be able to move an iterator through all the elements of a container. This can be satisfied by defining ++p and p++ for an iterator p.

There are more things an iterator could do, but nothing more it need do, at least, not for the purposes of a find function. Actually, the STL defines several levels of iterators of increasing capabilities, and we'll return to that matter later. Note, by the way, that an ordinary pointer meets the requirements of an iterator. Hence, you can rewrite the find_arr() function like this:

```
typedef double * iterator;
iterator find_ar(iterator ar, int n, const double & val)
{
    for (int i = 0; i < n; i++, ar++)
        if (*ar == val)
            return ar;
    return 0;
}
```

For the find_ll()function, you can define an iterator class that defines the * and ++ operators:

```
struct Node
{
    double item;
    Node * p_next;
};

class iterator
{
    Node * pt;
public:
    iterator() : pt(0) {}
    iterator (Node * pn) : pt(pn) {}
    double operator*() { return pt->item;}
    iterator& operator++()     // for ++it
    {
        pt = pt->next;
        return *this;
    }
    iterator operator++(int)   // for it++
    {
        iterator tmp = *this;
        pt = pt->next;
        return tmp;
    }
// ... operator==(), operator!=(), etc.
};
```

(To distinguish between the prefix and postfix versions of the ++ operator, C++ adopted the convention of letting operator++() be the prefix version and opera-tor++(int) be the postfix version; the argument is never used, hence needn't be given a name.)

The main point here is not how, in detail, to define the iterator class, but that with such a class, the second find function can be written like this:

```
iterator find_ll(iterator head, const double & val)
{
    iterator start;
    for (start = head; start!= 0; ++start)
        if (*start == val)
            return start;
    return 0;
}
```

This is very nearly the same as find_ar(). The point of difference is in how the two functions determine if they've reached the end of the values being searched. The find_ar() function uses an element count, while find_ll() uses a null value stored in the final node. Remove that difference, and you can make the two functions identical. For example, you could require that both the array and the linked list have one additional element after the last official element. That is, have both the array and the linked list have a past-the-end element, and end the search when the iterator reaches the past-the-end position. Then find_ar() and find_ll() will have the same way of detecting the end of data and become identical algorithms. Note that requiring a past-the-end element moves from making requirements upon iterators to making requirements upon the container class.

The STL follows the approach just outlined. First, each container class (vector, list, deque, and so on) defines an iterator type appropriate to the class. For one class, the iterator might be a pointer, for another, it might be an object. Whatever the implementation, the iterator will provide the needed operations, such as * and ++. (Some classes may need more operations than others.) Next, each container class will have a past-the-end marker, which is the value assigned to an iterator when it has been incremented one past the last value in the container. Have begin() and end() methods that return iterators to the first element in a container and to the past-the-end position. Have the ++ operation take an iterator from the first element to past-the-end, visiting every container element en route.

To use a container class, you don't need to know how its iterators are implemented nor how past-the-end is implemented. It's enough to know it does have iterators, that begin() returns an iterator to the first element and that end() returns an iterator to past-the-end. For example, suppose you want to print the values in a vector<double> object. Then you can do this:

```
vector<double>::iterator pr;
for (pr = scores.begin(); pr != scores.end(); pr++)
    cout << *pr << endl;
```

Here the line

```
vector<double>::iterator pr;
```

identifies pr as the iterator type defined for the vector<double> class. If you used the list<double> class template instead to store scores, you could use this code:

```
list<double>::iterator pr;
for (pr = scores.begin(); pr != scores.end(); pr++)
    cout << *pr << endl;
```

The only change is in the type declared for pr. Thus, by having each class define appropriate iterators and designing the classes in a uniform fashion, the STL lets you write the same code for containers having quite dissimilar internal representations.

Actually, as a matter of style, it's better to avoid using the iterators directly; instead, if possible, use an STL function, such as for_each(), that takes care of the details for you.

Let's summarize the STL approach. Start with an algorithm for processing a container. Express it in as general terms as possible, making it independent of data type and container type. To make the general algorithm work with specific cases, define iterators that meet the needs of the algorithm and place requirements on the container design. That is, basic iterator properties and container properties stem from requirements placed upon them by the algorithm.

KINDS OF ITERATORS

Different algorithms have different requirements for iterators. For example, a find algorithm needs the ++ operator to be defined so the iterator can step through the entire container. It needs read access to data but not write access. (It just looks at data and doesn't change it.) A sort algorithm, however, requires random access so that it can swap the two non-adjacent elements. If iter is an iterator, you can get random access by defining the + operator so that you can use expressions like iter + 10. Also, a sort algorithm needs to be able both to read and to write data.

The STL defines five kinds of iterators and describes its algorithms in terms of which kinds of iterators it needs. The five kinds are the *input iterator*, *output iterator*, *forward iterator*, *bidirectional iterator*, and *random access iterator*. For example, the find() prototype looks like this:

```
template<class InputIterator, class T>
InputIterator find(InputIterator first, InputIterator last, const T&
value);
```

This tells you that this algorithm requires an input iterator. Similarly, the prototype

```
template<class RandomAccessIterator>
void sort(RandomAccessIterator first, RandomAccessIterator last);
```

tells you that the sort algorithm requires a random access iterator.

All five kinds of iterators can be dereferenced (that is, the * operator is defined for them) and can be compared for equality (using the == operator, possibly overloaded) and inequality (using the != operator, possibly overloaded.) If two iterators test as equal, then dereferencing one should produce the same value as dereferencing the second. That is, if:

```
iter1 == iter2
```

is true, then the following also is true:

```
*iter1 == *iter2
```

Of course these properties hold true for built-in operators and pointers, so these requirements are guides for what you must do when overloading these operators for an iterator class. Now let's look at other iterator properties.

Input Iterator

The term "input" is used from the viewpoint of a program. That is, information going from the container to the program is considered input, just as information from a keyboard to the program is considered input. So an input iterator is one that can be used by a program to read values from a container. In particular, dereferencing an input iterator must allow a program to read a value from a container, but it needn't allow a program to alter that value. So algorithms that require an input iterator are algorithms that don't change values held in a container.

An input iterator has to allow you to access all the values in a container. It does so by supporting the ++ operator, both in prefix and suffix form. If you set an input operator to the first element in a container and increment it until reaching past-the-end, it will point to every container item once en route. Incidentally, there is no guarantee that traversing a container a second time with an input iterator will move through the values in the same order. Also, after an input iterator has been incremented, there is no guarantee that its prior value can still be dereferenced. Any algorithm based on an input iterator, then, should be a single-pass algorithm that doesn't rely upon iterator values from a previous pass or upon earlier iterator values from the same pass.

Note that an input iterator is a one-way iterator; it can increment, but it can't back up.

Output Iterator

Here the term "output" indicates that the iterator is used for transferring information from a program to a container. The output iterator is similar to the input iterator, except that dereferencing is guaranteed to allow a program to alter a container value, but not to read it. If the ability to write without reading seems strange, keep in mind that property also applies to output sent to your display; cout can modify the stream of characters sent to the display, but it can't read what's on the screen. The STL is general enough that its containers can represent output devices, so you can run into the same situation with containers. Also, if an algorithm modifies the contents of a container (for example, by generating new values to be stored) without reading the contents, there's no reason to require that it use an iterator that can read the contents.

In short, you can use an input iterator for single-pass, read-only algorithms and an output operator for single-pass, write-only algorithms.

Forward Iterator

Like the input and output iterators, the forward iterator uses only the ++ operators for navigating through a container. So it can only go forward through a container one element at a time. However, unlike input and output iterators, it always goes through a sequence of values in the same order. Also, after you increment a forward iterator, you still can dereference the prior iterator value and get the same value. These properties make multiple pass algorithms possible.

A forward iterator can allow you to both read and modify data, or it can allow you just to read it:

```
int * pirw;       // read-write iterator
const int * pir;  // read-only iterator
```

Bidirectional Iterator

Suppose you have an algorithm that needs to be able to traverse a container in both directions? For example, a reverse function could swap the first and last elements, increment the pointer to the first element, decrement the pointer to a second element, and repeat the process. A bidirectional iterator has all the features of a forward iterator and adds support for the two decrement operators (prefix and postfix).

Random Access Iterator

Some algorithms, such as sort and binary search, require the capability to jump directly to an arbitrary element of a container. This is termed random access and requires a random access iterator. It has all the features of a bidirectional iterator, plus it adds operations (like pointer addition) supporting random access and relational operators for ordering the elements. Table 15.3 lists the operations a random access iterator has beyond those of the bidirectional iterator. In this table, X represents a random iterator type, T represents the type pointed to, a and b are iterator values, n is an integer, and r is random iterator variable or reference.

Expressions like a + n are valid only if both a and a + n lie within the range of the container (including past-the-end).

TABLE 15.3
RANDOM ACCESS ITERATOR OPERATIONS

EXPRESSION	COMMENTS
a + n	points to the nth element after the one a points to
n + a	same as a + n
a - n	points to the nth element before the one a points to
r += n	equivalent to r = r + n
r -= n	equivalent to r = r - n
a[n]	equivalent to *(a + n)
b - a	the value of n such that b = a + n
a < b	true of b - a > 0
a > b	true if b < a
a >= b	true if !(a < b)
a <= b	true if !(a > b)

Iterator Hierarchy

You probably noticed that the iterator kinds form a hierarchy. A forward iterator has all the capabilities of an input iterator and of an output iterator plus its own capabilities. A bidirectional iterator has all the capabilities of a forward iterator plus its own capabilities. And a random access iterator has all the capabilities of a forward iterator plus its own capabilities. Table 15.4 summarizes the main iterator capabilities. In it, i is an iterator, n is an integer.

An algorithm written in terms of a particular kind of iterator can use that kind of iterator or any other iterator that has the required capabilities. So a container with, say, a random-access iterator can use an algorithm written for an input iterator.

Why all these different kinds of iterators? The idea is to write an algorithm using the iterator with the fewest requirements possible, allowing it to be used with the largest range of containers. Thus, the find() function, by using a lowly input iterator, can be used with any container containing readable values. The sort() function, however, by requiring a random access iterator, can be used just with containers that support that kind of iterator.

Note that the various iterator kinds are not defined types; rather, they are conceptual characterizations. As mentioned earlier, each container class defines a class scope typedef name called iterator. So the vector<int> class has iterators of type vector<int>::iterator. But the documentation for this class would tell you that vector iterators are random access iterators. That, in turn, allows you to use algorithms based

TABLE 15.4
ITERATOR CAPABILITIES

ITERATOR CAPABILITY	INPUT	OUTPUT	FORWARD	BIDIRECTIONAL	RANDOM ACCESS
dereferencing read	yes	no	yes	yes	yes
dereferencing write	no	yes	yes	yes	yes
fixed and repeatable order	no	no	yes	yes	yes
++i i++	yes	yes	yes	yes	yes
--i i--	no	no	no	yes	yes
i[n]	no	no	no	no	yes
i + n	no	no	no	no	yes
i - n	no	no	no	no	yes
i += n	no	no	no	no	yes
i -=n	no	no	no	no	yes

upon any iterator type because a random access iterator has all the iterator capabilities. Similarly, a `list<int>` class has iterators of type `list<int>::iterator`. The STL implements a doubly linked list, so it uses a bidirectional iterator. Thus, it can't use algorithms based on random access iterators, but it can use algorithms based on less demanding iterators.

Concepts, Refinements, and Models

The STL has several features, such as kinds of iterators, that aren't expressible in the C++ language. That is, although you can design, say, a class having the properties of a forward iterator, you can't have the compiler restrict an algorithm to only using that class. The reason is that the forward iterator is a set of requirements, not a type. The requirements could be satisfied by an iterator class you've designed, but it also can be satisfied by an ordinary pointer. An STL algorithm works with any iterator implementation that meets its requirements. STL literature uses the word *concept* to describe a set of requirements. Thus, there is an input iterator concept, a forward iterator concept, and so on. By the way, if you do need iterators for, say, a container class you're designing, the STL does include iterator templates for the standard varieties.

Concepts can have an inheritance-like relationship. For instance, a bidirectional iterator inherits the capabilities of a forward iterator. However, you can't apply the C++ inheritance mechanism to iterators. For example, you might implement a forward iterator as a class and a bidirectional iterator as a regular pointer. So, in terms of the C++ language, this particular bidirectional iterator, being a built-in type, couldn't be derived from a class. Conceptually, however, it does inherit. Some STL literature uses the term *refinement* to indicate this conceptual inheritance. Thus, a bidirectional iterator is a refinement of the forward iterator concept.

A particular implementation of a concept is termed a *model*. Thus, an ordinary pointer-to-`int` is a model of the concept random access iterator. It's also a model of forward iterator, for it satisfies all the requirements of that concept.

> " *STL literature uses the word concept to describe a set of requirements.* "

The Pointer as Iterator

Iterators are generalizations of pointers, and a pointer satisfies all the iterator requirements. Iterators form the interface for STL algorithms, and pointers are iterators, so STL algorithms can use pointers to operate upon non-STL containers. For example, you can use STL algorithms with arrays. Suppose `Receipts` is an array of `double` values, and you would like to sort in ascending order:

```
const int SIZE = 100;
double Receipts[SIZE];
```

The STL `sort()` function, recall, takes as arguments an iterator pointing to the first element in a container and an iterator pointing to past-the-end. Well, `&Receipts[0]` (or just `Receipts`) is the address of the first element, and `&Receipts[SIZE]` (or just `Receipts + SIZE`) is the address of the element following the last element in the array. Thus, the function call:

```
sort(Receipts, Receipts + SIZE);
```

sorts the array. C++, by the way, does guarantee that the expression `Receipts + n` is defined as long as the result lies in the array or one past the end.

Thus, the fact that pointers are iterators and that algorithms are iterator-based makes it possible to apply STL algorithms to ordinary arrays. Similarly, you can apply STL algorithms to data forms of your own design, providing you supply suitable iterators (which may be pointers or objects) and past-the-end indicators.

`copy()`, `ostream_iterator`, and `istream_iterator`

The STL provides some predefined iterators. To see why, let's establish some background. There is an algorithm (`copy()`) for copying data from one container to another. This algorithm is expressed in terms of iterators, so it can copy from one kind of container to another or even from or to an array, because you can use pointers into an array as iterators. For instance, the following copies an array into a vector:

```
int casts[10] = {6, 7, 2, 9 ,4 , 11, 8, 7, 10, 5};
vector<int> dice[10];
copy(casts, casts + 10, dice.begin());   // copy array to vector
```

The first two iterator arguments to `copy()` represent a range to be copied, and the final iterator argument represents the location to which the first item is copied. The first two arguments must be input iterators (or better), and the final argument must be an output iterator (or better). The `copy()` function overwrites existing data in the destination container, and the container has to be large enough to hold the copied elements. So you can't use `copy()` to place data in an empty vector, at least not without resorting to a trick to be revealed later.

Now suppose you wanted to copy information to the display. You could use `copy()` providing there was an iterator representing the output stream. The STL provides such an iterator with the `ostream_iterator` template. Using STL terminology, this template is a model of the output iterator concept. It is also an example of an *adapter*, a class or function that converts some other interface to an interface used by the STL. You can create an iterator of this kind by including the `iterator` (formerly `itera-tor.h`) header file and making a declaration:

```
#include <iterator>
...
ostream_iterator<int, char> out_iter(cout, " ");
```

The `out_iter` iterator now becomes an interface allowing you to use `cout` to display information. The first template argument (`int`, in this case) indicates the data type being sent to the output stream. The second template argument (`char`, in this case) indicates the character type used by the output stream. (Another possible value would be `wchar_t`.) The first constructor argument (`cout`, in this case), identifies the output stream being used. It also could be a stream used for file output, as discussed in Chapter 16, "Input, Output, and Files." The final character string argument is a separator to be displayed after each item sent to the output stream.

Older implementations use just the first template argument for the
`ostream_iterator`:
`ostream_iterator<int> out_iter(cout, " "); // older`
`                                           // implementation`

You could use the iterator like this:

```
*out_iter++ = 15;    // works like cout << 15 << " ";
```

For a regular pointer, this would mean assigning the value 15 to the pointed to location, and then incrementing the pointer. For this `ostream_iterator`, however, the
statement means send 15 and then a string consisting of a space to the output stream
managed by `cout`. Then get ready for the next output operation. You can use the iterator with `copy()` as follows:

```
copy(dice.begin(), dice.end(), out_iter);    // copy vector to output
stream
```

This would mean to copy the entire range of the `dice` container to the output stream,
that is, to display the contents of the container.

Or, you can skip creating a named iterator and construct an anonymous iterator
instead. That is, you can use the adapter like this:

```
copy(dice.begin(), dice.end(), ostream_iterator<int, char>(cout, " ") );
```

Similarly, the `iterator` header file defines an `istream_iterator` template for adapting `istream` input to the iterator interface. It is a model of input iterator. You can use
two `istream_iterator` objects to define an input range for `copy()`:

```
copy(istream_iterator<int, char>(cin),
     istream_iterator<int, char>(), dice.begin());
```

Like `ostream_iterator`, `istream_iterator` uses two template arguments. The first
indicates the data type to be read, and the second indicates the character type used by
the input stream. Using a constructor argument of `cin` means to use the input stream
managed by `cin`. Omitting the constructor argument indicates input failure, so the
above code means to read from the input stream until end-of-file, type mismatch, or
some other input failure.

Other Useful Iterators

The `iterator` header file provides some other special-purpose predefined iterator types
in addition to `ostream_iterator` and `istream_iterator`. They are `reverse_itera-`
`tor`, `back_insert_iterator`, `front_insert_iterator`, and `insert_iterator`.

Let's start with seeing what a reverse iterator does. In essence, incrementing a
reverse iterator causes it to decrement. Why not just decrement a regular iterator? The
main reason is to simplify using existing functions. Suppose you want to display the
contents of the `dice` container. As you just saw, you can use `copy()` and an
`ostream_iterator` to copy the contents to the output stream:

```
ostream_iterator<int, char> out_iter(cout, " ");
copy(dice.begin(), dice.end(), out_iter);  // display in forward order
```

Now suppose you want to print the contents in reverse order. (Perhaps you are performing time-reversal studies.) There are several approaches that don't work, but rather than wallow in them, let's go to one that does. The `vector` class has a member function called `rbegin()` that returns a reverse iterator pointing to past-the-end and a member `rend()` that returns a reverse iterator pointing to the first element. Because incrementing a reverse iterator makes it decrement, you can use the statement:

```
copy(dice.rbegin(), dice.rend(), out_iter); // display in reverse order
```

to display the contents backward. You don't even have to declare a reverse iterator.

Both `rbegin()` and `end()` return the same value (past-the-end), but as a different type (`reverse_iterator` versus `iterator`). Similarly, both `rend()` and `begin()` return the same value (an iterator to the first element), but as a different type.

There is a special compensation reverse pointers have to make. Suppose `rp` is a reverse pointer initialized to `dice.rbegin()`. What should `*rp` be? Since `rbegin()` returns past-the-end, you shouldn't try to dereference that address. Similarly, if `rend()` is really the location of the first element, `copy()` would stop one location earlier because the end of the range is not in a range. Reverse pointers solve both problems by decrementing first, then dereferencing. That is, `*rp` dereferences the iterator value immediately preceding the current value of `*rp`. If `rp` points to position six, `*rp` is the value of position five, and so on. Listing 15.7 illustrates using `copy()`, an `istream` iterator and a reverse iterator.

Listing 15.7 copy.cpp

```cpp
// copy.cpp -- copy() and iterators
#include <iostream>
#include <iterator>
#include <vector>
using namespace std;

int main()
{
    int casts[10] = {6, 7, 2, 9 ,4 , 11, 8, 7, 10, 5};
    vector<int> dice(10);
    // copy from array to vector
    copy(casts, casts + 10, dice.begin());
    cout << "Let the dice be cast!\n";
    // create an ostream iterator
    ostream_iterator<int, char> out_iter(cout, " ");
    // copy from vector to output
    copy(dice.begin(), dice.end(), out_iter);
    cout << endl;
    cout <<"Implicit use of reverse iterator.\n";
    copy(dice.rbegin(), dice.rend(), out_iter);
    cout << endl;
    cout <<"Explicit use of reverse iterator.\n";
    vector<int>::reverse_iterator ri;
    for (ri = dice.rbegin(); ri != dice.rend(); ++ri)
        cout << *ri << ' ';
    cout << endl;

    return 0;
}
```

Older implementations may use the `iterator.h` and `vector.h` header files instead. Also, older implementations may use `ostream_iterator<int>` instead of `ostream_iterator<int, char>`.

Here is the output:

```
Let the dice be cast!
6 7 2 9 4 11 8 7 10 5
Implicit use of reverse iterator.
5 10 7 8 11 4 9 2 7 6
Explicit use of reverse iterator.
5 10 7 8 11 4 9 2 7 6
```

> *If you have the choice of explicitly declaring iterators or of using STL functions to handle the matter internally, for instance, by passing an `rbegin()` return value to a function, take the latter course.*

If you have the choice of explicitly declaring iterators or using STL functions to handle the matter internally, for instance, by passing an `rbegin()` return value to a function, take the latter course. It's one less thing to do and one less opportunity to experience human fallibility.

The other three iterators (`back_insert_iterator`, `front_insert_iterator`, and `insert_iterator`) also increase the generality of the STL algorithms. Many STL functions are like `copy()` in that they send their results to a location indicated by an output iterator. Recall that

```
copy(casts, casts + 10, dice.begin());
```

copies values to the location beginning at `dice.begin()`. These values overwrite the prior contents in `dice`, and the function assumes that `dice` has enough room to hold the values. That is, `copy()` does not automatically adjust the size of the destination to fit the information sent to it. Listing 15.7 took care of that situation by declaring `dice` to have 10 elements, but suppose you don't know in advance how big `dice` should be? Or suppose you want to add elements to `dice` rather than overwrite existing ones?

The three insert iterators solve these problems by converting the copying process to an insertion process. Insertion adds new elements without overwriting existing data and uses automatic memory allocation to ensure the new information fits. A `back_insert_iterator` inserts items at the end of the container, while a `front_insert_iterator` inserts items at the front. Finally, the `insert_iterator` inserts items in front of the location specified as an argument to the `insert_iterator` constructor. All three are models of the output container concept.

There are restrictions. A back insertion iterator can be used only with container types that allow rapid insertion at the end. (Rapid means a constant time algorithm; the section on containers discusses this concept further.) The `vector` class qualifies. A front insertion iterator can be used only with container types allowing constant time insertion at the beginning. Here the `vector` class doesn't qualify. The insertion iterator doesn't have these restrictions. Thus, you can use it to insert material at the front of a vector. However, a front insertion iterator will do so faster for those container types that support it.

Remember

> **You can use an insert iterator to convert an algorithm that copies data to one that inserts data.**

These iterators take the container type as a template argument and the actual container identifier as a constructor argument. That is, to create a back insertion iterator for a vector<int> container called dice, you do this:

```
back_insert_iterator<vector<int> > back_iter(dice);
```

Declaring a front insertion iterator has the same form. An insertion iterator declaration has an additional constructor argument to identify the insertion location:

```
insert_iterator<vector<int> > insert_iter(dice, dice.begin() );
```

Listing 15.8 illustrates using two of these iterators.

Listing 15.8 inserts.cpp

```cpp
// inserts.cpp -- copy() and insert iterators
#include <iostream>
#include <string>
#include <iterator>
#include <vector>
using namespace std;

int main()
{
    string s1[4] = {"fine", "fish", "fashion", "fate"};
    string s2[2] = {"busy", "bats"};
    string s3[2] = {"silly", "singers"};
    vector<string> words(4);
    copy(s1, s1 + 4, words.begin());
    ostream_iterator<string, char> out(cout, " ");

    copy (words.begin(), words.end(), out);

    cout << endl;

// construct anonymous back_insert_iterator object

    copy(s2, s2 + 2, back_insert_iterator<vector<string> >(words));

    copy (words.begin(), words.end(), out);

    cout << endl;

// construct anonymous insert_iterator object

    copy(s3, s3 + 2, insert_iterator<vector<string> >(words,
words.begin()));

    copy (words.begin(), words.end(), out);

    cout << endl;

    return 0;
}
```

Remember

Older versions may use `list.h` and `iterator.h`. Also, older versions may use `ostream_iterator<int>` instead of `ostream_iterator<int,char>`.

Here is the output:

```
fine fish fashion fate
fine fish fashion fate busy bats
silly singers fine fish fashion fate busy bats
```

If you're feeling overwhelmed by all the iterator varieties, keep in mind that using them will make them familiar. Also keep in mind that these predefined iterators expand the generality of the STL algorithms. Thus, not only can `copy()` copy information from one container to another, it can copy information from a container to the output stream and from the input stream to a container. And you also can use `copy()` to insert material into another container. So you wind up with a single function doing the work of many. And because `copy()` is just one of several STL functions that use an output iterator, these predefined iterators multiply the capabilities of those functions, too.

KINDS OF CONTAINERS

The STL has both container concepts and container types. The concepts are general categories with names like container, sequence container, associative container, and so on. The container types are templates you can use to create specific container objects. The eleven container types are `deque`, `list`, `queue`, `priority_queue`, `stack`, `vector`, `map`, `multimap`, `set`, `multiset`, and `bitset`. (This chapter won't discuss `bitset`, which is a container for dealing with data at the bit level.) Because the concepts categorize the types, let's start with them.

The Container Concept

There is no type corresponding to the basic container concept, but the concept describes elements common to all the container classes. It's sort of a conceptual abstract base class—conceptual because the container classes don't actually use the inheritance mechanism. Or putting it another way, the container concept lays down a set of requirements that all STL container classes must satisfy.

A container is an object that stores other objects, which are all of a single type. The stored objects may be objects in the OOP sense, or they may be values of built-in types. Data stored in a container are *owned* by the container. That means when a container expires, so do the data stored in the container. (However, if the data are pointers, the pointed-to data does not necessarily expire.)

You can't store just any kind of object in a container. In particular, the type has to be *copy constructible* and *assignable*. Basic types satisfy these requirements as do class types unless the class definition makes one or both of the copy constructor and the assignment operator private or protected.

The basic container doesn't guarantee that its elements are stored in any particular order or that the order doesn't change, but refinements to the concept may add such guarantees. All containers do provide certain features and operations. Table 15.5 summarizes several of these common features. In the table, X represents a container type, such as vector, T represents the type of object stored in the container, a and b represent values of type X, and u represents an identifier of type X.

The complexity column describes the time needed to perform an operator. This table lists three possibilities, which, from fastest to slowest, are as follows:

- compile time
- constant time
- linear time

If the complexity is compile time, the action is performed during compilation and uses no execution time. A constant complexity means the operation takes place during runtime but doesn't depend upon the number of elements in an object. A linear complexity means the time is proportional to the number of elements. Thus, if a and b are containers, a == b has linear complexity because the == operation may have to be applied to each element of the container. Actually, that is a worst-case scenario. If two containers have different sizes, no individual comparisons need be made.

CONSTANT TIME AND LINEAR TIME COMPLEXITY

Consider a long narrow box filled with large packages arranged in a line, and suppose the box is open at just one end. Suppose my task is to unload the package at the open end. This is a constant time task. Whether there are 10 packages or a 1000 packages behind the one at the end makes no difference.

Now suppose my task is to fetch the package at the closed end of the box. This is a linear time task. If there are 10 packages altogether, I have to unload 10 packages to get the one at the closed end. If there are 100 packages, I have to unload 100 packages at the end. Assuming I'm a tireless worker who can move only one package at a time, that will take ten times longer.

Now suppose my task is to fetch an arbitrary package. It might happen that the package I'm supposed to get is the first one at hand. However, on the average, the number of packages I have to move is still proportional to the number of packages in the container, so the task still has linear time complexity.

Replacing the long narrow box with a similar box having open sides would change the task to constant time complexity, for then I could move directly to the desired package and remove it without moving the others.

The idea of time complexity describes the effect of container size on execution time but ignores other factors. If a superhero can unload packages from a box with one open end 1000 times faster than me, the task as executed by her still has linear time complexity. In this case, her linear time performance with a closed box (open end) would be faster than my constant time performance with an open box as long as the boxes didn't have too many packages.

TABLE 15.5
SOME BASIC CONTAINER PROPERTIES

EXPRESSION	RETURN TYPE	COMMENT	COMPLEXITY
`X::iterator`	iterator type pointing to T	any iterator category except output iterator	compile time
`X::value_type`	T	the type for T	compile time
`X u;`		creates 0-size container called u	constant
`X();`		creates 0-size anonymous container	constant
`X u(a);`		copy constructor	linear
`X u = a;`		same effect as `X u(a);`	
`(&a)->~X();`	void	apply destructor to every element of a container	linear
`a.begin()`	iterator	returns an iterator referring to first element of container	constant
`a.end()`	iterator	returns an iterator that is a past-the-end value	constant
`a.size()`	unsigned integral type	number of elements, equal to `a.end()` - `a.begin()`	constant
`a.swap(b)`	void	swap contents of a and b	constant
`a == b`	convertible to bool	true if a and b have the same size and each element in a is equivalent to (`==` is true) the corresponding element in b	linear
`a != b`	convertible to bool	same as `!(a == b)`	linear

Complexity requirements are characteristic of the STL. While the details of an implementation may be hidden, the performance specifications should be public so that you know the computing cost of doing a particular operation.

Sequences

You can refine the basic container concept by adding requirements. The *sequence* is an important refinement, for six of the STL container types (deque, list, queue, prior-ity_queue, stack, and vector) are sequences. (Recall that a queue allows elements to be added at the rear end and removed from the front. A double-ended queue, represented by deque, allows addition and removal at both ends.) The sequence concept adds the requirement that the iterator be at least a forward iterator. This, in turns, guarantees that the elements are arranged in a definite order that doesn't change from one cycle of iteration to the next.

The sequence also requires that its elements be arranged in strict linear order. That is, there is a first element, a last element, and each element but the first and last have exactly one element immediately ahead of it and one element immediately after it. An array and a linked list are examples of a sequence, while a branching structure (in which each node points to two daughter nodes) would not be.

Because elements in sequence have a definite order, operations such as inserting values at a particular location and erasing a particular range become possible. Table 15.6 lists these and other operations required of a sequence. The table uses the same notation as Table 15.5, with the addition of t representing a value of type T, that is, the type of value stored in the container, of n, an integer, and of p, q, i and j, representing iterators.

TABLE 15.6
SEQUENCE REQUIREMENTS

EXPRESSION	RETURN TYPE	COMMENTS
X a(n,t);		Declares a sequence a of n copies of value t
X(n, t)		Creates an anonymous sequence of n copies of value t
X a(i, j)		Declares a sequence a initialized to the contents of range [i,j)
X(i, j)		Creates an anonymous sequence initialized to the contents of range [i,j)
a.insert(p,t)	iterator	Inserts a copy of t before p
a.insert(p,n,t)	void	Inserts n copies of t before p
a.insert(p,i,j)	void	Insert copies of elements in the range [i,j) before p
a.erase(p)	iterator	Erases the element pointed to by p
a.erase(p,q)	iterator	Erases the elements in the range [p,q)
a.clear()	void	Same as erase(begin(), end())

Because the deque, list, queue, stack, and vector template classes all are models of the sequence concept, they all support the operators of Table 15.6. In addition there are operations that are available to some of these five models. When allowed, they have constant time complexity. Table 15.7 lists these additional operations.

Table 15.7 does merit a comment or two. First, you'll notice that a[n] and a.at(n) both return a reference to the nth element (numbering from 0) in a container. The difference is that a.at(n) does bounds checking and throws an out_of_range exception if n is outside the valid range for the container. Next, you might wonder why, say, push_front() is defined for list and deque and not vector. Suppose you want to insert a new value at the front of a vector of 100 elements. To make room, you have to move element 99 to position 100, and then move element 98 to position 99, and so on. This is an operation with linear time complexity because moving 100 elements would take 100 times as long as moving a single element. But the operations in Table 15.7 are supposed to be implemented only if they can be performed with constant time complexity. The design for lists and double-ended queues, however, allows an element to be added to the front without moving the other elements to new locations, so they can implement push_front() with constant time complexity. Figure 15.4 illustrates push_front() and push_back().

Let's take a closer look at the six sequence container types.

vector

You've already seen several examples using the vector template, which is declared in the vector header file. In brief, vector is a class representation of an array. The class provides automatic memory management that allows the size of a vector object to vary dynamically, growing and shrinking as elements are added or removed. It provides random access to elements. Elements can be added to or removed from the end in constant time, but insertion and removal from the beginning and the middle is a linear time operation.

TABLE 15.7
OPTIONAL SEQUENCE REQUIREMENTS

EXPRESSION	RETURN TYPE	MEANING	CONTAINER
a.front()	T&	*a.begin()	vector, list, deque
a.back()	T&	*−a.end()	vector, list, deque
a.push_front(t)	void	a.insert(a.begin(), t)	list, deque
a.push_back(t)	void	a.insert(a.end(), t)	vector, list, deque
a.pop_front(t)	void	a.erase(a.begin())	list, deque
a.pop_back(t)	void	a.erase(−a.end())	vector, list, deque
a[n]	T&	*(a.begin() + n)	vector, deque
a.at(n)	T&	*(a.begin() + n)	vector, deque

FIGURE 15.4
*push_front() and
push_back()*

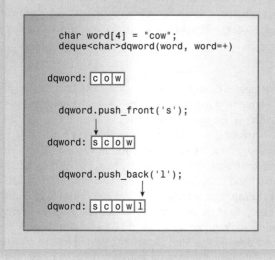

In addition to being a sequence, a vector also is a model of the *reversible container* concept. This adds two more class methods: rbegin() returns an iterator to the first element of the reversed sequence, and rend() returns a past-the-end iterator for the reversed sequence. So if dice is a vector<int> container and Show(int) is a function that displays an integer, the following code will first display the contents of dice in forward order and then in reverse order:

```
for_each(dice.begin(), dice.end(), Show);    // display in order
cout << endl;
for_each(dice.rbegin(), dice.rend(), Show);  // display in reversed order
cout << endl;
```

The iterator returned by the two methods is of a class scope type reverse_iterator. Incrementing such an iterator, recall, causes it to move through a reversible container in reverse order.

The vector template class is the simplest of the sequence types and is considered the type that should be used by default unless the program requirements are better satisfied by the particular virtues of the other types.

deque

The deque template class (declared in the deque header file) represents a double-ended queue, a type often called a *deque* (sounds like deck), for short. As implemented in the STL, it's a lot like a vector, supporting random access. The main difference is that inserting and removing items from the beginning of a deque object are constant-time operations instead of being linear-time operations the way they are for *vector*. So if most operations take place at the beginning and ends of a sequence, consider using a deque data structure.

The goal of constant time insertion and removal at both ends of a deque make the design of a deque more complex than that of a vector. Thus, while both offer random access to elements and linear time insertion and removal from the middle of a sequence, the vector should allow faster execution of these operations.

list

The list template class (declared in the list header file) represents a doubly linked list. Each element, other than the first and last, is linked to the item before it and the item following it, implying that a list can be traversed in both directions. The crucial difference between list and vector is that list provides for constant time insertion and removal of elements at any location in the list. (The vector template, recall, provides linear time insertion and removal except at the end, where it provides constant time insertion and removal.) Thus, vector emphasizes rapid access via random access, while a list emphasizes rapid insertion and removal of elements.

Like vector, list is a reversible container. Unlike vector, list does not support array notation and random access. Unlike a vector iterator, a list iterator remains pointing to the same element even after items are inserted into or removed from a container. Let's clarify this statement. Suppose you have an iterator pointing to the fifth element of a vector container. Then suppose you insert an element at the beginning of the container. All the other elements have be moved to make room, so after the insertion, the fifth element now contains the value that used to be in the fourth element. Thus the iterator points to the same location but different data. Inserting a new element into a list, however, doesn't move the existing elements; it just alters the link information. An iterator pointing to a certain item still points to the same item, but it may be linked to different items than before. Figure 15.5 illustrates this difference between vector and list.

The list template class has some list-oriented member functions in addition to those that come with sequences and reversible containers. Table 15.8 lists many of them. (For a complete list of STL methods and functions, see Appendix G.) The Alloc template parameter is one you normally don't have to worry about because it has a default value. Listing 15.9 illustrates these methods along with the insert() method.

TABLE 15.8
SOME LIST MEMBER FUNCTIONS

FUNCTION	DESCRIPTION
void merge(list<T, Alloc>& x)	Merges list x with the invoking list. Both lists must be sorted. The resulting sorted list is in the invoking list, and x is left empty. This function has linear time complexity.
void remove(const T & val)	Removes all instances of val from the list. This function has linear time complexity.
void sort()	Sorts the list using the < operator; the complexity is N log N for N elements.
void splice(iterator pos, list<T, Alloc> x)	Inserts the contents of list x in front of position pos, and x is left empty. This function has constant time complexity.
void unique()	Collapses each consecutive group of equal elements to a single element. This function has linear time complexity.

FIGURE 15.5

Effects of insertion on iterators

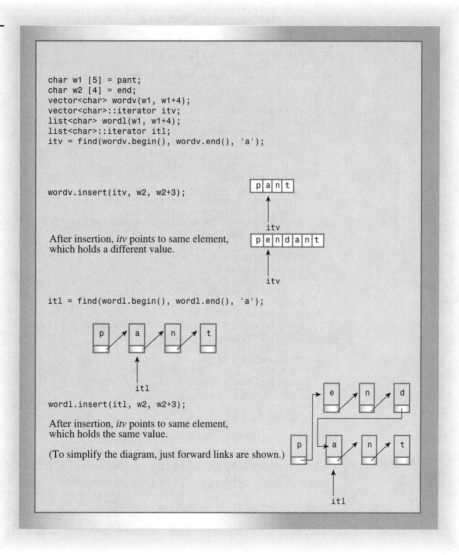

```
char w1 [5] = pant;
char w2 [4] = end;
vector<char> wordv(w1, w1+4);
vector<char>::iterator itv;
list<char> wordl(w1, w1+4);
list<char>::iterator itl;
itv = find(wordv.begin(), wordv.end(), 'a');


wordv.insert(itv, w2, w2+3);
```

After insertion, *itv* points to same element, which holds a different value.

```
itl = find(wordl.begin(), wordl.end(), 'a');




wordl.insert(itl, w2, w2+3);
```

After insertion, *itv* points to same element, which holds the same value.

(To simplify the diagram, just forward links are shown.)

Listing 15.9 list.cpp

```
// list.cpp -- using a list
#include <iostream>
#include <list>
#include <iterator>
using namespace std;

int main()
{
```

```
list<int> one(5, 2); // list of 5 2s
int stuff[5] = {1,2,4,8, 6};
list<int> two;
two.insert(two.begin(),stuff, stuff + 5 );
int more[6] = {6, 4, 2, 4, 6, 5};
list<int> three(two);
three.insert(three.end(), more, more + 6);

cout << "List one: ";
ostream_iterator<int,char> out(cout, " ");
copy(one.begin(), one.end(), out);
cout << endl << "List two: ";
copy(two.begin(), two.end(), out);
cout << endl << "List three: ";
copy(three.begin(), three.end(), out);
three.remove(2);
cout << endl << "List three minus 2s: ";
copy(three.begin(), three.end(), out);
three.splice(three.begin(), one);
cout << endl << "List three after splice: ";
copy(three.begin(), three.end(), out);
cout << endl << "List one: ";
copy(one.begin(), one.end(), out);
three.unique();
cout << endl << "List three after unique: ";
copy(three.begin(), three.end(), out);
three.sort();
three.unique();
cout << endl << "List three after sort & unique: ";
copy(three.begin(), three.end(), out);
two.sort();
three.merge(two);
cout << endl << "Sorted two merged into three: ";
copy(three.begin(), three.end(), out);
cout << endl;

return 0;
}
```

Remember

Older versions may use `list.h` and `iterator.h`. Also, older versions may use `ostream_iterator<int>` instead of `ostream_iterator<int,char>`.

Here is the output:

```
List one: 2 2 2 2
List two: 1 2 4 8 6
List three: 1 2 4 8 6 6 4 2 4 6 5
List three minus 2s: 1 4 8 6 6 4 4 6 5
List three after splice: 2 2 2 2 1 4 8 6 6 4 4 6 5
List one:
List three after unique: 2 1 4 8 6 4 6 5
List three after sort & unique: 1 2 4 5 6 8
Sorted two merged into three: 1 1 2 2 4 4 5 6 6 8 8
```

Program Notes The program uses the technique discussed earlier for using the general STL `copy()` function and an `ostream_iterator` object to display the contents of a container.

The main difference between `insert()` and `splice()` is that `insert()` inserts a copy of the original range into the destination, while `splice()` moves the original range into the destination. Thus, after the contents of `one` are spliced to `three`, `one` is left empty. (The `splice()` method has additional prototypes for moving single elements and a range of elements.) The `splice()` method leaves iterators valid. That is, if you set a particular iterator to point to an element in `one`, that iterator would still point to the same element after `splice()` relocated it in `three`.

Notice that `unique()` only reduces adjacent equal values to a single value. After the program executes `three.unique()`, `three` still contains two 4s and two 6s that weren't adjacent. But applying `sort()` and then `unique()` does limit each value to a single appearance.

There is a non-member `sort()` function (Listing 15.6), but it requires random access iterators. Because the trade-off for rapid insertion was giving up random access, you can't use the non-member `sort()` with a list. Therefore, the class includes a member version that works within the restrictions of the class.

The `list` Toolbox The `list` methods form a handy toolbox. Suppose, for example, that you have two mailing lists to organize. You could sort each list, merge them, and then use `unique()` to remove multiple entries.

The `sort()`, `merge()`, and `unique()` methods also each have a version accepting an additional argument to specify an alternative function to be used for comparing elements. Similarly, the `remove()` method has a version with an additional argument specifying a function used to determine whether or not an element is removed. These arguments are examples of predicate functions, a topic to which we'll return later.

queue

The `queue` template class (declared in the `queue` (formerly `queue.h` header file) is an adapter class. Recall that the `ostream_iterator` template is an adapter that allows an output stream to use the iterator interface. Similarly, the `queue` template allows an underlying class (`deque`, by default) to exhibit the typical queue interface.

The `queue` template is more restrictive than `deque`. Not only doesn't it permit random access to elements of a queue, the `queue` class doesn't even allow you to iterate through a queue. Instead, it limits you to the basic operations that define a queue. You can add an element to the rear of queue, remove an element from the front of a queue, view the values of the front and rear elements, check the number of elements, and test to see if the queue is empty. Table 15.9 lists these operations.

Note that `pop()` is a data removal method, not a data retrieval method. If you want to use a value from a queue, first use `front()` to retrieve the value, and then `pop()` to remove it from the queue.

TABLE 15.9
`queue` OPERATIONS

METHOD	DESCRIPTION
`bool empty() const`	Returns true if the queue is empty, and false otherwise.
`size_type size() const`	Returns the number of elements in the queue.
`T& front()`	Returns a reference to the element at the front of the queue.
`T& back()`	Returns a reference to the element at the back of the queue.
`void push(const T& x)`	Inserts x at the back of the queue.
`void pop()`	Removes the element at the front of the queue.

priority_queue

The `priority_queue` template class (also declared in the `queue` header file) is another adapter class. It supports the same operations as `queue`. The main difference is that the largest item gets moved to the front of the queue. (Life is not always fair, and neither are queues.) An internal difference is that the default underlying class is `vector`. You can alter the comparison used to determine what gets to the head of the queue by providing an optional constructor argument:

```
priority_queue<int> pq1;                    // default version
priority_queue<int> pq2(greater<int>);  // use greater<int> to order
```

The `greater<>()` function is a predefined function object discussed later in this chapter.

stack

Like queue, `stack` (declared in the `stack`—formerly `stack.h`—header file) is an adapter class. It gives an underlying class (`vector`, by default) the typical stack interface.

The `stack` template is more restrictive than `vector`. Not only doesn't it permit random access to elements of a stack, the `stack` class doesn't even allow you to iterate through a stack. Instead, it limits you to the basic operations that define a stack. You can push a value onto the top of a stack, pop an element from the top of a stack, view the value at the top of the stack, check the number of elements, and test to see if the stack is empty. Table 15.10 lists these operations.

TABLE 15.10
`stack` OPERATIONS

METHOD	DESCRIPTION
`bool empty() const`	Returns true if the stack is empty, and false otherwise.
`size_type size() const`	Returns the number of elements in the stack.
`T& top()`	Returns a reference to the element at the top of the stack.
`void push(const T& x)`	Inserts x at the top of the stack.
`void pop()`	Removes the element at the top of the stack.

Much as with `queue`, if you want to use a value from a stack, first use `top()` to retrieve the value, then use `pop()` to remove it from the queue.

ASSOCIATIVE CONTAINERS

The *associative container* is another refinement of the container concept. An associative container associates a value with a *key* and uses the key to find the value. For instance, the values could be structures representing employee information, such as name, address, office number, home and work phones, health plan, and so on, and the key could be a unique employee number. To fetch the employee information, a program would use the key to locate the employee structure. Recall that for a container X, in general, the expression `X::value_type` indicates the type of value stored in the container. For an associative container, the expression `X::key_type` indicates the type used for the key.

The strength of an associative container is that it provides rapid access to its elements. Like a sequence, an associative container allows you to insert new elements; however, you can't specify a particular location for the inserted elements. The reason is that an associative container usually has a particular algorithm for determining where to place data so that it can retrieve information quickly.

The STL provides four associative containers: `set`, `multiset`, `map`, and `multimap`. The first two types are defined in the `set` header file (formerly separately in `set.h` and `multiset.h`), and the second two types are defined in the `map` header file (formerly separately in `map.h` and `multimap.h`).

The simplest of the bunch is `set`; the value type is the same as the key type, and the keys are unique, meaning there is no more than one instance of a key in a set. Indeed, for `set`, the value is the key. The `multiset` type is like the `set` type except that it can have more than one value with the same key. For instance, if the key and value type are `int`, a `multiset` object could hold, say 1,2,2,2,3,5,7,7.

For the `map` type, the value type is different from the key type, and the keys are unique, with only one value per key. The `multimap` type is similar to `map`, except one key can be associated with multiple values.

There's too much information about these types to cover in this chapter (but Appendix G does list the methods), so let's just look at a simple example using `set` and a simple example using `multimap`.

A `set` Example

The STL `set` models several concepts. It is an associative set, it is reversible, it is sorted, and the keys are unique, so it can hold no more than one of any given value. Like `vector` and `list`, `set` uses a template parameter to provide the type stored:

```
set<string> A;   // a set of string objects
```

An optional second template argument can be used to indicate a comparison function or object to be used to order the key. By default, the `less<>` template (discussed later) is used. Older implementations may not provide a default value and thus require an explicit template parameter:

```
set<string, less<string> > A;   // older implementation
```

Consider the following code:

```
const int N = 6;
string s1[N] = {"buffoon", "thinkers", "for", "heavy", "can", "for"};
set<string> A(s1, s1 + N);   // initialize set A using a range from array
ostream_iterator<string, char> out(cout, " ");
copy(A.begin(), A.end(), out);
```

Like other containers, set has a constructor (see Table 15.6) that takes a range of iterators as arguments. This provides a simple way to initialize a set to the contents of an
array. Remember, the last element of a range is one past the end, and s1 + N points to
one position past the end of array s1. The output for this code fragment illustrates that
keys are unique (the string "for" appears twice in the array but once in the set) and
that the set is sorted:

```
buffoon can for heavy thinkers
```

Mathematics defines some standard operations for sets. The union of two sets is a set
that combines the contents of the two sets. If a particular value is common to both sets,
it appears just once in the union because of the unique key feature. The intersection of
two sets is a set consisting of those elements common to both sets. The difference
between two sets is the first set minus the elements common to both sets.

The STL provides algorithms supporting these operations. They are general functions
rather than methods, so they aren't restricted to set objects. However, all set objects
automatically satisfy the precondition for using this algorithm, namely, that the container be sorted. The set_union() function takes five iterators as arguments. The first
two define a range in one set, the second two a range in a second set, and the final iterator is an output iterator identifying a location to copy the resultant set. For example,
to display the union of sets A and B, you can do this:

```
set_union(A.begin(), A.end(), B.begin(), B.end(),
          ostream_iterator<string, char> out(cout, " "));
```

Suppose you want to place the result in a set C instead of displaying it. Then you
would want the last argument to be an iterator into C. The obvious choice is
C.begin(), but it doesn't work for two reasons. The first reason is that associative sets
treat keys as constant values, so the iterator returned by C.begin() is a constant iterator and can't be used as an output iterator. The second reason not to use C.begin()
directly is that set_union(), like copy(), overwrites existing data in a container and
requires the container have sufficient space to hold the new information. C, being
empty, does not satisfy that requirement. But the insert_iterator template discussed
earlier solves both problems. Earlier you saw that it converts copying to insertion.
Also, it models the output iterator concept, so you can use it to write to a container. So
you can construct an anonymous insert_iterator to copy information to C. The constructor, recall, takes the name of the container and an iterator as arguments:

```
set_union(A.begin(), A.end(), B.begin(), B.end(),
          insert_iterator<set<string> >(C, C.begin()));
```

The set_intersection() and set_difference() functions find the set intersection
and set difference of two sets, and they have the same interface as set_union().

Two useful set methods are `lower_bound()` and `upper_bound()`. The `lower_bound()` method takes a key as its argument and returns an iterator pointing to the first member of the set that is not less than the key argument. Similarly, the `upper_bound()` method takes a key as its argument and returns an iterator pointing to the first member of the set that is greater than the key argument. For example, if you had a set of strings, you could use these methods to identify a range encompassing all strings from `"b"` up to `"f"` in the set.

Because sorting determines where additions to a set go, the class has insertion methods that just specify the material to be inserted without specifying a position. If A and B are sets of strings, for example, you can do this:

> *Because sorting determines where additions to a set go, the class has insertion methods that just specify the material to be inserted without specifying a position.*

```
string s("tennis");
A.insert(s);                    // insert a value
B.insert(A.begin(), A.end());   // insert a range
```

Listing 15.10 illustrates these uses of sets.

Listing 15.10 set.cpp

```cpp
// set.cpp -- some set operations
#include <iostream>
#include <string>
#include <set>
#include <algorithm>
#include <iterator>
using namespace std;

int main()
{
    const int N = 6;
    string s1[N] = {"buffoon", "thinkers", "for", "heavy", "can", "for"};
    string s2[N] = {"metal", "any", "food", "elegant", "deliver","for"};

    set<string> A(s1, s1 + N);
    set<string> B(s2, s2 + N);

    ostream_iterator<string, char> out(cout, " ");
    cout << "Set A: ";
    copy(A.begin(), A.end(), out);
    cout << endl;
    cout << "Set B: ";
    copy(B.begin(), B.end(), out);
    cout << endl;

    cout << "Union of A and B:\n";
    set_union(A.begin(), A.end(), B.begin(), B.end(), out);
    cout << endl;

    cout << "Intersection of A and B:\n";
    set_intersection(A.begin(), A.end(), B.begin(), B.end(), out);
    cout << endl;

    cout << "Difference of A and B:\n";
    set_difference(A.begin(), A.end(), B.begin(), B.end(), out);
    cout << endl;
```

```
    set<string> C;
    cout << "Set C:\n";
    set_union(A.begin(), A.end(), B.begin(), B.end(),
        insert_iterator<set<string> >(C, C.begin()));
    copy(C.begin(), C.end(), out);
    cout << endl;

    string s3("grungy");
    C.insert(s3);
    cout << "Set C after insertion:\n";
    copy(C.begin(), C.end(),out);
    cout << endl;

    cout << "Showing a range:\n";
    copy(C.lower_bound("ghost"),C.upper_bound("spook"), out);
    cout << endl;

    return 0;
}
```

Remember

Older implementations may use `set.h`, `iterator.h`, **and** `algo.h`. **Older implementations may require** `less<string>` **as a second template argument for set. Also, older versions may use** `ostream_iterator<string>` **instead of** `ostream_iterator<string,char>`.

Here is the output:

```
Set A: buffoon can for heavy thinkers
Set B: any deliver elegant food for metal
Union of A and B:
any buffoon can deliver elegant food for heavy metal thinkers
Intersection of A and B:
for
Difference of A and B:
buffoon can heavy thinkers
Set C:
any buffoon can deliver elegant food for heavy metal thinkers
Set C after insertion:
any buffoon can deliver elegant food for grungy heavy metal thinkers
Showing a range:
grungy heavy metal
```

A `multimap` Example

Like `set`, `multimap` is a reversible, sorted, associative container. However, the key type is different from the value type, and a `multimap` object can have more than one value associated with a particular key.

The basic `multimap` declaration specifies the key type and the type of value stored as template arguments. For example, the following declaration creates a `multimap` object using `int` as the key type and `string` as the type of value stored:

```
multimap<int,string> codes;
```

An optional third template argument can be used to indicate a comparison function or object to be used to order the key. By default, the less<> template (discussed later) is used with the key type as its parameter. Older implementations may require this template parameter explicitly.

To keep information together, the actual value type combines the key type and the data type into a single pair. To do this, the STL uses a pair<class T, class U> template class for storing two kinds of values in a single object. If keytype is the key type and datatype is the type of the stored data, then the value type is pair<const keytype, datatype>. For instance, the value type for the codes object declared earlier is pair<const int, string>.

Suppose, for example, you wanted to store city names using the area code as a key. This happens to fit the codes declaration, which uses an int for a key and a string as a data type. One approach is to create a pair and then insert it:

```
pair<const int, string> item(213, "Los Angeles");
codes.insert(item);
```

Or you can create an anonymous pair object and insert it in a single statement:

```
codes.insert(pair<const int, string> (213, "Los Angeles"));
```

Because items are sorted by key, there's no need to identify an insertion location.

Given a pair object, you can access the two components by using the first and second members:

```
pair<const int, string> item(213, "Los Angeles");
cout << item.first << ' ' << item.second << endl;
```

What about getting information about a multimap object? The count() member function takes a key as its argument and returns the number of items having that key. There are lower_bound() and upper_bound() member functions that take a key and work as they did for set. There's an equal_range() member function that takes a key as its argument and returns iterators representing the range matching that key. In order to return two values, the method packages them into a pair object, this time with both template arguments being the iterator type. For example, the following would print a list of cities in the codes object with area code 718:

```
pair<multimap<KeyType, string>::iterator,
     multimap<KeyType, string>::iterator> range
                         = codes.equal_range(718);
cout << "Cities with area code 718:\n";
for (it = range.first; it != range.second; ++it)
    cout << (*it).second    << endl;
```

Listing 15.11 demonstrates most of these techniques. It also uses typedef to simplify some of the code writing.

Listing 15.11 multmap.cpp

```cpp
// multmap.cpp -- use a multimap
#include <iostream>
using namespace std;
#include <string>
#include <map>
#include <algorithm>

typedef int KeyType;
typedef pair<const KeyType, string> Pair;
typedef multimap<KeyType, string> MapCode;

int main()
{
    MapCode codes;

    codes.insert(Pair(415, "San Francisco"));
    codes.insert(Pair(510, "Oakland"));
    codes.insert(Pair(718, "Brooklyn"));
    codes.insert(Pair(718, "Staten Island"));
    codes.insert(Pair(415, "San Rafael"));
    codes.insert(Pair(510, "Berkeley"));

    cout << "Number of cities with area code 415: "
        << codes.count(415) << endl;
    cout << "Number of cities with area code 718: "
        << codes.count(718) << endl;
    cout << "Number of cities with area code 510: "
        << codes.count(510) << endl;
cout << "Area Code    City\n";
    MapCode::iterator it;
    for (it = codes.begin(); it != codes.end(); ++it)
        cout << "    " << (*it).first << "      "
            << (*it).second     << endl;

    pair<MapCode::iterator, MapCode::iterator> range
        = codes.equal_range(718);
    cout << "Cities with area code 718:\n";
    for (it = range.first; it != range.second; ++it)
        cout <<  (*it).second    << endl;

    return 0;
}
```

Remember

Older implementations may use `multimap.h` and `algo.h`. Older implementations may require `less<Pair>` as a third template argument for multimap. Also, older versions may use `ostream_iterator<string>` instead of `ostream_iterator <string,char>`. Borland's C++Builder 1.0 wants the const omitted from the `Pair` typedef.

Here is the output:

```
Number of cities with area code 415: 2
Number of cities with area code 718: 2
Number of cities with area code 510: 2
Area Code   City
   415      San Francisco
   415      San Rafael
   510      Oakland
   510      Berkeley
   718      Brooklyn
   718      Staten Island
Cities with area code 718:
Brooklyn
Staten Island
```

Function Objects (aka Functors)

Many STL algorithms use function objects, also known as *functors*. A functor is any object that can be used with ( ) in the manner of a function. This includes normal function names, pointers to functions, and class objects for which the ( ) operator is overloaded, that is, classes for which the peculiar-looking function operator()() is defined. For instance, you could define a class like this:

```
class Linear
{
private:
    double slope;
    double y0;
public:
    Linear(double _sl = 1, double _y = 0)
        : slope(_sl), y0(_y) {}
    double operator()(double x) {return y0 + slope * x; }
};
```

Then you could use Linear objects like functions:

```
Linear f1;
Linear f2(2.5, 10.0);
double y1 = f1(12.5);    // rhs is f1.operator()(12.5)
double y2 = f2(0.4);
```

Remember the for_each function? It applied a specified function to each member of a range:

```
for_each(books.begin(), books.end(), ShowReview);
```

In general, the third argument could be a functor, not just a regular function. Actually, this raises a question. How do you declare the third argument? You can't declare it as a function pointer, for a function pointer specifies the argument type. Because a container can contain about any type, you don't know in advance what particular argument type should be used. The STL solves that problem by using templates. The for_each prototype looks like this:

```
template<class InputIterator, class Function>
Function for_each(InputIterator first, InputIterator last, Function f);
```

The `ShowReview()` prototype was this:

```
void ShowReview(const Review &);
```

This makes the identifier `ShowReview` have the type `void (*)(const Review &)`, so that is the type assigned to the template argument `Function`.

FUNCTOR CONCEPTS

Just as the STL defines concepts for containers and iterators, it defines functor concepts:

- A *generator* is a functor that can be called with no arguments.
- A *unary function* is a functor that can be called with one argument.
- A *binary function* is a functor that can be called with two arguments.

For example, the functor supplied to `for_each()` should be a unary function because it is applied to one container element at a time.

Of course, these concepts come with refinements:

- A unary function that returns a `bool` value is a *predicate*.
- A binary function that returns a `bool` value is a *binary predicate*.

Several STL functions require predicate or binary predicate arguments. For instance, Listing 15.6 use a version of `sort()` that took a binary predicate as its third argument:

```
bool WorseThan(const Review & r1, const Review & r2);
...
sort(books.begin(), books.end(), WorseThan);
```

The `list` template has a `remove_if()` member that takes a predicate as an argument. It applies the predicate to each member in the indicated range, removing those elements for which the predicate returns true. For example, the following code would remove all elements greater than 100 from the list `three`:

```
bool tooBig(int n){ return n > 100; }
list<int> scores;
...
scores.remove_if(tooBig);
```

Incidentally, this last example shows where a class functor might be useful. Suppose you wanted to remove every value greater than 200 from a second list. It would be nice if you could pass the cut-off value to `tooBig()` as a second argument so you could use the function with different values, but a predicate can have but one argument. If, however, you design a `TooBig` class, you can use class members instead of function arguments to convey additional information:

```
template<class T>
class TooBig
{
private:
    T cutoff;
```

```
public:
    TooBig(const T & t) : cutoff(t) {}
    bool operator()(const T & v) { return v > cutoff; }
};
```

Here one value (v) is passed as a function argument while the second argument (cut-off) is set by the class constructor. Given this definition, you can initialize different TooBig objects to different cut-off values:

```
TooBig<int> f100(100);
list<int> froobies;
list<int> scores;
,,,
froobies.remove_if(f100);                    // use a named function object
scores.remove_if(TooBig<int>(200));          // construct a function object
```

Remember

The remove_if() method is a template method of a template class. Template methods are a recent extension to C++ template facilities (mainly because the STL needs them), and most compilers at the time of this writing haven't implemented them yet. However, there also is a non-member remove_if() function that takes a range (two iterators) and a predicate as arguments.

Suppose that you already had a template function with two arguments:

```
template <class T>
bool tooBig(const T & val, const T & lim)
{
    return val > lim;
}
```

You can use a class to convert it to a one-argument function object:

```
template<class T>
class TooBig2
{
private:
    T cutoff;
public:
    TooBig2(const T & t) : cutoff(t) {}
    bool operator()(const T & v) { return tooBig<T>(v, cutoff); }
};
```

That is, you can do the following:

```
TooBig2<int> tB100(100);
int x;
cin >> x;
if (tB100(x))    // same as if (tooBig(x,100))
    ...
```

So the call `tB100(x)` is the same as `tooBig(x,100)`, but the two-argument function is converted to a one-argument function object, with the second argument being used to construct the function object. In short, the class functor `TooBig2` is a function adapter, adapting a function to meet a different interface.

PREDEFINED FUNCTORS

The STL defines several elementary function objects. They perform actions such as adding two values, comparing two values for equality, and so on. They are provided to help support STL functions that take functions as arguments. For example, consider the `transform()` function. It has two versions. The first version takes four arguments. The first two are iterators specifying a range in a container. (By now you must be familiar with that approach.) The third is an iterator specifying where to copy the result. The final is a functor which is applied to each element in the range to produce each new element in the result. For example, consider the following:

```
const int LIM = 5;
double arr1[LIM] = {36, 39, 42, 45, 48};
vector<double> gr8(arr1, arr1 + LIM);
ostream_iterator<double, char> out(cout, " ");
transform(gr8.begin(), gr8.end(), out, sqrt);
```

This code would calculate the square root of each element and send the resulting values to the output stream. The destination iterator can be in the original range. For example, replacing `out` in the above example with `gr8.begin()` would copy the new values over the old values. Clearly, the functor used must be one that works with a single argument.

The second version uses a function that takes two arguments, applying it to one element from each of two ranges. It takes an additional argument, which comes third in order, identifying the start of the second range. For example, if `m8` were a second vec- `tor<double>` object and if `mean(double, double)` returned the mean of two values, the following would output the average of each pair of values from `gr8` and `m8`:

```
transform(gr8.begin(), gr8.end(), m8.begin(), out, mean);
```

Now suppose you want to add the two arrays. You can't use + as an argument because, for type `double`, + is a built-in operator, not a function. You could define a function to add two numbers and use it:

```
double add(double x, double y) { return x + y; }
...
transform(gr8.begin(), gr8.end(), m8.begin(), out, add);
```

But then you'd have to define a separate function for each type. It would be better to define a template, except you don't have to, because the STL already has. The `func-tional` (formerly `function.h`) header defines several template class function objects including one called `plus<>()`.

Using the `plus<>` class for ordinary addition is possible, if awkward:

```
#include <functional>
...
plus<double> add;  // create a plus<double> object
double y = add(2.2, 3.4); // using plus<double>::operator()()
```

But it makes it easy to provide a function object as an argument:

```
transform(gr8.begin(), gr8.end(), m8.begin(), out, plus<double>() );
```

Here, rather than create a named object, the code uses the `plus<double>` constructor to construct a function object to do the adding. (The parentheses indicate calling the default constructor; what's passed to `transform()` is the constructed function object.)

The STL provides function object equivalents for all the built-in arithmetic, relational, and logical operators. Table 15.11 shows the names for these functor equivalents. They can be used with the C++ built-in types or with any user-defined type that overloads the corresponding operator.

Older implementations use the name `times` instead of `multiplies`.

ADAPTABLE FUNCTORS AND FUNCTION ADAPTERS

The predefined functors of Table 15.11 are all *adaptable*. Actually, the STL has five related concepts, the *adaptable generator*, the *adaptable unary function*, the *adaptable binary function*, the *adaptable predicate*, and the *adaptable binary predicate*.

What makes a functor object adaptable is that it carries `typedef` members identifying its argument types and return type. The members are called `result_type`, `first_argument_type`, and `second_argument_type`, and they represent what they sound like. For instance, the return type of a `plus<int>` object is `plus<int>::result_type`.

"What makes a functor object adaptable is that it carries `typedef` members identifying its argument types and return type."

TABLE 15.11
OPERATORS AND FUNCTION OBJECT EQUIVALENTS

OPERATOR	FUNCTION OBJECT EQUIVALENT
+	plus
-	minus
*	multiplies
/	divides
%	modulus
-	negate
==	equal_to
!=	not_equal_to
>	greater
<	less
>=	greater_equal
<=	less_equal
&&	logical_and
||	logical_or
!	logical_not

The significance of a function object being adaptable is that it then can be used by function adapter objects which assume the existence of these `typedef` members. For instance, a function with an argument that is an adaptable functor can use the `result_type` member to declare a variable that matches the `functor`'s return type.

Indeed, the STL provides function adapter classes that use these facilities. For example, suppose you want to multiply each element of the vector gr8 by 2.5. That calls for using the `transform()` version with a unary function argument, like the

```
transform(gr8.begin(), gr8.end(), out, sqrt);
```

example shown earlier. The `multiplies()` functor can do the multiplication, but it's a binary function. So you need a function adapter that converts a functor with two arguments to one with one argument. The `TooBig2` example earlier showed one way, but the STL has automated the process with the `binder1st` and `binder2nd` classes, which convert adaptable binary functions to adaptable unary functions.

Let's look at `binder1st`. Suppose you have an adaptable binary function f2(). You can create a `binder1st` object that binds a particular value, call it val, to be used as the first argument to f():

```
binder1st(f2, val) f1;
```

Then, invoking f1(x) with its single argument returns the same value as invoking f2(x, val) with val as its first argument and f1()'s argument as its second argument. That is, f1(x) is equivalent to f2(val, x) except that it is a unary function instead of a binary function. The f2() function has been adapted. Again, this is possible only if f2() is an adaptable function.

This may seem a bit awkward. However, the STL provides the `bind1st()` function to simplify using the `binder1st` class. You give it the function name and value used to construct a `binder1st` object, and it returns an object of that type. For example, let's convert the binary function `multiplies()` to a unary function that multiplies its argument by 2.5. Just do this:

```
bind1st(multiplies<double>(), 2.5)
```

Thus, the solution to multiplying every element in gr8 by 2.5 and displaying the results is this:

```
transform(gr8.begin(), gr8.end(), out,
        bind1st(multiplies<double>(), 2.5));
```

The `binder2nd` class is similar, except that it assigns the constant to the second argument instead of the first. It has a helper function called `bind2nd` that works analogously to `bind1st`.

If an STL function calls for a unary function and you have an adaptable binary function that does the right thing, you can use `bind1st()` or `bind2nd()` to adapt the binary function to a unary interface.

Listing 15.12 incorporates some of recent examples into a short program.

Listing 15.12 funadap.cpp.

```cpp
// funadap.cpp -- using function adapters
#include <iostream>
using namespace std;
#include <vector>
#include <iterator>
#include <algorithm>
#include <functional>

const int LIM = 5;
int main()
{
    double arr1[LIM] = {36, 39, 42, 45, 48};
    double arr2[LIM] = {25, 27, 29, 31, 33};
    vector<double> gr8(arr1, arr1 + LIM);
    vector<double> m8(arr2, arr2 + LIM);
    ostream_iterator<double, char> out(cout, " ");
    copy(gr8.begin(), gr8.end(), out);
    cout << endl;
    copy(m8.begin(), m8.end(), out);
    cout << endl;

    transform(gr8.begin(), gr8.end(), m8.begin(), out, plus<double>());
    cout << endl;

    transform(gr8.begin(), gr8.end(), out, bind1st(multiplies<double>(),
2.5));
    cout << endl;

    return 0;
}
```

Remember

Older implementations may use `vector.h`, `iterator.h`, `algo.h`, and `function.h`. Older implementations may use `times` instead of `multiplies`.

Here is the output:

```
36 39 42 45 48
25 27 29 31 33
61 66 71 76 81
90 97.5 105 112.5 120
```

Algorithms

The STL contains many non-member functions for working with containers. You've seen a few of them already: `sort()`, `copy()`, `find()`, `for_each()`, `random_shuffle()`, `set_union()`, `set_intersection()`, `set_difference()`, and `transform()`. You've probably noticed they feature the same overall design, using iterators to identify data ranges to be processed and to identify where results are to go. Some also take a function object argument to be used as part of the data processing.

There are two main generic components to the algorithm function designs. First, they use templates to provide generic types. Second, they use iterators to provide a generic representation for accessing data in a container. Thus, the `copy()` function can work with a container holding type `double` values in an array, with a container holding `string` values in a linked list, or with a container storing user-defined objects in a tree structure, such as used by `set`. Because pointers are a special case of iterators, STL functions such as `copy()` can be used with ordinary arrays.

The `string` class, although not part of the STL, is designed with the STL in mind. For example, it has `start()` and `end()` members. Thus, it can use the STL interface.

The uniform container design allows there to be meaningful relations between containers of different kinds. For example, you can use `copy()` to copy values from an ordinary array to a `vector` object, from a `vector` object to a `list` object, and from a `list` object to a `set` object. You can use `==` to compare different kinds of containers, for example, `deque` and `vector`. This is possible because the overloaded `==` operator for containers uses iterators to compare contents, so a `deque` object and a `vector` object test as equal if they have the same content in the same order.

ALGORITHM GROUPS

The STL divides the algorithm library into four groups:

- Non-modifying sequence operations
- Mutating sequence operations
- Sorting and related operations
- Generalized numeric operations

The first three groups are described in the `algorithm` (formerly `algo.h`) header file, while the fourth group, being specifically oriented towards numeric data, gets its own header file, called `numeric`. (Formerly, they, too, were in `algol.h`.)

Non-modifying sequence operations operate on each element in a range. These operations leave a container unchanged. For instance, `find()` and `for_each()` belong to this category.

Mutating sequence operations also operate on each element in a range. As the name suggests, however, they can change the contents of a container. The change could be in values or in the order in which the values are stored. For instance, `transform()`, `random_shuffle()`, and `copy()` fall into this category.

Sorting and related operations include several sorting functions (including `sort()`) and a variety of other functions, including the set operations.

The numeric operations include functions to sum the contents of a range, calculate the inner product of two containers, calculate partial sums, and calculate adjacent differences. Typically, these are operations characteristic of arrays, so `vector` is the container most likely to be used with them.

Appendix G provides a complete summary of these functions.

GENERAL PROPERTIES

As you've seen again and again, STL functions work with iterators and iterator ranges. The function prototype indicates the assumptions made about the iterators. For example, the copy() function has this prototype:

```
template<class InputIterator, class OutputIterator>
OutputIterator copy(InputIterator first, InputIterator last,
                    OutputIterator result);
```

Because the identifiers InputIterator and OutputIterator are template parameters, they just as easily could have been T and U. However, the STL documentation uses the template parameter names to indicate the concept that the parameter models. So this declaration tells us that the range parameters must be input parameters or better and that the iterator indicating where the result goes must be an output parameter or better.

One way of classifying algorithms is on the basis of where the result of the algorithm is placed. Some algorithms do their work in place, others create copies. For example, when the sort() function is finished, the result occupies the same location that the original data did. So sort() is an *in-place algorithm*. The copy() function, however, sends the result of its work to another location, so it is a *copying algorithm*. The transform() function can do both. Like copy(), it uses an output iterator to indicate where the results go. Unlike copy(), transform() allows the output iterator to point to a location in the input range, so it can copy the transformed values over the original values.

Some algorithms come in two versions, an in-place version and a copying version. The STL convention is to append _copy to the name of the copying version. The latter version will take an additional output iterator parameter to specify the location to which to copy the outcome. For example, there is a replace() function with this prototype:

```
template<class ForwardIterator, class T>
void replace(ForwardIterator first, ForwardIterator last,
             const T& old_value, const T& new_value);
```

It replaces each instance of old_value with new_value. This occurs in place. Because this algorithm both reads from and writes to container elements, the iterator type has to be ForwardIterator or better. The copying version has this prototype:

```
template<class InputIterator, class OutputIterator, class T>
OutputIterator replace_copy(InputIterator first, InputIterator last,
             OutputIterator result,
             const T& old_value, const T& new_value);
```

This time the resulting data is copied to a new location given by result, so the read-only input iterator is sufficient for specifying the range.

Note that replace_copy() has an OutputIterator return type. The convention for copying algorithms is that they return an iterator pointing to the location one past that last value copied.

Another common variation is that some functions have a version that performs an action conditionally, depending upon the result of applying a function to a container element. These versions typically append _if to the function name. For example, replace_if() replaces an old value with a new value if applying a function to the old value returns a value of true. Here's the prototype:

```
template<class ForwardIterator, class Predicate class T>
void replace_if(ForwardIterator first, ForwardIterator last,
            Predicate pred, const T& new_value);
```

A predicate, recall, is the name of a unary function returning a bool value. There's also a version called replace_copy_if(). You probably can figure out what it does and what its prototype is like.

As with InputIterator, Predicate is a template parameter name and could just as easily be called T or U. However, the STL chooses to use Predicate to remind the user that the actual argument should be a model of the Predicate concept. Similarly, the STL use terms like Generator and BinaryPredicate to identify arguments that should model other function object concepts.

USING THE STL

" The STL components are tools, but they also are building blocks to create other tools. "

The STL is a library whose parts are designed to work together. The STL components are tools, but they also are building blocks to create other tools. Let's illustrate that with an example. Suppose you want to write a program that lets the user enter words. At the end, you'd like a record of the words as they were entered, an alphabetical list of the words used (capitalization differences ignored), and a record of how many times each word was entered. To keep things simple, assume the input contains no numbers or punctuation.

Entering and saving the list of words is simple enough. Following the example of Listing 15.5, you can create a vector<string> object and use push_back() to add input words to the vector:

```
vector<string> words;
string input;
while (cin >> input && input != "quit")
    words.push_back(input);
```

What about getting the alphabetic word list? You can use sort() followed by unique(), but that approach overwrites the original data because sort() is an in-place algorithm. There is an easier way that avoids this problem. Create a set<string> object, and copy (using an insert iterator) the words from the vector to the set. A set automatically sorts its contents, taking the place of calling sort(), and a set only allows one copy of a key, so that takes the place of calling unique(). Wait! The specification called for ignoring the case differences. One way to handle that is to use transform() instead of copy() to copy data from the vector to the set. For the transformation function, use one that converts a string to lowercase.

```
set<string> wordset;
transform(words.begin(), words.end(),
    insert_iterator<set<string> > (wordset, wordset.begin()), ToLower);
```

The `ToLower()` function is easy to write. Just use `transform()` to apply the `tolower()` function to each element in the string, using the string both as source and destination. Remember, `string` objects, too, can use the STL functions. Passing and returning the string as a reference means the algorithm works on the original string without having to make copies.

```
string & ToLower(string & st)
{
    transform(st.begin(), st.end(), st.begin(), tolower);
    return st;
}
```

To get the number of times each word appeared in the input, you can use the `count()` function. It takes a range and a value as arguments and returns the number of times the value appears in the range. You can use the `vector` object to provide the range and the `set` object to provide the list of words to count. That is, for each word in the set, count how many times it appears in the vector. To keep the resulting count associated with the correct word, store the word and the count as a `pair<const string, int>` object in a `map` object. The word will be the key (just one copy), and the count will be the value. This can be done in a single loop:

```
map<string, int> wordmap;
set<string>::iterator  si;
for (si = wordset.begin(); si != wordset.end(); si++)
    wordmap.insert(pair<string, int>(*si, count(words.begin(),
    words.end(), *si)));
```

Remember

Older STL implementations declare `count()` as type `void`. Instead of using a return value, you provide a fourth argument passed as a reference, and the number of items is added to that argument:

```
int ct = 0;
count(words.begin(), words.end(), *si), ct));        count
added to ct
```

The map class has an interesting feature—you can use array notation with keys serving as indices to access the stored values. For instance, `wordmap["the"]` would represent the value associated with the key `"the"`, which in this case is number of occurrences of the string `"the"`. Because the `wordset` container holds all the keys used by `wordmap`, you can use the following code as an alternative and more attractive way of storing results:

```
for (si = wordset.begin(); si != wordset.end(); si++)
    wordmap[*si] = count(words.begin(), words.end(), *si);
```

Because `si` points to a string in the `wordset` container, `*si` is a string and can serve as a key for `wordmap`. This code places both keys and values into the `wordmap` map.

Similarly, you can use the array notation to report results:

```
for (si = wordset.begin(); si != wordset.end(); si++)
    cout << *si << ": " << wordmap[*si] << endl;
```

If a key is invalid, the corresponding value is 0.

Listing 15.13 puts these ideas together and includes code to display the contents of the three containers (a vector with the input, a set with a word list, and a map with a word count).

Listing 15.13 usealgo.cpp

```cpp
//usealgo.cpp
#pragma warning (disable : 4786)
#include <iostream>
#include <string>
#include <vector>
#include <set>
#include <map>
#include <iterator>
#include <algorithm>
#include <cctype>
using namespace std;

string & ToLower(string & st);

int main()
{
    vector<string> words;
    cout << "Enter words (enter quit to quit):\n";
    string input;
    while (cin >> input && input != "quit")
        words.push_back(input);

    cout << "You entered the following words:\n";
    ostream_iterator<string,char> out(cout, " ");
    copy(words.begin(), words.end(), out);
    cout << endl;

    // place words in set, converting to lowercase
    set<string> wordset;
    transform(words.begin(), words.end(),
        insert_iterator<set<string> > (wordset, wordset.begin()),
        ToLower);
    cout << "\nAlphabetic list of words:\n";
    copy(wordset.begin(), wordset.end(), out);
    cout << endl;

    // place word and frequency in map
    map<string, int> wordmap;
    set<string>::iterator si;
    for (si = wordset.begin(); si != wordset.end(); si++)
        wordmap[*si] = count(words.begin(), words.end(), *si);

    // display map contents
    cout << "\nWord frequency:\n";
for (mi = wordmap.begin(); mi != wordmap.end(); mi++)

    for (si = wordset.begin(); si != wordset.end(); si++)
        cout << *si << ": " << wordmap[*si] << endl;

    return 0;
}
```

```
string & ToLower(string & st)
{
    transform(st.begin(), st.end(), st.begin(), tolower);
    return st;
}
```

Remember

Older implementations may use `vector.h`, `set.h`, `map.h`, `iterator.h`, `algo.h`, and `ctype.h`. Older implementations may require the `set` and `map` templates to use an additional `less<string>` template parameter. Older versions may use `ostream_iterator<string>` instead of `ostream_iterator<string,char>`. Older versions use the type `void count()` function mentioned earlier.

Here is a sample run:

```
Enter words (enter quit to quit):
The dog saw the cat and thought the cat fat
The cat thought the cat perfect
quit
You entered the following words:
The dog saw the cat and thought the cat fat The cat thought the cat
perfect

Alphabetic list of words:
and cat dog fat perfect saw that the thought

Word frequency:
and: 1
cat: 4
dog: 1
fat: 1
perfect: 1
saw: 1
that: 1
the: 4
thought: 2
```

The moral here is that your attitude when using the STL should be, how much code can I avoid writing myself? STL's generic and flexible design should save you lots of work. Also, the STL designers are algorithm people very much concerned with efficiency. So the algorithms are well-chosen and in-line.

Other Libraries

C++ provides some other class libraries that are more specialized than the examples covered in this chapter. The `complex` header file provides a `complex` class template for complex numbers, with specializations for `float`, `long`, and `long double`. The class provides standard complex number operations along with standard functions that can be used with complex numbers.

The `valarray` header file provides a `valarray` template class. This class template is designed to represent numeric arrays and provides support for a variety of numeric array operations, such as adding the contents of one array to another, applying math functions to each element of an array, and applying linear algebra operations to arrays.

Summary

C++ provides a powerful set of libraries that provide solutions to many common programming problems and the tools to simplify many more problems. The `string` class provides a convenient means to handle strings as objects. The class provides automatic memory management and a host of methods and functions for working with strings. For example, they allow you to concatenate strings, insert one string into another, reverse a string, search a string for characters or substrings, and perform input and output operations.

The `auto_ptr` template makes it easier to manage memory allocated by `new`. If you use an `auto_ptr` object instead of a regular pointer to hold the address returned by `new`, you don't have to remember to use the delete operator later. When the `auto_ptr` object expires, its destructor will call the delete operator automatically.

The Standard Template Library, or STL, is a collection of container class templates, iterator class templates, function object templates, and algorithm function templates that feature a unified design based on generic programming principles. The algorithms use templates to make them generic in terms of type of stored object and an iterator interface to make them generic in terms of the type of container. Iterators are generalizations of pointers.

The STL uses the term "concept" to denote a set of requirements. For example, the concept of forward iterator includes the requirements that a forward iterator object can be dereferenced for reading and writing, and that it can be incremented. Actual implementations of the concept are said to "model" the concept. For instance, the forward iterator concept could be modeled by an ordinary pointer or by an object designed to navigate a linked list. Concepts based on other concepts are termed "refinements." For instance, the bidirectional iterator is refinement of the forward iterator concept.

Container classes, such as `vector` and `set`, are models of container concepts, such as container, sequence, and associative container. The STL defines several container class templates: `vector`, `deque`, `list`, `set`, `multiset`, `map`, `multimap`, and `bitset`. It also defines adapter class templates `queue`, `priority_queue`, and `stack`; these classes adapt an underlying container class to give it the characteristic interface suggested by the adapter class template name. Thus, `stack`, although based, in default, on `vector`, allows insertion and removal only at the top of the stack.

Some algorithms are expressed as container class methods, but the bulk are expressed as general, non-member functions. This is made possible by using iterators as the interface between containers and algorithms. One advantage to this approach is that there need be just one `for_each()` or `copy()` function, and so on, instead of a separate version for each container. A second advantage is that STL algorithms can be used with non-STL containers, such as ordinary arrays, `string` objects, and any classes you design consistent with the STL iterator and container idiom.

Both containers and algorithms are characterized by the type of iterator they provide or need. You should check that the container features an iterator concept that supports the algorithm's needs. For example, the `for_each()` algorithm uses an input iterator, whose minimal requirements are met by all the STL container class types. But `sort()` requires random-access iterators, which not all container classes support. A container class may offer a specialized method as an option if it doesn't meet the requirements for a particular algorithm. For example, the `list` class has a `sort()` method based on bidirectional iterators, so it can use that method instead of the general function.

The STL also provides function objects, or functors, that are classes for which the `()` operator is overloaded; that is, for which the `operator()()` method is defined. Objects of such classes can be invoked using function notation but can carry additional information. Adaptable function objects, for example, have `typedef` statements identifying the argument types and the return value type for the function object. This information can be used by other components, such as function adapters.

The STL, by representing common container types and providing a variety of common operations implemented with efficient algorithms, all done in a generic manner, provides an excellent source of reusable code. You may be able to solve a programming problem directly with the STL tools, or you may be able to use them as building blocks to construct the solution you need.

The `complex` and `valarray` template classes support numerical operations for complex numbers and arrays.

Review Questions

1. Consider the following class declaration:

```
class RQ1
{
private:
    char * st;        // points to C-style string
public:
    RQ1() { st = new char [1]; strcpy(st,""); }
    RQ1(const char * s)
    {st = new char [strlen(s) + 1]; strcpy(st, s); }
    RQ1(const RQ1 & rq);
    {st = new char [strlen(rq.st) + 1]; strcpy(st, rq.st); }
    ~RQ1() {delete [] st};
    RQ & operator=(const RQ & rq);
    // more stuff
};
```

Convert this to a declaration using a `string` object instead. What methods no longer need an explicit definition?

2. Name at least two advantages `string` objects have over C-style strings in terms of ease-of-use.

3. Write a function that takes a reference to a `string` as an argument and which converts the `string` to all uppercase.

4. Which of the following are not examples of correct usage (conceptually or syntactically) of `auto_ptr`? (Assume the needed header files have been included.)

```
auto_ptr<int> pia(new int[20]);
auto_ptr<str> (new string);
int rigue = 7;
auto_ptr<int>pr(&rigue);
auto_ptr dbl (new double);
```

5. If you could make the mechanical equivalent of a stack that held golf clubs instead of numbers, why would it (conceptually) be a bad golf bag?

6. Why would a `set` container be a poor choice for storing a hole-by-hole record of your golf scores?

7. Since a pointer is an iterator, why didn't the STL designers simply use pointers instead of iterators?

8. Why didn't the STL designers simply define a base iterator class, use inheritance to derive classes for the other iterator types, and express the algorithms in terms of those iterator classes?

9. Give at least three examples of convenience advantages that a `vector` object has over an ordinary array.

10. If Listing 15.6 were implemented with `list` instead of `vector`, what parts of the program would become invalid? Could the invalid part be fixed easily? If so, how?

Programming Exercises

1. A palindrome is a string that is the same backwards as it is forwards. For example, "tot" and "otto" are rather short palindromes. Write a program that lets a user enter a string and which passes a reference to the string to a `bool` function. The function should return `true` if the string is a palindrome and `false` otherwise. At this point, don't worry about complications such as capitalization, spaces, and punctuation. That is, this simple version will reject "Otto" and "Madam, I'm Adam." Feel free to scan the list of string methods in Appendix F for methods to simplify the task.

2. Do the same problem as given in programming exercise 1, but do worry about complications such as capitalization, spaces, and punctuation. That is, "Madam, I'm Adam" should test as a palindrome. For example, the testing function could reduce the string to "madamimadam" and then test if the reverse is the same. Don't forget the useful `cctype` library. You may find an STL function or two useful, although not necessary.

3. You have to write a function with an old-style interface. It has this prototype:

```
int reduce(long ar[], int n);
```

The arguments are the name of an array and the number of elements in the array. The function sorts an array, removes duplicate values, and returns a value equal to the number of elements in the reduced array. Write the function using STL functions. (If you decide to use the general `unique()` function, note that it returns the end of the resulting range.) Test the function in a short program.

4. Do the same problem as described in programming exercise 3, except make it a template function:

```
template <class T>
int reduce(T ar[], int n);
```

Test the function in a short program using both a `long` instantiation and a `string` instantiation.

5. Redo the example shown in Listing 11.13 using the STL `queue` template class instead of the `Queue` class of Chapter 11.

6. A common game is the lottery card. The card has numbered spots of which a certain number are selected at random. Write a `Lotto()` function that takes two arguments. The first is the number of spots on a lottery card and the second the number of spots selected at random. The function returns a `vector<int>` object containing, in sorted order, the numbers selected at random. For example, you could use the function as follows:

```
vector<int> winners;
winners = Lotto(51,6);
```

This would assign to `winners` a vector containing six numbers selected randomly from the range 1 through 51. Note that simply using `rand()` doesn't quite do the job because it may produce duplicate values. Suggestion: Have the function create a vector containing all the possible values, use `random_shuffle()`, and then use the beginning of the shuffled vector to obtain the values. Also write a short program that lets you test the function.

7. Mat and Pat wish to invite their friends to a party. They ask you to write a program that does the following:

Lets Mat enter a list of his friends' names. The names are stored in a container and then displayed in sorted order.

Lets Pat enter a list of her friends' names. The names are stored in a second container and then displayed in sorted order.

Creates a third container that merges the two lists, eliminating duplicates, and displays the contents of this container.

Discussing C++ input and output (I/O, for short) poses a problem. On the one hand, practically every program uses input and output, and learning how to use them is one of the first tasks facing someone learning a computer language. On the other hand, C++ uses many of its more advanced language features to implement input and output, including classes, derived classes, function overloading, virtual functions, templates, and multiple inheritance. Thus, to really understand C++ I/O, you need to know a lot of C++. To get you started, the early chapters outlined the basic ways for using the `istream` class object `cin` and the `ostream` class object `cout` for input and output. Now we'll take a longer look at C++'s input and output classes, seeing how they are designed and learning how to control the output format. (If you've skipped a few chapters just to learn advanced formatting, you can skim the sections on that topic, noting the techniques and ignoring the explanations.)

The C++ facilities for file input and output are based on the same basic class definitions that `cin` and `cout` are based on, so this chapter uses the discussion of console I/O (keyboard and screen) as a springboard to investigating file I/O.

The ANSI/ISO C++ standards committee has worked to make C++ I/O more compatible with existing C I/O, and this has produced some changes from traditional C++ practices.

You will learn about the following in this chapter:

- The C++ view of input and output
- The `iostream` family of classes
- Redirection
- `ostream` class methods
- Formatting output
- `istream` class methods
- Stream states
- File I/O
- Using the `ifstream` class for input from files
- Using the `ofstream` class for output to files
- Using the `fstream` class for file input and output
- Command-line processing
- Binary files
- Random file access
- Incore formatting

An Overview of C++ Input and Output

Most computer languages build input and output into the language itself. For instance, if you look through the lists of keywords for languages like BASIC or Pascal, you'll see that PRINT statements, `writeln` statements, and the like are part of the language vocabulary. But neither C nor C++ have built input and output into the language. If you look through the keywords for these languages, you find `for` and `if`, but nothing relating to I/O. C originally left I/O to compiler implementers. One reason for this was to give implementers the freedom to design I/O functions that best fit the hardware requirements of the target computer. In practice, most implementers based I/O on a set of library functions originally developed for the UNIX environment. ANSI C formalized recognition of this I/O package, called the Standard Input/Output package, by making it a mandatory component of the standard C library. C++ also recognizes this package, so if you're familiar with the family of C functions declared in the `stdio.h` file, you can use them in C++ programs. (Newer implementations use the `cstdio` header file to support these functions.)

C++, however, relies upon a C++ solution rather than a C solution to I/O, and that solution is a set of classes defined in the `iostream` (formerly `iostream.h`) and `fstream` (formerly `fstream.h`) header files. This class library is not part of the formal language definition (`cin` and `istream` are not keywords); after all, a computer language defines rules for how to do things, such as create classes, and doesn't define what you should create following those rules. But, just as C implementations come with a standard library of functions, C++ comes with a standard library of classes. At first, that standard class library was an informal standard consisting solely of the classes defined in the `iostream` and `fstream` header files. The ANSI/ISO C++ committee decided to formalize this library as a standard class library and to add a few more standard classes, such as those discussed in Chapter 15. This chapter discusses standard C++ I/O. But first, let's examine the conceptual framework for C++ I/O.

STREAMS AND BUFFERS

A C++ program views input or output as a stream of bytes. On input, a program extracts bytes from an input stream, and on output, a program inserts bytes into the output stream. For a text-oriented program, each byte can represent a character. More generally, the bytes can form a binary representation of character or numeric data. The bytes in an input stream can come from the keyboard, but they also can come from a storage device, such as a hard disk, or from another program. Similarly, the bytes in an output stream can flow to the screen, to a printer, to a storage device, or to another program. A stream acts as an intermediary between the program and the stream's source or destination. This approach enables a C++ program to treat input from a keyboard in the same manner it treats input from a file; the C++ program merely examines the stream of bytes without needing to know from where the bytes come. Similarly, by using streams, a C++ program can process output in a manner independent of where the bytes are going. Managing input, then, involves two stages:

- Associating a stream with an input to a program

- Connecting the stream to a file

In other words, an input stream needs two connections, one at each end. The file-end connection provides a source for the stream, and the program-end connection dumps the stream outflow into the program. (The file-end connection can be a file, but it also can be a device, such as a keyboard.) Similarly, managing output involves connecting an output stream to the program and associating some output destination with the stream. It's like plumbing with bytes instead of water (see Figure 16.1).

Usually, input and output can be handled more efficiently by using a *buffer*. A buffer is a block of memory used as an intermediate, temporary storage facility for the transfer of information from a device to a program or from a program to a device. Typically, devices like disk drives transfer information in blocks of 512 bytes or more, while programs often process information one byte at a time. The buffer helps match these two disparate rates of information transfer. For instance, assume a program is supposed to count the number of dollar signs in a hard-disk file. The program could read one character from the file, process it, read the next character from the file, and so on. Reading a file a character at a time from a disk requires a lot of hardware activity and is slow. The buffered approach is to read a large chunk from the disk, store the chunk in the buffer, and read the buffer one character at a time. Because it is much quicker to read individual bytes of data from memory than from a hard disk, this

FIGURE 16.1

C++ input and output

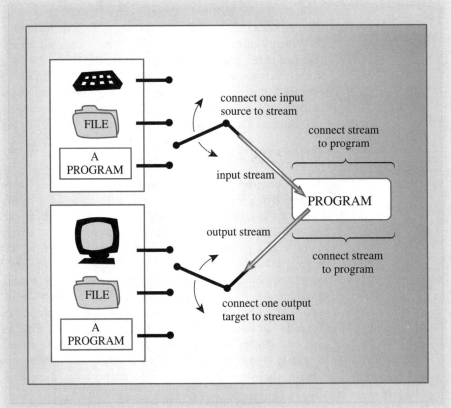

approach is much faster as well as easier on the hardware. Of course, after the program reaches the end of the buffer, the program then should read another chunk of data from the disk. The principle is similar to that of a water reservoir that collects megagallons of runoff water during a big storm and then feeds water to your home at a more civilized rate of flow (see Figure 16.2). Similarly, on output a program can first fill the buffer and then transfer the entire block of data to a hard disk, clearing the buffer for the next batch of output. This is called *flushing the buffer*. Perhaps you can come up with your own plumbing-based analogy for that process.

Keyboard input provides one character at a time, so in that case a program doesn't need a buffer to help match different data transfer rates. However, buffered keyboard input allows the user to back up and correct input before transmitting it to a program. A C++ program normally flushes the input buffer when you press [Enter]. That's why the examples in this book don't begin processing input until you press [Enter]. For output to the screen, a C++ program normally flushes the output buffer when you transmit a newline character. Depending upon the implementation, a program may flush input on

FIGURE 16.2

A stream with a buffer

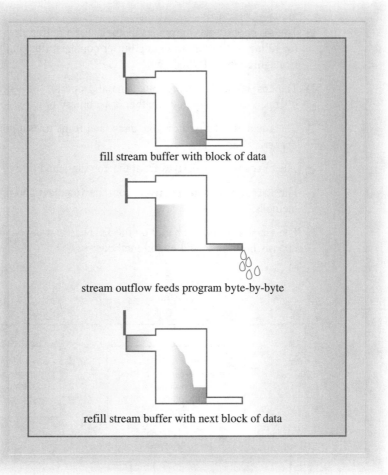

fill stream buffer with block of data

stream outflow feeds program byte-by-byte

refill stream buffer with next block of data

other occasions, too, such as impending input. That is, when a program reaches an input statement, it flushes any output currently in the output buffer. C++ implementations that are consistent with ANSI C should behave in that manner.

STREAMS, BUFFERS, AND THE `iostream` FILE

The business of managing streams and buffers can get a bit complicated, but including the `iostream` (formerly `iostream.h`) file brings in several classes designed to implement and manage streams and buffers for you. The newest version of C++ I/O actually defines class templates in order to support both char and wchar_t data. By using the typedef facility, C++ makes the char specializations of these templates mimic the traditional non-template I/O implementation. Here are some of those classes (see Figure 16.3):

- The `streambuf` class provides memory for a buffer along with class methods for filling the buffer, accessing buffer contents, flushing the buffer, and managing the buffer memory.

- The `ios_base` class represents general properties of a stream, such as whether it's open for reading and whether it's a binary or a text stream.

- The `ios` class is based on `ios_base`, and it includes a pointer member to a `streambuf` object.

- The `ostream` class derives from the `ios` class and provides output methods.

- The `istream` class also derives from the `ios` class and provides input methods.

- The `iostream` class is based on the `istream` and `ostream` classes and thus inherits both input and output methods.

FIGURE 16.3

Some I/O classes

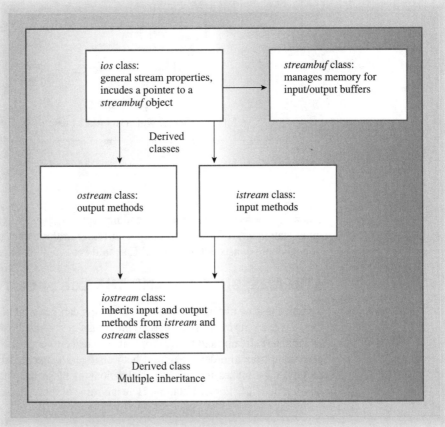

To use these facilities, you use objects of the appropriate classes. For example, use an `ostream` object such as `cout` to handle output. Creating such an object opens a stream, automatically creates a buffer, and associates it with the stream. It also makes the class member functions available to you.

REDEFINING I/O

C++ I/O has been revised a couple of ways. First, there's the change from `ostream.h` to `ostream`, with `ostream` placing the classes in the `std` namespace. Second, the I/O classes have been rewritten. To be an international language, C++ had to be able to handle international character sets that require a 16-bit character type. So the language added the 16-bit `wchar_t` (or "wide") character type to the traditional 8-bit `char` (or "narrow") type. Each type needs its own I/O facilities. Rather than develop two separate sets of classes, the standards committee developed a template set of I/O classes, including `basic_istream<charT, traits<charT> >` and `basic_ostream<charT, traits<charT> >`. The `traits<charT>` template, in turn, is a template class defining particular traits for a character type, such as its equivalent of a null character and EOF value. The standard provides `char` and `wchar_t` specializations of the I/O classes. For example, `istream` and `ostream` are `typedefs` for `char` specializations. Similarly, `wistream` and `wostream` are `wchar_t` specializations. For instance, there is a `wcout` object for outputting wide character streams. The `ostream` header file contains these definitions.

Certain type-independent information that used to be kept in the `ios` base class has been moved to the new `ios_base` class. This includes the various formatting constants such as `ios::fixed`, which now is `ios_base::fixed`. Also, `ios_base` contains some options that weren't available in the old `ios`.

In some cases, the change in the file name corresponds with the change in class definitions. In Microsoft Visual C++ 5.0, for example, you can include `iostream.h` and get the old class definitions or include `iostream` and get the new class definitions. However, such synchronization does not seem to be the general rule.

The C++ `iostream` class library takes care of many details for you. For instance, including the `iostream` file in a program creates eight stream objects (four for narrow character streams and four for wide character streams) automatically:

- The `cin` object corresponds to the standard input stream. By default, this stream is associated with the standard input device, typically a keyboard. The `wcin` object is similar, but works with the `wchar_t` type.

- The `cout` object corresponds to the standard output stream. By default, this stream is associated with the standard output device, typically a monitor. The `wcout` object is similar, but works with the `wchar_t` type.

● The `cerr` object corresponds to the standard error stream, which you can use for displaying error messages. By default, this stream is associated with the standard output device, typically a monitor, and the stream is unbuffered. This means that information is sent directly to the screen without waiting for a buffer to fill or for a newline character. The `wcerr` object is similar, but works with the `wchar_t` type.

● The `clog` object also corresponds to the standard error stream. By default, this stream is associated with the standard output device, typically a monitor, and the stream is buffered. The `wclog` object is similar, but works with the `wchar_t` type.

What does it mean to say an object represents a stream? Well, for example, when the `iostream` file declares a `cout` object for your program, that object will have data members holding information relating to output, such as the field widths to be used in displaying data, the number of places after the decimal to use, what number base to use for displaying integers, and the address of a `streambuf` object describing the buffer used to handle the output flow. A statement such as

```
cout << "Bjarne free";
```

places the characters from the string `"Bjarne free"` into the buffer managed by `cout` via the pointed-to `streambuf` object. The `ostream` class defines the `operator<<()` function used in this statement, and the `ostream` class also supports the `cout` data members with a variety of other class methods, such as the ones this chapter discusses later. Furthermore, C++ sees to it that the output from the buffer is directed to the standard output, usually a monitor, provided by the operating system. In short, one end of a stream is connected to your program, the other end is connected to the standard output, and the `cout` object, with the help of a type `streambuf` object, manages the flow of bytes through the stream.

REDIRECTION

The standard input and output streams normally connect to the keyboard and the screen. But many operating systems, including UNIX and MS-DOS, support redirection, a facility that lets you change the associations for the standard input and the standard output. Suppose, for example, you have an executable DOS C++ program called `counter.exe` that counts the number of characters in its input and reports the result. A sample run might look like this:

```
C>counter
Hello
and goodbye!
Control-Z                // simulated end of file
Input contained 19 characters.
C>
```

Here, input came from the keyboard, and output went to the screen.

With input redirection (<) and output redirection (>), you can use the same program to count the number of characters in the oklahoma file and to place the results in the cow_cnt file:

```
C>counter <oklahoma >cow_cnt
C>
```

The <oklahoma part of the command line associates the standard input with the oklahoma file, causing cin to read input from that file instead of the keyboard. In other words, the operating system changes the connection at the inflow end of the input stream, while the outflow end remains connected to the program. The >cow_cnt part of the command line associates the standard output with the cow_cnt file, causing cout to send output to that file instead of to the screen. That is, the operating system changes the outflow end connection of the output stream, leaving its inflow end still connected to the program. Both DOS (2.0 and later) and UNIX automatically recognize this redirection syntax. (UNIX and DOS 3.0 and later also permit optional space characters between the redirection operators and the file names.)

The standard output stream, represented by cout, is the normal channel for program output. The standard error streams (represented by cerr and clog) are intended for a program's error messages. By default, all three typically are sent to the monitor. But redirecting the standard output doesn't affect cerr or clog; thus if you use one of these objects to print an error message, a program will display the error message on the screen even if the regular cout output is redirected elsewhere. For instance, consider this code fragment:

```
if (success)
    cout << "Here come the goodies!\n";
else
{
    cerr << "Something horrible has happened.\n";
    exit(1);
}
```

If redirection is not in effect, whichever message is selected is displayed onscreen. If, however, the program output has been redirected to a file, the first message, if selected, would go to the file, but the second message, if selected, would go to the screen. By the way, some operating systems permit redirecting the standard error, too. In UNIX, for example, the 2> operator redirects the standard error.

Actually, the istream and ostream classes don't necessarily provide for redirection. The Borland C++ 3.1 implementation, for example, derives an istream_withassign class from the istream class for handling redirection, and cin is an istream_withassign object. Similarly, the cout object belongs to the ostream_withassign class, which is derived from ostream in a manner that allows output redirection. Otherwise, these standard objects use the same methods as their respective base classes. For simplicity, we'll refer to cin as an istream object and cout as an ostream object.

Output with `cout`

C++, we've said, considers output to be a stream of bytes. (If you use `wostream`, they will be 16-bit-wide bytes, but bytes nonetheless.) But many kinds of data in a program are organized into larger units than a single byte. An `int` type, for example, may be represented by a 2- or 4-byte binary value. And a `double` value may be represented by 8 bytes of binary data. But when you send a stream of bytes to a screen, you want each byte to represent a character value. That is, to display the number -2.34 on the screen, you should send the five characters -, 2, ., 3, and 4 to the screen, and not the internal 8-byte floating-point representation of that value. Therefore, one of the most important tasks facing the `ostream` class is converting numeric types, such as `int` or `float`, into a stream of characters that represents the values in text form. That is, the `ostream` class translates the internal representation of data as binary bit patterns to an output stream of character bytes. (Some day we may have bionic implants to enable us to interpret binary data directly. We leave that development as an exercise for the reader.) To perform these translation tasks, the `ostream` class provides several class methods. We'll look at them now, summarizing methods used throughout the book and describing additional methods that provide a finer control over the appearance of the output.

THE OVERLOADED << OPERATOR

Most often, this book has used `cout` with the `<<` operator, also called the *insertion* operator:

```
int clients = 22;
cout << clients;
```

In C++, as in C, the default meaning for the `<<` operator is the bitwise left-shift operator (see Appendix E). An expression such as `x<<3` means to take the binary representation of x and shift all the bits 3 units to the left. Obviously, this doesn't have a lot to do with output. But the `ostream` class redefines the `<<` operator through overloading to output for the `ostream` class. In this guise, the `<<` operator is called the insertion operator instead of the left-shift operator. (The left-shift operator earned this new role through its visual aspect, which suggests a flow of information to the left.) The insertion operator is overloaded to recognize all the basic C++ types:

- `unsigned char`
- `signed char`
- `char`
- `short`
- `unsigned short`
- `int`
- `unsigned int`

- long

- unsigned long

- float

- double

- long double

The `ostream` class provides a definition for the `operator<<()` function for each of the above types. (Functions incorporating operators into the name are used to overload operators, as discussed in Chapter 10.) Thus if you use a statement of the form

```
cout << value;
```

and if `value` is one of the preceding types, a C++ program can match it to an operator function with the corresponding signature. For example, the expression `cout << 88` matches the following method prototype:

```
ostream & operator<<(int);
```

Recall that this prototype indicates that the `operator<<()` function takes one type `int` argument. That's the part that matches the 88 in the previous statement. The prototype also indicates that the function returns a reference to an `ostream` object. That property makes it possible to concatenate output, as in the following old rock hit:

```
cout << "I'm feeling sedimental over " << boundary << "\n";
```

If you're a C programmer who has suffered through C's multitudinous % type specifiers and the problems that arise when you mismatch a specifier type to a value, using cout is almost sinfully easy. (And C++ input, of course, *is* cinfully easy.)

Output and Pointers

The `ostream` class also defines insertion operator functions for the following pointer types:

- const signed char *

- const unsigned char *

- const char *

- void *

C++ represents a string, don't forget, by using a pointer to the location of the string. The pointer can take the form of the name of an array of `char` or of an explicit `pointer-to-char` or of a quoted string. Thus all of the following `cout` statements display strings:

```
char name[20] = "Dudly Diddlemore";
char * pn = "Violet D'Amore";
cout << "Hello!";
cout << name;
cout << pn;
```

The methods use the terminating null character in the string to determine when to stop displaying characters.

C++ matches a pointer of any other type with type void * and prints a numerical representation of the address. If you want the address of the string, you have to typecast it to another type:

```
int eggs = 12;
char * amount = "dozen";
cout << &eggs;              // prints address of eggs variable
cout << amount;            // prints the string "dozen"
cout << (void *) amount;   // prints the address of the "dozen" string
```

Remember

Not all current C++ implementations have a prototype with the void * argument. In that case, you have to typecast a pointer to unsigned or, perhaps, unsigned long, if you wish to print the value of the address.

Output Concatenation

All the incarnations of the insertion operator are defined to return type ostream &. That is, the prototypes have this form:

```
ostream & operator<<(type);
```

(Here, *type* is the type to be displayed.) The ostream & return type means that using this operator returns a reference to an ostream object. Which object? The function definitions say that the reference is to the object used to evoke the operator. In other words, an operator function's return value is the same object that evokes the operator. For example, cout << "potluck" returns the cout object. That's the feature that lets you concatenate output using insertion. For instance, consider the following statement:

```
cout << "We have " << count << " unhatched chickens.\n";
```

The expression cout << "We have " displays the string and returns the cout object, reducing the statement to the following:

```
cout << count << " unhatched chickens.\n";
```

Then the expression cout << count displays the value of the count variable and returns cout, which then can handle the final argument in the statement (see Figure 16.4). This design technique really is a nice feature, which is why our examples of overloading the << operator in the previous chapters shamelessly imitate it.

THE OTHER ostream METHODS

Besides the various operator<<() functions, the ostream class provides the put() method for displaying characters and the write() method for displaying strings.

The put()method seems to be widely misimplemented. Traditionally, it had the following prototype:

```
ostream & put(char);
```

FIGURE 16.4

Output concatenation

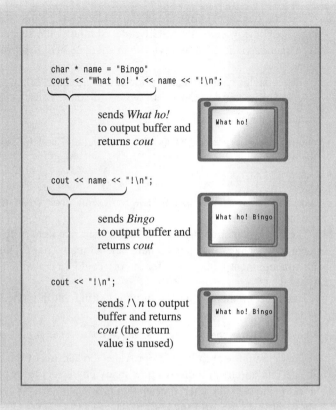

The current standard is equivalent, except it's templated to allow for wchar_t. You invoke it using the usual class method notation:

```
cout.put('W');      // display the W character
```

Here cout is the invoking object and put() is the class member function. Like the << operator functions, this function returns a reference to the invoking object, so you can concatenate output with it:

```
cout.put('I').put('t'); // displaying It with two put() calls
```

The function call cout.put('I') returns cout, which then acts as the invoking object for the put('t') call.

Given the proper prototype, you can use put() with arguments of numeric types other than char, such as int, and let function prototyping automatically convert the argument to the correct type char value. For instance, you could do the following:

```
cout.put(65);       // display the A character
cout.put(66.3);     // display the B character
```

The first statement converted the int value 65 to a char value and then displayed the character having 65 as its ASCII code. Similarly, the second statement converted the type double value 66.3 to a type char value 66 and displayed the corresponding character.

This behavior came in handy prior to C++ Release 2.0; at that time the language represented character constants with type int values. Thus, a statement such as

```cpp
cout << 'W';
```

would have interpreted 'W' as an int value, and hence displayed it as the integer 87, the ASCII value for the character. But the statement

```cpp
cout.put('W');
```

worked fine. Because current C++ represents char constants as type char, you now can use either method.

The implementation problem is that some compilers overload put() for three argument types: char, unsigned char, and signed char. This makes using put() with an int argument ambiguous, for an int could be converted to any one of those three types.

The write() method writes an entire string and has the following template prototype:

```cpp
basic_ostream<charT,traits>& write(const char_type* s, streamsize n);
```

The first argument to write() provides the address of the string to be displayed, and the second argument indicates how many characters to display. Using cout to invoke write() invokes the char specialization, so the return type is ostream &. Listing 16.1 shows how the write() method works.

Listing 16.1 write.cpp

```cpp
// write.cpp -- use cout.write()
#include <iostream>
using namespace std;
#include <cstring>  // or else string.h

int main()
{
    const char * state1 = "Ohio";
    const char * state2 = "Utah";
    const char * state3 = "Euphoria";

    int len = strlen(state2);
    cout << "Increasing loop index:\n";
    int i;
    for (i = 1; i <= len; i++)
    {
        cout.write(state2,i);
        cout << "\n";
    }

// concatenate output
    cout << "Decreasing loop index:\n";
    for (i = len; i > 0; i--)
```

```
        cout.write(state2,i) << "\n";

// exceed string length
    cout << "Exceeding string length:\n";
    cout.write(state2, len + 5) << "\n";

    return 0;
}
```

Here is the output:

```
Increasing loop index:
U
Ut
Uta
Utah
Decreasing loop index:
Utah
Uta
Ut
U
Exceeding string length:
Utah    E
```

Note that the `cout.write()` call returns the `cout` object. This is because the `write()` method returns a reference to the object that invokes it, and in this case, the `cout` object invokes it. This makes it possible to concatenate output, for `cout.write()` is replaced by its return value, `cout`:

```
cout.write(state2,i) << "\n";
```

Also, note that the `write()` method doesn't stop printing characters automatically when it reaches the null character. It simply prints how many characters you tell it to, even if that goes beyond the bounds of a particular string! In this case, the program brackets the string `"Utah"` with two other strings so that adjacent memory locations would contain data. Compilers differ in the order in which they store data in memory and in how they align memory. For instance, `"Utah"` occupies five bytes, but this particular compiler appears to align strings using multiples of four bytes, so `"Utah"` is padded out to eight bytes.

The `write()` method can also be used with numeric data. It doesn't translate a number to the correct characters; instead it transmits the bit representation as stored in memory. For instance, a 4-byte `long` value such as 560031841 would be transmitted as four separate bytes. An output device such as a monitor would then try to interpret each byte as if it were ASCII (or whatever) code. So 560031841 would appear onscreen as some 4-character combination, most likely gibberish. However, `write()` does provide a compact, accurate way to store data in a file. We'll return to this possibility later in this chapter.

FLUSHING THE OUTPUT BUFFER

Consider what happens as a program uses `cout` to send bytes on to the standard output. Because the `ostream` class buffers output handled by the `cout` object, output isn't

" If your implementation doesn't flush output when you want it to, you can force flushing by using one of two manipulators. "

sent to its destination immediately. Instead, it accumulates in the buffer until the buffer is full. Then the program *flushes* the buffer, sending the contents on and clearing the buffer for new data. Typically, a buffer is 512 bytes or an integral multiple thereof. Buffering is a great time-saver when the standard output is connected to a file on a hard disk. After all, you don't want a program to access the hard disk 512 times to send 512 bytes. It's much more effective to collect 512 bytes in a buffer and write them to a hard disk in a single disk operation.

For screen output, however, filling the buffer first is less critical. Indeed, it would be inconvenient if you had to reword the message "Press any key to continue" so that it consumed the prerequisite 512 bytes to fill a buffer. Fortunately, in the case of screen output, the program doesn't necessarily wait until the buffer is full. Sending a newline character to the buffer, for example, normally flushes the buffer. Also, as mentioned before, most implementations flush the buffer when input is pending. That is, suppose you have the following code:

```
cout << "Enter a number: ";
float num;
cin >> num;
```

The fact that the program expects input causes it to display the `cout` message (that is, flush the `"Enter a number: "` message) immediately, even though the output string lacks a newline. Without this feature, the program would wait for input without having prompted the user with the `cout` message.

If your implementation doesn't flush output when you want it to, you can force flushing by using one of two manipulators. The `flush` manipulator flushes the buffer, and the `endl` manipulator flushes the buffer and inserts a newline. You use these manipulators the way you would use a variable name:

```
cout << "Hello, good-looking! " << flush;
cout << "Wait just a moment, please." << endl;
```

Manipulators are, in fact, functions. For instance, you can flush the `cout` buffer by calling the `flush()` function directly:

```
flush(cout);
```

However, the `ostream` class overloads the `<<` insertion operator in such a way that the expression

```
cout << flush
```

gets replaced with the `flush(cout)` function call. Thus you can use the more convenient insertion notation to flush with success.

FORMATTING WITH cout

The `ostream` insertion operators convert values to text form. By default, they format values as follows:

- A type `char` value, if it represents a printable character, is displayed as a character in a field one character wide.

 Numerical integer types are displayed as decimal integers in a field just wide enough to hold the number and, if present, a minus sign.

 Strings are displayed in a field equal in width to the length of the string.

The default behavior for floating-point has changed. The following list details the differences between older and newer implementations:

 (Old Style) Floating-point types are displayed with six places to the right of the decimal, except that trailing zeros aren't displayed. (Note that the number of digits displayed has no connection with the precision to which the number is stored.) The number is displayed in fixed-point notation or else in E notation (see Chapter 3), depending upon the value of the number. Again, the field is just wide enough to hold the number and, if present, a minus sign.

 (New Style) Floating-point types are displayed with a total of six digits, except that trailing zeros aren't displayed. (Note that the number of digits displayed has no connection with the precision to which the number is stored.) The number is displayed in fixed-point notation or else in E notation (see Chapter 3), depending upon the value of the number. In particular, E notation is used if the exponent is 6 or larger or –5 or smaller. Again, the field is just wide enough to hold the number and, if present, a minus sign. The default behavior corresponds to using the standard C library function `fprintf()` with a `%g` specifier.

Because each value is displayed in a width equal to its size, you have to provide spaces between values explicitly; otherwise, consecutive values would run together.

There are several small differences between early C++ formatting and the current standard; we'll summarize them in Table 16.3 later in this chapter.

Listing 16.2 illustrates the output defaults. It displays a colon (:) after each value so you can see the width field used in each case. The program uses the expression 1.0/9.0 to generate a nonterminating fraction so you can see how many places get printed.

Remember

Not all compilers generate output formatted in accordance with the current standard. Also, the current standard allows for regional variations. For example, a European implementation can follow the continental fashion of using a comma instead of a period for displacing decimal fractions. That is, it may write 2,54 instead of 2.54. The locale library (header file `locale`) provides a mechanism for *imbuing* an input or output stream with a particular style, so a single compiler can offer more than one locale choice. This chapter will use the U.S. locale.

Listing 16.2 defaults.cpp

```cpp
// defaults.cpp -- cout default formats
#include <iostream>
using namespace std;
```

```
int main()
{
    cout << "12345678901234567890\n";
    char ch = 'K';
    int t = 273;
    cout << ch << ":\n";
    cout << t << ":\n";
    cout << -t <<":\n";

    double f1 = 1.200;
    cout << f1 << ":\n";
    cout << (f1 + 1.0 / 9.0) << ":\n";

    double f2 = 1.67E2;
    cout << f2 << ":\n";
    f2 += 1.0 / 9.0;
    cout << f2 << ":\n";
    cout << (f2 * 1.0e4) << ":\n";


    double f3 = 2.3e-4;
    cout << f3 << ":\n";
    cout << f3 / 10 << ":\n";

    return 0;
}
```

Here is the output:

```
12345678901234567890
K:
273:
-273:
1.2:
1.31111:
167:
167.111:
1.67111e+006:
0.00023:
2.3e-005:
```

Each value fills its field. Note that the trailing zeros of 1.200 are not displayed but that floating-point values without terminating zeros have six places to the right of the decimal displayed. Also, this particular implementation displays three digits in the exponent.

Changing the Number Base Used for Display

The ostream class inherits from the ios class, which inherits from the ios_base class. The ios_base class stores information describing the format state. For instance, certain bits in one class member determine the number base used, while another member determines the field width. By using *manipulators*, you can control the number base used to display integers. By using ios_base member functions, you can control the field width and the number of places displayed to the right of the decimal. Because the ios_base class is an indirect base class for ostream, you can use its methods with ostream objects (or descendants), such as cout.

Remember

The members and methods found in the `ios_base` class formerly were found in the `ios` class. Now `ios_base` is a base class to `ios`. In the new system, `ios` is a template class with `char` and `wchar_t` specializations, while `ios_base` contains the non-template features.

Let's see how to set the number base to be used in displaying integers. To control whether integers are displayed in base 10, base 16, or base 8, you can use the `dec`, `hex`, and `oct` manipulators. For instance, the function call

```
hex(cout);
```

sets the number base format state for the `cout` object to hexadecimal. Once you do this, a program will print integer values in hexadecimal form until you set the format state to another choice. Note that the manipulators are not member functions, hence they don't have to be invoked by an object.

Although the manipulators really are functions, you normally see them used this way:

```
cout << hex;
```

The `ostream` class overloads the `<<` operator to make this usage equivalent to the function call `hex(cout)`. Listing 16.3 illustrates using these manipulators. It shows the value of an integer and its square in three different number bases. Note that you can use a manipulator separately or as part of a series of insertions.

Listing 16.3 manip.cpp

```cpp
// manip.cpp -- using format manipulators
#include <iostream>
using namespace std;
int main()
{
    cout << "Enter an integer: ";
    int n;
    cin >> n;

    cout << "n       n*n\n";
    cout << n << "       " << n * n << " (decimal)\n";
// set to hex mode
    cout << hex;
    cout << n << "       ";
    cout << n * n << " (hexadecimal)\n";

// set to octal mode
    cout << oct << n << "       " << n * n << " (octal)\n";

// alternative way to call a manipulator
    dec(cout);
    cout << n << "       " << n * n << " (decimal)\n";

    return 0;
}
```

Here is some sample output:

```
Enter an integer: 13
n     n*n
13    169 (decimal)
d     a9 (hexadecimal)
15    251 (octal)
13    169 (decimal)
```

Adjusting Field Widths

You probably noticed that the columns in the preceding example don't line up; that's because the numbers have different field widths. You can use the width member function to place differently sized numbers in fields having equal widths. The method has these prototypes:

```
int width();
int width(int i);
```

The first form returns the current setting for field width. The second sets the field width to i spaces and returns the previous field width value. This allows you to save the previous value in case you want to restore the width to that value later.

The width() method affects only the next item displayed, and the field width reverts to the default value afterwards. For example, consider the following statements:

```
cout << '#';
cout.width(12);
cout << 12 << "#" <<  24 << "#\n";
```

Because width() is a member function, you have to use an object (cout, in this case) to invoke it. The output statement produces the following display:

```
#           12#24#
```

The 12 is placed in a field 12 characters wide at the right end of the field. This is called right-justification. After that, the field width reverts to the default, and the two # characters and the 24 are printed in fields equal to their own size.

Remember

The width() method affects only the next item displayed, and the field width reverts to the default value afterwards.

C++ never truncates data, so if you attempt to print a seven-digit value in a field width of 2, C++ expands the field to fit the data. (Some languages just fill the field with asterisks if the data doesn't fit. The C/C++ philosophy is that showing all the data is more important than keeping the columns neat; C++ puts substance before form.) Listing 16.4 shows how the width() member function works.

Listing 16.4 width.cpp

```
// width.cpp -- use the width method
#include <iostream>
```

> *Some languages just fill the field with asterisks if the data doesn't fit. The C/C++ philosophy is that showing all the data is more important than keeping the columns neat; C++ puts substance before form.*

```
using namespace std;

int main()
{
    int w = cout.width(30);
    cout << "default field width = " << w << ":\n";

    cout.width(5);
    cout << "N" <<':';
    cout.width(8);
    cout << "N * N" << ":\n";

    for (long i = 1; i <= 100; i *= 10)
    {
        cout.width(5);
        cout << i <<':';
        cout.width(8);
        cout << i * i << ":\n";
    }

    return 0;
}
```

Here is the output:

```
      default field width = 0:
  N:    N * N:
  1:        1:
 10:      100:
100:    10000:
```

The output displays values right-justified in their fields. The output is padded with spaces. That is, cout achieves the full field width by adding spaces. With right-justification, the spaces are inserted to the left of the values. The character used for padding is termed the *fill character*. Right-justification is the default.

Note that the program applies the field width of 30 to the string displayed by the first cout statement but not to the value of w. This is because the width() method affects only the next single item displayed. Also, note that w has the value 0. This is because cout.width(30) returns the previous field width, not the one to which it was just set. The fact that w is zero means that zero is the default field width. Because C++ always expands a field to fit the data, this one size fits all. Finally, the program uses width() to align column headings and data by using a width of five characters for the first column and a width of eight characters for the second column.

Fill Characters

By default, cout fills unused parts of a field with spaces. You can use the fill() member function to change that. For instance, the call

```
cout.fill('*');
```

changes the fill character to an asterisk. That can be handy for, say, printing checks so that recipients can't easily add a digit or two. Listing 16.5 illustrates using this member function.

Listing 16.5 fill.cpp

```cpp
// fill.cpp -- change fill character for fields
#include <iostream>
using namespace std;

int main()
{
    cout.fill('*');
    char * staff[2] = { "Waldo Whipsnade", "Wilmarie Wooper"};
    long bonus[2] = {900, 1350};

    for (int i = 0; i < 2; i++)
    {
        cout << staff[i] << ": $";
        cout.width(7);
        cout << bonus[i] << "\n";
    }

    return 0;
}
```

Here's the output:

```
Waldo Whipsnade: $****900
Wilmarie Wooper: $***1350
```

Note that, unlike the field width, the new fill character stays in effect until you change it.

Setting Floating-Point Display Precision

The meaning of floating-point precision depends upon the output mode. In the default mode, it means the total number of digits displayed. In the fixed and scientific modes, to be discussed soon, the precision means the number of digits displayed to the right of the decimal place. The precision default for C++, as you've seen, is 6. (Recall, however, that trailing zeros are dropped.) The precision() member function lets you select other values. For instance, the statement

```cpp
cout.precision(2);
```

causes cout to set the precision to 2. Unlike the case with width(), but like the case for fill(), a new precision setting stays in effect until reset. Listing 16.6 demonstrates precisely this point.

Listing 16.6 precise.cpp

```cpp
// precise.cpp -- set the precision
#include <iostream>
using namespace std;

int main()
{
    float price1 = 20.40;
    float price2 = 1.9 + 8.0 / 9.0;
```

```
        cout << "\"Furry Friends\" is $" << price1 << "!\n";
        cout << "\"Fiery Fiends\" is $" << price2 << "!\n";

        cout.precision(2);
        cout << "\"Furry Friends\" is $" << price1 << "!\n";
        cout << "\"Fiery Fiends\" is $" << price2 << "!\n";

        return 0;
    }
```

Remember

Older versions of C++ interpret the precision for the default mode as the number of digits to the right of the decimal instead of as the total number of digits.

Here is the output:

```
"Furry Friends" is $20.4!
"Fiery Fiends" is $2.78889!
"Furry Friends" is $20!
"Fiery Fiends" is $2.8!
```

Note that the third line doesn't print a trailing decimal point. Also, the fourth line displays a total of two digits.

Printing Trailing Zeros and Decimal Points

Certain forms of output, such as prices or numbers in columns, look better if trailing zeros are retained. For instance, the output to Listing 16.6 would look better as $20.40 than as $20.4. The `iostream` family of classes doesn't provide a function whose sole purpose is accomplishing that. However, the `ios_base` class provides a `setf()` (for *set flag*) function that controls several formatting features. The class also defines several constants that can be used as arguments to this function. For instance, the function call

```
    cout.setf(ios_base::showpoint);
```

causes `cout` to display trailing decimal points. Formerly, but not currently, it also causes trailing zeros to be displayed. That is, instead of displaying 2.00 as 2, `cout` will display it as 2.000000 (old C++ formatting) or 2. (current formatting) if the default precision of 6 is in effect. Listing 16.7 adds this statement to Listing 16.6.

Remember

If your compiler uses the `iostream.h` header file instead of `iostream`, you most likely will have to use `ios` instead of `ios_base` in `setf()` arguments.

In case you're wondering about the notation `ios_base::showpoint`, `showpoint` is a class scope static constant defined in the `ios_base` class declaration. Class scope means that you have to use the scope operator (`::`) with the constant name if you use the name outside a member function definition. So `ios_base::showpoint` names a constant defined in the `ios_base` class.

Listing 16.7 showpt.cpp

```cpp
// showpt.cpp -- set the precision, show trailing point
#include <iostream>
using namespace std;

int main()
{
    float price1 = 20.40;
    float price2 = 1.9 + 8.0 / 9.0;

    cout.setf(ios_base::showpoint);
    cout << "\"Furry Friends\" is $" << price1 << "!\n";
    cout << "\"Fiery Fiends\" is $" << price2 << "!\n";

    cout.precision(2);
    cout << "\"Furry Friends\" is $" << price1 << "!\n";
    cout << "\"Fiery Fiends\" is $" << price2 << "!\n";

    return 0;
}
```

Here is the output using the current formatting. Note that trailing zeros are not shown, but the trailing decimal point for the third line is shown.

```
"Furry Friends" is $20.4!
"Fiery Fiends" is $2.78889!
"Furry Friends" is $20.!
"Fiery Fiends" is $2.8!
```

How, then, can you display trailing zeros? To answer that question, we have to discuss the setf() function in more detail.

More About setf()

The setf() method controls several other formatting choices, so let's take a closer look at it. The ios_base class has a protected data member in which individual bits (called *flags* in this context) control different formatting aspects such as the number base or whether trailing zeros are displayed. Turning a flag on is called *setting the flag* (or bit) and means setting the bit to 1. (If you've ever had to set DIP switches to configure computer hardware, bit flags are the programming equivalent.) The hex, dec, and oct manipulators, for example, adjust the three flag bits that control the number base. The setf() function provides another means of adjusting flag bits.

The setf() function has two prototypes. The first is this:

```cpp
fmtflags setf(fmtflags);
```

Here fmtflags is a typedef name for a *bitmask* type (see Note) used to hold the format flags. The name is defined in the ios_base class. This version of setf() is used for setting format information controlled by a single bit. The argument is an fmtflags value indicating which bit to set. The return value is a type fmtflags number indicating the former setting of all the flags. You then can save that value if you later wish to

> *Keeping track of bits sounds (and is) tedious. However, you don't have to do that job; the ios_base class defines constants representing the bit values.*

restore the original settings. What value do you pass to setf()? If you want to set bit number 11 to 1, you pass a number having its number 11 bit set to 1. The return value would have its number 11 bit assigned the prior value for that bit. Keeping track of bits sounds (and is) tedious. However, you don't have to do that job; the ios_base class defines constants representing the bit values. Table 16.1 shows some of these definitions.

Remember

A bitmask type is a type used to store individual bit values. It could be an integer type, an enum, or an STL `bitset` container. The main idea is that each bit is individually accessible and has its own meaning. The `iostream` package uses bitmask types to store state information.

TABLE 16.1
FORMATTING CONSTANTS

CONSTANT	MEANING
ios_base::boolalpha	input and output bool values as true and false
ios_base::showbase	use C++ base prefixes (0,0x) on output
ios_base::showpoint	show trailing decimal point
ios_base::uppercase	use uppercase letters for hex output, E notation
ios_base::showpos	use + before positive numbers

Because these formatting constants are defined within the ios_base class, you must use the scope resolution operator with them. That is, use ios_base::uppercase, not just uppercase. Changes remain in effect until overridden. Listing 16.8 illustrates using some of these constants.

Listing 16.8 setf.cpp

```cpp
// setf.cpp -- use setf() to control formatting
#include <iostream>
using namespace std;

int main()
{
    int temperature = 63;

    cout << "Today's water temperature: ";
       cout.setf(ios_base::showpos);      // show plus sign
     cout << temperature << "\n";

       cout << "For our programming friends, that's\n";
    cout << hex << temperature << "\n"; // use hex
       cout.setf(ios_base::uppercase);    // use uppercase in hex
       cout.setf(ios_base::showbase);     // use 0X prefix for hex
    cout << "or\n";
```

```
        cout << temperature << "\n";
    cout << "How " << true << "!  oops -- How ";
    cout.setf(ios_base::boolalpha);
    cout << true << "!\n";

    return 0;
}
```

Remember

Older implementations may use `ios` instead of `ios_base`, and they may fail to provide a `boolalpha` choice.

Here is the output:

```
Today's water temperature: +63
For our programming friends, that's
3f
or
0X3F
How 1!  oops -- How true!
```

Note that the plus sign is used only with the base 10 version. C++ treats hexadecimal and octal values as unsigned; hence no sign is needed for them. (However, some implementations may still display a plus sign.)

The second `setf()` prototype takes two arguments and returns the prior setting:

```
fmtflags setf(fmtflags , fmtflags );
```

This overloaded form of the function is used for format choices controlled by more than one bit. The first argument, as before, is an `fmtflags` value containing the desired setting. The second argument is a value that first clears the appropriate bits. For instance, suppose setting bit 3 to 1 means base 10, setting bit 4 to 1 means base 8, and setting bit 5 to 1 means base 16. Suppose output is in base 10 and you want to set it to base 16. Not only do you have to set bit 5 to 1, you also have to set bit 3 to 0—this is called *clearing the bit*. The clever `hex` manipulator does both tasks automatically. The `setf()` requires a bit more work because you use the second argument to indicate which bits to clear and then use the first argument to indicate which bit to set. This is not as complicated as it sounds because the `ios_base` class defines constants (shown in Table 16.2) for this purpose. In particular, you should use the constant `ios_base::basefield` as the second argument and `ios::hex` as the first argument if you're changing bases. That is, the function call

```
 cout.setf(ios::hex, ios::basefield);
```

has the same effect as using the `hex` manipulator.

TABLE 16.2
ARGUMENTS FOR `setf(long, long)`

SECOND ARGUMENT	FIRST ARGUMENT	MEANING
`ios_base::basefield`	`ios_base::dec`	use base 10
	`ios_base::oct`	use base 8
	`ios_base::hex`	use base 16
`ios_base::floatfield`	`ios_base::fixed`	use fixed-point notation
	`ios_base::scientific`	use scientific notation
`ios_base::adjustfield`	`ios_base::left`	use left-justification
	`ios_base::right`	use right-justification
	`ios_base::internal`	left-justify sign or base prefix, right-justify value

The `ios_base` class defines three sets of formatting flags that can be handled this way. Each set consists of one constant to be used as the second argument and two to three constants to be used as a first argument. The second argument clears a batch of related bits; then the first argument sets one of those bits to 1. Table 16.2 shows the names of the constants used for the second `setf()` argument, the associated choice of constants for the first argument, and their meanings. For instance, to select left-justification, use `ios_base::adjustfield` for the second argument and `ios_base::left` as the first argument. Left-justification means starting a value at the left end of the field, and right-justification means ending a value at the right end of the field. Internal justification means placing any signs or base prefixes at the left of the field and the rest of the number at the right of the field. (Unfortunately, C++ does not provide a self-justification mode.)

Fixed-point notation means using the 123.4 style for floating-point values regardless of the size of the number, and scientific notation means using the 1.23e04 style regardless of the size of the number.

Under the current standard, both fixed and scientific notation have the following two properties:

- Precision means the number of digits to the right of the decimal rather than the total number of digits.

- Trailing zeros are displayed.

Under the older usage, trailing zeros are not shown unless `ios::showpoint` is set. Also, under older usage, precision always meant the number of digits to the right of the decimal, even in the default mode.

The `setf()` function is a member function of the `ios_base` class. Because that's a base class for the `ostream` class, you can invoke the function using the `cout` object. For example, to request left-justification, use this call:

```
ios_base::fmtflags old = cout.setf(ios::left, ios::adjustfield);
```

To restore the previous setting, do this:

```
cout.setf(old, ios::adjustfield);
```

Listing 16.9 illustrates further examples of using setf() with two arguments.

Remember

This program uses a math function, and some C++ systems don't automatically search the math library. For instance, some UNIX systems require that you do the following:

```
$ CC setf2.C -lm
```

The -lm option instructs the linker to search the math library.

Listing 16.9 setf2.cpp

```
// setf2.cpp -- use setf() with 2 arguments to control formatting
#include <iostream>
using namespace std;
#include <cmath>

int main()
{
    // use left justification, show the plus sign, show trailing
    // zeros, with a precision of 3
    cout.setf(ios_base::left, ios_base::adjustfield);
    cout.setf(ios_base::showpos);
    cout.setf(ios_base::showpoint);
    cout.precision(3);
    // use e-notation and save old format setting
    ios_base::fmtflags old = cout.setf(ios_base::scientific,
        ios_base::floatfield);
    cout << "Left Justification:\n";
    long n;
    for (n = 1; n <= 41; n+= 10)
    {
        cout.width(4);
        cout << n << "|";
        cout.width(12);
        cout << sqrt(n) << "|\n";
    }

    // change to internal justification
    cout.setf(ios_base::internal, ios_base::adjustfield);
    // restore default floating-point display style
    cout.setf(old, ios_base::floatfield);

    cout << "Internal Justification:\n";
    for (n = 1; n <= 41; n+= 10)
    {
        cout.width(4);
        cout << n << "|";
        cout.width(12);
        cout << sqrt(n) << "|\n";
    }

    // use right justification, fixed notation
    cout.setf(ios_base::right, ios_base::adjustfield);
```

```
    cout.setf(ios_base::fixed, ios_base::floatfield);
    cout << "Right Justification:\n";
    for (n = 1; n <= 41; n+= 10)
    {
        cout.width(4);
        cout << n << "¦";
        cout.width(12);
        cout << sqrt(n) << "¦\n";
    }

    return 0;
}
```

Here is the output:

```
Left Justification:
+1   ¦+1.000e+000 ¦
+11  ¦+3.317e+000 ¦
+21  ¦+4.583e+000 ¦
+31  ¦+5.568e+000 ¦
+41  ¦+6.403e+000 ¦
Internal Justification:
+  1¦+        1.00¦
+ 11¦+        3.32¦
+ 21¦+        4.58¦
+ 31¦+        5.57¦
+ 41¦+        6.40¦
Right Justification:
  +1¦      +1.000¦
 +11¦      +3.317¦
 +21¦      +4.583¦
 +31¦      +5.568¦
 +41¦      +6.403¦
```

Note how a precision of 3 causes the default floating-point display (used for internal justification in this program) to display a total of three digits, while the fixed and scientific modes display three digits to the right of the decimal.

The effects of calling setf() can be undone with unsetf(), which has the following prototype:

```
void unsetf(fmtflags mask);
```

Here mask is a bit pattern. All bits set to 1 in mask cause the corresponding bits to be unset. That is, setf() sets bits to 1 and unsetf() sets bits back to 0.

Standard Manipulators

Using setf() is not the most user-friendly approach to formatting, so C++ offers several manipulators to invoke setf() for you, automatically supplying the right arguments. You've already seen dec, hex, and oct. These manipulators, most of which are not available to older implementations, work like hex. For example, the statement

```
cout << left << fixed;
```

turns on left justification and the fixed decimal point option. Table 16.3 lists these along with several other manipulators.

Remember

> If your system supports these manipulators, take advantage of them; if it doesn't, you still have the option of using setf().

TABLE 16.3
SOME STANDARD MANIPULATORS

MANIPULATOR	CALLS
boolalpha	setf(ios_base::boolalpha)
noboolalpha	unset(ios_base::noboolalpha)
showbase	setf(ios_base::showbase)
noshowbase	unsetf(ios_base::showbase)
showpoint	setf(ios_base::showpoint)
noshowpoint	unsetf(ios_base::showpoint)
showpos	setf(ios_base::showpos)
noshowpos	unsetf(ios_base::showpos)
uppercase	setf(ios_base::uppercase)
nouppercase	unsetf(ios_base::uppercase)
internal	setf(ios_base::internal, ios_base::adjustfield)
left	setf(ios_base::left, ios_base::adjustfield)
right	setf(ios_base::right, ios_base::adjustfield)
dec	setf(ios_base::dec, ios_base::basefield)
hex	setf(ios_base::hex, ios_base::basefield)
oct	setf(ios_base::oct, ios_base::basefield)
fixed	setf(ios_base::fixed, ios_base::floatfield)
scientific	setf(ios_base::scientific, ios_base::floatfield)

The iomanip Header File

Setting some format values, such as the field width, can be awkward using the iostream tools. To make life easier, C++ supplies additional manipulators in the iomanip header file. They provide the same services we've discussed, but in a notationally more convenient manner. The three most commonly used are setprecision() for setting the precision, setfill() for setting the fill character, and setw() for setting the field width. Unlike the manipulators discussed previously, these take arguments. The setprecision() manipulator takes an integer argument specifying the precision, the setfill() takes a char argument indicating the fill character, and the setw() manipulator takes an integer argument specifying the field width. Because they are manipulators, they can be concatenated in a cout statement. This makes the setw() manipulator particularly convenient when displaying several columns of values. Listing 16.10 illustrates this by changing the field width and fill character several times for one output line. It also uses some of the newer standard manipulators.

Remember

This program uses a math function, and some C++ systems don't automatically search the math library. For instance, some UNIX systems require that you do the following:

```
$ CC iomanip.C -lm
```

The `-lm` option instructs the linker to search the math library. Also, older compilers may not recognize the new standard manipulators such as `showpoint`. In that case, you can use the `setf()` equivalents.

" This makes the setw() manipulator particularly convenient when displaying several columns of values. "

Listing 16.10 iomanip.cpp

```cpp
// iomanip.cpp -- use manipulators from iomanip
// some systems require explicitly linking the math library
#include <iostream>
using namespace std;
#include <iomanip>
#include <cmath>

int main()
{
    // use new standard manipulators
    cout << showpoint << fixed << right;

    // use iomanip manipulators
    cout << setw(6) << "N" << setw(14) << "square root"
         << setw(15) << "fourth root\n";

    double root;
    for (int n = 10; n <=100; n += 10)
    {
        root = sqrt(n);
        cout << setw(6) << setfill('.') << n << setfill(' ')
             << setw(12) << setprecision(3) << root
             << setw(14) << setprecision(4) << sqrt(root)
             << "\n";
    }

    return 0;
}
```

Here is the output:

```
    N   square root   fourth root
....10        3.162        1.7783
....20        4.472        2.1147
....30        5.477        2.3403
....40        6.325        2.5149
....50        7.071        2.6591
....60        7.746        2.7832
....70        8.367        2.8925
....80        8.944        2.9907
....90        9.487        3.0801
...100       10.000        3.1623
```

Now you can produce neatly aligned columns. Note that this program produces the same formatting with either the older or current implementations. Using the `showpoint` manipulator causes trailing zeros to be displayed in older implementations, and using the `fixed` manipulator causes trailing zeros to be displayed in current implementations. Using `fixed` makes the display fixed-point in either system, and in current systems it makes precision refer to the number of digits to the right of the decimal. In older systems, precision always has that meaning, regardless of the floating-point display mode.

Table 16.4 summarizes some of the differences between older C++ formatting and the current state. One moral of this table is that you shouldn't feel baffled if you run a sample program you've seen somewhere and the output format doesn't match what is shown for the example.

TABLE 16.4
FORMATTING CHANGES

FEATURE	OLDER C++	CURRENT C++
`precision(n)`	Display n digits to the right of the decimal point	Display a total of n digits in the default mode, and display n digits to the right of the decimal point in fixed and scientific modes
`ios::showpoint`	Display trailing decimal point and trailing zeros	Display trailing decimal point
`ios::fixed, ios::scientific`		Show trailing zeros (also see comments under `precision()`)

Input with `cin`

Now it's time to turn to input and getting data into a program. The `cin` object represents the standard input as a stream of bytes. Normally, you generate that stream of characters at the keyboard. If you type the character sequence 1998, the `cin` object extracts those characters from the input stream. You may intend that input to be part of a string, to be an `int` value, to be a `float` value, or to be some other type. Thus extraction also involves type conversion. The `cin` object, guided by the type of variable designated to receive the value, must use its methods to convert that character sequence into the intended type of value.

Typically, you use `cin` as follows:

```
cin >> value_holder;
```

Here `value_holder` identifies the memory location in which to store the input. It can be the name of a variable, a reference, a dereferenced pointer, or a member of a structure or of a class. How `cin` interprets the input depends on the data type for `value_holder`. The istream class, defined in the `iostream` header file, overloads the `>>` extraction operator to recognize the following basic types:

- `signed char &`

- `unsigned char &`

- `char &`

- `short &`

- `unsigned short &`

- `int &`

- `unsigned int &`

- `long &`

- `unsigned long &`

- `float &`

- `double &`

- `long double &`

These are referred to as *formatted input functions* because they convert the input data to the format indicated by the target.

A typical operator function has a prototype like the following:

```
istream & operator>>(int &);
```

Both the argument and the return value are references. A reference argument (see Chapter 9) means that a statement such as

```
cin >> staff_size;
```

causes the `operator>>()` function to work with the variable `staff_size` itself rather than with a copy, as would be the case with a regular argument. Because the argument type is a reference, `cin` is able to modify directly the value of a variable used as an argument. The statement above, for example, directly modifies the value of the `staff_size` variable. We'll get to the significance of a reference return value in a moment. First, let's examine the type conversion aspect of the extraction operator. For arguments of each type in the preceding list of types, the extraction operator converts the character input to the indicated type of value. For instance, suppose `staff_size` is type `int`. Then the compiler matches the

```
cin >> staff_size;
```

to the following prototype:

```
istream & operator>>(int &);
```

The function corresponding to that prototype then reads the stream of characters being sent to the program, say, the characters 2, 3, 1, 8, and 4. For a system using a 2-byte int, the function then converts these characters to the 2-byte binary representation of the integer 23184. If, on the other hand, staff_size had been type double, cin would use the operator>>(double &) to convert the same input into the 8-byte floating-point representation of the value 23184.0.

The istream class also overloads the >> extraction operator for character pointer types:

- signed char *

- char *

- unsigned char *

For this type of argument, the extraction operator reads the next word from input and places it at the indicated address, adding a null character to make a string. For instance, suppose you have this code:

```
cout << "Enter your first name:\n";
char name[20];
cin >> name;
```

If you respond to the request by typing Hilary, the extraction operator places the characters Hilary\0 in the name array. (As usual, \0 represents the terminating null character.) The name identifier, being the name of a char array, acts as the address of the array's first element, making name type char * (pointer-to-char).

The fact that each extraction operator returns a reference to the invoking object lets you concatenate input, just as you can concatenate output:

```
char name[20];
float fee;
int group;
cin >> name >> fee >> group;
```

Here, for example, the cin object returned by cin >> name becomes the object handling fee.

HOW cin >> VIEWS INPUT

The various versions of the extraction operator share a common way of looking at the input stream. They skip over white space (blanks, newlines, and tabs) until they encounter a nonwhite-space character. This is true even for the single-character modes (those in which the argument is type char, unsigned char, or signed char), which is not true of C's character input functions (see Figure 16.5). In the single-character modes, the >> operator reads that character and assigns it to the indicated location. In the other modes, the operator reads in one unit of the indicated type. That is, it reads everything from the initial nonwhite-space character up to the first character that doesn't match the destination type.

> *" The various versions of the extraction operator share a common way of looking at the input stream. They skip over white space (blanks, newlines, and tabs) until they encounter a nonwhite-space character. "*

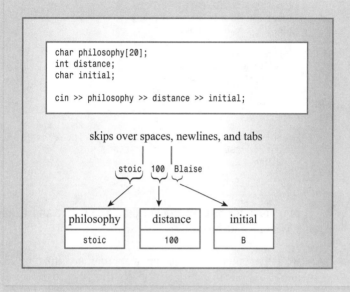

FIGURE 16.5

`cin >>` *skips over white space*

```
char philosophy[20];
int distance;
char initial;

cin >> philosophy >> distance >> initial;
```

skips over spaces, newlines, and tabs

stoic 100 Blaise

philosophy	distance	initial
stoic	100	B

For example, consider the following code:

```
int elevation;
cin >> elevation;
```

Suppose you type the following characters:

```
-123Z
```

The operator will read the -, 1, 2, and 3 characters, because they are all valid parts of an integer. But the Z character isn't valid, so the last character accepted for input is the 3. The Z remains in the input stream, and the next `cin` statement will start reading at that point. Meanwhile, the operator converts the character sequence -123 to an integer value and assigns it to `elevation`.

It can happen that input fails to meet a program's expectation. For example, suppose you entered Zcar instead of -123Z. In that case, the extraction operator leaves the value of `elevation` unchanged and returns the value zero. (More technically, an `if` or `while` statement evaluates an `istream` object as `false` if it's had an error state set—we'll discuss this in more depth later in this chapter.) The `false` return value allows a program to check whether input meets the program requirements, as Listing 16.11 shows.

Listing 16.11 check_it.cpp

```cpp
#include <iostream>
using namespace std;
```

```
int main()
{
    cout.precision(2);
    cout << showpoint << fixed;
    cout << "Enter numbers: ";

    double sum = 0.0;
    double input;
    while (cin >> input)
    {
        sum += input;
    }

    cout << "Last value entered = " << input << "\n";
    cout << "Sum = " << sum << "\n";
    return 0;
}
```

Remember

> **If your compiler doesn't support the `showpoint` and `fixed` manipulators, use the `setf()` equivalents.**

Here's the output when some inappropriate input (-123Z) sneaks into the input stream:

```
Enter numbers: 200.0
1.0E1 -50 -123Z 60
Last value entered = -123.00
Sum = 37.00
```

Because input is buffered, the second line of keyboard input values didn't get sent to the program until we typed ⌐Enter⌐ at the end of the line. But the loop quit processing input at the Z character, because it didn't match any of the floating-point formats. The failure of input to match the expected format, in turn, caused the expression `cin>> input` to evaluate to `false`, thus terminating the `while` loop.

STREAM STATES

Let's take a closer look at what happens for inappropriate input. A `cin` or `cout` object contains a data member (inherited from the `ios_base` class) that describes the *stream state*. A stream state (defined as type `iostate`, which, in turn, is a bitmask type, such as described earlier) consists of the three `ios_base` elements: `eofbit`, `badbit`, or `failbit`. Each element is a single bit that can be 1 (*set*) or 0 (*cleared*). When a `cin` operation reaches the end of a file, it sets the `eofbit`. When a `cin` operation fails to read the expected characters, as in the example above, it sets the `failbit`. I/O failures, such as trying to read a non-accessible file or trying to write to a write-protected diskette, also can set `failbit` to 1. The `badbit` element is set when some undiagnosed failure may have corrupted the stream. (Implementations don't necessarily agree about which events set `failbit` and which set `badbit`.) When all three of these state bits are set to 0, everything is fine. Programs can check the stream state and use that information to decide what to do next. Table 16.5 lists these bits along with some ios_base methods that report or alter the stream state. (Older compilers don't provide the two exceptions() methods.)

TABLE 16.5
STREAM STATES

MEMBER	DESCRIPTION
eofbit	Set to 1 if end-of-file reached.
badbit	Set to 1 if the stream may be corrupted; for instance, there could have been a file read error.
failbit	Set to 1 if an input operation failed to read the expected characters or an output operation failed to write the expected characters.
goodbit	Just another way of saying 0.
good()	Returns true if the stream can be used (all bits are cleared).
eof()	Returns true if eofbit is set.
bad()	Returns true if badbit is set.
fail()	Returns true if badbit or failbit is set.
rdstate()	Returns the stream state.
exceptions()	Returns a bit mask identifying which flag causes an exception to be thrown.
exceptions(iostate ex)	Sets which states will cause clear() to throw an exception; for instance, if ex is eofbit, then clear() will throw an exception if eofbit is set.
clear(iostate s)	Sets the stream state to s; the default for s is 0 (goodbit); throws a basic_ios::failure exception if rdstate() & exceptions()) != 0.
setstate(iostate s)	Calls clear(rdstate() ¦ s). This sets stream state bits corresponding to those bits set in s; other stream state bits are left unchanged.

Setting States

Two of the methods in Table 16.5, clear() and setstate(), are similar. Both reset the state, but in a different fashion. The clear() method sets the state to its argument. Thus, the call

```
clear();
```

uses the default argument of 0, which clears all three state bits (`eofbit`, `badbit`, and `failbit`). Similarly, the call

```
clear(eofbit);
```

makes the state equal to `eofbit`; that is, the `eofbit` is set and the other two state bits are cleared.

The `setstate()` method, however, affects only those bits that are set in its argument. Thus, the call

```
setstate(eofbit);
```

sets `eofbit` without affecting the other bits. So if `failbit` were already set, it stays set.

Why would you reset the stream state? For a program writer, the most common reason is to use `clear()` with no argument to reopen input after encountering mismatched input or end-of-file; whether or not doing so makes sense depends on what the program is trying to accomplish. You'll see some examples shortly. The main purpose for `setstate()` is to provide a means for input and output functions to change the state. For example, if `num` is an `int`, the call

```
ccin >> num;  // read an int
```

can result in `operator>>(int &)` using `setstate()` to set `failbit` or `eofbit`.

I/O and Exceptions

Suppose, say, an input function sets `eofbit`. Does this cause an exception to be thrown? By default, the answer is no. However, you can use the `exceptions()` method to control how exceptions are handled.

First, here's some background. The `exceptions()` method returns a bitfield with three bits corresponding to `eofbit`, `failbit`, and `badbit`. Changing the stream state involves either `clear()` or `setstate()`, which uses `clear()`. After changing the stream state, the `clear()` method compares the current stream state to the value returned by `exceptions()`. If a bit is set in the return value and the corresponding bit is set in the current state, `clear()` throws a `basic_ios::failure` exception. This would happen, for example, if both values had `badbit` set. It follows that if `exceptions()` returns `goodbit`, no exceptions are thrown.

The default setting for `exceptions()` is `goodbit`, that is, no exceptions thrown. However, the overloaded `exceptions(iostate)` function gives you control over the behavior:

```
cin.exceptions(badbit);  // setting badbit causes exception to be thrown
```

The bitwise OR operator (`|`), as discussed in Appendix E, allows you to specify more than one bit. For example, the statement

```
cin.exceptions(badbit | eofbit);
```

results in an exception being thrown if either `badbit` or `eofbit` subsequently is set.

Stream State Effects

An `if` or `while` test such as

```
while (cin >> input)
```

tests as `true` only if the stream state is good (all bits cleared). If a test fails, you can use the member functions in Table 16.5 to discriminate among possible causes. For example, you could modify the central part of Listing 16.11 to look like this:

```
while (cin >> input)
{
    sum += input;
}
if (cin.eof())
    cout << "Loop terminated because EOF encountered\n";
```

Setting a stream state bit has a very important consequence: The stream is closed for further input or output until the bit is cleared. For instance, the following code won't work:

```
while (cin >> input)
{
    sum += input;
}
cout << "Last value entered = " << input << "\n";
cout << "Sum = " << sum << "\n";
cout << "Now enter a new number: ";
cin >> input;    // won't work
```

If you want a program to read further input after a stream state bit has been set, you have to reset the stream state to good. This can be done by calling the `clear()` method:

```
while (cin >> input)
{
    sum += input;
}
cout << "Last value entered = " << input << "\n";
cout << "Sum = " << sum << "\n";
cout << "Now enter a new number: ";
cin.clear();          // reset stream state
while (!isspace(cin.get()))
    continue;         // get rid of bad input
cin >> input;         // will work now
```

Note that it is not enough to reset the stream state. The mismatched input that terminated the input loop still is in the input queue, and the program has to get past it. One way is to keep reading characters until reaching white space. The `isspace()` function (see Chapter 6) is a `cctype` function that returns true if its argument is a white space character. Or you can discard the rest of the line instead of just the next word:

```
while (cin.get() != '\n')
    continue;  // get rid rest of line
```

This example assumes that the loop terminated because of inappropriate input. Suppose, instead, the loop terminated because of end-of-file or because of a hardware failure. Then the new code disposing of bad input makes no sense. You can fix matters by using the `fail()` method to test whether the assumption was correct. Because, for historical reasons, `fail()` returns true if either `failbit` or `badbit` is set, the code has to exclude the latter case.

```
while (cin >> input)
{
    sum += input;
}
cout << "Last value entered = " << input << "\n";
cout << "Sum = " << sum << "\n";
cout << "Now enter a new number: ";
if (cin.fail() && !cin.bad() ) // failed because of mismatched input
{

    cin.clear();        // reset stream state
    while (!isspace(cin.get()))
        continue;      // get rid of bad input
}
else // else bail out
{
    cout << "I cannot go on!\n";
    exit(1);
}
cout << "Now enter a new number: ";
cin >> input;  // will work now
```

OTHER `istream` CLASS METHODS

Chapters 3, 4, and 5 discuss the `get()` and `getline()` methods. As you may recall, they provide the following additional input capabilities:

- The `get(char &)` and `get(void)` methods provide single-character input that doesn't skip over white space.

- The `get(char *, int, char)` and `getline(char *, int, char)` functions read entire lines by default rather than single words.

These are termed *unformatted input functions* because they simply read character input as it is without skipping over white space and without performing data conversions.

Let's look at these two groups of `istream` class member functions.

Single-Character Input

When used with a *char* argument or no argument at all, the `get()` methods fetch the next input character, even if it is a space, tab, or newline character. The `get(char & ch)` version assigns the input character to its argument, while the `get(void)` version uses the input character, converted to an integer type, typically `int`, as its return value.

Let's try `get(char &)` first. Suppose you have the following loop in a program:

```
int ct = 0;
char ch;
cin.get(ch);
while (ch != '\n')
{
    cout << ch;
    ct++;
    cin.get(ch);
}
cout << ct << '\n';
```

Next, suppose you type the following optimistic input:

```
I C++ clearly.⌷Enter⌷
```

Pressing the ⌷Enter⌷ key sends this input line to the program. The program fragment will first read the `I` character, display it with `cout`, and increment `ct` to 1. Next, it will read the space character following the `I`, display it, and increment `ct` to 2. This continues until the program processes the ⌷Enter⌷ key as a newline character and terminates the loop. The main point here is that, by using `get(ch)`, the code reads, displays, and counts the spaces as well as the printing characters.

Suppose, instead, that the program had tried to use `>>`:

```
int ct = 0;
char ch;
cin >> ch;
while (ch != '\n')     // FAILS
{
    cout << ch;
    ct++;
    cin >> ch;
}
cout << ct << '\n';
```

First, the code would skip the spaces, thus not counting them and compressing the corresponding output to this:

```
IC++clearly.
```

Worse, the loop would never terminate! Because the extraction operator skips newlines, the code would never assign the newline character to `ch`, so the `while` loop test would never terminate the loop.

The `get(char &)` member function returns a reference to the `istream` object used to invoke it. This means you can concatenate other extractions following `get(char &)`:

```
char c1, c2, c3;
cin.get(c1).get(c2) >> c3;
```

First, `cin.get(c1)` assigns the first input character to `c1` and returns the invoking object, which is `cin`. This reduces the code to `cin.get(c2) >> c3`, which assigns the second input character to `c2`. The function call returns `cin`, reducing the code to `cin >> c3`. This, in turn, assigns the next nonwhite-space character to `c3`. Note that `c1` and `c2` could wind up being assigned white space, but `c3` couldn't.

If `cin.get(char &)` encounters the end of a file, either real or simulated from the keyboard (Ctrl-Z for DOS, Ctrl-D at the beginning of a line for UNIX), it does not assign a value to its argument. This is quite right, for if the program has reached the end of the file, there is no value to be assigned. Furthermore, the method calls `set-state(failbit)`, which causes `cin` to test as `false`:

```
char ch;
while (cin.get(ch))
{
    // process input
}
```

As long as there's valid input, the return value for `cin.get(ch)` is `cin`, which evaluates as `true`, so the loop continues. Upon reaching end-of-file, the return value evaluates as `false`, terminating the loop.

The `get(void)` member function also reads white space, but it uses its return value to communicate input to a program. So you would use it this way:

```
int ct = 0;
char ch;
ch = cin.get();        // use return value
while (ch != '\n')
{
    cout << ch;
    ct++;
    ch = cin.get();
}
cout << ct << '\n';
```

Some older C++ implementation functions don't provide this member function.

The `get(void)` member function returns type `int` (or some larger integer type, depending upon the character set and locale). This makes the following invalid:

```
char c1, c2, c3;
cin.get().get() >> c3;  // not valid
```

Here `cin.get()` returns a type `int` value. Because that return value is not a class object, you can't apply the membership operator to it. Thus you get a syntax error. However, you can use `get()` at the end of an extraction sequence:

```
char c1;
cin.get(c1).get();   // valid
```

The fact that `get(void)` returns type `int` means you can't follow it with an extraction operator. But, because `cin.get(c1)` returns `cin`, it makes it a suitable prefix to `get()`. This particular code would read the first input character, assign it to `c1`, and then read the second input character and discard it.

Upon reaching the end-of-file, real or simulated, `cin.get(void)` returns the value `EOF`, which is a symbolic constant provided by the `iostream` header file. This design feature allows the following construction for reading input:

```
int ch;
while ((ch = cin.get()) != EOF)
{
    // process input
}
```

You should use type `int` for `ch` instead of type `char` here because the value `EOF` may not be expressed as a `char` type.

Chapter 5 describes these functions in a bit more detail, and Table 16.6 summarizes the features of the single-character input functions.

TABLE 16.6
`cin.get(ch)` VERSUS `cin.get()`

PROPERTY	cin.get(ch)	ch = cin.get()
method for conveying input character	assign to argument `ch`	use function return value to assign to `ch`
function return value for character input	reference to a class `istream` object	code for character as type `int` value
function return value at end-of-file	converts to `false`	EOF

Which Form of Single-Character Input?

Given the choice of >>, `get(char &)`, and `get(void)`, which should you use? First, decide whether you want input to skip over white space or not. If skipping white space is more convenient, use the extraction operator >>. For instance, skipping white space is convenient for offering menu choices:

```
cout  << "a. annoy client       b. bill client\n"
      << "c. calm client        d. deceive client\n"
      << "q.\n";
cout  << "Enter a, b, c, d, or q: ";
char ch;
cin >> ch;
while (ch != 'q')
{
    switch(ch)
    {
        ...
    }
    cout << "Enter a, b, c, d, or q: ";
    cin >> ch;
}
```

To enter, say, a b response, you type b and press ⎋Enter⎋, generating the two-character response of b\n. If you used either form of `get()`, you would have to add code to process that \n character each loop cycle, but the extraction operator conveniently skips it. (If you've programmed in C, you've probably encountered the situation in which the newline appears to the program as an invalid response. It's an easy problem to fix, but it is a nuisance.)

If you want a program to examine every character, use one of the `get()` methods. For instance, a word-counting program could use white space to determine when a word came to an end. Of the two `get()` methods, the `get(char &)` method has the classier interface. The main advantage of the `get(void)` method is that it closely resembles the standard C `getchar()` function, letting you convert a C to a C++ program by including `iostream` instead of `stdio.h`, globally replacing `getchar()` with `cin.get()`, and globally replacing C's `putchar(ch)` with `cout.put(ch)`.

String Input: `getline()`, `get()`, and `ignore()`

Next, let's review the string input member functions introduced in Chapter 4. The `getline()` member function and the third version of `get()` both read strings, and both have the same function signature (simplified here from the more general template declaration):

```
istream & get(char *, int, char = '\n');
istream & getline(char *, int, char = '\n');
```

The first argument, recall, is the address of the location to place the input string. The second argument is one greater than the maximum number of characters to be read. (The additional character leaves space for the terminating null character used in storing the input as a string.) If you omit the third argument, each function reads up to the maximum characters or until it encounters a newline character, whichever comes first.

For example, the code

```
char line[50];
cin.get(line, 50);
```

reads character input into the character array `line`. The `cin.get()` function quits reading input into the array after encountering 49 characters or, by default, after encountering a newline character, whichever comes first. The chief difference between `get()` and `getline()` is that `get()` leaves the newline character in the input stream, making it the first character seen by the next input operation, while `getline()` extracts and discards the newline character from the input stream.

Chapter 4 illustrated using the default form for these two member functions. Now let's look at the final argument, which modifies the function's default behavior. The third argument, which has a default value of `'\n'`, is the termination character. Encountering the termination character causes input to cease even if the maximum number of characters hasn't been reached. So, by default, both methods quit reading input if they reach the end of a line before reading the allotted number of characters. Just as in the default case, `get()` leaves the termination character in the input queue, while `getline()` does not.

Listing 16.12 demonstrates how `getline()` and `get()` work. It also introduces the `ignore()` member function. It takes two arguments: a number specifying a maximum number of characters to read and a character that acts as a terminating character for input. For example, the function call

```
cin.ignore(80, '\n');
```

reads and discards the next 80 characters or up through the first newline character, whichever comes first. The prototype provides defaults of 1 and EOF for the two arguments, and the function return type is `istream &`:

```
istream & ignore(int = 1, int = EOF);
```

The function returns the invoking object. This lets you concatenate function calls, as in the following:

```
cin.ignore(80, '\n').ignore(80, '\n');
```

Here the first `ignore()` method reads and discards one line, and the second call reads and discards the second line. Together the two functions read through two lines. Now check out Listing 16.12.

Listing 16.12 get_fun.cpp

```cpp
// get_fun.cpp -- using get() and getline()
#include <iostream>
using namespace std;
const int Limit = 80;

int main()
{
    char input[Limit];

    cout << "Enter a string for getline() processing:\n";
    cin.getline(input, Limit, '#');
    cout << "Here is your input:\n";
    cout << input << "\nDone with phase 1\n";

    char ch;
    cin.get(ch);
    cout << "The next input character is " << ch << "\n";

    if (ch != '\n')
        cin.ignore(Limit, '\n');    // discard rest of line

    cout << "Enter a string for get() processing:\n";
    cin.get(input, Limit, '#');
    cout << "Here is your input:\n";
    cout << input << "\nDone with phase 2\n";

    cin.get(ch);
    cout << "The next input character is " << ch << "\n";

    return 0;
}
```

> **Remember**
>
> The Microsoft Visual C++ 5.0 `iostream` version of `getline()` has a bug causing the display of the next output line to be delayed until you after you enter the data requested by the undisplayed line. The `iostream.h` version, however, works properly.

Here is a sample program run:

```
Enter a string for getline() processing:
Please pass
me a #3 melon!
Here is your input:
```

```
Please pass
me a
Done with phase 1
The next input character is 3
Enter a string for get() processing:
I still
want my #3 melon!
Here is your input:
I still
want my
Done with phase 2
The next input character is #
```

Note that the getline() function discards the # termination character in the input, while the get() function does not.

Unexpected String Input

Some forms of input for get(char *, int) and getline() affect the stream state. As with the other input functions, encountering end-of-file sets eofbit, and anything that corrupts the stream, such as device failure, sets badbit. Two other special cases are no input and input that meets or exceeds the maximum number of characters specified by the function call. Let's look at those cases now.

If either method fails to extract any characters, the method places a null character into the input string and uses setstate() to set failbit. (Older C++ implementations don't set failbit if no characters are read.) When would a method fail to extract any characters? One possibility is if an input method immediately encounters end-of-file. For get(char *, int), another possibility is if you enter an empty line:

```
char temp[80];
while (cin.get(temp,80))  // terminates on empty line
    ...
```

Interestingly, an empty line does not cause getline() to set failbit. That's because getline() still extracts the newline character, even if it doesn't store it. If you want a getline() loop to terminate on an empty line, you can write it this way:

```
char temp[80];
while (cin.getline(temp,80) && temp[0] != '\0') // terminates on empty
line
```

Now suppose the number of characters in the input queue meets or exceeds the maximum specified by the input method. First, consider getline() and the following code:

```
char temp[30];
while (cin.getline(temp,30))
```

The getline() method will read consecutive characters from the input queue, placing them in successive elements of the temp array, until (in order of testing) EOF is encountered, the next character to be read is the newline character, or until 29 characters have been stored. If EOF is encountered, `eofbit` is set. If the next character to be read is a newline character, that character is read and discarded. And if 29 characters were read, `failbit` is set, unless the next character is a newline. Thus, an input line of 30 characters or more will terminate input.

   Now consider the `get(char *, int)` method. It tests the number of characters first, end-of-file second, and for the next character being a newline third. It does not set the `failbit` flag if it reads the maximum number of characters. Nonetheless, you can tell if too many input characters caused the method to quit reading. You can use `peek()` (see the next section) to examine the next input character. If it's a newline, then `get()` must have read the entire line. If it's not a newline, then `get()` must have stoped before reaching the end. This technique doesn't necessarily work with `getline()` because `getline()` reads and discards the newline, so looking at the next character doesn't tell you anything. But if you use `get()`, you have the option of doing something if less than an entire line is read. The next section includes an example of this approach. Meanwhile, Table 16.7 summarizes some of the differences between older C++ input methods and the current situation.

TABLE 16.7
CHANGES IN INPUT BEHAVIOR

METHOD	OLDER C++	CURRENT C++
`getline()`	Doesn't set `failbit` if no characters are read.	Sets `failbit` if no characters are read (but newline counts as a character read).
	Doesn't set `failbit` if maximum number of characters are read.	Sets `failbit` if maximum number of characters are read and more are still left in the line.
`get(char *, int)`	Doesn't set `failbit` if no characters are read.	Sets `failbit` if no characters are read.

OTHER `istream` METHODS

   Other `istream` methods include `read()`, `peek()`, `gcount()`, and `putback()`. The `read()` function reads a given number of bytes, storing them in the specified location. For instance, the statement

```
char gross[144];
cin.read(gross, 144);
```

" *The peek( )*
function returns
the next
character from
input without
extracting from
the input
stream. "

reads 144 characters from the standard input and places them in the gross array. Unlike getline() and get(), read() does not append a null character to input, so it doesn't convert input to string form. The read() method is not primarily intended for keyboard input. Instead, it most often is used in conjunction with the ostream write() function for file input and output. The method's return type is istream &, so it can be concatenated as follows:

```
char gross[144];
char score[20];
cin.read(gross, 144).read(score, 20);
```

The peek() function returns the next character from input without extracting from the input stream. That is, it lets you peek at the next character. Suppose you wanted to read input up to the first newline or period, whichever comes first. You can use peek() to peek at the next character in the input stream in order to judge whether to continue or not:

```
char great_input[80];
char ch;
int i = 0;
while ((ch = cin.peek()) != '.' && ch != '\n')
    cin.get(great_input[i++]);
great_input [i] = '\0';
```

The call to cin.peek() peeks at the next input character and assigns its value to ch. Then the while loop test condition checks that ch is neither a period nor a newline. If this is the case, the loop reads the character into the array and updates the array index. When the loop terminates, the period or newline character remains in the input stream, positioned to be the first character read by the next input operation. Then the code appends a null character to the array, making it a string.

The gcount() method returns the number of characters read by the last unformatted extraction method. That means characters are read by a get(), getline(), ignore(), or read() method but not by the extraction operator (>>), which formats input to fit particular data types. For instance, suppose you've just used cin.get(myarray, 80) to read a line into the myarray array and want to know how many characters were read. You could use the strlen() function to count the characters in the array, but it would be quicker to use cin.gcount() to report how many characters were just read from the input stream.

The putback() function inserts a character back in the input string. The inserted character then becomes the first character read by the next input statement. The putback() method takes one char argument, which is the character to be inserted, and it returns type istream &, which allows the call to be concatenated with other istream methods. Using peek() is like using get() to read a character, then using putback() to place the character back in the input stream. However, putback() gives you the option of putting back a character different from the one just read.

Listing 16.13 uses two approaches to read and echo input up to, but not including, a # character. The first approach reads through the # character and then uses putback() to insert the character back in the input. The second approach uses peek() to look ahead before reading input.

Listing 16.13 peeker.cpp

```cpp
// peeker.cpp -- some istream methods
#include <iostream>
using namespace std;
#include <cstdlib>                    // or stdlib.h

int main()
{

// read and echo input up to a # character
    char ch;

    while(cin.get(ch))            // terminates on EOF
    {
        if (ch != '#')
            cout << ch;
        else
        {
            cin.putback(ch);      // reinsert character
            break;
        }
    }

    if (!cin.eof())
    {
        cin.get(ch);
        cout << '\n' << ch << " is next input character.\n";
    }
    else
    {
        cout << "End of file reached.\n";
        exit(0);
    }

    while(cin.peek() != '#')      // look ahead
    {
        cin.get(ch);
        cout << ch;
    }
    if (!cin.eof())
    {
        cin.get(ch);
        cout << '\n' << ch << " is next input character.\n";
    }
    else
        cout << "End of file reached.\n";

    return 0;
}
```

Here is a sample run:

I used a #3 pencil when I should have used a #2.
I used a
is next input character.
3 pencil when I should have used a
is next input character.

PROGRAM NOTES

Let's look more closely at some of the code. The first approach uses a `while` loop to read input. The expression `(cin.get(ch))` returns 0 on reaching the end-of-file condition, so simulating end-of-file from the keyboard terminates the loop. If the # character shows up first, the program puts the character back in the input stream and uses a break statement to terminate the loop.

```
while(cin.get(ch))                 // terminates on EOF
{
    if (ch != '#')
        cout << ch;
    else
    {
        cin.putback(ch);   // reinsert character
        break;
    }
}
```

The second approach is simpler in appearance:

```
while(cin.peek() != '#')        // look ahead
{
    cin.get(ch);
    cout << ch;
}
```

The program peeks at the next character. If it is not the # character, the program reads the next character, echoes it, and peeks at the next character. This continues until the terminating character shows up.

Now let's look, as promised, at an example (Listing 16.14) that uses `peek()` to determine whether or not an entire line has been read. If only part of a line fits in the input array, the program discards the rest of the line.

Listing 16.14 truncate.cpp

```
// truncate.cpp -- use get() to truncate input line, if necessary
#include <iostream>
using namespace std;
const int SLEN = 10;
inline void eatline() { while (cin.get() != '\n') continue; }
int main()
{
    char name[SLEN];
    char title[SLEN];
    cout << "Enter your name: ";
    cin.get(name,SLEN);
    if (cin.peek() != '\n')
        cout << "Sorry, we only have enough room for "
                << name << endl;
    eatline();
    cout << "Dear " << name << ", enter your title: \n";
    cin.get(title,SLEN);
    if (cin.peek() != '\n')
        cout << "We were forced to truncate your title.\n";
    eatline();
```

```
    cout << " Name: " << name
         << "\nTitle: " << title << endl;

    return 0;
}
```

Here is a sample run:

```
Enter your name: Stella Starpride
Sorry, we only have enough room for Stella St
Dear Stella St, enter your title:
Astronomer Royal
We were forced to truncate your title.
 Name: Stella St
Title: Astronome
```

Note that the following code makes sense whether or not the first input statement read the entire line:

```
while (cin.get() != '\n') continue;
```

If `get()` reads the whole line, it still leaves the newline in place, and this code reads and discards the newline. If `get()` reads just part of the line, this code reads and discards the rest of the line. If you didn't dispose of the rest of the line, the next input statement would begin reading at the beginning of the remaining input on the first input line. With this example, that would have resulted in the program reading the string `arpride` into the `title` array.

File Input and Output

"The C++ I/O class package handles file input and output much as it handles standard input and output."

Most computer programs work with files. Word processors create document files. Database programs create and search files of information. Compilers read source code files and generate executable files. A file itself is a bunch of bytes stored on some device, perhaps magnetic tape, perhaps an optical disk, floppy disk, or hard disk. Typically, the operating system manages files, keeping track of their locations, their sizes, when they were created, and so on. Unless you're programming on the operating system level, you normally don't have to worry about those things. What you do need is a way to connect a program to a file, a way to have a program read the contents of a file, and a way to have a program create and write to files. Redirection (as discussed earlier this chapter) can provide some file support, but it is more limited than explicit file I/O from within a program. Also, redirection comes from the operating system, not from C++, so it isn't available on all systems. We'll look now at how C++ deals with explicit file I/O from within a program.

The C++ I/O class package handles file input and output much as it handles standard input and output. To write to a file, you create a stream object and use the `ostream` methods, such as the `<<` insertion operator or `write()`. To read a file, you create a stream object and use the `istream` methods, such as the `>>` extraction operator or `get()`. Files require more management than the standard input and output, however. For instance, you have to associate a newly opened file with a stream. You can open a file in read-only mode, write-only mode, or read-and-write mode. If you write to a file, you may wish to create a new file, replace an old file, or add to an old file. Or you may wish to move back and forth through a file. To help handle these tasks, C++ defines several new classes in the `fstream` (formerly `fstream.h`) header file, including an `ifstream` class for file input and an `ofstream` class for file output. C++ also defines an `fstream` class for simultaneous file I/O. These classes are derived from the classes in the `iostream` header file, so objects of these new classes will be able to use the methods you've already learned.

SIMPLE FILE I/O

Suppose you want a program to write to a file. You need to do the following:

- Create an `ofstream` object to manage the output stream.

- Associate that object with a particular file.

- Use the object the same way you would use `cout`; the only difference is that output goes to the file instead of to the screen.

To accomplish this, begin by including the `fstream` header file. Including this file automatically includes the `iostream` file for most, but not all, implementations, so you may not have to include `iostream` explicitly. Then declare an `ofstream` object:

```
ofstream fout;        // create an ofstream object named fout
```

The object's name can be any valid C++ name, such as `fout`, `outFile`, `cgate`, or `didi`.

Next, you need to associate this object with a particular file. You can do so by using the `open()` method. Suppose, for example, you want to open the `cookies` file for output. You would do the following:

```
fout.open("cookies");  // associate fout with cookies
```

You can combine these two steps (creating the object and associating a file) into a single statement by using a different constructor:

```
ofstream fout("cookies");  // create fout object and associate with
cookies
```

Once you've gotten this far, use `fout` (or whatever name you choose) in the same manner as `cout`. For instance, if you want to put the words `Dull Data` into the file, you can do the following:

```
fout << "Dull Data";
```

Indeed, because `ostream` is a base class for the `ofstream` class, you can use all the `ostream` methods, including the various insertion operator definitions and the formatting methods and manipulators. The `ofstream` class uses buffered output, so the program allocates space for an output buffer when it creates an `ofstream` object like `fout`. If you create two `ofstream` objects, the program creates two buffers, one for each object. An `ofstream` object like `fout` collects output byte-by-byte from the program;

then, when the buffer is filled, it transfers the buffer contents en masse to the destination file. Because disk drives are designed to transfer data in larger chunks, not byte-by-byte, the buffered approach greatly speeds up the transfer rate of data from a program to a file.

Opening a file for output this way creates a new file if there is no file of that name. If a file by that name exists prior to opening it for output, the act of opening it truncates it so that output starts with a clean file. Later you'll see how to open an existing file and retain its contents.

Remember

Opening a file for output in the default mode automatically truncates the file to zero size, in effect disposing of the prior contents.

The requirements for reading a file are much like those for writing to a file:

1. Create an `ifstream` object to manage the input stream.

2. Associate that object with a particular file.

3. Use the object the same way you would use `cin`.

The steps for doing so are similar to those for writing to a file. First, of course, include the `fstream` header file. Then declare an `ifstream` object, and associate it with the file name. You can do so in two statements or one:

```
// two statements
ifstream fin;            // create ifstream object called fin
fin.open("jellyjar.dat"); // open jellyjar.dat for reading
// one statement
ifstream ifs("jamjar.dat"); // create ifs and associate with jamjar.dat
```

You now can use `fin` or `ifs` much like `cin`. For instance, you can do the following:

```
char ch;
fin >> ch;               // read a character from the jellyjar.dat file
char buf[80];
fin >> buf;              // read a word from the file
fin.getline(buf, 80);   // read a line from the file
```

Input, like output, is buffered, so creating an `ifstream` object like `fin` creates an input buffer which the `fin` object manages. As with output, buffering moves data much faster than byte-by-byte transfer.

The connections with a file are closed automatically when the input and output stream objects expire—for example, when the program terminates. Also, you can close a connection with a file explicitly by using the `close()` method:

```
fout.close();   // close output connection to file
fin.close();    // close input connection to file
```

Closing such a connection does not eliminate the stream; it just disconnects it from the file. However, the stream management apparatus remains in place. For instance, the `fin` object still exists along with the input buffer it manages. As you'll see later, you can reconnect the stream to the same file or to another file.

Meanwhile, let's look at a short example. The program in Listing 16.15 asks you for a file name. It creates a file having that name, writes some information to it, and closes the file. Closing the file flushes the buffer, guaranteeing that the file is updated. Then the program opens the same file for reading and displays its contents. Note that the program uses fin and fout in the same manner as cin and cout.

Listing 16.15 file.cpp

```cpp
// file.cpp -- save to a file
#include <iostream> // not needed for many systems
using namespace std;
#include <fstream>

int main()
{
    char filename[20];

    cout << "Enter name for new file: ";
    cin >> filename;

// create output stream object for new file and call it fout
    ofstream fout(filename);

    fout << "For your eyes only!\n";        // write to file
    cout << "Enter your secret number: ";   // write to screen
    float secret;
    cin >> secret;
    fout << "Your secret number is " << secret << "\n";
    fout.close();            // close file

// create input stream object for new file and call it fin
    ifstream fin(filename);
    cout << "Here are the contents of " << filename << ":\n";
    char ch;
    while (fin.get(ch))      // read character from file and
        cout << ch;          // write it to screen
    cout << "Done\n";
    fin.close();

    return 0;
}
```

Here is a sample run:

```
Enter name for new file: pythag
Enter your secret number: 3.14159
Here are the contents of pythag:
For your eyes only!
Your secret number is 3.14159
Done
```

If you check the directory containing your program, you should find a file named pythag, and any text editor should show the same contents that the program output displayed.

OPENING MULTIPLE FILES

You may require that a program open more than one file. The strategy for opening multiple files depends upon how they will be used. If you need two files open simultaneously, you need to create a separate stream for each file. For instance, a program that collates two sorted files into a third file would create two ifstream objects for the two input files and an ofstream object for the output file. The number of files you can open simultaneously depends on the operating system, but it typically is on the order of 20.

However, you may plan to process a group of files sequentially. For instance, you may wish to count how many times a name appears in a set of ten files. Then you can open a single stream and associate it with each file in turn. This conserves computer resources more effectively than opening a separate stream for each file. To use this approach, declare a stream object without initializing it and then use the open() method to associate the stream with a file. For instance, this is how you could handle reading two files in succession:

```
ifstream fin;            // create stream using default constructor
fin.open("fat.dat");     // associate stream with fat.dat file
...                      // do stuff
fin.close();             // terminate association with fat.dat
fin.clear();             // reset fin (may not be needed)
fin.open("rat.dat");     // associate stream with rat.dat file
...
fin.close();
```

We'll look at an example shortly, but first, let's examine a technique for feeding a list of files to a program in a manner that allows the program to use a loop to process them.

COMMAND-LINE PROCESSING

File-processing programs often use command-line arguments to identify files. Command-line arguments are arguments that appear on the command line when you type a command. For example, to count the number of words in some files on a UNIX system, you would type this command at the UNIX prompt:

```
wc report1 report2 report3
```

Here wc is the program name, and report1, report2, and report3 are file names passed to the program as command-line arguments.

C++ has a mechanism for letting a program access command-line arguments. Use the following alternative function heading for main():

```
int main(int argc, char *argv[])
```

The argc argument represents the number of arguments on the command line. The count includes the command name itself. The argv variable is a pointer to a pointer to a char. This sounds a bit abstract, but you can treat argv as if it were an array of pointers to the command-line arguments, with argv[0] being a pointer to the first character of a string holding the command name, argv[1] being a pointer to the first character of a string holding the first command-line argument, and so on. That is, argv[0] is the first string from the command line, and so on. For instance, suppose you have the following command line:

```
wc report1 report2 report3
```

Then argc would be 4, argv[0] would be wc, argv[1] would be report1, and so on. The following loop would print each command-line argument on a separate line:

```
for (int i = 1; i < argc; i++)
    cout << argv[i] << "\n";
```

Starting with i = 1 just prints the command-line arguments; starting with i = 0 would also print the command name.

Command-line arguments, of course, go hand-in-hand with command-line operating systems like DOS and UNIX. Other setups may still allow you to use command-line arguments:

- Many DOS and Windows IDEs (integrated development environments) have an option for providing command-line arguments. Typically, you have to navigate through a series of menu choices leading to a box into which you can type the command-line arguments. The exact set of steps varies from vendor to vendor and from upgrade to upgrade, so check your documentation.

- DOS IDEs and many Windows IDEs can produce executable files that run under DOS or in a DOS window in the usual DOS command-line mode.

- Under Symantec C++ for the Macintosh and under Metrowerks CodeWarrior for the Macintosh, you can simulate command-line arguments by placing the following code in your program:

```
...
#include <console.h> // for emulating command-line arguments
int main(int argc, char * argv[])
{
    argc = ccommand(&argv); // yes, ccommand, not command
    ...
```

When you run the program, the ccommand() function places a dialog box onscreen with a box in which you can type the command-line arguments. It also lets you simulate redirection.

Listing 16.16 combines the command-line technique with file stream techniques to count characters in those files listed on the command line.

Listing 16.16 count.cpp

```cpp
// count.cpp -- count characters in a list of files
#include <iostream>
using namespace std;
#include <fstream>
#include <cstdlib>          // or stdlib.h
// #include <console.h>     // for Macintosh
int main(int argc, char * argv[])
{
    // argc = ccommand(&argv);        // for Macintosh
    if (argc == 1)          // quit if no arguments
    {
    cerr << "Usage: " << argv[0] << " filename[s]\n";
    exit(1);
    }

    ifstream fin;           // open stream
    long count;
    long total = 0;
    char ch;

    for (int file = 1; file < argc; file++)
    {
    fin.open(argv[file]);   // connect stream to argv[file]
    count = 0;
    while (fin.get(ch))
        count++;
    cout << count << " characters in " << argv[file] << "\n";
    total += count;
    fin.clear();            // needed for some implementations
    fin.close();            // disconnect file
    }
    cout << total << " characters in all files\n";

    return 0;
}
```

Remember

Some implementations require using `fin.clear()` while others do not. It depends on whether associating a new file with the `fstream` object automatically resets the stream state or not. In does no harm to use `fin.clear()` even if it isn't needed.

On a DOS system, for example, you could compile Listing 16.16 to an executable file called count.exe. Then sample runs could look like this:

```
C>count
Usage: c:\count.exe filename[s]
C>count paris rome
3580 characters in paris
4886 characters in rome
8466 characters in all files
C>
```

Note that the program uses cerr for the error message. A minor point is that the message uses argv[0] instead of count.exe:

```
cerr << "Usage: " << argv[0] << " filename[s]\n";
```

This way, if you change the name of the executable file, the program will automatically use the new name.

Suppose you pass a bogus file name to the count program. Then the input statement fin.get(ch) will fail, terminating the while loop immediately, and the program will report 0 characters. But you can modify the program to test whether it succeeded in linking the stream to a file. That's one of the matters we'll take up next.

STREAM CHECKING AND is_open()

The C++ file stream classes inherit a stream-state member from the ios_base class. This member, as discussed earlier, stores information reflecting the stream status: all is well, end-of-file has been reached, I/O operation failed, and so on. If all is well, the stream state is zero (no news is good news). The various other states are recorded by setting particular bits to 1. The file stream classes also inherit the ios_base methods that report about the stream state and that were summarized earlier in Table 16.5. You can monitor conditions with these stream-state methods. For instance, you can use the good() method to see that all the stream state bits are clear. However, newer C++ implementations have a better way to check if a file has been opened—the is_open() method. You can modify the program in Listing 16.16 so that it reports bogus file names and then skips to the next file by adding a call to fin.is_open() to the for loop as follows:

```
for (int file = 1; file < argc; file++)
{
    fin.open(argv[file]);

// Add this
    if (!fin.is_open())
    {
        cerr << "Couldn't open file " << argv[file] << "\n";
        continue;
    }
// End of addition

    count = 0;
    while (fin.get(ch))
        count++;
    cout << count << " characters in " << argv[file] << "\n";
    total += count;
    fin.clear();
    fin.close();    // disconnect file
}
```

The fin.is_open() call returns false, if the fin.open() call fails. In that case, the program warns you of its problem, and the continue statement causes the program to skip the rest of the for loop cycle and start with the next cycle.

In the past, the usual tests for successful opening of a file were the following:

```
if(!fin.good()) ... // failed to open
if (!fin) ...       // failed to open
```

The `fin` object, when used in a test condition, is converted to `false` if `fin.good()` is `false` and to `true` otherwise, so the two forms are equivalent. However, there is a circumstance that these tests fail to detect, which is attempting to open a file using an inappropriate file mode (see the File Modes section). The `is_open()` method catches this form of error along with those caught by the `good()` method. However, older implementations do not have `is_open()`.

FILE MODES

The file mode describes how a file is to be used: read it, write to it, append it, and so on. When you associate a stream with a file, either by initializing a file stream object with a file name or by using the `open()` method, you can provide a second argument specifying the file mode:

```
ifstream fin("banjo", mode1);  // constructor with mode argument
ofstream fout();
fout.open("harp", mode2);      // open() with mode arguments
```

The `ios_base` class defines an openmode type to represent the mode; like the `fmtflags` and `iostate` types, it is a bitmask type. (In the old days, it was type `int`.) You can choose from several constants defined in the `ios_base` class to specify the mode. Table 16.8 lists the constants and their meanings. C++ file I/O has undergone several changes to make it compatible with ANSI C file I/O.

TABLE 16.8
FILE MODE CONSTANTS

CONSTANT	MEANING
`ios_base::in`	Open file for reading.
`ios_base::out`	Open file for writing.
`ios_base::ate`	Seek to end-of-file upon opening file.
`ios_base::app`	Append to end-of-file.
`ios_base::trunc`	Truncate file if it exists.
`ios_base::binary`	Binary file.

If the `ifstream` and `ofstream` constructors and the `open()` methods each take two arguments, how have we gotten by using just one in the previous examples? As you probably have guessed, the prototypes for these class member functions provide default values for the second argument (the file mode argument). For instance, the `ifstream open()` method and constructor use `ios_base::in` (open for reading) as the default value for the mode argument, while the ofstream open() method and constructor use ios_base::out ¦ ios_base::trunc (open for writing and truncate the file) as the default. The bitwise OR operator (¦), discussed in Appendix E, is used to combine two bit-values into a single value that can be used to set both bits. The fstream class doesn't provide a mode default, so you have to provide a mode explicitly when creating an object of that class.

Note that the ios_base::trunc flag means an existing file is truncated when opened to receive program output; that is, its previous contents are discarded. While this behavior commendably minimizes the danger of running out of disk space, you probably can imagine situations in which you don't want to wipe out a file when you open it. C++, of course, provides other choices. If, for instance, you want to preserve the file contents and add (append) new material to the end of the file, you can use the ios_base::app mode:

```
ofstream fout("bagels", ios_base::out ¦ ios_base::app);
```

Again, the code uses the ¦ operator to combine modes. So ios_base::out ¦ ios_base::app means to invoke both the out mode and the app mode (see Figure 16.6).

FIGURE 16.6
Some file-opening modes

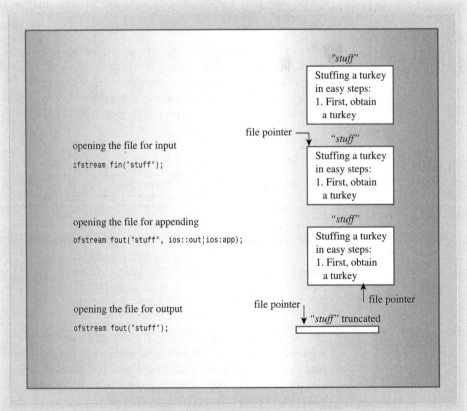

Expect to find some differences among older implementations. For instance, some allow you to omit the ios_base::out in the above example, and some don't. If you aren't using the default mode, the safest approach is to provide all the mode elements explicitly. Some don't support all the choices in Table 16.7, and some may offer choices beyond those in the table. One consequence of these differences is that you may have to make some alterations in the following examples to do them on your system. The good news is that the development of the C++ standard is providing greater uniformity.

C++ defines parts of file I/O in terms of ANSI C standard I/O. A C++ statement like

```
ifstream fin(filename, c++mode);
```

is implemented using the C fopen() function:

```
fopen(filename, cmode);
```

Here *c++mode* is a type openmode value, such as ios_base::in, and *cmode* is the corresponding C mode string, such as "r". Table 16.9 shows the correspondence between C++ modes and C modes. Note that ios_base::out by itself causes truncation but that it doesn't cause truncation when combined with ios_base::in. Unlisted combinations, such as ios_base::in ¦ ios_base::trunc, prevent the file from being opened.

TABLE 16.9
C++ AND C FILE-OPENING MODES

C++ MODE	C MODE	MEANING
ios_base::in	"r"	Open for reading.
ios_base::out	"w"	(Same as ios_base::out ¦ ios_base::trunc).
ios_base::out ¦ ios_base::trunc	"w"	Open for writing, truncating file if it already exists.
ios_base::out ¦ ios_base::app	"a"	Open for writing, append only.
ios_base::in ¦ ios_base::out	"r+"	Open for reading and writing, with writing permitted anywhere in the file.
ios_base::in ¦ ios_base::out ¦ ios_base::trunc	"w+"	Open for reading and writing, first truncating file if it already exists.
c++mode ¦ ios_base::binary	"*cmode*b"	Open in *c++mode* or corresponding *cmode* and in binary mode; for example, ios_base::in ¦ ios_base::binary becomes "rb".
c++mode ¦ ios_base::ate	"*cmode*"	Open in indicated mode and go to end of file. C uses a separate function call instead of a mode code. For example, ios_base::in ¦ ios_base::ate translates to the mode and the C function call fseek(file, 0, SEEK_END).

Note that both `ios_base::ate` and `ios_base::app` place you (or, more precisely, a file pointer) at the end of the file just opened. The difference between the two is that the `ios_base::app` mode allows you to add data to the end of the file only, while the `ios_base::ate` mode merely positions the pointer at the end of the file.

Clearly, there are many possible combinations of modes. We'll look at a few representative ones.

Appending to a File

Let's begin with a program that appends data to the end of a file. The program will maintain a file containing a guest list. When the program begins, it will display the current contents of the file, if it exists. It can use the `good()` method after attempting to open the file to check if the file exists. Next, the program will open the file for output using the `ios_base::app` mode. Then it will solicit input from the keyboard to add to the file. Finally, the program will display the revised file contents. Listing 16.17 illustrates how to accomplish these goals. Note how the program uses the `is_open()` method to test if the file has been opened successfully.

Remember

File I/O was perhaps the least standardized aspect of C++ in its earlier days, and many older compilers don't quite conform to the current standard. Some, for example, used modes such as `nocreate` that are not part of the current standard. Also, only some compilers require the `fin.clear()` call before opening the same file a second time for reading.

Listing 16.17 append.cpp

```cpp
// append.cpp -- append information to a file
#include <iostream>
using namespace std;
#include <fstream>
#include <cstdlib>        // (or stdlib.h) for exit()

const char * file = "guests1.dat";
const int Len = 40;
int main()
{
    char ch;

// show initial contents
    ifstream fin;
    fin.open(file);

    if (fin.is_open())
    {
        cout << "Here are the current contents of the "
            << file << " file:\n";
        while (fin.get(ch))
```

```
            cout << ch;
        }
        fin.close();

// add new names
    ofstream fout(file, ios::out | ios::app);
    if (!fout.is_open())
    {
        cerr << "Can't open " << file << " file for output.\n";
        exit(1);
    }

    cout << "Enter guest names (enter a blank line to quit):\n";
    char name[Len];
    cin.get(name, Len);
    while (name[0] != '\0')
    {
        while (cin.get() != '\n')
            continue;    // get rid of \n and long lines
        fout << name << "\n";
        cin.get(name, Len);
    }
    fout.close();

// show revised file
    fin.clear();      // not necessary for some compilers
    fin.open(file);
    if (fin.is_open())
    {
        cout << "Here are the new contents of the "
            << file << " file:\n";
        while (fin.get(ch))
            cout << ch;
    }
    fin.close();

    return 0;
}
```

Here's a sample first run. At this point the `guests.dat` file hasn't been created, so the program doesn't preview the file.

```
Enter guest names (enter a blank line to quit):
Sylvester Ballone
Phil Kates
Bill Ghan

Here are the new contents of the guests.dat file:
Sylvester Ballone
Phil Kates
Bill Ghan
```

Next time the program is run, however, the `guests.dat` file does exist, so the program does preview the file. Also, note that the new data is appended to the old file contents rather than being replaced.

```
Here are the current contents of the guests.dat file:
Sylvester Ballone
Phil Kates
Bill Ghan
Enter guest names (enter a blank line to quit):
Greta Greppo
LaDonna Mobile
Fannie Mae

Here are the new contents of the guests.dat file:
Sylvester Ballone
Phil Kates
Bill Ghan
Greta Greppo
LaDonna Mobile
Fannie Mae
```

You should be able to read the contents of `guest.dat` with any text editor.

Binary Files

When you store data in a file, you can store the data in text form or in binary format. Text form means you store everything as text, even numbers. For instance, storing the value –2.324216e+07 in text form means storing the 13 characters used to write this number. That requires converting the computer's internal representation of a floating-point number to character form, and that's exactly what the << insertion operator does. Binary format, however, means storing the computer's internal representation of a value. That is, instead of storing characters, store the 64-bit `double` representation of the value. For a character, the binary representation is the same as the text representation—the binary representation of the character's ASCII code. For numbers, however, the binary representation is much different from the text representation (see Figure 16.7).

Each format has its advantages. The text format is easy to read. You can use an ordinary editor or word processor to read and edit a text file. You easily can transfer a text file from one computer system to another. The binary format is more accurate for numbers, because it stores the exact internal representation of a value. There are no conversion errors or round-off errors. Saving data in binary format can be faster because there is no conversion and because you may be able to save data in larger chunks. And the binary format usually takes less space, depending upon the nature of the data. Transferring to another system can be a problem, however, if the new system uses a different internal representation for values. In that case, you (or someone) may have to write a program to translate one data format to another.

Let's look at a more concrete example. Consider the following structure definition and declaration:

```
struct planet
{
    char name[20];       // name of planet
    double population;   // its population
    double g;            // its acceleration of gravity
};
planet pl;
```

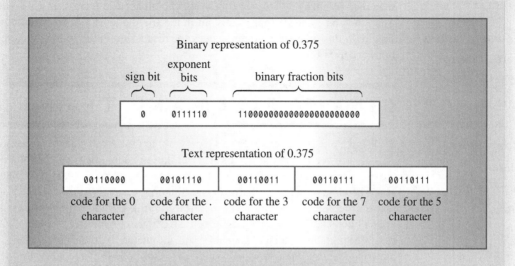

FIGURE 16.7

Binary and text representation of a floating-point number

To save the contents of the structure p1 in text form, you can do this:

```
ofstream fout("planets.dat", ios_base::app);
fout << pl.name << " " << pl.population << " " << pl.g << "\n";
```

Note that you have to provide each structure member explicitly by using the membership operator, and you have to separate adjacent data for legibility. If the structure contained, say, 30 members, this could get tedious.

To save the same information in binary format, you can do this:

```
ofstream fout("planets.dat", ios_base::app | ios_base::binary);
fout.write( (char *) &pl, sizeof pl);
```

This code saves the entire structure as a single unit, using the computer's internal representation of data. You won't be able to read the file as text, but the information will be stored more compactly and precisely than as text. And it certainly is easier to type the code. This approach made two changes:

- It used a binary file mode.

- It used the write() member function.

Let's examine these changes more closely.

" Using a binary file mode causes a program to transfer data from memory to a file, or vice versa, without any hidden translation taking place. "

Some systems, such as DOS, support two file formats: text and binary. If you want to save data in binary form, you'd best use the binary file format. In C++ you do so by using the `ios_base::binary` constant in the file mode. If you want to know why you should do this on a DOS system, check the discussion in the following note on Binary Files and Text Files.

BINARY FILES AND TEXT FILES

Using a binary file mode causes a program to transfer data from memory to a file, or vice versa, without any hidden translation taking place. Such is not necessarily the case for the default text mode. For instance, consider DOS text files. They represent a newline with a two-character combination: carriage return, linefeed. Macintosh text files represent a newline with a carriage return. UNIX files represent a newline with a linefeed. C++, which grew up on UNIX, also represents a newline with a linefeed. For portability, a DOS C++ program automatically translates the C++ newline to a carriage return, linefeed when writing to a text mode file; and a Macintosh C++ program translates the newline to a carriage return when writing to a file. When reading a text file, these programs convert the local newline back to the C++ form. The text format can cause problems with binary data, for a byte in the middle of a `double` value could have the same bit pattern as the ASCII code for the newline character. Also, there are differences in how end-of-file is detected. So you should use the binary file mode when saving data in binary format. (UNIX systems have just one file mode, so on them the binary mode is the same as the text mode.)

To save data in binary form instead of text form, you can use the `write()` member function. This method, recall, copies a specified number of characters from memory to a file. We used it earlier to copy text, but it will copy any type data byte-by-byte with no conversion. For instance, if you pass it the address of a `long` variable and tell it to copy 4 characters, it will copy the 4 bytes constituting the `long` value verbatim to a file and not convert it to text. The only awkwardness is that you have to typecast the address to type pointer-to-`char`. You can use the same approach to copy an entire planet structure. To get the number of bytes, use the `sizeof` operator:

```
fout.write( (char *) &pl, sizeof pl);
```

This statement goes to the address of the `pl` structure and copies the 36 bytes (the value of `sizeof pl` expression) beginning at this address to the file connected to `fout`.

To recover the information from a file, use the corresponding `read()` method with an `ifstream` object:

```
ifstream fin("planets.dat", ios_base::binary);
fin.read((char *) &pl, sizeof pl);
```

This copies `sizeof pl` bytes from the file to the `pl` structure. This same approach can be used with classes that don't use virtual functions. In that case, just the data members are saved, not the methods. (Also, see the note in Programming Exercise 4.)

Remember

> The `read()` and `write()` member functions complement each other. Use `read()` to recover data that has been written to a file with `write()`.

Listing 16.18 uses these methods to create and read a binary file. In form, the program is similar to Listing 16.17, but it uses `write()` and `read()` instead of the insertion operator and the `get()` method. It also uses manipulators to format the screen output.

Remember

> Although the binary file concept is part of ANSI C, some C and C++ implementations do not provide support for the binary file mode. The reason for this oversight is that some systems only have one file type in the first place, so you can use binary operations such as `read()` and `write()` with the standard file format. Therefore, if your implementation rejects `ios_base::binary` as a valid constant, just omit it from your program. If your implementation doesn't support the `fixed` manipulator, you can use `cout.setf(ios_base::fixed, ios_base::floatfield)`. Symantec C++ 8 requires replacing (twice)
>
> `while (fin.read((char *) &pl, sizeof pl))`
>
> with the following:
>
> `while (fin.read((char *) &pl, sizeof pl) && !fin.eof())`

Listing 16.18 binary.cpp

```
#include <iostream> // not required by most systems
using namespace std;
#include <fstream>
#include <iomanip>
#include <cstdlib>  // (or stdlib.h) for exit()

inline void eatline() { while (cin.get() != '\n') continue; }
struct planet
{
    char name[20];      // name of planet
    double population;  // its population
    double g;           // its acceleration of gravity
};

const char * file = "planets.dat";

int main()
{
    planet pl;
    cout << fixed <<right;
```

```
// show initial contents
    ifstream fin;
    fin.open(file, ios::in |ios::binary);   // binary file
    //NOTE: some systems don't accept the ios::binary mode
    if (fin.is_open())
    {
    cout << "Here are the current contents of the "
        << file << " file:\n";
    while (fin.read((char *) &pl, sizeof pl))
        {
        cout << setw(20) << pl.name << ": "
            << setprecision(0) << setw(12) << pl.population
            << setprecision(2) << setw(6) << pl.g << "\n";
        }
    }
    fin.close();

// add new data
    ofstream fout(file, ios::out | ios::app | ios::binary);
    //NOTE: some systems don't accept the ios::binary mode
    if (!fout.is_open())
    {
        cerr << "Can't open " << file << " file for output:\n";
        exit(1);
    }

    cout << "Enter planet name (enter a blank line to quit):\n";
    cin.get(pl.name, 20);
    while (pl.name[0] != '\0')
    {
        eatline();
        cout << "Enter planetary population: ";
        cin >> pl.population;
        cout << "Enter planet's acceleration of gravity: ";
        cin >> pl.g;
        eatline();
        fout.write((char *) &pl, sizeof pl);
        cout << "Enter planet name (enter a blank line "
                "to quit):\n";
        cin.get(pl.name, 20);
    }
    fout.close();

// show revised file
    fin.clear();     // not required for some implementations, but won't
                     // hurt
    fin.open(file, ios::in | ios::binary);
    if (fin.is_open())
    {
    cout << "Here are the new contents of the "
        << file << " file:\n";
    while (fin.read((char *) &pl, sizeof pl))
        {
        cout << setw(20) << pl.name << ": "
            << setprecision(0) << setw(12) << pl.population
            << setprecision(2) << setw(6) << pl.g << "\n";
        }
    }
```

```
    }
    fin.close();

    return 0;
}
```

Here is a sample initial run:

```
Enter planet name (enter a blank line to quit):
Earth
Enter planetary population: 5962000000
Enter planet's acceleration of gravity: 9.81
Enter planet name (enter a blank line to quit):

Here are the new contents of the planets.dat file:
            Earth:    5932000000  9.81
```

And here is a sample follow-up run:

```
Here are the current contents of the planets.dat file:
            Earth:    5932000000  9.81
Enter planet name (enter a blank line to quit):
Bill's Planet
Enter planetary population: 23020020
Enter planet's acceleration of gravity: 8.82
Enter planet name (enter a blank line to quit):

Here are the new contents of the planets.dat file:
      Earth:            5932000000  9.81
      Bill's Planet:    23020020    8.82
```

You've already seen the major features of the program, but let's reexamine an old point. The program uses this code (in the form of the inline `eatline()` function) after reading the planet's g value:

```
while (cin.get() != '\n') continue;
```

This reads and discards input up through the newline character. Consider the next input statement in the loop:

```
cin.get(pl.name, 20);
```

If the newline had been left in place, this statement would read the newline as an empty line, terminating the loop.

RANDOM ACCESS

For our last example, let's look at random access. This means moving directly to any location in the file instead of moving through it sequentially. The random access approach is often used with database files. A program will maintain a separate index file giving the location of data in the main data file. Then it can jump directly to that location, read the data there, and perhaps modify it. This approach is done most simply if the file consists of a collection of equal-sized records. Each record represents a related collection of data. For instance, in the preceding example, each file record would represent all the data about a particular planet. A file record corresponds rather naturally to a program structure or class.

We'll base our example on the binary file program in Listing 16.18, because the `planet` structure provides a pattern for a file record. To add to the creative tension of programming, the example will open the file in a read-and-write mode so that it can both read and modify a record. You can do this by creating an `fstream` object. The `fstream` class derives from the `iostream` class, which, in turn, is based on both `istream` and `ostream` classes, so it inherits the methods of both. It also inherits two buffers, one for input and one for output, and synchronizes the handling of the two buffers. That is, as the program reads the file or writes to it, it moves both an input pointer in the input buffer and an output pointer in the output buffer in tandem.

The example will do the following:

1. Display the current contents of the `planets.dat` file.

2. Ask which record you wish to modify.

3. Modify that record.

4. Show the revised file.

A more ambitious program would use a menu and a loop to let you select from this list of actions indefinitely, but this version will perform each action just once. This simplified approach allows you to examine several aspects of read-write files without getting bogged down in matters of program design.

Remember

This program assumes that the `planets.dat` file already exists and was created by the `binary.cpp` program.

The first question to answer is what file mode to use. In order to read the file, you need the `ios_base::in` mode. For binary I/O, you need the `ios_base::binary` mode. (Again, on some non-standard systems you can omit, indeed, you may have to omit, this mode.) In order to write to the file, you need the `ios_base::out` or the `ios_base::app` mode. However, the append mode allows a program to add data to the end of the file only. The rest of the file is read-only; that is, you can read the original data, but not modify it—so you have to use `ios_base::out`. As Table 16.9 indicates, using the in and out modes simultaneously provided a read/write mode, so you just have to add the binary element. As mentioned earlier, you use the ¦ operator to combine modes. Thus you need the following statement to set up business:

```
finout.open(file,ios_base::in ¦ ios_base::out ¦ ios_base::binary);
```

Next, you need a way to move through a file. The `fstream` class inherits two methods for this: `seekg()` moves the input pointer to a given file location, and `seekp()` moves the output pointer to a given file location. (Actually, because the `fstream` class uses buffers for intermediate storage of data, the pointers point to locations in the buffers, not in the actual file.) You also can use `seekg()` with an `ifstream` object and `seekp()` with an `ostream` object. Here are the `seekg()` prototypes:

```
basic_istream<charT,traits>& seekg(off_type, ios_base::seekdir);
basic_istream<charT,traits>& seekg(pos_type);
```

As you can see, they are templates. This chapter will use a template specialization for the char type. For the char specialization, the two prototypes are equivalent to the following:

```
istream & seekg(streamoff, ios_base::seekdir);
istream & seekg(streampos);
```

The first prototype represents locating a file position measured, in bytes, as an offset from a file location specified by the second argument. The second prototype represents locating a file position measured in bytes from the beginning of a file.

TYPE ESCALATION

When C++ was young, life was simpler for the seekg() methods. The streamoff and streampos types were typedefs for some standard integer type, such as long. However, the quest for creating a portable standard had to deal with the realization that an integer argument might not provide enough information for some file systems, so streamoff and streampos were allowed to be structure or class types so long as they allowed some basic operations, such as using an integer value as an initialization value. Next, the old istream class was replaced with the basic_istream template, and streampos and streamoff were replaced with template-based types pos_type and off_type. However, streampos and streamoff continue to exist as char specializations of pos_type and off_type. Similarly, you can use wstreampos and wstreamoff types if you use seekg() with a wistream object.

Let's take a look at the arguments to the first prototype of seekg(). Values of the streamoff type are used to measure offsets, in bytes, from a particular location in a file. The streamoff argument represents the file position in bytes measured as an offset from one of three locations. (The type may be defined as an integral type or as a class.) The seek_dir argument is another integer type defined, along with three possible values, in the ios_base class. The constant ios_base::beg means measure the offset from the beginning of the file. The constant ios_base::cur means measure the offset from the current position. The constant ios_base::end means measure the offset from the end of the file. Here are some sample calls, assuming fin is an ifstream object:

```
fin.seekg(30, ios_base::beg);    // 30 bytes beyond the beginning
fin.seekg(-1, ios_base::cur);    // back up one byte
fin.seekg(0, ios_base::end);     // go to the end of the file
```

Now let's look at the second prototype. Values of the streampos type locate a position in a file. It can be a class, but, if so, the class includes a constructor with a streamoff argument and a constructor with an integer argument, providing a path to convert both types to streampos values. A streampos value represents an absolute location in a file measured from the beginning of the file. You can treat a streampos position as if it measures a file location in bytes from the beginning of a file, with the first byte being byte 0. So the statement

```
fin.seekg(112);
```

locates the file pointer at byte 112, which would be the 113th byte in the file. If you want to check the current position of a file pointer, you can use the tellg() method for input streams and the tellp() methods for output streams. Each returns a streampos value representing the current position, in bytes, measured from the beginning of the file. When you create an fstream object, the input and output pointers move in tandem, so tellg() and tellp() return the same value. But if you use an istream object to manage the input stream and an ostream object to manage the output stream to the same file, the input and output pointers move independently of one another, and tellg() and tellp() can return different values.

You can then use seekg() to go to the file beginning. Here is a section of code that opens the file, goes to the beginning, and displays the file contents:

```
fstream finout;       // read and write streams
finout.open(file,ios::in ¦ ios::out ¦ios::binary);
//NOTE: Some UNIX systems require omitting ¦ ios::binary
int ct = 0;
if (finout.is_open())
{
    finout.seekg(0);     // go to beginning
    cout << "Here are the current contents of the "
        << file << " file:\n";
    while (finout.read((char *) &pl, sizeof pl))
    {
        cout << ct++ << ": " << setw(20) << pl.name << ": "
        << setprecision(0) << setw(12) << pl.population
        << setprecision(2) << setw(6) << pl.g << "\n";
    }
    if (finout.eof())
        finout.clear(); // clear eof flag
    else
    {
        cerr << "Error in reading " << file << ".\n";
        exit(1);
    }
}
else
{
    cerr << file << " could not be opened -- bye.\n";
    exit(2);
}
```

This is similar to the start of Listing 16.18, but there are some changes and additions. First, as just described, the program uses an fstream object with a read-write mode, and it uses seekg() to position the file pointer at the start of the file. (This isn't really needed for this example, but it shows how seekg() is used.) Next, the program makes the minor change of numbering the records as they are displayed. Then it makes the following important addition:

```
if (finout.eof())
    finout.clear(); // clear eof flag
```

```
else
{
    cerr << "Error in reading " << file << ".\n";
    exit(1);
}
```

The problem is that once the program reads and displays the entire file, it sets the eofbit element. This convinces the program that it's finished with the file and disables any further reading of or writing to the file. Using the clear() method resets the stream state, turning off eofbit. Now the program can once again access the file. The else part handles the possibility that the program quit reading the file for some reason other than reaching the end-of-file, such as a hardware failure.

The next step is to identify the record to be changed and then change it. To do this, the program asks the user to enter a record number. Multiplying the number by the number of bytes in a record yields the byte number for the beginning of the record. If record is the record number, the desired byte number is record * sizeof pl:

```
cout << "Enter the record number you wish to change: ";
long rec;
cin >> rec;
eatline();               // get rid of newline
if (rec < 0 || rec >= ct)
{
    cerr << "Invalid record number -- bye\n";
    exit(3);
}
streampos place = rec * sizeof pl;  // convert to streampos type
finout.seekg(place);     // random access
```

The variable ct represents the number of records; the program exits if you try to go beyond the limits of the file.

Next, the program displays the current record:

```
finout.read((char *) &pl, sizeof pl);
cout << "Your selection:\n";
cout << rec << ": " << setw(20) << pl.name << ": "
<< setprecision(0) << setw(12) << pl.population
<< setprecision(2) << setw(6) << pl.g << "\n";
if (finout.eof())
    finout.clear();      // clear eof flag
```

After displaying the record, the program lets you change the record:

```
cout << "Enter planet name: ";
cin.get(pl.name, 20);
eatline();
cout << "Enter planetary population: ";
cin >> pl.population;
cout << "Enter planet's acceleration of gravity: ";
cin >> pl.g;
finout.seekp(place);     // go back
finout.write((char *) &pl, sizeof pl) << flush;

if (finout.fail())
{
    cerr << "Error on attempted write\n";
    exit(5);
}
```

The program flushes the output to guarantee that the file is updated before proceeding to the next stage.

Finally, to display the revised file, the program uses seekg() to reset the file pointer to the beginning. Listing 16.19 shows the complete program. Don't forget that it assumes that a planets.dat file created using the binary.cpp program is available.

Remember

The older the implementation, the more likely it is to run afoul of the standard. Some systems don't recognize the binary flag. Symantec C++ appends the new input instead of replacing the indicate record. Also, Symantec C++ requires replacing (twice)

```
while (fin.read((char *) &pl, sizeof pl))
```

with the following:

```
while (fin.read((char *) &pl, sizeof pl) && !fin.eof())
```

Listing 16.19 random.cpp

```cpp
// random.cpp -- random access to a binary file
#include <iostream>         // not required by most systems
using namespace std;
#include <fstream>
#include <iomanip>
#include <cstdlib>          // (or stdlib.h) for exit()

struct planet
{
    char name[20];        // name of planet
    double population;    // its population
    double g;             // its acceleration of gravity
};

const char * file = "planets.dat";  // ASSUMED TO EXIST (binary.cpp
example)
inline void eatline() { while (cin.get() != '\n') continue; }

int main()
{
    planet pl;
    cout << fixed <<right;

// show initial contents
    fstream finout;       // read and write streams
    finout.open(file,ios::in | ios::out |ios::binary);
    //NOTE: Some UNIX systems require omitting | ios::binary
    int ct = 0;
    if (finout.is_open())
    {
        finout.seekg(0);     // go to beginning
        cout << "Here are the current contents of the "
            << file << " file:\n";
```

```
        while (finout.read((char *) &pl, sizeof pl))
        {
            cout << ct++ << ": " << setw(20) << pl.name << ": "
            << setprecision(0) << setw(12) << pl.population
            << setprecision(2) << setw(6) << pl.g << "\n";
        }
        if (finout.eof())
            finout.clear(); // clear eof flag
        else
        {
            cerr << "Error in reading " << file << ".\n";
            exit(1);
        }
    }
    else
    {
        cerr << file << " could not be opened -- bye.\n";
        exit(2);
    }

// change a record
    cout << "Enter the record number you wish to change: ";
    long rec;
    cin >> rec;
    eatline();              // get rid of newline
    if (rec < 0 || rec >= ct)
    {
        cerr << "Invalid record number -- bye\n";
        exit(3);
    }
    streampos place = rec * sizeof pl;  // convert to streampos type
    finout.seekg(place);    // random access
    if (finout.fail())
    {
        cerr << "Error on attempted seek\n";
        exit(4);
    }

    finout.read((char *) &pl, sizeof pl);
    cout << "Your selection:\n";
    cout << rec << ": " << setw(20) << pl.name << ": "
    << setprecision(0) << setw(12) << pl.population
    << setprecision(2) << setw(6) << pl.g << "\n";
    if (finout.eof())
        finout.clear();     // clear eof flag

    cout << "Enter planet name: ";
    cin.get(pl.name, 20);
    eatline();
    cout << "Enter planetary population: ";
    cin >> pl.population;
    cout << "Enter planet's acceleration of gravity: ";
    cin >> pl.g;
    finout.seekp(place);    // go back
    finout.write((char *) &pl, sizeof pl) << flush;
    if (finout.fail())
```

```
        {
            cerr << "Error on attempted write\n";
            exit(5);
        }

// show revised file
    ct = 0;
    finout.seekg(0);                // go to beginning of file
    cout << "Here are the new contents of the " << file
         << " file:\n";
    while (finout.read((char *) &pl, sizeof pl))
    {
        cout << ct++ << ": " << setw(20) << pl.name << ": "
             << setprecision(0) << setw(12) << pl.population
             << setprecision(2) << setw(6) << pl.g << "\n";
    }
    finout.close();

    return 0;
}
```

Here's a sample run based on a `planets.dat` file that has had a few more entries added since you last saw it:

```
Here are the current contents of the planets.dat File:
0:      Earth:          5333000000      9.81
1:      Bill's Planet: 23020020         8.82
2:      Trantor:        58000000000     15.03
3:      Trellan:        4256000         9.62
4:      Freestone:      3845120000      8.68
5:      Taanagoot:      350000002       10.23
6:      Marin:          232000          9.79
Enter the record number you wish to change: 2
Your selection:
2:      Trantor:        58000000000     15.03
Enter planet name: Trantor
Enter planetary population: 59500000000
Enter planet's acceleration of gravity:  10.53
Here are the new contents of the planets.dat file:
0:      Earth:          5333000000      9.81
1:      Bill's Planet: 23020020         8.82
2:      Trantor:        59500000000     10.53
3:      Trellan:        4256000         9.62
4:      Freestone:      3845120000      8.68
5:      Taanagoot:      350000002       10.23
6:      Marin:          232000          9.79
```

Using the techniques in this program, you can extend it to allow you to add new material and delete records. If you were to expand the program, it would be a good idea to reorganize it by using classes and functions. For example, you could convert the `planet` structure to a class definition; then overload the `<<` insertion operator so that `cout << pl` displays the class data members formatted as in the example.

Incore Formatting

" That is, you can use the same `ostream` methods you've used with `cout` to write formatted information into a `string` object, and you can use `istream` methods such as `getline()` to read information from a `string` object. "

The `iostream` family supports I/O between the program and a terminal. The `fstream` family uses the same interface to provide I/O between a program and a file. The C++ library also provides an `sstream` family that uses the same interface to provide I/O between a program and a `string` object. That is, you can use the same `ostream` methods you've used with `cout` to write formatted information into a `string` object, and you can use `istream` methods such as `getline()` to read information from a `string` object. The process of reading formatted information from a `string` object or of writing formatted information to a `string` object is termed *incore* formatting. Let's take a brief look at these facilities. (The `sstream` family of `string` support supersedes a `strstream.h` family of `char`-array support.)

The `sstream` header file defines an `ostringstream` class derived from the `ostream` class. (There also is a `wostringstream` class based on `wostream` for wide character sets.) If you create an `ostringstream` object, you can write information to it, which it stores. You can use the same methods with an `ostringstream` object that you can with `cout`. That is, you can do something like the following:

```
ostringstream outstr;
double price = 55.00;
char * ps = " for a copy of the draft C++ standard!";
outstr.precision(2);
outstr << fixed;
outstr << "Pay only $" << price << ps << end;
```

The formatted text goes into a buffer, and the object uses dynamic memory allocation to expand the buffer size as needed. The `ostringstream` class has a member function, called `str()`, which returns a `string` object initialized to the buffer's contents:

```
string mesg = outstr.str();    // returns string with formatted
information
```

Using the `str()` method "freezes" the object, and you no longer can write to it. Listing 16.20 provides a short example.

Listing 16.20 strout.cpp

```
// strout.cpp -- incore formatting (output)
#include <iostream>
using namespace std;
#include <sstream>
#include <string>
int main()
{
    ostringstream outstr;   // manages a string stream

    string hdisk;
    cout << "What's the name of your hard disk? ";
    getline(cin, hdisk);
    int cap;
    cout << "What's its capacity in MB? ";
    cin >> cap;
    // write formatted information to string stream
    outstr << "The hard disk " << hdisk << " has a capacity of "
```

```
                << cap << " megabytes.\n";
    string result = outstr.str();    // save result
    cout << result;                  // show contents

    return 0;
}
```

Here's a sample run:

```
What's the name of your hard disk? Rocky
What's its capacity in MB? 2425
The hard disk Rocky has a capacity of 2425 megabytes.
```

The `istringstream` class lets you use the `istream` family of methods to read data from an `istringstream` object, which can be initialized from a `string` object. Suppose `facts` is a `string` object. To create an `istringstream` object associated with this string, do the following:

```
istringstream instr(facts);    // use facts to initialize stream
```

Then you use `istream` methods to read data from `instr`. For instance, if `instr` contained a bunch of integers in character format, you could read them as follows:

```
int n;
int sum = 0;
while (instr << n)
    sum += num;
```

Listing 16.21 uses the overloaded `>>` operator to read the contents of a string one word at a time.

Listing 16.21 strin.cpp

```
// strin.cpp -- formatted reading from a char array
#include <iostream>
using namespace std;
#include <sstream>
#include <string>
int main()
{
    string lit = "It was a dark and stormy day, and "
                 " the full moon glowed brilliantly. ";
    istringstream instr(lit);    // use buf for input
    string word;;
    while (instr >> word)        // read a word a time
        cout << word << endl;
    return 0;
}
```

Here is the program output:

```
It
was
a
dark
and
```

```
stormy
day,
and
the
full
moon
glowed
brilliantly.
```

In short, `istringstream` and `ostringstream` classes give you the power of the `istream` and `ostream` class methods to manage character data stored in strings.

What Now?

If you have worked your way through this book, you should have a good grasp of the rules of C++. However, that's just the beginning in learning this language. The second stage is learning to use the language effectively, and that is the longer journey. The best situation to be in is a work or learning environment that brings you into contact with good C++ code and programmers. Also, now that you know C++, you can read books that concentrate on more advanced topics and upon object-oriented programming. Appendix H lists some of these resources.

In addition to increasing your understanding of C++ in general, you may wish to learn about specific class libraries. Microsoft, Borland, and Symantec, for example, offer extensive class libraries to facilitate programming for the Windows environment, and Symantec and Metrowerks offer similar facilities for Macintosh programming.

Summary

A stream is a flow of bytes into or out of a program. A buffer is a temporary holding area in memory that acts as an intermediary between a program and a file or other I/O devices. Information can be transferred between a buffer and a file using large chunks of data of the size most efficiently handled by devices like disk drives. And information can be transferred between a buffer and a program in a byte-by-byte flow that often is more convenient for the processing done in a program. C++ handles input by connecting a buffered stream to a program and to its source of input. Similarly, C++ handles output by connecting a buffered stream to a program and to its output target. The `iostream` and `fstream` files constitute an I/O class library that defines a rich set of classes for managing streams. C++ programs that include the `iostream` file automatically open eight streams, managing them with eight objects. The `cin` object manages the standard input stream, which, by default, connects to the standard input device, typically a keyboard. The `cout` object manages the standard output stream, which, by default, connects to the standard output device, typically a monitor. The `cerr` and `clog` objects manage unbuffered and buffered streams connected to the standard error device, typically a monitor. These four objects have four wide-character counterparts named `wcin`, `wcout`, `wcerr`, and `wclog`.

The I/O class library provides a variety of useful methods. The `istream` class defines versions of the extraction operator (>>) that recognize all the basic C++ types and that convert character input to those types. The `get()` family of methods and the `getline()` method provide further support for single-character input and for string input. Similarly, the `ostream` class defines versions of the insertion operator (<<) that recognize all the basic C++ types and that convert them to suitable character output. The `put()` method provides further support for single-character output. The `wistream` and `wostream` classes follow similar support for wide characters.

You can control how a program formats output by using `ios_base` class methods and by using manipulators (functions that can be concatenated with insertion) defined in the `iostream` and `iomanip` files. These methods and manipulators let you control the number base, the field width, the number of decimal places displayed, the system used to display floating-point values, and other elements.

The `fstream` file provides class definitions that extend the `iostream` methods to file I/O. The `ifstream` class derives from the `istream` class. By associating an `ifstream` object with a file, you can use all the `istream` methods for reading the file. Similarly, associating an `ofstream` object with a file lets you use the `ostream` methods to write to a file. And associating an `fstream` object with a file lets you employ both input and output methods with the file.

To associate a file with a stream, you can provide the file name when initializing a file stream object or you can first create a file stream object and then use the `open()` method to associate the stream with a file. The `close()` method terminates the connection between a stream and a file. The class constructors and the `open()` method take an optional second argument that provides the file mode. The file mode determines such things as whether the file is to be read and/or written to, whether opening a file for writing truncates it or not, whether attempting to open a nonexistent file is an error or not, and whether to use the binary or text mode.

A text file stores all information in character form. For instance, numeric values are converted to character representations. The usual insertion and extraction operators, along with `get()` and `getline()`, support this mode. A binary file stores all information using the same binary representation the computer uses internally. Binary files store data, particularly floating-point values, more accurately and compactly than text files, but they are less portable. The `read()` and `write()` methods support binary input and output.

The `seekg()` and `seekp()` functions provide C++ random access for files. These class methods let you position a file pointer relative to the beginning of a file, relative to the end, or relative to the current position. The `tellg()` and `tellp()` methods report the current file position.

The `sstream` header file defines `istringstream` and `ostringstream` classes that let you use `istream` and `ostream` methods to extract information from a string and to format information placed into a string.

Review Questions

1. What role does the `iostream` file play in C++ I/O?

2. Why does typing a number such as 121 as input require a program to make a conversion?

3. What's the difference between the standard output and the standard error?

4. Why is `cout` able to display various C++ types without being provided explicit instructions for each type?

5. What feature of the output method definitions allows you to concatenate output?

6. Write a program that requests an integer and then displays it in decimal, octal, and hexadecimal form. Display each form on the same line in fields that are 15 characters wide, and use the C++ number base prefixes.

7. Write a program that requests the information shown below and that formats it as shown:

```
Enter your name: Billy Gruff
Enter your hourly wages: 12
Enter number of hours worked: 7.5
First format:
                    Billy Gruff: $      12.00:  7.5
Second format:
Billy Gruff                    : $12.00     :7.5
```

8. Consider the following program:

```cpp
//rq16-8.cpp
#include <iostream>
using namespace std;

int main()
{
    char ch;
    int ct1 = 0;

    cin >> ch;
    while (ch != 'q')
    {
        ct1++;
        cin >> ch;
    }

    int ct2 = 0;
    cin.get(ch);
    while (ch != 'q')
    {
        ct2++;
        cin.get(ch);
    }
    cout << "ct1 = " << ct1 << "; ct2 = " << ct2 << "\n";

    return 0;
}
```

What does it print, given the following input:

```
I see a q Enter
I see a q Enter
```

Here Enter signifies pressing the Enter key.

9. Both of the following statements read and discard characters up to and including the end of a line. In what way does the behavior of one differ from that of the other?

```
while (cin.get() != '\n')
    continue;
cin.ignore(80, '\n');
```

Programming Exercises

1. Write a program that counts the number of characters up to the first $ in input and that leaves the $ in the input stream.

2. Write a program that copies your keyboard input (up to simulated end-of-file) to a file named on the command line.

3. Write a program that copies one file to another. Have the program take the file names from the command line. Have the program report if it cannot open a file.

4. Write a program that opens two text files for input and one for output. The program concatenates the corresponding lines of the input files, using a space as a separator, and writing the results to the output file. If one file is shorter than the other, the remaining lines in the longer file are also copied to the output file. For example, suppose the first input file has these contents:

```
eggs kites donuts
balloons hammers
stones
```

And suppose the second input file has these contents:

```
zero lassitude
finance drama
```

Then the resulting file would have these contents:

```
eggs kites donuts zero lassitude
balloons hammers finance drama
stones
```

5. Mat and Pat wish to invite their friends to a party, much as they did in Chapter 15, Programming Exercise 5, except now they want a program that uses files. They ask you to write a program that does the following:

Reads a list of Mat's friends' names from a text file called `mat.dat`, which lists one friend per line. The names are stored in a container and then displayed in sorted order.

Reads a list of Pat's friends' names from a text file called `pat.dat`, which lists one friend per line. The names are stored in a container and then displayed in sorted order.

Merges the two lists, eliminating duplicates, and stores the result in the file `matnpat.dat`, one friend per line.

6. Consider the class definitions of Programming Exercise 5 in Chapter 13. If you haven't yet done that exercise, do so now. Then do the following:

Write a program that uses standard C++ I/O and file I/O in conjunction with data of types `employee`, `manager`, `fink`, and `highfink`, as defined in Chapter 13, Programming Exercise 5. The program should be along the general lines of Listing 16.17 in that it should let you add new data to a file. The first time through, the program should solicit data from the user, then show all the entries, and then save the information in a file. On subsequent uses, the program should first read and display the file data, then let the user add data, and then show all the data. One difference is that data should be handled by an array of pointers to type `employee`. That way, a pointer can point to an employee object or to objects of any of the three derived types. Keep the array small to facilitate checking the program:

```
const int MAX = 10;     // no more than 10 objects
...
employee * pc[MAX];
```

For keyboard entry, the program should use a menu to offer the user the choice of which type of object to create. The menu will use a switch to use `new` to create an object of the desired type and to assign the object's address to a pointer in the `pc` array. Then that object can use the virtual `setall()` function to elicit the appropriate data from the user:

```
pc[i]->setall();  // invokes function corresponding to type of object
```

To save the data to a file, devise a virtual `writeall()` function for that purpose:

```
for (i = 0; i < index; i++)
    pc[i]->writeall(fout);// fout ofstream connected to output file
```

Remember

Use text I/O, not binary I/O, for this exercise. (Unfortunately, virtual objects include pointers to tables of pointers to virtual functions, and `write()` copies this information to a file. An object filled by using `read()` from the file gets weird values for the function pointers, which really messes up the behavior of virtual functions.) Use a newline to separate each data field from the next; this makes it easier to identify fields on input.

The tricky part is recovering the data from the file. The problem is, how can the program know whether the next item to be recovered is an employee object, a manager object, a fink type, or a highfink type? One approach is, when writing the data for an object to a file, precede the data with an integer indicating the type of object to follow. Then, on file input, the program can read the integer and then use a switch to create the appropriate object to receive the data:

```
enum classkind{Employee, Manager, Fink, Highfink}; // in class header
...
while((fin >> classtype).get(ch)){ // newline separates int from data
    switch(classtype) {
        case Employee  : pc[i] = new employee;
                       : break;
```

Then you can use the pointer to invoke a virtual getall() function to read the information:

```
pc[i++]->getall();
```

A
Number Bases

Our method for writing numbers is based on powers of 10. For instance, consider the number 2468. The 2 represents 2 thousands, the 4 represents 4 hundreds, the 6 represents 6 tens, and the 8 represents 8 ones:

$$2468 = 2 \times 1000 + 4 \times 100 + 6 \times 10 + 8 \times 1$$

One thousand is $10 \times 10 \times 10$, which can be written as 10^3, or 10 to the 3rd power. Using this notation, we can write the preceding relationship this way:

$$2468 = 2 \times 10^3 + 4 \times 10^2 + 6 \times 10^1 + 8 \times 10^0$$

Because our number notation is based on powers of 10, we refer to it as base 10, or decimal, notation. One can just as easily pick another number as a base. C++ lets you use base 8 (octal) and base 16 (hexadecimal) notation for writing integer numbers. (Note: 10^0 is 1, as is any nonzero number to the zero power.)

Octal Integers

Octal numbers are based on powers of 8, so base 8 notation uses the digits 0–7 in writing numbers. C++ uses a 0 prefix to indicate octal notation. Thus, 0177 is an octal value. You can use powers of 8 to find the equivalent base 10 value:

$$
\begin{aligned}
0177 \text{ (octal)} \quad &= 1 \times 8^2 + 7 \times 8^1 + 7 \times 8^0 \\
&= 1 \times 64 + 7 \times 8 + 7 \times 1 \\
&= 127 \text{ (decimal)}
\end{aligned}
$$

The UNIX operating system often uses octal representation of values, which is why C++ and C provide octal notation.

Hexadecimal Numbers

Hexadecimal numbers are based on powers of 16. That means 10 in hexadecimal represents the value $16 + 0$, or 16. To represent the values between 9 and hexadecimal 16, you need a few more digits. Standard hexadecimal notation uses the letters a–f for that purpose. C++ accepts either lowercase or uppercase versions of these characters, as shown in Table A.1.

C++ uses a 0x or 0X notation to indicate hexadecimal notation. Thus, 0x2B3 is a hexadecimal value. To find its decimal equivalent, you can evaluate the powers of 16:

$$
\begin{aligned}
\text{0x2B3 (hex)} \quad &= 2\times16^2 + 11\times16^1 + 3\times16^0 \\
&= 2\times256 + 11\times16 + 3\times1 \\
&= 691 \text{ (decimal)}
\end{aligned}
$$

Hardware documentation often uses hexadecimal notation to represent values such as memory locations and port numbers.

Binary Numbers

Whether you use decimal, octal, or hexadecimal notation for writing an integer, the computer stores it as a binary, or base 2, value. Binary notation uses just two digits, 0 and 1. As an example, 10011011 is a binary number. Note, however, that C++ doesn't provide for writing a number in binary notation. Binary numbers are based on powers of 2:

$$
\begin{aligned}
10011011 \quad &= 1\times2^7 + 0\times2^6 + 0\times2^5 + 1\times2^4 + 1\times2^3 \\
&\quad + 0\times2^2 + 1\times2^1 + 1\times2^0 \\
&= 128 + 0 + 0 + 16 + 8 + 0 + 2 + 0 \\
&= 154
\end{aligned}
$$

Binary notation makes a nice match to computer memory, in which each individual unit, called a bit, can be set to off or on. Just identify the off setting with 0 and the on setting with 1. Memory commonly is organized in units called bytes, with each byte being 8 bits. The bits in a byte are numbered corresponding to the associated power of 2. Thus, the rightmost bit is bit number 0, the next bit is bit 1, and so on. Figure A.1, for example, represents a 2-byte integer.

TABLE A.1
HEXADECIMAL DIGITS

HEXADECIMAL DIGITS	DECIMAL VALUE	HEXADECIMAL DIGITS	DECIMAL VALUE
a or A	10	d or D	13
b or B	11	e or E	14
c or C	12	f or F	15

FIGURE A.1

A two-byte integer value

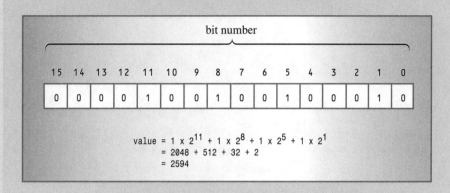

B

C++ Keywords

Keywords are identifiers that form the vocabulary of a programming language. They may not be used for other purposes, such as serving as a variable name. The following list shows C++'s keywords; not all of them are currently implemented. Keywords shown in boldface are also keywords in ANSI C.

asm	**auto**	bool	**break**	case
catch	**char**	class	**const**	const_cast
continue	**default**	delete	**do**	**double**
dynamic_cast	**else**	**enum**	explicit	**extern**
false	**float**	**for**	friend	**goto**
if	inline	**int**	**long**	mutable
namespace	new	operator	private	protected
public	**register**	reinterpret_cast	**return**	short
signed	**sizeof**	**static**	static_cast	**struct**
switch	template	this	throw	true
try	**typedef**	typeid	typename	**union**
unsigned	using	virtual	**void**	**volatile**
wchar_t	**while**			

1

C

The ASCII Character Set

Computers store characters using a numeric code. The ASCII code (American Standard Code for Information Interchange) is the most commonly used code in the United States. C++ lets you represent most single characters directly, by including the character in single quotation marks, as in `'A'` for the A character. You can also represent a single character by using the octal or hex code preceded by a backslash; for instance, `'\012'` and `'\0xa'` both represent the linefeed (LF) character. Such escape sequences can also be part of a string, as in `"Hello,\012my dear"`.

When used as a prefix in the following table, the ^ character denotes using a `Ctrl` key.

DECIMAL	OCTAL	HEX	BINARY	CHARACTER	ASCII NAME
0	0	0	00000000	^@	NUL
1	01	0x1	00000001	^A	SOH
2	02	0x2	00000010	^B	STX
3	03	0x3	00000011	^C	ETX
4	04	0x4	00000100	^D	EOT
5	05	0x5	00000101	^E	ENQ
6	06	0x6	00000110	^F	ACK
7	07	0x7	00000111	^G	BEL
8	010	0x8	00001000	^H	BS
9	011	0x9	00001001	^I	HT
10	012	0xa	00001010	^J	LF
11	013	0xb	00001011	^K	VT

Table Continued…

DECIMAL	OCTAL	HEX	BINARY	CHARACTER	ASCII NAME
12	014	0xc	00001100	^L	FF
13	015	0xd	00001101	^M	CR
14	016	0xe	00001110	^N	SO
15	017	0xf	00001111	^O	SI
16	020	0x10	00010000	^P	DLE
17	021	0x11	00010001	^Q	DC1
18	022	0x12	00010010	^R	DC2
19	023	0x13	00010011	^S	DC3
20	024	0x14	00010100	^T	DC4
21	025	0x15	00010101	^U	NAK
22	026	0x16	00010110	^V	SYN
23	027	0x17	00010111	^W	ETB
24	030	0x18	00011000	^X	CAN
25	031	0x19	00011001	^Y	EM
26	032	0x1a	00011010	^Z	SUB
27	033	0x1b	00011011	^esc	ESC
28	034	0x1c	00011100	^\	FS
29	035	0x1d	00011101	^]	GS
30	036	0x1e	00011110	^^	RS
31	037	0x1f	00011111	^_	US
32	040	0x20	00100000	space	SP
33	041	0x21	00100001	!	
34	042	0x22	00100010	"	
35	043	0x23	00100011	#	
36	044	0x24	00100100	$	
37	045	0x25	00100101	%	
38	046	0x26	00100110	&	
39	047	0x27	00100111	'	
40	050	0x28	00101000	(	
41	051	0x29	00101001	)	
42	052	0x2a	00101010	*	
43	053	0x2b	00101011	+	
44	054	0x2c	00101100	'	
45	055	0x2d	00101101	-	
46	056	0x2e	00101110	.	
47	057	0x2f	00101111	/	
48	060	0x30	00110000	0	
49	061	0x31	00110001	1	
50	062	0x32	00110010	2	
51	063	0x33	00110011	3	
52	064	0x34	00110100	4	
53	065	0x35	00110101	5	
54	066	0x36	00110110	6	

DECIMAL	OCTAL	HEX	BINARY	CHARACTER	ASCII NAME
55	067	0x37	00110111	7	
56	070	0x38	00111000	8	
57	071	0x39	00111001	9	
58	072	0x3a	00111010	:	
59	073	0x3b	00111011	;	
60	074	0x3c	00111100	<	
61	075	0x3d	00111101	=	
62	076	0x3e	00111110	>	
63	077	0x3f	00111111	?	
64	0100	0x40	01000000	@	
65	0101	0x41	01000001	A	
66	0102	0x42	01000010	B	
67	0103	0x43	01000011	C	
68	0104	0x44	01000100	D	
69	0105	0x45	01000101	E	
70	0106	0x46	01000110	F	
71	0107	0x47	01000111	G	
72	0110	0x48	01001000	H	
73	0111	0x49	01001001	I	
74	0112	0x4a	01001010	J	
75	0113	0x4b	01001011	K	
76	0114	0x4c	01001100	L	
77	0115	0x4d	01001101	M	
78	0116	0x4e	01001110	N	
79	0117	0x4f	01001111	O	
80	0120	0x50	01010000	P	
81	0121	0x51	01010001	Q	
82	0122	0x52	01010010	R	
83	0123	0x53	01010011	S	
84	0124	0x54	01010100	T	
85	0125	0x55	01010101	U	
86	0126	0x56	01010110	V	
87	0127	0x57	01010111	W	
88	0130	0x58	01011000	X	
89	0131	0x59	01011001	Y	
90	0132	0x5a	01011010	Z	
91	0133	0x5b	01011011	[	
92	0134	0x5c	01011100	\	
93	0135	0x5d	01011101	]	
94	0136	0x5e	01011110	^	
95	0137	0x5f	01011111	_	
96	0140	0x60	01100000	`	

Table Continued…

DECIMAL	OCTAL	HEX	BINARY	CHARACTER	ASCII NAME
97	0141	0x61	01100001	a	
98	0142	0x62	01100010	b	
99	0143	0x63	01100011	c	
100	0144	0x64	01100100	d	
101	0145	0x65	01100101	e	
102	0146	0x66	01100110	f	
103	0147	0x67	01100111	g	
104	0150	0x68	01101000	h	
105	0151	0x69	01101001	i	
106	0152	0x6a	01101010	j	
107	0153	0x6b	01101011	k	
108	0154	0x6c	01101100	l	
109	0155	0x6d	01101101	m	
110	0156	0x6e	01101110	n	
111	0157	0x6f	01101111	o	
112	0160	0x70	01110000	p	
113	0161	0x71	01110001	q	
114	0162	0x72	01110010	r	
115	0163	0x73	01110011	s	
116	0164	0x74	01110100	t	
117	0165	0x75	01110101	u	
118	0166	0x76	01110110	v	
119	0167	0x77	01110111	w	
120	0170	0x78	01111000	x	
121	0171	0x79	01111001	y	
122	0172	0x7a	01111010	z	
123	0173	0x7b	01111011	{	
124	0174	0x7c	01111100			
125	0175	0x7d	01111101	}	
126	0176	0x7e	01111110	~	
127	0177	0x7f	01111111	del, rubout	

Operator Precedence

Operator precedence determines the order in which operators are applied to a value. C++ operators come in 18 precedence groups, which are presented in Table D.1. Those in group 1 have the highest precedence, and so on. If two operators apply to the same operand (something upon which an operator operates), the operator with the higher precedence applies first. If the two operators have the same precedence, C++ uses associativity rules to determine which operator binds more tightly. All operators in the same group have the same precedence and the same associativity, which is either left to right (L–R in the table) or right to left (R–L in the table). Left-to-right associativity means to apply the left-hand operator first, while right-to-left associativity means to apply the right-hand operator first.

Some symbols, such as * and &, are used for more than one operator. In such cases, one form is *unary* (one operand) and the other form is *binary* (two operands), and the compiler uses the context to determine which is meant. The table labels operator groups unary or binary for those cases in which the same symbol is used two ways. Here are some examples of precedence and associativity:

```
3 + 5 * 6
```

The * operator has higher precedence than the + operator, so it is applied to the 5 first, making the expression 3 + 30, or 33.

```
120 / 6 * 5
```

Both / and * have the same precedence, but these operators associate from left to right. That means the operator to the left of the shared operand (6) is applied first, so the expression becomes 20 * 5, or 100.

```
char * str = "Whoa";
char ch = *str++;
```

Both the unary * and the ++ operators have the same precedence, but they associate right-to-left. This means the increment operator operates upon str and not *str. That is, the operation increments the pointer, making it point to the next character, rather than altering the character pointed to. However, because ++ is the postfix form, the pointer is incremented after the original value of *str is assigned to ch. Therefore, this expression assigns the character W to ch and then moves str to point to the h character.

TABLE D.1
C++ OPERATOR PRECEDENCE AND ASSOCIATIVITY

PRECEDENCE	OPERATOR	ASSOC.	MEANING
1	::		scope resolution operator
	(expression)		grouping
2	()	L–R	function call
	()		value construction, that is, *type (expr)*
	[]		array subscript
	->		indirect membership operator
	.		direct membership operator
	const_cast		specialized type cast
	dynamic_cast		specialized type cast
	reinterpret_cast		specialized type cast
	static_cast		specialized type cast
	typeid		type identification
	++		increment operator, postfix
	--		decrement operator, postfix
3 (all unary)	!	R–L	logical negation
	~		bitwise negation
	+		unary plus (positive sign)
	-		unary minus (negative sign)
	++		increment operator, prefix
	--		decrement operator, prefix
	&		address
	*		dereference (indirect value)
	()		type cast, that is, *(type) expr*
	sizeof		size in bytes
	new		dynamically allocate storage
	new []		dynamically allocate array
	delete		dynamically free storage
	delete []		dynamically free array
4	.*	L–R	member dereference
	->*		indirect member dereference
5 (all binary)	*	L–R	multiply
	/		divide
	^		modulus (remainder)

PRECEDENCE	OPERATOR	ASSOC.	MEANING
6 (all binary)	+	L–R	addition
	-		subtraction
7	<<	L–R	left shift
	>>		right shift
8	<	L–R	less than
	<=		less than or equal to
	>=		greater than or equal to
	>		greater than
9	==	L–R	equal to
	!=		not equal to
10 (binary)	&	L–R	bitwise AND
11	^	L–R	bitwise XOR (exclusive OR)
12	¦	L–R	bitwise OR
13	&&	L–R	logical AND
14	¦¦	L–R	logical OR
15	=	R–L	simple assignment
	*=		multiply and assign
	/=		divide and assign
	%=		take remainder and assign
	+=		add and assign
	-=		subtract and assign
	&=		bitwise AND and assign
	^=		bitwise XOR and assign
	¦=		bitwise OR and assign
	<<=		left shift and assign
	>>=		right shift and assign
16	:?	R–L	conditional
17	throw	L–R	throw exception
18	,	L–R	combine two expressions into one

In order to avoid terminal obesity, the main text of this book doesn't cover two groups of operators. The first group consists of the bitwise operators, which let you manipulate individual bits in a value; these operators were inherited from C. The second group consists of two-member dereferencing operators; they are C++ additions. This appendix briefly summarizes these operators.

Bitwise Operators

The bitwise operators operate upon the bits of integer values. For example, the left-shift operator moves bits to the left, and the bitwise negation operator turns each one to a zero, and each zero to a one. Altogether, C++ has six such operators: <<, >>, ~, &, ¦, and ^.

THE SHIFT OPERATORS

The left-shift operator has the following syntax:

```
value << shift
```

Here `value` is the integer value to be shifted, and `shift` is the number of bits to shift. For example:

```
13 << 3
```

means shift all the bits in the value 13 three places to the left. The vacated places are filled with zeros, and bits shifted past the end are discarded (see Figure E.1).

Because each bit position represents a value twice that of the bit to the right (see Appendix A), shifting one bit position is equivalent to multiplying the value by 2. Similarly, shifting two bit positions is equivalent to multiplying by 2^2, and shifting n positions is equivalent to multiplying by 2^n.

The left-shift operator provides a capability often found in assembly languages. However, an assembly left-shift operator directly alters the contents of a register, while the C++ operator produces a new value without altering existing values. For instance, consider the following:

```
int x = 20;
int y = x << 3;
```

This code doesn't change the value of x. The expression x << 3 uses the value of x to produce a new value, much as x + 3 produces a new value without altering x.

If you want to use the left-shift operator to change the value of a variable, you also have to use assignment. You can use regular assignment or the <<= operator, which combines shifting with assignment.

```
x = x << 4;        // regular assignment
y <<= 2;           // shift and assign
```

FIGURE E.1

Left-shift operator

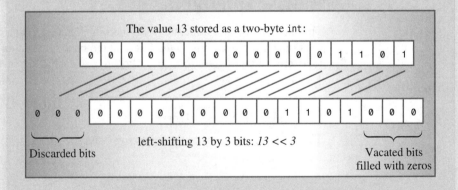

The value 13 stored as a two-byte int:

| 0 | 0 | 0 | 0 | 0 | 0 | 0 | 0 | 0 | 0 | 0 | 0 | 1 | 1 | 0 | 1 |

left-shifting 13 by 3 bits: *13 << 3*

Discarded bits

Vacated bits filled with zeros

The right-shift operator (>>), as you might expect, shifts bits to the right. It has the following syntax:

```
value >> shift
```

Here value is the integer value to be shifted, and shift is the number of bits to shift. For example:

```
17 >> 2
```

means shift all the bits in the value 17 two places to the right. For unsigned integers, the vacated places are filled with zeros, and bits shifted past the end are discarded. For signed integers, vacated places may be filled with zeros or else with the value of the original leftmost bit. The choice depends upon the implementation (see Figure E.2).

Shifting one place to the right is equivalent to integer division by 2. In general, shifting n places to the right is equivalent to integer division by 2^n.

C++ also defines a shift-and-assign operator if you wish to replace the value of a variable by the shifted value:

```
int q = 43;
q >>= 2;                 // replace 43 by 43 >> 2, or 10
```

On some systems, using left- and right-shift operators may produce faster integer multiplication and division by 2 than using the division operator, but as compilers get better at optimizing code, such differences are fading.

FIGURE E.2

Right-shift operator

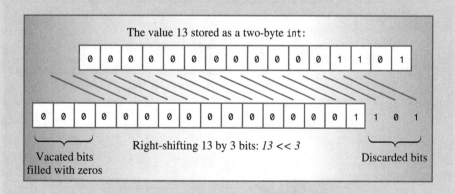

The value 13 stored as a two-byte int:

| 0 | 0 | 0 | 0 | 0 | 0 | 0 | 0 | 0 | 0 | 0 | 0 | 1 | 1 | 0 | 1 |

| 0 | 0 | 0 | 0 | 0 | 0 | 0 | 0 | 0 | 0 | 0 | 0 | 0 | 1 | 1 | 0 | 1 |

Vacated bits filled with zeros

Right-shifting 13 by 3 bits: *13 << 3*

Discarded bits

THE LOGICAL BITWISE OPERATORS

The logical bitwise operators are analogous to the regular logical operators, except they apply to a value on a bit-by-bit basis rather than to the whole. For instance, consider the regular negation operator (!) and the bitwise negation operator (~). The ! operator converts a true (or non-zero) value (nonzero) to false and a false value to true. The ~ operator converts each individual bit to its opposite (1 to 0 and 0 to 1). For instance, consider the unsigned char value of 3:

```
unsigned char x = 3;
```

The expression !x has the value 0. To see the value of ~x, write it in binary form: 00000011. Then convert each 0 to 1 and each 1 to 0. This produces the value 11111100, or in base 10, the value 252 (see Figure E.3) .

The bitwise OR operator (¦) combines two integer values to produce a new integer value. Each bit in the new value is set to 1 if one or the other, or both, of the corresponding bits in the original values is set to 1. If both corresponding bits are 0, then the final bit is set to 0 (see Figure E.4).

Table E.1 summarizes how the ¦ operator combines bits.

TABLE E.1
VALUE OF b1 ¦ b2

BIT VALUES	B1 = 0	B1 = 1
b2 = 0	0	1
b2 = 1	1	1

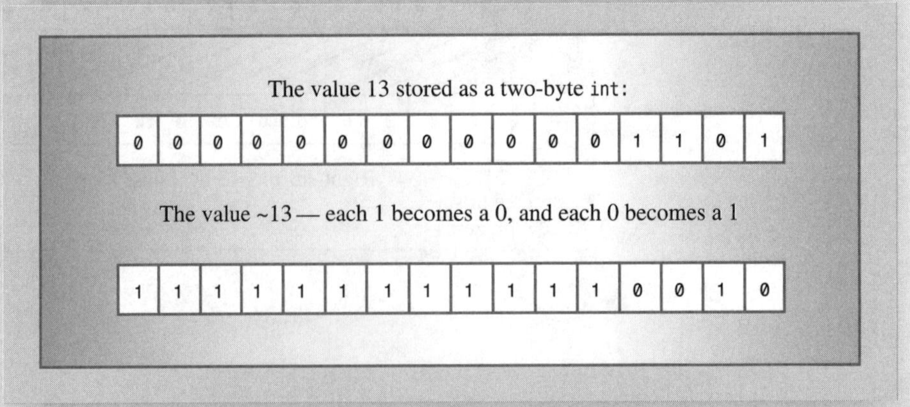

FIGURE E.3
Bitwise negation operator

The value 13 stored as a two-byte int:

0	0	0	0	0	0	0	0	0	0	0	0	1	1	0	1

The value ~13 — each 1 becomes a 0, and each 0 becomes a 1

1	1	1	1	1	1	1	1	1	1	1	1	0	0	1	0

FIGURE E.4

The bitwise OR operator

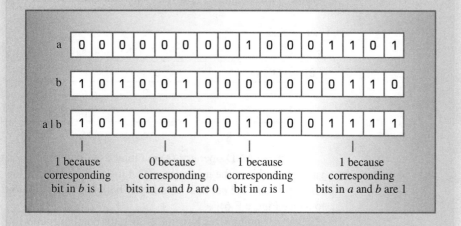

The bitwise XOR operator (^) combines two integer values to produce a new integer value. Each bit in the new value is set to 1 if one or the other, but not both, of the corresponding bits in the original values is set to 1. If both corresponding bits are 0 or both are 1, the final bit is set to 0 (see Figure E.5).

FIGURE E.5

The bitwise XOR operator

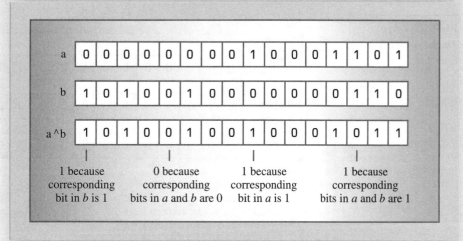

Table E.2 summarizes how the ^ operator combines bits.

TABLE E.2
VALUE OF b1 ^ b2

BIT VALUES	B1 = 0	B1 = 1
b2 = 0	0	1
b2 = 1	1	0

The bitwise AND operator (&) combines two integer values to produce a new integer value. Each bit in the new value is set to 1 only if both of the corresponding bits in the original values are set to 1. If either or both corresponding bits are 0, the final bit is set to 0 (see Figure E.6).

Table E.3 summarizes how the & operator combines bits.

TABLE E.3
VALUE OF b1 & b2

BIT VALUES	B1 = 0	B1 = 1
b2 = 0	0	0
b2 = 1	0	1

FIGURE E.6

The bitwise AND operator

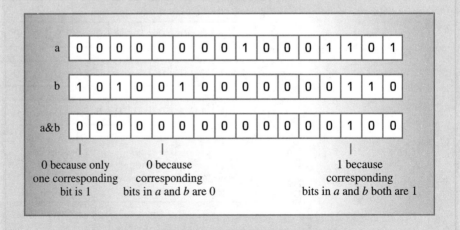

A FEW COMMON BITWISE TECHNIQUES

Often, controlling hardware involves turning particular bits on or off or checking their status. The bitwise operators provide the means to perform such actions. We'll go through the methods quickly.

In the following examples, `lottabits` represents a general value, and `bit` represents the value corresponding to a particular bit. Bits are numbered from right to left, beginning with bit 0, so the value corresponding to bit position n is 2^n. For example, an integer with only bit number 3 set to 1 has the value 2^3 or 8. In general, each individual bit corresponds to a power of 2, as described for binary numbers in Appendix A. So `bit` will be a power of 2 corresponding to a particular bit being set to 1 and all other bits set to 0.

Turning a Bit On

The following two operations each turn on the bit in `lottabits` corresponding to the bit represented by `bit`:

```
lottabits = lottabits | bit;
lottabits |= bit;
```

Each sets the corresponding bit to 1 regardless of the former value of the bit. That's because ORing 1 with either 0 or 1 produces a 1. All other bits in `lottabits` remain unaltered. That's because ORing 0 with 0 produces a 0, and ORing 0 with 1 produces a 1.

Toggling a Bit

The following two operations each toggle the bit in `lottabits` corresponding to the bit represented by `bit`. That is, they turn the bit on if it is off, and they turn it off if it is on:

```
lottabits = lottabits ^ bit;
lottabits ^= bit;
```

XORing 1 with 0 produces 1, turning an off bit on, and XORing 1 with 1 produces 0, turning an on bit off. All other bits in `lottabits` remain unaltered. That's because XORing 0 with 0 produces a 0, and XORing 0 with 1 produces a 1.

Turning a Bit Off

The following two operations each turn off the bit in `lottabits` corresponding to the bit represented by `bit`:

```
lottabits = lottabits & ~bit;
lottabits &= ~bit;
```

These statements turn the bit off regardless of its prior state. First, the operator ~bit produces an integer with all its bits set to 1 except the bit that originally was set to 1; that bit becomes a 0. ANDing a 0 with any bit results in 0, thus turning that bit off. All other bits in lottabits are unchanged. That's because ANDing a 1 with any bit produces the value that bit had before.

Testing a Bit Value

Suppose you wish to determine whether the bit corresponding to bit is set to 1 in lottabits. The following test does not necessarily work:

```
if (lottabits == bits)          // no good
```

That's because even if the corresponding bit in lottabits is set to 1, so might other bits be set to 1. The equality above is true only when *only* the corresponding bit is 1. The fix is to first AND lottabits with bit. This produces a value that is 0 in all the other bit positions, because 0 AND any value is 0. Only the bit corresponding to the bit value is left unchanged, because 1 AND any value is that value. Thus the proper test is this:

```
if (lottabits & bit == bits)       // testing a bit
```

Member Dereferencing Operators

Before discussing the member dereferencing operators, we need to provide a bit of background. C++ lets you define pointers to members of a class, but the process is not simple. To see what's involved, let's look at an example class that raises some problems:

```
class example
{
private:
    int feet;
    int inches;
public:
    example();
    example(int ft);
    ~example();
    void show_in();     // display inches member
    example operator+(example &ex);
};
```

Now suppose that you wish to define a pointer to the inches member of this class. The following attempt fails:

```
int * pi = &inches;     // not valid C++
```

It fails because `inches` is not type `int`. Because `inches` is declared in the class, it has class scope. Therefore, the type for `inches` must also specify the class to which the member belongs. To make the declaration valid, you have to use the scope operator to identify the class for the pointer and for the member:

```
int example::* pi = &example::inches;     // valid C++
```

In this declaration the phrase `int example::*` is the type "pointer-to-int member of example class." The expression `&example::inches` means "the address of the `inches` member of the `example` class."

You can use this form of declaration in member functions or in friend functions. The `pi` pointer acts like a class member in that it must be invoked with a class object. This is where the member dereferencing operators come in. For example, suppose `ex` is an `example` object declared in a member function. To access the `inches` member of `ex`, you can use the standard `ex.inches` notation. But you can also use the `.*` operator with the `pi` pointer:

```
cout << ex.inches;                // display the inches member
cout << ex.*pi;                   // ditto
```

That is, the `.` operator accesses a member using the member name, while the `.*` member accesses a member using a pointer to that member.

Similarly, suppose `px` is a pointer to an `example` object. Then you can use the `->` operator to access the `inches` member by name or by using the `->*` dereferencing operator to access `inches` via a pointer to a member:

```
px = &ex;                  // px a pointer to an example object
cout << px->inches;        // display the inches member
cout << px->*pi;           // ditto
```

Note that `px` is a pointer to an entire object, while `pi` is a pointer to a class member.

To see how these new operators work in practice, let's use them in a slightly round-about way of implementing the `operator+()` function. The function adds two objects. One object is an argument to the function. Because it is an object, not a pointer, you can use the `.*` operator to access the `inches` member. The other object is the invoking object, which, you recall, is represented by the pointer `this`. Hence you can use the `->` operator with it, as shown in the next code segment:

```
example example::operator+(example &ex)
{
    example sum;

    int example::*pi = &example::inches;
    // point to an inches member of example class

    sum.inches = ex.*pi + this->*pi;
    sum.feet = 12 * sum.inches;
    return sum;
}
```

Here `ex.*pi` represents the `inches` member of `ex` and `this->*pi` represents the inches member of the object to which `this` points. Note that `*pi` is used like a member name.

Listing E.1 provides the rest of the method definitions and a `main()` function that uses the class.

Listing E.1 memb_pt.cpp

```cpp
// memb_pt.cpp -- dereferencing pointers to class members
#include <iostream>
using namespace std;

class example
{
private:
    int feet;
    int inches;
public:
    example();
    example(int ft);
    ~example();
    void show_in();
    example operator+(example &ex);
};

example::example()
{
    feet = 0;
    inches = 0;
}

example::example(int ft)
{
    feet = ft;
    inches = 12 * feet;
}

example::~example()
{
}

void example::show_in()
{
    cout << inches << " inches\n";
}

example example::operator+(example &ex)
{
    example sum;

    int example::*pi = &example::inches;
    // point to an inches member of example class

    sum.inches = ex.*pi + this->*pi;
    sum.feet = 12 * sum.inches;
```

```
        return sum;
    }

    int main()
    {
        example car(15);
        example van(20);
        example garage;

        garage = car + van;
        car.show_in();
        van.show_in();
        garage.show_in();

        return 0;
    }
```

Here is a sample run:

```
180 inches
240 inches
420 inches
```

The `string` class is based on a template definition:

```
template<class charT, class traits = char_traits<charT>,
               class Allocator = allocator<charT> >
class basic_string {...};
```

Here `charT` represents the type stored in the string. The `traits` parameter represents a class that defines necessary properties a type must possess to be represented as a string. For example, it should have a `length()` method that returns the length of a string represented as an array of type `charT`. The end of such an array is indicated by the value `charT(0)`, the generalization of the null character. (The expression `charT(0)` is a type cast of 0 to type `charT`. It could be just a 0, as it is for type `char`, or, more generally, it could be an object created by a `charT` constructor.) The class also includes methods for comparing values, and so on. The `Allocator` parameter represents a class to handle memory allocation for the string. The default `allocator<charT>` template uses new and delete in the standard ways.

There are two predefined specializations:

```
typedef basic_string<char> string;
typedef basic_string<wchar_t> wstring;
```

These specializations, in turn, use the following specializations:

```
char_traits<char>
allocator<char>
char_traits<wchar_t>
allocator<wchar_t>
```

You can create a `string` class for some type other than `char` or `wchar_t` by defining a traits class and using the `basic_string` template.

Thirteen Types and a Constant

The `basic_string` template defines several types that are used later in defining the methods:

```
typedef traits                                 traits_type;
typedef typename traits::char_type             value_type;
typedef Allocator                              allocator_type;
typedef typename Allocator::size_type          size_type;
typedef typename Allocator::difference_type    difference_type;
typedef typename Allocator::reference          reference;
typedef typename Allocator::const_reference    const_reference;
typedef typename Allocator::pointer            pointer;
typedef typename Allocator::const_pointer      const_pointer;
```

Note that `traits` is a template parameter that will correspond to some specific type, such as `char_traits<char>`; `traits_type` will become a `typedef` for that specific type. The notation:

```
typedef typename traits::char_type        value_type;
```

means that `char_type` is a type name defined in the class represented by `traits`. The keyword `typename` is used to tell the compiler that the expression `traits::char_type` is a type. For the string specialization, for example, `value_type` will be `char`.

The `size_type` is used like `size_t`, except it measures the size of a string in terms of stored type. For the string specialization, that would be in terms of `char`, in which case `size_type` is the same as `size_t`. It is an unsigned type.

The `difference_type` is used to measure the distance between two elements of a string, again in units corresponding to the size of a single element. Typically, it would be a signed version of the type underlying `size_type`.

For the char specialization, pointer will be type char *, and reference will be type char &. However, if you create a specialization for a type of your own design, these types (pointer and reference) could refer to classes that have the same properties as the more basic pointers and references.

To allow STL algorithms to be used with strings, the template defines some iterator types:

```
typedef (models random access iterator)              iterator;
typedef (models random access iterator)              const_iterator;
typedef std::reverse_iterator<iterator>              reverse_iterator;
typedef std::reverse_iterator<const_iterator>        const_reverse_iterator;
```

The template defines a static constant:

```
static const size_type npos = -1;
```

Because size_type is unsigned, assigning a value of −1 actually amounts to assigning the largest possible unsigned value to npos. This value corresponds to 1 greater than the largest possible array index.

Data Information, Constructors, and So On

Constructors can be described in terms of the effects they have. Because the private portions of a class can be implementation-dependent, these effects should be described in terms of information available as part of the public interface. Table F.1 lists several methods whose return values can be used to describe the effects of constructors and of other methods. Note that much of the terminology is from the STL.

Be careful of the differences among begin(), rend(), data(), and c_str(). All relate to the first character in a string, but in different ways. The begin() and rend() methods return iterators, which are generalizations of pointers, as described in the Chapter 15 discussion of the STL. In particular, begin() returns a model of a forward iterator, and rend() a copy of a reverse iterator. Both refer to the actual string managed by the string object. (Because the string class uses dynamic memory allocation, the actual string contents need not be inside the object, so we use the term *manage* to describe the relationship between object and string.) You can use the methods that return iterators with the iterator-based algorithms of the STL. For instance, you can use the STL transform() function to convert the elements of a string to uppercase:

```
string word;
cin >> word;
transform(word.begin(), word.end(), toupper);
```

TABLE F.1
SOME `string` DATA METHODS

METHOD	RETURNS
begin()	An iterator to the first character in a string (also available in a `const` version, which returns a `const` iterator)
end()	An iterator that is the past-the-end value (also available n a `const` version)
rbegin()	A reverse iterator that is the past-the-end value (also available in a `const` version)
rend()	A reverse iterator that refers to the first character (also available in a `const` version)
size()	The number of elements in a string, equal to the distance from `begin()` to `end()`
length()	The same as `size()`
capacity()	The allocated number of elements in a string
max_size()	The maximum allowable size of a string
data()	A pointer of type `const charT*` to the first element of an array whose first `size()` elements equal the corresponding elements in the string controlled by `*this`. The pointer should not be assumed to be valid after the string object itself has been modified.
c_str()	A pointer of type `const charT*` to the first element of an array whose first `size()` elements equal the corresponding elements in the string controlled by `*this` and whose next element is the `trait::eos()` character for the `charT` type. The pointer should not be assumed to be valid after the string object itself has been modified.
get_allocator()	A copy of the allocator object used to allocate memory for the string object.

The data() and c_str() methods, on the other hand, do return ordinary pointers. Furthermore, the returned pointers point to the first element of an *array* holding the string characters. This array can be, but need not be, a copy of the original string managed by the string object. (The internal representation used by the string object can be an array, but it doesn't have to be.) Because it is possible that the returned pointers do point to the original data, they are const, so they can't be used to alter the data. Also, the pointers are not guaranteed to be valid after the string is modified; this reflects that they may point to the original data. The difference between data() and c_str() is that the array c_str() points to is terminated with a null character (or equivalent), while data() just guarantees the actual string characters are present. Thus, the c_str() method can be used, for example, as an argument to a function expecting a C-style string:

```
string file("tofu.man");
ofstream outFile(file.c_str());
```

Similarly, `data()` and `size()` could be used with a function that expects to receive a pointer to an array element and a value representing the number of elements to process:

```
string vampire("Do not stake me, oh my darling!");
int vlad = byte_check(vampire.data(), vampire.size());
```

An implementation could choose to represent a `string` object's string as a dynamically allocated C-style string and to implement the forward iterator as a `char *` pointer. In that case, the implementation could choose to have `begin()`, `data()`, and `c_str()` all return the same pointer. But it could just as legitimately (if not as easily) return references to three different data objects.

Table F.2 lists the six constructors and one destructor for the `basic_string` template class. Note that all six constructors have an argument of the following form:

```
const Allocator& a = Allocator()
```

Recall that the term `Allocator` is the template parameter name for an allocator class to manage memory. The term `Allocator()` is the default constructor for that class. Thus, the constructors, by default, use the default version of the allocator object, but they give you the option of using some other version of the allocator object. Let's examine the constructors individually.

DEFAULT CONSTRUCTOR

The default constructor is this:

```
explicit basic_string(const Allocator& a = Allocator());
```

TABLE F.2
string CONSTRUCTORS

CONSTRUCTOR AND DESTRUCTOR PROTOTYPES

`explicit basic_string(const Allocator& a = Allocator());`
`basic_string(const charT* s, const Allocator& a = Allocator());`
`basic_string(const basic_string& str, size_type pos = 0,`
`    size_type n = npos, const Allocator& a = Allocator());`
`basic_string(const charT* s, size_type n,`
`    const Allocator& a = Allocator());`
`basic_string(size_type n, charT c, const Allocator& a = Allocator());`
`template<class InputIterator>`
`basic_string(InputIterator begin, InputIterator end,`
`    const Allocator& a = Allocator());`
`~basic_string();`

Typically, you would accept the default argument and would use the constructor to create empty strings:

```
string bean;
wstring theory;
```

The following relations hold after the constructor is called:

- The data() method returns a non-null pointer to which 0 can be added.
- The size() method returns 0.
- The return value for capacity() is not specified.

CONSTRUCTOR USING AN ARRAY

The next constructor lets you initialize a string object from a C-style string; more generally, it lets you initialize a charT specialization from an array of charT values:

```
basic_string(const charT* s, const Allocator& a = Allocator());
```

To determine how many characters to copy, the constructor applies the traits::length() method to the array pointed to by s. (The pointer s shall not be a null pointer.) For example, the statement

```
string toast("Here's looking at ya, kid.");
```

initializes the toast object using the indicated character string. The traits::length() method for type char will use the null character to determine how many characters to copy.

The following relations hold after the constructor is called:

- The data() method returns a pointer to the first element of a copy of the array s.
- The size() method returns a value equal to traits::length().
- The capacity() method returns a value at least as large as size().

CONSTRUCTOR USING PART OF AN ARRAY

The next constructor lets you initialize a string object from part of a C-style string; more generally, it lets you initialize a charT specialization from part of an array of charT values:

```
basic_string(const charT* s, size_type n, const Allocator& a =
                Allocator());
```

This constructor copies a total of n characters from the array pointed to by s to the constructed object. Note that it doesn't stop copying if s has fewer characters than n. If n exceeds the length of s, the constructor will interpret the contents of memory following the string as if they held data of type charT.

The constructor requires that s is not a null pointer and that n < npos. (Recall that npos is a static class constant equal to the maximum possible number of elements in a string.) If n equals npos, the constructor throws an out_of_range exception. (Because n is of type size_type and npos is the maximum size_type value, n cannot be greater than npos.) Otherwise, the following relations hold after the constructor is called:

- The data() method returns a pointer to the first element of a copy of the array s.

- The size() method returns n.

- The capacity() method returns a value at least as large as size().

COPY CONSTRUCTOR

The copy constructor provides several arguments with default values:

```
basic_string(const basic_string& str, size_type pos = 0,
            size_type n = npos, const Allocator& a = Allocator());
```

Calling it with only a basic_string argument initializes the new object to the string argument:

```
string mel("I'm ok!");
string ida(mel);
```

Here ida would get a copy of the string managed by mel.

The optional second argument pos specifies a location in the source string from which to begin the copying:

```
string att("Telephone home.");
string et(att, 4);
```

Position numbers begin with 0, so position 4 is the p character. Thus, et is initialized to "phone home."

The optional third argument n specifies the maximum number of characters to copy. Thus,

```
string att("Telephone home.");
string pt(att, 4, 5);
```

will initialize pt to the string "phone". However, this constructor will not go past the end of the source string, so it actually copies a number of characters equal to the lesser of n and of str.size() - pos.

This constructor requires that pos <= str.size(); if this is not the case, it throws an out_of_range exception. Otherwise, letting copy_len represent the lessor of n and of str.size() - pos, the following relations hold after the constructor is called:

- The data() method returns a pointer to a copy of copy_len elements copied from the string str, starting with position pos in str.

- The size() method returns copy_len.

- The capacity() method returns a value at least as large as size().

CONSTRUCTOR USING n COPIES OF A CHARACTER

The next constructor creates a string object consisting of n consecutive characters all having the value c:

```
basic_string(size_type n, charT c, const Allocator& a = Allocator());
```

The constructor requires that n < npos. If n equals npos, the constructor throws an out_of_range exception. Otherwise, the following relations hold after the constructor is called:

- The data() method returns a pointer to the first element of a string of n elements, each set to c.

- The size() method returns n.

- The capacity() method returns a value at least as large as size().

CONSTRUCTOR USING A RANGE

The final constructor uses an iterator-defined range in the style of the STL:

```
template<class InputIterator>
basic_string(InputIterator begin, InputIterator end,
             const Allocator& a = Allocator());
```

The begin iterator points to the element in the source at which copying begins, and end points to one past the last location to be copied.

You can use this form with arrays, strings, or STL containers:

```
char cole[40] = "Old King Cole was a merry old soul.";
string title(cole + 4, cole + 8);
vector<char> input;
char ch;
```

```
while (cin.get(ch) && ch != '\n')
    input.push_back(ch);
string str_input(input.begin(), input.end());
```

In the first use, `InputIterator` is evaluated to type `const char *`. In the second use, `InputIterator` is evaluated to type `vector<char>::iterator`.

The following relations hold after the constructor is called:

- The `data()` method returns a pointer to the first element of a string formed from copying elements from the range [`begin`, `end`).

- The `size()` method returns the distance between `begin` and `end`. (The distance is measured in units equal to the size of data type obtained when the iterator is dereferenced.)

- The `capacity()` method returns a value at least as large as `size()`.

MEMORY MISCELLANY

Several methods deal with memory, for example, clearing memory contents, resizing a string, adjusting the capacity of a string. Table F.3 lists some memory-related methods.

TABLE F.3
SOME MEMORY-RELATED METHODS

METHOD	EFFECT
`void resize(size_type n)`	Throws an `out_of_range` exception if n > npos. Otherwise, changes size of string to n, truncating the end of the string if n < `size()` and padding the string with `charT(0)` characters if n > `size()`.
`void resize(size_type n, charT c)`	Throws an `out_of_range` exception if n > npos. Otherwise, changes size of string to n, truncating the end of the string if n < `size()` and padding the string with the character c if n > `size()`.
`void reserve(size_type res_arg = 0)`	Sets `capacity()` to greater than or equal to `res_arg`. Because this reallocates the string, it voids previous references, iterators, and pointers into the string.
`void clear()`	Removes all characters from a string.
`bool empty() const`	Returns true if `size() == 0`.

String Access

There are four methods for accessing individual characters, two using the [ ] operator, and two using the at( ) method:

```
reference operator[](size_type pos);
const_reference operator[](size_type pos) const;
reference at(size_type n);
const_reference at(size_type n) const;
```

The first operator[]( ) method allows you to access an individual element of a string using array notation; it can be used to retrieve or alter the value. The second operator[ ] method can be used with const objects, and it can be used only to retrieve the value:

```
string word("tack");
cout << word[0];      // display the t
word[3] = 't';        // overwrite the k with a t
const ward("garlic");
cout << ward[2];  // display the r
```

The at( ) methods provide similar access, except the index is provided in function argument notation:

```
string word("tack");
cout << word.at(0);    // display the t
```

The difference (besides that of syntax) is that the at( ) methods provide bounds checking and throw an out_of_range exception if pos >= size( ). Note that pos is type size_type, which is unsigned, therefore a negative value is impossible for pos. The operator[]( ) methods don't do bounds checking, so the behavior is undefined if pos >= size( ), except that the const version returns the null character equivalent if pos == size( ).

Thus you get a choice between safety (using at( ) and testing for exceptions) or execution speed (using array notation).

There also is a function that returns a new string that is a substring of the original:

```
basic_string substr(size_type pos = 0, size_type n = npos) const;
```

It returns a string that's a copy of the string starting at position pos and going for n characters or to the end of the string, whichever comes first. For example, the following initializes pet to "donkey":

```
string message("Maybe the donkey will learn to sing.");
string pet(message.substr(10, 6));
```

Basic Assignment

There are three overloaded assignment methods:

```
basic_string& operator=(const basic_string& str);
basic_string& operator=(const charT* s);
basic_string& operator=(charT c);
```

The first assigns one string object to another, the second assigns a C-style string to a string object, and the third assigns a single character to a string object. Thus, all of the following operations are possible:

```
string name("George Wash");
string pres, veep, source;
pres = name;
veep = "Road Runner";
source = 'X';
```

String Searching

The `string` class provides six search functions, each with four prototypes. Let's describe them briefly.

THE `find()` FAMILY

Here are the `find()` prototypes:

```
size_type find (const basic_string& str, size_type pos = 0) const;
size_type find (const charT* s, size_type pos = 0) const;
size_type find (const charT* s, size_type pos, size_type n) const;
size_type find (charT c, size_type pos = 0) const;
```

The first member returns the position of the beginning of the first occurrence of the substring str in the invoking object; with the search beginning at position pos. If the substring is not found, the method returns npos.

```
string longer("That is a funny hat.");
string shorter("hat");
size_type loc1 = longer.find(shorter);        // sets loc1 to 1
size_type loc2 = longer.find(shorter, loc1 + 1); // sets loc2 to 16
```

Because the second search begins at position 2 (the a in That), the first occurrence of hat it finds is near the end of the string. To test for failure, use the string::npos value:

```
if (loc1 == string::npos)
    cout << "Not found\n";
```

The second method does the same thing except it uses an array of characters instead of a `string` object as the substring.

The third method does the same as the second, except it uses only the first n characters of the string s. The effect is the same as using the `basic_string(const charT* s, size_type n)` constructor and using the resulting object as the string argument to the first form of `find()`.

The fourth method does the same as the first except it uses a single character instead of a string object as the substring.

THE `rfind()` FAMILY

The `rfind()` methods have these prototypes:

```
size_type rfind(const basic_string& str, size_type pos = npos) const;
size_type rfind(const charT* s, size_type pos = npos) const;
size_type rfind(const charT* s, size_type pos, size_type n) const;
size_type rfind(charT c, size_type pos = npos) const;
```

These methods work like the analogous `find()` methods, except they find the last occurrence of a string or character that starts at or before position pos. If the substring is not found, the method returns npos.

```
string longer("That is a funny hat.");
string shorter("hat");
size_type loc1 = longer.rfind(shorter);         // sets loc1 to 16
size_type loc2 = longer.rfind(shorter, loc1 - 1); // sets loc2 to 1
```

THE `find_first_of()` FAMILY

The `find_first_of()` methods have these prototypes:

```
size_type find_first_of(const basic_string& str, size_type pos = 0)
          const;
size_type find_first_of(const charT* s, size_type pos, size_type n)
          const;
size_type find_first_of(const charT* s, size_type pos = 0) const;
size_type find_first_of(charT c, size_type pos = 0) const;
```

These methods work like the corresponding `find()` methods except instead of looking for a match of the entire substring, they look for the first match for any single character in the substring.

```
string longer("That is a funny hat.");
string shorter("fluke");
size_type loc1 = longer.find_first_of(shorter); // sets loc1 to 10
size_type loc2 = longer.find_first_of("fat");   // sets loc2 to 2
```

The first occurrence of any of the five characters of fluke, in longer is the f in funny.
The first occurrence of any of three characters of fat in longer is the a in That.

THE `find_last_of()` FAMILY

The `find_last_of()` methods have these prototypes:

```
size_type find_last_of (const basic_string& str,
                         size_type pos = npos) const;
size_type find_last_of (const charT* s, size_type pos, size_type n)
          const;
size_type find_last_of (const charT* s, size_type pos = npos) const;
size_type find_last_of (charT c, size_type pos = npos) const;
```

These methods work like the corresponding `rfind()` methods except instead of looking for a match of the entire substring, they look for the last match for any single character in the substring.

```
string longer("That is a funny hat.");
string shorter("hat");
size_type loc1 = longer.find_last_of(shorter);  // sets loc1 to 18
size_type loc2 = longer.find_last_of("any");     // sets loc2 to 17
```

The last occurrence of any of the three letters of hat in longer is the t in hat. The last
occurrence of any of the three characters of any in longer is the a in hat.

THE `find_first_not_of()` FAMILY

The `find_first_not_of()` methods have these prototypes:

```
size_type find_first_not_of(const basic_string& str,
                            size_type pos = 0) const;
size_type find_first_not_of(const charT* s, size_type pos,
                            size_type n) const;
size_type find_first_not_of(const charT* s, size_type pos = 0) const;
size_type find_first_not_of(charT c, size_type pos = 0) const;
```

These methods work like the corresponding `find_first_of()` methods, except they
search for the first occurrence of any character not in the substring.

```
string longer("That is a funny hat.");
string shorter("This");
size_type loc1 = longer.find_first_not_of(shorter);    // sets loc1 to 2
size_type loc2 = longer.find_first_not_of("Thatch"); // sets loc2 to 4
```

The a in That is the first character in longer that does not appear in This. The first
space in the longer string is the first character not present in Thatch.

THE `find_last_not_of()` FAMILY

The `find_last_not_of()` methods have these prototypes:

```
size_type find_last_not_of (const basic_string& str,
                            size_type pos = npos) const;
size_type find_last_not_of (const charT* s, size_type pos,
                            size_type n) const;
size_type find_last_not_of (const charT* s, size_type pos = npos) const;
size_type find_last_not_of (charT c, size_type pos = npos) const;
```

These methods work like the corresponding `find_last_of()` methods, except they search for the first occurrence of any character not in the substring.

```
string longer("That is a funny hat.");
string shorter("That.");
size_type loc1 = longer.find_last_not_of(shorter);     // sets loc1 to 15
size_type loc2 = longer.find_last_not_of(shorter, 10); // sets loc2 to 10
```

The last space in `longer` is the last character in `longer` that does not appear in `shorter`. The `f` in the `longer` string is the last character not present in `shorter` found up through position 10.

Comparison Methods and Functions

The string class offers methods and functions for comparing two strings. First, here are the method prototypes:

```
int compare(const basic_string& str) const;
int compare(size_type pos1, size_type n1,
            const basic_string& str) const;
int compare(size_type pos1, size_type n1,
            const basic_string& str,
            size_type pos2, size_type n2) const;
int compare(const charT* s) const;
int compare(size_type pos1, size_type n1,
            const charT* s, size_type n2 = npos) const;
```

These methods use a `traits::compare()` method defined for the particular character type used for the string. The first method returns a value less than 0 if first string precedes the second string according to the ordering supplied by `traits::compare()`. It returns 0 if the two strings are the same, and it returns a value greater than 0 if the first string follows the second. If two strings are identical to the end of the shorter of the two strings, the shorter string comes before the longer string.

```
string s1("bellflower");
string s2("bell");
string s3("cat");
int a1 = s1.compare(s3); // a1 is < 0
int a2 = s1.compare(s2); // a2 is < 0
```

The second method is like the first, except that it just uses n1 characters starting from position pos1 in the first string for the comparison.

```
string s1("bellflower");
string s2("bell");
int a2 = s1.compare(0,4s2); // a2 is 0
```

The third method is like the first, except that it just uses n1 characters starting from position pos1 in the first string and n2 characters starting from position pos2 in the second string for the comparison.

The fourth method is like the first, except it uses a string array instead of a string object for the second string.

The fifth method is like the third, except it uses a string array instead of a string object for the second string.

The non-member comparison functions are overloaded relational operators:

```
operator==()
operator<()
operator<=()
operator>()
operator>=()
operator!=()
```

Each operator is overloaded so that it can compare a string object to a string object, a string object to a string array, and a string array to a string object. They are defined in terms of the compare() method, so they provide a notationally more convenient way of making comparisons.

String Modifiers

The string class provides several methods for modifying strings. Most come with an abundance of overloaded versions so that they can be used with string objects, string arrays, individual characters, and iterator ranges.

APPENDING AND ADDING

You can append one string to another by using the overloaded += operator or by using an append() method. All throw a length_error exception if the result would be longer than the maximum string size. The += operators let you append a string object, a string array, or an individual character to another string:

```
basic_string& operator+=(const basic_string& str);
basic_string& operator+=(const charT* s);
basic_string& operator+=(charT c);
```

The append() methods also let you append a string object, a string array, or an individual character to another string. In addition, they let you append part of a string object by specifying an initial position and a number of characters to append or else by specifying a range. You can append part of a string by specifying how many characters of the string to use. The version for appending a character lets you specify how many instances of that character to copy.

```
basic_string& append(const basic_string& str);
basic_string& append(const basic_string& str, size_type pos,
                     size_type n);
template<class InputIterator>
  basic_string& append(InputIterator first, InputIterator last);
basic_string& append(const charT* s, size_type n);
basic_string& append(const charT* s, size_type n);
basic_string& append(size_type n, charT c);  // append n copies of c
```

Here are a couple of examples:

```
string test("The");
test.append("ory");  // test is "Theory"
test.append(3,'!');  // test is "Theory!!!"
```

The operator+() function is overloaded to enable string concatenation. The overloaded functions don't modify a string; rather, they create a new string consisting of one string appended to a second. The addition functions are not member functions, and they allow you to add a string object to a string object, a string array to a string object, a string object to a string array, a character to a string object, and a string object to a character. Here are some examples:

```
string st1("red");
string st2("rain");
string st3 = st1 + "uce";  // st3 is "reduce"
string st4 = 't' + st2;    // st4 is "train"
string st5 = st1 + st2;    // st5 is "redrain"
```

MORE ASSIGNMENT

In addition to the basic assignment operator, the string class provides assign() methods, which allow you to assign a whole string or a part of a string or a sequence of identical characters to a string object.

```
basic_string& assign(const basic_string&);
basic_string& assign(const basic_string& str, size_type pos,
                     size_type n);
basic_string& assign(const charT* s, size_type n);
basic_string& assign(const charT* s);
basic_string& assign(size_type n, charT c); // assign n copies of c
template<class InputIterator>
  basic_string& assign(InputIterator first, InputIterator last);
```

Here are a couple of examples:

```
string test;
string stuff("set tubs clones ducks");
test.assign(stuff, 1, 5);    // test is "et tu"
test.assign(6, '#');         // test is "######"
```

INSERTION METHODS

The insert() methods let you insert a string object, string array, character, or several characters into a string object. The methods are similar to the append() methods, except they take an additional argument indicating where to insert the new material. This argument may be a position or an iterator. The material is inserted before the insertion point. Several of the methods return a reference to the resulting string. If pos1 is beyond the end of the target string or if pos2 is beyond the end of the string to be inserted, a method throws an out_of_range exception. If the resulting string will be larger than the maximum size, a method throws a length_error exception.

```
basic_string& insert(size_type pos1, const basic_string& str);
basic_string& insert(size_type pos1, const basic_string& str,
                     size_type pos2, size_type n);
basic_string& insert(size_type pos, const charT* s, size_type n);
basic_string& insert(size_type pos, const charT* s);
basic_string& insert(size_type pos, size_type n, charT c);
iterator insert(iterator p, charT c = charT());
void insert(iterator p, size_type n, charT c);
template<class InputIterator>
  void insert(iterator p, InputIterator first, InputIterator last);
```

ERASE METHODS

The erase() methods remove characters from a string. Here are the prototypes:

```
basic_string& erase(size_type pos = 0, size_type n = npos);
iterator erase(iterator position);
iterator erase(iterator first, iterator last);
```

The first form removes the character from position pos to n characters later, or the end of the string, whichever comes first. The second removes the single character referenced by the iterator position and returns an iterator to the next element, or, if there are no more elements, returns end(). The third removes the characters in the range [first, last) (that is, including first and up to but not including last). The method returns an iterator to element following the last element erased.

REPLACEMENT METHODS

The various replace() methods identify part of a string to be replaced and identify the replacement. The part to be replaced can be identified by an initial position and a character count or by an iterator range. The replacement can be a string object, a string array, a particular character duplicated several times. Replacement string objects and arrays can further be modified by indicating a particular portion, using a position and a count, just a count, or an iterator range.

```
basic_string& replace(size_type pos1, size_type n1,
            const basic_string& str);
basic_string& replace(size_type pos1, size_type n1,
            const basic_string& str, size_type pos2, size_type n2);
basic_string& replace(size_type pos, size_type n1, const charT* s,
            size_type n2);
basic_string& replace(size_type pos, size_type n1, const charT* s);
basic_string& replace(size_type pos, size_type n1,
            size_type n2, charT c);
basic_string& replace(iterator i1, iterator i2, const basic_string& str);
basic_string& replace(iterator i1, iterator i2,
            const charT* s, size_type n);
basic_string& replace(iterator i1, iterator i2, const charT* s);
basic_string& replace(iterator i1, iterator i2,
            size_type n, charT c);
template<class InputIterator>
  basic_string& replace(iterator i1, iterator i2,
                    InputIterator j1, InputIterator j2);
```

Here is an example:

```
string test("Take a right turn at Main Street.");
test.replace(7,5,"left"); // replace right with left
```

OTHER MODIFYING METHODS: copy() AND swap()

The copy() method copies a string object, or part thereof, to a designated string array:

```
size_type copy(charT* s, size_type n, size_type pos = 0) const;
```

Here s points to the destination array, n indicates the number of characters to copy, and pos indicates the position in the string object from which copying begins. Copying proceeds for n characters or until the last character in the string object, whichever comes first. The function returns the number of characters copied. The method does not append a null character, and it is up to the programmer to see that the array is large enough to hold the copy.

The swap() method swaps the contents of two string objects using a constant time algorithm:

```
void swap(basic_string<charT,traits,Allocator>&);
```

Output and Input

The `string` class overloads the `<<` operator to display string objects. It returns a reference to the `istream` object so that output can be concatenated:

```
string claim("The string class has many features.");
cout << claim << endl;
```

The `string` class overloads the `>>` operator so that you can read input into a string:

```
string who;
cin >> who;
```

Input terminates on end-of-file, reading the maximum number of characters allowed in a string, or on reaching a white space character. (The definition of whitespace will depend on the character set and upon the type `charT` represents.)

There are two `getline()` functions. The first has this prototype:

```
template<class charT, class traits, class Allocator>
basic_istream<charT,traits>& getline(basic_istream<charT,traits>& is,
            basic_string<charT,traits,Allocator>& str, charT delim);
```

It reads characters from the input stream `is` into the string `str` until encountering the `delim` delimiter character, reaching the maximum size of the string, or encountering end-of-file. The `delim` character is read (removed from the input stream), but not stored. The second version lacks the third argument and uses the newline character (or its generalization) instead of `delim`:

```
string str1, str2;
getline(cin, str1);        // read to end-of-line
getline(cin, str2, '.');   // read to period
```

G

The STL Methods and Functions

The STL aims to provide efficient implementations of common algorithms. It expresses these algorithms in general functions that can be used with any container satisfying the requirements for the particular algorithm and in methods that can be used with instantiations of particular container classes. This appendix assumes that you have some familiarity with the STL, such as might be gained from reading Chapter 15. Thus, it assumes you know about iterators and constructors, for example.

Members Common to All Containers

All containers define the types in Table G.1. In this table, X is a container type, such as vector<int>, and T is the type stored in the container, such as int.

The class definition will use a typedef to define these members. You can use these types, to declare suitable variables. For example, the following takes a round-about way to replace the first occurrence of "bonus" in a vector of string objects with "bogus" in order to show how you can use member types to declare variables.

TABLE G.1
TYPES DEFINED FOR ALL CONTAINERS

TYPE	VALUE
`X::value_type`	T, the element type
`X::reference`	Behaves like `T &`
`X::const_reference`	Behaves like `const T &`
`X::iterator`	Iterator type pointing to T, behaves like `T *`
`X::const_iterator`	Iterator type pointing to const T, behaves like `const T *`
`X::difference_type`	Signed integral type used to represent the distance from one iterator to another; for example, the difference between two pointers
`X::size_type`	Unsigned integral type `size_type` can represent size of data objects, number of elements, and subscripts

```
vector<string> input;
    string temp;
    while (cin >> temp && temp != "quit")
        input.push_back(temp);
    vector<string>::iterator want=
        find(input.begin(), input.end(), string("bonus"));
    if (want != input.end())
    {
        vector<string>::reference r = *want;
        r = "bogus";
    }
```

This code makes r a reference to the element in input to which want points.

These types also can be used in more general code in which the type of container and element are generic. For example, suppose you want a min() function that takes as its argument a reference to a container and returns the smallest item in the container. This assumes that the < operator is defined for the value type and that you don't want to use the STL min_element() algorithm, which uses an iterator interface. Because the argument could be vector<int> or list<string> or deque<double>, use a template with a template parameter, such as Bag, to represent the container. So the argument type for the function will be const Bag & b. What about the return type? It should be the value type for the container, that is, Bag::value_type. However, at this point, Bag is just a template parameter, and the compiler has no way of knowing that the value_type member is actually a type. But you can use the typename keyword to clarify that a class member is a typedef:

```
vector<string>::value_type st;    // vector<string> a defined classs
typename Bag::value_type m;       // Bag an as yet undefined type
```

For the first definition, the compiler has access to the vector template definition, which states that value_type is a typedef. For the second definition, the typename keyword promises that the combination `Bag::value_type` is a `typedef`. These considerations lead to the following definition:

```
template<typename Bag>
typename Bag::value_type min(const Bag & b)
{
    typename Bag::const_iterator it;
    typename Bag::value_type m = *b.begin();
    for (it = b.begin(); it != b.end(); ++it)
        if (*it < m)
            m = *it;;
    return m;
}
```

All containers also contain the member functions or operations listed in Table G.2. Again, X is a container type, such as `vector<int>`, and T is the type stored in the container, such as `int`. Also, a and b are values of type X.

The > operator for a container assumes that the > operator is defined for the value type. A lexicographical comparison is a generalization of alphabetical sorting. It compares two containers element by element until encountering an element in one container that doesn't equal the corresponding element in the other container. The containers then compare the same as those elements; for example, if the element in the first container is less than the element in the second container, the first container precedes the second. If two containers compare equal until one runs out of elements, the shorter container precedes the longer.

TABLE G.2
METHODS DEFINED FOR ALL CONTAINERS

METHOD/OPERATION	DESCRIPTION
`begin()`	Returns an iterator to the first element
`end()`	Returns an iterator to past-the-end
`rbegin()`	Returns a reverse iterator to past-the-end
`rend()`	Returns a reverse iterator to first element
`size()`	Returns number of elements
`maxsize()`	Returns the size of the largest possible container
`empty()`	Returns `true` if the container is empty
`swap()`	Swaps the contents of two containers
`==`	Returns `true` if two containers are the same size and have the same elements in the same order
`!=`	`a != b` is the same as `!(a == b)`
`<`	Returns true if a lexicographically precedes b
`>`	`a > b` is the same as `b < a`
`<=`	`a <= b` is the same as `!(a > b)`
`>=`	`a >= b` is the same as `!(a < b)`

Additional Members for Vectors, Lists, and Deques

Vectors, lists, and deques are all sequences, and they all have the methods listed in Table G.3. Again, X is a container type, such as vector<int>, and T is the type stored in the container, such as int, a is a value of type X, t is a value of type X::value_type, i and j are input iterators, q2 and p are iterators, q and q1 are dereferenceable iterators (you can apply the * operator to th935), and n is a integer of X::size_type.

Table G.4 lists methods common to two out of the three sequence classes.

TABLE G.3
METHODS DEFINED FOR VECTORS, LISTS, AND DEQUES

METHOD	DESCRIPTION
a.insert(p,t)	Inserts a copy of t before p; returns an iterator pointing to the inserted copy of t. The default value for t is T(), that is, the value used for type T in the absence of explicit initialization.
a.insert(p,n,t)	Inserts n copies of t before p; no return value.
a.insert(p,i,j)	Inserts copies of the elements in range [i,j] before p, no return value.
a.resize(n,t)	If n > a.size(), inserts n - a.size() copies of t before a.end(); t has a default value of T(), that is, the value used for type T in the absence of explicit initialization. If n < a.size(), the elements following the nth element are erased.
a.assign(i,j)	Replaces the current contents of a with copies of the elements in range [i,j].
a.assign(n,t)	Replaces the current contents of a with n copies of t. The default value for t is T(), the value used for type T in the absence of explicit initialization.
a.erase(q)	Erases the element pointed to by q; returns an iterator to the element that had followed q.
a.erase(q1,q2)	Erases the elements in the range [q1,q2]; returns an iterator pointing to the element q2 originally pointed to.
a.clear()	Same as erase(a.begin(), a.end()).
a.front()	Returns *a.begin() (the first element).
a.back()	Returns *--a.end() (the last element).
a.push_back(t)	Inserts t before a.end().
a.pop_back()	Erases the last element.

TABLE G.4
METHODS DEFINED FOR SOME SEQUENCES

METHOD	DESCRIPTION	CONTAINER
a.push_front(t)	Inserts a copy of t before the first element.	list, deque
a.pop_front()	Erases the first element.	list, deque
a[n]	Returns *(a.begin() + n).	vector, deque
a.at(n)	Returns *(a.begin() + n), throws out_of_range exception if n > a.size().	vector, deque

The list template additionally has the methods in Table G.5. Here, a and b are list containers, and T is the type stored in the list, such as int, t is a value of type T, i and j are input iterators, q2 and p are iterators, q and q1 are dereferenceable iterators, and n is a integer of X::size_type.

TABLE G.5
ADDITIONAL METHODS FOR LISTS

METHOD	DESCRIPTION
a.splice(p,b)	Moves the contents of list b to list a, inserting them before p.
a.splice(p,b,i)	Moves the element in list b pointed to by i to before position p in list a.
a.splice(p,b,i,j)	Moves the elements in range [i,j] of list b to before position p in list a.
a.remove(const T& t)	Erases all elements in list a having the value t.
a.remove_if(Predicate pred)	Given that i is an iterator into the list a, erases all values for which pred(*i) is true. (A Predicate is a Boolean function or function object, as discussed in Chapter 15.)
a.unique()	Erases all but the first element from each group of consecutive equal elements.
a.unique(BinaryPredicatebin_pred)	Erases all but the first element from each group of consecutive elements for which bin_pred(*i, *(i - 1)) is true. (A BinaryPredicate is a Boolean function or function object, as discussed in Chapter 15.)
a.merge(b)	Merges the contents of list b with list a using the < operator defined for the value type. If an element in a is equivalent to an element in b, the element from a is placed first. List b is empty after the merge.
a.merge(b, Compare comp)	Merges the contents of list b with list a using the comp function or function object. If an element in a is equivalent to an element in b, the element from a is placed first. List b is empty after the merge.
a.sort()	Sorts list a using the < operator.
a.sort(Compare comp)	Sorts list a using the comp function or function object.
a.reverse()	Reverses the order of the elements in list a.

Additional Members for Sets and Maps

Associative containers, of which sets and maps are models, have a Key template parameter and a Compare template parameter indicating, respectively, the type of the key used to order the contents and the function object, termed a *comparison object*, used to compare key values. For the set and multiset containers, the stored keys are the stored values, so the key type is the same as the value type. For the map and multimap containers, the stored values of one type (template parameter T) are associated with a key type (template parameter Key), and the value typc is pair<const Key, T>. Associative containers introduce additional members to describe these features, as listed in Table G.6.

Associative containers provide the methods listed in Table G.7. In general, the comparison object need not require that values with the same key are identical; the term *equivalent keys* means that two values, which may or may not be equal, have the same key. In the table, X is a container class, a is an object of type X. If X uses unique keys (that is, is a set or map), a_uniq is an object of type X. If X uses multiple keys (that is, is a multiset or multimap), a_eq is an object of type X. As before, i and j are input iterators referring to elements of value_type, [i, j) is a valid range, p and q2 are iterators to a, q and q1 are dereferenceable iterators to a, [q1, q2) is a valid range, t is a value of X::value_type (which may be a pair). Also, k is a value of X::key_type.

STL Functions

The STL algorithm library, supported by the algorithm and numeric header files, provides a large number of non-member, iterator-based template functions. As discussed in Chapter 15, the template parameter names are chosen to indicate what concept particular parameters should model. For example, ForwardIterator is used to indicate that a parameter should, at the minimum, model the requirements of a forward iterator, and Predicate is used to indicate a parameter that should be a function object with one argument and a bool return value. The standard divides the algorithms into four groups: non-modifying sequence operations, mutating sequence operations, sorting and related operators, and numeric operations. The term *sequence operation* indicates the function, takes a pair of iterators as arguments to define a range, or sequence, to be operated upon. The term *mutating* means the function is allowed to alter the container.

TABLE G.6
TYPES DEFINED FOR ASSOCIATIVE CONTAINERS

TYPE	VALUE
X::key_type	Key, the key type
X::key_compare	Compare, which has a default value of less<key_type>
X::value_compare	A binary predicate type that is the same as key_compare for set and multiset and which supplies ordering for the pair<const Key, T> values in a map or multimap
X::mapped_type	T, the type of the associated data (map and multimap only)

TABLE G.7
METHODS DEFINED FOR SETS, MULTISETS, MAPS, AND MULTIMAPS

METHOD	DESCRIPTION
`a.key_comp()`	Returns the comparison object used in constructing a.
`a.value_comp()`	Returns an object of the `value_compare` type.
`a_uniq.insert(t)`	Inserts the value t into the container a if and only if a does not yet contain a value with an equivalent key. The method returns a value of type `pair<iterator,bool>`. The `bool` component is `true` if insertion occurred and `false` otherwise. The iterator component points to the element whose key is equivalent to the key of t.
`a_eq.insert(t)`	Inserts t and returns an iterator pointing to its location.
`a.insert(p,t)`	Inserts t using p as a hint to where `insert()` should begin its search. If a is a container with unique keys, insertion takes place if and only if a doesn't contain an element with an equivalent key; otherwise, insertion takes place. Whether or not insertion takes place, the method returns an iterator pointing to the location with an equivalent key.
`a.insert(i,j)`	Inserts elements from the range `[i,j]` into a.
`a.erase(k)`	Erases all elements in a whose keys are equivalent to k and returns the number of elements erased.
`a.erase(q)`	Erases the element pointed to by q.
`a.erase(q1,q2)`	Erases the elements in the range `[q1,q2]`.
`a.clear()`	Same as `erase(a.begin(), a.end())`.
`a.find(k)`	Returns an iterator pointing to an element whose key is equivalent to k; returns `a.end()` if no such element is found.
`a.count(k)`	Returns the number of elements having keys equivalent to k.
`a.lower_bound(k)`	Returns an iterator to the first element with a key not less than k.
`a.upper_bound(k)`	Returns an iterator to the first element with a key greater than k.
`a.equal_range(k)`	Returns a pair whose first member is `a.lower_bound(k)` and whose second member is `a.upper_bound(k)`.
`a.operator[](k)`	Returns a reference to the value associated with the key k (map containers only).

NON-MODIFYING SEQUENCE OPERATIONS

Table G.8 summarizes the non-modifying sequence operations. Arguments are not shown, and overloaded functions are listed just once. A fuller description including the prototypes follows the table. Thus, you can scan the table to get an idea of what a function does and then look up the details if you find the function appealing.

TABLE G.8
NON-MODIFYING SEQUENCE OPERATIONS

FUNCTION	DESCRIPTION
for_each()	Applies a non-modifying function object to each element in a range.
find()	Finds the first occurrence of a value in a range.
find_if()	Finds the first value satisfying a predicate test criterion in a range.
find_end()	Finds the last occurrence of a subsequence whose values match the values of a second sequence. Matching may be by equality or by applying a binary predicate.
find_first_of()	Finds the first occurrence of any element of a second sequence that matches a value in the first sequence. Matching may be by equality or be evaluated with a binary predicate.
adjacent_find()	Finds the first element that matches the element immediately following it. Matching may be by equality or be evaluated with a binary predicate.
count()	Returns the number of times a given value occurs in a range.
count_if()	Returns the number of times a given value matches values in a range, with a match determined by using a binary predicate.
mismatch()	Finds the first element in one range that does not match the corresponding element in a second range and returns iterators to both. Matching may be by equality or be evaluated with a binary predicate.
equal()	Returns true if each element in one range matches the corresponding element in a second range. Matching may be by equality or be evaluated with a binary predicate.
search()	Finds the first occurrence of a subsequence whose values match the values of a second sequence. Matching may be by equality or by applying a binary predicate.
search_n()	Finds the first subsequence of n elements that each match a given value. Matching may be by equality or by applying a binary predicate.

Now let's look at the prototypes. Pairs of iterators indicate ranges, with the chosen template parameter name indicating the type of iterator. As usual, a range of the form [first, last) goes from first up to, but not including last. Some functions take two ranges, which need not be in the same kind of container. For example, you can use equal() to compare a list to a vector. Functions passed as arguments are function objects, which can be pointers (of which function names are an example) or objects for which the () operation is defined. As in Chapter 15, a predicate is a Boolean function with one argument, and a binary predicate is a Boolean function with two arguments. (The functions need not be type bool as long as they return a 0 value for false and a non-zero for true.)

```
template<class InputIterator, class Function>
Function for_each(InputIterator first, InputIterator last, Function f);
```

The for_each() function applies function object f to each element in the range [first, last). It also returns f.

```
template<class InputIterator, class T>
InputIterator find(InputIterator first, InputIterator last, const T& value);
```

The find() function returns an iterator to the first element in the range [first, last) that has the value value.

```
template<class InputIterator, class Predicate>
InputIterator find_if(InputIterator first, InputIterator last,
                      Predicate pred);
```

The find_if() function returns an iterator it to the first element in the range [first, last) for which the function object call pred(*i) is true.

```
template<class ForwardIterator1, class ForwardIterator2>
ForwardIterator1 find_end(ForwardIterator1 first1, ForwardIterator1 last1,
                          ForwardIterator2 first2, ForwardIterator2 last2);
template<class ForwardIterator1, class ForwardIterator2,
         class BinaryPredicate>
ForwardIterator1 find_end(ForwardIterator1 first1, ForwardIterator1 last1,
                          ForwardIterator2 first2, ForwardIterator2 last2,
                          BinaryPredicate pred);
```

The find_end() function returns an iterator it to the last element in the range [first1, last1) that marks the beginning of a subsequence that matches the contents of the range [first2, last2). The first version uses the == operator for the value type to compare elements. The second version uses the binary predicate function object pred to compare elements. That is, elements pointed to by it1 and it2 match if pred(*it1, *it2) is true.

```
template<class ForwardIterator1, class ForwardIterator2>
ForwardIterator1 find_first_of(
                   ForwardIterator1 first1, ForwardIterator1 last1,
                   ForwardIterator2 first2, ForwardIterator2 last2);

template<class ForwardIterator1, class ForwardIterator2,
         class BinaryPredicate>
ForwardIterator1 find_first_of(
                   ForwardIterator1 first1, ForwardIterator1 last1,
                   ForwardIterator2 first2, ForwardIterator2 last2,
                   BinaryPredicate pred);
```

The find_first_of() function returns an iterator it to the first element in the range [first1, last1) that matches any element of the range [first2, last2). The first version uses the == operator for the value type to compare elements. The second version uses the binary predicate function object pred to compare elements. That is, elements pointed to by it1 and it2 match if pred(*it1, *it2) is true.

```
template<class ForwardIterator>
ForwardIterator adjacent_find(ForwardIterator first, ForwardIterator last);

template<class ForwardIterator, class BinaryPredicate>
ForwardIterator adjacent_find(ForwardIterator first, ForwardIterator last,
                              BinaryPredicate pred);
```

The adjacent_find() function returns an iterator it to the first element in the range [first1, last1) such that the element matches the following element. The function returns last if no such pair is found. The first version uses the == operator for the value type to compare elements. The second version uses the binary predicate function object `pred` to compare elements. That is, elements pointed to by `it1` and `it2` match if `pred(*it1, *it2)` is true.

```
template<class InputIterator, class T>
iterator_traits<InputIterator>::difference_type count(
                InputIterator first, InputIterator last, const T& value);
```

The `count()` function returns the number of elements in the range [`first`, `last`) that match the value `value`. The `==` operator for the value type is used to compare values. The return type is an integer type large enough to contain the maximum number of items the container can hold.

```
template<class InputIterator, class Predicate>
iterator_traits<InputIterator>::difference_type count_if(
                InputIterator first, InputIterator last, Predicate pred);
```

The `count if()` function returns the number of elements in the range [`first`, `last`) for which the function object `pred` returns a true value when passed the element as an argument.

```
template<class InputIterator1, class InputIterator2>
pair<InputIterator1, InputIterator2> mismatch(InputIterator1 first1,
                    InputIterator1 last1, InputIterator2 first2);

template<class InputIterator1, class InputIterator2, class BinaryPredicate>
pair<InputIterator1, InputIterator2> mismatch(InputIterator1 first1,
                    InputIterator1 last1, InputIterator2 first2,
                    BinaryPredicate pred);
```

This version of the `mismatch()` function finds the first element in range [`first1`, `last1`) that doesn't match the corresponding element in the range beginning at `first2` and returns a pair holding iterators to the two mismatching elements. If no mismatch is found, the return value is `pair<last1, first2 + (last1 - first1)>`. The first version uses the `==` operator to test matching. The second version uses the binary predicate function object `pred` to compare elements. That is, elements pointed to by `it1` and `it2` don't match if `pred(*it1, *it2)` is false.

```
template<class InputIterator1, class InputIterator2>
bool equal(InputIterator1 first1, InputIterator1 last1,
            InputIterator2 first2);

template<class InputIterator1, class InputIterator2, class BinaryPredicate>
bool equal(InputIterator1 first1, InputIterator1 last1,
            InputIterator2 first2, BinaryPredicate pred);
```

The `equal()` function returns `true` if each element in the range [`first1`, `last1`) matches the corresponding element in the sequence beginning at `first2` and `false` otherwise. The first version uses the `==` operator for the value type to compare elements. The second version uses the binary predicate function object `pred` to compare elements. That is, elements pointed to by `it1` and `it2` match if `pred(*it1, *it2)` is true.

```
template<class ForwardIterator1, class ForwardIterator2>
ForwardIterator1 search(ForwardIterator1 first1, ForwardIterator1 last1,
                        ForwardIterator2 first2, ForwardIterator2 last2);

template<class ForwardIterator1, class ForwardIterator2,
         class BinaryPredicate>
ForwardIterator1 search(ForwardIterator1 first1, ForwardIterator1 last1,
                        ForwardIterator2 first2, ForwardIterator2 last2,
                        BinaryPredicate pred);
```

The search() function finds the first occurrence in the range [first1, last1) that matches the corresponding sequence found in range [first2, last2). It returns last1 if no such sequence is found. The first version uses the == operator for the value type to compare elements. The second version uses the binary predicate function object pred to compare elements. That is, elements pointed to by it1 and it2 match if pred(*it1, *it2) is true.

```
template<class ForwardIterator, class Size, class T>
ForwardIterator  search_n(ForwardIterator first, ForwardIterator last,
                          Size count, const T& value);

template<class ForwardIterator, class Size, class T, class BinaryPredicate>
ForwardIterator1 search_n(ForwardIterator first, ForwardIterator last,
                          Size count, const T& value, BinaryPredicate pred);
```

The search_n() function finds the first occurrence in the range [first1, last1) that matches the sequence consisting of count consecutive occurrences of value. It returns last1 if no such sequence is found. The first version uses the == operator for the value type to compare elements. The second version uses the binary predicate function object pred to compare elements. That is, elements pointed to by it1 and it2 match if pred(*it1, *it2) is true.

MUTATING SEQUENCE OPERATIONS

Table G.9 summarizes the mutating sequence operations. Arguments are not shown, and overloaded functions are listed just once. A fuller description including the prototypes follows the table. Thus, you can scan the table to get an idea of what a function does; then look up the details if you find the function appealing.

Now let's go to the prototypes. As you saw earlier, pairs of iterators indicate ranges, with the chosen template parameter name indicating the type of iterator. As usual a range of the form [first, last) goes from first up to, but not including last. Functions passed as arguments are function objects, which can be function pointers or objects for which the () operation is defined. As in Chapter 15, a predicate is a Boolean function with one argument, and a binary predicate is a Boolean function with two arguments. (The functions need not be type bool as long as they return a 0 value for false and a non-zero for true.) Also, as in Chapter 15, a unary function object is one taking a single argument, and a binary function object is one taking two arguments.

TABLE G.9
MUTATING SEQUENCE OPERATIONS

FUNCTION	DESCRIPTION
`copy()`	Copies elements from a range to a location identified by an iterator.
`copy_backward()`	Copies elements from a range to a location identified by an iterator. Copying begins at the end of the range and proceeds backwards.
`swap()`	Exchanges two values stored at locations specified by references.
`swap_ranges()`	Exchanges corresponding values in two ranges.
`iter_swap()`	Exchanges two values stored at locations specified by iterators.
`transform()`	Applies a function object to each element in a range (or to each pair of elements in a pair of ranges), copying the return value to the corresponding location of another range.
`replace()`	Replaces each occurrence of a value in a range with another value.
`replace_if()`	Replaces each occurrence of a value in a range with another value if a predicate function object applied to the original value returns true.
`replace_copy()`	Copies one range to another, replacing each occurrence of a specified value with another value.
`replace_copy`	Copies one range to another, replacing each value for which a predicate function object is true with an indicated value.
`fill()`	Sets each value in a range to an indicated value.
`fill_n()`	Sets n consecutive elements to a value.
`generate()`	Sets each value in a range to the return value of a generator, which is a function object that takes no arguments.
`generate_n()`	Sets the first n values in a range to the return value of a generator, which is a function object that takes no arguments.
`remove()`	Removes all occurrences of an indicated value from a range and returns a past-the-end iterator for the resulting range.
`remove_if()`	Removes all occurrences of values for which a predicate object returns true from a range and returns a past-the-end iterator for the resulting range.
`remove_copy()`	Copies elements from one range to another, omitting elements that equal a specified value.
`remove_copy_if()`	Copies elements from one range to another, omitting elements for which a predicate function object returns true.
`unique()`	Reduces each sequence of two or more equivalent elements in a range to a single element.
`unique_copy()`	Copies elements from one range to another, reducing each sequence of two or more equivalent elements to one.
`reverse()`	Reverses the elements in a range.
`reverse_copy()`	Copies a range in reverse order to a second range.
`rotate()`	Treats a range as a circular ordering and rotates the elements left.
`rotate_copy()`	Copies one range to another in a rotated order.
`Random_shuffle()`	Randomly rearranges the elements in a range.
`partition()`	Places all the elements that satisfy a predicate function object before all elements that don't.
`stable_partition()`	Places all the elements that satisfy a predicate function object before all elements that don't. The relative order of elements in each group is preserved.

```
template<class InputIterator, class OutputIterator>
OutputIterator copy(InputIterator first, InputIterator last,
                    OutputIterator result);
```

The copy() function copies the elements in the range [first, last) into the range [result, result + (last - first)). It returns result + (last - first), that is, an iterator pointing one past the last copied-to location. The function requires that result not be in the range [first, last), that is, the target can't overlap the source.

```
template<class BidirectionalIterator1, class BidirectionalIterator2>
BidirectionalIterator2 copy_backward(BidirectionalIterator1 first,
        BidirectionalIterator1 last, BidirectionalIterator2 result);
```

The copy_backward() function copies the elements in the range [first, last) into the range [result -(last - first), result). Copying begins with the element at last -1 being copied to location result - 1, and proceeds backwards from there to first. It returns result - (last - first), that is, an iterator pointing one past the last copied-to location. The function requires that result not be in the range [first, last). However, because copying is done backwards, it is possible for the target and source to overlap.

```
template<class T> void swap(T& a, T& b);
```

The swap() function exchanges values stored at two locations specified by references.

```
template<class ForwardIterator1, class ForwardIterator2>
ForwardIterator2 swap_ranges(
                        ForwardIterator1 first1, ForwardIterator1 last1,
                        ForwardIterator2 first2);
```

The swap_ranges() function exchanges values in the range [first1, last1) with the corresponding values in the range beginning at first2. The two ranges should not overlap.

```
template<class ForwardIterator1, class ForwardIterator2>
void iter_swap(ForwardIterator1 a, ForwardIterator2 b);
```

The iter_swap() function exchanges values stored at two locations specified by iterators.

```
template<class InputIterator, class OutputIterator, class UnaryOperation>
OutputIterator transform(InputIterator first, InputIterator last,
OutputIterator result, UnaryOperation op);
```

This version of transform() applies the unary function object op to each element in the range [first, last) and assigns the return value to the corresponding element in the range beginning at result. So *result is set to op(*first), and so on. It returns result + (last - first), that is, the past-the-end value for the target range.

```
template<class InputIterator1, class InputIterator2,
        class OutputIterator, class BinaryOperation>
OutputIterator transform(InputIterator1 first1, InputIterator1 last1,
                        InputIterator2 first2, OutputIterator result,
                        BinaryOperation binary_op);
```

This version of `transform()` applies the binary function object op to each element in the range [`first1`, `last1`) and to each element in the range [`first2`, `last2`) and assigns the return value to the corresponding element in the range beginning at `result`. So `*result` is set to op(`*first1`, `*first2`), and so on. It returns `result + (last - first)`, the past-the-end value for the target range.

```
template<class ForwardIterator, class T>
void replace(ForwardIterator first, ForwardIterator last,
          const T& old_value, const T& new_value);
```

The `replace()` function replaces each occurrence of the value `old_value` in the range [`first`, `last`) with the value `new_value`.

```
template<class ForwardIterator, class Predicate, class T>
void replace_if(ForwardIterator first, ForwardIterator last,
             Predicate pred, const T& new_value);
```

The `replace()_if` function replaces each value `old` in the range [`first`, `last`) for which `pred(old)` is true with the value `new_value`.

```
template<class InputIterator, class OutputIterator, class T>
OutputIterator replace_copy(InputIterator first, InputIterator last,
      OutputIterator result,const T& old_ value, const T& new_ value);
```

The `replace_copy()` function copies the elements in the range [`first`, `last`) to a range beginning at `result`, but substituting `new_value` for each occurrence of `old_value`. It returns `result + (last - first)`, the past-the-end value for the target range.

```
template<class Iterator, class OutputIterator, class Predicate, class T>
OutputIterator replace_copy_if(Iterator first, Iterator last,
      OutputIterator result, Predicate pred, const T& new_ value);
```

The `replace_copy_if()` function copies the elements in the range [`first`, `last`) to a range beginning at `result`, but substituting `new_value` for each value `old` for which `pred(old)` is true. It returns `result + (last - first)`, the past-the-end value for the target range.

```
template<class ForwardIterator, class T>
void fill(ForwardIterator first, ForwardIterator last, const T& value);
```

The `fill()` function sets each element in the range [`first`, `last`) to value.

```
template<class OutputIterator, class Size, class T>
void fill_n(OutputIterator first, Size n, const T& value);
```

The `fill_n()` function sets each of the first n elements beginning at location `first` to value.

```
template<class ForwardIterator, class Generator>
void generate(ForwardIterator first, ForwardIterator last,
            Generator gen);
```

The generator() function sets each element in the range [first, last) to gen(), where gen is a generator function object, that is, one that takes no arguments. For example, gen can be a pointer to rand().

```
template<class OutputIterator, class Size, class Generator>
void generate_n(OutputIterator first, Size n, Generator gen);
```

The generator_n() function sets each of the first n elements in the range beginning at first to gen(), where gen is a generator function object, that is, one that takes no arguments. For example, gen can be a pointer to rand().

```
template<class ForwardIterator, class T>
ForwardIterator remove(ForwardIterator first, ForwardIterator last,
                       const T& value);
```

The remove() function removes all occurrences of value from the range [first, last) and returns a past-the-end iterator for the resulting range. The function is stable, meaning the order of the unremoved elements is unaltered.

Remember

Because the various remove() and unique() functions are not member functions and also because they aren't restricted to STL containers, they can't reset the size of a container. Instead, they return an iterator indicating the new past-the-end location. Typically, the removed items simply are shifted to the end of the container. However, for STL containers you can use the returned iterator and one of the erase() methods to reset end().

```
template<class ForwardIterator, class Predicate>
ForwardIterator remove_if(ForwardIterator first, ForwardIterator last,
                          Predicate pred);
```

The remove_if() function removes all occurrences of values val for which pred(val) is true from the range [first, last) and returns a past-the-end iterator for the resulting range. The function is stable, meaning the order of the unremoved elements is unaltered.

```
template<class InputIterator, class OutputIterator, class T>
OutputIterator remove_copy(InputIterator first, InputIterator last,
                           OutputIterator result, const T& value);
```

The remove_copy() function copies values from the range [first, last) to the range beginning at result, skipping instances of value as it copies. It returns a past-the-end iterator for the resulting range. The function is stable, meaning the order of the unremoved elements is unaltered.

```
template<class InputIterator, class OutputIterator, class Predicate>
OutputIterator remove_copy_if(InputIterator first, InputIterator last,
                              OutputIterator result, Predicate pred);
```

The remove_copy_if() function copies values from the range [first, last) to the range beginning at result, but skipping instances of val for which pred(val) is true as it copies. It returns a past-the-end iterator for the resulting range. The function is stable, meaning the order of the unremoved elements is unaltered.

```
template<class ForwardIterator>
ForwardIterator unique(ForwardIterator first, ForwardIterator last);
```

```
template<class ForwardIterator, class BinaryPredicate>
ForwardIterator unique(ForwardIterator first, ForwardIterator last,
                       BinaryPredicate pred);
```

The unique() function reduces each sequence of two or more equivalent elements in a range [first, last) to a single element and returns a past-the-end iterator for the new range. The first version uses the == operator for the value type to compare elements. The second version uses the binary predicate function object pred to compare elements. That is, elements pointed to by it1 and it2 match if pred(*it1, *it2) is true.

```
template<class InputIterator, class OutputIterator>
OutputIterator unique_copy(InputIterator first, InputIterator last,
                           OutputIterator result);
```

```
template<class InputIterator, class OutputIterator,
         class BinaryPredicate>
OutputIterator unique_copy(InputIterator first, InputIterator last,
                           OutputIterator result, BinaryPredicate pred);
```

This version of unique_copy() copies elements from a range [first, last) to the range beginning at result, reducing each sequence of two or more identical elements to a single element. It returns a past-the-end iterator for the new range. The first version uses the == operator for the value type to compare elements. The second version uses the binary predicate function object pred to compare elements. That is, elements pointed to by it1 and it2 match if pred(*it1, *it2) is true.

```
template<class BidirectionalIterator>
void reverse(BidirectionalIterator first, BidirectionalIterator last);
```

The reverse() function reverses the elements in the range [first, last) by invoking swap(first, last - 1), and so on.

```
template<class BidirectionalIterator, class OutputIterator>
OutputIterator reverse_copy(BidirectionalIterator first,
                            BidirectionalIterator last,
                            OutputIterator result);
```

The reverse copy() function copies the elements in the range [first, last) to the range beginning at result in reverse order. The two ranges should not overlap.

```
template<class ForwardIterator>
void rotate(ForwardIterator first, ForwardIterator middle,
            ForwardIterator last);
```

The rotate() function performs a left-rotate on the elements in the range [first, last). The element at middle is moved to first, the element at middle + 1 to first + 1, and so on. The elements preceding middle are wrapped around to the end of the container so that the element at first follows that formerly at last - 1.

```
template<class ForwardIterator, class OutputIterator>
OutputIterator rotate_copy(ForwardIterator first, ForwardIterator middle,
                           ForwardIterator last, OutputIterator result);
```

The rotate_copy() function copies the elements in the range [first, last) to the range beginning at result using the rotated sequence described for rotate().

```
template<class RandomAccessIterator>
void random_shuffle(RandomAccessIterator first,
                    RandomAccessIterator last);
```

This version of the random_shuffle() function shuffles the elements in the range [first, last). The distribution is uniform; that is, each possible permutation of the original order is equally likely.

```
template<class RandomAccessIterator, class RandomNumberGenerator>
void random_shuffle(RandomAccessIterator first, RandomAccessIterator last,
                    RandomNumberGenerator& random);
```

This version of the random_shuffle() function shuffles the elements in the range [first, last). The function object random determines the distribution. Given n elements, the expression random(n) should return a value in the range [0,n).

```
template<class BidirectionalIterator, class Predicate>
BidirectionalIterator partition(BidirectionalIterator first,
                                BidirectionalIterator last,
                                Predicate pred);
```

The partition() function places each element whose value val is such that pred(val) is true before all elements that don't meet that test. It returns an iterator to the position following that last position holding a value for which the predicate object function was true.

```
template<class BidirectionalIterator, class Predicate>
BidirectionalIterator stable_partition(BidirectionalIterator first,
                                       BidirectionalIterator last,
                                       Predicate pred);
```

The stable_partition() function places each element whose value val is such that pred(val) is true before all elements that don't meet that test. The function preserves the relative ordering within each of the two groups. It returns an iterator to the position following that last position holding a value for which the predicate object function was true.

SORTING AND RELATED OPERATIONS

Table G.10 summarizes the sorting and related operations. Arguments are not shown, and overloaded functions are listed just once. Each function has a version that uses < for ordering elements and a version that uses a comparison function object for ordering elements. A fuller description including the prototypes follows the table. Thus, you can scan the table to get an idea of what a function does, then look up the details if you find the function appealing.

TABLE G.10
SORTING AND RELATED OPERATIONS

FUNCTION	DESCRIPTION
sort()	Sorts a range.
stable_sort()	Sorts a range, preserving the relative order of equivalent elements.
partial_sort()	Partially sorts a range, providing the first *n* elements of a full sort.
partial_sort_copy()	Copies a partially sorted range to another range.
nth_element()	Given an iterator into a range, finds the element that would be there if the range were sorted, and places that element there.
lower_bound()	Given a value, finds the first position in a sorted range before which the value can be inserted while maintaining the ordering.
upper_bound()	Given a value, finds the last position in a sorted range before which the value can be inserted while maintaining the ordering.
equal_range()	Given a value, finds the largest subrange of a sorted range such that the value can be inserted before any element in the subrange without violating the ordering.
binary_search()	Returns true if a sorted range contains a value equivalent to a given value, and false otherwise.
merge()	Merges two sorted ranges into a third range.
inplace_merge()	Merges two consecutive sorted ranges in place.
includes()	Returns true if every element in one set also is found in another set.
set_union()	Constructs the union of two sets, which is a set containing all elements present in either set.
set_intersection()	Constructs the intersection of two sets, which is a set containing only those elements found in both sets.
set_difference()	Constructs the difference of two sets, which is a set containing only those elements found in the first set but not the second.
set_symmetric_difference()	Constructs a set consisting of elements found in one set or the other, but not both.
make_heap	Converts a range to heap.
push_heap()	Adds an element to a heap.
pop_heap()	Removes the largest element from a heap.
sort_heap()	Sorts a heap.
min()	Returns the lesser of two values.
max()	Returns the greater of two values.
min_element()	Finds the first occurrence of the smallest value in a range.

FUNCTION	DESCRIPTION
`max_element()`	Finds the first occurrence of the largest value in a range.
`lexicographic_compare()`	Compares two sequences lexicographically, returning `true` if the first sequence is lexicographically less than the second, and `false` otherwise.
`next_permutation()`	Generates the next permutation in a sequence
`previous_permutation()`	Generates the preceding permutation in a sequence.

The functions in this section determine the order of two elements by using the < operator defined for the elements or by using a comparison object designated by the template type `Compare`. If `comp` is an object of type `Compare`, then `comp(a,b)` is a generalization of `a < b` and returns `true` if `a` precedes `b` in the ordering scheme. If `a < b` is false and `b < a` also is false, `a` and `b` are equivalent. A comparison object must provide at least *strict weak ordering*. This means the following:

The expression `comp(a,a)` must be false, a generalization of the fact that a value can't be less than itself. (This is the strict part.)

If `comp(a,b)` is true and `comp(b,c)` is true, then `comp(a,c)` is true (that is, comparison is a transitive relationship).

If `a` is equivalent to `b`, and `b` is equivalent to `c`, then `a` is equivalent to `c` (that is, equivalency is a transitive relationship).

If you think of applying < to integers, then equivalency implies equality, but this doesn't have to hold for more general cases. For example, you could define a structure with several members describing a mailing address and define a `comp` comparison object that orders the structures according to zip code. Then any two addresses with the same zip code would be equivalent but not equal.

Now let's go to the prototypes. We'll divide this section into several subsections. As you saw earlier, pairs of iterators indicate ranges, with the chosen template parameter name indicating the type of iterator. As usual a range of the form [`first`, `last`) goes from `first` up to, but not including, `last`. Functions passed as arguments are function objects, which can be pointers or objects for which the `()` operation is defined. As you learned in Chapter 15, a predicate is a Boolean function with one argument, and a binary predicate is a Boolean function with two arguments. (The functions need not be type `bool` as long as they return a 0 value for false and a non-zero for true.) Also, as in Chapter 15, a unary function object is one taking a single argument, and a binary function object is one taking two arguments.

Sorting

First, let's examine the sorting algorithms.

```
template<class RandomAccessIterator>
void sort(RandomAccessIterator first, RandomAccessIterator last);
```

```
template<class RandomAccessIterator, class Compare>
void sort(RandomAccessIterator first, RandomAccessIterator last,
          Compare comp);
```

The sort() function sorts the range [first, last) in increasing order, using the value type < operator for comparison. The first version uses < and the second uses the comparison object comp to determine the order.

```
template<class RandomAccessIterator>
void stable_sort(RandomAccessIterator first, RandomAccessIterator last);
```

```
template<class RandomAccessIterator, class Compare>
void stable_sort(RandomAccessIterator first, RandomAccessIterator last,
                 Compare comp);
```

The stable_sort() function sorts the range [first, last) preserving the relative order of equivalent elements. The first version uses < and the second uses the comparison object comp to determine the order.

```
template<class RandomAccessIterator>
void partial_sort(RandomAccessIterator first, RandomAccessIterator middle,
                  RandomAccessIterator last);
template<class RandomAccessIterator, class Compare>
void partial_sort(RandomAccessIterator first, RandomAccessIterator middle,
                  RandomAccessIterator last, Compare comp);
```

The partial_sort() function partially sorts the range [first, last). The first middle - first elements of the sorted range are placed in the range [first, middle), and the remaining elements are unsorted. The first version uses < and the second uses the comparison object comp to determine the order.

```
template<class InputIterator, class RandomAccessIterator>
RandomAccessIterator partial_sort_copy(InputIterator first,
                                       InputIterator last,
                                       RandomAccessIterator result_first,
                                       RandomAccessIterator result_last);
```

```
template<class InputIterator, class RandomAccessIterator, class Compare>
RandomAccessIterator partial_sort_copy(
                InputIterator first, InputIterator last,
                RandomAccessIterator result_first,
                RandomAccessIterator result_last,
                Compare comp);
```

The partial_sort_copy() function copies the first n elements of the sorted range [first, last) to the range [result_first, result_first + n). The value of n is the lesser of last - first and result_last - result_first. The function returns result_first + n. The first version uses < and the second uses the comparison object comp to determine the order.

```
template<class RandomAccessIterator>
void nth_element(RandomAccessIterator first, RandomAccessIterator nth,
                 RandomAccessIterator last);
```

```
template<class RandomAccessIterator, class Compare>
void nth_element(RandomAccessIterator first, RandomAccessIterator nth,
                 RandomAccessIterator last, Compare comp);
```

The nth_element() function finds the element in range [first, last) that would be at position nth were the range sorted, and it places that element at position nth. The first version uses < and the second uses the comparison object comp to determine the order.

Binary Search

The algorithms in the binary search group assume the range is sorted. They only require a forward iterator but are most efficient for random iterators.

```
template<class ForwardIterator, class T>
ForwardIterator lower_bound(ForwardIterator first, ForwardIterator last,
                            const T& value);

template<class ForwardIterator, class T, class Compare>
ForwardIterator lower_bound(ForwardIterator first, ForwardIterator last,
                            const T& value, Compare comp);
```

The lower_bound() function finds the first position in a sorted range [first, last) in front of which value can be inserted without violating the order. It returns an iterator pointing to this position. The first version uses < and the second uses the comparison object comp to determine the order.

```
template<class ForwardIterator, class T>
ForwardIterator upper_bound(ForwardIterator first, ForwardIterator last,
                            const T& value);

template<class ForwardIterator, class T, class Compare>
ForwardIterator upper_bound(ForwardIterator first, ForwardIterator last,
                            const T& value, Compare comp);
```

The upper_bound() function finds the last position in a sorted range [first, last) in front of which value can be inserted without violating the order. It returns an iterator pointing to this position. The first version uses < and the second uses the comparison object comp to determine the order.

```
template<class ForwardIterator, class T>
pair<ForwardIterator, ForwardIterator> equal_range(
    ForwardIterator first, ForwardIterator last, const T& value);

template<class ForwardIterator, class T, class Compare>
pair<ForwardIterator, ForwardIterator> equal_range(
    ForwardIterator first, ForwardIterator last, const T& value,
    Compare comp);
```

The equal_range() function finds the largest subrange [it1, it2) in a sorted range [first, last) such that value can be inserted in front of any iterator in this range without violating the order. The function returns a pair formed of it1 and it2. The first version uses < and the second uses the comparison object comp to determine the order.

```
template<class ForwardIterator, class T>
bool binary_search(ForwardIterator first, ForwardIterator last,
                   const T& value);

template<class ForwardIterator, class T, class Compare>
bool binary_search(ForwardIterator first, ForwardIterator last,
                   const T& value, Compare comp);
```

The `binary_search()` function returns `true` if the equivalent of `value` is found in the sorted range [`first`, `last`) and `false` otherwise. The first version uses < and the second uses the comparison object `comp` to determine the order.

Remember

> Recall that if < is used for ordering, values a and b are equivalent if both a < b and b < a are false. For ordinary numbers, equivalency implies equality, but this is not the case for structures sorted on the basis of just one member. Similarly, if the comparison object `comp` is used for ordering, equivalency means both `comp(a,b)` and `comp(b,a)` are false. (This is a generalization of the statement that a and b are equivalent if a is not less than b and b is not less than a.)

Merging

The merging functions assume ranges are sorted.

```
template<class InputIterator1, class InputIterator2,
        class OutputIterator>
OutputIterator merge(InputIterator1 first1, InputIterator1 last1,
                     InputIterator2 first2, InputIterator2 last2,
                     OutputIterator result);

template<class InputIterator1, class InputIterator2,
        class OutputIterator, class Compare>
OutputIterator merge(InputIterator1 first1, InputIterator1 last1,
                     InputIterator2 first2, InputIterator2 last2,
                     OutputIterator result, Compare comp);
```

The `merge()` function merges elements from sorted range [`first1`, `last1`) and from sorted range [`first2`, `last2`), placing the result in the range starting at `result`. The target range should not overlap either of the merged ranges. When equivalent elements are found in both ranges, elements from the first range precede elements of the second. The return value is the past-the-end iterator for the resulting merge. The first version uses < and the second uses the comparison object `comp` to determine the order.

```
template<class BidirectionalIterator>
void inplace_merge(BidirectionalIterator first,
        BidirectionalIterator middle, BidirectionalIterator last);

template<class BidirectionalIterator, class Compare>
void inplace_merge(BidirectionalIterator first,
        BidirectionalIterator middle, BidirectionalIterator last,
        Compare comp);
```

The `inplace_merge()` function merges two consecutive sorted ranges—[`first`, `middle`) and [`middle`, `last`)—into a single sorted sequence stored in the range [`first`, `last`). Elements from the first range will precede equivalent elements from the second range. The first version uses < and the second uses the comparison object `comp` to determine the order.

Set Operations

Set operations work with all sorted sequences, including set and multiset. For containers holding more than one instance of a value, such as multiset, definitions are generalized. A union of two multisets contains the larger number of occurrences of each element, and an intersection contains the lesser number of occurrences of each element. For example, suppose multiset A contains the string "apple" seven times and multiset B contains the same string four times. Then the union of A and B will contain seven instances of "apple" and the intersection will contain four instances.

```
template<class InputIterator1, class InputIterator2>
bool includes(InputIterator1 first1, InputIterator1 last1,
            InputIterator2 first2, InputIterator2 last2);

template<class InputIterator1, class InputIterator2, class Compare>
bool includes(InputIterator1 first1, InputIterator1 last1,
            InputIterator2 first2, InputIterator2 last2, Compare comp);
```

The includes() function returns true if every element in range [first2, last2) also is found in the range [first1, last1) and false otherwise. The first version uses < and the second uses the comparison object comp to determine the order.

```
template<class InputIterator1, class InputIterator2,
        class OutputIterator>
OutputIterator set_union(InputIterator1 first1, InputIterator1 last1,
                        InputIterator2 first2, InputIterator2 last2,
                        OutputIterator result);

template<class InputIterator1, class InputIterator2,
        class OutputIterator, class Compare>
OutputIterator set_union(InputIterator1 first1, InputIterator1 last1,
                        InputIterator2 first2, InputIterator2 last2,
                        OutputIterator result, Compare comp);
```

The set_union() function constructs the set that is the union of the ranges [first1, last1) and [first2, last2) and copies the result to the location pointed to by result. The resulting range should not overlap either of the original ranges. The function returns a past-the-end iterator for the constructed range. The union is the set containing all elements found in either or both sets. The first version uses < and the second uses the comparison object comp to determine the order.

```
template<class InputIterator1, class InputIterator2,
        class OutputIterator>
OutputIterator set intersection(
                        InputIterator1 first1, InputIterator1 last1,
                        InputIterator2 first2, InputIterator2 last2,
                        OutputIterator result);

template<class InputIterator1, class InputIterator2,
        class OutputIterator, class Compare>
OutputIterator set_intersection(
                        InputIterator1 first1, InputIterator1 last1,
                        InputIterator2 first2, InputIterator2 last2,
                        OutputIterator result, Compare comp);
```

The `set_intersection()` function constructs the set that is the intersection of the ranges [first1, last1) and [first2, last2) and copies the result to the location pointed to by `result`. The resulting range should not overlap either of the original ranges. The function returns a past-the-end iterator for the constructed range. The intersection is the set containing those elements common to both sets. The first version uses < and the second uses the comparison object `comp` to determine the order.

```
template<class InputIterator1, class InputIterator2,
         class OutputIterator>
OutputIterator set_difference(InputIterator1 first1, InputIterator1 last1,
                              InputIterator2 first2, InputIterator2 last2,
                              OutputIterator result);

template<class InputIterator1, class InputIterator2,
         class OutputIterator, class Compare>
OutputIterator set_difference(InputIterator1 first1, InputIterator1 last1,
                              InputIterator2 first2, InputIterator2 last2,
                              OutputIterator result, Compare comp);
```

The `set_difference()` function constructs the set that is the difference of the ranges [first1, last1) and [first2, last2) and copies the result to the location pointed to by `result`. The resulting range should not overlap either of the original ranges. The function returns a past-the-end iterator for the constructed range. The difference is the set containing those elements found in the first set but not in the second. The first version uses < and the second uses the comparison object `comp` to determine the order.

```
template<class InputIterator1, class InputIterator2,
         class OutputIterator>
OutputIterator set_symmetric_difference(
                         InputIterator1 first1, InputIterator1 last1,
                         InputIterator2 first2, InputIterator2 last2,
                         OutputIterator result);
template<class InputIterator1, class InputIterator2,
         class OutputIterator,
         class Compare>
OutputIterator set_symmetric_difference(
                         InputIterator1 first1, InputIterator1 last1,
                         InputIterator2 first2, InputIterator2 last2,
                         OutputIterator result, Compare comp);
```

The `set_symmetric_difference()` function constructs the set that is the symmetric difference of the ranges [first1, last1) and [first2, last2) and copies the result to the location pointed to by `result`. The resulting range should not overlap either of the original ranges. The function returns a past-the-end iterator for the constructed range. The symmetric difference is the set containing those elements found in the first set but not in the second and those elements found in the second set but not the first. It's the same as the difference between the union and the intersection. The first version uses < and the second uses the comparison object `comp` to determine the order.

Heap Operations

A *heap* is a common data form with the property that the first element in a heap is the largest. Whenever the first element is removed or any element is added, the heap may have to be arranged to maintain that property. A heap is designed so that these two operations are done efficiently.

```
template<class RandomAccessIterator>
void make_heap(RandomAccessIterator first, RandomAccessIterator last);

template<class RandomAccessIterator, class Compare>
void make_heap(RandomAccessIterator first, RandomAccessIterator last,
               Compare comp);
```

The make_heap() function makes a heap of the range [first, last). The first version use < to determine the ordering, while the second version uses the comp comparison object.

```
template<class RandomAccessIterator>
void push_heap(RandomAccessIterator first, RandomAccessIterator last);

template<class RandomAccessIterator, class Compare>
void push_heap(RandomAccessIterator first, RandomAccessIterator last,
               Compare comp);
```

The push_heap() function assumes that the range [first, last - 1) is a valid heap, and it adds the value at location last - 1 (that is, one past the end of the assumed valid heap) into the heap, making [first, last) a valid heap. The first version use < to determine the ordering, while the second version uses the comp comparison object.

```
template<class RandomAccessIterator>
void pop_heap(RandomAccessIterator first, RandomAccessIterator last);

template<class RandomAccessIterator, class Compare>
void pop_heap(RandomAccessIterator first, RandomAccessIterator last,
              Compare comp);
```

The pop_heap() function assumes that the range [first, last) is a valid heap. It swaps the value at location last - 1 with the value at first and makes the range [first, last - 1) a valid heap. The first version use < to determine the ordering, while the second version uses the comp comparison object.

```
template<class RandomAccessIterator>
void sort_heap(RandomAccessIterator first, RandomAccessIterator last);

template<class RandomAccessIterator, class Compare>
void sort_heap(RandomAccessIterator first, RandomAccessIterator last,
               Compare comp);
```

The sort_heap() function assumes the range [first, last) is a heap and sorts it. The first version uses < to determine the ordering, while the second version uses the comp comparison object.

Minimum and Maximum

The minimum and maximum functions return the minimum and maximum values of pairs of values and of sequences of values.

```
template<class T> const T& min(const T& a, const T& b);

template<class T, class Compare>
const T& min(const T& a, const T& b, Compare comp);
```

The min() function returns the lesser of two values. If the two values are equivalent, it returns the first value. The first version uses < to determine the ordering, while the second version uses the comp comparison object.

```
template<class T> const T& max(const T& a, const T& b);
template<class T, class Compare>
const T& max(const T& a, const T& b, Compare comp);
```

The max() function returns the lesser of two values. If the two values are equivalent, it returns the first value. The first version uses < to determine the ordering, while the second version uses the comp comparison object.

```
template<class ForwardIterator>
ForwardIterator min_element(ForwardIterator first, ForwardIterator last);

template<class ForwardIterator, class Compare>
ForwardIterator min_element(ForwardIterator first, ForwardIterator last,
                            Compare comp);
```

The min_element() function returns the first iterator it in the range [first, last) such that no element in the range is less than *it. The first version uses < to determine the ordering, while the second version uses the comp comparison object.

```
template<class ForwardIterator>
ForwardIterator max_element(ForwardIterator first, ForwardIterator last);

template<class ForwardIterator, class Compare>
ForwardIterator max_element(ForwardIterator first, ForwardIterator last,
                            Compare comp);
```

The max_element() function returns the first iterator it in the range [first, last) such that there is no element that *it is less than. The first version uses < to determine the ordering, while the second version uses the comp comparison object.

```
template<class InputIterator1, class InputIterator2>
bool lexicographical_compare(InputIterator1 first1, InputIterator1 last1,
                             InputIterator2 first2, InputIterator2 last2);

template<class InputIterator1, class InputIterator2, class Compare>
bool lexicographical_compare(InputIterator1 first1, InputIterator1 last1,
                             InputIterator2 first2, InputIterator2 last2,
                             Compare comp);
```

The lexicographical_compare() function returns true if the sequence of elements in range [first1, last1) is lexicographically less than the sequence of elements in range [first2, last2) and false otherwise. A lexicographical comparison compares the first element of one sequence to the first of the second, that is, it compares *first1 to *first2. If *first1 is less than *first2, the function returns true. If *first2 is less than *first1, the function returns false. If the two are equivalent, comparison proceeds to the next element in each sequence. This process continues until two corresponding elements are not equivalent or until the end of a sequence is reached. If two sequences are equivalent until the end of one is reached, the shorter sequence is less. If the two sequences are equivalent and of the same length, neither is less, so the function returns false. The first version of the function uses < to compare elements and the second version uses the comp comparison object. The lexicographic comparison is a generalization of an alphabetic comparison.

Permutations

A permutation of a sequence is a reordering of the elements. For instance, a sequence of three elements has six possible orderings, because you have a choice of three elements for the first element. Choosing a particular element for the first position leaves a choice of two for the second, and one for the third. For example, the six permutations of the digits 1, 3, and 5 are as follows:

123 132 213 232 312 321

In general, a sequence of n elements has $n * (n-1) * \ldots * 1$, or $n!$ possible permutations.

The permutation functions assume that the set of all possible permutations can be arranged in lexicographical order, as in the example of six permutations above. That means, in general, that there is a specific permutation that precedes and follows each permutation. For example, 213 immediately precedes 232, and 312 immediately follows it. However, the first permutation (123 in the example) has no predecessor, and the last permutation (321) has no follower.

```
template<class BidirectionalIterator>
bool next_permutation(BidirectionalIterator first,
                      BidirectionalIterator last);

template<class BidirectionalIterator, class Compare>
bool next_permutation(BidirectionalIterator first,
                      BidirectionalIterator last, Compare comp);
```

The next_permutation() function transforms the sequence in range [first, last) to the next permutation in lexicographic order. If the next permutation exists, the function returns true. If it doesn't exist (that is, the range contains the last permutation in lexicographic order), the function returns false and transforms the range to first permutation in lexicographic order. The first version uses < to determine the ordering, while the second version uses the comp comparison object.

```
template<class BidirectionalIterator>
bool prev_permutation(BidirectionalIterator first,
                      BidirectionalIterator last);

template<class BidirectionalIterator, class Compare>
bool prev_permutation(BidirectionalIterator first,
                      BidirectionalIterator last, Compare comp);
```

The previous_permutation() function transforms the sequence in range [first, last) to the previous permutation in lexicographic order. If the previous permutation exists, the function returns true. If it doesn't exist (that is, the range contains the first permutation in lexicographic order), the function returns false and transforms the range to last permutation in lexicographic order. The first version uses < to determine the ordering, while the second version uses the comp comparison object.

NUMERIC OPERATIONS

Table G.11 summarizes the numeric operations, which are described by the numeric header file. Arguments are not shown, and overloaded functions are listed just once. Each function has a version that uses < for ordering elements and a version that uses a comparison function object for ordering elements. A fuller description including the prototypes follows the table. Thus, you can scan the table to get an idea of what a function does; then look up the details if you find the function appealing.

```
template <class InputIterator, class T>
T accumulate(InputIterator first, InputIterator last, T init);

template <class InputIterator, class T, class BinaryOperation>
T accumulate(InputIterator first, InputIterator last, T init,
            BinaryOperation binary_op);
```

The accumulate() function initializes a value acc to init; then it performs the operation acc = acc + *i (first version) or acc = binary_op(acc, *i) (second version) for each iterator i in the range [first, last) in order. It then returns the resulting value of acc.

```
template <class InputIterator1, class InputIterator2, class T>
T inner_product(InputIterator1 first1, InputIterator1 last1,
                InputIterator2 first2, T init);

template <class InputIterator1, class InputIterator2, class T,
class BinaryOperation1, class BinaryOperation2>
T inner_product(InputIterator1 first1, InputIterator1 last1,
                InputIterator2 first2, T init,
                BinaryOperation1 binary_op1, BinaryOperation2 binary_op2);
```

TABLE G.11
SORTING AND RELATED OPERATIONS

FUNCTION	DESCRIPTION
accumulate()	Calculates a cumulative total for values in a range.
inner_product()	Calculates the inner product of two ranges.
partial_sum()	Copies partial sums calculated from one range into a second range.
adjacent_difference()	Copies adjacent differences calculated from elements in one range to a second range.

The `inner_product()` function initializes a value acc to init; then it performs the operation acc = *i * *j (first version) or acc = binary_op(*i, *j) (second version) for each iterator i in the range [first1, last1) in order and each corresponding iterator j in the range [first2, first2 + (last1 - first1)). That is, it calculates a value from the first elements from each sequence, then from the second elements of each sequence, and so on, until it reaches the end of the first sequence. (Hence the second sequence should be as least as long as the first.) The function then returns the resulting value of acc.

```
template <class InputIterator, class OutputIterator>
OutputIterator partial_sum(InputIterator first, InputIterator last,
                           OutputIterator result);

template <class InputIterator, class OutputIterator,
          class BinaryOperation>
OutputIterator partial_sum(InputIterator first, InputIterator last,
                           OutputIterator result,
                           BinaryOperation binary_op);
```

The `partial_sum()` function assigns *first to *result, *first + *(first + 1) to *(result + 1), (first version) or binary_op(*first, *(first + 1)) to *(result + 1) (second version, and so on. That is, the nth element of the sequence beginning at result contains the sum (or binary_op equivalent) of the first n elements of the sequence beginning at first. The function returns the past-the-end iterator for the result. The algorithm allows result to be first, that is, it allows the result to be copied over the original sequence, if desired.

```
template <class InputIterator, class OutputIterator>
OutputIterator adjacent_difference(InputIterator first, InputIterator last,
                                   OutputIterator result);

template <class InputIterator, class OutputIterator, class BinaryOperation>
OutputIterator adjacent_difference(InputIterator first, InputIterator last,
                                   OutputIterator result,
                                   BinaryOperation binary_op);
```

The `adjacent_difference()` function assigns *first to the location result (*result = *first). Subsequent locations in the target range are assigned the differences (or binary_op equivalent) of adjacent locations in the source range. That is, the next location in the target range (result + 1) is assigned *(first + 1) - *first (first version) or binary_op(*(first + 1), *first) (second version, and so on. The function returns the past-the-end iterator for the result. The algorithm allows result to be first, that is, it allows the result to be copied over the original sequence, if desired.

Selected Readings

Booch, Grady. *Object-Oriented Analysis and Design*. Second Edition. Redwood City, CA: Benjamin/Cummings, 1994.

This book presents the concepts behind OOP, discusses OOP methods, and presents sample applications. The examples are in C++.

Ellis, Margaret A., and Bjarne Stroustrup. *The Annotated C++ Reference Manual*. Reading, MA: Addison-Wesley, 1990.

This book, usually called the ARM, serves as a base document for the ANSI/ISO C++ standard committee. It's not a book for learning the language, but it answers most technical questions about how the language works. The book doesn't cover all the additions made by the ANSI/ISO committee.

Meyers, Scott. *Effective C++: 50 Specific Ways to Improve Your Programs and Designs,* Second Edition. Reading, MA: Addison-Wesley, 1998.

This book is aimed at programmers who already know C++, and it provides 50 rules and guidelines. Some are technical, such as explaining when you should define copy constructors and assignment operators. Others are more general, such as discussing is-a and has-a relationships.

Meyers, Scott. *More Effective C++: 35 New Ways to Improve Your Programs and Designs*. Reading, MA: Addison-Wesley, 1996.

This book continues in the tradition of *Effective C++,* clarifying some of the more obscure aspects of the language and showing how to accomplish various goals, such as designing smart pointers. It reflects the additional experience C++ programmers have gained the last few years.

Murray, Robert B. *C++ Strategies and Tactics*. Reading, MA: Addison-Wesley, 1993.

This book aims to help a new or intermediate C++ programmer learn to use the language effectively. It discusses classes, inheritance, templates, exceptions, and a few other topics, offering practical advice and describing common techniques.

Stroustrup, Bjarne. *The C++ Programming Language.* Third Edition. Reading, MA: Addison-Wesley, 1997.

Stroustrup created C++, so this is the definitive text. However, it's most easily digested if you already have some knowledge of C++. It not only describes the language, it also provides many examples of how to use it as well as discussions of OOP methodology. Successive editions of this book have grown with the language, and this edition includes a discussion of standard library elements such as the STL and strings.

Stroustrup, Bjarne. *The Design and Evolution of C++.* Reading, MA: Addison-Wesley, 1994.

If you're interested in learning how C++ evolved and why it is the way it is, read this book.

The ISO/ANSI standard

At the time of this writing, the Committee Draft 2 of December 1996 (CD2) is available for $50 from the following address:

American National Standards Institute

11 W. 42nd St.

New York, NY 10036

It's also available in ASCII, PostScript, HTML , and Adobe Acrobat PDF formats from the following two web sites:

```
http://www.setech.com/x3.html
http://www.maths.warwick.ac.uk/c++/pub/
```

The following FAQ (*F*requently *A*sked *Q*uestions) site may have more current information:

```
http://reality.sgi.com/austern/std-c++/faq.html
```

Chapter 2

1. They are called functions.

2. It causes the contents of the `iostream` file to be substituted for this directive before final compilation.

3. It makes definitions made in the `std` namespace available to a program.

4. `cout << "Hello, world\n";`

5. `int cheeses;`

6. `cheeses = 32;`

7. `cin >> cheeses;`

8. `cout << "We have " << cheeses << " varieties of cheese\n";`

9. It tells us that the function `froop()` expects to be called with one argument, which will be type `double`, and that the function will return a type `int` value.

10. You don't use `return` in a function when the function has return type `void`.

Chapter 3

1. Having more than one integer type lets you choose the type best suited to a particular need. For instance, you could use short to conserve space, long to guarantee storage capacity, or find that a particular type speeds up a particular calculation.

2.
```
short rbis = 80;              // or short int rbis = 80;
unsigned int q = 42110;       // or unsigned q = 42110;
unsigned long ants = 3000000000;
```

Remember

Note: Don't count on int being large enough to hold 3000000000.

3. C++ provides no safeguards to keep you from exceeding integer limits.

4. The constant 33L is type long, while the constant 33 is type int.

5. The two statements are not really equivalent, although they have the same effect on some systems. Most important, the first statement assigns the letter A to grade only on a system using the ASCII code, while the second statement also works for other codes. Second, 65 is a type int constant, while 'A' is a type char constant.

6. Here are four ways:

```
char c = 88;
cout << c << "\n";           // char type prints as character
cout.put(char(88));          // put() prints char as character
cout << char(88) << "\n";    // new-style type cast value to char
cout << (char)88 << "\n";    // old-style type cast value to char
```

7. The answer depends on how large the two types are. If long is 4 bytes, there is no loss. That's because the largest long value would be about 2 billion, which is 10 digits. Because double provides at least 15 significant figures, no rounding would be needed.

8.
   a. 8 * 9 + 2 is 72 + 2 is 74
   b. 6 * 3 / 4 is 18 / 4 is 4
   c. 3 / 4 * 6 is 0 * 6 is 0
   d. 6.0 * 3 / 4 is 18.0 / 4 is 4.5
   e. 15 % 4 is 3

9. Either of the following work:

```
int pos = (int) x1 + (int) x2;
int pos = int(x1) + int(x2);
```

Chapter 4

1.

> a. `char actors[30];`
>
> b. `short betsie[100];`
>
> c. `float chuck[13];`
>
> d. `long double dipsea[64];`

2. `int oddly[5] = {1, 3, 5, 7, 9};`

3. `int even = oddly[0] + oddly[4];`

4. `cout << ideas[1] << "\n";   // or << endl;`

5.

```
char lunch[13] = "cheeseburger"; // number of characters + 1
```

  or

```
char lunch[] = "cheeseburger";  // let the compiler count elements
```

6.

```
struct fish {
    char kind[20];
    int weight;
    float length;
};
```

7.

```
fish petes =
{
    "trout",
    13,
    12.25
};
```

8.

```
enum Response {No, Yes, Maybe};
```

9.

```
double * pd = &ted;
cout << *pd << "\n";
```

10.

```
float * pf = treacle;   // or = &treacle[0]
cout << pf[0] << " " << pf[9] << "\n";
            // or use *pf and *(pf + 9)
```

11.

```
unsigned int size;
cout << "Enter a positive integer: ";
cin >> size;
int * dyn = new int [size];
```

12. Yes, it is valid. The expression `"Home of the jolly bytes"` is a string constant, hence it evaluates as the address of the beginning of the string. The cout object interprets the address of a `char` as an invitation to print a string, but the type cast (`int *`) converts the address to type pointer-to-int, which is then printed as an address. In short, the statement prints the address of the string.

13.

```
struct fish
{
    char kind[20];
    int weight;
    float length;
};

fish * pole = new fish;
cout << "Enter kind of fish: ";
cin >> pole->kind;
```

14. Using `cin >> address` causes a program to skip over white space until it finds nonwhite space. It then reads characters until it encounters white space again. Thus, it will skip over the newline following the numeric input, avoiding that problem. On the other hand, it will read just a single word, not an entire line.

Chapter 5

1. An entry-condition loop evaluates a test expression before entering the body of the loop. If the condition initially is false, the loop never executes its body. An exit-condition loop evaluates a test expression after processing the body of the loop. Thus, the loop body is executed once even if the test expression initially is false. The `for` and `while` loops are entry-condition loops, and the `do while` loop is an exit-condition loop.

2. It would print the following:

```
01234
```

Note that the cout << "\n"; is not part of the loop body (no braces).

3. It would print the following:

```
0369
12
```

4. It would print the following:

```
6
8
```

5. It would print the following:

```
k = 8
```

6. It's simplest to use the *= operator:

```
for (int num = 1; num <= 64; num *= 2)
    cout << num << " ";
```

7. You enclose the statements within paired braces to form a single compound statement, or block.

8. Yes, the first statement is valid. The expression 1,024 consists of two expressions—1 and 024—joined by a comma operator. The value is the value of the right-hand expression. This is 024, which is octal for 20, so the declaration assigns the value 20 to x. The second statement also is valid. However, operator precedence causes it to be evaluated as follows:

```
(y = 1), 024;
```

That is, the left expression sets y to 1, and the value of the entire expression, which isn't used, is 024, or 20.

9. The cin >> ch form skips over spaces, newlines, and tabs when it encounters them. The other two forms read these characters.

Chapter 6

1. Both versions give the same answers, but the if else version is more efficient. Consider what happens, for instance, when ch is a space. Version 1, after incrementing spaces, tests to see whether the character is a newline. This wastes time because the program already has established that ch is a space and hence could not be a newline. Version 2, in the same situation, skips the newline test.

2. Both ++ch and ch + 1 have the same numerical value. But ++ch is type char and prints as a character, while ch + 1, because it adds a char to an int, is type int and prints as a number.

3. Because the program uses ch = '$' instead of ch == '$', the combined input and output looks like this:

```
Hi!
H$i$!$
$Send $10 or $20 now!
S$e$n$d$ $ct1 = 9, ct2 = 9
```

Each character is converted to the $ character before being printed the second time. Also, the value of the expression ch = $ is the code for the $ character, hence nonzero, hence true; so ct2 is incremented each time.

4.

  a. `weight >= 115 && weight < 125`

  b. `ch == 'q' ¦¦ ch == 'Q'`

  c. `x % 2 == 0 && x != 26`

  d. `donation >= 1000 && donation <= 2000 ¦¦ guest == 1`

  e. `(ch >= 'a' && ch <= 'z') ¦¦(ch >= 'A' && ch <= 'Z')`

5. Not necessarily. For instance, if x is 10, then !x is 0 and !!x is 1. However, if x is a bool variable, then !!x is x.

6.

```
(x < 0)? -x : x
```

7.

```
switch (ch)
{
    case 'A': a_grade++;
              break;
    case 'B': b_grade++;
              break;
    case 'C': c_grade++;
              break;
    case 'D': d_grade++;
              break;
    default:  f_grade++;
              break;
}
```

8. If you use integer labels and the user types a noninteger such as q, the program hangs up because integer input can't process a character. But if you use character labels and the user types an integer such as 5, character input will process 5 as a character. Then the default part of the switch can suggest entering another character.

9. Here is one version:

```
int line = 0;
char ch;
while (cin.get(ch) && ch != 'Q')
{
    if (ch == '\n')
    line++;
}
```

Chapter 7

1. The three steps are defining the function, providing a prototype, and calling the function.

2.

    a. `void igor(void);`

    b. `float tofu(int n);   // or  float tofu(int);`

    c. `double mpg(double miles, double gallons);`

    d. `long summation(long harray[], int size);`

    e. `double doctor(const char * str);`

    f. `void ofcourse(boss dude);`

    g. `char * plot(map *pmap);`

3.

```
void set_array(int arr[], int size, int value)
{
    for (int i = 0; i < size; i++)
        arr[i] = value;
}
```

4.

```
double biggest (const double foot[], int size)
{
    double max;
    if (size < 1)
    {
        cout << "Invalid array size of " << size << "\n";
        cout << "Returning a value of 0\n";
        return 0;
    }
    else    // not necessary because return terminates program
    {
        max = foot[0];
        for (int i = 1; i < size; i++)
            if (foot[i] > max)
                max = foot[i];
        return max;
    }
}
```

5. We use the `const` qualifier with pointers to protect the original pointed-to data from being altered. When a program passes a fundamental type such as an `int` or `double`, it passes it by value so that the function works with a copy. Thus, the original data is already protected.

6.

```
int fill_array(double ar[], int limit)
{
    double temp;
    for (int i = 0; i < limit; i++)
    {
        cout << "Enter value #" << i + 1 << ": ";
        if (!(cin >> temp))      // non-numeric input
        {
            cin.clear();         // reset input
            while (cin.get() != '\n')
                continue;        // get rid of old input
            break;
        }
        ar[i] = temp;
    }
    return i;
}
```

7. A string can be stored in a char array, it can be represented by a string constant in double quotation marks, and it can be represented by a pointer pointing to the first character of a string.

8.

```
int replace(char * str, char c1, char c2)
{
    int count = 0;
    while (*str)        // while not at end of string
    {
        if (*str == c1)
        {
            *str = c2;
            count++;
        }
        str++;          // advance to next character
    }
    return count;
}
```

9. Because C++ interprets "pizza" as the address of its first element, applying the * operator yields the value of that first element, which is the character p. Because C++ interprets "taco" as the address of its first element, it interprets "taco"[2] as the value of the element two positions down the line; that is, as the character c. In other words, the string constant acts the same as an array name.

10. To pass it by value, just pass the structure name glitz. To pass its address, use the address operator &glitz. Passing by value automatically protects the original data, but it takes time and memory. Passing by address saves time and memory but doesn't protect the original data unless you use the const modifier for the function parameter. Also, passing by value means you can use ordinary structure member notation, but passing a pointer means you have to remember to use the indirect membership operator.

11.

```
int judge (int (*pf)(const char *));
```

Chapter 8

1. Short, non-recursive functions that can fit in one line of code.

2.

  a. `void song(char * name, int times = 1);`

  b. None. Only prototypes contain the default value information.

  c. Yes, providing you retain the default value for `times`:

  ```
  void song(char * name = "O, My Papa", int times = 1);
  ```

3. You can use either the string `"\""` or the character `'"'` to print a quotation mark. The following functions show both methods:

```
#include <iostream.h>
void iquote(int n)
{
    cout << "\"" << n << "\"";
}

void iquote(double x)
{
    cout << '"' << x << '"';
}

void iquote(const char * str)
{
    cout << "\"" << str << "\"";
}
```

4.

  a. This function shouldn't alter the structure members, so use the `const` qualifier.

  ```
  void show_box(const box & container)
  {
      cout << "Made by " << container. maker << "\n";
      cout << "Height = " << container.height << "\n";
      cout << "Width = " << container.width << "\n";
      cout << "Length = " << container.length << "\n";
      cout << "Volume = " << container.volume << "\n";
  }
  ```

  b.

  ```
  void set_volume(box & crate)
  {
      crate.volume = crate.height * crate.width * crate.length;
  }
  ```

5.

   a. This can be done using a default value for the second argument:

   ```
   double mass(double d, double v = 1.0);
   ```

   It can also be done by overloading:

   ```
   double mass(double d, double v);
   double mass(double d);
   ```

   b. You can't use a default for the repeat value because you have to provide default values from right to left. You can use overloading:

   ```
   void repeat(int times, const char * str);
   void repeat(const char * str);
   ```

   c. You can use function overloading:

   ```
   int average(int a, int b);
   double average(double x, double y);
   ```

   d. You can't do this one because both versions would have the same signature.

   e. At least one version must be defined as a static function in one of the files:

   ```
   static int average(int a, int b);        // definition in file 1
   static double average(int a, int b);     // definition in file 2
   ```

6.

```
template<class T>
T max(T t1, T t2)   // or T max(const T & t1, const T & t2)
{
    return t1 > t2? t1 : t2;
}
```

7.

```
template<> box max(box b1, box b2)
{
    return b1.volume > b2.volume? b1 : b2;
}
```

8.

   a. homer is automatically an automatic variable.

   b. secret should be defined as an external variable in one file and declared using extern in the second file.

   c. topsecret should be defined as a static external variable by prefacing the external definition with the keyword static.

   d. beencalled should be defined as a local static variable by prefacing a declaration in the function with the keyword static.

9. A using-declaration makes a single name from a namespace available, and it has the scope corresponding to the declarative region in which the using-declaration occurs. A using-directive makes all the names in a namespace available. When you use a using-directive, it is as if you declared the names in the smallest declarative region containing both the using-declaration and the namespace itself.

Chapter 9

1. A class is a definition of a user-defined type. A class declaration specifies how data is to be stored, and it specifies the methods (class member functions) that can be used to access and manipulate that data.

2. A class represents the operations one can perform on a class object with a public interface of class methods; this is abstraction. The class can use private visibility (the default) for data members, meaning that the data can be accessed only through the member functions; this is data hiding. Details of the implementation, such as data representation and method code, is hidden; this is encapsulation.

3. The class defines a type, including how it can be used. An object is a variable or other data object, such as that produced by new, created and used according to the class definition. The relationship is the same as that between a standard type and a variable of that type.

4. If you create several objects of a given class, each object comes with storage for its own set of data. But all the objects use the one set of member functions. (Typically, methods are public and data members are private, but that's a matter of policy, not of class requirements.)

5.

Remember

Note: The program uses `cin.get(char *, int)` instead of `cin >>` to read names because `cin.get()` reads a whole line instead of just one word (see Chapter 4).

```cpp
#include <iostream>
using namespace std;

// class definition
class BankAccount
{
private:
    char name[40];
    char acctnum[25];
    double balance;
public:
    BankAccount(char * client, char * num, double bal = 0.0);
    void set(void);
    void show(void) const;
```

```
    void deposit(double cash);
    void withdraw(double cash);
};
```

6. A class constructor is called when you create an object of that class or when you explicitly call the constructor. The class destructor is called when the object expires.

7. Note that you need to include `cstring` or `string.h` in order to use `strncpy()`.

```
BankAccount::BankAccount(char * client, char * num, double bal)
{
    strncpy(name, client, 39);
    name[39] = '\0';
    strncpy(acctnum, num, 24);
    acctnum[24] = '\0';
    balance = bal;
}
```

Keep in mind that default arguments go in the prototype, not in the function definition.

8. A default constructor is one with no arguments or else with defaults for all the arguments. Having one enables you to declare objects without initializing them, even if you've already defined an initializing constructor. It also allows you to declare arrays.

9.

```
// stock3.h
#ifndef _STOCK3_H_
#define _STOCK3_H_

class Stock
{
private:
    char company[30];
    int shares;
    double share_val;
    double total_val;
    void set_tot() { total_val = shares * share_val; }
public:
    Stock();                // default constructor
    Stock(const char * co, int n, double pr);
    ~Stock() {}             // do-nothing destructor
    void buy(int num, double price);
    void sell(int num, double price);
    void update(double price);
    void show() const;
    const Stock & topval(const Stock & s) const;
    int numshares() const { return shares; }
    double shareval() const { return share_val; }
    double totalval() const { return total_val; }
    const char * co_name() const { return company; }
};
```

10. The `this` pointer is a pointer available to class methods. It points to the object used to invoke the method. Thus `this` is the address of the object, and `*this` represents the object itself.

Chapter 10

1. Here's a prototype for the class definition file and a function definition for the methods file:

```
// prototype
Stonewt operator*(double mult);

// definition -- let constructor do the work
Stonewt Stonewt::operator*(double mult)
{
    return Stonewt(mult * pounds);
}
```

2. A member function is part of a class definition and is invoked by a particular object. The member function can access members of the invoking object implicitly, without using the membership operator. A friend function is not part of a class, so it's called as a straight function call. It can't access class members implicitly, so it has to use the membership operator applied to an object passed as an argument.

3. It has to be a friend to access private members, but it doesn't have to be a friend to access public members.

4. Here's a prototype for the class definition file and a function definition for the methods file:

```
// prototype
friend Stonewt operator*(double mult, const Stonewt & s);

// definition -- let constructor do the work
Stonewt operator*(double mult, const Stonewt & s)
{
    return Stonewt(mult * s.pounds);
}
```

5. The following five operators cannot be overloaded:

```
sizeof  .  .*  ::  ? :
```

6. These operators must be defined by using a member function.

7. Here is a possible prototype and definition:

```
// prototype and inline definition
operator double () {return mag;}
```

Note, however, that it makes better sense to use the `magval()` method than to define this conversion function.

Chapter 11

1.

    a. The syntax is fine, but this constructor leaves the `str` pointer uninitialized. The constructor should either set the pointer to NULL or use `new []` to initialize the pointer.

    b. This constructor does not create a new string; it merely copies the address of the old string. It should use `new []` and `strcpy()`.

    c. It copies the string without allocating the space to store it. It should use `new char[len + 1]` to allocate the proper amount of memory.

2. First, when an object of that type expires, the data pointed to by the object's member pointer remains in memory, using space and remaining inaccessible because the pointer has been lost. That can be fixed by having the class destructor delete memory allocated by `new` in the constructor functions. Second, after the destructor deletes such memory, it may wind up trying to delete it twice if a program initialized one such object to another. That's because the default initialization of one object to another copies pointer values but does not copy the pointed-to data, producing two pointers to the same data. The solution is to define a class copy constructor that causes initialization to copy the pointed-to data. Third, assigning one object to another can produce the same situation of two pointers pointing to the same data. The solution is to overload the assignment operator so that it copies the data, not the pointers.

3. C++ automatically provides the following member functions:

- A default constructor if you define no constructors

- A copy constructor if you don't define one

- An assignment operator if you don't define one

- A default constructor if you don't define one

- An address operator if you don't define one

The default constructor does nothing, but it allows you to declare arrays and uninitialized objects. The default copy constructor and the default assignment operator use memberwise assignment. The default destructor does nothing. The implicit address operator returns the address of the invoking object (that is, the value of the `this` pointer).

4. The `personality` member should be declared either as a character array or as a pointer-to-char. Or you could make it a `String` object. Here are two possible solutions, with changes (other than deletions) in boldface.

```
#include <iostream>
#include <cstring>
using namespace std;
class nifty
```

```
{
private: // optional
    char personality[40];    // provide array size
    int talents;
public: // needed
// methods
    nifty();
    nifty(const char * s);
    friend ostream & operator<<(ostream & os, const nifty & n);
};    // note closing semicolon

nifty::nifty()
{
    personality[0] = '\0';
    talents = 0;
}

nifty::nifty(const char * s)
{
    strcpy(personality, s);
    talents = 0;
}

ostream & operator<<(ostream & os, const nifty & n)
{
    os << n.personality << '\n';
    os << n.talent << '\n';
    return os;
}
```

Or you could do this:

```
#include <iostream>
#include <cstring>
using namespace std;
class nifty
{
private: // optional
    char * personality;    // create a pointer
    int talents;
public: // needed
// methods
    nifty();
    nifty(const char * s);
    nifty(const nifty & n);
    ~nifty() { delete personality; }
    nifty & operator=(const nifty & n) const;
    friend ostream & operator<<(ostream & os, const nifty & n);
};    // note closing semicolon

nifty::nifty()
{
    personality = NULL;
    talents = 0;
}

nifty::nifty(const char * s)
{
    personality = new char [strlen(s) + 1];
```

```
        strcpy(personality, s);
        talents = 0;
    }

    ostream & operator<<(ostream & os, const nifty & n)
    {
        os << n.personality << '\n';
        os << n.talent << '\n';
        return os;
    }
```

5.

   a.

```
Golfer nancy; // default constructor
Golfer lulu(Little Lulu); // Golfer(const char * name, int g)
Golfer roy(Roy Hobbs, 12); // Golfer(const char * name, int g)
Golfer * par = new Golfer; // default constructor
Golfer next = lulu; // Golfer(const Golfer &g)
Golfer hazard = "Weed Thwacker"; // Golfer(const char * name, int
g)
*par = nancy; // default assignment operator
nancy = "Nancy Putter";// Golfer(const char * name, int g), then
                        // the default assignment operator
```

Remember

Note: Some compilers will additionally call the default assignment operator for statements #5 and #6.

   b. The class should define an assignment operator that copies data rather than addresses.

Chapter 12

1. The public members of the base class become public members of the derived class. The protected members of the base class become protected members of the derived class. The private members of the base class are inherited, but cannot be accessed directly. The answer to review question 2 provides the exceptions to these general rules.

2. The constructor's methods are not inherited, the destructor is not inherited, the assignment operator is not inherited, and friends are not inherited.

3. You would still be able to use the value of an element, but you no longer could assign to it:

```
ArrayDb tosanjose[4];
double n = tosanjose[2];    // ok
tosanjose[1] = 68.8;        // no longer valid
```

The method execution would be slowed a bit because the return statement would involve copying the object.

4. Constructors are called in the order of derivation, with the most ancestral constructor called first. Destructors are called in the opposite order.

5. Yes, every class requires its own constructors. If the derived class adds no new members, the constructor may have an empty body, but it must exist.

6. Only the derived class method is called. It supersedes the base class definition. A base class method is called only if the derived class does not redefine the method. However, you really should declare as virtual any functions that will be redefined.

7. The derived class should define an assignment operator if the derived class constructors use the *new* or new [] operator to initialize pointers that are members of that class. More generally, the derived class should define an assignment operator if the default assignment is incorrect for derived class members.

8. Yes, you can assign the address of an object of a derived class to a pointer to the base class. You can assign the address of a base object to a pointer to a derived class (downcasting) only by making an explicit type cast, and it is not necessarily safe to use such a pointer.

9. Yes, you can assign an object of a derived class to an object of the base class. Any data members new to the derived type are not passed to the base type, however. The program will use the base class assignment operator. Assignment in the opposite direction (base to derived) is possible only if the derived class defines a conversion operator, which is a constructor having a reference to the base type as its sole argument.

10. It can do so because C++ allows a reference to a base type to refer to any type derived from that base.

11. Passing an object by value invokes the copy constructor. Because the formal argument is a base class object, the base class copy constructor is invoked. The copy constructor has as its argument a reference to the base class, and this reference can refer to the derived object passed as an argument. The net result is producing a new base class object whose members correspond to the base class portion of the derived object.

12. Passing an object by reference instead of by value enables the function to avail itself of virtual functions. Also, passing an object by reference instead of by value may use less memory and time, particularly for large objects. The main advantage of passing by value is that it protects the original data, but you can accomplish the same end by passing the reference as a const type.

13. If head() is a regular function, then ph->head() invokes Corporation::head(). If head() is a virtual function, then ph->head() invokes PublicCorporation::head().

14. First, the situation does not fit the *is-a* model, so public inheritance is not appropriate. Second, the definition of area() in House hides the Kitchen version of area() because the two methods have different signatures.

Chapter 13

1.

class Bear	class PolarBear	public, a polar bear is a kind of bear
class Kitchen	class Home	private, a home has a kitchen
class Person	class Programmer	public, a programmer is a kind of person
class Person	class HorseAndJockey	private, a horse and jockey team contains a person
class Person, class Automobile	class Driver	Person public because a driver is a person; Automobile private because a driver has an automobile

2.

```
Gloam::Gloam(int g, const char * s) : glip(g), fb(s) { }
Gloam::Gloam(int g, const Frabjous & f) : glip(g), fb(f) { }
// note: the above uses the default Frabjous copy constructor
void Gloam::tell()
{
    fb.tell();
    cout << glip << '\n';
}
```

3.

```
Gloam::Gloam(int g, const char * s)
            : glip(g), Frabjous(s) { }
Gloam::Gloam(int g, const Frabjous & f)
            : glip(g), Frabjous(f) { }
// note: the above uses the default Frabjous copy constructor
void Gloam::tell()
{
    Frabjous::tell();
    cout << glip << '\n';
}
```

4.

```
class Stack<Worker *>
{
private:
    enum {MAX = 10};          // constant specific to class
    Worker * items[MAX];      // holds stack items
    int top;                  // index for top stack item
public:
    Stack();
    Boolean isempty();
    Boolean isfull();
    Boolean push(const Worker * & item); // add item to stack
    Boolean pop(Worker * & item);        // pop top into item
};
```

5.

```
ArrayTP<String> sa;
StackTP< ArrayTP<double> > stck_arr_db;
ArrayTp< StackTP<Worker *> > arr_stk_wpr;
```

6. If two lines of inheritance for a class share a common ancestor, the class winds up with two copies of the ancestor's members. Making the ancestor class a virtual base class to its immediate descendants solves that problem.

Chapter 14

1.

a. The friend declaration should be as follows:

```
friend class clasp;
```

b. This needs a forward declaration so that the compiler can interpret void snip(muff &):

```
class muff;    // forward declaration
class cuff {
public:
    void snip(muff &) { ... }
    ...
};
class muff {
    friend void cuff::snip(muff &);
    ...
};
```

c. First, the cuff class declaration should precede the muff class so that the compiler can understand the term cuff::snip(). Second, the compiler needs a forward declaration of muff so that it can understand snip(muff &).

```
class muff;    // forward declaration
class cuff {
public:
    void snip(muff &) { ... }
    ...
};
class muff {
    friend void cuff::snip(muff &);
    ...
};
```

2. No. For A to have a friend that's a member function of B, the B declaration must precede the A declaration. A forward declaration is not enough, for it would tell A that B is a class, but it wouldn't reveal the names of the class members. Similarly, if B has a friend that's a member function of A, the complete A declaration must precede the B declaration. These two requirements are mutually exclusive.

3. The only access to a class is through its public interface, which means the only thing you can do with a Sauce object is call the constructor to create one. The other members (soy and sugar) are private by default.

4. Suppose function `f1()` calls function `f2()`. A return statement in `f2()` causes program execution to resume at the next statement following the `f2()` function call in function `f1()`. A throw statement causes the program to back up through the current sequence of function calls until it finds a try block that directly or indirectly contains the call to `f2()`. This might be in `f1()` or in a function that called `f1()`, and so on. Once there, execution goes to the next matching catch block, not to the first statement after the function call.

5. You should arrange the catch blocks in the order of most derived class to least derived.

6. For sample #1, the `if` condition is true if pg points to a `Superb` object or to an object of any class descended from `Superb`. In particular, it is also true if pg points to a `Magnificent` object. In sample #2, the `if` condition is true only for a `Superb` object, not for objects derived from `Superb`.

7. The `dynamic_cast` operator only allows upcasting in a class hierarchy, while a `static_cast` operator allows both upcasting and downcasting. The `static_cast` operator also allows conversions from enumeration types to integer types and vice versa.

Chapter 15

1.

```
#include <string>
using namespace std;
class RQ1
{
private:
    string st;        // a string object
public:
    RQ1() : st("") {}
    RQ1(const char * s) : st(s) {}
    ~RQ1() {};
// more stuff
};
```

The explicit copy constructor, destructor, and assignment operator no longer are needed because the `string` object provides its own memory management.

2. You can assign one string object to another. A string object provides its own memory management so that you normally don't have to worry about a string exceeding the capacity of its holder.

3.

```
#include <string>
#include <cctype>
using namespace std;
void ToUpper(string & str)
{
```

```
        for (int i = 0; i < str.size(); i++)
            str[i] = toupper(str[i]);
    }
```

4.

```
auto_ptr<int> pia= new int[20];   // wrong, use with new, not new[]
auto_ptr<str>(new string);        // wrong, no name for pointer
int rigue = 7;
auto_ptr<int>(&rigue);            // wrong, memory not allocated by new
auto_ptr dbl (new double);        // wrong, omits <double>
```

5. The LIFO aspect of a stack means you might have to remove a lot of clubs before reaching the one you need.

6. The set will store just one copy of each value, so, say, five scores of 5 would be stored as a single 5.

7. Using iterators allows one to use objects with a pointer-like interface to move through data organized in fashions other than an array, for example, data in a doubly-linked list.

8. The STL approach lets STL functions be used with ordinary pointers to ordinary arrays as well as with iterators to STL container classes, thus increasing generality.

9. You can assign one `vector` object to another. A `vector` manages its own memory, so you can insert items into a vector and have it resize itself automatically. By using the `at()` method, you can get automatic bounds checking.

10. The two `sort()` functions and the `random_shuffle()` function require a random-access iterator, while a `list` object just has a bidirectional iterator. You can use the list template class `sort()` member functions instead of the general-purpose functions to do the sorting, but there is no member function equivalent to `random_shuffle()`. However, you could copy the list to a vector, shuffle the vector, and copy the results back to the list. (At the time of this writing, most compilers have not yet implemented the `sort()` member function that takes a Compare object as its argument. Also, the Microsoft Visual C++ 5.0 implementation of the `list` class has some bugs that prevent making the suggested conversions.)

Chapter 16

1. The `iostream` file defines the classes, constants, and manipulators used to manage input and output. These objects manage the streams and buffers used to handle I/O. The file also creates standard objects (`cin`, `cout`, `cerr`, and `clog` and their wide-character equivalents) used to handle the standard input and output streams connected to every program.

2. Keyboard entry generates a series of characters. Typing 121 generates three characters, each represented by a 1-byte binary code. If the value is to be stored as type int, these three characters have to be converted to a single binary representation of the value 121.

3. By default, both the standard output and the standard error send output to the standard output device, typically a monitor. If you have the operating system redirect output to a file, however, the standard output connects to the file instead of to the screen, but the standard error continues to be connected to the screen.

4. The ostream class defines a version of the operator<<() function for each basic C++ type. The compiler interprets an expression like

```
cout << spot
```

as the following:

```
cout.operator<<(spot)
```

It then can match this method call to the function prototype having the same argument type.

5. You can concatenate output methods that return type ostream &. This causes the invoking of a method with an object to return that object. The returned object can then invoke the next method in a sequence.

6.

```
//rq16-6.cpp
#include <iostream>
#include <iomanip>
using namespace std;

int main()
{
    cout << "Enter an integer: ";
    int n;
    cin >> n;
    cout << setw(15) << "base ten" << setw(15)
         << "base sixteen" << setw(15) << "base eight" << "\n";
    cout.setf(ios::showbase);    // or cout << showbase;
    cout << setw(15) << n << hex << setw(15) << n
         << oct << setw(15) << n << "\n";

    return 0;
}
```

7.

```
//rq15-7.cpp
#include <iostream>
#include <iomanip>
using namespace std;

int main()
{
```

```
        char name[20];
        float hourly;
        float hours;

        cout << "Enter your name: ";
        cin.get(name, 20).get();
        cout << "Enter your hourly wages: ";
        cin >> hourly;
        cout << "Enter number of hours worked: ";
        cin >> hours;

        cout.setf(ios::showpoint);
        cout.setf(ios::fixed, ios::floatfield);
        cout.setf(ios::right, ios::adjustfield);
// or cout << showpoint << fixed << right;
        cout << "First format:\n";
        cout << setw(30) << name << ": $" << setprecision(2)
             << setw(10) << hourly << ":" << setprecision(1)
             << setw(5) << hours << "\n";
        cout << "Second format:\n";
        cout.setf(ios::left, ios::adjustfield);
        cout << setw(30) << name << ": $" << setprecision(2)
             << setw(10) << hourly << ":" << setprecision(1)
             << setw(5) << hours << "\n";

        return 0;
    }
```

8. Here is the output:

```
ct1 = 5; ct2 = 9
```

The first part of the program ignores spaces and newlines; the second part doesn't. Note that the second part of the program begins reading at the newline character following the first q, and it counts that newline as part of its total.

9. The `ignore()` form falters if the input line exceeds 80 characters. In that case it only skips the first 80 characters.

Index

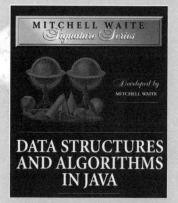